ENVIRONMENTAL PSYCHOLOGY

ENVIRONMENTAL PSYCHOLOGY: MAN AND HIS PHYSICAL SETTING

Edited by
HAROLD M. PROSHANSKY
WILLIAM H. ITTELSON
LEANNE G. RIVLIN

Environmental Psychology Program
The City University of New York

HOLT, RINEHART AND WINSTON, INC.
New York   Chicago   San Francisco   Atlanta   Dallas
Montreal   Toronto   London   Sydney

The poem "Domed Edifice" is reprinted by permission of Atheneum Publishers from *Types of
Shape* by John Hollander. Copyright © 1967,
1969 by John Hollander. It originally appeared
in the *Columbia University Forum*.

PREFACE

Books focused on scientific theory and research are written from the point of view of any one of a number of objectives: to serve as a specialized college text; to communicate new concepts and findings to other investigators; to clarify and order a problem domain characterized by contradictory findings and diverse points of view; or to accomplish some combination of these. The present volume, *Environmental Psychology: Man and His Physical Setting,* was written with still another and perhaps more specific purpose in mind—a purpose that took on increasing significance for the editors over a period of almost a decade while they were engaged in empirical research of this nature.

During this period of time, the term *environmental psychology* was employed with greater and greater frequency by various researchers and theorists, whose primary conceptual and empirical interests were focused on understanding the relationship between the physical environment and the behavior of man. However, to the questions "What is environmental psychology?" and "What kind of research and thinking goes on in this field?" the "on the spot" accounts of one or more of the editors were hardly satisfying for those social scientists, architects, and designers who had more than a passing interest in the field. By the same token, with the exception of a small number of published reports on actual environmental psychological research and the very many more highly general discussions of specific problems, such as urban design and behavior, there was no single source that provided an ordered and comprehensive picture of this emerging field of inquiry. Indeed it was for this reason that, long before the editors decided to prepare the present volume, they assembled, kept up to date, and widely distributed a bibliography of empirical and theoretical journal articles and books relevant to environmental psychology.

Of course such bibliographies are of inordinate value not only to those researchers and applied professionals whose interests lie outside a given scientific field and who need to learn more about it, but also to those investigators already immersed in the area who desire to keep abreast of the newest theoretical conceptions, empirical findings, and basic controversial issues. For the newcomer interested in learning more about environmental psychology, however, reading the relevant literature falls far short if he needs an encompassing and coherent picture of this field. This is true for a number of interrelated reasons.

The fact that the field is new, undeveloped, and interdisciplinary in character has resulted in a "relevant body of literature" which is both widely dispersed and highly varied in the nature and level of the problems, concepts, and methods discussed. This literature consists of not only the writings of psychologists, sociologists, and anthropologists, but also those of architects, urban planners, geographers, interior designers, and still others skilled in and concerned with the design of the physical environment. For the novice and indeed perhaps no less for those already involved in environmental psychology, the relevant literature taken as a whole can only present a picture of confusion. It is difficult not to emerge with the view that what characterizes this field is a conglomeration of remotely related, if not seemingly unrelated, discussions of research and theory about man's relationship to his physical environment.

The primary purpose of our book should now be clear: to define and establish the substantive and conceptual boundaries of the field of environmental psychology. Our desire was to establish some order in an array of diverse problems, conceptions, and findings that to the uninitiated seemed to show little if any theoretical coherence. However, our efforts were not only being directed at the uninitiated. For the investigator already involved in research in environmental psychology—including ourselves —there was a strong need for someone "to take inventory" and to provide an interim "progress report" on this new but rapidly growing field. As we already noted, investigators and theorists from a variety of social science and design disciplines could be designated as "environmental psychologists" at least in terms of the nature of the problems they defined for themselves or the

issues they raised. And yet in any number of instances, it was evident that many were unaware of the work being done by others. The numerous requests for our "bibliography of the field," from those whose own work was already cited in this bibliography, clearly suggested that this was indeed the case.

How could our purposes be achieved? From the beginning of our endeavor a book of readings seemed most appropriate; by the judicious sampling of the widely dispersed relevant literature, it would allow us to bring together *in one place* the variety of concepts, methods, theoretical orientations, and empirical research findings that characterize the field. Furthermore, if this sampling of the literature and the subsequent organization of these selected papers were guided by a conceptual framework designed to define and establish the boundaries of the field of environmental psychology, then our primary purpose for the volume would be served. But for a new, undeveloped interdisciplinary field, this did not seem to be enough. For this reason we decided to include with these readings especially prepared interstitial material in the form of introductions to each major section, including a general Introduction at the beginning of the book. Our introductions do not summarize the selected papers that follow each introduction. Their purpose, broadly stated, is to highlight for the reader those major issues and questions—particularly as they relate to the status of the field —which will permit him to see the relationships not only among the papers in a given section but also among those in different sections of the volume. Finally, we also included as part of the readings some of our own theoretical and research papers based on a systematic program of research into the effects of psychiatric ward design on patient behavior. These papers also provide some perspective with respect to the substantive and empirical character of environmental psychology.

Making selections for a book of readings is a painful task. Regardless of the organizing framework or the criteria to be employed, the editor is invariably confronted with the dilemma of choosing among two or more equally relevant and worthwhile papers. The present volume was no exception. Since there are clearly limits to the number of readings one can include in a reader directed to research, we had to omit many provocative and significant papers from our book. It is true, however, that this was far more the case for theoretical or general discussion papers relevant to environmental psychology than it was for those reporting on systematic research. Indeed there were very few of the latter, and even that small number of them available was limited to an even smaller number of problem areas (hospital design, playground design, and so forth), rather than being widely distributed over many such areas. For this reason we included in our selections some that report "findings" based on what social scientists, environmental designers, and others have "experienced" or observed in given physical settings. Given our desire to provide a substantive definition of environmental psychology by highlighting its major concepts and problem areas, it seemed reasonable in the light of the newness of the field to make use of any kind of evidence, anecdotal as well as systematic. Our search for data, therefore, ranged far and wide— from scientific journals to architectural and environmental trade magazines to novels and autobiographical accounts.

And even in the search for discussions of concept, theory, and approach we did not confine ourselves to the view of the social scientist or the behaviorally oriented environmental designer. Although there was no dearth of discussions by these individuals, the greater majority of them called for "concept and theory" rather than actually attempting their formulation. For this reason we again ranged far and wide in our search, considering the views and interpretations of social practitioners, community leaders, urban planners, and others.

Writing and putting together a book of readings, perhaps more than any other kind of volume, depends on the cooperation and skill of many other people beside the editors. Our expressions of gratitude, however, should begin with respect to the two institutions whose direct support in the way of funds and facilities made this book pos-sible. Over a period of years, the National Institute of Mental Health has supported our continuing efforts to understand the relationships between the physical design of a psychiatric ward and patient and staff behavior on that ward. Of importance was the willingness of NIMH to allow us to go beyond this specific research task, so that we could deepen as well as extend our knowledge of problems in environmental psychology by preparing and writing the present volume. Thus the library of articles, monographs, and books which we established, the preparation of the bibliography we referred to earlier, and most importantly the ever necessary clerical and research assistance for all aspects of such an endeavor, were all made possible by the continuing grants we received from the federal government. Both this book and the papers by the authors included in this volume grew directly out of this National Institute of Mental Health support (Grants 5 R11 MH 00220, 1 R11 MH 02497, 5 R01 MH 14858, and 7 R01 MH 15569).

We also owe a great deal to the Graduate Center of the City University of New York. By its annual research grants to faculty it has enabled us to increase our research and clerical staff at critical periods, and it has also endorsed our proposed library in environmental psychology by providing us with the necessary space. Without such support it is not unlikely that the present volume would have been long delayed and perhaps not completed at all. If, as we have already indicated, the purpose of our book is to define and establish "the reality" of the field of environmental psychology, then it can be said that the Graduate Center of the City University of New York, and more specifically our colleagues in the PhD program in psychology accepted and implemented that reality well before we could prove it by means of the present volume. In the spring of 1967 they approved the addition of environmental psychology as an area of specialization for graduate students in the PhD program in psychology. With a number of advanced seminars given as part of the curriculum of this specialization area, there was now a need to provide students as well as trained researchers with a more elaborate and coherent description of *Environmental Psychology*.

The doctoral students on our research staff played important roles in the preparation of our book. Aside from the usual editorial assistance, they were of incalculable aid in the final decisions we made about alternative selections; in our development of the conceptual scheme for organizing the presentation of the selected readings; and in some instances in the rewriting and integrating into a single selection the bits and pieces taken from a number of sources. Special thanks goes to Dr. Frank Stallone who was almost continuously involved with us in the preparation and writing of the book. We are no less grateful to our other graduate students, Mr. Ronald Barazani, Mrs. Arza Churchman, Mrs. Linda Klau, Mrs. Miriam Leibman, and Mrs. Caralee Roberts for their considerable assistance in the various phases of preparing and writing the book. All of these students must be thanked in still another way. Each one of them, including Dr. Maxine Wolfe, was involved in the data collection and analysis phase of the editors' own empirical research reported in a number of chapters in this volume.

With the number of individuals involved in preparing and writing this book, someone had to keep track of and coordinate all of the activities. In this regard we wish to express our very considerable gratitude to Mrs. Mona Carp, our Research Administrative Aide for many years, who was involved in and assumed responsibility for all of the paper work connected with this endeavor. Her intelligence, devotion, and great energy more than compensated for the buzzing confusion introduced by three editors involved in research and administration as well as in the attempt to edit and write a book. By way of clerical assistance, we would also like to thank Miss Bonnie Kalem and Miss Carol Greene who typed a number of the empirical and theoretical papers written for this volume by the editors.

We have reserved for last any reference to the many colleagues in environmental psychology, who either by word or deed, contributed to our understanding in this area and therefore to the writing of this book. We not only wish to thank all of the authors who willingly allowed us to include their writings in it, but also all whose provocative discussions with us helped to sharpen, clarify, and indeed establish our conception of the field of environmental psychology. Since there are far too many of the latter to cite by name, we must simply say that without their stimulation and indeed great encouragement this book would probably never have been prepared.

H. M. P.
W. H. I.
L. G. R.

CONTENTS

ix

Behavioral Concepts

eg.
① Territoriality
② Privacy

Problems Social Interaction

DOMED EDIFICE

John Hollander

Closure
surmounts the
strange open ways
that even an interior
may inherit or a dark chamber
achieve through partial ruin Such
unpierced coverings hold dominion for
ever over minded regions below as the
sky does above our heightened eyes that strive to measure
and contend Not like the sole fiery lord rising wide over
azure ramparts nor Madame M queen of all the minor purple
distances her dust penetrated her silver honor intact Not
like the stony rule of starlight raining in apertures cut
to admit the once—unruined gods But from this distance or
this angle our sunlit or unlit domes govern their domains
as a skull tells its soft protectorate <u>I am clamped above
you for your own good and behold there is still visionary
room above you</u> We have lain below we who scanning all the
unquiet ceilings of day and night know every zenith to be
limned on the inner surface of some one of our domes our many
unopening skies We have strained Our parched eyes water only by our
lowering of them into depths of darkness and touch toward our bottom doom

INTRODUCTION

At first glance it might appear that a book on environmental psychology is not in need of an introduction. Interest in environment has become so intense that the mere mention of the word sometimes seems justification for any endeavor. But intense interest in the environmental sciences is so very recent, and they are proliferating at such a remarkable rate, that we think it desirable to indicate at the outset in a very general way what "environmental psychology" means to us, why we think it represents a fruitful field for study, and what characteristics justify considering it as a distinctive subject matter. Environmental psychology can only be understood and defined, however, in the context of the environmental sciences in general—the larger body of studies concerned with the consequences of man's manipulation of his environment.

Man the builder, man the conqueror of his environment, form such a central place in the human self-image that we sometimes forget that, when man seeks to modify his environment, he is actually doing something which is a biological commonplace. All living organisms engage in a complex interchange with their environments in the course of which they modify, and are modified by, what they encounter. Some such interchange is essential for the maintenance of life and usually is involved in definitions of the concept of life itself. Living necessarily involves changes wrought on the environment by the organism, changes that may subsequently alter the organism itself, chemically, biologically, or behaviorally. In plants and primitive organisms, the interchange is of a most elementary form. The activity of the organism may change, for example, the chemical nature of the medium, and this change in turn may alter the range of possible activities of the organism. A dynamic equilibrium of some kind must be reached, or the organism perishes. More complex organisms engage in more complex interchanges—hunting, fishing, building, destroying, transporting, reproducing—and respond to environmental changes in more complex and varied ways.

It is quite clear that life on this planet depends on a delicate ecological balance among many forms of life at all levels of complexity. Each organism contributes to and takes from its surroundings in such a way that an overall equilibrium is maintained. Upset this equilibrium at any point and monumental consequences ensue. Each organism, and each group of diverse organisms, must somehow achieve an environment that all find at least

1

reasonably congenial if it is to survive. Only today, and slowly, is man coming to recognize that this great imperative of nature applies as much to him as to the creatures from whose study he has gained this knowledge. We can no longer blindly change the world about us, ignoring the consequences of change, without threatening our own survival as a species.

The malleability of the environment in the face of the cumulative onslaught of groups of organisms has long been recognized as an important biological fact. The archaic view of a fixed environment that organisms must adapt to or perish is being replaced by a view that emphasizes the organism's creative role in shaping his own environment. Although the extent to which man shapes his environment is unique, in a sense man's relative impact on his immediate environment is perhaps less than that of some other organisms on theirs. Certain insects, for example, may live their entire life span in a totally artificial, insect-made environment without once coming upon undefiled nature—a fate that, happily, is still reserved for relatively few humans. The absolute magnitude of man's effect on his environment needs no documentation, however. Through his efforts, the entire face of the globe is being transformed at a rapidly increasing rate.

Closely related to its magnitude is the complexity of man's relationship with his environment. It is both physically and biologically complex. Vast and permanent changes in the composition of the earth's crust and atmosphere, widespread changes in the ecological equilibrium of huge numbers and many forms of life, will have a complex and unpredictable influence on all forms of human activity. From the viewpoint of the social sciences, man's social and psychological environment is largely a product of his own creation, and he, in turn, is fundamentally influenced by this product. Indeed, the social effect on man of the environment he himself has created may prove to be the most important aspect of this relationship. For in the long run of history, the product becomes the master. Man has produced modifications in his environment that have set irreversible evolutionary trends in motion.

The magnitude and complexity of man's effect on his environment would be little more than an interesting biological curiosity were it not for man's capacity to predict the consequences of his behavior. This characteristic makes it possible for him to do more than blindly operate on the environment; it permits planned manipulation of the environment.

Man the builder is also man the planner. But for the most part man's planning, with respect to the environment, has been limited to the physical effects of his alterations. Understanding and predicting the effects of these manipulations upon himself, while operationally inseparable from the fact of manipulation, have tended to be separated conceptually and, until quite recently, largely ignored.

The capacity to predict the consequences of behavior, in addition to making planning possible, has another and perhaps further-reaching significance. It places on man a responsibility for his behavior which is biologically unique, and Simpson (1966) suggests that it is the biological basis for an ethical sense. But whether we accept it as a moral imperative or simply as a necessary condition for survival, it is evident that the scope of man's manipulations of his environment makes essential an understanding of the consequences of these manipulations for human life itself.

This is precisely the task that the environmental sciences have set for themselves—the study of the consequences of environmental manipulations on man. As this study progresses, our ability to predict and control these consequences will increase. We will know what results will follow a particular environmental manipulation, and we will know how to produce any particular result. In short, we will understand the consequences of environmental change. Understanding consequences does not, however, lead to choice among alternatives without a commitment, as well, to a choice of goals. Any decision to attack the environment in any particular way involves, at least implicitly, a particular goal.

The decoration of a room, the design of a building, and the choice of a site for a housing project are all based ultimately on decisions about the kinds of behaviors one wishes to foster or to discourage. In these cases, the goal may be clear while the design decisions to implement them are largely intuitive and only incidentally and occasionally based on verifiable facts. In other cases the design decisions may be relatively clear while the goal is indistinct, as in the conflict between scenic beauty and needed electric power, or between the economics of the automotive industry and the safety and health of the rider and the person who breathes exhaust fumes. In the overwhelming majority of cases, however, it is probably true that the complex relationships between design and policy decisions on the one hand and their human consequences on the other are but little understood and rarely even thought of.

The broad topic of societal goals cannot be avoided in a complete discussion of the environmental sciences, since knowledge of the consequences of environmental manipulation implies choice among those consequences. In this sense, environmental studies are involved in the determination of both short- and long-term societal goals. Such studies recognize that every action shapes its own consequences. The choice of means and the choice of ends are inseparable, both in theory and in practice. In planning for the totality of human needs, hard and irreversible choices must be made as to where we are going, as well as how we will get there. And as environmental sciences result in a concomitant technology, the goals society sets for itself will themselves be one of the many products of technology, as well as the bases for selection among technologies.

This is, of course, a rather grand undertaking for sciences as new and untried as the environmental sciences, whose very existence as legitimate fields of study is often questioned. "One of the newest fads in Washington— and elsewhere—is 'environmental science'," say the editors of *Science*. "Lacking specific definition, it embraces every science—physical, natural, social—for all of these deal with man's surroundings and their influence and impact upon him." From this point of view, to speak of environmental sciences is to be at best redundant. Environmental sciences have not discovered the environment, nor are they pioneers in dealing with problems of man's environment. Science has always been interested in the environment; indeed it is impossible to imagine a science which is not a science of the environment. In this sense all science is environmental, and there is nothing new or distinctive in the body of studies labeled "environmental."

From another point of view, however—one that is gradually taking shape within certain areas of the environmental sciences, and that is reflected in the selections of this book—this reasoning is only partially valid; it applies only partially to some of the many types of studies that have assumed the mantle of environmental science in the past decade or so. From this point of view, study of the environment is not synonymous with environmental science. All science studies the environment. Environmental sciences, as we use the term, are characterized by certain distinctive features that set them off as embracing a definite subject matter.

First and most obvious, the environment that is of primary concern to the environmental sciences is a limited and particular one. Every science may study the environment, but the environmental sciences undertake investigations specifically of the man-ordered or man-defined environment, that is, aspects of the setting that have in some way been modified by man. Instead of asking, "What has nature wrought?" the environmental sciences ask, "What has man done to his natural heritage?" The modifications that man has imposed on his physical environment in the past, those he is undertaking now, and those he plans for the future represent the unifying reference of the environmental sciences.

Certainly these sciences do not suffer from a shortage of raw material to study. It is probably true that today no place on earth is untouched by man's hand. And it is almost certain that in the future every place on earth will be significantly altered by his efforts. One is tempted to write, "altered for better or worse." That almost compelling addendum points to a second characteristic common to the environmental sciences: their scientific problems grow out of pressing social problems. Take away the social issue and the scientific problem ceases to exist; at least, it ceases to excite the interest and the energies of the environmental scientist. The recognition that man can alter his environment favorably or unfavorably is a crucial identifying feature of the environmental sciences, which bear a unique value orientation. Indeed, they owe their very existence to a value judgment. We have already emphasized the close relationship between the environmental sciences and the goals of society. Here we suggest that this relationship is one of the identifying features of environmental science.

Of course this does not mean that environmental science is any less "scientific" or "objective" than other sciences. It does not appear to need any new scientific principles or procedures. We would suggest, however, that one cannot fully understand the environmental sciences without taking into consideration their particular and universally held value orientation. Similarly, although the environmental sciences have grown out of pressing social problems, it is a mistake to think of them strictly as applied science. Their value orientation undoubtedly commits them to a greater interest in future technologies than some of the more traditional sciences would claim. But it has become abundantly clear that the solution of environmental problems requires a vast addition to our store of basic scientific knowledge, and the environmental sciences are actively addressing themselves to this end.

Perhaps the relative lack of knowledge about environmental problems stems in part from a characteristic they seem to share. Not one of them fits neatly into an established scientific discipline. Each demands a multi-disciplinary approach. Unfortunately, it is clear that after years of interest in interdisciplinary problems, we are still far from any effective understanding of how to deal with them. We do not yet know how to handle problems whose solutions require knowledge that can only be gleaned from the empty interstices between disciplines. The multidisciplinary nature of the environmental sciences represents both one of their chief identifying features and one of their major challenges.

③

interdisciplinary (?) as well ?

A final common feature of the environmental sciences is that in them man, above all else, is the measure. Perhaps this follows as a necessary corollary of what has already been said, but it merits separate attention. No matter how remote from man some of the aspects of an environmental problem may appear, the study of man is a crucial part of the study of every environmental problem. Man's importance is self-evident in such pressing problems as air pollution and urban design. We suggest that the study of man as part of the field of inquiry is one of the necessary defining features of all the environmental sciences.

④

In summary, the environmental sciences, as we understand them, have four identifying and defining characteristics. They deal with the man-ordered and -defined environment; they grow out of pressing social problems; they are multidisciplinary in nature; and they include the study of man as an integral part of every problem. In short, the environmental sciences are concerned with human problems in relation to an environment of which man is both victim and conqueror.

Summary

⋇

Ultimately all environmental sciences are concerned to a greater or lesser extent with questions of human behavior. They must then turn to environmental psychology, which can be characterized, in keeping with our general discussion, as the study of human behavior in relation to the man-ordered and -defined environment. While this statement may serve as a concise description of environmental psychology, however, it poses rather than answers the question of definition. The enormous complexities inherent in this study are only gradually becoming apparent as greater effort is devoted to it.

Is there, at present, an adequate definition of environmental psychology? We think not. There are, in general, two ways in which the definition of a field of study may be stated. One—and in the long run, the only really satisfactory way—is in terms of theory. And the simple fact is that as yet there is no adequate theory, or even the beginnings of a theory, of environmental psychology on which such a definition might be based. As in any other new scientific field, however, researchers and theorists move quickly to conceptualize particular problems, to suggest broader theoretical formulations, and in general to recommend and design the theoretical future of the field. Some of these attempts at theory are presented in Part One, and in the introduction to Part One the difficulties in establishing a theory of environmental psychology are discussed.

The second approach to definition—a much less satisfying but much more feasible one—is operational: environmental psychology is what the environmental psychologists do. This book provides such a definition. Although we have had to omit many specific subjects of interest to the environmental psychologist, as well as many notable papers in the areas of study we have chosen, we have attempted to point to the major problem areas that, taken together, constitute environmental psychology.

In this sense, the table of contents is an approach to an operational definition of environmental psychology. Enclosed between an opening section on theory and a closing one on methodology, the reader finds four major problem areas that spell out very broadly the domain of environmental psychology. Part Two, on basic psychological processes in relation to the environment, reveals that much fundamental thinking in psychology needs to be reevaluated in the light of growing knowledge about environmental influences. Basic psychological concepts, such as learning, perception, cognition, and emotion, derive from processes that can be understood fully only in relation to their environmental context. To attain this kind of understanding is one of the important tasks for environmental psychology. Part Three deals with behavioral concepts that have meaning only in relation to the environment. Territoriality and privacy, for example, refer to ways in which the individual organizes his environment in order to satisfy some specific needs. As the field expands, other fruitful concepts of this nature will be developed. Part Four deals with problems of social interaction, which, although it has long been recognized as an important area for psychological study, has only recently been treated in the full environmental context. Here also, old concepts are being newly clarified, and revised or wholly new concepts are emerging. Part Five deals with environmental planning and explores the contribution that environmental psychology can make to this important and complex field.

These four divisions, then, together with those on theory and methodology, constitute the domain of environmental psychology. Clearly, however, the book does not exhaust the problems relevant to the field. Many specific problems have been omitted for lack of space; others because they have not yet been empirically studied; and still others because they have yet to be clearly identified and conceptualized. The table of contents provides an outline for a definition of environmental psychology, but the book itself does not claim to include the entire field.

One other feature emerges from an examination of the table of contents. The work that we have chosen to subsume under the heading "environmental psychology" originates in a variety of disciplines. Among the authors are sociologists, anthropologists, psychiatrists, geographers, biologists, designers, architects, and others. We hope they will be willing to accept the title of environmental psychology—if not for themselves, at least for the work represented here. A unifying theme appears in these papers: all deal in one way or another with the relationship between behavior and the man-defined environment, and in its simplest form, that is what environmental psychology is all about.

REFERENCE:

Simpson, G. G. Biological nature of man. *Science*, April 22, 1966, **152**, 472–478.

PART ONE

Theoretical Conceptions and Approaches

As we noted in the introduction, the structure of interrelated concepts, assumptions, and principles required for a theoretical definition of environmental psychology simply does not exist. This absence should not be construed to mean, however, that environmental psychologists are opposed or indifferent to theory. On the contrary, as the selections in Part One attest, they are very much concerned with concepts and theory for purposes of analysis and systematic research. What then is the problem?

From one point of view it is simply enough to say that environmental psychology is a very new field, clearly still in its infancy. Indeed some would argue that it is more embryo than infant and that its real development has yet to begin. But no scientific field emerges full-grown. It develops slowly, in most instances haltingly, by means of a process in which analytical concepts are organized into a coherent and viable theoretical system supported by a firm foundation of empirical findings. However, to point to the newness of environmental psychology as a field of inquiry is merely to beg the question of its limitations in theoretical structure.

Like any other environmental science concerned with cogent social problems, environmental psychology is necessarily a multidisciplinary field of inquiry. Its focus on behavior in relation to physical settings defined or ordered by man precludes the possibility of any more limited approach. As we noted in the introduction, man's social problems express the complexity of his existence in a complex and changing environment. They have no simple solutions because what determines them is not simple. Problems in the nature of air pollution, the urban ghetto, and the loss of individual privacy are multicausal in character. They are rooted in a pattern of interrelated determinants that express the human condition at varyingly complex levels of social organization. And herein lies the critical requirement that environmental psychology be multidisciplinary in its approach, a requirement that creates many of its difficulties in establishing a viable theoretical structure and, therefore, in undertaking meaningful research.

In considering the relationship between physical setting and human behavior, the environmental psychologist is confronted with the special

7

problem of deciding which of the various levels of human or social organization he should undertake to conceptualize and study. This relationship can be defined and analyzed, for example, at the level of the individual who experiences as well as behaves in the physical environment. At this level, inner experience in the form of perceptions, feelings, values, and underlying motivations assumes considerable significance both in determining the meaning of the environment for the individual and in evoking responses to it. So significant a relationship between environment and behavior is clearly suggested by the papers presented in Part Two and also by some of them in Part One.

An important digression must be made here. It is possible to assume from the name "environmental psychology" that the psychological or individual level of analysis is the primary, if not sole, theoretical orientation of the field. This is not true. What binds the various presentations in this volume together is not concern with the behavior of the individual, but rather with behavior in general, that is, with behavior as it is expressed at all levels of social organization.

The fact is that the individual can never really develop and live in social isolation. His experience is defined by his membership in a variety of face-to-face groups and still larger social units. At this level of analysis one can ask, reflecting the approach of the sociologist and the social psychologist, how normative patterns of behavior and the group structure in which they are embedded influence and are influenced by the physical environment in which social groups exist. Here the unit of analysis is not the experiencing individual, but rather the characteristic pattern—of behavior, values, or standards—that comprises the organized nature of group life. The significance of this approach is implicit, if not explicit, in many of the papers in this and later parts of the book.

There remains a still more encompassing kind of social organization. Groups are organized into even larger social systems that may take the form of a community or even a nation. Here the approach of the sociologist, anthropologist, and political scientist assumes a theoretical role of major importance. How an urban community "lives its life" in terms of intergroup relations, economic productivity, political process, and other institutional activities can be studied in relation to the physical setting of the community and, more particularly, the design of its neighborhoods, parks, recreational areas, and so on. Parts Four and Five present several papers that express this theoretical orientation to problems concerning the relationships between the physical environment and human behavior.

If human behavior in relation to the physical setting can only be understood by analyzing it at all levels of social organization, then from a theoretical point of view there is no physical environment apart from human experience and social organization. The physical environment that man constructs is as much a social phenomenon as it is a physical one. Man's constructed world, whether it is a school, hospital, apartment, community, or highway, is simply a particular expression of the social system that generally determines his activities and his relationships with others. Furthermore, the individual's response to his physical world is never determined solely by the properties of the structures and events that define it. Spaces, their properties, the people in them, and the activities that involve these people represent significant systems for the individual participant and thereby influence his responses to the physical setting. "Crowding," for example, either for the member or the observer of the crowd, is not simply a matter of the density of persons in a given space. For the crowded person, at least, the experience of "being crowded" depends also to some degree on the people crowding him, the activity going on, and his previous experience involving numbers of people in similar situations.

Interdisciplinary theory, in either a single research problem or an entire field of study, is fraught with many difficulties. A single theorist or researcher can seldom embody the concepts, theoretical orientations, and methodological approaches of the various levels and kinds of analysis needed. Problems in environmental psychology are analyzed in accordance with the theorist's definition of the problem. Researchers vary in their fundamental training in and orientation to man-and-environment phenomena, and hence in the problems they define for themselves, in the questions they ask, and in conceptual and methodological orientations they have for answering their questions. To be concerned, for example, with the "loss of privacy" among the inhabitants of an urban ghetto in no way confines an investigator to a particular definition of his problem. Privacy is not merely an individual psychological event. It is also a socio-psychological, economic, sociological, and architectural-design phenomenon related to the organization of groups, institutional practices, and structural and substantive properties of physical settings.

Two things are suggested by this discussion. First, as already noted in the introduction, environmental psychology is an emergent discipline that must evolve as an interdisciplinary superstructure of theoretical constructs and principles rooted in the basic formulations and empirical findings of many separate disciplines. Second, this superstructure can emerge only from the *cooperative* theoretical and empirical endeavors of the researchers representing these various disciplines.

Interdisciplinary cooperation, however, entails its own set of problems that must be overcome before the needed theoretical superstructure can even begin to take shape. Many of the social science disciplines upon which environmental psychology must rest have not themselves established a coherent theoretical structure supported by a firm foundation of empirical findings. It is true that the many methodological and theoretical developments in the fields of psychology, social psychology, anthropology, sociology, economics, and political science during the last two decades have contributed to a vast "explosion of knowledge" in these areas. But as yet there is little evidence that this knowledge is cumulative or capable of being integrated to reveal solutions to social problems in cause-and-effect terms.

Many behavioral concepts employed in the various social sciences have evolved out of research endeavors in limited empirical contexts. To what extent they will be useful for the analysis of problems in environmental psychology remains to be seen. Clearly, additional concepts and refinement and elaboration of existing ones will be needed. Perhaps what is even more striking is the fact that conceptual integration has yet to be achieved even between any two of the existing social science disciplines, for example, between psychology and sociology. Whether such integration is possible while the theorists of each discipline tend to evolve concepts and theories that ignore the problems and conceptions of the others is a question that has already been asked by those interested in achieving an integrated behavioral science (Landau, Proshansky, & Ittelson, 1962).

To ask why the various behavioral science disciplines have not cooperated more touches upon a host of issues that concern the structure of science as a social institution and the professional and organizational consequences of this structure. Apart from these issues, however—and they need not concern us here—it can be said that in terms of the simple requirement for theoretical communication between disciplines, such cooperation is not easily achieved. More is involved than a mere lack of familiarity with conceptual tools and methodological orientations of each discipline with the others. Differences in levels of analysis, styles of formulating concepts and problems, and empirical procedures tend to limit fruitful cooperation between two fields.

For environmental psychology this difficulty is compounded by the fact that its interdisciplinary focus extends beyond the boundaries of the social sciences. For some of its problems it must also rely on concepts and data from the natural sciences, and for others it must embrace the thinking and orientation of the architect, designer, geographer, urban planner, conservationist, and ecologist.

Architects, designers, and urban planners concerned with relationships between the physical environment and behavior have themselves occasionally assumed the mantle of the environmental psychologist. Some of the articles in Part One, for example, show architects and designers embracing a behavioral orientation. But what of the reverse, or more importantly, how do we make use of the architect's and designer's concepts and principles to establish relationships between the physical setting and the behavior of the individual? Their concepts and principles may well be of limited value in understanding how people relate to the physical world—in much the same way that existing conceptual tools for the analysis of individual and group behavior may prove useless for this purpose, or for that matter for the analysis of any complex social problem. It is enough at the moment, however, that the environmental psychologist and the architect and designer stand poised for a cooperative and integrated attack on such problems. How their work will be achieved and what direction it will take are questions that have yet to be answered.

Whatever the difficulties for environmental psychology in establishing a general theoretical framework of its own, there are no shortcuts of "conceptual gimmicks" that will readily resolve these difficulties. But this statement is not meant to be pessimistic. It merely describes what is and has been true in the development of any new field of inquiry, and particularly those whose phenomena must necessarily be defined in interdisciplinary terms. At this juncture—in spite of the ever-increasing pressures of government officials, and administrators seeking solutions to community, educational, and industrial problems—the environmental psychologist can only explore and grope along his way. He needs a level of theory that has meaning for specific but significant empirical events and that allows for the possibility of systematic research with respect to these events. The value of this research will lie not so much in its ability to solve particular problems as in its potential for a mutual correction process: theory provides the basis for understanding facts, and facts in turn have the capacity for modifying theory.

REFERENCE:

Landau, M., Proshansky, H., & Ittelson, W. H. The interdisciplinary approach and the concept of behavioral science. In N. F. Washburne (Ed.), *Decisions, values and groups*. Proceedings of a Conference of the Air Force Office of Scientific Research at the University of New Mexico. New York: Pergamon Press, 1962. Vol. 2. Pp. 7–24.

1 In Search of Theory

A. E. Parr

Since a large part of the input into our minds, from the day we are born, comes from the perception of our environment, it would be entirely illogical to assume that our surroundings do not have a great deal to do with the development of our mental powers, patterns and prowess. The presence and importance of such influences emanating from the milieu is borne out by all evidence available from studies of animals under controlled conditions, from human experiments with artificial sensory deprivations, from psychiatric experience, and from psychological, pedagogic and sociological observations of human behavior. The merits of the work already done are great, but the sum total of precisely defined information is very slight— barely sufficient to warn about the dangers that may lurk in the perceptual habitat, but utterly inadequate to establish usable guidelines for those who design our environments.

The designers, on their part, have contributed to the deficiencies by their failure to live up to the requirements of their oft-declared high purpose of embracing psychological problems, as well as the physical ones, in their efforts to provide for our needs.

From *Arts and Architecture*, Sept. 1965, 82, 14–16. Reprinted by permission of the author and publisher.

These sins of omission seem to stem from a combination of negligence and arrogant assumption that the knowledge needed for the proper environmental care and feeding of men's souls is already at the designer's command by virtue of his intuition. The devotion of modern architects to the study of the physical properties of materials, and of structural features, is well known and universally acknowledged. But it is difficult to find any evidence of equally vigorous encouragement, promotion or sponsorship of investigations into the stresses of the mind that their own designs might create or alleviate. Such matters have been left to artistic conviction without benefit of research, perhaps in a subconscious and mistaken fear that knowledge of the dynamic principles of harmony and pitch might hobble a composer's creative genius.

It is the purpose of the following remarks to attempt to offer some tactical suggestions for a first approach toward the achievement of the over-all aims of our inquiry. It is hoped that the reader will bear in mind that even the sum of all tactical measures can never present the neat, compact and complete intellectual structure of a statement of faith and final intent.

Valid conclusions about the direct influence of the inanimate environment upon human feeling, thought and action demand that very careful distinctions be made between spontaneous and contrived or coerced behavior. As a ridiculously obvious example one may mention the fact that the flow of traffic in a one-way street is no indication of a directional spell cast by architectural configurations. Unfortunately, the situation is only very rarely as simple and evident as this, and very painstaking analysis and controls will often be required.

The scale and complexity of urban existence make it clear from the start that neither field observations nor experiments, alone, will suffice. Both must be combined. It is impossible to evaluate a single factor without control of the others. It is equally impossible to feel sure of having discovered all the factors, and their manifold interactions, without observations on the full scale on which they operate in "real" life.

In order to apply experimental results to the understanding of uncontrived behavior, and in order to design experiments for such purposes, it is necessary to determine the form and dimensions of space in which an individual normally interacts with his environment when not constrained by experimental conditions. Two magnitudes of space are involved.

Territory is the space which a person, as an individual, or as a member of a close-knit group (e.g., family, gang), in joint tenancy, claims as his or their own, and will "defend." There is a considerable literature on territoriality in the animal kingdom, and some, but very far from enough on human territoriality.

Orbit is a term I use to define the much wider concept of the space through which an individual habitually or occasionally roams. The orbit may contain two or more territories (e.g. home, office) in addition to all other space traversed or only irregularly occupied by the individual.

Both territories and orbits have to be analyzed in considerable detail with regard to frequency and duration of tenure or transience in their various sectors, and to the freedom or restraint of the various senses in the perception of the environment. On a path traversed exclusively by automobile, vision offers virtually the only channel of sensory contact with the exterior surroundings, in a situation that is actually very similar to the contrived circumstances of certain experiments in animal psychology. But it would be a reckless oversimplification to

assume that the only distinction that needs to be made would be the separation of transients by car from residents on foot or in rocking chairs.

An investigation of orbits and territories is not merely essential to other studies, it also involves interesting problems and possibilities of its own, of which some may be mentioned here.

Not long ago stores and office buildings were the joint occupants of a central business district in most cities. The wives did an important part of their shopping in the district in which their husbands worked, made their purchases, and had their meals away from home. The orbits of husbands and wives were largely identical, and each was fully acquainted with the territories of the other. The automobile and the suburban shopping center have put an end to this.

Although the rapidly spreading new pattern has been remarked upon by many commentators, quantitative records of the attending behavioral changes seem woefully lacking. Data should be gathered on the age, sex, income level and occupations of the individuals, and on the type, size, and environs of the urban communities in which the orbits of housewives and children are separating more and more from the orbits of husbands, single women, and "working" wives. Comparisons between cities and metropolitan regions now at different stages of technical progress and industrialization might help us to reconstruct the recent past in places where it is already too late to obtain a clear picture from the records. The history of our adjustments to changing circumstances has a momentum of its own, and a comprehension of days gone by may be quite essential for an understanding of times to come.

Included in the new order of things is also the intriguing phenomenon of a reversal of orbits that may be brought about when large business concerns move their offices into remote, rustic isolation, while drawing most of their workers from distantly surrounding towns and cities. Does the work-a-day ambience of green landscapes increase or reduce the appreciation of urban surroundings, and the need for week-end escape? Is there, or is there not, a positive correlation between preference for office work and preference for city living? It is time to find out.

In an entirely free relationship increasing uniformity of surroundings may conceivably affect territory in entirely opposite ways, depending upon circumstances and personality. The individual might roam over a larger territory in search of satisfactions that are more thinly spread through environment, or the reduced awards of venturing might, instead, cause a confinement of activities within a shrinking area. Factual observation of these reactions would be of great practical and theoretical interest, particularly if the data would permit correlation with psychological traits.

In adults the dimensions of territories and orbits are commonly set by practical considerations and do, therefore, not represent unfettered responses to the environment. But in children and animals the behavior is likely to be predominantly impulsive, clearly reflecting their spontaneous reactions to circumstances. A study of the extent of territory in relation to density of perceptual inventory among children and the higher animals would, therefore, be of great interest. A special aspect of this inquiry might also take the form of an analysis of the proportions of their free time that children will voluntarily spend indoors and outdoors in relation to indoor and outdoor perceptual inventories.

Many of the factors involved in environmental psychology will only manifest themselves in circumstances that offer room for experience, response and choice of action on a scale that it would be physically and economically impossible to duplicate under experimental conditions. The refinement and evaluation of cinematic and other techniques for the creation of simulated experiences are, therefore, an essential prerequisite for the conduct of a well-rounded research program. Such methods are already used in testing the psychological aspects of highway design, and for a great variety of investigations which would, incidentally, also advance the evaluation of simulation techniques.

Many subjective and some qualitatively objective claims have been made for the mental and emotional impact of the forms, dimensions and contents of space. These assertions should be tested by actual exposure of adequate samples of individuals to extensive modifications of the interior of the research facility, with and without the introduction of various solid shapes within the inclosure. All the transformations of space and contents should be fully recorded on simulator film for comparison between the reactions of those actually present, and of others who may be made to feel as though they were.

From such general studies to specific inquiries into various aspects of proxemics is only a very short step. For example, by placing people in the reality of progressively reduced space one may observe the syndrome of responses loosely described as claustrophobia. These observations should then be compared with the physiological as well as the conscious reactions to the same series of simulated experiences of space. This might ultimately lead to the development of standardized simulation sequences that might provide a form of quantitative measurement of a person's psychological space requirements. When the basic method has been worked out it will not only be applicable to the assessment of individual idiosyncracies, but will be readily adaptable for the study of culturally or biologically determined general attitudes toward space. For environmental design it will be particularly important to study the effects of the form and the dimensions of space, as separate variables, including a comparison between contraction and obstruction of the void.

The evaluation tests and experiments that can be conducted in contained space will of necessity be limited to a scale that will not allow a direct approach to the more comprehensive problems of environmental design. The next step must, therefore, be a refinement and appraisal of techniques for the creation of simulated experiences of outdoor situations. Perfection of the means of illusion can probably be achieved most rapidly and most economically by concentrating upon the imitation of an outdoor location close at hand, regardless of whether or not the scene offers an interesting subject for other studies. But, as soon as an adequate method of simulation has been obtained, its potentialities and limitations in free application to any situation calling for study must be assessed. Among other lines of inquiry this task might involve a general study of cognitive and affective responses to simulated and to real experiences of actual cities and cityscapes.

An adequate collection of simulator films and other devices representative of city environments of all kinds from all parts of the world should be assembled as quickly as possible, but even the images of a few contrasting urban surroundings would suffice to get a research program on its way. Comparisons should be made of reactions to simulated cityscapes observable in (a) persons entirely unacquainted with the places imitated; (b) persons of the same background having spent some time in the environment shown, including, whenever possible, members of group (a) who may subsequently have visited or moved to the location; and (c) native residents. When distant locations are contrasted (e.g. Tokyo, Milan, London, New York) intercultural as well as intrasocial and personality differences can be examined. When contrasting situations belonging to the same cultural tradition and geographically near each other are available, they offer the advantage of making it possible to include actual visits in the experimental procedure.

Responses to the cityscape also find an easily recorded expression in pedestrian traffic patterns. The driver of a car is always conscious of the forces of momentum and the physical strains created by changes of speed and direction. This awareness acts as a strong inhibitor of free, spontaneous responses to environmental attractions or aversions, even when traffic conditions do not provide other compelling limitations of choice. But this does not apply to the person on foot. Pedestrian traffic patterns are, therefore, much more strongly subject to the free play of personal preferences for, or subconscious reaction to, milieu than are the other aspects of life in the street, and these patterns should be carefully studied and compared with the patterns of variation of perceptual inventories in the surroundings, with due consideration of other variables such as sun and shade and the human herd.

Any experienced traveler knows that the development of fatigue often seems to bear little relationship to the amount of physical exertion, while it is strongly influenced by the stimulating, insipid or enervating qualities of the surroundings. There are cities where we can walk all day without weariness, and others where lethargy sets in after a short stroll. The tiredness we feel at any time is a composite measure of physical toil and psychosomatic fatigue. To the extent that psychosomatic fatigue is a wasteful product of a maladapted perceptual environment it should be a task of environmental design to effect a cure and an elimination of the evil in the cities of our future. But first we must learn more about the phenomenon itself. This ought not to be too difficult.

Groups of people, particularly children, could be taken on separate trips into contrasting surroundings, while their behavior is being closely observed and recorded, with intermittent or continuing instrument tests, and with particular attention being paid to evidence of drowsiness from underactivity or genuine weariness from being overactivated. Each environment should be experienced in several different ways: with the participants enjoying complete pedestrian freedom of action; by exploration on foot but with physical action uniformly and narrowly circumscribed; by leisurely observation from a vehicle; and by simulator techniques.

A special chapter in the study of psychosomatic fatigue might be devoted to an investigation of the psychological effects of the presence of visible obstacles, such as columns, which restrict the abstract freedom of movement without interfering with any concrete, practical need of such freedom. Architectural criticism is full of references to the desirability of entirely imaginary senses of freedom created by the proper manipulation of space, but objective psychological studies of the phenomenon are not referred to. The entire relationship between mental and practical needs for freedom of choice is crying for clarification.

If visible obstructions may produce tension, there is also reason to suspect that landmarks, directional topographic design, and redundancies in the perceptual inventory of our surroundings, may have relaxing and reassuring properties. But the claims made for the faults or merits of such features are not backed by sufficient, and sufficiently objective, research. More precise knowledge is needed for practical application to environmental design.

There are indications that a diminishing perceptual inventory causes a majority of people to increase their speed of movement, whether on foot or by car. But the phenomenon has not yet been sufficiently explored to produce results that can be taken into consideration in planning our milieu. Personality differences between the accelerating majority and the unaffected or decelerating minority should be looked into. By gathering enough data to establish, at least, a quasi-quantitative understanding of the relationship between inventory and locomotor response, we would also lay the foundations for a much-needed method of measuring perceptual inventory by spectator reaction.

To one who has sat in the driver's seat through a highway simulator test it seems clear that our subconscious is completely persuaded by the counterfeit experience. It takes considerable effort of will for reason to regain control over our emotional responses and physical reflexes, while the "show" is still on. This gives reason to hope that a subject placed in a similar device for feigned exploration of cityscapes and interiors—at pedestrian as well as vehicular speeds, controlled by the observer's own foot or feet—will react spontaneously to the psychological abundance or shortages of the unfolding visual inventories. If this hope is well founded, the relationship between contents and projection-speed of the simulator film would provide data that could be used both for the assessment of environmental design and of personality traits.

The procedure suggested in the foregoing paragraph might also become one of the means of investigating the relationship between speed of locomotion and mode of esthetic appreciation and recall. At a pedestrian rate of progress, the inanimate environment is seen, remembered and enjoyed or deplored as a sequence of static forms. With increasing speed of movement there is an increasing awareness of changes in perspectives as a continuous process, performing a choreography in which the movement itself becomes a recognizable element of form. Experiments could be made to compare the

ability to recognize scenes repeated or imitated by still projection, and by projection pretending to different velocities of spectator movement, in relation to the haste or tardiness of personal progress during previous exposure to the same surroundings. Possible changes in the esthetic ratings of environmental configurations according to celerity of passage should also be looked into.

Research in animal behavior has revealed a positive relationship between mental performance and perceptual diversity of milieu. In man, only short-term experiments with reversible effects are permissible. But it would seem well worth investigating whether school records and other sociological data show any correlation with the perceptual paucity or abundance of home and territory. Conversely, inquiries should be made into the frequency of erratic and unpredictable behavior among both animals and man in increasingly homogeneous and predictable surroundings. Excursions with children at relatively spontaneous age levels might offer useful information, along with observations on behavior in enclosed and controlled space. It has been postulated that growing perceptual monotony of the urban milieu may contribute to the rise of juvenile delinquency. General statistics and case histories should give evidence upon this possibility.

When we consider the modern simplification of forms and surfaces, the omission or removal of applied ornamentations, of exterior stairways, railings and other features that used to be commonplace, we realize that the eye level of the viewer makes less and less difference in the appearance of the view. It seems natural to wonder what effects, if any, this progressive elimination of visual clues to growing up may have upon the minds and personalities of succeeding generations.

Architectural adjustments to climate are almost universally treated as though they involved only the simple and obvious physical problems of heat, light, shade, insulation and air conditioning. Nevertheless, it seems beyond dispute that the perceptual image of a building has a lot to do with the sense of well-being it may generate. Houses and cityscapes that look cool and inviting during the hot summer, may look chilly and forbidding in winter, adding to the psychological discomforts of the cold season. The basic assumption is, of course, generally accepted and equally generally disregarded. The region around the Great Lakes, and especially around Lake Michigan, is particularly rich in striking, and often highly esteemed, examples of architectural disregard for the psychological effects of extreme seasonal ranges of climatic conditions. Responses to simulated and actual architecture and cityscapes should be obtained at different times of the year, and under different temperature and weather conditions. From such observations it should be possible to gain a rational approach to the problems of climate and environmental design.

Other things permitting, the individual will choose his surroundings according to the preferences and demands of his own personality. When he exercises his choice, there will unavoidably be a feed-back from his selection to the psychological mechanism that made it. This implies a two-way relationship between mind and milieu in which the environment might well prove to be a determinant, as well as a product, of attitude and personality. A comparative study of applicants, day students, dormitory students, and graduates of romantically or functionally designed colleges, in sylvan, small-town, suburban, or metropolitan precincts, should be extremely interesting. But this is only one example of numerous special situations that invite research on the problems of environment and character formation.

2 The Anthropology of Space: An Organizing Model

Edward T. Hall

The term proxemics is used to define the interrelated observations and theories of man's use of space. His use of space, however, can only be understood in terms of a

This selection is a slightly condensed version of Chapters 9 and 10 from *The Hidden Dimension* by Edward T. Hall. Copyright © 1966 by Edward T. Hall. Reprinted by permission of Doubleday & Company, Inc.

multilevel analysis of its manifestations and related determinants. Thus, *infraculture* applies to behavior on lower organizational levels that underlies culture and is rooted in man's biological past. It is a part of the proxemic classification system and implies a specific set of levels of relationships with other parts of the system. A second proxemic manifestation, the *precultural*, refers to the physiological base shared by all human beings, to which culture gives structure and meaning, and to which the scientist must inevitably refer in comparing the proxemic patterns of Culture A with those of Culture B. The *pre*cultural is very much in the present. The third, the *micro*cultural level, is the one on which most proxemic observations are made. Proxemics as a manifestation of microculture has three aspects: fixed-feature, semifixed-feature, and informal.

FIXED-FEATURE SPACE

Fixed-feature space is one of the basic ways of organizing the activities of individuals and groups. It includes material manifestations as well as the hidden, internalized designs that govern behavior as man moves about on this earth. Buildings are one expression of fixed-feature patterns, but buildings are also grouped together in characteristic ways as well as being divided internally according to culturally determined designs. The layout of villages, towns, cities, and the intervening countryside is not haphazard but follows a plan which changes with time and culture.

Even the inside of the Western house is organized spatially. Not only are there special rooms for special functions—food preparation, eating, entertaining and socializing, rest, recuperation, and procreation—but for sanitation as well. *If*, as sometimes happens, either the artifacts or the activities associated with one space are transferred to another space, this fact is immediately apparent. People who "live in a mess" or a "constant state of confusion" are those who fail to classify activities and artifacts according to a uniform, consistent, or predictable spatial plan. At the opposite end of the scale is the assembly line, a precise organization of objects in *time* and *space*.

Actually the present internal layout of the house, which Americans and Europeans take for granted, is quite recent. As Philippe Ariès (1962) points out in *Centuries of Childhood*, rooms had no fixed functions in European houses until the eighteenth century. Members of the family had no privacy as we know it today. There were no spaces that were sacred or specialized. Strangers came and went at will, while beds and tables were set up and taken down according to the moods and appetites of the occupants. Children dressed and were treated as small adults. It is no wonder that the concept of childhood and its associated concept, the nuclear family, had to await the specialization of rooms according to function and the separation of rooms from each other. In the eighteenth century, the house altered its form. In French, *chambre* was distinguished from *salle*. In English, the function of a room was indicated by its name—bedroom, living room, dining room. Rooms were arranged to open into a corridor or hall, like houses into a street. No longer did the occupants pass through one room into another. Relieved of the Grand Central Station atmosphere and protected by new spaces, the family pattern began to stabilize and was expressed further in the form of the house.

Goffman's *Presentation of Self in Everyday Life* (1959) is a detailed, sensitive record of observations on the relationship of the façade that people present to the world and the self they hide behind it. The use of the term façade is in itself revealing. It signifies recognition of levels to be penetrated and hints at the functions performed by architectural features which provide screens behind which to retire from time to time. The strain of keeping up a façade can be great. Architecture can and does take over this burden for people. It can also provide a refuge where the individual can "let his hair down" and be himself.

The fact that so few businessmen have offices in their homes cannot be solely explained on the basis of convention and top management's uneasiness when executives are not visibly present. I have observed that many men have two or more distinct personalities, one for business and one for the home. The separation of office and home in these instances helps to keep the two often incompatible personalities from conflicting

and may even serve to stabilize an idealized version of each which conforms to the projected image of both architecture and setting.

The relationship of fixed-feature space to personality as well as to culture is nowhere more apparent than in the kitchen. When micro-patterns interfere as they do in the kitchen, it is more than just annoying to the women I interviewed. My wife, who has struggled for years with kitchens of all types, comments on male design in this way: "If any of the men who designed this kitchen had ever worked in it, they wouldn't have done it this way." The lack of congruence between the design elements, female stature and body build (women are not usually tall enough to reach things), and the activities to be performed, while not obvious at first, is often beyond belief. The size, the shape, the arrangement, and the placing in the house all communicate to the women of the house how much or how little the architect and designer knew about fixed-feature details.

Man's feeling about being properly oriented in space runs deep. Such knowledge is ultimately linked to survival and sanity. To be disoriented in space is to be psychotic. The difference between acting with reflex speed and having to stop to think in an emergency may mean the difference between life and death—a rule which applies equally to the driver negotiating freeway traffic and the rodent dodging predators. Lewis Mumford (1961) observes that the uniform grid pattern of our cities "makes strangers as much at home as the oldest inhabitants." Americans who have become dependent on this pattern are often frustrated by anything different. It is difficult for them to feel at home in European capitals that don't conform to this simple plan. Those who travel and live abroad frequently get lost. An interesting feature of these complaints reveals the relationship of the layout to the person. Almost without exception, the newcomer uses words and tones associated with a personal affront, as though the town held something against him. It is no wonder that people brought up on either the French radiating star or the Roman grid have difficulty in a place like Japan where the entire fixed-feature pattern is basically and radically different. In fact, if one were to set out to design two systems in contrasts, it is hard to see how one could do better. The European systems stress the lines, which they name; the Japanese treat the intersecting points technically and forget about the lines. In Japan, the intersections but not the streets are named. Houses instead of being related in space are related in time and numbered in the order in which they are built. The Japanese pattern emphasizes hierarchies that grow around centers; the American plan finds its ultimate development in the sameness of suburbia, because one number along a line is the same as any other. In a Japanese neighborhood, the first house built is a constant reminder to the residents of house #20 that #1 was there first.

Some aspects of fixed-feature space are not visible until one observes human behavior. For example, although the separate dining room is fast vanishing from American houses, the line separating the dining area from the rest of the living room is quite real. The invisible boundary which separates one yard from another in suburbia is also a fixed-feature of American culture or at least some of its subcultures.

Architects traditionally are preoccupied with the visual patterns of structures—what one sees. They are almost totally unaware of the fact that people carry around with them internalizations of fixed-feature space learned early in life. It isn't only the Arab who feels depressed unless he has enough space but many Americans as well. As one of my subjects said: "I can put up with almost anything as long as I have large rooms and high ceilings. You see, I was raised in an old house in Brooklyn and I have never been able to accustom myself to anything different."

The important point about fixed-feature space is that it is the mold into which a great deal of behavior is cast. It was this feature of space that the late Sir Winston Churchill referred to when he said: "We shape our buildings and they shape us." During the debate on restoring the House of Commons after the war, Churchill feared that departure from the intimate spatial pattern of the House, where opponents face each other across a narrow aisle, would seriously alter the patterns of government. He may not have been the first to put his finger on the influence of fixed-feature space, but its effects have never been so succinctly stated.

One of the many basic differences between cultures is that they extend different anatomical and behavioral features of the human organism. Whenever there is cross-cultural borrowing, the borrowed items have to be adapted. Otherwise, the new and the old do not match, and in some instances, the two patterns are completely contradictory. For example, Japan has had problems integrating the automobile into a culture in which the lines between points (highways) receive less attention than the points. Hence, Tokyo is famous for producing some of the world's most impressive traffic jams. The automobile is also poorly adapted to India, where cities are physically crowded and the society has elaborate hierarchical features. Unless Indian engineers can design roads that will separate slow pedestrians from fast-moving vehicles, the class-conscious drivers' lack of consideration for the poor will continue to breed disaster. Even Le Corbusier's great buildings at Chandigarh, capital of Punjab, had to be modified by the residents to make them habitable. The Indians walled up Corbusier's balconies, converting them into kitchens! Similarly, Arabs coming to the United States find that their own internalized fixed-feature patterns do not fit American housing. Arabs feel oppressed by it—the ceilings are too low, the rooms too small, privacy from the outside inadequate, and views non-existent.

It should not be thought, however, that incongruity between internalized and externalized patterns occurs only between cultures. As our own technology explodes, air conditioning, fluorescent lighting, and soundproofing make it possible to design houses and offices without regard to traditional patterns of windows and doors. The new inventions sometimes result in great barnlike rooms where the "territory" of scores of employees in a "bull pen" is ambiguous.

SEMIFIXED-FEATURE SPACE

Several years ago, a talented and perceptive physician named Humphry Osmond was asked to direct a large health and research center in Saskatchewan. His hospital was one of the first in which the relationship between semifixed-feature space and behavior was clearly demonstrated. Osmond had noticed that some spaces, like railway waiting rooms, tend to keep people apart. These he called sociofugal spaces. Others, such as the booths in the old-fashioned drugstore or the tables at a French sidewalk café, tend to bring people together. These he called sociopetal (1957). The hospital of which he was in charge was replete with sociofugal spaces and had very few which might be called sociopetal. Furthermore, the custodial staff and nurses tended to prefer the former to the latter because they were easier to maintain. Chairs in the halls, which would be found in little circles after visiting hours, would soon be lined up neatly in military fashion, in rows along the walls.

One situation which attracted Osmond's attention was the newly built "model" female geriatrics ward. Everything was new and shiny, neat and clean. There was enough space, and the colors were cheerful. The only trouble was that the longer the patients stayed in the ward, the less they seemed to talk to each other. Gradually, they were becoming like the furniture, permanently and silently glued to the walls at regular intervals between the beds. In addition, they all seemed depressed.

Sensing that the space was more sociofugal than sociopetal, Osmond put a perceptive young psychologist, Robert Sommer, to work to find out as much as he could about the relationship of furniture to conversations. Looking for a natural setting which offered a number of different situations in which people could be observed in conversations, Sommer selected the hospital cafeteria, where 36 by 72-inch tables accommodated six people (1959). As Figure 2-1 indicates, these tables provided six different distances and orientations of the bodies in relation to each other. Fifty observational sessions in which conversations were counted at controlled intervals revealed that: *F–A* (cross corner) conversations were twice as frequent as the *C–B* (side by side) type, which in turn were three times as frequent as those at *C–D* (across the table). No conversations were observed by Sommer for the other positions. ... other words, corner situa-

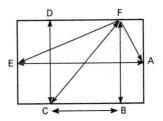

Figure 2–1. F–A, across the corner; C–B, side by side; C–D, across the table; E–A, from one end to the other; E–F, diagonally the length of the table; C–F, diagonally across the table.

tions with people at right angles to each other produced six times as many conversations as face-to-face situations across the 36-inch span of the table, and twice as many as the side-by-side arrangement.

The results of these observations suggested a solution to the problem of gradual disengagement and withdrawal of the old people. Both Osmond and Sommer had noted that the ward patients were more often in the *B–C* and *C–D* relationships (side by side and across) than they were in the cafeteria, and they sat at much greater distances. In addition, there was no place to put anything, no place for personal belongings. The only territorial features associated with the patients were the bed and the chair. As a consequence, magazines ended up on the floor and were quickly swept up by staff members. Enough small tables so that every patient had a place would provide additional territoriality and an opportunity to keep magazines, books, and writing materials. If the tables were square, they would also help to structure relationships between patients so that there was a maximum opportunity to converse.

The small tables were moved in and the chairs arranged around them. At first, the patients resisted. They had become accustomed to the placement of "their" chairs in particular spots, and they did not take easily to being moved around by others. The staff kept the new arrangement reasonably intact until it was established as an alternative rather than an annoying feature to be selectively inattended. When this point had been reached, a repeat count of conversations was made. The number of conversations had doubled, while reading had tripled, possibly because there was now a place to keep reading material. Similar restructuring of the dayroom met with the same resistances and the same ultimate increase in verbal interaction.

At this point, three things must be said. Conclusions drawn from observations made in the hospital situation just described are not universally applicable. That is, across-the-corner-at-right-angles is conducive *only* to: (a) conversations of certain types between (b) persons in certain relationships and (c) in very restricted cultural settings. Second, what is sociofugal in one culture may be sociopetal in another. Third, sociofugal space is not necessarily bad, nor is sociopetal space universally good. What *is* desirable is flexibility and congruence between design and function so that there is a variety of spaces, and people can be involved or not, as the occasion and mood demand. The main point of the Canadian experiment for us is its demonstration that the structuring of semifixed features can have a profound effect on behavior and that this effect is measurable. This will come as no surprise to housewives who are constantly trying to balance the relationship of fixed-feature enclosures to arrangement of their semifixed furniture. Many have had the experience of getting a room nicely arranged, only to find that conversation was impossible if the chairs were left nicely arranged.

It should be noted that what is fixed-feature space in one culture may be semifixed in another, and vice versa. In Japan, for example, the walls are movable, opening and closing as the day's activities change. In the United States, people move from room to room or from one part of a room to another for each different activity, such as eating, sleeping, working, or socializing with relatives. In Japan, it is quite common for the person to remain in one spot while the activities change. The Chinese provide us with further opportunities to observe the diversity of human treatment of space, for they assign to the fixed-feature category certain items which Americans treat as semifixed. Apparently, a guest in a Chinese home *does not move his chair* except at the host's suggestion. To do so would be like going into someone else's home and moving a screen or even a partition. In this sense, the semifixed

nature of furniture in American homes is merely a matter of degree and situation. Light chairs are more mobile than sofas or heavy tables. I have noted, however, that some Americans hesitate to adjust furniture in another person's house or office. Of the forty students in one of my classes, half manifested such hesitation.

Many American women know it is hard to find things in someone else's kitchen. Conversely, it can be exasperating to have kitchenware put away by well-meaning helpers who don't know where things "belong." How and where belongings are arranged and stored is a function of microcultural patterns, representative not only of large cultural groups but of the minute variations on cultures that make each individual unique. Just as variations in the quality and use of the voice make it possible to distinguish one person's voice from another, handling of materials also has a characteristic pattern that is unique.

INFORMAL SPACE

We turn now to the category of spatial experience, which is perhaps most significant for the individual because it includes the distances maintained in encounters with others. These distances are for the most part outside awareness. I have called this category *informal space* because it is unstated, not because it lacks form or has no importance. Indeed informal spatial patterns have distinct bounds, and such deep, if unvoiced, significance that they form an essential part of the culture. To misunderstand this significance may invite disaster.

Birds and mammals not only have territories which they occupy and defend against their own kind but they have a series of uniform distances which they maintain from each other. Hediger (1955) has classified these as flight distance, critical distance, and personal and social distance. Man, too, has a uniform way of handling distance from his fellows. With very few exceptions, flight distance and critical distance have been eliminated from human reactions. Personal distance and social distance, however, are obviously still present.

How many distances do human beings have and how do we distinguish them? What is it that differentiates one distance from the other? The answer to this question was not obvious at first when I began my investigation of distances in man. Gradually, however, evidence began to accumulate indicating that the regularity of distances observed for humans is the consequence of sensory shifts.

One common source of information about the distance separating two people is the loudness of the voice. Working with the linguistic scientist George Trager, I began by observing shifts in the voice associated with changes in distance. Since the whisper is used when people are very close, and the shout is used to span great distances, the question Trager and I posed was, How many vocal shifts are sandwiched between these two extremes? Our procedure for discovering these patterns was for Trager to stand still while I talked to him at different distances. If both of us agreed that a vocal shift had occurred, we would then measure the distance and note down a general description. The result was the eight distances described in *The Silent Language* (1959).

Further observation of human beings in social situations convinced me that these eight distances were overly complex. Four were sufficient; these I have termed intimate, personal, social, and public (each with its close and far phase). My choice of terms to describe various distances was deliberate. Not only was it influenced by Hediger's work with animals (1955) indicating the continuity between *infra*culture and culture but also by a desire to provide a clue as to the types of activities and relationships associated with each distance, thereby linking them in peoples' minds with specific inventories of relationships and activities. It should be noted at this point that *how people are feeling toward each other* at the time is a decisive factor in the distance used. Thus people who are very angry or emphatic about the point they are making will move in close, they "turn up the volume," as it were, by shouting. Similarly—as any woman knows—one of the first signs that a man is beginning to feel amorous is his move closer to her. If the woman does not feel similarly disposed she signals this by moving back.

The following descriptions of the four distance zones have been compiled from observations and interviews with non-contact, middle-class, healthy adults, mainly natives of the northeastern seaboard of the United States. A high percentage of the subjects were men and women from business and the professions; many could be classified as intellectuals. The interviews were effectively neutral; that is, the subjects were not noticeably excited, depressed, or angry. There were no unusual environmental factors, such as extremes of temperature or noise. These descriptions represent only a first approximation. They will doubtless seem crude when more is known about proxemic observation and how people distinguish one distance from another. It should be emphasized that these generalizations are not representative of human behavior in general—or even of American behavior in general—but only of the group included in the sample. Negroes and Spanish Americans as well as persons who come from southern European cultures have very different proxemic patterns.

Each of the four distance zones described below has a near and a far phase. It should be noted that the measured distances vary somewhat with differences in personality and environmental factors. For example, a high noise level or low illumination will ordinarily bring people closer together.

INTIMATE DISTANCE

At intimate distance, the presence of the other person is unmistakable and may at times be overwhelming because of the greatly stepped-up sensory inputs. Sight (often distorted), olfaction, heat from the other person's body, sound, smell, and feel of the breath all combine to signal unmistakable involvement with another body.

Intimate Distance—Close Phase. This is the distance of love-making and wrestling, comforting and protecting. Physical contact or the high possibility of physical involvement is uppermost in the awareness of both persons. The use of their distance receptors is greatly reduced except for olfaction and sensation of radiant heat, both of which are stepped up. In the maximum contact phase, the muscles and skin communicate. Pelvis, thighs, and head can be brought into play; arms can encircle. Except at the outer limits, sharp vision is blurred. When close vision is possible within the intimate range—as with children—the image is greatly enlarged and stimulates much, if not all, of the retina. The detail that can be seen at this distance is extraordinary. This detail plus the cross-eyed pull of the eye muscles provide a visual experience that cannot be confused with any other distance. Vocalization at intimate distance plays a very minor part in the communication process, which is carried mainly by other channels. A whisper has the effect of expanding the distance. The vocalizations that do occur are largely involuntary.

Intimate Distance—Far Phase (distance: six to eighteen inches). Heads, thighs, and pelvis are not easily brought into contact, but hands can reach and grasp extremities. The head is seen as enlarged in size, and its features are distorted. Ability to focus the eye easily is an important feature of this distance for Americans. The iris of the other person's eye seen at about six to nine inches is enlarged to more than life-size. Small blood vessels in the sclera are clearly perceived, pores are enlarged. Clear vision (15 degrees) includes the upper or lower portion of the face, which is perceived as enlarged. The nose is seen as over-large and may look distorted, as will other features such as lips, teeth, and tongue. Peripheral vision (30 to 180 degrees) includes the outline of head and shoulders and very often the hands.

Much of the physical discomfort that Americans experience when foreigners are inappropriately inside the intimate sphere is expressed as a distortion of the visual system. One subject said, "These people get so close, you're cross-eyed. It really makes me nervous. They put their face so close it feels like they're *inside you*." At the point where sharp focus is lost, one feels the uncomfortable muscular sensation of being cross-eyed from looking at something too close. The expressions "Get your face *out* of mine" and "He shook his fist *in* my face" apparently express how many Americans perceive their body boundaries.

At six to eighteen inches the voice is used but is normally held at a very low level or even a whisper. As Martin Joos (1962), the linguist, describes it, "An intimate utterance

pointedly avoids giving the addressee information from outside of the speaker's skin. The point . . . is simply to remind (hardly 'inform') the addressee of some feeling . . . inside the speaker's skin." The heat and odor of the other person's breath may be detected, even though it is directed away from subject's face. Heat loss or gain from other person's body begins to be noticed by some subjects.

The use of intimate distance in public is not considered proper by adult, middle-class Americans even though their young may be observed intimately involved with each other in automobiles and on beaches. Crowded subways and buses may bring strangers into what would ordinarily be classed as intimate spatial relations, but subway riders have defensive devices which take the real intimacy out of intimate space in public conveyances. The basic tactic is to be as immobile as possible and, when part of the trunk or extremities touches another person, withdraw if possible. If this is not possible, the muscles in the affected areas are kept tense. For members of the non-contact group, it is taboo to relax and enjoy bodily contact with strangers! In crowded elevators the hands are kept at the side or used to steady the body by grasping a railing. The eyes are fixed on infinity and are not brought to bear on anyone for more than a passing glance.

It should be noted once more that American proxemic patterns for intimate distance are by no means universal. Even the rules governing such intimacies as touching others cannot be counted on to remain constant. Americans who have had an opportunity for considerable social interaction with Russians report that many of the features characteristic of American intimate distance are present in Russian social distance. However, Middle Eastern subjects in public places do not express the outraged reaction to being touched by strangers which one encounters in American subjects.

PERSONAL DISTANCE

"Personal distance" is the term originally used by Hediger (1955) to designate the distance consistently separating the members of non-contact species. It might be thought of as a small protective sphere or bubble that an organism maintains between itself and others.

Personal Distance—Close Phase (distance: one and a half to two and a half feet). The kinesthetic sense of closeness derives in part from the possibilities present in regard to what each participant can do to the other with his extremities. At this distance, one can hold or grasp the other person. Visual distortion of the other's features is no longer apparent. However, there is noticeable feedback from the muscles that control the eyes. The reader can experience this himself if he will look at an object eighteen inches to three feet away, paying particular attention to the muscles around his eyeballs. He can feel the pull of these muscles as they hold the two eyes on a single point so that the image of each eye stays in register. Pushing gently with the tip of the finger on the surface of the lower eyelid so that the eyeball is displaced will illustrate clearly the work these muscles perform in maintaining a single coherent image. A visual angle of 15 degrees takes in another person's upper or lower face, which is seen with exceptional clarity. The planes and roundness of the face are accentuated; the nose projects and the ears recede; fine hair of the face, eyelashes, and pores is clearly visible. The three-dimensional quality of objects is particularly pronounced. Objects have roundness, substance, and form unlike that perceived at any other distance. Surface textures are also very prominent and are clearly differentiated from each other. Where people stand in relation to each other signals their relationship, or how they feel toward each other, or both. A wife can stay inside the circle of her husband's close personal zone with impunity. For another woman to do so is an entirely different story.

Personal Distance—Far Phase (distance: two and a half to four feet). Keeping someone at "arm's length" is one way of expressing the far phase of personal distance. It extends from a point that is just outside easy touching distance by one person to a point where two people can touch fingers if they extend both arms. This is the limit of physi-cal domination in the very real sense. Beyond it, a person cannot easily "get his hands on" someone else. Subjects of personal interest and involvement can be discussed at this distance. Head size is perceived as normal and details of the other person's features are clearly visible. Also easily seen are fine details of skin, gray hair, "sleep" in the eye, stains on teeth, spots, small wrinkles, or dirt on clothing. Foveal vision covers only an area the size of the tip of the nose or one eye, so that the gaze must wander around the face (*where the eye is directed* is strictly a matter of cultural conditioning). Fifteen-degree clear vision covers the upper *or* lower face, while 180-degree peripheral vision takes in the hands and the whole body of a seated person. Movement of the hands is detected, but fingers can't be counted. The voice level is moderate. No body heat is perceptible. While olfaction is not normally present for Americans, it is for a great many other people who use colognes to create an olfactory bubble. Breath odor can sometimes be detected at this distance, but Americans are generally trained to direct the breath away from others.

SOCIAL DISTANCE

The boundary line between the far phase of personal distance and the close phase of social distance marks, in the words of one subject, the "limit of domination." Intimate visual detail in the face is not perceived, and nobody touches or expects to touch another person unless there is some special effort. Voice level is normal for Americans. There is little change between the far and close phases, and conversations can be overheard at a distance of up to twenty feet. I have observed that in overall loudness, the American voice at these distances is below that of the Arab, the Spaniard, the South Asian Indian, and the Russian, and somewhat above that of the English upper class, the Southeast Asian, and the Japanese.

Social Distance—Close Phase (distance: four to seven feet). Head size is perceived as normal; as one moves away from the subject, the foveal area of the eye can take in an ever-increasing amount of the person. At four feet, a one-degree visual angle covers an area of a little more than one eye. At seven feet the area of sharp focus extends to the nose and parts of both eyes; or the whole mouth, one eye, and the nose are sharply seen. Many Americans shift their gaze back and forth from eye to eye or from eyes to mouth. Details of skin texture and hair are clearly perceived. At a 60-degree visual angle, the head, shoulders, and upper trunk are seen at a distance of four feet; while the same sweep includes the whole figure at seven feet.

Impersonal business occurs at this distance, and in the close phase there is more involvement than in the distant phase. People who work together tend to use close social distance. It is also a very common distance for people who are attending a casual social gathering. To stand and look down at a person at this distance has a domineering effect, as when a man talks to his secretary or receptionist.

Social Distance—Far Phase (distance: seven to twelve feet). This is the distance to which people move when someone says, "Stand away so I can look at you." Business and social discourse conducted at the far end of social distance has a more formal character than if it occurs inside the close phase. Desks in the offices of important people are large enough to hold visitors at the far phase of social distance. Even in an office with standard-size desks, the chair opposite is eight or nine feet away from the man behind the desk. At the far phase of social distance, the finest details of the face, such as the capillaries in the eyes, are lost. Otherwise, skin texture, hair, condition of teeth, and condition of clothes are all readily visible. None of my subjects mentioned heat or odor from another person's body as detectable at this distance. The full figure—with a good deal of space around it—is encompassed in a 60-degree glance. Also, at around twelve feet, feedback from the eye muscles used to hold the eyes inward on a single spot falls off rapidly. The eyes and the mouth of the other person are seen in the area of sharpest vision. Hence, it is not necessary to shift the eyes to take in the whole face. During conversations of any significant length it is more important to maintain visual contact at this distance than it is at closer distances.

Proxemic behavior of this sort is culturally conditioned and entirely arbitrary. It is also binding on all concerned. To fail to hold the other person's eye is to shut him out and bring conversation to a halt, which is why people who are conversing at this distance can be observed craning their necks and leaning from side to side to avoid intervening obstacles. Similarly, when one person is seated and the other is standing, prolonged visual contact at less than ten or twelve feet tires the neck muscles and is generally avoided by subordinates who are sensitive to their employer's comfort. If, however, the status of the two parties is reversed so that the subordinate is seated, the other party may often come closer.

At this distant phase, the voice level is noticeably louder than for the close phase, and it can usually be heard easily in an adjoining room if the door is open. Raising the voice or shouting can have the effect of reducing social distance to personal distance.

A proxemic feature of social distance (far phase) is that it can be used to insulate or screen people from each other. This distance makes it possible for them to continue to work in the presence of another person without appearing to be rude. Receptionists in offices are particularly vulnerable as most employers expect double duty: answering questions, being polite to callers, as well as typing. If the receptionist is less than ten feet from another person, even a stranger, she will be sufficiently involved to be virtually compelled to converse. If she has more space, however, she can work quite freely without having to talk. Likewise, husbands returning from work often find themselves sitting and relaxing, reading the paper at ten or more feet from their wives, for at this distance a couple can engage each other briefly and disengage at will. Some men discover that their wives have arranged the furniture back-to-back—a favorite sociofugal device of the cartoonist Chick Young, creator of "Blondie." The back-to-back seating arrangement is an appropriate solution to minimum space because it is possible for two people to stay uninvolved if that is their desire.

PUBLIC DISTANCE

Several important sensory shifts occur in the transition from the personal and social distances to public distance, which is well outside the circle of involvement.

Public Distance—Close Phase (distance: twelve to twenty-five feet). At twelve feet an alert subject can take evasive or defensive action if threatened. The distance may even cue a vestigial but subliminal form of flight reaction. The voice is loud but not full-volume. Linguists have observed that a careful choice of words and phrasing of sentences as well as grammatical or syntactic shifts occur at this distance. Martin Joos's choice of the term "formal style" is appropriately descriptive: "Formal texts . . . demand advance planning . . . the speaker is correctly said to think on his feet" (1962). The angle of sharpest vision (one degree) covers the whole face. Fine details of the skin and eyes are no longer visible. At sixteen feet, the body begins to lose its roundness and to look flat. The color of the eyes begins to be imperceivable; only the white of the eye is visible. Head size is perceived as considerably under life-size. The 15-degree lozenge-shaped area of clear vision covers the faces of two people at twelve feet, while 60-degree scanning includes the whole body with a little space around it. Other persons present can be seen peripherally.

Public Distance—Far Phase (distance: twenty-five feet or more). Thirty feet is the distance that is automatically set around important public figures. An excellent example occurs in Theodore H. White's *The Making of the President 1960* when John F. Kennedy's nomination became a certainty. White is describing the group at the "hideaway cottage" as Kennedy entered:

> Kennedy loped into the cottage with his light, dancing step, as young and lithe as springtime, and called a greeting to those who stood in his way. Then he seemed to slip from them as he descended the steps of the split-level cottage to a corner where his brother Bobby and brother-in-law Sargent Shriver were chat-

ting, waiting for him. The others in the room surged forward on impulse to join him. Then they halted. A distance of perhaps 30 feet separated them from him, but it was impassable. They stood apart, these older men of long-established power, and watched him. He turned after a few minutes, saw them watching him, and whispered to his brother-in-law. Shriver now crossed the separating space to invite them over. First Averell Harriman; then Dick Daley; then Mike DiSalle, then, one by one, let them all congratulate him. Yet no one could pass the little open distance between him and them uninvited, because there was this thin separation about him, and the knowledge they were there not as his patrons but as his clients. They could come by invitation only, for this might be a President of the United States (1961, p. 171).

The usual public distance is not restricted to public figures but can be used by anyone on public occasions. There are certain adjustments that must be made, however. Most actors know that at thirty or more feet the subtle shades of meaning conveyed by the normal voice are lost as are the details of facial expression and movement. Not only the voice but everything else must be exaggerated or amplified. Much of the nonverbal part of the communication shifts to gestures and body stance. In addition, the tempo of the voice drops, words are enunciated more clearly, and there are stylistic changes as well. Martin Joos's *frozen style* is characteristic: "Frozen style is for people who are to remain strangers" (1962). The whole man may be seen as quite small and he is perceived in a setting. Foveal vision takes in more and more of the man until he is entirely within the small circle of sharpest vision. At which point—when people look like ants—contact with them as human beings fades rapidly. The 60-degree cone of vision takes in the setting while peripheral vision has as its principal function the altering of the individual to movement at the side.

WHY "FOUR" DISTANCES?

In concluding this description of distance zones common to our sample group of Americans a final word about classification is in order. It may well be asked: Why are there four zones, not six or eight? Why set up any zones at all? How do we know that this classification is appropriate? How were the categories chosen?

The scientist has a basic need for a classification system, one that is as consistent as possible with the phenomena under observation and one which will hold up long enough to be useful. Behind every classification system lies a theory or hypothesis about the nature of the data and their basic patterns of organization. The hypothesis behind the proxemic classification system is this: it is in the nature of animals, including man, to exhibit behavior which we call territoriality. In so doing, they use the senses to distinguish between one space or distance and another. The specific distance chosen depends on the transaction; the relationship of the interacting individuals, how they feel, and what they are doing. The four-part classification system used here is based on observations of both animals and men. Birds and apes exhibit intimate, personal, and social distances just as man does.

Western man has combined consultative and social activities and relationships into one distance set and has added the public figure and the public relationship. "Public" relations and "public" manners as the Europeans and Americans practice them are different from those in other parts of the world. There are implicit obligations to treat total strangers in certain prescribed ways. Hence, we find four principal categories of relationships (intimate, personal, social, and public) and the activities and spaces associated with them. In other parts of the world, relationships tend to fall into other patterns, such as the family/non-family pattern common in Spain and Portugal and their former colonies or the caste and outcast system of India. Both the Arabs and the Jews also make sharp distinctions between people to whom they are related and those to whom they are not. My work with Arabs leads me to believe that they employ a system for the organization of informal space which is very different from what I observed in the United States. The relationship of the Arab peasant or fellah to his sheik or to God is not a public relationship. It is close and personal without intermediaries.

Until recently man's space requirements were thought of in terms of the actual amount of air displaced by his body. The fact that man has around him as extensions of his personality the zones described earlier has generally been overlooked. Differences in the zones—in fact their very existence—became apparent only when Americans began interacting with foreigners who organize their senses differently so that what was intimate in one culture might be personal or even public in another. Thus for the first time the American became aware of his own spatial envelopes, which he had previously taken for granted.

The ability to recognize these various zones of involvement and the activities, relationships, and emotions associated with each has now become extremely important. The world's populations are crowding into cities, and builders and speculators are packing people into vertical filing boxes—both offices and dwellings. If one looks at human beings in the way that the early slave traders did, conceiving of their space requirements simply in terms of the limits of the body, one pays very little attention to the effects of crowding. If, however, one sees man surrounded by a series of invisible bubbles which have measurable dimensions, architecture can be seen in a new light. It is then possible to conceive that people can be cramped by the spaces in which they have to live and work. They may even find themselves forced into behavior, relationships, or emotional outlets that are overly stressful. Like gravity, the influence of two bodies on each other is inversely proportional not only to the square of the distance but possibly even the cube of the distance between them. When stress increases, sensitivity to crowding rises—people get more on edge—so that more and more space is required as less and less is available.

REFERENCES:

Ariès, P. *Centuries of childhood*. New York: Knopf, 1962.
Goffman, E. *The presentation of self in everyday life*. Garden City, N.Y.: Doubleday, 1959.
Hall, E. T. *The silent language*. Garden City, N.Y.: Doubleday, 1959.
Hediger, H. *Studies of the psychology and be-*

havior of captive animals in zoos and circuses. London: Butterworth, 1955.

Joos, M. The five clocks. *International Journal of American Linguistics*, 1962, **28**, 127–133.

Mumford, L. *The city in history.* New York: Harcourt, Brace, 1961.

Osmond, H. Function as the basis of psychiatric ward design. *Mental Hospitals* (Architectural Supplement), 1957, **8**, 23–29.

Sommer, R. Studies in personal space. *Sociometry*, 1959, **22**, 247–260.

White, T. H. *The making of the president 1960.* New York: Atheneum, 1961.

3 The Influence of the Physical Environment on Behavior: Some Basic Assumptions

Harold M. Proshansky, William H. Ittelson, and Leanne G. Rivlin

Environmental psychology is a new field of scientific inquiry born of social necessity. At the present time it lacks a theoretical structure that would permit us to define it in theoretical terms, and we can only attempt to define it by pointing to the events or phenomena it studies. Its essential concern is with man's relationship to his physical environment, and more particularly to the physical environment that he himself has "created." There is no question that in the last century man has transformed the face of the earth and the nature of his own existence. But it is no less true that in the very fruits of this transformation—man's conquest of his physical environment through modern technology—lie the seeds of his own destruction in the form of overpopulation, water and air pollution, urban deterioration, depletion of natural resources, and other fundamental environmental problems. The inexorable pressures created by the need for solutions to these kinds of problems gave rise to environmental psychology.

Our own interest in problems of this nature began approximately ten years ago in response to a rather direct, but far from simple, request. We were asked, as psychologists, to undertake research that would, it was hoped, answer the question of how to design psychiatric facilities with a therapeutic atmosphere and influence on social interactions that would facilitate the treatment of institutionalized mental patients. To ask this question and expect it to be answered by systematic research involves a host of questionable assumptions concerning the state of knowledge of psychologists, not alone of environmental psychologists. It assumes, for example, that psychologists and other social scientists already understand the role of the physical environment in mediating complex social interactions. More importantly, it takes for granted the existence of an acknowledged body of principles for the treatment of mental illness that would permit the derivation of propositions about the nature of the "atmosphere" and social interactions that should be induced by the hospital setting in order to maximize the therapeutic effects of treatment.

Because such knowledge did not in fact exist, we had no choice but to postpone the question of how to design therapeutically effective psychiatric facilities. Perhaps the major problem that confronted us, and indeed that continues to plague researchers in all of the behavioral science fields, is the absence of a conceptually adequate definition of the environment, not to mention a unified theory of the nature of the environment. To effect changes in behavior by modifying the physical setting requires just such a definition or theory. To implement, for example, the commonly held view that the physical environment of the psychiatric patient should be "warm," "friendly," and "reassuring" requires an understanding of just how physical environment is related to other kinds of human environments, that is, to psychological and social environments.

As psychologists, we of course turned to psychology in an initial attempt to define and conceptualize man's environment. What we soon found out—and perhaps knew from the beginning—was that modern psychology could offer little guidance. Notwithstanding its concern with, and contribution to, establishing relationships between the behavior of the individual and the nature of the environment, its objective was far more empirical than theoretical; far more in establishing specific regularities of behavior than in understanding the environmental context that at least in part determined them. For this reason it can be said that the field still stands at the periphery of the problem of defining the environment and has yet to come directly to grips with it.

One of its two major approaches defines the environment in purely physical and objective terms, and the other—a phenomenological orientation—essentially denies the significance of the physical environment. Each has ignored the basic task of conceptualizing the environment within the framework of its own approach. But even if these two approaches were to attempt such a definition, a basic difficulty would still remain because each approach overlooks a class of significant parameters—namely, those defined by the other. The objective approach to the environment, which has its roots in experimental psychophysics and Watsonian behaviorism, has fragmented the physical environment into discrete quantifiable stimuli whose specific functional relationship to experience and behavior it has sought. This approach is essential to establishing the dimensions and nature of human psychological functions, such as perceiving, thinking, learning, and feeling. It has taught us much about some of the fundamental properties of these functions, but by no means so much that we understand man's integrated, on-going, and purposive behavior in a complex social setting. The question of the *patterning* of the basic dimensions of the physical environment, such as light and sound, as the source of such behavior has yet to be seriously considered. And more importantly, the significance of meaning, understanding, and other cognitive processes as another class of influences on this behavior, the very essence of the phenomenological approach, is repudiated by definition.

It should be apparent that at the level of human interaction in any given social setting and for any purpose, the individual responds not to a diffusion of proximal and distal light and sound waves, shapes and structures, objects and spaces, but to *another person*, engaged in a specific *activity* in a specific *place* for a specific *purpose*. Physical settings—simple or complex—evoke complex human responses in the form of feelings, attitudes, values, expectancies, and desires, and it is in this sense as well as in their known physical properties that their relationships to human experience and behavior must be understood.

The phenomenological approach to the environment, that is, an approach to the environment not as it is but at it is *experienced*, was first expressed by Koffka's concept of the "behavioral environment" (1935) and later developed more fully by Lewin's field-theory conception of the life-space (1936). Behavior springs not from the objective properties of the stimulus world "out there," but from that world transformed into an "inner world" or psychological environment by an inherently cognizing organism. Other theorists have subsequently drawn heavily on this formulation (Murray, 1938; Murphy, 1947; Barker, 1963; Krech & Crutchfield, 1948; and others), but in each instance the attempt, if any, to provide an adequate conceptualization of the environment has fallen far short of the mark.

An understanding of the psychological environment itself would require at least a study of how this environment comes into being, the processes by which the individual perceives, cognizes, and creates it, and more critically, the role played by the physical environment in all these processes. Clearly, a major task of any attempt to conceptualize the human environment must include the relationship between the person's physical world and the world he "constructs" from it, as well as between the latter and human behavior and experience.

Given this state of affairs in the field of environmental psychology, it should be quite evident why we had to retreat so quickly and so far from the original question of how to design psychiatric facilities that would improve the therapeutic process. Not unlike other researchers in environmental psychology and other inchoate scientific fields of inquiry, we asked a far more simple and direct, but nonetheless basic, question: Does the physical setting of a psychiatric ward induce identifiable and consistent patterns of behavior in the patients and staff who occupy and use it? To speak of modifying human behavior by changing the physical environment—whether a psychiatric ward, a school room, an urban community, or any other physical setting—not only assumes that a relationship between the two exists but that the relationship is rooted in the stability and consistency of human responses to the physical environment. Whether or not we explicitly stated this assumption when we took the first empirical step in our research program is not important. What is important is that, explicitly or implicitly, this assumption determined our initial research effort. Let us look at this first research step briefly before considering the assumption in more detail.

We began our research by "mapping" the behavior of all of the patients and staff on two psychiatric wards in a large municipal hospital located in a low-income area of a major urban community. The two wards, one male and the other female, constituted the single psychiatric floor of the hospital. Each ward had about 25 beds and consisted of a 138-foot-long corridor on which were three bedrooms for three patients each and three others accommodating six patients each. A dayroom at the center of the ward and an enclosed solarium at the far end were the established social areas. The patients were Negroes, whites, and Puerto Ricans from the low-income area surrounding the hospital; they were admitted for diagnosis and short-range treatment (shock, drugs, psychotherapy, etc.) for a period of generally less than three months.

The mapping of the two wards was done by a team of trained observers who recorded the activities of patients and staff, including where and when they occurred, which and how many individuals were involved, and how long they lasted. Observations were made on a time-sample basis of 15-minute intervals during the morning, afternoon, and evening of each day for a period of four to five weeks. The categories of observation, derived from an earlier pilot study, included such activities as sitting alone, personal hygiene, talking, standing alone, pacing, and reading. These in fact were the activities first observed in the patients during the pilot study. To begin our research, then, we focused on behavior that was overt, easily observable, and related to the use of the various areas of the ward.

On the basis of these data and the derivation of more general analytic categories of behavior from them, for example, "social,"

"isolated passive," and "isolated active," we derived behavioral maps of the wards. A detailed account of the technique of constructing behavioral maps and of their various uses, based on investigations of the psychiatric wards of the hospital noted above and still another, rather different general hospital that was studied concurrently, is presented elsewhere in this volume (Article 65). Here we need only note that the percentage values for each intersection of columns designating the various areas on the ward with rows representing the established analytic categories of behavior provided us with a quantitative behavioral map of the wards. By comparing these maps from day to day, from week to week, and even over more extended periods of time (months and years), we found clear evidence to support the following assumption:

Assumption 1: Human behavior in relation to a physical setting is enduring and consistent over time and situation; therefore, the characteristic patterns of behavior for that setting can be identified.

Indeed what emerged was not simply that patients generally carried out certain activities in certain places, and at certain times of the day, but that in general the relative frequency of activities for a given ward area, such as bedroom or solarium, both alone and in comparison with other areas, showed a constancy over time. This finding, combined with other information we had, led us to conclude not only that characteristic, stable patterns of behavior can be identified in relation to the physical setting of the ward, but that these patterns of response actually resist change.

We have noted that patients on these wards generally stayed somewhat less than three months. Continual admission of new patients and discharge or transfer of others was the rule rather than the exception in any week. What our behavioral maps revealed to us, therefore, was not merely that patients ate, slept, interacted, paced, withdrew, and engaged in other activities in characteristic fashions, places, and times, but that these space utilization patterns persisted regardless of the patients involved. Here then is a corollary to our first assumption: other things being equal, patterns of behavior in response to a physical setting persist regardless of the individuals involved. We call this the *continuity of behavior*.

But to return to the assumption itself for a moment, we must answer an argument that will surely arise. It will be said that the data in support of Assumption 1 confirm merely a "self-evident truth," that not only is the stability of human behavior generally assumed but its regularity in relation to particular physical environments is a patent aspect of human existence. We grant this argument at least some merit in that we never doubted the validity of the assumption either before or during our first empirical investigation. But the behavioral scientist must continue to test and systematize his more "self-evident" assumptions, especially with respect to problem areas that are relatively untouched by systematic research—and this is clearly the case for environmental research as we define it here.

A more vulnerable aspect of the argument that the regularity or stability of psychiatric patient behavior in relation to physical space is self-evident is its implication that the nature of this regularity is also self-evident. It implies that given bedrooms, dining rooms, dayrooms, and bathrooms, such places are necessarily where patients must sleep, eat, recreate, and take care of bodily needs. Our data not only reveal that this assumption is only partially true, but more importantly, establish that it oversimplifies the relationship between human behavior and the physical setting. What we found was that bedrooms were used consistently for socializing and eating as well as for sleeping; the dining room not only for eating but also for patterned social interaction; the dayroom and solarium for social withdrawal as well as for social interaction; and so on.

What we have learned, then, from our initial research efforts is that how and for what purpose individuals use space is by no means a simple reflection of the functional nature of that space determined either by its physical design or its administrative "label." This finding confronts us with a patent conclusion and an inescapable paradox. The conclusion is simple enough: the

rational planning of physical settings for specific purposes and groups before they are constructed must be tested against the actual use of these settings after they are constructed and in operation. Without such "testing" it is impossible to accumulate knowledge for influencing human behavior by purposeful organization of physical space. The paradox that follows is that systematic studies to evaluate the effectiveness of physical settings after they are in operation are rare—if indeed they exist at all.

Stability and regularity are not the only characteristics of patient behavior in relation to physical space that are observed on the ward. What is observed, if one spends any time on the ward observing a given area for a period of time and then moving on to another, is the diversity and constant flux of patient activity. By design, of course, activities *at any given moment* vary from one ward area to the next. Watching TV can only occur where there is TV, and sleeping in bed can only occur in bedrooms. Yet both our behavioral maps and our day-to-day observations clearly reveal diversity within each area as well as between areas. The dayroom, for example, was used for eating, games, social withdrawal, reading, social interaction, and still other activities. And for any one of these kinds of behavior, diversity was no less true. Patients eat or play games in different parts of the dayroom, with varied numbers of patients interacting in different ways. Conversely, eating or games were found in other sectors of the ward, in various combinations of patient numbers.

But if a given area is observed for a brief period of time, say five or ten minutes, patient activity or behavior is seen to change continuously. When the duration of an activity is included in our behavioral maps, we learn that in general patient activities do not last long. Even when an activity is maintained, however, change occurs. Two patients in conversation may be joined by a third, or they may move to the opposite side of the room, or even sit silently after conversing for awhile. A patient reading in the dayroom may move to his bedroom to escape increasing noise as more people enter. This kaleidoscope of human activity, of course, is not limited to the psychiatric ward; it characterizes social interaction in every setting. The smaller the unit of behavioral analysis, the finer the details recorded, the more likely we are to find diversity and change in relation to physical setting.

Assumption 2: Human behavior in relation to physical setting reveals diversity over space at any given moment and continuous variability in any given space over time.

The diversity and continuity of patient behavior in the psychiatric ward are by no means unlimited. Stated differently, the patient's freedom of choice—or the freedom of choice of any individual in any physical setting—has defined limits. The physical design of the ward limits choice of behavior. The patient could not, for example, sleep in the solarium since neither a bed nor a couch was there. And if he decided to sleep on the floor, he would be confronted with the restraints of the regulation requiring patients to sleep in assigned beds. Perhaps an even greater obstacle to freedom of choice is the presence of other patients. A seat occupied by one patient cannot be occupied by another; and if all the seats in the dayroom are taken, the patient may have to go elsewhere to eat his lunch or read his book. Where there are six patients in a bedroom, as in the hospital wards we mapped, the restrictions on freedom of choice for each are even more apparent.

We began observing the ward with deliberately limited research objectives. The task we set ourselves was to relate patient and staff activities to "places" on the ward. Observed behavior was viewed simply as a function of the immediate physical setting in which it occurred, although we knew that this was a gross oversimplification of the causal relationship between space and behavior. Clearly other kinds of variables were involved, but given the paucity of previous research and the exploratory nature of our own, both conceptually and methodologically, we had no choice but to proceed in this fashion. Yet these other variables became more conspicuous the longer they remained at the periphery of our research interest.

For example, the patients on the wards consisted of roughly equal numbers of Puerto Ricans, whites, and Negroes. To be aware of these ethnic differences was also to be aware that the physical setting had, in a very real sense, a "past" and a "future" as well as a "present." The kinds of responses it evoked were rooted not only in the nature of the immediate properties of the ward structure, but also in the past home and hospital experiences of the three groups and in their expectations about hospital settings. While it is true that the observed consistencies of behavior on the ward persisted in the face of a changing patient population, it is also true that the population remained ethnically and culturally homogeneous. Two questions for subsequent investigation immediately arose, however. To what extent would comparisons of the space utilization patterns of the three ethnic groups reveal systematic differences? Would their general patterns of response to the physical setting show variation when compared to the response patterns of another population that varied in ethnic background or social class?

If a physical setting is not bound by time, our experiences on the ward revealed that it is no more bound by space. We found that shifts in patient and staff behavior in relation to the physical setting were sometimes determined by administrative decisions made in other parts of the hospital or beyond the hospital walls. Administrative decisions can alter the nature of the physical setting and in this respect influence patient behavior. Decisions concerning the number of patients on a ward, whether security should be tight or lax, the ratio of staff to patients, or even approval of appropriations for a new psychiatric ward have important consequences for behavior on the kind of ward we studied. Any physical setting, whether a psychiatric ward, a living room, an apartment house, a school classroom, a neighborhood, or a city, is part of a larger and more encompassing physical setting, which it therefore influences and is influenced by. This is true because physical settings and the broader structures that encompass them are themselves expressions of correspondingly inclusive and interlocking social systems.

Assumption 3: The physical setting that defines and structures any concrete situation is not a closed system; its boundaries are not fixed either in space or in time.

A physical setting, like the behavior of individuals in response to it that we described in Assumptions 1 and 2, is characterized by continuous changes amidst regularity and stability. Not only is it an open system subject to external space and time determinants, but for any given perceiver, it includes other people and their behavior, as well as walls, doors, corridors, colors, and the like. The physical properties of a room are a function not only of its decoration but also of the number of people in it, the arrangement of its furniture, and even the amount of light it has. A room with six people in it is not physically identical with the same room with two people in it; even when the number of people remains constant, its perceived structure may vary with their behavior.

If a physical setting is an open system characterized simultaneously by change and stability, then its organization is *dynamic*. The behavior of patients and staff on a psychiatric ward and all of the specific physical settings in which it occurs are *interdependent*. Closing off an inadequately heated recreation room increases the possibility of maintaining comfortable temperatures in other parts of the ward; but it also increases patient density in these areas, which in turn may increase room temperatures to the point of discomfort. In our study, a poorly furnished and often overheated solarium was infrequently used by patients, so that the dayroom, the only other specifically designated recreation area, was busy and often crowded.

Assumption 4: Behavior in relation to a physical setting is dynamically organized: a change in any component of the setting has varying degrees of effects on all other components in that setting, thereby changing the characteristic behavior pattern of the setting as a whole.

Whether or not the degree of activity or crowding in the dayroom of the ward we studied was in fact determined to some extent by avoidance of the solarium was an empirical question we attempted to ask somewhat later in our research program. At the entrance to the long corridor that ran the length of the ward was the nurses' station, and at the other end of the corridor was the solarium with the various sized bedrooms, the dayroom, bathroom, and other areas located between these two points. The solarium was used very little, even though it contained a television set. Avoidance of it clearly resulted to some degree from its location at the extreme end of the ward, but far more from its sparse furnishings, uncomfortable temperatures, and the intense sunlight that poured through a bank of uncovered windows. The activities that took place there were primarily sitting alone in the far corners of the room and conversations involving two or more patients sitting on a hard wooden bench. The bench was the one stable piece of furniture in the room, as the occasional chairs that also belonged there appeared and disappeared.

Given these circumstances we systematically studied the effects of increasing the physical comforts of the solarium on activity in it and in other areas of the ward. We hypothesized that such a change, accomplished by refurnishing the solarium, would increase the use of this ward area and concurrently decrease the activity in other areas. We added attractive furniture, drapes, and other accessories to the solarium and imposed experimental controls to the extent that is possible in a field setting. The data resulting from before-and-after comparisons of frequency and duration of activities in various areas of the ward confirmed our hypothesis. The changes made in the solarium kept patients in it for longer periods of time and correspondingly decreased use of other ward areas. Although the reader is referred to Article 43 for details of this investigation and its findings with respect to specific activities, one finding bears directly on the dynamically organized character of a physical setting.

Standing alone in a state of preoccupation and detachment is not unusual behavior in psychiatric patients. Often isolated places are selected specifically for this kind of withdrawal. Before we experimentally changed the solarium, this behavior occurred in it some 40 percent of the time it was observed on the ward; it was seen in the dayroom somewhat less frequently—35 percent of the time, and least frequently—26 percent of the time—in the corridor. After the solarium was redecorated, the locus of this behavior shifted radically to the opposite end of the corridor near the nurses' station. Standing alone occurred 80 percent of the time in this area and roughly only 10 percent of the time in the solarium or the dayroom. This finding, although clearly related to our first assumption of the stability and regularity of behavior in a physical setting, led to our assumption of what we have designated as the "conservation of behavior."

Assumption 5: When a change in a physical setting is not conducive to a pattern of behavior that has been characteristic of the setting, that behavior will express itself at a new time or locus.

If, as we have already suggested, the many objects, places, events, and people that make up a physical setting are interdependent, then it should be possible to induce the same or equivalent changes in many different ways. In our investigation, we were able to effect a decrease in the activity of the dayroom by changing the furnishings of the solarium. The same change could have been achieved in many other ways: by decreasing the number of patients admitted to the ward; by scheduling use of the dayroom at different times for different groups of patients; or by simply moving some of the activities, furniture, or diversions from the dayroom to other parts of the ward.

Assumption 6: Changes in the characteristic behavior patterns of a physical setting can be induced by changing the physical, social, or administrative structures that define that setting.

If Assumption 6 seems self-evident, then because of its very special importance, especially for those concerned with planned changes in the environment, it only becomes more compelling. What it tells us is not simply, for example, that overcrowding on a ward can be eliminated by building another ward or by reducing the number of patients

admitted to the ward. It also tells us that a great deal of consideration should be given to determining what method is most appropriate for dealing with the problem. In many instances it is wasteful to solve problems of this kind by physical change when other methods are available. It is well known, for example, that architects spend a great deal of ingenuity and money constructing buildings that are structurally flexible, but greater flexibility can often be obtained through administrative (and budgetary) flexibility.

We began this discussion by indicating that the primary focus of environmental psychology was "man's relationship to his physical environment." For purposes of analysis and research, this working definition and its implications are both useful and necessary. We now must consider whether these implications can help us to understand the concept of "environment." However useful and necessary it is for purposes of analysis and research, the definition and what it implies conceptually about the nature of the environment are clearly misleading.

To speak of man's behavior in relation to the physical environment—or for that matter any kind of environment—implies that a dichotomy can be made between the person on the one hand and the environment on the other. Theoretically, however, such a distinction is untenable. There is only the total environment, of which man is simply one kind of component in relationships with other kinds of components. Indeed it can be asserted, again from a theoretical point of view, that man does not exist except in his relationships to all the other components of a given environmental situation. The psychiatric patient, for example, is a component of the psychiatric hospital environment, and he derives his meaning from the physical setting that contains him, the psychiatrists who treat him, the people who visit him, the people who wait on him, and so on.

To use the term "physical environment" as we have been using it implies that there are other kinds of environments. And so there are. Again, for purposes of analysis and research, it is possible to extract from the total environment a social, physical, or even personal or psychological environment. Yet these are not separate environments but different ways of analyzing the same situation. And even for purposes of analysis, the physical environment, perhaps more than any other kind, does not exist except in relation to the total environment. In speaking of the physical setting of the ward, the physical setting was not simply its physical space, its design, and the inanimate objects that occupy it. For any individual in this setting, it also included other people, their behavior, and the social context that defined what the space was for, who would use it, and what should and should not happen in it.

For purposes of analysis, we could ask what effects changing the solarium physically could have on patient behavior. But the changes were not simply "physical," but also social, administrative, and psychological. Each patient observed not just new furniture but "meanings" that defined the intentions of others with respect to his own behavior. New furniture meant, for example, that the hospital administration expected patients to use the solarium, or that patients should engage in certain recreational activities suggested by the furniture and its arrangement.

Whether we speak of the total environment, or "man and his environment," or the "physical environment" or some other part of it extracted for purposes of analysis, the same set of assumptions previously discussed prevails. In each instance we must assume an open, dynamic system, not bound by space or time, that is both structured and constantly changing. And if we consider the interrelationships among these properties, and the fact that theoretically there is only a single "inclusive environment," then it is clear that this inclusive environment is a total process in which all components participate and are defined by their enduring and changing relationships with each other.

Assumption 7: The environment is an active and continuing process whose participating components define and are defined by the nature of the interrelationships among them at a given moment and over time.

A number of significant implications can be drawn from Assumption 7. But it is important first to stress that whatever the mode of analysis, all components are defined by their participation in the environmental process. A "psychiatric patient" component can be identified only because of its defined relationships to such other components (also in defined relationships to each other) as "psychiatrist," "psychiatric ward," "nurse," "visitor," and so on. *No component is seen as an entity existing "in" an "environment" composed of the others.* What this suggests is that we never encounter the components except as participants in some situation. We abstract characteristics that show some continuity across a variety of situations and label these as entities. To give them greater reality than the situations from which they are abstracted is to commit what Whitehead has called the "fallacy of misplaced concreteness."

If we again consider Assumption 7, particularly in its emphasis on the environment as an active, continuous process of interacting and interrelated components, an important implication is immediately discernible. Whatever component is abstracted for purposes of analysis and study, it is clearly evident that that component is both cause and effect. It not only acts upon other components and thereby changes them, but in so doing it changes the environment and thereby induces changes in itself. Any component, in acting on other components, is necessarily acting on itself. Environmental process, therefore, is not a direct causal sequence, but one of reciprocal or circular feedback.

Assumption 8: Every component of the environment interacts or has defined relationships with every other component in two ways: (a) it acts on all other aspects, and (b) it is acted upon by all other aspects and in particular, receives the consequences of its own action in terms of a changed environmental situation.

The significance of Assumption 8 can be illustrated in a psychiatric ward situation. An administrative decision to increase the number of patients beyond some *optimum* point will have effects throughout the ward. Such a decision will affect not only the social setting but the physical setting as well. Indeed it is because of changes in the latter, resulting in crowding of bedrooms and other areas of the ward, that interpersonal relationships between patients and between patients and staff may deteriorate to the point of open conflict. Under these circumstances the administrative person who made the decision to increase the number of patients may now be forced to make a new set of decisions in order to handle the negative consequences of his original directive.

Perhaps the most obvious implication that can be drawn from the definition of the environment in Assumption 7 as a dynamic process of interacting components is that the environment is unique at any given moment. It is never at rest. To stand as an alert observer in a psychiatric ward—or in any other physical setting—is to experience the variability, and indeed the uniqueness, of the environment from one moment to the next. This uniqueness, however, is as much a function of place as of time. Thus, two wards on two different floors may be identically structured and furnished, but the environment on those two wards in actual situations will necessarily be quite different.

Assumption 9: The environment is unique at any given time and place.

The uniqueness of the environment can be conceived of in still a third sense. We have already suggested that while the environment is a total process, components can be abstracted for the purposes of analysis and investigation. Thus, although man and his environment are inseparable, the two can be and are distinguished for just these purposes. And this can be done in order to investigate either of two kinds of problems. The environment, in effect, can be analyzed from either of two vantage points, although in both instances it is the individual who is studied. In one case, the individual, as a component of the total environmental process, is investigated in order to provide us with a greater understanding of this process. The scientist, as the observer, stands outside the environment and gathers data on the persons who participate in it with this objective in mind. In the second case, the environmental process is studied from a "first person" point of view, that is, from the standpoint of the individual who is a *participant* in the process. And research undertaken from this vantage point provides a basis for understanding the nature not only of the environmental process, but also of the participant or individual (a component defined as an entity) from whose viewpoint this process is being examined.

These two methodological orientations toward understanding environmental process reflect the theoretical dualism of the *objective* and *phenomenological* approaches, which we considered earlier in this article. We reiterate our original position: both analytic approaches are necessary for a full understanding of the environmental situation. At this point in our discussion, it is the participant rather than the observer orientation that concerns us.

Assumption 10: The study of environmental process from the point of view of a particular participant in that process creates a situation dichotomized into participant, on the one hand, and all other environmental components, on the other.

Our investigation of patient behavior in relation to the physical setting of the psychiatric ward by definition distinguished between patients and other components of the total psychiatric ward environment. Furthermore, all of the behavioral mapping based on observation was an attempt to understand environmental process from the observer's or bystander's point of view rather than from the participant's. Later in our research program we began to extend our methodology to include the participant to some degree. We attempted to understand the environmental process of the two psychiatric wards by gathering data based on how specific patients perceived the physical setting.

At one point in our mapping studies, we interviewed the patients as well as observed them. We asked them to describe the settings in which various activities took place, what they liked and disliked about the physical setting, what changes they would like to make in the ward design, and other related issues. In a later longitudinal study, we questioned patients about the physical setting of the wards when they entered the hospital, during their stay, and after they were discharged. Our objective was not simply to establish the particular ward environment of each participant but to trace the changes in this environment over time. We found, of course, similarities in these patients' views of the ward, their feelings about its physical arrangement, and indeed their evaluations of particular areas. In fact these similarities, especially with respect to the patients' perception of where various activities took place and whom they involved, were not inconsistent with the behavioral maps we made on the basis of systematic observation.

Clear differences in patients' views of the ward were also evident, however. Each patient saw the ward setting, its activities, the other patients, and the staff in terms that were to some degree unique. Assumption 9 tells us that any environment is unique at a given time and place, but it is now evident that, given the *same* time and place, participants in the environmental process view "all other environmental components" in this situation in both unique and similar fashions.

Assumption 11: Although there is only one environmental situation, there are as many surroundings as there are components from whose point of view the process can be examined.

No two components in the environmental process can occupy the same place in it, and therefore, the surroundings or view of the environment of each is necessarily unique at any given time. But even if it were possible for space and time to be identical for two participants, the surroundings of each would still be unique. Each participant reflects properties that express not only his unique interrelationships with other participants in the immediate environmental setting, but also the pattern of interrelationships experienced in other settings at other times. The variations we described in the way the patients on the same ward viewed their physical surroundings were rooted to no small degree in differences in previous hospital experiences, sociocultural background, attitudes toward mental illness, and a host of other factors.

Taken together, our interview and mapping data of the psychiatric patients we investigated gave us an important insight into how each of them viewed his surroundings. What we learned from the interviews—and this was true of all the patients studied—was that they were largely unaware of the physical structure of the ward in terms of its detail and, more particularly, in terms of having clear-cut opinions, sharp preferences or convictions, or desires to change it. The physical surroundings of the ward seemed to be "neutral" and to enter into awareness only when difficulties were encountered. Psychiatric patients are not alone in being mostly oblivious of their physical surroundings under conditions of quiescence and stability. All people are. It is only when temperature, sound, light, space, colors, and other design and structural aspects of the physical environment deviate from some adaptation level that the environment or some aspect of it intrudes upon consciousness.

Assumption 12: Seen from the viewpoint of the participant in the environmental process, the surroundings typically are "neutral"; they enter into awareness only when they deviate from some adaptation level.

It would be wrong to assume that an exception to this generalization occurs when an individual confronts a new physical setting. It might be argued that even though a new setting were optimum in all respects, including temperature, light, sound, space, and color, in order to move about and participate in it, a person's awareness of this setting must necessarily be heightened. But this case reflects our assumption because it includes a deviation from some adaptation level in the unfamiliar environment. The participant's awareness grows out of the fact that until he learns the structure of the setting and how to use it, his adaptation to it has not been established.

One more assumption deserves to be stated explicitly. Taken together, our interview data and our observations of patient behavior on the ward conspicuously revealed that however unaware the patient may be of his physical environment, his behavior at all times is greatly influenced by it. To be unaware of an environment is by no means to be unmoved by it, and in fact there is considerable discrepancy between our awareness of our surroundings and our behavior in relation to them.

Assumption 13: Although the participant remains largely unaware of his surroundings in the environmental process, these surroundings continue to exert considerable influence on his behavior.

Now that we have completed our list of assumptions, we must provide the reader with the proper theoretical and research perspective for them. It cannot be stressed too strongly that although the assumptions have been presented rather formally, in no sense are they meant to represent a rationally articulated and integrated theoretical structure. At best they are a set of general propositions about the nature of the environment and the way it should be studied. Yet they have more than heuristic value for a field as new as environmental psychology.

Some of them suggest important sources of variables in relationships between physical setting and the behavior of the person. Assumption 3, for example, which states that the physical setting is not a closed system, emphasizes the importance of past experiences and the broader social system for such relationships. Still others point to relationships between variables that can be formulated in more specific terms for testing in particular social settings. Assumption 12, for example, leads us to ask how the relationship between experienced difficulty in the physical setting and awareness of that setting is influenced by the specific nature of the setting. Is there a level of difficulty at which awareness of the physical setting begins to decrease? The concept of "environmental adaptation" in relation to awareness is still another way of stating this problem.

Perhaps the greatest value of many of the assumptions lies in the warning they give against environmental research that fails to recognize the complexity of the phenomena studied. Most, if not all, of the assumptions point to the need for investigations that are willing to discard the relatively simple cause-and-effect paradigm that typifies some of the more laboratory-oriented behavioral science research. Many of the assumptions make it clear that such an approach, at least at the present stage of knowledge about behavior in relation to space, provides useless information. Others bring us back to a point we have made frequently: the total environmental process can and should be studied from different vantage points and at different levels of analysis. This means, of course, that only a multidisciplinary approach can lead to a viable theory of, and a fruitful body of knowledge in, environmental psychology.

REFERENCES:

Barker, R. G. *The stream of behavior.* New York: Appleton-Century-Crofts, 1963.

Koffka, K. *Principles of Gestalt psychology.* New York: Harcourt, Brace, 1935.

Krech, D., & Crutchfield, R. S. *Theory and problems of social psychology.* New York: McGraw-Hill, 1948.

Lewin, K. *Principles of topological and vector psychology.* New York: McGraw-Hill, 1936.

Murphy, G. *Personality.* New York: Harper, 1947.

Murray, H. *Explorations in personality.* New York: Oxford University Press, 1938.

4 Space, Territory and Human Movements

David Stea

We tend to regard space, in the designed environment, as defined by physical barriers which are erected to restrict motion and the reception of visual and auditory stimuli. In fact, it is also defined by the behavior of organisms occupying the space. The characteristics of their spatial behavior are many, but several similar ones have been grouped under the general heading "territoriality."

In describing organisms lower than man, we speak of certain spatial volumes as individual and collective territories, and further define these in terms of the animal's inclination to defend them against intruders and to "aggress" against these intruders when they violate the boundaries of his territory. In civilized man, aggression is highly socialized, so we cannot always use this form of overt behavioral expression as an index. Neverthe-

From *Landscape*, Vol. 15, No. 1, Autumn 1965, pp. 13–16. Reprinted by permission of the author and publisher.

less, we have reason to believe that "territorial behavior," the desire both to possess and occupy portions of space, is as pervasive among men as among their animal forebears —witness the attitude of slum-area street gangs toward their "turf." There is some suggestion, coming largely from the animal world, that territorial possession is not less fundamental than sexual possession, as had originally been supposed, but is equally or even more fundamental. Our legal code bears little resemblance to organic and behavioral evolution, but recent changes in certain statutes would seem to be in accord, to stretch a point, with the new behavioral view: for example, in most states you may still shoot a man with relative impunity if he attempts to run away with your household possessions but not if he runs away with your wife. It appears, too, that private property is likely to be the most tenacious sacred cow of western civilization. The reason certainly does not lie in utility *per se,* for there is no intrinsic reason why objects and spaces held as individual property have more utility than objects and spaces open to the use of many.

When space is held collectively by men, their behavior regarding it greatly resembles the behavior of animals defending their individual territories. Hostility is overt and socialized individual patterns of aggression in men are collectively released. When our own tribe engages in this behavior we call it patriotism; when another does the same, we call it nationalism or aggression. Often, we merely advertise our possession by means of an obvious *display,* not unlike the vocalizations of common song birds; in former centuries we rattled swords—now we rattle bombs.

But, as previously indicated, territorial manifestations exist on smaller levels too, on levels more readily amenable to empirical investigation. And it is my contention that these smaller territories are in some way affected or shaped by the designed environment; if the designed environment changes, the territory may also change.

Suppose we take a fraction of the real world, of the existing environment, and subject it to examination. As an example rich with theoretical promise, let us look at a hypothetical large business concern. The firm, located in a major city, occupies several closely spaced tall buildings, each consisting of many offices. It employs a wide variety of people: there is a small executive pinnacle, inaccessible to almost everyone, and a broad base of managerial personnel, sales engineers, investment analysts, accountants, clerks, draftsmen, maintenance crews, etc. The company has provided an environment which takes care of most of the employees' diurnal needs: there are libraries, cafeterias, a restaurant, snack bars and areas for active and passive relaxation within its buildings.

The system of behavioral actions and interactions within this building constitutes a legitimate subculture, in anthropological terms, and the membership of this subculture is highly varied. For the purpose of the present discussion, I exclude the lowest echelons (janitors, messenger boys, etc.) and the highest echelons (president and vice-presidents). Among the working staff, the former have no permanent place within the design; the latter can frequently (but not always) alter the design to suit themselves. Most of these inhabitants occupy fixed places within the environment whose physical aspects they cannot markedly alter. In inhabiting a given portion of space, they necessarily identify with it; regardless of who, in a strictly legal sense, owns the furniture, the individual comes to regard that portion of space centering about his desk and working area as conceptually "his." He symbolizes the fact and degree of this possession by the number and arrangement of his personal effects, by the detailed nature of his image of the space and by the attitude he adopts, while occupying it, towards visitors.

Let me digress briefly, in order to suggest the beginnings of a conceptual framework. First, we shall call the element of space described above the *territorial unit,* and the individual who "dwells" within it the inhabitant. This is not his *only* territorial unit; he has one at home and also, perhaps, in his car, but it is the office with which we are now concerned. It should be noted that, however physically separated, all these territorial units are conceptually close to one another.

The inhabitant of such a unit must be distinguished from the *occupant* who is in (but does not possess) the territory of another, and the occasional *visitor*.

When the individual leaves his territorial unit, his behavior makes two other important behavioral characteristics of space evident. The first is *personal space* (described by E. T. Hall, 1966), defined as a small circle in physical space, with the individual at its center and a culturally-determined radius. The second is the *territorial cluster,* enclosing those people (or other territorial units) frequently visited and the paths taken to reach them. Each of the individuals in this cluster has his own cluster, too, and the set consisting of the original cluster and these others is loosely termed a *territorial complex*. The three "stationary" territories just described are schematically summarized in Figure 4-1. Some territorial clusters are simply clusters of territorial units; others are genuine collective territories, viewed as "ours" by their members.[1]

---

[1] Both *stationary* and *moving* territory have been defined; similarly, with respect to either form of territory, the individual participant may be either stationary or moving. Moreover, the space may be either *individual* (personal space, territorial unit), or *collective* (some territorial clusters and territorial complexes), and *formal* (professional) or *informal* (social) on the collective level. Further, these spaces are held to possess certain properties which we can summarize as: shape, size, number of units, extensiveness and types of boundary, differentiation (detail), relatedness and so on.

If the little circles representing territorial units are thought of as the cross-sections of columns conceptually linking several of the same individual's territorial clusters (home, office, etc.), this reflects the similarity, mentioned earlier, among the territorial units in a variety of physical locations. The resulting three-dimensional diagram bears a marked resemblance to graphic descriptions of Kurt Lewin's behavioral "field theory" or "topological psychology," but there is an important difference: while the territorial hierarchy is behaviorally *defined*, it represents, for any given location, a set of physical entities. It is hypothesized that its shape and extensiveness are frequently determined by elements of the designed environment. To cite an extreme case from our office example, a minor supervisory accountant may be physically in closest proximity to an individual directly above him on the next floor, a person with whom, at most, he has few contacts and whom he may never even have met.

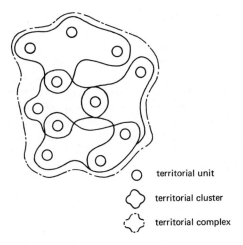

	territorial unit
	territorial cluster
	territorial complex

Figure 4–1

Our major interest is in territorial changes and their effects, but change cannot be asserted without defining the situation that existed before the change. A variety of techniques exists for asserting contributory aspects of behavior. In examining the office situation, sociometric choice and other inventories can be used to identify the personnel with whom an individual interacts, for example, thus determining the size, shape and boundedness of the cluster. The individual, it may be assumed, also possesses a mental map or environmental image of the space represented by the cluster; using techniques similar to those employed by Kevin Lynch (1960) in his investigation of the conceptual form of cities, we can determine the perceived nature of units, clusters and complexes, and of the paths connecting them.

The changes take two forms: behavior change and design change. Our hypothesis, in most general terms, is that changing the defining characteristics of territory changes the behavior that occurs within it and, conversely, that changes in behavior lead to changes in territory. We are less interested in the cause-and-effect aspects of this than simply in the relationship; we may even ask: "What change in behavior, with physical aspects of design held constant, is equivalent to a given change in design?"

Having theorized at length, let us consider some problems of the physical aspects of office design in particular and, later, of environmental design in general. The most commonplace example involves that ubiquitous piece of office furniture, the file cabinet. File cabinets are often quite tall, and it is sometimes impossible to see over them; they provide good visual and acoustical insulation. They are good social insulators too, and alteration in their positions, once territorial boundaries have become firmly established, often produces considerable confusion.

But the situations are often more complex. In the past few years German architects have developed a radical approach to the treatment of office spaces which they term *bürolandschaft* (office landscape). This system for office planning is distinguished by a lack of subspace-defining walls and barriers and an intentionally amorphous arrangement of furniture (actually determined from work flow and desired communication and circulation patterns). One of its claimed advantages is flexibility but this is nothing new in concept. To see flexibility in *practice* is something else again since studies of offices performed in the past indicate that many so-called "flexible" partitions remain fixed from the day of their installation. The psychological reluctance to change may be more precisely termed a reluctance to alter territorial boundaries.

The designers of *bürolandschaft* seem to recognize that there is a certain discomfort associated with sharing a large space with so many people for a large part of each day; and they have sought to alleviate the problem by providing floor coverings of domestic finish, by facing desks in different directions to afford a modicum of privacy, by removing patterned auditory stimulation and by adding extensive acoustical insulation to supplement the constant noise level of an air-conditioning system. This environmental manipulation is in line with findings that too-quiet open spaces can be disturbing after a period of time. American designers have been more concerned with removing patterned visual stimulation than patterned auditory stimulation, through the use of opaque but unsubstantial partitions. The German *bürolandschaft* designers assumed, on the other hand, that in a constantly varying visual environment, any individual event

will be less disturbing (e.g., a fellow worker departing for a "coffee break"). Since German workers typically take breaks at will, this form of environmental variation is a recurring event in their surroundings; such is not the case in American offices, where work pauses are highly regimented.

But visual chaos is one of the less important potentially adverse consequences of open offices in America. If we assume that a more regimented system of control is also more threatening, and that the greater the supervisory pressure, the greater the need for physical territorial boundaries, then the possibility of acute "employee insecurity" must be faced. In this regard, the following example is outstanding:

Richards and Dobyns's article in *Human Organization* (1957) describes a territorial cluster almost entirely dependent for its existence upon aspects of design. The cluster in this case was the Vouchercheck Filing Unit of a large insurance company. The Unit consisted of six fulltime and three part-time employees, all engaged in document filing and locating. The external territorial boundaries were clearly defined: one of the walls was enclosed in steel mesh, giving the unit its nickname "The Cage" and this frontier was further reinforced with a row of filing cabinets, their effective height increased with stacks of pasteboard boxes. One door gave access to the Audit Division, of which the Cage was a part, and another opened onto the outside corridor. Its "cluster" nature was indicated by the *esprit* and general effectiveness of the team and by their attitudes toward the various items of company property surrounding them (furniture, pencils, pads, rulers and so on) which the workers regarded as collectively theirs. Further, they possessed a privilege—a status symbol—denied to other workers in the division: one Cage-member would go out during the afternoon, when the mood struck the group, and bring back "snacks" for the remainder.

When the company relocated two divisions together on one floor, the Cage's topography was altered in several apparently small ways:

(1) The territory was slightly reduced in size; (2) the protective file-cabinet barrier was removed, allowing an external super-

visor visual access into the territorial interior; (3) access to the outside corridor was removed; (4) disposition of their territorial property was taken out of their control; and (5) arrangement of territorial units within the cluster was altered. The result of an increased opportunity for external regimentation was increased regimentation in fact, a loss of the primary status symbol and, inevitably, greatly decreased morale and a nearly catastrophic reduction in work efficiency. Thus, as the external boundaries of the territory became increasingly permeable, this miniature social system lost its autonomy; and, as autonomy was lost, psychological stress resulted from a reduction in the number of alternative behaviors available to the members, restrictions in freedom of movement and a loss of "overt behavior symbols of in-group uniqueness." In other words, with the alteration in the shape, size, boundedness and differentiation of the territorial cluster and of the territorial units came marked alteration in the behavior of the individual members.

A. E. Parr (1964–65) stressed the importance of *variability* in the environment, the need for change, for variety in what might be termed the stimulus field. The overall suggestion is that, unless forcibly restrained, most higher organisms engage in an active process of seeking this variability if it cannot be found in the immediate surroundings. Of course, many sources other than the designed environment may provide such stimuli. A man's work, if varied and interesting, may more than adequately compensate for an unvaried and uninteresting working space. Work is obviously so very important to so very many people that we might better ask the question (in light of Paul Goodman's (1964) identification of the apparent pointlessness of the wage-earning tasks in which a large proportion of the population engage): "How does the environment compensate for the 'boredom' of the office job?" Our hypothesis is that the bored worker engages in active stimulus-seeking behavior and, in the terminology of the framework developed earlier, enlarges the boundaries of his territorial cluster without increasing the number of territorial units actively included. Perhaps he takes only more frequent and more farflung coffee breaks, but he may

also take many prolonged and apparently purposeless trips to a library located in another of the company's buildings. He may pick up social acquaintances along the way and may even attempt to acquire professional contacts in this (to him) remote area of the organizational landscape to give further excuses for his ramblings. The result is often termed restlessness, under the assumption that if we attach a name to a phenomenon we can then file it away and forget it (which is what usually happens).

The territorial cluster in the office, as it has been described, seems a static thing. But the cluster cannot exist without *movement* within it, nor the complex without movement among clusters. Human movement within the cluster, the complex, the building and the city is closely related to the general problem of topographical orientation (location, navigation, pathfinding, etc.). When we ask whether an individual is well-oriented, we are in fact asking whether he is oriented at all, how long he took to become oriented, the process by which he became oriented and the techniques he uses to *maintain* this orientation.

This relates to what some architects may mean when they speak of space and sense of space, to the problem of the familiar path in the *Umwelt* (phenomenal world) described by Jakob von Uexküll (1957) three decades ago. Thirty years later, John Barlow (1964) suggested that von Uexküll's three sensory spatial cues could be reduced to two: sense of direction and sense of distance. From recent experiments with human and animal subjects, we know that humans are not the only ones who tend to alter their familiar paths in retracing a point-to-point route. But we do not really know very much about the variables controlling the *establishing* of familiar paths in designed environments. That no two human *Unwelten* are the same implies that even two *objectively identical* familiar paths are *subjectively* different. The difficulty one experiences in finding one's way about a city on the basis of directions given by a friend has its parallel in the confusion engendered by first contact with modern office environments. Architects deplore directional signs, but they seem unable or unwilling to design environments to which most participants orient with ease; in the end, signs must be provided anyway.

Both the uniqueness of the office environment and its communality with other spaces may be made clearer by comparing it with an environment whose function is quite distinct: the museum. The two broad behavioral classes we have mentioned—territoriality and topographical orientation—play very different roles in the office and the museum. The office is designed primarily for the worker, not the visitor, and to the worker both territory and orientation are important. The museum is designed for the visitor, not the worker, and to the visitor, as a very occasional inhabitant of the museum space, territory is of no importance, and orientation, unless he is in a hurry, is perhaps of much less pressing importance than in the office. In the office, paths and goals are usually quite distinct; thus corridors serve only as quick-communication channels between working areas for men and material. In the museum, both the path and the goal are important; indeed, they are often indistinguishable, and the designer's usual elimination of corridors in favor of a network of interconnected galleries is a recognition of this.

But the designer's desire to provide an "exciting experience" for the participant is often realized in the museum, often frustrated in the office, where the 40-hour-a-week worker rapidly becomes habituated to the design elements which excite the occasional visitor. This does not negate my original thesis; it simply reiterates that the intuitions of the designer are frequently inadequate to cope with the subtle contributions of the designed environment to behavior.

REFERENCES:

Barlow, J. S. Inertial navigation as a basis for animal navigation. *The Journal of Theoretical Biology*, 1964, **6**, 76–117.

Goodman, P. *Utopian essays and practical proposals.* New York: Random House, 1964.

Hall, E. T. *The hidden dimension.* Garden City, N.Y.: Doubleday, 1966.

Lynch, K. *The image of the city.* Cambridge, Mass.: MIT Press, 1960.

Parr, A. E. Environmental design and psychology. *Landscape*, 1964–1965, **14**, No. 2.

Richards, C. B., & Dobyns, H. F. Topography and culture: The case of the changing cage. *Human Organization*, 1957, **16**, 16–20.

Von Uexküll, J. A stroll through the world of animals and men. In Claire H. Schiller (Ed.), *Instinctive behavior: The development of a modern concept.* New York: International Universities Press, 1957.

5 The Goodness of Fit and Its Source

Christopher Alexander

I. THE GOODNESS OF FIT

The ultimate object of design is form. The reason that iron filings placed in a magnetic field exhibit a pattern—or have form, as we say—is that the field they are in is not homogeneous. If the world were totally regular and homogeneous, there would be no forces, and no forms. Everything would be amorphous. But an irregular world tries to compensate for its own irregularities by fitting itself to them, and thereby takes on form.[1] D'Arcy Thompson (1959, p. 16) has even called form the "diagram of forces" for the irregularities. More usually we speak of these irregularities as the functional origins of the form.

The following argument is based on the assumption that physical clarity cannot be achieved in a form until there is first some programmatic clarity in the designer's mind and actions; and that for this to be possible, in turn, the designer must first trace his design problem to its earliest functional origins and be able to find some sort of pat-

Reprinted by permission of the publishers from Christopher Alexander, *Notes on the Synthesis of Form*, Cambridge, Mass.: Harvard University Press, Copyright, 1964, by the President and Fellows of Harvard College.

[1] The source of form actually lies in the fact that the world tries to compensate for its irregularities as economically as possible. This principle, sometimes called the principle of least action, has been noted in various fields: notably by Le Chatelier, who observed that chemical systems tend to react to external forces in such a way as to neutralize the forces; also in mechanics as Newton's law, as Lenz's law in electricity, again as Volterra's theory of populations. See Mayer (1877).

tern in them. I shall try to outline a general way of stating design problems which draws attention to these functional origins, and makes their pattern reasonably easy to see.

It is based on the idea that every design problem begins with an effort to achieve fitness between two entities: the form in question and its context.[2] The form is the solution to the problem; the context defines the problem. In other words, when we speak of design, the real object of discussion is not the form alone, but the ensemble comprising the form and its context. Good fit is a desired property of this ensemble which relates to some particular division of the ensemble into form and context.[3]

There is a wide variety of ensembles which we can talk about like this. The biological ensemble made up of a natural organism and its physical environment is the most familiar: in this case we are used to describing the fit between the two as well-adaptedness (see Darwin, 1947; Cannon, 1939; Ashby, 1960). But the same kind of objective aptness is to be found in many other situations. The ensemble consisting of a suit and tie is a familiar case in point; one tie goes well with a certain suit, another goes less well (see Köhler, 1938, p. 96). Again, the ensemble may be a game of chess, where at a certain stage of the game some moves are more appropriate than others because they fit the context of the previous moves more aptly (see de Groot, 1956; Wittgenstein, 1953, p. 15). The ensemble may be a musical composition— musical phrases have to fit their contexts too: think of the perfect rightness when Mozart puts just *this* phrase at a certain point in a sonata (see Wertheimer, 1933, 1934). If the ensemble is a truck-driver plus

a traffic sign, the graphic design of the sign must fit the demands made on it by the driver's eye. An object like a kettle has to fit the context of its use, and the technical context of its production cycle (Holm & Larsen, 1953). In the pursuit of urbanism, the ensemble which confronts us is the city and its habits. Here the human background which defines the need for new buildings, and the physical environment provided by the available sites, make a context for the form of the city's growth. In an extreme case of this kind, we may even speak of a culture itself as an ensemble in which the various fashions and artifacts which develop are slowly fitted to the rest (see Collins, 1959).

The rightness of the form depends, in each one of these cases, on the degree to which it fits the rest of the ensemble (see Ozenfant, 1952, pp. 340–341; Koffka, 1935, pp. 638–644).

We must also recognize that no one division of the ensemble into form and context is unique. Fitness across any one such division is just one instance of the ensemble's internal coherence. Many other divisions of the ensemble will be equally significant. Indeed, in the great majority of actual cases, it is necessary for the designer to consider several different divisions of an ensemble, superimposed, at the same time.

Let us consider an ensemble consisting of the kettle plus everything about the world outside the kettle which is relevant to the use and manufacture of household utensils. Here again there seems to be a clear boundary between the teakettle and the rest of the ensemble, if we want one, because the kettle itself is a clearly defined kind of object. But I can easily make changes in the boundary. If I say that the kettle is the wrong way to heat domestic drinking water anyway, I can quickly be involved in the redesign of the entire house, and thereby push the context back to those things outside the house which influence the house's form. Alternatively I may claim that it is not the kettle which needs to be redesigned, but the method of heating kettles. In this case the kettle becomes part of the context, while the stove perhaps is form.

There are two sides to this tendency designers have to change the definition of the

---

[2] The symmetry of this situation (i.e., the fact that adaptation is a mutual phenomenon referring to the context's adaptation to the form as much as to the form's adaptation to its context) is very important.

[3] At later points where I use the word "system," this always refers to the whole ensemble. However, some care is required here, since many writers refer to that part of the ensemble which is held constant as the environment, and call only the part under adjustment the "system." For these writers my form, not my ensemble, would be the system.

problem. On the one hand, the impractical idealism of designers who want to redesign entire cities and whole processes of manufacture when they are asked to design simple objects is often only an attempt to loosen difficult constraints by stretching the form-context boundary.

On the other hand, this way in which the good designer keeps an eye on the possible changes at every point of the ensemble is part of his job. He is bound, if he knows what he is doing, to be sensitive to the fit at several boundaries within the ensemble at once. Indeed, this ability to deal with several layers of form-context boundaries in concert is an important part of what we often refer to as the designer's sense of organization. The internal coherence of an ensemble depends on a whole net of such adaptations. In a perfectly coherent ensemble we should expect the two halves of every possible division of the ensemble to fit one another.

It is true, then, that since we are ultimately interested in the ensemble as a whole, there is no good reason to divide it up just once. We ought always really to design with a number of nested, overlapped form-context boundaries in mind. Indeed, the form itself relies on its own inner organization and on the internal fitness between the pieces it is made of to control its fit as a whole to the context outside.

However, since we cannot hope to understand this highly interlaced and complex phenomenon until we understand how to achieve fit at a single arbitrarily chosen boundary, we must agree for the present to deal only with the simplest problem. Let us decide that, for the duration of any one discussion, we shall maintain the same single division of a given ensemble into form and context, even though we acknowledge that the division is probably chosen arbitrarily. And let us remember, as a corollary, that for the present we shall be giving no deep thought to the internal organization of the form as such, but only to the simplest premise and aspect of that organization: namely, that fitness which is the residue of adaptation across the single form-context boundary we choose to examine.

The form is a part of the world over which we have control, and which we decide to shape while leaving the rest of the world as it is. The context is that part of the world which puts demands on this form; anything in the world that makes demands of the form is context. Fitness is a relation of mutual acceptability between these two. In a problem of design we want to satisfy the mutual demands which the two make on one another. We want to put the context and the form into effortless contact or frictionless coexistence.

We now come to the task of characterizing the fit between form and context. Let us consider a simple specific case.

It is common practice in engineering, if we wish to make a metal face perfectly smooth and level, to fit it against the surface of a standard steel block, which is level within finer limits than those we are aiming at, by inking the surface of this standard block and rubbing our metal face against the inked surface. If our metal face is not quite level, ink marks appear on it at those points which are higher than the rest. We grind away these high spots, and try to fit it against the block again. The face is level when it fits the block perfectly, so that there are no high spots which stand out any more.

This ensemble of two metal faces is so simple that we shall not be distracted by the possibility of multiple form-context boundaries within it. There is only one such boundary worth discussion at a macroscopic level, that between the standard face (the context), and the face which we are trying to smooth (the form). Moreover, since the context is fixed, and only the form variable, the task of smoothing a metal face serves well as a paradigm design problem. In this case we may distinguish good fit from bad experimentally, by inking the standard block, putting the metal face against it, and checking the marking that gets transferred. If we wish to judge the form without actually putting it in contact with its context, in this case we may also do so. If we define levelness in mathematical terms, as a limitation on the variance which is permitted over the surface, we can test the form itself, without testing it against the context. We can do this because the criterion for levelness is, simultaneously, a description of the required form, and also a description of the context.

Consider a second, slightly more complex

example. Suppose we are to invent an arrangement of iron filings which is stable when placed in a certain position in a given magnetic field. Clearly we may treat this as a design problem. The iron filings constitute a form, the magnetic field a context. Again we may easily judge the fit of a form by placing it in the magnetic field, and watching to see whether any of the filings move under its influence. If they do not, the form fits well. And again, if we wish to judge the fit of the form without recourse to this experiment, we may describe the lines of force of the magnetic field in mathematical terms, and calculate the fit or lack of fit. As before, the opportunity to evaluate the form when it is away from its context depends on the fact that we can give a precise mathematical description of the context (in this case the equations of the magnetic field).

In general, unfortunately, we cannot give an adequate description of the context we are dealing with. The fields of the contexts we encounter in the real world cannot be described in the unitary fashion we have found for levelness and magnetic fields. There is as yet no theory of ensembles capable of expressing a unitary description of the varied phenomena we encounter in the urban context of a dwelling, for example, or in a sonata, or a production cycle.

Yet we certainly need a way of evaluating the fit of a form which does not rely on the experiment of actually trying the form out in the real world context. Trial-and-error design is an admirable method. But it is just real world trial and error which we are trying to replace by a symbolic method, because real trial and error is too expensive and too slow.

The experiment of putting a prototype form in the context itself is the real criterion of fit. A complete unitary description of the demands made by the context is the only fully adequate nonexperimental criterion. The first is too expensive, the second is impossible: so what shall we do?

Let us observe, first of all, that we should not really expect to be able to give a unitary description of the context for complex cases: if we could do so, there would be no problems of design. The context and the form are complementary. This is what lies behind D'Arcy Thompson's (1959) remark that the form is a diagram of forces. Once we have the diagram of forces in the literal sense (that is, the field description of the context), this will in essence also describe the form as a complementary diagram of forces. Once we have described the levelness of the metal block, or the lines of force of the magnetic field, there is no conceptual difficulty, only a technical one, in getting the form to fit them, because the unitary description of the context is in both cases also a description of the required form.

In such cases there is no design problem. *What does make design a problem in real world cases is that we are trying to make a diagram for forces whose field we do not understand.*[4] Understanding the field of the context and inventing a form to fit it are really two aspects of the same process. It is because the context is obscure that we cannot give a direct, fully coherent criterion for the fit we are trying to achieve; and it is also its obscurity which makes the task of shaping a well-fitting form at all problematic. What do we do about this difficulty in everyday cases? Good fit means something, after all—even in cases where we cannot give a completely satisfactory field-like criterion for it. How is it, cognitively, that we experience the sensation of fit?

If we go back to the procedure of leveling metal faces against a standard block, and think about the way in which good fit and bad fit present themselves to us, we find

---

[4] The concept of an image, comparable to the ideal field statement of a problem, is discussed by Miller, Galanter, & Pribram (1960). The "image" is presented as something present in every problem solver's mind, and used by him as a criterion for the problem's solution and hence as the chief guide in problem planning and solving. In the majority of interesting cases, however, I do not believe that such an image exists psychologically, so that the testing paradigm described by Miller et al. is therefore an incorrect description of complex problem-solving behavior. In interesting cases the solution of the problem cannot be tested against an image, because the search for the image or criterion for success is actually going on at the same time as the search for a solution. Miller does make a brief comment acknowledging this possibility on pp. 171–172. He also agreed to this point in personal discussions at Harvard in 1961.

a rather curious feature. Oddly enough, the procedure suggests no direct practical way of identifying good fit. We recognize bad fit whenever we see a high spot marked by ink. But in practice we see good fit only from a negative point of view, as the limiting case where there are no high spots.

Our own lives, where the distinction between good and bad fit is a normal part of everyday social behavior, show the same feature. If a man wears eighteenth-century dress today, or wears his hair down to his shoulders, or builds Gothic mansions, we very likely call his behavior odd; it does not fit our time. These are abnormalities. Yet it is such departures from the norm which stand out in our minds, rather than the norm itself. Their wrongness is somehow more immediate than the rightness of less peculiar behavior, and therefore more compelling. Thus even in everyday life the concept of good fit, though positive in meaning, seems very largely to feed on negative instances; it is the aspects of our lives which are obsolete, incongruous, or out of tune that catch our attention.

The same happens in house design. We should find it almost impossible to characterize a house which fits its context. Yet it is the easiest thing in the world to name the specific kinds of misfit which prevent good fit. A kitchen which is hard to clean, no place to park my car, the child playing where it can be run down by someone else's car, rainwater coming in, overcrowding and lack of privacy, the eye-level grill which spits hot fat right into my eye, the gold plastic doorknob which deceives my expectations, and the front door I cannot find, are all misfits between the house and the lives and habits it is meant to fit. These misfits are the forces which must shape it, and there is no mistaking them. Because they are expressed in negative form they are specific, and tangible enough to talk about.

The same thing happens in perception. Suppose we are given a button to match, from among a box of assorted buttons. How do we proceed? We examine the buttons in the box, one at a time; but we do not look directly for a button which fits the first. What we do, actually, is to scan the buttons, rejecting each one in which we notice some discrepancy (this one is larger, this one darker, this one has too many holes, and so on), until we come to one where we can see no differences. Then we say that we have found a matching one. Notice that here again it is much easier to explain the misfit of a wrong button than to justify the congruity of one which fits.

When we speak of bad fit we refer to a single identifiable property of an ensemble, which is immediate in experience, and describable. Wherever an instance of misfit occurs in an ensemble, we are able to point specifically at what fails and to describe it. It seems as though in practice the concept of good fit, describing only the absence of such failures and hence leaving us nothing concrete to refer to in explanation, can only be explained indirectly; it is, in practice, as it were, the disjunction of all possible misfits.[5]

With this in mind, I should like to recommend that we should always expect to see the process of achieving good fit between two entities as a negative process of neutralizing the incongruities, or irritants, or forces, which cause misfit (see Köhler, 1938, p. 345, pp. 329–360).[6]

It will be objected that to call good fit the absence of certain negative qualities is no more illuminating than to say that it is the presence of certain positive qualities.

[5] It is not hard to see why, if this is so, the concept of good fit is relatively hard to grasp. It has been shown by a number of investigators, for example, Bruner et al. (1958), that people are very unwilling and slow to accept disjunctive concepts. To be told what something is not is of very little use if you are trying to find out what it is. See also Hovland & Weiss, 1953.

[6] There is, to my mind, a striking similarity between the difficulty of dealing with good fit directly, in spite of its primary importance, and the difficulty of the concept zero. Zero and the concept of emptiness, too, are comparatively late inventions (clearly because they too leave one nothing to hold onto in explaining them). Even now we find it hard to conceive of emptiness as such: we only manage to think of it as the absence of something positive. Yet in many metaphysical systems, notably those of the East, emptiness and absence are regarded as more fundamental and ultimately more substantial than presence. This is also connected with the fact, now acknowledged by most biologists, that symmetry, being the natural condition of an unstressed situation, does not require explanation, but that on the contrary it is asymmetry which needs to be explained.

However, though the two are equivalent from a logical point of view, from a phenomenological and practical point of view they are very different.[7] In practice, it will never be as natural to speak of good fit as the simultaneous satisfaction of a number of requirements, as it will be to call it the simultaneous nonoccurrence of the same number of corresponding misfits.

Let us suppose that we did try to write down a list of all possible relations between a form and its context which were required by good fit. (Such a list would in fact be just the list of requirements which designers often do try to write down.) In theory, we could then use each requirement on the list as an independent criterion, and accept a form as well fitting only if it satisfied all these criteria simultaneously.

However, thought of in this way, such a list of requirements is potentially endless, and still really needs a "field" description to tie it together. Think, for instance, of trying to specify all the properties a button had to have in order to match another. Apart from the kinds of thing we have already mentioned, size, color, number of holes, and so on, we should also have to specify its specific gravity, its electrostatic charge, its viscosity, its rigidity, the fact that it should be round, that it should not be made of paper, etc., etc. In other words, we should not only have to specify the qualities which distinguish it from all other buttons, but we should also have to specify all the characteristics which actually made it a button at all.

Unfortunately, the list of distinguishable characteristics we can write down for the button is infinite. It remains infinite for all practical purposes until we discover a field description of the button. Without the field description of the button, there is no way of reducing the list of required attributes to finite terms. We are therefore forced to

economize when we try to specify the nature of a matching button, because we can only grasp a finite list (and rather a short one at that). Naturally, we choose to specify those characteristics which are most likely to cause trouble in the business of matching, and which are therefore most useful in our effort to distinguish among the objects we are likely to come across in our search for buttons. But to do this, we must rely on the fact that a great many objects will not even come up for consideration. There are, after all, conceivable objects which are buttons in every respect except that they carry an electric charge of one thousand coulombs, say. Yet in practice it would be utterly superfluous, as well as rather unwieldy, to specify the electrostatic charge a well-matched button needed to have. No button we are likely to find carries such a charge, so we ignore the possibility. The only reason we are able to match one thing with another at all is that we rely on a good deal of unexpressed information contained in the statement of the task, and take a great deal for granted (see Bruner, 1958, p. 166).

In the case of a design problem which is truly problematical, we encounter the same situation. We do not have a field description of the context, and therefore have no intrinsic way of reducing the potentially infinite set of requirements to finite terms. Yet for practical reasons we do need some way of picking a finite set from the infinite set of possible ones. In the case of requirements, no sensible way of picking this finite set presents itself. From a purely descriptive standpoint we have no way of knowing which of the infinitely many relations between form and context to include, and which ones to leave out.

But if we think of the requirements from a negative point of view, as potential misfits, there is a simple way of picking a finite set. This is because it is through misfit that the problem originally brings itself to our attention. We take just those relations between form and context which obtrude most strongly, which demand attention most clearly, which seem most likely to go wrong. We cannot do better than this. If there were some intrinsic way of reducing the list of requirements to a few, this would mean in essence that we were in possession of a field

[7] For the idea that departures from closure force themselves on the attention more strikingly than closure itself, and are actually the primary data of a certain kind of evaluative experience, and for a number of specific examples, see Wertheimer (1935). What I have been describing as misfits are described by Wertheimer as *Leerstellen* or emptiness. The feeling that something is missing, and the need to fill whatever is incomplete (*Lückenfullung*), are discussed.

description of the context: if this were so, the problem of creating fit would become trivial, and no longer a problem of design. We cannot have a unitary or field description of a context and still have a design problem worth attention.

In the case of a real design problem, even our conviction that there is such a thing as fit to be achieved is curiously flimsy and insubstantial. We are searching for some kind of harmony between two intangibles: a form which we have not yet designed, and a context which we cannot properly describe. The only reason we have for thinking that there must be some kind of fit to be achieved between them is that we can detect incongruities, or negative instances of it. The incongruities in an ensemble are the primary data of experience. If we agree to treat fit as the absence of misfits, and to use a list of those potential misfits which are most likely to occur as our criterion for fit, our theory will at least have the same nature as our intuitive conviction that there is a problem to be solved.

The results of this chapter, expressed in formal terms, are these. If we divide an ensemble into form and context, the fit between them may be regarded as an orderly condition of the ensemble, subject to disturbance in various ways, each one a potential misfit. Examples are the misfits between a house and its users, mentioned earlier. We may summarize the state of each potential misfit by means of a binary variable. If the misfit occurs, we say the variable takes the value 1. If the misfit does not occur, we say the variable takes the value 0. Each binary variable stands for one possible kind of misfit between form and context.[8] The value this variable takes, 0 or 1, describes a state of affairs that is not either in the form alone or in the context alone, but a relation between the two. The state of this relation, fit

or misfit, describes one aspect of the whole ensemble. It is a condition of harmony and good fit in the ensemble that none of the possible misfits should actually occur. We represent this fact by demanding that all the variables take the value 0.

The task of design is not to create form which meets certain conditions, but to create such an order in the ensemble that all the variables take the value 0. The form is simply that part of the ensemble over which we have control. It is only through the form that we can create order in the ensemble.

II. THE SOURCE OF GOOD FIT

We must now try to find out how we should go about getting good fit. Where do we find it? What is the characteristic of processes which create fit successfully?

It has often been claimed in architectural circles that the houses of simpler civilizations than our own are in some sense better than our own houses (Brodrick, 1954; Sumner, 1908). While these claims have perhaps been exaggerated, the observation is still sometimes correct. I shall try to show that the facts behind it, if correctly interpreted, are of great practical consequence for an intelligently conceived process of design.

Let us consider a few famous modern houses for a moment, from the point of view of their good fit. Mies Van der Rohe's Farnsworth house, though marvelously clear, and organized under the impulse of certain tight formal rules, is certainly not a triumph economically or from the point of view of the Illinois floods (Hilbersheimer, 1956, p. 63). Buckminster Fuller's geodesic domes have solved the weight problem of spanning space, but you can hardly put doors in them. Again, his dymaxion house, though efficient as a rapid-distribution mass-produced package, takes no account whatever of the incongruity of single free-standing houses set in the acoustic turmoil and service complexity of a modern city (Marks, 1960, pp. 110–133). Even Le Corbusier in the Villa Savoie, for example, or in the Marseilles apartments, achieves his clarity of form at the expense of certain elementary comforts and conveniences (Collins, 1960).

Laymen like to charge sometimes that

---

[8] In case it seems doubtful whether all the relevant properties of an ensemble can be expressed as variables, let us be quite clear about the fact that these variables are not necessarily capable of continuous variation. Indeed, it is quite obvious that most of the issues which occur in a design problem cannot be treated numerically, as this would require. A binary variable is simply a formal shorthand way of classifying situations; it is an indicator which distinguishes between forms that work and those that do not, in a given context.

these designers have sacrificed function for the sake of clarity, because they are out of touch with the practical details of the housewife's world, and preoccupied with their own interests. This is a misleading charge. What is true is that designers do often develop one part of a functional program at the expense of another. But they do it because the only way they seem able to organize form clearly is to design under the driving force of some comparatively simple concept.

On the other hand, if designers do not aim principally at clear organization, but do try to consider all the requirements equally, we find a kind of anomaly at the other extreme. Take the average developer-built house; it is built with an eye for the market, and in a sense, therefore, fits its context well, even if superficially. But in this case the various demands made on the form are met piecemeal, without any sense of the overall organization the form needs in order to contribute as a whole to the working order of the ensemble.

Since everything in the human environment can nowadays be modified by suitable purchases at the five and ten, very little actually has to be taken care of in the house's basic organization. Instead of orienting the house carefully for sun and wind, the builder conceives its organization without concern for orientation, and light, heat, and ventilation are taken care of by fans, lamps, and other kinds of peripheral devices. Bedrooms are not separated from living rooms in plan, but are placed next to one another and the walls between them then stuffed with acoustic insulation.

The complaint that macroscopic clarity is missing in these cases is no aesthetic whim. While it is true that an individual problem can often be solved adequately without regard for the fundamental physical order it implies, we cannot solve a whole net of such problems so casually, and get away with it. It is inconceivable that we should succeed in organizing an ensemble as complex as the modern city until we have a clear enough view of simpler design problems and their implications to produce houses which are physically clear as total organizations.

Yet at present, in our own civilization, house forms which are clearly organized and also satisfactory in all the respects demanded by the context are almost unknown.

If we look at a peasant farmhouse by comparison, or at an igloo, or at an African's mud hut, this combination of good fit and clarity is not quite so hard to find. Take the Mousgoum hut, for instance, built by African tribesmen in the northern section of the French Cameroun (Office de la Recherche Scientifique Outre-Mer, 1952). Apart from the variation caused by slight changes in site and occupancy, the huts vary very little. Even superficial examination shows that they are all versions of the same single form type, and convey a powerful sense of their own adequacy and nonarbitrariness.

Whether by coincidence or not, the hemispherical shape of the hut provides the most efficient surface for minimum heat transfer, and keeps the inside reasonably well protected from the heat of the equatorial sun. Its shape is maintained by a series of vertical reinforcing ribs. Besides helping to support the main fabric, these ribs also act as guides for rainwater, and are at the same time used by the builder of the hut as footholds which give him access to the upper part of the outside during its construction. Instead of using disposable scaffolding (wood is very scarce), he builds the scaffolding in as part of the structure. What is more, months later this "scaffolding" is still there when the owner needs to climb up on it to repair the hut. The Mousgoum cannot afford, as we do, to regard maintenance as a nuisance which is best forgotten until it is time to call the local plumber. It is in the same hands as the building operation itself, and its exigencies are as likely to shape the form as those of the initial construction.

Again, each hut nestles beautifully in the dips and hollows of the terrain. It must, because its fabric is as weak structurally as the earth it sits on, and any foreignness or discontinuity caused by careless siting would not have survived the stresses of erosion. The weather-defying concrete foundations which we rely on, and which permit the arbitrary siting of our own houses, are unknown to the Mousgoum.

The grouping of the huts reflects the social order of their inhabitants. Each man's hut is surrounded by the huts of his wives and his subservients, as social customs require—

and in such a way, moreover, that these subsidiary huts also form a wall round the chief's hut and thereby protect it and themselves from wild beasts and invaders.

This example shows how the pattern of the building operation, the pattern of the building's maintenance, the constraints of the surrounding conditions, and also the pattern of daily life, are fused in the form. The form has a dual coherence. It is coherently related to its context. And it is physically coherent.

This kind of dual coherence is common in simple cultures. Yet in our own culture the only forms which match these simpler forms for overall clarity of conception are those we have already mentioned, designed under the impulse of very special preoccupations. And these forms, just because they derive their clarity from simplification of the problem, fail to meet all the context's demands. It is true that our functional standards are higher than those in the simple situation. It is true, and important to remember, that the simple cultures never face the problems of complexity which we face in design. And it is true that if they did face them, they would probably not make any better a showing than we do (Brodrick, 1954, p. 101). When we admire the simple situation for its good qualities, this doesn't mean that we wish we were back in the same situation. The dream of innocence is of little comfort to us; our problem, the problem of organizing form under complex constraints, is new and all our own. But in their own way the simple cultures do their simple job better than we do ours. I believe that only careful examination of their success can give us the insight we need to solve the problem of complexity. Let us ask, therefore, where this success comes from.

To answer this question we shall first have to draw a sharp and arbitrary line between those cultures we want to call simple, for the purposes of argument, and those we wish to classify with ours. I propose calling certain cultures unselfconscious, to contrast them with others, including our own, which I propose to call selfconscious.

Of course, the contrast in quality between the forms produced in the two different kinds of culture is by no means as marked as I shall suggest. Nor are the two form-making processes sharply distinguished, as my text pretends. But I have deliberately exaggerated the contrast, simply to draw attention to certain matters, important and illuminating in their own right, which we must understand before we can map out a new approach to design. It is far more important that we should understand the particular contrast I am trying to bring out, than that the facts about any given culture should be accurate or telling. This is not an anthropological treatise, and it is therefore best to think of the first part of the following discussion simply as a comparison of two descriptive constructs, the unselfconscious culture and the selfconscious culture.

The cultures I choose to call "unselfconscious" have, in the past, been called by many other names—each name chosen to illuminate whatever aspect of the contrast between kinds of culture the writer was most anxious to bring out. Thus they have been called "primitive," to distinguish them from those where kinship plays a less important part in social structure (Radcliffe-Brown, 1925); "folk," to set them apart from urban cultures (Redfield, 1947); "closed," to draw attention to the responsibility of the individual in today's more open situation (Popper, 1950); "anonymous," to distinguish them from cultures in which a profession called "architecture" exists (Moholy-Nagy, 1957).

The particular distinction I wish to make touches only the last of these: the method of making things and buildings. Broadly, we may distinguish between our own culture, which is very selfconscious about its architecture, art, and engineering, and certain specimen cultures which are rather unselfconscious about theirs.[9] The features

[9] Of course, although selfconsciousness, as I shall define it, does tend to affect many aspects of culture at once, we certainly know of cases where cultures are highly selfconscious in some respects, yet quite unselfconscious in others. It is especially important to avoid any suggestion of evolution here (to the effect that all cultures are at first unselfconscious, and become uniformly less so as they grow more mature). The fact is that selfconsciousness is differently directed in different cultures; some people give their closest attention to one sort of thing, some to another. See Mauss (1935).

which distinguish architecturally unselfconscious cultures from selfconscious ones are easy to describe loosely. In the unselfconscious culture there is little thought about architecture or design as such. There is a right way to make buildings and a wrong way; but while there may be generally accepted remedies for specific failures, there are no general principles comparable to Alberti's treatises or Le Corbusier's. Since the division of labor is very limited, specialization of any sort is rare, there are no architects, and each man builds his own house (see Summer, 1908, pp. 3–4; Lévy-Bruhl, 1925, pp. 109–116; Brown, 1958, pp. 272–273; Whorf, 1953).

The technology of communication is underdeveloped. There are no written records or architectural drawings, and little intercultural exchange. This lack of written records and lack of information about other cultures and situations means that the same experience has to be won over and over again generation after generation—without opportunity for development or change. With no variety of experience, people have no chance to see their own actions as alternatives to other possibilities, and instead of becoming selfconscious, they simply repeat the patterns of tradition, because these are the only ones they can imagine. In a word, actions are governed by habit (Redfield, 1947). Design decisions are made more according to custom than according to any individual's new ideas. Indeed, there is little value attached to the individual's ideas as such. There is no special market for his inventiveness. Ritual and taboo discourage innovation and self-criticism. Besides, since there is no such thing as "architecture" or "design," and no abstractly formulated problems of design, the kinds of concept needed for architectural self-criticism are too poorly developed to make such self-criticism possible; indeed the architecture itself is hardly tangibly enough conceived as such to criticize.

To be sure that such a distinction between unselfconscious and selfconscious cultures is permissible, we need a definition which will tell us whether to call a culture unselfconscious or selfconscious on the basis of visible and reportable facts alone. We find a clearly visible distinction when we look at the way the crafts of form-building are taught and learned, the institutions under which skills pass from one generation to the next. For there are essentially two ways in which such education can operate, and they may be distinguished without difficulty.

At one extreme we have a kind of teaching that relies on the novice's very gradual exposure to the craft in question, on his ability to imitate by practice, on his response to sanctions, penalties, and reinforcing smiles and frowns. The great example of this kind of learning is the child's learning of elementary skills, like bicycle riding. He topples almost randomly at first, but each time he does something wrong, it fails; when he happens to do it right, its success and the fact that his success is recognized make him more likely to repeat it right (Skinner, 1938; Gillin & Gillin, 1948, p. 80). Extended learning of this kind gives him a "total" feeling for the thing learned—whether it is how to ride a bicycle, or a skill like swimming, or the craft of housebuilding or weaving. The most important feature of this kind of learning is that the rules are not made explicit, but are, as it were, revealed through the correction of mistakes.

The second kind of teaching tries, in some degree, to make the rules explicit. Here the novice learns much more rapidly, on the basis of general "principles." The education becomes a formal one; it relies on instruction and on teachers who train their pupils, not just by pointing out mistakes, but by inculcating positive explicit rules. A good example is lifesaving, where people rarely have the chance to learn by trial and error. In the informal situation there are no "teachers," for the novice's mistakes will be corrected by anybody who knows more than he. But in the formal situation, where learning is a specialized activity and no longer happens automatically, there are distinct "teachers" from whom the craft is learned.

These teachers, or instructors, have to condense the knowledge which was once laboriously acquired in experience, for without such condensation the teaching problem would be unwieldy and unmanageable. The teacher cannot refer explicitly to each single mistake which can be made, for even if there were time to do so, such a list could not be learned. A list needs a structure for mnemonic purposes (Bruner, 1960, p. 24). So the teacher invents teachable rules within which he accommodates as much of his unconscious training as he can—a set of shorthand principles.

In the unselfconscious culture the same form is made over and over again; in order to learn form-making, people need only learn to repeat a single familiar physical pattern. In the selfconscious culture new purposes are occurring all the time; the people who make forms are constantly required to deal with problems that are either entirely new or at best modifications of old problems. Under these circumstances it is not enough to copy old physical patterns. So that people will be able to make innovations and modifications as required, ideas about how and why things get their shape must be introduced. Teaching must be based on explicit general principles of function, rather than unmentioned and specific principles of shape.

I shall call a culture unselfconscious if its form-making is learned informally, through imitation and correction. And I shall call a culture selfconscious if its form-making is taught academically, according to explicit rules (Hall, 1959).

Now why are forms made in the selfconscious culture not so well fitting or so clearly made as those in the unselfconscious culture? In one case the form-making process is a good one, in the other bad. What is it that makes a form-making process good or bad?

In explaining why the unselfconscious process is a good one, hardly anyone bothers, nowadays, to argue the myth of the primitive genius, the unsophisticated craftsman supposedly more gifted than his sophisticated counterpart. The myth of architectural Darwinism has taken its place (Sumner, 1908, p. 54; Radcliffe-Brown, 1952, pp. 7–9). Yet though this new myth is more acceptable, in its usual form it is not really any more informative than the other.

It says, roughly, that primitive forms are good as a result of a process of gradual adaptation—that over many centuries such forms have gradually been fitted to their cultures by an intermittent though persistent series of corrections. But this explanation is vague hand-waving.[10] It doesn't tell us what it is that prevents such adaptation from taking place successfully in the selfconscious culture, which is what we want to know most urgently. And even as an explanation of good fit in the unselfconscious culture, the raw concept of adaptation is something less than satisfactory. If forms in an unselfconscious culture fit now, the chances are that they always did. We know of no outstanding differences between the present states and past states of unselfconscious cultures; and this assumption, that the fit of forms in such cultures is the result of gradual adjustment (that is, improvement) over time, does not illuminate what must actually be a dynamic process in which both form and context change continuously, and yet stay mutually well adjusted all the time.

To understand the nature of the form-making process, it is not enough to give a quick one-word account of unselfconscious form-making: adaptation. We shall have to compare the detailed inner working of the unselfconscious form-making process with that of the selfconscious process, asking why one works and the other fails. Roughly speaking, I shall argue that the unselfconscious process has a structure that makes it homeostatic (self-organizing), and that it therefore consistently produces well-fitting forms, even in the face of change. And I shall argue that in a selfconscious culture the homeostatic structure of the process is broken down, so that the production of forms which fail to fit their contexts is not only possible, but likely.

We decided in the last section that to describe fit and misfit between form and context, we must make a list of binary variables, each naming some one potential misfit which may occur.

Whether a form-making process is self-conscious or unselfconscious, these misfit

---

[10] The archeological evidence is so thin that any pseudo-Darwinian accounts based on it cannot be more than highly general and rather doubtful fictions.

variables are always present, lingering in the background of the process, as thoughts in a designer's mind, or as actions, criticisms, failures, doubts. Only the thought or the experience of possible failure provides the impetus to make new form.

At any moment in a form-making process, whether the form is in use, a prototype, as yet only a sketch, or obsolete, each of the variables is in a state of either fit or misfit. We may describe the state of all the variables at once by a row of 1's and 0's, one for each variable: for instance, for twenty variables, 00100110101110110000 would be one state. Each possible row of 1's and 0's is a possible state of the ensemble.

As form-making proceeds, so the system of variables changes state. One misfit is eradicated, another misfit occurs, and these changes in their turn set off reactions within the system that affect the states of other variables. As form and culture change, state follows state. The sequence of states which the system passes through is a record or history of the adaptation between form and context. The history of the system displays the form-making process at work. To compare unselfconscious and selfconscious form-making processes, we have only to examine the kinds of history which the system of variables can have in these two processes. As we shall see, the kinds of history which the system can have in the unselfconscious and selfconscious processes are very different.

We shall perhaps understand the idea of a system's history best if we make a simple picture of it.[11]

Imagine a system of a hundred lights. Each light can be in one of two possible states. In one state the light is on. The lights are so constructed that any light which is on always has a 50–50 chance of going off in the next second. In the other state the light is off. Connections between lights are constructed so that any light which is off has a 50–50 chance of going on again in the next second, provided at least one of the lights it is connected to is on. If the lights it is directly connected to are off, for the

time being it has no chance of going on again, and stays off. If the lights are ever all off simultaneously, then they will all stay off for good, since when no light is on, none of the lights has any chance of being reactivated. This is a state of equilibrium. Sooner or later the system of lights will reach it.

This system of lights will help us understand the history of a form-making process. Each light is a binary variable, and so may be thought of as a misfit variable. The off state corresponds to fit; the on state corresponds to misfit. The fact that a light which is on has a 50–50 chance of going off every second, corresponds to the fact that whenever a misfit occurs efforts are made to correct it. The fact that lights which are off can be turned on again by connected lights, corresponds to the fact that even well-fitting aspects of a form can be unhinged by changes initiated to correct some other misfit because of connections between variables. The state of equilibrium, when all the lights are off, corresponds to perfect fit or adaptation. It is the equilibrium in which all the misfit variables take the value 0. Sooner or later the system of lights will always reach this equilibrium. The only question that remains is, how long will it take for this to happen? It is not hard to see that apart from chance this depends only on the pattern of interconnections between the lights.

Let us consider two extreme circumstances.

1. On the one hand, suppose there are no interconnections between lights at all. In this case there is nothing to prevent each light's staying off for good, as soon as it goes off. The average time it takes for all the lights to go off is therefore only a little greater than the average time it takes for a single light to go off, namely 2^1 seconds or 2 seconds.

2. On the other hand, imagine such rich interconnections between lights that any one light still on quickly rouses all others from the off state and puts them on again. The only way in which this system can reach adaptation is by the pure chance that all 100 happen to go off at the same moment. The average time which must elapse before this happens will be of the order of 2^{100} seconds, or 10^{22} years.

[11] This example is based on one given in Ashby (1960).

The second case is useless. The age of the universe itself is only about 10^{10} years. For all intents and purposes the system will never adapt. But the first case is no use either. In any real system there are interconnections between variables which make it impossible for each variable to adapt in complete isolation. Let us therefore construct a third possibility.

3. In this case suppose there are again interconnections among the 100 lights, but that we discern in the pattern of interconnections some 10 principal subsystems, each containing 10 lights. The lights within each subsystem are so strongly connected to one another that again all 10 must go off simultaneously before they will stay off; yet at the same time the subsystems themselves are independent of one another as wholes, so that the lights in one subsystem can be switched off without being reactivated by others flashing in other subsystems. The average time it will take for all 100 lights to go off is about the same as the time it takes for one subsystem to go off, namely 2^{10} seconds, or about a quarter of an hour.

Of course, real systems do not behave so simply. But fifteen minutes is not much greater than the two seconds it takes an isolated variable to adapt, and the enormous gap between these magnitudes and 10^{22} years does teach us a vital lesson. No complex adaptive system will succeed in adapting in a reasonable amount of time unless the adaptation can proceed subsystem by subsystem, each subsystem relatively independent of the others.

This is a familiar fact. It finds a close analogy in the children's sealed glass-fronted puzzles which are such fun and so infuriating. The problem, in these puzzles, is to achieve certain configurations within the box: rings on sticks, balls in sockets, pieces of various shapes in odd-shaped frames—but all to be done by gentle tapping on the outside of the box. Think of the simplest of these puzzles, where half a dozen colored beads, say, are each to be put in a hole of corresponding color.

One way to go about this problem would be to pick the puzzle up, give it a single energetic shake, and lay it down again, in the hope that the correct configuration would appear by accident. This all-or-nothing method might be repeated many thousand times, but it is clear that its chances of success are negligible. It is the technique of a child who does not understand how best to play. Much the easiest way—and the way we do in fact adopt under such circumstances—is to juggle one bead at a time. Once a bead is in, provided we tap gently, it is in for good, and we are free to manipulate the next one that presents itself, and we achieve the full configuration step by step. When we treat each bead as an isolable subsystem, and take the subsystems independently, we can solve the puzzle.

If we now consider the process of form-making, in the light of these examples, we see an easy way to make explicit the distinction between processes which work and those which don't.

Let us remind ourselves of the precise sense in which there is a system active in a form-making process. It is a purely fictitious system. Its variables are the conditions which must be met by good fit between form and context. Its interactions are the causal linkages which connect the variables to one another. If there is not enough light in a house, for instance, and more windows are added to correct this failure, the change may improve the light but allow too little privacy; another change for more light makes the windows bigger, perhaps, but thereby makes the house more likely to collapse. These are examples of inter-variable linkage. If we represent this system by drawing a point for each misfit variable, and a link between two points for each such causal linkage, we get a structure which looks something like that which appears in Figure 5-1.

Now, let us go back to the question of adaptation. Clearly these misfit variables, being interconnected, cannot adjust inde-

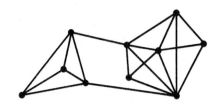

Figure 5–1

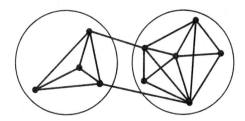

Figure 5–2

pendently, one by one. On the other hand, since not all the variables are equally strongly connected (in other words there are not only dependences among the variables, but also *independences*), there will always be subsystems like those circled in Figure 5-2, which can, in principle, operate fairly independently.

We may therefore picture the process of form-making as the action of a series of subsystems, all interlinked, yet sufficiently free of one another to adjust independently in a feasible amount of time. It works, because the cycles of correction and recorrection, which occur during adaptation, are restricted to one subsystem at a time.

We shall not be able to see, directly, whether or not the unselfconscious and selfconscious form-making processes operate by subsystems. Instead we shall infer their modes of operation indirectly.

The greatest clue to the inner structure of any dynamic process lies in its reaction to change. A culture does not move from one change to the next in discrete steps, of course. New threads are being woven all the time, making changes continuous and smooth. But from the point of view of its effect on a form, change only becomes significant at that moment when a failure or misfit reaches critical importance—at that moment when it is recognized, and people feel the form has something wrong with it. It is therefore legitimate, for our purpose, to consider a culture as changing in discrete steps.

We wish to know, now, how the form-making process reacts to one such change. Whether a new, previously unknown misfit occurs or a known one recurs, in both cases, from our point of view, some one variable changes value from 0 to 1. What, precisely, happens when a misfit variable takes the

value 1? How does the process behave under this stimulus?

Let us go back for a moment to our system of 100 lights. Suppose the system is in a state of fit—that is, all the lights are switched off. Now imagine that every once in a while one light gets switched on by an outside agent, even though no others are on to activate it. By waiting to see what happens next, we can very easily deduce the inner nature of the system, even though we cannot see it directly. If the light always flashes just once, and then goes off again and stays off, we deduce that the lights are able to adapt independently, and hence that there are no interconnections between lights. If the light activates a few other lights, and they flash together for a while, and then switch themselves off, we deduce that there are subsystems of interconnected lights active. If the light flashes and then activates other lights until all of them are flashing, and they never settle down again, we deduce that the system is unable to adapt subsystem by subsystem because the interconnections are too rich.

The solitary light switched on by an external agent is the occasional misfit which occurs. The reaction of the system to the disturbance is the reaction of the form-making process to the misfit. If we detect the active presence of subsystems in a process, we may then argue (by induction, as it were) that this is fully responsible for the good fit of the forms being produced by the process. For if good forms can always be adjusted correctly the moment any slight misfit occurs, then no sequence of changes will destroy the good fit ever (at least while the process maintains this character); and provided there was good fit at some stage in the past, no matter how remote (the first term of the induction), it will have persisted, because there is an active stability at work. If, on the other hand, a form-making process is such that a minor culture change can upset the good fit of the forms it produces, then any well-fitting forms we may observe at one time or another fit only by accident; and the next cultural deflection may once more lead to the production of badly fitting forms.

It is the inner nature of the process which

counts. The vital point that underlies the discussion is that the form-builders in unselfconscious cultures respond to small changes in a way that allows the subsystems of the misfit system to work independently—but that because the selfconscious response to change cannot take place subsystem by subsystem, its forms are arbitrary.

REFERENCES:

Ashby, W. R. Design for a brain (2nd ed.) New York: Wiley, 1960.
Brodrick, R. H. Grass roots. Architectural Review, 1954, 115, 101–111.
Brown, R. Words and things. Glencoe, Ill.: The Free Press, 1958.
Bruner, J. S., Goodnow, J. J., & Austin, G. A. A study of thinking. New York: Wiley, 1958.
Bruner, J. S. The process of education. Cambridge, Mass.: Harvard University Press, 1960.
Cannon, W. B. The wisdom of the body. New York: W. W. Norton, 1939.
Collins, P. Biological analogy. Architectural Review, 1959, 126, 303–306.
Collins, P. Not with steel and cement. Manchester Guardian Weekly, Jan. 14, 1960.
Darwin, C. The origin of species. New York: E. P. Dutton, 1947.
de Groot, A. D. Über das Denken des Schachspielers. Rivista di psicologia, 1956, 50, 90–91.
Gillin, J. L., & Gillin, J. P. Cultural sociology. New York: 1948.
Hall, E. T. The silent language. New York: Doubleday, 1959.
Hilbersheimer, L. Mies van der Rohe. Chicago: P. Theobald, 1956.
Holm, K. L., & Larsen, C. T. Development index. Ann Arbor: University of Michigan Press, 1953.
Hovland, C. L., & Weiss, W. Transmission of information concerning concepts through positive and negative instances. Journal of Experimental Psychology, 1953, 45, 175–182.
Koffka, K. Principles of Gestalt psychology. London: Harcourt, Brace, 1935.
Köhler, W. The place of value in a world of facts. New York: Liveright, 1938.
Lévy-Bruhl, L. How natives think. London: G. Allen and Unwin, 1925.
Marks, R. W. The dymaxion world of Buckminster Fuller. New York: Reinhold, 1960.
Mauss, M. Les techniques du corps. Journal de psychologie, 1935, 32, 271–293.
Mayer, A. Geschichte des prinzipsder isleinsten action. Leipzig, 1887.
Miller, G. A., Galanter, E., & Pribram, K. H. Plans and the structure of behavior. New York: Holt, Rinehart and Winston, 1960.
Moholy-Nagy, S. Native genius in anonymous architecture. New York: Horizon Press, 1957.
Office de la Recherche Scientifique Outre-Mer. L'Habitat aux Cameroun. Paris: 1952.
Ozenfant, A. Foundations of modern art. New York: Dover, 1952.
Popper, K. R. The open society and its enemies. Princeton, N.J.: Princeton University Press, 1950.
Radcliffe-Brown, A. R. Structure and function in primitive society. Glencoe, Ill.: The Free Press, 1925.
Redfield, R. The folk society. American Journal of Sociology, 1947, 52, 298–308.
Skinner, B. F. The behavior of organisms. New York: Appleton-Century, 1938.
Sumner, W. G. Folkways. Boston: Ginn, 1908.
Thompson, D. W. On growth and form, (2nd ed.) Cambridge, Eng.: Cambridge University Press, 1959.
Wertheimer, M. Zu dem problem der unterscheidung von einzelinhalt und teil. Zeitschrift für Psychologie, 1933, 129, 356.
Wertheimer, M. On truth. Social Research, 1934, 1, 144.
Wertheimer, M. Some problems in ethics. Social Research, 1935, 2, 352 ff.
Whorf, B. L. Linguistic factors in the terminology of Hopi architecture. International Journal of American Linguistics, 1953, 19, 141.
Wittgenstein, L. Philosophical investigations. Oxford: Blackwell, 1953.

6 The Dynamics of Behavior-Contingent Physical Systems[1]

Raymond G. Studer

In his analysis of scientific revolutions, Thomas Kuhn (1962) identifies characteristics of scientific development which may have relevance for the environmental design community. He argues that what gives continuity to disparate research activities in a particular scientific area is the pervasive recognition of a *paradigm*. Historically the process of arriving at a firm research consensus is extremely arduous. Once acquired, however, the shared paradigm permits the more esoteric type of research which is characteristic of mature scientific status. The developmental pattern of a mature science, Kuhn points out, is the successive transition from one paradigm to another via revolution. The design community cannot be said to

From G. Broadbent and A. Ward (Eds.), Portsmouth College of Technology Symposium on Design Methods, Portsmouth, England. London: Messrs. Lund Humphries Ltd., 1969.

[1] Aspects of this research and preparation of this manuscript were partially supported by Contract CST-408, U. S. Bureau of Standards, Institute for Applied Technology.

have experienced a revolution in this sense, but it has seen the need to identify a research consensus. Collectively we seek a paradigm.

The following remarks are intended to suggest the basis for a paradigm of sorts. As such, they are necessarily and frankly quite broad and somewhat theoretical. Hopefully something of the real world comes through, for there may be useful implications for environmental design and research. Whatever else might be gained, the search for a paradigm almost immediately makes explicit and conspicuous the nature of our ignorance, a fact which will be made abundantly clear many times throughout this presentation. In this regard one can take heart in Karl Popper's suggestion that "It might be well for all of us to remember that while differing widely in the various little bits we know, in our infinite ignorance we are all about equal" (Popper, 1959). The underlying objective in these formulations is the accommodation, or integration, of two generally emerging, but hitherto tenuously connected ideas: a more lucid epistemology of the man-made environment, and more effective design methods. This is obviously a period of great attitudinal change within the design community, and the Zeitgeist embodies an impressive array of concepts which are both highly innovative and disparate. In such a milieu it is often difficult to know where one's own ideas begin and another's end. The intention here is to both build upon, and refute, certain aspects of recent work in design method (e.g., C. Alexander, 1964). If this is the case, so much the better, for it suggests that the design disciplines may at last be moving toward a research consensus, one whereby knowledge—not of products but processes—becomes cumulative.

The move to externalize, evaluate and model more viable design procedures is having a trenchant effect. The potential success and/or failure of these various efforts has led this researcher to become less concerned with the methods of formal synthesis per se, and more concerned with the precepts which guide problem formulation. The reasons for this concern are quite obvious. Our understanding of, and mode of conceptualizing, the problem space has a profound

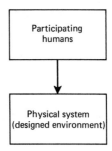

Figure 6–1

effect upon internal procedures, not to mention the resultant product. To put it another way, there is the distinct possibility that a designer, or method, may operate quite effectively while solving the *wrong problem!*

These arguments are based upon the proposition that what is critically needed in environmental design is a unit of analysis with dimensions which are both relevant and empirically accessible. "Relevance" has meant many things for designers, but in terms of this historical situation an acceptable unit must have relevance in terms of the *participating organism(s)* (see Figure 6-1).

The most commonly accepted unit for design purposes is "human need." Such a concept has relevance perhaps; what it lacks is empirical substance. That is, we cannot observe need, but can only infer its existence through observation of its empirical counterpart, *behavior* (see Figure 6-2). Human behavior appears to be the more correct unit of analysis; it has characteristics which

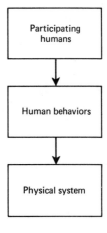

Figure 6–2

are relevant, empirically verifiable, and operationally definable. Assuming behavior as the class of independent variables—an index of biological and nonbiological need—what are the implications for environmental design?

A behavior-contingent paradigm challenges not only the concept of "need," but conventional problem space descriptions and boundaries generally. "Building," "urban core," "house," "city," "school," "room," and so forth are conceptual entities which may have little relevance in the description of appropriate problem spaces. These historically preconditioned terms obviously bias and inhibit both the logical and behavioral aspects of problem-solving; but more important, they describe the *wrong class* of variables. That is, physical characteristics are defined (in intension[2] as it were) in a manner which begs the very (design) question which a viable design process is intended to answer. The "building type" mentality thus assures that the problem space is arbitrarily described and prematurely closed, and that the behavioral goals of the inhabitants are constrained without ever having been analyzed. A new taxonomy of problem formulation is in order, one which objectifies with greater fidelity the implicit continuum of highly differentiated events—the ordered variety—which characterizes human life in a particular context. A behavior-contingent approach then rejects the stereotyped "list of physical requirements" in favor of a more basic and relevant taxonomy. The detection, isolation and structure of environmental problems grow out of an analysis of human behavior systems. It is only through an analysis of this class of variables that quantities, qualities and relationships of elements in the *designed environment* (Studer, 1966) can be properly determined. A designed environment is essentially a system of energy-matter elements which are interposed between a collection of human participants and antithetical forces in the general, impinging milieu, i.e., the designed environment complement. When properly config-

[2] See B. Russell (1956) on intensional and extensional definitions.

ured, these energy-matter elements produce and support the various activities required to meet the goals of the human participants under analysis. That is, the designed environment can be analyzed as a *prosthetic* phenomenon. It functions prosthetically in two distinct but interrelated modes: (1) it is *physiologically* prosthetic in that it supports behavioral goals through maintenance of required (behaviorally correlated) physiological states, and (2) it is *behaviorally* prosthetic (Lindsley, 1964) in that it intentionally configures specific behavioral topographies.

We need no particular label for such physical systems, and it adds nothing to our understanding of the substance of the problem, or its solution, to assign them. Indeed it is in response to the linguistic amorphism which abounds within the design community that generic concepts are used throughout this presentation. When the term "designed environment" or "physical system" is used, for example, this should not be construed as a self-conscious attempt to promote a more esoteric jargon. It is rather a straightforward recognition that terms such as "architecture" and "buildings" are too restrictive and dissimilar in conventional meaning to adequately characterize the intended phenomena.

The systems which must be accommodated in a behavior-contingent approach are rather easily identified, at least in general terms. They are, however, very difficult to realize. The conceptual and technical issues which must eventually be dealt with involve the following operations, each of which will be briefly discussed (see Figure 6-3):

1. Defining the requisite behavior system
2. Specifying the requisite physical system
3. Realizing the requisite physical system
4. Verifying the resultant environment-behavior system

ASPECTS OF A BEHAVIOR-CONTINGENT APPROACH

Defining the requisite behaviors to be accommodated in a particular problem situation has not traditionally been an aspect of

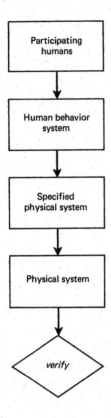

Figure 6–3

concern in design method. It is an essential aspect, however, and the implicit operations must come to be better understood. One quite naturally seeks an approach with empirical substance. Careful observation and extensive interviews with the potential users would therefore seem to yield the kind of behavioral data required. Naturalistic observations of, and verbal reports from, the human participants (or class of them) to be re-accommodated are obviously important and necessary to gain insight into a problem situation. Such information alone, however, will not produce the requisite behaviors, because what is being observed (and responded to) is a physical setting which is ostensibly in a state of malfunction. If this were not the case no problem situation would exist. The task of identifying behaviors for environmental design is not fundamentally empirical, but *normative*. Like the economist, the environmental designer "does not try to prescribe *what* people ought to want—he is not normative in

that sense—but he does try to prescribe *how* they should go about getting what they want" (G. A. Miller, 1964). Objectifying and identifying the values and purpose of a particular subculture can sometimes be a difficult and delicate procedure. Without such information, however, no environmental problem can be conceptualized. In other words, it might be said that a collection of humans with no identifiable purpose can have no identifiable problems. Indeed every interacting collection of humans, whether large, small, formal or informal, evolves and maintains itself in response to some explicit or implicit purpose. James G. Miller defines purpose as follows:

> By the information input of its charter, or genetic input, or by changes in behavior brought about by rewards and punishments from its suprasystem, a system develops a preferential hierarchy of values that . . . determine its preference for one internal steady state value rather than another. This is its purpose [Miller, 1965].

A human organization's purpose in turn delimits its goals and the kinds of behaviors required to accommodate them. Beyond the difficult questions involved in identifying values and purpose, the task of extensionally, or operationally, defining a human organization's goals in terms of a behavioral network is a complex proposition with highly technical ramifications. Because no inductive procedure seems possible (see comments above), defining the requisite behavior system in a particular problem situation is essentially a problem of *design*. It is a problem of (behavioral) design in the sense that no deterministic procedures exist for delineating a behavior system for a given set of goals (see Figure 6-4). This behavior system design is constrained by the physiological and psychological characteristics of the population under analysis. It is also constrained by the cultural suprasystem within which the population, or participating humans, must operate. Fortunately, some powerful analytic tools are becoming available which can assist the conceptualization of behavior systems for environmental design. These include, for example, the inter-

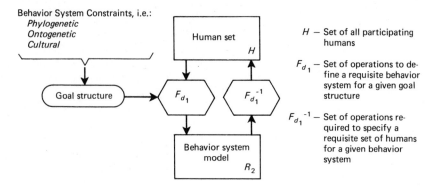

Figure 6–4

related resources of: behavior-oriented organization theory (March & Simon, 1958), information network theory (J. Rothstein, 1954) and simulation of human groups (Guetzkow, 1962). Indeed any heuristic or algorithm which facilitates the solution of multiple outcome problems has relevance for this kind of design task. The result could be called the *behavior system model* (see R_2 in Figure 6-5).

It is only after a behavior system has been conceptualized—in response to the organization's purpose(s), goals and subgoals—that the very existence of a physical problem can be determined. Without a proper behavioral analysis we are not only likely to misstructure physical problems, but may also misclassify them as well. That is, we often see a problem as physical when it is another aspect of the environment which is causing behavioral dissonance. A physical problem exists if and only if there is disequilibrium between requisite behaviors and the designed environment. The tests (see Figure 6-5, "Test 1") which must be applied to determine physical dissonance include: (1) systematically comparing the conceptualized requisite behavior system (R_2) to the extant system (R_1) in order to detect disparities (according to certain tolerance thresholds), and (2) determining whether or not these disparities are attributable to elements in the physical system (S_1^{de}). Dysfunction may, in fact, be attributable to some other

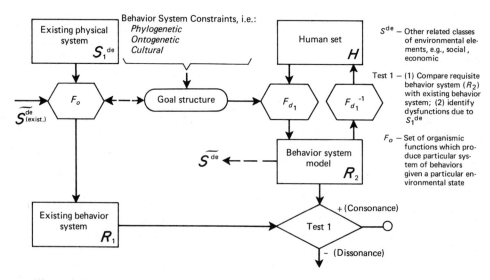

Figure 6–5

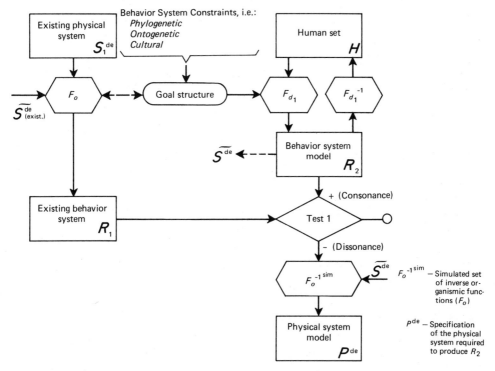

Figure 6–6

aspect of the environment $(\widetilde{S^{de}})$,[3] e.g., social, economic, educational, etc. (Ostensibly tests for evaluating dissonance in other stimulus domains would proceed similarly.) If such tests indicate the existence of a physical dysfunction, an alternative environment (P^{de}) must be conceptualized (see Figure 6-6).

Specifying the requisite physical system consists of systematically correlating conceptual elements of an environmental system (P^{de}) with conceptual elements of a behavioral system (R_2). What must be described is a specific (designed) environment-behavior interface. Describing such an interface in a comprehensive integrated and functional sense assumes the resources of a

comprehensive, integrated and functional science of behavior. No such science exists. We all understand this, and are presumably attempting, in one way or another, to do something about it. What is required is empirical evidence and a language for describing functional mappings between elements in these two systems. These kinds of mappings are difficult to come by, which is probably what leads psychologist Robert Sommer (1966) to conclude that "the entire art of design rests on empirical underpinnings so weak that no consensus exists about what arrangements are efficient, beautiful, or even relevant to a given activity."

The phenomena to be described (in P^{de}) are quantities, qualities, and relationships in the spatial environment. Specification of these physical requirements is in essence a model of the system of physical contingencies which will produce the requisite state of behavioral affairs. If such a proposition seems obscure it is because we have yet to develop a functional language for describing such systems—for mapping the interface— at the appropriate levels of precision. Like

[3] The misclassification of environmental problems is not in the least uncommon. An industrial firm may construct additional quantities of space, when the actual conflicts result from inventory and/or sales policies. Insufficient space quantities are often identified as the source of dysfunction in educational environments, when the real problem may grow out of an inappropriate and ineffective teaching system.

all abstract language systems, it must facilitate descriptions which are sufficiently explicit and unambiguous, while admitting many concrete (real world) interpretations.

The nature of this interface model will ultimately depend not only upon a great deal of incomplete empirical evidence, but also upon the system, theory or paradigm found to be, or believed to be, most viable in explaining the etiology of human behavior (Marx & Hillix, 1963). There must be a commitment to those resources in the behavioral sciences which one considers most adequate and reliable. It is well known that there are controversies, and that there are several competing paradigms in the behavioral sciences. Designers, if they are genuinely and technically interested in accommodating human requirements, must be drawn into these controversies. They must become knowledgeable of the issues and, of course, familiar with those techniques which have been found successful.

Why are resources in the behavioral sciences so difficult to assimilate for our purposes? Beyond the fact that the data are simply not in, the behavioral scientist has a mission (and a language) quite unlike the designer's. In the laboratory he usually deals with the isolation and control of a few variables, with small and fragmented samples of behavior. Even when investigating larger samples he usually examines stimulus domains other than the designed environment, e.g., interpersonal relations, and he isolates only those aspects which he chooses to examine. With but few exceptions, he deals with analysis. The designer, on the other hand, must deal with environment-behavior complexes as they come. He must understand wholes, large and complex behavioral continuums; he deals with synthesis. The environmental designer daily attempts to accommodate a level of behavioral complexity which no scientific analysis has ever approached in a unitary and functional sense (or in a mode required for environmental design). In selecting phenomena to study, the behavioral scientist generally has two choices. He can investigate a multivariate situation which reflects somewhat the complexities of real life. The price usually paid for such a choice is, of course, imprecise control of variables and ambiguity regarding the functional relations between environmental and behavioral events.

> Real life with its multiplicity of variables may present interactions not readily observed in simpler laboratory experiments . . . [but] the ultimate scientific test of theoretical principles is an experimental one, and real-life models should serve as guides rather than criteria or objectives [Marx & Hillix, 1963].

The most scientifically prestigious data are produced in experimental situations which are artificially impoverished in order to observe the effects on behavior of single (environmental) variable manipulation. The resulting data are reliable, replicable and predictable, but they are highly limited. In terms of real-world application this is the behavioral scientist's dilemma—but it is also our dilemma.

Before we have the capability to control, predict and explain human behavior at the levels required for environmental design we must come to understand a greater breadth of phenomena along what Brunswik identifies as the environment-environment continuum (Brunswik, 1952) (see Figure 6-7). Brunswik was somewhat unsuccessful in making a sound scientific case for his "probabilistic functionalism," but he did identify the level of understanding which seems necessary in applications to environmental design. The behavioral sciences cannot yet deliver reliable resources at this level, and designers must operate with a great deal less. Like many others attempting to apply resources in the behavioral sciences, this researcher's own views of this complexity of means are not entirely resolved. At this juncture they are generally as follows.[4] Behavioral science, like any science, seeks not "truth," but a useful way of organizing experience. Designers are primarily interested in resources describing orderly relations

---

[4] It is extremely important to note here that these particular views on the nature of the (designed) environment-behavior interface neither validate nor invalidate the arguments for a behavior-contingent paradigm. There are obviously several competing systems or theories within which one could interpret the operations denoted in Figure 6-6 (F_0^{-1s1m}).

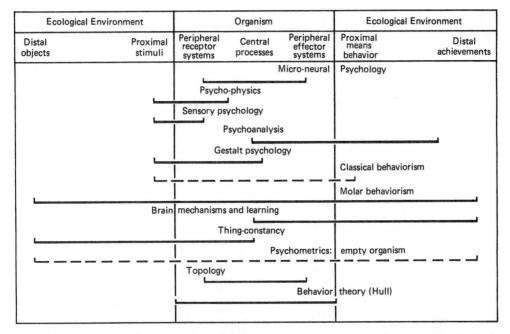

Figure 6–7. The place of representative schools and problems of psychology on the basic psychological unit defined by Brunswik. (From R. Barker, 1960.)

within which human behavioral events (as affected by elements in the designed environment) can be explained, predicted and controlled. When attempting to apply what behavioral science has to offer, designers are justified in selecting those resources which are (technically) most relevant to an environmental design context. Questions regarding a behavioral theory's comprehensiveness—its "aesthetic" qualities—are something to be worked out at another level, e.g., within the behavioral science community.

It is generally held by those who study such matters that a person's behavior is caused by three interdependent classes of phenomena: genetic endowment, history of interaction with the environment, and the existing environment. A skilled surgeon or a biogeneticist can exert effective control over the first; a comprehensive account of the second would also yield a high level of control. Designers, however, exert influence only upon the existing environment. The existing environment, needless to say, is composed of many subsystems, e.g., social and economic—and the designed environment (i.e., those limited energy-

matter variables under the direct control of the environmental designer). This subsystem includes some fairly significant behavior-controlling variables,[5] but little in the way of a scientifically based understanding has developed.

Designers are essentially interested in the fact, beyond any theory which explains it, that particular physical states will produce discrete and predictable behavioral states. For environmental design purposes, our interest in intervening organismic variables is quite limited. This is true *provided* we have resources by which behavior can be effectively predicted and controlled via manipulation of variables within the effective domain of the designer. In order to specify the characteristics of an appropriate physical system we must obviously understand the psychophysical limits of processing incoming stimuli (Dember, 1963). Beyond this, however, the exclusive interest on the part of some designers in perception as a basic

[5] That designers control human behavior is an undisputable empirical fact. The issue is not whether they *ought* to control but whether this control is to be exerted via accidental contingencies or upon understood techniques.

resource is in many ways misdirected[6] (Studer, 1967).

Let us look at the nature of the interface problem. A desired behavioral state (R_2) has been specified. The participants have not been previously emitting this particular system of behaviors but another (R_1) (otherwise no environmental problem would exist). It is desired that they will. They have quite diverse, generally unspecified behavioral histories, and the problem is one of specifying an environmental configuration which will produce, with the highest probability, the specified state of behavioral events. What this clearly describes is a *learning* situation, i.e., the acquisition of, or modification toward, a new system of behaviors.

There is a branch of psychology which has developed resources which seem particularly relevant to this kind of problem. An *operant* behavioral analysis (Skinner, 1953) deals exclusively with events and elements in the environment, i.e., temporal and spatial relations between behavior and its *consequences*. Extensive and highly controlled laboratory experiments have isolated and defined orderly relations among three classes of variables in the environment which have relevance in controlling and predicting human behavior. These are: (1) the situation, or *stimuli*, (2) the behavior, or *response*, and (3) the consequence, or *reinforcer*. Predictable response probability comes about when reinforcing consequences are made *contingent* upon a particular behavior in a particular situation. The manipulation of these *contingencies of reinforcement* brings about a change in the organism that we call learning. The designed environment can be viewed, and programmed, as a *learning system* (Studer, forthcoming), a system in which energy-matter variables are arranged to bring about the requisite state of behavioral affairs.

Some behavioral scientists contend that humans appear to behave *as though* influenced not only by contingencies in the extant environment, but also by a structured hypothesis concerning future environmental-behavioral states (Miller, Galanter & Pribram, 1960). This hypothesis is constantly revised in response to events as they occur in the real world. Such *planning* behavior is probably explicable for the most part in terms of a history of interaction with the environment. The environment appears to reinforce this planning behavior in that survival apparently favors the organism which anticipates future events. If this interpretation is correct, no additional constructs seem to be required beyond extensive refinement of the operant framework mentioned above. In any event this is a phenomenon to be better understood if response probability is to be more accurately predicted. Some researchers explain anticipatory behavior as a phenomenon whereby a human constructs a model of the environment, runs the model faster than the environment, and predicts that the environment will behave as the model does (Galanter & Gerstenhaber, 1956). If this is the case, prior knowledge of the participant's "environmental model"[7] would give the designer important data regarding probable response patterns. In order to make such information available to a design analysis it must obviously be somehow *externalized*, and this can be a rather formidable task.

Finally, it would seem that formal models which correlate environmental and behavioral variables are an eventual necessity in the behavior-contingent approach. The ability to precisely describe and manipulate variables in order to delineate the (designed) environment-behavior interface is fundamental to a clear and precise understanding of physical requirements at the appropriate levels (see above comments on a descriptive language). Reliable mathematical models, as they are developed and generalized to describe a greater breadth of behavioral phenomena, can hopefully be

---

[6] That is, unless the behavioral consequences of such investigations are examined, it is difficult to see their relevance for environmental organization. Two common errors occur when designers turn to perceptual investigations, when: (1) they confuse conceptual and perceptual phenomena, and (2) they (quite selectively) seek "scientific" support for their aesthetic beliefs and dogmas.

[7] This term seems tentatively preferable to that of "image," which has been used to connote all manner of metaphysical things.

utilized to express the functional mappings required (to describe P^{de}).

Realizing the physical system in the real world is, of course, that aspect which has been most extensively investigated, and a more sophisticated understanding of these processes is emerging. At this level in the process new complications arise as the requisite physical states (P^{de}) come under the influence of another class of variables. These impinge when the system is analyzed in a particular spatial-temporal (geographic) context. Such variables might be classified as "external" constraints (see Figure 6-8). A solution has been adequately realized when matter and energy have been ordered so as to accommodate these "external" constraints, as well as the previously conceptualized quantitative, qualitative and relational requirements.

Sophisticated investigations of both the normative (logical) and behavioral (empirical) aspects of environmental problem-solving have and will produce tools which greatly increase our capacity to deal with the complexities of physical synthesis. For purposes of this explication one need not go too deeply into this aspect of the process, except to note that the procedure seems to be one of successive approximations toward a specific real-world system via the following states:

1. An abstract description of the requisite environment-behavior interface (P^{de})
2. A description of the same interface, but made more specific as a result of accommodating the "external" constraints related to a particular spatial-temporal context
3. A series of analogues or simulations of the real-world system at greater and greater levels of specificity, each iteration terminating in a test for consonance with respect to the requisite behavior system
4. Final realization of the physical system (S_2^{de})

One of the generally agreed-upon characteristics of creative problem-solving is that it occurs with the discovery, or invention, of entirely new patterns of relationships, and avoidance of preconceived contexts. The behavior-contingent approach may help both the normative and behavioral aspects of problem-solving in at least three ways: (1) the taxonomy of independent variables, i.e., units of behavior, tend to minimize preconception in terms of known physical configurations; (2) this class of variables suggests a systematic "linking" procedure (Studer, 1966); and (3) behavioral variables can be defined in very small (single class) units, thus increasing the probability that new conflict-free patterns of relationships can be more easily generated.

Verification of the physical system in the real world has never been demanded of, or by, the design community. One consequence of this is a conspicuous lack of cumulative knowledge regarding either the viability of design methods, or the effects of resultant artifacts upon the humans who interact with them. Unless verification (that a clearly defined problem has in fact been solved) becomes an integral and systematic aspect of design method, the whole enterprise is frankly specious.

A procedure for testing or verifying (see Figure 6-9) the functioning environment-behavior system, or ensemble, is possible if and only if the class of independent variables has been explicitly delineated and is empirically accessible. Behavior has such dimensions, and the test procedure would include the following:

1. What system of behavior is being emitted (R_3)?
2. Compare this system to the requisite system (R_2).
3. Do these two systems fit within defined tolerances?
4. If there are intolerable dissonances, are these attributable to variables in the designed (physical) environment (S^{de}), or other stimulus domains ($\widetilde{S^{de}}$), e.g., social, economic, and so forth?
5. If dissonances are within defined tolerances, the physical solution is confirmed.

Such tests as these present no particularly difficult conceptual problems. They do, however, embody difficult technical problems.

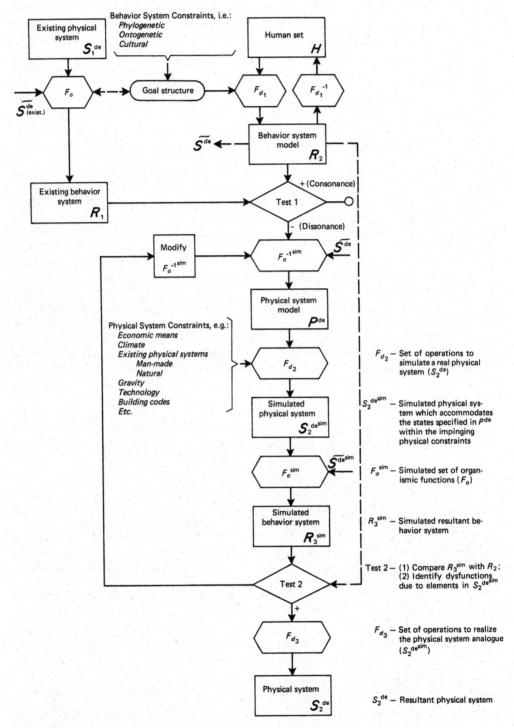

Figure 6–8

66

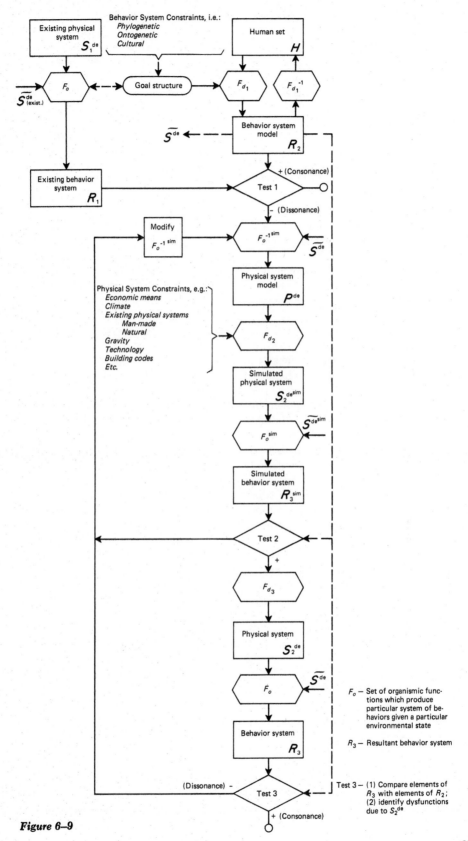

Figure 6-9

Most important among these is the monitoring and analysis of relevant variables. If the ensemble is found to be in inordinate disequilibrium, a difficult and embarrassing situation arises in terms of existing modes of thinking.

THE DYNAMICS OF ENVIRONMENT-BEHAVIOR SYSTEMS

The above issues, and characteristics of behavior-contingent physical systems, have been discussed in greater detail elsewhere (Studer, 1962, 1966, 1967). There are additional aspects—certain intrinsic complications—which must be examined before the required states can be properly understood and actually realized.

The arguments for a behavior-contingent paradigm are compelling, but limited resources in the behavioral sciences make the actualization of these operations probabilistic at best. The need for expanded and intensive behavioral research is well known, but there is another kind of difficulty. Implicit in the above, as in most discussions of this sort, is the underlying assumption that the ensemble would exist, once realized, in a steady state. The material result of this sort of thinking has produced what Serge Chermayeff has referred to as the "disposal problem." This steady-state assumption is clearly erroneous. Such systems are, in fact, highly variable along several time scales. Within the design disciplines, there is an emerging awareness of the desirability to produce systems which are more open-ended and adaptable. This "felt need" should, however, be made more technically explicit, lest we confuse the "image" with the substantive problem. In terms of the previous comments, the sources of variability are identifiable. These include (see Figure 6-9): (1) changes in the organization's goal structure, (2) changes in physical impingements, (3) changes in other stimulus domains, and (4) changes in the human organism.

The goals of human organizations inevitably change. A culture, subculture, industrial organization and even families often alter their purpose(s) and redirect their goals. Such alterations may be in response to both external and internal events. An industrial organization may enter or abandon a certain market area (an aspect of the larger economic milieu). A governmental organization may redefine its mission in response to a mandate from the operating culture or subculture. Also, the economic status, changing membership or social impingements can produce an altered goal structure within families. When a human organization's purpose(s) and goals vary, new behaviors are required. If the physical system remains constant, disequilibrium occurs.

Changes in "external" *physical* constraints can induce considerable dissonance in the ensemble. New man-made and natural physical configurations can, for example, affect the ensemble in unpredictable ways. These new external states, because they produce a new set of relations, often result in an unforeseen disparity between requisite behaviors and the designed environment. The addition or deletion of adjacent structures in the milieu can critically alter the sonic, luminous, thermal, and other relevant aspects. New systems of circulation to, from and nearby can greatly affect the impinging environment and thus the overall equilibrium in similar ways.

Other *stimulus domains*, e.g., social and economic, can go out of equilibrium in ways which also have a critical effect on requisite physical states. The social environment, for example, is usually subject to unforeseen external or internal forces which can produce interpersonal or intergroup conflict. If such conflicts become critical, it may be found that social equilibrium can be reestablished only by altering the physical system. For example, dissonance may be relieved by restructuring and/or delineating certain territorial boundaries (Hall, 1966). The aversive consequences brought about when such adjustments cannot be made produce serious immediate and long-term effects on the participants' behavior.

The most interesting, pervasive and complicated source of variability is change in the participating *humans*. For purposes of design the human participant is customarily considered to exhibit steady-state response probabilities in the presence of a given physical setting. Findings in the behavioral sciences do not justify this assumption. Indeed they do not, as a rule, furnish directives for producing physical settings which are either optimal *or* time independent. Rather they deal with relationships, i.e., dependencies, amongst relevant variables. Such dependencies are not static or absolute, as many design strategies assume, but are subject to changing probabilities along a continuum. Variability in the human participants brought about by the interdependent effects of adaptation, deprivation states and particularly learning have a significant and inevitable impact upon the environment-behavior interface. These changes in the participants in turn affect equilibrium in the ensemble.

Behavior is greatly modified as a person *adapts* to an environment which is, for example, visually, sonically or socially noisy. In experimental situations, the effects of environmental manipulations cannot be properly assessed until stable behavioral *base lines* have been established; that is, until the organism adapts to the experimental situation. Behavior before and after adaptation differs greatly. It is also well known that response probability varies when a stimulus situation (either conditioned or unconditioned) becomes satiating, i.e., when environmental elements lose their effect on behavior with sustained contact. Constant overexposure of participants to an impressive external (or internal) vista provides an interesting example. When such reinforcing events are indiscriminately and/or grossly introduced, their effect is diminished with time.

A more remote possibility of organismic variability is that of gross physiological[8] change. When persons grow older or become disabled we observe a number of prosthetic devices appearing in the environment, e.g., hearing aids, wheelchairs, ramps, special lifts, and so forth. Unforeseen changes in human metabolic, perceptual or skeletal-musculature systems demand new

behavior and/or physical configuration if the goals of the organization remain constant.

The above organismic changes are possible and frequently occur, but the most interesting and important source of variability is brought about by *learning*. One is likely to satiate in undifferentiated, low-information environments. Highly complex settings can, on the other hand, produce disoriented and ineffective behavior; that is, until one learns—comes under the influence of—its ordering principles. Laboratory experiments (and common sense) indicate that response probability, and the requisite stimulus configuration, change with time and context. Modifying behavior toward a viable or specified state, that is, effective *stimulus control*,[9] and the acquisition of appropriate (and behavior-influencing) *stimulus discriminations*[10] involve multiple, varying presentations. Programmed instruction provides an interesting and relevant example. The new technology of teaching (Holland, 1960) is based upon a principle whereby extant behavioral capacities are modified through a series of modest steps of increasing difficulty. Appropriate responses to complex, high-information environments generally come about as an organism acquires increasingly complex repertoires. An environment which reinforces these acquisitions is one which is constantly modified.

The reality of day-to-day events produces still further complications for the environmental designer. Superimposed upon the basic learning functions above are effects brought about when social and other classes of contingencies modify a participant's perception of, and response to, aspects of the designed environment. A positively reinforcing series of social encounters which are related in a particular way to aspects of the designed environment will greatly modify

---

[8] All the organismic changes mentioned herein produce physiological changes. What is intended here is a situation in which the physiology is so altered that it becomes an overriding consideration.

[9] When a behavior is reinforced in the presence of certain stimuli there is a higher probability that this particular behavior will occur in their presence in the future. Response to these similar conditions is called stimulus control (Terrace, 1966).

[10] A situation in which an organism, having been reinforced in the presence of particular stimuli, comes to discriminate these (and respond to them in a somewhat consistent way).

response probabilities within it. Aversive social events will modify this in yet another way.[11] Indeed the participants' varying histories of environmental interaction add a complicated dimension generally. It is because of such histories, on the other hand, that effective behavior in most designed environments is possible at all.

These phenomena of organismic variability are basic and well known. One need go no further into the complexities of them to realize that the requisite system of physical elements is, in effect, *highly variable* if behavioral equilibrium is to be maintained.

To recapitulate, the sources of variability in the ensemble include the interdependent effects of: (1) changes in the organization's goal structure, (2) changes in the external physical constraints, (3) changes in other (internal) stimulus domains, and (4) changes in the participating humans. These sources of conflict and variability remind us that human systems are above all *dynamic*. The precise characteristics of this dynamism are, within the context of present knowledge, extremely unpredictable. The paradox encountered by designers as they attempt to accommodate the dynamic human problem with a static formal solution, i.e., "architecture," is a familiar one. What must be decided is whether or not increasingly complex, technologically sophisticated cultures really tolerate the resulting conflicts indefinitely. The "crisis" mentality[12] within the design community is generally overstated and has produced little more than platitudes. It must be conceded, on the other hand, that highly complex ecological systems can go out of equilibrium with little advance warning.

THE ADAPTATION INTERFACE

The arguments for well-fitting designed environments are dismissed as pedantic by some on the grounds that the human organism is, in fact, highly adaptive. He will prevail, it is insisted, regardless of our design decisions. There is a great deal of truth in this. The human is endowed with a marvelously adaptive physiology, and he does emit highly adaptive behavior in designed environments. Species whose behavior was excessively stereotyped, i.e., failed to respond differentially to varying environmental conditions, are obviously no longer with us (Sidman, 1960). A continuously changing milieu insures a high level of adaptive behavior in humans, forcing as it does the emission of a wide variety of behavior in our repertories.

In general, however, the simplistic notion (held by many designers unfortunately) that man is "infinitely adaptable" is critically erroneous. Both common sense and excellent laboratory data indicate that there are limits to adaptability. We already know that certain modes and intensities of environmental dissonance can produce physiological and behavioral disintegration long before an organism can adapt to them (Solomon et al., 1961). There is obviously a great deal more to be learned about the more subtle side effects brought about by environments which are biologically and extrabiologically dissonant. Long-term ethological studies of lower organisms in stressful environments (Calhoun, 1966), for example, command serious attention. One question which could be asked is what adaptive states have the greatest utility. A conflicting environment may be overcome via adaptation, but the new organismic state could be found undesirable in terms of long-range demands (Dubos, 1965). For example, a person continuously subjected to very loud sounds may adapt but become less sensitive to lesser sounds. The resulting adaptive state, i.e., deafness to certain intensities, could be critically dysfunctional in other environmental contexts.

The real issue here is that the human participant may, in fact, and usually does, survive both physiologically and psychologically in dysfunctioning environments. He may, however, fail to attain his defined goals. It must be remembered that it is not survival alone which defines environmental requirements, but the human *goal structure*, and this includes a great deal more.

---

[11] A way which is not "equal and opposite" but one which requires a more complex analysis.

[12] By this is meant the persistent warning from designers that humanity is most certainly doomed unless man takes drastic action to improve his "visual" surroundings. John Beshers (1962) has labeled this simplistic notion as "architectural determinism."

A second and more sophisticated argument against well-fitting physical systems says that a certain level of conflict with the environment is essential to the survival and well-being of an organism, human or otherwise. Evolution appears to favor the organism which survives stress and hardship. Taken to an extreme, such an argument would, on a medical front, ostensibly legislate against immunization altogether, on the grounds that a new disease could annihilate future generations made vulnerable by not having survived smallpox. The argument does have merit, however, and if a certain level of conflict has utility for human well-being, then it requires careful attention. It must be systematically included as an important aspect of the problem space, since we could hardly leave such a fundamental requirement to chance. There are several questions involved here. How much and what kind of stress is desirable? Also, how much energy should a human expend simply overcoming conflict in the designed environment—what are the risks? There is obviously a rather delicate balance between well-fitting and inordinately stressful environments. We might call this the *adaptation interface*. It is not a phenomenon which can be understood in ethical or speculative terms. It is rather another of the many areas requiring the attention of a scientific analysis.

MAINTENANCE OF ENVIRONMENT-BEHAVIOR SYSTEMS

These comments outlining the complexities of behavioral accommodation—the many ways that environment-behavior systems can go out of equilibrium—are not intended as nihilistic. Neither do they suggest that we should abandon the behavior-contingent paradigm. They do suggest that designers and design methods have not been altogether realistic in dealing with the human dynamic, i.e., changing, requirement states. Variability of the several interdependent systems—the sources of dissonance—presents an extremely complex problem if we are to realize well-fitting systems. Beyond this, our knowledge of human behavioral phenomena is generally impoverished. As a consequence of these two kinds of difficul-ties, our ability to conceptualize, order, specify and realize appropriate physical settings is highly problematic. This is true regardless of how effective our design method per se. Clearly the designer is committed to a problem-solving situation of great *uncertainty*.[13] Uncertainty obviously does not preclude action, but have we really faced this uncertainty in our formulations, that is, beyond the simplistic demand for "flexibility"?

The behavioral sciences are developing resources which move beyond folk wisdom. As we come to understand the technical basis for the vast uncertainty facing designers, we must also come to question generally the *solution-oriented* precepts held by most conscientious designers and methodologists. In spite of my obvious enthusiasm for the behavior-contingent approach, it must be conceded that our ability to respond incisively within the bounds of present knowledge is critically limited. We haven't the conceptual tools, nor do we have an adequate empirical understanding to precisely correlate environmental and behavioral variables. But more important is the undeniable fact that the human problem changes in most instances, before a physical solution to it can be realized! In short, the goals implicit in seeking "the solution" should be *abandoned*. The quest for this elusive entity has too often led to physical settings based either upon information-rich but steady-state requirement systems, or information-poor generalizations. Our design goals should be redirected so as to respond more directly and realistically to the dynamics of human systems. We must address the problems of unpredictable response configurations, the adaptation interface, and the general maintenance of the environment-behavior ensemble—on a *continuing* basis. An environmental solution, considering the uncertainties involved, should not be viewed as a solution at all, but a complex *hypothesis*. No matter how refined, a (behavior-contingent) physical system can be nothing more than a hypothesis, which can be verified only when placed in its real-world setting.

---

[13] That is, his efforts are constrained by a limited knowledge of behavioral causes, by what he can predict concerning future requirements and by limited methodological tools generally.

Furthermore, it must be reformulated each time relevant constraints vary. Designed environments, then, should be viewed as *experiments* in which relevant variables—either behavioral or environmental—are manipulated (either by the participants or others) to move the system toward a state of consonance with respect to the goal structure in effect. Figure 6-10 denotes the hypothetical characteristics of an environment-behavior system moving toward a state of equilibrium. This process is assumed and denoted as a generalized learning configuration. In such a situation the environment, the participants and the decision-makers produce a complex information-decision system, one which constantly responds to dissonances with respect to a specified goal structure and requisite behaviors. It should be noted that under such circumstances, the characteristics of the ensemble change as it becomes asymptotic to an equilibrium state. If such systems do in fact behave this way, it is clear that preasymptotic and postasymptotic aspects require physical systems with significantly different levels of adaptability. In Figure 6-11 we see such a hypothetical ensemble, perhaps on a greater time scale, in which the organization's goal structure is periodically modified.

The suggestion that we abandon "solutions" in favor of experimental contexts may seem subversive to traditional views of design, and a somewhat austere response to the designer's dilemma. In light of the realities of human processes, however, the com-

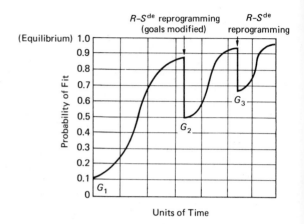

Figure 6–11. Hypothetical R–S^{de} accommodation with variable goal structure.

mitment to finite-state design objectives is not justified. Indeed we will no doubt come to understand that the experiment *is* the solution. A design effort committed to human well-being is one which seeks an environmental setting which is systematically linked and responsive to human variability. It is one which is constantly refined, constantly adapting to (quantitative and qualitative) dissonance—constantly moving toward a state of equilibrium.

The above argues for a more appropriate response to the human dynamic; beyond this, however, we obviously need a much better understanding of environment-behavior relationships generally. Competent, laboratory-trained psychologists are beginning to examine larger behavioral samples in larger, more complex environments. They seek to further verify and extrapolate from successful laboratory situations. Naturalistic observations in real environments have led to interesting and important insights (Barker, 1960; Sommer, 1966). These must, however, be supplemented with the rigorous kind of data which can only be obtained in an experimental analysis. In the near future millions will be spent to create expanded laboratory settings, and billions will be spent for environments which don't work behaviorally. It would appear that these two efforts can be consolidated for the good of all. The designer and behavioral scientist have complementary goals, and in many instances designed environments could and

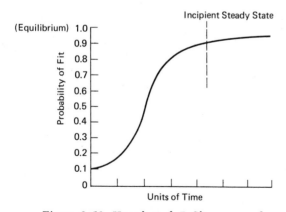

Figure 6–10. Hypothetical R–S^{de} accommodation with constant goal structure.

should become experimental in a more rigorous and systematic sense. Manipulations required to bring an ensemble into equilibrium also yield invaluable data concerning the environment-behavior interface generally. Such data should, therefore, be carefully recorded, stored and analyzed. Designer-behavioral scientist collaboration has not been particularly successful. In a properly conceptualized environment-behavior setting these two can interact in a meaningful and productive context.

CONCLUSIONS

To summarize the points presented, there is a great need within the design community for a paradigm, a framework to facilitate more viable designed environments, to implement findings in other disciplines, and to assess developments in design research. In order to evolve such a framework, the basis for formulating design problems should be reexamined. Fundamental to this is the identification of a viable unit of analysis. The generally accepted unit human "need" lacks the required dimensions, and it is suggested that units of behavior describe a more fundamental taxonomy of problem formulation. The practice of formulating problems in terms of "buildings" and other preconceived concepts should be abandoned in favor of more relevant problem spaces which are detected, isolated, structured and realized through an analysis of human behavioral systems. Requisite behavior systems cannot be defined empirically but must be essentially designed in response to the participants' physiological and psychological capacities, and to their goals. Given a requisite system of behaviors, the problem of specifying a correlated system of physical contingencies is one of describing a particular environment-behavior interface—a formidable undertaking considering the limited conceptual and empirical resources available. Realization of the appropriate physical system depends not only upon the problem-solving repertoires of an individual designer, but also upon methodological tools which are now being developed and refined. Before environmental design can become a truly viable enterprise, it is essential that the physical product be verified. Because units of behavior can be well defined and empirically observed, they form a reliable basis for verifying the physical results. Our capacity to conceptualize and solve environmental problems is generally limited by our problem-solving tools and knowledge of behavioral processes. Beyond this, however, are the intrinsic limitations of predicting future sources of environment-behavior dysfunction, i.e., changing goals, external physical constraints, other stimulus domains and participating organisms. Because of our empirical and conceptual limitations, and because the human problem changes almost before its solution can be actualized, long-term, well-fitting environments are, with present tools and knowledge, unrealizable. Under the circumstances we should abandon the finite state, problem-solving commitment in favor of realizing experimental settings which respond to disequilibrium on a continuing basis. This shift in design objectives will not only insure more integral and appropriate physical settings, but provide an effective context for acquiring critically needed information concerning environment-behavior relations generally.

Designed environments, then, should be both conceptualized and realized as dynamic systems capable of moving toward more appropriate states. They should be viewed as experiments to test hypotheses and record relevant aspects. The conceptual schema presented earlier (see Figure 6-9) embodies the general characteristics required, and with one minor adjustment (see Figure 6-12), physical systems can be conceptualized as dynamic. That is, the resultant behavior system (R_3) becomes (at the completion of all tests and manipulations to realize a physical state) the "existing" behavioral system (R_1). The entire process is thus analyzable as an iterative one. An integral component of such systems would be an information and control system which would have the capability to perform or assist the following operations:

1. Identifying and testing the consequences of the organization's goal structure

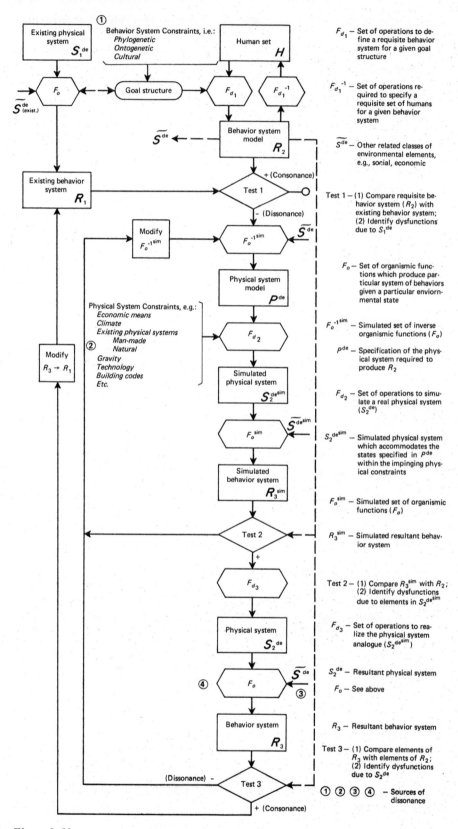

Figure 6–12

74

2. Reprogramming requisite behaviors in response to changes in the goal structure
3. Reprogramming contingent physical configurations
4. Monitoring behavioral and physical configurations
5. Testing for dissonance within the ensemble
6. Improving predictions (short, intermediate and long-range) by simulating future behavioral and environmental aspects. (These simulations would be based upon past histories of the ensemble and/or hypotheses concerning future configurations.)
7. Analyzing data obtained from particular isolated experiments to (a) upgrade the ensemble and/or (b) gain general knowledge concerning the environment-behavior interface
8. Interfacing with, and communicating, these phenomena to human decision-makers at the appropriate stages

Such an information and control system assumes an on-line, digital computation capability—hardware and software—of some sophistication. Such tools are, however, realizable within existing or soon to be developed technology.

While quite outside the scope of this presentation, it should be noted that a behavior-contingent approach implies new modes of physical technology. It suggests subsystems open-ended and highly adaptive along a continuum. There has never been any serious question regarding our ability to produce physical systems of great technical sophistication. The limitations have not really been so much technological as conceptual. A culturally conditioned predilection for "permanence" in our artifacts, for example, may have low utility in accommodating environmental requirements for highly dynamic, technologically sophisticated cultures. Innovative attempts to accommodate well-fitting environment-behavior systems at the levels suggested herein may provide the necessary link to our latent technology, and to the greater physical design freedom implicit in highly developed, mass-production capabilities.

REFERENCES:

Alexander, C. *Notes on the synthesis of form,* Cambridge, Mass.: Harvard University Press, 1964.

Barker, R. G. Ecology and motivation, *Nebraska Symposium on Motivation,* Lincoln, Nebr.: University of Nebraska Press, 1960.

Beshers, J. M. *Urban social structure,* Glencoe, Ill.: Free Press, 1962.

Brunswik, E. *The conceptual framework of psychology,* Chicago: University of Chicago Press, 1952.

Calhoun, J. The role of space in animal sociology, *Journal of Social Issues,* 1966, **4,** 46–58.

Dubos, R. *Man adapting,* New Haven, Conn.: Yale University Press, 1965.

Dember, W. *The psychology of perception,* New York: Holt, Rinehart and Winston, 1963.

Fitch, J. M. The aesthetics of function, *New York Academy of Sciences Journal,* 1965, **128,** 706–714.

Galanter, E., & Gerstenhaber, M. On thought: The extrinsic theory, *Psychological Review,* 1956, **63,** 218–227.

Guetzkow, H. (Ed.) *Simulation in social science,* Englewood Cliffs, N.J.: Prentice-Hall, 1962.

Hall, E. T. *The hidden dimension,* Garden City, N.Y.: Doubleday, 1966.

Holland, J. G. Teaching machines: An application of principles from the laboratory, *Journal of the Experimental Analysis of Behavior,* 1960, **30,** 275–287.

Kuhn, T. *The structure of scientific revolutions,* Chicago: University of Chicago Press, 1962.

Lindsley, O. R. Geriatric behavioral prosthesis, in R. Kastenbaum (Ed.), *New Thoughts on Old Age,* New York: Springer, 1964, Pp. 41–60.

March, J., & Simon, H. *Organizations,* New York: Wiley, 1958.

Marx, M. H., & Hillix, W. *Systems and theories in psychology,* New York: McGraw-Hill, 1963.

Miller, G. A. *Mathematics and psychology,* New York: Wiley, 1964.

Miller, G. A., Galanter, E., & Pribram, K. *Plans and the structure of behavior,* New York: Holt, Rinehart and Winston, 1960.

Miller, J. G. Living systems: Basic concepts, *Behavioral Science,* 1965, **10,** 193–237.

Popper, K. *The logic of scientific discovery,* New York: Basic Books, 1959.

Rothstein, J. Information, organization and systems, *IRE Transactions on Information Theory,* 1954, 64–66.

Russell, B. Definition of number, in J. R. Newman (Ed.), *The world of mathematics,* New York: Simon and Schuster, 1956, Pp. 537–543.

Sidman, M. *Tactics of scientific research,* New York: Basic Books, 1960.

Skinner, B. F. *Science and human behavior,* New York: Macmillan, 1953.

Sommer, R. Man's proximate environment, *Journal of Social Issues,* 1966, **22,** 59–70.

Solomon, P., *et al. Sensory deprivation: A symposium held at the Harvard Medical School,*

Cambridge, Mass.: Harvard University Press, 1961.

Studer, R. G. Alexander's notes on the synthesis of form, *Architectural Association Journal*, 1965, **80**, 260–262.

Studer, R. G. On environmental programming, *Architectural Association Journal*, 1966, **81**, 290–296.

Studer, R. G. Experimental analysis of the programmed instruction environment, Programmed Instruction Project, Harvard University, Sept. 1962.

Studer, R. G. Behavior manipulation in designed environments, *Connection*, publication of the Graduate School of Design, Harvard University, 1967, **5**(1), 7–13.

Studer, R. G., & Stea, D. Environmental programming and human behavior, *Journal of Social Issues*, 1966, **22**, 127–136.

Terrace, H. S. Stimulus control, in W. Honig (Ed.), *Operant behavior: Areas of research and application*, New York: Appleton-Century-Crofts, 1966, Pp. 271–344.

Ulrich, R., Stachnik, T., & Mabry, J. *Control of human behavior*, Glenview, Ill.: Scott, Foresman and Co., 1966.

7 Experiential Bases for Aesthetic Decision

James Marston Fitch

A fundamental weakness in most discussions of aesthetics is the failure to relate it to experiential reality. Most literature on aesthetics tends to isolate it from this matrix of experience, to discuss the aesthetics process as though it were an abstract problem in logic.

Art and architectural criticism suffers from this conceptual limitation. This finds expression in a persistent tendency to discuss art forms and buildings as though they were exclusively visual phenomena. This leads to serious misconceptions as to the actual relationship between the artifact and the human being. Our very terminology reveals this misapprehension: we speak of art as having "spectators," artists as having "audiences." This suggests that man exists in some dimension quite separate and apart from his artifacts; that the only contact between the two is this narrow channel of

From *Annals of the New York Academy of Sciences*, 1965, **128**, 706–714. Reprinted by permission of the author and The New York Academy of Sciences.

vision or hearing; and that this contact is unaffected by the environmental circumstances in which it occurs. The facts are quite otherwise and our modes of thought should be revised to correspond to them.

Art and architecture, like man himself, are totally submerged in an exterior environment. Thus they can never be felt, perceived, experienced in anything less than multi-dimensional totality. A change in one aspect or quality of the environment inevitably affects our response to, and perception of, all the rest. The primary significance of a painting may indeed be visual; or of a concert, sonic: but perception of these art forms occurs in a situation of experiential totality. Recognition of this is crucial for aesthetic theory, above all for architectural aesthetics. Far from being based narrowly upon any single sense of perception like vision, architectural aesthetics actually derives from the body's *total* response to, and perception of, its external physical environment. It is literally impossible to experience architecture in any "simpler" way. *In architecture, there are no spectators: there are only participants.* The body of architectural criticism which pretends otherwise is based upon photographs of buildings and not actual exposure to architecture at all.

Life is coexistant and coextensive with the external natural environment in which the body is submerged. The body's dependence upon this external environment is absolute—in the fullest sense of the word, *uterine.* And yet, unlike the womb, the external natural environment does not afford optimum conditions for the existence of the individual. The animal body, for its survival, maintains its own special internal environment. In man, this internal environment is so distinct in its nature and so constant in its properties that it has been given its own name, "homeostasis." Since the natural environment is anything but constant in either time or space, the contradictions between internal requirements and external conditions are normally stressful. The body has wonderful mechanisms for adjusting to external variations, e.g., the eye's capacity to adjust to enormous variations in the luminous environment or the adjustability of the heat-exchange mechanism of the skin. But the limits of adaptation are sharp and obdurate. Above or below them, an ameliorating element, a "third" environment, is required.

Before birth, the womb affords this to the foetus. But man, once born into the world, enters into a much more complex relationship with his external environment. Existence now is on two distinct levels, simultaneously and indissolubly connected, the metabolic and the perceptual (Figure 7-1). The metabolic process remains basic. It is at once a "preconscious" state and the material basis of consciousness. Many of life's fundamental processes transpire at this level: heartbeat, respiration, digestion, hypothalmic heat exchange controls, etc. Metabolic disturbance occurs only when the external environment begins to drop below the minimal, or rise above the maximal, requirements of existence. And sensual perception of the external environment comes into play only *after* these minimal requirements are met. (As a matter of fact, loss of consciousness is one of the body's characteristic responses to environmental stress— drop in oxygen or pressure, extremes of heat and cold, etc.)

Metabolic process then is clearly the precondition to sensory perception, just as sensory perception is the material basis of the aesthetic process. But the aesthetic process only begins to operate maximally, i.e., as a uniquely human faculty, when the impact upon the body of all environmental forces is held within tolerable limits (limits which, as we have said, are established by the body itself). Thus, we can construct a kind of experiential spectrum of stress. The

The Relationship between Man and His Environment

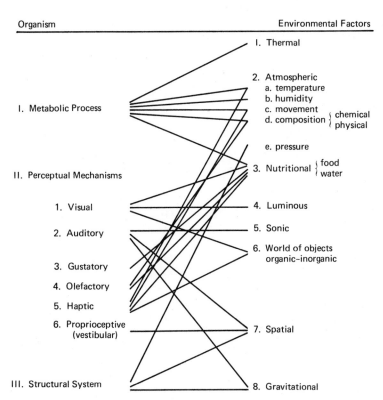

Figure 7–1. The relationship between the metabolic process and its environmental support is literally uterine. And since the process is the substructure of consciousness, sensory perception of changes in the environment in which the body finds itself is totally dependent upon satisfaction of the body's minimal metabolic requirements.

work of psychiatrists like Dr. George Ruff (1963) at the University of Pennsylvania establishes the lower end of this spectrum: sensory overloading is destructive, first of balanced judgments, then of rationality itself. But the other end of this spectrum proves equally destructive. Investigations of the effects of sensory deprivation, such as those carried on by Dr. Philip Solomon (1963) of the Harvard Medical School, indicate that too little environmental stress (and hence too little sensory stimulation) is as deleterious to the body as too much. Volunteer subjects for Dr. Solomon's experiments were reduced to gibbering incoherence in a matter of a few hours by being isolated from all visual, sonic, haptic and thermal stimulation.

Psychic satisfaction with a given situation is thus directly related to physiologic well-being, just as dissatisfaction must be related to discomfort. A condition of neither too great nor too little sensory stimulation permits the fullest exercise of the critical faculties upon that situation or any aspect of it. But even this proposition will not be indefinitely extensible in time. As one investigator (Heron, 1957) has observed in a recent paper (significantly entitled *The Pathology of Boredom*): "variety is not the spice of life; it is the very stuff of it." The psychosomatic equilibrium which the body always seeks is dynamic, a continual resolution of opposites. Every experience has built-in time limits. Perception itself has thresholds. One is purely quantitative: the ear cannot perceive sounds above 18,000 cycles per second; the eye does not perceive radiation below 3,200 Angstroms. But another set of thresholds are functions of time: constant exposure to steady stimulation at some fixed level will ultimately deaden perception. This is true of many odors, of "white" sounds and of some aspects of touch.

Of course, even more important facts prevent any mechanistic equating of physical comfort with aesthetic satisfaction. For while all human standards of beauty and ugliness stand ultimately upon a bedrock of material existence, the standards themselves vary astonishingly. All men have always been submerged in the environment. All men have always had the same sensory apparatus for perceiving changes in its qualities and dimensions. All men have always had the same central nervous system for analyzing and responding to the stimuli thus perceived. The physiological limits of this experience are absolute and intractable. Ultimately, it is physiology, and not culture, which establishes the levels at which sensory stimuli become traumatic. With such extremes—high temperatures, blinding lights, cutting edges and heavy blows, noise at blast level, intense concentrations of odor—experience goes beyond mere perception and becomes somatic stress. Moreover, excessive loading of any one of these senses can prevent a balanced assessment of the total experiential situation. (A temperature of 120 degrees F. or a sound level of 120 decibels can render the most beautiful room uninhabitable.) But as long as these stimuli do not reach stressful levels of intensity, rational assessment and hence aesthetic judgments are possible. Then formal criteria, derived from personal idiosyncrasy and socially-conditioned value judgments, come into play.

The value judgments that men apply to these stimuli, the evaluation they make of the total experience as being either beautiful or ugly, will vary: measurably with the individual, enormously with his culture. This is so clearly the case in the history of art that it should not need repeating. Yet we constantly forget it. Today, anthropology, ethnology and archaeology alike show us the immense range of aesthetically satisfactory standards which the race has evolved in its history: from cannibalism to vegetarianism in food; from the pyramid to the curtain wall in architecture; from polygamy and polyandry to monogamy and celibacy in sex; from hoopskirt to bikini in dress. Yet we often act, even today, as if our own aesthetic criteria were absolutely valid instead of being, as is indeed the case, absolutely relative for all cultures except our own.

Our aesthetic judgments are substantially modified by non-sensual data derived from social experience. This again can be easily confirmed in daily life. It is ultimately our faith an antiseptic measures that makes the immaculate white nurses, uniforms and spotless sheets of the hospitals so reassuring. It is our knowledge of their cost which exaggerates the visual difference between diamonds and crystal, or the gustatory difference between the flavor of pheasant and chicken. It is our knowledge of Hitler Germany which has converted the swastika from the good luck sign of the American Indians to the hated symbol of Nazi terror. All sensory perception is modified by consciousness. Consciousness applies to received stimuli, the criteria of digested experience, whether acquired by the individual or received by him from his culture. The aesthetic process cannot be isolated from this matrix of experiential reality. It constitutes, rather, a quintessential evaluation of and judgment on it.

Once in the world, man is submerged in his natural external environment as completely as the fish in water. Unlike the fish in his aqueous abode, however, he has developed the capacity to modify it in his favor. Simply as an animal, he might have survived without this capacity. Theoretically, at least, he might have migrated like the bird or hibernated like the bear. There are even a few favored spots on earth, like Hawaii, in which biological survival might have been possible without any modification. But, on the base of sheer biological existence, man builds a vast superstructure of institutions, processes and activities: and these could not survive exposure to the natural environment even in those climates in which, biologically, man could.

Thus man was compelled to invent architecture in order to become man. By means of it he surrounded himself with a new environment, tailored to his specifications; a "third" environment interposed between himself and the world. Architecture is thus *an instrument whose central function is to intervene in man's favor.* The building—and, by extension, the city—has the function of lightening the stress of life; of taking the raw environmental load off man's shoulders; of permitting *homo fabricans* to focus his energies upon productive work.

The building, even in its simplest forms, invests man, surrounds and encapsulates him at every level of his existence, metabolically and perceptually. For this reason, it must be regarded as a very special kind of container (Figure 7-2). Far from offering solid, impermeable barriers to the natural environment, its outer surfaces come more and more closely to resemble permeable membranes which can accept or reject any environmental force. Again, the uterine analogy; and not accidentally, for with such convertibility in the container's walls, man can modulate the play of environmental forces upon himself and his processes, to guarantee their uninterrupted development, in very much the same way as the mother's body protects the embryo. Good architecture must thus meet criteria much more complex than those applied to other forms of art. And this confronts the architect, especially the contemporary architect, with a formidable range of subtle problems (Figure 7-3).

All architects aspire to give their clients beautiful buildings. But "beauty" is not a discrete property of the building: it describes, rather, the client's response to the building's impact upon him. This response is extremely complex. Psychic in nature, it is based upon somatic stimulation. Architecture, even more than agriculture, is the most environmental of man's activities. Unlike the other forms of art—painting, music, dance—its impact upon man is total. Thus the aesthetic enjoyment of an actual building cannot be merely a matter of vision (as most criticism tacitly assumes). It can only be a matter of total sensory perception. And that perceptual process must in turn have adequate biological support. To be truly satisfactory, the building must meet *all* the body's requirements, for it is not just upon the eye but upon the whole man that its impact falls.

From this it follows also that the architect has no direct access to his client's subjective existence: the only channels of communication open to him are objective, somatic. Only by manipulating the physical properties of his environment—heat, air, light, color, odor, sound, surface and space—can the architect communicate with his client at all. And only by *doing it well*, i.e., meeting all man's requirements, objective and subjective, can he create buildings which men may find beautiful.

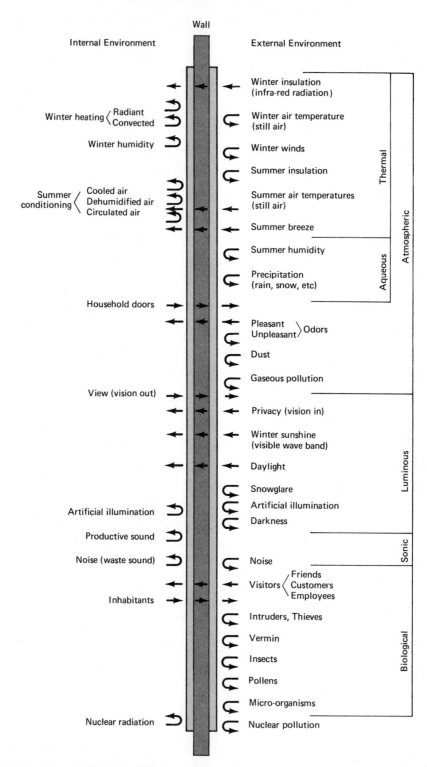

Figure 7–2. The building wall can no longer be considered as an impermeable interface separating the meso- and macro-environments. Rather it must be conceived of as a selectively permeable membrane, capable of sophisticated response to a wide range of environmental forces. Like the uterus, its task is the modulation of these forces in the interest of the building's inhabitants—i.e., creation of a third or meso-environment designed in their favor.

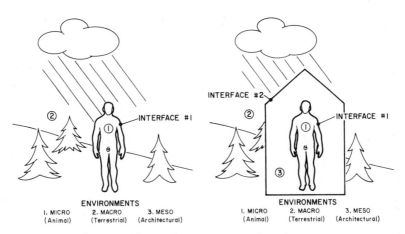

Figure 7–3. In civilization, relations between man and environment occur across two inter-faces. This relationship is manipulated in his favor by clothing along the surface of his epidermis (1) and by architecture as the boundary of his "built" environment (2). By thus lifting gross environmental loads, a greater portion of his energies can be focussed on socially productive work.

The matter by no means ends here, however. The architect builds not merely for man at rest, man in the abstract. Typically, he builds for man at work. And this confronts him with another set of contradictions. For work is not a "natural" activity, as Hannah Arendt (1959) has brilliantly reminded us. Labor, according to her definition, is "natural"—that is, the use of the whole body to meet its biological needs, to feed it, bathe it, dress it, protect it from attack. Work, on the other hand, is "unnatural"—the use of the hand and the brain to produce the artificial, non-biological world of human artifice (skyscrapers, textbooks, paintings, space ships, highways, symphonies and pharmaceuticals). Both levels of human activity are, of course, fundamental to civilization and the world of work can only exist as a superstructure on the world of labor. But insofar as we share the world of labor with the beasts, it

can fairly be described as both natural and subhuman. Only the world of work, of human thought and artifice, is truly human.

This distinction is not so fine as it might at first appear: it has important consequences for architectural design. For if the architect ever builds for the wholly "natural" man, it will be only in his house, at his biological activities of resting, eating, love-making and play. Most other modern building types involve man at work, engaged in a wide spectrum of "unnatural" processes. Each of these involves stress. Stress, as we have seen, comes either from too much or too little stimulation, from sensory "over-loading" and "underloading" alike. Biological man requires a dynamic balance, a golden mean between extremes. But modern work knows no such requirements: on the contrary, for maximum output and optimum quality, it sometimes implies environments of absolute constancy (e.g., pharmaceuticals, printing) and often requires extreme conditions never met in nature (e.g., high-temperature metallurgy, cobalt radiation therapy, etc.).

When plotted, these two sets of requirements will seldom lie along the same curve. From this it follows that architecture must meet two distinctly different sets of environmental criteria—those of man at some "unnatural" task, and those of the "unnatural" process itself.

Variety may indeed be the very stuff of man's natural life. But most of our human activities are, to a greater or lesser extent, "unnatural." From the moment we place the young child in kindergarten, we are imposing "unnatural" tasks upon him—placing his eyesight, his posture, his capacity for attention under quite abnormal stress. And this situation grows more acute throughout his education and his normal working life. As an adult, his biological existence is linked to processes which are never completely congruent with his own. Often they involve work which is fractionalized, repetitive and hence often unintelligible to the individual; often, the processes are actually dangerous to him. Only in agriculture does he confront work whose "natural" environment, rhythms and wholeness correspond to his own; but only six out of one hundred American workers are involved nowadays in this work.

The child at school faces a situation not qualitatively different from his father on the job: namely, to accomplish a given amount of work in a given time. Ideally, his physical growth and intellectual development should be steady and parallel. His rate of development should be as high at the end of his school day as at its beginning. In reality, of course, this is impossible. His energies flag as the day advances and nothing but play, food and rest will restore them. The question for architects is how should the classroom intervene in his favor? How to manipulate his external environment so that his learning advances with optimum speed and minimum stress?

It should be immediately apparent that the child's requirements are dynamic and imply a dynamic relationship with his classroom. No classroom should confront the child with a fixed set of day-long environmental norms, e.g., 72°F. air, 50 percent humidity, 60 foot lamberts at desk top, 45 decibels of sound. Far from being held at some fixed level, the probability is that environmental conditions should be continually changing. *But this change cannot be casual or statistically indeterminate* (if change alone were all that was required, the class could be held in a nearby meadow). It must be a *designed* response to the child's changing requirements. The child may well need less heat at 2 p.m. than at 9 a.m. At day's end he may need less humidity and more oxygen; he may require more light and a different color; he may need a chair that gives a different posture or sound levels higher or lower than the morning. Whatever the requirements are, they could only derive from the child himself, in the experiential circumstances of study. They cannot be met by mechanistic engineers (windowless classrooms, "steady state" controls) nor by formalistic architects who design as though visual perception is the whole of experience.

But the symbiotic relationship between the architectural container and the men and processes contained is nowhere clearer than in the modern hospital. Here we find every degree of biological stress, including that of birth and of death. Here we find a wide range of highly specialized technologies, each with its own environmental requirements. And here we find the narrowest margins for error of any building type: here success or failure are literally matters of life or death. Here, if anywhere, we can observe the integral connections of metabolic function and aesthetic response as shown in Figure 7–1.

The seriously ill patient—above all, the major surgery case—will traverse the full experiential spectrum during his stay at the hospital. Stress will be greatest under surgery. His relationship with his environment can be almost wholly defined in somatic terms. Since he is under total anesthesia, there is no aesthetic aspect to his experience. (It is interesting, in this connection, to note that the two words anesthesia and aesthetic have a common origin in the Greek word meaning "to feel" or "to perceive.")

His gradual process of convalescence—through the recovery room, intensive nursing, regular nursing and ambulatory state, on up to discharge—traverses the full spectrum of experience. Precisely as the metabolic crisis diminishes so will his aesthetic response rise to the front of consciousness. Colors, lights, noises, and odors which he was too ill to notice can now become major factors of experience. And their satisfactory manipulation becomes a matter of active therapy.

The surgeon and his staff too will meet their greatest period of stress during surgery. At this juncture their requirements will be opposed to those of the patient. Where the latter requires warm moist air (and anti-explosive measures demand even higher humidities), the staff under nervous tension should ideally be submerged in dry, cool air. But since stress for them is of limited duration while any added load might be disastrous for the patient, the room's thermo-atmospheric environment is usually designed in the latter's favor. The staff sweats and suffers and recovers later. On the other hand, the luminous environment of the operating room must be wholly designed in the surgeon's favor (and no contradiction is raised because of the patient's lack of consciousness). The color of the walls, of the uniforms, even of the towels is quite as important to visual acuity of the surgeon as the lighting fixtures themselves.

Thus, every decision made in design of the operating room will be based upon functional considerations, objectively evaluated. The very nature of the intervention prohibits any abstractly "aesthetic" considerations. The margin of safety is too narrow to allow the architect the luxury of any formalistic decisions based upon subjective preferences. In varying degrees, this situation will obtain in other specialized areas of the hospital. And it will increase as the hospital comes to be regarded not merely as a container for men and processes but as being itself an actual instrument of therapy. There are many evidences of this tendency already: the hyperbaric chamber where barometric pressure and oxygen content are manipulated in the treatment of both circulatory disorders and gas gangrene; the

metabolic surgery suites where body temperatures are reduced to slow the metabolic rate before difficult surgery; the use of saturated atmospheres for serious cases of burn; artificially-cooled, dry air to lighten the thermal stress on cardiac cases; the use of electrostatic precipitation and ultraviolet radiation to produce completely sterile atmospheres for difficult respiratory ailments or to prevent cross-infection from contagious diseases. Here the building is not merely manipulating the natural environment in the patient's favor but actually creating totally new environments with no precedent in nature as specific instruments of therapy.

The exact point in hospitalization at which these environmental manipulations cease to be purely therapeutic and become merely questions of comfort or satisfaction, i.e., the point at which they cease to be functional and become aesthetic problems, is not easy to isolate. Objectionable odors, disturbing noises and lights; uncomfortable beds; lack of privacy; hot, humid atmosphere—all these will work against "beauty" in the hospital room. They may also delay convalescence. We cannot hope to make modern medical procedures "pretty" and the well-adjusted patient will probably want to leave the hospital as soon as possible under any circumstances. All the more reason, then, that every external factor be analyzed as objectively as possible, with a view to removing all unnecessary stress.

All of this suggests the possibility of establishing, much more precisely than ever before, an objective basis for aesthetic decision. It would be mistaken to attach too much importance to aesthetics in hospital design; but it would be equally foolish to minimize it. It cannot, in any case, be avoided. Everything the architect does, every form he adopts or material he specifies, has aesthetic repercussions. His problem is thus not Hamlet's: to act or not to act. It is rather to act wisely, understanding the total consequences of his decision.

A monograph such as this is an appropriate place in which to formulate such a proposition. For if the architect's aesthetic standards are to be placed on a firmer factual basis than the one on which they now stand, he will need the help of physiologists and psychologists to do it. Architecture needs a much more systematic and detailed investigation of man's actual psychosomatic relationship with his environment than has yet been attempted, at least in architecture. It is not at all accidental that we can find the broad lines of such research appearing in the field of aerospace medicine. For man can only penetrate space by encapsulating himself in a container of terrestial environment. And to accomplish this he must ask fundamental questions: what, actually, *is* this environment? What specifically is its effect upon us? What *is* its relation to human pleasure and delight?

In the design of the space vehicle, for example, it is no longer possible to say where problems of simple biological survival leave off and more complex questions of human satisfaction begin. Clearly, they constitute different ends of one uninterrupted spectrum of human experience. It is very probable that the upper end of this spectrum, involving as it does man's innermost subjective existence, can never be fully explored or understood. But it could certainly be far better understood than it is today, even among architects and doctors.

American society today employs some 270 distinct building types to provide the specialized environments required by its multiform activities. Most of them embody contradictions which must be resolved at two different levels: first between the persons and processes contained and then between their container and the natural environment. Respect for these two conditions is mandatory if the building is to be operationally successful. And yet, respect for these two conditions will often leave the architect with little room in which he can manipulate the building for purely formal, i.e., aesthetic, ends.

Most contemporary failures in architecture (and they are very many) stem either from a failure to understand this situation or else from a refusal to come to terms with it. Of course, no building can grow like an organism. Architects do not work with living tissue, with its powers of cellular division and genetic memory. In this sense, buildings must always be designed by men and these men will always bring to the task preconceived ideas of what forms they ought to assume. As Ernst Fischer (1963), the Austrian philosopher, has said, a good honey bee will often put a bad architect to shame. "But what from the very first distinguishes the most incompetent of architects from the best of bees is that the architect has built a cell in his head before he constructs it in wax." Good or bad, beautiful or ugly, the building is always the expression of somebody's creative ambitions. Today, more than ever in history, these ambitions must be contained, structured and disciplined by objectively verifiable terms of reference.

REFERENCES:

Arendt, H. *The human condition.* New York: Doubleday, 1959.
Fischer, E. *The necessity of art.* New York: Pelican Books, 1963.
Heron, W. The pathology of boredom. *Scientific American,* 1957, **196.**
Ruff, G. Lecture delivered at School of Architecture, Columbia University, New York, October 29, 1963.
Solomon, P. Sensory deprivation and psychological stress. Lecture delivered at Columbia University, New York, November 12, 1963.

8 A Theory of Urban Form

Kevin Lynch and Lloyd Rodwin

The principal concern of the physical planner is to understand the physical environment and to help shape it to serve the community's purposes. An outsider from some other discipline would ordinarily assume that such a profession had developed some ideas concerning the diverse effects of different forms of the physical environment (not to mention the reverse effects of nonphysical forces on the environment itself). And he might be equally justified in expecting that intellectual leaders in the profession had been assiduously gathering evidence to check and reformulate these ideas so that they might better serve the practitioners in the field. A systematic considera-

Reproduced by permission of the *Journal of the American Institute of Planners* (November 1958, Volume XXIV, No. 4) and the authors.

tion of the interrelations between urban forms and human objectives would seem to lie at the theoretical heart of city planning work.

But the expectation would bring a wry smile to the face of anyone familiar with the actual state of the theory of the physical environment. Where has there been any systematic evaluation of the possible range of urban forms in relation to the objectives men might have? Although most attempts at shaping or reshaping cities have been accompanied by protestations of the ends towards which the shapers are striving, yet in fact there is usually only the most nebulous connection between act and protestation. Not only are goals put in a confused or even conflicting form, but also the physical forms decided upon have very little to do with these goals. Choice of form is most often based on custom, or intuition, or on the superficial attraction of simplicity. Once constructed, forms are rarely later analyzed for their effectiveness in achieving the objectives originally set.

What does exist is some palliative knowledge and rules of thumb for designing street intersections, neighborhoods, and industrial areas, for separating different land uses, distinguishing different traffic functions, or controlling urban growth. Analysis of urban design is largely at the level of city parts, not of the whole. The prevailing views are static and fragmentary. When ideal models are considered, they take the form of utopias. These serve to free the imagination, but are not substitutes for adequate analysis.

There are some reasons for this unsatisfactory situation. The profession is still quite young, and most of its energies are concentrated in professional practice. The men in the field are far too preoccupied with practical problems to fashion new concepts. The profession itself developed from fields like architecture and civil engineering which have not been research minded. The professionals in the universities have taught practical courses and spent much of their time in outside practice. Research and theory under these circumstances were expendable. In the rough and tumble of daily operations, preliminary notions such as economic base studies, land use master plans, neigh-borhood design, or zoning and subdivision controls serve a reasonably useful function.

But the planner's situation is changing rapidly. Most of our population now lives in metropolitan regions, and the metropolitan trend is still continuing. There is not only increasing dissatisfaction with our cities, but also an awareness that it is possible to make them more delightful and more efficient places in which to live and work. Tremendous public support has been generated by organizations like The American Council to Improve Our Neighborhoods. Housing, road building, and urban renewal programs are also providing powerful instruments for the transformation of our metropolitan environment. These changing circumstances and values are interesting symptoms of the age of leisure.

The planner's tools and concepts are being subjected to a severe test by this growing demand for action. Something better than rule of thumb and shrewd improvisation is required if his services are to warrant public appreciation. In short, we need better ideas, better theory. Formulated operationally, such theory can be tested, revised, and ultimately verified. Even if initially inadequate, theories can help to develop and extend our ideas, to make them more precise, embracing, and effective. Unless planners can devise more powerful ideas for understanding and controlling the physical environment, they are not likely, and perhaps do not deserve, to be treated as more than lackeys for the performance of routine chores.

POSSIBLE ANALYTICAL APPROACHES

It is not easy to create theories "full blown." Effective theories, as a rule, are products of many men's efforts constantly reworked into a more general and more systematic form. It is also hard to locate the best starting place. In tackling the problems of the physical environment one can employ a number of approaches ranging from the descriptive to the genetic, from problem-solving to process and function analyses. All have certain advantages and disadvantages.

Description is the most obvious approach,

and perhaps the weakest, standing alone. To describe the physical environment more accurately is an important aim; but since these descriptive possibilities are endless, it is difficult to be sure what is and what is not crucial or relevant. Description works best when there is enough familiarity with significance to permit vividness and terse accuracy. Too little is known about the form of the physical environment, or even about the appropriate analytical categories for analyzing these forms, to handle effective description. Description alone, moreover, yields little insight as to the underlying mechanism of operation.

Studying how the physical environment is transformed might be another approach. The nature of the changes can be recorded, the difficulties and directions in transition, the conditions associated with the changes, and the various social, economic, and political processes by which the alteration takes place. Often the historical, comparative, and genetic approaches are the best ways of following the dynamics of the physical environment. But there are limitations too; and these lie in the difficulty of disentangling the strategic variables which should be examined and of understanding the mechanism of change.

Another approach, now most current, is pragmatic. Each case can be considered more or less unique. The emphasis is on problem solving, or on shaping or reshaping the physical environment to eliminate specific difficulties or to achieve specific effects. Limited generalizations or rules can be formulated; but the tendency is to emphasize the uniqueness of each problem and the inapplicability of "stratospheric generalizations." The advantage here is the "realism"; the weakness is the handicap implicit in the assumption that general ideas and theories are of almost no value as guides for dealing with specific cases or classes of cases.

A more abstract variant of problem solving might be a study of the goal-form relationship. This approach is concerned with how alternative physical arrangements facilitate or inhibit various individual and social objectives. It is an approach directly keyed to action; it would, if perfected, sug-gest optimum forms or a range of them, once aspirations had been clarified and decided upon. Its weakness is its static nature; and its strength lies in the emphasis on the clear formulation of goals and on the probable effects of various forms of physical organization. The more that is learned about these effects, the more light will be shed on the process and perhaps even on the mechanism of change. Similarly, descriptive techniques and genetic and historical approaches might prove more effective if the emphasis were on objectives and if the evidence sought were related to the effectiveness of the environment in serving these ends. Problem solving, too, might be more systematic, less haphazard and subject to rules of thumb, if it were grounded on more solid knowledge of goal-form relationships.

This paper proposes to set forth an approach to such a theory. It will therefore necessarily deal first with the problem of analyzing urban form, secondly with the formulation of goals, and thirdly with the techniques of studying the interrelations between such forms and goals.

CRITERIA FOR ANALYTICAL CATEGORIES OF URBAN FORM

Since the work on urban form has been negligible, the first task is to decide what it is and to find ways of classifying and describing it that will turn out to be useful both for the analysis of the impact on objectives and for the practical manipulation of form. Without a clear analytical system for examining the physical form of a city, it is hardly possible to assess the effect of form or even to change it in any rational way. The seemingly elementary step of formulating an analytical system is the most crucial. Upon it hangs all the rest; and while other questions, such as the statement of objectives or the analysis of effects, may be partly the task of other disciplines, the question of city form cannot be passed off.

There are a number of criteria which a workable system must meet. First, it must apply to cities and metropolitan areas and be significant at that scale. This is simply an arbitrary definition of our particular sphere of interest, but it conceals an important distinction. There are many environmental effects which operate at larger scales (such as the influence of climate or the distribution of settlement on a national level), and even more which are effective at a smaller scale (such as the decoration of a room or the siting of a group of houses). Cities are too often regarded simply as collections of smaller environments. Most traditional design ideas (shopping centers, neighborhoods, traffic intersections, play spaces, etc.) reflect this tendency. It is usually assumed that well-designed neighborhoods, with good roads and sufficient shopping and industry, automatically produce an optimum settlement. As another example, many planners are likely to think that a beautiful city is simply the sum of a large series of small areas which are beautiful in themselves.

But this may be no more true than that a great building is a random collection of handsome rooms. Every physical whole is affected not only by the quality of its parts, but also by their total organization and arrangement. Therefore, the first criterion for form analysis is that it identify form qualities which are significant at the city or metropolitan scale, that is, which can be controlled at that scale and which also have different effects when arranged in different patterns that are describable at that scale. This criterion excludes, without in any way denying their importance, such features as intercity spacing (describable only beyond the city level) or the relation of the front door of a house to the street (which is hard to describe on the city scale unless uniform, difficult to control at that level, and whose city-wide pattern of distribution would seem to be of no importance).

The second criterion is that categories must deal solely with the physical form of the city or with the distribution of activities within it; and that these two aspects must be clearly and sharply separated. City and regional planners operate primarily upon the physical environment, although mindful of its complex social, economic, or psycho-logical effects. They are not experts in all the planning for the future that a society engages in, but only in planning for the future development of the physical and spatial city: streets, buildings, utilities, activity distributions, spaces, and their interrelations. Although cries of dismay may greet such a reactionary and "narrow" view, the currently fashionable broader definitions lead in our judgment only to integrated, comprehensive incompetence.

A planner in this sense is aware that the final motive of his work is its human effect, and he should be well grounded, for example, in the interrelation between density and the development of children in our society. He must be quite clear that the physical or locational effects may often be the least important ones, or operate only in conjunction with other circumstances. Above all, he has to understand that the very process of achieving his proposed form, the way in which the group decides and organizes itself to carry it out, may turn out to be the most decisive effect of all. Nevertheless, he takes the spatial environment as the focus of his work, and does not pretend to be a sociologist, an economist, an administrator, or some megalomaniacal super-combination of these.

Physical form and the spatial distribution of activities in the city are partly contained in the traditional "land use" categories of the planning field. Unfortunately, these categories are analytically treacherous.

It is true that their very ambiguity is often useful in field operation, where they can be made to mean what the user wants them to mean. But for theoretical study these categories thoroughly confound two distinct spatial distributions: that of human activity, or "use" proper, and that of physical shape. The traditional concept of "single-family residential use," for example, unites a certain kind of activity: family residence (and its concomitant features of eating, sleeping, child-rearing, etc.) with a type of isolated physical structure, called a "house," which is traditionally allied with this activity. This works tolerably well in a homogeneous society, as long as people behave with docility and continue to reside in families in these houses. But if they should choose to sleep in buildings we call factories, then the whole system would be in danger. Even under present circumstances "mixed uses," or structures used now for storage, now for selling, now for religious meetings, cause trouble.

The pattern of activities and the physical pattern are often surprisingly independent of each other, and they must be separated analytically if we are to understand the effect of either. In practice, planners operate primarily upon the physical pattern, while often aiming to change the activity pattern via the physical change. Only in the negative prohibitions of some parts of the zoning ordinance do planners operate directly upon the activity pattern itself. By sharp distinction of the two, it is possible to explore how activity pattern and physical pattern interact, and which (if either) has significant effects in achieving any given objective.

This paper, however, will develop primarily the notion of the urban physical pattern, leaving the question of the activity pattern for another effort. This is done not to prejudge the relative importance of the two, but for clarity of analysis and because at present most planners operate primarily upon the physical rather than the activity patterns. The time may come, of course, when city planners may manipulate the distribution of activities in an equally direct manner. Even should this time not come and should our influence on activities continue to be indirect, it would be important to know the consequences of activity distribution.

Such nonspatial factors as the range of family income, political organization, or the social type of a city are excluded by this second criterion. This paper will also exclude factors such as the distribution of work place versus sleeping place or the quantity of flow on city streets. These latter are activity categories, properly considered under their own heading.

A third criterion of our analytical system, which adds to the problems of constructing it, is that it must be applicable to all types of urban settlement, used by any human culture. An American city, a Sumerian settlement, or a future Martian metropolis must all be capable of being subsumed under it. The categories must reach a level of generality that might be unnecessary in simply considering present-day cities in the United States. Not only is this necessary for complete analysis, but also by making our categories truly general we may uncover new form possibilities not now suspected. For example, dwelling-units-per-acre cannot be used as a basic descriptive measure, since some settlements may not have sleeping areas organized into dwelling units. (The fact of having such an organization, of course, may be part of a physical description.)

A fourth criterion is that the categories must eventually be such that they can be discovered or measured in the field, recorded, communicated, and tested. Lastly, the crucial test: all the factors chosen for analysis must have significant effect on whatever goals are important to the group using the facilities and must encompass all physical features significant for such goals.

Our aim is to uncover the important factors that influence the achievement of certain human objectives. Therefore the categories allowable here will depend upon the objectives chosen and on the threshold of effect considered significant. The categories used might shift with each new study. It is necessary, however, to set up one system of form categories so that comparisons may be made from one study to another. Therefore one must begin by considering the familiar human purposes and by guessing what physical features might be significant for those purposes. Subsequent analysis and testing will undoubtedly modify the categories based on this criterion.

In summary, the criteria for an analytic system of city form are that the categories of analysis must:

1. Have significance at the city-wide scale, that is, be controllable and describable at that level.
2. Involve either the physical shape or the activity distribution and not confuse the two.
3. Apply to all urban settlements.
4. Be capable of being recorded, communicated, and tested.

5. Have significance for their effect on the achievement of human objectives and include all physical features that are significant.

PROPOSED ANALYTICAL SYSTEM

While several types of analytical systems might be considered, we have attempted to develop a set of abstract descriptions of the quality, quantity, or spatial distribution of various features, of types that are present in some form in all settlements. The abstractness of this system makes it difficult to conceptualize. It also divides up the total form of city, although not spatially, and it therefore raises the problem of keeping in mind the interrelations among categories. But for generality, clarity, and conciseness —and perhaps even for fresh insights—it seems to be the preferable method and will be followed in the rest of this paper.

A system for activity pattern would probably require a description of two basic aspects: flows of men and goods, on the one hand, and, on the other, the spatial pattern of more localized activities such as exchange, recreation, sleeping, or production. Although this side of the analysis will be omitted in order to concentrate on physical pattern, a similar breakdown is feasible in the physical form description: (a) the flow *system*, excluding the flow itself; and (b) the distribution of adapted space, primarily sheltered space.

These are quite similar to the familiar duet of land use and circulation, with the content of activity removed. It may be remarked that an overtone of activity still remains, since the physical facilities are divided between those primarily used for flow, and those accommodating more fixed activities. This is a very convenient division, however, and seems to be a regular feature of all settlements.

There are many cases, of course, in which a given physical space is used both for flow and for other activities. Usually the other activities are alongside the flow, or sometimes intermixed with it, and here the space must be subdivided, or simply counted in both categories. Occasionally there may be a cyclical shift in use, as when a road is shut off for a street dance. Then, if this is important, a temporal shift of the facility from one category to another must be made. It is even conceivable that a city could contain mobile facilities in which both circulation and other activities are performed simultaneously, on the analogy of the ocean liner. But perhaps that can be faced when it happens on a scale that would be significant in a city.

Except for these difficulties, then, the division into flow system and adapted space is a convenient one. The former is usually easy to identify, and includes all the roads, paths, tubes, wires, canals, and rail lines, which are designed to facilitate the flow of people, goods, wastes, or information. The latter category, that of adapted spaces, although it seems tremendously broad, has sufficient basic similarity to be treated as an entity. It consists of all spaces that have been adapted in some way to be useful for some one or several significant noncirculatory activities.

In this country's climate, the key spaces of this nature are those enclosed and with a modified climate, that is, the city's "floor space." Elsewhere enclosure may be less important. Almost everywhere, however, the adaptation includes some modification of the ground plane, even to the cultivation of a field; and the key activities are often likely to take place in at least sheltered, if not enclosed, spaces. But in any case, the fundamental thing done to our physical environment, besides providing means for communication, is to provide spaces for various activities, to adapt the quality of those spaces, and to distribute them in an over-all pattern.

Since many of the primary adaptations of a space, such as enclosure or the provision of a smooth, level, hard, dry ground plane, are useful for many different activities, spaces are often used interchangeably. A "store-front" may be used as a store, an office, a church, a warehouse, or even a family residence. This interchangeability argues for the usefulness and necessity of generalizing adapted space into one category. Within it, one may dissect as much as necessary, dividing enclosed floor space from open space, picking out tall structures from the floor space category, or hard-surfaced lots from total open space. Occasionally, purely for convenience, it may be necessary to use activity-oriented names, such as "office structure," or "parking lot." But, whenever this is done, reference is being made solely to a physical type and not to its use.

Each one of these two general categories, flow system and adapted space, could also be broken down in a parallel way for more exact analysis.

1) Element Types: The basic types of spaces and of flow facilities can be described qualitatively in their most significant aspects, including the extent to which the different types are differentiated in character, or to which they grade into each other.

2) Quantity: The quantities of houses or streets, in length or capacity or size, can then be enumerated, to give total capacity and scale.

3) Density: Next the intensity with which spaces or channels are packed into a given unit area can be stated; as a single quantity, if uniform, but more likely as ranges of intensity and as average and typical intensities. This is a familiar idea when applied to adapted space, particularly enclosed space, as is exemplified in the concept of the floor-area ratio. The same idea could be applied to the circulation system, calculating intensity as the flow capacity which passes in any direction through a small unit area and mapping the variation of this ratio (as in potential vehicles per hour-acre).

4) Grain: The extent to which these typical elements and densities are differentiated and separated in space can be defined as coarse or fine in terms of the quantity of a given type that is separated out in one cluster, and sharp or blurred in terms of the manner of separation at the boundary. Thus, house and factory building types might typically be separated in one city into large pure clusters, sharply differentiated at the edges; while in another town the grain might be very fine and the transitions generally blurred. Again, the outdoor spaces might be blurred and undifferentiated or, in the circulation system, footpaths and vehicular pavements might be sharply and coarsely separated. Essentially, this quality refers to the typical local interrelations between similar or dissimilar elements, but without reference as yet to total pattern.

5) Focal Organization: The spatial arrangement and interrelation of the key points in the total environment can be examined. These might be the density peaks, the concentrations of certain dominant building types, the key open spaces, or the termini or basic intersections of the circulation systems. Consideration of the arrangement of such key points is often a shorthand method of expressing total pattern.

6) Generalized Spatial Distribution: This could be taken as a catchall which included the entire analysis. What is meant here is the gross pattern in two- (or three-) dimensional space, as might be expressed on a greatly simplified map or model. It would include such items as outline (or the shape of the city with reference to the noncity) and the broad pattern of zones occupied by the basic element and density types. One city might have a single central density peak; another a circle cut by pie-shaped zones of "factory" buildings; another a flow system on a rectangular grid; still another might have a uniform pattern of small interconnecting enclosed outdoor spaces surrounded by a deep belt of free-flowing space punctuated by tall masses. Such a description would be needed whenever the notation of type, quantity, density, grain, and pattern of key points was insufficient to describe the significant total pattern.

Finally, of course, it would be necessary to interrelate the two basic categories, to show where the flow termini came with reference to the density peaks, for example, or to relate the pattern of the flow system to the general open space pattern.

The method given above is proposed as a basic system of analyzing a city's form in accordance with the original criteria. It does not try to cover all the physical features of a city, which are endless, but concentrates on those considered significant at that scale.

Only systematic testing in real cities will indicate whether all the important features are included.

AN EXAMPLE OF THE ANALYTICAL SYSTEM

Since this system may be difficult to follow in the abstract, it will perhaps clarify the proposal to use it in describing an imaginary settlement named Pone. Like any town, Pone is best described by the use of both words and precise drawings, but here words and a simple sketch must suffice.

a) Pone is made up of six types of adapted space: dirt-floored rooms, 20 by 20 feet, roofed with thatch and enclosed by adobe, each structure being free standing: concrete-floored shed spaces, 75 feet by up to 300 feet, in corrugated iron, sometimes single and sometimes in series horizontally; multistory concrete structures containing from fifty to two hundred 10 by 10 foot rooms; walled-in cultivated spaces of rectangular shape, varying from ½ to 3 acres; walled, stone-paved spaces pierced by paths; irregular bare dust-covered spaces which take up the remainder of the area. Pone has four types of flow channels: four-foot dirt paths, unenclosed; thirty-foot cobbled roads, enclosed in semicircular tubes of corrugated iron; an interconnecting waterproof system of four-inch pipes; and some telegraph wires.

b) There are ten thousand adobe rooms, totaling 4,000,000 square feet; fifty shed spaces, totaling 1,000,000 square feet; and four multistory structures, with 40,000 square feet of floor space. There are five thousand cultivated spaces occupying 5,000 acres, two walled and paved open spaces of 10 acres each; and the leftover dust covers 1,200 acres. There are three miles of cobbled road, each with a capacity of 400 mulecarts per hour in both directions; and 60 miles of dirt path, each able to carry 2,000 persons per hour in either direction. There are 20 miles of pipe and 2 miles of wire.

c) Density of adobe rooms varies continuously from a floor-area ratio of 0.003 to 0.3; that of the sheds from 0.3 to 0.9 (with a tendency to group at the two extremes),

while the tall structures are uniformly at 5.0. Road-capacity density varies from a peak of 1,600 carts per hour-acre to a low of 20; path-capacity density varies from 4,000 persons per hour-acre to 50.

d) The three types of enclosed space are sharply differentiated and separated in plan. Cultivated spaces are mixed coarsely with the adobe rooms, while the irregular dusty areas are finely distributed throughout. Roads and paths are sharply separated and do not interconnect except at the shed spaces. Any intersections are at separated grades. They are also coarsely separated, since the roads are associated with the shed spaces.

Wires and pipes follow along paths. Pipes are dispersed, but wires serve only sheds and the multistory structures.

e) Focal points in this organization are the two rectangular paved open spaces. The first is central to the area of adobe rooms, and is the focus of converging paths. It corresponds to the peak of room density and to one of the peaks of path density. The other focal point is flanked by the multistory structures, occurs at another convergence and density peak of the path system, and is touched upon by the road system. Here occurs the major terminus and interchange point of that road system. The wire lines all pass through a central switchboard in one of the multistoried structures. The pipe lines have a single source just beyond the town boundary.

f) The settlement is round and compact, with no holes. The multistoried structures and second focus occur at the center, with the sheds occupying a narrow pie-shaped sector outwards from this. The focus of room density is slightly off center. The road system is a rectangular grid of irregular spacing, tying to the sheds, to the second focal point, and, by a single line, to the outside. The path system is irregular and capillary, but converges and intensifies at the two focal points, as noted above (see Figure 8-1).

In theory (and particularly if we could use more drawings) we now know enough of the physical form to judge its value for various basic purposes at the city level of significance. One is tempted to object: Isn't

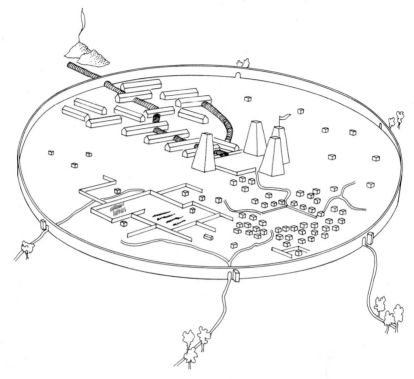

Figure 8–1

this meaningless, if one knows nothing of the life that is going on within that form? Lifeless, yes, and saying little or nothing about the society of Pone (though one may make some guesses); but yet adequate, if you want to test its cost, or productive efficiency (given some productive system), or comfort (given some standards). Certainly it is the first step in trying to disentangle the effects of physical form per se, and the first step even if one wants to study the results of physical form in relation to activity pattern, or social organization, or politics. (To describe New York City in this way would, of course, take a few more pages.)

PROBLEMS OF GOAL FORMULATION

What will be the goals against which we will test this city? Unfortunately for a neat and workmanlike job, they might be almost anything. One group inhabiting Pone might find it highly satisfactory, another might find it useless or even dangerous, all depending on their several purposes and the variations in their cultures. Is there any method by which relevant goals might be set out and related to these environmental shapes? Unhappily for the reader, we now find that we must digress to consider the problems of setting up a goal system. Only after this is done will it be possible to return to the implications of the forms themselves.

The possible goals must first be considered. This may cause some confusion, since such a collection is not likely to be consistent or unified. It must be distinguished from a goal *system*, i.e., a set of selected objectives which are coherent, unified, and capable of guiding action. Construction of such a system is the desirable result of considering goal possibilities, but it can only be brought to completion by a particular group in a particular situation. Thus the possible range of goals might include both the preservation of individual life at all costs and also the maximization of human sacrifice. A particular system would have to choose, or, more probably, settle upon some intermediate stand; and this stand should be related to its other objectives.

Probably the most confusing aspect of this question is not the infinite number of goal possibilities, but rather their range of generality. Some objectives, such as "goodness," may seem to regulate almost every action, but to do so in such a vague and generalized way as to be of little help in choice. Others, such as the goal of having all children say "please" when asking for things at the table, are very clear in their implications for action, but quite limited in their application and their consequences. These two goals are interconnected only by a long chain of explanations, situations, and interactions. It is difficult to be sure that one follows from the other and hard to weight their relative importance in relation to other goals.

To avoid such confusions, it is important that any one goal system should contain only objectives which are at approximately the same level of generality. We may smile when someone admonishes a child to "be good, and keep your fingernails clean!" But we are also exhorted to build city additions that will be good places to live in and will keep valuations high. In many cases, of course, there may be no real confusion, as when the second point is the true objective and the first is only a verbal blind.

Similarly, it is meaningless to consider beauty and fresh paint as alternative objectives: they do not operate at the same level. Each objective may in its turn be looked upon as a means of attaining some objective higher up the scale of generality. Shouting at recruits may be considered a means of overawing them, with the goal of developing obedience, which is itself directed to the building of a disciplined military force, having as its objective the winning of wars, which may be thought of as a way to gain security. When constructing a rational system for guidance in any particular situation, what must be built up is a connected hierarchy of goals, considering possible alternatives only at the same level of generality and checking lower levels for their relevance to upper levels of the system.

The more general objectives have the advantage of relative stability: they are applicable to more situations for larger groups over longer spans of time. They have the corresponding disadvantages of lack of precision and difficulty of application in any specific problem. Very often, in goal systems of real life, such general objectives may have very little connection with objectives farther down the list, being, rather, top-level show pieces, or covers for hidden motives. The operating goals are then the intermediate ones, those which actually regulate action. To develop a rational set of goals, however, the connection must be sought out, or the motives that are the true generalized goals must be revealed. The aim is to produce a system that is as coherent as possible, although this again is rare in reality.

Since reference back to very general goals is a painful one intellectually, most actions must be guided by intermediate, more concrete, objectives, which can be referred to more quickly. Only the most serious steps warrant reference to fundamentals, while everyday decisions depend on customs and precepts that are actually low-level goals. City building is important enough to be referred back to more than simple precepts; but even here decisions cannot always be brought up to the highest level of generality, since the analysis is so complex. Therefore reliance must be placed upon goals of an intermediate level. But these intermediate goals should be periodically checked for their relevance to more general objectives and to the changing situation, as well as for consistency among themselves.

It is a besetting sin to "freeze" upon rather specific goals and thus risk action irrelevant to a new situation. If it is observed, for example, that growing cities have been prosperous ones, attention may focus upon increase of population size as an objective. Actions will be directed toward stimulating growth, regardless of any consequences of dislocation, instability, or cost. Industries may be brought in which will depress the wage level and the general prosperity, because no one has stopped to examine the objectives that lie behind the growth objective, i.e., to ask the simple question: "Why do we want to grow?" Because of this continuous tendency to fix upon goals at too specific a level, it is a wise habit to challenge current goals by always pushing them back at least one step up the ladder of generality.

CRITERIA FOR THE CHOICE OF GOALS

What will be the criteria for the choice of goals in our case? If they are rational, they should be internally consistent. There should, moreover, be some possibility of moving toward their realization, now or in the future. Otherwise they are simply frustrating. To have operational meaning, they must be capable of being contradicted, thus permitting a real choice. And finally, the goals must be relevant to city form, since there are many human objectives which are little affected by environmental shape. Therefore, given one's basic values and the values of the culture in which one is operating, it is necessary to develop a set of useful intermediate objectives which are consistent, possible, operational, and relevant to the task in hand.

Devising such objectives is difficult; and it is not made easier by the fact that a planner is an individual responsible for actions or recommendations in an environment used by large numbers of people. He is not concerned simply with his own values, nor even with their interaction with the values of another individual with whom he can communicate, which is the situation of the architect with a single client. The planner's client is a large group, a difficult client to talk to, often incoherent, and usually in some conflict with itself.

To some extent the planner can rely on democratic processes to establish group objectives; to some extent he must use sociological techniques to uncover them. Often he is forced, or thinks he is forced, to rely upon his own intuition as to group objectives—a most hazardous method, since the planner is himself likely to be a member of a rather small class of that society. In any event, he must make every effort to understand his own values, as well as to uncover and clarify the goals of the society he is working for.

His troubles do not stop here. Even if he had perfect knowledge of group goals, and they proved to form a completely consistent system, he is still faced with the issue of relating them to his own personal values. He cannot be solely the handmaiden of the group, but has some responsibility (should he differ) to urge upon them a modification of their goal system or to acquaint them with new alternatives. He has a complicated role of leader and follower combined and must resolve this for himself. This is true of many other professional groups.

And should the public goals, as is most likely, prove to be internally inconsistent or in transition, then the planner must mediate these conflicts and changes. He must find the means of striking a balance and the way of preparing for the new value to come without destroying the old value still present.

But to all these everyday woes we can at the moment simply shrug our theoretical shoulders. Give us a consistent and operational system of objectives, a system possible and relevant and organized properly by levels, and we will show you the environmental forms to achieve these objectives. If your goals are superficial or shortsighted, so much the worse. That is your concern, not ours.

In western culture, general and accepted goals would probably cluster around the worth of the individual human being, around the idea of man as the measure, with an emphasis on future results and yet on the importance of process as well as final achievement. Basic values for the individual might include such things as:

a) Health, equilibrium, survival, continuity, adaptability.
b) Coherence, meaning, response.
c) Development, growth, stimulus, choice, freedom.
d) Participation, active use of powers, efficiency, skill, control.
e) Pleasure, comfort.

Upon the basis of such generalities, one can make for himself (or for his group) a set of broad goals. One way of conveniently organizing such goals may be the following:

a) Regarding the relation of men and objects: Those goals
  1) having to do with direct functioning: biological or technical goals, such as the achievement of an en-

vironment which sustains and prolongs life;

2) having to do with sensuous interactions: psychological or esthetic goals, such as the creation of an environment which is meaningful to the inhabitant.

b) Regarding the relation of men and men: Those goals

1) having to do with interpersonal relations: sociological and psychological goals, such as constructing surroundings which maximize interpersonal communications;

2) or having to do with group functioning: social goals such as survival and continuity of the group.

It is important to see that a mere listing of objectives is insufficient even at this generalized level, if a policy of relative emphasis is not also included. Any real action may work for one goal and against the other, or be more or less helpful in relation to another action. Yet the choice must be made. Therefore a statement of objectives must be accompanied by a statement of relative importance: that, for example, group survival is valued above individual survival, although both are valued. More precisely, it will have to be said that, in such-and-such a circumstance, group survival is more valued.

Since attainment of human objectives almost always entails the use of scarce resources, the next level of objectives are the economic. In their most general form, they can be described as the attainment of ends with the maximum economy of means, while keeping or making the resource level as high as possible. In all these general objectives, moreover, there is an intertwining of means and ends, of process and final achievement. Particularly where "final" achievement may be as long delayed or even as illusory as it is in city development, the attainment of objectives may be affected more by the process itself than by the final form that is being sought.

But the goal system at this level, however consistent and relevant, is still too general for effective application to city-form decisions. Moving down to lower levels for specific guidance, how can one define a "meaningful environment," for example, or

the limits within which interpersonal communication is to be maximized?

It would be possible to move down the ladder step by step, ending with some such rule as "all buildings should by their exterior form reveal to any adult inhabitant of average education and intelligence their principal internal use," or even ". . . to accomplish this, the following building types shall have the following shapes. . . ." The latter is undoubtedly an example of "misplaced concreteness"; but even the former poses problems in relating it back to the general descriptive categories of city form that were developed above. How does the "meaningfulness" of structure relate to density, or grain, or focal organization? In coming down the ladder of specificity we may find we have slipped away from relevance to form at the city scale, or have developed precepts which have multiple and complex effects on the various categories of city form.

Since the formulation of specific objectives is unavoidable, it would be preferable that they be reorganized by being grouped in terms of their relevance to the descriptive categories. Such organization is simply a tactical move, but a crucial one. It involves running through the list of descriptive categories of city form, and choosing (by intuition or prior experience) those general objectives that seem most relevant to that aspect of form.

For example, the following general goals are probably affected in some important way by the "grain" of adapted spaces in an urban settlement:

a) Optimum interpersonal communication.

b) Maximum choice of environment for the individual.

c) Maximum individual freedom in construction.

d) Optimum esthetic stimulus.

e) Maximum productive efficiency.

f) Maximum productive flexibility.

g) Minimum first cost.

h) Minimum operating cost.

By thus selecting and grouping our general goals, a hypothesis is being asserted, that, for example, "the grain of city facilities has significant (if unknown) effect on the first cost of constructing them." Such hypotheses may prove untrue, in which case the group of goals must be revised or, equally likely, it may indicate that some other objective not originally listed is also significantly affected and must be added to the list.

One objective may be significantly affected by more than one form quality and will thus appear in more than one group. Another objective may be little influenced by any one quality alone, but rather by the nature of the combination of two or more, such as the total effect of grain and density together. This is a separate point, to which we will later return.

The critical nature of the form categories previously selected now becomes apparent, since they impose their pattern upon the entire investigation. If they are not in themselves highly significant, or if they are inconsistent or poorly organized, the work must be redone. Nevertheless, by bringing in the relation to form thus early in our consideration of objectives, a much more economical and systematic attack is possible. The objectives not only contain hypotheses of relevancy, but are really turning into action questions, for example: "What grain of spaces gives a minimum first cost?"

It must be made clear that, if physical forms are considered in isolation, such action questions are not answerable. No relation between grain and first cost can be established until a construction process is postulated. Or, for another example, the impact of the grain of spaces on interpersonal communication depends also on the activity occupying those spaces. Nevertheless, once given a construction process or an activity distribution which is held constant during the test, then the differential impact of various grain alternatives can be analyzed. Thus, in a given activity context, the results of various physical patterns might be studied. Often, a principal result of a given physical pattern may occur via the manner in which it changes an activity distribution, given an assumption as to a fixed association between certain forms and certain activities.

The same limitations apply to the study of activity patterns in isolation, which are meaningless without reference to the facilities available for communication, insulation, and so on. Eventually, there would be a more complex level of analysis, in which both activity distribution and form might be allowed to vary simultaneously. Even here, however, a general cultural context is still required.

Once the general goals are arranged in terms of the type, quantity, density, grain, focal organization, and pattern of the adapted spaces and the flow system (and in the process just those objectives have been selected out which may be most critically affected by these qualities), and once a general context of culture and activity has been chosen, a more concrete level of analysis is possible. The level should be specific enough to say that "city A is closer to this objective than city B." The meaning of terms must be put in an operational, and often quantitative, way. For example, "what density of spaces allows a reasonable journey from home to work" might become: "what density (or densities) allows 75 percent of the population to be within 30 minutes' time distance of their place of work, providing no more than 10 percent are less than 5 minutes away from their work place?" Different city models could now be tested by this criterion.

Not all goals could be put in this quantitative form, of course. But they would at least have a testable wording, such as "what is the density at which there is maximum opportunity for interpersonal communication within the local group, without destroying the ability of the individual to achieve privacy when desired?" Such formulations are likely to contain the words maximum, or minimum, or optimum.

The caution must be repeated that, while satisfyingly specific, such goals require continuous rechecking for relevance to the general goals and the changing situation. The home-to-work objective, for example, is simply a definition of the original word "reasonable." Next year, or in India, it might be different.

GOAL FORM INTERACTION

Having established an analytical system of urban form and groups of objectives cast in relevant operational terms, the next problem we have is the interaction of form with goal.

One might begin either by considering the grain of adapted space and the objectives significantly related to it, or, alternatively, a fundamental objective and the form aspects related to it. If one of the goals is minimum first cost, for example, are the shed spaces of Pone cheaper to build when concentrated as they are in a coarse grain than if they were dispersed throughout the adobe spaces in a fine grain? Or, perhaps, does the grain of dispersion make no difference whatever? Undoubtedly, the effect of grain on cost may differ for different types of space. For example, while the grain of shed spaces was critical because they were built by mass site fabrication methods, the grain of adobe spaces might be indifferent, since they were put up singly by hand in any case. Or it might be found that dispersion of the multistory spaces among the shed spaces did not affect their cost, but dispersion among the adobe spaces did. Only in certain cases could generalizations as to grain, per se, be made. More often, the grain of a certain type of adapted space would have to be the subject of a conclusion.

The grain of the shed spaces may also affect productive efficiency. To test this, one may assume a type of activity, a given productive system, similar to the assumption of construction methods to test the cost implications. To do so does not mean that activity distribution slips in by the back door; we are still testing the impact of one or another physical quality upon the functioning of an activity which is held constant during the test. That is, given a factory system of production, which operates more easily in the wide-span shed spaces of Pone than anywhere else in the city, is that productive system more efficient if all the sheds are close together or if they are dispersed?

In this manner, the goal implications of grain could be analyzed, testing each for relevance and effect, and ending by a search to see if significant goals have been left out. If this system is successful, one should be able to say that, given such-and-such a culture, this particular grain gives best results if your goal system has these particular elements and emphases, and another grain would be better for another system. Alternatively, the objective of minimum first cost could be explored throughout all its ramifications, resulting in a statement that, given a certain culture, this particular total urban form can be constructed at a minimum first cost.

These are final stage results, difficult to attain. Partial, and still useful, conclusions are more likely, such as: if this is the contemporary American society, and if the *only* goal is productive efficiency, then here is the grain to use for this type of adapted space (or: there are several equally good distributions or, perhaps, the grain is of no consequence). Of course, the answer is likely to be still more qualified. One may have to add that this grain is best in a city of small size, another in the larger city; or that optimum grain cannot be separated from density or pattern.

One further note must be made. The *process* of achieving goals or of reshaping form is, in cities, as important as the long-range goal or form. Building a new city of a specific shape may have vital side-effects on the administrative acts and organization required; sequence of development has as much to do with cost as final density. Moreover, one may have important goals which have to do mainly with the process itself, for example, that development decisions be arrived at democratically, or that people be allowed to participate in planning their dwellings, regardless of the final result.

The goal-form method, then, consists in ordering form analysis and definition of objectives so that their interrelation can be considered in a systematic and rational manner. It helps to pose the problem. There it blesses the investigator, and drops him in the mud. It has no further bearing on the analysis of any given interrelation. Each such analysis is likely to be unique and to demand its own method of solution. One might be amenable to mathematical methods; another, to sociological tools; a third, solvable only by subjective analysis; a fourth, by full-scale field tests. There is no guarantee, of course, that the fifth may be solvable at all. What is proposed is merely a way of attacking the central problems of cities in a methodical way.

This "merely," however, may in time open up new possibilities, simply because the problems are more precisely put. If the important physical properties of cities can be clearly defined, and if an operational standard can be set, such as one regarding commuting times, we may be able to study the implications of complex forms by means of new mathematical methods or with such aids as the high-speed computers.

COMPLEX FORM AND GOAL RELATIONSHIPS

If form qualities and goals could be analyzed and disposed of one by one, then in time a complete structure could be built with relative ease. Unfortunately (and this is perhaps the most vulnerable point of the system) physical patterns and goals have a habit of complex interaction. There is not one goal, but many; and the presence of other goals influences the force of the original one. The city forms, which we have herded into arbitrary categories to make our analysis possible, in truth make one pattern. It is not always easy to discuss the impact of grain without specifying density or size. The consequences of the distribution of adapted spaces rest partly on the flow system allied with it.

Thus there are frequently situations where a given goal may not only be influenced by more than one form aspect, but also may at times be affected by such an intimate interaction of aspects that there is no separable cause. A convenient system of notation for such a situation might be as follows, imagining that we are concerned with five goals, A, B, C, D, and E, which have the relationships with form shown in Figure 8-2.

Achievement of goal is influenced by:

A—(1) space type; (2) flow system size.
B—(1) space, density, and grain combined; (2) focal organization of space and flow system combined.
C—(1) space, size, and flow system pattern combined.
D—(1) grain of flow system; (2) density of space and flow system combined.
E—(1) grain of space, and density and focal organization of flow system all combined.

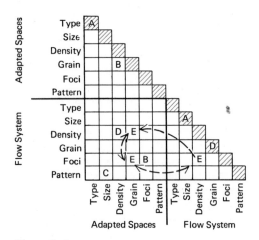

Figure 8–2

Here the appearance of a goal in the top diagonal (shaded squares) indicates that it relates to a single form quality at a time. Elsewhere its appearance shows that it is influenced by a pair of form qualities that must be considered together. One goal is shown (E) which is effected by an inseparable combination of three, and must therefore be shown as a connected triangle. If a three-dimensional notation system were used, it could occupy a single solid cube. Higher interactions would require more complicated notations.

This figure would change, of course, as the system of descriptive categories was modified. It is simply a convenient way of reminding ourselves what must be taken into account in studying goal-form interaction. It indicates, incidentally, that in this particular case two aspects of form (space pattern and flow system type) happen to be the ones that have no bearing on any goal. All the rest are involved in one way or another.

Probably these analytical methods could handle situations where pairs of qualities were involved. Triads of qualities become much more difficult, and many more are likely to make analysis impossible. Some questions may therefore be answerable, and others may resist our best efforts.

To complete the example, consider the city of Pone again. The people of Pone are simple-minded; they have few wants. They have only three goals relevant to city form:

1) Maximum individual privacy, when not producing.
2) Maximum defensibility in war.
3) Maximum productive efficiency.

In case of conflict, goal 2 takes precedence, then goal 3. The Ponians are a simple and a rather grim people.

These goals are set in the following situation: the town produces various kinds of simple consumer goods, which it exports to the surrounding countryside in return for raw materials. This production is most easily carried out in the shed spaces, directed by control functions in the multistory spaces. But the town also produces a large part of its food supply in the cultivated spaces within its limits. Other life functions, beyond production and distribution, are traditionally carried out in the adobe rooms or in the paved open spaces. Wars are fought by ground action, with simple short-range weapons, and may occur suddenly.

The following matrix indicates the probable relevancy of various form aspects to the three goals:

That is, objective 1 is affected by the type, density, and grain of adapted spaces, all acting singly. Objective 2 is influenced by the pattern of spaces and by the density, grain and focal organization of the flow system, acting singly. It is also the prey of the combined action of the size and density of the adapted spaces. This is true because, although the larger the city the greater the defensive army that could be raised for war and the higher the density the more compact the defensive perimeter, yet in combination they may work in another way. A large, very dense city might quickly succumb to food shortages, owing to the lack of adequate internal cultivated spaces. Therefore the optimum solution is likely to be a function of size in relation to density. Finally, objective 3 is related to the type and grain of spaces and the type and density of the flow system, acting singly, plus the combined effect of the spatial and flow-system focal organizations. The matrix indicates that the size and pattern of the flow system are meaningless to the Ponians (see Figure 8-3).

The analysis on all these separate points

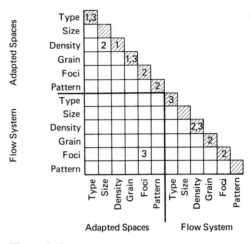

Figure 8–3

could then be carried through and the total balance struck, comparing the actual form of Pone with any other forms within the reach of this people. One might come out with some such conclusion as: given these goals, the actual form is probably the optimum available, with the following modifications:

a) For the privacy objective, a new type of space should be substituted for the single-room adobe space.

b) For the defense objective, a better balance of size and density could be struck, particularly if the unused dust spaces were eliminated. Furthermore, if the capacity density of the flow system were stepped up and the system dispersed at finer grain throughout the settlement, then defense would be simplified.

c) For the production objective, an increase in flow capacity-density would also facilitate efficiency.

As was stated at the beginning, the high planners of Pone would also have gone on to a study of the consequences of the activity distribution in the city, and they would have ended with a higher level study of the interrelation of activity and form. But probably the reader has had enough.

EVALUATION

Application of this method to a modern metropolis would obviously be far more complicated and, necessarily, more fragmentary. But the basic technique should still be applicable, though it would call for descriptions at a larger scale and goals less precisely formulated. Since the whole technique is analytical, a study of isolated parts, it will tend to give first approximations, rather coarse conclusions bristling with "ifs." It would nevertheless be the elementary knowledge upon which much more refined, and in particular much more fluid and integrated methods could be constructed.

To the student of the physical environment, perhaps the most attractive features of goal-form studies are the new possibilities for research and theory. Regardless of the inadequacy of our present formulations there is a need to test and explore both the range and appropriateness of form categories. Hardly anything is known of how they interact and what the possibilities are for substitution. And instead of fragmentary notions, such as the differentiation of traffic networks, the separation or mixing of land uses, and the organization of neighborhood units, there is the prospect of a general theory of urban form for the city as a whole. If some measure of success is achieved in developing such a general theory, it should not prove too difficult to fit these miscellaneous doctrines into this broader framework, especially since these doctrines purport to modify city form in line with some more or less definite objectives.

Goal-form studies also suggest a new lead for examining city planning history. Instead of the traditional historical survey of civic design accomplishments, the adequacy of urban forms might be examined in the light of some of the major goals of different cultures. The same approach might be applied with profit to current history. Significant contemporary plans for communities might be studied to see how adequately the goals are formulated and how explicitly they are related to the physical forms proposed.

The essence of progress for most disciplines lies in finding ways of systematizing as well as extending present knowledge. Goal-form studies offer a springboard for city and regional planning to achieve this extension and synthesis.

But aside from the elegance or logic of the theoretical framework, such an analytical system may find its ultimate usefulness in providing the raw material for planning decisions. Eventually it should tell the planner: "If your only aim is productive efficiency, and if other elements are like this, and if your society does not change, then this form is the best one yet found to do the job." This is the underpinning for what in part must remain a complex art, an art yet beyond the determinability of scientific knowledge in three ways. First, in that the more complex interactions are most likely to elude rigorous theory and depend on personal judgment. Second, because the method is indifferent to the choice of values, and the choice or clarification of objectives is a fundamental part of the art of planning. And thirdly, because the method can do no more than test form alternatives previously proposed. The creative task of imagining new form possibilities, as in all other realms of art and science, lies beyond it, although the analytical system may be suggestive in this work.

PART TWO

Basic Psychological Processes
and the Environment

Discussions of environmental influences on human behavior frequently emphasize vast environments and their influence on all mankind. This emphasis is apparent in Part One, in which most of the theoretical orientations address themselves, quite properly, to broad questions of human survival and enrichment in an increasingly man-made world. It is also true, however, that the smaller environment in which an individual functions may have as far-reaching effects on him as the larger environment has on all of human society. It therefore seems appropriate to include in this volume a group of articles devoted to basic psychological processes in relation to the environment.

What are usually taken to be the basic processes of psychology can be determined by examining any introductory text. Chapter headings typically list perception, cognition, memory, learning, affect, and sometimes a few others. These have traditionally been considered the elementary processes that, in various combinations, produce the functioning adult human. But this elementaristic and fragmentary approach seems increasingly inadequate as the interrelationships among these processes reveal themselves to be extremely complex. At the same time, the boundaries among the processes are becoming increasingly hard to define.

The relationship between perception and cognition is an example. During much of its history, psychology, with infrequent exceptions, treated this problem by refusing to recognize its existence. Perception was studied from the standpoint of what we might call, with some license, the external mechanism of the process. Insofar as cognition was considered in relation to perception, it was summed up by the ancient dictum, "seeing is believing." The road to the cognitive or belief system was through the perceptual process. Approximately two decades ago psychology repealed its ancient pronouncement and reversed the law. "Believing is seeing" became the keynote of a generation of perceptual studies. No longer did perception mirror an external world that we believed because we saw it; instead, it mirrored our innermost values and produced a world that we saw precisely because we believed in it. Today, of course, we know that neither of these views is correct because both are predicated on the incorrect assumption that we are dealing with two separate and isolated systems, perception and cognition, having certain fixed and unidirectional contacts.

In considering basic psychological processes we do not, therefore, commit ourselves to the traditional categories of perception, cognition, and so on. The only assumption the material in this section makes is that man actively extracts information from the environment, processes it, and utilizes it. How he does this, what kinds of information are used, and how they are processed constitute the questions of concern to environmental psychology in the study of basic psychological processes.

Perhaps the most limiting position a psychological study can take is to treat man as a fixed entity who functions in, but is unchanged by, his surroundings. Such an approach makes it necessary to attribute to the inherent nature of the organism properties that may in fact be reflections of the environmental situation, or of a particular set of relationships between the individual and the environment. Environmental psychology does not question that man is a sensing and responding organism, that like all living things he is differentially sensitive to various aspects of his surroundings and responds differentially to them. But it does suggest that our knowledge of human psychological functioning has been limited by an approach that sees the environment as the context within which behavior takes place rather than as itself an integral part of behavior.

In general, the traditional study of basic psychological processes has been aimed at finding an assumed underlying nature of the organism, and environmental manipulations have been used primarily as a means of eliciting this information. This has been equally true whether the theoretical assumptions behind the study are phenomenological or behavioral. The environment has typically been used as a means of testing the limits of the organism and thus of plotting the parameters of a great many psychological processes. Much extremely useful information has been learned in this way, but it is becoming increasingly clear that this knowledge helps us little in understanding and predicting man as an active participant in complex environmental situations. Only recently have increasingly large numbers of investigators come to realize that most situations do not test the limits of man's receptor and response capabilities. Far more frequently there is a great deal of redundancy, in which a large number of equivalent modes of behaving are equally possible.

This fact has long been recognized in complex psychological functioning, such as adult personality structure, which represents one particular pattern out of many potential, functionally equivalent ones for dealing with a series of external contingencies. But it has only recently been acknowledged in the basic psychological processes. Cognitive styles, for example—the ways individuals characteristically organize their thought processes—are not direct reflections of the nature of the organism but rather represent preferred strategies the individual has developed over long periods of time.

From the standpoint of environmental psychology, therefore, the important psychological processes are not only those which represent the limits of the organism but also those which actually are exhibited in concrete environmental situations. This is perhaps no more than a statement of a fundamental principle of environmental psychology—that psychological processes manifest themselves only in specific environmental contexts. What we have learned about the nature of human psychological functioning is not necessarily a reflection of the inherent nature of the organism but is perhaps more frequently an indication of the demands made upon the organism by the environment.

If this line of thinking is correct, then two further principles for environmental psychology emerge—first, that a full knowledge of basic psychological processes requires a sampling of all possible environments, and second, that what appear to be basic properties of the organism may, in fact, be contingent upon the environmental context. These two interrelated principles form the basis for the environmental psychologist's approach to basic psychological processes. The first principle tells us that if we want to know how the normal human functions we must study him in environments that are representative of those in which behavior actually occurs. The second principle suggests that what we find in such an investigation might have been different had the environmental situations been different. In short what we are seeking, as Simon (1969) has pointed out, are not fixed laws of behavior but rather contingent relationships, that is, a science of "systems that, given different circumstances, might be quite other than they are."

The need for representative sampling of environments has been recognized by many investigators, although only relatively recently, and the importance of environmental influences has, of course, long been stressed. This approach has been influential, however, primarily only in relation to the more complex psychological processes, such as personality formation and social behavior. And even here, relatively little importance has been attributed to the physical environment as such. The environmental approach has certainly not been dominant in the study of basic psychological processes, such as perception, cognition, and learning. In spite of the vast amount of work that has been done in these areas there does not exist a large body of findings directly pertinent to this section. The selections offered here, therefore, have been chosen to suggest the flavor of work in this area. Some of them indicate past work done on specific psychological processes in specific environmental situations, but they grew out of very different theoretical concerns from those underlying this volume. Many of the selections antedate the current concern with environmental problems. Others explicitly address themselves to contemporary problems, but are offered here more as intimations of work that needs to be done than as reflections of existing accomplishments.

Part Two is therefore largely programmatic and to a certain extent evangelical in intent. It points out what may well be the most significant task before environmental psychology—to study the role of environmental contingencies in forming what is taken to be human nature, past contingencies leading to the man of today and future contingencies pointing the way to the man of tomorrow.

REFERENCE:

Simon, H. A. *The sciences of the artificial.* Cambridge, Mass.: M.I.T. Press, 1969.

9 Two Processes in Perceptual Learning[1]

Franklin P. Kilpatrick

It can be stated categorically that learning plays a role in visual space perception, even though there is considerable disagreement concerning the importance of that role. The author has placed extreme emphasis on the side of learning (e.g., Kilpatrick, 1952a, 1952b; Kilpatrick & Ittelson, 1953) in contrast to some other views (e.g., Gibson, 1950; Koffka, 1935; Köhler, 1947; Pratt, 1950). Perhaps, though, it would prove profitable to lay aside, at least for a time, the question of "how much?" and pay a bit more attention to the question of "how?"

Work with monocular distorted rooms designed by Adelbert Ames, Jr. (Ittelson, 1952) has led the author to the formulation of certain notions concerning possible learning processes involved in visual space perception. Such rooms were built originally as an empirical test of a limited case of the hypothesis of equivalent configurations, that is, for the case of a three-dimensional object monocularly observed (Ittelson & Kilpatrick, 1952). A monocular distorted room is nonrectangular, but built in such a way that each part of the room subtends the same

From *The Journal of Experimental Psychology,* 1954, **47,** 362–370. Reprinted by permission of the author and publisher.

[1] The research reported in this paper was supported by the Office of Naval Research as a portion of a larger project initiated by the Professional Division, Bureau of Medicine and Surgery. However, the opinions expressed are the author's, and should not be construed as representing the opinions or policy of the naval service.

visual angle at the nodal point of an eye placed at the chosen observation point as would the corresponding part of a particular rectangular room (reference room) observed from the same point. If this prescription is followed, the stimulus pattern on *O*'s retina will be the same for the distorted room, of whatever shape, and the undistorted reference room, except, of course, for very slight differences due to unavoidable defects in construction and inability to place *O*'s eye *exactly* at the prescribed observation point. Viewed by a naive *O* with one eye from the prescribed location, such distorted rooms are perceived as being like the reference room, that is, "normal" or very nearly "normal" in shape. Sloping walls are seen as vertical, sloping floors and ceilings are seen as level, and windows of different sizes and shapes are seen as being alike. Apparently no amount of time spent in just looking at such a static configuration has any effect in altering the way in which it is seen. However, and this is the important point for the purposes of this paper, *O* can *learn to see* more and more of the distorted shape of the room, even though the stimulus pattern on his retina remains unchanged.

Occurrence of this learned alteration in visual space perception was first noted in connection with the behavioral testing of *O*'s perception of a distorted room. The *O* is given a wand and asked to touch various parts of the room while keeping his eye at the observation point; he is initially unsuccessful in his efforts. His actions are those which would work in an undistorted room, and are in accord with the verbal reports of how the room is seen. Gradually, however, as he continues to act with the wand and to experience the consequences of his actions, he becomes increasingly successful in touching various parts of the room. More important, Os reported that concurrent with this experience, there was an alteration of the appearance of part or all of the room in the direction of its true shape. These initial findings were substantiated by several hundred observations in undergraduate laboratory classes and elsewhere.

Hoffman (1953) was the first to deal with and measure the phenomenon in controlled experiments. His findings verified the earlier observational results, and showed further that the perceptual alteration was gradual and tended to increase with added practice, at least within the limits of the relatively small amounts of practice his Os had. In this experiment, distorted rooms were used as a means of obtaining evidence concerning two theoretical formulations in the area of learning in visual space perception.

STATEMENT OF THE PROBLEM

It was briefly suggested in an earlier paper (Ittelson & Kilpatrick, 1952) that the perceptual modification that occurs in the distorted rooms involves at least two learning processes, overlapping and affecting one another, but logically and perhaps experimentally distinguishable nevertheless.

Reorganizational learning.—The first process is one in which an unconscious reweighting of visual cues occurs. Unavoidably present in every such room are cues that we are able to perceive in ways not in harmony with the dominant percept; thus they have the potential of functioning as "give-away" cues. These cues, which "give away" to some degree the distortions present in the room but are not at first utilized, are given greater and greater weight as the incompatibilities between the original percept and the consequences of the practice continue to be registered, with the result that changes in the apparent shape of the room occur. The cues referred to are those which are present because of minor, and almost impossible to correct, defects in construction, lighting, placement of O's eye, etc.; also, of course, they may be deliberately introduced. Probably "reorganizational learning"

is not the ideal name for this process, but it does suggest that what is learned is a new way of organizing into a whole the complex of previously established cue-percept relationships. It is the usual explanation offered for perceptual modification such as that in the distorted room, and probably few people would argue that such a process does not occur.

Formative learning.—The second process, which we shall call "formative learning," is, however, far more crucial than the first in terms of perceptual theory. It is believed to consist of an actual learned alteration in the way in which a given stimulus pattern is perceived, a new perception which is not dependent on the utilization of give-away cues. It is a learning process in which the perception of the basic configuration related to that particular distorted room, the reference room, or equivalent distorted rooms of any shape, is modified. Reorganizational learning shakes up and rearranges the marbles in the bag; formative learning puts new marbles in the bag, and, if we are correct in our view, explains how most, if not all, of the marbles got in the bag in the first place.

From this two-process theory certain deductions concerning perceptual learning in distorted rooms may be made and tested as a means of checking the adequacy of the theory. If one had two or more equivalent rooms of different shapes and O were given sufficient training at one of them (Room 1) to perceive to some degree its true shape, and were then transferred to an equivalent room of an entirely different shape (Room 2), one would expect the following:

a. If the only learning that took place was reorganizational, that is, dependent on give-away cues, there would be no transfer of the newly learned percept from Room 1 to Room 2, because no give-away cues to the Room 1 shape could be available in Room 2. Thus, Room 2 would be seen as normal after the Room 1 learning.

b. If, on the other hand, as the theory states, formative learning is also involved, there should be some transfer of the newly learned percept. That is, one would expect

Room 2 to be seen as "normal" no longer, but to be seen at least to some degree as being shaped like Room 1.

The major purpose of this experiment was to show, if possible, that formative learning does occur in visual space perception.

A second problem in theory was included in the experiment since a rough check on its adequacy could be included without much trouble. This second problem is concerned with the role of action. The author (1952a, 1952b) and others (Ames, 1951; Cantril, 1950; Ittelson, 1951) with a similar point of view have stated that actions and their consequences are instrumental in the "construction" of what we see. What exactly is meant by action has not been well specified, but the implication has always been, probably intentionally, that it means gross, overt bodily activity, the doing of something. This implies that one's perception of a distorted room would remain unmodified, or very nearly so, if he merely observed the room's interior while someone else carried out the prescribed action, such as feeling around the interior of the room with a wand. Of course, O would not be completely inactive under these conditions. There would be eye movement and minor bodily adjustments, but generally speaking his activity would be minimized to an extent that, on the basis of theory as stated, the author would be forced to predict that little or no perceptual learning would occur under such circumstances.

METHOD

Apparatus

The basic apparatus consisted of three rooms designed to be monocularly equivalent, two of them distorted and one a 4×4-ft. cubical room (the "normal" or N room). One of the distorted rooms is larger on O's left than on his right (the L room), and the other is larger at the top than at the bottom (the T room).[2] In constructing the three

[2] Construction drawings are contained in Ittelson, 1951.

rooms used in this experiment great care was taken to eliminate nonequivalent visual cues such as grain in the wood, nail or screw heads, shiny reflecting surfaces, etc. The interiors were painted a flat gray with the exception of the window panels, which were painted a flat black. Plywood panels were placed over the fronts of the rooms. The rooms were arranged in a blacked-out experimental room so that their fronts formed a U, the distorted rooms facing one another, and the front of the N room forming the bottom of the U.

Lighting for each room was from a number of 7-w. bulbs placed inside the room along the top of the front panel, above O's head and out of his visual field. Extreme care was taken to equate the brightnesses of all parts of each room, and to equate the rooms with each other.

An armless straight-back swivel chair on casters, on which O sat straddling the seat and facing the back of the chair, was provided. A face piece at the top of the chair back provided a means of guiding O's face to the observation position and of preventing undue head movement. In the front panel of each room an oval opening was cut that was just large enough to admit O's nose and allow him to observe the interior of the room with the right eye when his nose was as far down and to the left as it would go. This use of a nose rest permitted more accurate placement of the eye than would a chin rest. Since these observation holes were at the same height in each of the rooms, a single adjustment of the face piece sufficed for all. Thus O could be moved from room to room while seated on the chair, and in each case simply putting his face back in the face piece insured the proper observational position.

The L room, which was to be the practice room, was provided with some additional equipment. A number of sponge rubber balls, covered with scotch tape so as not to mark the interior of the room when thrown against the walls, were provided. A small spotlight on a swivel was pointed into the room through a hole slightly to the left and above the observation hole. It was placed as near to the observation point as possible so that the alteration in the visual angle subtended by the spot as it was aimed at various parts of the room would be very little from O's point of view. This spot of light, about 3 in. in diameter when the spotlight was aimed at a point directly opposite the hole into which it was inserted, served as a target at which to throw the balls. A light bamboo wand 4 ft. long and covered with several thicknesses of flannel at one end was also provided. In addition, most of the bottom third of the front panel was cut out to permit both O and E to have free access to the interior of the room with their hands.

A tape recorder was also used.

Observers

The Os were 12 young adults, 10 males and 2 females, all with normal vision without glasses.

Procedure

Equivalence testing.—In order to be sure that any distortions in appearance of the rooms following the learning sessions could be attributed to learning, it was necessary first to establish for each O that the L, N, and T rooms were, in fact, equivalent and all seen as "normal" under the prescribed conditions. This was done through equivalence testing conducted immediately prior to the learning sessions for each O.

The O first was shown line drawings of the L, T, and N rooms, and their shapes were fully described. He was told that he would be seated in a chair and moved from room to room, that he would be given two looks at each of them, and that his task in each case was simply to identify the room as L, N, or T. Then a mask was placed over his left eye, he was led with his eyes closed into the blacked-out experimental room, seated in the chair, and given two 10-sec. looks at each of the three rooms, the order of these six looks being randomly determined. Following the viewing and attempted identification, he was asked to describe how the rooms looked and, if he had felt he could tell them apart, the ways in which they looked different.

The results show that the rooms are seen as normal and are monocularly equivalent under the prescribed viewing conditions; thus, any different results following a learning session may be treated as change in perception, provided one trusts O's reports in both instances. Of the 72 room identifications, 51 were incorrect and 21 were correct. This is just slightly worse than chance. Of the 21 correct identifications, 15 were of the N room; this is not surprising in view of the fact that all 12 of the Os stated after viewing that the rooms all looked alike, that is, quite normal. In fact, almost half of the Os either "gave up" or else disbelieved E, three responded "normal" all six times and two others did so five times in spite of having been told in advance that they would view each of the three rooms twice. The L room was correctly identified four times, twice by the same O. He stated, however, that he was just guessing and that it looked normal. The T room was correctly identified only twice, and then by different Os.

The learning sessions.—All learning sessions were conducted at the L room, and consisted of a number of throws of the ball at the spot of light at various locations on the back wall, and of tracing the outline of the back wall four times with the wand. Half of the Os, the action group (Group A), tossed the ball and manipulated the wand themselves. The other half, the no-action group (Group NA), merely observed the interior of the L room while E or his assistant threw the ball or handled the stick. The O was asked to call out "hit" when he saw the ball hit the spot. This was not done for data purposes, but simply as a device to maintain O's interest and motivation.

There were four learning sessions separated by rest periods of about 2 min. Immediately after each learning session, O was asked to observe and describe the interior of one of the three rooms: the L room after Session 1, the L room again after Session 2, the N room or the T room after Session 3, and the remaining room after Session 4. Half of the Os saw the T room after the third session and the N room after the fourth; for the other half the order was the reverse. All assignment to groups and orders was random.

Room descriptions were elicited in a standard way with the instruction, "Please describe the shape of the room as you see it; that is, not how you might guess or know it to be, but how you actually see it." It was desired that every O describe at least the back wall, the windows in the back wall, the floor, and the ceiling, so omissions were filled in with questions in the form, "How does (the back wall) look to you?" All instructions, questions, and answers were tape-recorded and transcribed verbatim for analysis.

When the Os were moved from the L room to one of the others, they knew they were being shifted to either the N or the T room, but not which one.

The four learning sessions differed only in the ball throwing; in Session 1 there were five throws at each of five positions of the spot, in Session 2 there were five throws at nine positions, in Session 3 there were three throws at nine positions, and Session 4 was the same as Session 3.

Postexperimental interview.—Following the final observation, O was asked to discuss the nature of his experiences, particularly any alterations in what he saw and any discrepancies that he felt existed between what he saw and what he otherwise judged to be so. This material also was tape-recorded and transcribed.

RESULTS

The main results of the experiment are summarized in Table 9-1. Of the six Os in Group A, five reported modification in the appearance of the L room after the first learning session. All six reported such modification for the L room after the second session. There were marked individual differences in both amount and type of change reported, but in all cases the change was in the direction of the true shape of the room. All six reported seeing to a marked degree the slope of the floor, and five of the six reported additional changes, such as the slope of the ceiling, the shape and slant of the back wall, the difference in size and shape of the two windows in the back wall, etc.

These alterations in appearance carried over to both the N and the T rooms,[3] according to Os' reports, for five of the six Os in the case of the N room, and for all six in the case of the T room. Both the N and the T rooms were seen, at least to some degree, as having the shape of the L room, with only a single exception. In 9 of the 11 instances in which there was such carryover, the Os said that they saw slightly less of the L-room appearance at the N or T rooms than they had at the L room, but that it was clear and unequivocal nevertheless. In the other two instances no reduction in perceived L-room shape was reported. In Os' reports the N and T rooms were described as looking as though the floor sloped down to the left, and in most cases one or more other L-room appearances; such as ceiling sloping up to the left, back wall receding to the left, etc., were described.

A few illustrative excerpts from the protocols follow.

1. Observer C. S. viewing N room after Learning Session 3:

   E. How does the floor look?
   O. It looks as if it slants down to the left.
   E. How does the ceiling look?
   O. It slants up to the left some.
   E. How about the windows?
   O. The left window of the center panel looks larger and like it is slanting down to the left on the bottom.
   E. Anything else you can tell me about the appearance of the room?
   O. Well, I think it does give the appearance of being like the room that slants to the left, quite a lot.

2. G. S. viewing the T room after Learning Session 3:

   E. How does the floor look?
   O. The floor seems to tilt down toward the left.

[3] Perhaps it should be pointed out that this phenomenon is not at all analogous to classical figural aftereffect. The "transferred" configuration is not different, "compensatory," or "opposite," but is, to the degree that transfer occurs, like the learned configuration. In addition, visual fixation is not involved. Satiation or statistical theories of figural aftereffect should not be invoked as explanations for this phenomenon, as they clearly do not apply.

Table 9-1 Reported Changes in Appearance of the Three Rooms after Learning Sessions for the Action Group ($N = 6$) and the No-Action Group ($N = 6$)

Condition of Observation	Reported Room Appearance			
	A Group		NA Group	
	No Change	Changed in One or More Aspects	No Change	Changed in One or More Aspects
L room				
After 1st learning session	1	5	2	4
After 2nd learning session		6		6
Transfer				
At the N room	1	5	2	4
At the T room		6	1	5

E. How about the ceiling?

O. The ceiling tilts up and to the left.

E. How about the back wall?

O. It seems to slant quite a little bit. Back to the left.

3. P. B. viewing the N room after Learning Session 4:

O. Well, the floor slopes down towards— down towards the bottom left-hand, you know, the far left-hand corner. Again the corner up at the right looks closer to me than the corner at the left and it looks shorter than the corner at the left. The ceiling looks like it's going up towards the left-hand side.

The results for Group NA were substantially the same as for Group A. Four of the six *O*s reported alterations in the appearance of the L room after Learning Session 1, and all six did so after Learning Session 2. Four of the six reported carry-over to the N room, and five of the six to the T room. However, these results plus a comparative examination of the protocols strongly suggest that the perceptual alteration was slightly less in speed and amount and that there was somewhat less carry-over to the N and T rooms than for Group A.

The replies to questions in the postexperimental interviews provide convincing evidence that *O*s experienced marked changes in visual space perception and reported what they saw. Here is an example that is perhaps more concise than most, but otherwise typical.

O. It progressively got more distorted as the experiment went on. I could tell some difference in the back wall and in the ceiling and floor. The ceiling seemed to be the slowest to come along, though. It seemed to be normal for quite a time there and then I began to see a difference —it began to slope, I think, upwards and to the left.

E. This is an actual change in how it looked?

O. That's right.

The evidence obtained in this experiment would seem to point to several rather clearcut conclusions.

1. Marked alterations in visual space perception did occur as a consequence of the learning sessions. Every *O* did learn to see the L room in more nearly its true shape even though the stimulus configuration presented to his eye remained unchanged, thus confirming earlier findings.

2. This perceptual learning tends to increase with increasing amounts of practice in this situation.

3. The almost unanimous carry-over of the newly learned percept to both the N and the T rooms provides strong confirmation for the basic hypothesis that formative learning does occur. The *O*s did learn to see differently the basic visual configuration related to all three rooms, independently of giveaway cues. We may infer that any properly constructed room based on the same reference room would have been seen the same way, regardless of its actual shape.

4. The evidence that the carry-over from the L room to the N and T rooms was not complete suggests that give-away cues func-

tioning below the level of awareness also played a role in the learning. It seems likely that reorganizational learning did occur in the L room, but the cues on which it depended were not available in the N and T rooms. Only give-away cues to the N or the T shapes would be available in those rooms. Also, the protocols provide some evidence that the learning sessions resulted in a generalized increase in the saliency of give-away cues, not only for the L room, but for the other rooms as well. These factors would work against the carry-over of the newly learned percept.

5. The notion that gross overt action is necessary for such perceptual modification to occur is clearly wrong. The amount of action indulged in by Group NA was at a minimum, yet there was very little less perceptual learning than in Group A. A more adequate formulation of the role of action in perceptual learning is called for.

DISCUSSION

It would be easy to speculate at length concerning the significance of these findings and conclusions for perceptual learning in general. However, it is felt that much more evidence is needed before any such ambitious project is undertaken. This discussion will be confined to a very few notions concerning reorganizational and formative learning, the role of action in perceptual learning, and the use of the distorted rooms in the controlled study of factors involved in learning in visual space perception.

It appears probable that both the reorganizational and formative processes are at work in almost any instance of perceptual learning; however, the formative process may be thought of as more fundamental in the sense that it is the one on which the expansion and development of our perception of our world depends. If we consider perceiving as acting, as responding, then we might say that reorganizational learning is simply the reshuffling of old previously learned responses; formative learning is the acquiring of new ones. Of course, the matter is not this simple, as there is no doubt an intimate and complex relationship between the two processes so that they affect one another differently under different circum-

stances. Perhaps if give-away cues are sufficiently available to permit an adequate and stable perceptual reorganization to be arrived at easily and quickly, formative learning related to the basic configuration may not occur because it becomes unnecessary. On the other hand, when the reorganizational process occurs to some degree but not enough to provide such adequate reorganization, it probably facilitates formative learning through helping to stabilize the learned modification as it occurs.

Implicit in the above is the suggestion that formative perceptual learning is gradual and not subject to sudden shifts; for it, continuity is the rule. Reorganizational learning, on the other hand, probably proceeds in sudden shifts. A hitherto unutilized cue becomes effective, with a consequent sudden alteration in perception. Reorganizational learning *need not* give the impression of discontinuity since the shifts may be so small as to conceal their nature; but it *may* do so, as in the case of hidden pictures, the rotating trapezoid (Ames, 1951), etc.

Let us turn now to the problem of the role of action in perceptual learning. A more adequate formulation might be that some degree of perceptual modification occurs whenever certain aspects of the total process of perceiving are out of harmony with others in terms of carrying out some purpose, and this means both across modalities and within a single modality. Action merely serves the function of bringing the organism into contact with the cues that give rise to the disharmony; if the cues are made available in other ways, e.g., through the actions of others, the conditions necessary for perceptual learning will have been fulfilled. One might also add that probably the modification generally tends toward an organization which has more functional value in the sense of providing a better bet based on experience about "what happens next."

It should be pointed out that this reformulation does not appreciably diminish the importance of the role of action in perceptual learning. Apparently perceptual learning requires that a relevant set of sequential events be set in motion in such a way that successive impingements on the learning organism will be attended to and related over time to one another, to expectations, and to purposes. Only in rare circumstances, such as in an experiment, will these conditions even be approximated unless the learner is the operator. An operator other than the learner can provide the necessary sequence of conditions if he knows enough about what the learner perceives, what he expects, what he is attending to and will attend to, etc., but these factors will be known imperfectly in the first place and are continually changing in a unique way for the learner as the sequence of events proceeds. Thus, only when the learner is the operator can the conditions for perceptual alteration be maximized.

Discussion of the use of the distorted rooms as a means of investigating learning in visual space perception necessitates some preliminary remarks about previous work. Research involving postoperative cataract cases, the use of prism, aniseikonic, and inversion lenses, and the employment of unstructured or ambiguous pictures or objects would seem to have contributed most heavily to our knowledge in this area. However, certain limitations in these investigations must be noted. The cataract and lens researches are, in general, characterized by lack of experimental control of the factors involved in the perceptual learning; the other experiments have generally involved rather sudden shifts from one fairly stable perceptual organization to another and made analysis of the processes involved in the change rather difficult. Perhaps a valuable supplement to these would be the use of the distorted rooms. They provide a clear-cut instance of learning in visual space perception gradual enough to be described or measured at intervals as it proceeds, and one in which such factors as amount of practice, kind of practice, motivation, advance knowledge, number and kind of conflicting visual cues available, etc. might be varied systematically and checked for effects. Also, they permit reorganizational and formative perceptual learning to be separated for experimental treatment.

SUMMARY

The experiment reported in this paper was designed primarily to distinguish between two hypothesized perceptual learning processes, reorganizational and formative. A secondary purpose was to test the notion that gross overt physical action on the part of the learner is a necessary condition for perceptual learning.

Three small rooms, one cubical and two distorted, were used as basic apparatus. After experimentally demonstrating that the rooms are monocularly equivalent and seen as "normal" or cubical prior to learning, learning sessions were conducted at one of the distorted rooms. Six Os (the action group) tossed balls at a target and felt around the room with a wand while observing its interior monocularly; and six Os (the no-action group) observed the room's interior while E's assistant tossed the balls and manipulated the wand.

For all 12 Os, the learning sessions resulted in reported alteration in appearance of the distorted room in which the practice occurred; 11 of the 12 Os reported that this alteration in appearance carried over to one or both of the other two rooms, but generally with a decrement. This transfer of the newly learned percept was as predicted and was interpreted as evidence that formative as well as reorganizational perceptual learning occurs. Some probable characteristics and relations of these two learning processes were discussed.

The positive results from the no-action group were clearly contrary to hypothesis, and a modified formulation concerning the role of action in perceptual learning was outlined.

Finally, it was pointed out that rooms of the kind used in this experiment provide a means for investigating many aspects of learning in visual space perception.

REFERENCES:

Ames, A., Jr. Visual perception and the rotating trapezoidal window. *Psychological Monographs*, 1951, **65**, No. 7 (Whole No. 324).
Cantril, H. The *"why"* of man's experience. New York: Macmillan, 1950.
Gibson, J. *The perception of the visual world.* Boston: Houghton Mifflin, 1950.
Hoffman, E. L. The role of action in defining and changing visual perception. Unpublished doctor's dissertation, Princeton University, 1953.
Ittelson, W. H. The constancies in perceptual theory. *Psychological Review*, 1951, **58**, 285–294.
Ittelson, W. H. *The Ames demonstrations in*

perception. Princeton: Princeton University Press, 1952.

Ittelson, W. H., & Kilpatrick, F. P. Equivalent configurations and the monocular and binocular distorted rooms. In F. P. Kilpatrick (Ed.), *Human behavior from the transactional point of view.* Hanover, N.H.: Institute for Associated Research, 1952.

Kilpatrick, F. P. Assumptions and perception: three experiments. In F. P. Kilpatrick (Ed.), *Human behavior from the transactional point of view.* Hanover, N.H.: Institute for Associated Research, 1952a.

Kilpatrick, F. P. Statement of theory. In F. P. Kilpatrick (Ed.), *Human behavior from the transactional point of view.* Hanover, N.H.: Institute for Associated Research, 1952b.

Kilpatrick, F. P., & Ittelson, W. H. The size-distance invariance hypothesis. *Psychological Review,* 1953, **60,** 223–231.

Koffka, K. *Principles of Gestalt psychology.* New York: Harcourt, Brace, 1935.

Köhler, W. *Gestalt psychology.* New York: Liveright, 1947.

Pratt, C. C. The role of past experience in visual perception. *Journal of Psychology,* 1950, **30,** 85–107.

10 The Constancies in Perceptual Theory[1]

William H. Ittelson

I

We live and act in a world which we perceive as relatively stable in spite of the ever-changing impingements on our sense organs. This fact becomes a problem to those interested in evolving simplified conceptual explanatory systems. It has interested philosophers of all times and has troubled psychologists for the last several decades. Whatever may be the ultimate evaluation of psychological theorists, on one statement all can agree. It is the fact of perceptual constancy which makes effective behavior possible, from the simplest action to the most complex, from walking across the street to striving for a sane social order. Without some degree of constancy mere survival would be impossible.

From *The Psychological Review,* 1951, **58,** 285–294. Reprinted by permission of the author and publisher.

[1] The author wishes to express his indebtedness to Adelbert Ames, Jr., and to Hadley Cantril for the theoretical orientation of this paper. For a more general, and more adequate, statement see especially Cantril (1950).

As most commonly used in psychological literature, constancy refers to the similarity between specific apparent properties (such as the size, shape, or color) of two or more objects producing different proximal stimuli, with emphasis on the correspondence between these perceived properties and the actual properties of the objects. The objects need not be viewed simultaneously and indeed may be the same object viewed at different times. This fact leads directly to the continuous viewing of the same object, which is related to effects that can be termed continuity as opposed to constancy (Koffka, 1935, p. 304). In actual experience, however, continuity is the rule, and constancy, as traditionally investigated, merely represents a sample picked out for study from the more general experienced continuity. In this paper, therefore, any behavior which tends to preserve the continuity and stability of the perceived world in the face of ever-changing relationships between observer and environment will be labeled "constancy."

The perceptual constancies are studied experimentally by comparing the relevant characteristics of the percept with those of the object (Boring, 1942; Woodworth, 1938). If perception remains constant as stimulation changes, then clearly there can be no constant relationship between stimulation and perception. The substitution of perceptual constancy for the rejected constancy hypothesis introduces a confusion of terms which, although deplored by some, may eventually be judged quite apposite. For Gestalt theory remains primarily concerned with stimulation-to-percept relationships and, in a sense, merely assumes a constant geometrical distortion in place of the constancy hypothesis, of which the law of *Prägnanz* can be seen as an elaboration. While such geometrical constancy is becoming seriously challenged by recent work on the role of subjective determinants in perception (*cf.,* for example, Bruner, 1950), more functionally oriented psychologists, taking a cue from behaviorism, have shifted the focus of interest from perceptual constancy to object or thing constancy with all that this implies in terms of conceptual and experimental reorientation.

The study of constancy by comparisons

of object with percept has not escaped methodological criticism. The frequently used constancy ratio (Brunswik, 1949; Thouless, 1931) offers the paradox of ratios greater than one, *i.e.*, over-constancy, which clearly must be considered as much an "error" as under-constancy. This objection has been met by the substitution of correlations (Brunswik, 1940), which give a more meaningful measure of the extent to which the organism is in functional rapport with its environment. The most serious limitation of such measures of correspondence is that they channel interest away from the means by which the organism achieves constancy toward a description of the final achievement. Far from being viewed as a limitation, however, this one-sided emphasis is hailed as crucial by those who would adhere strictly to the narrow definition of constancy in terms of percept and object comparisons, and who would, for example, rule out the Gestalt studies in constancy on the ground that they are "not properly concerned with 'distal' object relationships" (Bruner, 1950, p. 58). It will be one of the primary arguments of this paper that the creation of such an artificial dichotomy makes the attainment of an adequate solution impossible. Constancy is functional only in so far as veridical distal relationships are established. (We shall return to this statement later in an effort to pluck the verbal plumage and reveal the behavioral meat beneath.) It is dangerous, however, to forget that such relationships are achievements of an acting organism, and that the means by which they are achieved are as much a part of the problem as are the relationships themselves. Constancy mechanisms and constancy achievements are inseparable. Any complete theory of perceptual constancy must encompass all its aspects.

II

A simple laboratory demonstration may serve to illustrate this point.[2] Let us photograph an ordinary playing card and repro-

duce it in three different sizes, one double-size, one normal-size, and one half-size. If we now view the double-sized card with one eye from a distance of, for example, eight feet, the card alone being illuminated in an otherwise dark room, it will appear to be only four feet from us and of normal size. Similarly, the half-sized card placed at four feet will appear to be of normal size and at a distance of eight feet, while the normal-sized card placed at six feet will indeed appear to be a normal card at a distance of six feet. We are thus confronted with three cards physically spaced from the observer in the order *small-normal-large* but seen in the reverse order, *large-normal-small*, and of physical sizes *small-normal-large* but seen in size as *normal-normal-normal*. Clearly by any definition of constancy calling for correspondence between perceived and objective properties this performance is the very antithesis of constancy behavior.

If we now make two slight changes in the above described configuration, the performance becomes quite different. In place of the half-sized card let us substitute a wrist watch in a rectangular case of the same size and shape as the small card, and in place of the double-sized card substitute the cover of a pocket magazine which is of the same size and shape as the large card. This new arrangement, when viewed with one eye as described above, presents us with three objects in both physical and apparent order *watch-card-magazine*, and both physical and apparent sizes *watch-card-magazine*. This performance therefore is typical of perceptual constancy. These relationships are summarized in Table 10-1.[3]

This demonstration raises many questions of relevance to perceptual theory (Ames, 1946; Hastorf, 1950; Ittelson, 1951; Ittelson & Ames, 1950; Lawrence, 1949; Smith, 1952). We are here concerned only with its relationship to the problem of problemization in the study of perceptual constancy. With reference to a narrow definition of

[2] What follows is a description of one of a series of perceptual demonstrations designed by Adelbert Ames, Jr. The author is grateful to Mr. Ames for permission to report this demonstration.

[3] The description in the text, and as summarized in the table, is of the ideal performance. Careful records have been taken for a group of observers. The typical performance closely approximates that indicated in the table, and even extreme deviations from this typical performance are closer to it than to any of the other possibilities.

Table 10-1 Apparent Sizes and Distances in Two Monocularly Viewed Configurations (Size and Distance of Normal Playing Card Taken as Unity)[a]

Test object	Visual angle	Actual size	Apparent size	Actual distance	Apparent distance
		Condition I			
Half card	¾	½	1	⅔	1⅓
Normal card	1	1	1	1	1
Double card	1½	2	1	1⅓	⅔
		Condition II			
Wrist watch	¾	½	½	⅔	⅔
Normal card	1	1	1	1	1
Magazine	1½	2	2	1⅓	1⅓

[a] Condition I shows deviation from, and Condition II agreement with, conventionally defined "constancy."

constancy, in terms of percept-to-object correlations, we must view as different the performances under the two conditions. In the one case we have constancy, in the other we do not. Similarly, as isolated responses to isolated stimuli from which behavior in the isolated situations may be predicted, they are different. Behavior in the one case will be successful and in the other unsuccessful. On the other hand, the two cases are certainly identical in terms of the perceptual processes involved. One cannot maintain that a constancy mechanism was operating in the one instance and not in the other. In order to avoid labeling the same performance both constancy and non-constancy, we must seek a conceptualization which will encompass both aspects, viz., the intra-organism constancy mechanism as well as the functional relationship between organism and environment. Such a conceptualization can be reached only by recognizing that object-to-percept and response-to-goal are not one-way roads. Neither are they completely isolated from each other, but rather represent two abstracted aspects of the same continuing process in which they are mutually affecting each other.

III

There have, of course, been many attempts to link these two aspects conceptually. Every investigator, no matter which isolated aspect may initially dominate his thinking, has eventually found it impossible completely to ignore the other. Two major lines of thought may be traced, although it is fully recognized that such an oversimplified presentation does violence to many views which cannot be classified so neatly. One line of approach is primarily concerned with perceptual mechanisms. It may call upon the generalized configurational or field effects introduced by the Gestalt psychologists or upon specific mutually cancelling processes which leave the resultant perception unchanged. This latter type of explanation has been of recurring popularity since its early statement by Wheatstone, who noted that in his mirror stereoscope "the perceived magnitude of an object . . . diminishes as the inclination of the [optic] axes becomes greater, while the distance remains the same; and it increases, when the inclination of the axes remains the same, while the distance diminishes. When both these conditions vary inversely, as they do in ordinary vision when the distance of an object changes, the perceived magnitude remains the same" (Wheatstone, 1852, p. 507). This quotation may be compared with more recent statements of the same type of explanation by, for example, Wallach (1948), Schlosberg (1950), and Gibson (1950), as well as with the general Gestalt treatment of invariance (Koffka, 1935). This approach has sought fixed laws of perception, usually natively or innately determined, and has considered the high degree of functional validity shown by perceptions to be fortuitous and fortunate. For example, to say that "luckily we are so made, and the world is so made, *that under the normal conditions of life* there exists in general a definite correspondence between our perceptions and the objects or the physical events which give rise to them" (Michotte, 1946, p. 217) is but to state in its most extreme form a view which is representative of this approach (Koffka, 1935, p. 305). The emphasis on the uniqueness of normal conditions holds throughout. Truth is to be had for the looking; seeing *is* believing, provided the conditions are auspicious.

The other major tradition specifically concerned with the constancies has followed a diametrically opposed orientation. It has consistently been impressed with the very obvious need for, and attainment of, functionally useful responses. It has concentrated on the observation of such responses and the specification of the conditions which arouse them (Boring, 1946; Brunswik, 1944). When questioned as to the intra-organism processes which mediate effective response to extra-organism factors, it either is not interested or is content to accept functional effectiveness as itself a sufficient explanatory principle. An unspecified evolutionary theory is implied here, and the fortuitous and fortunate implications are not missing.[4]

Attempts to account for the perceptual constancies along one or the other of these two general approaches have not been completely successful, nor have they met with universal acceptance, simply because neither approach deals with the whole problem. And attempts to pick and choose various parts from each in an effort to fit together the parts thus selected into some sort of jigsaw pattern, as advocates of eclecticism would have us do, can be adequate only if the initial artificial separation of the problem has not distorted it beyond recognition.

> "Indeed!" said Mr. Pickwick; "I was not aware that that valuable work contained any information respecting Chinese metaphysics."
> "He read, sir," rejoined Pott, laying his hand on Mr. Pickwick's knee, and looking round with a smile of intellectual superiority, "he read for metaphysics under the letter M, and for China under the letter C, and combined his information, sir!" (Dickens, p. 789.)

If instead, all phases of constancy behavior are treated as merely different aspects abstracted out of a unitary whole, no aspect of which would exist except for the whole, an adequate conceptualization seems possible (Cantril, Ames, Hastorf, & Ittelson, 1949). In this view functional effectiveness is mediated by the perceptual constancies, and constancy is in turn mediated by functional behavior. The stimulus-to-response phase of behavior has long been studied in psychology. This must now be supplemented by the parallel study of the effect of the response on the receptor system, *i.e.*, the response-to-stimulus sequence. Such a study may well lead to a reconsideration of the meaning of stimulus in psychological theory.

[4] This common point of view, which sees one or another aspect of constancy phenomena as a more or less chance occurrence, is carried to a *reductio ad absurdum* in much recent work in which the attempt seems to be made to prove that perceptual constancy is achieved *in spite of* the organism's best efforts to avoid it! By superimposing motivational or personality factors on unspecified perceptual processes, which are then removed from consideration after being mollified with some such high-sounding title as "autochthonous," this approach has concentrated on displaying distortions of perception. The resulting contradiction in terms, which finds motivational factors called upon to account for essentially nonfunctional behavior, is still further emphasized when perceptual distortion is used as an explanatory principle to account for the functional nature of perceiving.

IV

Action and perception are inseparably related. An evaluation of the many theoretical attempts to link perception and action is a major study in itself and cannot be pursued in detail at this time. Suffice it to say that we are here referring neither to the mental acts of the Act Psychologists, nor to the kinesthetic cues which interested many of the early empiricists and functionalists, nor to the incipient motor responses of the motor theorists, nor to the overt, observable motor responses so dear to the behaviorists, although all these may properly be seen as among the historical antecedents of the position presented in this paper.

Rather, "action" as used here is more adequately defined in the homely words of the dictionary, "the doing of something." The perceiving of something and the doing of something are treated as two abstracted aspects of a continuing process of living, no one aspect of which can be understood without reference to the others. Dewey and Bentley have noted that the "differences between perception and manipulation seemed striking to the earlier stages of the development of psychology, but today's specialization of inquiry should not lose sight of their common behavioral status" (1949, p. 299). And it is only in terms of this common behavioral status that such currently popular phrases as the "distal focusing of perception" take on any meaning. Reference to veridical distal relationships means nothing unless it means that perception and manipulation have been mutually consistent.

A clear recognition of the unity of perception and action enables us to achieve a conceptualization which does not rest on a meaningless a priorism, and at the same time avoids what Whitehead has termed the "Berkeleyan Dilemma," from which one readily descends to "a complete scepticism which was not in Berkeley's own thought."

There are two types of answer to this sceptical descent. One is Dr. Johnson's. He stamped his foot on a paving-stone, and went on his way satisfied with its reality. . . . The other type of answer was first given by Kant. We must distinguish between the general way he set about constructing his answer to Hume, and the details of his system, which in many respects are highly disputable. The essential point of his method is the assumption that "significance" is an essential element in concrete experience. The Berkeleyan dilemma starts with tacitly ignoring this aspect of experience, and thus with putting forward, as expressing experience, conceptions of it which have no relevance to fact. In the light of Kant's procedure, Johnson's answer falls into its place; it is the assertion that Berkeley has not correctly expounded what experience in fact is.

Berkeley himself insists that experience is significant, indeed three-quarters of his writings are devoted to enforcing this position. But Kant's position is the converse of Berkeley's, namely that significance is experience. . . . For Berkeley the significance is detachable from the experience[5] (Whitehead, 1925, pp. 11–12).

"What is significance?" Whitehead then asks. "Significance is the relatedness of things. To say that significance is experience, is to affirm that perceptual knowledge is nothing else than an apprehension of the relatedness of things." This relatedness of things, in the view presented in this paper, is revealed through action, or more precisely, action provides the concrete, operational definition of the relatedness of things, with reference to a particular space and time framework. Perception, then, is the product of the continual recording of the relatedness of things as defined by action. Perception is the apprehension of significance.

The psychological consequence of action, then, is a change of significance—change, because the relatedness of things is ever changing. The perceiver himself operates within the process and his very perceiving and acting constitute part of the relatedness of things. However, change is relative, and some significances are relatively stable and enduring, that is, have a high probability of recurring (Brunswik, 1943; Helmholtz, 1925; Tolman & Brunswik, 1935). Perceiving is, therefore, the apprehending of probable significances. It is predictive in function, or, as Ames has expressed it, perceptions are prognostic directives for action (1946).

Out of the relatively stable significances, as determined by the relative effectiveness of actions, a pattern of unconscious assumptions is built. These assumptions may be conceptualized variously as relatively stable ways of reacting, as patterns of probable

---

[5] And, we might add, for most psychologists who have sought an empiricist explanation. The most extreme example of detaching significance from experience is undoubtedly to be found in Titchener's context theory of meaning which set a fashion from which much of psychology has yet to emancipate itself.

significances, as value systems, or as concepts as to the nature of the objective world, which have been constructed through active participation in living, and may be considered as weighted averages of past experiences.[6] The sum total of assumptions which the individual makes as to the nature and significances of the external world constitutes his assumptive world (Cantril, 1950; Cantril, Ames, *et al.*, 1949; Ittelson, 1951; Kilpatrick, 1950). The assumptive world of any particular individual at any particular time determines his perceptions, that is, provides him with predictions of probable significances. His assumptive world is, therefore, in a very real sense, the only world which he knows. And since the assumptive world of each individual is to a certain extent unique, to that extent each one of us resembles Thurber's spy, who reported that what he had seen was "something very much like nothing anyone had seen before."

V

Such an approach makes possible a more adequate understanding of the perceptual constancies. Consider, for example, the constancies which are encountered in the study of depth perception. The most commonly cited case undoubtedly is size constancy, which, it is universally agreed, is dependent on the proper estimation of distance (Boring, 1942; Carr, 1935; Gibson, 1950; Koffka, 1935; Vernon, 1937). Apparent size equals objective size only when apparent distance equals objective distance; or, in other words, size constancy and distance constancy are inseparably related, and both are essential for functional effectiveness.[7]

[6] Since these weights are a function of the situation, no fixed hierarchy can be established apart from specific conditions.

[7] It is interesting to speculate as to why distance constancy is not included among the constancies commonly studied. Certainly the relative independence from specific proximal stimulation shown by apparent distance is at least as striking as that shown by size, for example. Size constancy, however, of all the constancies, has provoked the most interest simply because it astounds the most people. And this astonishment can probably be traced to an unacknowledged but binding conceptual link to the Lockeian primary qualities.

But apparent size is only one of the constancies dependent on apparent distance. Changes in many other important aspects of the perceived properties of objects are related to deviations from distance constancy, *i.e.*, to cases in which apparent distance does not correspond to actual distance. At least apparent size, shape, orientation in space and possibly brightness (Ames, 1946; Gibson, 1950; Holway & Boring, 1941; Thouless, 1931; Vernon, 1937) can be shown to be dependent on apparent distance. Apparent distance, however, is in turn dependent on size, shape, orientation in space, and brightness (Ames, 1946; Bartley, 1950; Donders, 1864; Gibson, 1950; Ittelson, 1951; Ittelson & Ames, 1950) so that analogous statements can be made reversing the direction of the effect. If the apparent size, shape, orientation, and brightness of an object deviate from the objective size, shape, etc., then both the apparent absolute distance of the object and the apparent relative distances of various parts of the object will deviate from the corresponding objective distances (Ames, 1946; 1951; Hastorf, 1950; Ittelson, 1951; Kilpatrick, 1950). Apparent "thingness" and the apparent distance of the thing are complexly interdependent. There seems to be no reason for asserting the invariable primacy of one over the other.

There is, in fact, no aspect of depth perception which cannot be shown to be interdependent on all other aspects. There is no basis for asserting that some aspects are independent and some dependent, that some serve as cause and others as effect. Any apparent property can be altered in many ways: by varying impingements directly related to that aspect, by changing impingements related to other aspects which in turn are related to that aspect, or by keeping impingements constant and altering significances attributed to the impingements (Hastorf, 1950; Ittelson, 1951; Kilpatrick, 1950; Kilpatrick & Ittelson, 1951; Smith, 1952). The individual makes sense out of the intrinsically meaningless impingements by assessing their significance in terms of his assumptive world. He endeavors to create in the present a world which as closely as possible resembles his world of the past and which therefore gives him a feeling of surety that he can act effectively in the future. He does so not only because he wants to, but because he has no other alternative; this is the only world which he can know (*cf.* Ames, 1951; Cantril, 1950).

It should be further pointed out that the effects described above, which apply to the perception of static objects, become immensely more complicated when movement is introduced. For example, the factor of relative movement (parallax) becomes important. Everything said above with respect to the static constancies applies in this case. Relative apparent distance is very strongly dependent on parallax indications (Graham, Baker, *et al.*, 1948). However, if apparent relative distances deviate from objective relative distances, parallax indications become perceptually related to apparent movements which deviate markedly from the corresponding objective movements (Ames, 1946, 1951; Kilpatrick, 1950). The number of apparent properties (in terms of which constancies can be specified) also increases to include such aspects as the speed and direction of movement. In addition, the relative importance of the static constancies changes. For example, static apparent size and shape can readily be altered by varying either apparent distance or objective size and shape, but when movement is introduced there is a strong tendency to see the moving object as constant in shape and size (Hastorf, 1950; Ittelson, 1951; Kilpatrick, 1950; Kilpatrick & Ittelson, 1951; Smith, 1952). It may well be, therefore, as suggested earlier, that the static constancies are special cases derived from the more commonly experienced movement and continuity.

VI

A conceptualization of the perceptual constancies such as that outlined in the preceding sections can be extended into other areas of human behavior. We are able thereby to resolve the paradox which has found those psychologists most concerned with studying the functional effectiveness of man in his total environmental surroundings, *i.e.*, social, personality, and clinical psychologists, frequently neglecting the role of such supremely functional behavior as that represented by the constancies, although they are actively concerned with analogous problems variously conceptualized in terms of prejudice, stereotype, frame of reference, suppression, etc. The probable reason these psychologists have not found the conventional treatment of perceptual constancy to be of value in their disciplines lies in the definition of constancy in terms of correspondence between objective and apparent properties. Much of what might properly be labeled constancy-behavior in social and personality studies lies outside this definition, and indeed consists of maintaining a stable perceptual world which in one or more ways deviates markedly from the objective world. This contradiction disappears (and incidentally leaves room for a more adequate definition of the reality to which we are often told we must all adjust) when we define constancy-behavior as the attempt of the individual to create and maintain a world which deviates as little as possible from the world which he has experienced in the past, which is the only world he knows, and which offers him the best possible chance of acting effectively and continuing to experience the particular satisfactions which he seeks out of living.

This view, incidentally, enables us to account for the maladaptive behavior evidenced by individuals whose perceptions quite grossly disagree with the objective situation. Such conditions are readily established in the perceptual laboratory: for example, one may cite the distorted room of Ames (1946; Cantril, 1950), or the tilting room—tilting chair of Witkin (1949). Some writers profess to see an element of stupidity in behavior in such situations (Bruner & Krech, 1950, p. 59; Witkin, 1949, p. 40). However, in the conceptualization presented in this paper, such errors, far from being stupid, represent the best possible and hence wisest attempt to interpret the perceptual situation in terms of the individual's assumptive world, with its host of weightings and probabilities relating the results of past actions to similar situations. To go contrary to the dictates of this accumulated experience, even though in any particular instance it may be wrong, would indeed be stupid.

VII

It may be fitting, in a paper devoted to constancy, to close with a few remarks on change. The conceptualization presented here has stressed the functional importance of constancy as well as the psychological mechanism by which constancy is achieved. Behavior will be random and ineffective unless it takes off from some relatively stable and determined foundation. Once the situation changes, however, in such a way that this foundation ceases to be the best possible one on which to base action, preserving it (*i.e.*, constancy) ceases to be of functional value. As outlined above, the consequence of action is a change in the individual's assumptive world, either reinforcing or modifying it. The consequence of consistently ineffective action will therefore be an alteration of the assumptive world in the direction of a relatively stable, but changed, pattern of assumptions with resulting new constancies appropriate for effective action in the new situation. Paradoxical as it may seem, change is the midwife at the birth of constancy. As the world changes, so must we.

REFERENCES:

Ames, A., Jr. Some demonstrations concerned with the origin and nature of our sensations (what we experience). A laboratory manual (preliminary draft). Hanover, N.H.: Hanover Institute, 1946 (mimeographed).

Ames, A., Jr. Visual perception and the rotating trapezoidal window. *Psychological Monographs*, 1951, **65**, Whole No. 324.

Bartley, S. H. *Beginning experimental psychology*. New York: McGraw-Hill, 1950.

Boring, E. G. Size constancy and Emmert's law. *American Journal of Psychology*, 1940, **53**, 293–295.

Boring, E. G. *Sensation and perception in the history of experimental psychology*. New York: Appleton-Century, 1942.

Boring, E. G. The perception of objects. *American Journal of Physics*, 1946, **14**, 99–107.

Bruner, J. S., & Krech, D. (Eds.) *Perception and personality*. Durham, N.C.: Duke University Press, 1950.

Brunswik, E. Thing constancy as measured by correlation coefficients. *Psychological Review*, 1940, **47**, 69–78.

Brunswik, E. Organismic achievement and environmental probability. *Psychological Review*, 1943, **50**, 255–272.

Brunswik, E. Distal focussing of perception: Size constancy in a representative sample of situations. *Psychological Monographs*, 1944, **56**, Whole No. 254.

Brunswik, E. Systematic and representative design of psychological experiments. *Proceedings of the Berkeley Symposium: Mathematical Statistics and Probability*. Berkeley: University of California Press, 1949.

Cantril, H. *The "why" of man's experience*. New York: Macmillan, 1950.

Cantril, H., Ames, A., Jr., Hastorf, A. H., & Ittelson, W. H. Psychology and scientific research. *Science*, 1949, **110**, 461–464, 491–497, 512–522.

Carr, H. *An introduction to space perception*. New York: Longmans, 1935.

Dewey, J., & Bentley, A. F. *Knowing and the known*. Boston: Beacon, 1949.

Dickens, C. *The posthumous papers of the Pickwick Club*. Philadelphia: Macrae Smith.

Donders, F. C. *Accommodation and refraction of the eye*. (Trans. from author's manuscript by W. D. Moore.) London: New Sydenham Society, 1864.

Gibson, J. J. *The perception of the visual world*. Boston: Houghton Mifflin, 1950.

Graham, C. H., Baker, K. E., Hecht, M., & Lloyd, V. V. Factors influencing thresholds of monocular movement parallax. *Journal of Experimental Psychology*, 1948, **38**, 205–223.

Hastorf, A. H. The influence of suggestion on the relationship between stimulus size and perceived distance. *Journal of Psychology*, 1950, **29**, 195–217.

Helmholtz, H. *Physiological optics*. (Trans. by J. P. C. Southall, 1866.) Optical Society of America, 1925, Vol. III.

Holway, A. H., & Boring, E. G. Determinants of apparent visual size with distance variant. *American Journal of Psychology*, 1941, **54**, 21–37.

Ittelson, W. H. Size as a cue to distance. *American Journal of Psychology*, 1951, **64**, 54–67, 188–202.

Ittelson, W. H., & Ames, A., Jr. Accommodation, convergence, and their relation to apparent distance. *Journal of Psychology*, 1950, **30**, 43–62.

Kilpatrick, F. P. The role of assumptions in perception. Unpublished Ph.D. thesis, Princeton University, 1950.

Kilpatrick, F. P., & Ittelson, W. H. Three demonstrations involving the visual perception of movement. *Journal of Experimental Psychology*, 1951, **42**, 394–402.

Koffka, K. *Principles of Gestalt psychology*. New York: Harcourt, Brace, 1935.

Kohler, W. *Gestalt psychology*. New York: Liveright, 1947.

Lawrence, M. *Studies in human behavior*. Princeton, N.J.: Princeton University Press, 1949.

Michotte, A. *La perception de la causalité*. Paris: Vrin, 1946.

Pratt, C. C. The role of past experience in visual perception. *Journal of Psychology*, 1950, **30**, 85–107.

Schlosberg, H. A note on depth perception, size

constancy, and related topics. *Psychological Review,* 1950, **57,** 314–317.

Smith, W. M. A study of the influence of past experience on apparent size and distance. *American Journal of Psychology,* 1952, **65,** 389–403.

Thouless, R. S. Phenomenal regression to the real object. *British Journal of Psychology,* 1931, **21,** 339–359; **22,** 1–30.

Tolman, E. C., & Brunswik, E. The organism and the causal texture of the environment. *Psychological Review,* 1935, **42,** 43–77.

Vernon, M. D. *Visual perception.* Cambridge, Eng.: Cambridge University Press, 1937.

Wallach, H. Brightness constancy and the nature of achromatic colors. *Journal of Experimental Psychology,* 1948, **38,** 310–324.

Wheatstone, C. Contributions to the physiology of vision. Part the second. *Philosophical Magazine,* 1852, Series 4, **3,** 504–523.

Whitehead, A. N. *The principles of natural knowledge.* Cambridge, Eng.: Cambridge University Press, 1925.

Witkin, H. A. Perception of body position and of the position of the visual field. *Psychological Monograph,* 1949, **63,** Whole No. 302.

Woodworth, R. *Experimental psychology.* New York: Holt, 1938.

11 The Effects of Reward and Punishment on Perception

Harold Proshansky and Gardner Murphy

The traditional dualism of "perception" versus "action," or more broadly, the separation of cognitive activity from behavior, has an extraordinary capacity to resist the unifying tendencies of contemporary biology and psychology. After the usual formal acceptance of a monistic view of the organism, the experimenter often proceeds into his laboratory to study perception in terms of a group of categories almost entirely unrelated to those employed when studying motor acts. Thus, for example, the whole psychology of skill, in which the various forms of learning curves are analyzed and compared, suggests almost no transfer to the concepts and methods used in the study of perception and thought. The unity of the organism would suggest, however, that

From *The Journal of Psychology,* 1942, **13,** 295–305. Reprinted by permission of the authors and publisher.

whatever principles are of value in the understanding of the laws of motor response are of some pertinence in understanding the laws of perception. It is the hypothesis of the present paper that we *learn to perceive* in much the same way that we *learn to act.*

Learning curves for perceptual development can be discovered in which the various stages in consolidation of the responses correspond in some measure to stages in the consolidation of motor patterns. If this be true, a cardinal principle of motor learning, the effectiveness of reward and punishment, should be pertinent to the psychology of perception. It is our thesis that perception develops by virtue of its capacity to mediate adjustments, to serve needs; and that it may reasonably be expected to show the basic learning phenomena, including trial and error and the consolidation of successful phases of response. This is not to assert pretentiously that the dynamics of trial and error, or of reward and punishment, or of configuration, are fully understood, but only that the empirical principles evident in motor learning are also evident in perceptual learning. Our purpose is simply to demonstrate, as far as one brief experiment can do so, that perception develops positively in the direction of reward, tending away from the region of failure.

It may well be asked if the problem of perceptual learning has not already been abundantly studied. The reward-and-punishment situation has indeed often been utilized in training the subject to report on what he perceives; namely, in instances where the subject must acquire the skill to make correct estimates, and by means of knowledge of results tends toward the reduction of errors. Such experiments illustrate in several respects the typical learning curve that is characteristic of motor learning. But there are two features of the usual experiment on "learning to report" which seem to us to obscure the issue, because they involve types of overt behavior which prevent the experimenter from understanding what is happening to perception itself. In the usual experiment, the subject is trained so that his estimates achieve a pattern which is not only socially correct (accepted by experimenter and other subjects), but is *behaviorally useful* to him. The subject will learn what judgment is "appropriate," as in the case when we say, *"It looks like A, but I know it is really B."* As the subject is rewarded (perhaps only by hearing "right"), his results come closer to the desired pattern. In this classical type of experiment the subject *verbalizes his estimates* during the training period of the experiment. His verbal responses change, but exact knowledge about what he perceives is withheld.

Perception, however, has other functions besides mediating correct reports. For one thing, it often fulfills a drive directly; one perceives as one wishes to perceive. One perceives in a way which has proved to be satisfying, or "rewarding." Our present problem stems from this ability of individuals to perceive things in a manner which is compatible with their *wishes* and *attitudes*. The general term used to describe this tendency to perceive, recall, or think in drive-determined fashion is "autism"; the term has, for example, been used extensively by Bartlett (1932).

Sherif (1936) has been perhaps the most widely quoted contemporary writer to present representative material on the problem of autism. His *Psychology of Social Norms* shows how the autistic processes may be established within the individual through interaction with other persons. The general conclusion that one obtains from these investigations is that autistic processes are continually operating within the individual. In a simple everyday situation, such as reading a newspaper, this process operates. The individual obtains from the newspaper largely that material which is compatible with his attitudes.

The problem now arises as to the relation between the *learning process* and the process of autism. The answer is that most of the existing experimental work on autism relates to the individual *after* a given autistic process had been built up. On the contrary, we intend, by means of the reward-and-punishment situation, to build up what might be termed a "restricted autism" in the individual, such that we can be confident that he will react to certain specified situations in a certain desired manner. If our procedure gives significant results, it may be possible to proceed to build up more complex autistic systems within the individual.

For the purpose, it is necessary to work with a relatively unstructured situation in which the subject's perception is determined in considerable measure by his antecedent training and his present attitude. This unstructured situation must be repeatedly renewed in such fashion that certain aspects of the situation are strengthened through reward and others weakened through punishment. Any convenient everyday laboratory device for visual, auditory, or tactual perception of a poorly structured field will serve the purpose. Such procedures as have been used by Bartlett and Sherif for the study of frames of reference which give structure and meaning to otherwise poorly structured situations will be suitable.

SUBJECTS

The experimental subjects were 11 college students of approximately 17 years of age. Most of them were freshmen, and none had gone farther than the sophomore year. None of them had had any course in psychology. They were naïve about the experiment. Of these, eight were experimental subjects and three control subjects.

APPARATUS AND PROCEDURE

Our apparatus consisted of lines, weights, and a mechanism to produce the auto-kinetic effect.

Nine lines were drawn in black india ink on pieces of 8" x 6" white cardboard. There were three "long" lines, one 7", one 6", and one 5". Three other lines, 3½", 3", and 2½" long respectively, were called for convenience "intermediate" lines, though they are not uniformly "intermediate" between the long and the short (their use will be explained below). There were three "short" lines, one 4", one 3", and one 2".

Nine weights were made by filling cigarette cans, about 3½″ high, with buckshot. The "large" weights were 24 oz., 20 oz., and 16 oz. The "intermediate" weights were 13 oz., 12 oz., and 11 oz. The "small" weights were 12 oz., 8 oz., and 4 oz.

The third item, for the auto-kinetic effect, included a small bulb attached to a block of wood, and covered with a can. The can had a tiny hole in it which allowed a small point of light to be seen by the subject (in the darkroom). In the testing period, it was necessary that this light actually be made to move. This was done by sliding the block of wood in a crevice made in a baseboard.

When the subject had to make estimates concerning the lengths of the lines, it was necessary that the room be semi-dark. This was provided by a 2.5 mm. bulb burning in the corner of the darkroom. The room was so dark that it was difficult for the subjects to see the stimulus lines. However, by means of a rheostat, the bulb was made to provide more light for those subjects who complained that they could not see the lines at all.

The proper form of reward and punishment to use was the chief problem. At first it was felt that perhaps a shock would serve as the punishment and candy as the reward. However, upon questioning these subjects, it was concluded that they would probably resent the shock and tire of the candies. It was finally decided that perhaps the best reward and punishment would be in terms of money. Each time the subject was to be "rewarded" he received 15 cents, and each time he was to be "punished" he lost 15 cents. It was impressed upon the subject that each time he received money as reward, it was his to keep, and that he must pay money back as punishment; moreover, that if at a given session he won 30 cents or 45 cents he might have to pay it back at some time in the course of the experiment as a result of "punishment." As the experiment progressed, it was found advisable to make larger payments while keeping the punishment at the original level. Thus, at the termination of the study the experimenters found themselves $9.00 in the red. Reward and punishment in the form of money may fail when the amounts are trivial, yet succeed when the active interest of the subjects is maintained.

PROCEDURE

The experiment consisted of three periods: a pre-training period, a training period, and a post-training period.

1. Procedure for the Experimental Group

In each session of the pre-training period (two sessions a week for five weeks), the subjects were asked to give estimates of the lengths of all the lines and the magnitudes of all the weights, and to report in which direction the light moved.

The training period extended over seven weeks, two sessions per week. The procedure was as follows: The subjects were asked to perceive the lines, the weights, and the light without making any overt response. For each "long" line as defined above, each "heavy" weight, or light which moved to the right, the subject received a reward, and for each "short" line, "small" weight, and light which moved to the left, he received a punishment. For the "intermediate" stimuli, he was sometimes rewarded, sometimes punished, according to a "planned haphazard" schedule. It was impressed upon the subject that he was not to make any overt responses, but just to perceive.

The third part of our experiment was a final testing period. Each subject was again asked to estimate each of the intermediate lines and weights, and also the direction in which the light moved. At each session the subject perceived a single light at three different positions. At each position, he was asked to determine in which direction the light moved.

2. Procedure for the Control Group

The pre- and post-training periods for the control group were identical with those for the experimental group. During the training period, the members of this group were neither rewarded nor punished, but were simply shown the lines, the weights, and the light.

Table 11-1 Means for All Lines and All Weights

		1	2	3	4	5	6	7	8
					Subjects				
		Lines							
M	Pre-Training	4.2	4.2	4.7	4.7	4.4	4.6	4.4	4.1
	Post-Training	5.1	5.6	5.4	6.2	5.7	5.3	5.2	5.3
SD	Pre-Training	2.3	2.1	2.4	2.3	2.0	2.6	2.4	2.3
	Post-Training	1.5	2.3	2.4	3.2	2.5	2.7	2.6	3.4
		Weights							
M	Pre-Training	17.1	15.2	13.5	14.0	17.0	14.2	10.4	16.4
	Post-Training	20.0	18.9	17.8	18.4	16.4	17.1	13.9	17.8
SD	Pre-Training	8.8	7.0	9.0	7.0	7.0	6.0	6.0	7.5
	Post-Training	9.8	6.5	9.5	7.3	6.8	7.5	6.8	7.5
		Critical ratios for shifts							
	Lines	3.3	3.8	1.7	3.0	3.4	1.5	1.3	2.4
	Weights	3.4	3.1	2.7	3.6	.5	2.2	3.1	1.1

Results of three control subjects

		Lines						*Lines*		
		1	2	3				1	2	3
M	Pre-Training	4.9	5.3	4.3		SD	Pre-Training	2.3	1.7	2.6
	Post-Training	4.5	5.2	4.7			Post-Training	2.0	1.4	2.4
		Weights								
M	Pre-Training	21.4	15.8	18.0		SD	Pre-Training	9.2	7.0	8.0
	Post-Training	19.6	13.9	18.4			Post-Training	6.5	5.4	7.3

RESULTS

The means are given in Table 11-1 for the comparison of each subject's total estimations of lines and of weights for the pre-training period and the post-training period. The responses for all subjects in the pre-training period are compared with those in the post-training period, the control group being compared with the experimental group in Table 11-2.

The *group results* give a pre-training mean of 4.4 in line estimates for the experimental group; 5.5 in the post-training period. This difference gives a critical ratio of 5.0. Of eight experimental subjects, four showed significant differences in the expected direction between the pre-training and post-training estimates of the lines. In

the other four cases, the differences were also in the expected direction, but not individually significant. In the control group we found that our results were identical for the two periods (*CR*, 0).

Table 11-2 Group Results

	Lines		*Weights*	
	M	SD	M	SD
	Experimental			
Pre-Training	4.4	1.4	12.6	5.3
Post-Training	5.5	1.3	17.5	4.9
Critical Ratio	5.0		5.3	
	Control			
Pre-Training	4.8	1.9	18.4	5.7
Post-Training	4.8	2.3	17.3	6.2
Critical Ratio	0		.8	

Results with the weights were similar. Of eight experimental subjects, four showed significant differences in the expected direction. While not individually significant, the other four subjects tended also in the expected direction. Experimental mean for the pre-training period, 12.6; for the post-training period, 17.5, CR, 5.3; CR for the controls, 0.8.

Among a total of 162 judgments (lines and weights combined), in only five cases did a subject's judgment fall below his mean (for the line or weight) of the pre-training period. Even in those extreme cases in which subjects greatly exaggerated in the pre-training period, the same subjects increased the exaggeration after training. In one case, a subject gave an estimate of 12 inches for a five-inch line. Of three control subjects, only one produced a higher mean either in line or weight estimates in the post-training period. The same individual did this in line and weight estimates. In both cases the increase was small and far below the level of significance.

With the auto-kinetic effect, it was found during the course of the experiment that a major source of error was operating. The experiment was arranged so that this effect would occur during the pre- and post-training periods. During the training period the light was moved so as to train the subject in the desired direction. The source of error arose from the fact that the auto-kinetic effect was so marked that it took place also during the *training period* to a degree masking the training itself. Thus, though we moved the light to the right, the subject often commented on its moving in other directions. Although the subjects were instructed not to make any overt responses, they invariably commented during the period of the auto-kinetic effect, and thus revealed the source of error. We could obviously not hope to build a perceptual pattern within the individual if we could not control what he perceived.

DISCUSSION

What factors other than autism might have operated within the individual to produce these distortions in perception? One obvious danger is that we might have been training an overt verbal performance rather than an autistic system. Did the subject actually perceive the lines in a manner induced by our training, or was he just responding in terms of successful overt reports? The best answer is that the subjects frequently complained that it was impossible to perceive the stimuli. If the effect of the training was to modify the verbal response alone by means of rewards and punishments, the subjects would have responded immediately without too much interest in the lines themselves. Our subject constantly asked the experimenter during the post-training series to provide enough light to give some conception of the lengths of the lines. The same sort of thing occurred in the case of the weights. If a subject was set to respond verbally in a certain fashion because of rewards and punishments, the natural thing would have been to give an immediate response and get the process over with. In every case, however, our subjects handled the weights and took their time before responding. We cannot say that change in the motor set, in the direction of altered verbal tendencies, was completely absent; but we can say that if it was operating its effect was too small to be observed.

It will be recalled that with the "intermediate" stimuli the subjects were sometimes rewarded, sometimes punished. This seems to have served the purpose of breaking up a rational attack, a verbal "key" for mastering the problem; the subject could not formulate a rule for reward and punishment, and was perhaps rendered more passive.

A question arises as to the degree of naïveté of our subjects. Thrice during the course of the experiment the subjects were asked for introspections. It was only in the third inquiry that we came across one subject who had "caught on" to one aspect of the experiment. He remarked, *"I know that when the light goes to the right I am rewarded, and when to the left I am punished."* This was the only individual and the only report suggesting knowledge of the purpose of the experiment.

One of the most frequent difficulties with which the psychologist is faced is the question of cues from the experimenter. We sought to combat it by telling the subject as little about the experiment as possible, and by minimizing conversation. Directions were given only at the beginning of the three periods of the experiment. In order to prevent the subject from getting an idea as to the purpose of the experiment, written rather than oral instructions were given.

Is there a tendency in some individuals to exaggerate continually and progressively, such that our method of pre- and post-training periods gives an opportunity for increasing scores aside from the actual effects of training? This point cannot be completely answered; it may, however, be noted that it would be odd if this tendency were prevalent among all of the experimentals, and markedly so in four cases, while it is not present significantly in any of the controls.

Further experiments are planned in which autistic tendencies will be established in relation to more complex social situations. However, before we can attempt any experiments of a complex nature it is necessary that we corroborate our results. We intend first to repeat our experiment with certain modifications. These modifications will relate to the reward-and-punishment situation, the stimuli and other factors.

The subsequent experiment will then be more complex. We are going to attempt to establish autistic tendencies in social conflict situations. But not to leap too far in our next attempt, our social conflict situations will be on a simple level, and presented in a simple manner. Our method will aim to permit the individual's autistic tendencies to be built up by means of ambiguous pictures involving social conflicts. We will continue to use the reward-and-punishment situation. This reward-and-punishment situation is a typical laboratory arrangement, and certainly not true to life. Yet this is what we wish, because we do not profess to know how autistic tendencies are actually built up.

From this artificial reward-and-punishment situation we can then proceed to situations more real to life. For these more complex experiments, we shall have to enter the field of child psychology, in which perhaps basic, and more naïve, attitudes can be studied in the process of formation.

SUMMARY AND CONCLUSIONS

The purpose of the experiment was to build up by rewards and punishments a tendency to perceive in a predetermined manner, i.e., to induce an autism in the individual. Eleven college students served as subjects. The experiment was divided into three periods: a pre-training period in which lines and weights were estimated, a training period in which money was given in association with certain percepts and taken away in association with other percepts, and a post-training period physically identical with the first.

The experimental subjects showed, in the post-training series, significant shifts in estimates of lines and weights in the direction of the percepts which had been rewarded.

The control subjects showed no significant shifts in perception.

Such large and uncontrolled auto-kinetic effects appeared in the training series as to vitiate the post-training data.

Further experiments are planned in which autistic tendencies will be established in relation to social conflict situations.

REFERENCES:

Bartlett, F. C. *Remembering*. Cambridge, Eng.: Cambridge University Press, 1932.
Sherif, M. *The psychology of social norms*. New York: Harper, 1936.

12 Excerpts from Motivation Reconsidered: The Concept of Competence

Robert W. White

NEEDS FOR EXCITEMENT AND NOVELTY

Human experience provides plentiful evidence of the importance of reducing excessive levels of tension. Men under wartime stress, men under pressure of pain and ex-

From *Psychological Review*, 1959, **66**, 313–324. Reprinted by permission of the author and publisher.

treme deprivation, men with excessive work loads or too much exposure to confusing social interactions, all act as if their nervous systems craved that utterly unstimulated condition which Freud once sketched as the epitome of neural bliss. But if these same men be granted their nirvana they soon become miserable and begin to look around for a little excitement. Human experience testifies that boredom is a bad state of affairs about which something must be done. Hebb (1949) has been particularly insistent in reminding us that many of our activities, such as reading detective stories, skindiving, or driving cars at high speeds, give clear evidence of a need to raise the level of stimulation and excitement. Men and animals alike seem at times bent on increasing the impact of the environment and even on creating mild degrees of frustration and fear. Hebb and Thompson (1954) reflect upon this as follows:

> Such phenomena are, of course, well known in man: in the liking for dangerous sports or roller coasters, where fear is deliberately courted, and in the addiction to bridge or golf or solitaire, vices whose very existence depends upon the level of difficulty of the problems presented and an optimal level of frustration. Once more, when we find such attitudes toward fear and frustration in animals, we have a better basis for supposing that we are dealing with something fundamental if a man prefers skis to the less dangerous snowshoes, or when we observe an unashamed love of work (problem solving and frustration included) in the scientist, or in the businessman who cannot retire. Such behavior in man is usually accounted for as a search for prestige, but the animal data make this untenable. It seems much more likely that solving problems and running mild risks are inherently rewarding, or, in more general terms, that the animal will always act so as to produce an optimal level of excitation (Hebb and Thompson, 1954, p. 551).

The concept of optimal stimulation has been developed by Leuba (1955), who sees it as helpful in resolving some of the problems of learning theory. Believing that most theorizing about motivation has been based upon "powerful biological or neurotic drives," Leuba bids us look at the much more common learning situations of nursery, playground, and school, where "actions which increase stimulation and produce excitement are strongly reinforced, sometimes to the dismay of parents and teachers." He proposes that there is an optimal level of stimulation, subject to variation at different times, and that learning is associated with movement toward this optimal level, downward when stimulation is too high and upward when it is too low. A similar idea is expressed by McReynolds (1956) concerning the more restricted concept of "rate of perceptualization." Monotonous conditions provide too low a rate, with boredom; excessive stimulation produces too high a rate, with disruptive excitement; the optimal rate yields the experience of pleasure. These ideas are now amply supported by recent experimental work on sensory deprivation (Lilly, 1956; Hebb, 1958).

In recent papers Young (1949, 1955) has argued for an hedonic theory of motivation, one in which affective processes "constitute a form of primary motivation." According to Young's theory, "an organism behaves so as to maximize positive affective arousal (delight, enjoyment) and to minimize negative arousal (distress)." McClelland (1953) has offered a version of hedonic theory which is of particular value in understanding the significance of novelty. Affective arousal occurs when a stimulus pattern produces a discrepancy from the existing adaptation level. Small discrepancies produce pleasant affect and a tendency to approach; large ones produce unpleasantness and a tendency toward avoidance. The child at play, like the young chimpanzee and the exploring rat, needs frequent novelty in the stimulus field in order to keep up his interest—in order to maintain pleasant discrepancies from whatever adaptation level he has reached. Hebb's (1949) theory of the neurological correlates of learning also deals with novelty, though in a somewhat different way. He equates sustained interest with a state of neural affairs in which "phase sequences" are relatively complex and are growing, in the sense of establishing new internal relations. Such a state follows most readily from a stimulus field characterized by difference-in-sameness; that is, containing much that is familiar along with certain features that are novel. If the field is entirely familiar, phase sequences run off quickly, are short-circuited, and thus fail to produce sustained interest. Hebb's theory, which has the engaging quality of being able to explain why we enjoy reading a detective story once but not right over again, expresses in a neurological hypothesis the familiar fact that well-learned, habituated processes do not in themselves greatly interest us. Interest seems to require elements of unfamiliarity: of something still to be found out and of learning still to be done.

It seems to me that these contributions, though differing as to details, speak with unanimity on their central theme and would force us, if nothing else did, to reconsider seriously the whole problem of motivation. Boredom, the unpleasantness of monotony, the attraction of novelty, the tendency to vary behavior rather than repeating it rigidly, and the seeking of stimulation and mild excitement stand as inescapable facts of human experience and clearly have their parallels in animal behavior. We may seek rest and minimal stimulation at the end of the day, but that is not what we are looking for the next morning. Even when its primary needs are satisfied and its homeostatic chores are done, an organism is alive, active, and up to something.

DEALING WITH THE ENVIRONMENT

If we consider things only from the viewpoint of affect, excitement, and novelty, we are apt to overlook another important aspect of behavior, its effect upon the environment. Moving in this direction, Diamond (1939) invites us to consider the motivational properties of the sensorineural system, the apparatus whereby higher animals "maintain their relations to the environment." He conceives of this system as demanding stimulation and as acting in such a manner as to "force the environment to stimulate it." Even if one thinks only of the infant's exploring eyes and hands, it is clear that the main direction of behavior is by no means always that of reducing the impact of stimulation. When the eyes follow a moving object, or when the hand grasps an object which it has touched, the result is to preserve the stimulus and to increase its effect. In more elaborate explorations the consequence of a series of actions may be to vary the manner in which a stimulus acts upon the sense organs. It is apparent that the exploring, manipulating child produces by his actions precisely what Hebb's theory demands as a basis for continuing interest: he produces differences-in-sameness in the stimulus field.

In a critical analysis of Freud's views on the reality principle, Charlotte Bühler (1954) makes a strong case for positive interests in the environment, citing as evidence the responsiveness and adaptiveness of the newborn baby as well as the exploratory tendencies of later months. The problem is worked out in more detail by Schachtel (1954) in a paper on focal attention. Acts of focal attention are characteristically directed at particular objects, and they consist of several sustained approaches "aimed at active mental grasp" while excluding the rest of the field. These qualities can be observed even in the infant's early attempts to follow a moving object with his eyes, and they show more clearly in his later endeavors to learn how objects are related both to himself and to one another. Such behavior bespeaks "a relatively autonomous capacity for object interest." Schachtel makes the proposal that this interest is pursued precisely at those times when major needs are in abeyance. High pressure of need or anxiety is the enemy of exploratory play and is a condition, as every scientist should know, under which we are unlikely to achieve an objective grasp of the environment. Low need pressure is requisite if we are to perceive objects as they are, in their constant character, apart from hopes and fears we may at other times attach to them. Schachtel doubts that "the wish for need-satisfaction alone would ever lead to object perception and to object-oriented thought." Hence an autonomous capacity to be interested in the environment has great value for the survival of a species.

Being interested in the environment implies having some kind of satisfactory interaction with it. Several workers call attention to the possibility that satisfaction might lie in having an effect upon the environment, in dealing with it, and changing it in various ways. Groos (1901), in his classical analysis of play, attached great importance to the child's "joy in being a cause," as shown in making a clatter, "hustling things about," and playing in puddles where large and dramatic effects can be produced. "We demand a knowledge of effects," he wrote, "and to be ourselves the producers of effects." Piaget (1952) remarks upon the child's special interest in objects that are affected by his own movements. This aspect of behavior occupies a central place in the work of Skinner (1953), who describes it as "operant" and who thus "emphasizes the fact that the behavior *operates* upon the environment to generate consequences." These consequences are fed back through the sense organs and may serve to reinforce behavior even when no organic needs are involved. A rat will show an increased tendency to press a bar when this act produces a click or a buzz. A baby will continue to investigate when his efforts produce rattling or tinkling sounds or sparkling reflections from a shiny object. The young chimpanzees in Welker's experiment spent the longest time over objects which could be lighted or made to emit sounds. Skinner finds it "difficult, if not impossible, to trace these reinforcing effects to a history of conditioning." "We may plausibly argue," he continues, "that a capacity to be reinforced by any feedback from the environment would be biologically advantageous, since it would prepare the organism to manipulate the environment successfully before a given state of deprivation developed."

COMPETENCE AND THE PLAY OF CONTENTED CHILDREN

A backward glance at our survey shows considerable agreement about the kinds of behavior that are left out or handled poorly by theories of motivation based wholly on organic drives. Repeatedly we find reference to the familiar series of learned skills which starts with sucking, grasping, and visual exploration and continues with crawling and walking, acts of focal attention and perception, memory, language and thinking, anticipation, the exploring of novel places and objects, effecting stimulus changes in the environment, manipulating and exploiting the surroundings, and achieving higher levels of motor and mental coordination. These aspects of behavior have long been the province of child psychology, which has attempted to measure the slow course of their development and has shown how heavily their growth depends upon learning. Collectively they are sometimes referred to as adaptive mechanisms or as ego processes, but on the whole we are not accustomed to cast a single name over the diverse feats whereby we learn to deal with the environment.

I now propose that we gather the various kinds of behavior just mentioned, all of which have to do with effective interaction with the environment, under the general heading of competence. According to Webster, competence means fitness or ability, and the suggested synonyms include capability, capacity, efficiency, proficiency, and skill. It is therefore a suitable word to describe such things as grasping and exploring, crawling and walking, attention and perception, language and thinking, manipulating and changing the surroundings, all of which promote an effective—a competent —interaction with the environment. It is true, of course, that maturation plays a part in all these developments, but this part is heavily overshadowed by learning in all the more complex accomplishments like speech or skilled manipulation. I shall argue that it is necessary to make competence a motivational concept; there is a *competence motivation* as well as competence in its more familiar sense of achieved capacity. The behavior that leads to the building up of effective grasping, handling, and letting go of objects, to take one example, is not random behavior produced by a general overflow of energy. It is directed, selective, and persistent, and it is continued not because it serves primary drives, which indeed it cannot serve until it is almost perfected, but because it satisfies an intrinsic need to deal with the environment.

No doubt it will at first seem arbitrary to

propose a single motivational conception in connection with so many and such diverse kinds of behavior. What do we gain by attributing motivational unity to such a large array of activities? We could, of course, say that each developmental sequence, such as learning to grasp or to walk, has its own built-in bit of motivation—its "aliment," as Piaget (1952) has expressed it. We could go further and say that each item of behavior has its intrinsic motive—but this makes the concept of motivation redundant. On the other hand, we might follow the lead of the animal psychologists and postulate a limited number of broader motives under such names as curiosity, manipulation, and mastery. I believe that the idea of a competence motivation is more adequate than any of these alternatives and that it points to very vital common properties which have been lost from view amidst the strongly analytical tendencies that go with detailed research.

In order to make this claim more plausible, I shall now introduce some specimens of playful exploration in early childhood. I hope that these images will serve to fix and dramatize the concept of competence in the same way that other images—the hungry animal solving problems, the child putting his finger in the candle flame, the infant at the breast, the child on the toilet, and the youthful Oedipus caught in a hopeless love triangle—have become memorable focal points for other concepts. For this purpose I turn to Piaget's (1952) studies of the growth of intelligence from its earliest manifestations in his own three children. The examples come from the first year of life, before language and verbal concepts begin to be important. They therefore represent a practical kind of intelligence which may be quite similar to what is developed by the higher animals.

As early as the fourth month, the play of the gifted Piaget children began to be "centered on a result produced in the external environment," and their behavior could be described as "rediscovering the movement which by chance exercised an advantageous action upon things" (1952, p. 151). Laurent, lying in his bassinet, learns to shake a suspended rattle by pulling a string that hangs

from it. He discovers this result fortuitously before vision and prehension are fully coordinated. Let us now observe him a little later when he has reached the age of three months and ten days.

> I place the string, which is attached to the rattle, in his right hand, merely unrolling it a little so that he may grasp it better. For a moment nothing happens. But at the first shake due to chance movement of his hand, the reaction is immediate: Laurent starts when looking at the rattle and then violently strikes his right hand alone, as if he felt the resistance and the effect. The operation lasts fully a quarter of an hour, during which Laurent emits peals of laughter (Piaget, 1952, p. 162).

Three days later the following behavior is observed:

> Laurent, by chance, strikes the chain while sucking his fingers. He grasps it and slowly displaces it while looking at the rattles. He then begins to swing it very gently, which produces a slight movement of the hanging rattles and an as yet faint sound inside them. Laurent then definitely increases by degrees his own movements. He shakes the chain more and more vigorously and laughs uproariously at the result obtained (Piaget, 1952, p. 185).

Very soon it can be observed that procedures are used "to make interesting spectacles last." For instance, Laurent is shown a rubber monkey which he has not seen before. After a moment of surprise, and perhaps even fright, he calms down and makes movements of pulling the string, a procedure which has no effect in this case, but which previously has caused interesting things to happen. It is to be noticed that "interesting spectacles" consist of such things as new toys, a tin box upon which a drumming noise can be made, an unfolded newspaper, or sounds made by the observer such as snapping the fingers. Commonplace as they are to the adult mind, these spectacles enter the infant's experience as novel and apparently challenging events.

Moving ahead to the second half of the first year, we can observe behavior in which the child explores the properties of objects and tries out his repertory of actions upon them. This soon leads to active experimentation in which the child attempts to provoke new results. Again we look in upon Laurent, who has now reached the age of nine months. On different occasions he is shown a variety of new objects—for instance a notebook, a beaded purse, and a wooden parrot. His carefully observing father detects four stages of response: (a) visual exploration, passing the object from hand to hand, folding the purse, etc.; (b) tactile exploration, passing the hand all over the object, scratching, etc.; (c) slow moving of the object in space; (d) use of the repertory of action: shaking the object, striking it, swinging it, rubbing it against the side of the bassinet, sucking it, etc., "each in turn with a sort of prudence as though studying the effect produced" (1952, p. 255).

Here the child can be described as applying familiar tactics to new situations, but in a short while he will advance to clear patterns of active experimentation. At 10 months and 10 days Laurent, who is unfamiliar with bread as a nutritive substance, is given a piece for examination. He manipulates it, drops it many times, breaks off fragments and lets them fall. He has often done this kind of thing before, but previously his attention has seemed to be centered on the act of letting go. Now "he watches with great interest the body in motion; in particular, he looks at it for a long time when it has fallen, and picks it up when he can." On the following day he resumes his research.

He grasps in succession a celluloid swan, a box, and several other small objects, in each case stretching out his arm and letting them fall. Sometimes he stretches out his arm vertically, sometimes he holds it obliquely in front of or behind his eyes. When the object falls in a new position (for example on his pillow) he lets it fall two or three times more on the same place, as though to study the spatial relation; then he modifies the situation. At a certain moment the swan falls near his mouth; now he does not suck it (even though this object habitually serves this purpose), but drops it three times

more while merely making the gesture of opening his mouth (Piaget, 1952, p. 269).

These specimens will furnish us with sufficient images of the infant's use of his spare time. Laurent, of course, was provided by his studious father with a decidedly enriched environment, but no observant parent will question the fact that babies often act this way during those periods of their waking life when hunger, erotic needs, distresses, and anxiety seem to be exerting no particular pressure. If we consider this behavior under the historic headings of psychology we shall see that few processes are missing. The child gives evidence of sensing, perceiving, attending, learning, recognizing, probably recalling, and perhaps thinking in a rudimentary way. Strong emotion is lacking, but the infant's smiles, gurgles, and occasional peals of laughter strongly suggest the presence of pleasant effect. Actions appear in an organized form, particularly in the specimens of active exploration and experimentation. Apparently the child is using with a certain coherence nearly the whole repertory of psychological processes except those that accompany stress. It would be arbitrary indeed to say that one was more important than another.

These specimens have a meaningful unity when seen as transactions between the child and his environment, the child having some influence upon the environment and the environment some influence upon the child. Laurent appears to be concerned about what he can do with the chain and rattles, what he can accomplish by his own effort to reproduce and to vary the entertaining sounds. If his father observed correctly, we must add that Laurent seems to have varied his actions systematically, as if testing the effect of different degrees of effort upon the bit of environment represented by the chain and rattles. Kittens make a similar study of parameters when delicately using their paws to push pencils and other objects ever nearer to the edge of one's desk. In all such examples it is clear that the child or animal is by no means at the mercy of transient stimulus fields. He selects for continuous treatment those aspects of his environment which he finds it possible to affect in some way. His behavior is selective, directed, persistent—in short, motivated.

Motivated toward what goal? In these terms, too, the behavior exhibits a little of everything. Laurent can be seen as appeasing a stimulus hunger, providing his sensorium with an agreeable level of stimulation by eliciting from the environment a series of interesting sounds, feels, and sights. On the other hand we might emphasize a need for activity and see him as trying to reach a pleasurable level of neuromuscular exercise. We can also see another possible goal in the behavior: the child is achieving knowledge, attaining a more differentiated cognitive map of his environment and thus satisfying an exploratory tendency or motive of curiosity. But it is equally possible to discern a theme of mastery, power, or control, perhaps even a bit of primitive self-assertion, in the child's concentration upon those aspects of the environment which respond in some way to his own activity. It looks as if we had found too many goals, and perhaps our first impulse is to search for some key to tell us which one is really important. But this, I think, is a mistake that would be fatal to understanding.

We cannot assign priority to any of these goals without pausing arbitrarily in the cycle of transaction between child and environment and saying, "This is the real point." I propose instead that the real point is the transactions as a whole. If the behavior gives satisfaction, this satisfaction is not associated with a particular moment in the cycle. It does not lie solely in sensory stimulation, in a bettering of the cognitive map, in coordinated action, in motor exercise, in a feeling of effort and of effects produced, or in the appreciation of change brought about in the sensory field. These are all simply aspects of a process which at this stage has to be conceived as a whole. The child appears to be occupied with the agreeable task of developing an effective familiarity with his environment. This involves discovering the effects he can have on the environment and the effects the environment will have on him. To the extent that these results are preserved by learning, they build up an increased competence in dealing with the environment. The child's play can thus be viewed as serious business, though to him it is merely something that is interesting and fun to do.

Bearing in mind these examples, as well as the dealings with environment pointed out by other workers, we must now attempt to describe more fully the possible nature of the motivational aspect of competence. It needs its own name, and in view of the foregoing analysis I propose that this name be *effectance*.

EFFECTANCE

The new freedom produced by two decades of research on animal drives is of great help in this undertaking. We are no longer obliged to look for a source of energy external to the nervous system, for a consummatory climax, or for a fixed connection between reinforcement and tension-reduction. Effectance motivation cannot, of course, be conceived as having a source in tissues external to the nervous system. It is in no sense a deficit motive. We must assume it to be neurogenic, its "energies" being simply those of the living cells that make up the nervous system. External stimuli play an important part, but in terms of "energy" this part is secondary, as one can see most clearly when environmental stimulation is actively sought. Putting it picturesquely, we might say that the effectance urge represents what the neuromuscular system wants to do when it is otherwise unoccupied or is gently stimulated by the environment. Obviously there are no consummatory acts; satisfaction would appear to lie in the arousal and maintaining of activity rather than in its slow decline toward bored passivity. The motive need not be conceived as intense and powerful in the sense that hunger, pain, or fear can be powerful when aroused to high pitch. There are plenty of instances in which children refuse to leave their absorbed play in order to eat or to visit the toilet. Strongly aroused drives, pain, and anxiety, however, can be conceived as overriding the effectance urge and capturing the energies of the neuromuscular system. But effectance motivation is persistent in the sense that it regularly occupies the spare waking time between episodes of homeostatic crisis.

In speculating upon this subject we must bear in mind the continuous nature of behavior. This is easier said than done; habitually we break things down in order to understand them, and such units as the reflex arc, the stimulus-response sequence, and the single transaction with the environment seem like inevitable steps toward clarity. Yet when we apply such an analysis to playful exploration we lose the most essential aspect of the behavior. It is constantly circling from stimulus to perception to action to effect to stimulus to perception, and so on around; or, more properly, these processes are all in continuous action and continuous change. Dealing with the environment means carrying on a continuing transaction which gradually changes one's relation to the environment. Because there is no consummatory climax, satisfaction has to be seen as lying in a considerable series of transactions, in a trend of behavior rather than a goal that is achieved. It is difficult to make the word "satisfaction" have this connotation, and we shall do well to replace it by "feeling of efficacy" when attempting to indicate the subjective and affective side of effectance.

It is useful to recall the findings about novelty: the singular effectiveness of novelty in engaging interest and for a time supporting persistent behavior. We also need to consider the selective continuance of transactions in which the animal or child has a more or less pronounced effect upon the environment—in which something happens as a consequence of his activity. Interest is not aroused and sustained when the stimulus field is so familiar that it gives rise at most to reflex acts or automatized habits. It is not sustained when actions produce no effects or changes in the stimulus field. Our conception must therefore be that effectance motivation is aroused by stimulus conditions which offer, as Hebb (1949) puts it, difference-in-sameness. This leads to variability and novelty of response, and interest is best sustained when the resulting action affects the stimulus so as to produce further difference-in-sameness. Interest wanes when action begins to have less effect; effectance

motivation subsides when a situation has been explored to the point that it no longer presents new possibilities.

We have to conceive further that the arousal of playful and exploratory interest means the appearance of organization involving both the cognitive and active aspects of behavior. Change in the stimulus field is not an end in itself, so to speak; it happens when one is passively moved about, and it may happen as a consequence of random movements without becoming focalized and instigating exploration. Similarly, action which has effects is not an end in itself, for if one unintentionally kicks away a branch while walking, or knocks something off a table, these effects by no means necessarily become involved in playful investigation. Schachtel's (1954) emphasis on focal attention becomes helpful at this point. The playful and exploratory behavior shown by Laurent is not random or casual. It involves focal *attention* to some object—the fixing of some aspect of the stimulus field so that it stays relatively constant—and it also involves the focalizing of *action* upon this object. As Diamond (1939) has expressed it, response under these conditions is "relevant to the stimulus," and it is change in the *focalized* stimulus that so strongly affects the level of interest. Dealing with the environment means directing focal attention to some part of it and organizing actions to have some effect on this part.

In our present state of relative ignorance about the workings of the nervous system it is impossible to form a satisfactory idea of the neural basis of effectance motivation, but it should at least be clear that the concept does not refer to any and every kind of neural action. It refers to a particular kind of activity, as inferred from particular kinds of behavior. We can say that it does not include reflexes and other kinds of automatic response. It does not include well-learned, automatized patterns, even those that are complex and highly organized. It does not include behavior in the service of effectively aroused drives. It does not even include activity that is highly random and discontinuous, though such behavior may be its most direct forerunner. The urge toward competence is inferred specifically from behavior that shows a lasting focalization and that has the characteristics of exploration and experimentation, a kind of variation within the focus. When this particular sort of activity is aroused in the nervous system, effectance motivation is being aroused, for it is characteristic of this particular sort of activity that it is selective, directed, and persistent, and that instrumental acts will be learned for the sole reward of engaging in it.

Some objection may be felt to my introducing the word *competence* in connection with behavior that is so often playful. Certainly the playing child is doing things for fun, not because of a desire to improve his competence in dealing with the stern hard world. In order to forestall misunderstanding, it should be pointed out that the usage here is parallel to what we do when we connect sex with its biological goal of reproduction. The sex drive aims for pleasure and gratification, and reproduction is a consequence that is presumably unforeseen by animals and by man at primitive levels of understanding. Effectance motivation similarly aims for the feeling of efficacy, not for the vitally important learnings that come as its consequence. If we consider the part played by competence motivation in adult human life we can observe the same parallel. Sex may now be completely and purposefully divorced from reproduction but nevertheless pursued for the pleasure it can yield. Similarly, effectance motivation may lead to continuing exploratory interests or active adventures when in fact there is no longer any gain in actual competence or any need for it in terms of survival. In both cases the motive is capable of yielding surplus satisfaction well beyond what is necessary to get the biological work done.

In infants and young children it seems to me sensible to conceive of effectance motivation as undifferentiated. Later in life it becomes profitable to distinguish various motives such as cognizance, construction, mastery, and achievement. It is my view that all such motives have a root in effectance motivation. They are differentiated from it through life experiences which emphasize one or another aspect of the cycle of transaction with environment. Of course, the motives of later childhood and of adult life are no longer simple and can almost never be referred to a single root. They can acquire loadings of anxiety, defense, and compensation; they can become fused with unconscious fantasies of a sexual, aggressive, or omnipotent character; and they can gain force because of their service in producing realistic results in the way of income and career. It is not my intention to cast effectance in the star part in adult motivation. The acquisition of motives is a complicated affair in which simple and sovereign theories grow daily more obsolete. Yet it may be that the satisfaction of effectance contributes significantly to those feelings of interest which often sustain us so well in day-to-day actions, particularly when the things we are doing have continuing elements of novelty.

THE BIOLOGICAL SIGNIFICANCE OF COMPETENCE

The conviction was expressed at the beginning of this paper that some such concept as competence, interpreted motivationally, was essential for any biologically sound view of human nature. This necessity emerges when we consider the nature of living systems, particularly when we take a longitudinal view. What an organism does at a given moment does not always give the right clue as to what it does over a period of time. Discussing this problem, Angyal (1941) has proposed that we should look for the general pattern followed by the total organismic process over the course of time. Obviously this makes it necessary to take account of growth. Angyal defines life as "a process of self-expansion"; the living system "expands at the expense of its surroundings," assimilating parts of the environment and transforming them into functioning parts of itself. Organisms differ from other things in nature in that they are "self-governing entities" which are to some extent "autonomous." Internal processes govern them as well as external "heteronomous" forces. In the course of life there is a relative increase in the preponderance of internal over external forces. The living system expands, assimilates more of the environment, transforms its surroundings so as to bring them under greater control. "We may say," Angyal writes, "that the general dynamic trend of the organism is toward an increase of autonomy. . . . The human being has a characteristic tendency toward self-determination, that is, a tendency to resist external influences and to subordinate the heteronomous forces of the physical and social environment to its own sphere of influence." The trend toward increased autonomy is characteristic so long as growth of any kind is going on, though in the end the living system is bound to succumb to the pressure of heteronomous forces.

Of all living creatures, it is man who takes the longest strides toward autonomy. This is not because of any unusual tendency toward bodily expansion at the expense of the environment. It is rather that man, with his mobile hands and abundantly developed brain, attains an extremely high level of competence in his transactions with his surroundings. The building of houses, roads and bridges, the making of tools and instruments, the domestication of plants and animals—all qualify as planful changes made in the environment so that it comes more or less under control and serves our purposes rather than intruding upon them. We meet the fluctuations of outdoor temperature, for example, not only with our bodily homeostatic mechanisms, which alone would be painfully unequal to the task, but also with clothing, buildings, controlled fires, and such complicated devices as self-regulating central heating and air conditioning. Man as a species has developed a tremendous power of bringing the environment into his service, and each individual member of the species must attain what is really quite an impressive level of competence if he is to take part in the life around him.

REFERENCES:

Angyal, A. *Foundations for a science of personality.* New York: Commonwealth Fund, 1941.

Bühler, Charlotte. The reality principle. *American Journal of Psychotherapy,* 1954, **8**, 626–647.

Diamond, S. A. A neglected aspect of motivation. *Sociometry,* 1939, **2**, 77–85.

Groos, K. *The play of man.* (Trans. by E. L. Baldwin) New York: D. Appleton, 1901.

Hebb, D. O. *The organization of behavior.* New York: Wiley, 1949.

Hebb, D. O. The motivating effects of exteroceptive stimulation. *American Psychologist,* 1958, **13**, 109–113.

Hebb, D. O., & Thompson, W. R. The social significance of animal studies. In G. Lindzey (Ed.), *Handbook of social psychology.* Cambridge, Mass.: Addison-Wesley, 1954, Ch. 15.

Leuba, C. Toward some integration of learning theories: The concept of optimal stimulation. *Psychological Reports,* 1955, **1**, 27–33.·

Lilly, J. C. Mental effects of reduction of ordinary levels of physical stimuli on intact, healthy persons. *Psychiatric Research Reports,* 1956, **5**, 1–9.

McClelland, D. D., Atkinson, J. W., Clark, R. A., & Lowell, E. L. *The achievement motive.* New York: Appleton-Century, 1953.

McReynolds, P. A restricted conceptualization of human anxiety and motivation. *Psychological Reports,* 1956, **2**, 293–312. Monogr. Suppl. 6.

Piaget, J. *The origins of intelligence in children.* (Trans. by M. Cook) New York: International Universities Press, 1952.

Schachtel, E. G. The development of focal attention and the emergence of reality. *Psychiatry,* 1954, **17**, 309–324.

Skinner, B. F. *Science and human behavior.* New York: Macmillan, 1953.

Young, P. T. Food-seeking drive, affective process, and learning. *Psychological Review,* 1949, **56**, 98–121.

Young, P. T. The role of hedonic processes in motivation. In M. R. Jones (Ed.), *Nebraska symposium on motivation.* Lincoln, Nebr.: University of Nebraska Press, 1955. Pp. 193–238.

13 Spatial Meaning and the Properties of the Environment

Robert Beck

Perception of the environment requires man to interpret the physical and social components of his stimulus field. Such an area of inquiry falls congruently into the disciplines of geography and psychology, which are concerned, respectively, with the physical properties of the stimulus field and with personal attributes arising out of functional and

From *Environmental Perception and Behavior,* edited by David Lowenthal, Research Paper #109, Department of Geography, The University of Chicago, 1967. Reprinted by permission of the author and publisher.

symbolic transactions between men and that field. These transactions further lead to the establishment of group attitudes, beliefs, and values associated with various domains of the environmental field. The physical and interpersonal properties of the environment are distributed in space, and personal environmental space is shaped by the configuration of these properties. Personal systems of spatial meaning may yield important insights into individual perceptions of the environment.

The theory of spatial meaning includes insights from many disciplines. It requires some consideration of the philosophy and logic of space. The question, "Is space inherently or experientially derived?" must be answered before questions concerning developmental spatial articulation can even be formulated. That space is personal and has unique meaning for the individual is clear from the existential-psychiatric literature on the psychopathology of experienced space, and from the brilliant spatial-phenomenological speculations of such men as Binswanger (1947), Straus (1963), and Minkowski (1939). The work of artists, art critics, and anthropologists likewise yield categories important for an interpretation of space in psychological terms. The painter, the sculptor, the architect, the city planner, are all professional manipulators of the spatial field, translators of spatial meaning into tangible structures; their systems of spatial terminologies are invaluable in the study of spatial meaning. The linguistic spatial expressions and notation systems of other cultures may also be tapped as sources of a spatial grammar.

In the developmental articulation of the self with environment, and the subsequent differentiation of the environment itself into increasingly discrete and heterogeneous parts, percept and concept are conjoined. Each of the sensory modalities breaks down phenomena into sets of components. The progressive delineation of forms in space is a basic part of this process. Spatial reference and orientation systems—for example, up-down, left-right, horizontal-vertical, dense-diffuse, open-delineated, forward-backward, near-far, symmetrical-asymmetrical—are not mere geometrical abstractions, but meaningful properties of individual environments. The six cardinal directions are not endowed with equivalent meaning for us; up and down, front and back, left and right, have particular values because we happen to be a special kind of bilaterally symmetrical terrestrial animal. As Lowenthal (1961) has stated, "It is one contingent fact about the world that we attach very great importance to things having their tops and bottoms in the right places; it is another contingent fact that we attach more importance to their having fronts and backs in the right places than their left and right sides." In fact, people adapt more rapidly to distorting spectacles that invert up and down than to those that invert right and left.

The spatial field is differentially charged with meaning from individual to individual; and particular configurations of the spatial field may be important clues to personality. As a sacred grove has historical-religious significance for a whole people, so individuals acquire and integrate spatial axes and orientations which become personal styles. Spatial styles are analogous to characteristic conceptual, expressive, and other personal styles, which are built word upon word, action upon action. Such styles are carried as unique personality attributes. As these spatial styles become more and more a part of the personality structure of the individual, space is slowly divided into definitive zones and directions with intuitive meanings and an expressive character of their own.

Whole cultures, through the use of myth, render certain spatial configurations distinct and important. According to Cassirer (1953), "Myth arrives at spatial determinations and differentiations only by lending a peculiar mythical accent to each 'region' in space, to the 'here' and 'there', the rising and setting of the sun, the 'above' and 'below'." In Greece, myth flooded, embraced the relation of man and land, the meaning the land had for him. To quote Scully (1962):

. . . not only were certain landscapes indeed regarded by the Greeks as holy and expressive of certain Gods, or rather as embodiments of their presence, but . . . the temples and the subsidiary buildings of their sanctuaries were so formed in themselves, and so placed in relation to the landscape and to each other as to enhance, develop, and sometimes even contradict, the basic meaning that was felt in the land. . . . Therefore, no study of Greek temples can be purely morphological, of form without theme . . . since in Greek art, the two are one. The form is the meaning.

Let us return to the development of spatial meaning and its relation to the geographical environment. As meaning is acquired, it clothes the perceptual world. The infant's active exploration of his physical environment—pushing, pulling, grasping, thrusting—endows space with a primitive concrete meaning. But the infant passes through stages of involvement with different kinds of space. At first the baby is placed on his stomach (facing down), then on his back (facing up).[1] In the crawling stage, the infant lives in the horizontal plane—his line of sight and mode of exploration are highly uniplanar, action occurs toward and away from objects at his own level of height.

Later the child raises his head, and eventually stands up; he enters the space of the vertical plane—up and down become coordinated, right and left gain more freedom. As the child structures space and forms object relations, innumerable spatial connotations develop. About the same time the acquisition of binocular vision expands the two-dimensional into the three-dimensional world. The distinction of symmetrical from non-symmetrical relations comes later still.

The concrete primitive meaning of physical exploration is supplemented and elaborated by the use and function of objects. Meaning is derived from a satisfaction of needs, needs which have spatial qualities. Food-objects, tool-objects, danger-objects, pleasure or love objects acquire special significance for the child. Mother is too *close* or *far away*; food is consumed (put *inside* or spit *out*); tools move, are used in certain directions—they dig *in*, they move *vertically, horizontally*; one maintains *distance from* or is curiously attracted *toward* fire, punishment, danger.

Concepts of spatial meaning thus derive from individual modes and styles of perception. Indeed, meaning and perception are inseparable. Allport (1955) has summarized the Brunswik-Ames concept of perception as "the process of apprehending probable significances. . . . Basic to the process is the fact that the organism has built up certain assumptions about the world in which it lives. These assumptions which are largely *unconscious* lead to . . . the attaching of significances to cues."

We do, in fact, build up "assumptions," expectancies of the world which lead to meaning systems; but these meaning systems are derived from a particular *kind* of world. "Kind" refers to the dominant geographical-spatial construction of the environment. Each people is exposed to a unique spatial environment; for example, the world of one population may be predominantly vertical, that of another horizontal, and this *verticality* or *horizontality* becomes the dominant source for *spatial* assumptions.

The study of spatial distributions, real and perceived, is the cornerstone of investigations of interactions between humans and their physical environments. "The perception of what has been called space is the basic problem of all perception," as Gibson (1950) remarks. "Space perception is . . . the first problem to consider, without a solution for which the other problems remain unclear."

There are three basic kinds of space. *Objective space* is the space of physics and mathematics, measured by universal standards along dimensions of distance, size, shape, and volume. *Ego space* (these are the operations of the ego which make logical objective space) is the individual's adaptation of observed to objective space, to produce a coherent and logically consistent view of sizes, shapes, and distances. *Immanent space* is inner, subjective space, the space of the unconscious, of dreams, of fantasy; it includes the spatial styles and orientations of the individual, and the ingrained spatial notation systems of whole cultures. This is the basic space imposed upon us by the anatomy of our bodies. Consequently, it is also the space involved in the image of our body.

---

[1] This will vary, of course, with the child-rearing practices of a particular culture.

Spatial styles, like any other attributes of personality, are the result of prolonged and complex exchanges between the individual and his environment—and hence derive from all three kinds of space defined above. For experimental convenience, spatial typologies may be broken down into a number of simple dichotomous variables, of which five are considered below:

1. *Diffuse Space vs. Dense Space.* Diffuse space has a spread-apart, scattered quality; dense space suggests compactness, compression, smaller distances between objects.

2. *Delineated vs. Open Space.* Delineated space refers to bounded, constricted, contained, contracted, or centripetal space; open space suggests inward and outward movement, spatial penetration, liberty, and freedom.

3. *Verticality vs. Horizontality.* These are vectors in different spatial planes.

4. *Right and Left in the Horizontal Plane.* These are the two vectors of the horizontal plane.

5. *Up and Down in the Vertical Plane.* These are the two vectors of the vertical plane.

Personal spatial systems may be observed through preferences expressed for symbols representing individual spatial parameters. A recent study (Beck, 1964) employs a Spatial Symbols Test, in which pairs of figures composed of simple geometrical shapes, points, and lines represent the five dichotomous variables described above. Subjects were asked to choose the symbol figure they prefer or like better of *each* of 67 pairs.

The Spatial Symbols Test was administered to 611 subjects. Table 31-1 shows the distribution of responses by age and by profession. The younger subjects were drawn from suburban grammar, junior high, and high schools in the Midwest. Professional psychologists and social workers, including students, were from academic institutions throughout the United States. A factor analysis of the entire sample indicates that five principal clusters of variables accounted for 83 percent of the variance of preference response. Table 13-2 shows the item makeup

Table 13-1 Distribution of the Total Sample

Age Group (yrs.)	N
5– 6	66
9–10	66
13–14	57
17–18	58
	247

Professional Group	N
Academic Psychologists	28
Placement Psychologists	31
Student Psychologists	172
Academic Social Workers	05
Placement Social Workers	15
Student Social Workers	94
Geographers	19
	364

Total Population = 611

of each cluster and the degree of inter-item correlation within each cluster. The number of test items used is reduced from 67 to 50; that is, 17 items are not related to any of the clusters. And, each cluster is composed of items representative of a single predicted spatial parameter.

To determine if developmental processes, as hypothesized, were influential in the acquisition of spatial styles, factor analyses were performed on each age and professional group. The results are present in Table 13-3. (The number of clusters which emerge increases from 5 to 13 years.) The clusters which appear at 5–6 years are composed of items coming from all five spatial scales. It appears that spatial preferences at this age belie an undifferentiated spatial meaning. In short, our five differentiated parameters are seen by young children as fused into a single system. Of the 32 items composing the two clusters, 22 represent the spatial planes (Left-Right; Up-Down; Horizontal-Vertical). This is in line with Cassirer's (1953) hypothesis that left and right and up and down represent the child's first spatial differentiation, and the Piaget and Inhelder (1956) formulation that topological space precedes projective space in development.

Table 13-2 Factor Analysis of the Total Population ($N = 611$)

Item Number	Factor I Correlation	Scale	Item Number	Factor III Correlation	Scale
					Horizontal-Vertical
03	—.60	Diffuse-Dense	08	—.46	"
06	—.58	"	16	—.30	"
11	—.57	"	21	—.34	"
14	—.32	"	27	—.28	"
18	—.61	"	34	—.29	"
23	—.42	"	37	—.39	"
25	—.72	"	41	—.59	"
29	—.76	"	44	—.57	"
31	—.47	"	61	—.56	"
40	—.63	"	67	—.65	"
43	—.68	"			
46	—.68	"		Factor IV	
48	—.64	"			
52	—.53	"	04	—.40	Left-Right
58	—.57	"	07	—.35	"
64	—.63	"	12	—.24	"
66	—.57	"	30	—.31	"
			36	—.40	"
			45	—.54	"
	Factor II		50	—.57	"
		Open-Delineated	56	—.63	"
10	.45		59	—.25	"
15	.35	"			
17	.49	"		Factor V	
24	.37	"			
26	.41	"	09	—.40	Up-Down
28	.35	"	13	—.29	"
33	.32	"	22	—.30	"
38	.32	"	35	—.40	"
47	.29	"	53	—.34	"
49	.36	"	63	—.33	"
55	.56	"			
62	.75	"			

At 9–10 years, the item clusters increase from two to three. Two clusters are now dominated by items coming from a single scale. Spatial differentiation is increasing, and this age is marked by the appearance of an essentially Diffuse-Dense cluster, perhaps a spatial signal of the development of object relations, of an increasing sense of self as distinct from other. When the 9–10 population is divided by sex, the males largely resemble the younger population, while the females, perhaps because of their earlier physical maturation, conform more to the 13–14 year old group. By the age of 13, 5 clusters appear, each composed of items from a single scale. Now space is fully differentiated, relevant and meaningful.

Spatial experience apparently leads to differentiated spatial meaning. If this is the case, a sample of geographers might be expected to display unusual ability to differentiate space. The factor analysis of geographers' responses to the Spatial Symbols Test (see Table 13-4) includes the only bipolar factors (4 and 5) to appear in any population tested. This indicates that in two kinds of spatial items, Left-Right and Up-Down, geographers commonly reverse reference point and variant—they are apt to see an item otherwise considered Left as constituting Right, and items generally chosen as Up as constituting Down, and vice versa. In dealing with spatial planes, geographers are either capable of differentiating space

Table 13-3 Factor Composition in Sub-Populations of the Sample

Group	Number of Factors	Composition		
5–6	2	Factor I:	8 items	Left-Right
			5 items	Open-Delineated
			4 items	Horizontal-Vertical
			2 items	Dense-Diffuse
			2 items	Up-Down
		Factor II:	3 items	Up-Down
			3 items	Horizontal-Vertical
			2 items	Left-Right
			2 items	Dense-Diffuse
			1 item	Open-Delineated
9–10	3	Factor I:	15 items	Diffuse-Dense
			4 items	Open-Delineated
			1 item	Horizontal-Vertical
		Factor II:	7 items	Left-Right
			3 items	Up-Down
			2 items	Horizontal-Vertical
			1 item	Dense-Diffuse
		Factor III:	5 items	Left-Right
			4 items	Up-Down
13–14	5	Factor I:	17 items	Dense-Diffuse
		Factor II:	10 items	Open-Delineated
		Factor III:	9 items	Left-Right
		Factor IV:	7 items	Up-Down
		Factor V:	9 items	Horizontal-Vertical
17–18	5	Factor I:	16 items	Dense-Diffuse
		Factor II:	8 items	Left-Right
		Factor III:	7 items	Open-Delineated
		Factor IV:	8 items	Horizontal-Vertical
		Factor V:	5 items	Up-Down
Social Workers	5	Conforms to scale		
Psychologists	5	Conforms to scale		
Geographers	5	Conforms to scale		

to a finer degree than any other tested group, or are unable to make any stable discriminations—a spatial-occupational hazard!

Finally, what is the meaning of spatial symbol choices, as indicated by preference for one pole or the other within each scale? Scale means and standard deviations for our three professional groups are presented in Table 13-5. (Within each profession, the Spatial Symbols Test discriminates between students and the academic-professional group, and in some instances between the academics and professionals.) Geographers exhibit *very strong* preferences for Diffuse, Delineated, and Right, but are rather ambivalent with regard to Up vs. Down and

Horizontal vs. Vertical. On the Diffuse-Dense and Open-Delineated scales their scores are grossly and significantly different from the rest of the population. They have the highest preference for Horizontal of any group except social worker students. Geographers' ambivalence for Up vs. Down is augmented by the low score scatter (S.D. = .94). Geographers' preference for Left is not unlike the rest of the population (psychologists excepted).

Beyond this brief summary, little can be added. The cognitive and personality correlates of the scales are still in doubt. There is, as yet, no analysis of cross-validating materials. It is abundantly clear that differ-

Table 13-4 Factor Analysis of the Geographers

	Factor I			Factor III	
Item Number	Correlation	Scale	Item Number	Correlation	Scale
					Horizontal-
03	.62	Diffuse-Dense	08	−.55	Vertical
06	.55	"	16	−.46	"
11	.58	"	21	−.58	"
14	.71	"	27	−.39	"
18	.43	"	34	−.63	"
23	.36	"	37	−.77	"
25	.70	"	41	−.41	"
29	.82	"	44	−.82	"
31	.85	"	61	−.66	"
40	.65	"	67	−.55	"
43	.45	"			
46	.56	"		Factor IV	
48	.62	"			
52	.67	"	04	+.83	Left-Right
64	.91	"	07	−.35	"
66	.73	"	30	−.40	"
			32	+.82	"
	Factor II		42	+.76	"
			45	−.63	"
		Open-	65	+.34	"
10	.44	Delineated			
15	.35	"		Factor V	
17	.52	"			
24	.61	"	01	−.29	Up-Down
26	.31	"	09	−.40	"
28	.54	"	19	+.35	"
33	.71	"	35	+.38	"
38	.60	"	39	+.39	"
47	.39	"	53	−.40	"
49	.47	"	37	+.68	"
55	.75	"	60	+.35	"
62	.62	"			

Table 13-5 Scale Means and Standard Deviations in Three Professional Groups

		Total Population	Psychologists			Social Workers			Geographers
			Stud.	Faculty	Professionals	Stud.	Faculty	Professionals	
Diffuse	Mean	10.37	9.86	12.21	10.65	11.40	10.32	10.00	12.58
	S.D.	4.38	4.12	3.54	4.10	4.60	4.15	3.00	4.30
Open	Mean	5.32	6.30	8.23	7.50	4.90	4.15	4.00	4.32
	S.D.	2.15	2.11	2.25	2.34	2.38	2.02	1.50	2.21
Horizontal	Mean	5.32	4.32	5.25	5.30	5.70	5.05	5.00	5.68
	S.D.	2.28	2.15	2.50	2.37	2.45	1.86	1.00	3.13
Down	Mean	2.57	2.51	3.15	3.04	2.60	3.18	3.00	3.00
	S.D.	1.23	1.62	2.25	1.83	.99	1.05	1.50	.94
Left	Mean	3.28	2.97	2.42	2.55	3.00	3.80	4.00	3.74
	S.D.	1.62	1.54	1.60	1.31	1.84	1.72	2.00	1.48

ent professions, age groups, and sexes approach and use spatial variables in significantly varying ways, and hence have differing spatial styles as defined here. But the psychological meaning of space is yet to be determined, and spatial approaches to the perception of the environment require greater elaboration and further classification.

REFERENCES:

Allport, G. W. *Becoming: Basic considerations for a psychology of personality.* New Haven, Conn.: Yale University Press, 1955.

Beck, R. A comparative study of spatial meaning. Unpublished Master's thesis. University of Chicago, 1964.

Binswanger, L. Traum und existenze. In *Ausgewahlte Vorhage uns Aufsatze.* Bern: A. Flancke, 1947.

Cassirer, E. *The philosophy of symbolic forms.* New Haven, Conn.: Yale University Press, 1953.

Gibson, J. J. *Perception of the visual world.* Boston, Mass.: Houghton Mifflin, 1950.

Lowenthal, D. Geography, experience and imagination: Towards a geographical epistemology. *Annals of the Association of American Geographers,* 1961, **51**, 241–260.

Minkowski, E. *Le temps vécu.* Paris, 1939.

Piaget, J., & Inhelder, B. *The child's conception of space.* (Translated by F. J. Langdon and J. L. Lunzer), London: Routledge and Kegan Paul, 1956.

Straus, E. *The primary world of senses.* Glencoe, Ill.: Free Press, 1963.

Scully, V. *The earth, the temple and the gods.* New Haven, Conn.: Yale University Press, 1962.

14 Function and Meaning in the Physical Environment

J. Ruesch and W. Kees

The human *functions of communication* serve the purpose of mediating information across the boundary lines of the human organism or the group organization. Specifically, they solve the problem of how events outside an organism or an organization are represented in terms of information on the inside, and how events on the inside are

From *Nonverbal communication.* Berkeley and Los Angeles: Univ. of Calif. Press, 1964. Reprinted by permission of the authors and publisher.

relayed to the outside. The functions of communication include:

Perception—that is, the reception of incoming signals

Evaluation, which also involves memory and the retention of past experiences as well as decision making

Transmission and expression of information.

For our present purposes we shall be concerned primarily with the processes of perception and transmission, and among the processes of perception with *visual perception* in particular (see Blake and Ramsey, 1951). The human eye is an unparalleled distance receiver, but effective visual perception is relatively late in developing. The child's exploration begins with its immediate environment and moves gradually to more distant objects. Only at the age of five or six do children begin to perceive with some spontaneity such remotely situated objects as airplanes, birds in flight, or ships on the horizon. Not only are the eyes distance receivers, but the number of objects and persons encompassed at a single glance is large. Unlike our hands, which, equipped with the end organs of touch, can explore only a few things at any one time, the act of scanning the horizon creates a situation in which the observer often needs to decide which particular object or person within range should be focused upon or regarded at greater length. Of particular relevance here is the concept of cue, which may be defined as a perception having problem-solving properties. For example, some of the cues in the perception of space (Graham, 1951) are the relative size of objects, the interposition of objects in front of each other, linear perspective of convergent or divergent lines, the presence or absence of texture such as occurs in aerial views, differences in light and shade, as well as those cues related to stereoscopic vision and ocular convergence sensations. Movement in space is perceived by the eye with the help of differences in angular velocity between the fixated moving object and other stationary objects. Both apparent movement—stimuli appearing at intervals in different places but arising from stationary objects—and real movement of actual objects are assessed by such cues as the length of pause between stimuli, duration of exposure, distance between stimuli, and color differences.

Or so perception psychology has it. In terms of communication, however, perception is treated along with evaluation and transmission as components of a single unit. In *social action*, for example, the self is always proprioceptively as well as exteroceptively perceived as part of the situation. Perception in such terms is inseparable from evaluation. Movement is not conceived as proceeding from one point in space to another point—or simply from A to B; the self is additionally considered as a triangulation point. Movement is then assessed as toward or away from the self, or the self on a line of action or away from it. Similarly, distance is not judged in terms of specific physical measurement, but also in terms of biological implications—for example, whether a goal is within walking or reaching distance. In the assessment of social actions, therefore, one or more persons comprise the permanent points of orientation, and events are dealt with not only in terms of their physical characteristics but also in terms of their human origins and impact. Considerations of such an approach illuminate a striking difference between the cultural anthropologist and the novelist on the one hand and the physicist and the sociologist on the other. The former observe, interpret, and act upon events with the human being as the central and permanent frame of reference. The latter treat the individual human being either as an organism made up of molecules or as an anonymous particle in large social structures.

For the communication specialist, the individual still has an identity, and all kinds of information may have relevance; consequently he is primarily interested in the symbolic and referential properties of events. When a person observes a series of events and then wishes to make a statement about them, such a statement has to be represented by signs that are comprehensible to others. The technical aspects of this process are referred to as *codification*. In human interaction the most frequent codification systems are: personal appearance and dress;

gestures; such ordinary actions as those connected with eating and drinking; traces of activity such as footprints and material objects; and simple sounds, spoken words, and written words. Thus any action or thing may have symbolic properties and represent some other event. Knowledge and information enable the human being to reconstruct past events, understand present events, and to predict and anticipate those of the future.

When communicating with each other, people not only exchange messages containing information that refers to outside events, but they also exchange messages referring to the communication process itself. These *metacommunicative messages* include:

The specific instructions given by a sender about the way messages ought to be interpreted and the respective interpretations made by the receiver

Implicit instructions contained in what is commonly referred to as role

Institutionalized instructions, either explicit or implicit, that are inherent in the structure of social situations and the rules governing the flow of messages.

When a person has expressed an idea in words to others, a reaction is necessarily expected. And this reaction contributes to clarify, extend, or alter the original idea. *Feedback*, therefore, refers to the process of correction through incorporation of information about effects achieved. When a person perceives the results produced by his own actions, the information so derived will influence subsequent actions. Feedback of information thus becomes a steering device upon which learning and the correction of errors and misunderstandings are based (Wiener, 1948; 1950).

In short, people communicate by making statements (Ruesch, 1953). These statements are signals that are coded in various prearranged ways. When they impinge upon earlier impressions, they become signs. These signs, in the strictest sense of the word, exist only in the minds of people, because their interpretation is based upon prior agreements. A statement becomes a message when it has been perceived and interpreted by another person. Finally, when sender and receiver can consensually validate an interpretation, then communication has been successful.

Within the framework of modern communication theory, communicative actions are conceived of as events that occur in a certain *context*. The perception and evaluation of signals, both spatial and temporal, cannot be separated from the perception and evaluation of the situation in which they occur. A present-day study of communication, therefore, does not aim at compiling a dictionary of gestures or other motions, but instead emphasizes all possible information about the physical and social settings in which the exchange of messages takes place. In addition to considering symbolic movements and gestures and practical, adaptive actions with communicative value, such a study must take into account all those objects with which human beings surround themselves and which affect social interaction.

To document nonverbal communication, we have chosen and limited ourselves to *visually perceivable codifications*. The majority of the illustrations to be used are from photographs made in the San Francisco Bay area in 1953 and 1954. In our photographic expeditions we wandered from one section to another in an attempt to record human activities and the traces of existence in a variety of situations. Candid and often very rapid shooting was used to capture some of the intentional and unintentional statements made by people as we found them, and by the shopkeepers, decorators, architects, and private home owners whose establishments and houses we saw. We used natural lighting whenever possible. Reflections on store windows or other such blemishes typical of either natural conditions or traces of living were photographed much as any pedestrian might see them.

THE ROLE OF CONTEXT IN THE INTERPRETATION OF ACTION

The unity of the thirteenth century was contrasted by Henry Adams (1904) with twentieth-century multiplicity. It may well be that our contemporary concern with social structure and interpersonal relations should be regarded as an attempt to bring some order into the complexities and discrepancies of modern life. Today almost everyone becomes involved in undesired and often changing roles, and many must carry on an incessant struggle for identity. The fluidity of modern life, with its reduction of the personal, almost forces individuals to use functional concepts related to the identification of social situations and social roles. These concepts help the individual to establish a temporary operational definition of the identity of the participants, thus facilitating initial interaction.

The recognition of *roles* is implemented through the perception and interpretation of a variety of strategic cues. The speediest assignment of a role becomes possible when custom or circumstance determines the use of uniforms and one person is able to address another as "Officer," "Waiter," "Nurse," or "Sergeant." Roles may be indicated also through material objects; tools, implements, and machines sometimes identify such persons as welders, musicians, or brakemen. Sometimes a variety of cues throws light on the identification of members of particular trades—when uniforms, props, movements, and even language characteristics contribute to identification. Usually, however, such identification is far more complex, since any one person may fulfill multiple roles at the same time—roles defined in terms of age, sex, occupation, family position, citizenship—and may shift through a number of such transient roles as those of a pedestrian, passenger, spectator, or consumer. The cues singled out and fixed upon are also determined not only by the subjective needs and expectations of the participants but by the total context of the situation. For example, a waiter is not —needless to say—addressed as "Waiter" when he is in any other than his professional context.

Roles are *multipolar phenomena* regulating the communication systems of two or more persons. In some situations one pole of the role system is specified and the other is fluid. The concept of role of a traffic officer fixes his relationship to those he directs, whereas the drivers and pedestrians have more latitude of action and the possibility of changing their own roles. Such asymmetries are less common in two-person situations where the reciprocal roles of mother and child, husband and wife, or pilot and navigator are more rigidly defined. Two-person relationships are a function of the context in which they occur, and may be superseded or crisscrossed by other interpersonal relations. In nonverbal communication, the interpretation of mutual roles serves the purpose of clarifying the verbal, gestural, and action messages that people consciously convey to each other—hence, roles are also *metacommunicative statements*. Those who are quick to recognize roles and are aware of the shifting nature of roles are at an advantage in dealing with social situations. The number of misunderstandings that occur through a failure to recognize a change in role is staggering. For example, at one moment a man may talk and act as a father, in the next in his capacity as a husband, and then again as a tennis player. Others who participate in the conversation may or may not follow these shifts with comprehension. It is scarcely accidental that some of the most worldly and discerning of novelists—for example, Henry James, Marcel Proust, Ford Madox Ford, Gustave Flaubert, Thomas Marin, E. M. Forster, Conrad Aiken, and F. Scott Fitzgerald—are continuously and even obsessively preoccupied with the concept of role and its importance in shaping the incongruities, ironies, and tragedies of human existence. James' *The Sacred Fount* (1910) takes the awareness of role as its subject matter almost with a vengeance, as does Flaubert's *Bouvard and Pécuchet* (1954); its significance for individual representatives of two cultures is extremely marked in Forster's *A Passage to India* (1924).

Relationships as defined through roles are not limited to individuals, but are meaningful in identifying *groups* vis-à-vis each other—for example, spectators and players, labor and management, and civilians and soldiers. In such circumstances individual identity is submerged and persons are regarded as members of large organizations. Since large groups rarely interact with each other—except perhaps in time of war—spokesmen for each group transact business in the name of their organizations. Upon the skillful implementation of shifting roles at such levels may depend strikes, trade treaties, international tension, and possibly war.

A particular kind of role is expressed through the symbols of *status and prestige*. Society is vertically stratified, and whatever names are used to denote prestige groups and social classes, the identification marks of status differences are known and recognized. In one culture, they may distinguish peasant from nobleman or party member from nonmember; in our culture, they are the signs that identify lower, middle, and upper classes. Although people congregate socially in separate groups, by necessity they must cross class boundaries as well. The manager of a factory deals with his employees, the battalion commander "mixes" with his soldiers while on duty, and the teacher as a matter of course interacts with his students. Although such confrontations continually occur, status characteristics are carefully preserved and identified by dress or uniform or are conveyed by marks of age, sex, skill, or wealth. Just as roles are communicative statements without which verbal communication as we know it would be impossible, symbols of status explain aspects of power and prestige—imaginary or real—that an individual possesses or wishes to suggest he may possess.

In the practice of communication, we are continually assessing our material surroundings, making attempts at identifying others and their roles, their status, and their group membership in order to arrive at a kind of diagnosis that will combine all these features into an integral pattern: the *social situation*. In the truest sense, it is the social situation that determines the context and nature of any communicative exchange. It would be unthinkable for anyone to disrobe in the middle of Park Avenue, even though wearing a bathing suit, but such an activity would pass without a glance at Coney Island. Such a strict definition of behavior takes into account not only implementations but the kind and style of verbal communication as well. Such settings as night clubs, conference rooms, Turkish baths, and vestry rooms rigidly define what may or may not be said or done.

Once a social situation has been identi-

Figure 14–1

fied, persons automatically apply *rules* of behavior they feel to be pertinent. These rules may be determined in part by the action itself, particularly when the application of inappropriate rules might result in personal inconvenience or even injury or death. On other occasions misinterpretation or violation of rules may bring about reprimands, social ostracism, or civil censure. However, personal survival would not be possible if we could not occasionally break, modify, or improvise rules. This is particularly true when one social situation merges into another.

Just as scientists in modern field theory have distinguished between field forces—that is, the parameters of the system—and variables that pertain to the action itself, so do we all distinguish between social context and communicative action. Whereas the parameters of a communicative situation are defined through physical and social context, roles, and rules, the process under observation is defined by the activity of signaling. The parameters thus become interpretive devices—that is, metacommunicative devices—for the understanding of the signals.

CODIFICATION IN MATERIAL TERMS

Signaling by means of word, gesture, or other action by no means exhausts the possibilities of communication; on the contrary, a whole series of situations exists in which people influence, guide, and direct each other by means of signals that are embedded in the material environment. Objects as systems of codification are used pervasively in every walk of life—in business and at home, ranging from household gadgets to articles of furniture. Architectural style, interior decoration, and lighting conditions, for example, also play significant parts in communication. Thus there is little doubt that the nonverbal and often unconscious exchange of messages codified in material terms fulfills all the criteria of language; for brevity's sake, we shall subsequently refer to it as *object language.*

The language of objects is outspokenly used in the world of trade, where shop windows and commercial exhibits are arranged with the undisguised purpose of attracting customers. Rarely if ever does a verbal description achieve the same effect as an exhibit of merchandise; no merchant would attempt to influence his customers through the display and arrangement of things if it were not for the fact that the success of such nonverbal methods can be evaluated in terms of dollars and cents. In this field, consequently, no conjecture is involved. The intent to influence and sell is unconcealed. And the fact that objects on display are bought would indicate that the desired effect is frequently achieved. Objects for commercial display, as they appear in showcases and store windows, usually convey brief and simple statements; in private homes, statements through objects become

more complex and the intentions of the owners far less open and transparent.

The effects that objects achieve in terms of their communicative value are dependent not only upon arrangement but also upon variations of *material, shape, and surface.* Any material evokes tactile and thermal images—of smoothness, roughness, hardness, softness, coldness, and warmth. Wood, metal, brick, and textiles produce a variety of anticipations of touch sensations. Wood against wood, metal against brick, a stiffened fabric against a soft and pliable one—all set up "chords" of tactile images that often produce sharp and immediate physical and emotional reactions. Metal may be highly polished or finished with a dull patina; containers may be opaque, translucent, or transparent. Surfaces—whether raised, carved, rough, or smooth—when exposed to light reflections, are likely not only to express the moods of those who shaped them, but also to suggest such subtle and abstract manners as interpenetration or merely the simple adjoining of boundaries.

Once an object exists, it may be used in a variety of ways. A trash receptacle can be identified by its design, and a hole in its top instructs, "Put your trash through this opening." The one in Figure 14–2 announces, through its weathered state, some idea of its age and use; the handles indicate that it can be lifted, carried, and tossed. The *arrangement* of similarly shaped objects reinforces or attenuates the impression made by the single object. Several rounded and hollow articles enhance the impression of containment and maneuverability. For example, the display of stockings, mounted on several models of legs cut off below the knee, puts over the idea of stockings, legs, quality, diversity, and whatever other connotations the spectator wishes to assign to it. Form is conveyed not only through the shape of the individual object, but also by way of the character of a layout. Buttons, for example, framed in ordered rows as if they were collectors' items, suggest plentiful supply, ready availability, specialization; and to some they may hold the promise of expert service.

Although standardization has limited expression through personal craftsmanship, an

Figure 14–2

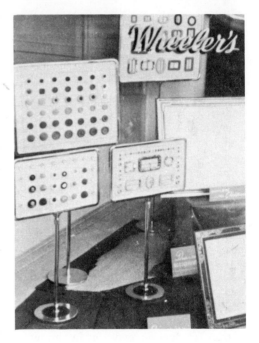

object can nonetheless be connected with the personality of its maker; or it can be connected with its owner; or a combination of objects may be linked to the person who made the arrangement. The selection of objects and the nature of their grouping constitute nonverbal expressions of thoughts, needs, conditions, or emotions. Thus, when people shape their surroundings, they introduce man-made *order*. Such arrangements may follow a rigid geometrical order based on symmetry or repetition from which randomness is carefully excluded. In other arrangements, even in carefully arranged display, order may occasionally be disturbed through true accident; an object or a carton of food may move from its place and remain where it fell. Between these extremes are several other possibilities. A comfortable state of informality may be achieved by throwing cushions customarily used outdoors into a wicker basket in the living room; a shop may hint at its readiness to deliver goods by displaying flowers as though they had been casually tossed into the window.

Order implies the notion of arrangement of parts into a *whole*. When a person has to deal with thousands of separate items, whether they are objects or pieces of information, his problem is one of simplification. In object language the arrangement of many small items into a whole achieves brevity and compactness of expression, just as abstraction unites many subordinate thoughts into an overall idea. A variety of methods may be used to achieve such a whole.

The codification of ideas in material terms, in regard to both small objects and more sizable constructions, is largely related to notions of order. But, unlike the order dictated by logic, *the order of objects* depends largely upon physical reality. The laws of physics determine the construction of an object. The material determines its appearance and usage. Human needs dictate an object's function and shape. Agreements between people govern the manner of arrangement of several objects, and during any historical period these styles were known to most people within a particular cultural group. Thus there was possible a shared understanding of the use and interpretation of object language. However, above and beyond all this, and in a way similar to pictorial representation, objects can become a kind of international language. In the last analysis, practical objects are relatively free of the limitations imposed by class, caste, and race; instead they are controlled by considerations of a more universal nature: the ability to serve men at a given time for a given purpose.

APPEAL AND SOCIAL CONTROL THROUGH MATERIAL THINGS

Verbal commands, suggestions, and hints are common ways of influencing people in a direct manner. However, the resistance to such approaches increases with insistence and repetition—drawbacks that are less likely to present themselves when indirect and nonverbal methods of influence are employed. Such methods involve three principal lines of approach: the first involves exhibiting objects with an implicit appeal to perception; the second involves the arrangement of articles in such a way that they can be used or tried out, where the appeal is essentially kinesthetic and muscular; and the third involves control of the traffic lanes on the highways, sidewalks, and interiors of stores or houses. All three methods involve control of social situations by using the predictable needs of human beings for specific ends or by arranging physical facilities in the hope that people will not bother to change them. Who shall meet whom, when, where, and perhaps for how long can thus be determined in advance.

APPEAL TO PERCEPTION

Stores and places of entertainment not only must identify themselves so that the customers can come to see them; in turn they must, if they wish to survive, *appeal selectively* to customers who need their goods and services. The specialty store in particular has the task of attracting customers whose needs and interests may result in a business transaction.

An initial distinction among potential customers lies in differentiating men and women, the old and the young, workmen and luxury trade. Women, for example, are not likely to be interested in engines; indeed, most women consider an engine or a boat more of a competitor than an object of curiosity. Exhibitions of hardware or motor parts will not usually stop a woman passing on the street. Men, in contrast, rarely look at window displays of "foundation garments," except surreptitiously. Jewelers and other luxury stores make a particular appeal to persons currently interested in a member of the opposite sex.

The cues that serve as recognition signals for a *particular clientele* are of considerable subtlety, and are often implicit in the arrangement of display as a whole. The mural in front of Dougherty's bar has as its subject matter a woodland lake scene. It not only covers the entire front, making its point about privacy, but also, in one of its details—the meeting of the elks—has something to say about isolation as a problem of lonely people in a big city. The permanence of the mural gets over the idea that it is an anchorage for neighborhood regulars. In contrast, the South Pacific island atmosphere offered by a fashionable restaurant beckons both the Pacific traveler and the sentimentalist; the artists' bar extends an invitation to those who want to throw off the yoke of conformity and rub elbows with actual or would-be Bohemians; the shopper for antiques is alerted by the elegant formality of the lettering, the symmetry of the building, and the classic art motif.

The problem of facilitating the meeting of buyers and sellers is met only through cues of mutual identification, since some people tend to react more to the *line of approach*—the "how" of action—than to marks of identity—the "what" of action. The line of approach is expressed sometimes with greater urgency in the intimations of doorways, which set the expectations of those who enter. To promise, disappoint, intimidate, guide, or restrict people in their thoughts and actions is an art in itself; the

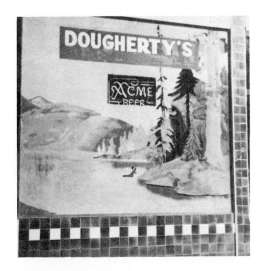

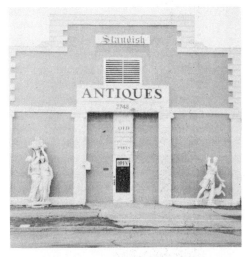

Figure 14–3

efficient interpretation of such statements frequently lies in going far beyond their literal meaning. In addition, to overcome the feelings of anxiety, indecision, and reserve that frequently arise when people are asked to commit themselves before they are familiar with a situation, many establishments extend special invitations through conspicuously displayed signs and notices. A commercial establishment may express its special concerns by assuming a specific line of approach defining the social techniques and forms of relatedness. What is suggested here is not exclusiveness of identity but conformity in terms of action.

The whitewash lettering announces the changing variety of merchandise in the sec-

ondhand store. The unobstructed view into the store invites rummaging for "finds" inside. The verbal announcement of Mary's hamburgers indicates, through the presence of the flowers and the handwritten sign, that atmosphere as well as food goes into the making of a restaurant, and that this one is homelike, personal, and improvised. The airline's display takes the line that the destination advertised is one of lush foliage where a hula girl eagerly awaits the passenger.

Various *dimensions* may be used to evoke fantasies and bodily sensations. Three-dimensional dummies, clothed or unclothed, do not seem to convey sensations of warmth or sensuality. To produce such effects, dec-

Figure 14-4

orators usually fall back on photographs or paintings. However, the idea of sensuality can sometimes be relayed to the spectator by the isolation of parts of the body or clothing, leaving it to the individual's capacity for fantasy to fit bodies into clothing and to complete what is left unexpressed. Apparently a two-dimensional reproduction or a three-dimensional facsimile in close-up perspective is more effective for such purposes than an elaborate naturalistic model that acts as a hindrance to fantasy.

DESIGN FOR MEETING

The life of domestic animals is, among other things, controlled through the erection of fences, flap doors, or the placement of food and water in particular locations. Although the control of human situations is implemented through verbal and nonverbal actions, manipulation of barriers, openings, and other physical arrangements is rather helpful. Meeting places can be appropriately rigged so as to regulate human traffic and, to a certain extent, the network of communication. An auditorium in which chairs are placed in parallel rows, where people cannot face each other, is unlikely to provoke much discussion; an amphitheater, on the contrary, makes a lively discussion more probable, because people are able to see each other.

Even particular kinds of human interaction are frequently steered, facilitated, or modified by the *physical nature of establishments*, which may indicate where possible meetings may occur—in a car, on a sidewalk, or in a store. Announcements of special meeting places for the transaction of particular tasks are recognizable through their strategic location and special format—in lettering, shape, and color. Although the

Figure 14–5

content of the statements may be expressed in words, recognition from a distance is based upon nonverbal cues. The post office announces, through a particular type of hood, the existence of a mailbox specifically designed for the motorist. Since this is an innovation, the government feels the necessity of pointing out its use in verbal terms as well. The fire department, in keeping with the emergency nature of its function, is more succinct. The point is implied that any person, after breaking the glass and pushing the button, will meet the representatives of the fire department at this spot a few minutes later. The very architecture of the drive-in is designed to allow the customer to enjoy the customary surroundings of his car without the effort of getting out or dressing for the occasion. However, if the customer is of a more gregarious and enterprising nature, he is still free to park his car and eat inside.

Meeting places are not confined to outdoors. The interiors of both stores and houses are honeycombed with potential sites for interpersonal activities. Physical arrangements elicit expectations; they may instruct to some degree: "This, and not that"; "Here, not there." Most stores make sure that their customers are immediately confronted by merchandise. By being forced to walk between displays of merchandise, the customers are informed of what is available. Care is taken to place chairs and tables for comfort at strategic locations, and in full view of the merchandise, with a salesman or salesgirl in readiness to take the order.

In private homes, arrangements of *furniture* and accessory objects likewise designate and control the "where" and "how" of interaction. Such factors as the nature of the lighting, the placing of tables, and the grouping of chairs and couches may further modify interpersonal exchanges. Chairs

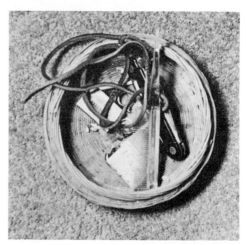

Figure 14–6

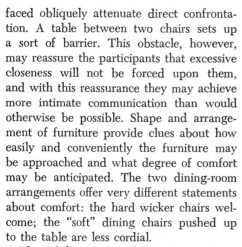

faced obliquely attenuate direct confrontation. A table between two chairs sets up a sort of barrier. This obstacle, however, may reassure the participants that excessive closeness will not be forced upon them, and with this reassurance they may achieve more intimate communication than would otherwise be possible. Shape and arrangement of furniture provide clues about how easily and conveniently the furniture may be approached and what degree of comfort may be anticipated. The two dining-room arrangements offer very different statements about comfort: the hard wicker chairs welcome; the "soft" dining chairs pushed up to the table are less cordial.

The subdivision of a house into separate rooms creates physical and psychological barriers that force the residents to stake out *private corners* for themselves. The usual bachelor quarters are in themselves one big private corner, but in a family dwelling these special places are reduced to diminutive size. The lady's dressing table, for example, is organized around principles that are not challenged by the other members of the household, and hence stakes its claim as a place of refuge. The private corner contains a statement of sufferance as well as of resistance: would the boxer be allowed his special place on the couch if he were not decorative? A unique phenomenon—a sort of communal private corner—

is the little straw basket dish, about which one of the owners explained: "That is where we empty our pockets."

REFERENCES:

Adams, H. *Mont St. Michel and Chartres.* Boston and New York: Houghton Mifflin, 1904.

Blake, R. R., & Ramsey, G. V. *Perception: An approach to personality.* New York: Ronald Press, 1951.

Flaubert, G. *Bouvard and Pécuchet.* (Translated by T. W. Earp & G. W. Stonier). Norfolk, Conn.: New Directions, 1954.

Forster, E. H. *A passage to India.* New York: Harcourt, Brace, 1924.

Graham, H. C. Visual perception. In S. S. Stevens (Ed.), *Handbook of experimental psychology.* New York: Wiley, 1951. Pp. 868–920.

James, H. *The sacred fount.* New York: Scribners, 1910.

Ruesch, J. Synopsis of the theory of human communication. *Psychiatry,* 1953, **16,** 215–243.

Wiener, N. *Cybernetics, or control and communication in the animal and the machine.* New York: Wiley, 1948.
Wiener, N. *The human use of human beings.* Boston: Houghton Mifflin, 1950.

15 Some Psychological Theory and Predictions of Cultural Differences

M. H. Segall, D. T. Campbell, and M. J. Herskovits

While the proposition that culture influences perception is highly plausible, there exist very few cross-cultural data that unequivocally support this point of view. On the other hand, a considerable accumulation of studies report, almost without exception, cultural differences in behavior that could very well indicate differences in perception. As a result, even without substantiation in full, the prevailing view in the cross-cultural literature is that perceptual responses are subject to cultural influences. Recognizing both the plausibility of the proposition and the difficulties encountered in attempts to substantiate it, we undertook in 1956 to formulate a theoretical rationale that would predict specific kinds of differences in illusion susceptibility, and we then embarked on a cross-cultural study that found them. This paper will be devoted to a discussion of that rationale and of related theoretical issues.

Most generally, our interest in cultural differences in perception relates to the nativist-empiricist controversy that has long existed in perceptual theorizing. As we stated when the study was proposed:

> Not only will the findings be of interest to those concerned with the comparative study of culture, they will also contribute to the theory of perception, particularly

From *The Influence of Culture on Visual Perception* by Marshall H. Segall, Donald T. Campbell and Melville J. Herskovits, copyright © 1966, by The Bobbs-Merrill Company, Inc., reprinted by permission of the authors and publishers.

with respect to the role of experience. Currently there are a number of lines of development in the theory of visual perception which create a new interest in the nativist-empiricist controversy. There is new evidence which emphasizes the role of early visual experience in setting the base for adult perceptual processes. Clearly relevant to this topic would be findings on perceptual illusions among peoples whose visual worlds are quite different from that of the European (Herskovits, Campbell, and Segall, 1956, p. 2).

As this excerpt implies, data from the psychological laboratory that support an empiricistic theory of perception enhance the expectation of finding cross-cultural differences in perception. Conversely, of course, cross-cultural data that demonstrate perceptual differences would provide support for an empiricistic theory and weaken the nativists' case. Allport and Pettigrew (1957, p. 105) referred to the nativist-empiricist issue in their report of research with Zulu children and the rotating trapezoidal illusion:

> To gain light on this dispute psychologists have often asked, "How about primitive peoples?" If we can find a tribe or a culture where relevant past experience can be ruled out, we can then determine whether the perception resembles that of Western peoples. If it does so, then the argument for nativism is presumably stronger.

Then Allport and Pettigrew added a caveat:

> . . . we do not believe that comparative perceptual studies on Western and on primitive peoples can solve this particular riddle.

While the caveat is appropriate, we would stress the relevance of data like those collected by Allport and Pettigrew to the central issue of the nativist-empiricist controversy, namely, the manner and extent of experiential influence on visual perception. Although cross-cultural data may not settle the issue, there are classes of such data that could substantially illuminate the problem. In the study manual we prepared for our fieldworkers we summarized our conceptualization of the problem as follows:

> If the cross-cultural differences in extent of illusion are found, the initial explanatory effort would be focused on differences in the usual visual environment. For this reason, it is very important that details of the visual environment of each group be recorded on the form provided. Such details include the typical form of houses, the maximum distance at which objects are typically viewed, whether or not vistas over land or water occur, typical games, skills, artistic training, and other aspects of culture that might affect habits of inference from line drawings.
>
> Two cultural factors are to be of particular significance for this investigation. In the carpentered western world such a great proportion of artifacts are rectangular that the habit of interpreting obtuse and acute angles as rectangular surfaces extended in space is a very useful one. Such an inference pattern would generate many of the line illusions here tested. In a culture where rectangles did not dominate, this habit might be absent. Similarly, elliptical retinal images are interpreted as circles extended in the third dimension. This inference pattern might be absent where objects are truly elliptical in cross-section.
>
> Another cultural factor which might be related to illusions is two-dimensional representation of three-dimensional objects. Perspective drawing is a most pervasive feature of Euroamerican culture. It is a substantial feature of the visual world from childhood on. Children in this culture from a very early age attempt to make representations of this kind themselves. The technique or conventions involved may be related to the habits of inference which some illusions illustrate (Herskovits, Campbell, and Segall, 1956, pp. 2–3).

It should now be clear that from the start our general theoretical position has been that if cross-cultural differences in responses to perceptual illusions were found, they would reflect learned differences in perceptual habits. Thus the discovery of such differences would lend support to an empiricist theory of visual perception. Let us now spell out this position in detail.

THE NATIVIST-EMPIRICIST CONTROVERSY

Two decades ago, Boring termed the nativist-empiricist controversy "one of the two dreariest topics in experimental psychology" (1942, p. 28). However, his review of the topic indicated that no matter how fruitless the controversy may have appeared at times during its long history—particularly as manifested in the speculative efforts of the eighteenth and nineteenth centuries—many issues involved in theories of space-perception had not yet been fully resolved. Subsequent reviews of the controversy, provided by Gibson (1950), Hilgard (1951), Allport (1955), and Hochberg (1957), among others, make it clear that however dull or fruitless the controversy may have seemed, it is not dead. Moreover, as Hochberg notes,

> . . . the perception of space, depth, and distance is frequently treated in the textbooks as a solved problem. Despite the fact that some restricted areas of precise and applicable knowledge exist, however, the basic problems in this area are completely *unsolved* and we must launch a fresh attack on what is historically one of the oldest of the systematic problems of psychology (1957, p. 83).

In 1950 Gibson introduced his treatment of visual perception by stating that

> . . . the perception of what has been called space is the basic problem of all perception. Space perception is . . . the first problem to consider, without a solution for which other problems remain unclear. That a solution is lacking, most psychologists would agree.

And in very concise terms Gibson states the problem.

> The physical environment has three dimensions; it is projected by light on a sensitive surface of two dimensions; it is perceived nevertheless in three dimensions. How can the lost third dimension be restored in perception? This is the problem of how we perceive space (1950, p. 2).

Allport points out that the nativist-empiricist controversy, as it applies to space-perception, is not an all-or-none issue.

> Scarcely anyone, now or earlier, would be found on the nativist side with respect to all the phenomena of perception (1955, p. 86).

It is also true that scarcely any of the modern-day empiricists would entirely rule out certain perceptual potentials that seem to be part of the human biological endowment. Hilgard, in an advocacy of the role of learning in perception, admits that

> . . . the side of the nativists in the argument has a good deal of support (1951, p. 96).

Our view on this general issue represents essentially a "moderate" empiricist position, one that hypothesizes that the pattern of visual experiences in the lifetime of a person can *modify* his perceptions of objects in space. These modifications might not be drastic, but they are subtly manifested in tendencies to perceive the world in accord with pervasively learned expectations. Such phenomena as size- and shape-constancies and the distorted room phenomena (Ames, 1949; Cantril, 1950; Kilpatrick, 1952; Ittelson, 1960) seem to us, as to their originators, obvious examples of perceptual tendencies shaped largely by experience.

This view seems to us to be shared by most contemporary theorists of perception, even by those, e.g., Gibson (1950, 1960) and Pratt (1950), who perhaps give less weight to experience than most. For example, Gibson, while emphasizing that many perceptual responses do not require prior learning, acknowledges that experience contributes to perception:

> The perceiver who has observed the world from many points of view, as we say, is literally one who has traveled about and used his eyes. That is, he has looked at the furniture of the earth from many station points. The more he has done so, the more likely it is that he has isolated the invariant properties of things —the permanent residue of the changing perspectives (1960, p. 220).

Closest to the view that has shaped the present research is that of Brunswik and the Ames group, for whom perception is "the process of apprehending probable significances." Allport has succinctly summarized this position as follows: In the process of perceiving an object, the past experience of the organism plays an important part. Basic to the perception process ". . . is the fact that the organism has built up certain *assumptions* about the world in which it lives. These assumptions, which are usually *unconscious* [result in] the attaching of significances to cues" (1955, pp. 278–279).

Our general theoretical position can perhaps best be epitomized by Brunswik's phrase "ecological cue validity" (Brunswik and Kamiya, 1953; Brunswik, 1956).[1] It involves some general assumptions that Brunswik summarized as "probabilistic functionalism." It is hypothesized that the visual system is functional in general, although not in every specific utilization. The modes of operation are what they are because they are useful in the statistical average of utilizations.

When this is applied to optical illusions, it is hypothesized that the illusion taps a process that is in general functional, although it is misleading in the particular instance because of "ecological unrepresentativeness"; that is, this type of situation is unlike the general run of situations to which the process is functionally adapted and adaptive. Thus, in the illusion of induced movement, it is ecologically unusual for the great bulk of the visual environment to move while a small segment remains fixed. If one creates such a situation artificially, a compelling illusion, or mistaken judgment, occurs. For some constant errors or illusions, we accept nonfunctional explanations, for example, the attribution of perceptual errors to the coarse grain of the retinal mosaic of

[1] Note here a difference in our use of the term "ecological" from that common in anthropology. Following Brunswik, and in some consistency with sociological and evolutionary theory, we use the term to refer to the total environment, including both man-made artifacts and the natural environment of flora, fauna, and geological structure. Anthropological usage restricts the term "ecology" to the latter.

rods and cones, the finite speed of neural transmission, etc. But illusions of both types require an hypothesis as to why they should be so, and for complex total processes of the kind under study here, the anatomical-limitation approach is not judged to be plausible.

It might be argued that the term "perceptual illusion" is essentially meaningless since all perception, insofar as it is not strictly stimulus determined, is "illusory." It might be further argued that since the sensing organism functions as a transducer, so that the attributes of sensations and of external stimuli are never identical, perception is *never* stimulus determined. On the basis of a similar line of thought, Mueller (1965) argues that it is misleading to speak of perceptual illusions as if they constituted a separate class of visual-response phenomena. Boring, too, has argued (1942, p. 245) that when the general laws of perception are known, the illusions also will be understood. Still, we find the concept of "illusion" useful in designating those infrequent cases in which one mode of cognition (e.g., unaided vision) is persistently, and in a constant direction, in disagreement with the collective product of other modes of cognition, such as measurement, superimposition, vision aided by reduction screens, and sighting along tilted surfaces. Although it is little remarked upon, in the great bulk of cases visual estimates of magnitude are useful and nondeceptive. Error of fine degree is, of course, present, but by emphasizing systematic bias, or constant error, the psychologist readily distinguishes between problems of illusion and problems of acuity.

Historically, there has been great concern with various geometric figures and with "illusory," or nonveridical, perceptual responses to them. As Boring pointed out (1942, p. 239), "a knowledge of the prin-ciples governing the abnormal perception of extent (as in the case of perceptual illusions) would certainly help with the understanding of the normal cases."

Comprehensive reviews of various theoretical accounts of the best-known illusions are available (e.g. Sanford, 1908; Woodworth, 1938; Boring, 1942; Osgood, 1953; Allport, 1955, and others). Two of the accounts described in these reviews are exceedingly relevant to the present research. Brentano (1892, 1893) thought that a significant feature of the Müller-Lyer figure (Figure 15-1) was the fact that the context segments are made up of lines forming acute and obtuse angles with the horizontal comparison segments. He argued that acute angles tend to be overestimated and obtuse angles underestimated and that such misestimates of the angles in the Müller-Lyer figure would result in a compression or expansion of the horizontal segments.

The rationale for including the Müller-Lyer figure in our research is based upon a theoretical interpretation that bears some similarity to Brentano's explanation of this figure. Boring (1942) describes another explanation, attributed to Thiery (1895, 1896), which perhaps comes even closer to the view that will be presented below. According to Boring, Thiery referred the phenomenon to perspective. He saw the illusion in the third dimension, as a sawhorse. The acute-angled figure would be a sawhorse with the legs extending away from the observer and with the back near and hence relatively small, whereas the obtuse-angled figure would be a sawhorse with the legs approaching the observer, with the belly far away and therefore relatively large.

The view that optical illusions are products of the same processes that mediate normal visual achievements is, as we have just seen, not at all peculiar to Brunswik.

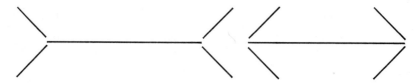

Figure 15–1. The Müller-Lyer illusion.

It is at least implicit in the bulk of older discussions of optical illusions, including those of Brentano and Thiery cited above. A modern revival of these older empiricist perspective theories emphasizes the role of perceptual constancy and, in particular, constancy scaling as factors contributing to the optical illusions (Tausch, 1954; Holst, 1957; Gregory, 1962, 1963; and Green and Hoyle, 1963). For example, Gregory (1962, p. 16), argues that the mechanism of constancy scaling "could produce distortion if it were misplaced, and that all the known illusions have features which commonly indicate depth by perspective. It is also clear in every case that the illusions go the right way; those parts of the figures which would normally be further away in 3-D space appear too large in the illusion figures."

Moreover, the psychologist and physiologist of the visual system are keenly aware of the inferential, hypothetical, fallible, problematic nature of perception. External objects are in no sense directly known, and any simple visual system is equivocal in that it gives identical readings for widely disparate external events. Brunswik, for example, emphasized that actual, functional visual systems, in confronting this problem, use many cues applied in combination. He emphasized that even cues of only partial, or probabilistic, validity would be useful in reducing equivocality in complex, cue-rich natural settings. Optical-illusion situations, however, typically lack this richness and hence help to isolate a single cue, but under conditions not typical of its normal utilization. In a prototypic study, therefore, Brunswik and Kamiya (1953) attempted to compute—from analyses of photographs of typical scenes of numerous discrete objects —the "ecological cue validity" of various Gestalt principles of visual organization. These cues (proximity, similarity, continuity, and so forth) have been demonstrated by the Gestalt psychologists to contribute to the organization of elements of the visual field. They are interpreted by Brunswik to be cues as to which sense-data segments belong together as cosymptoms of a single object. He finds cue validity correlations on the order of .20, and judges that these low but statistically significant, functionally de-

pendent cue validities are useful, and in fact used, in the visual inference system.

Thus, our theoretical system hypothesizes (1) *that the visual perceptual system uses numerous cues of low and probabilistic (but still positive) validity*, and (2) *that optical illusions demonstrate the function of normally useful cues but provide atypical visual performance settings*. In other words, psychological factors affect the probability that certain inference tendencies rather than others will be acquired and that under certain unusual conditions these tendencies will lead to nonveridical perceptions. So-called geometric illusions provide examples of such unusual conditions.

This orientation obviously calls for specific hypotheses of ecology-function relationships. In the long run the theory must point to the specific ecological cue validities being misexploited in each optical illusion. This task is an unfinished one. Its incompleteness is the major source of weakness in the explanations offered here. However, *afunctional* explanations are regarded as weaker and as implicitly invoking "inexplicability" as an explanation. Chance, coincidence, and so forth are plausible on occasion, but not for learned functions based upon numerous opportunities for differential reinforcement nor even for innate functions involving many complex genetic factors.

The next step in our reasoning is a direct extension of the ecological cue validity theory: (3) *if human groups differ in their visual inference tendencies, it is because their visual environments differ*; that is, the cues in their ecologies have different validities. Accepting this implication leads us to regard our theoretical task as unfinished until we can point to ecological differences that functionally relate to the perceptual inference differences. We assume that neither by learning nor by genetic selection would populations have come to differ on these perceptual processes unless the ecological validities of the processes differed.

It should be noted that owing to modern genetic theory it is no longer possible to explain "inexplicable" group differences, when plausible environmental explanations are lacking, by attributing them to arbitrary genetic differences. Most manifest structural features and their related functional processes are determined by scores of genes. On these genes, each human population is heterozygous and differs from other populations only in relative allele or gene frequencies. These specific gene frequencies are maintained by selection pressures. Populations of the size we are concerned with do not differ from one another unless selection pressures differ. Selection-pressure differences would result where different environments made different structures and processes optimal. In the case of the perceptual processes under study, this would require theories as to how ecological differences made different perceptual functions optimal. Such theories would likewise be useful in explaining learned differences, for the ecology that edits mutation and genetic recombination is usually also the ecology that edits the trial-and-error processes of learning, unless the ecology has been undergoing rapid change.

Thus today, both empiricist theories, based upon a learning process, and hereditary theories, based upon a mutation-recombination selection process, require functional theories relating process to ecology. The "inexplicability" of a group difference is no longer an argument favoring the choice of a hereditary as opposed to an empiricist or learning explanation.

The final step in our preliminary argument is (4) *that given a hereditary and a learning explanation that both fit the data, the learning (empiricist) explanation is the more plausible.* Since the experimental psychology evidence on perception that justifies this position is not generally known, it seems fitting to sample the literature here. Two classes of studies are involved, with both human and animal data for each.

There are, first, the studies of effects of the lack of visual experience in infancy. For human beings, these studies come from cases where surgical operations have given sight to those who have lacked it from birth or early infancy (Latta, 1904; Senden, 1932; Hebb, 1949; and London, 1960). These studies uniformly report that the interpretation of visual data has to be learned; that even for the identification of simple shapes familiar to touch, there is no matching of visual outline with tactual outline until a process of looking-while-touching has taken place; that even when objects can be identified as discrete, the perception of distance is lacking, with most objects being seen as near. Without learning, then, the visual data provide a "blooming, buzzing confusion," to use William James's famous phrase.

As for animals, Riesen's (1947, 1958) studies of chimpanzees show that experimentally induced infantile restrictions of visual input (total absence of light stimulation or absence of form stimuli) produce comparable defects, and defects that are typically overcome more slowly than those in humans. More recent work with animals shows that, over and above the presence or absence of visual stimuli, early experience with *particular* visual objects and forms facilitates the subsequent perceptual discrimination of these forms (e.g., Gibson, Walk, Pick, and Tighe, 1959).

The most recent account of the postoperative behavior of a human adult who was blind, or near-blind, almost from birth was provided by Gregory and Wallace (1963). We cite it at some length, for it is a particularly fascinating case history, with findings of considerable relevance to the present topic. The patient, possessing preoperative vision "not sufficiently good to be of any material use to him for orientation or recognition of objects . . . appears from all accounts to have led the life of a blind person throughout his life" (Gregory and Wallace, 1963, pp. 12–13). At the age of 52, two successful corneal transplants provided him with vision. He was first examined by the authors 48 days after the first operation (the second had also been completed). Subsequently, until the patient's death 19 months later, numerous observations and tests were made. The results of these observations led the authors to conclude that this patient acquired visual perception far more rapidly than did earlier cases reviewed by Senden (1932) and the authors thus reopen the question of just how much *learning to perceive* is a factor in the postoperative adjustment of such patients.

Be that as it may, certain of the authors' observations point to the conclusion that numerous visual inference habits readily detected in normal-sighted persons were not part of the patient's postoperative behavioral repertory. We will sample a few of these.

When he sat down he would not look round or scan the room with his eyes; indeed he would generally pay no attention to visual objects unless his attention were called to them. (Gregory and Wallace, 1963, p. 16. This observation was made during the initial interview with the patient, 48 days after his sight was restored.)

We were even more surprised when he named correctly a magazine we had with us. It was in fact *Everybody's* (for January 17th, 1959) and had a large picture of two musicians dressed in striped pullovers. *Although he named the magazine correctly, he could make nothing of the picture* (p. 16, our italics).

At the time we first saw him, he did not find faces "easy" objects. He did not look at a speaker's face, and made nothing of facial expressions (p. 17).

As in previous cases (Latta, 1904), he experienced marked scale distortion when looking down from a high window (p. 17).

It is also worth noting that reflections fascinated him and continued to do so for at least a year after the operation (p. 18).

Although the patient showed a striking ability to recognize objects already familiar to him by touch—and thus displayed considerable, and in certain respects surprising, bimodal transfer—it is clear from several of the authors' observations that certain normal perceptual abilities were very likely not present for some time after the operation. Most notable is the suggestion implicit in these observations that the ability to interpret the two-dimensional representation of objects was not present immediately upon the patient's acquisition of sight. He also apparently was unable to perceive depth in real space accurately, at least under certain conditions.

Of greatest relevance to our present topic are the patient's responses to several tests of illusion susceptibility. On the Hering illusion, the Zollner illusion, the Poggendorf illusion, the Necker cube illusion, and the Müller-Lyer illusion, all administered during the second postoperative month, the patient displayed either no illusion susceptibility at all or a degree of susceptibility considerably less marked than that typical of normal observers. On the other hand, with the Ames distorted room, the only illusion in this set that is literally three dimensional, the patient displayed what appears to be normal illusion susceptibility. The authors' comment on the two-dimensional optical illusions and the patient's responses to them is particularly instructive.

The illusion figures presented here seem to produce distortion of visual space by evoking constancy which is inappropriate to the flat plane (visible as a textured surface) on which the figures lie. On this view, we might say that the anomalous results obtained for S. B. show that these figures did not serve to evoke constancy scaling for him, and thus the illusions were absent (p. 19).

We are impressed with Gregory's and Wallace's illusion data and their inference that the patient may have lacked the opportunity to learn the perceptual habits that underlie the illusions.

The second line of research pointing to an empiricist explanation for cue-utilization differences involves the experimental disarrangement of normal visual input by distorting lenses. The oldest continuing research on this concerns inverted retinal images (Stratton, 1896; Ewert, 1930; Snyder and Pronko, 1952). In sum, these studies show rapid improvement of performance during prolonged wearing of the inverting lenses, disruption of performance when the lenses are removed, and, for the first and last studies at least, occasional loss of phenomenal awareness of visual image inversion. A similar study with rhesus monkeys (Foley, 1938) showed both the improvement of performance and its disruption after lens removal, although performance improvement with the lenses was perhaps not as marked as for human subjects. Considering the short periods of visual experience involved (8 days, 15 days, and 29 days for the humans; 7 days for the monkeys), these studies show a remarkable degree of plasticity in the visual system.

Other research involves lenses providing less drastic disturbances: for example, the curvature of straight lines; displacement of images right or left, near or far; segmentation of the visual field by split-color lenses; etc. (Gibson, 1933; Kohler, 1951, as reported in Hochberg, 1957; Held and Schlank, 1959; Held and Bossom, 1961). These studies show adaptation occurring within an hour, with the phenomenal visual field returning completely to normal; the subsequent removal of the lenses is accompanied by illusory distortions complementary to those that the lenses originally produced. It is Held's view that the achievement of eye-hand coordination under these conditions requires active eye-hand coordination experience. Held and Bossom (1961) emphasize the similarity between these results and those of the infantile-deprivation literature and the uniform evidence of greater plasticity in humans than in lower animals.

A final relevant line of evidence comes from the Gestalt psychologists themselves, who have tended in general to be advocates of the nativist position. In research on "figural aftereffects," i.e., distortion in the perception of the position and size of lines and dots following prolonged fixation of other figures, aftereffects persisting for months have been found to result from inspection times amounting to less than a few hours (Köhler and Wallach, 1944; Köhler and Fishback, 1950a, 1950b).

The visual perception of objects distributed in space comes to us with such vivid directness and clarity that it is hard to imagine that vision is affected by learning. The evidence provided by the research cited here shows that naïve introspection, or phenomenal absolutism, is wrong; that in fact, the visual "given" is articulated, in general and in detail, by learned inference systems.

SPECIFIC HYPOTHESES BASED ON THE ECOLOGICAL CUE VALIDITY CONCEPT

Thus far, our explanatory efforts have remained at a fairly general level. The basic line of argument has included the following concepts: ecological cue validity; multiple-cue-utilization under probabilistic levels of validity; ecological differences corresponding to cue-utilization differences; and higher plausibility for learning than for hereditary explanations of cue-utilization differences. In what follows we state our specific hypotheses as to how ecological differences might relate to visual-inference differences. At this more specific level we offer three hypotheses on: (1) *the carpentered world,* (2) *the foreshortening of receding horizontals,* and (3) *symbolizing three dimensions in two.* In this context, we can then predict cross-cultural differences in susceptibility to several geometric illusions.

The Carpentered-World Hypothesis

From 1880 to 1910, when visual line illusions were a principal preoccupation of the most active psychologists of Europe and America, the dominant interpretation was that they were by-products of a tendency to see the lines as representing three-dimensional extent. Sanford (1908) is particularly thorough on the subject and may be taken to represent this literature and this interpretation:

> The tendency to see things spatially is so inveterate that a moderate suggestion of perspective is sufficient to introduce differences in apparent distance and so of apparent size. . . . Certain arrangements of lines tend . . . to take on a three-dimensional interpretation. This may happen with oblique lines in drawings on paper. . . . This tendency to perceive oblique angles as perspective pictures of right angles is perhaps connected with the tendency to overestimate small angles, and underestimate large ones (pp. 215–217).

Our version of this hypothesis can best be described by applying it to the Sander parallelogram, an example of which is shown in Figure 15-2. For this drawing, the well-established tendency—at least of Western or Westernized respondents—is to judge the diagonal on the respondent's left as longer than it really is. This bias is understandable if one perceives a nonorthogonal parallelogram drawn on a flat surface as the representation of a rectangular surface extended

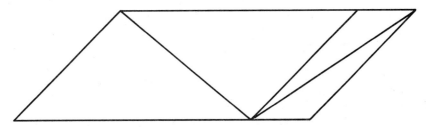

Figure 15–2. The Sander parallelogram illusion.

in space. Given such a tendency, it is clear that the represented *distance* covered by the left diagonal is greater than the represented distance covered by the right diagonal.

A tendency such as this constitutes a habit of inference that has great ecological validity—and great functional utility—in highly carpentered environments. Western societies provide environments replete with rectangular objects; these objects, when projected on the retina, are represented by nonrectangular images. For people living in carpentered worlds, the tendency to interpret obtuse and acute angles in retinal images as deriving from rectangular objects is likely to be so pervasively reinforced that it becomes automatic and unconscious relatively early in life. For those living where man-made structures are a small portion of the visual environment and where such structures are constructed without benefit of carpenters' tools (saw, plane, straightedge, tape measure, carpenter's square, spirit level, plumb bob, chalk line, surveyor's sight, etc.), straight lines and precise right angles are a rarity. As a result, the inference habit of interpreting acute and obtuse angles as right angles extended in space would not be learned, at least not as well.

The application of this line of reasoning to the Müller-Lyer illusion is somewhat more complicated. We again assume, however, that among persons raised in a carpentered world there would be a tendency to perceive the Müller-Lyer figure, shown in Figure 15-1, as a representation of three-dimensional objects extended in space. In this instance, the two main parts of the drawing represent two objects. On the right, for example, if the horizontal segment were perceived as the representation of the

edge of a box, it would be a *front edge;* while on the left, if the horizontal segment were perceived as the edge of another box, it would be the *back edge* along the inside of the box. Hence, the right-hand horizontal would "have to be" shorter than the drawing makes it out to be, and the left-hand horizontal would "have to be" longer. This line of speculation is similar to that of Thiery (1895). In the example given here, and in the explanatory device offered by Thiery, the assumption is made that the diagonal segments are perceived as "really" meeting the horizontal segments at 90-degree angles, as they might if those diagonals were meant to represent lines extended in space.

Even if the alleged differences in phenomenal distance of the two horizontals are not apparent, the habits of inference involved may generate the illusion, according to an interpretation given by Brentano (1892, 1893). Brentano saw the central process in the Müller-Lyer and related illusions as one of orthogonalizing angles, of exaggerating acute angles and reducing obtuse angles. Such a tendency would be a useful part of an inference system in which two-dimensional retinal patterns and pictures were interpreted as three dimensional. This orthogonalizing tendency would introduce distortions in the figure, which would be distributed over all parts. One can imagine the process as a turning of the diagonals into the vertical around their own centers, thus compressing the horizontal in this figure ◄————► and stretching it in this ►————◄. Central nervous system processes in which the extension of a line along its own axis occurs readily, while the horizontal displacement of a whole line meets with resistance, would provide a basis for this distribution of the effects of the distortional process of orthogonalizing.

While Brentano, Thiery, Sanford, and the others were not aware of and were not attempting to explain group differences, their mode of interpreting the "normal case" provides a specific basis for anticipating group differences under the general theory of ecological cue validity. We can make this theory more explicit by stating the ideal kinds of ecological data for testing the hypothesis. One could photograph the views of regard of children to get a sample of photographs representative of all waking hours, seasons, and age levels. Identifying all the junctures of lines, one would then compute the percentages of acute and obtuse angles on the surface of the photograph that had been generated by right angles in the objects represented (some of the angles would, of course, represent objective acuteness and obtuseness). Crude estimates of the relative carpenteredness or relative rectangularity could be made for the environments of different cultural groups.

We can in general assert that European and American city dwellers have a much higher percentage of rectangularity in their environments than any residents of non-Europeanized cultures. It also seems highly probable that within the United States, or within Europe, or within Africa, rural residents live in less carpentered visual environments than urban ones (even if their houses and furnishings are equally carpentered) because they are out of doors more of the time. On similar grounds, it seems probable that residents of a cold climate have a more carpentered visual environment than residents of a hot climate if their climate leads the former groups to spend more of their time indoors. And within the non-Europeanized cultures studied in this research, we would expect square-house cultures to be more rectangular in visual environment than round-house cultures.

This carpentered-world hypothesis is the basis of our predictions of cross-cultural differences in response to the Sander parallelogram and Müller-Lyer illusions. For a perspective drawing included in our materials (Figure 15-3), the same line of reasoning would hold, but to a lesser extent. Thus, for two figures, the Sander parallelogram and the Müller-Lyer figure, and in part for the perspective drawing, we would predict on the basis of the carpentered-world hypothesis that people who live in non-Western environments would be *less* susceptible than Western peoples to the illusions typically noted with these figures.[2]

The Foreshortening of Receding Horizontals

By this awkward title we designate the relatively greater foreshortening of those lines in the horizontal plane that extend away from the observer more or less *parallel* to his line of regard (in comparison, equally long lines in the horizontal plane that are more or less *transverse* to his line of regard appear as much less shortened). Consider the view of a sidewalk one yard wide and marked off in squares one yard long. Look first at the square at your feet. Now look at a square 50 yards away. In terms of retinal image (or extent on the surface of a photograph), while all dimensions of the square are reduced in the 50-yard case, the edges parallel to the line of regard are foreshortened; that is, they are proportionately shorter, in relation to their actual length, than the transverse edges.

Woodworth (1938, p. 645) states the theory concisely: ". . . a short vertical line in a drawing may represent a relatively long horizontal line extending away from the observer. The horizontal-vertical illusion can be explained by supposing the vertical

---

[2] Ames, in his explanation of the illusory oscillation of the rotating trapezoidal window, employs an hypothesis that also places emphasis on the carpenteredness of the environment.

In his past experience the observer, in carrying out his purposes, has on innumerable occasions had to take into account and act with respect to rectangular forms, e.g., going through doors, locating windows, etc. On almost all such occasions, except in the rare case when his line of sight was normal to the door or window, the image of the rectangular configuration formed on his retina was trapezoidal. He learned to interpret the particularly characterized retinal images that exist when he looks at doors, windows, etc., as rectangular forms. Moreover, he learned to interpret the particular degree of trapezoidal distortion of his retinal images in terms of the positioning of the rectangular form to his particular viewing point (Ames, 1951, p. 14).

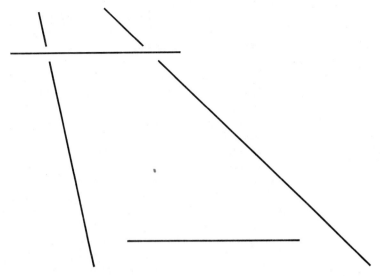

Figure 15–3. The perspective drawing illusion.

to represent such a foreshortened horizontal line." Sanford (1908, p. 238) cites Hering (1861–64, p. 355) and Lipps (1891, p. 221) as hypothesizing "an unconscious allowance for foreshortening, acquired through preponderating experience with squares lying in planes inclined with regard to the plane of vision."

To this theory we add the observation that such an inference habit would have varying cue validities in varying ecologies. Let us consider the most valid extreme—a man living without a house on a flat plain devoid of trees, posts, or poles. Into this plain, furrows have been plowed. For this man the only source of verticals on the retinal image are furrows in the horizontal plane extending away from him. These re-

ceding horizontals parallel to his line of regard are much more foreshortened than the transverse horizontals. For such a person there would be great ecological validity in the inference habit of interpreting vertical retinal extensions as greatly foreshortened lines in the horizontal plane extending along the line of regard. This person should be maximally subject to the horizontal-vertical illusions (Figure 15-4 and 15-5).

Such an inference habit would have much less utility for the dweller in a rain forest or jungle, away from vistas over water or land, in which the largest real surfaces in the visual regard are, in fact, vertical, with tree trunks and hanging vines the commonest source of retinal verticals. Dwellers in canyon bottoms are in a similar ecology—

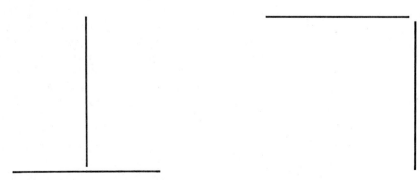

Figure 15–4. The horizontal-vertical illusion (⊥).

Figure 15–5. The horizontal-vertical illusion (⊐).

as would be one who grew up in a courtyard surrounded by the towering walls of apartments if the tendency of apartment-house areas to have long straight streets did not keep them from this extreme. For most regions, rural residents should have a greater degree of susceptibility to the horizontal-vertical illusion than urban residents. In comparable out-of-doors environments with predominantly open fields, warm-climate residents should be more susceptible than cold-climate residents. (Quantitative scorings from photographs would again be required for determinate statements.)

Most important, the cross-cultural differences to be expected for the horizontal-vertical illusion are not identical to those expected for the three other illusions discussed above.

Symbolizing Three Dimensions in Two

Another dominant ecological factor relevant to the line illusions relates to the pervasive use of symbols on paper in many societies. While most of this symbolization is connected with the representation of language, from the very beginning much of it has been employed for a more iconic representation of space, as in maps and figures of persons, animals, and other objects. Within such representational drawing, an increasingly dominant portion over the last thousand years has involved the deliberate effort to represent three-dimensional spatial arrays on the two-dimensional surface of paper, canvas, or wall.

To repeat, it is hard for us as Westerners to realize that the tradition of representing three dimensions in two has the character of an arbitrary linguistic convention. Hudson (1960) has shown that one who is not familiar with this communicative intent does not find this "language" at all obvious. In many respects, it is a language that has to be learned, like any other.

But this may overstate the case somewhat. As Gibson correctly notes, ". . . it does not seem reasonable to assert that the use of perspective in paintings is merely a convention, to be used or discarded by the painter as he chooses" (1960, p. 227). What *is* arbitrary is the *decision* to represent three

dimensions in two. Once this useful arbitrary convention has been invented, the optimally efficient device is, no doubt, to imitate the retinal display, to produce a two-dimensional frontal display that generates a retinal display most comparable to that generated by the three-dimensional display that is the topic of the message. Leonardo da Vinci's success in anticipating the photograph indicates how nonarbitrary his principles were. The arbitrariness equally present in painting and photography lies in the decision to represent three dimensions in two.

In the course of distinguishing between the visual field and the visual world, Gibson (1952, p. 149) has pointed to the influence of this cultural tradition:

> The visual field . . . is simply the pictorial mode of visual perception, and it depends . . . not on conditions of stimulation but on conditions of attitude. The visual field is a product of the chronic habit of civilized men of seeing the world as a picture (1952, p. 149).

In a similar vein, Hochberg (1961) has emphasized the role of artists, from Leonardo da Vinci to Adelbert Ames, in developing our inventory of cues of depth perception.

This cultural convention relates to the present problem because of the way in which one learns to receive and to send such messages. Frequent exposure to pictures and picture books in childhood and the resultant learning to interpret perspective drawings and photographs are conditions that would contribute to the tendency to interpret acute and obtuse angles as right angles, and hence increase susceptibility to the Müller-Lyer illusion and the Sander parallelogram. (Depending upon the contents, picture experience might also affect the horizontal-vertical illusions, but we are not prepared to say how.) Traditions of nonrepresentational decoration on two-dimensional surfaces, on the other hand, can lead to inference habits of taking two-dimensional drawings "literally," of taking the surface lines in themselves as the "objects" of perceptual inference rather than as mere communicative indicators of three-dimensional objects not actually present. In cultures with such traditions, susceptibility to the Müller-Lyer illusion and the Sander parallelogram should be low.

Learning to communicate by this means, learning to draw good perspective drawings of boxes, tables, houses, etc., is an ecological condition of presumably *opposite* effect. The child's first efforts to draw the box in front of him are impeded by his compulsion to draw all of the angles as right angles. It is only by effort and training that he learns to note "what is in front of his eyes," that is, that several of the rectangular sides of the box are represented in the field of vision by obtuse and acute angles. The artist's devices (for example, sighting across a pencil or brush held at arm's length to get the appropriate retinal-angle size) are techniques employed to overcome the distracting tendency to draw things as "we know they are" rather than "as they appear." As a result, artists are less subject to the constancy effects, or "phenomenal regression to the real object" (Thouless, 1932). Our inference is that they should also be less susceptible to the Müller-Lyer and Sander illusions, although as far as we know, this has not been tested.

Incidentally, it is on this ground of learning how to represent three dimensions in two that we would explain the universally noted lesser susceptibility to these two illusions of adults as compared with children (Wohlwill, 1960). This "superiority" of adults is, of course, supported by their quite general superiority in ability tasks of all kinds, their greater analytic skill, their greater compensation for known distortions, etc.

SUMMARY OF OUR ATTEMPTS TO EXPLAIN GEOMETRIC OPTICAL ILLUSIONS

1. The so-called optical illusions result, at least in part, from learned habits of inference that possess ecological cue validity.

2. In different physical and cultural environments, different habits of inference are likely to be acquired, reflecting the differing ecological validities.

3. For figures constructed of lines meeting in nonrectangular junctions, there will be a learned tendency among persons dwell-ing in carpentered environments to rectangularize those junctures, to perceive the figures in perspective, and to interpret them as two-dimensional representations of three-dimensional objects. Such a tendency produces, or at least enhances, the Müller-Lyer illusion and the Sander parallelogram illusion. Since the tendency is assumed to have more ecological validity for peoples in Western, or carpentered, environments, it is predicted that Western peoples will be more susceptible to these illusions than peoples dwelling in uncarpentered environments.

4. The horizontal-vertical illusion results from a tendency to counteract the foreshortening of lines extending into space away from a viewer, so that the vertical in the drawing that is the stimulus for the illusion is interpreted as representing a longer line. Since the tendency has more ecological validity for peoples living mostly outdoors in open, spacious environments, it is predicted that such people will be *more* susceptible than Western peoples in urban environments. On the other hand, some non-Western groups should be *less* susceptible to the illusions, e.g., rain forest or canyon dwellers.

5. Learning to interpret drawings and photographs should enhance some of these illusions, whereas learning to produce drawings representing three dimensions should reduce the illusions.

REFERENCES:

Allport, F. H. *Theories of perception and the concept of structure.* New York: Wiley, 1955.

Allport, G. W., & Pettigrew, T. F. Cultural influence on the perception of movement: The trapezoidal illusion among Zulus. *Journal of Abnormal and Social Psychology,* 1957, **55,** 104–113.

Ames, A., Jr. *Nature and origin of perception.* Hanover, N.H.: The Hanover Institute, 1949.

Boring, E. G. *Sensation and perception in the history of experimental psychology.* New York: Appleton-Century, 1942.

Brentano, F. Uber ein optisches Paradoxen. *Z. Psychol. Physiol. Sinnesorgane,* 1892, **3,** 349–358.

Brentano, F. Uber ein optisches Paradoxen. *Z. Psychol. Physiol. Sinnesorgane,* 1893, **5,** 61–82.

Brunswik, E. *Perception and the representative design of psychological experiments.* Berkeley, Calif.: University of California Press, 1956.

Brunswik, E., & Kamiya, J. Ecological cue validity of proximity and other Gestalt factors. *American Journal of Psychology*, 1953, **66**, 20–32.

Cantril, H. *The "why" of man's experience.* New York: Macmillan, 1950.

Ewert, P. H. A study of the effect of inverted retinal stimulation upon spatially coordinated behavior. *Genetic Psychology Monographs*, 1930, **7**, 177–363.

Foley, J. P., Jr. Observation on the effect of prolonged inverted retinal stimulation upon spatially coordinated behavior in the rhesus monkey (Macaca mulatta). *Psychological Bulletin*, 1938, **35**, 701–702.

Gibson, E. J., Walk, R. D., Pick, H. L., & Tighe, T. J. The effect of prolonged exposure to visual patterns on learning to discriminate similar and different patterns. *Journal of Comparative and Physiological Psychology*, 1959, **51**, 584–587.

Gibson, J. J. Adaptation, after-effect and contrast in the perception of curved lines. *Journal of Experimental Psychology*, 1933, **16**, 1–31.

Gibson, J. J. *The perception of the visual world.* Boston: Houghton Mifflin, 1950.

Gibson, J. J. The visual field and the visual world: A reply to Professor Boring. *Psychological Review*, 1952, **59**, 149–151.

Gibson, J. J. Pictures, perspective, and perception. *Daedalus*, 1960, **89**, 216–227.

Green, R. T., & Hoyle, E. M. The Poggendorff Illusion as a constancy phenomenon. *Nature*, 1963, **200**, 611–712.

Gregory, R. L. How the eyes deceive. *The Listener*, 1962, **18**, 15–16.

Gregory, R. L. Distortion of visual space as inappropriate constancy scaling. *Nature*, 1963, **199**, 678–680.

Gregory, R. L., & Wallace, J. G. Recovery from early blindness. *Experimental Psychology Monographs* (Cambridge, England), 1963, Whole No. 2.

Hebb, D. O. *The organization of behavior.* New York: Wiley, 1949.

Held, R., & Bossom, J. Neonatal deprivation and adult rearrangement: Complimentary techniques for analysing plastic sensory-motor coordinations. *Journal of Comparative and Physiological Psychology*, 1961, **54**, 33–37.

Held, R., & Schlank, M. Adaptation to disarranged eye-hand coordination in the distance dimension. *American Journal of Psychology*, 1959, **72**, 603–605.

Hering, E. *Beiträge zur Physiologie.* Vol. 5. Leipzig: W. Englemann, 1861–1864. P. 355.

Herskovits, M. J., Campbell, D. T., & Segall, M. H. *Materials for a cross-cultural study of perception.* Evanston, Ill.: Program of African Studies, Northwestern University, 1956.

Hilgard, E. The role of learning in perception. In R. R. Blake & G. V. Ramsey (Eds.), *Perception: An approach to personality.* New York: Ronald Press, 1951.

Hochberg, J. E. Effects of the Gestalt revolution: The Cornell symposium on perception. *Psychological Review*, 1957, **64**, 73–84.

Hochberg, J. E. Visual world and visual field: *Perception, sensation and pictorial observation.* Personal communication, 1961, mimeographed.

Holst, E. von. Aktive Leistungen der menschlichen Gesichtswahrnehmung. *Studium Generale*, 1957, **10**, 231–243.

Hudson, W. Pictorial depth perception in subcultural groups in Africa. *Journal of Social Psychology*, 1960, **52**, 183–208.

Ittelson, W. H. *Visual space perception.* New York: Springer, 1960.

Kilpatrick, F. P. (Ed.). *Human behavior from the transactional point of view.* Princeton, N.J.: Institute for Associated Research, 1952.

Köhler, W., & Fishback, J. The destruction of the Müller-Lyer illusion in repeated trials. I. An examination of two theories. *Journal of Experimental Psychology*, 1950 (a), **40**, 267–281.

Köhler, W., & Fishback, J. The destruction of the Müller-Lyer illusion in repeated trials. II. Satiation patterns and memory traces. *Journal of Experimental Psychology*, 1950 (b), **40**, 398–410.

Köhler, W., & Wallach, H. Figural after-effects: An investigation of visual processes. *Proceedings of American Philosophical Society*, 1944, **88**, 269–357.

Kohler, I. Uber Aufbau und Wandlugen der Wahrnermungswelt. *Oesterr. Akad. Wiss. Philos-Histor. Kl., Sitz.-Ber.*, 1951, **227**, 1–118.

Latta, R. Notes on a case of successful operation for congenital cataract in an adult. *British Journal of Psychology*, 1904, **1**, 135–150.

Lipps, T. *Aesthetische Faktoren der Raumanschauung. Beitrage zur Psychologie und Physiologie der Sinnesorgane.* Hamburg and Leipzig, 1891. Pp. 219–307.

London, I. G. A Russian report on the postoperative newly seeing. *American Journal of Psychology*, 1960, **73**, 478–482.

Mueller, C. G. *Sensory psychology.* Englewood Cliffs, N.J.: Prentice-Hall, 1965.

Osgood, C. E. *Method and theory in experimental psychology.* New York: Oxford University Press, 1953.

Pratt, C. C. The role of past experience in visual perception. *Journal of Psychology*, 1950, **30**, 85–107.

Riesen, A. H. The development of visual perception in man and chimpanzee. *Science*, 1947, **106**, 107–108.

Riesen, A. H. Plasticity of behavior: Psychological aspects. In H. F. Harlow and C. N. Woolsey (Eds.), *Biological and biochemical bases of behavior.* Madison: University of Wisconsin Press, 1958. Pp. 425–450.

Sanford, E. C. *A course in experimental psychology. Part I: Sensation and perception.* Boston: Heath, 1908.

Senden, M. von. *Raum und Gestaltauffaussung bei operietan Blindgebornen vor und nach der Operation.* Leipzig: Barth, 1932. Translated by P. Heath, *Space and sight.* Glencoe, Ill.: Free Press, 1960.

Snyder, F. W., & Pronko, N. H. *Vision with spatial inversion.* Wichita, Kansas: University of Wichita Press, 1952.

Stratton, G. M. Some preliminary experiments in vision without inversion of the retinal image. *Psychological Review*, 1896, **3**, 611–617.

Tausch, R. Optische Tauschungen als artifizielle Effekto der Gestaltungsprozeesse von Grössenund Formenkonstanz in der natürlichen Raumwahrnehmung. *Psychologische Forschung*, 1954, **24**, 299–348.

Thiery, A. Uber geometrische-optische Tauschungen. *Philos. Studien*, 1895, **11**, 307–370.

Thiery, A. Uber geometrische-optische Tauschungen. *Philos. Studien*, 1896, **12**, 67–126.

Thouless, R. H. Individual differences in phenomenal regression. *British Journal of Psychology*, 1932, **22**, 217.

Wohlwill, J. F. Developmental studies of perception. *Psychological Bulletin*, 1960. **57**, 249–288.

Woodworth, R. S. *Experimental psychology*. New York: Holt, 1938.

PART THREE

Individual Needs in the Organization of the Environment

Man is both a physical object and a living organism, and it is in the interplay between these two aspects of his nature that his relationship to the physical world is revealed. As a physical object characterized by size, density, and shape, he necessarily occupies space in his environment. Indeed, in this respect, he does not differ from any other component of the environment. As a constituent element, he both acts upon his physical environment and is acted upon by it. Because he is a living organism, however, his influence on his physical surroundings goes far beyond his being an object found in them.

As a living organism he is a *cause* as well as a consequence of his physical environment. He *experiences* and therefore is influenced by this environment, but in no small measure these consequences are of his own making. Man can alter his physical environment either by direct manipulation of it or of its organization, or by simply shifting and changing his own position in it. For the individual, it is not only what he does to his physical setting—rearranging it, adding or subtracting objects from it, or destroying it—that has phenomenological consequences for him, but also what he does to himself in relation to this setting. Man is a readily mobile, goal-directed organism. Where he goes, how he positions himself, whether he is lying down or sitting up, and indeed even how long he occupies a given space in the pursuit of his goals are all factors that contribute to what he experiences as his physical setting in a given behavioral context.

These characteristics of man in relation to his physical environment, however, are also true of many other animal forms. They also are goal-directed and mobile, and thereby capable of manipulating their physical environment or changing their position in it. What makes man distinctive are his cognitive capacities. He not only "sees" but applies meaning to what he sees, and on this basis he can link the present with the past and extend both into the future. These capacities permit him to deepen and extend his control of his environment beyond the immediate situation. He is not situation bound, either in what he perceives or in how he behaves. Conscious planning, based on the ability to integrate accumulated knowledge of the past with reasoned, anticipated outcomes in the future, is the distinctive mark of the human animal.

If man is a rational animal, there seem to be limits to his rationality. He can neither see nor foretell all. And it is indeed true that

> The best laid schemes o' mice an' men
> Gang aft a-gley.

Technological advances in the attempt to improve human existence seem always to carry the seeds of a new set of human problems that in many instances portend even greater threats. There are unexpected as well as expected consequences of a planned scientific technology that often suggest that man's control of his environment is almost illusory. Although man's capacity to plan his future undoubtedly has limits, how much of his failure is a function of inadequate use of this capacity is a critical question in its own right.

The focus of the selections that follow, however, is not on how man thinks and plans, but on what he wants. The question of what are man's fundamental needs has been asked since the beginning of recorded history and undoubtedly before that as well. Psychologists, sociologists, and other behavioral scientists have been no less moved to raise this question than theologians, philosophers, and political scientists have been. Attempts to reduce all of human motivation to one or a small number of fundamental needs have been no more successful than attempts to catalogue or classify the myriad of human desires. What has emerged in recent years is a consensus among behavioral scientists that human needs are many and varied, and that their sum and substance depends on where and how particular groups of individuals are socialized.

Attempts among behavioral scientists to establish a basic "human nature" in terms of innate drives, commonly referred to as primary drives, have borne little fruit. Some innate, tissue-connected drives are basic in the sense that they involve the preservation of the organism—for example, hunger, thirst, and respiration—but others, such as sex, are also rooted in the physiology of the individual and yet their frustration in no sense threatens his existence as an individual. Furthermore, there is more than a little evidence that persistent frustration of complex social motives, such as the need for esteem or for affiliation, may be just as threatening to a person's well being as the failure to satisfy such tissue-related drives as hunger and thirst.

What all of this suggests is that the distinction between the primary drives and the more complex secondary or learned social motives is more apparent than real. All human drives, both primary and secondary, are in the last analysis the product of the individual's experiences in a series of sociocultural systems—the family, neighborhood, geographical region, and so on. The intensity of the person's hunger or sex drive, the objects that satisfy it, the means of achieving these objects, and even his responses to frustrations of these drives are as much a function of human socialization as are the secondary or more complex social motives.

What does such a view mean for the environmental psychologist? If we think in terms of the hunger motive, for example, then the assumption that all human needs and their properties reflect the process of socialization leads to a very important consequence. The individual not only learns to satisfy his need for food in particular ways with particular food objects, but he learns to satisfy it in particular places. Usually, he wants to eat specific foods at particular times—but these satisfactions are not independent of the physical setting. He is not merely unwilling to eat his dinner in the bathroom or in a dank cellar. The kitchen, dining room, or porch may also have to be warm (or cool), clean, light, or relatively quiet. Similarly, the satisfaction of other bodily functions—whether thirst, rest, elimination, or sex— also depends on matters pertaining to the nature and condition of the physical setting.

It follows that man's hunger drive is not a simple unidimensional structure. Indeed, it subsumes any number of specific needs, including those that define *where* and how he shall satisfy his desires for food. The significance of needs with respect to physical setting, whether for food, elimination, or rest, is only revealed when they are not easily and routinely satisfied. The urban dweller is not satisfied in a rural setting when he is required to use an outhouse rather than a room with modern toilet facilities, and he may even experience difficulty sleeping in the unusual stillness of the country.

An important implication for environmental psychology can be drawn from our analysis of human motivation in relation to properties of the physical setting. Some of the papers in Part Three deal with the problem of privacy; it should be evident at this point that the individual's need for privacy can be regarded as a learned motive acquired in the process of socialization of some of his primary drives. The person—at least in a complex industrial society—needs to be alone when performing certain bodily functions. A physical setting that permits him to be unobserved becomes a significant need in its own right.

There are many needs or types of needs for privacy, however, and the task of defining privacy is by no means a simple matter. The privacy required to carry out certain bodily functions cannot be equated with the need to be free from external distractions in order to be creative or productive (Westin, 1967). Each of these privacy needs must have been learned under different conditions, and each is satisfied by somewhat different properties of the physical setting.

The need for privacy for creativity or productivity is far afield from the primary drives discussed earlier. The more complex social motives of the individual—his need not only to be creative or productive, but also for status, recognition, security, and affiliation—are directly rooted in the values of his social system, and the latter in turn expresses itself in the child-rearing practices of the society. But here again it is important from the point of view of the environmental psychologist not to obscure the complexity of any of these secondary motives by assuming that it is a simple unidimensional characteristic. The individual's need for status or affiliation, for example, may be evidenced in a variety of situations and activities, in relation to different individuals, and in each instance it may be aroused and satisfied under very specific conditions.

For the environmental psychologist, the question of such social needs as the need for success or affiliation must be asked in specific terms: Success in what endeavor? Friendship with whom and under what circumstances? And in every instance in which questions of this nature are answered, the specific need of the individual is expressed more precisely in terms of a given social context in which he behaves according to a defined social role. For example, the individual seeks success in his profession, or as a parent, a citizen of the community, a golfer, and so on. In a complex society an individual plays many social roles, some that endure throughout his lifetime (the sex role) and others for a given period (the role of student).

What the person learns is not merely a set of behaviors that characterize a given social role, but the social context, including the physical setting, in which the role is to occur. Parental roles are played primarily in the home, medical roles in the hospital, the educational role of the teacher in the classroom, the secretarial role in the office setting. For any given role, the person not only learns to behave in certain ways and to expect certain behavior from others, but also has expectations about the nature and conditions of the physical setting in which he is to play the role. Thus in the case of the development of complex social motives, derived needs with respect to the nature of the physical setting clearly emerge.

This assumption receives considerable support if we consider the phenomenon of *territoriality*, still another concept considered in a number of the articles in Part Three. Although territoriality—not unlike privacy—reveals itself in a variety of circumstances, the fact remains that in many instances the person's need to define and control a given space, area, or object represents his attempt to play a given social role. Only teachers have access to the faculty lunch room and the right to prevent students from using it. And, although the office secretary owns neither her desk nor her typewriter, only she has the right to use them and the privilege of denying their use to others.

The selections that follow are concerned not only with privacy and territoriality, but with still other phenomena. Personal space and crowding reflect the inextricable relationship between the behavior of the person and the nature of his physical environment. For each case, however, the analysis we provide here offers a necessary approach that can be summarized in the following terms: (1) both primary and secondary needs or motives reflect the process of human socialization; (2) the socialization of these needs necessarily includes the development of "physical setting needs," that is, needs that express desired properties of given physical settings in the attempt to satisfy day-to-day motivations, including hunger, good job performance, and parental role; (3) physical setting needs are in most instances mediational or instrumental in character, and provide the basis for understanding the emergence in the individual of such complex, environment-related phenomena as privacy, territoriality, personal space, and others.

REFERENCE:

Westin, A. F. *Privacy and freedom*. New York: Atheneum, 1967.

16 Freedom of Choice and Behavior in a Physical Setting

Harold M. Proshansky, William H. Ittelson, and Leanne G. Rivlin

For the social sciences, particularly those concerned with man's relations to other men, the physical environment has been conceived as a given, rather than as a source of parameters for understanding human behavior. Urban settings, for example, are distinguished from suburban or rural settings, or the "ghetto" from the more affluent areas of a community, but more for their contrasting properties as social systems or complex social contexts than for the differences between them as organized physical settings. The scientific literature abounds in descriptions of ghettos as a prelude to examining them as sociocultural systems generating given sets of values and relevant behaviors. But systematic studies of the behavioral consequences of ghettos as physical settings are rare indeed.

Even at a more circumscribed level of analysis—a neighborhood, an apartment, or a business office—the physical setting is no less taken for granted. It is assumed to set the stage for and perhaps define the actors' roles with respect to particular human relationships and activities; but for any given setting there are countless variations in design and substance that are generally ignored in the attempts to establish the factors that facilitate or hinder the prescribed behaviors.

It is reasonable to ask why physical setting has been neglected in the theory and research of social scientists. In our judgment, it is rooted in more fundamental considerations than those of priority or theoretical predilection. Increasingly the term "physical environment" is used to refer to the man-made environment: to the physical environment that is planned, constructed, and changed by man on the basis of a continually evolving scientific technology whose limits are by no means in sight. To the social scientist no less than to the casual observer, the success of this technology has suggested, at least until the last decade, that the problem of man's control of his physical environment was solved and that each planned technological advance would produce corresponding favorable changes in man's existence. From the social scientist's point of view, the ability of modern technology to plan and construct a large variety of physical settings to meet the specification of any number of human functions, activities, and relationships meant that the effects of the physical environment were predictable and controllable. An appropriately designed physical setting could be expected to evoke, or at least to serve as the locus of, a range of expected behaviors whose variations could be studied as a function not of physical parameters but of those complex social and psychological determinants that are rooted in all human activities and relationships. Thus, for the child to learn, he needs to feel at ease, comfortable, and secure. It follows, therefore, that schools must be light, airy, colorful, and roomy, and beyond that how and whether the child learns will depend on psychological and social determinants.

During the past ten years both the citizen and the scientist have been compelled to take a second look at their man-made world. The physical environment assumes a new significance once it is viewed against the backdrop of pressing and urgent problems created by the inexorable progress of modern technology. The fruits of this progress are bitter as well as sweet, as evidenced by the existence of urban slums, water and air pollution, depletion of natural resources, congestion and crowding in the city, and any number of other contemporary evils. For the first time scientists of all persuasions are being asked to reexamine the physical world that they have in part created. Yet they are being asked to do more than simply provide solutions to these environmental problems.

To solve one set of environmental problems does not preclude the emergence of others as still greater technological advances are made. The concern with solving problems of a man-made environment has increasingly led to the more fundamental questions of why did it happen and what can be done to prevent new problems from occurring. What has emerged is an emphasis on predicting and understanding the consequences of the physical environment for the behavior of the individual, and this emphasis in turn has called attention to the social scientist, his theory, concepts, and methods. The result has been the new interdisciplinary field of inquiry, environmental psychology. The definition of this field and the conceptual and methodological problems inherent in its interdisciplinary character need not concern us here. What is of immediate interest is a consideration of some of the major concepts made prominent by the recent interest in the relationship between the physical environment and the behavior of the individual.

The concepts of privacy, territoriality, and crowding are used frequently and interrelatedly to describe a class of environmental problems or to explain behavior in relation to these problems. Their frequent use, however, is not evidence of a theoretical viability evolved in a context of sustained systematic research, but rather of the preliminary attempts of a new field of inquiry to define its problem areas and establish its conceptual structure. Since little if any systematic research with respect to these phenomena exists, we are not even afforded empirical definitions in the form of the conceptual restraints that emerge from specified operational procedures.

It is our purpose in the discussion that follows to consider briefly the status and meaning of the concepts of privacy, territoriality, and crowding as reflected in their use in the current literature and to suggest the value of introducing "freedom of choice" as a unifying concept that can help to organize and make clear the definitions of the other terms. Our concern is with concepts used in discussing the behavior and experience of the individual in relation to the nature and organization of the physical environment. Whether privacy is a "right of the individual," whether cities are growing more or less crowded, and whether individuals are seeking autonomy through territoriality are not of immediate interest. Furthermore, whether these processes can function as motivations, and whether freedom of choice can be used as a superordinate

motivational concept, as Brehm has suggested, are not within the province of this discussion. Before more complex questions can be approached, the underlying concepts must be clarified.

We begin this conceptualization with three propositions.

1. Man, in almost all instances and situations, is a cognizing and goal-directed organism.

This proposition is generally accepted by behavioral scientists; indeed, it lies at the root of all modern theories that attempt to explain man's behavior either generally or in terms of specific social settings. While the proposition is obvious, it is important to stress the fact that the individual's behavior is guided not only by the goals he seeks, but also by his cognitive processes, that is, by the way he reads and interprets or even imagines his environment. Each individual interprets and gives meaning to his environment, and to this extent the real differences among individuals and groups lie not in how they behave but in how they perceive.

2. Man's attempts at need satisfaction always involve him in interactions and exchanges with his physical environment.

Since man himself is one physical component of a total environment in any given setting, it follows that any attempt on his part to change his state must involve him, because he is also a goal-directed and cognizing organism, in an interchange or interaction with other physical components of the environment. However obvious this statement, it has been virtually ignored in attempts to understand the behavior of the individual. Social scientists have taken the physical environment for granted. It has served merely as a mediating context in which need satisfaction and social interaction take place, rather than as a source of influence in its own right. In modern psychological and sociological research literature, not only are physical settings seldom described, but the individual does not seem to have the capacity to move or to change his physical environment. It appears that man is not a motor animal.

We can state Propositions 1 and 2 in

somewhat different fashion. Taken together they tell us that the individual in most instances is an aroused and active organism who defines, interprets, and searches his physical environment for relevant ways of achieving his goals. He must often first seek subsidiary goals in order to achieve primary ones. To achieve solitude, he may first have to find the right place at the right time. To read a book in a library, he may first have to find the book, then find a place to sit, and then position himself so that he can read effectively. Trite as these examples seem, they illustrate quite accurately the goal-directed, cognizing character of man in transactions with his physical environment. Furthermore, even in the instance of the individual seeking to achieve complex social goals, the achievement of any one of them involves a myriad of subsidiary need satisfactions depending on the kinds of mundane transactions with the physical environment we have described. It is this view of man that leads us to our third and final propostion.

3. *In any situational context, the individual attempts to organize his physical environment so that it* maximizes *his freedom of choice.*

Freedom of choice is a critical aspect of man's behavior in relation to his physical environment. Whatever the primary purpose that brings the individual to a given physical setting, the setting must not only have the capacity to satisfy the primary need and other relevant subsidiary needs, but it must also allow for goal satisfactions that are only remotely related to the major purpose. The individual who comes to the library to read needs not only the particular books and the appropriate facilities; he may also need a water fountain, a toilet, and perhaps a place to smoke. Any physical setting that provides many alternatives for the satisfaction of a primary purpose and the satisfaction of related and unrelated subsidiary purposes obviously provides considerable freedom of choice.

In an established physical setting the individual will position himself so that he can both accurately cognize and move freely in it in order to achieve goal satisfactions. The individual must know his environment in order to search in it and use it appropriately in the pursuit of particular goals or objectives. Of course, a familiar setting in which the individual routinely satisfies particular needs is less likely to reveal the person's continuing adaptation in these respects. On the other hand, in any new setting or where a familiar setting changes, the person will in some implicit fashion reorganize his relationship to the physical environment so that his freedom of choice is maximized.

The extent of the person's freedom of choice in a given physical setting depends not only on the enduring structure and design of that setting, but on what happens in it from one moment to the next. Changes in light, sound, and temperature may either increase or decrease freedom of choice in, for example, a library, recreation room, living room, or office. If a hospital room is improperly lighted, the patient may be unable to read; and if the other patient in his semiprivate room is too noisy, he may not be able to concentrate on writing a letter. The mere presence of other people may reduce freedom of choice if the individual either cannot or will not carry on particular activities in the presence of others.

If the structure of the physical setting precludes the possibility of a desired behavior or range of behaviors, relatively permanent alterations in the physical surroundings may be undertaken. In this way the range of choices available is expanded. Of course, every expansion of possibilities through environmental manipulation at the same time precludes other choices, setting in motion the never-ending effort to organize the environment in ways that will maximize freedom of choice within the range of existing purposes and needs.

Freedom of choice involves much more than freedom from environmental constraints, but we are here concerned with the environmental context and particularly with freedom of choice in relation to the concepts of privacy, territoriality, and crowding. Our thesis is easily stated. We start with Westin's (1967) definition of privacy as "the claim of individuals, groups or institutions to determine for themselves when, how, and to what extent information about them is communicated to others." These are the objective defining conditions for privacy; if an individual believes these conditions are met, he will experience a sense of privacy. Clearly the specific circumstances under which this sense of privacy is experienced vary widely, but in all cases psychological privacy serves to maximize freedom of choice, to permit the individual to feel free to behave in a particular manner or to increase his range of options by removing certain classes of social constraints.

Anecdotal evidence of the importance of privacy in the daily existence of individuals in a complex society is readily available. Descriptions of the lack of privacy—and its consequences—among those who live in a ghetto are reported by Lewis (1961; 1965), Goodwin (1964), and Schorr (1966). There are, of course, many other situations in which crowding combined with social isolation evokes a strong sense of the loss of privacy. Vischer (1919) reports that the main complaint of French and German prisoners during World War I was that constant contact with other prisoners engendered a lack of privacy. From Vischer's account it is clear that the prisoners' response to the continual presence of others, irritability and resentment, revealed in excessive criticism of others and boasting about themselves was an attempt to maintain identity in the face of a complete lack of privacy. In a very different setting, the *kibbutz* or communal settlement, Weingarten (1955) reports that some smaller settlements did not survive because a small number of individuals were unable to continue living with each other in an isolated setting. Communal life can lead to frustration and tension if the continual awareness of other persons in the setting and the constant exposure to public opinion result in a sense of loss of privacy.

The crucial role of privacy in any attempt to understand man's relationship to a manmade world is not to be disputed. However, as Pastalan suggests (1968), this concept has not been examined in a systematic attempt to generate theoretical and empirical data. Privacy, as it is currently treated in the literature, is not a simple, unidimensional concept with an easily identifiable

class of empirical referents. Indeed the question, "What is privacy?" can evoke a wide range of conceptions, not all of which are directly relevant to questions concerning the design and organization of the physical setting. And for those conceptions that are directly relevant, differences in emphasis and approach still remain. Yet with all this, decisions involving the design, organization, and use of space are still made as if the meaning of privacy was clear, and its implications for the development and functioning of the individual and groups of individuals in a variety of physical settings were fully understood.

Westin's discussion of privacy reveals the full complexity of the uses of this concept. As a political scientist sensitive to the changing nature of American sociopolitical structure in relation to the freedom of the individual, he states his definition in normative value terms. To speak of privacy as a claim of the individual is meaningful primarily in a democratic society, and this fact, for the political scientist, raises a host of questions: To what extent does the individual in America actually enjoy this right? What factors in American society facilitate its expression? What factors inhibit it? Considering the design and organization of the physical environment in the light of the changing character of the urban setting, we may even ask if, given this right, people can achieve privacy.

For the environmental psychologist and sociologist, the question of the individual's right to make decisions about his privacy is less important than the question of the function of privacy for the individual. To understand the relationship between the individual's behavior and the physical environment, it is important to establish what his needs are with respect to privacy and what he expects his physical world to be like in the light of these needs. Experience already tells us that cultural and subcultural factors play a role in what individuals want and expect in the realm of privacy. Whatever the needs of individuals in this respect, still another task for the environmental psychologist is to specify by means of theory and research the conditions under which these needs are aroused and satisfied.

Finally, there remains the no less crucial question of what consequences follow from persistent frustration of human needs for privacy, or whether there are any conditions under which privacy ceases to be important?

The significance of questions concerning individual needs and expectancies in privacy is revealed by Westin's analysis of privacy into four basic states and four related functions. As we have already suggested, privacy subsumes various classes of empirical events, and Westin's analytical schema bears this out. The four basic states he suggests are solitude, intimacy, anonymity, and reserve.

Solitude is the state of privacy in which the person is alone and free from the observation of other persons. The key words here are "observation of other persons," for the person is still subject to auditory, olfactory, and tactile stimuli as well as to other sensations in the form of pain, heat, and cold. Solitude, then, is a state of complete isolation from the observation of others, and is almost identical with privacy as defined by Chermayeff and Alexander (1963).

Intimacy refers to the type of privacy sought by members of a dyad or larger group that seeks to achieve maximally personal relationships between or among its members, who are, for example, husband and wife, family members, peers, and so on. Here the requirements for privacy go beyond mere freedom from external observation. There is an attempt to minimize all sensory input from outside the boundaries of an appropriate physical setting.

Anonymity is a state in which the individual seeks and achieves freedom from identification and surveillance in a public setting, for example, in the street, in a park, on the subway, or at an artistic event. To be self-consciously aware of direct and deliberate observation in public is to lose the ease and relaxation that is often sought in such a setting.

Reserve, Westin's final state of privacy, in a sense is not only the most complex of the four states psychologically but its requirements lie more in the nature of interpersonal relationships than in the nature and organization of the physical setting. Stated simply, reserve is the state of privacy allowing each person, even in the most intimate situations, not to reveal certain aspects of himself that are either too personal, shameful, or profane. To achieve reserve, individuals in group situations must each claim it for himself and respect it in others.

In discussing functions of the various states of privacy, Westin again establishes a fourfold classification. A basic function of privacy is to protect and maintain the individual's need for *personal autonomy*, which is a sense of individuality and conscious choice in which the individual controls his environment, including his ability to have privacy when he desires it. Privacy, whether through solitude, intimacy, or anonymity, may serve the function of *emotional release*. Both social and biological factors create tension in everyday life, so that from the point of view of physical and mental health, people need periods of privacy for various types of emotional release.

Privacy affords the individual the opportunity for *self-evaluation*. To take stock of himself in the light of the continuing stream of information received in his day-to-day experience, the person must remove himself from these events so that he can integrate and assimilate the information they present. Indeed, in a state of solitude or withdrawal during reserve, the individual not only processes information but also makes plans by interpreting it, recasting it, and anticipating his subsequent behaviors. Finally, Westin sees privacy serving the function of *limited and protected communication*, which in turn serves two important needs for the individual. First, it meets his need to share confidences and intimacies with individuals he trusts, and second, it establishes a psychological distance in all types of interpersonal situations when the individual desires it or when it is required by normative role relationships. Clearly in many role relationships psychological distance or limited communication is required and may be achieved through physical arrangements such as private offices, "for teachers only," or "for officers only."

Westin's analytical schema for privacy is both provocative and useful, if only because it asks what privacy is and what its critical dimensions are. On the other hand, like other preliminary analytical schemes, it can be criticized. For example, the four states of privacy are not always conceptually clear or consistent with each other. "Solitude" describes the state of the individual's relationship to the physical environment—that is, he is not observed by others—rather than his experience of solitude. On the other hand, "intimacy" defines a very close relationship between people in terms of psychological distance, which is achieved by seclusion from others. Yet this classification overlooks certain kinds of small groups, such as juries, in which members are only formally related to each other because of their involvement in a common task and in which privacy is a necessity and intimacy frowned upon.

Still another problem in Westin's states and functions of privacy is the fact that the relationships among the four states are not considered. It might be useful to distinguish between individual states of privacy (solitude and anonymity) and group states of privacy (intimacy and reserve). It is also apparent that intimacy and reserve are closely related forms of privacy. Intimacy is a state of privacy achieved by two or more individuals, whereas reserve is a limiting condition placed on that privacy by each of the "intimate" members of the group. Both intimacy and reserve not only involve the group as the unit of analysis, but in each instance privacy can only be achieved if all members of the group agree to achieve it. An intimate state of privacy involving two individuals depends on both agreeing to exercise the right to exclude others, and without such mutual consent intimacy does not exist. Similarly reserve is a form of privacy that depends on the consensus of the members of the group to accept a limitation on the information about self provided by the others. As with other social-psychological conceptions, the application of a concept mainly derived from an individual level of analysis to phenomena at the group level of analysis can lead to conceptual confusion.

The conceptualization of the psychological function of privacy as increasing the individual's freedom of choice in a particular situation by giving him control over what,

how and to whom he communicates information about himself offers a starting point for the resolution of some of the issues in the study of privacy. This approach takes into account, for example, the paradoxical fact that privacy is essentially a social phenomenon and that it includes the freedom to communicate differently with different individuals and groups. Westin's states of privacy specify certain socially prescribed conditions under which various types of behaviors become acceptable. Although the conditions and the behaviors vary widely, they all have in common the property of maximizing the choices open to the individual.

The functions of privacy that Westin lists—autonomy, emotional release, self-evaluation, and protected communication—similarly have in common the function of providing conditions under which the individual is able to behave in ways that produce these consequences. The overall function of privacy thus is to increase the range of options open to the individual so that he can behave in ways appropriate to his particular purposes. In this context, the "need for privacy" is seen as the need to maximize freedom of choice, to remove constraints and limitations on behavior, of which those social constraints subsumed under the heading "lack of privacy" represent an important segment.

One way to achieve this desired freedom of choice is through the ability to control what goes on in defined areas of space that are significant for the behavior of the individual. In recent years the concept of territoriality has been very much in vogue in discussions of man's relationship to his physical environment. Drawing heavily on the work of animal psychologists or ethologists, it has been assumed, implicitly if not explicitly, that man too lays claim to his piece of ground, which he will defend against intruders. Because he occupies it, he has the right to determine who may or may not enter "his" physical domain.

There is no need for us to review the growing literature on territoriality in lower organisms. The volumes by Lorenz (1966) and Ardrey (1966) and the papers by Leyhausen (1965) and others answer this purpose. What emerges from all of the existing research, both systematic and informal, is clear and unassailable evidence that various species of infrahumans stake out a territory that they will defend against intruders in order to protect their young, obtain food, carry out mating patterns, and generally preserve the species by establishing appropriate ecological balances. The question that arises, of course, is where man fits into this picture.

Man too gives clear evidence of territorial behavior. Human beings no less than lower organisms define particular boundaries of the physical environment and assume the right to determine who can and who cannot move across these boundaries. Whether we speak of a man's home, the turf of the streetcorner gang, a secretary's desk in an administrative office, or the locker given to an elementary school teacher for her belongings, we find evidence of behavior that can be subsumed by the concept of territoriality. On the other hand, the analogy with territorial behavior in infrahuman species quickly reaches its limit. For example, much apparently territorial behavior in humans involves the concept of private property. To assume that such behavior serves the same functions in man as in lower organisms, or that it is rooted in man in innately determined biological mechanisms, simply ignores the properties that distinguish man from all other groups of living organisms. Whatever the complex social behavior of man under consideration, and regardless of its essential origins in biology, in every instance it has been so inextricably tied to man's direct socializing and broader cultural experiences that the biological or animal analogy must necessarily be discarded.

What function does human territoriality serve? Another way of putting this question is to ask under what conditions territorial behavior may arise. Man is both a living organism and a physical object. To exist and survive as a living organism, indeed to be free of physical discomfort or pain, he requires a minimum amount of physical space. Under conditions that threaten to eliminate or reduce this minimum, we can expect territorial needs to be aroused and ex-

pressed. Thus, under conditions of severe spatial restriction, the tendency to push others away and to arrange oneself properly may be basic expressions of territoriality as a means of reducing pain and discomfort.

The functioning individual, however, requires another kind of minimum space in order to survive. The individual needs more than the minimum space that guarantees that others will not touch him and that allows him to breathe, move, and carry on in recurrent transient situations. He must be able to move freely within and between physical settings to satisfy not only his hunger, thirst, sex, and other biological drives, but also his needs for affiliation, achievement, success, and other complex social motives. In this sense, then, and under given circumstances, the individual may have to define a large enough space for himself to permit the satisfaction of these drives and motives, including those that are sociospatial in nature.

Such a need may explain, for example, the findings of studies of territoriality in two very different settings. In a study of psychiatric patients in a hospital ward, Esser et al. (1965) found many specific instances of territoriality. Some patients claimed particular seats in a dayroom as theirs and they regarded them as off-limits for all other patients. In another investigation, reported by Altman and Haythorn (1967), nine pairs of sailors who were initially strangers to each other, were studied over a ten-day period during which each pair lived in a small room and had no outside contacts. The men showed a gradual increase in territorial behavior and a tendency toward social withdrawal. At the beginning, the observed territoriality was expressed by fixed geographical areas, for example, part of a room, and highly personal objects, such as a bed or the side of a table. Later it extended to more mobile and less personal things, such as chairs.

Territoriality of this kind was more rigidly maintained in the case of pairs of sailors who both were either high or low in dominance characteristics than among pairs of sailors who were compatible in this respect, that is, one was high and the other low in dominance. In the study by Esser and his associates, dominance tendencies were also found to determine territoriality, but in this case, territoriality both reflected and maintained a relatively stable dominance hierarchy.

In both settings, it should be remembered, individuals were confined to a single area (a room or a ward) and were socially isolated from other settings and groups of people. Need satisfactions of all kinds, social as well as biological, were necessarily limited to whatever resources existed within the confines of the restricted physical setting. To be dominant or to be high in the dominance hierarchy of these settings was to have potential control of these resources. However, the actual realization of these resources depended on the instrumentality of behaviors which guaranteed that defined spaces and objects would always be available, what we have called territoriality. Indeed, territoriality, whether achieved through dominance, mutual consent, aggression, or administrative authority, establishes which individuals have access to what areas of a physical setting, and therefore, to what extent the needs of each will be satisfied.

Territoriality in man is not limited to situations involving social isolation and confinement. On the contrary, it is a ubiquitous phenomenon, although its manifestations may be less apparent in everyday physical settings. Territorial behavior is instrumental in the definition and organization of various role relationships. The prescriptions for social and occupational roles often include the meaning and use of particular objects and spatial areas for carrying out these role assignments. In many instances a social or occupational role establishes exclusive or near-exclusive use and control of a given space or setting. Only doctors and nurses—not patients—have access to the drug cabinet in a hospital; the boss's office is off-limits to everyone except his secretary and his executive assistant when he is not in it; the high school teachers' cafeteria is not open to students. Control of specific territories and the role relationships between people are closely interrelated.

The development and maintenance of an identity in the individual does not depend entirely on how others react to his be-

haviors, skills, and achievements. It is also a matter of places and things, and the acquisition of both serves to define and evaluate the identity of the person for himself and for others. The loss of valued objects or places, or unwilling separation from familiar physical settings for long periods of time, may contribute to a blurring or even a loss of identity.

Territoriality is thus one means of establishing and maintaining a sense of personal identity. This fact may in part explain why, under conditions of social isolation, territorial behavior will in time manifest itself. The socially isolated pairs of sailors in the Altman and Haythorn (1967) study may have laid claim to particular places, beds, and chairs not merely to guarantee the satisfaction of biological and social needs, but also to preserve a sense of personal identity. Removed from their usual physical settings and confined to a single setting in which social interaction was severely curtailed, these men may have needed a more or less primitive and continuing definition of self through ownership of places and things. Not unrelated is the unprovoked declaration by the pre-nursery or nursery school child that a friend can no longer play with his toys. The young child is likely to behave in this fashion even when his self-esteem or personal identity is threatened by events unrelated to his interaction with the other child.

These considerations suggest that territoriality in humans is probably quite different from the primitive, biologically determined behavior observed in many animal studies. Territoriality in humans, defined as achieving and exerting control over a particular segment of space, seems always to be instrumental to the achievement of a more primary goal. We have suggested that the inner determinant of territorial behavior in the individual is his desire to maintain or achieve privacy. Territoriality thus becomes one mechanism whereby he can increase the range of options open to him and maximize his freedom of choice in the given situation.

Under conditions commonly described as "crowded," control over one's territory may be severely limited. "Crowding" is a ubiquitous phenomenon of modern urban life, and it is not always evidence of a major social ill. Indeed, crowding is an inherent quality of the urban setting that may lend excitement and a sense of participation for those within it.

When does crowding represent a significant social problem? Given the population explosion and the urban crisis, discussions of the crowded city, home, ghetto, school, highway, hospital, mental institution, and subway have become commonplace. In these instances it is clear enough why crowding is a problem. Some settings chronically contain excessive crowd densities that have immediate and long-range detrimental effects on individuals within them. There is no need to document the already extensive anecdotal literature on the effects of crowding in the ghetto (Lewis, 1961, 1965) and elsewhere (Biderman et al., 1963).

To the extent that the optimum number of individuals in a physical setting can be maintained or achieved by increasing or redesigning the available space, we can expect the negative effects of crowding to be reduced. What, however, *is* the optimum number of individuals for a neighborhood, community, school, classroom, hospital ward, or any other physical setting? For an institutional setting that is currently in use, it would be easy to assume that the optimum number of individuals equals the number of available facilities—for example, the seats in a classroom, the beds in a hospital ward, and so on. But such an approach really begs the question, although a classroom with 35 seats provides a less desirable learning atmosphere for 50 students than for 35.

The problem of crowding, however, goes beyond this oversimplified, objective approach. A setting may be crowded even when individuals and facilities are equal in number. What our previous discussion suggests is that crowding must be seen as a psychological as well as an objectively-viewed social phenomenon. Its conceptualization as both a cause and a consequence of modern urban life must go beyond the question of the number of persons in a given space. How a space is organized, for what purposes it is designated, and what kinds of activities are involved—all are factors that contribute to the phenomenology of crowding.

Crowding may be pleasurable as well as painful. Some people thrill to the excitement of the crowded city. Other things being equal, a large crowd is a good indication at the theater, stadium, beach, or party. An office area intended to induce a sense of belonging among its occupants may require more clerical desks than is desirable from the point of view of maximum task efficiency. Of course, crowded areas that have positive effects, or that are enjoyed because they are crowded, are often described in terms that avoid the word "crowded." In most cases physical settings described as crowded are meant to have negative connotations. They are experienced as unpleasant or even painful.

For purposes of conceptual analysis it is important to ask under what circumstances the individual experiences a sense of being crowded. Physical settings have normative properties. Whether or not the individual experiences them as crowded depends on what he has experienced in the past and therefore expects in the present. Regardless of apparent discomfort or frustration because of the numbers of persons involved, the individual may experience no sense of being crowded because this is what he expects and regards as desirable. Cultural and subcultural differences in the use and organization of space, including differences in acceptable levels of crowd density, have only recently been emphasized (Hall, 1966; Rivlin et al., 1968; Lucas, 1964). The very great density of crowds that characterizes the Tokyo subways, with "slick" coats sold to passengers to facilitate their progress through the hordes of other riders—suggests that the normative adjustments in the use of space are indeed unusual. Similarly, disconfirmation of culturally established expectancies in the use of space may induce a sense of crowding. If custom prescribes that a task should be performed in a given setting with a given number of individuals, any increase in this number may be experienced as crowding by each person in the situation.

It is important to note, however, that failure to confirm normative expectations with respect to space never contributes to a sense of crowding alone, but always changes other aspects of the situation as well. To find that space cannot be used as one expects means more to the individual than just a lack of expectancy fulfillment. The addition of a second person to an office may mean many other things for the original occupant: that he can no longer behave in exactly the same fashion; that he must accommodate his working habits to those of another; and that in fact what was once his must be shared with another.

This suggests that perhaps a more significant factor underlies the individual's sense of being crowded. He may feel crowded to the extent that he is frustrated in the pursuit of his goals in a given physical setting by simply the presence of others. For the patient hospitalized in a double room, the presence of one other patient who disturbs his sleep may cause him to regard his room as crowded. For those waiting in line to eat at their favorite restaurant, the sense of being crowded may be much less if 20 people before them are seated within 15 minutes than if only two or three people ahead of them are not seated for an hour.

Of course we should not overlook the obvious. The phenomenology of crowding must take into account sheer physical discomfort or pain under circumstances in which people are in fact packed like sardines in a can. The jammed rush-hour subway in many urban centers or even the crowded shopping centers during particular holiday seasons are cases in point. The fact that crowdedness has become the norm for these settings doesn't mean that they do not cause the individual to feel crowded when he is in them. His acceptance of these situations should not be construed as absence of discomfort or pain. Acceptance is a form of adaptation to negative situations in which the individual's willingness to act to change the situation is neutralized; his ability to experience the pain and discomfort they induce is not, although over long periods of time the intensity of these feelings may be reduced.

Crowding as a psychological phenomenon, then, is only indirectly related to mere numbers or densities of people. It is possible to feel crowded in the presence of few people or not crowded in the presence of many. The significant element appears to be frustration in the achievement of some purpose because of the presence of others. Crowding is thus directly related to privacy and territoriality. Crowding occurs when the number of people an individual is in contact with is sufficient to prevent him from carrying out some specific behavior and thereby restricts his freedom of choice.

Freedom of choice then becomes a key concept in understanding privacy, territoriality, and crowding. We have suggested that the psychological significance of privacy, whether it is achieved by structuring the physical environment or by learning to relate in specific ways to others who are continuously present, is its capacity to maximize the individual's freedom of choice. Whether for reasons of personal autonomy, emotional release, or self-evaluation, the individual in privacy can satisfy these needs on his own terms. The presence of others is not merely distracting but inhibiting. Other things being equal, privacy affords the individual the opportunity, in both thought and action, to attempt any and all alternatives and to make his choice accordingly. The significance of freedom of choice in the individual's relation to his physical environment is no less evident with respect to territorial behavior. To the degree to which the individual can lay claim to and secure an area or an object, he maximizes his freedom of choice to perform any behavior relevant to that area or object. When he controls the available alternatives and the means to these alternatives, he can achieve privacy and satisfy other relevant needs. Invasion of his territory reduces his freedom of choice. Similarly, the number of persons in a physical setting is experienced by an individual as crowding when it results in the perhaps less than conscious realization that his freedom of choice is reduced by the presence of others, or even of one other person.

The importance of these considerations for anyone concerned with physical space and man's behavior in the most general terms is clearly and succinctly expressed by

Doxiadis (1968), who sees the individual's freedom of choice as an essential determinant in the planning and organization of cities.

> We must learn how to plan and build our cities in such a way as to give all of us the maximum choices. Since our cities restrict, because of their structure, the total number of our choices . . . we must study the type of structure that eliminates the smallest number of alternatives. To achieve this we must conceive the best type of life and then build the structure that allows the best function in the sense of a maximum of choices [p. 22].

Whether the individual's freedom of choice represents a decision to use the least crowded of a variety of routes, to read in his bedroom rather than the living room, or to formulate any of many other decisions that he faces each day, broadening the available possibilities open to him can only enhance his dignity and human qualities, making him less an automaton and more a fulfilled individual.

REFERENCES:

Altman, I., & Haythorn, W. W. The ecology of isolated groups. *Behavioral Science,* 1967, **12,** 169–182.

Ardrey, R. *The territorial imperative: A personal inquiry into the animal origins of property and nations.* New York: Atheneum, 1966.

Biderman, A. D., Lovria, M. & Bacchus, J. *Historical incidents of extreme overcrowding.* Washington, D.C.: Bureau of Social Science Research, 1963.

Brehm, J. W. *A theory of psychological reactance.* New York: Academic Press, 1966.

Chermayeff, S., & Alexander, C. *Community and privacy: Toward a new architecture of humanism.* New York: Doubleday, 1963.

Doxiadis, C. A. Man and the space around him. *Saturday Review,* December 14, 1968, pp. 21–23.

Esser, A. H., Chamberlain, A. S., Chapple, E. D., & Kline, N. S. Territoriality of patients on a research ward. In J. Wortis (Ed.), *Recent advances in biological psychiatry,* Vol. VII. New York: Plenum Press, 1965. Pp. 36–44.

Goodwin, J. What is a slum? *The Independent,* February 1964, p. 4.

Hall, E. T. *The hidden dimension.* New York: Doubleday, 1966.

Lewis, O. *The children of Sanchez.* New York: Vintage, 1961.

Lewis, O. *Five families.* New York: New American Library, 1965.

Leyhausen, P. The communal organization of solitary mammals. *Symposium of the Zo-*

ological Society of London, April 1965, No. 14, 249–263.

Lorenz, K. *Aggression.* New York: Harcourt, Brace & World, 1966.

Lucas, R. C. *The recreational capacity of the Quetico-Superior Area.* U.S. Forest Service Research Paper LS-15. Lake States Forest Experiment Station, St. Paul, Minn.: 1964.

Pastalan, L. A. *Privacy as an expression of human territoriality.* Unpublished paper. University of Michigan, 1968.

Rivlin, L. G., Proshansky, H. M., & Ittelson, W. H. *An experimental study of the effects of changes in psychiatric ward design on patient behavior.* Offset. City University of New York, 1968.

Schorr, A. L. *Slums and social insecurity.* U.S. Department of Health, Education, and Welfare. Social Security Administration. Research Report No. 1, U.S. Government Printing Office, 1966.

Vischer, A. L. *Barbed wire disease.* London: John Bale and Davidson, 1919.

Weingarten, M. *Life in a Kibbutz.* New York: Reconstructionist Press, 1955.

Westin, A. F. *Privacy and freedom.* New York: Atheneum, 1967.

17 The Communal Organization of Solitary Mammals

Paul Leyhausen

INTRODUCTION

Normally we do not think of solitary animals as forming a community of any kind except for the very limited purposes and periods of propagation. Perhaps this is true of a great number of species, even some mammals, as for example the hamster, the red squirrel, the badger (Eibl-Eibesfeldt, 1950, 1953, 1958) and the wolverine (Krott, 1959). However, if we want to examine more closely what relationships might possibly exist between individuals of an allegedly solitary mammalian species, we are in a very bad position indeed. For the main reason why so many mammals are said to be solitary seems to be that they can only be shot one at a time. Very little field work has been done on such species; field workers—for reasons not to be discussed here—

From *Symposium of the Zoological Society of London,* 1965, No. 14, 249–263. Reprinted by permission of the author and the publisher, the Zoological Society of London.

have concentrated on mammals living in social groups or herds. Hence some of my arguments will be of a highly speculative nature. The only justification is my hope that they may help to arouse more interest in the life of solitary mammals and that more field observations will be made over long periods of time and in sufficient detail.

MAMMALIAN TERRITORIES

As far as I know, the existence of a social pattern into which individual, solitary lives might be woven has never seriously been considered. The basis for any such pattern could be found in territorial behaviour. This was first observed in birds, and bird territories have been studied most fully. When similar behaviour was discovered in other vertebrates as well, the characteristics of bird territories were at first thought to apply universally. They have been thoroughly listed and reviewed by Nice (1941). If we exclude colony breeders from our considerations, it may broadly be stated that the breeding territories of most birds—and for that matter fishes—start from a centre which is occupied by the owner, who afterwards stakes out his claim in serious or ritualized fights with occupants of nearby centres, so that after a while territory boundaries can be mapped out quite precisely, each territory owner as a rule keeping to his own boundaries (Curio, 1959; Greenberg, 1947; Kirchshofer, 1953; Kluyver, 1955; Koenig, 1951; Lind, 1961; Tinbergen & Kluyver, 1953).

Hediger (1949) pointed out that, to mammals, it is not so much an occupied area which is important as a number of points of interest—first-order homes, second-order homes, places for feeding, rubbing, resting, sunbathing, etc. All these places are connected by an elaborate network of paths, along which the territory owner travels according to a more or less strict daily, or seasonal, or otherwise determined routine. The areas enclosed by the pathways, though more or less familiar, are seldom or never used. These concepts have been corroborated and elaborated in detail by the studies of Dasmann & Taber (1956) and Graf (1956) on territorialism in North American deer.

The distinction made by Burt (1943) between home range as an area regularly used by the animal and territory as an area (usually smaller than and situated within the home range) defended against intruding or trespassing conspecifics is not borne out by free-ranging domestic cats, because they behave inconsistently; for a full discussion of these concepts see Kaufmann (1962). The terminology adopted for the purpose of this paper is a synthesis between that of Hediger and of Kaufmann.

One outstanding feature of most mammalian territories—the only exception I know being that of the hamster (Eibl-Eibesfeldt, 1958)—is that mammals are not usually in a position to survey the whole of their territory all the time and to spot intruders or trespassers almost instantaneously, because of the nature of the habitat and of inferior methods of locomotion (as compared with birds). This is usually thought to be sufficient explanation of the often considerable overlap of adjacent territories and the shared use of paths running through border areas (Hediger, 1948, 1949, 1951; Eibl-Eibesfeldt, 1958; Krott, 1959; Krott & Krott, 1963; Hall, 1962a, 1962b; Koenig, 1960; Kaufmann, 1962; Wynne-Edwards, 1962).

Gustav Kramer (1950) was the first to point out that, in territorial animals, the fixation of an individual in a definite locality obviously facilitates the recognition of this individual by its neighbours. All territorial animals have a good memory for localities and their spatial relationships. Hence they probably "label" the conspecifics encountered by the locality where the encounter took place. This is perhaps of minor importance in species like most song-birds, where neighbours are in almost continuous vocal/auditory contact, but is likely to play a major role under conditions prevailing for solitary mammals, as described above.

Attention has always been focused on the fact that territories in general owe their existence to repulsive forces within the animals, which tend to space out individuals as far apart as possible, and students of territory and territorial behaviour have been almost completely absorbed by studying hostile or agonistic behaviour. However, it has long been known that in cases where there is a small population of territorial birds inhabiting a very wide area that is well suited to all conceivable needs of the species, the individuals or pairs are not spaced out evenly as far from each other as the inhabitable area would allow. Clearly there is, in many species at least, not only a minimum but also a maximum size of territory (Kluyver, 1955; Koenig, 1951; Tinbergen & Kluyver, 1953; for review see Wynne-Edwards, 1962). Many authors have noted the fact and expressed their belief that there must be some agent which keeps a population from dispersing beyond any possibility of contact, but although, as I have already mentioned, dispersing forces have been studied intensively, there has as yet been no attempt to make a close study of the counteracting forces and modes of behaviour which allow a population of solitary individuals to retain contact with each other. Fights, threat displays and the like are very conspicuous and therefore more easily observed in the field than hypothetical centripetal tendencies which, if they can be affirmed, are certainly of a less theatrical nature. To detect them it would be necessary to make an uninterrupted, continuous day and night record of a selected population of solitary mammals. As far as I know this has so far never been done, and the only people who ever seriously set out to do it were my collaborator R. Wolff and myself—on free-ranging domestic cats! The result of this little survey has been published elsewhere (Leyhausen & Wolff, 1959). As measured against the standards set out above, we failed: it was an impossible job. To follow a single cat around day and night without losing sight of it, and keep a complete record of all its movements, encounters, etc., requires at least three well-trained, physically fit and inexhaustible observers, plus a lot more equipment than we could command at the time. We carefully selected an isolated farm-house situated in a clearing in a very hilly region. There were two resident cats, and another one in a farm some 600 yards away. Sufficient data were collected for only one of the residents, to form a picture from which we hope no essential feature is missing: even these data were not complete. However, both of us had previously made extensive observations on cat populations under free-ranging conditions, Wolff in two suburbs of Hamburg, myself in the gardens facing the back of my parents' home in Bonn, of some cats in Wales, of a small population in a garden area in Zurich where I lived for approximately two and a half years, and of some individually known cats which night after night populated a small square on the outskirts of Paris. Combined, this was a sizeable amount of data, and our observations confirmed each other in most details. Part of our data fitted well with traditional theories but some simply did not seem to make sense. When we had completed the study, we did not feel it amounted to much in itself and only reluctantly published it, mainly in order to elicit comment and to interest other field workers with perhaps better resources and more time to spend. But on re-examination of our old records, and in the light of old and recent observations and experiments on caged cats, the once odd and ill-fitting pieces suddenly fell into place, and what had previously seemed contradictory became comprehensible. Hence I am quite confident that the picture I shall outline briefly is correct in its essentials.[1]

SOCIAL AND TERRITORIAL BEHAVIOUR IN THE DOMESTIC CAT

Individual cats own a territory which tallies roughly with Hediger's description of the average mammalian territory: a first-order home, usually a room or even a special corner in a room of the house where they live, and a home range which consists of a varying number of more or less regularly visited localities connected by an elaborate network of pathways (1948). To draw a line through the outer points of this network and call this the boundary of the home range would be a purely abstract procedure. The concept of such a boundary cannot be based on the actual behaviour of the animals, as we shall presently see. The immediate surroundings of the first-order home,

---

[1] I am grateful to Dr. Rosemarie Wolff for generously allowing me to use her invaluable records.

as for example the house and the garden, are entirely familiar to the resident cat; it uses practically every part of them and there are usually several places in them for resting, sunbathing, keeping watch, etc. Beyond this limited home area the paths mentioned above lead to places for hunting, courting, contests and fighting, and other activities. To each of these places there is usually more than one path. The areas between the paths are rarely used, if at all. The places the paths lead to must not, of course, be thought of as mere points. Hunting grounds, for example, like clearings in a wood or freshly cut wheat fields where mice are abundant, may cover areas bigger than the home area, and in the course of time the cat investigates them thoroughly.

There are two snags, however, in our attempt to use observations on free-ranging domestic cats as a kind of substitute for the observation of true wild solitary mammals: (i) domestic cats are not allowed to choose or control their own density of numbers, and as a rule they are not allowed to select their first-order home freely; (ii) their behaviour has been changed in various respects during the course of domestication. Important with regard to territorial behaviour is the fact that domestic cats are less repulsive to one another than their wild relatives and in most cases can be brought to share a home area and often even the first-order home with one or more other cats (Leyhausen, 1956, 1962). At first this might seem to be a serious disadvantage, but probably it is simply that the special circumstances mentioned above have brought out more clearly the cohesive factors within the population which are certainly at work in wild populations as well.

As stated above, it is quite normal for the pathway-network of neighbouring cats to overlap, and overlap in this case means the common use of pathways and also of hunting-grounds and sometimes other commodities such as sites for sunbathing and look-out posts. However, common use normally does not mean simultaneous use. In their daily routine, the animals avoid direct encounters, and even cats sharing a home keep separate in the field. According to Hediger many species achieve this by following a rather definite timetable, scheduled like a railway timetable so as to make collisions unlikely. Wolff's and my observations have so far failed to produce any positive evidence that the daily routine of domestic cats is subject to such a definite schedule. Where there is a strong tendency towards being in a certain place at the same time every day, this is usually due to human influence, for example, feeding time. Thus the cat population (up to a dozen or more) of the Welsh farms I saw, gathered about milking time at the barn door or the cowshed to collect their daily ration of milk. Of course, this does show that cats are quite capable of keeping to a time schedule. Our failure to observe anything of the kind in free-ranging cats which are not influenced by human time-fixing does not mean that it could not occur—and, indeed, does occur in captive groups (see below).

Cats seem to regulate their traffic mainly by visual contact. It is often possible to observe one cat watching another moving along a path some distance away—say anything from thirty to one hundred yards—until it is out of sight. Some time afterwards, the watching cat can usually be seen using the same path. On occasion I have observed two cats approaching a kind of cat crossroads from different directions. If they had gone on they would have met almost precisely at the crossing. Both sat down and stared at each other, looking deliberately away from time to time. The deadlock is eventually broken, either by one cat moving on towards the crossing while the other is looking away, hesitantly at first, then speeding up and trotting hastily away as soon as it has passed the point nearest to the other cat; or after a while both move off almost simultaneously in the direction from which they originally came. In all these remote visual-contact (or control) cases, it is very rare indeed for one of the animals to walk right up to the other in order to drive it away or, if it does not move, to attack it. If, however, the animals suddenly and unexpectedly find themselves face to face, a clash of some sort may result. In this way a ranking order is established between neighbours. There is rarely more than one serious fight between any two adult animals; usually any subsequent close-range encounter will develop almost at once into a chase, with the animal which had been defeated in the previous fight taking to flight, and the victorious one chasing and slashing out at the other if it gets close enough. Females are, on the whole, less tolerant of each other than males. However, the kind of ranking order thus produced does not develop into a rigid social hierarchy within the population. Although the victorious cat is sometimes permitted to visit and inspect the territory and even the first-order home of the defeated one unchallenged, it does not make a habit of this and it does not take over the other's home range. Nor is its superiority valid at any place and at any time. If the inferior cat has already entered a commonly used passage before the superior cat arrives on the scene, the latter will sit down and wait until the road is clear; if it does not, its superiority may be challenged successfully. In one case, for example, two females had established homes in two adjacent rooms of the house. The normally superior one had kittens, which enhanced her superiority still further. She wanted to cross into the adjacent room but her neighbour was sitting in the doorway, and when she tried to pass the other spat at her and blocked her path. So she did not fight, but retreated a little way and waited. After a while her neighbour moved away from the doorway, the mother cat crossed and was afterwards tolerated by the resident and in no way inhibited in her investigation of the room. Likewise a superior cat will not normally drive away an inferior one which is already occupying the superior cat's favourite resting place or look-out post. Sometimes the clashes and chasings involved in establishing a locality-priority-dependent hierarchy produce a lasting and irreconcilable hate between two neighbours, so that the superior one chases and hits the other on sight. But this is by no means the rule. Not only is the superior animal allowed to pay visits to the home area of the inferior one, but the latter may also trespass on the former's ground. They may hunt over the same area at the same time, keeping on an average some fifty yards apart, depending on the ground and the vegetation. They do

so deliberately, even when there is no other reason for being so close together. This was particularly obvious in the Welsh farm populations. After collecting their daily milk, the animals walked off one by one to their hunting grounds. Normally they were not fed by the farmers but had to sustain themselves, largely by catching and eating rabbits which lived in vast numbers in the hedges bordering the fields. Although rabbits seemed to abound everywhere, it was usual to see two or three cats hunting within thirty to seventy yards of each other, rather than one lone cat.

At nightfall there is often something which I can only describe as a social gathering. Males and females come to a meeting-place adjacent to or situated within the fringe of their territories and just sit around. This has no connection with the mating season, which I am excluding from my description throughout. They sit, not far apart —two to five yards or even less—some individuals even in actual contact, sometimes licking and grooming each other. There is very little sound, the faces are friendly and only occasionally an ear flattens or a small hiss or growl is heard when an animal closes in too much on a shy member of the gathering. Apart from this there is certainly no general hostility, no threat displays can be seen except perhaps for a tom parading a little just for fun. I could observe this particularly well and on many occasions in the Paris population. The gathering would go on for hours, sometimes (probably as a forewarning of the mating season) all night. But usually by about midnight or shortly after the cats had retired to their respective sleeping quarters. There can be no doubt that these meetings were on a friendly, sociable footing, although members of these same populations could at other times be seen chasing each other wildly or even fighting. Indeed, such an urge for social "togetherness" exists also in those wild species in which, according to all available observations, mutual repulsion is much stronger than it is in domestic cats. They are, therefore, better capable of close friendship with humans than with conspecifics. A human with sufficient knowledge and understanding can have all the social attractiveness of a conspecific without necessarily possessing its repulsiveness (Leyhausen, 1956).

So far I have been dealing mainly with the behaviour of the females. Resident males are different in that, normally, they are even more tolerant towards trespassers. Their aggressiveness is of course accentuated during the mating season, but this has no relation to territory or home range in the proper sense. Fierce defence of the home and the home area is usually exhibited only by females rearing a litter. Adult tom-cats meeting for the first time are liable to engage in fierce fighting regardless of the season. But once it has been decided which is the stronger or the more tenacious, courageous fighter of the two, they settle their arguments thereafter by display and avoid serious fighting. It is therefore possible to put several adult tom-cats, so far strangers to one another, with a number of females in a comparatively small cage, and after a few days of bitter fights there is peace, even when one or more females come on heat. The males may show their threat display but they will rarely engage in actual fighting. Several times I have seen a shifting of rank between the two top cats of such a caged crowd effected by display alone. In an earlier paper (1956) I interpreted all this as a consequence of the animals being forced to live so close together all day that they expended their aggressiveness in "small change" all the time and therefore had no opportunity to build up an aggressive urge strong enough to lead to and sustain actual fighting. This may still play a part, but I am quite certain that a similar process occurs in free-ranging tom-cats and that, after some initial fighting, those who pass the test and are not completely defeated and reduced to pariahs form a kind of order or establishment, ruling a great area in brotherhood. They gather in friendly convention as described above, and even in the mating season seldom fight to the bitter end. Such fights as take place between members of the establishment seem mostly to have a mock or *pro forma* quality. The picture is strikingly different if, within the established neighbourhood, there is a young tom just crossing the line from adolescence to maturity. The established tom-cats of the vicinity, singly or in twos and threes, will come to his home and yell their challenge to him to come out and join the brotherhood, but first to go through the initiation rites. The challenge is not the piercing, up-and-down caterwauling of the threat display but rather softer and seems to have a good deal of purr in it, as if it were not merely challenging but also coaxing. In fact, the sound is hardly discernible from the call by which a tom tries to entice a female in heat to meet him. If the youngster lets himself be persuaded, hard and prolonged fighting ensues. This is in fact the situation in which most really bitter fights occur. And since the novice, who feels his strength growing from day to day, will not accept defeat as any sensible adult would, he will at first be beaten up and often more or less badly injured. But the wounds have hardly closed before he hurries to battle again, and after a year or so, if he survives and is not beaten into total submission, he will have won his place within the order and the respect of his brethren.

It must be noted that, while the territorial ranking order is relative and does not deprive the weak of all rights, the ranking order of the tom-cat brotherhood is an absolute one and is valid wherever and whenever two members meet. But the strongest male normally does not, as is often assumed, become a tyrant, dominating and excluding all others from courting and mating. I have known female cats, free-ranging and in cage situations, remaining faithful to inferior males from one heat period to the next for years. And at least with caged animals I know for certain that the dominant male never made any serious attempt to interfere. The whole social system as described above seems to me designed to ensure that the greatest possible number of strong and healthy males has an almost equal chance of reproduction, rather than to favour exclusively a single dominating individual. Such a situation arises only if, and when, there is one male so overpoweringly superior, in both physique and energy, that he does not find another tom-cat fit to challenge his dominance. For what I rather poetically described above as the "brotherhood" is in fact nothing mythical, but rests on a very real balance of power, risks and deterrents. It can be formed only if there are several males of almost equal strength, so that victories and defeats are decided by a narrow margin and it might cost a higher ranking male his superiority if he provoked an inferior so far as to make him actually fight.

Before describing the interaction of the hierarchical dichotomy in caged cat societies, I must make a few remarks on what is called territory marking. Many authors have described how territorial mammals mark their territories by scent, sound, scratching posts, etc. The usual interpretation attributed to this sort of behaviour is that the animal is setting up a warning signal, with the intention of scaring away trespassers and potential intruders. I do not know whether this scaring-off function of an olfactory mark has been established beyond doubt in a species of solitary mammal. In cats I have certainly never observed anything suggesting such an interpretation. Cats, predominantly males but also most females, have a habit of spraying their urine against trees, poles, shrubs, walls, etc., and afterwards they often rub their face in it and then the face against other things. No cat has been observed to go up to the mark made by another, sniff it and then retreat. What they almost invariably do is sniff the mark carefully and at leisure, and then either move on quite unconcernedly or put their own mark over it. There is not the slightest hint that the original marking has anything like an intimidating effect. Of course, this is no proof that this is never the case; but there must be at least one other function if not more. One may be to avoid unexpected encounters and sudden clashes, another to tell who is ahead on the road and how far, and whether he can be met if required. However, this is pure speculation and my data do not so far allow me to single out or reject any of the possibilities. The odds are that all of them play their part depending on the situation. But I should like to stress the point that we must not deny territorial behaviour to cats because their markings do not, or only moderately, function as deterrents.

When I first (1956) described the structure of artificial cat societies in cages, I found that there was usually a dominant male and frequently, though not always, one or two animals, male or female, which were so subdued that they hardly dared breathe, and which I called "pariahs." There was some ranking order among the rest of the population, but it seemed very indefinite and unstable. My explanation then was that cats, as essentially solitary animals, simply lack the capacity to build a stable society. When the existence of two different types of ranking dawned upon me, two facts emerged: (i) it is actually possible to find evidence for such a dualism. At the food bowl, for example, an absolute rank order is observed. Narrow passages and preferred resting places may, in a sense, belong to top cats, and inferior cats often leave them when the superior one approaches, but if they do not there is no quarrel; and, in particular, the cat already in a passage has the right of way regardless of its status within the absolute hierarchy. Also, there is sometimes a prerogative related to the time of day. Some cats, for example, make full use of the floor for running and playing in the morning, others in the evening, and it is "their" time, when they are superior to all others which happen to come their way, again regardless of their absolute ranking. (ii) There is a direct relationship between the balance of absolute and relative hierarchy, and population density. The more crowded the cage is, the less relative hierarchy there is. Eventually a despot emerges, "pariahs" appear, driven to frenzy and all kinds of neurotic behaviour by continuous and pitiless attack by all the others; the community turns into a spiteful mob. They all seldom relax, they never look at ease, and there is continuous hissing, growling and even fighting. Play stops altogether and locomotion and exercise are reduced to a minimum.

It should be noted that all statements so far are based on plain observation and, although they seem reliable enough qualitatively, there has as yet been no quantitative investigation. In the near future, however, I hope to make a detailed quantitative study by means of a new photographic recording device.

DISCUSSION, WITH SPECIAL REFERENCE TO HUMAN SOCIETIES

I believe that this basic dualism of social hierarchy is present in many other mammals, and that the interaction of the two and the possibility of the weight shifting from one to the other lies at the root of the ability of some species either to lead solitary, territorial lives or to live in small or even quite large groups. But as individual territories shrink and the group emerges, a group territory is formed. Davis (1942) found that the social behaviour of various species of the family of Crotophaginae represents successive steps in a phylogenetic change from individual to group territory. In a number of mammalian species, however, the change need not be brought about by a slow, phylogenetic process, the faculty for both solitary and group life being inherent to the individual. Ecological and perhaps other circumstances determine what kind of social structure a population will have. The North African lion was, as far as one can make out from the reports of hunters and travellers, a solitary animal, living at the most in pairs. This seems also to be true of the West African lion in many regions. Yet in the East African plains, lions live in groups sometimes numbering more than twenty members (Guggisberg, 1961). The same principle seems also to govern the life—both within the group and among the groups—of species, such as the wolf, which habitually live in small groups (Armitage, 1962). In Murie's description (1944) we find examples of strong leadership at times and of relative tolerance and indulgence at others when the rights of the weak are well and, I might almost say, deliberately respected by the strong. In striking contrast are the observations of Schenkel (1947), who describes the social behaviour of wolves in an overcrowded captivity situation in exactly the same way as I have for the overcrowded cat community.

I should also like to suggest that the fact that territorial dominance in mammals depends on locality and time might help to settle controversies between various observers with regard to territoriality in some species. Hediger (1951) reports territorial behaviour in bull hippopotami; Grzimek (1956) and Verheyen (1954) deny this. Likewise it has always been assumed, and has also been confirmed by field observations, that black and brown bears are territorial animals (Meehan, 1961; Meyer-Holzapfel, 1957). Yet Krott & Krott (1963) frantically deny even the remotest possibility of territoriality in bears and describe the species as being "socially indifferent" (social neutral). It has, I hope, become sufficiently clear from the above that the only mammal one could conceivably speak of as being socially indifferent is a dead one. Apart from this ill-chosen term, I think once again that the controversy may find its solution in the way I have already explained. Only after studying a population for a long period and following the individuals at all times and through all situations will one be able to make a correct and proportional assessment of their social interaction and relationships.

Just as mammals that normally live solitary lives often seem to have a faculty for changing to some form of group life, so many, if not all, mammals normally living in groups and even large herds seem to me to possess a faculty in the reverse direction. The wapiti for example is territorial in some habitats and non-territorial in others (Altmann, 1952; Graf, 1956). I therefore believe that, even in mammals living in herds and not occupying territories in the strict sense, both forms of social hierarchy could be traced, if only the attention of observers were focused on the point. And in that case I should predict that absolute rank order would predominate over relative rank order, the bigger the herd, and the less there is a tendency to subdivide it into small groups.

Although I have no special knowledge of the social life of monkeys and apes, I suggest that here again the hierarchical dichotomy could be found. There would be, perhaps almost exclusive, predominance of absolute hierarchy in monkeys living in large bands, like the rhesus (Chance, 1959; Chance & Mead, 1953), and a more proportionate balance between the two in monkeys living in smaller groups like the South Indian macaque (Nolte, 1955) or the langur (Jay, 1962, 1963). Whatever the results of pertinent observation of monkey life may be, I feel sure that the dichotomy exists basically in man and can be observed in all kinds of human social organizations; I am also convinced that the well-being and even the survival of our species depends on a proper balance between the two types of hierarchy.

In an earlier paper (1954) I gave numerous examples of the fact that in all sorts of human social organization territorial behaviour in various forms, both unadorned and sublimated, plays a role which it would be hard to overestimate (Meyer-Holzapfel, 1952; Nippold, 1954; Schmidt, 1937). I described in some detail that, under the conditions of overcrowding prevailing in prisoner-of-war camps, exactly the same symptoms developed as those described above in overcrowded captive cat and wolf communities. I showed that the same symptoms are becoming increasingly conspicuous in modern mass communities. In that sense, the cynical definition of psychoanalysis, as the main symptom of the illness of which it pretends to be the cure, is one hundred percent correct. My conclusion was that space in its physical or—if I may say so—biological form, not in a sublimated or figurative sense only, is indispensable for the biological, and particularly for the psychological and mental health of humans in a human society. For these reasons overcrowding is a menace to mankind long before general and insurmountable food shortage sets in. The increase in human numbers is not primarily a food problem, it is a psychological, sociological, mental health problem—in short, a humanist problem. And we have to realise that human nature sets a far narrower limit to human adaptability to overcrowding than is commonly believed today.

This I could see as a fact in 1954, but at that time I had no idea why it should be so. The key was given me by Wynne-Edwards (1962) when he formulated and elaborated the principle that natural selection has produced various kinds of social organization because they replace direct competition for the basic needs of life by competition for other goals (i.e., social goals in the widest sense). This controls numbers before the basic necessities of life become so scarce that they need be competed for, thus guaranteeing that the numbers of a given species are kept at an optimum level. Group selection (Wynne-Edwards, 1962) and the mechanisms which are involved in intraspecific balance of numbers do not operate in a void. Other factors, especially ecological ones, are taken into account and their more or less constant presence is "relied upon." If, for instance, a species is suddenly freed of practically all predators, the balance of numbers may break down completely. To what extent the numerical control mechanisms depend on such partial elimination and other environmental factors, and whether these feedback systems are of a direct or an indirect nature, probably varies greatly from species to species. On the whole one might guess that short-lived animals, with an enormous rate of reproduction and regular elimination, can make do with more direct methods of control, i.e., food supply might directly affect numbers, whereas long-lived species have to keep a balance of numbers over longer periods and cannot readily adapt their density to short-term fluctuations in the food situation. In such cases an indirect influence based on the average situation over many cycles comes into operation, and this is precisely the function of what Wynne-Edwards calls "conventional competition." In any case, an all too drastic change in such conditions as have been so far "taken into account" in the process of evolving the "homeostatic machine" that they are practically working parts of it, will result in a breakdown of the machine as a whole. This is what happened to our own species during the last few centuries—a mere nothing of time, phylogenetically speaking. The natural biological instruments for balancing our numbers have been reduced to ineffectiveness by man's rational powers and inventions. But our nature has not basically changed. We do not want to suffer from diseases, we do not want our old people to die sooner or our babies to die before they grow up. We certainly cannot wish to restore the original system for balancing numbers. Yet we cannot bear to become more and more numerous and to be in a crowd wherever we turn. The only human and humane answer is to evolve and make effective use of rational, scientific means to restore the balance.

The other point I did not realise in 1954 was the dichotomy of social hierarchy.[2] I am fully aware that there may be many cases in which the line between territorial or relative dominance (relative hierarchy) and absolute dominance (absolute hierarchy) cannot be drawn as neatly as I have done for the sake of argument. Yet there can be no doubt that the constructive antagonism between the two forms one of the most effective mechanisms for balancing numbers by means of "conventional competition" (Wynne-Edwards, 1962). In human history endless examples can be found; constructive balance between the two marks the periods of peaceful and prosperous development. Perhaps I may reformulate here what I said when describing the cat community, in order to make plain its potentialities for the interpretation of human organizations. Territorial dominance gives

[2] I owe an apology to Dr. Peter Marler, whose important work (1955a, 1955b, 1956, 1957) on fighting in chaffinches escaped my notice while preparing this paper. Marler found both forms of social rank order in his birds and came very close to realising the potentialities of their interaction; in the chaffinch, however, they seem not to exist simultaneously but to be exchanged for each other according to season, with transitional stages in between. I fully agree with Marler that it is not two different types of aggressiveness underlying the dichotomy, but typically differing factors of the internal and external situation. These, especially the internal ones, undergo seasonal changes in the chaffinch but co-exist, to some extent at least, in some mammals. However Marler's statement that fighting is not sought after "for fun" and does not lead to appetitive behaviour if not properly released for some time certainly must not be applied generally. I do not know about birds, but many fish and mammals *do* seek a releasing situation for fighting when they are "in the mood."

the individual, or individual family, superiority over all or almost all other members of the community in certain places and at certain times; it stands for the rights and liberty of the individual. It enables the individual to enter a community and cooperate in it with other individuals, as a separate member in his own right, regardless of his status in the absolute hierarchy of that community. On the other hand, absolute ranking order ultimately makes leadership and law possible, law being originally the will of the leader or overlord.

What it may lead to if territorial behaviour runs free of any control by a superimposed absolute order can be amply illustrated, for instance, from the history of exploration and settlement in North America. At the other extreme, the result of unchecked absolute hierarchy is tyranny, when individuals or organizations have acquired excessive power and succeeded in reducing individual liberty more and more in favour of the "common good." In crowded societies, both have a strong tendency to combine and to squash the individual into an anonymous cipher. Sometimes the problem of crowding has been solved socially by the emergence of an élite of "free citizens" or princes, who established among themselves a community based on proper balance between relative and absolute dominance, reducing the rest of the population to the status of mere domestic animals. Striking examples of this were the city-states of ancient Greece and the medieval princedoms of central Europe. Whenever the absolute hierarchy grew too oppressive, rebellions and revolutions were the inevitable course of events. And the coercion exerted by the underlying mechanism described can hardly be better illustrated than by the fact that the great revolution rising in the name of "liberté, égalité, fraternité" set up its own tyranny as soon as it had won victory. This was not because of the wickedness of some of the revolutionary leaders, but was the inevitable consequence of crowding and crowd management, and it is not by chance that under similar circumstances wicked leaders are almost automatically swept into power.

I do not want to oversimplify matters.

There is no question of hierarchical antagonism being the one and only agent of human history. All I wish to stress is that it has been *one* agent, and that the fact that it has a biological foundation and forms an indispensable and indestructible part of human nature has hitherto been utterly neglected. The shift of balance between the two orders of dominance is only possible within limits. The range of such a shift is species-specific and represents the density tolerance of a species as defined by this particular mechanism. It seems, unfortunately, that these limits are not hard and fast, so that it is possible for density unobtrusively to increase too much if it is strongly favoured by other factors. Since the human mind is adapted to life in a small group and to co-operating in a neighbourly manner with a small number of other groups, it is often incapable in a modern mass society of singling out individuals for social partnership. In the midst of an anonymous crowd it is faced with hopeless loneliness.

In modern mass democracy, "mass" and "democracy" are incompatible because crowding favours absolute hierarchy to a degree where it becomes tyranny. Democracy has one of its indispensable biological roots in relative hierarchy. Almost daily we can observe how the liberty and free enterprise of the individual are drastically diminished because of the priority given to the communal good, whatever that may be or may be believed to be. Anyone who owns a piece of land and wants to erect on it a house suiting his own needs and taste will know what I mean. The words "own" and "property" have long lost their original meaning. We accept this, rationally and morally, as inevitable and therefore "good." But our nature will not accept it, and open or latent crisis will ensue. This road leads to either rebellion and violence, or neurosis, or both. There is no other remedy than to re-establish the balance of numbers in human societies and quickly to find effective means of controlling them at the optimum level.

Modern psychology and sociology have for far too long been obsessed by the idea that maladjustment between individual and society is almost exclusively due to a faulty construction of the individual, who must therefore be helped to adjust to the demands of a society which is taken as a more or less unalterable system of conditions. In the present situation this is decidedly the wrong way of looking at the problem; as history clearly teaches, societies and their structures have undergone rapid changes all the time, and there is no reason to assume that adaptive changes could not be effected by conscious human effort. But phylogeny has left us with a set human nature, with a basic construction of the species, which cannot be altered at will and needs enormous periods of time for harmonious evolution. For practical purposes, and in striking contrast to common belief even by scientists, the limits within which the individual can adapt and stay healthy are rather narrow and cannot be changed without interfering with the basic pattern of human nature itself, that is, without danger of destroying the species. We should therefore stop striving vainly to adapt the individual to the impossible demands of a society which regards itself as an end instead of a means to a better and happier life for the individual. We should conscientiously proceed towards altering societies and their structures in order to adapt them —to *re*-adapt them—to human nature. One of the most effective means to this end would be to pursue a policy of birth control which would gradually reduce our numbers in some parts of the world and in all others ensure that they do not exceed a certain level.

There can be little doubt that the balance between relative and absolute dominance has been *one* of the mechanisms which controlled human density under primitive conditions. It is, within limits, capable of responding to ecological feed-back, but can presumably work to some extent, perhaps for only a limited period of time, without such feed-back; it is probably capable of functioning again if its basic functional requirements are restored. A close study of this and other mechanisms which form part of the "homeostatic machine" will perhaps enable us to define objectively "density tolerance" and "desirable or optimum level of density" in our own species.

REFERENCES:

Altmann, M. Social behavior of elk, *Cervus canadensis* Nelsoni, in the Jackson Hole area of Wyoming. *Behaviour*, 1952, **4**, 116–143.

Armitage, K. B. Social behaviour of a colony of the yellow-bellied marmot (*Marmota flaviventris*). *Animal Behaviour*, 1962, **10**, 319–331.

Burt, W. H. Territoriality and home range concepts as applied to mammals. *Journal of Mammals*, 1943, **24**, 346–352.

Chance, M. R. A. What makes monkeys sociable? *New Scientist*, 1959, **5**, 520–523.

Chance, M. R. A., & Mead, A. P. Social behaviour and primate evolution. *Symposium of the Society for Experimental Biology*, 1953, No. 7, 395–439.

Curio, E. Verhaltensstudien am Trauerschnapper. *Zeitschrift für Tierpsychologie*, 1959, Beiheft **3**.

Dasmann, R. F., & Taber, R. D. Behavior of Columbian black-tailed deer with reference to population ecology. *Journal of Mammals*, 1956, **37**, 143–164.

Davis, D. E. The phylogeny of social nesting habits in the Crotophaginae. *Quarterly Review of Biology*, 1942, **17**, 115–134.

Eibl-Eibesfeldt, I. Über die Jugendentwicklung des Verhaltens eines männlichen Dachses (*Meles meles* L.) unter besonderer Berückichtigung des Speiles. *Zeitschrift für Tierpsychologie*, 1950, **7**, 327–355.

Eibl-Eibesfeldt, I. Zur Ethologie des Hamsters (*Cricetus cricetus* L). *Zeitschrift für Tierpsychologie*, 1953, **10**, 204–254.

Eibl-Eibesfeldt, I. Das Verhalten der Nagetiere. *Handbuch Zoologie Berlin*, 1958, **8**, Lfg 12, Teil 10 (13), 1–88.

Graf, W. Territorialism in deer. *Journal of Mammals*, 1956, **37**, 165–170.

Greenberg, B. Some relations between territory, social hierarchy, and leadership in the green sunfish (*Lepomis cyanellus*). *Physiological Zoology*, 1947, **20**, 267–299.

Grzimek, B. Einige Beobachtungen an Wildtieren in Zentral-Afrika. *Zeitschrift für Tierpsychologie*, 1956, **13**, 143–150.

Guggisberg, C. A. W. *Simba. The life of the lion.* London: Bailey Bros. & Swinfen, 1961.

Hall, K. R. L. Numerical data, maintenance activities and locomotion of the wild Chacma baboon, *Papio ursinus*. *Proceedings of the Zoological Society of London*, 1962a, **139**, 181–220.

Hall, K. R. L. The sexual, agonistic and derived social behaviour patterns of the wild Chacma baboon, *Papio ursinus*. *Proceedings of the Zoological Society of London*, 1962b, **139**, 283–327.

Hediger, H. Kleine Tropen-Zoologie. *Acta tropica Basel*, 1948, Suppl. 1, 1–182.

Hediger, H. Säugetier-Territorien und ihre Markierung. *Bijdragen tot de Dierkunde*, 1949, **28**, 172–184.

Hediger, H. Observations sur la psychologie animale dans les Parcs nationaux du Congo belge. *Explorations des Parcs nationaux Albert, Miss. Hediger & Verschuren*, 1951, 1, 1–194.

Jay, P. C. Aspects of maternal behavior among langurs. *Annals of the New York Academy of Science*, 1962, **102**, 468–476.

Jay, P. C. Ecologie et comportement social du langur commun des Indes, *Presbytis entellus. Terre et la Vie*, 1963, **110**, 50–65.

Kaufmann, J. H. Ecology and social behaviour of the coati, *Nasua Narica*, on Barro Colorado Island, Panama. *University of California Publications in Zoology*, 1962, **60**, 95–222.

Kirschshofer, R. Aktionssystem des Maulbrüters, *Haplochromis desfontainesii*. *Zeitschrift für Tierpsychologie*, 1953, **10**, 297–318.

Kluyver, H. N. Das Verhalten des Drosselrohrsangers. *Acrocephalus arundinaceus* (L.), am Brutplatz mit besonderer Berücksichtigung der Nestbautechnik und der Rivierhauptung. *Ardea*, 1955, **43**, 1–50.

Koenig, L. Das Aktionssystem des Siebenschläfers (*Glis glis* L.) *Zeitschrift für Tierpsychologie*, 1960, **17**, 427–505.

Koenig, O. Das Aktionssystem der Bartmeise II. *Österreichische Zoologie Zeitschrift*, 1951, **3**, 247–325.

Kramer, G. Über individuell und anonym gebundene Gemeinschaften der Tiere und Menschen. *Studium generale*, 1950, **3**, 565–572.

Krott, P. *Der Vielfrab* (*Gulo gulo* L. *1758*). Jena, 1959.

Krott, P. & Krott, G. Zum Verhalten des Braunbären (*Ursus arctos* L. 1758) in den Alpen. *Zeitschrift für Tierpsychologie*, 1963, **20**, 160–206.

Leyhausen, P. Vergleichendes über die Territorialität bei Tieren und den Raumanspruch des Menschen. *Homo*, 1954, **5**, 116–124.

Leyhausen, P., & Wolff, R. Das Revier einer Hauskatze. *Zeitschrift für Tierpsychologie*, 1959, **16**, 666–670.

Leyhausen, P. Domestikationsbedingte Verhaltenseigentumlichkeiten der Hauskatze. *Zeitschrift für Tierzuchtung und Zuchturgsbiologie*, 1962, **77**, 191–197.

Marler, P. Studies of fighting in chaffinches: Behaviour in relation to the social hierarchy. *British Journal of Animal Behavior*, 1955a, 3, 111–117.

Marler, P. Studies of fighting in chaffinches: The effect on dominance relations of disguising females as males. *British Journal of Animal Behavior*, 1955b, 3, 137–146.

Marler, P. Studies of fighting in chaffinches: Proximity as a cause of aggression. *British Journal of Animal Behavior*, 1956, 4, 23–30.

Marler, P. Studies of fighting in chaffinches: Appetitive and consummatory behaviour. *British Journal of Animal Behavior*, 1957, 5, 29–37.

Meehan, W. R. Observations on feeding habits and behavior of grizzly bears. *American Midland Naturalist*, 1961, **65**, 409–412.

Meyer-Holzapfel, M. Das Verhalten der Baren (Ursidae). *Handbuch Zoologie Berlin*, 1957, 8, Lfg 8, Teil 10 (17), 1–28.

Murie, A. *The wolves of Mount McKinley.* Washington, D.C.: U. S. Department of the Interior, 1944.

Nice, M. The role of territory in bird life. *American Midland Naturalist*, 1941, **26**, 441–487.

Nippold, W. *Die Anfänge des Eigentums bei den Naturvölkern und die Entstehung des Privateigentums.* s'Gravenhage, 1954.

Nolte, A. Field observations on the daily routine and social behaviour of common Indian monkeys with special reference to the bonnet monkey (*Macaca radiata* Geoff). *Journal of the Bombay Natural History Society,* 1955, **53**, 177–184.

Schenkel, R. Ausdrucksstudien an Wölfen. *Behaviour,* 1947, **1**, 81–130.

Schmidt, W. *Das Eigentum auf den ältesten Stufen der Menschheit I.* Münster: Westf, 1937.

Tinbergen, L., & Kluyver, H. N. Territory and the regulation of density in titmice. *Archives Néerlandaises de Zoologie,* 1953, **10**, 265–289.

Verheyen, R. Monographie ethologique de l'hippopotame (*Hippopotamus amphibius* Linné). *Institute des Parcs Nationaux du Congo Belge.* (Explorations des Parcs Nationaux Albert), 1954.

Wynne-Edwards, V. C. *Animal dispersion in relation to social behaviour.* Edinburgh and London: Oliver & Boyd, 1962.

18 The Role of Space in Animal Sociology

John B. Calhoun

The distribution of resources through the environment, the localization of objects eliciting responses, and the presence of barriers to movement or perception at a distance, represent primary circumstances moulding the evolution and maturation of social behavior. I shall summarize the formulations of the role of such variables, which have developed from my research (Calhoun, 1956a, 1956b, 1958, 1962, 1963, 1964, 1966) over the past 20 years, and place in perspective to them a few insights apparent from the wide literature on the ecology and evolution of mammals.

From any point, such as where there occurs a concentration of food, it often happens that some other kind of object may be distributed at varying distances from this primary locus of orientation. Such situations are common to the experience of anyone observing animals in their native

From *The Journal of Social Issues,* 1966, **22**, 46–58. Reprinted by permission of the author and publisher.

habitats. However, despite such extensive experience, it was only after reading Stewart (1948) and Zipf (1949) that I was able to conceive of a more rigorous approach to this general problem. I constructed a very simple environment (Figure 18-1) in which several groups of domesticated inbred house mice were permitted to reside, each group separately.

At one side of a 225 sq. ft. pen a single opening gave access to a smaller pen containing an abundant supply of food, water, and nesting material. This became the primary center of orientation. On the opposite side of the room there stood a stand with shelves at four levels above the floor. A single ramp connected one end of each shelf to the floor. From the ramp end of each shelf four nest boxes were equally spaced along its length.

On each shelf five kinds of data were recorded which reflected single responses, groups of related responses, or physiological

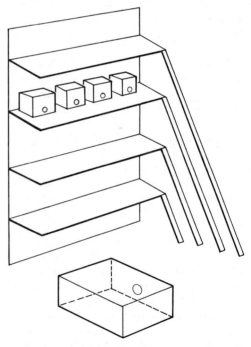

Figure 18–1. Diagrammatic representation of mouse-habitat. A four shelf stand, with four boxes on each shelf, formed the two-dimensional space over which mice spread their activities after visiting the small pen in the foreground in which were located the sources of food, water, and nesting material.

states. These were (1) defecation in boxes, (2) defecation beside boxes, (3) boxes entered during periods of activity, (4) mouse found "sleeping" in box, and (5) grams of nesting material deposited in box. These categories are here simply designated as behaviors. Regardless of type of behavior, it took place most frequently on the shelf nearest the floor, or near the next box at the ramp end of shelves. Toward higher shelves, or toward boxes farther out from the ramp end, the frequency of behaviors declined. An exception to this rule applied to the highest shelf or to the farthest box along a shelf from its ramp end. The increase in behaviors taking place at these more distant points included the sum of behaviors which would have taken place at even more distant points had not this absence of opportunity, or barrier effect, been present. Heightened goal orientation, such as when sleep follows entering a nest box as opposed to merely brief visits during periods of exploration, caused accentuated use of boxes on lower shelves or near the ramp end of shelves, with concomitant more rapid decline in use of more distant boxes.

This influence of distance upon behavior alters social contact. The mean group size per box in the 2nd, 3rd, and 4th box from the ramp along shelves was respectively only 0.84, 0.65, and 0.56 of that in the box nearest the ramp. Likewise, the mean size of groups per box on the 2nd, 3rd, and 4th shelves were respectively only 0.46, 0.43, and 0.57 that per box on the lowest shelf. Furthermore, as groups of mice residing in such systematically structured habitats in turn become socially structured, the more dominant members concentrated their activities in areas nearer to the primary site of orientation, the food-water nesting material pen enclosure, while still retaining their basic pattern of visiting all points but with fewer visitations to more distant points. In contrast, this normal pattern becomes partially disrupted for subordinate individuals; they tended to spend a disproportionate amount of time in places more distant from the major locus of orientation. This process accentuates the probability of associations among higher ranking individuals or among lower ranking ones. Very comparable results have been obtained with both wild and domesticated Norway rats.

It became imperative to gain more precise insight into the behavior of single individuals with regard to distance before it was possible to understand how this could affect social behavior. The basic tool in such study has been a long narrow alley with a starting compartment at one end containing food and water. Automatic recording provided a history of each trip out and back. Even when the alley was barren of structures except its walls, roof, and floor, and the rat introduced into it had a prior life history of living only in a smaller barren cage, it would, nevertheless, make a number of trips out into the alley. For each unit of distance more trips terminated nearest the starting compartment, with successively fewer at each farther location. A negative exponential equation of the form $\log_e y = a - bx$, where y is number of trips and x is distance of termination adequately describes the data (see Figure 18-2).

Furthermore, examination of long sequences of terminations of trips reveals that the distance at which any specific one is terminated is independent of that of the prior or succeeding one. This strongly indicates that in such constant surroundings the length, in effect the duration, of any trip is solely determined by some random signal

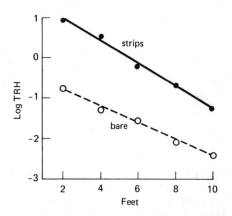

Figure 18–2. Frequency of trips of varying lengths in structured and unstructured alleys. (Ordinate: TRH = trips per rat per hour. Abscissa: Distance of termination of trips. Mean trips per hour = 6.31 in the structured alley vs. 1.17 in the bare alley.)

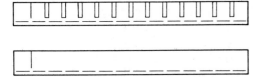

Figure 18–3. Cross-section side views of activity alleys. The lower represents a bare alley, while the upper one represents an alley structured with a pad of paper at each foot interval from the home compartment. The starting or home compartment is at the left end of each.

from the central nervous system such that, no matter how long a trip has already continued, the same probability still exists that it will terminate within a fixed further amount of time.

Such a barren alley can be structured by placing pads of paper strips at regular intervals (Figure 18-3). When this is done, the rat will make repeated trips out into the alley for paper with which it constructs a nest. Everything said above about the behavior of a rat in a barren alley applies to that in the structured one. However, many more trips are made and the probability of terminating trips increases (Figure 18-2). Thus, relevantly structuring the environment must modify central nervous system activity by increasing the probability of initiation of an appropriate behavioral state, while at the same time increasing the probability of it terminating. This latter effect results in the rat spending more time near its major point of orientation, its "home" cage compartment.

Now, we may turn from this one-dimensional environment to that of the normal, essentially two-dimensional one of such small mammals as mice and shrews in their field or forest habitat. Most such mammals have a single nest or burrow, or a few closely neighboring ones. From such a region the individual roams out and back for the various resources it needs for its daily life. Ecologists designate as the animal's "home range" the total space encompassed by such wanderings from and back to such a home base. Over most such home ranges every object meeting some need has roughly the same probability of being encountered within each relatively smaller sub-unit of

space. In this general sense, resources can be said to be uniformly distributed over the range on the average.

When one records the places at which an individual makes specific responses and plots them, it is found that the number of responses per unit area declines with distance from home (Figure 18-4). Interestingly enough this distribution over space is quite adequately described by the bivariate normal distribution function. (See Calhoun, 1964, for proof that the distribution of responses in two-dimensional space conforms to the bivariate normal distribution function rather than to the univariate normal distribution function.) That is to say: 39 percent of the responses will occur within a 1σ distance from the home range center, 86 percent within a 2σ distance, and 99 percent within a 3σ distance. Sigma here in terms of the equation for the bivariate normal distribution function is merely some appropriate measure of distance in feet or meters.

How, then, do we make the insights developed in the one-dimensional environment helpful in appreciating an animal's use of space in a two-dimensional one? It will be helpful to clarify a conclusion relating to

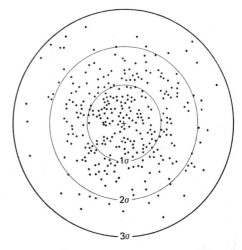

Figure 18–4. Diagrammatic representation of the distribution of responses in two-dimensional space about a central home site, marked by a +. Response points are normally distributed with reference to both their x and y coordinate dimensions and thus fit the bivariate normal distribution.

obtaining and transport of nesting material mentioned above for one-dimensional environments. In such activity a single rat may make several hundred trips with only a few seconds intervening between successive trips. Three consecutive trips might terminate with strips taken from the 7th, 3rd, and 10th distance, respectively. In each case the rat will have passed by two or more opportunities to stop and get a piece of paper to take back to its nest-in-process-of-construction. Obviously, the rat is highly motivated, as evidenced by the many consecutive transport trips without much time for other behaviors intervening between trips. In fact, motivation here becomes synonymous with the probabilities of starting and continuing trips. It may only be concluded that as long as the stimuli in the environment—here the paper strips—remain essentially unvarying, the rat is blind to them in the sense of not being able to respond to any specific pad it passes until the central nervous system sends out the signal which terminates the outward trip. Only then can it attend to the neighboring relevant stimuli.

Furthermore, it was observed in the alley that the amount of time a rat vacillated back and forth about the point where its trip terminated, was proportional to the distance (duration) at which the trip terminated. Now, taking only these two conclusions, (1) that there is a constant probability of a trip terminating no matter how long it has already persisted, and (2) that amount of wandering at the end of a trip is proportional to the length of the trip before it terminates, it is possible to develop from them an equation for the distribution of responses about a home site in a two-dimensional environment that is so similar to the bivariate normal distribution function that we are never likely to get any empirical set of data that would permit us to decide which one describes home range best. Because of this agreement one is then led to the conclusion (despite the inherent circular reasoning necessary until other more direct experimental confirmation is available) that mammals are perceptually "blind" to constant stimuli during outward excursions, and perceptually "cognizant" of them during the wanderings about at the end of trips.

This is not to say that a domesticated rat couldn't react to a flashing light, suddenly facing it on an outward trip, or a wild mouse or shrew couldn't detect a relatively unusual or foreboding stimulus, such as a weasel, if it were to encounter one.

You will also note that I am jumping back and forth from data relating first to domesticated mice or rats and then again to wild mice or shrews. The inherent assumption is that we are here dealing with processes equally applicable to mice or men, or to cats or bats, for that matter. But I shall actually, in the next few paragraphs, be concerned rather specifically with small mammals, such as mice and shrews, which in terms of the ecological situations they face are the closest we can come to the types of primitive mammals from which most mammals, including ourselves, trace their ancestry.

Here, we return to the two-dimensional home range. Over the course of evolution the "metronomes" of the central nervous system which normally control the start of excursions, their termination, and the cutting in of periods of heightened awareness, must be attuned to opportunities for relevant behavior provided by the environment. Otherwise animals would die of starvation. This whole built-in process of the central nervous system is reflected in the measure of its home range. Animals having more scattered resources will evolve the CNS function which reduces the probability of terminating trips, and in other ways increases their home range; thus they will be assured of adequate resources.

However, if we take the circular area encompassed by a 3σ radius about an animal's home as its home range, for at least 99 percent of its responses are included within this area, it is apparent that, were any individual alone in a habitat, it would make very ineffective use of its home range. Resources toward the periphery would be very ineffectively utilized simply because the individual rarely gets there. Evolution tends to produce species whose behavior makes more optimal use of avenues for behavior—including use of resources—available to them. More effective use of resources can most readily come about, in the early stages of evolution, by the several members of a population shifting their homes closer together so that their home ranges overlap.

It may be shown that when homes of neighbors are 2σ apart, and when all homes are uniformly distributed over the available space, that the accompanying overlapping will produce a nearly equivalent impact on every unit of space, while still providing the maximal separation of individuals compatible with such effective use of space.

Studies of small mammals in their natural habitat provide fairly good substantiation of the above concepts about home range. If the ideal pattern of distribution of home sites for such fairly asocial small mammals is as described above, some very interesting social relationships between any individual and his associates become apparent. Take any such individual. He will have six nearest neighbors, and lines connecting their homes form a hexagon. Due to the considerable overlapping of their home ranges, he will, by chance alone, fairly frequently encounter them. Likewise, he will have 12 next-nearest neighbors, and lines connecting their homes will form a larger hexagon about the central animal's home. Due to the much lesser overlapping of ranges of these 12 with the one central individual we are considering, they will encounter him less frequently, and so know him less well than do his six nearest neighbors.

At this level of social evolution each individual is sufficiently antagonistic to his neighbors to assure that neighboring home sites are approximately 2σ distance apart. Yet this force of dispersal becomes counteracted by the opposite one of attraction, in proportion to the probability of neighbors contacting each other by chance. This causes animals to shift their homes slightly toward each other. Some few individuals in a large population will each have attracted toward their own home site the home sites of all of their six nearest neighbors. This represents the first basic tendency toward group formation. The central animal will become the dominant member of this dispersed group of seven individuals. He will also have attracted toward him some of his next-nearest neighbors, but some of them will shift their home away from his toward the home of some other individual who, by a comparable process, is also gaining dominance. In this stochastic process of attraction, each animal becoming a dominant center will, on the average, attract toward him 5 of his 12 next-nearest neighbors, in addition to all of his 6 nearest neighbors. Thus, on the average, each of these primordial dispersed groups, which I have designated as a "constellation," will contain 12 individuals, consisting of a socially dominant individual and eleven associates who shift the sites of their homes toward his.

From this stage of loose aggregation of slightly clumped, but still quite dispersed home sites, there is an abrupt transition to species customarily living as compact groups of about 12 adults. This number applies to a host of species as divergent as the Norway rat, howler monkeys, or man in his more primitive state as represented by the bushmen of the Kalahari Desert. My essential thesis thus holds that the stochastic process involved in developing the most effective use of resources by relatively asocial species will normally favor the evolution of species living as compact groups averaging 12 adults.

Professor Glen McBride of the University of Queensland (in a discussion with him during February 1964) has pointed out that other optimum group sizes can evolve by this process. If a species with dispersed home sites suddenly comes to live in an environment with a much greater density, or abundance of resources, home sites will tend to approach each other more closely and thus there will develop much more overlap of home ranges. Any one animal will encounter more associates. Related to the extent of such new abundance of resources, the optimum group size characterizing the evolving species will become one of the expanding series of 27, 48, 75, 108. . . . Domestication of the chicken has thus changed its heredity to be most nearly compatible to living in groups of 48.

Once a species has developed the capacity to live as members of a compact group, they then become subject to being further influenced by another change in their physical environment. The members of most such compact groups do not always remain together. Individuals make independent excursions away from the group or away from the site to which all return to sleep. During such excursions an individual may encounter some locally abundant resource, which in fact may be found in only a few places of the now-shared home range of the group. Even by chance, two individuals may find themselves simultaneously at the same such site, while responding to the resources available at it. Whenever this happens, there is the opportunity for each individual to become a secondary reinforcer for the other. As such secondary reinforcement becomes established, animals actively seek out places for satisfying such primary drives as hunger or thirst where others of their kind have already assembled.

When several such sites are scattered over the range of a group, some will more likely be encountered than others. Gradually, all members of the group will assemble at the one place, where other factors affecting movement make it more likely to be encountered. Here each individual can be assured of the greatest likelihood of encountering others, of fulfilling its acquired secondary drive of needing to be near others. In time, all other sites within the group's range will be ignored. Each individual may pass by one or more sites where food and water can be obtained in order to reach the one site where it most likely will find others of its species. It is as if food is no longer food merely because it has the correct visual and olfactory characteristics—there must also be other members of the respondent's own species standing nearby.

For the same reason that the ranges of individuals overlap, so do the ranges of neighboring groups. Thus, as the members of one group begin to spend an inordinate amount of time at one place, the several neighboring groups nearest to it may likewise be attracted to this one place. I have called this process the development of a behavioral sink. In a state of nature it may cause at least seven times the optimum number of animals to assemble at one place, with a resulting accompanying array of abnormal behaviors developing. Prominent among these are nearly total dissolution of all maternal behavior, predominance of homosexuality, and marked social withdrawal to the point where many individuals appear to be unaware of their associates despite their close proximity.

I have shown how this behavioral sink, with all its manifestations, can be induced to develop under experimental conditions with domesticated Norway rats. Such a behavioral sink also came to characterize Virginia deer, when after the mid-1930's large amounts of hay and grain were placed at widely separated points throughout the severe winter months.

The behavioral sink also has its time aspects. Where there is only a single site of a resource, or where attachment to one of several sites has developed through the process described above, it may happen that so many individuals aggregate at the site that each may interfere with the opportunity for his associates to obtain the resource available at that site. At least this will be so unless the individuals present spread their activities out over time.

For rats, just the opposite happens. In another of my experimental situations, one or two narrow parallel channels led to a source of water. In the one-channel situation, two rats could go in side by side. In the two-channel situation, a rat on one side would find water available only if another rat was at the opposite source of water. In both situations there was the opportunity for one rat to associate presence of another with his obtaining water. When 16, 24, or 36 rats were placed in a pen containing such a situation, the characteristic response became one where, when one rat went to get water, most of his associates would also rush over and attempt to crowd into the narrow channels. Under such circumstances most failed to secure any water. After awhile, all would go away and sleep for quite awhile even though most had received no water. This process would be repeated over and over again. Most rats lost considerable weight or died from lack of water, even though the source was vacant from use most of the time, so that there was ample opportunity for drinking. Such is the time aspect of the behavioral sink.

Through the course of evolution, many species must have been subjected to the behavioral sink process often enough to threaten their survival as a species. Those which survived must have become genetically transformed into another species capable of maintaining the basic integrity of each individual despite the persisting crowding. On a theoretical basis this integrity is bought at the price of reduced social awareness. Each individual must be endowed with an heredity facilitating a diminution in the intensity, frequency, and complexity of responses to associates, and a reduction in the necessity for learned responses. The buffalo and the caribou of the American plains and tundra represent such forms. They have long since gone down a path of evolution forever barring them from the door to cultural evolution.

The physical environment has also fostered the evolution of other species which have followed along a quite different path but one that similarly precludes any future possibility of cultural evolution for them. In evolution it seems as though all possible paths, all possible opportunities, will be exploited. One of these is the abundant source of food under the surface of the earth—a mass of roots and rhizomes equal to that of plants above the surface, as well as the myriad invertebrates subsisting on the living and decaying underground plant material.

On every continent mammals have ducked under the surface and remained there. There is the marsupial mole in Australia. Mole-like Insectivora or gopher-like Rodentia occur across the other continents. Typically, each adult constructs its own subterranean network of tunnels without connections to those of its neighbors. There these troglodytes spend their lives, each alone, buffered from the sight, sounds, smells, and social stimuli churning in the world above. Contact among adults is restricted to the minimum required for copulation at the rare periods when the female is receptive. Shortly after weaning, the mother ejects her young from the home burrow to seek their own maze-like cell. Such is the culmination of evolution accompanying the stimulus deprivation associated with accommodating to the subterranean source of food. This whole process of accommodating to stimulus deprivation, including its end state, I wish now to designate as the "behavioral vacuum."

Research on the behavior of animals may provide insight into the human condition with regard to either its evolution or its present circumstances. The utility of such insights depends upon there being a relationship between the present human condition and its antecedents in simpler forms of mammals, or on the fact that comparable processes characterize both man and lower forms. Research on the behavior and sociology of animals other than man stems from two opposing perspectives. First, from the direct study of man insights develop which culminate in a paradigm amenable to exploration through the use of animal subjects. Second, on the basis of the knowledge of the evolution and natural history of a particular species one examines more rigorously the processes affecting the species in its natural setting or devises more controlled settings which will permit the process or phenomenon to be expressed in a more precise or exaggerated manner. This latter approach often produces insights not previously recognized on the human level, or which if seriously recognized may be seen in a different relationship to other processes. Those of us who are engaged in research on animals from this second point of view can only point out certain insights which we believe merit the consideration of those of our colleagues whose concern is directly with man.

For example, I have mentioned briefly here the explanation, developed in detail elsewhere, for the finding that so many species of mammals, up through the primates, live in compact groups of about twelve adults. By virtue of his biological heritage, *Homo sapiens* appears to have been long related, and presumably adjusted to, a way of life that was most harmonious when the population was fragmented into small social groups of about twelve adults. For this reason it behooves us to examine what restrictions upon culture such biological heritage may impose. From a theoretical point of view (Calhoun, 1964, 1967) a long heritage of a particular group size imposes the necessity for an intensity and frequency of interaction with associates commensurate with the stochastics of the relatively closed system of that size group. Furthermore, I have shown that, when we increase the group size of rats above that of about twelve, which does characterize the species in its native state, all members exhibit both physical and psychological withdrawal to a greater degree than may be anticipated for individuals in a customary sized group. Thus we may suspect that if man does have a biological heritage most compatible with life in a relatively closed small social group, then a major function of culture may be to schedule contacts such that their frequency will approximate that which characterized life in the smaller, more closed social group of a much earlier stage of biological and cultural evolution.

These concepts relating to group size serve as background to others more directly related to the import of the physical environment. As noted above, the physical configuration of the environment, including the prevalence of stimuli which might elicit responses, can increase the likelihood either of an animal following a solitary way of life or, on the other hand, of it joining with its fellows in large massed groups even when much nearby similarly structured space remains relatively unused. These observations merely raise the question whether there are comparable situations on the human scene which may lead to either excessive isolation or excessive aggregations, either of which would alter the frequency of interaction. Judged by both mathematically derived formulations and observations on animals, such changes in frequency of interaction lead to types of social organization which I would judge to be completely incompatible with a cultural context of life such as characterizes man.

There is one final possible relevance of these studies on animals to the human situation. Merely increasing the number of relevant stimuli increased the number of excursions which rats made into their environment, where they engaged in responses appropriate to these stimuli. This raises a question, not yet answered even with animal experimentation, but still worth keeping in mind with regard to man's physical environment: Can responses to inanimate objects be equated with those to members of his own species with reference to an apparent need for a certain number of satisfactory social interactions per unit time? If there exists such an interchangeability between physical and social response eliciting objects, then the complexity of the physical environment must be evaluated against the existing social organization.

REFERENCES:

Calhoun, J. B. A comparative study of the social behavior of two inbred strains of house mice. *Ecological Monographs*, 1956a, **26**, 81–103.

Calhoun, J. B. Behavior of house mice with reference to fixed points of orientation. *Ecology*, 1956b, **37**, 287–301.

Calhoun, J. B. Social welfare as a variable in population dynamics. *Symposium of Quantitative Biology*, 1958, **22**, 339–356.

Calhoun, J. B. A behavioral sink. In E. Bliss (Ed.), *Roots of behavior*. New York: Paul Hoeber, 1962.

Calhoun, J. B. *The ecology and sociology of the Norway rat*, U.S. Dept. of Health, Education, and Welfare, Public Health Service, Pub. No. 1008, Washington, D.C.: GPO, 1963.

Calhoun, J. B.: The social use of space. In W. Mayer & R. Van Gelder (Eds.), *Physiological mammalogy*. New York: Academic Press, 1964.

Calhoun, J. B. Ecological factors in the development of behavioral anomalies. In J. Zubin (Ed.), *Comparative psychopathology*. New York: Grune and Stratton, 1967.

Stewart, J. Q. Concerning social physics. *Scientific American*, 1948, **178**, 20–23.

Zipf, G. K. *Human behavior and the principle of least effort*. Cambridge, Mass.: Addison-Wesley, 1949.

19 The Social Environment

René Dubos

1. PHYSIOLOGICAL RESPONSES TO POPULATION DENSITY

The word crowd has unpleasant connotations. It evokes disease, pestilence, and group-generated attitudes often irrational and either too submissive or too aggressive. Congested cities call to mind unhealthy complexions and harassed behavior; city crowds are accused of accepting despotic power and of blindly engaging in acts of violence. In contrast, rural areas and small towns are thought to foster health and

From René Dubos, *Man Adapting*. New Haven, Conn.: Yale University Press, 1965, pp. 100–109. Reprinted by permission of the author and publisher.

freedom. The legendary Arcadia and the Utopias of all times are imagined as comfortably populated by human beings enjoying vast horizons. The nature and history of man are far too complex, of course, to justify such generalizations, but there is some truth nevertheless in the belief that crowding generates problems of disease and behavior. However, these problems are poorly understood and their formulation is rendered even more difficult by a number of oversimplified and erroneous concepts inherited from the late nineteenth century.

During the Industrial Revolution, the crowding in tenements, factories, and offices was associated with tremendous increases in morbidity and mortality rates. Along with malnutrition, the various "fevers" were the most obvious causes of ill health. Epidemic outbreaks and chronic forms of microbial disease constituted the largest medical problems of the late nineteenth century because they were extremely prevalent, not only among the economically destitute but also among the more favored classes. The new science of microbiology that developed during that period provided a theory that appeared sufficient at first sight to explain the explosive spread of infection. The germ theory made it obvious that crowding facilitates the transfer of microbes from one person to another, and this led to the reasonable conclusion that the newly industrialized communities had been caught in a web of infection, resulting from the increase in human contacts.

The expression "crowd diseases" thus became, and has remained ever since, identified with a state of affairs conducive to the rapid spread of infective agents, particularly under unsanitary conditions. Epidemiologists have built their science on the hypothesis that the pattern of microbial diseases in a given community of animals or men is determined by the channels available for the spread of microbes. In reality, however, the rise and fall of animal populations, both in confined environments and in the field, present aspects that cannot be entirely accounted for by these classical concepts of epidemiology. The reason, as we shall now see, is that crowding has several independent effects. On the one hand, it facilitates the spread of infective agents; on the other hand, it also modifies the manner in which men and animals respond to the presence of these agents and thereby increases indirectly the prevalence and severity of microbial disease. In fact, crowding affects the response of the individual and social body, not only to infection, but also to most of life's stresses.

In many species, the numbers of animals increase continuously from year to year until a maximum population density is reached; then suddenly an enormous mortality descends. This phenomenon, known as "population crash," has long been assumed to be caused by epidemics corresponding to those which have been so destructive in the course of human history, for example plague or yellow fever. Indeed, several different kinds of pathogens have been found to attack animal populations at the time of the crash. Pasteurellae and salmonellae are among the bacterial organisms that used to be most commonly incriminated; two decades ago a particular strain of *Mycobacterium muris* (the vole bacillus), isolated from field mice in England, was thought for a while to be responsible for population crashes in these rodents. Now that viruses have taken the limelight from bacteria, they in turn have been made responsible for occurrences of widespread mortality in several animal species.

It has become apparent, however, that the relation between population crashes and microbial diseases is far less clear than was once thought. On the one hand, several different types of pathogens can be associated with crashes in a given animal species. On the other hand, there are certain crashes for which no pathogen has been found to account for the pathological picture. These puzzling observations have led to the theory that the microbial diseases associated with population crashes are but secondary phenomena, and that the primary cause is a metabolic disturbance.

Food shortages, or at least nutritional deficiencies, were long considered as a probable cause of drastic population decline. It is well known, in fact, that when wild animals multiply without check under natural conditions they exhaust their food supply, lose weight, and bear fewer young; this occurs for example when their predators are eliminated. However, a poor nutritional state can hardly account alone for population crashes. Its effect is rather to limit reproduction, either by failure of conception or by abortion; the overall result is an automatic adjustment of population size to the food supply instead of a massive crash. In fact, drastic population declines commonly occur even when the food supply is abundant.

The trend during recent years has been to explain population crashes by a "shock disease" related in some obscure way to overactivity of the adrenopituitary system. A notorious example of this type of crowd disease is the mass migration of the Norwegian lemmings from the mountaintops of Scandinavia. According to an ancient Norwegian belief, the lemmings periodically experience an irresistible "collective urge" either to commit suicide or to search for their ancestral home on the lost Atlantic Continent, and consequently they march unswervingly into the sea. In reality, such migrations take place whenever the lemmings become overcrowded, a situation that occurs every third or fourth year, as each mating pair produces 13 to 16 young annually. The migration of Norwegian lemmings was so massive in 1960–61 that a steamer entering the Trondheim Fjord took one hour to pass through a two-mile-long pack of swimming and sinking rodents!

Although the nature of the initial stimulus that prompts the lemmings to migrate is not understood, crowding is almost certainly one of its aspects. As the rodents become more and more crowded they fall victims to a kind of mass psychosis. This results in a wild scrambling about that, contrary to legend, is not necessarily a march toward the sea but merely random movement. The animals die, not by drowning, but from metabolic derangements associated with stress; lesions are commonly found in the brain and the adrenals.

Profound changes have also been observed to occur at more or less regular intervals in the population of snowshoe hares. According to a classical description, these animals observed in Minnesota during periods of crash

. . . characteristically died in convulsive seizures with sudden onset, running movements, hind leg extension, retraction of the head and neck, and sudden leaps with clonic seizures upon alighting. Other animals were typically lethargic or comatose. . . . This syndrome was characterized primarily by decrease in liver glycogen and a hypoglycemia preceding death. Petechial or ecchymotic brain hemorrhages, and congestion and hemorrhage of the adrenals, thyroid, and kidneys were frequent findings (Deevey, 1960).

Interestingly enough, many of the signs and symptoms observed in wild animals dying during population crashes have been reproduced in the laboratory by subjecting experimental animals to crowding and other forms of stress. Voles placed for a few hours a day during a month in cages containing another pair of aggressive voles eventually died, but not of wounds. The main finding at necropsy was a marked increase in the weight of their adrenals and spleen and a decrease in the weight of the thymus. Similar findings have been made in captive and wild rats.

Crowding can act as a form of stress in most species of experimental animals. In chickens, mice, rats, and voles, it causes an enlargement of the adrenals chiefly through cellular hyperplasia in the cortical areas; in addition it interferes with both growth and reproductive function.

Crowding affects many other biological characteristics of animal population; for example, the reproducibility of the response to various abnormal states, such as barbiturate anaesthesia, is affected by population density. The toxicity of central nervous system stimulants such as amphetamine is remarkably enhanced when the animals are placed in a crowded environment; central depressants protect to some degree against this aggregation effect. The experimental hypertension produced in rats bearing regenerating adrenals is increased by crowding, and coronary arteriosclerosis develops more rapidly and more intensely in chickens that are grouped than in animals kept isolated.

Field studies of voles in England have revealed the puzzling fact that their population continues to fall the year after the crash. It would appear, therefore, that the reduced viability responsible for the crash is transmitted from one generation to another. This finding is compatible with other observations which indicate that crowding of the mother affects the physical development and behavior of the offspring.

The response to almost any kind of stimulus can be modified by crowding, as is illustrated by the production of experimental granuloma. Cotton pellets impregnated with turpentine were introduced subcutaneously into groups of mice that were then either caged individually or in groups. The granulomas that developed in the grouped mice weighed 19 percent less than in the other animals, a result probably due to the fact that the greater adrenocortical activity in the grouped mice had exerted a suppressive effect on the inflammatory reaction.

It is probable that the effect of crowding on tissue response accounts for the decrease in resistance to infection. In order to put this hypothesis to the test, mice were infected with a standardized dose of *Trichinella* and then were either isolated in individual jars or caged in groups immediately after infection. When these mice were sacrificed 15 days later, it was found that all the grouped animals had large numbers of worms (15 to 51) in their intestines, whereas only 3 out of 12 of the isolated animals showed any sign of infection. Although exposure to infection had been identical, crowding had therefore increased the ability of trichinella to invade the intestinal wall, probably by decreasing the inflammatory response to the parasite. Analogous observations have been made with regard to infantile diarrhea of mice. The incidence of clinical signs of this disease remains small or is nil when the population density in the animal room is low, but it increases as the colony approaches peak production. The infection is endemic in most colonies, but the disease does not become overt until the animals are crowded.

The groupings of several organisms of one given species has certainly many physiological consequences more subtle than those mentioned above. One such curious effect has been observed in male ducks kept constantly either in the dark or exposed to artificial light for periods of over two years. In both cases, these abnormal conditions of light exposure resulted in marked disturbances of the sexual cycles, which were no longer in phase with the seasonal rhythms. However, the animals within each group exhibited a remarkable synchronism of testicular evolution, thus revealing a "group effect" on sexual activity that was independent of light, of season, and of the presence of animals of the opposite sex.

2. TERRITORIALITY, DOMINANCE, AND ADAPTATION TO CROWDING

As we have just seen, the epidemiology of "crowd" diseases involves factors other than those affecting the spread of infectious agents. Association with other living things modifies the total response of the organism to the various environmental forces and thereby affects susceptibility to a multiplicity of noxious influences, including infection.

A quantitative statement of population density is not sufficient, however, to forecast the effects of crowding on human beings or animals. Even more important than numbers of specimens of a given species per unit area is the manner in which each particular person or animal responds to the other members of the group under a given set of conditions. The response to population density is determined in large part by the history of the group and of its individual members; furthermore, it may be favorable or unfavorable, depending upon the circumstances.

Many types of rodents, such as laboratory rats and mice, prefer to be somewhat crowded. In fact, individually housed rats and mice usually behave in a more "emotional" or "frightened" manner than their group-housed counterparts; they are also less able to adapt to a variety of experimental procedures such as food restriction, food selection, or cold stress. Isolated mice are less able than grouped mice to overcome the disturbances in intestinal ecology caused by antimicrobial drugs and other physiological disturbances (unpublished observations). The practice of mutual cleaning accelerates wound healing in many animal species, and isolation has unfavorable effects on the behavior and personality structure of animals and man.

In most animal species, probably in all, each group develops a complex social organization based on territoriality and on a social hierarchy comprising subordinate and dominant members, the so-called pecking order. The place of each animal in the hierarchy is probably determined in part by anatomical and physiological endowments and in part by the history of the group. In any case, the behavioral differences that result from the pecking order eventually bring about anatomical and physiological differences far more profound than those initially present. For example, the dominant animals usually have larger adrenals than the subordinates and they grow more rapidly because they have more ready access to food. It appears also that in rhesus monkeys the young males issued from females with a high social rank have a better chance than other males to become dominant in the colony.

Under a given set of conditions, the relative rank of each individual animal is fairly predictable. Social competition is often restricted to the male sex, the reproductive fortunes of the female being determined by the status of the male which selects her. Females associated with subordinate males in experimental populations may entirely fail to reproduce. However, the pecking order is valid only for well-defined environmental conditions. For example, each canary bird is dominant in the region near its nest; and similarly chickens in their home yard win more combats than strangers to that yard. The successes of animals on their own territorial grounds bring to mind the better performance of baseball teams on their home fields.

Successful competition within the group naturally confers advantages. The despot has first choice with regard to food and mates, and its position may even increase its resistance to certain forms of stress such as infection. In a particular experiment involving tenches, one fish in the group was found to dominate the whole territory and to be the first one to feed. This dominance had such profound physiological consequences that when all the tenches were in-fected with trypanosomes, the infection disappeared first from the dominant fish. When this fish was removed from the tank, fighting started among those remaining; the fish that became dominant in the new grouping in its turn had first access to the food, and soon got rid of its trypanosome infection.

The phenomenon of dominance has a social meaning which transcends the advantages that it gives to the dominant individuals. Acceptance of the hierarchical order reduces fighting and other forms of social tensions and thus provides a stability that is beneficial to the group as a whole. In an undisturbed organized flock of chickens, for example, the individual animals peck each other less frequently and less violently, eat more, maintain weight better, and lay more eggs than do chickens in flocks undergoing social reorganization through removal of some animals or addition of new ones. Furthermore, the subordinate animals do not suffer as much as could be expected from their low rank in the pecking order. There is no direct competition for food or for mates in the well-organized group; the subordinates readily yield their place to the dominants at the feeding box; they exhibit no sexual interest, often behaving as if they were "socially castrated." Thus, the establishment of an accepted hierarchy in a stable group of animals almost eliminates the stresses of social tension and results in a kind of social homeostasis.

Needless to say, there are limits to the protective efficacy social organization can provide against the dangers created by high population density. Excessive crowding has deleterious effects even in the most gregarious rodents. When laboratory rats are allowed to multiply without restriction in a confined space, an excess of food being available at all times, they develop abnormal behavior with regard to mating, nest building, and care of the young as soon as the population becomes too dense. However, such conditions of life are extremely artificial. Under the usual conditions of rodent life in the wild, animals migrate or are killed when the population becomes too large for the amount of food available.

Although man is a gregarious animal,

sudden increases in population density can be as dangerous for him as they are for animals. The biological disturbances created during the Industrial Revolution by lack of sanitation and by crowding in tenements and factories were aggravated by the fact that most members of the new labor class had immigrated from rural areas and were totally unadapted to urban life. In contrast, the world is now becoming more and more urbanized. Constant and intimate contact with hordes of human beings has come to constitute the "normal" way of life, and men have eagerly adjusted to it. This change has certainly brought about all kinds of phenotypic adaptations that are making it easier for urban man to respond successfully to situations that in the past constituted biological and emotional threats.

There may be here an analogy with the fact that domesticated animals do not respond to various types of threatening situations in the laboratory as do wild animals of the same or related species. In any case, the effects of crowding on modern urban man are certainly very different from those experienced by the farmer and his family when they were first and suddenly exposed a century ago to the city environment of industrialized societies.

The readiness with which man adapts to potentially dangerous situations makes it unwise to apply directly to human life the results of experiments designed to test the acute effects of crowding on animals. Under normal circumstances, the dangerous consequences of crowding are mollified by a multiplicity of biological and social adaptations. In fact, crowding per se, that is, population density, is probably far less important in the long run even in animals than is the intensity of the social conflicts, or the relative peace achieved after social adjustments have been made. As already mentioned, animal populations in which status differences are clearly established are likely to reach a greater size than those in which differences in rank are less well defined.

Little is known concerning the density of population or the intensity of stimulation that is optimum in the long run for the body and the mind of man. Crowding is a relative term. The biological significance of population density must be evaluated in the light of the past experience of the group concerned, because this experience conditions the manner in which each of its members responds to the others as well as to environmental stimuli and trauma.

Laying claim to a territory and maintaining a certain distance from one's fellow are probably as real biological needs in man as they are in animals, but their expressions are culturally conditioned. The proper distance between persons in a group varies from culture to culture. People reared in cultures where the proper distance is short appear "pushy" to those coming from social groups where propriety demands greater physical separation. In contrast, the latter will appear to the former as behaving in a cold, aloof, withdrawn, and standoffish manner. Although social anthropologists have not yet adequately explained the origin of these differences, they have provided evidence that ignorance of them in human relations or in the design of dwellings and hospitals can have serious social and pathological consequences.

The problems posed by crowding in human populations are thus more complex than those which exist in animal populations because they are so profoundly conditioned by social and cultural determinants. Indeed, there is probably no aspect of human life for which it is easier to agree with Ortega y Gasset that "man has no nature. What he has is a history." Most experimental biologists are inclined to scorn discussions of mob psychology and related problems because they feel that the time is not yet ripe for scientific studies on the mechanisms of collective behavior. Yet the phrase "mob psychology" serves at least to emphasize that the response of human beings to any situation is profoundly influenced by the structure of the social environment.

The numerous outbreaks of dancing manias that occurred in Europe from the fourteenth to sixteenth century constitute a picturesque illustration of abnormal collective behavior; such an event was witnessed by P. Breughel the Elder and became the subject of one of his most famous paintings, "The Saint Vitus Dancers," now in Vienna. Even today, revivalists, tremblers and shakers often outdo the feats of the medieval performers during the dancing manias. And millions of people can still be collectively bewitched by the antics of a Hitler or other self-proclaimed prophet, to whom they yield body and soul. What happens in the mind of man is always reflected in the diseases of his body. The epidemiology of crowd diseases cannot be completely understood without knowledge of mob psychology.

REFERENCE:

Deevey, E. S. The hare and the haruspex: A cautionary tale. *American Scientist*, 1960, 48, 415–429.

20 Territoriality of Patients on a Research Ward

Aristide H. Esser, Amparo S. Chamberlain, Eliot D. Chapple, and Nathan S. Kline

The dispersion of animal groups in space shows territorial factors that control their survival and the social structure within them. Animals in groups can be ranked according to dominance, and the top animal maintains his position through possessing more territory or food than his fellow animals. So general are these phenomena throughout the entire animal kingdom that they are regarded as critical in the evolutionary process.

In our search for objective criteria to describe the behavior of patients on a psychiatric ward, we have come to realize the importance of information on how patients use space, and on the relationship of this usage to rank in the group hierarchy. Better patients on the ward, "the elite" as we called them until recently, are regarded by the staff as leaders and initiators; there is no question of their dominance.

Patient Ro, for instance, functions more adequately than any other patient on the

From J. Wortis (Ed.), *Recent Advances in Biological Psychiatry*, 1965, 7, 36–44. Reprinted by permission of the authors and publisher.

ward. When there is work in the sheltered workshop, he acts as foreman. He helps with serving at mealtime and does such side chores as taking care of the urine collection in the morning. Although he has no particular chair that he calls his own, he can sit wherever he pleases and, without applying force, he can oust another patient from a chair if he wants it. In addition, since he has more property than most, he controls to a great extent which patient receives a cigarette, a piece of candy, or a soda. Such patients probably exist on every ward. Their position is rarely challenged because of their value in the ward's functioning. One of the incidents that occurs when dominance is not absolute is conflict between two patients close together in the ward dominance hierarchy.[1]

However, there are other patients, like Mn, whose dominance is low and whose position in the hierarchy has not been as firmly established; these men may maintain definite territories[2] in the ward. Patient Mn is withdrawn, almost mute, and initiates interaction only to ask for a cigarette or light, generally in a characteristic nonverbal manner. When he isn't pacing the hall, he sits in a chair in the TV room, apparently hallucinating. We became aware of his defensive behavior when one of our nurse-observers, having seen from the central one-way glass observation booth that he wanted a cigarette, came out and went to his chair to hand him one. As she neared him, he rose, struck her with his right fist, and then resumed his crouched seating position. In the following weeks, he repeated this behavior on two occasions when a fellow patient and a staff member unwittingly came within striking distance of "his" chair. Staff and patients have learned to avoid him when he is in this corner; otherwise, he cannot be considered an aggressive patient.

In order to define and measure how our 22 schizophrenic patients express themselves in these nonverbal ways, that is, in their

[1] "Dominance hierarchy" is a term used to describe power structure in monkey colonies.

[2] "Territory," in animal ecology, refers to a place that is habitually used and defended by the animal.

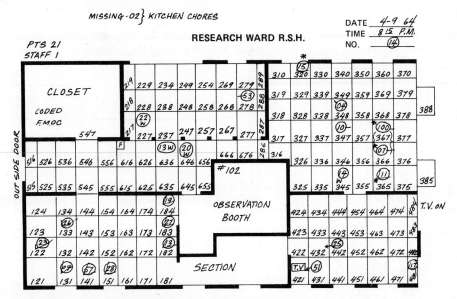

Figure 20–1. Distribution of territories on the ward.

spatial relations and in establishing their relative dominance positions, we have developed two main types of observation.

The first is what we call "location observation." To facilitate precise recordings of each patient's position, we have marked the floor of our Research Ward into 3 × 3 ft grids. The adjoining enclosed yard is marked off in the same way, but this presentation will deal only with observations done on the ward.

On observation days, we start between 8 and 9 o'clock in the morning and make observations every subsequent half hour. Using a rubber stamp with a pointed end, the observers in the booth record on preprinted plans (Figure 20-1) the square on which each person (including staff) is and what direction he is facing. To this record is added, in simple code, what his postural position is, the work or activity in which he is engaged, and with whom he is interacting, if at all. The information from these maps is then transformed into numerical code and entered on card format for our computer.

Our second method of investigating the problem of dominance and territoriality is by recording the interactional behavior of the individual patients. We observe continuously the interactional behavior of one patient at a time, sometimes up to a total of 10 hours a day. As long as the patient is on the day ward, we observe when and for how long he interacts with specific patients or staff members and we also note who initiated the interaction.

The dominance hierarchy of the patients on our ward is determined on the basis of their interactional behavior in the following manner:[3]

First, from the location observations, we summarize all patient-patient and patient-staff contacts in matrix form. These discrete data suffice to rank the patient in the ward hierarchy on the basis of (a) his total number of patient-patient contacts, (b) his total number of patient-staff contacts, and (c) the total number of different patients he contacted. The main rank order is derived by averaging these three suborders.

Second, on the basis of continuous observation of each patient's interactional behavior, he is ranked according to (1) his total interaction durations, and (2) his initiative. Three suborders are formulated for the first criterion by discriminating between (a) total interaction time, (b) total patient-patient interaction time, and (c)

[3] For the methodology and validation of this hierarchy, see A. H. Esser and E. D. Chapple, "Interactional hierarchy and power structure on a psychiatric ward" (in preparation).

| PATIENTS | | | USE OF AVAILABLE SPACE | | | | |
| Rank # | Code Name | Code # | Dayroom Areas | | | | |
			1	2	3	4	5 & 6
1	Ro	007					
2	Rz	013					
3	Ss	056					
4	Fa	058		■			■
5	Da *	052					
6	Fr *	057					
7	Ga	019					
8	Kl *	002			□		
9	St *	022	■		□	■	■
10	Fn	015	□	□		■	■
11	Cp	020				□	■
12	Bk +	004					□
13	El +	009	■			■	
14	Jb *	014					
15	Mn *	017	■	■		□	
16	Rd	018				■	
17	Fd	010	■				
18	Pl *	011		■			
19	Ms *	003			□		
20	Bn	051				□	
21	La	053		□			
22	Mo	055	■			■	

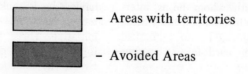

□ – Areas with territories

■ – Avoided Areas

* and + – – In cases of ties, seniority on the ward determined who ranked higher.

Figure 20–2. Dominance hierarchy and the use of space.

total time of informal patient-staff contacts. For the second criterion, we rank the patient on the basis of the percentages of time he took the initiative in these three contact situations, which again yields three suborders. The two groups of suborders are averaged separately and the results again averaged to give us the second main rank order.

These two rank orders, one based on discrete data on interaction and the other based on continuous data, show good internal consistency. Our final dominance hierarchy for the study period presented here is an average of both. To give a clinical impression of the constituents of this dominance hierarchy, we can say that the top third consists of patients who all have good verbal contact. The bottom third of the hierarchy contains five practically nonverbal patients.

The data presented here concern 330 location observations obtained during 16 out of 20 weeks at the beginning of last year. In this period our sheltered workshop did not operate, and no major change in our patient or staff population took place. The only change in the ward conditions was that half of the patients changed from drug to placebo medication or vice versa halfway through the study period. The measure of control that we exercise over our ward environment is described elsewhere (Simpson & Kline, 1962; Chapple et al., 1963; Esser et al., 1964).

From our location observations, we ascertained where each patient kept himself. If he was not present in an area for more than 5% of the observations, he was considered to have avoided this room. If he was in an area for more than one third of the observations, we looked for a particular square or group of squares where he might have spent more than 75% of the time he was seen in that area. Such a place is called a territory, and our manner of arriving at it ensures that the patient has been at that spot for at least 25% of all the observations. Patient Mn, mentioned earlier, possesses a territory in which he was observed in over 70% of all observations.

Figure 20-2 ranks the patients according to their position in the dominance hierarchy and gives an impression of how many areas

some patients avoided and which patients possessed a territory. There are 10 patients, with one exception all belonging to the lower two thirds of the dominance hierarchy, who avoid one or more areas. Of these patients, 6 possess a territory. Of the 12 patients who avoid no rooms, the 7 who have no territories belong to the top third of the hierarchy, except for one case. The remaining 5 who do possess a territory show a majority belonging to the bottom third of the hierarchy.

We may try to generalize from Figure 20-2 by saying that the patients in the upper third of the hierarchy are free to move wherever they want and do not seem to need to establish ownership of a spot. Patients in the middle third of the hierarchy show restrictions of range, and seem in need of occupying territories with a great chance for contact, i.e., those located in the main flow of traffic that comes through the ward entrance (see patients Bk, Fn, St, Kl, and El in Figure 20-3). The patients in the bottom third of the hierarchy are moderately restricted in range and find themselves secluded spots in which to withdraw with a markedly lower chance of being contacted (see patients La, Ms, Mn, and Bn in Figure 20-3). Of course, the fact that the dominance hierarchy was determined by measurements of interactional behavior lends credibility to this general statement.

We tried to find out whether the combination of restricted range and location of territories in the pathway of the main ward traffic, which characterizes the middle third of the hierarchy, might lead to more frequent involvement in aggressive acts on their part. To do so, we went back to our clinical records for the 4-month period in which these observations were made. We simply collected from these records all occasions in which patients were mentioned as having been involved in any hostile behavior, ranging from physical assault to verbal altercation. We did not try to determine whether the patient initiated the fight or not. We found that the patients could easily be grouped into three categories: those who were never mentioned, those who were occasionally involved in fights, and

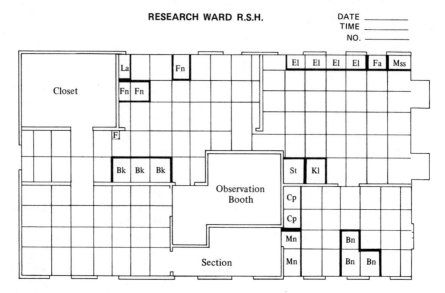

Figure 20–3. Plan of the ward used for location observations.

those who regularly displayed aggressive behavior. The distribution of these different categories of aggressiveness in the dominance hierarchy is shown in Figure 20-4.

It is immediately evident that our hypothesis, i.e., that fighting would occur most in the middle third of the hierarchy, does not hold. Instead, there seem to be two groups of "fighters," one in the upper half of the hierarchy and one in the lower half. The data reveal that these two groups fight almost exclusively among themselves or with patients lowest in the hierarchy. This in turn led us to suspect that the members of these two groups probably maintain unstable positions in the dominance hierarchy. Thus, they would fight either with patients with about equal dominance positions or with those patients in the lowest ranks from whom they have nothing to fear. Two factors appear to determine instability in dominance rank among our patients. In the first place, we noticed that recently admitted patients tend to fight more frequently than the older inhabitants of the ward. Second, we know from clinical experience that patients who change from active drug to placebo medication or vice versa undergo profound behavioral changes. Figure 20-4 shows which patients can be classified in one or both of these groups. As can be seen, instability in dominance position is related to aggressive

behavior in 10 out of 12 cases. Also, the factors contributing to instability seem to characterize the two groups of "fighters" mentioned earlier.

Two patients (Cp and Rd in Figure 20-4), who should have been aggressive but are not, form an exception to this rule. Although we cannot offer a definitive explanation for this negative relationship, it is perhaps relevant that both these patients stayed in rooms having an average of only 70% as many people at any one time as did the areas of the "fighters." Both patients have idiosyncratic problems: Cp has a marked latency of response that would reduce the chance of conflict; he waits about 4–6 seconds before he reacts in a standard interview situation, the longest delay recorded in any of our patients. For patient Rd, who spoke only Spanish, the impossibility of interacting verbally with any of the other patients could well have kept him out of trouble.

In closing, we may say that although most of the aggressive behavior on our ward is generated among patients whose position in the dominance hierarchy is not stable, it is also true that of those patients who possess territories, only 3 fail to show aggressive behavior. On the basis of the data presented here, no conclusion can be drawn as to how possession of territories and instability in the dominance hierarchy are related.

Patients			Factors		Measure of Aggression	
Rank #	Name	Code #	1	2	Occasional	Regular
1	Ro	007				
2	Rz	013				
3	Ss	056		+		
4	Fa	058	+	+		
5	Da	052				■
6	Fr	057	+			
7	Ga	019	+	+		
8	Kl	002		+		■
9	St	022	+	+		
10	Fn	015				■
11	Cp	020	+	+		
12	Bk	004				■
13	El	009				■
14	Jb	014		+		
15	Mn	017	+	+		
16	Rd	018	+	+		
17	Fd	010		+		
18	Pl	011		+		
19	Mss	003				■
20	Bn	051				■
21	La	053				■
22	Mo	055				■

Figure 20–4. Factors related to instability in dominance hierarchy and aggressive behavior. Factor 1—less than 3 months on the ward at start of study period; Factor 2—change from drug to placebo or vice versa halfway through study period.

DISCUSSION

We have tried to present our data within the framework of terminology derived from studies of free-ranging animal colonies, especially monkeys. "Territory," as defined in animal ecology, is an area habitually used and defended by the animal. "Dominance hierarchy" in adult monkeys is an easily ascertainable phenomenon; one need only watch to see which monkeys are frequently groomed and occupy the feeding and resting grounds of their choice.

Comparable behavior studies of human groups are impossible in noninstitutionalized surroundings, since the range of man over a lifetime has increased far beyond simple life in colonies. However, once the normal human range is restricted, as happens with people who live in an enforced community, such aspects of group interaction as aggressiveness can be related to territorial behavior and the fight for a stable position in the dominance hierarchy. For instance, in a prison, an army outpost, a Polaris submarine on patrol, and in our case, a mental hospital, outbursts of aggressiveness easily occur when one person encroaches upon another.

Our data show that a person's instability in the dominance hierarchy and his possession of a territory are both related to aggressive behavior. Conversely, a person whose position in the hierarchy is established and who does not occupy a specific spot will not show aggressive behavior. We might postulate that an initial instability in dominance position, caused for example by recent admission to the ward, will lead to in-fighting until either a dominance position at the top is reached, or a territory is established. Nonaggressive patients without territories in the lower dominance positions have such low tenacity that they continually cede their place to higher ranking individuals, and thus are chased around all of the available space.

We are currently developing a comprehensive system of computer programs (of which part has recently become operational) that will enable us to follow on a weekly basis the evolving dominance relationships and the manipulation of space by the patients. Apart from enabling us to pinpoint by quantitative means where the causes of friction among patients—and eventually staff—lie, and to change undesirable territorial patterns by manipulating the physical structure of the ward, these computer analyses will give us insight into the cohesive and dissociative functions of the members of the patient-staff community. Clinical applications of these findings might become possible for other psychiatric wards.

Of course, we do not want to imply that all aggressive behavior can be explained in these ways. Evidently there are personality characteristics that enter into the picture. An important one of these is the phenomenon of "personal space," which particularly in the schizophrenic seems to be crucial. We think, in fact, that most of our patients show an avoidance and not an aggressive reaction to intrusions on their personal space outside their territory. This reaction might be comparable to the startle of an animal once it is approached within its so-called flight distance. We are currently determining whether data concerning the personal space of normals (Sommer, 1959; 1962) are different from the findings in our schizophrenic population. When our opinion is confirmed that schizophrenics are "personal space sensitive," we will be able to use our distance measurements on the ward to help us in the clinical estimation of patient mental state.

Finally, we found in our data that some patients avoid rooms with many people (for example, patients Cp and Rd mentioned earlier), and we are trying to determine whether there is a possible connection with the findings on animals in crowded conditions. We have started to investigate the possibility of determining daily urinary catecholamine excretion in all our patients. The technical difficulties associated with accurate frequent determinations have limited our progress in this area.

SUMMARY

Combination of data on exact geographical locations, discrete instants of verbal interaction, continuous interaction recording, and incidence of aggression of chronic patients on a psychiatric ward has led to the following conclusions:

1. Only half of our patients make use of all available space on the day ward.

2. Half of these patients, and half of the patients who restrict their use of the available space, occupy specific territories. An example of the defensive behavior associated with the possession of such a spot is given for a patient who was seen in 273 out of 330 location observations to be in that spot. Of the 11 patients possessing a territory, 8 showed involvement in aggressive acts.

3. For those patients whose position in the dominance hierarchy on the ward has not been firmly established, the chances increase that they will become involved in aggressive incidents. Of 12 such patients, only 2 were not involved in aggressive acts.

The importance of the findings in animal ecology for the study of institutionalized groups is discussed. Possible uses of our methodology and results—for clinical management of patients, for research into ward structure and group cohesion, and for the study of "personal space"—are outlined.

REFERENCES:

Chapple, E. D., Chamberlain, A. S., Esser, A. H., & Kline, N. S. The measurement of activity patterns of schizophrenic patients. *Journal of Nervous and Mental Disease*, 1963, **137**, 259–268.

Esser, A. H., Chamberlain, A. S., Chapple, E. D., & Kline, N. S. Productivity of chronic schizophrenics in a sheltered workshop: A quantitative evaluation of the effects of drug therapy. *Comprehensive Psychiatry*, 1965, **6**, 41–50.

Simpson, G., & Kline, N. S. A new type of psychiatric research ward. *American Journal of Psychiatry*, 1962, **119**, 511–514.

Sommer, R. Studies in personal space. *Sociometry*, 1959, **22**, 247–260.

Sommer, R. The distance for comfortable conversation. *Sociometry*, 1962, **25**, 111–116.

21 Personal Space and the Body-Buffer Zone[1]

Mardi J. Horowitz, Donald F. Duff, and Lois O. Stratton

Measurements of personal space, the area immediately surrounding an individual, demonstrate its reality and its function as a body-buffer zone in interpersonal transactions.

From the *Archives of General Psychiatry*, December, 1964, **11**, 651–656. Reprinted by permission of the authors and publisher.

[1] This study was aided by Contract Nonr-222 (51) (NR 105 156) between the Office of Naval Research, Department of the Navy, and the University of California School of Medicine, San Francisco.

Portions of this paper were read before the meetings of the Western Division, American Psychiatric Association, San Francisco, Sept. 27–29, 1963; and the San Francisco Psychoanalytic Society, Feb. 10, 1964.

The opinions or assertions contained herein are the private ones of the authors and are not to be construed as official or as necessarily reflecting the views of the Medical Department of the Navy or of the Naval Service at large.

The idea of personal space entered behavioral science with ethologic studies of territoriality (Howard, 1920; Hediger, 1955). Subsequently, anthropologists noted that human spatial use was an important variable in studying cultural patterns (Hall, 1959). The psychiatric literature rarely refers to space, yet it is artfully and intuitively used by psychotherapists: closeness and distance, as well as the relative position of the patient and therapist, are modulated in therapy.

Clinical observations, aided by interaction painting (Horowitz, 1963) and topographic mapping of individual and group utilization of space, led to the predictions that: (1) there would be a certain reproducible distance which persons impose between themselves and objects or persons, and (2) in certain schizophrenic patients this distance would be relatively increased. To test these predictions, four experimental situations were designed. In the interest of clarity, each method with the results will be presented separately.

METHODS AND RESULTS

Experiment 1. Frontal Approach Distances.
—At the US Naval Hospital, Oakland, 19 patients with an established diagnosis of schizophrenia and 19 nonschizophrenic enlisted men of similar age, rank, and cultural background were told that their equilibrium was to be studied. Actually, measurements of the distance left between themselves and an object and a person were taken when they stopped their approach as they walked across a room. The object was a hatrack of semihuman proportions on which a coat was hung. The person was a staff member of the same sex as the subject. The instructions were: "Walk over to Smith (or the hatrack) while we check your equilibrium." Upon cessation of the movement, the distance between the subject's toes and the base of the hatrack or toes of the person approached was recorded on three successive frontal approaches. Square tiles on the floor were used as the scale. Analysis of the results revealed that both groups would approach the object significantly closer than they would approach the person.

As Shakow (1963) pointed out, schizophrenic patients in *any* behavioral experiment often show greater interindividual variability than do control groups. In addition to increased variability of response, the schizophrenic group had significantly greater mean distance from the object than the nonschizophrenic group; there was no significant difference between the groups in the approach to a person (Table 21-1).

Experiment 2. Multidirectional Approach Distances.
—The purpose of the second experiment was to select two groups of women with a known difference in their relationships with people to see if their sense of personal space around the body circumference would differ. The subjects consisted of a group of ten schizophrenic females from the In-Patient Service at the Langley Porter Neuropsychiatric Institute (San Francisco) and a group of ten female volunteer workers from the University of California Medical Center (San Francisco).

The subjects were asked to make separate approaches to three different objects: (1) a hatrack, (2) a male, and (3) a female. These approaches were repeated on three different days, with the subjects approaching each of the "objects" in eight different ways, as follows: (1) walking frontwards, (2) backwards, (3) sideways (right and left), and (4) walking at an angle to the "objects" (right and left frontwards, right and left backwards). Since these eight ap-

Table 21-1 Frontal Approach Distances (Inches)

	Object		Person	
Measurements	Schizophrenic	Nonschizophrenic	Schizophrenic	Nonschizophrenic
Mean	6.4	3.1	10.0	8.3
Median	1.5	1.2	7.3	9.0
Range	72–0	9–0	54–1	18–1
P*	<0.01		N.S.	

* The P comparing the approach to an object vs. the approach to a person was <0.02 for the schizophrenic group and <0.0001 for the nonschizophrenic group; all values were determined by the Wilcoxon Paired Replicates Ranks test (Wilcoxon, 1949, pp. 5–7).

Table 21-2 Multiple Approach Distance: Mean of Direct Measures of Each Aspect of Approach (Inches)

Subject	To	Front	Back	Side		Front		Back	
				R	L	R	L	R	L
Schizophrenic	Object	2.4	3.6	3.7	4.2	1.7	1.5	2.1	1.8
	Male	9.8	6.7	9.1	10.6	9.3	8.6	7.6	9.6
	Female	10.2	5.4	8.1	9.6	9.9	5.7	8.5	7.8
Nonschizophrenic	Object	1.6	3.0	3.7	3.3	1.4	1.7	2.7	2.2
	Male	6.2	3.6	7.4	7.3	5.9	5.3	5.0	4.7
	Female	4.8	6.8	7.7	6.4	5.3	4.9	4.5	4.3
P^*	Object	NS	NS	NS	NS	NS	NS	NS	NS
	Male	<0.01	NS	NS	<0.01	<0.01	<0.01	<0.01	<0.01
	Female	<0.01	NS	NS	<0.01	<0.01	<0.01	<0.01	<0.01

* P values determined by Rank Sum test (Dixon, 1957, p. 289).

proaches were made to each of the three "objects" (male, female, hatrack), there was a total of 24 approaches per session, or a grand total of 72 approaches per subject. The order of approaching the "object" was selected at random for every session.

The subjects were seated across the room from the investigators and were read these instructions: "This is a study about the way people walk. You are simply to walk in your own natural manner, and we shall observe you and take notes. Try to relax, because we are interested in your own natural gait. After the test is finished, you may ask questions about the purpose of the study." The specific directions for the eight approaches were as follows: "Stand and walk over to Mr. A (Miss B, or the object) and then return to your seat." This instruction was varied so that each of the subject's approaches presented a different bodily aspect selected at random. If the subject asked when she should stop walking she was told, "As soon as you come to (Mr. A, Miss B) the hatrack."

When the subject stopped moving, the distance between the subject's feet and those of the test "object" was recorded. Nine inch square tiles on the floor were used as the measuring scale. The total number of steps taken by the subject, the number of eye aversions, physical contacts, and verbalizations or gestures were also recorded. As was seen in Experiment 1, both groups approached closer to the inanimate object (Table 21-2).

The individual measures from each of the eight approaches were plotted on a graph around a figure representing a top view of the subject's body. Connected, these eight points formed an irregular circle around the subject which was designated as the "body-buffer zone." Each subject had three graphs: one representing the buffer zones with respect to the inanimate object; another with respect to the animate "object" —male; and the third with respect to the animate "object"—female. In each graph were three buffer zones—one for each day the subject was studied. The area of each buffer zone was measured with a compensating polar planimeter. Figure 21-1 depicts the mean of the approach for all three days.

As shown in Table 21-3, the schizophrenic group had a significantly greater buffer-zone area for the approach to persons in each trial. Both groups approached the inanimate object closer than the male or female; no significant difference between approaches to male or female was found in either group.

The schizophrenic group approached significantly closer to the male on Day 3: this was the only significant intertrial difference in either group (Table 21-4).

To determine if differences between groups were due solely to a greater variability within the schizophrenic group, a test was run by taking the closest approach to each of the "objects" for each of the eight approaches, regardless of the day on which it occurred, and connecting these points to make the smallest possible buffer

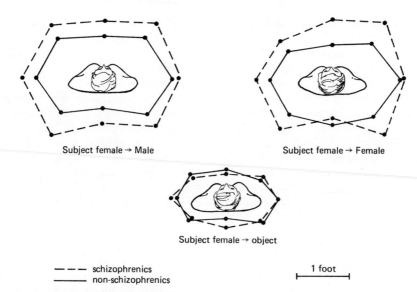

Subject female → Male   Subject female → Female

Subject female → object

——— schizophrenics   1 foot
——— non-schizophrenics

Figure 21–1. Mean of approach distances.

Table 21-3 Multiple Approach Distance: Comparison of Areas by Days (Square Inches)

Mean	To	Schizo-phrenic	Non-schizo-phrenic	P^*
Day 1	Object	225	205	NS
	Male	697	400	0.001
	Female	616	371	0.002
Day 2	Object	236	225	NS
	Male	629	374	0.001
	Female	608	350	0.001
Day 3	Object	218	219	NS
	Male	505	365	0.05
	Female	522	368	0.01

* P values determined by the Rank Sum test (Dixon, 1957, p. 289).

Table 21-4 Multiple Approach Distance: Comparison of Areas, Day 1 Vs. Day 3 (Square Inches)

Subject	To	Day 1	Day 3	P^*
Schizo-phrenic	Object	225	218	NS
	Male	697	505	0.05
	Female	616	522	NS
Nonschizo-phrenic	Object	205	219	NS
	Male	400	365	NS
	Female	371	368	NS

* P values determined by the Wilcoxon Paired Replicates Ranks test (Wilcoxon, 1949, pp. 5–7).

zone for each subject. Using these *closest* approach distances, the schizophrenics still had significantly greater ($P < 0.01$) buffer-zone areas than did the volunteer workers.

The schizophrenic group took more steps to cover the same distances and more frequently averted their eyes from the "objects" than did the volunteers ($P < 0.01$). The schizophrenic group made fewer body contacts with the inanimate and animate "objects" than did the volunteer workers ($P < 0.01$).

Experiment 3. <u>Approaches to Male and Female</u>. A somewhat similar approach technique was used at the naval hospital, with instructions modified to correspond with the real topic of the study: *feelings about space.* The ten active-duty hospital corpsmen who were subjects were told to approach a person known to them until they just began to feel uncomfortable about closeness. They were further instructed to move either backward or forward after the approach until they reached a point where, to move any closer would make them feel a little uneasy. As in the experiment just described the subjects approached first a male and then a female, the same persons in every instance, presenting each time another of the eight aspects of their own bodies. Next, they frontally approached the eight similar aspects of the body of the male and female with the same criterion of where to stop. The shoulder girth circumference was used to record accurately with a tape measure the shortest body-to-body distance in each of the eight aspects. The results were recorded graphically, the points connected, and the area enclosed was measured with a compensating polar planimeter.

Subjects using personal comfort as a criterion placed greater distances between themselves and the male as compared with their distances from a female (Table 21-5). The group outline of the buffer zone demonstrated surprisingly regular contours and regular differences between the sexes (Figures 21-2, 21-3). Note in Figure 21-2 that those aspects of the body for which the approach distances did not differ significantly are the posterior aspects of the subject where looking behavior is partially in-

hibited. The areas of the two techniques were comparable.

Experiment 4. *Self-Rating of Personal Space.*

—In order to determine whether or not self-ratings would produce results similar to the foregoing methods, silhouettes of a nondescript male figure, seen from above, frontally and in profile, were mimeographed separately on 8 × 10 inch white paper. Twenty-five schizophrenic and 25 nonschizophrenic male enlisted men were asked to draw a line around the figures which showed the distance they liked to keep between themselves and others in ordinary conversations or approaches. The area of each zone drawn was measured with a compensating polar planimeter. The schizo-

Table 21-5 Multiple Approach of Subjects to Male and Female (Inches)

8 Aspects of Subject to Front of Person	Mean Distances		
	To Male	To Female	P*
Front	22	17	0.02
Back	15	12	NS
Right	13	10	0.002
Left	12	10	0.01
Rt Front	19	14	0.05
Lft Front	18	14	0.01
Rt Back	11	9	NS
Lft Back	11	8	NS
Area	1,200 sq in	720 sq in	
Front of Subject to 8 Aspects of Person			
Front	24	20	0.05
Back	17	13	0.02
Right	10	7	0.05
Left	10	7	NS
Rt Front	21	15	0.001
Lft Front	19	14	0.001
Rt Back	16	12	0.01
Lft Back	15	11	0.001
Area	1,300 sq in	630 sq in	

* P values determined by the Sign test (Dixon, 1957, p. 280).

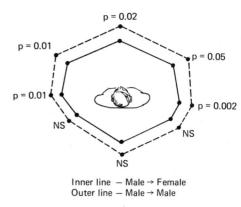

Inner line — Male → Female
Outer line — Male → Male

Figure 21–2. Mean of approach distances: eight aspects of subject to front of person.

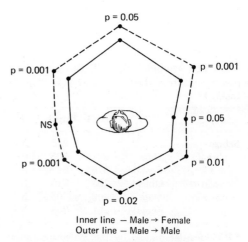

Inner line — Male → Female
Outer line — Male → Male

Figure 21–3. Mean of approach distances: front of subject to eight aspects of person.

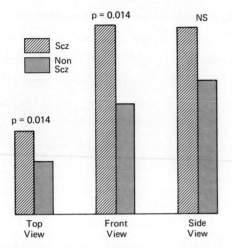

Figure 21–4. Self-ratings: bar graphs of mean planimeter readings. Probability was determined by sign test.

phrenic group had a significantly greater area around each view of the silhouette than did the nonschizophrenic group (Figure 21-4).

COMMENT

Several hypotheses emerge from these findings:

1. Individuals tend to keep a characteristic distance between themselves and other people and inanimate objects.

2. This distance is shorter with nonthreatening inanimate objects than with persons.

3. These distances, especially for persons, tend to be greater in schizophrenic groups.

4. Experimental methods are available for studying spatial behavior.

5. An area of personal space appears to surround every individual, which seems to be reproducible and may be regarded as an immediate *body-buffer zone.*

In *The Ego and the Id* Freud wrote: "The ego is first and foremost a body ego: it is not merely a surface entity, but is itself the projection of a surface" (Freud, 1927). Many psychoanalysts have commented on the importance of the development of the body image to early ego formation (Hartmann et al., 1946; Bernfeld,

1929; Schilder, 1950). Bender (1952) and Schilder (1950) regarded an internal concept of the spatial organization of the world to be part of the body image. In considering the immediate body-buffer zone as a separate facet of the body image, the body-image constellation would be regarded as comprising not only an internalized projection of the body's boundary and position but also a sensitized projection of the immediate area around the body.

William James (1950) observed long ago that we feel as if we extend into contiguous material. One example of this is our feeling for the periphery of our automobiles. We know where our car's fenders and bumpers are in about the same way as we sense the position and boundaries of our bodies in space. The body-buffer zone idea suggests that one's concept of self can extend into nonmaterial space as well.

This body-buffer zone facet of the body image would have a transactional quality; it would depend on nearby individuals and one's attitudes toward them, as well as on such internal-drive derivatives as oral-dependency needs and aggressive conflicts. *Thus, the size, shape, and penetrability of the buffer zone would depend on immediate interpersonal events as well as on the current ego state and motivational state of the individual.*

There is some linguistic support for this concept. The everyday phrases, "to keep at arms length," "get off my toes (back, or neck)," "he gets under my skin," and "he is beside himself," express feelings through the metaphors of personal space. Also, in many cultures space is measured in bodily units such as "the foot," "the fathom (the breadth reached by the extended arms)," and "the cubit (elbow to extended middle finger)."

The apparent alteration of the shape, size, and permeability of the body-buffer zone in schizophrenic subjects requires further investigation and validation. Mahler (1958) theorized that in the psychotic child the crucial stage of body-image differentiation from the mother may be untenable or undeveloped, and that this may be responsible for a defective sense of reality. Goldfarb (1961) noted the compulsive overconcern with space and the impaired awareness of the body image in schizophrenic children. Sarvis (1960) reported that a child with organically-determined loss of the sense of body boundaries due to temporal-lobe damage was especially preoccupied with binding and enclosing space. Quite probably, then, developmental factors will prove pertinent in the further study of man's spatial behavior.

SUMMARY

Clinical observation of human spatial behavior has led to experimental studies of personal space. The subjects tested approached nonthreatening inanimate objects closer than persons. A group notorious for interpersonal withdrawal and avoidance, i.e., psychiatric patients with a diagnosis of schizophrenia, tended to place greater distances around themselves than did nonschizophrenic groups. From these observations, a hypothesis emerged that each human being has, as part of his body-image constellation, an internal projection of the space immediately around him. We tentatively call this the body-buffer zone. The size, shape, and penetrability of this buffer zone probably depend on immediate interpersonal events, current ego and drive states, and the individual's psychologic and cultural history. This hypothesis and the effect of the variables on human spatial behavior warrant further study.

REFERENCES:

Bender, L. Child psychiatric techniques. Springfield, Ill.: Charles C Thomas, 1952.
Bernfeld, S. Psychology of the infant. New York: Coward-McCann, Inc., 1929.
Dixon, W. J., & Massey, F. J., Jr. Introduction to statistical analysis. (2nd ed.). New York: McGraw-Hill, 1957.
Freud, S. Ego and id. London: Hogarth, 1927.
Goldfarb, W., & Mintz, I. Schizophrenic child's reactions to time and space. Archives of General Psychiatry, 1961, 5, 535–543.
Hall, E. T. The silent language. New York: Doubleday, 1959.
Hartmann, H., Kris, E., & Lowenstein, R. M. Comments on formation of psychic structure. The psychoanalytic study of the child, Vol. 2. New York: International Universities Press, 1946.
Hediger, H. Studies of psychology and behaviour of captive animals in zoos and circuses. New York: Criterion Books, 1955.
Horowitz, M. J. Graphic communication: Study of interaction painting with schizophrenics. American Journal of Psychotherapy, 1963, 117, 230–237.
Howard, H. E. Territory in bird life. London: Collins, 1920.
James, W. Principles of psychology. New York: Dover Publications, 1950.
Mahler, M. S. Autism and symbiosis, two extreme disturbances of identity. International Journal of Psychoanalysis, 1958, 39, 77–83.
Sarvis, M. A. Psychiatric implications of temporal lobe damage. In The psychoanalytic study of the child, Vol. 15. New York: International Universities Press, 1960.
Schilder, P. The image and appearance of the human body. New York: International Universities Press, 1950.
Shakow, D. Psychological deficit in schizophrenia. Behavioral Science, 1963, 8, 275–305.
Wilcoxon, F. Some rapid approximate statistical procedures. New York: American Cyanamid Company, 1949.

22 Mental Effects of Reduction of Ordinary Levels of Physical Stimuli on Intact, Healthy Persons

John C. Lilly [1]

INTRODUCTION

We have been seeking answers to the questions of what happens to a brain and its contained mind in the relative absence of physical stimulation. In neurophysiology, this is one form of the question: Freed of normal efferent and afferent activities, does the activity of the brain soon become that of coma or sleep, or is there some inherent mechanism which keeps it going, a pacemaker of the "awake" type of activity? In psychoanalysis, there is a similar, but not identical problem. If the healthy ego is freed of reality stimuli, does it maintain the secondary process, or does primary process take over? That is, is the healthy ego independent of reality or dependent in some fashion, in some degree, on exchanges with the surroundings to maintain its structure?

From Psychiatric Research Reports, 1956, 5, 1–9. Reprinted by permission of the author and publisher.

[1] National Institutes of Mental Health, Public Health Service, Department of Health, Education and Welfare, Washington, D.C.

In seeking answers, we have found pertinent autobiographical literature and reports of experiments by others, and have done experiments ourselves. The experiments in isolation have been done on animals, but are not recounted in detail here; parenthetically, the effect on very young animals can be an almost completely irreversible lack of development of whole systems, such as those necessary for the use of vision in accomplishing tasks put to the animal. No truly neurophysiological isolation experiments on either animals or man have yet been done.

AUTOBIOGRAPHICAL ACCOUNTS

The published autobiographical material has several drawbacks: In no case is there a sizeable reduction of all possibilities of stimulation and action; in most cases, other factors add complications to the phenomena observed. We have collected 18 autobiographical cases from the polar and sea-faring literature (see References) which are more frank and revealing than most. We have interviewed two persons who have not published any of their material. In this account, we proceed from rather complicated situations to the more simple ones, i.e., from a maximum number of factors to the most simple experimental situation.

From this literature we have found that isolation per se acts on most persons as a powerful stress. The effects observed are similar to those of any extreme stress, and other stressful factors add their effects to those of isolation to cause mental symptoms to appear more rapidly and more intensely. As is well known, stresses other than isolation can cause the same symptoms to appear in individuals in an isolated group.

Taking our last point first, we have the account by Walter Gibson (1953) given in his book *The Boat*. This is the case in which four persons out of an initial 135 survived in a lifeboat in the Indian Ocean in World War II. Gibson gives a vivid account of his experiences, and the symptoms resulting from loss of hope, dehydration, thirst, intense sunburn, and physical combat. Most of the group hallucinated rescue

planes and drank salt water thinking it fresh; many despaired and committed suicide; others were murdered; and some were eaten by others. The whole structure of egos were shaken and recast in desperate efforts at survival. (It is interesting to note that many of those who committed suicide tried to sink the boat by removing the drain plugs before jumping overboard, *i.e.*, sink the boat [and other persons] as well as the self; this dual destruction may be used by some of the non-surviving solitary sailors; see below.)

I cite this case because it gives a clue as to what to expect in those who do survive isolation in other conditions: Gibson survived—how? He says: (1) by previous out-of-doors training in the tropical sun for some years; (2) by having previously learned to be able to become completely passive (physically and mentally); (3) by having and maintaining the conviction that he would come through the experience; and, we add, (4) by having a woman, Doris Lim, beside him, who shared his passivity and convictions.

In all cases of survivors of isolation, at sea or in the polar night, it was the first exposure which caused the greatest fears and hence the greatest danger of giving way to symptoms; previous experience is a powerful aid in going ahead, despite the symptoms. Physical passivity is necessary during starvation, but, in some people, may be contraindicated in social isolation in the absence of starvation. In all survivors, we run across the inner conviction that he or she will survive, or else there are definite reassurances from others that each will be rescued. In those cases of a man and a woman together, or even the probability of such a union within a few days, there is apparently not only a real assurance of survival, but a love of the situation can appear. (Such love can develop in a solitaire; see below.) Of course, such couples are the complete psychological antithesis of our major thesis of complete isolation; many symptoms can be avoided by healthy persons with such an arrangement.

Solitary sailors are in a more complex situation than the group of polar isolates. The sailing of a small boat across oceans requires a good deal of physical exertion, and the situation may be contaminated by a lack of sleep which can also cause symptoms. The solitary sailors, of which Joshua Slocum and Alain Bombard are outstanding examples, relate that the first days out of port are the dangerous ones; awe, humility, and fear in the face of the sea are most acute at this time (Slocum, 1948; Bombard, 1953). Bombard states that if the terror of the first week can be overcome, one can survive. Apparently, many do not survive this first period. Many single-handed boats have not arrived at their trans-oceanic destination. We have clues as to the causes from what sometimes happens with two persons on such crossings. There are several pairs of ocean-crossing sailors in which one of the couple became so terror-stricken, paranoid, and bent on murder and/or suicide, that he had to be tied to his bunk.

Once this first period is past, other symptoms develop, either from isolation itself or from isolation plus other stresses. In the South Atlantic, Joshua Slocum had a severe gastro-intestinal upset just before a gale hit his boat; he had reefed his sails, but should have taken them down. Under the circumstances, he was unable to move from the cabin. At this point he saw a man take over the tiller. At first he thought it was a pirate, but the man reassured him and said that he was the pilot of the Pinta and that he would take his boat safely through the storm. Slocum asked him to take down sail, but the man said, no, they must catch the Pinta ahead. The next morning Slocum recovered, and found his boat had covered 93 miles on true course, sailing itself. (His boat was quite capable of such a performance; he arranged it that way for long trips without his hand at the helm.) In a dream that night the pilot appeared and said he would come whenever Slocum needed him. During the next three years the helmsman appeared to Slocum several times, during gales.

This type of hallucination—delusion—seems to be characteristic of the strong egos who survive: a "savior" type of hallucination rather than a "destroyer" type. Their inner conviction of survival is projected thoroughly.

Other symptoms that appear are: superstitiousness (Slocum thought a dangerous reef named M Reef was lucky because M is the 13th letter of the alphabet and 13 was his lucky number. He passed the reef without hitting it. Bombard thought the number of matches necessary to light a damp cigarette represented the number of days until the end of the voyage. He was wrong several times); intense love of any living things (Slocum was revolted at the thought of killing food-animals, especially a goat given to him at one port. Ellam and Mudie became quite upset after catching and eating a fish that had followed the boat all day, and swore off further fish-eating: Ellam and Colin, 1953); conversations with inanimate objects (Bombard had bilateral conversations with a doll mascot); and a feeling that when one lands, one had best be careful to listen before speaking to avoid being considered insane (Bernicot refused an invitation to dinner on another yacht after crossing the Atlantic alone, until he could recapture the proper things to talk about: Bernicot, 1953). The inner life becomes so vivid and intense that it takes time to readjust to the life among other persons and to reestablish one's inner criteria of sanity. (When placed with fellow prisoners, after 18 months in solitary confinement, Christopher Burney was afraid to speak for fear that he would show himself to be insane. After several days of listening he recaptured the usual criteria of sanity, and then could allow himself to speak: Burney, 1952).

Life alone in the polar night, snowed-in, with the confining surroundings of a small hut is a more simple situation. However, there are other complicating factors: extreme cold, possibilities of carbon monoxide poisoning, collapse of the roof, etc. Richard Byrd (1938), in his book *Alone*, recounts in great detail his changes in mental functioning, and talks of a long period of CO poisoning resulting in a state close to catatonia. I refer you to his book for details. He experienced, as did Slocum and many others, an oceanic feeling, the being "of the universe," at one with it.

Christiane Ritter (*A Woman in the Polar Night*, 1954) was exposed to isolation for periods up to 16 days at a time. She saw a monster, hallucinated her past as if in bright sunshine, became "at one" with the moon, and developed a monomania to go out over the snow. She was saved by an experienced Norwegian who put her to bed and fed her lavishly. She developed a love for the situation and found great difficulty in leaving Spitzbergen. For a thorough and sensitive account of symptoms, I recommend her book to you.

From these examples and several more (see References), we conclude the following:

(1) Published autobiographies are of necessity incomplete. Social taboos, discretion to one's self, suppression and repression of painful or uncomfortable material, secondary elaboration, and rationalization severely limit the scope of the material available. (Interviews with two men, each of whom lived alone in the polar night, confirm this impression.)

(2) Despite these limitations, we find that persons in isolation experience many, if not all, of the symptoms of the mentally ill.

(3) In those who survive, the symptoms can be reversible. How easily reversible, we do not know. Most survivors report, after several weeks exposure to isolation, a new inner security and a new integration of themselves on a deep and basic level.

(4) The underlying mechanisms are obscure. It is obvious that inner factors in the mind tend to be projected outward, that some of the mind's activity which is usually reality-bound now becomes free to turn to fantasy and ultimately to hallucination and delusion. It is as if the laws of thought are projected into the realm of the laws of inanimate matter and of the universe. The primary process tends to absorb more and more of the time and energy usually taken by the secondary process. Such experiences either lead to improved mental functioning or to destruction. Why one person takes the healthy path and another person the sick one is not yet clear.

Experiments to clarify the necessary conditions for some of these effects have been done. One of the advantages of the experimental material is that simpler conditions can be set up and tested, and some of the additional stresses of natural life situations can be eliminated.

EXPERIMENTAL ISOLATION

The longest exposure to isolation on the largest number of subjects has been carried out in Dr. Donald Hebb's Department of Psychology at McGill University by a group of graduate students. We started a similar project independently with different techniques at the National Institute of Mental Health. In the Canadian experiments, the aim is to reduce the *patterning* of stimuli to the lowest level; in ours, the objective is to reduce the *absolute intensity* of all physical stimuli to the lowest possible level.

In the McGill experiments, a subject is placed on a bed in an air-conditioned box with arms and hands restrained with cardboard sleeves, and eyes covered completely with translucent ski goggles. The subjects are college students motivated by payment of $20 per day for as long as they will stay in the box. An observer is present, watching through a window, and tests the subject in various ways verbally through a communication set.

In our experiments, the subject is suspended with the body and all but the top of the head immersed in a tank containing slowly flowing water at 34.5° C. (94.5° F.), wears a blacked-out mask (enclosing the whole head) for breathing, and wears nothing else. The water temperature is such that the subject feels neither hot nor cold. The experience is such that one tactually feels the supports and the mask, but not much else; a large fraction of the usual pressures on the body caused by gravity are lacking. The sound level is low; one hears only one's own breathing and some faint water sounds from the piping; the water-air interface does not transmit air-borne sounds very efficiently. It is one of the most even and monotonous environments I have experienced. After the initial training period, no observer is present. Immediately after exposure, the subject writes personal notes on his experience.

At McGill, the subjects varied considerably in the details of their experiences. However, a few general phenomena appeared. After several hours, each subject found that it was difficult to carry on organized, directed thinking for any sustained period. Suggestibility was very much increased. An extreme desire for stimuli and action developed. There were periods of thrashing around in the box in attempts to satisfy this need. The borderline between sleep and awakedness became diffuse and confused. At some time between 24 and 72 hours most subjects couldn't stand it any longer and left. Hallucinations and delusions of various sorts developed, mostly in those who could stay longer than two days.

The development of hallucinations in the visual sphere followed the stages seen with mescaline intoxication. When full-blown, the visual phenomena were complete projections maintaining the three dimensions of space in relation to the rest of the body and could be scanned by eye and head movements. The contents were surprising to the ego, and consisted of material like that of dreams, connected stories sharing past memories and recent real events. The subjects' reactions to these phenomena were generally amusement and a sense of relief from the pressing boredom. They could describe them vocally without abolishing the sequences. A small number of subjects experienced doubling of their body images. A few developed transient paranoid delusions, and one had a seizure-like episode after five days in the box with no positive EEG findings for epilepsy.

Our experiments have been more limited both in numbers of subjects and duration of exposures. There have been two subjects, and the longest exposure has been three hours. We have much preliminary data, and have gained enough experience to begin to guess at some of the mechanisms involved in the symptoms produced.

In these experiments, the subject always has a full night's rest before entering the tank. Instructions are to inhibit all movements as far as possible. An initial set of training exposures overcomes the fears of the situation itself.

In the tank, the following stages have been experienced:

(1) For about the first three-quarters of an hour, the day's residues are predominant. One is aware of the surroundings, recent problems, etc.

(2) Gradually, one begins to relax and more or less enjoy the experience. The feeling of being isolated in space and having nothing to do is restful and relaxing at this stage.

(3) But slowly, during the next hour, a tension develops which can be called a "stimulus-action" hunger; hidden methods of self-stimulation develop: twitching muscles, slow swimming movements (which cause sensations as the water flows by the skin), stroking one finger with another, etc. If one can inhibit such maneuvers long enough, intense satisfaction is derived from later self-stimulations.

(4) If inhibition can win out, the tension may ultimately develop to the point of forcing the subject to leave the tank.

(5) Meanwhile, the attention is drawn powerfully to any residual stimulus: the mask, the suspension, each come in for their share of concentration. Such residual stimuli become the whole content of consciousness to an almost unbearable degree.

(6) If this stage is passed without leaving the tank, one notices that one's thoughts have shifted from a directed type of thinking about problems to reveries and fantasies of a highly personal and emotionally charged nature. These are too personal to relate publicly, and probably vary greatly from subject to subject. The individual reactions to such fantasy material also probably varies considerably, from complete suppression to relaxing and enjoying them.

(7) If the tension and the fantasies are withstood, one may experience the furthest stage which we have yet explored: projection of visual imaginery. I have seen this once, after a two and one-half hour period. The black curtain in front of the eyes (such as one "sees" in a dark room with eyes closed) gradually opens out into a three-dimensional, dark, empty space in front of the body. This phenomenon captures one's interest immediately, and one waits to find out what comes next. Gradually forms of the type sometimes seen in hypnogogic states appear. In this case, they were small, strangely shaped objects with self-luminous

borders. A tunnel whose inside "space" seemed to be emitting a blue light then appeared straight ahead. About this time, this experiment was terminated by a leakage of water into the mask through a faulty connector on the inspiratory tube.

It turns out that exposures to such conditions train one to be more tolerant of many internal activities. Fear lessens with experience, and personal integration can be speeded up. But, of course, there are pitfalls here to be avoided. The opposite effects may also be accelerated in certain cases. Fantasies about the experience (such as the illusion of "return to the womb," which is quite common) are dispelled; one realizes that at birth we start breathing air and hence cannot "return to the womb." One's breathing in the tank is extremely important: as a comforting, constant safeguard and a source of rhythmic stimulation.

In both the McGill experiments and in ours, certain aftereffects are noted: The McGill subjects had difficulty in orienting their perceptual mechanisms; various illusions persisted for several hours. In our experiments, we notice that after emersion the day apparently is started over. That is, the subject feels as if he has just arisen from bed afresh; this effect persists, and the subject finds he is out of step with the clock for the rest of that day. He also has to readjust to social intercourse in subtle ways. The night of the day of the exposure he finds that his bed exerts great pressure against his body. No bed is as comfortable as floating in water.

Experiments such as these demonstrate results similar to that given above for solitary polar living and sailing alone. If one is alone long enough and at levels of physical and human stimulation low enough, the mind turns inward and projects outward its own contents and processes; the brain not only stays active despite the lowered levels of input and output, but accumulates surplus energy to extreme degrees. In terms of libido theory, the total *amount* of libido increases with time of deprivation; body-libido reaches new high levels. If body-libido is not discharged somatically, discharge starts through fantasy; but apparently this is neither an adequate mode

nor can it achieve an adequate rate of discharge in the presence of the rapidly rising level. At some point a new threshold appears for more definite phenomena of regression: hallucinations, delusions, oceanic bliss, etc. At this stage, given any opportunities for action or stimulation by external reality, the healthy ego seizes them and re-establishes more secondary processes. Lacking such opportunities for a long enough interval of time, re-organization takes place, how reversibly and how permanently we do not yet know.

Apparently even healthy minds act this way in isolation. What this means to psychiatric research is obvious: We have yet to obtain a full, documented picture of the range available to the healthy human adult mind; some of the etiological factors in mental illness may be clarified and sharpened by such research. Of course, this is a limited region of investigation. We have not gone into details about loss of sleep, starvation, and other factors which have great power in changing healthy minds to sick ones. I think that you can see the parallels between these results and phenomena found in normal children and in psychotics. And, if we could give you a more detailed account, possible explanations of the role of isolation factors in involuntary indocrination and its opposite, psychotherapy, would be more evident.

REFERENCES:

Small, M. H. On some psychical relations of society and solitude. *Pedagogical Seminary,* 1900, **7**, No. 2.

SOLITARY SAILORS

Bernicot, L. *The voyage of Anahita—single-handed round the world.* London: Rupert Hart-Davis, 1953.
Bombard, A. *The voyage of the Heretique.* New York: Simon and Schuster, 1953.
Ellam, P., & Colin, M. *Sopranino.* New York: W. W. Norton and Co., Inc., 1953.
Merrien, J. *Les Navigateurs solitaires.* Paris: Editiones Denoel, 1954.
Merrien, J. *Lonely voyagers.* New York: G. P. Putnam's Sons, 1954.
Slocum, J. *Sailing alone around the world.* London: Rupert Hart-Davis, 1948.

DRASTIC DEGREES OF STRESS

Gibson, W. *The boat.* Boston: Houghton Mifflin Co. (The Riverside Press), 1953.

LIVING IN THE POLAR NIGHT

Byrd, R. E. *Alone.* New York: G. P. Putnam's Sons, 1938.
Courtauld, A. Living alone under polar conditions. *The Polar Record*, 1932, No. 4.
Ritter, C. *A woman in the polar night.* New York: E. P. Dutton and Co., Inc., 1954.
Scott, J. M. *Portrait of an ice cap with human figures.* London: Chatto and Windus, 1953.

FORCED ISOLATION AND CONFINEMENT

Burney, C. *Solitary confinement.* New York: Coward-McCann, Inc., 1952.
Stypulkowski, Z. *Invitation to Moscow.* London: Thames and Hudson, 1951.

THE DEAF AND THE BLIND

Bartlet, J. E. A. A case of organized visual hallucinations in an old man with cataract, and their relation to the phenomena of the phantom limb. *Brain*, 1951, **74**, 363–373.
Collingswood, H. W. Adventures in silence. New York: *The Rural New Yorker*, 1923.
Ormond, A. W. Visual hallucinations in sane people. *British Medical Journal*, 1925, **2**, 376–378.

EXPERIMENTAL ISOLATION

Heron, W., Bexton, W. H., & Hebb, D. O. Cognitive effects of a decreased variation to the sensory environment. *The American Psychologist*, 1953, **8**, 366.

23 The Ecology of Isolated Groups[1]

Irwin Altman and William W. Haythorn

This study reports on social activity and "territoriality" behavior of isolated and confined groups. It is part of a larger program concerned with performance effectiveness, stress reactions, and interpersonal exchange

From *Behavioral Science*, 1967, **12**, 169–182. Reprinted by permission of the author and publisher.

[1] From Bureau of Medicine and Surgery, Navy Department, research task, MF 022.01.03-1002. The opinions and statements contained herein are those of the writers and are not to be construed as official or reflecting the views of the Navy Department or the Naval Service at large. The authors wish to thank William N. Colson, John Graham, and Judith Rhodes for their invaluable assistance in the collection and analysis of data.

processes that occur in social isolation (Altman and Haythorn, 1965, in press; Haythorn and Altman, 1967; Haythorn, Altman, and Myers, 1966).

A fairly extensive literature exists on spatial habits, territoriality, and effects of overcrowding of lower animals, but relatively little empirical work has examined human use of space (Sommer, 1959; Little, 1965). What is available includes a few studies of clinical populations and some sociological and social psychological investigations.

Most animals in the wild state exhibit territoriality, which may include preventing other animals, especially of the same species, from entering a geographical area. (Hediger, 1950, 1955; Howard, 1948.) That disturbances in territorial and ecological distributions of animals result in behavior pathology and even physiological malfunctioning has been well documented (Calhoun, 1956, 1962; Christian, Flyger, and Davis, 1960; Christian, 1961; Errington, 1957).

Several studies have found differences in territoriality and spatial habit patterns of clinical and normal populations. For example, schizophrenics exhibited territorial behavior in joint-interaction painting with a therapist, which was alternately lowered and raised as rapport was established and disrupted (Horowitz, 1963). They also maintained greater than normal distances between themselves and objects (including people), and often confused boundaries between animate and inanimate objects and between the self and the not-self (Horowitz, Duff, and Stratton, 1963; Horowitz, Duff, and Stratton, undated). Thus, definition of "own" territory and preferred distance between self and others appears to be an important correlate of emotional malfunctioning. Sommer (1959) found differences in seating habits of clinical and normal populations, and Winick and Holt (1961) report that types of chairs, seating arrangements, chair colors and shapes, and so on, are responded to in significant ways by therapy patients. Without attempting to establish causal links, it seems that personal space factors are important correlates of social-emotional states for humans as well as for other animals.

Spatial and role relationships have also been demonstrated to affect interaction patterns in small groups (Steinzor, 1950; Bass and Klubeck, 1952; Sommer, 1961, 1965; Little, 1965). Group members arrange themselves to maximize interaction potential with a leader (Sommer, 1961) and tend to interact with those they face (Steinzor, 1950). Little (1965) found personal distance in social relationships to vary as a function of friendship, again suggesting the linkage of social-emotional relationships and spatial habits. That these linkages are culturally specific is abundantly evident from the work of Hall (1959, 1963, 1966).

The present study compared spatial habits of pairs of men socially isolated in a small room for ten days with those of matched nonisolated groups. Of particular interest were territoriality patterns with respect to beds, chairs, and parts of the room, and social distances maintained by teammates in free-time activities. It was anticipated that isolated and nonisolated groups and groups formed according to different personality compositions would differ in spatial behavior. Prior research had shown that incompatibility and compatibility of dyad members on need affiliation, need dominance, need achievement, and dogmatism affected performance, stress, and interpersonal exchange in isolation (Altman and Haythorn, 1965, in press; Haythorn and Altman, 1967; Haythorn, et al., 1966).

PROCEDURE

Subjects

Eighteen pairs of volunteer sailors were selected to meet personality composition criteria on need affiliation, need achievement, need dominance, and dogmatism, discussed below. Nine matched pairs were assigned to isolation and nonisolation control conditions. Ss within a dyad were relative strangers 17–21 years of age with an average I.Q. of 100 and were matched as closely as possible in age, education, and similar demographic variables.

Isolation and Control Conditions

The isolation area was a 12′ by 12′ room equipped with bunks, toilet, cabinet, table, and chairs. For recreation, Ss had playing cards, a checker game, and limited reading materials. Isolated pairs received no mail and did not have radios, watches, or calendars. Groups worked two hours in the morning, three hours in the afternoon, and one hour in the evening on three tasks. The remaining time was free. Controls followed the same schedule, but lived in barracks, ate at the base mess, and had room breaks between tasks. After work, they were free to use base recreation facilities.

Personality Composition of Groups

Personality composition effects were assessed within a Greco-Latin square experimental design (Figure 23-1). Each cell represents a dyad defined by the personality characteristics of the two members. For example, the upper left cell represents a pair of men homogeneously high on dogmatism, need achievement, and need affiliation, and homogeneously low on need dominance. Ss in the upper or lower tertiles on the Rokeach Dogmatism Scale (Rokeach, 1960) and on relevant scales of the Edwards Personal Preference Schedule (Edwards, 1959) were selected. The design was repeated under isolation and nonisolation conditions, yielding a total of eighteen dyads.

Measures of Spatial Behavior

To tap spatial behavior, sampling of the following was accomplished:

Objects and Side of Table. This refers to specific objects with which S was in contact, such as table, chair, bed, bathroom, and their locations around the table in the room. Each room had a red and green leather chair, identical except for color. Red vs. green chair usage, top vs. bottom bunk usage, and positions around the table were used to measure territoriality.

Activity. Behavior samples were categorized into: personal and room chores (washing,

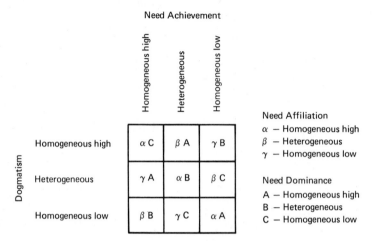

Figure 23–1. Greco-Latin square experimental design.

combing hair, shining shoes, cleaning the room, and so forth); bed asleep; solitary recreation (playing solitaire, reading, writing letters, drawing); solitary nonrecreation (bed awake, quiet, smoking); joint recreation (playing cards, playing checkers); talking. For analysis purposes these were grouped into percentage of time spent asleep, together and alone for three three-day blocks of the experiments.[2]

Spatial data were collected every day for 20 minutes during a one and a half-hour free time block in the morning and afternoon. For isolation groups five additional five-minute samples were taken in the early morning and evening, at a rate of one sample per hour. (Controls were not confined to the room during these times.) Observers recorded behavior every other minute, yielding three observations for five-minute periods and ten observations for twenty-minute periods.

Indices of Territoriality

Territoriality was defined in terms of the degree of consistent and mutually exclusive use of particular chairs, beds, or sides of the

table by dyad members.[3] Table 23-1 presents illustrative data and formulae developed in this study to compute territoriality indices. To determine computational logic for each dyad, that is, the general direction of exclusive object usage, we inspected the data to locate the most consistent diagonal pattern. In those few cases where directionality was not clear, combined data for all days were used. Thus it is possible to have negative scores, as in the third group, where there was a Day 1 and Day 3 preference for the red chair by Man 1 and the green chair by Man 2, and a reversal during the intermediate day block. To eliminate negative scores, a constant of 50 or 100 was added, depending on the particular score used.

Two territoriality indices were calculated for chairs, beds, and sides of the table. In addition to an unadjusted score, based on the simple subtraction procedure of formula 1, it was felt desirable to adjust for frequency of use of objects. For example, two sets of data could show high and identical territoriality—that is, dyad members always using different chairs and beds—but because of differences in amount of chair vs.

---

[2] Three additional categories of spatial behavior did not yield fruitful data or were redundant with the preceding, that is, body position (standing, sitting, lying), mutual body position (face-to-face, back-to-back, and so on), eye contact between Ss (full, partial, none, and so forth).

[3] In animal ecology the term "territoriality" ordinarily implies an active response to intrusion. Strictly speaking, our use of the term in this study is not necessarily restricted to intrusion and defense but also includes preferences by Ss for areas and objects.

Table 23-1 Procedure for Computing Territoriality Indices

Man	Day Block					
	1		2		3	
	red chair (rc)	green chair (gc)	(rc)	(gc)	(rc)	(gc)
Group 1						
1	0	49°	0	36°	0	43°
2	9°	0	17°	0	4°	0
Group 2						
1	17	22°	17	19°	1	16°
2	26°	18	12°	25	20°	0
Group 3						
1	14°	2	1°	19	20°	1
2	1	23°	24	2°	0	14°

1. Unadjusted territoriality index = $(rc - gc + 50)$: For each man for established direction of territoriality, that is, for group 1, man $1 = (49 - 0 + 50) = 99$; for group 2, man $2 = (22 - 17 + 50) = 55$.

2. Adjusted territoriality index = $(rc - gc/n \times 100) + 100$: For group 1, man 1 = $(49 - 0/49 \times 100) + 100 = 200$; for group 2, man 2 = $(22 - 17/39 \times 100) + 100 = 113$.

° Indicates main directions of territoriality.

bed usage, such a pattern would be masked. To account for this possibility, the unadjusted territoriality score was divided by the number of cases upon which the observations were based. Analyses were based on both scores.

RESULTS

Isolation-Control Differences in Territoriality

Tables 23-2 and 23-3 and Figure 23-2 summarize analyses of bed, chair, and side-of-table territoriality for isolation and control groups over day blocks of the experiment. Isolation groups showed an early preference for particular beds, with relatively little intrusion by teammates into each other's sleeping space. While bed territoriality dropped over time, the decline was

not statistically significant. For chairs and locations around the table there was less establishment of territorial rights in the early days. However, by Days 4–6 of the experiment (Day Block 2), isolates had clear preferences for sitting in particular places around the table which persisted thereafter. A similar pattern obtained for chairs although it developed somewhat more slowly.

Control groups showed a different history, with increasing territoriality occurring only for beds. During early days they exchanged bunks readily, but eventually ended up at a level of territoriality equivalent to isolates. On the other hand, controls established clear initial delineation as to chair and side-of-table usage, which then significantly declined over days. Thus, social isolation was associated with continuously high or growing territoriality for all areas and objects, while nonisolation was accompanied by gradually declining territoriality in two cases and rising territoriality in the other (beds).

Isolation-Control Differences in Social Activities

Analyses were conducted on three classes of free-time activities—asleep, alone (quiet or solitary recreation), and together (talking or joint recreation). As shown in Table 23-4, significant F-ratios were found for Activities, Isolation-control × Activities, and Isolation-control × Days × Activities. From Figure 23-3 it can be seen that, over days, members of isolated groups gradually withdrew from one another. While relative amount of time spent asleep remained constant, there was a significant decline in together activities from early to later days and a significant elevation in time spent alone. In fact, by the end of isolation, Ss engaged in about one and a half times more solitary than joint activities, whereas at the beginning of isolation the distribution of free time into these activities was roughly equivalent.

In contrast, at both the beginning and end of the experiment, controls spent equal time in joint and solitary activities, although there was an elevation in solitary and a

Table 23-2 Analyses of Variance of Chair and Bed Territoriality Behavior

Source of Variance	df	MS^a	MS^b	F^a	F^b
Isolation-Control (I-C)	1	11,137.0	436.3	2.36	2.93
Ss within dyads	18	4,709.3	148.9		
Days	2	1,652.0	207.8	1.26	3.90*
IC × Days	2	532.7	115.8	<1	2.17
Ss within × Days	36	1,307.8	53.2		
Chair-Bed	1	10,347.3	2,625.0	2.31	5.50*
IC × Chair-Bed	1	9,480.4	172.5	2.12	<1
Ss within × Object	18	4,477.0	477.0		
Day × Chair-Bed	2	2,397.0	117.0	2.04	1.74
IC × Day × Chair-Bed	2	23,115.2	1,164.7	19.69***	17.31***
Ss within × Day × Chair-Bed	72	1,173.7	67.3		

* $p < .05$
** $p < .01$
*** $p < .001$
^{a} refers to the adjusted territoriality index. See Table 23-1.
^{b} refers to the unadjusted territoriality index. See Table 23-1.

Table 23-3 Analyses of Variance of Side-of-Table Territoriality Behavior

Source of Variance	df	MS^a	MS^b	F^a	F^b
Isolation-Control (IC)	1	546.8	1,014.4	<1	1.86
Ss within dyads	18	3,895.5	545.8		
Days	2	3,977.1	218.1	4.15*	2.73
IC × Days	2	14,528.6	886.0	10.93***	11.10**
Ss within × Days	36	1,329.4	79.8		

* $p < .05$
** $p < .01$
*** $p < .001$
^{a} refers to the adjusted territoriality index. See Table 23-1.
^{b} refers to the unadjusted territoriality index. See Table 23-1.

decline in joint activities in the middle days. Thus, controls did not exhibit the continuously increasing withdrawal from one another which was characteristic of isolates. Controls and isolates both showed level amounts of sleep throughout the experiment, with controls significantly higher. Taken together, the territoriality and social activity data suggest that isolates may have begun drawing a psychological and spatial "cocoon" around themselves, gradually doing more things alone and in their own part of the room.

A similar pattern of withdrawal held for nighttime activities of isolated groups. Time spent alone increased and time spent together decreased over days, although the *absolute* amount of joint activity was higher at night and higher than solitary activities. By the end of the experiment, nighttime alone and together activities were approximately the same.

Group Composition and Territoriality Behavior

The Greco-Latin square analysis apportions the between-subjects variance according to need affiliation, need dominance, need achievement, and dogmatism composition differences, in addition to isolation-control conditions. The most significant territoriality findings occurred for affiliation and dominance. Table 23-5 presents means associated with a significant IC × Chair-bed × Dominance × Day interaction ($F = 3.26$, $p < .05$).

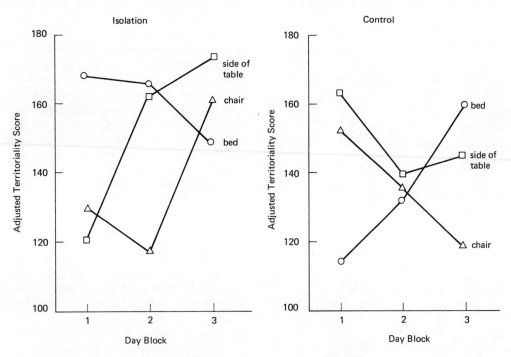

Figure 23–2. Territoriality patterns of isolation and control groups.

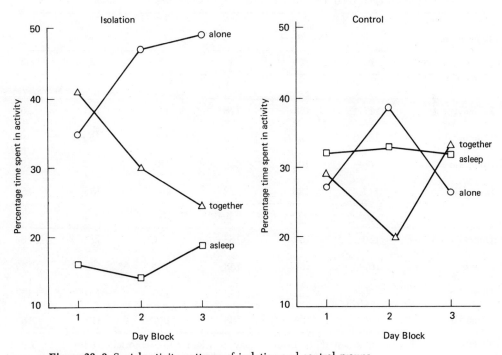

Figure 23–3. Social activity patterns of isolation and control groups.

Table 23-4 Analysis of Variance of Social Activities

Source of Variance	df	MS	F
Isolation-Control	1	1.9	<1
Ss within groups	18	19.4	
Days	2	24.1	<1
IC × Days	2	7.5	<1
Ss within × Days	36	33.5	
Activities (alone-together-asleep)	2	8,848.5	15.88[***]
IC × Activities	2	12,744.0	22.87[***]
Ss within × Activities	36	557.1	
Days × Activities	4	1,917.2	4.25[**]
IC × Days × Activities	4	1,845.4	4.09[**]
Ss within × Days × Activities	72	450.6	

[*] $p < .05$
[**] $p < .01$
[***] $p < .001$

For dominance, homogeneously high dyads (hi dom) represented an incompatible, competitive relationship, whereas the heterogeneous composition (hetero dom) was a hypothetically compatible, complementary relationship. The homo low dom dyads were intermediate with regard to compatibility, not because of competitive conflict, but because of absence of anyone to provide group structure (Altman and Haythorn, 1965; Haythorn, et al., 1966; Haythorn and Altman, 1967).

In both isolation and control conditions incompatible hi dom dyads rose in chair territoriality over days (significant only for isolates), as did low dom groups. On the other hand, compatible hetero dom dyads declined in chair territoriality in both isolation and control conditions, ending up significantly lower than the other compositions. These results indicate that incompatibility on dominance was associated with increasing chair territoriality, while compatibility led to gradually declining territoriality.

Table 23-5 Mean Chair-Bed Territoriality Scores for Dominance Compositions

Compositions	Isolation Day Block			Control Day Block		
	1	2	3	1	2	3
			Chair			
Homo Hi	147	128 [*]	178 [**]	144	155	158 [*]
Hetero	181[b] [*]	121	113 [**]	168[b]	150 [*]	97 [**]
Homo Lo	68[b] [**]	105 [**]	200	81 [**]	112 [*]	165
Homo Hi	147	128 [*]	178	144	155	158
			Bed			
Homo Hi	150	162	165	106[b]	117 [*]	163
Hetero	167[a]	167	158	101 [**]	180 [**]	172
Homo Lo	200[ab] [*]	183[a] [*]	132	139	104 [*]	154
Homo Hi	150	162	165	106[b]	117	163

This table is based on a significant IC × Dom × Day × Chair-Bed territoriality term, $F = 3.26$, $p < .05$.
Differences between means were tested by the Duncan Multiple Range Test.
[*] indicates significance at $p < .05$.
[**] indicates significance at $p < .01$.
[a] indicates significant differences between matched isolation and control groups at $p < .05$ or better.
[b] indicates significant Day Block 1 and Day Block 3 differences at $p < .05$ or better.

For beds, hi dom dyads gradually increased in territoriality (significant only for controls), while hetero and low dom groups in isolation declined through days (significant only for low dom groups). Also, hetero and low dom control dyads increased in bed territoriality. Thus, all compositions rose in bed territoriality in control conditions and either declined or were stable in isolation.

These data indicate that the findings reported earlier concerning the general isolate elevation in chair territoriality over days were more characteristic of *incompatible isolated dominance groups* and do not necessarily apply to all socially isolated groups. For beds, however, a generally more constant level of territoriality was maintained in isolation, except for low dom groups who showed a decline.

No particular pattern occurred for side-of-table territoriality except that low dom groups gradually came to prefer particular locations, perhaps indicating, along with their rising chair territoriality, an attempt to provide structure to the environment.

Table 23-6 presents means associated with a significant IC × Chair-bed × Affiliation × Days interaction term ($F = 2.76$, $p < .05$). Generally, the isolated hetero aff composition, hypothetically incompatible, had higher chair and bed territoriality than homo hi aff groups, although differences were not always statistically reliable. It is also interesting that hetero aff isolates were either continuously high in territoriality throughout the experiment (for beds) or rose over days (chairs), while homo high aff Ss either declined or remained at a low level. Control hetero and hi aff groups evidenced no particular temporal pattern for chairs, although they exhibited increasing bed territoriality. The isolated low aff dyads showed sharp boundary definition, with rising chair territoriality over days and a consistently differential usage of beds. No differences were found for side-of-table measures of territoriality.

These results suggest again that the generally higher territoriality levels shown by isolated groups, considered earlier, are further associated with either incompatibility

Table 23-6 Mean Territoriality Scores for Affiliation Compositions

Compositions	Isolation Day Block			Control Day Block		
	1	2	3	1	2	3
			Chair			
Homo Hi	131	91^a **	125	153	155	165
Hetero	128	175^a **	167	147	122	133 **
Homo Lo	136 *	88^a **	198^a	156^b	138 **	60
Homo Hi	131	91^a	125	153	155	165
			Bed			
Homo Hi	150^{ab}	133 **	98^a **	78^b *	128	161
Hetero	183^a	200	166	108^b *	162	185
Homo Lo	183	179^a	191 **	158 *	111	143
Homo Hi	150	133	98	78^b	128	161

This table is based on significant IC × Aff × Day × Chair-Bed territoriality term, $F = 3.42$, $p < .05$.
Differences between means were tested by the Duncan Multiple Range Test.
* indicates significance at $p < .05$.
** indicates significance at $p < .01$.
^{a} indicates significant differences between matched isolation and control groups at $p < .05$ or better.
^{b} indicates significant Day Block 1 and Day Block 3 differences at $p < .05$ or better.

or low affiliation and dominance needs, and are less evident for more compatible compositions. The other composition variables, dogmatism and need achievement, did not yield clear-cut territoriality differences.

Group Composition and Activities

Activity analyses for the various compositions compared *alone, together,* and *asleep* behavior. Both affiliation and achievement yielded significant IC × Composition × Activity × Day terms ($F = 5.02$, $p < .01$; $F = 2.29$, $p < .05$, respectively) and similar patterns of means (see Tables 23-7 and 23-8).

In general, the data suggest withdrawal of members of incompatible isolated hetero aff and hetero ach dyads from one another. Table 23-7 indicates that hetero aff isolates spent more time alone and less together than the other compositions during the first six days, and spent more time asleep throughout the ten days (reliably so only during the last Day Block). Low aff isolates

gradually withdrew from one another as days progressed, spending less time in joint and more time in solitary activities. From these data it can be concluded that the overall reduction in Together and elevation in Alone activities by isolates, reported earlier, is more characteristic of those incompatible or low in affiliation needs, and is not necessarily typical of isolates in general.

The achievement means in Table 23-8 are generally consistent with the above, that is, hetero ach isolates engaged in fewer joint activities and/or spent more time alone or asleep than more compatible homo hi and low ach groups. They also spent significantly more time alone throughout the ten days than their matched controls.

Activity findings for dominance and dogmatism comparisons are counter to the preceding and suggest that incompatible isolates spent more time together and less time alone than compatible compositions. Means associated with IC × Composition × Activity terms for dominance (Table

Table 23-7 Activity Patterns of Affiliation Compositions

Activity	Compositions	Isolation Day Block			Control Day Block		
		1	2	3	1	2	3
Alone	Homo Hi	36.1	47.2	49.7	23.4	36.3	37.6
	Hetero	45.9	55.4	49.0	33.3	46.0	29.3
	Homo Lo	29.3^b	41.3	51.8	31.1	36.0	15.7
	Homo Hi	36.1	47.2	49.7	23.4	36.3	37.6
Together	Homo Hi	43.6	33.9	33.6	43.5	30.2	22.2
	Hetero	23.1 **	17.8 *	14.1	36.0 *	13.8	29.0
	Homo Lo	56.7^{ab}	42.5^a	29.6^a	13.5 **	19.1	54.6 **
	Homo Hi	43.6	33.9	33.6	43.5	30.2	22.2
Asleep	Homo Hi	13.8	11.7	10.7^a *	29.3	30.8	38.5
	Hetero	25.6	23.7	33.6	20.6 **	38.2	35.7
	Homo Lo	10.7^a	11.1^a	15.4	51.5^b	35.7	29.0
	Homo Hi	13.8	11.7	10.7	29.3	30.8	37.5

This table is based on a significant IC × Aff × Activity × Day interaction, $F = 5.02$, $p < .01$. Differences between means were tested by the Duncan Multiple Range Test.
* indicates significance at $p < .05$.
** indicates significance at $p < .01$.
^{a} indicates significant differences between matched isolation and control groups at $p < .05$ or better.
^{b} indicates significant Day Block 1 and Day Block 3 differences at $p < .05$ or better.

Table 23-8 Activity Patterns of Achievement Compositions

Activity	Compositions	Isolation Day Block			Control Day Block		
		1	2	3	1	2	3
Alone	Homo Hi	36.4^b *	53.6	56.1^a	38.5	58.3 **	22.8
						**	
	Hetero	53.6^a	46.0^a	49.9^a	20.9	17.5	19.7
		**				*	
	Homo Lo	21.2	44.4	44.4	28.3	42.6	40.1
	Homo Hi	36.4	53.6	56.1	38.5	58.3	22.8
Together	Homo Hi	45.3	30.8	37.0	29.6	24.1	38.8
		*		*			
	Hetero	18.3	23.4	11.7^a	32.6	27.4 *	50.8
		**					**
	Homo Lo	59.8^{ab}	40.0^a	28.6	30.8	11.7	16.0
							*
	Homo Hi	45.3	30.8	37.0	29.6	24.1	38.8
Asleep	Homo Hi	13.2	10.7	6.1^a	25.9	15.1	33.0
				*		**	*
	Hetero	23.1	24.6^a	29.3	40.7	46.9 *	28.0
	Homo Lo	13.8^a	11.1^a	24.3	34.8	42.8	42.2
						*	
	Homo Hi	13.2	10.7	6.1	25.9	15.1	33.0

This table is based on a significant IC × Achievement × Activity × Day interaction, $F = 2.29$, $p < .05$.
Differences between means were tested by the Duncan Multiple Range Test.
* indicates significance at $p < .05$.
** indicates significance at $p < .01$.
a indicates significant differences between matched isolation and control groups at $p < .05$ or better.
b indicates significant Day Block 1 and Day Block 3 differences at $p < .05$ or better.

23-9) and dogmatism yielded significant F-ratios ($F = 22.33$, $p < .001$; $F = 18.50$, $p < .001$, respectively). The high dom isolates spent less time alone and more time together than either the hetero or homo low dom groups (significant only for the latter), with an opposite pattern in the control condition. Furthermore, they also were more socially active than their controls. The results are generally similar for dogmatism with the hetero dogma isolates alone less than either of the other compositions and together more than the homogeneous groups.

These results indicate one pattern of social activity for affiliation and achievement compositions in isolation, and an opposite pattern for dogmatism and dominance. The former show incompatibles withdrawing from one another, whereas dominance and dogmatism incompatibles in isolation increased their joint activities.

DISCUSSION

Socially isolated and nonisolated groups behaved very differently with regard to territoriality and social activities. Those isolated for ten days showed continually high, exclusive, nonreciprocal use of particular beds from the outset, a not too surprising finding. Territoriality for specific chairs and areas (positions around the table) was low at first but steadily grew as days in isolation progressed. This might tend to happen on the basis of habit alone, but the interesting aspect of the problem is the degree to which it happened differentially as a function of experimental manipulations, both situational and compositional.

For isolates, developmental patterns were different, with bed territoriality established first, followed by side-of-table and finally by chair territoriality. Perhaps two factors as-

Table 23-9 Activity Patterns for Dominance Groups

Activity	Compositions	Isolation		Control	
Alone	Homo Hi	34.9		44.0 *	
	Hetero	43.3 *		27.9	
	Homo Lo	57.0 **	**	24.2	
Together	Homo Hi	34.9		44.0	
	Homo Hi	46.4	**	20.4	
	Hetero	36.6 **		24.6 **	
	Homo Lo	15.3 **	**	42.2 **	
Asleep	Homo Hi	46.4		20.4	
	Homo Hi	15.2	**	33.7	
	Hetero	12.0	**	42.0 *	
	Homo Lo	24.8		27.4	
	Homo Li	15.2		33.7	

This table is based on a significant IC × Dominance × Activity interaction, $F = 22.33$, $p < .001$.
Difference between means were tested by the Duncan Multiple Range Test.
* indicates significance at $p < .05$.
** indicates significance at $p < .01$.

sociated with beds led to this rapid and persistent jurisdictional behavior. First, beds possess a high degree of personal character associated with olfactory cues, body contact, amount of time spent there, and general cultural practices regarding the inviolability and sanctity of a person's bed, bedding, and pillow. Second, beds were located in a fixed geographical region, an extremely critical aspect of animal territoriality. The next order of territoriality occurred for areas around the table, which became pronounced by the second 3-day block. Red and green chair preferences became strong next and reached their peak during the final days of isolation. Side-of-table territoriality may have developed more rapidly because it entailed a fixed geographical area, while chair territoriality involved movable objects. Furthermore, sides of the table may have assumed importance because of unique cues associated with a specific geographical position such as wall arrangements, lighting, visual configurations, and so on.

Isolates also exhibited gradual withdrawal and increased "cocooning" behavior in social activities. While amount of time asleep remained constant, they spent more and more time alone through days and less time together—phenomena often qualitatively described in reports of groups in naturalistic isolated situations such as the Antarctic.

Controls showed a different pattern, with chair and side-of-table territoriality high at first, but dropping dramatically over days. On the other hand, bed territoriality was initially low but gradually rose, eventually reaching a level comparable to isolates. They may have first perceived the isolation room as a work area only and a minor part of their total environment. Our procedure fostered this expectancy by allowing them access to base mess, recreation, and barracks facilities. Controls appear to have established territoriality in accord with such a set, initially focusing on aspects of the room relevant to work—sides of the table and chairs. As time passed, however, it may have become clear that much free time would be spent in the room, and that they could sleep or lie on the beds. As this perception evolved, the functional value and importance of beds may have increased, leading to growing bed territoriality. This hypothesis is parsimonious with qualitative observations and other data suggesting that controls were actually isolated to some extent and experienced a significant elevation in subjective stress (Haythorn et al., 1966). Thus they may have begun, toward the tenth day of the experiment, to perceive the situation much as isolates did at the beginning.

While these data attest to spatial behavior differences across environments, the conclusion that "men in isolation develop territorial behavior and withdraw from one another" is an oversimplification, as demonstrated by personality composition analyses according to need achievement, need affiliation, need dominance, and dogmatism. There were several interactions indicating the "cocoon-like syndrome" to be associated with incompatibility on certain personality variables but not on others. As shown in Figure 23-4, the results fall into relatively unique patterns of territoriality and activity

Object Orientation

Point of Reference		People DOMINANCE[b]	Ideas/Things DOGMATISM	Activity result High social[a] activity
	Egocentric			
	Sociocentric	AFFILIATION	ACHIEVEMENT	Low social activity
	Territoriality[c]	High	Low	
	Result	Territoriality	Territoriality	

[a] High social activity refers to results indicating either a greater amount of time together, a lower amount of time spent alone, or both, by incompatible vs. compatible isolated compositions.

[b] For Dominance, incompatibles were homo high dyads; for all other personality characteristics, hetero dyads represented incompatibility.

[c] High territoriality refers to results suggesting elevated bed, chair, or side of table territoriality by incompatible isolated compositions compared to the other compositions in general or in later periods of the experiment.

Figure 23–4. Integrative model and summary of results of incompatibility effects in isolation.

for each composition variable. Incompatibility on dominance, for isolation groups, yields data suggestive of active interpersonal interaction and high territoriality. Ss dealt with one another socially to a great extent, but probably competitively in view of their possessiveness about territories. The relationship might be characterized as active, competitive, and volatile. That this portrayal has some validity is suggested by the fact that two isolation groups were unable to complete the ten-day period, attributable to the stresses of the situation (Altman and Haythorn, in press), and that both had members high on dominance. The third high group exhibited severe interpersonal conflict, but completed the experiment.

The profile of incompatible affiliation dyads was different. While incompatibility here was also associated with elevated territoriality (hetero aff vs. hi aff groups), there was marked social withdrawal. Heterogeneous affiliation groups had a relatively subdued, quiet, and private relationship, in which members bore one another in relative silence, at a distance, and from their own territories. Thus, while both exhibited high territoriality, affiliation incompatibility involved social withdrawal (movement *away* from one another), whereas dominance incompatibility led to a noisy, volatile, aggressive relationship (movement *against* one another).

Incompatibility on dogmatism and achievement had dissimilar patterns from the above, characterized by no differential territorial behavior among compositions. They were distinguished from one another,

however, with incompatible dogmatism Ss displaying active social interaction and heterogeneous achievement members withdrawing socially from one another. Dogmatism incompatibility, then, yielded a socially active, nonterritorial relationship while achievement incompatibility resulted in a more socially passive relationship, also without significant jurisdictional allocation of objects and areas of the room.

To develop a more general conceptualization, properties underlying the four personality variables which may have led to the obtained findings were hypothesized (see Figure 23-4). The four personality characteristics were classified as primarily dealing either with "people" or "ideas and/or things" (object orientation dimension), and as involving "egocentric" or "sociocentric" points of reference. Thus, dominance and affiliation both refer to interpersonal characteristics, that is, orientations toward people, whereas dogmatism and achievement primarily involve personal orientations to ideas, tasks, and "things." Examining rows of the figure, dominance and dogmatism both have an "egocentric" reference point, in the sense of reflecting primary concern for the self in relation to other people (dominance) or to ideas and/or things (dogmatism). The high need dominance dyad is a competitive situation in which each member is concerned with getting the other to do what *he* wants. The highly dogmatic individual regards *his* view of things as the correct and most important view, a position not likely to be accepted by his partner in the hetero dogma dyad, resulting in competition or conflict with regard to task structuring, beliefs, and problem-solving approaches. Affiliation and achievement, on the other hand, have in common a "sociocentric" reference point, in the sense of reflecting degree of concern for the joint roles of the self and other people as social entities (affiliation), or as members of task-oriented groups (achievement). The high need affiliation individual contributes to the satisfaction of the affiliative needs of other high aff people in pursuing satisfaction of his own needs, and the high need achiever in a group setting similarly contributes to the need satisfaction of other high ach individuals in pursuing his own concern with the group's *raison d'être*, the task or mission. In both cases, the point of reference is more towards the contribution the individual makes to others than is the case with either dominance or dogmatism. In both cases, the heterogeneous (incompatible) dyad is more aptly described as incongruent than as competitive or conflicting, since the two individuals have dissimilar needs that are likely to be frustrated in the situation, but not because of what the other man does. Rather, the frustration for the high aff or high ach member of the pair derives from what the other man doesn't do, which seems quite different from the nature of the incompatible compositions on the other two variables.

This analysis is congruent with some existing approaches to personality functioning (Schutz, 1958; Harvey, Hunt, and Schroder, 1961). Schutz's emphasis on interpersonal needs of control and affection maps directly with our classification of dominance and affiliation. Proceeding counterclockwise in Figure 23-4, high dogmatism represents the Harvey et al. system I personality (high authoritarian in interpersonal relationships, concretistic in cognitive style); high dominance reflects system II types (manipulative, egocentric, and concerned with interpersonal control); high affiliation represents system III personality types (group oriented, interested in avoiding overt interpersonal conflict); achievement crudely represents their system IV personality organization (abstract, interest in people as information sources).

From this general conceptualization, one might expect dominance and affiliation to be associated with territoriality because they involve "people"-oriented characteristics, with incompatibility yielding interpersonal barriers. Dogmatism and achievement incompatibility should not yield any particular territoriality pattern because they have no direct bearing on interpersonal relationships. For the other dimension, dominance and dogmatism incompatibility are presumably associated with high social activity because of Ss' attempts to maintain their own positions (either interpersonal or ideational). Because incompatibility on affiliation and achievement implies lack of common goal, nonbonding, exclusion, and so on, but not direct competition or struggle for control, the observed withdrawal of the parties from one another might be reasonably expected. While this conceptualization is post hoc, it fits the data fairly well and is congruent with other approaches regarding interpersonal functioning.

The data of the present study also indicate the importance of individual differences in personality, as well as interpersonal composition factors, on territorial and social activity behavior. For example, members of low affiliation groups tended to withdraw socially from one another and to exhibit high territorial behavior. Also, groups with low dominance members showed little initial, but eventually strong, territoriality behavior, perhaps reflecting an early reticence to dominate one another but a later need to counteract environmental stress through territorial structuring.

To summarize, the present experiment indicated that a condition of social isolation, in which pairs of men were isolated from society for ten days, led to a gradual increase in territorial behavior with respect to areas and objects in the environment and to a general pattern of social withdrawal. There also seemed to be a developmental sequence of territoriality behavior, with fixed geographic areas and highly personal objects subject to jurisdictional control first and more mobile, less personal objects somewhat later. The effects of social isolation on territoriality and social activities also interacted with group personality composition.

Incompatibility on traits directly associated with interpersonal matters—dominance and affiliation—resulted in high territoriality. Incompatibility on characteristics primarily relevant to orientation to ideas and objects —achievement and dogmatism—did not produce unusual territoriality behavior.

For social activities, personality incompatibilities on "egocentric" characteristics (dominance and dogmatism) were associated with strong and active member interactions. Incompatibility on characteristics such as affiliation and achievement, which involve a "sociocentric" reference point, led to withdrawal rather than heightened social interaction.

REFERENCES:

Altman, I., & Haythorn, W. W. Interpersonal exchange in isolation. *Sociometry*, 1965, **28**, 411–426.

Altman, I., & Haythorn, W. W. The effects of social isolation and group composition on performance. *Human Relations*, 1967, **20** (4), 313–340.

Bass, B. M., & Klubeck, S. Effects of seating arrangement on leaderless group discussions. *Journal of Abnormal and Social Psychology*, 1952, **47**, 724–727.

Calhoun, J. B. A comparative study of the social behavior of two inbred strains of house mice. *Ecological Monograph*, 1956, **26**, 81–103.

Calhoun, J. B. Population density and social pathology. *Scientific American*, 1962, **306**, 139–148.

Christian, J. J. Phenomena associated with population density. *Proceedings of the National Academy of Science*, 1961, **47**, 428–449.

Christian, J. J., Flyger, V., & Davis, D. C. Factors in the mass mortality of a herd of sika deer *cervus nippon*. *Chesapeake Science*, 1960, **1**, 79–95.

Edwards, A. L. *Edwards Personal Preference Schedule Manual.* (Revised edition.) New York: Psychological Corporation, 1959.

Errington, P. L. Of population cycles and unknowns. *Cold Springs Symposia on Quantitative Biology*, 1957, **22**.

Hall, E. T. *The silent language.* New York: Doubleday, 1959.

Hall, E. T. A system for the notation of proxemic behavior. *American Anthropologist*, 1963, **65**, 1003–1026.

Hall, E. T. *The hidden dimension.* New York: Doubleday, 1966.

Harvey, O. J., Hunt, D. E., & Schroder, H. M. *Conceptual systems and personality organizations.* New York: John Wiley, 1961.

Haythorn, W. W., & Altman, I. Personality factors in isolated environments. In M. H. Appley & R. Trumbull (Eds.), *Psychological stress.* New York: Appleton-Century-Crofts, 1967. Pp. 363–386.

Haythorn, W. W., Altman, I., & Myers, T. I. Emotional symptomatology and subjective stress in isolated pairs of men. *Journal of Experimental Research in Personality*, 1966, **1**, 290–305.

Hediger, H. *Wild animals in captivity.* London: Butterworths Scientific Publications, 1950.

Hediger, H. *Studies of the psychology and behavior of captive animals in zoos and circuses.* New York: Criterion Books, 1955.

Horowitz, M. J. Graphic communication: A study of interaction painting with schizophrenics. *American Journal of Psychotherapy*, 1963, **17**, 230–239.

Horowitz, M. J., Duff, D. F., & Stratton, L. O. The body-buffer zone in normal and schizophrenic persons. Paper read at the Western Divisional meeting of the American Psychiatric Association, San Francisco, California, September 1963.

Horowitz, M. F., Duff, D. F., & Stratton, L. O. Territoriality in man. Mimeographed report, the Clinical Investigation Center and the Neuropsychiatric Service, U. S. Naval Hospital, Oakland, California, undated.

Howard, D. *Territory and bird life.* London: Collins Publishing Company, 1948.

Little, K. B. Personal Space. *Journal of Experimental and Social Psychology*, 1965, **1**, 237–247.

Rokeach, M. *The open and closed mind.* New York: Basic Books, 1960.

Schutz, W. *FIRO: A three-dimensional theory of interpersonal behavior.* New York: Holt, Rinehart, & Winston, 1958.

Steinzor, B. The spatial factor in face to face discussion groups. *Journal of Abnormal and Social Psychology*, 1950, **45**, 552–555.

Sommer, R. Studies in personal space. *Sociometry*, 1959, **22**, 247–260.

Sommer, R. Leadership and group geography. *Sociometry*, 1961, **24**, 99–110.

Sommer, R. Further studies of small group ecology. *Sociometry*, 1965, **28**, 337–348.

Winick, C., & Holt, H. Seating position as nonverbal communication in group analysis. *Psychiatry*, 1961, **24**, 171–182.

24 Jurisdiction: An Ecological Concept

Philip D. Roos

THE SETTING OF SHIPBOARD TERRITORIALITY

In late summer of 1961, President Kennedy called up a number of military reserve units in response to the "Berlin crisis." As a member of one such unit, I served ten months on a ship here called the USS *Oswald A.*

From *Human Relations*, 1968, **21**, 75–84. Reprinted by permission of the author and publisher.

Powers (a pseudonym). The *Powers* is slightly over 300 feet long and almost 37 feet wide at its widest point. The ship's World War II complement was 220 officers and men; on this cruise, about 190 were aboard. While the situation and the crew were far from typical, there is good reason to believe that this did not affect the phenomena studied.

The crew of a warship is divided horizontally by rank and vertically by a complex division of labor. There are six enlisted ranks (ranging from seaman or fireman apprentice to chief petty officer) and approximately two dozen enlisted specialties. Some specialties, such as postal clerk or disbursing clerk, had but one member; others, such as Boilertenders and Machinist's Mates, had 20 or more.

Each such shipboard work group typically had a territory in the form of a room (a "space") where most group members do much of their work. The room generally contains the equipment necessary for that work, be it sonar consoles or typewriters. When possible, those in a particular work group also spend their leisure time in this space, improving its comfort as much as the Navy and their resources allow. Other members of the crew, whether officers or enlisted men, do not enter the territory except on business or by invitation from one of the work group. Intruders on business stand and generally leave when their business is concluded even though lower ranking members of the work group may remain seated. This is only the most obvious way in which a group controls its territory. [Other common forms of territorial behavior include, but are by no means restricted to, locked doors (the keys to which could easily be, but never are, stolen), asking intruders to state their business, using the territory to store personal belongings (against formal regulations), taking great pains with the appearance of the space, and even rarely asking intruders to leave.]

Such territories are of course common enough in civilian life. In many cultures, the family has a home. People work at *their* desks, offices, fields, shops, etc. People cathect their territories and resist invasions

of their privacy. They use their territories to increase power, comfort, and control.

JURISDICTION: A SERENDIPITOUS CONCEPT

Some social psychologists and anthropologists have begun to use ethological spatial concepts such as territoriality and personal space in describing human behavior. (Examples include Esser, 1965, pp. 37–44; Felipe, 1966, pp. 206–14; Goffman, 1961; Hall, 1961, 1966; Sommer, 1959, pp. 247–60.) E. R. Leach strongly criticizes such conceptual analogies.

> But can we take fish and birds as our models? In observing how animals behave we can only record what they do and the circumstances in which they do it; we know nothing about their feelings and motives. But when we discuss human behavior our objectivity is fogged by subjective private experience. It may be perfectly sensible to describe the action of a baboon in baring its teeth towards an opponent as "an aggressive gesture." For the Chinese government to authorize the firing of a nuclear rocket may also be properly described as "an aggressive gesture." But to argue that the two behaviors are comparable in anything except a purely metaphorical sense is just nonsense. Yet this is precisely what both our authors are up to all the time. (1966, p. 8.)

> It is true that living human beings, both as individuals and as groups, do on occasion exhibit symptoms resembling the "territoriality" displayed by various species of birds and fish, but this human behavior is not a species characteristic, and this makes all the difference. It is optional not "instinctive" behavior. (1966, p. 12.)

We cannot know whether human territoriality is the product of genes or culture, or, more likely, of some combination. It does appear to be a pervasive human characteristic. Hall (1961, 1966) has demonstrated repeatedly how pervasive and how far from normal consciousness human spatial behavior is.

But the social scientist who uses an analogy must be sensitive to where that analogy breaks down and why. In my research on a small warship, I was able to apply ethological concepts, particularly territory (see Burt, 1943, pp. 346–52; Carpenter, 1958, pp. 224–50), to the behavior of Navy enlisted men with some success. (See Roos, 1963, 1967.)

Some space-oriented behavior, however, could not be treated in ethological terms. The substantive reasons for this are discussed below. Formally, such a breakdown is inherent in the nature of analogical reasoning: the analogy is usually only partial. In describing territorial behavior, the topological aspect is generally omitted. The concepts of home, territory, and range can be topologically interpreted as a series of closed figures of increasing size, one within the next. (Some animals do have more than one home or territory within their range, or, more frequently, more than one home or nest within a territory or core area.[1] This only complicates the topology without changing the essentials.) Life on shipboard admits of no such topologically simple interpretation. Territories are scattered all over the ship, and are divided by passageways common to everyone.

As a result of a ship's design, the high density of personnel, and the intricate social structure, not all shipboard spatial behavior can be dealt with in terms of territoriality and personal space. A large part of such residual behavior can be dealt with as "jurisdiction." This legal term has passed over into ordinary usage and the dictionary defines it as:

. . . 2. authority or power in general. 3. the range of authority. 4. the territorial range of authority. . . . (Webster's, 1957, p. 795.)

While animals (and sailors) defend some spaces more or less continuously, the term jurisdiction covers the temporary defense of space (generally for a specific, instrumental purpose and not because the space "belongs" to its defenders), or the defense of some object or commodity which involves at most an instrumental attempt to secure the surrounding space. Jurisdictional like territorial behavior has the social function of helping to order shipboard life. The working sailor needs some protection from general shipboard duties if he is to get his specialized job done. His jurisdiction gives him a mandate (cf. Hughes, 1957, p. 78) to do so with minimal disturbance.

We can speak of two distinct types of jurisdictions:

(1) over a space for a specific, and rather short, time, and

(2) over things which may or may not be dispensed.

TEMPORARY TERRITORIES OR JURISDICTIONS OVER SPACE

Animals generally stay in their home ranges for extended periods, if not their entire lifetimes. Migrating animals return to the same places every year. Within such ranges, animals may defend space—physical, personal, or both. Temporary control of physical areas is generally irregularly placed in time and space. Human beings who establish temporary territories generally do so at regular intervals and at the same place. They may occupy a place at a bar for certain hours on certain days of the week (Cavan, 1966, Chs, 5, 10) or, like professors, hold office hours which are regular within a term but vary from term to term.[2]

---

[1] I use "range" as the total area traversed; "territory" as the area defended; "core area" as the area preponderantly occupied; and "home" as the area slept in. I realize that there is considerable disagreement about these terms and that not all of them apply to any one species. But neither of these problems affects the essential topological interpretation which is implicit in animal studies only because it is so obvious.

[2] Professor Goffman suggests that temporary territories may be distinguished from jurisdictions. Territories are defended on two grounds: "you keep off" and "it is mine." Jurisdictions are controlled only on the former ground; no claim of ownership, no matter how transitory, is made. A bus seat, while I am sitting on it, is a temporary territory, not a jurisdiction. In practice, this distinction often breaks down, particularly when a person has repeated jurisdiction. (Personal communication.)

On a ship, jurisdiction over a physical space is most often associated with cleaning and painting. The ship is divided into areas so precisely delimited that someone is responsible for each surface. A few of the men who sleep in each berthing compartment clean it (except in chiefs' and officers' quarters); the mess cooks clean the mess deck. Territories are cleaned by their work groups and all other places are assigned to one work group or another. The most enlightening example is "field day"—a period devoted to cleaning and polishing. In theory, field day comes each Friday; in practice, less often. During field day, all normal work ceases (except operation of the ship at sea). Since first class and chief petty officers and commissioned officers are exempt from field day, they are free to go anywhere out of the workers' way. Even those officers or chiefs who would walk casually through an area during everyday cleaning generally make their excuses when passing through on field day. Field day generally involves scrubbing bulkheads (walls), ladders (stairs), and decks (floors), shining brightwork, and waxing decks covered with asphalt tile. On the morning after field day, the captain and executive officer each inspect half the ship.

During field day virtually every part of the ship was roped off. Although it was generally physically possible to pass through the ropes, they did give men some control over their assigned area. This partially symbolic control was not essential—except when cleaning decks or ladders—since workers could stand aside. Their bitter reaction to intrusions, however, indicates territorial behavior. Because this behavior did not extend beyond keeping others out for the time of cleaning and the following inspection (when scheduled), it seems useful to distinguish it from the more fully fleshed territoriality described above. At other times, the man who snarled, "Secured!" would be unconcerned about what happened to the area.

By the afternoon of field day, the ship's company became somewhat more mobile. Several areas would be finished and, more significantly, some officers and chiefs would feel the inactivity weighing upon them. Since decks were done last, this was a critical point: no one wanted his scrubbed deck walked on before it was waxed and buffed. With only one buffer available to enlisted men, and with much of the ship's interior decking covered with asphalt tile, this often meant a long wait. While waiting, men might stand at the various entrances to their area in an attempt to block all traffic. My area (generally cleaned by 3 or 4 men) was particularly subject to heavy travel since the wardroom, galley, mess deck (two entrances) and three entrances to other places opened from it. The only solution was to wax and guard half the area while waiting for the buffer, then wax and buff the rest when the buffer was obtained. Because there was no set rotation for the use of the buffer, one member of each group had to search the ship for it, and then "get in line" for its use. This increased traffic forced men all over the ship to increase their attempts to control their areas.

Saturday morning brought an orgy of last minute tidying before the inspection. These were typical of what must be general in total institutions: the inspecting officers' habits soon became obvious, and the cleaners learned which areas required special attention or permitted relative neglect. (Sailors who cleaned their own group's territory might, however, clean to the satisfaction of a more finicky petty officer.) In addition to the spaces themselves, lockers were inspected, though rarely, for the quantity, quality, marking, and arrangement of clothing. The crew was occasionally inspected for cleanliness of body, etc. No two of these inspections ever coincided, so the sailor always had a place for discrepant articles (*e.g.*, civilian clothes, pornography). In Melville's day, inspections of personal possessions and person commonly coincided (Melville, 1959, p. 278). Thus, one improvement in Naval habitability is that the self, which may perhaps be considered as residing partly in the territory and the nest (bunk and locker) as well as in the body, now always has two places to retreat to during inspection of the third.

"Neatness," as it is called, is a most important shipboard value. Nevertheless, cleaning and painting are, as in the civilian world, done by lower status people. On a ship, those who clean have many other duties to perform. This lack of specialization is not found in most organizations and institutions, where most people can generally ignore cleaning activity. Although use and cleaning of a space can be partially phased on a ship, the crowded conditions and the extraordinary amount of dirt make cleanliness a more or less constant effort. In business establishments or schools, the time of day for cleaning is different from the time of day for transacting business or holding classes. The personnel who do the cleaning are different than those engaged in furthering organizational goals. In total institutions, inmates may be briefly removed from areas to allow a relatively small custodial group to clean. The distinction between territory and jurisdiction (or temporary territory) is, if anything, more clean-cut in these civilian examples. Those who exercise jurisdiction (for janitorial purposes) displace those who exercise territorial prerogatives (e.g., employees—who usually have higher status—or inmates—who usually have lower status).

In field day we see only one aspect of territorial defense: "you keep off." The "this is mine" aspect is missing. Even this overt control necessary on a ship is generally absent from schools and businesses. Field day is thus an intermediate case between a full-fledged territoriality and the smooth jurisdiction of much civilian janitoring. And it is the feature of overt control that shows one point at which the analogy to animals tends to break down. It makes no sense to speak of the jurisdiction of one animal at a social distance from others aside from its normal personal space. It does make sense to speak of the jurisdiction of a lone janitor as quite distinct from (and larger than) his personal space. Of course, the place of cleaning behavior in the social structure, whether in military or civilian life, is very different than the place of temporary spatial defense in the structure of an animal's life. But in using the analogy in the first place we implicitly ignore structural implications, so that

it would be inconsistent to bring them in again solely to make distinctions.

JURISDICTION OVER THINGS

Some objects and information pass out of the control of an individual or group permanently. I call these _commodities._ Other objects pass out of control only temporarily; these I call _equipment_. In both cases, individuals and groups behave spatially toward objects.

Commodities are generally small things, passed from hand to hand and often consumed in use (_e.g._, soap). They can usually be put away or locked up. Equipment is usually _there_—physically built into the situation. The individuals and groups who use it come and go. While the major illustrations presented again come from the warship, they are highly similar to more familiar instances in everyday life.

Commodities

On shipboard, the Storekeeper (SK) is basically responsible for ordering, obtaining, and storing supplies for all departments. The three or four SK's aboard the _Powers_ worked in a Supply Office (which had room for only two to work at once) and in various storerooms.

Increasingly, SK's are becoming responsible for storerooms which hold such items as spare parts and office supplies. On the _Powers_, SK's had taken over the office supplies storeroom from the Yeomen (clerks) before activation; storerooms for electronics and engineering repair parts were taken over in the second and fifth months of activation respectively.

The bureaucratic motivation for this change in Naval policy is not difficult to understand: having technicians manage their own spare parts is an inefficient use of relatively expensive manpower. Further, the technician is obviously less committed to good supply procedures than to maintaining his equipment. He may be wasteful or slovenly with Navy material or use them for social exchanges. (For example, Electronics Technicians—ET—handling their own spare parts will normally use them to repair personally owned radios and TV's.) In sum, the character of control differs with the occupational commitment of the controllers.

Inventory control is considered a burden, although it is reasonable to expect groups to resent SK's taking over their storerooms. The ET's fought two battles with the SK's over different aspects of control. Both disputes were resolved by the officers and each side prevailed once; later conflict mostly involved such routine matters as waking up SK's for parts in the middle of the night. The engineers did resent the takeover of their storeroom, which contained spares for all Engineering specialties. This held both specific spare parts with stock numbers in the Federal Catalog, and generally useful objects lacking stock numbers. The latter had to be discarded when the SK's took over, as there was no way to classify and index them. The engineers thus had the melancholy task of throwing overboard bolts, gaskets, valves, etc.—some felt that the truly useful items were at the bottom of the sea, while those that remained were relatively useless.

Similar situations abound in civilian life. The parts man in a large automobile repair shop is obviously committed to keeping his stock under control, while the mechanics who come to him are under pressure to do repairs in reasonable time. The parts man's jurisdiction stops, in theory, when he hands the part to the mechanic. But, like the SK, he may feel obliged to be certain that the part goes where it is intended and not, for example, into the car of the mechanic's friend.

Certain kinds of information are commodities which have a more limited circulation and then a broader circulation. On the ship, radiomen and some officers know where the ship is going before others do. If there is enough time, there may then be a period of rumor and increasing certainty, and finally the whole crew is officially notified. In civilian life there are some kinds of "inside information" which are typically known by a few people before they become public knowledge. In these cases, the "thing" some have jurisdiction over is not a material substance but is not otherwise different from other commodities.

Thus far I have discussed commodities infused with positive feelings, and this would appear to be the more common case, at least on shipboard. Jurisdictions also exist over negatively valued objects. The nursing profession has successfully eliminated the handling of routine human wastes. Orderlies who now deal with these materials dispose of them expeditiously. Negatively valued objects are not dealt with in ethology. Animals don't have "jobs" which require them to "handle" such things as slops and excreta.[3]

Equipment

Of several possible Naval examples of jurisdiction over equipment, the matter of electronic repairs is perhaps most illuminating. Sailors typically perform minor service and repair on their own equipment, while major overhaul is left to civilians in a shipyard. Equipment is generally located in a space which is already the territory of a particular group—e.g., boilers, operated and maintained by Boilertenders, are in the boilerrooms—and servicing does not usually entail the entry of other crew members.

Electronic equipment is the most complicated found aboard older ships. On the *Powers*, for a variety of reasons, ET's spent more time repairing radar equipment than any other kind. It is Navy policy to ask operators to repair their own equipment. ET's thus are beginning to look upon themselves as a sort of "Board of Electronic Appeals." This is obviously not good for intergroup morale, but it does illustrate our concepts nicely.

Combat Information Center (CIC) was the Radarmen's territory. When off duty, they congregated there to smoke, talk, and play cards. When one or more of the many pieces of equipment broke down, ET's arrived. As they opened up the equipment

---

[3] I am indebted to Professor Erving Goffman for this insight as well as helpful comments on the rest of the paper.

and used their test gear, the small amount of space available for humans diminished. Nevertheless, the Radarmen present would often stay, continuing their activities. Thus, the ET's worked at their jurisdiction and the Radarmen worked or rested in their territory. Unfortunately, these two groups got in each other's way. To add to the difficulty, a whole series of breakdowns occurred during underway training when the whole crew was working harder than usual. On several occasions, when the ship was operating all day and returning to the harbor at night, the ET's worked until midnight or later, getting up for an early reveille to do it all over again. Under these conditions, it is not surprising that tempers flared in CIC. After some days, the division officer stepped in and ordered the Radarmen out of CIC while gear was worked on.

In this instance territory gave way to jurisdiction. The Radarmen's reluctance to leave indicates the strength of their attachment to the territory. But the overriding importance of jurisdictional demands is evident in the decisive way the division officer sided with the ET's.

Jurisdictions over things present phenomena unknown to the ethologists. This is so for the very basic reason that humans use tools. A successful technology requires that tools be serviced and used where appropriate. At times, technological jurisdictions override what appears to the outsider as the organization's primary function. In the scarcity economy of some mental hospitals, technicians and those who control scarce goods and services become more powerful than the line staff who treat patients (Cumming, 1956, pp. 361–9). For many analytic purposes the two kinds of jurisdictions over things may merge, as in the mental hospital. But jurisdiction over commodities seems more widespread and more available as a source of "secondary adjustments" (Goffman, 1961, ch. 3).

DISCUSSION

Human behavior invariably has symbolic or cultural content. Ethological analogies deemphasize this content. While it is possible to shed much light on space-oriented behavior without venturing into the meanings of things, such a view can be no more than partial. The use of analogy from outside human experience may lead to some mistaken examples. Hall uses "hot bunking" on submarines (the use of a bed by more than one person, seriatum) as an instance of the objectionability of another's—but not one's own—body heat (1966, p. 55). While he may well be correct, in this case there are other strong objections closer to the submariner's awareness. "Hot bunking" (a) does not conform with cultural norms concerning sleeping; (b) is an invasion of virtually the only place a submariner can call his own; and (c) is formally considered a privation by the Navy and is visited only on lower ranking enlisted men and then only when necessary. A more germane investigation of this point would involve finding out how frequently (if ever) and under what circumstances couples sharing double beds exchange sides for sleeping.

More generally it is safe to say that all objects and spaces may have some symbolic value—they may be coveted, disdained, used, saved, squandered, traded, admired, disposed of, etc. While animals react to spaces and objects in a variety of ways, they lack the immense repertory of response which humans display. Much of this repertory is of everyday interest to people. Social scientists use analogy as one means of seeing familiar phenomena in an unfamiliar light. But they must remember that this new light does not remove the validity of older lights cast on the same places. (See, for example, Theodoreson, 1961 and Riecken & Homans, 1954.)

It would be convenient if we could systematically distinguish jurisdiction from territory. But the characteristics of animal territoriality, let alone human territoriality, are not universally agreed on. In this paper I have argued that territorial behavior maximizes control over space to enhance positive values. Jurisdiction, on the other hand, is generally forced onto an individual or group by the structural nature of their specific social surroundings. Duties often imply responsibility which, in turn, may imply interest. The extent and quality of the interest depend upon numerous factors: Does the jurisdiction approximate territory, as in giving the potential for power, influence, comfort or control? Or is it negatively valued and therefore to be disposed of (as in the bedpan example)? Does the responsibility entailed by a jurisdiction have major consequences for a person's social standing or is it something (like cleaning an area unlikely to be inspected) with, at most, implications only in one's internal conversation? Such are only a few of the questions that can be raised in the analysis of human spatial behavior.

REFERENCES:

Burt, W. H. Territoriality and home range concepts as applied to mammals. *Journal of Mammalogy*, 1943, 24, 346–352.

Carpenter, C. R. Territoriality: A review of concepts and problems. In A. Roe & G. G. Simpson (Eds.), *Behavior and evolution.* New Haven, Conn.: Yale University Press, 1958.

Cavan, S. *Liquor license.* Chicago: Aldine, 1966.

Cumming, E. & Cumming, J. The locus of power in a large mental hospital. *Psychiatry*, 1956, 19, 361–369.

Esser, A. H., Chamberlain, A. S., Chapple, E. D., & Kline, N. S. Territoriality of patients on a research ward. In J. Wortis (Ed.), *Recent advances in biological psychiatry.* New York: Plenum Press, 1965.

Felipe, N. & Sommer, R. Invasion of personal space. *Social Problems*, 1966, 14, 206–214.

Goffman, E. *Asylums.* Garden City, N.Y.: Doubleday, 1961.

Hall, E. T. *The silent language.* Greenwich, Conn.: Fawcett, 1961.

Hall, E. T. *The hidden dimension.* Garden City, N.Y.: Doubleday, 1966.

Hughes, E. C. *Men and their work.* Glencoe, Ill.: The Free Press, 1958.

Leach, E. R. Review of K. Lorenz, *On aggression. New York Review of Books*, July 10, 1966, 8–12.

Leach, E. R. Review of R. Ardrey, *The territorial imperative. New York Review of Books*, July 10, 1966, 8–12.

Melville, H. *White jacket, or the world in a man-of-war.* New York: Grove Press, 1959. Originally published in 1850.

Riecken, H. W. & Homans, G. C. Psychological aspects of social structure. In G. Lindzey (Ed.), *Handbook of social psychology.* Cambridge, Mass.: Addison-Wesley, 1954.

Roos, P. D. On the social micro-ecology of a small warship. Microfilm No. 67-3 deposited at the Clearinghouse for Sociological Literature, Department of Sociology, University of Wisconsin, Milwaukee, 1967.

Sommer, R. Studies in personal space. *Sociometry*, 1959, 22, 247–260.

Theodoreson, G. A. (Ed.) *Studies in human ecology.* Evanston, Ill.: Row, Petersen & Co., 1961.

Webster's New World Dictionary. College edition. New York: World Publishing, 1957.

25 Neighbour on the Hearth

Leo Kuper

The adage that an Englishman's home is his castle suggests a home fortified against neighbours and the world at large. Nothing could be less descriptive of much of contemporary English urban housing. In a very real sense, the general layout of the Braydon Road residential unit[1] and the design of its steel houses introduce an awareness of neighbours even within the inner sanctum.

PARTY NEIGHBOURS

The first involuntary link between neighbours is by ear, and this is a common feature of modern urban English housing. At evening, in place of the melodious notes recorded by the poets—"The curfew tolls the knell of parting day"—there is the quite unique and unforgettable noise of the neighbour's wife scratching at her grate with a poker, and the sudden rush of sound as the radio is tuned and quickly hushed. Dawn is heralded by the sound of wood being chopped, and the clatter of the neighbour's grate. Over week-ends other noises spell out the activities of the unseen neighbour. The husband is being handy; you follow his movements round the house; his daughter is picking out her favourite notes on the upper reaches of the piano, single notes exuberantly sprinkled with random combinations. On rare party nights, or at Christmas, the virtuoso, your neighbour's wife, takes over the piano, and explores her memory of old tunes, largely with the right hand, but

From Leo Kuper (Ed.), *Living in Towns.* London: The Cresset Press, 1953, Chapter 2. Reprinted by permission of the author and publisher.

[1] Braydon Road is a residential unit of ninety families in the urban area of Houghton, a neighborhood unit on the outskirts of Coventry.

sometimes accompanied by a few belated chords with the left. Some sounds are difficult to place. Was that knocking at your front door or at your neighbour's front door? And it may be necessary to take a rapid inventory of all the members of your household—which is by no means difficult, since the even lower standards of insulation within the house have the effect of charting with most detailed intimacy all movements —and to analyse carefully the direction of the sound before deciding: "No, that was not our Jennie coughing; it must be Janice Carter." A sort of non-electrical radar process! Only one sound is quite unambiguous, and that is the water returning to the cisterns when the closet has been used. It fills the house with an avalanche of noise. No wonder, then, that many of our informants appreciate an outdoor closet, more especially if there are young children in the house.

In the Braydon Road residential unit, this close auditory linkage of neighbours is promoted by the design of the houses, which are semi-detached, and so arranged that most of the activities of the residents are carried out in the rooms immediately adjoining the dividing or party wall (see Figure 25-1).

The houses are described as nontraditional, but this refers to the material and methods of construction; they are permanent prefabricated steel houses. The interior arrangement of space, however, follows traditional lines and conforms to one of the models (the two-storey semi-detached, three-bedroomed house), provided in the Housing Manual issued by the Ministry of Health for the guidance of local authorities, and extensively reproduced throughout the country. At the outer ends of the house are the front doors, which give direct access to hallway and staircase. These, together with the kitchen, the bathroom and the small third bedroom, lie furthest away from the party wall, and therefore do not serve as insulating barriers between the two semi-detached units. The main living-rooms, on the other hand, the large lounge and dining recess downstairs, and the first and second bedrooms upstairs, are distributed along the party wall. In the first bedroom, a number of factors combine to fix the placing of the double bed. This is almost invariably with the head towards the middle of the party wall, an arrangement contemplated by the architect as indicated both in his sketches, which show the distribution of the main items of furniture, and also in the position of the electric light pull. Hence, of a winter's evening the party neighbours (as we shall describe the occupants of a pair of semi-detached houses), sit in their three-piece suites around the open grate, separated only by the narrow line of the party wall. And at night, the connubial heads lie, each on their own side of the partition.

Through the party wall, a variety of noises enter. We are not concerned with the problem of the standard of insulation of this wall. Our main interest is in the reactions of residents to these intimacies of noise, whatever the objective measure of the degree of insulation may be, since it is their reactions which are the basis of relations with neighbours. This introduces an element of variability, because of the different characteristics of the residents. Some are particularly sensitive to sounds, more especially those which they cannot control. "It's noises from *other* people that distress us." And they complain: "It's terrible, you can hear everything." Mrs. Hayes says of one such sensitive neighbour, that "when I clean my mirror, it bangs against the wall, and she knocks back. My husband says it's best to ignore people like that." Others enjoy noise associated with neighbours: "I don't feel so lonely when I know there's somebody about," and, "It's company in one way to hear noises." Again, the party neighbours may be particularly quiet. They play the radio so low, that it is hard to believe they can hear the broadcasts; they speak quietly, quarrel in subdued tones, and their children are brought up in the tradition that children should be seen and not heard. In these circumstances, there is little neighbouring by ear. "You wouldn't know they had any children." "You wouldn't think anybody was living next door." This does not imply more effective insulation, but simply that the neighbouring unit houses one of the more muted patterns of the English way of life. And quite apart from this

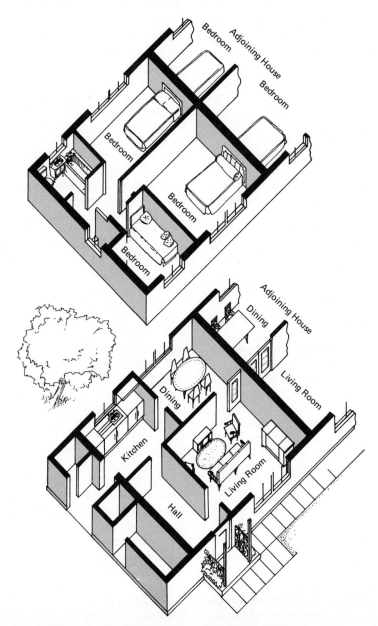

Figure 25–1. First floor plan (*top*) and ground floor plan (*bottom*).

variability among residents, there is seasonal change, with greater vulnerability to sound in open-windowed summer.

Developing our picture of neighbour linkage by ear from the comments of the residents, we find that it is possible in these houses to entertain a neighbour's wife by playing her favourite records with the gramophone tuned to loud, or to mind her child or invite her to tea, all through the party wall. Residents are aware of many "vicinal" noises, extending from the unusual clamour of birthday celebrations to the sound of the daily routine. Informants mention the wireless, the baby crying at night, coughing, shoes dropped at bedtime, children running up and down the stairs or on the bedroom floors, strumming at the piano, and laughing or loud talk. In the connubial bedroom, the intimations from the neighbour may be shocking: "You can even hear them use the pot; that's how bad it is. It's terrible"; or disturbing: "I heard them having a row in bed. One wanted to read, and the other one wanted to go to sleep. It's embarrassing to hear noises in bed, so I turned my bed the other way round" (that is, away from the architecturally preordained position). "I like to read in bed and I'm light of hearing, so it disturbs me to hear them talk"; or a little inhibiting: "You sometimes hear them say rather private things, as, for example, a man telling his wife that her feet are cold. It makes you feel that *you* must say private things in a whisper"; and, "It does make you feel a bit restrained, as if you ought to walk on tiptoe into your bedroom at night." Usually, however, only a murmur is conveyed, and that there may be some curiosity is indicated in the frequent comments: "You can't hear the actual words," or, "You can't distinguish what they say." These sounds do not always remain in their own natural element. Sometimes they materialise: "When they had the television at first, the noise used to rattle our ornaments"; and, in another case, the vibration shook a photograph off the sideboard. Or again, the party neighbours "nearly sent us crazy last week end. Their children played football upstairs and the whitewash came off our ceiling. They were reported for noise"—though not by our informant.

Yet many residents, while aware of vicinal noises, do not complain of them. This forbearance is not only an expression of British fortitude, of the "we can take it" spirit; there is also active adjustment between neighbours. This adjustment has two aspects —control over noise in the neighbour's house, and control over noise in one's own home. In the first case, the neighbour is approached, either indirectly by dropping a hint, knocking at the party wall, or directly, if the relationship is such as to allow of the discussion of difficulties without quarrelling; the real trouble arises when one of the neighbours is reserved, unapproachable, shy, or generally difficult. In the second case, there is a censoring of noises within the home by identification with the neighbours and their problems. It is in this sense

more particularly that your neighbour sits on your own hearth. Thus, the arrangement of furniture may be influenced by neighbourly considerations; the radio or the piano is moved from the party wall. If the family is not already very quiet, it may be necessary to curb the children, to tone down the husband's games with them, to play the piano only in the daytime, to close doors softly, and generally to be as quiet as possible.

This consideration for neighbours, and identification with them, may be carried very far indeed. Mrs. Carroll tells us that her neighbour's vacuum interferes with her wireless, "so I suppose mine does with hers. I try to do my vacuuming quickly." And Mrs. Leek comments that when they know that Mr. Donnelly, the party neighbour, is in bed, "we keep quiet so as not to disturb him. He's on the opposite shift to my husband." The Loudens, similarly, hardly play their wireless at all, when their party neighbours are on night shift. Inability to control noises within the house, as for example, bronchial coughs, babies crying at night, or a Welsh husband who joins in with singing on the wireless, may give rise to uneasiness or even anxiety. Perhaps there is something in the comment made by one informant that she heard her neighbour's visitors, because they spoke much louder, due, she supposed, to the fact that "they may be used to brick houses." Her assumption that brick houses are better insulated than steel houses may not be correct; but the inference from her statement is that residents learn to adjust to the degree of insulation provided by their homes, and this is supported by our data. It raises the important question, with which we are not concerned in this study, of the effects of house design on personality. *What are the consequences of the particular standards of insulation against sound for the personality development of the residents and more especially of their children?*

SIDE NEIGHBOURS

The link with party neighbours is, to be sure, not entirely auditory. They are also seen, but only well out in the garden or coming into the house. And of the visual

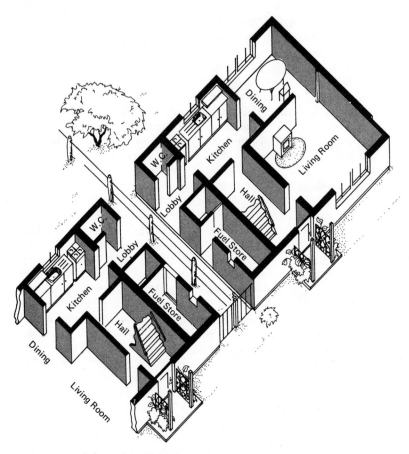

Figure 25–2. Ground floor plan, adjacent houses.

links, the most important is between side neighbours (see Figure 25-2).

The front doors of the houses have no handles (a deliberate omission in many English houses), and if the doors are properly closed, it is necessary to use a latchkey. Partly for this reason, but mainly to keep the front hall clean, most families walk round to the side of the house and into a narrow lane. This lane is divided into two by what is virtually a symbolic fence, made of strands of wire attached to artificial stone pillars. From each side of the lane, there is access to a semi-detached house through a corridor, which is part of the house structure. A water-closet and fuel shed flank the corridor, which leads into the kitchen. Beyond the kitchen is the dining recess, and if both kitchen doors are open, an unimpeded view is obtained from the lane right through to the recess. The lanes are narrow, and the

side neighbours (or occupants of the houses adjoining a common lane) are quite readily vulnerable by broomstick, as we had occasion to observe in a neighbouring unit with a similar house type. One morning, our attention was attracted by a great clamour of two women (side neighbours), and by the clash of shattering glass. Mrs. O'Grady's broomstick had that moment crashed through Mrs. Hemming's kitchen door. We joined the women in Mrs. O'Grady's house and took notes of the discussion, one of the few situations in which the investigator's notebook is quite irrelevant to rapport. Mrs. Hemming was in a state close to hysteria, and complained that Mrs. O'Grady's son had thrown dirt into her kitchen, and so she threw dirt back again. Mrs. O'Grady, calm, very much in the ascendant, said she had no intention of breaking the glass in the kitchen door, but "she's a misery to live by. Being childish, she throws dirt back in here and hits my baby. I never interfere with her. I don't notice her on the street. She says my kids wasn't brought up proper, just dragged up. When I was pally with her she wouldn't let the children fight it out, as I said they should." Mrs. Hemming confirms the former friendship, and asserts that she is not going to pay 22s. 8d. a week to live by Mrs. O'Grady; on the other hand, she has no intention of moving. Mr. O'Grady, on night shift and disturbed in his sleep, introduces his pyjama'd contribution, and finally, after many heated exchanges, the parties agree to put up a trellis between the side entries. Seven months later, this had not been done. A neighbour reports that "for about six months after the quarrel they did not speak to each other; they avoided each other at their back doors." (This is, incidentally, a considerable feat, involving reconnaissance every time the housewife plans an exit from her house.) "About six weeks ago they became friendly again. They talked, and then there was a little mutual visiting, but about three weeks ago they had a slight quarrel and dropped each other again."

This incident illustrates in somewhat dramatic fashion the intimate linking of houses by the side entry. The strength of this link varies with siting arrangements. Only eight semi-detached houses have side entries directly opposite each other. For the most part, the houses are slightly staggered, with the result that side entries are taken out of the line which allows of visual contact from dining recess to dining recess. Nevertheless, the extreme intimacy of this siting aspect only disappears in the case of the corner houses, of the top houses which close off the cul-de-sac, and in a row of ten semi-detached houses in which the units are set back the full width of the house and separated by brick walls.

The close proximity of side neighbours may affect enjoyment of the amenities of the downstairs water-closet. A sex factor sometimes enters. Mr. Brown comments that: "It's embarrassing for women when men are in the next garden." One informant clearly wished to eliminate from her social personality any suggestion of natural functions: "I

may only be going to clean it (the closet) or wash it, but it's all the same to them. For all they know, I may be going to the toilet."

The side entry not only gives access to the house, and to the fuel shed and closet. It is also the way out from the house into the garden. The kitchen doors lead into the dining recess or into the corridor; there is no back door to the garden. Hence it is through the side entry that men and children come and go, and the housewife is in and out with the carpet, laundry and ashes. As a result, it is impossible for residents not to be keenly aware of side neighbours:

"When one goes out the back way, one is immediately right on top of one's neighbours"; "as soon as she comes out of her door, we are face to face"; "being so near, people can see the sort of things you have and want to borrow them"; "we are putting up a partition. Every time you open the back door, you see your neighbour. Children quarrel, and with the unbroken view, it makes it difficult to keep the peace."

The second involuntary link is thus between side neighbours. But these links with side and party neighbours, are elements in a wider system of neighbour contacts, made possible or inevitable by the general layout of the residential unit.

CUL-DE-SACS AND CLOISTERS

The main components of the layout of Braydon Road are four cul-de-sacs (B, C, D, and E on Figure 25-3). Three have seven pairs of houses and one has eight. These cul-de-sacs are arranged on either side of a large plot of land which extends from an exit road, Barnett Avenue, to the lower end of the residential unit. They are widest where they abut on to this open piece of land, and narrow in staggered steps. On the plan they look a little like the open mouth of a crocodile. One cul-de-sac is closed off at its furthest end from the open land by two pairs of houses, and the remainder each by one pair. Binding the residential area together and excluding access to the outside world except through the exit road, is a straight line of eight semi-detached houses

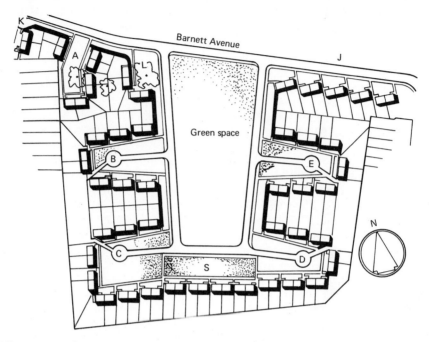

Figure 25–3. The Braydon Road Residential Unit, Coventry.

(S on our sketch), which joins the lower cul-de-sacs, C and D. At the upper end, in Barnett Avenue, there is a certain irregularity. On one side of the open strip are the five deeply staggered pairs, separated by brick walls, which we have already mentioned (J on the sketch); these are not in a cul-de-sac setting, and face a large undeveloped tract of land. The opposite side of Barnett Avenue consists of three groupings. L has four semi-detached units, arranged in a right angle at the corner of a grassed rectangle, with a large tree in the centre. A is quite irregular; four pairs of houses and a brick wall, which takes the place of the fifth pair in the original design, are distributed around three sides of something approximating a rectangular grassed court, which also features a tree. The final group, K, is one pair, and alone of all the houses shares with the J area direct access to the outside world.

The cul-de-sacs and the square give the impressions of a very intimate arrangement of houses. Density of development is not high by current standards—about eight houses to the acre. Yet the open spaces and houses are so organised as to achieve the same result as a layout at high density. And

a number of design elements contribute to make the residents accessible to each other visually at the fronts of their houses. The living-rooms have large glass windows directly overlooking the cul-de-sacs. These windows start at a low level from the ground, and at a convenient height for children to climb through from the inside or to peer into from the outside. Curtains are draped a little behind the windows, and back of them is the box-like shape of the living-room. The effect is not unlike that of a stage setting. Here, the family may seek to make its debut to the outside world by a display of possessions. And conversely through these windows neighbours gain some inside knowledge of the family's life. In fact, it is quite difficult for neighbours to avoid seeing into each other's homes, because no barriers are interposed. Separate front gardens were eliminated to enable the architect to handle the open spaces as a whole and to safeguard his design from the disturbing fences, privet hedges, trellises and other features of suburban gardens. In their place are narrow unfenced strips of ground, which run parallel to the house and may be cultivated by the tenants; large common forecourts; entry roads in the four cul-de-sacs, kept down to about twelve feet, ending in a large circle and so sited that the houses can be reached only on foot; and finally, narrow footpaths close beside the fronts of the houses and giving access to front doors and side entries. All these elements combine with the large front windows to link the houses into an involuntary community of the eye. Hence, it is possible to sit in the Canning's living-room and to tell the time by the clock in the house over the way. The Burtons' boy, aged 8, complains that he was seen in his pyjamas by the little girl across the road. One woman likes to watch people get off the bus some distance away and to follow their movements as they approach the steel houses; our own field workers were under this same constant observation, and there is a feeling among residents that neighbours know when they receive callers. The inside space of these cul-de-sacs makes an ideal playground for children. The entry road, with its circle and lamp-post, is an effective cricket pitch, almost as if it were specially designed by the architect to train wicket keepers, because behind the lamp-post wicket loom the large windows of the living-rooms. And often of an afternoon, the women will sit at the front windows, watch their children at play, and observe the activities in the cul-de-sac. For a person sensitive to neighbours' reactions the effect may be rather like the tele-screen described by Orwell in his novel *Nineteen Eighty-Four*. It is as if all actions and even thoughts are being observed. Thus, Mr. Dudley tells us: "There is no privacy. . . . You look across at the houses there—they must feel as though you are looking at them. You look out of the bed-room windows into their bedrooms. . . . You turn the corner coming home and everybody's eyes are on you in the cul-de-sac. For the amount you pay it's degrading —especially to old residents of Coventry, who knew the town as it used to be." And Mrs. Dudley relates her embarrassment when she kissed her mother in the street: "Then I thought everybody would be making fun of me up here. They don't do that sort of thing here."

A community of the eye links not only the houses within the cul-de-sac, but also houses in adjoining areas through the back gardens. These, again, are divided from each other only symbolically, by strands of wire. To give a more pleasing impression of the area, brick walls were built parallel to the large central plot of land in such a manner as to prevent passers-by looking into the back gardens. The effect of this is to create a sort of cloister knitting together houses in adjacent areas (see Figure 25-4). This is the cloister of the wash line, of baby's napkins, and of men's and women's and children's clothes, and of household linen. It provides opportunities also for empirical research, as we found in a quarrel between two women because one had disclosed how often her neighbour changed her bed linen. Here too, is a field of activity for the men: gardeners discuss their plans, complain of the builders' rubble and clay in the soil, exchange plants, give presents of vegetables, and sometimes start hedges and rustic fences for greater privacy. It is an area of family recreation, and in some sense of communal living, because there are no effective physical barriers to keep children and dogs, and for that matter, adult residents, from wandering freely into adjoining gardens.

Facing these back gardens are the windows of the kitchen, the dining recess, and an upstairs room. Hence it is not only the area of back-garden living which is drawn together, but also some aspects of the inside domestic life. And so there are complaints of lack of privacy in the dining recess. "It's not very nice to be seen eating." Or a woman may be embarrassed because neighbours might see her husband wearing a vest in the dining recess, though she herself has no objection to it. Or there is general discomfort: "You don't really feel free to walk about the house as you like." And again, in the same way that a person can be seen by neighbours it is sometimes difficult to avoid looking at them. When in the kitchen, "Every time you look up, you're looking at the one across, and you have to look somewhere."

PLANNED AND UNPLANNED CONSEQUENCES

Many of these consequences of the layout were not intended by the architects. At this stage it is difficult to get information

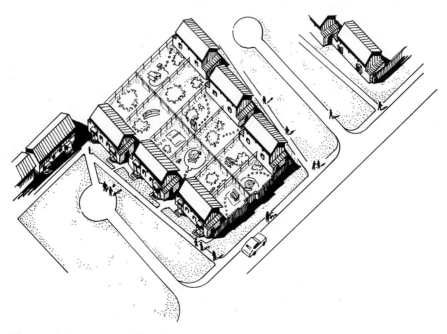

Figure 25–4. Layout providing for screened back gardens.

in detail as to the considerations which were the basis of the decisions taken. A general impression of these deciding factors can, however, be gained from the resultant layout. An architect town-planner described to us what he regarded as its distinctive features, in the conventional phrases of his profession. He selects first the experiments in the third dimension (the building along the contours and the staggering of houses, giving an interesting skyline and play of shapes), and in the fourth dimension (that of movement, with constantly changing vistas and relationships between gable ends and façade as you walk). There is safety for the children in the segregation of foot and motor traffic, in the generous use of forecourts, and in the treatment of development roads. Urbanity and neighbourliness are suggested by the controlled architectural treatment. Asserting "the need for the perception of community in immediately recognisable terms," he finds the solution in *street* architecture and cites, as a good example, the Square A. Here, inspired (or accidental) use of existing hedgerow tree gives individuality to the group, and with its constant change of colour, foliage, its at-

traction of bird life, secures an added awareness of natural processes within the urban setting: this too, in the grassed square, full of daisies. The effect of enclosure is simply achieved by linked walls and slightly rising ground. (Note the medieval village, with closely clustered cottages, and its friendly containing effect to the field worker returning home from the open country and limitless sky.) Colour wash can be used to suggest "our street—the one with red walls."

Some such considerations certainly entered into the layout of the area. Perhaps there is an occasional overstatement in this account of the architectural "mystique"; certainly, the large brick wall in Square A was a last-minute compromise and replaced a projected house. But there was clearly the intention to create a more intimate and secluded area of living, to provide safety for the children, and to pursue, in the third and fourth dimensions, some of the aesthetic satisfactions of contemporary architecture. These are the planned objectives which the architect realised in the Braydon Road residential unit. But flowing from these objectives are the unanticipated results, the unplanned consequences, which have the effect of drawing neighbours together in a great variety of linkages.

We may illustrate this by reference to some of the unplanned consequences of staggering the houses. The widened mouths of the main cul-de-sacs increase the distance between neighbours at the front, but bring the back windows more closely together; and tenants in these outer houses are more keenly aware of their proximity to back-garden neighbours. Conversely, the staggering of the houses, in the interior of the cul-de-sac, reduces the distance at the front while increasing the length of the back gardens; among these tenants of the inside houses there are frequent comments of overlooking at the front. Again the large irregular gardens of some of the top houses have the effect of insulating tenants from back-garden contacts, and similarly, in the deeply staggered houses of Area J, awareness of side neighbours is greatly diminished. There is a general tendency for the awareness of neighbours to be determined by siting factors, a result certainly not envisaged by the architect.

This relationship between siting factors and awareness of neighbours is influenced by a number of factors. Residents vary in their use of the house; it makes a difference to this awareness of neighbours if most activities are confined to the back of the house, and the front living-room is preserved as a sort of ceremonial parlour, or on the other hand, if there is no money to furnish the recess, and the front room is used as an all-purpose room, or again, if the tenants and their neighbours are keen or indifferent gardeners. Moreover, people vary in their requirements for privacy.

The attitude to privacy, in particular, throws much light on the different reactions of residents to the auditory and visual linkages. For those who like to hear and be heard, to see and be seen, the physical conditions of Braydon Road are no problem: their difficulties lie in the "queer" behaviour and demands of residents, whose standards of privacy are high. For the "queer" residents, on the other hand, Braydon Road imposes the need of a variety of adjustments. The control of other people's noise is a somewhat intractable problem: if an approach cannot be made to neighbours, or does not produce the required result, the only solution may be to move from area to area in search of quiet neighbours. Some defence against being seen is provided by the use of window curtains, of lace or net, to supplement the inadequate draped curtains, and by hedges and rustic fences in the back gardens. We have commented on the consideration shown by some residents in the control of noise within their own homes. This consideration extends also to seeing, so that residents will restrain the almost reflex action of looking into windows and doorways, and sometimes pretend not to notice their neighbours. But the control of one's own noise and visual impressions is not exclusively a recognition of social responsibilities: it serves the further function of securing for residents their standards of privacy, by keeping domestic activities from the public ear, and by demonstrating that more intimate contact is not desired.

The siting factors, with their planned and unplanned consequences, only provide a potential base for neighbour relations. There is no simple mechanical determination by the physical environment. The extent to which the awareness of neighbours will develop into active social relationships depends on the characteristics of the residents, their attitudes to neighbouring, their status,[2] aspirations, and their general compatibility. We will not be able to understand either the patterns of these social relationships nor the contribution of elements in the house design and the general siting arrangements, without an analysis of population characteristics, attitudes and status aspirations.

[2] I am using the word "status" in the everyday sense of "social standing," and not with the sociological or legal connotation of "institutionalized position."

26 The Ecology of Privacy

Robert Sommer[1]

Indispensable to many library patrons is a feeling of privacy, of being able to read and take notes without disturbing others or being disturbed by them. Few places make as strict a demand upon the physical setting to guarantee privacy as the library reading area. The library is one of the few public institutions in which interaction between people is actively discouraged. Museums, art galleries, and government buildings permit conversation which, in the view of many librarians, would prevent the concentration that readers require to get maximum benefit from library facilities. Undoubtedly there are some library patrons who prefer to chat as they read and students who prefer groups rather than individual studying. New libraries on university campuses often contain special rooms to satisfy the needs of more gregarious readers as well as to get them out of the way of students who prefer quiet and solitude while they study. Although silence and respect for others can be encouraged and maintained through official regulations, social disapproval, and staff surveillance, these tasks become much easier and sometimes unnecessary in the proper library environment. The purpose of this article is to discuss the part played by the library environment in regulating interaction between people.

The writer's interest in man-environment systems began some years ago in the field of hospital design. In that area it was necessary to design rooms, lounges, and other facilities for people largely unable to alter

Reprinted from *The Library Quarterly*, 1966, 36, 234–248, by permission of The University of Chicago Press and the author.

[1] I am indebted to Nancy Felipe, Mary Juncker, Linda Larson, Faye Nixon, Pamela Pearce, and Melva Rush for their assistance. This study was supported in part by a grant from the U.S. Office of Education, HEW.

their environments themselves. One aspect of being a hospital patient is a passivity in the face of the environment, an inability to move the bed or change the drapes if they are unsatisfactory. The major effort of these studies was directed to the social areas, such as lounges, day rooms, and solariums, where it was common to find rows of chairs lined up against the walls, which made it difficult if not impossible for patients to converse. Out of these observations came several attempts to increase conversation by making the room, to use Osmond's term (1959), *sociopetal* (literally "bringing people together") instead of *sociofugal* ("keeping people apart"). We found that sociopetal arrangements of tables and chairs could increase materially the amount of conversation between patients (Sommer and Ross, 1958). This work suggested the potential role that environment might play in other settings.

Since that time we have studied classrooms, cafeterias, bus stations, and, more recently, libraries, with the hope of learning how the arrangement of people affects what goes on between them. We have at one time or another used methods of direct observation, interview, questionnaires, and occasionally experiments. Much of our work is based on the premise that spatial behavior is largely unconscious and unverbalized, a "silent language," to use Hall's phrase (1959). It therefore would be more profitable to observe space usage directly rather than to ask people what sorts of arrangements they prefer. This is not to deny the value of opinion surveys, for we have done them ourselves as well as profited from the results of surveys done elsewhere, but rather to emphasize that systematic observations of reader behavior are necessary too. Library reports are very rich in entrance and exit statistics, which show how many people come in and how many books are checked out, but there is a real gap in knowledge when it comes to what goes on during the reader's stay in the library. Meier (1963) recently showed that the official circulation statistics grossly underestimated the true circulation of books at the University of Michigan library. Though it was against library rules, the students sought books from one another rather than check for required reading materials on the appropriate shelf. Meier concluded that these policies devised by the students increased book use to a level 30–40 percent greater than the amount the librarians had estimated on the basis of operating statistics. The new college study based at Amherst, almost a classic in its field, showed the high percentage of readers in a college library who made no use whatever of the collection but rather confined their studies to books they had brought with them (Stoke et al., 1960). It was apparent that the library was serving as a study hall, a function that could have been filled by study facilities in other buildings, perhaps dormitories or convertible classroom space. This sort of finding, which has many important implications for library design, can be derived only from a study of user behavior in the library.

The present observations took place at the main library building of the University of California, Davis. The library contains approximately 400,000 volumes and serves a population of 8,000 students as well as faculty members. The library operates on the open-stack plan, and access and circulation are controlled at two exit desks. We are concerned here primarily with three public reading areas—the periodical, reserve, and reference rooms. The pattern here follows that found elsewhere (cf. the Amherst, Dartmouth, and Michigan studies) in that the vast majority of students in these public reading areas is there to study and use materials brought with them rather than the collection. A library-staff member stated that probably 90 percent or more of the readers in these areas were studying their own materials, and three years of direct observation of these areas tend to support this conclusion.

RESULTS

We began our observations in the library reserve room, a large room (twenty-nine by eighty-three feet) containing thirty-three small rectangular tables, each with four chairs, two per side. The observations took

place at times when there was a choice of seats and were made by an undergraduate student, David Addicott. Of those students who entered the room alone, 64 percent sat alone, 26 percent sat diagonally across from another student, while only 10 percent sat directly opposite or beside another student. These results, the opposite of findings in lounges and cafeterias where conversation was encouraged, led to an extended series of observations in this room and other study areas (Sommer, 1965). These observations confirmed the hypothesis that people who came alone did indeed prefer to sit alone. When room density reached one per table, then the next preferred arrangement was diagonal seating. That is, two people occupied a table in such a way that neither sat alongside or opposite the other. In the periodical room, which contains four-chair and six-chair tables, we ranked the six-chair tables on a sociality continuum. At the top (see Figure 26-1) is the most sociofugal arrangement, and at the bottom is the side-by-side arrangement which was the most sociopetal. A majority of those pairs who sat side by side were observed to converse or otherwise interact during the brief observation period.

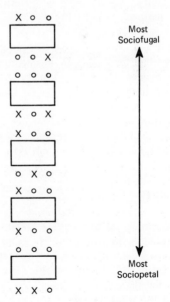

Figure 26–1. Sociality continuum for six-chair table.

At this point we turned our attention to the largest study area in the building, the reference room. This is a very large high-ceilinged room containing eighteen large, heavy wooden tables (four by sixteen feet) each surrounded by twelve chairs, six to a side. The table tops slope upward five degrees from each side to form a central apex to make it easier to rest books and more difficult to talk across the table. Lighting, provided by large fluorescent globes suspended from the ceiling, is very good and homogeneous throughout the room for the entire day. The large windows on the north side are more than nine feet up the wall and do not let direct sunlight fall on the tables at any time. Lighting should not be an important consideration in a student's decision about where to sit in the room. There is generous spacing between the long tables so that people can walk by without disturbing those already seated. The design of this room is instructive in that it reflects the methods still extant in developing job specifications for the architect. Certain features, such as the large overhead lights, were undertaken as a contrast to the situation at Berkeley which, at the time, used dark wooden paneling and small individual study lamps. There were also individual design features favored by the campus librarian, such as the slanted table tops intended to keep students from distracting one another. The librarian also visited approximately twenty university libraries throughout the country before the design specifications were written.

To determine the patterns of occupation and succession in the reference room, an observer arrived at 8:00 A.M. when the room first opened and using a number sequence, recorded where each of the first occupants sat and the sex of each person. These observations ran from 8:00–8:45 A.M. on sixty-one week-day mornings. We found that approximately four-fifths of those students who were among the first ten occupants and came alone sat at empty tables. The same is true for the sixty-nine pairs, people who entered the room together, among the first ten occupants. Furthermore, there is a strong trend among the first individuals to gravi-

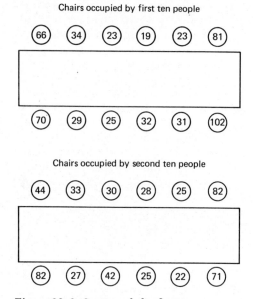

Chairs occupied by first ten people

Chairs occupied by second ten people

Figure 26–2. Seating of the first ten occupants at reference-room tables.

tate to the end chairs at the table (see Figure 26-2). The number in each circle refers to the number of times that place at a table was chosen by one of the first ten or second ten people during the duration of observations.

The situation at zero density is clear: the first occupants tend to sit one per table at an end chair if they come alone or two per table if both arrive together. We then examined our seating diagram to learn where the next person at the table would sit. There were 401 instances where a student sat at a table already occupied by a lone student. Figure 26-3 shows the seats protected when one person occupies a given location. Essentially this is where a stranger will not sit unless room density is very high. We also undertook another seventy-one observations at other times of the day. These were all "instantaneous" cross-sectional observations in which the writer entered the room at random times during the day and recorded seating of all those individuals present. What this method gains in simplicity is balanced by a lack of knowledge about what went on previously at the table. At any given moment we have no record where previous occupants sat, although it

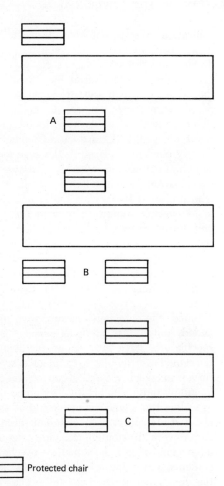

Protected chair

Figure 26–3. Seats protected at each of three table locations.

is possible, like the astronomer who infers the presence of an unknown planet from unusual deviations in the orbits of adjacent planets, to hypothesize where a previous occupant must have sat to account for an unusual arrangement at the table. Figure 26-3 shows that when one person occupied an end chair, the other person is likely to be found at the middle or far end of the table. When one individual occupies the B position, the other occupant is likely to be found in a far end chair. When one occupant is found at C, the second person occupies *any* of the end chairs. Our diagrams also disclosed 113 pairs who conversed at one time or another (who were excluded from the preceding tabulations). Of this number of conversing pairs, 82 percent were

seated side by side, 12 percent were seated directly across from one another, and 6 percent were people alongside one another with an empty chair in between or catty-cornered across from one another.

QUESTIONNAIRE STUDIES

A library also has a subjective meaning for its patrons, an image or stereotype as a cold or warm, friendly or unfriendly, personal or impersonal place. This image or connotation has an effect on people's reactions to a library, albeit sometimes an indirect effect. One study found that in communities where hospital bond issues failed in public election, the hospital was frequently regarded as a cold and impersonal place (Roemer and White, 1960). There are several techniques that can be used to measure these images, and they can be exceedingly useful to librarians. One method is the semantic differential developed by Charles Osgood (1957) and his associates at the University of Illinois. The semantic differential explores the connotations of a concept, the way it appears subjectively to a person, in contrast to its denotative meaning, which relates to the objective referent (the height of the building, its color, room size, etc.). Osgood found that the major dimensions of connotative meaning are value (expressed by the good-bad scale), activity (expressed by the active-passive scale), and potency (expressed by the strong-weak scale).

One hundred and three students in an introductory psychology class were asked to rate the library reference room along nine different scales, these scales representing each of the three major dimensions of meaning. Figure 26-4 shows that the room is seen as good and valuable, probably because of its associations with scholarly activity, though it is not particularly beautiful. It is also seen as a somewhat large area containing many people but that they tend to move slowly.

Two additional surveys were undertaken to compare the reference room with other library study areas. In the first, 103 students in another introductory psychology class were asked the following questions: If you

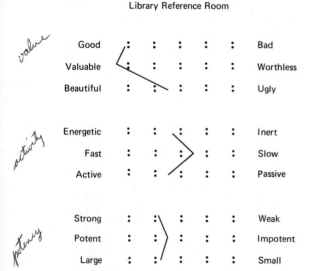

Figure 26–4. Semantic profile of the reference room.

went alone to the library to study for a midterm examination, where would you go to study? What do you like about this place?

In tabulating the replies, a distinction was made between public study areas (including the reference, periodical, and reserve rooms) and semiprivate areas such as the tables in the stacks or individual study carrels. Since some librarians maintain that practically all patrons prefer individual study carrels to large public areas (Ellsworth, 1965), it is instructive to note that 49 of the 103 students indicated one of the public areas as their first choice. Their explanations reflected a need to be with people (to maintain a social distance in the sense that biologists use the term) as well as to be away from them. The spaciousness, increased activity, and general atmosphere were the most frequent reasons why people chose the large public areas, while less common answers included the lighting, long tables, proximity of reference books, and ease of access and egress. Some comments showed a distaste for small, cramped areas, while others specifically rejected complete quiet as a prerequisite for study. There seem to be some students who feel the need for activity or social stimulation around them, particularly the presence of other people studying, in order to maintain their con-

centration. We do not know the extent to which this is related to extroversion or other-directedness. Fifty years ago social psychologists described the "social increment" and the ways in which the presence of other people stimulated a person to greater activity. Animal biologists have found that a sated chicken will start eating again if a hungry chicken is placed in the cage alongside him. However, what is desirable for some patrons is not suitable for all. Those who preferred the private and semi-private areas overwhelmingly mentioned the quiet *and* fewer distractions. Visual distractions seemed as important as auditory distractions in bringing people to the private areas; almost as many mentioned the disturbance of people coming in and out as mentioned noise.

Since the previous survey was open-ended, only those students who chose a specific area gave their reason for liking it. It seemed worthwhile to conduct a second survey in which a large group of students, including those who habitually studied there as well as those who did not would be asked about study spaces. Two different questionnaires were distributed randomly among a large class of 205 introductory psychology students, 101 being asked specifically about the library periodical room and a classroom building in the evening when the rooms were unoccupied, and 104 being asked about the value of the library reference room and the student-union cafeteria between meals as study places. The replies showed distinct preferences for certain areas: the unoccupied classroom building in the evening was preferred by 49 percent, the library reference room by 47 percent, the library periodical room by 22 percent, and the cafeteria between meals by 6 percent. The desirable and undesirable features of each study area are summarized in Table 26-1. The replies can be divided into those involving social, cultural, or psychological factors, on the one hand, and those involving physical or architectural features, on the other. Of the 223 desirable features of study places mentioned by the students, 63 percent involved social factors, while 37 percent involved non-human or physical factors, including such items as table arrangement,

Table 26-1

A. Desirable Features of Study Areas

	Library Reference Room	Library Periodical Room	Student Union Cafeteria	Classroom Building (Evenings)
A. Social or psychological factors:				
More quiet	30	6	2	28
Fewer distractions, less movement	9	2	0	16
Less crowded	2	0	1	14
More privacy	0	1	0	3
Academic atmosphere	9	0	0	0
Friendly atmosphere	3	3	1	2
Miscellaneous social factors	0	0	2	6
Total	53	12	6	69
B. Physical factors:				
Table arrangement, size, shape, etc.	18	5	0	5
Good (internal) lighting	10	6	0	6
Good ventilation, cool	4	0	1	5
Near reference materials	6	1	0	0
Roomy, large, open	3	1	0	0
Comfortable chairs	2	0	0	2
Miscellaneous physical factors	1	0	0	7
Total	44	13	1	25

B. Undesirable Features of Study Areas

	Library Reference Room	Library Periodical Room	Student Union Cafeteria	Classroom Building (Evenings)
A. Social or psychological factors:				
Distractions, activity	18	24	8	2
Too noisy	10	14	7	0
Too crowded	4	8	5	2
Too social, friendly	1	0	5	0
Too quiet	1	3	0	2
Miscellaneous social factors	0	2	1	0
Total	34	51	26	6
B. Physical factors:				
Poor table arrangement, size, shape, etc.	7	2	0	6
Poor lighting	5	6	2	0
Xerox noise	0	5	0	0
Room too large	3	2	0	0
Uncomfortable chairs	0	1	2	0
Miscellaneous physical factors	1	0	0	3
Total	16	16	4	9

ventilation, lighting, etc. The undesirable features show this trend even more, since 72 percent of the reasons involved social factors and only 28 percent involved physical factors.

The implications of this finding for librarians are interesting. In one sense, social and cultural factors are more readily under the librarian's control than the physical aspects of the environment. Generally it is cheaper to alter rules and regulations then to renovate rooms and buildings. However, the social and the architectural features of the environment are interrelated. The distraction from people entering and leaving originates from social rather than physical features of environment, but the distraction can be minimized or eliminated by properly designed study carrels, table dividers, and desk arrangements. The fact that reader complaints center on social rather than physical factors can mean either that the latter have been adequately provided for or that social stimuli are generally more distracting than physical ones. A recent study by McBride, King, and James (1965) has shown that people are more emotionally involved, as measured by their galvanic skin response, by pictures of human faces than by pictures of non-human objects, and the same applies to being touched by a human hand compared to being touched by a feather or other non-human object.

About half the students (forty-nine) felt that the reference room was a good place to study, thirty-eight said it was not, and sixteen did not know. Of those who liked the reference room, their major reasons in the order of frequency were the quiet, long slanted tables with space to spread out, the good lighting, freedom from distractions, and studious atmosphere. Twenty students specifically mentioned the tables and, of this number, thirteen explicitly mentioned the slant of the tables as a desirable feature. The main reason given by the students was that the slight inclination made reading easier. The major reason for not wanting to study in the reference room was the distraction of people entering and leaving. Almost twice as many students mentioned the distraction from movement as mentioned noise.

Some of the answers shed additional light on the students' perception of a good study place. The atmosphere of the reference room is described in these comments:

> The large room and high ceilings put me in a studying mood. I think the size of the room contributes to its quietness and enhances studying.

> I like the atmosphere of the old building with its high ceiling, large tables,

and chairs. This I suppose is my sentimental idea of what a real college is like —old and wise and used, not modern.

> It provides a suitable environment for academic endeavor. Also seeing all the other students busy as bees gives me an incentive, and I really feel an urge to study which I don't get in the dorms at all.

Some students preferred the public reading areas because there were *fewer* distractions than in the carrels or stacks. Here are two answers that illustrate the apparent paradox of greater distraction in low-density area:

> Since there are many distractions in the large rooms they seem less disturbing, whereas on the more quiet floors one distraction will disturb the entire remainder trying to study.

> I like the reference room because the tables supply adequate room, the chairs are comfortable, and probably most important is that there are enough people going in and out so that when someone walks in it isn't abnormal and it doesn't interrupt your studying.

These comments make me recall the finding in a British hospital that there were more complaints about noise in the private rooms than in the semiprivate or ward rooms. Apparently the greater amount of background stimulation in the ward rooms minimized the disturbance from external noise, but against the silence of the private rooms, every sound or movement stood out.

TERRITORIAL DEFENSE

Readers protect their privacy in many ways, some offensive and others defensive. The former are based on the notion that "the best defense is a good offense" and include both threat positions and threat postures. Position refers to an individual's location with reference to external coordinates; posture refers to his particular stance. Librarians are also familiar with the use of physical objects, such as coats, handbags, books, personal belongings, which are used to mark out individual territories. A table space can be defended by position, posture, territorial markers, or some combination of the three.

These are more than academic considerations as indicated by librarians' complaints about room capacity lowered by empty chairs "staked out" by students occupied elsewhere. Territorial possession is another reason why empty classrooms are not always successful as study halls during the evening hours. Conceivably the number of empty chairs in classrooms could accommodate all those students who wanted to study, but what happens in fact is that the first student in a room takes possession of it and subsequent students stay away. Stuart Stoke and his associates (1960) report that "the standard custom seems to award the whole classroom to the first student to take possession by squatter's rights. By looking sufficiently annoyed when other students try to study there, the first usually succeeds in maintaining his solitude. A classroom building which will take care of 800 students in classes may house only 23–50 in study." The effectiveness with which a student can keep intruders away depends upon population pressure on the room. We conducted a small experiment along these lines in a student soda fountain which contained ten small side rooms. We stationed a young girl who appeared to be studying at one of the three tables in the room. When the pressure for seats became heavy, she was unable to protect the entire room although she was able to defend successfully the three empty chairs at her particular table.

To learn something of the difference between two available methods of insuring privacy, offensive display and avoidance, a brief questionnaire was constructed which presented the student with table diagrams containing six, eight, and ten chairs respectively (see Figure 26-5). There were two forms to the questionnaire which were distributed randomly within a class of forty-five students. Twenty-four students were given avoidance instructions: "If you wanted to be as far as possible from the distraction of other people, where would you sit at the table?" Twenty-one other students in the same class were shown the same diagrams and given the offensive-display instructions: "If you wanted to have the table to yourself, where would you sit to discourage anyone else from occupying it?"

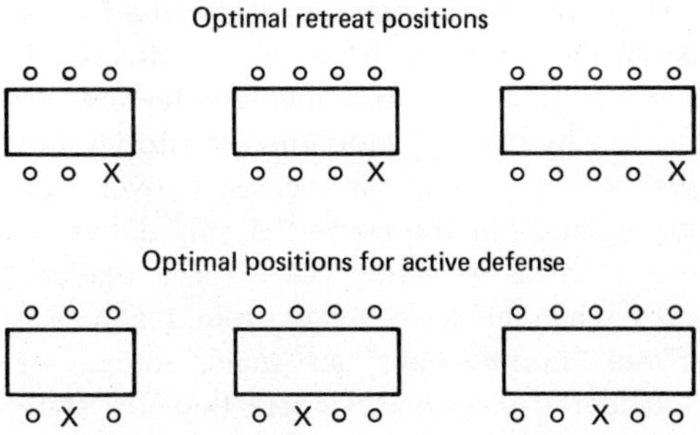

Figure 26–5. Optimal offensive and defensive positions.

Even though both sets of instructions were aimed at insuring privacy, the two tactics produced a striking difference in seats chosen. Those students who wanted to sit by themselves as far as possible from other people overwhelmingly chose the *end* chairs; those students who wanted to keep others away from the table almost unanimously chose the *middle* chair.

The utility of each tactic, offensive display or active retreat, depends in large measure on predictions of future room density. Occupying the middle seat at a table may keep people away when densities are low, but once the room begins to fill up, the man in the middle runs the risk of being completely surrounded. At high densities an end chair, which provides at least one side without people, is a more effective way of gaining privacy. The size of rooms and tables also has an effect; other things being equal it is easier to defend a small room or table than a large one. Privacy also can be increased by erecting barriers between areas. Studies in offices, army barracks, and dormitories have shown that barriers decrease communication between units while increasing it within units (Blake et al., 1956). Barriers also can be used to regulate room density. Partitions between reading areas at a table will insure that no more than, for example, six individuals occupy one side of a table. These barriers protect personal space and permit two people to sit side by side at very close distances without physical contact. By permitting greater physical closeness without psychological discomfort, barriers increase the upper limit of comfortable room density. Such barriers need not be ponderous or weighty objects. A small raised strip down the center of the table can effectively serve as a barrier and increase feelings of privacy by defining individual territories and preventing unnecessary conflict over "no man's land" in the center. A raised barrier can serve as a resting place for a reader's eyes when he looks away from his books. These "study breaks" are major sources of accidental intrusion. Barriers that are symbolic rather than physical impediments to movement also can regulate interaction. Subtle color changes or painted lines can define individual territories almost as well as raised partitions.

The finding described earlier, that the first occupants in the reference room gravitate to end chairs, can be interpreted in the light of our discussion of territorial defense. These data suggest that avoidance defensive positions are more widely used than offensive displays. Undoubtedly this has some connection with student's anticipation of future room density. If we studied a place where room density rarely exceeded one per table, we would predict more use of the central chairs by the first occcupants. In the reference room a person's territory does not extend very far down the table. He has almost no influence over what happens at the opposite end of the table. For example, we have found that sexual segregation is a characteristic feature of campus life. If one observes students riding bicycles, eating in the cafeteria, or lolling on the grass, it is more common to see girls with girls and boys with boys than to see mixed groups. This is a function of the dormitory living arrangements as well as the special-interest groups on campus (home-economics majors are largely female, engineering majors are largely male, etc.). In the reserve room and periodical room with small four- and six-chair tables, there is sexual segregation in seating. When room density reaches approximately one per table, a newcomer in either room is twice as likely to sit with someone of his own sex than with someone of the opposite sex. However, when we look at the long tables in the reference room, a very different picture emerges. The second person at a long table, who typically sits at the opposite end, is equally likely to sit at a table occupied by someone of opposite sex as someone of his own sex. To use the term of the sociologists, the occupant so far away at the other end of the table is a "non-person," and his sex or other personal characteristics are unimportant.

DISCUSSION

The previous section has shown the ways in which readers find privacy in public. It is entirely possible that at some future time every reader will have his own area protected visually and aurally from other library patrons with access to the collection and a centralized data storage and retrieval area through various electronic aids. On the other hand, almost all present library structures as well as those being planned make provision for public reading areas. Rovelstad (1958) speaks enthusiastically of the openness of new small college libraries that allow for areas rather than for rooms with fixed walls and of the flow of space throughout the building with the subsequent intermingling of students and books. This openness is emphasized by Wheeler (cited by Rovelstad), who attempts to break down the barriers between the library and the outside through the use of extensive glass exteriors. If we look outside of the United States, we find that the public reading area is far from out of date. In Soviet libraries, for example, reading rooms seating over two hundred are not uncommon in many of the larger libraries (Horecky, 1959). There is every indication that the quest for reader privacy still must be the active concern of librarians. From our studies we find that social stimuli are a major source of distraction for readers, and unwanted eye contact must be avoided by allowing each reader to have a territory that does not overlap that of his neighbor as well as a neutral place where he can rest his eyes during pauses and breaks. The sight of other people studying is not ordinarily distracting to most readers. For some it seems to exert a dynamogenic effect on their motivation. The connection between disturbing noise and public areas is not as simple as it seems at first. There is some evidence not only from our own study but from those conducted in other settings that noise stands out more and is more distracting against a background of silence than against one of general ordered activity. Some firms have found it necessary to pipe in white noise to overcome the coldness and non-human quality of fully sound-proofed and quiet areas where any movement or noise disturbs the entire office. The ideal library would not be one with all individual study rooms or all open areas but, instead, would contain a diversity of spaces that would meet the needs of introverts and extroverts, lone studiers and group studiers, browsers and day-long researchers. It is a serious mistake to assume that all people have the same spatial needs. We have seen this in other settings, for example, the English doctor in a rural Saskatchewan hospital who maintained that all patients needed the privacy of single rooms but whose patients, it was learned during interviewing, rarely had enjoyed the luxury of private rooms at any time in their lives and were scared to death of staying alone in the hospital. Some interesting outcomes can be produced when introverts design facilities for extroverts or vice versa. There are also cultural differences involved in spatial usage that must be considered. The anthropologist Edward Hall (1959) has shown how the English typically require more space than Frenchmen or Spaniards. An Englishman talking to a Frenchman often feels that the latter is coming too close, breathing down his neck, or hissing in his face, while the Frenchman wonders why this cold Englishman keeps moving back. I remember the conversation with an intelligent farm wife who maintained she would never live in an apartment because she could not stand the idea of people above her and below her. The implication is clear that we should hesitate to impute our own spatial needs to other people unless we know something of their backgrounds, temperament, etc. Such knowledge can come from interviewing and direct observation of the client group. By seeing the extent to which people seek isolation when they have the opportunity, we can gain some understanding of the sorts of facilities that are needed. There is also room for serious systematic experimentation in the design of library facilities. This would involve building facilities with a goal of learning something—trying one arrangement for a year and then switching to another arrangement, systematically observing reader behavior all the while. Such observation can be done quickly, discreetly, and without any upset at all.

All this should not be taken to suggest that privacy is the sole or even the major goal of library design. Though it is a major factor to be taken into account in planning individual study areas, there are other parts of the library where informal and spontaneous interaction can be encouraged. Though it presents certain problems in the form of maintenance and care of books, the use of coffee facilities or automatic food-vending machines in certain designated areas of the library *where books are available* should be explored. There is no inherent reason why a man during his lunch hour could not satisfy his intellect as well as his stomach. A library should not be a museum for dead books or a paper warehouse but a center of intellectual life in the community. I am *not* advocating a separate dungeon-like coffee room somewhere in the basement of the building but, rather, a major open browsing room with books and lounge chairs as well as coffee and sandwiches. Conversation would be encouraged in this room, and both the sound-proofing and the arrangement should favor small conversational groups. Just as the railroads had smoking cars as well as cars for non-smokers, people who wanted complete silence could find it elsewhere in the library, but those who like to talk about a book while they read would have a place to go. There is no question but that a stimulating book arouses energy and tension which requires release. Sometimes this is done by sharp exclamation of agreement or disagreement or by underlining some crucial passage (a practice keenly discouraged by librarians when the books are library property), but it is intensely frustrating to acquire insight in a public place without being allowed to exclaim "Ah-ha!"

Meier (1963), who studied student behavior in an open-stack area of the University of Michigan Library, used particularly by students from large classes seeking specific books, found that each book taken off the shelf was used by an average of two people before it was returned and that closed reserve books were used almost three times despite regulations to the contrary. The standard student strategy upon entering the library was to seek out someone from the class rather than look for the required reading on its appropriate shelf because it was more likely that information as to the actual location could be obtained from the student than from the particular shelf. It was also noted that the collective use of books was not uncommon. Meier concluded that the socializing that was so discouraged (by the library staff) appeared to be vital for achieving a high level of book use at peak periods, and these informal student practices increased book use to a level perhaps 30–40 percent greater than the amount the librarians had estimated on the basis of operating statistics.

I hope this brief digression clarifies the intent of this article. Its aim has been to discuss the connection between privacy and the physical environment, without necessarily setting up privacy as an absolute value in itself. Gregariousness as well as privacy has a place in a library serving as a community intellectual resource. However, in those areas where privacy is desired, it is important to know the architectural and design characteristics that favor it. Such information can be obtained best by observing how people arrange themselves when they have some choice as to seats. When there is limited choice, properly designed facilities to insure individual privacy are of crucial importance.

SUMMARY

A series of observational, questionnaire, and experimental studies was undertaken to learn how readers found privacy in public reading areas of a university library. The first readers in the room gravitated to the end chairs at separate tables. The seats alongside a person or the seat directly across from him were rarely occupied except at times of high density. Individual readers marked out territories in various ways, using personal belongings and positioning of their own chair. Privacy can be obtained by offensive display or by avoidance procedures. In view of the large area that must be protected and the high population density at times, the majority of patrons used avoidance techniques.

Questionnaire studies showed that about half of a group of university students preferred the large public reading areas to the stacks. The replies indicated that some readers need to be with people, although direct eye contact is avoided. Most of the reported distraction came from human sources rather than physical aspects of the environment such as ventilation, lighting, etc. The implications of these findings for library design were discussed.

REFERENCES:

Blake, R., Rhead, C. C., Wedge, B., & Mouton, J. S. Housing architecture and social interaction. *Sociometry,* 1956, **19,** 133–139.

Ellsworth, R. The college and university library as a building type. *American Library Association Journal,* May 1965, 69–72.

Hall, E. T. *The silent language.* Garden City, N.Y.: Doubleday, 1959.

Horecky, P. L. *Libraries and bibliographic centers in the Soviet Union.* Bloomington: Indiana University Publication, 1959.

McBride, G., King, M. G., & James, J. W. Social proximity effects of galvanic skin response. *Journal of Psychology,* 1965, **61,** 153–157.

Meier, R. L. Information input overload: Features of growth in communications-oriented institutions. *Libri,* 1963, **13,** 1–44.

Osgood, C. E., Suci, G. J., & Tannenbaum, P. *The measurement of meaning.* Urbana: University of Illinois Press, 1957.

Osmond, H. The relationship between architect and psychiatrist. In C. Goshen (Ed.), *Psychiatric architecture.* Washington, D.C.: American Psychiatric Association, 1959.

Roemer, M. L., & White, R. F. Community attitudes toward hospitals. *Hospital Management,* 1960, **89,** 37–39.

Rovelstad, H. College and university library buildings. In W. S. Yenawine (Ed.), *Contemporary library design.* Syracuse, N.Y.: Syracuse University Press, 1958.

Sommer, R. Further studies of group ecology. *Sociometry,* 1965, **28,** 337–348.

Sommer, R., & Ross, H. Social interaction on a geriatrics ward. *International Journal of Social Psychiatry,* 1958, **4,** 128–133.

Stoke, S. M., et al., *Student reactions to study facilities.* Amherst, Mass.: Committee on Cooperation, 1960.

27 Privacy and Crowding in Poverty

Oscar Lewis

As I grew older, I became more aware of the restrictions one had to put up with when a whole family lived in a single room. In my case, because I lived in fantasy and liked to daydream, I was especially annoyed by having my dreams interrupted. My brothers would bring me back to reality with, "Hey, what's the matter with you! You look dopey." Or I'd hear my father's voice, "Wake up, you. Always in the clouds! Get moving, fast!"

Coming back to earth, I had to forget the pretty home I was imagining and I looked at our room with more critical eyes. The crude dark wardrobe, so narrow it reminded me of a coffin, was crowded with the clothing of five, seven or nine people, depending upon how many were living there at the time. The chiffonier, too, had to serve the entire family. Dressing and undressing without being seen was a problem. At night, we had to wait until the light was out or undress under the blanket or go to sleep in our clothing. Antonia cared least about being seen in her slip, but Paula, Marta and I were very modest. Roberto, too, would get up in the morning wrapped in his blanket and go into the kitchen to dress. We women wouldn't dress until the men and children went out so we could close the door. But there was always someone wanting to get in, impatiently banging and telling us to hurry. We could never dawdle.

It would have been a great luxury to be able to linger at the mirror to fix my hair or to put on make-up; I never could because of the sarcasm and ridicule of those in the room. My friends in the Casa Grande complained of their families in the same way. To this day, I look into the mirror hastily,

as though I were doing something wrong. I also had to put up with remarks when I wanted to sing, or lie in a certain comfortable position or do anything that was not acceptable to my family.

Living in one room, one must go at the same rhythm as the others, willingly or unwillingly—there is no way except to follow the wishes of the strongest ones. After my father, Antonia had her way, then La Chata, then my brothers. The weaker ones could approve or disapprove, get angry or disgusted but could never express their opinions. For example, we all had to go to bed at the same time, when my father told us to. Even when we were grown up, he would say, "To bed! Tomorrow is a work day." This might be as early as eight or nine o'clock, when we weren't at all sleepy, but because my father had to get up early the next morning, the light had to be put out. Many times I wanted to draw or to read in the evening, but no sooner did I get started when, "To bed! Lights out!" and I was left with my drawing in my head or the story unfinished.

During the day it was Antonia who chose the radio programs we all had to listen to; in the evenings it was my father. We especially hated the Quiz Kids (*los niños Catedráticos*) because my father would say, "A child of eight and he knows so much . . . and you donkeys, you don't want to study. Later you'll be sorry." When my father or Antonia were not at home, how we would fight over the radio!

If La Chata was in charge of the house, she lorded it over us in her own way. She made us wait in the courtyard until she finished cleaning and sometimes, due to the cold, I would have to go to the toilet. She would refuse to open the door and I would jump up and down yelling, for all the neighbors to hear, "Ay, La Chata, let me in. I have to go. I can't stand it any longer." Then she would get even by leaving the front door open so that the passers-by in the courtyard could see my feet under the door of the toilet. I would try to hide my feet and would beg her to please shut the front door. But she'd say, "Oh, who's going to notice a kid."

The toilet, with its half-door, gave us

almost no privacy. It was so narrow that La Chata had to go in sidewise and leave the shutter ajar in order to sit down. Antonia would always crack some joke about the person using the toilet. If Manuel stayed in too long, as he usually did, she would say, "Cut it short or shall I bring you the scissors?" To me she'd say, "Are you still there? I thought you were already in San Lazaro." San Lazaro is the exit of the city sewage system and she meant that I had fallen into the drainpipe. Other times I was the one who gave trouble. I would tease Roberto when he was in the toilet by opening the front door, saying the smell was too strong. He would shout angrily, "Close that door or you'll see what happens." But I would escape into the courtyard before he came out. Or when someone was in the toilet I would begin dancing in front of the door and yelling that I had to go in. I remember Manuel coming out holding his magazine or comics between his teeth, pulling up his pants, looking daggers at me. Antonia never came out until she was ready, no matter how much of a scandal was made, and often were the times when I had to chase everyone out of the room so that I could use the chamber pot.

Sometimes the jokes were rude. Antonia was constipated and suffered very much from gas. She tried to hold it but often she just laughed and said, "Why should I hold it in if it gives me stomach aches." But if any of us went to the toilet for that reason she would joke about it, "How hoarse you are . . . you have a cough, pal." And we might say, "And when you go on like a machine gun at night we can even see your blanket rising." When we were little and someone made a noise my father would laugh and say, "Ay, who was that? It must have been a rat." But later he would scold harshly and send the guilty one to the toilet. When he was not present, Manuel and Roberto would carry on by calling each other names like "slob" or "pig" and making each other blush for shame. If no one commented, we usually passed over a slip and paid no attention to it.

But these annoyances were insignificant compared to that of being scolded in the presence of everyone else. I often thought that if my father had berated me in private,

I would not have minded so much. But everyone heard the awful things he said to me, even though they pretended not to, and it hurt and shamed me more. My sisters and brothers felt the same way. When one of us was scolded, the others felt equally punished. My father's words would build up little by little, until they covered us and made us fall in a crisis of tears. . . .

While I was going to school, I forgot my troubles. All I thought about was having work later, having clothes, continuing my studies, and fixing up my house nicely, as I had always dreamed about. "I would like our next-door neighbor to move," I thought, "and my father to take that room. I would help him have the wall between knocked down and that room would be used as a living room, with a fireplace, a nice day-bed suite, the floor waxed and the walls fixed up. Then we would have a place to entertain our friends. The same with the kitchen —the two in one, with a nice gas stove, knives and forks, curtains, and some big flower pots with green plants all the way to the front door. The bedroom would have its window on the street. And if thieves wanted to come in? Well, we would have bars put over the window. There would be a record player and nice lamps. I would help my *papá* pay for the labor and everything."

My ideal was to see my family united and happy. I dreamed of helping my brothers and sisters and of bringing them consolation so that they would not feel the way I did. Whenever my father made Roberto cry, everything within me rebelled and shouted: "No! It isn't fair." But I always remained silent. My heart ached seeing my brother in a corner of the kitchen with his head lowered, the tears rolling down his cheeks. Then I would say, "Don't mind *papá*, he's angry." Or I would motion to my brothers to go out into the courtyard so as not to hear my father any more.

My father's words were destructive to everyone, but Roberto was the one who felt them most deeply. Manuel preferred to become cynical. He remained silent while my father scolded him, but after a few minutes he would raise his head and go out into the courtyard, whistling. Finally, he began to turn his back on my father and leave immediately. Roberto remained rooted to the spot and cried.

I believe that this is what gave rise to my desire to help my brothers and my sister. I wanted to be (what a dreamer I was!) the one who guided and counseled them. For Manuel, I dreamed up the career of lawyer or teacher. For Roberto, I wanted the career of an architect or engineer. By that time my father would not work so much. I dreamed of winning the lottery so that I could buy him a farm and chickens and have nice upholstered furniture. At night he would sit in his easy chair in front of the fireplace, with his robe and slippers on, surrounded by all of his children (four) and he would think or say to us, "These are my children, my creation. I educated them!" I lived in hopes that all these things would come about some day.

28 Privacy and the Bathroom

Alexander Kira

While all of us need to perform the same basic bodily functions and while we all have more or less similar needs for personal hygiene facilities, the ultimate makeup and distribution of these facilities is obviously quite variable beyond a certain point and is dependent upon a great variety of factors, psychological as well as purely functional: family size, family life cycle, household composition, socio-economic status, personal values, attitudes, privacy requirements, etc. While the most obvious determinant of need might appear to be simply number, i.e., family size and composition, this rarely is more than a multiplier, except in the most extreme cases. Perhaps the single most important aspect is composed of our various privacy requirements, which cause us to insist on individual time/space use of facilities. In fact, if it were not for privacy

Adapted from *The Bathroom: Criteria for Design*, pp. 55–57 and 93–99. Ithaca, N.Y.: Center for Housing and Environmental Studies, Cornell University, 1966. Used with permission from the author and publisher.

requirements, it is doubtful that, in the average home, use-problems alone would regularly result in overcrowding or in the need for more than one set of basic facilities. The recognition of, and adherence to, privacy demands has often resulted in the adoption of a fairly strictly observed policy with respect to the use of a bathroom which has to be shared by family members:

> The fact that the middle-class family rises almost together, and has few bathrooms, has resulted in a problem for it, which has been resolved by a very narrowly prescribed ritual for many of them —a bathroom ritual. They have developed set rules and regulations which define who goes first (according to who must leave the house first), how long one may stay in, what are the penalties for overtime, and under what conditions there may be a certain overlapping of personnel (Bossard and Boll, 1950, pp. 113–114).[1]

The concept of privacy is an infinitely complex and variable phenomenon and embraces a number of aspects. First, we must consider the philosophical and psychological aspects of privacy and second, we must consider the practical operational aspects of how we obtain this privacy.

MODESTY AND INDIVIDUAL PRIVACY

Since the entire sex/elimination amalgam is something we tend to think of as "dirty" and something to be somewhat ashamed of, we also tend to want to hide and disguise our involvement with it, i.e., we seek privacy for it. We seek this privacy beginning with our language usage: we cannot even state directly what our needs are or where we wish to go, and once there we resort to all sorts of stratagems to avoid anyone's knowing where we are or what we are about.

Probably the most common, obvious, and

[1] In this connection, also see: Langford, Marilyn, *Personal Hygiene Attitudes and Practices in 1000 Middle-Class Households*, Ithaca, N.Y.: Cornell University Agricultural Experiment Station Memoir 393, 1965, pp. 23–25, for a discussion of the particulars of bathroom sharing practices.

clear-cut example of the sex/elimination linkage is to be found in our culture's insistence on privacy on a sexual basis, i.e., men's and women's rooms, which guarantee complete privacy from the opposite sex but only limited privacy from members of the same sex. It is also likely that it is because of this sex linkage that our culture virtually guarantees a person privacy for elimination. Significantly, the only substantial exceptions to this unspoken guarantee are in the case of married persons, where the sexual-privacy aspect is not always observed and in the case of very young children who have not yet learned the rules (Langford, 1965). Otherwise, however, if the bathroom is shared by members of the family, the tendency is to respect both the sexual segregation and privacy for elimination functions.

The consequences of such a guaranteed privacy situation are not always favorable, however. Some persons, for example, come to rely on it so heavily that it becomes an effective triggering mechanism for elimination functions, and is essential for normal responses. Although the following observation was made almost thirty years ago it is just as applicable today as it was then:

> It is unfortunate that false modesty also places a heavy burden upon our intestinal functions. From early childhood we are taught to see in excretory functions of the body something debasing and evil. Instead of considering them in the same natural way that we think of eating, drinking, and sleeping, we come to regard them with a sense of shame or guilt. Many people with rectal trouble or constipation defer consultation with a physician because the disorders pertain to the "unmentionables" (Aaron, 1938, p. 39).

Similarly, as almost anyone who has ever had to provide a urine specimen can testify, modesty and privacy play a big role in our ability to perform.

SOCIAL PRIVACY

On the other hand, the guarantee of privacy has also led to situations where the privacy has been exploited for a variety of non-hygiene purposes, most generally, simply for its own sake. This category might be termed "socially useful," and be defined as that circumstance in which the person's activity is common knowledge (i.e., elimination) and therefore his right to pursue it in peace is inviolable and, most significantly, free from any questioning or social censure. It will be noted that this usage represents a species of "having your cake and eating it too," for it is necessary to establish one's destination (lack of privacy) in order to be assured of privacy! This device is commonly used at work, where generally any interruption is a welcome one, and where a mild prolongation is the rule, especially if one has not finished reading the morning paper. Or, it may be used as a delaying tactic at school when a pupil may ask to be excused when the questioning gets to be dangerously close. It also serves as a popular means of escape from family noise, quarrels, pressures, or, sometimes simply from a person's own activities, without arousing any feelings of guilt.

It must be noted, of course, that there are exceptions: persons who accord only partial respect to these conventions; most generally, those who are compulsive about their work and who cannot bear to let any time go to waste; those who maintain telephones in their bathrooms; or those who insist on carrying on business conversations with associates they happen to encounter.

STATUS PRIVACY

There is still a third circumstance that must be acknowledged: where elimination functions are overtly recognized and where privacy must be guaranteed because of it, and, because of station. This is based on the recognition that the elimination processes are human, universal, and in a sense, the "great leveler" of all mankind. King, prime minister, movie queen, or stock boy— all have identical biological needs, and all are *equal* before the imperious demands of Nature. This is best exemplified, perhaps, by the well-known European expression: "I'm going where even the Kaiser must go on foot," i.e., to the bathroom. The converse of this is, of course, that the "great" must have privacy in such circumstances; hence, we have the "executive washroom" and the private washroom for the board chairman. Similarly, in military situations, the first preparations made for a visiting Field Marshall are to erect a private facility so that he does not have to share the normal communal and semi-public accommodations. Involved, of course, is the preservation of the image and, in some situations, maintaining the security of the personage and guaranteeing his freedom from importunities by the less exalted.

This notion of preserving the image is, in fact, quite common, as we saw earlier, since it is simply another facet of the privacy-demand and accounts, at least in part, for the status generally attached to the relative privacy, or sole use, of hygiene facilities. We find instances of this in any number of situations: in the number of bathrooms a house has, in the "star's" dressing room which must have a private bath, in the "first-class" European hotel, and in first-class air travel, which has one facility for every 6 or 7 passengers instead of one for every 20 or 30 passengers as in tourist class.

DEGREE OF PRIVACY

The state or condition of privacy is also relative and there are a number of degrees of it which are obtainable or which may be desired. Specifically, with reference to the bathroom, it is possible to establish three major categories: (1) privacy of being heard but not seen, (2) privacy of not being seen or heard, and (3) privacy of not being seen, heard, or sensed, i.e., that other people should not even be aware of your whereabouts or your intended behaviour. It is probably fair to say, however, that these categories represent degrees of tolerable privacy rather than degrees of desired privacy, in the sense that given a choice, we would for these purposes probably always select maximum privacy. The degree of tolerable privacy obviously varies enormously depending upon the activity and the particular individual.

The degree of privacy we insist on, or tolerate, influences the various ways in which we physically create the state of privacy: the location of the bathroom relative to other areas of the house; the specific location of the entrance; the acoustical treatment of the space; the location and size of the bathroom windows; the extent to which facilities are intended to be for the sole use of one person, and the extent to which facilities may be shared, with or without compartmentation of some sort.

It must be noted in this connection that compartmentation is widely regarded as a means of securing greater privacy. This may or may not be true depending upon a variety of factors, including the type of compartmentation, i.e., where the compartment is entered from, whether the partitions are floor to ceiling, whether there is a full door. In terms of the kind of partial compartmentation of a single basic space commonly found today, compartmentation offers privacy, of a sort, *only* in those circumstances where none was had before, i.e., a single, minimal bath which was shared in use. If a bathroom was not shared, then a greater degree of privacy was available before—unless the compartmentation is so thorough as to amount to a separate facility—because such compartmentation usually assumes that the bathroom previously unshared may now be shared. The suitability of this device obviously depends upon the degree of privacy we are concerned about. It is important, therefore, that the degree of privacy desired and the type of compartmentation be specifically defined in each instance.

In certain instances, it is possible that compartmentation may be desired in order to satisfy a particular kind of personal need, unrelated to privacy in the strict sense. It may be that in some cases the performance of certain functions in what is essentially an open space, i.e., a large bathroom, may cause one to feel as though the activity were being performed "out in the open." One survey respondent, for example, commented that she preferred the shower to the tub because pulling the curtain gave her a greater sense of privacy (did she mean security?). It is quite likely that by association we have come to feel the need to have a tight, wrapped-around or "snug" space for certain hygiene functions, just as we have strong feelings about the suitability and appropriateness of other spaces for other functions.

PRIVACY AND THE INDIVIDUAL

Identity. Since the dawn of time, man has searched in various ways to answer the question, who am I? This quest for a personal sense of identity seems to be a fundamental aspect of man's nature and is certainly a fundamental tenet of modern psychology, which is becoming increasingly concerned with this question. Until very recently, our Western culture has also laid great stress upon the importance of the individual and upon self-expression. Basic, however, to the development, and the maintenance, of a strong personal identity is privacy, both in a conceptual as well as an operational sense. In its simplest form it involves "aloneness," or freedom from the presence and demands of others. It also, however, involves the concept of possession —a "mineness"—of time, space, property, each of which serve as a measure of our uniqueness and our self-expression.

> . . . through habituation and teaching, the mother reproduces in the child her own needs, in this case the need for privacy which inevitably brings with it related needs. Now the child grows up needing time to himself, a room of his own, freedom of choice, freedom to plan his own time, and his own life. He will brook no interference and no encroachment. He will spend his wealth installing private bathrooms in his house, buying a private car, a private yacht, private woods and a private beach, which he will then people with his privately chosen society (Lee, 1956, p. 339).

It may be noted, however, that there are today strong societal counter-pressures for conformity and togetherness, which exist side by side with our tendency toward individuality and which, it is suggested, are the cause of much of the personal conflict in contemporary society. So that on the one hand, we will, in general, buy the same clothes, car, and house as everyone else in our peer group, but they must, on the other hand, still be "ours" in a very personal and private sense. To a varying degree, therefore, we tend in some cases to measure our sense of identity by the number and quality of things we can call ours, and by which others can identify us.

Privacy and privateness, therefore, sustain our sense of individual identity to such a degree that removal of them has demonstrable effects on the personality, which in some cases may be quite serious. This very direct relationship between privacy and privateness and the opportunity for self-expression, individuality, and personal identity has long been recognized by a variety of institutions who have quite deliberately set about to remove privacy and privateness in order to minimize individual identity so as to foster, or force, a strong group identity. Examples of such institutional behaviour may be found in a number of very familiar and common instances, chiefly those institutions which are highly structured and authoritarian: the military, prisons, and some educational and religious institutions. Each of these focuses its deprivatory attentions on certain common targets, those aspects which, in fact, most of us normally use to give evidence of our individuality: clothing, the arrangement of the hair, possessions, and privacy in certain activities. The G.I. haircut, the nun's habit, the schoolboy's cap all serve the same function, as does the wearing of a *uniform* (the very word itself is significant), and the substitution of a number or a brother or a sister for one's own name. Similarly, the prohibition on personal possessions, the common sleeping, eating, and hygiene facilities, all serve to reinforce the relative unimportance and anonymity of the individual.

That the technique is more or less effective is beyond doubt, although it may be questioned whether it is always desirable. The military latrines and medical inspections have long been infamous for their effects, either humorous or tragic, on individuals who found it exceedingly painful to make the necessary adjustments. In many cases, the adjustments can also result in more or less severe psychopathologies. This seems to be particularly true of sudden and enforced privacy deprivation which commonly occurs during catastrophies, or war, when people are forced into a prolonged and un-accustomed intimacy. This is also true of many institutional settings such as schools, prisons, or hospitals.

Privacy deprivation, however, is not a phenomenon which is limited to institutions; it is a very common feature, and a major problem, in most of the slum housing around the world. Even the average American house today, as demonstrated earlier in this report, offers instances of it. The open-planning and multi-purpose rooms combined with small size—all intended to encourage family unity and cohesiveness—have in many instances produced irritation and a variety of anti-social behaviour. Chapin observes:

> The sentiment of self-respect, the re-spect for self as an individual with status, can hardly thrive when the person is con-tinuously open to pressures of the pres-ence of many others in the household. Privacy is needed for thinking, reflection, reading and study, and for aesthetic en-joyment and contemplation. Intrusions on the fulfillment of personal desires need to be shut off in order to avoid the in-ternal tensions that are built up from the frustrations, resentments, and irritations of continual multiple contacts with others (Chapin, 1951, p. 165).

This particular aspect of privacy has come to have a particular significance for our con-sideration of the bathroom. Because there is a strong social sanction for obtaining pri-vacy from others for personal hygiene ac-tivities, the bathroom has gradually assumed a special, privileged, "off-limits" character. In the majority of homes today the bath-room, moreover, is the only such space in the house. Partly, this is the result of present house planning practise and partly, it is the result of changes in child-rearing, which is considerably more permissive than it used to be. Children, by and large, may now be heard as well as seen, and are not required to knock or ask permission to visit their parents' room nor to maintain a respectful silence if the parents are busy. The result is that, by extension or usurpation, the privileged character of the bathroom is used to obtain privacy for a variety of emotional purposes which have nothing to do with

personal hygiene: sulking, crying, day-dreaming, or seeking relief from one's social role. Chapin and a number of other com-mentators have noted that:

> . . . there is often need to escape from the compulsions of one's social role, to be able to retire from the role of parent, spouse, relative or child, as the case may be. A window may be closed against outside noise; a door may be shut to block demands of others for advice, consola-tion, help, or gossip; the radio or tele-vision set may be turned off to eliminate distracting claims on attention . . . (Chapin, 1951, p. 165).

It may also be noted in this regard that the bathroom is also a common place in which suicides occur, presumably because it guar-antees freedom from interruption.

Privacy, Embarrassment and Shame. We also seek privacy from others in an opera-tional sense so that we may be spared em-barrassment or shame: in this case, with respect to personal hygiene functions. Shame or embarrassment can be defined as an outer-directed response: a fear of what we know, or imagine, others think or feel with respect to a variety of circumstances. We may also feel shame or embarrassment when we fail publicly to live up to our own image or the image which others hold of us. Thus, we are embarrassed when the wrong person walks into the bathroom by mistake or when one's body/beauty image is faulty: for ex-ample, flat-chested, pimply, or when caught picking one's nose in public. In this respect, adolescents have a strong privacy need, for during this period bodily changes create an acute body awareness and often result in sensitivity and embarrassment. The endless experiments with grooming and the time thus spent are also contributory factors to their privacy needs.

We also exhibit modest behaviour out of deference to the unknown reactions of other persons. For example, we may take great pains and resort to all sorts of strategems to avoid being heard in the bathroom simply because we don't know whether or not we might otherwise embarrass other people. In actual practice, however, it becomes extremely difficult to sort out the basic motivations which lead us to seek privacy in a particular situation or which cause us to be uncomfortable if deprived of it. It is likely too that, many times, the basic motivation is a compound of deference to others' sensibilities, to social norms, to our own self-image, and to our self-esteem.

PRIVACY AND SOCIETY

Social Role. Perhaps the most obvious social component of privacy is that of role and relationship. This is particularly applicable to the preceding discussion of embarrassment since in many cases embarrassment is not caused by the presence of just any person, but rather, by the presence of specific culturally prohibited categories of people. What is an acceptable behaviour and privacy relationship between a child and a child may not be between that child and a parent, or between children of different sexes, etc. With respect to personal hygiene functions the obvious breaks come along sex, age, and relationship lines (Langford, 1965). There are, however, a great many other possible differentiating points depending upon the particular matter in question: for example, age, rank, status, occupation, etc. There are, for example, a number of "privileged" roles in our society; among them are the physician, the nurse, the dressmaker, hairdresser, and some sales people, each of whom is exempted from the general social rules with respect to privacy of the body. Such exemption also carries with it, of course, certain obligations with respect to the manner in which this knowledge is obtained and how much, if any, of it may be transmitted to others. The situation of the physician, for example, is different from that of the woman who sells foundation garments and each in turn is different from that of the husband, or wife.

Cultural Norms. In addition to its purely personal and internalized aspects, privacy is also a value in a cultural and socio-economic sense, and to a large extent is, therefore, a learned response to particular social situations. Privacy in these terms becomes a necessary condition for acceptable social be-

haviour, i.e., we must have privacy in certain instances in order that we do not violate cultural norms which specify that certain things be done in private. Such cultural norms can vary widely, both from culture to culture and from age to age, or from one segment to another within a given culture. As an illustration, one can refer to: the respectively opposed attitudes of the Japanese and the French toward kissing in public, the veil worn by Moslem women, the codpiece worn by the men in the middle ages, etc. Similarly, much of LeCorbusier's residential work, while much admired, would be unacceptable by American standards, and building codes, for a lack of internal privacy. Conversely, Europeans are always amazed at the American custom of leaving windows uncovered at night.

SOCIO-ECONOMIC ASPECTS

Norms, even within a culture, are also variable depending upon socio-economic status and family values. In the lowest socio-economic group, for example, where crowded living conditions force a lack of privacy (and where privacy has, in all likelihood, never been experienced) privacy norms are much less severe than they are in situations where they are a realistic societal requirement.

> Upper-class girls, most of whom had their own individual bathrooms, reacted with interest when told of middle-class procedures (bathroom scheduling) in this respect. The lower-class girls were amazed that such a thing was necessary. Probably privacy, which they had never had, and over-fastidiousness were not family values which made such arrangements important (Bossard & Boll, 1950, p. 114).

At the upper end of the socio-economic scale, however, one sometimes finds that privacy demands are carried to what may well be their ultimate conclusion: a total privacy which can then be manipulated for a variety of purposes. There are situations, for example, where all the facets of daily living are treated as an art and where only the most carefully contrived and carefully controlled images are permitted to obtain, i.e., what is sometimes regarded as the ultimate in good breeding and civilized behaviour. Here, role and format are everything, leading to separate bedrooms, bathrooms, and sitting rooms, where people come together only when fully prepared and "on stage." This applies equally to speech, display of emotions, manner of dress, and to privacy demands, particularly with respect to the necessary intimate details of one's life. In these situations, the privacy demand may also be regarded as being based on a sense of aesthetics. In the survey, for example, the highest socio-economic group indicated the greatest desire for compartmented baths, even though they, by virtue of having several baths, presumably had least need for it, and indeed, indicated the least desire for bathroom privacy, per se (Langford, 1965).

REFERENCES:

Aaron, H. *Our common ailment.* New York: Dodge Publishing Co., 1938.

Bossard, J. H. S., & Boll, E. S. *Ritual in family-living.* Philadelphia: University of Pennsylvania Press, 1950.

Chapin, F. S. Some housing factors related to mental hygiene. *Journal of Social Issues,* 1951, 8, Nos. 1 and 2.

Langford, M. *Personal hygiene attitudes and practices in 1000 middle-class households.* Ithaca, N.Y.: Cornell University Agricultural Experiment Station Memoir 393, 1965.

Lee, D. Are basic needs ultimate? In C. Kluckhohn and H. A. Murray (Eds.), *Personality in nature, society and culture.* (2nd ed.) New York: Alfred A. Knopf, 1956.

PART FOUR
Social Institutions and Environmental Design

Recently the press gave considerable attention to a huge housing complex nearing completion in New York City. Described as the country's largest cooperative apartment development, it consists of 15,382 units in 35 buildings. Eventually it will contain about 60,000 persons in what is regarded as a relatively low-cost form of housing. What makes this apartment development interesting to environmental psychology, and in particular to an understanding of social institutions and environmental design, is the raging controversy it aroused even before the first building had been occupied. For some, this form of housing is a panacea, the answer to urban housing problems. For others, it is a wasteland, a vast jungle of buildings that is neither aesthetically pleasing nor socially satisfying.

From the viewpoint of environmental psychology, both the praise and the criticism rest on very limited evidence and point up the tremendous difficulty facing the evaluation of cities, buildings, schools, and various other social institutions. For example, those praising the project emphasize economy—and the units certainly are not expensive. They see this form of housing as meeting the pressing need for really middle-class apartments in urban areas. Critics, on the other hand, suggest that the planners have failed to balance economic advantages against the nature of the neighborhood created, the physical form the housing takes, the social interactions (or lack of them) that will occur—in essence the quality of life that is likely to develop in such housing. They see the construction meeting few of the needs of the occupants other than the rudimentary need for shelter. They suggest not only that it is the creation of a massive conglomeration of people living in a noncommunity, but that it occurs at the expense of existing neighborhoods, since it is likely to filter off large numbers of white, middle-class families from the surrounding areas. They see the potential destruction of old, established neighborhoods and a proliferation of ghetto slums.

Without pretending to have the answers, environmental psychology, in particular the study of the effects of environmental design on social institutions, does lead toward a basis for evaluating the effects of a particular construction on the behavior of its occupants. At the heart of the evaluation

277

of the effects of any design on behavior is the social process underlying the man-construction interrelationship.

One of the basic assumptions the behavioral scientist makes is that human activity can only be understood within the context of an organized social environment—the family, the school, the hospital, the business organization, the community. The importance of these institutions is obvious. They provide not only for the socialization and control of individuals, but also for their growth and development. It is essential, therefore, that a book concerned with environmental psychology consider not only how individual psychological processes interrelate with various aspects of the physical environment (as previous sections of this book have done), but also how these interrelationships are conditioned by the social matrix in which they occur.

It must be emphasized here, as it has been before, that the environment is not to be regarded as a container in which the occupant perceives, interacts, and reacts but rather as part of a complex interchange in which both the person and the setting are affected. Such a dynamic relationship is likely to alter the goals of the institution, the social relationships of the inhabitants, and the physical setting itself, if not through changes in the physical materials, then through the development of imaginary barriers, defined by use. This complex interchange between individual and environment can only be regarded as a system, a dynamic process from which all factors emerge altered.

For many years, the physical setting per se has not been a direct interest of behavioral scientists. They have concentrated upon the effects of selected stimuli emanating from a setting on the subjects studied. When social scientists have been concerned with the effects of institutions on behavior, they have considered the physical setting as a mediating influence, without specifying details of the process. Limitations on theory in environmental psychology are in large part a result of the tendency to relegate the physical environment to the role of a mediating variable or a given. Clearly, we cannot consider the effects of institutions without broadening our perspective and, in the process, evolving some theory. Thus a large scale housing project is not the place where a specific form of social interaction will occur, but rather a participant, along with its occupants, in a dynamic process; people, buildings, and neighborhood are affected by the interaction. All aspects of the behavior of the inhabitants may be touched by the setting, and therefore the environment cannot be considered either a passive agent or a mediator.

For the environmental psychologist, the study of social institutions in their environmental context is both the most difficult challenge and the most promising avenue for an effective contribution to the planning disciplines. The problems of incorporating a myriad of variables—physical, physiological, social, psychological, historical—into a meaningful and useful conceptual schema are enormous, as the papers in this volume amply convey. Furthermore, the practical difficulties of conducting research in institutional settings are great. Since research and evaluation are seldom integral parts of the operation of institutions, the researcher rarely has the power to control the variables he is studying. And yet in spite of these difficulties interest in environmental research in institutional settings has grown rapidly in recent years. It has been given impetus by just such situations as the evaluation of the housing project discussed at the beginning of this introduction. Clearly, there is need for a better understanding of how the environment can participate in the effective functioning of institutions that are growing in size and complexity.

At the present stage of development in environmental psychology, very few systematic research efforts have been reported. Instead, as the selections that follow indicate, considered speculation is far more common. There is concern, for example, about the role complex psychological needs such as privacy and territoriality (discussed in Part Three) play in various social settings such as the home, the hospital, the school, and so on. There has been discussion of the need of individuals for a sense of "spatial identity" and some work to demonstrate this need (see Article 35). There is also concern about the implicit assumptions underlying a given environmental design. The design of school buildings is a case in point. Approaches to education in the past several decades have moved toward a conception of the pupil as one who actively participates in the learning process rather than one who passively acquires material by rote. Certain environmental changes have paralleled this change in emphasis. Desks and chairs are no longer anchored to the floor, and teachers no longer stand on raised platforms. Instead, flexible arrangements, designed to facilitate pupil involvement, are now provided. This approach is thought to be more successful than older ones, yet there is little concrete evidence of the success or failure of these designs in terms of the basic goals of education. What is most compelling today is the realization, by administrators of schools, hospitals, and other institutions, of the critical importance of the physical setting on the effectiveness of their institutions. They raise questions regarding the size of classrooms and hospital bedrooms, the design of play and recreational facilities, that were not a prime concern years ago, and the demand for research to help provide answers is a major influence on the growth of environmental psychology.

To discover the process by which environmental decisions are made and to assess the validity of the assumptions underlying these decisions are goals of the researcher in environmental psychology. However, the lack of definitive theory in the disciplines to which environmental psychology is closely related—psychology, sociology, psychiatry, education, urban planning, and others—has hindered the environmental researcher. In the absence of a commonly accepted theoretical framework for understanding the learning process, for example, it is difficult to establish criteria for judging the behavioral consequences of a particular school environment. Similarly, until psychiatry advances to the point where the goals of therapy can be stated explicitly, it will be difficult to assess the therapeutic value of a given psychiatric ward design. What is the therapeutic impact, if any, of an environmental design that facilitates social contacts among patients? Is the patient's self-esteem enhanced when he has a "territory" that he can call his own? In what ways does the emotionally disturbed individual differ from others in the structuring of his environment, and in the need for structure? Until we develop some conception of the functions of housing, we cannot effectively evaluate any form of shelter, or the incidental functions of the neighborhood in which the housing is located.

While the environmental researcher can begin to address himself to the question of the behavioral consequences of a particular design, he cannot assess the relevance of these behavioral data to the social institution in question as long as the goals of the institution are not clearly stated. He is therefore compelled to select the most promising approach from a welter of possible strategies, and he gets limited assistance from supporting disciplines. In the hospitals we have studied, we have been able to demonstrate through observation techniques that the physical design of the wards greatly influences patients' behavior. For example, the size of the bedroom affects the activities that are likely to take place there; the private room tends to elicit the widest variety of behaviors, and the multioccupancy room is more likely to evidence the isolated, withdrawal type of behavior. What kind of behavior is desirable from the hospital's viewpoint depends on its own goals, and we have found these goals difficult to determine. In many cases, they vary with the particular staff role, administrators, physicians, or floor personnel. Other cases appear to involve conflicting or unexpressed goals, as in the need to protect the patient from himself (and the community from the patient), yet at the same time to give him a sense of dignity and some freedom of choice. Structurally, conflicts of goals create serious problems and make the task of finding physical solutions most difficult. Cases in which goals have influenced the design of an institution— for example, L'Institut Marcel Rivière described by Sivadon (Article 42) and the institutions planned by Osmond (Article 55) and Izumi (Article 56)—provide rare opportunities to evaluate architectural effectiveness. The close relationship, still unusual, between explicit goals and physical design that these institutions evidence is probably a model for the future.

The ultimate practical goal of environmental research in specific, organized social contexts is to distinguish between characteristics of the environment that facilitate attainment of organizational goals from those that obstruct or impede such attainment and to clarify the processes underlying the effect of the environment on the goals. It should be emphasized, however, that given the limitations we have already noted, the present level of theoretical development and empirical knowledge does not permit specification of optimal physical conditions, nor is it likely to in the near future. The task of current research is rather to help to determine how and in what direction institutions change as their occupants interact with the environment.

This does not imply that we cannot consider the relationship between social institutions and environmental design. Rather, it suggests the need for a close examination of the issues and a delineation of areas for future work. At the present stage of its development, environmental psychology probably needs more descriptive rather than experimental studies, although the latter are certainly not impossible. For example, although we do not pretend to be able to describe the optimal school environment, we can describe school behavior in a specific setting—and perhaps explain why the particular behavior we observe occurs—rather than some other form. We can determine the patterns of school behavior elicited in a flexible seating arrangement as compared with those seen in a fixed seating arrangement, and the patterns seen in a large dormitory as opposed to those in a private bedroom in a hospital. We can also begin to uncover the subtle attitudinal changes in the school or hospital staff and occupants made by the conditions in which they live and work and the extent to which these people alter the environment given to them.

Clearly, we can cover a very wide scope in considering the interaction between environmental design and social institutions. In Part Four, our own work, our own interests, and the more conspicuous institutional studies of others of necessity provide the organizing framework. Many areas are excluded, not because they are unimportant, but rather because space limitations have confined us to a few issues only. For example, the complicated and important problems associated with transportation have been excluded, except as they are covered in selections dealing with urban problems. Our sampling of topics here is clearly suggestive rather than exhaustive; it tends to favor areas of work that are readily available to psychological study.

The articles in this section are organized topically rather than in terms of a basic schema. We have selected them with a view toward demonstrating how we are thinking about various themes, but in Part Four and elsewhere neither we nor the authors presented provide definitive answers. We begin with natural settings, yet in no sense do these environments represent pure, untouched nature. Rather, they are less complicated, less man-altered settings than the vast complexities of the city and its various agencies and institutions. For the environmental psychologist, such settings provide a rich natural laboratory. The natural environment actually is more complex than it appears, when an individual, with his various needs and attitudes, either observes or utilizes a particular natural setting. Yet the very perception of a natural setting is conditioned by the accumulation of experiences in both natural and man-made situations. What seems open to an urban dweller might seem quite constricting to a farmer. What is desirable to an urban vacationer clearly may not meet the needs of residents of rural areas. These reactions reflect accumulated experience through which information communicated by the environment has been distilled and distinctively interpreted, resulting in judgments about environmental quality. Part Two, on basic psychological processes, demonstrates how some of these environmental reactions develop.

Urban settings raise more troubling questions, largely because their rapid proliferation carries the seeds of a vast number of social problems. Increasingly we see references to environmental crises, environmental failure (Huxtable, 1968), and environmental stress (see Duhl, 1963). The implication is clear that the physical environment, in this case the poor quality urban setting, is capable of eliciting extreme and disordered reactions. The physical environment is held responsible for many of the symptoms of social as well as physical disorders of urban dwellers, especially those in the ghetto slum areas. In previous parts of this volume we considered such problems as the need for privacy, the effects of overcrowding, and the need of individuals to exercise some control over their surroundings. We feel that all of these, and other factors too, are at the basis of the breakdown of many urban areas; yet our belief is based largely upon speculation. Important too, but perhaps to a lesser degree, is the need for a closer appraisal of suburban life. The search for a city of reasonable size (certainly never an ideal one) will lie somewhere between the available extremes. The recent return to the city of many suburbanites suggests that life in the suburbs was far from ideal. In fact, the population movement from city to suburbs, suburbs to city is largely a reflection of the failure of the environment; people are choosing among various evils. Yet the truly mobile people are only a small minority who are economically and socially free to live where they want to. For the vast majority there is no such freedom. Restrained by severe economic limitations as well as by the social prejudices of others, their potential living areas are highly restricted—usually to the already overcrowded ghetto slums in both urban and suburban areas. We can only speculate what the effects of such restrictions are. We know it is at the heart of many educational and social problems. What it means for the individual to know that he is really unable to alter his physical setting in any substantial way can only be a matter of conjecture. If we regard the freedom to choose one's physical setting and the freedom to control this setting as essential features of the healthy life, their absence must be a critical defect for occupants of a closed, fixed, and harsh environment.

The application of our ideas about the pervasive effects of physical design to specific institutions highlights many of the issues previously discussed. To some extent we can say more about the effects of a particular institutional form on behavior than we can about housing and urban planning in general. In many instances, the specific institution—school, hospital, prison, or office—has been a microcosm for applied research, since it offers a degree of control of some of the factors relevant to the use of space that is impossible in the larger urban setting. As we have indicated, research is still far from controlling all relevant factors. Perhaps an open and self-conscious declaration of research needs is a first step in our understanding of some of the problems of our constructed world.

REFERENCES:

Duhl, L. *The urban condition: People and policy in the metropolis.* New York: Basic Books, 1963.

Huxtable, A. L. *The New York Times*, November 25, 1968, p. 43.

29 An Appreciation of the Earth

Stephen H. Dole

We take our home for granted most of the time. We complain about the weather, ignore the splendor of our sunsets, the scenery, and the natural beauties of the lands and seas around us, and cease to be impressed

Reprinted by permission of the publisher, from Stephen H. Dole, *Habitable Planets for Man* (Waltham, Mass.: Blaisdell Publishing Company, A Division of Ginn and Company, 1964).

by the diversity of living species that the Earth supports. This is natural, of course, since we are all products of the Earth and have evolved in conformity with the existing environment. It is our natural habitat, and all of it seems very commonplace and normal. Yet how different our world would be if some of the astronomical parameters were changed even slightly.

Suppose that, with everything else being the same, the Earth had started out with twice its present mass, giving a surface gravity of 1.38 times Earth normal. Would the progression of animal life from sea to land have been so rapid? While the evolution of marine life would not have been greatly changed, land forms would have to be more sturdily constructed, with a lower center of mass. Trees would tend to be shorter and to have strongly buttressed trunks. Land animals would tend to develop heavier leg bones and heavier musculature. The development of flying forms would certainly have been different, to conform with the denser air (more aerodynamic drag at a given velocity) and the higher gravity (more lifting surface necessary to support a given mass). A number of opposing forces would have changed the face of the land. Mountain-forming activity might be increased, but mountains could not thrust so high and still have the structural strength to support their own weight; raindrop and stream erosion would be magnified, but the steeper density gradient in the atmosphere would change the weather patterns; wave heights in the oceans would be lower, and spray trajectories would be shortened, resulting in less evaporation and a drier atmosphere; and cloud decks would tend to be lower. The land-sea ratio would probably be smaller. The length of the sidereal month would shorten from 27.3 to 19.4 days (if the Moon's distance remained the same). There would be differences in the Earth's magnetic field, the thickness of its crust, the size of its core, the distribution of mineral deposits in the crust, the level of radioactivity in the rocks, and the size of the ice caps on islands in the polar regions. Certainly man's counterpart (assuming that such a species would have evolved in this environment) would be quite different in appearance and have quite different cultural patterns.

Conversely, suppose that the Earth had started out with half its present mass, resulting in a surface gravity of 0.73 times Earth normal. Again the course of evolution and geological history would have changed under the influences of the lower gravity, the thinner atmosphere, the reduced erosion by falling water, and the probably increased level of background radiation due to more crustal radioactivity and solar cosmic particles. Would evolution have proceeded more rapidly? Would the progression from sea to land and the entry of animal forms into the ecological niches open to airborne species have occurred earlier? Undoubtedly animal skeletons would be lighter, and trees would be generally taller and more spindly; and again, man's counterpart, evolved on such a planet, would be different in many ways.

What if the inclination of the Earth's equator initially had been 60 degrees instead of 23.5 degrees? Seasonal weather changes would then be all but intolerable, and the only climatic region suitable for life as we know it would be in a narrow belt within about 5 degrees of the equator. The rest of the planet would be either too hot or too cold during most of the year, and with such a narrow habitable range, it is probable that life would have had difficulty getting started and, once started, would have tended to evolve but slowly.

Starting out with an inclination of 0 degrees would have influenced the course of development of the Earth's life forms in only a minor way. Seasons would be an unknown phenomenon; weather would undoubtedly be far more predictable and constant from day to day. All latitudes would enjoy a constant spring. The region within 12 degrees of the equator would become too hot for habitability but, in partial compensation, some regions closer to the poles would become more habitable than they are now.

Suppose the Earth's mean distance from the Sun were 10 percent less than it is at present. Less than 20 percent of the surface area (that between latitudes 45 degrees and 64 degrees) would then be habitable. Thus there would be two narrow land regions favorable to life separated by a wide and intolerably hot barrier. Land life could evolve independently in these two regions. The polar ice would not be present, so the ocean level would be higher than it is now, thus decreasing the land area.

If the Earth were 10 percent farther away from the Sun than it is, the habitable regions would be those within 47 degrees of the equator. (The present limit of habitability is assumed to be, on an average, within 60 degrees of the equator.)

If the Earth's rotation rate were increased so as to make the day 3 hours long instead of 24 hours, the oblateness would be pronounced, and changes of gravity as a function of latitude would be a common part of a traveler's experience. Day-to-night temperature differences would become small.

On the other hand, if the Earth's rotation rate were slowed to make the day 100 hours in length, day-to-night temperature changes would be extreme; weather cycles would have a more pronounced diurnal pattern. The Sun would seem to crawl across the sky, and few life forms on land could tolerate either the heat of the long day or the cold of the long night.

The effects of reducing the eccentricity of the Earth's orbit to 0 (from its present value of 0.0167) would be scarcely noticeable. If orbital eccentricity were increased to 0.2 without altering the length of the semi-major axis (making perihelion coincide with summer solstice in the Northern Hemisphere to accentuate the effects), the habitability apparently would not be affected in any significant manner.

Increasing the mass of the Sun by 20 percent (and moving the Earth's orbit out to 1.408 astronomical units to keep the solar constant at its present level) would increase the period of revolution to 1.54 years and decrease the Sun's apparent angular diameter to 26 minutes of arc (from its present 32 minutes of arc). Our primary would then be a class F5 star with a total main-sequence lifetime of about 5.4 billion years. If the age of the solar system were 4.5 billion years, then the Earth, under these conditions, could look forward to another billion years of history. Since neither of these numbers is known to the implied accuracy, however, a 10 percent error in each in the wrong direction could mean that the end was very near indeed. An F5 star may well be more "active" than our Sun, thus producing a higher exosphere temperature in the planetary atmosphere; but this subject is so little understood at present that no conclusions can be drawn. Presumably, apart from the longer year, the smaller apparent size of the Sun, its more pronounced whiteness, and the "imminence" of doom, life could be much the same.

If the mass of the Sun were reduced by 20 percent (this time decreasing the Earth's orbital dimensions to compensate), the new orbital distance would be 0.654 astronomical unit. The year's length would then become 0.59 year (215 days), and the Sun's apparent angular diameter, 41 minutes of arc. The primary would be of spectral type G8 (slightly yellower than our Sun is now) with a main-sequence lifetime in excess of 20 billion years. The ocean tides due to the primary would be about equal to those due to the Moon; thus spring tides would be somewhat higher and neap tides lower than they are at present.

What if the Moon had been located much closer to the Earth than it is, say, about 95,000 miles away instead of 239,000 miles? The tidal braking force would probably have been sufficient to halt the rotation of the Earth with respect to the Moon, and the Earth's day would equal its month, now 6.9 days in length (sidereal). Consequently, the Earth would be uninhabitable.

Moving the Moon farther away than it is would have much less profound results: the month would merely be longer and the tides lower. Beyond a radius of about 446,000 miles, the Earth can not hold a satellite on a circular orbit.

Increasing the mass of the Moon by a factor of 10 at its present distance would have an effect similar to that of reducing its distance. However, the Earth's day and month would then be equal to 26 days. Decreasing the Moon's mass would affect only the tides.

What if the properties of some of the other planets of the solar system were changed? Suppose the mass of Jupiter were increased by a factor of 1050, making it essentially a replica of the Sun. The Earth could still occupy its present orbit around the Sun, but our sky would be enriched by the presence of an extremely bright star, or second sun, of magnitude −23.7, which would supply at most only 6 percent as much heat as the Sun. Mercury and Venus could also keep their present orbits; the remaining planets could not, although those exterior to Saturn could take up new orbits around the new center of mass.

All in all, the Earth is a wonderful planet to live on, just the way it is. Almost any change in its physical properties, position, or orientation would be for the worse. We are not likely to find a planet that suits us better, although at some future time there may be men who prefer to live on other planets. At the present time, however, the Earth is the only home we have; we would do well to conserve its treasures and to use its resources intelligently.

30 The American Scene[1]

David Lowenthal

Face to face with the look of his own country, the well-traveled American is characteristically dismayed. Henry James, more than most others, viewed the American scene at the turn of the century with outright distaste. After his twenty-five years abroad, America seemed bleak and raw, except at Harvard College, where the mellow tones of the older buildings allowed him to hope that "we are getting almost ripe, . . . beginning to begin, and we have that best sign of it, . . . that we make the vulgar, the very vulgar, think we are beginning to end" (James, 1907, p. 61). If the American scene was elsewhere deplorable, it was because American society was unformed, American taste untutored. James attributed the sordid shabbiness of New Hampshire's wayside farms and people to "the suppression of the two great factors of the familiar English landscape, the squire and the parson" (James, 1907, p. 23). That America seemed such "an ugly . . . wintering, waiting, world" was a consequence, he believed, of "the vast general unconsciousness and indiffer-

From *Geographical Review*, 1968, **58**, 61–88. Reprinted by permission of the author and publisher.

[1] This paper is condensed and revised from a lecture delivered at the Graduate School of Design, Harvard University, in November, 1966. It is part of a longer work in preparation. The author acknowledges with gratitude the assistance of the John Simon Guggenheim Memorial Foundation, for a fellowship in 1965–1966, and his indebtedness for the title to Henry James's book (1907).

ence" (James, 1946, pp. 461 and 464) about its appearance; things looked as they did because almost no one cared.

A pioneer conservationist decided a century ago that although others "think that the earth made man, man in fact made the earth" (Lowenthal, 1958, p. 248). This insight was ecological, but the statement is as true esthetically. Landscapes are formed by landscape tastes. People see their surroundings through preferred and accustomed glasses and tend to make the world over as they see it. Such preferences long outlast geographical reality. Thus the English, although now mainly "town-birds through and through," still think of rural England as their true home; for them, Browning's chaffinch still sings on an orchard bough (Lowenthal & Prince, 1965).

IMAGES AND STEREOTYPES

The American scene, as much as any other, mirrors a long succession of idealized images and visual stereotypes. Let us examine a few historic responses to that scene and see how they are reflected in contemporary landscape and townscape.

A literary historian has categorized typical Eastern reactions to Western landscapes in terms of *vastness, astonishment, plenitude* (owing to the apparent inexhaustibility of wildlife), *incongruity* (the contrast between landscapes fit for the gods and their mean and petty human inhabitants), and *melancholy* (owing to the absence or transience of man and his works; Jones, 1964, pp. 379–386). But such responses were not new, nor were they confined to the West. They were equally appropriate in early settlements in the East, in forest as in prairie, in the salt marshes of Massachusetts as in the Sierras. America has usually struck visitors as vast, wild, and empty, formless and unfinished, and subject to violent extremes. A few examples will illustrate each trait.

Size

No aspect of the American scene is more notorious than the scale of the landscape and the size of objects in it. Eyes accustomed to European vistas and artifacts may take years to adjust, as one visitor put it, to "the unnerving bigness of everything" in America (Shepheard, 1963). " 'Too big,' said one of our Frenchmen, peering a mile down into the Grand Canyon; but he was wrong. In England something of that size would be absurd, but there it is in scale (although the American woman who wrote in the visitors' book before us 'Very pretty' was probably cutting it down to size too far)" (Seddon, 1962). The initial shock is the same in every kind of landscape; "the streets remain streets, the mountains mountains, and the rivers rivers—and yet one feels at a loss before them, simply because their scale is such that the normal adjustment of man-to-environment becomes impossible" (Lévi-Strauss, 1961, p. 83).

So it has seemed from the start. Weary weeks on the Atlantic, eyes strained between sky and ocean, did not habituate travelers to the continental scale of America. They expected monotony from the sea, but not from the land. West Indian landforms contrasted pleasantly with the solitude of the voyage. But the continent itself dismayed them; instead of circumnavigable islands, America proved to be an intractable hunk of land, more and more alien, interminable, and unrewarding the farther they moved into it. And it conformed less and less with European preconceptions about promised lands, visions chiefly Arcadian, insular, and small-scale. The long search for the Northwest Passage was more than a yearning for the fabled East; it was also an expression of active distaste for the American impediment. Only the trapper, the lumberman, the religious fanatic, and the most optimistic imperialist waxed enthusiastic over the endless forest and swamps, the prairies and deserts, of North America.

Limitless frontiers did attract a few. Jefferson (1955, p. 19) thought the "smooth blue horizon" seen where the Potomac clove the Blue Ridge was a view "worth a voyage across the Atlantic." Eighteenth-century fashion admired panoramic views and primitive nature; many paid homage to America on both counts. But they enjoyed landscapes more as set pieces than as real places. The

botanist Bartram dutifully gazed "with rapture and astonishment . . . [at the] amazing prospect of grandeur" in the southern Appalachians yet confided he felt as lonely as Nebuchadnezzar, "constrained to roam in the mountains and wilderness" (Van Doren, n.d., pp. 292–293).

America has continued to affect folk as "huge, vague, breeding as much fear as hope" (Dangerfield, 1965, p. 26). The hero alone in space has been a central theme in American literature since Cooper's "Leatherstocking Tales." And spaciousness is also a cardinal quality of American landscape paintings. The people in those landscapes are dwarfed by nature, seldom an integral part of the scene. Even the genre figures of Bingham, Eakins, and Mount seem dominated by their environments.

The classic reaction to American space is that of Rölvaag's pioneer wife, who dreaded the "endless plain . . . [that] stretched far into the Canadian north, God alone knows how far from the Mississippi River to the western Rockies. . . . Endless . . . beginningless. A grey waste . . . an empty silence . . . a boundless cold [where] snow fell; . . . a universe of nothing but dead whiteness" (1927, p. 241). Today's resident is apt to feel the same way. As a native of Bismarck put it, "We look out over all the space and figure, hell, it's too big for us, it's too wide, there's too much of it, and we get gloomy. Your North Dakota man can get good and gloomy" (Hamburger, 1965, p. 8).

"The American imitates nature, with whose great works he is in constant communication," said an observer a century ago. "Only an appreciation of the grandeur of such a fall as that of Niagara, could fit a man to construct the bridge that spans its river" (Miller, 1965, p. 304). Eighteenth-century European scientists had earlier asserted that nature and man in the New World were more puny than in the Old. "In America, there is not an animal that can be compared to the elephant," asserted Buffon (in Chinard, 1947, pp. 30–31), and "all the animals which have been transported from Europe . . . the horse, the ass, the sheep, the goat, the hog, etc., have become smaller. . . . [All species] shrink and diminish under a niggardly sky and an unprolific land, thinly peopled with wandering savages." Jefferson and others took great pains to refute these taunts, citing the elk and the moose, and mammoth bones discovered in Ohio.

Pride thus paved the way for a cult of bigness. The dinosaur became emblematic. Americans soon boasted that they had the largest animals, the longest rivers, the highest mountains, the tallest trees. And they created gargantuan structures to match. New York skyscrapers and the Golden Gate and Verrazano bridges reflect ambitions of the same order as that of the medieval cathedral builders who aimed at record heights. The best-known American structures are monumental. Boulder Dam, Fort Knox, the Mormon Temple, the Empire State Building are admired less for their efficiency or beauty than for their size. Size is preferred even in things that might be better small. But local planners can hardly be blamed for thinking big when the biggest projects get the largest federal allocations. They "want to see big, really important open spaces," as one planner put it, lest their funds be "wasted and frittered away on a bunch of little playgrounds and parks" (Whyte, n.d., p. 26).

The mania for bigness reached its peak at the turn of the century. "Make no little plans," Daniel Burnham (1955, p. 201) urged his fellow architects, "make big plans." That they did so is evident in Newport's "cottages," Roosevelt's Sagamore Hill, with foundations twenty feet thick, and the Flatiron Building in New York, deliberately designed "to dwarf the 'ordinary' buildings around" it (Gowans, 1964, p. 380). But the later progressive architects liked plenty of room too. And Americans still build as though bigger were always better.

The prevailing gridiron pattern, with straight streets at right angles, also accentuates size and space. In New York, Sartre's (1957, pp. 119 and 122) "glance met nothing but space. It slid over blocks of identical houses . . . to lose itself in empty space, at the horizon. . . . The moment you set foot on" a Manhattan avenue "you understand that it has to go on to Boston or Chicago." In smaller towns the grid emphasizes every

aspect of the terrain and draws the eye away from the houses out to the lonely horizon.

(2) Wildness

The nature of America, like its scale, leaves the spectator alone in an alien world—alien both in what it contains and in what it lacks. America is still full of unfamiliar, undomesticated, unclassifiable things, "a waste and howling wilderness," as Michael Wigglesworth (1871–1873, p. 83; see Heimert, 1953) described it in the seventeenth century, "where none inhabited but hellish fiends, and brutish men."

Even more than these strange shapes and species, the virtual absence of man's artifacts appalled viewers. Indians were few, nomadic, ephemeral; their works scarcely detracted from the powerful impression of emptiness. Melancholy amid "dreary wastes and awful solitude," two eighteenth-century poets conjured up future kingdoms to people the forlorn continent (Freneau & Brackenridge, 1957, p. 9). But even in southern New England, the longest settled, most densely populated and socially domesticated corner of the country, the sense of wilderness still endures. An English bird watcher in a nature reserve near Groton, Massachusetts, suddenly became conscious that he was "on a vast continent—exotic, tropical, rich in the possibility of surprises undreamed of in Shropshire." By English standards the woods and undergrowth seemed chaotic and impenetrable. The very absence of dreaded snakes, groundhogs, and wolves struck him as sinister, the silence foreboding. He moved along more rapidly, stumbled against a stump, fell, could not get up for fright. "What kind of a fool are you?" he asked himself. "Do you really imagine you are in any danger, here within five miles of America's most exclusive school?" But the answer was yes (Ellis, 1960, p. 24). After all, even a resident like John Hersey (1953, p. 50) has characterized summertime Connecticut as an "equatorial jungle."

Perhaps the most cogent summary of American wildness is Gertrude Stein's (1936, pp. 17–18): "In the United States there is more space where nobody is than where anybody is. That is what makes America what it is." To be sure, other countries have uninhabited wildernesses; those of Tibet, of Chile, of Algeria, for example, may be more extensive. What gives American emptiness its special poignance is its pervasiveness in ordinary landscapes. In a night train on the outskirts of a Kansas town, the traveler realizes that "beyond is America . . . and no one there. . . . It's only ten, fifteen minutes since you've left a thriving town but life has already been swallowed up in that ocean of matter which is and will remain as wild as it was made" (Barzun, 1954, p. 3).

Over much of the country, man and his structures seem to be insignificant or temporary features of the landscape. Even the sturdy New England farmhouse looks to many Europeans "like a temporary wooden structure hastily erected against the elements and marauding savages" (Alsop, 1962, p. 10). But it is in the metropolis that impermanence is most sharply felt. An English essayist recalls "lonely moments in some American city at night when you are on the edge of nightmare" and begin to fear that the place is "no more than a huddle of people . . . round a camp fire who will have packed up and moved on . . . in the morning" (Pritchett, 1965, p. 155).

Formlessness

Compared with Old World landscapes, those of America appear generally ragged, indefinite, and confused; parts stand out at the expense of a unified whole. Over much of the country topographic features are large, vague, and indefinitely structured, and vegetation tends to cloak patterns of terrain. The quality of American light is also partly responsible for the absence of clearly defined structure. Frequently bright, hard, undiminished by moisture, it seems to separate and isolate features rather than to join and compose them.

Man's structures mirror nature. Boundaries between city and country are blurred and smudged. Localities neither begin nor end, and little seems fixed. Unfenced, "the little houses sit lightly, barely engaged with

the ground and the landscape," as Banham (1961, p. 305) has put it: Le Corbusier (1964) felt that the absence of framing walls and fences gave the American landscape a pleasing amplitude. But most observers tend, with Henry James (1907, pp. 161–162), to inveigh against "this diffused vagueness of separation . . . between the . . . [place] you are in and the . . . [place] you are not in," and to deplore "the indefinite extension of all spaces . . . ; the enlargement of every opening, . . . the substitution of . . . far perspectives and resounding voids for enclosing walls."

Visual flux, with continual rebuilding, is the rule in the skyscraper city. As Kouwenhoven (1961) argues, "the logic of cage construction" is that of something "always complete but never finished." He concludes that America "is not an artifact; . . . America is process."

But the process produces artifacts, even if they are not rooted in place. They create America's most distinctive look—casual chaos. A French anthropologist (Lévi-Strauss, 1961, p. 99) provides a classic account of the genesis of the vacant lot: "Patches of dead ground . . . were once owned, and once briefly worked, by Man. Then he went off somewhere else and left behind him a battleground strewn with the relics of his brief tenure. . . . [On it] there has arisen a new, disorderly, and monotonous vegetation." From railroad cutting to riverbank, from city park to town dump, this landscape engulfs the country. More ragged than the primeval wilderness, it divides and subverts any ordered scene. Hence Dickens' (1957, p. 116) description of an open space in Washington as "a melancholy piece of waste ground with frowzy grass, which looks like a small piece of country that has taken to drinking, and has quite lost itself."

Extremes

America also strikes observers as subject to terrifying—or exhilarating—extremes. Nature here is not only on a larger scale but more violent than the early settlers had ever experienced. They endured torrid summers and bitter winters and despairingly noted savage vagaries of climate. Within this framework of excess, tornado, flood, and drought often wreaked havoc. And extremes are not confined to climate and weather; a modern visitor remarks that "the whole of American life is tempered by the threats of . . . overwhelming natural excesses. . . . In almost every State there are turbulences of scenery, grotesque formations or things of feverishly exaggerated size" (Morris, 1962, p. 41).

Sounds as well as sights tend toward excess. Early travelers mistook the roaring rush of passenger pigeons for tornadoes. They described rivers as angry, violent, fierce, reckless, headstrong, flowing with deafening turmoil. Beyond was silence; wide grasslands swallowed sounds as if they had never been uttered. On the Arkansas prairies Thomas Nuttall (1905, p. 205) remarked that "no echo answers the voice, and its tones die away in boundless and enfeebled undulations." Silence made the scene inhumanly lonely. On a wide plain near Pittsburgh a German novelist a century ago found "absolutely nothing. . . . Far and wide there was not a bird, not a butterfly, not the cry of an animal, not the hum of an insect" (Kürnberger, 1926, p. 301).

Such extremes stimulated some folk as they depressed others. But all felt that nature was of a different order in the New World than in the Old. The physical fundament seemed not only larger but less malleable.

To the excesses of nature have been added those of man. In their buildings, as in their behavior, Americans resemble the landscape they inhabit—exaggerated, vehement, powerful, unpredictable.

INSIDERS AND OUTSIDERS

Vast and wild, teeming yet lonely, formless, violent, and extreme—no wonder America seemed to the first Europeans like the original Creation, now chaos, now garden. "In the beginning all the world was America," John Locke said (1924, p. 140); the phrase conveys the threat as well as the promise of the New World. This was a land that simultaneously attracted and repelled, but in the end had to be brought to terms.

Empty, it must be filled; unfinished, it must be completed; wild, it must be tamed.

To the Elizabethans, America was simply a vision; to the settlers that vision was a challenge requiring action. Action became so strong a component of the American character that landscapes were often hardly seen at all; they were only acted on. Immediate necessity made a mockery of mere contemplation. To wrest a living from the soil, to secure frontiers against hostile forces, seemed to demand full attention. Appreciation of the landscape itself, apart from its practical uses, was disdained as pointless and effete.

The irrelevance of "scenic values" to real life is dramatized by Mark Twain (1929). After a typical tourist blurb about majestic panoramas, Twain turns around and derides the tourist view as artificial, self-conscious, above all ignorant. The tourist only enjoys the view because he is an outsider and doesn't understand it. Before he becomes familiar with the Mississippi, Twain's pilot enjoys the stock responses to a glowing sunset on the silvery water. But after he learns the river, he looks at the same scene "without rapture" and comments, "This sun means that we are going to have wind tomorrow; . . . that slanting mark on the water refers to a bluff reef which is going to kill somebody's steamboat one of these nights; . . . that silver streak in the shadow of the forest is the 'break' from a new snag" (pp. 79–80).

Perception of *scenery* is open only to those who have no real part to play in the landscape. Those who know it and work in it have to concentrate on the humdrum realities; "the choice is between the mawkish sentiments of the passengers and the bleak matter-of-factness of the pilot" (Marx, 1964, p. 324). Asked to be pilot or passenger, what red-blooded American would hesitate? We are all pilots, happy only when we are steering some ship, whether it is plow or airplane. We disdain the mere onlooker and dismiss his opinion of the landscape. What right has a passive spectator to impose his judgment? However drab a hotel or ugly a junkyard may seem to the passerby, if it fulfills its function there is no ground for complaint. A dealer may arrange his layout to attract customers, but not for beauty alone. We do not prettify the rugged face of workaday America in order to enjoy its looks.

In short, the landscape is worthy of its hire. Its ultimate critics are its residents, not its visitors. Such is the lesson of William James's "On a Certain Blindness in Human Beings" (1958).

> Journeying in the mountains of North Carolina, I passed by a large number of "coves" . . . which had been newly cleared and planted. The impression on my mind was one of unmitigated squalor. The settler had . . . cut down the more manageable trees, and left their charred stumps. . . . The larger trees he had girdled and killed . . . and had set up a tall zigzag rail fence around the scene of his havoc. . . . Finally, he had irregularly planted the intervals between the stumps and trees with Indian corn. . . . The forest had been destroyed; and what has "improved" it out of existence was hideous, a sort of ulcer, without a single element of artificial grace to make up for the loss of Nature's beauty.

Then a mountaineer told James, "Why, we ain't happy here, unless we are getting one of these coves under cultivation."

> I instantly felt that I had been losing the whole inward significance of the situation. . . . To me the clearings [were] . . . naught but . . . a mere ugly picture on the retina. . . . But, when *they* looked on the hideous stumps, what they thought of was personal victory. The chips, the girdled trees, and the vile split rails spoke of honest sweat, persistent toil and final reward.

And he points his moral: "The spectator's judgment is sure to miss the root of the matter, and to possess no truth" (pp. 149–169; see also Lowenthal, 1962–1963).

Many Americans would still agree. The editor of *Landscape* derides "beautification" as empty and idle. Abandon "the spectator stance," he urges, and ask instead what chances the landscape offers "for making a living . . . for freedom of choice of action . . . for meaningful relationships"—all emphatically *non*visual standards. And he con-

cludes that "we should never tinker with the landscape without thinking of those who live in the midst of it. . . . What the spectator wants or does not want is of small account" (Jackson, 1963–1964).

The epitome of functionalism in landscape, perhaps, is the state capitol grounds of Oklahoma City: no trees, gardens, fountains, or other humdrum frivolities adorn the mall, but "a maze of oil derricks, . . . all pumping away." It has been proposed that the capitol itself should sport a derrick set in the rotunda with its top jutting up through the nonexistent dome, "so that everybody could see who was boss in Oklahoma City" (Hamburger, 1965, pp. 194–195).

A rare protest against the purely monetary view of landscape appears in a utopian novel of a generation ago. Americans, the author notes, "ruined lovely views by unsightly structures. It never occurred to anyone that an ordinary view was worth saving when put into competition with a commercial interest." In the writer's utopia, by contrast, "no farmer merely farms but is an artist in landscape architecture as well. . . . [They] consider how the field will look when [plants] first come up through the earth, and when they are full grown . . . and when they are dead and when they are stubble. . . . What interested them was the effect upon a certain view. . . . They looked upon their whole farm as a great living canvas" (Wright, 1958, pp. 297–298).

IDEAL VERSUS REALITY

Most Americans reserve such esthetic considerations for select landscapes only. Thus the comment of a visitor from the Great Plains on first seeing the Hudson River Highlands: "It looks like scenery should look!" (Kahn, 1966). The gulf between ideal and reality, between "how things *ought* to look" and the easy acceptance of surroundings not remotely resembling that ideal—this cleavage takes many forms. Each illumines a facet of national behavior of value for environmental design and planning. (I do not mean to imply that any of these is unique to this country, only that they are clearly recognizable as American attitudes.) Let us look briefly at a few of them.

The Present Sacrificed to the Glorious Future

Americans build for tomorrow, not for today. They "*love* their country, not, indeed, *as it is*, but *as it will be*," a traveler noted in the 1830's; "they do not love the land of their fathers; but they are sincerely attached to that which their children are destined to inherit" (Grund, 1837). A New York State settler challenged an eighteenth-century visitor to "return in ten years and you will not recognize this . . . wild and savage [district]. Our humble log houses will be replaced by fine dwellings. Our fields will be fenced in, and the stumps will have disappeared" (Crèvecoeur, 1964, p. 493). In similar fashion I was taken in 1966 to see the view from the roof of a new building at the University of California, Los Angeles, where my hosts ignored the actual campus as it looks today and instead described how it *would* look in 1980.

The current American scene is not a finished landscape, but an embryo of future greatness. Meanwhile we endure protracted labor pains. Vast areas of our cities are occupied by wrecking crews and bulldozers, sand and gravel, rubble and structural elements—semipermanent wastelands dedicated to Tomorrow. A large proportion of the cityscape is in painful gestation at any time. The vaguest tidings of Urban Renewal, if sufficiently sweetened and sign-posted, persuade the citizen to suffer the laying waste of his city for years on end. At the Manhattan end of the Brooklyn Bridge, fifteen acres have been scheduled for total demolition since 1956, but new buildings are not to be finished until 1970—that is, half a generation. This aspect of urban progress long ago caught Tocqueville's attention (1956–1957, p. 56). He was dismayed that those clearing ground for the city of Washington "have already rooted up trees for ten miles around lest they should interfere with the future citizens of this imaginary metropolis."

Living in the future, Americans are predisposed to accept present structures that are makeshift, flimsy, and transient, obsolete from the start. "Downtowns and suburbs still bear the imprint of frontier-camp design," Pushkarev (1966, p. 111) points out. Elevated transit lines, overhead wiring, exterior fire escapes, are among the fixtures that stem from that spirit. We live in throw-away stage sets.

But the habit of discarding buildings almost as soon as they are put up has its compensations. "If something is built wrong," writes an observer of Los Angeles, "it doesn't matter much. Everyone expects it to come down in a decade or two" (Rand, 1966, p. 56). Because we invest so lightly in our buildings, we can—and do—experiment easily. Innovations embellish the whole countryside.

The Present Diminished by Contrast with an Idealized Past[2]

Old Sturbridge Village, the Minute Man National Historic Monument, the Trustees of Reservations, the Society for the Preservation of New England Antiquities—such Massachusetts-based institutions all testify to our wish to preserve, and if necessary to manufacture, an idealized Historyland as a sanctuary from the awful present. That past includes not only historic buildings and places but also a pastoral countryside and a sublime wilderness.

These romantic tastes are by no means unique to America. What is striking is how fast they took root here, after our initial rejection of whatever was old or natural. As early as 1844 the American Art Union promoted the sale of Hudson River School paintings as an antidote to the abysmal environment of city folk: "a painted landscape is almost essential to preserve a healthy tone to the spirits, lest they forget in the wilderness of bricks . . . the pure delights of nature and a country life" (Ward, 1966, p. 64). And this at a time when the countryside was half an hour's walk from New York City!

Hudson River paintings still inspire moral exhortation. The village of Garrison-on-Hudson recently exhibited dozens of colorful paintings by Cole, Kensett, Durand, and Church in its picturesque railroad station.

[2] See David Lowenthal, 1966.

In another room, labeled "Chamber of Horrors," a revolving spotlight flickered over black-and-white photographs of the bleak contemporary scene—litter in and along the river, abandoned shacks and piers, garbage dumps, decaying industries. A recorded commentary urged visitors to remake the river as it used to be. No one questioned whether the nineteenth-century Hudson really conformed to the painters' views of it; no one seemed to doubt that the present scene was one of unmitigated blight. Funds raised by the exhibit will be used, appropriately, for reconstructing a Hudson River sloop—not a replica of any specific ship, but an ideal nautical composite.

The preferred past is history expurgated and sanitized. When Walt Disney unveiled his new model of nineteenth-century New Orleans at Disneyland in 1966, he was not entirely satisfied with the mayor of New Orleans' remark that it looked "just like home." "Well," Disney replied, "it's a lot cleaner" (*New York Times*, 1966).

The visitor to historic sites seldom cares whether he is looking at a real relic or a fake. A Charleston resident contends that "if you point to an alley and say 'Catfish Row,' visitors are perfectly satisfied and return North happy" (Hamburger, 1965, p. 32). As a promoter of Lincoln's supposed birthplace remarked in the 1890's, "Lincoln was born in a log cabin, weren't he? Well, one cabin is as good as another" (Hosmer, 1965, p. 141). Even a replica of Uncle Tom's fictional cabin meets the demand for historic atmosphere.

As treasured heritages, History and Nature are not only altered to fit "a dream-image of an immutable past" (Whitehill, 1966, p. 44); they have also become objects of isolated pleasure and reverence, fenced off and enshrined in historical museums and wilderness preserves, out of touch with the rest of the landscape. By contrast with the idealized past, the present workaday environment is considered not worth looking at.

Nature is likewise thought preferable to artifice. The favored landscapes are wild; landscapes altered or disturbed or built on by man are considered beneath attention or beyond repair. Adoration of the wilderness, like idealization of the past, focuses attention on the remote and the special to the neglect of the nearby and the familiar (Lowenthal, 1964).

Conservationist organizations contrast sordid scenes dominated by man with lovely landscapes devoid of human activity—telegraph poles versus trees, a mass of people versus a mass of sand. The implication is clear: man is dreadful, nature is sublime. Yet Americans do not take so dim a view of human activities as the English, whose feelings are epitomized in Cowper's sanctimonious—and mistaken—apothegm that "God made the country, and man made the town" (Cowper, 1814, p. 40). From the start Americans have considered themselves chosen people—not mere servants in the great task of transforming nature, but junior partners to the Deity, and sometimes more than that. Watching the conversion of an old farm into a luxurious estate an onlooker remarked, "It just goes to show you what God could have done if He'd had money" (Morris, 1946, p. 40).

Individual Features Emphasized at the Expense of Aggregates

"Featurism," as defined by an Australian architect, is "the subordination of the essential whole and the accentuation of selected separate features. . . . A featurist city has little or no consistency of atmospheric quality and plenty of numbers on the guide map directing the visitor to features of interest. . . . Each new building is determined to be arresting" (Boyd, 1960, pp. 9–11).

Accentuation of features is perhaps less deliberate in America than in Australia. But it has been pervasive since the first settlements. Weak relationships mark even the old New England clustered villages. The houses may be homogeneous in style, but they are fragmented by distance and by the absence of any binding framework. As an English observer put it, they stand out around their central greens "like plucked chickens." Other places are only collections of heterogeneous buildings marooned in wastelands. It is the same in cities. No office structure in New York lines up its cornice or parapet with another. New York's Lever and Seagram buildings are "each elegantly and humanely designed within its boundaries," but they are separated, the visitor notes, by "a rush of cars, browbeaten shrubs, dumb pavements. . . . The art of making a pattern in the environment is entirely neglected" (Nairn, 1965, pp. 13 and 3).

Features of interest often lack all connectivity. Americans glory in the most arcane juxtapositions, as is suggested by a sightseeing advertisement for the "Only Tour in Key West That Will Take You to the Following Points of Interest: Monument of Cesar Romero's Grandfather—Gold Star Mothers' Monument—Home of Tennessee Williams—May Sands Elementary School—The Tree That Bears the Fruit on Its Trunk —The Oddest House—Or the Most Artistic House in Key West—The Unique Cigar Makers Home—The Miracle Tree—A Visit to the City Cemetery—Maine Monument —The Gun Turret of the Maine" (*New Yorker*, 1965).

Hunger and impatience help to account for disconnectedness. In America, as Henry James (1907) explained, a place "has had to have something for everybody, since everybody arrives famished; it has had to . . . produce on the spot the particular romantic object demanded. . . . It has had to have feature at any price . . . which accounts . . . for the general rather eruptive and agitated effect."

Noting the contrast between our new buildings and the subtopia around them, an English architect asked his American colleagues "how it was that they could see their splendid, shining buildings put up in surroundings that would make a Balkan sanitary inspector blench." They replied that "it was surprising what you could get used to, and anyway they were so busy doing architecture they had not yet had the time to worry about the spaces between" (Casson, 1957, p. 36). But the condition has other roots: our fluid social structure, our disposable dwellings, the absence of strong local ties.

The tendency to concentrate on features is promoted, too, by the American sky, which tends to highlight specific objects and to stretch distances. In American paintings space is not a palpable atmosphere, but an empty, shapeless void. Instead of clouds framing a landscape, "a cloudless sky descends to lengthen the reaches of river, field, or pavement" (McCoubrey, 1963, pp. 115–116). In Andrew Wyeth's canvases, for example, things and people are seen alone; he invests both the animate and the inanimate "with an air of detachment, by cutting the objects off from the whole" (Schroeder, 1965, p. 562). The industrial landscapes of Hopper and Sheeler have the same isolating quality, their structures seeming to inhabit a void.

But American structures sometimes fit together in an unselfconscious manner. House types in a small town, neon signs along a highway, the skyscrapers of Manhattan, relate to one another in a fashion celebrated in the paintings of Charles Demuth, Stuart Davis, and Robert Rauschenberg (Jellicoe, 1966), which organize a large number of seemingly unrelated things in a single comprehensive design.

The Nearby and the Typical Neglected for the Remote and the Spectacular

The National Parks were originally set up to enshrine the freaks and wonders of nature, and park literature still touts the Grand Canyon, the Grand Tetons, Yellowstone, and Yosemite as unique. If they were typical, who would bother to go and see them? And so with the works of man. If they are not unique, they are valueless, quickly passed by and soon forgotten. Litchfield, in the western Connecticut highlands, is heralded as the *ne plus ultra* of Federalist gracious living, while a score of nearby villages of almost equal grace go nearly unnoticed. Their counterparts in neighboring New York State, crossroad and railroad villages with massive, high-gabled roofs, remain unappreciated as visual entities because no architectural accolade has come to the individual houses.

In the West, neglect of the general in favor of a single focus of merit goes further still. Half a century ago Puget Sound boasted several attractive cities and many livable towns. Seattle alone is still alive. Up and down the coast the moribund harbors and decayed buildings of Bellingham and Port Angeles, Everett and La Conner, speak not only of the passing of enterprise, but of the feebleness of local spirit. The sense of neglect and abandonment is keenest in Tacoma, the region's second city, which used to be thought of as a Boston to Seattle's New York. The Tacoman sense of identity is now about on a par with that of Yonkers or Hoboken. Once the most glamorous city in the Pacific Northwest, Tacoma today appeals to one refugee from the East mainly "because it's such a *nothing* town. This gives it a real charm" (Michener, 1966, p. 46; see also Wolfe, 1963).

Where urban visual qualities *are* a matter of pride, Americans are apt to allude to the general setting rather than to anything near at hand. Seattleites daily admire Mount Rainier, fifty miles away, while ignoring the tawdriness under their noses. Above the smog in the Berkeley Hills people enjoy the lights of San Francisco, fifteen miles across the Bay. The greatest feature of Jersey City is the New York skyline. And New Yorkers themselves appreciate Gotham mainly when they desert the squalid streets to circumnavigate Manhattan at fifty miles an hour on an elevated parkway.

Long ago Tocqueville (1956–1957) noted that Americans built "some monuments on the largest scale" and also "a vast number of inconsiderable productions," but that "between these two extremes there is a blank." The long-run effect of the cult of uniqueness is the same as that of museumizing history and nature. The features most admired are set apart and deluged with attention; the rest of the country is consigned to the rubbish heap.

Scenic Appreciation—Serious and Self-Conscious

For many people "seeing" is an activity of specific purpose and fixed duration, as in the cartoon of the maid, about to draw curtains across the window, who turns to ask, "Is Madam through with the moon?" We dichotomize experience as we zone places: certain intervals are set aside for looking at things; the rest of the time we are blind.

From these habits of mind and sight scenic views inevitably take their character. Americans enhance preferred views by landscaping, and highlight them with identifying markers. But scenic promoters do not merely inform the traveler that he is now crossing Chipmunk Creek or ascending Hogback Hill; they give him a thumbnail sketch of the geology and natural history of the area, a disquisition on the domestic economy of the Indians, and an arrow on a trunk pointing out the route of Washington's retreat or Grant's advance. The signs along Virginia's Skyline Drive are so numerous, prominent, artful, and information-laden that the conscientious traveler is not so much seeing a landscape as reading a book or viewing a museum diorama.

Like exits from a modern highway, the scenic experience is not only signposted but numbered; to get the most out of a landscape, one is supposed to see a prearranged sequence, as along Boston's Freedom Trail. But the art of ordering experience is most fully developed for views of nature. "A trail should have a definite purpose," the Forest Service (1965, p. 51) notes. "Upon reaching his goal, the traveler should have a feeling of accomplishment . . . of having 'found' most of the interest points along the way, of having struggled to the top of the overlook where he can rest and enjoy his prize—the scenic view spread out before him."

Where nature lacks such stimuli, man must provide them. Thus a well-known landscape architect "improved" a New Hampshire hill which hotel guests used to saunter up for the view. Blocking off the easy path with hemlocks, he located a new trail "steeply up the roughest, wildest part of the hillside. . . . Pulling themselves from rock to rock, they [the guests] carefully pick their way until they finally break out at the very top. They have made it! Nothing, they may think, as they rest enjoying the view, is more exhilarating than mountain climbing" (Simonds, 1961, pp. 30–31). Climbing has become an end in itself, tending less to enhance than to supersede looking.

The well-blazed trail, the obstacle-course mentality, and the segregation of scenery within quotation marks tend ultimately to make any scenic view appear contrived. In such circumstances, to "beautify" is merely to plug in replicas of esthetic treasures, like the giant-size billboard copy of Gainsborough's "Blue Boy" along a New Jersey highway. We destroy by overemphasis as surely as by neglect and vandalism.

Comments on the American scene are often doctrinaire and imprecatory. City and country, suburb and slum, whatever critics see appalls them. The loss of natural and historic treasures; the ubiquity of litter, both the used-up old and the shoddy new; the absence of vital or well-integrated human landscapes—these are defects on which designers have moralized at length. Many of the remedies they recommend would require wholesale reform of American character and behavior. But values are no easier to alter than habitats. The present vogue for beautification is skin-deep; a few petunias along Pennsylvania Avenue are hardly harbingers of a design renaissance. People are not suddenly going to wake up and demand a better environment.

It used to be said that "the views of nature held by any people determine all their institutions" (Emerson, 1950, p. 548). But it may make more sense to stand this statement on its head: our whole way of life determines our views of nature. To be effective, therefore, planning and design should be grounded on intimate knowledge of the ways people think and feel about environment; this calls for a substantial familiarity with social and intellectual history, with psychology and philosophy, with art and anthropology. All these fields contribute to our knowledge of how we see the world we live in, how vision and value affect action, and how action alters institutions.

Beyond such knowledge still other unknowns confront us. To what extent are people aware of their surroundings at all, and when and where? How much do we really see at home, on vacation, on the way to or from work, in field or factory, office or classroom? Let us try to look around wherever we are—not necessarily with close attention to form or detail, but fleetingly, musingly, dreamily, provocatively, *any* way, just as long as we see *something*. For "without vision the people perish."

REFERENCES:

Alsop, S. America the ugly. *Saturday Evening Post,* June 23, 1962, pp. 8, 10.
Banham, R. Urbanism: USA. *Architectural Review,* 1961, 130, 303–305.
Barzun, J. *God's country and mine.* Boston: Little & Brown, 1954.
Boyd, R. *The Australian ugliness.* Melbourne: Melbourne University Press, 1960.
Burnham, D. H., as quoted in C. Tunnard and H. H. Reed, *American skyline: The growth and form of our cities and towns.* Boston, 1955.
Casson, H. Critique of our expanding "Subtopia." *New York Times Magazine,* October 27, 1957.
Chinard, G. Eighteenth century theories on America as a human habitat. *Proceedings of the American Philosophical Society,* 1947, 91, 27–57.
Cowper, W. The task. Book i, The sofa. In *Poems.* London, 1814, Vol. 2.
Crevecoeur, M-G. S. *Journey into Northern Pennsylvania and the State of New York* (in French, 1801, translated by Clarissa Spencer Bostelmann). Ann Arbor, Mich., 1964.
Dangerfield, G. The way West: A review of Daniel Boorstin's *The Americans. New York Times Book Review,* October 31, 1965, pp. 24, 26.
Dickens, C. *American notes, and pictures from Italy* (1842 and 1846). London, New York, Toronto: Oxford University Press, 1957.
Ellis, H. F. A walk in Massachusetts. *New Yorker,* July 2, 1960, pp. 22–24.
Emerson, R. W. English traits (1856). In *The selected writings of Ralph Waldo Emerson.* New York: Modern Library T14, 1950. Pp. 523–690.
Freneau, P., & Brackenridge, H. H. The rising glory of America, as quoted in H. N. Smith, *Virgin land.* New York: Vintage Books, 1957.
Gowans, A. *Images of American living.* Philadelphia and New York: Lippincott, 1964.
Grund, F. J. *The Americans in their moral, social, and political relations.* Vol. 2. London: Longman, 1837. Pp. 263–264.
Hamburger, P. *An American notebook.* New York: Knopf, 1965.
Heimert, A. Puritanism, the wilderness, and the frontier. *New England Quarterly,* 1953, 26, 361–382.
Hersey, J. *The Marmot drive.* New York: Popular Library, 1953.
Hosmer, C. B., Jr. *Presence of the past.* New York: Putnam, 1965. P. 141.
Jackson, J. B. Notes and comments. *Landscape,* 1963–1964, 13, 1–3.
James, H. *The American scene.* New York and London: Harper, 1907.
James, H. *The American scene.* Edited by W. H. Auden. New York, 1946.
James, W. On a certain blindness in human beings. In *Talks to teachers on psychology: And to students on some of life's ideals.* 1899. (Republished: New York; The Norton Library, 1958. Pp. 149–169.)

Jefferson, T. *Notes on the State of Virginia* (1787). Ed. by W. Peden. Chapel Hill, N.C.: University of North Carolina Press, 1955.

Jellicoe, G. A. *Studies in landscape design.* Vol. 2. London, New York, Toronto: Oxford University Press, 1966.

Jones, H. M. *O strange new world.* New York: Viking Press, 1964.

Kahn, E. J., Jr. The Hudson River. *Holiday,* 1966, **40**, 40–55, 83–89.

Kouwenhoven, J. A. What's "American" about America. In *The beer can by the highway.* Garden City, N.Y., 1961. Pp. 39–73.

Kurnberfer, F. Der Amerika-müde (1855), as quoted in D. A. Dondore, *The prairie and the making of Middle America: Four centuries of description.* Cedar Rapids, Iowa: Torch Press, 1926.

Le Corbusier, C-E. *When the cathedrals were white* (translated by Francis E. Hyslop, Jr.). New York, London, Toronto: McGraw-Hill Paperbacks, 1964.

Lévi-Strauss, C. *Tristes tropiques* (translated by John Russell). New York: Criterion Book, 1961.

Locke, J. Essay concerning the true original extent and end of civil government. In *Two treatises of government* (1690). London: Everyman, 1924.

Lowenthal, D. *George Perkins Marsh: Versatile Vermonter.* New York: Columbia University Press, 1958.

Lowenthal, D. Not every prospect pleases: What is our criterion for scenic beauty? *Landscape,* 1962–1963, **12**, 19–23.

Lowenthal, D. Is wilderness "Paradise Enow"? Images of nature in America. *Columbia University Forum,* 1964, **7**, 34–40.

Lowenthal, D. The American way of history. *Columbia University Forum,* 1966, **9**, 27–32.

Lowenthal, D., & Prince, H. C. English landscape tastes. *Geographical Review,* 1965, **55**, 186–222.

Marx, L. *The machine in the garden.* London: Oxford University Press, 1964.

McCoubrey, J. W. *American tradition in painting.* New York: George Braziller, 1963.

Michener, C. T. Why would anyone want to live in Tacoma? *Seattle,* 1966, **3**, 18–25, 46–47.

Miller, P. *The life of the mind in America.* New York: Harcourt, Brace & World, 1965.

Morris, J. *Coast to coast.* New York: Simon & Schuster, 1962.

Morris, L. Remaking America: The lake makers. *Holiday,* 1946, **1**, 46–48.

Nairn, I. *The American landscape.* New York: Random House, 1965.

New scene at Disneyland simulates New Orleans. *New York Times,* July 26, 1966.

Nuttall, T. A journal of travels into the Arkansas Territory during the year 1819 (Philadelphia, 1821). In R. G. Thwaites (Ed.), *Early Western travels 1748–1846.* Vol. 13. New York: AMS Press, 1905.

Only tour in Key West that will take you to the following points of interest. *New Yorker,* May 29, 1965.

Pritchett, V. S. Second steps. *New Statesman,* July 30, 1965, pp. 155–156.

Pushkarev, B. Scale and design in a new environment. In *Who Designs America?* (Ed. by L. B. Holland). Garden City, N.Y.: Anchor Original, 1966. Pp. 86–119.

Rand, C. L. A., the ultimate city: I. upward and outward. *New Yorker,* October 1, 1966, pp. 56–65+.

Rölvaag, O. E. *Giants in the earth* (1927) (translated by Lincoln Colcord and O. E. Rölvaag). New York, Evanston, London: Perennial Library, 1965.

Sartre, J-P. New York, the colonial city. In *Literary and Philosophical Essays* (translated by Annette Michelson). New York: Philosophical Library, 1957. Pp. 118–124.

Schroeder, F. E. H. Andrew Wyeth and the transcendental tradition. *American Quarterly,* 1965, **17**, 559–567.

Seddon, G. Hurricane view of U. S. London: *Observer,* November 18, 1962.

Shepheard, P. A Philadelphia Enquirer. *Listener,* May 9, 1963, 787–789.

Simonds, J. O. *Landscape architecture: The shaping of man's natural environment.* New York: McGraw-Hill, 1961.

Stein, G. *The geographical history of America.* New York: Random House, 1936.

Tocqueville, A. de. *Democracy in America* (in French, 1835–1840). Vol. 2 (translated by Henry Reeve, revised by Francis Bowen, ed. by Phillips Bradley). New York: Vintage Books, 1956–1957.

Twain, M. *Life on the Mississippi* (1875). New York and London: Harper, 1929.

The American Outdoors, *U. S. Forest Service Miscellaneous Publication No. 1000.* Washington, D.C., 1965.

Van Doren, M. *Travels of William Bartram* (1791). New York: Dover Publications, n.d., Pp. 292–293.

Ward, J. W. The politics of design. In L. B. Holland (Ed.), *Who designs America?* Garden City, N.Y.: Anchor Original, 1966. Pp. 51–85.

Whitehill, W. M. Promoted to glory. . . . In *With heritage so rich: A report of a special committee on historic preservation. . . .* New York, 1966. Pp. 35–44.

Whyte, W. H. The politics of open space. In A. J. W. Sheffey (Ed.), *Resources, the metropolis, and the landgrant university: Proceedings of the Conference on Natural Resources,* University of Massachusetts, January–May 1963. University of Massachusetts, College of Agriculture, Cooperative Extension Service, Publ. **410**, n.d., pp. 22–27.

Wigglesworth, M. God's controversy with New-England (1662). *Proceedings of the Massachusetts Historical Society,* 1871–1873.

Wolfe, M. R. *Towns, time, and regionalism.* Seattle: University of Washington, Dept. of Urban Planning, Urban Planning and Development Series, 1963.

Wright, A. T. *Islandia.* New York and Toronto: New American Library, 1958.

31 User Concepts of Wilderness and Their Implications for Resource Management

Robert C. Lucas

USER CONCEPTS OF WILDERNESS

The view of resources as physically defined entities has been effectively criticized, and in its place a view of resources as objects culturally perceived as useful has been advanced (see Zimmerman, 1951).

This view has now been widely accepted, but, for many topics, its use has not involved much change in research methods. Most often the use of the cultural perception concept has only involved recognizing technology's role in redefining resources—uranium, taconite, aspen pulpwood, and so on. However, the impact of a culturally defined concept of resources on the study of recreational resources is more substantial. Recreational resources can scarcely be studied except in perceptual terms. This is particularly true of a resource so elusive and subjective as wilderness.

What is a recreational resource and, particularly, what is wilderness? Planners, researchers, legislators, and administrators have struggled with these questions. They have made assumptions, often unconsciously, about user concepts and perceptions as they have defined resources. Their definitions aim at objectivity and permanency, and yet most of our ideas about scenery and wilderness are young and changeable.

A little over a century ago concepts of wilderness and scenery were nearly the opposite of today's (Lowenthal, 1962). The New England wilderness was described as hideous and desolate (Nash, 1963). Mountains and wild landscapes were detested,

and Niagara Falls was called "hideous, outrageous, terrible" (Huth, 1957). The attractive landscapes were soft, fertile lands, improved by human husbandry—in Europe especially those with ancient historical associations (Lowenthal, 1962). Gardens were formal—geometric and architectural. The French Voyageurs in the 18th century called part of the present Minnesota-Ontario border "le beau pays"—the beautiful country. But "le beau pays" was not the modern rocky canoe country. It was farther west, part of a glacial lake plain, level, often open, and reminiscent of farmland (Olson, 1963).

Changing religious, philosophical, and scientific ideas, and perhaps also changes in the appearance of the humanized landscape influenced this reversal. The reversal is so complete now that when I asked one of my university classes which landscape they preferred—rolling southern Minnesota farmland or Wyoming's Grand Tetons—they laughed.

The view of wilderness as a resource in its own right, rather than as land to be developed, was probably also tied to the "closing of the frontier" and ideas, such as historian Frederick Jackson Turner's, that the frontier had shaped American character. Increasing urbanization likely also contributed to the re-evaluation of the wilderness. More and more city people were cut off from former contacts with the land, and may have felt a loss of continuity and security.

Among the first appeals for public action to set aside wilderness was one made by George Catlin, the painter of Indians, in 1833; another by Thoreau followed shortly thereafter (Huth, 1957). George Perkins Marsh made a similar plea later (Marsh, 1882). The first park reservations, Yosemite and Yellowstone, probably owe much to these ideas. The act establishing Yellowstone stated that the Secretary of Interior should "Provide for the preservation from injury or spoilation, of all timber, mineral deposits, natural curiosities, or wonders within said park, and their retention in their natural condition." This seems to contain the germ of the wilderness idea, but not unequivocally. There is no indication that these parks were to have large roadless areas, in particular.

The Adirondack Forest Preserve in New York was established and the words "forever wild" were applied to it in law in 1885, but the original purpose was more to prevent timber exploitation than to preserve wilderness as a positive good (Thompson, 1963).

Specific wilderness reservations seem only about a generation old. Aldo Leopold, Arthur Carhart, and Robert Marshall all had a hand in the designation of national forest wilderness areas. Three areas were established in the 1920s, but almost all of the present wilderness came with a rush in the 1930s. Now there are over 80 areas and close to 15 million acres, most in the West. Regulations have shifted and numerous wilderness bills seek to further formalize the wilderness, especially in national forests and national parks.

AN EXAMPLE OF USER CONCEPTS

All of the national forest wilderness is defined by a line on a map. But does this correspond to what the public sees as "the wilderness?" And what is the visitors' "wilderness" like?

The answers to these questions were sought by the Lake States Forest Experiment Station in a study of the Quetico-Superior Area in 1960–61.[1] Half of the Quetico-Superior is in Minnesota—the Boundary Waters Canoe Area of the Superior National Forest. This is the only large Forest Service wilderness-type area in the eastern half of the country. The other half is in Ontario-Quetico Provincial Park. Together they form a rocky, rolling, lake-studded forest land about as big as Yellowstone National Park—3,000 square miles. It is often called simply, "the canoe country," but motorboat travel is almost as common as canoeing.

Besides its almost unique eastern location, the Quetico-Superior is unique in combining logging and primitive recreation. All of Quetico Park and two-thirds of the Boundary Waters Canoe Area are open to timber

harvest except in zones around lakes, streams, and portage trails. Because of limited markets there is very little cutting in Quetico, but about 15 percent of the Boundary Waters Canoe Area has been logged or timber contracted for cutting since 1945.

The total Quetico-Superior study concerned itself with use distribution estimates, use projections, and recreational carrying capacity in an aesthetic, rather than physical, sense. As part of the carrying capacity investigation, the visitors' perception of wilderness was investigated.

Three aspects of wilderness perception were studied: the importance of the area's wilderness qualities as an attraction, the area considered wilderness, and the amounts and types of use considered appropriate in the wilderness. Almost 300 groups of visitors of all types were interviewed. The sample was randomly distributed across the area and throughout the summer season.

We found great differences in wilderness views. Groups differed on all three aspects studied. However, the variation was greatly reduced when visitors were classified on the basis of the type of recreation they were engaging in. People come to the area in substantial numbers to take canoe trips, stay in the resorts or summer cabins (most are just outside the area and the few inside are being removed), camp in roadside campgrounds around the designated area, or travel by boat and camp on the waterways. The major division, though, was between the canoeists and the others, almost all of whom used motorboats. This does not mean that type of recreation caused differences in perception. The type of recreation chosen stands rather as a fairly good summary expression of a cluster of motives and abilities —which in turn have been substantially influenced in many ways.

Wilderness was most important as an attraction for canoeists (Table 31-1). Sample groups were asked, "Does this area (defined on a map) have some characteristics which caused you to come here rather than some other vacation region?" All answers were remote" were classified as wilderness qualities. This is not a direct measure of appeal, but it is thought to serve as an index of wilderness' relative importance to visitors.

---

[1] This section of the study is reported in considerable detail in a forthcoming publication by the Lake States Forest Experiment Station, *The Recreational Capacity of the Quetico-Superior.*

Table 31-1 Percent of Parties Citing Wilderness Qualities as a Basis for Choice of the Area

Type of recreationist	Number of sample groups	Percent citing wilderness qualities
CANOEISTS:	84	71
Paddlers	63	75 .
Motorized	21	62
OTHERS:	196	40
Auto campers	86	49
Boat campers	23	35
Resort guests	57	39
Private cabin users	21	10
Day use	9	33

The differences between types were significant at the .005 level tested by chi-square.

Canoeists, especially those not using outboard motors, cited some wilderness quality about twice as often as most other types of visitors. Car campers were next highest in their interest in wilderness. It may be significant that only half of the car campers used boats, compared to almost 100 percent of the other types.

The canoeists saw a much smaller area as wilderness than did other types of visitors (Figure 31-1). All sample groups were asked first where they had been (most interviews were with parties just completing their visits, and all were near the end of the stay). Later they were asked, "Do you feel that you are in 'the wilderness' now? Where did members of your group feel 'the wilderness' began?" The question seemed to be accepted as reasonable and relevant almost without exception—there were no "don't know" answers. Wilderness was not defined, and respondents did not ask for definitions. Answers ranged from a few "never reached the wilderness" replies to a few who placed wilderness gateways in central Minnesota, over 100 miles back down the road. The information on areas visited by sample groups was combined with their wilderness threshold to produce a "wilderness vote" for each area (lake, stretch of river, or section of highway). These "votes," or wilder-recorded and adjectives such as "primitive, uncivilized, rugged, wild, uncommercialized, ness/nonwilderness classifications, were aggregated for each area. There were 48 ratings for the most-used lake, and only one for many lightly used places. The aggre-

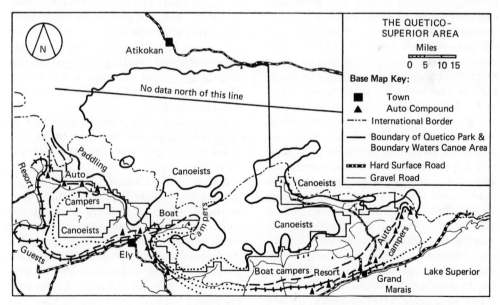

Figure 31–1. The area considered wilderness by at least 50 percent of the visitors in each of the four major user types. The area in the interior—that is, away from the roads and generally to the north of the line for each user type—was rated as "wilderness" by 50 to 100 percent of the visitors of that type reaching the area. The dotted portions of the lines indicate data were lacking, and subjective estimates have been made, based on 1960 data.

gated votes were then mapped for each major type of use.

The area considered wilderness by the paddling canoeists was smaller than the established area in Minnesota. This was true even for the area only 10 percent classed as wilderness. Only one small area outside the canoe area was included, although a substantial area outside Quetico Park was in-. cluded.

Sufficient data were available for maps of three other user types—auto campers,.. boat campers, and resort guests. All three maps were essentially the same. These visitors—largely motorboaters—saw a large wilderness, including about as much land around the canoe area as the canoe area itself (Figure 31-1).

What are the characteristics of these dif-. fering wildernesses? In general, canoeists, were more sensitive to other uses and to .. developments than boaters. The canoeists excluded roads, but the boaters did not. These roads varied in standards; many sections were narrow, winding, hilly, and gravelled. A very few were the same but asphalt paved, and some were paved, 50-mile-an-hour roads but with billboards and developments very limited. Boaters usually excluded the small towns and felt the wilderness began a few miles down the road. All sorts of roads seemed included in the boaters' wilderness, although a substantial number mentioned "the end of the blacktop" as the beginning of their wilderness and a little over half objected to straightening and paving roads when directly asked.

Recreational use seemed particularly important in influencing the canoeists' wilderness image. Heavily used areas were much less often considered wilderness. The most heavily used lake (over half of all canoeists started their trips there) was classed as nonwilderness by all 23 canoeist groups sampled there. The Spearman rank correlation coefficient between season-long use for each area and percent of paddling groups considering that area wilderness was −0.42. Parties were asked if they had been bothered by crowding on the waterways; 34 percent of the canoeists said, "Yes."

Boaters tolerated much heavier use. Only 8 percent reported that they were bothered by crowding on the water, but wilderness perception still dwindled with increasing visitors. The rank correlation of use and wilderness ratings for boaters was −0.37.

The type of use encountered was critical for canoeists but much less so for boaters. Canoeists felt strongly that motorboats were inappropriate in a wilderness. Almost two-thirds reported that they disliked meeting boats. Perhaps even more revealing, the canoeists' wilderness ratings for lakes with comparable total numbers of visitors were two or three times as high where boats were absent. Boaters actually preferred meeting canoeists to fellow motorboaters, but the difference was not great.

Remoteness—distance from the access point or end of the road—did not have any apparent effect on wilderness perception. This was contrary to expectations. Lakes were grouped as follows: first lakes reached from accesses, second, third, fourth, and fifth. Light use was associated with just as high a wilderness vote on first or second lakes as on fourth or fifth. Rank order correlation coefficients of use and wilderness rating were not significantly different for the five classes of remoteness.

The unique logging (the only important commodity use) seemed less detracting than heavy or inappropriate recreational use. There was little awareness of timber cutting in the area. In total, about 12 percent of the visitors reported noticing evidence of logging in or around the area. Some of this observation was logging truck traffic outside the area's boundaries. About 4 percent objected to what they saw—or one-third of those noticing cutting. But much of the area is not being logged now, and use is heaviest away from logging areas. It is possible use is light because of logging, but most people did not know there was any cutting. Furthermore unlogged southern parts of the canoe area were lightly used as was the south central logged area (use showed a strong northward orientation). Groups sampled near logging had noticed it in 46 percent of the cases, and 13 percent (less than one-third) found it objectionable. Canoeists observed logging less often than boaters, but found it more objectionable (about half of those encountering logging disliked it).

In summary, it appears that visitors do have rather clear wilderness perceptions, that variation in perception is large, but that much variation is associated with type of recreation chosen.

A similar study was made in Ontario's Algonquin Provincial Park in 1963 (Priddle). Algonquin is also a large lakeland reservation but is more heavily used, both for recreation and timber, than the Quetico-Superior. Canoeists and boaters differed in the same general ways, and wilderness ratings were lower, as would be expected from the heavier use. The parallel findings bolster confidence in the validity of the approach.

IMPLICATIONS FOR RESOURCE MANAGEMENT

User concepts alone are not a prescription for resource management. The analogy to the drawbacks in letting stockmen set their own grazing quotas on public lands has been pointed out (Burton & Kates, 1964). In fact, it would be impossible to give every recreationist what he says he wants at every time and place. Some desires conflict. Some wishes, if met now, would affect the resource so that the wishes could not be met in the future. Some people may want technically impossible conditions, such as continuous sunshine. Outdoor recreation is not a free good, obviously, and its allocation is an economic problem in the broadest sense of the term.

User concepts are an essential part of recreation resource management, however. To play this role, user concepts need to be interpreted in the light of long-term goals, other demands, and feasibility or costs. The identification and definition of desirable outdoor recreation settings are where the sort of user concepts I have illustrated become most useful. If it is assumed that the goal of recreation resource management is to provide a range of opportunities among which people may choose as freely as possible, then there are other pieces in the puzzle. Information is needed on relative demand for and value of different opportunities now and in the future. With knowledge of demand and user concepts of desirable resource—size of area, and type and intensity of recreational and nonrecreational use, in particular—needs could be established and weighed against other demands for the same

resources. In this sort of over-all resource allocation, other approaches seem needed, but user concepts of resources and, specifically, wilderness may be useful in allocation of resources between competing forms of recreation, and in assessing possibilities of integrating some nonrecreational uses.

The findings reported for the Quetico-Superior and generally confirmed in Algonquin Park imply that wilderness is not just one segment of this range of opportunities. There are different wildernesses. The dichotomy, which the various wilderness bills would perpetuate, between wilderness in one class and all other land in another class, may be unfortunate. A variety of wilderness recreation settings, in terms of ease of access and facilities, degree of restriction of nonrecreational uses, and limits on type and amount of recreational use, seems to be implied.

This does not necessarily mean the present wilderness areas should be converted into various sorts of semiwilderness. The maintenance of variety would seem to include a need for relatively undisturbed wilderness at one end of the range, and reducing this area seems dubious in view of projections of demand for wilderness-type recreation. All the evidence seems to point toward a greater relative growth in wilderness recreation than for recreation in general. The early projections by Marion Clawson imply this in the much higher projected increases in demand for resource-based areas (Clawson, 1959). The projections made for ORRRC (Outdoor Recreation Resources Review Commission) show wilderness use increasing more than eightfold by the year 2000 compared to less than a threefold increase for all outdoor recreation and a fourfold growth for camping in general.[2] (These projects are from different ORRRC study reports using somewhat different projection methods, and comparabil-

[2] Wilderness use projections are from University of California Wildland Research Center, *Wilderness and Recreation—A Report on Resources, Values, and Problems* (Outdoor Recreation Resources Review Commission Study Report 3), Washington, D.C., 1962, p. 236. Other projections are from Outdoor Recreation Resources Review Commission, *Outdoor Recreation for America*, Washington, D.C., 1962, pp. 46, 220.

ity is not complete.) Official Forest Service use estimates from 1946 to 1963 also showed wilderness use climbing most rapidly —in terms of man-days, the best measure of use, twice as fast as all other recreational use.[3]

If these trends and projections have any validity, and if there are truly "diminishing returns" in increasing use of the wilderness, as the data seem to show, a serious problem lies ahead. Rationing recreational use, accepting lower quality experiences, or expanding wilderness would be possible responses, singly or in many combinations.

User wilderness concepts are relevant to all three possible responses. User concepts make possible evaluation of rationing recreational use in terms of at least some measure of its effect on the quality of the use. Expansion might be considered, at least in part, in terms of adding various types of semiwilderness. This is probably much more feasible than establishing more strictly wilderness areas, and might actually produce more satisfaction for more people at less cost to society.

Some of the semiwilderness might serve as a buffer zone for existing wilderness. If some types of users are less attracted by wilderness, as is true of motorboaters in the canoe area, and if these groups also see a large wilderness outside the heart of the wild country, it might be possible to provide what they are seeking in an outer zone of semiwilderness, and exclude them from stricter wilderness. This sort of separation could reduce conflict between incompatible uses, increase wilderness core capacity, and thus reduce the need for rationing use. In fact, for the less demanding visitors (boaters in the canoe area), who accept heavier use, rationing in the buffer zone might be avoided for a long time.

Other semiwilderness might be based on the recognition that escape from mechanized recreation and crowds of people is more important in some users' concepts of wilder-

ness than are pre-Columbian ecological conditions, and could be zoned for primitive recreation while allowing some logging, grazing, and dams.

There may be considerable scope for improving the integration of commodity uses and primitive recreation in both kinds of semiwilderness. Logging is probably most critical. Screening and scheduling cutting could probably reduce exposure to logging greatly, and education might reduce the reaction to exposure. New logging technology might also reduce the prominence of cuttings on the landscape. Helicopters could eliminate or reduce roads, for example. Slash could be chipped. Cutting could also be modified to increase recreational benefits. For example, in some forest types a proportion of trees that would normally be harvested might be left to soften the scene, and clear-cut blocks might be smaller or more irregularly shaped than is usual. All of these modifications carry costs, but they would probably cost less than foregoing all commodity uses and they might increase total recreational returns substantially. Do we have the ingenuity to really explore the possibilities of this sort of multiple use?

The idea of various classes of wilderness and semiwilderness is not new. Robert Marshall, the founder of the Wilderness Society, proposed two classes of land—primeval and wilderness—in 1933 (Marshall, 1933). What he called "wilderness" would have provided an opportunity for primitive unmechanized recreation, but this land also would have been carefully logged, grazed, and so on. Semiwilderness, in addition to wilderness, has been suggested more recently by the Outdoor Recreation Resources Review Commission, the University of California Research Center in the ORRRC Study Report dealing with wilderness, and by Arthur Carhart (1961) in a recreational land use planning monograph.

What may be at least partly new is empirical support for an old idea. Also, the study of user perception of wilderness may provide a new approach to implementing wilderness variety.

Putting the idea of varied wilderness into practice effectively, however, would require

[3] Wilderness man-days increased from 406,000 in 1946 to 2,751,900 in 1963—a 578 percent increase. Total man-days use of all other national forest areas grew from 33,200,000 to 123,750,000 in the same period—a 272 percent increase.

more knowledge than we now have. More understanding would be needed in the Quetico-Superior to define boundaries between zones and set use and development standards for the zones. The relation of recreational use to wilderness quality should be defined, and I believe it could be. Other areas with differing landscapes and types of use would need new research, but the same framework may apply. The paddling purist in the canoe country may be comparable to the backpacker in the mountains. The pack-string hunter may be somewhat comparable to the motor canoe fisherman, and the jeep and scooter driver to the boat camper. There probably are some important differences, also. Possible routes of travel may be more concentrated, and more distant areas visible, than on the Canadian Shield.

Greater diversity in wilderness management will demand a good deal of planning and administrative effort, but maintaining the status quo may lead to even more complicated problems.

REFERENCES:

Burton, I., & Kates, R. W. Symposium: Perception and natural resources, Foreword. *Natural Resources Journal*, 1964, **3**, 378.

Carhart, A. H. *Planning for America's wildlands*. 1961.

Clawson, M. The crisis in outdoor recreation. *American Forests*, March and April, 1959.

Huth, H. Nature and the American. Berkeley, Calif.: University of California Press, 1957.

Lowenthal, D. Not every prospect pleases— What is our criterion for scenic beauty? *Landscape*, 1962–1963, **12**, 19–23.

Marsh, G. P. *The earth as modified by human action*. New York: Scribners, 1882.

Nash, R. W. The American wilderness in historical perspective. *Forest History*, 1963, **6**, 3.

Olson, S. F. *Runes of the north*. New York: Knopf, 1963.

Outdoor Recreation Resources Review Commission. *Outdoor recreation for America*. Washington, D.C., 1962.

Priddle, G. Unpublished master's thesis. Clark University, Worcester, Mass., 1963.

Thompson, R. C. Politics in the wilderness: New York's Adirondack Forest Preserve. *Forest History*, 1963, **6**, 14–23.

University of California Wildland Research Center, *Wilderness and recreation—A report on resources, values, and problems*. Outdoor Recreation Resources Review Commission Study Report 3, Washington, D.C., 1962.

Zimmermann, E. W. *World resources and industries*. New York: Harper, 1951.

32 Life Styles and Urban Space

Anselm Strauss

The spatial complexity and the social diversity of any city are linked in exceedingly subtle ways. An examination of such connections will force confrontation of a very thorny problem: how are the various urban social worlds related to specified spaces, areas, and streets of a city?

Technical sociological interest in this kind of inquiry dates back to the studies of Robert Park (1925) and "the Chicago school" of urban research. Chicago's ethnic diversity was so striking, and the spatial dispersal of these populations over the face of the city was so marked, that the Chicago sociologists evolved a series of studies of ethnic (and other) worlds located in urban space. They invented a corresponding set of terms to link space and social structure.[1] The point was, as Park said, that "In the course of time every section and quarter of the city takes on something of the character and qualities of its inhabitants. Each separate part of the city is inevitably stained with the peculiar sentiments of its population."

This kind of sociological inquiry had its roots in two kinds of tradition: one was scientific—the biological study of ecological communities; the other was popular—the colorful journalistic accounts of urban social worlds. (Park himself had been a journalist before he became a professor.) Journalistic exploration of the city, as presented in full-length book form, goes back at least to mid-nineteenth century, somewhat before the full tide of urban reform. Reform itself brought countless investigations of the less palatable

Reprinted with permission of The Macmillan Company from *Images of the American Life*, by Anselm Strauss. © The Free Press, a Corporation, 1961.

[1] "Natural area" was one such concept: "Natural areas" were areas produced without planning by the natural course of laying down railroads, parks, boulevards, and by the topographical features of the city. Communities often tended to be coterminous with the boundaries of natural areas (see Park, 1925).

aspects of metropolitan life, some of these rather more accurate and less luridly written than contemporary journalistic descriptions which sagacious publishers continued to offer a public hungry for images of how the other halves lived (see Browne, 1869; Campbell, Knox, and Brynes, 1895; McCabe, 1868, 1881; Smith, 1868). The reader comfortably sitting at home peered into the hovels of the poor, rubbed elbows with the rich, and was fleeced by the professionally wicked. He imaginatively walked streets he would never dream of frequenting, visiting places he would otherwise shrink from visiting, and listened to the speech of vulgar and uncouth persons whose actual company would have caused him untold embarrassment.

What the sociologists later did was not so much to add accuracy, and certainly not color, to the reformer's and journalist's accounts as to study more systematically the "cultures" of particular urban communities and to relate the communities to the spatial structure of the entire metropolis. Later they became especially interested in the spatial distribution and social organization of social classes, particularly in our smaller cities.

Some of this sociological research is related to our specific interest in the spatial representations of urban populations. First, we shall observe certain aspects of several studies in order to find modes of analyzing and ordering the spatial representations of the respective urban communities. The major ordering principle to be utilized will be the city themes characteristically found in novels about urban life.

One of the persistent themes of these novels has been the search for some viable metropolitan existence by migrants with rural or small town backgrounds. Many ethnic communities formerly found in our great cities were composed of men and women drawn from the villages and farms of Europe. In some instances, emigrants from the same village clustered along a single American street, seeking somehow to reconstitute at least the non-physical aspects of village life. Among the most intriguing sociological descriptions of such an ethnic community is one by Christen Jonassen (1949). A summary description of the Nor-

wegians of New York City will serve to illustrate a subtle rural symbolism of space.

The Norwegians who settled in New York City after 1830 came mainly from the coastal districts of Norway. That country remained unindustrialized during the last century, and even today it is among the least densely settled of Western nations. According to Jonassen, the Norwegians are "for the most part nature lovers and like green things and plenty of space about them" (Jonassen, 1949, p. 34). The original immigrants settled in such an area near the ship docks, although for occupational, as well as for "nature loving" motives. Over the decades the Norwegian colony clung to the shoreline, but gradually moved down it as deterioration set in and as invaders of lower status arrived on the scene. Jonassen believes that the continuous gradual retreat of the colony to contiguous areas was possible as long as land suiting their rural values remained available. Recently the colony has been driven into a spatial and symbolic box, its back to the ocean, for there is no further contiguous land to which to move. For this reason, Norwegians have begun to make the kind of jumps to non-contiguous areas so characteristic of other immigrant groups. Norwegians are now moving to sites that still retain some rural atmosphere (Staten Island and certain places in New Jersey and Connecticut). Among the newspaper excerpts which Jonassen quotes are two which help to illustrate his contention that the Norwegians symbolize their residential districts in rural terms (Jonassen, 1949, pp. 40–41). One man writes:

> I arrived in America in 1923, eight years old. I went right to Staten Island because my father lived there and he was a shipbuilder at Elco Boats in Bayonne, New Jersey, right over the bridge. I started to work with my father and I am now foreman at the shipyard where we are now building small yachts. . . . I seldom go to New York because I don't like large cities with stone and concrete. Here are trees and open places.

Another Norwegian declares:

> I like it here [Staten Island] because it reminds me of Norway. Of course, not

Bergen, because we have neither Floyen nor Ulrik nor mountains on Staten Island, but it is so nice and green all over the summer. I have many friends in Bay Ridge in Brooklyn, and I like to take trips there, but to tell the truth when I get on the ferry on the way home and get the smell of Staten Island, I think it's glorious.

This representation of land, redolent with rural memories, is no doubt paralleled by the spatial representations of other rural migrants to large urban centers. Polish citizens of our cities live—quite literally—in local parishes, whether their protestant neighbors recognize this or not. In some instances the parish was settled as a village, set down near a railroad yard or a factory. Although the expanding metropolis has caught up and surrounded the parish, the invisible village still exists for at least the older of its inhabitants.

Another persistent theme found in novels about city life is that cities are conducive to personal demoralization and are characterized by the destructive impersonality of their relationships: cities are sites, in a word, that are characteristically inhabited by anomic people. In the novels, these people are ex-rural people. During the 1920's, Harvey Zorbaugh described one area of Chicago, many of whose residents subscribed to this view of the city (see Zorbaugh, 1929, pp. 69–86; Firey, 1947, pp. 290–322). The area was one of furnished rooms in houses long abandoned by their former well-to-do owners. Zorbaugh described the residents of these rooms as 52 percent single men, 10 percent women, "and 38 percent are couples, 'married,' supposedly with 'benefit of clergy.' The rooming-house area is a childless area. Yet most of its population is . . . between twenty and thirty-five." This population was tremendously mobile: a turnover took only four months. Characteristically, the rooming house was "a place of anonymous relationships. One knows no one, and is known by no one. One comes and goes as one wishes, does very much as one pleases, and as long as one disturbs no one else, no questions are asked." (Zorbaugh gives documents showing how great this anonymity can be.) The depths of loneliness experienced by some are illustrated by the experiences of a girl from William Allen White's home-town of Emporia, Kansas, who after some months in this area

began to look at my life in Chicago. What was there in it, after all. My music was gone. I had neither family nor friends. In Emporia there would at least have been neighborhood clubs or the church. But here there was neither. Oh, for someone or something to belong to!

She belonged to no groups. People treated her "impersonally . . . not a human touch at all." Bitterly, she remarks that: "The city is like that. In all my work there had been the same lack of personal touch. In all this city of three million souls I knew no one, cared for no one, was cared for by no one." Another resident of the area reported that he was so totally alone that "there were evenings when I went out of my way to buy a paper, or an article at a drug store— just for the sake of talking a few minutes with someone." In the heart of the rooming house area there was a bridge over a lagoon, which became known as "Suicide Bridge," because so many of these people had used it as a way out of their anguish. Although not all the residents of such an urban area are lonely and demoralized, or have a corresponding perspective on city life, it seems reasonable to hypothesize that this kind of perspective would be found there with great frequency. It would be found with much less frequency in many other urban areas. These anomic urbanites, we may suppose, have little knowledge of other sectors of the city (except downtown), and must believe that all of the city and its people are much like the city and the people that they have already encountered.

It seems unnecessary to say much about the opposite of anomie: the creative use of privacy. People who seek escape from the confines of their small towns or from their equally oppressive urban families have traditionally flocked to those sections of cities known as "villages," "towertowns," "near North Sides," and other bohemian and quasi-bohemian areas. Here are found the people who wish privileged privacy: prostitutes, homosexuals, touts, criminals, as well as artists, café society, devotées of the arts, illicit lovers—anybody and everybody who is eager to keep the small-town qualities of the metropolis at a long arm's length. (Some smaller cities, of course, do not have such a bohemian section; see Ware, 1935; Zorbaugh, 1929, pp. 87–104.) The inhabitants do not necessarily intend to live here forever; the area is used by many who plan to settle down later in more conventional areas when they will then engage in more generally socially approved pursuits: "There's at least a year in everybody's life when he wants to do just as he damn pleases. The 'village' is the only place where he can do it without sneaking off in a hole by himself" (Zorbaugh, 1929, p. 99).

Closely related to the urban perspective of privileged privacy is, of course, the view that the city is a place to be enjoyed; and many of the residents of these urban areas are there because they believe that enjoyment and excitement are most easily obtained there. Other city dwellers may visit an area for temporary enjoyment and temporary privacy; the more or less permanent residents of the area merely want or need more of these qualities, or are perhaps wiser about how to get them.

Sociological studies of other urban communities likewise lend themselves to plausible interpretation of what may be the predominant spatial representations held by inhabitants of those communities. Walter Firey's study of Beacon Hill in Boston, for instance, demonstrates how deep an allegiance the Hill's upper class inhabitants may feel for that locale, an allegiance based upon immense respect for family inheritance and tradition, all intertwined with class pride. As one lady expressed it, "Here as nowhere else in Boston has the community spirit developed, which opens itself to the best in the new, while fostering with determination all that is fine and worth keeping in the old" (Firey, 1947, p. 121). Firey describes how close to the residences of the rich cluster the apartments and rooms of bohemian groups, a conjunction frequently found. Here they could "enjoy the 'cultural atmosphere' of Beacon Hill as well as the *demi-monde* bohemian flavor of the north slope." Beacon Hill, however, was at one

time in danger of a bit too many of these exotic groups, and so in further remarks of the lady already quoted we may hear a note of querulous warning:

> Beacon Hill is not and never can be temperamental, and those seeking to find or create there a second Greenwich Village will meet with obstacles in the shape of an old residence aristocracy whose ancestors have had their entries and exits through those charming old doorways for generations. . . . Those who dwell there [are] drawn together for self-defense.

The point of view of invading, but more conventional, upwardly mobile groups is given us by other sociological researches that supplement the information yielded by countless novels. The predominant meanings of the terrain for such populations are fairly self-evident: they are well illustrated by an apocryphal story about a university professor who had moved into an elite neighborhood perched atop one of the city's prominent hills. He was able to purchase a house a bit below the top. His investment was much more than financial. But the continual surge of populations to the city's outer rim is in some part an effort to find "nicer" parts of the city to live in; and a fair number of sociological researches have managed to trace the movements of various ethnic groups across the city, as their members moved upward on the social scale. Sometimes those groups that are impinged upon regard the invaders as a nuisance and sometimes as a danger, especially if the invaders are colored. We have fewer studies of how the invaders feel when they are invaded or surrounded by people whom they in turn consider dangerous, but such a volume as Cayton's and Drake's *Black Metropolis* carries hints here and there that some colored people are fully as afraid of their neighbors as are the whites.[2]

---

[2] A colored student of mine once interviewed the residents of a city block, all Negro, and found a number of migrants from the South whose predominant outlook on the city was a mixture of rural animosity against the city and a view that life all around them was dangerous. Their street and home were a veritable island in a sea of threat.

Few of the studies which I have cited are focused upon the more subtle meanings of space for the city's residents; but most studies pick up something of how people symbolize, and so perceive and use, the land upon which they are quartered. The studies tell us considerably less about the meanings and uses of near and distant urban areas; neither do they sketch, except for the smaller cities, a symbolic map of the entire metropolis. The only exceptions to this statement are attempts to zone the city, from the center to the periphery, roughly by social class. Such maps would depict how the many populations symbolize the city as a whole including various of its areas, and would attempt to draw together the collective representations of the more important city areas for many populations. The data and concepts necessary for making such maps do not exist. The investigation is, I suggest, worthwhile if one assumes that symbolic representations of space are associated with the use—or avoidance of use—of space.

The city, I am suggesting, can be viewed as a complex related set of symbolized areas. Any given population will be cognizant of only a small number of these areas: most areas will lie outside of effective perception; others will be conceived in such ways that they will hardly ever be visited, and will indeed be avoided. When properly mapped, any given area will be symbolized by several populations, from just a few to dozens. The sociological studies of less complex areas more satisfactorily discover the meanings of areal space than studies of areas that are used by many populations for diverse reasons. One has only to compare what is known about simple residential areas, like ethnic or suburban communities, with the Rush Street night club rows and 43rd Street theater areas of our cities.

How can we best begin to talk about urban spaces in terms of their symbolic as well as economic and ecological functions? A language for talking about the latter has been developed by the fields of urban ecology, urban geography, and urban economics, but none has been formed for the former. Consider for instance the downtown areas of our cities. Studies of the central district make clear that this district

has two centers: one defined by the focus of lines of communication, the other by the focus of lines of transportation. With the first center is associated the merchandising of credits; with the second is associated the merchandising of consumers goods and services at retail. Which of these is to be taken as the most significant center depends upon which of the two associated functions . . . characterize the economy of the central city (Johnson, 1951, p. 483).

These economic functions are manifested on certain important streets and in certain well-known buildings in the downtown area. The downtown is par excellence an area for financial and retail service—and the latter may include cultural services performed by museums and orchestras.

Yet one has only to observe closely a special city like Washington to perceive that a very considerable area of the central city is set aside for overtly ceremonial functions. A broad green belt contains the nation's ritual sites: the monuments and memorials, the Capitol, the Library of Congress and the Archives with their priceless national manuscripts on hushed display. Boston too has its historic ceremonial areas, and so does Philadelphia (the latter city has recently sought to make its monuments more visible and to give them a more dignified and attractive visual setting).

American cities as a rule do not have the elaborate ceremonial, or symbolically tinged areas downtown that many European cities possess. Cities on the Continent often evolved from medieval towns, which meant that the town's main market nestled alongside the cathedral. In time the markets grew and became the modern business district encompassing or moving from the original central market site. The church area likewise acquired, and often retained, additional functions visibly performed in additional churches, administrative buildings, and cultural institutions. In German cities, for instance, this area is often referred to as the *altstadt* (old city), since it is often coterminous with the site of earlier settlement; and it is sometimes sentimentally called the city's heart. This ceremonial area, however, does not always occupy a space separate from the central business district. In cities like Frankfurt and Hanover, the ceremonial area does exist apart; and when those areas were destroyed by the bombing during the war, the administrative and residential buildings were rebuilt in ceremonial styles, and business structures were kept off the area. But in cities like Nuremburg and Cologne, the central business district is embedded in, or superimposed upon revered ceremonial terrain. In both cities a rich symbolism is associated with the medieval street plan of the inner city. The streets themselves are considered, in some sense, sacred, and may not, quite aside from financial considerations, be tampered with. Although the area cradled within Nuremberg's famed medieval walls was terribly bombed during the war, the entire area was rebuilt thereafter with the conscious intention of recapturing the flavor of old Nuremberg; and the height and color of the buildings in the business district which lies within the walls have been carefully controlled to maintain the illusion of an old city. In Cologne, the street plan is so sacred that planners, after the war, have experienced great frustration in trying to provide for the flow of traffic because the city's street plan may not be altered. Such a city as Essen is much more like most American cities, for it grew quickly during the late nineteenth century from a village to a modern industrial city; hence it did not have any great investment in treasured buildings or inviolable street plans. Its central district was rebuilt with relative freedom and with no obvious ceremonial features.

These European examples illustrate that symbolic functions (or "services," if one wishes to retain the language of economics) go on coterminously with economic and ecological functions. One can see the point dramatically illustrated by the relaxed people who stroll up and down Fifth Avenue in New York City during any fine evening. Then this beautiful shopping street is used as a promenade of pleasure, and window shopping is part of the enjoyment. During the day, most New Yorkers who rush across or along it are too preoccupied with other affairs to use the street for viewing and promenading, but even during the busiest hours of the day one can observe people using the street and its shops exclusively for pleasure. The significance of Fifth Avenue is not merely a matter of economics or of ecology, and its symbolic meanings, we may assume, are multitudinous.

Just as the downtown area, and even single streets, are differentiated by economic function, so we may regard them as differentiated by symbolic function. This statement has implications that are not immediately apparent. A convenient way to begin seeing these implications is to examine closely a single important downtown street. It will probably be used simultaneously by several different kinds of populations, distinguishable by dress and posture. Other kinds of people will be wholly, or to a considerable extent, missing. (These may be found on other streets; for instance, the wealthier customers and strollers will be found on upper Fifth Avenue rather than below 42nd Street.) Just as several types of economic services can be found cheek by jowl on the same street, so may there be several symbolic functions performed by the same street. A restaurant there may serve expensive food; it may also serve leisure and a sense of luxury. Close by, another type of establishment may cater to another taste, an activity not entirely reducible to economic terms. The street may attract people who seek glamour, adventure, escape from a humdrum life, and who, though they may not spend a cent, feel wholly or partly satisfied by an evening on the street. The larger the downtown area, the more obviously districted will be the various economic and symbolic functions. A city as large as Chicago, for instance, has a separate hotel row, a separate elite shopping boulevard, a separate financial canyon; and on these streets may be seen different types of architecture, different types of clients and servicing agents, and different types of activities. During the evening some of the symbolic, if not indeed the economic, functions change on identical streets; that is, people are using different institutions, or using the same ones a little differently. The sociological question is always: "Who is found in such an area or on such a street, doing what, for what purposes, at any given hour?"

Over the years a downtown street can

change wholly in economic and symbolic function, as the center of town moves or as the city center grows larger and hence more differentiated. However, in American cities, some downtown streets seem to retain a remarkable affinity for the same kind of businesses, clients, visitors, and pleasure-seekers. Streets acquire and keep reputations. They evoke images in the minds of those who know these reputations; and presumably these images help attract and repel clients and visitors. From time to time, as the downtown district becomes more differentiated, functions break off from one street and become instituted on another. Thus in Chicago, upper Michigan Avenue was opened with some fanfare during the present century, drawing away elite shops and shoppers from the more centrally located and famed State Street section. One can, if he is sufficiently imaginative, therefore, view the downtown area of any city as having different historical depths. This is easier to see in Asiatic or European cities; for instance, in Tokyo there are ancient streets, with both new and old functions, and newer streets as well. In American cities, history tends to be lost more quickly; but even here some residents are more aware of street histories than other townspeople, and derive satisfactions from knowing about the past as they walk the street; it is, one might add, not too much to claim that they perceive the street differently from someone who does not know its past.[3] Here is an elderly Chicago lady speaking:

I am looking from the window of my office in the London Guaranty Building, on the very site of Fort Dearborn. I look from one window up the Chicago River, past the new Wacker Drive, once South Water Street, where my grandfather was a commission merchant. . . . A short distance south of the Wacker Drive, my father sat in the office of his bank and made his first loans to the merchants who were even then building their grain elevators and establishing a center for the meat industry of the world (Bowen, 1926, pp. 224–225).

Not everyone has personal and familial memories so intertwined with street histories. On the other hand, it is perhaps more characteristic of American urban memories than of European or of Asiatic that one's own personal memories are relied upon to supply temporal depth to city streets and districts. For the more obviously historic areas like the Boston Commons, personal memories are buttressed with folklore and textbook history.

To continue now with the complex symbolic functions of certain downtown streets, it is clearly observable that certain streets draw several different kinds of populations. The term "locale" shall refer to such a street. A street like Rush Street in Chicago, for example, is a locale where in the evening one may find—on the street and in the many restaurants and bars—a variety of customers, servicing agents, and visitors. Rush Street has its own atmosphere, as many people have observed, compounded of all these people and all these institutions. It is one of the glamour streets of Chicago. There one can see, if one has an eye for them, prostitutes, pimps, homosexuals, bisexuals, upper class men and women, university students, touts, artists, tourists, business men out for a good time with or without girl friends, young men and women dating, people of various ethnic backgrounds, policemen, cabbies—the entire catalogue is much longer. Rush Street is a locale where people from many different urban worlds, with many styles of urbanity, pass each other, buy services from each other, talk to one another, and occasionally make friends with one another. Like animals using the same bit of land, people on Rush Street can interact almost subliminally, demanding nothing of each other, making no contracts with each other, merely passing each other or sitting near each other. But the interaction can also be contractual and

---

[3] Donald Horton has supplied this amusing and revealing anecdote. Many years ago O. Henry wrote a story of which the scene was laid in Grove Court in Greenwich Village. Those living there then were working-class people and artists. They were succeeded by Irish men and women, who in turn were replaced by the present generation of middle-class intellectuals. One family of the latter group speaks of itself as "First Settlers" because it was among the earliest of this population to settle there. Frequently devotees of O. Henry's writing seek out Grove Court, only to be disappointed that a pump which was featured in his "Last Leaf" has been removed.

exploitative, as when prostitutes find clients or pickpockets find marks. But most important, perhaps, there can occur at such locales a more sociable, more lasting kind of contact between peoples drawn from different worlds. It is at places like Rush Street that the orbits of many worlds intersect, so that persons may learn something of the ways of another world. In locales, as the orbits intersect, the physical segregation of these urban worlds is at a minimum.[4]

Other streets in the city are inhabited and visited by persons drawn from just a few social worlds. Think, for instance, of the main street in a Polish area down whose length one can see only Polish people. The area may be visited occasionally by outsiders or patrolled by a non-Polish policeman; but for the most part, especially at night, this is a street which quite literally belongs to the residents of the parish. (If anything, the side streets are even more insular.) Let us call such a street or area, where intersect only a minimum number of social worlds, a "location." At a location, the physical segregation of the people of a social world is maximized. Here they can openly indulge in ceremonial and ritual gestures; here they may speak a foreign language without shame. For it is here that an urban world is seen in the form of relatively public activities based on relatively widely shared symbols. It is here, too, that the outsider really knows that he is an outsider; and if he wishes to become an insider, he knows that he must learn the appropriate ways of this world. This kind of area, too, is characterized by quite exclusive, or semiexclusive, spaces, as anyone who has entered a Polish tavern, to be eyed by the "regulars," knows. In the streets of such an area, the stranger is quickly spotted.

Some outsiders occasionally visit such locations by design, going as tourists who are "slumming"; or they may go on flying visits for particular services, as conventioneers are said to visit Negro areas for quick trips to houses of prostitution. But a person may find himself in a more or less closed location quite without design, and respond with delight, with aversion, or with another emotion to seeing the strange world "at home." If the outsider does not see the world on its home terrain, then he can only see some of its members in action at some more public locale, as when one observes certain people downtown at a restaurant, and experiences the same kinds of reactions or gets the same impressions of them that he might get if he visited these people—whether they are poor or rich, ethnic or native citizens—at their own more local haunts.

However, some city dwellers, by virtue of their work, are frequent visitors to a number of different locations. Jazz musicians, salesmen of some kinds, policemen, and bill collectors cross many lines of normal spatial and social segregation—in a certain restricted way, at least. Their occasional roles bring them to these locations where in the course of servicing clients they may also become spectators of local acts, or on occasion participate in them.

The names "locale" and "location" are polar terms with many intervening steps between them.[5] The main street of any city's Negro area is a locale—the side streets are a location—although somewhat fewer

---

[4] World famous streets and boulevards occasionally stimulate the writing of books about themselves. J. B. Kerfort (1911) wrote one about Broadway. Some of his feeling for the multiplicity of members of social worlds present at this locale is vividly suggested by his opening lines: "I was leaning, one afternoon, on the stone rail . . . that surrounds the fifty-second story of one of the downtown office towers, looking dreamily down into the chasm of Broadway. . . . A man alongside of me volunteered a remark. . . . 'They look like ants, don't they.' . . . From dawn to dark—and after —it . . . was lined with ascending and descending insects. What if, just once, one were to make the long journey up that crooked and curving highway, challenging every human ant one met, stopping him, rubbing antennae with him, sensing the sources he derived from, the ends he aimed at, the instincts he obeyed, the facts he blinked at, the illusions he hugged— getting, in short, the essence of his errand? Suppose one covered the dozen miles in eleven days and held two hundred thousand interviews by the way. Suppose, when one reached the heights of Harlem, one set down and took stock of what one had learned?" What one had learned can only mean that the worlds of so many of these people are different from one's own.

[5] I am greatly indebted to Howard S. Becker for these distinctions which were then further explored by the two of us.

orbits of social worlds perhaps intersect there than at the main street of the downtown area. Even at a location the orbits of members of the predominant social world necessarily crosscut the orbits of members of some other worlds: even the most isolated elderly lady of an ethnic enclave occasionally meets an outsider, however brief and superficial the contact. Most people's orbits, of work and of play, take them beyond their immediate residential neighborhoods. Nevertheless, we need not be surprised that most people use and know only a limited number of spatial sectors of their city and know very little about the people who frequent those areas. In a large city, unquestionably most spatial segments will be only vaguely conceived, virtually geographic blurs. The places where the orbits of life take a city dweller will have special meanings to him.

The concept of "orbit" permits us to say something about space that the earlier sociologists did not make clear or obscured. The point turns about the relations of space to social worlds. The Chicago sociologists, for instance, were alternatively struck by the ecological features of urban communities and by the social color of the communities themselves. Robert Park (1936) attempted to relate these two kinds of observation by talking about "ecological order" and a "moral order," maintaining uncertainly sometimes that they were interrelated and sometimes that the ecological sustained the moral. When the human ecologists later turned away from a sharp focus upon the "moral order," certain other sociologists like Walter Firey criticized them for ignoring the probable role played by the moral or cultural side of society in ordering ecological relationships. The tenor of Firey's criticism is conveyed by an opening passage from his book (1947):

Since its emergence as a definite field of research, ecology has developed a number of distinct theories, each of which has tried to bring a conceptual order out of man's relationships with physical space. When these theories are subjected to a careful analysis their differences turn out to be, in large part, variations upon a single conception of the society-space relationship. Briefly, this conception ascribes to space a determinate and invariant influence upon the distribution of human activities. The socially relevant qualities of space are thought to reside in the very nature of space itself, and the territorial patterns assumed by social activities are regarded as wholly determined by these qualities. There is no recognition, except in occasional fleeting insights, that social values may endow space with qualities that are quite extraneous to it as a physical phenomenon. Moreover, there is no indication of what pre-conditions there may be to social activities becoming in any way linked with physical space.

Firey's answer was to contend and try to establish that cultural factors influenced ecological, or locational, processes. Human ecologists have gone their way fairly unaffected by this species of criticism, although the issue seems still to be alive.

It is not my intent to do more than comment on this issue as a background to my own discussion of spatial representations. The chief efficacy of the term "orbit" is that it directs attention to the spatial movements of members of social worlds. Some worlds are relatively bounded in space, their members moving within very narrow orbits, like the immigrant mothers already mentioned. The members of other social worlds, such as the elite world of any large metropolis, move in orbits that take in larger sections of the city as well as encompass sections of other cities—foreign as well as domestic. In any genuine sense, it can be said that the members of such a world live not only, say, in the Gold Coast area, but also elsewhere for part of the year—in a favorite resort, in a fine suburb, in Paris, or in all four places.

The important thing about any given urban world is not that it is rooted in space. That is merely what often strikes the eye first, just as it attracted the attention of the nineteenth-century journalists and the twentieth-century sociologists. What is important about a social world is that its members are linked by some sort of shared symbolization, some effective channels of communication. Many urban worlds are diffusely organized, difficult to pin down definitely in space since their members are scattered through several, or many, areas of the city. An FM station, for instance, may draw devoted listeners to its classical programs from a half dozen areas in the city. The worlds of art or fashion or drama may find expression in particular institutions located downtown, but their members are scattered about the face of the city. These are but a few of the urban worlds to which one may belong. (As Tomatsu Shibutani (1955) has commented: "Each social world . . . is a culture area, the boundaries of which are set neither by territory nor by formal group membership but by the limits of effective communication.") The important thing, then, about a social world is its network of communication and the shared symbols which give the world some substance and which allow people to "belong" to "it." Its institutions and meeting places must be rooted somewhere, even if the orbits of the world's members do take them to many other sites in the city (just as the jazz musician moves about the city on jobs, and ends up in favorite bars for "kicks" and for job information). The experiences which the members have in those areas stem from, and in turn affect, their symbolic representations of those areas. Of an area which they never visit, they have no representations unless someone in their circle has visited it, and has passed along some representation of it. In sum: the various kinds of urban perspectives held by the residents of a city are constructed from spatial representations resulting from membership in particular social worlds.

REFERENCES:

Bowen, L. de K. *Growing up with a city*. New York: The Macmillan Co., 1926.

Browne, J. *The great metropolis, A mirror of New York*. Hartford, Conn.: American Publishing Co., 1869.

Campbell, H., Knox, T. W., & Brynes, T. *Darkness and light, or lights and shadows of New York life*. Hartford, Conn.: Hartford Publishing Co., 1895.

Cayton, H., & Drake, S. *Black metropolis*. New York: Harcourt Brace, 1945.

Firey, W. *Land use in Central Boston*. Cambridge, Mass.: Harvard University Press, 1947.

Johnson, E. The function of the central business district in the metropolitan community. In P. Hatt and A. Riess (Eds.), *Reader in urban sociology* (1st ed.). Glencoe, Ill.: The Free Press, 1951.

Jonassen, C. Cultural variables in the ecology of an ethnic group. *American Sociological Review*, 1949, **14**, 32–41.

Kerfort, J. B. *Broadway*. Boston: Houghton Mifflin, 1911.

McCabe, J. *The secrets of the great city*. Philadelphia: Jones Bros., 1868.

McCabe, J. *New York by sunlight and gaslight*. Philadelphia: Hubbard Bros., 1881.

Park, R. *The city*. Chicago: University of Chicago Press, 1925.

Park, R. Human ecology. *American Journal of Sociology*, 1936, **42**, 1–15.

Shibutani, T. Reference groups as perspectives. *American Journal of Sociology*, 1955, **60**, 566.

Smith, M. H. *Sunshine and shadow in New York*. Hartford, Conn.: J. B. Burr & Co., 1868.

Ware, C. *Greenwich Village*. Boston: Houghton Mifflin, 1935.

Zorbaugh, H. *The gold coast and the slum*. Chicago: University of Chicago Press, 1929.

33 The Uses of Sidewalks: Contact

Jane Jacobs

Reformers have long observed city people loitering on busy corners, hanging around in candy stores and bars and drinking soda pop on stoops, and have passed a judgment, the gist of which is: "This is deplorable! If these people had decent homes and a more private or bosky outdoor place, they wouldn't be on the street!"

This judgment represents a profound misunderstanding of cities. It makes no more sense than to drop in at a testimonial banquet in a hotel and conclude that if these people had wives who could cook, they would give their parties at home.

The point of both the testimonial banquet and the social life of city sidewalks is precisely that they are public. They bring together people who do not know each other in an intimate, private social fashion and in most cases do not care to know each other in that fashion.

Nobody can keep open house in a great city. Nobody wants to. And yet if interest-

From *Death and Life of Great American Cities*, by Jane Jacobs. © Copyright 1969 by Jane Jacobs. Reprinted by permission of Random House, Inc., and the author.

ing, useful and significant contacts among the people of cities are confined to acquaintanceships suitable for private life, the city becomes stultified. Cities are full of people with whom, from your viewpoint, or mine, or any other individual's, a certain degree of contact is useful or enjoyable; but you do not want them in your hair. And they do not want you in theirs either.

Considering city sidewalk safety, it is necessary that there should be, in the brains behind the eyes on the street, an almost unconscious assumption of general street support when the chips are down—when a citizen has to choose, for instance, whether he will take responsibility, or abdicate it, in combating barbarism or protecting strangers. There is a short word for this assumption of support: trust. The trust of a city street is formed over time from many, many little public sidewalk contacts. It grows out of people stopping by at the bar for a beer, getting advice from the grocer and giving advice to the newsstand man, comparing opinions with other customers at the bakery and nodding hello to the two boys drinking pop on the stoop, eying the girls while waiting to be called for dinner, admonishing the children, hearing about a job from the hardware man and borrowing a dollar from the druggist, admiring the new babies and sympathizing over the way a coat faded. Customs vary: in some neighborhoods people compare notes on their dogs; in others they compare notes on their landlords.

Most of it is ostensibly utterly trivial but the sum is not trivial at all. The sum of such casual, public contact at a local level—most of it fortuitous, most of it associated with errands, all of it metered by the person concerned and not thrust upon him by anyone—is a feeling for the public identity of people, a web of public respect and trust, and a resource in time of personal or neighborhood need. The absence of this trust is a disaster to a city street. Its cultivation cannot be institutionalized. And above all, *it implies no private commitments.*

I have seen a striking difference between presence and absence of casual public trust on two sides of the same wide street in East Harlem, composed of residents of roughly the same incomes and same races. On the old-city side, which was full of public places and the sidewalk loitering so deplored by Utopian minders of other people's leisure, the children were being kept well in hand. On the project side of the street across the way, the children, who had a fire hydrant open beside their play area, were behaving destructively, drenching the open windows of houses with water, squirting it on adults who ignorantly walked on the project side of the street, throwing it into the windows of cars as they went by. Nobody dared to stop them. These were anonymous children, and the identities behind them were an unknown. What if you scolded or stopped them? Who would back you up over there in the blind-eyed Turf? Would you get, instead, revenge? Better to keep out of it. Impersonal city streets make anonymous people, and this is not a matter of esthetic quality nor of a mystical emotional effect in architectural scale. It is a matter of what kinds of tangible enterprises sidewalks have, and therefore of how people use the sidewalks in practical, everyday life.

The casual public sidewalk life of cities ties directly into other types of public life, of which I shall mention one as illustrative, although there is no end to their variety.

Formal types of local city organizations are frequently assumed by planners and even by some social workers to grow in direct, common-sense fashion out of announcements of meetings, the presence of meeting rooms, and the existence of problems of obvious public concern. Perhaps they grow so in suburbs and towns. They do not grow so in cities.

Formal public organizations in cities require an informal public life underlying them, mediating between them and the privacy of the people of the city. We catch a hint of what happens by contrasting, again, a city area possessing a public sidewalk life with a city area lacking it, as told about in the report of a settlement-house social researcher who was studying problems relating to public schools in a section of New York City:

Mr. W—— [principal of an elementary school] was questioned on the effect of J—— Houses on the school, and the up-rooting of the community around the school. He felt that there had been many effects and of these most were negative. He mentioned that the project had torn out numerous institutions for socializing. The present atmosphere of the project was in no way similar to the gaiety of the streets before the project was built. He noted that in general there seemed fewer people on the streets because there were fewer places for people to gather. He also contended that before the projects were built the Parents Association had been very strong, and now there were only very few active members.

Mr. W——— was wrong in one respect. There were not fewer places (or at any rate there was not less space) for people to gather in the project, if we count places deliberately planned for constructive socializing. Of course there were no bars, no candy stores, no hole-in-the-wall *bodegas*, no restaurants in the project. But the project under discussion was equipped with a model complement of meeting rooms, craft, art and game rooms, outdoor benches, malls, etc., enough to gladden the heart of even the Garden City advocates.

Why are such places dead and useless without the most determined efforts and expense to inveigle users—and then to maintain control over the users? What services do the public sidewalk and its enterprises fulfill that these planned gathering places do not? And why? How does an informal public sidewalk life bolster a more formal, organizational public life?

To understand such problems—to understand why drinking pop on the stoop differs from drinking pop in the game room, and why getting advice from the grocer or the bartender differs from getting advice from either your next-door neighbor or from an institutional lady who may be hand-in-glove with an institutional landlord—we must look into the matter of city privacy.

Privacy is precious in cities. It is indispensable. Perhaps it is precious and indispensable everywhere, but most places you cannot get it. In small settlements everyone knows your affairs. In the city everyone does not—only those you choose to tell will know much about you. This is one of the attributes of cities that is precious to most city people, whether their incomes are high

or their incomes are low, whether they are white or colored, whether they are old inhabitants or new, and it is a gift of great-city life deeply cherished and jealously guarded.

Architectural and planning literature deals with privacy in terms of windows, overlooks, sight lines. The idea is that if no one from outside can peek into where you live—behold, privacy. This is simple-minded. Window privacy is the easiest commodity in the world to get. You just pull down the shades or adjust the blinds. The privacy of keeping one's personal affairs to those selected to know them, and the privacy of having reasonable control over who shall make inroads on your time and when, are rare commodities in most of this world, however, and they have nothing to do with the orientation of windows.

Anthropologist Elena Padilla, author of *Up from Puerto Rico*, describing Puerto Rican life in a poor and squalid district of New York, tells how much people know about each other—who is to be trusted and who not, who is defiant of the law and who upholds it, who is competent and well informed and who is inept and ignorant—and how these things are known from the public life of the sidewalk and its associated enterprises. These are matters of public character. But she also tells how select are those permitted to drop into the kitchen for a cup of coffee, how strong are the ties, and how limited the number of a person's genuine confidants, those who share in a person's private life and private affairs. She tells how it is not considered dignified for everyone to know one's affairs. Nor is it considered dignified to snoop on others beyond the face presented in public. It does violence to a person's privacy and rights. In this, the people she describes are essentially the same as the people of the mixed, Americanized city street on which I live, and essentially the same as the people who live in high-income apartments or fine town houses, too.

A good city street neighborhood achieves a marvel of balance between its people's determination to have essential privacy and their simultaneous wishes for differing degrees of contact, enjoyment or help from the people around. This balance is largely made up of small, sensitively managed details, practiced and accepted so casually that they are normally taken for granted.

Perhaps I can best explain this subtle but all-important balance in terms of the stores where people leave keys for their friends, a common custom in New York. In our family, for example, when a friend wants to use our place while we are away for a week end or everyone happens to be out during the day, or a visitor for whom we do not wish to wait up is spending the night, we tell such a friend that he can pick up the key at the delicatessen across the street. Joe Cornacchia, who keeps the delicatessen, usually has a dozen or so keys at a time for handing out like this. He has a special drawer for them.

Now why do I, and many others, select Joe as a logical custodian for keys? Because we trust him, first, to be a responsible custodian, but equally important because we know that he combines a feeling of good will with a feeling of no personal responsibility about our private affairs. Joe considers it no concern of his whom we choose to permit in our places and why.

Around on the other side of our block, people leave their keys at a Spanish grocery. On the other side of Joe's block, people leave them at the candy store. Down a block they leave them at the coffee shop, and a few hundred feet around the corner from that, in a barber shop. Around one corner from two fashionable blocks of town houses and apartments in the Upper East Side, people leave their keys in a butcher shop and a bookshop; around another corner they leave them in a cleaner's and a drug store. In unfashionable East Harlem keys are left with at least one florist, in bakeries, in luncheonettes, in Spanish and Italian groceries.

The point, wherever they are left, is not the kind of ostensible service that the enterprise offers, but the kind of proprietor it has.

A service like this cannot be formalized. Identifications . . . questions . . . insurance against mishaps. The all-essential line between public service and privacy would be transgressed by institutionalization. Nobody in his right mind would leave his key in such a place. The service must be given as a favor by someone with an unshakable understanding of the difference between a person's key and a person's private life, or it cannot be given at all.

Or consider the line drawn by Mr. Jaffe at the candy store around our corner—a line so well understood by his customers and by other storekeepers too that they can spend their whole lives in its presence and never think about it consciously. One ordinary morning last winter, Mr. Jaffe, whose formal business name is Bernie, and his wife, whose formal business name is Ann, supervised the small children crossing at the corner on the way to P.S. 41, as Bernie always does because he sees the need; lent an umbrella to one customer and a dollar to another; took custody of two keys; took in some packages for people in the next building who were away; lectured two youngsters who asked for cigarettes; gave street directions; took custody of a watch to give the repair man across the street when he opened later; gave out information on the range of rents in the neighborhood to an apartment seeker; listened to a tale of domestic difficulty and offered reassurance; told some rowdies they could not come in unless they behaved and then defined (and got) good behavior; provided an incidental forum for half a dozen conversations among customers who dropped in for oddments; set aside certain newly arrived papers and magazines for regular customers who would depend on getting them; advised a mother who came for a birthday present not to get the ship-model kit because another child going to the same birthday party was giving that; and got a back copy (this was for me) of the previous day's newspaper out of the deliverer's surplus returns when he came by.

After considering this multiplicity of extra-merchandising services I asked Bernie, "Do you ever introduce your customers to each other?"

He looked startled at the idea, even dismayed. "No," he said thoughtfully. "That would just not be advisable. Sometimes, if I know two customers who are in at the same time have an interest in common, I bring up the subject in conversation and let them carry it on from there if they want to. But oh no, I wouldn't introduce them."

When I told this to an acquaintance in a suburb, she promptly assumed that Mr. Jaffe felt that to make an introduction would be to step above his social class. Not at all. In our neighborhood, storekeepers like the Jaffes enjoy an excellent social status, that of businessmen. In income they are apt to be the peers of the general run of customers and in independence they are the superiors. Their advice, as men or women of common sense and experience, is sought and respected. They are well known as individuals, rather than unknown as class symbols. No; this is that almost unconsciously enforced, well-balanced line showing, the line between the city public world and the world of privacy.

This line can be maintained, without awkwardness to anyone, because of the great plenty of opportunities for public contact in the enterprises along the sidewalks, or on the sidewalks themselves as people move to and fro or deliberately loiter when they feel like it, and also because of the presence of many public hosts, so to speak, proprietors of meeting places like Bernie's where one is free either to hang around or dash in and out, no strings attached.

Under this system, it is possible in a city street neighborhood to know all kinds of people without unwelcome entanglements, without boredom, necessity for excuses, explanations, fears of giving offense, embarrassments respecting impositions or commitments, and all such paraphernalia of obligations which can accompany less limited relationships. It is possible to be on excellent sidewalk terms with people who are very different from oneself, and even, as time passes, on familiar public terms with them. Such relationships can, and do, endure for many years, for decades; they could never have formed without that line, much less endured. They form precisely because they are by-the-way to people's normal public sorties.

"Togetherness" is a fittingly nauseating name for an old ideal in planning theory. This ideal is that if anything is shared among people, much should be shared. "Together-

ness," apparently a spiritual resource of the new suburbs, works destructively in cities. The requirement that much shall be shared drives city people apart.

When an area of a city lacks a sidewalk life, the people of the place must enlarge their private lives if they are to have anything approaching equivalent contact with their neighbors. They must settle for some form of "togetherness," in which more is shared with one another than in the life of the sidewalks, or else they must settle for lack of contact. Inevitably the outcome is one or the other; it has to be; and either has distressing results.

In the case of the first outcome, where people do share much, they become exceedingly choosy as to who their neighbors are, or with whom they associate at all. They have to become so. A friend of mine, Penny Kostritsky, is unwittingly and unwillingly in this fix on a street in Baltimore. Her street of nothing but residences, embedded in an area of almost nothing but residences, has been experimentally equipped with a charming sidewalk park. The sidewalk has been widened and attractively paved, wheeled traffic discouraged from the narrow street roadbed, trees and flowers planted, and a piece of play sculpture is to go in. All these are splendid ideas so far as they go.

However, there are no stores. The mothers from nearby blocks who bring small children here, and come here to find some contact with others themselves, perforce go into the houses of acquaintances along the street to warm up in winter, to make telephone calls, to take their children in emergencies to the bathroom. Their hostesses offer them coffee, for there is no other place to get coffee, and naturally considerable social life of this kind has arisen around the park. Much is shared.

Mrs. Kostritsky, who lives in one of the conveniently located houses, and who has two small children, is in the thick of this narrow and accidental social life. "I have lost the advantage of living in the city," she says, "without getting the advantages of living in the suburbs." Still more distressing, when mothers of different income or color or educational background bring their children to the street park, they and their children are rudely and pointedly ostracized. They fit awkwardly into the suburbanlike sharing of private lives that has grown in default of city sidewalk life. The park lacks benches purposely; the "togetherness" people ruled them out because they might be interpreted as an invitation to people who cannot fit in.

"If only we had a couple of stores on the street," Mrs. Kostritsky laments. "If only there were a grocery store or a drug store or a snack joint. Then the telephone calls and the warming up and the gathering could be done naturally in public, and then people would act more decent to each other because everybody would have a right to be here."

Much the same thing that happens in this sidewalk park without a city public life happens sometimes in middle-class projects and colonies, such as Chatham Village in Pittsburgh for example, a famous model of Garden City planning.

The houses here are grouped in colonies around shared interior lawns and play yards, and the whole development is equipped with other devices for close sharing, such as a residents' club which holds parties, dances, reunions, has ladies' activities like bridge and sewing parties, and holds dances and parties for the children. There is no public life here, in any city sense. There are differing degrees of extended private life.

Chatham Village's success as a "model" neighborhood where much is shared has required that the residents be similar to one another in their standards, interests and backgrounds. In the main they are middle-class professionals and their families.[1] It has also required that residents set themselves distinctly apart from the different people in the surrounding city; these are in the main also middle class, but lower middle class, and this is too different for the degree of chumminess that neighborliness in Chatham Village entails.

The inevitable insularity (and homogeneity) of Chatham Village has practical con-

sequences. As one illustration, the junior high school serving the area has problems, as all schools do. Chatham Village is large enough to dominate the elementary school to which its children go, and therefore to work at helping solve this school's problems. To deal with the junior high, however, Chatham Village's people must cooperate with entirely different neighborhoods. But there is no public acquaintanceship, no foundation of casual public trust, no cross-connections with the necessary people—and no practice or ease in applying the most ordinary techniques of city public life at lowly levels. Feeling helpless, as indeed they are, some Chatham Village families move away when their children reach junior high age; others contrive to send them to private high schools. Ironically, just such neighborhood islands as Chatham Village are encouraged in orthodox planning on the specific grounds that cities need the talents and stabilizing influence of the middle class. Presumably these qualities are to seep out by osmosis.

People who do not fit happily into such colonies eventually get out, and in time managements become sophisticated in knowing who among applicants will fit in. Along with basic similarities of standards, values and backgrounds, the arrangement seems to demand a formidable amount of forbearance and tact.

City residential planning that depends, for contact among neighbors, on personal sharing of this sort, and that cultivates it, often does work well socially, if rather narrowly, *for self-selected upper-middle-class people.* It solves easy problems for an easy kind of population. So far as I have been able to discover, it fails to work, however, even on its own terms, *with any other kind of population.*

The more common outcome in cities, where people are faced with the choice of sharing much or nothing, is nothing. In city areas that lack a natural and casual public life, it is common for residents to isolate themselves from each other to a fantastic degree. If mere contact with your neighbors threatens to entangle you in their private lives, or entangle them in yours, and if you cannot be so careful who your neighbors are as self-selected upper-middle-class peo-

[1] One representative court, for example, contains as this is written four lawyers, two doctors, two engineers, a dentist, a salesman, a banker, a railroad executive, a planning executive.

ple can be, the logical solution is absolutely to avoid friendliness or casual offers of help. Better to stay thoroughly distant. As a practical result, the ordinary public jobs —like keeping children in hand—for which people must take a little personal initiative, or those for which they must band together in limited common purposes, go undone. The abysses this opens up can be almost unbelievable.

For example, in one New York City project which is designed—like all orthodox residential city planning—for sharing much or nothing, a remarkably outgoing woman prided herself that she had become acquainted, by making a deliberate effort, with the mothers of every one of the ninety families in her building. She called on them. She buttonholed them at the door or in the hall. She struck up conversations if she sat beside them on a bench.

It so happened that her eight-year-old son, one day, got stuck in the elevator and was left there without help for more than two hours, although he screamed, cried and pounded. The next day the mother expressed her dismay to one of her ninety acquaintances. "Oh, was that *your* son?" said the other woman. "I didn't know whose boy he was. If I had realized he was *your* son I would have helped him."

This woman, who had not behaved in any such insanely calloused fashion on her old public street—to which she constantly returned, by the way, for public life—was afraid of a possible entanglement that might not be kept easily on a public plane.

Dozens of illustrations of this defense can be found wherever the choice is sharing much or nothing. A thorough and detailed report by Ellen Lurie, a social worker in East Harlem, on life in a low-income project there, has this to say:

> It is . . . extremely important to recognize that for considerably complicated reasons, many adults either don't want to become involved in any friendship-relationships at all with their neighbors, or, if they do succumb to the need for some form of society, they strictly limit themselves to one or two friends, and no more. Over and over again, wives repeated their husband's warning:

> "I'm not to get too friendly with anyone. My husband doesn't believe in it."

> "People are too gossipy and they could get us in a lot of trouble."

> "It's best to mind your own business."

> One woman, Mrs. Abraham, always goes out the back door of the building because she doesn't want to interfere with the people standing around in the front. Another man, Mr. Colan . . . won't let his wife make any friends in the project, because he doesn't trust the people here. They have four children, ranging from 8 years to 14, but they are not allowed downstairs alone, because the parents are afraid someone will hurt them.[2] What happens then is that all sorts of barriers to insure self-protection are being constructed by many families. To protect their children from a neighborhood they aren't sure of, they keep them upstairs in the apartment. To protect themselves, they make few, if any, friends. Some are afraid that friends will become angry or envious and make up a story to report to management, causing them great trouble. If the husband gets a bonus (which he decided not to report) and the wife buys new curtains, the visiting friends will see and might tell the management, who, in turn, investigates and issues a rent increase. Suspicion and fear of trouble often outweigh any need for neighborly advice and help. For these families the sense of privacy has already been extensively violated. The deepest secrets, all the family skeletons, are well known not only to management but often to other public agencies, such as the Welfare Department. To preserve any last remnants of privacy, they choose to avoid close relationships with others. This same phenomenon may be found to a much lesser degree in non-planned slum housing, for there too it is often necessary for other reasons to build up these forms of self-protection. But it is surely true that this withdrawing from the society of others is much more extensive in planned housing. Even in England, this suspicion of the neighbors and the ensuing aloofness was found in studies of planned towns. Perhaps this pattern is nothing more than an elaborate group mechanism to protect and preserve inner dignity in

2 This is very common in public projects in New York.

the face of so many outside pressures to conform.

Along with nothingness, considerable "to-getherness" can be found in such places, however. Mrs. Lurie reports on this type of relationship:

> Often two women from two different buildings will meet in the laundry room, recognize each other; although they may never have spoken a single word to each other back on 99th Street, suddenly here they become "best friends." If one of these two already has a friend or two in her own building, the other is likely to be drawn into that circle and begins to make her friendships, not with women on her floor, but rather on her friend's floor.
>
> These friendships do not go into an ever-widening circle. There are certain definite well-traveled paths in the project, and after a while no new people are met.

Mrs. Lurie, who works at community organization in East Harlem, with remarkable success, has looked into the history of many past attempts at project tenant organization. She has told me that "togetherness," itself, is one of the factors that make this kind of organization so difficult. "These projects are not lacking in natural leaders," she says. "They contain people with real ability, wonderful people many of them, but the typical sequence is that in the course of organization leaders have found each other, gotten all involved in each other's social lives, and have ended up talking to nobody but each other. They have not found their followers. Everything tends to degenerate into ineffective cliques, as a natural course. There is no normal public life. Just the mechanics of people learning what is going on is so difficult. It all makes the simplest social gain extra hard for these people."

Residents of unplanned city residential areas that lack neighborhood commerce and sidewalk life seem sometimes to follow the same course as residents of public projects when faced with the choice of sharing much or nothing. Thus researchers hunting the secrets of the social structure in a dull gray-area district of Detroit came to the unexpected conclusion there was no social structure.

34 Housing and Its Effects

Alvin L. Schorr

IS THERE A CAUSAL RELATIONSHIP?

Whether housing affects people and how are old questions. They were examined in Glasgow about 1870, when the city took power to clear land and "reconstitute" neighborhoods. Examining the effects on people who were moved, J. B. Russell found himself perplexed in a way that seems painfully modern. Finding conclusions difficult, he wrote:

> A gutter-child from the Bridgegate is a very complicated production. . . . The evil which the Improvement Trust sets itself to remedy was worked in successive generations, and the good which it desires to effect cannot be exhausted in a period short of the life of one generation, if not of several (Ferguson, Thomas, & Pettigrew, 1954, p. 183).

That we have not come very far beyond this conclusion in a century may be a product of several factors. First, personal experiences testify so dramatically to the effect of housing that one is encouraged to approach research in somewhat patronizing fashion. Second, the motivation to conduct research has been chiefly to produce political action. The ideas that are useful for moving legislatures—crime, immorality, and ability to pay taxes—are too mixed and, over time, too inconsistent to probe very deeply into human behavior. Third, approached for theoretical purposes, the question of the effect of housing presents difficult problems of definition and method. Does housing mean the house or the neighborhood, and are they separable? Is it at all possible to

From *Slums and Social Insecurity*, U. S. Department of Health, Education, and Welfare, Social Security Administration, Division of Research and Statistics, 1966, Research Report No. 1, pp. 7–31. Reprinted by permission of the author and publishers.

disentangle the physical facts of housing from the family's image of it, and what is the relative importance of each?

Weighing the net meaning of all the evidence that is available, one must conclude that the placement of houses and apartments in relation to one another and to the total city (downtown, suburban) clearly influences family and social relationships. Though there is no solid evidence, there is at least a hint of the effect of such factors as internal physical arrangement and space per person. In one direction the evidence is overwhelming: *extremely poor* housing conditions perceptibly influence behavior and attitudes.

Let us list the forms in which these effects of housing may be found. A division into three types of effects will be useful. First, some effects are caused by housing, in the sense that both house and neighborhood are included in the term. In this sense, we shall discuss the effect of housing when it is viewed as a symbolic extension of one's self, as a factor in increasing or minimizing stress, as a cause of good or ill health, and as a factor in feelings of satisfaction. A second type of effect may be attributed to physical housing alone—its space, its state of repair, its facilities, and its arrangement. Such physical conditions may influence privacy, child-rearing practices, and housekeeping or study habits. Finally, other effects may flow from the neighborhood or its relationship to the rest of the city. Effects really cannot be divided neatly into three like this; the division is a matter of convenience and emphasis only.

EFFECTS OF HOUSE AND NEIGHBORHOOD

Housing and Self-Perception.—El Fanguito, in San Juan, P.R., was known, before it was cleared, as the largest slum[1] in the world.

[1] The term "slum" has been used to describe houses, neighborhoods, and people—and conditions that are physical, moral, and social. Here, slum means a house that is dilapidated, lacking in facilities, or overcrowded to a point that seriously interferes with health, safety, or the reasonable conduct of family life. Housing in an area where slums predominate is considered slum housing even if otherwise satisfactory.

But many residents neglected to mention it when researchers asked them to name a slum (Back, 1962). The first redevelopment proposal in the city of Milwaukee, announced in 1947, was defeated by residents. One woman's statement was reported by the *Milwaukee Journal*: "Slums, they call us. Why that's a terrible word—those are our homes, our shrines. We live there" (Woodbury, 1953, p. 379). The inertia, not to say intransigence, of those slum residents who resist being moved in one city after another makes it plain that they do not view their surroundings with the same contempt as city planners and municipal officials. Slum neighborhoods may serve other functions that are useful to residents—we shall be discussing these at greater length—but one factor at work is that house and place are regarded as extensions of one's self. In the words of a study in the Chelsea area of New York:

> Housing . . . has represented much more than physical structures. Housing is/has become a subject of highly charged emotional content: a matter of strong feeling. It is the symbol of status, of achievement, of social acceptance. It seems to control, in large measure, the way in which the individual, the family, perceives him/itself and is perceived by others (Hudson Guild, 1960, p. 60).

Thus, one evaluates his surroundings far from objectively, and himself in terms of his surroundings. How indeed call a house a slum if this is to tell the tenant he is a slum dweller!

To the middle-class reader, the social elements that are involved in identifying himself with his housing may be evident. These are the common coinage of deciding where to live: Who is accepted there? Are they my kind of people? Is it a step up or down? What will it do for me and my children? Whom shall I meet? The physical elements of self-evaluation may not be so evident. Indeed, it has been suggested that our culture tends to put out of mind the deep personal significance of what has been called the "nonhuman environment." It is interesting and perhaps also just that psychoanalysts are among the first to bring back to our minds a relationship that more primitive societies understand. Harold F. Searles (1960, p. 335) writes:

> It seems to me that, in our culture, a conscious ignoring of the psychological importance of the non-human environment exists simultaneously with a (largely unconscious) *overdependence upon* that environment. I believe that the actual importance of that environment to the individual is so great that he *dare* not recognize it. Unconsciously it is felt, I believe, to be not only an intensely important conglomeration of things *outside* the self, but also a large and integral *part* of the self.

If physical surroundings are a mirror to us all, they will reflect an especially disturbing image to the people who, lacking the simplest amenities, are made aware of the riches that others quite normally own and consume.

The reciprocal effects of housing and self-evaluation may flow in two directions. On one hand, people who feel they are worth more may avoid slums or low-status neighborhoods, if this is at all possible. Thus Moss Hart, assured of the success of his first play, moved his family within hours, leaving behind apartment, furniture, and clothing. Hart (1959, p. 437) wrote:

> Each piece of furniture in the cramped dim room seemed mildewed with a thousand double-edged memories. The ghosts of a thousand leaden meals hovered over the dining room table. The dust of countless blackhearted days clung to every crevice of the squalid ugly furniture I had known since childhood.

Who are the people who are eager to improve their housing? Studies show them to be the young, the families who are ambitious for their children, the people who wish to improve their status. As this listing may suggest, it appears that acceptance of change is a family rather than an individual attribute (Back, 1962; Rossi, 1955; Rubin, Orzack, & Tomlinson, 1959). The physical move is a social move, an evidence of aspiration and a functional step in improving one's social or economic situation.

On the other hand, living in poor housing itself influences self-evaluation and motivation. This is the heart of the question we are dealing with, whether causality moves *from* housing *to* attitudes and behavior. A good deal has been written about the pessimism that is common to poor people, the readiness to seize the present satisfaction and let the future care for itself, and the feeling that one is controlled by rather than in control of events (Kluckhohn & Spiegel, 1954). Indeed, so well do we understand these feelings that it has become necessary to be reminded that there is considerable variability, not to say aspiration, among even the very poor (Lewis, 1961; Rohrer, Edmonson, Lief, Thompson, & Thompson, 1960). Studies of families living in deteriorated neighborhoods make the same point: pessimism and passivity present the most difficult barriers to rehabilitating neighborhoods or relocating families.

However, where vigorous effort has gone into upgrading neighborhoods—in Chicago, Baltimore, New Orleans, and Miami—observers have seen people "who dropped their old, fatalistic attitudes and embraced new feelings of pride and optimism. . . ." (Millspaugh & Breckenfeld, 1958, p. 61). This observation should not be exaggerated; only some people, more in Baltimore and fewer in Miami, responded. Scientifically controlled studies give more ambiguous evidence about the effect of changing housing on self-evaluation. The two or three that have been done do not appear to span an adequate period of time, nor do they have adequate instruments to measure motivation and self-evaluation. It seems clear that families who have improved their housing feel they have improved their situation and status (Chapin, 1955; Wilner, Walkley, Pinkerton, & Tayback, 1960, Ch. 17). A substantial, controlled sample of families who moved to improved housing showed higher "general morale" but no change in aspirations (Wilner et al., 1960).

Certain factors appear to operate selectively to determine who will respond to a change in housing. Apparently, improvement has to go beyond the simplest physical facilities before a change in attitude shows. That is, while sheer physical need continues to occupy the family's attention, attitude is not affected (Millspaugh & Breckenfeld, 1958; Back, 1962). Even when their parents are not responding at all, children change their feelings about "the whole of life"—a change particularly noticeable in school (Millspaugh & Breckenfeld, 1958; Jackson, 1955). There is evidence that children who are rehoused are "considerably more likely to be promoted at a normal pace . . ." (Wilner & Walkley, 1962; Wilner, Walkley, Pinkerton & Tayback, 1962, p. 11). Another factor is that opportunity needs to be genuinely present; otherwise indifference or escapist activities offer equally acceptable retreats (Davis, 1946; Sarchet, 1958, p. 111). There needs, finally, to be some basic educational and cultural attainment; in a sense, this is another way of saying that opportunity must be genuinely present.

Stress.—In attempting to describe the link between culture and personality, while both are changing, stress appears to be a useful concept. For example, it has been proposed that migration from a rural to an urban setting places "excessive adjustive burdens" on migrants. Insofar as these stresses cannot be absorbed by the individual or the group with which he surrounds himself, he will show some form of ill health (Cassel, Patrick, & Jenkins, 1960). How housing affects families and individuals is a special form of the same general question, and stress has been offered as a tie. That is, housing may affect behavior by contributing to or dissipating stress. The use of such an intervening concept has at least two advantages over attempts to relate housing inadequacies (noise, for example) directly to behavioral consequences (irritability). It accounts for differences in reaction between individuals of the same general background. In other words, it introduces the idea that some people have more effective adjustive mechanisms than others—patently a factor that influences reactions. Second, it accounts for the effect of certain factors which would not otherwise appear to be relevant (the relation of filth to migraine headaches, for example).

Almost any housing quality that affects individuals may be interpreted as stressful—crowding (Davis, 1946), dilapidation and cockroaches (Berle, 1958), or a high noise level (Mumford, 1961, p. 473). Two further stressful factors are social isolation and inadequate space. There is some evidence that aged people who live alone are more likely to require psychiatric hospitalization than those living with families. Accumulating research suggests "that any environment which tends to isolate an individual from others offers a stress that will lead to distinguishable personality changes . . ." (Lemkau, 1955, p. 381; Faris, 1951). The adequacy of internal space will be considered at greater length later. For the moment, it is significant that the amount of space per person and the way space is arranged to promote or interfere with privacy have been related to stress. Though the point is mentioned frequently in the literature, it has perhaps been put most cogently by James S. Plant. Plant (1930, p. 853) refers to—

> . . . the mental strain arising from constantly having to "get along" with other people. . . . In the strain of having constantly to adapt to others there is a continuous challenge to the integrity of [the child's defenses] and the child gives to us beautifully the irritable, restless, insecure picture which proclaims this ever-present threat. Often adults feel the strain of having to adjust to others if they are persistently in a group for a period of time. We see children who have never known any other situation.

We speak here of a reaction to extreme stimulation, without attempting to distinguish between attitudes of one socioeconomic class and another. In dealing specifically with internal space, we shall see that such a distinction is important.

Health.—Particularly in studies that correlate poor housing with poor health, substantial evidence links the two together. We may accept as causally related those illnesses for which correlations are demonstrated *and* the mechanisms that are operating are well understood. Wilner, Walkley, Pinkerton, & Tayback (1956, Ch. 17) have offered a classification of these:

1. Acute respiratory infections (colds, bronchitis, grippe), related to multiple use

of toilet and water facilities, inadequate heating or ventilation, inadequate and crowded sleeping arrangements.

2. Certain infectious diseases of childhood (measles, chickenpox, and whooping cough), related to similar causal factors.

3. Minor digestive diseases and enteritis (typhoid, dysentery, diarrhea), related to poor facilities for the cold storage of food and to inadequate washing and toilet facilities.

4. Injuries resulting from home accidents, related to crowded or inadequate kitchens, poor electrical connections, and poorly lighted and unstable stairs.

5. Infectious and noninfectious diseases of the skin, related to crowding and facilities for washing.

Other diseases that, one may be confident, may be caused by poor housing include lead poisoning in children from eating scaling paint (New York Academy of Medicine, 1954) and pneumonia and tuberculosis (Pond, 1957). It is not surprising, therefore, to find that morbidity and mortality rates also correlate with adequacy of housing. With understandable exceptions—for example, an increase in infectious illness among young people newly exposed to one another (Wilner et al., 1960)—controlled studies confirm that improved housing reduces the incidence of illness and death (Wilner & Walkley, 1962).

Satisfaction.—Satisfaction is a somewhat different type of effect from those that have so far been discussed. Concepts such as health and optimism, though subjectively experienced, retain a degree of consistency from one group to another. Satisfaction is defined entirely by the current situation. Though the questions may vary from study to study, in each study "satisfaction" is defined as the answer to one or more specific questions: "Do you have complaints about this housing development?" "Do you like living here? Much? Little?" Consequently, satisfaction means only what each question means in the context in which it is asked. Used in association with other kinds of observations, measures of satisfaction provide additional leads and insights regarding

experience with housing. They are therefore used with some frequency.

Satisfaction may be defined as the absence of complaint, when opportunity for complaint is provided, or as an explicit statement that the person likes his housing. In these senses, satisfaction has at one time or another been shown to be positively related to the following housing characteristics: a set of beliefs about one's house, as distinguished from its physical properties (Mogey & Morris, 1960); the market value of the house (Riemer, 1945); ownership as opposed to rental (Back, 1962); one's neighbors or one's view of them (Rossi, 1955); close friendship or kinship ties in the neighborhood (Fried & Gleicher, 1961); space per person (Riemer, 1945; Cottam, 1951); the number of rooms per family (Mogey & Morris, 1960); the availability of space for separate uses (Chapin, 1938; Chapin, 1951); the possession of a kitchen or bathroom of one's own (Mogey & Morris, 1960); and the absence of certain deficiencies (vermin, etc.) (Wilner, Walkley, & Cook, 1955). Frequently such findings are based on correlations, but are confirmed, when confirmation is sought, by studies that follow families from poor to improved housing.

The relationship between such housing characteristics and satisfaction is plausible; unfortunately paradoxical findings also turn up. For example, the residents of a defense housing project, though their houses were more commodious, were less satisfied than residents of a project for student veterans (Kennedy, 1950). Evidently, the circumstances under which families move into housing has an overriding influence on their attitude. Again, 6 percent of a small group of white-collar workers and 21 percent of a group of semiskilled and unskilled workers had been living with relatives. However, complaints about overcrowding flowed in the opposite direction. Twenty-nine percent of the white-collar group and 6 percent of the semiskilled and unskilled complained that they were overcrowded (Dean, 1951). It has been argued that this represents a class difference in evaluation of privacy (Rosnow, 1961). A final example: People living in crowded accommodations turned out, on the average, to be more satisfied than people who were less crowded. It is suggested that those who were dissatisfied had managed to improve their accommodations and only the comparatively satisfied were still crowded (Back, 1962).

Thus, it appears that housing influences satisfaction, but within the limits of several general qualifications. First, satisfaction expresses a relationship between where a person has lived and his current housing. Thus, one man may be less satisfied with a mansion than another man with a small apartment, depending on where each lived earlier. Second, the housing that people want (and about whose lack they will complain) is related to what seems to them to be practical. Practicality, in turn, does not reach too far from what a family already has. "Needs," writes Svend Riemer (1951, p. 148), "appear, are satisfied, and fade out, only to make place for new needs." Finally, there is not one housing satisfaction but several. General "residential satisfaction," "house satisfaction," and "neighbor satisfaction" have been identified as important (Mogey & Morris, 1960). Any specific factor under consideration may disappear in or be canceled out by the effect of another factor.

EFFECTS OF PHYSICAL HOUSING

We turn now to the effects that may be attributed to physical housing alone. Most research attention has been paid to the adequacy of internal space—or its inadequacy, which is crowding. A number of signs suggest that crowding is the key housing factor affecting low-income families. Measures of maladjustment to the home are "most strikingly" related to crowding (Riemer, 1945). The need for more space is the dominant reason that families, when they can afford it, change one house or apartment for another (Rossi, 1955). Crowding appears to be the major housing characteristic that influences health (Pond, 1957). The effects of crowding have been more extensively investigated than other housing qualities, though perhaps only because crowding is more easily measured.

Crowding has been measured in a variety of ways. A count of persons per bed, used

in Great Britain in the 19th century, does now seem to be out of date. Thus does the demise of standards in itself reflect progress. The American Public Health Association some years ago established space requirements by number of square feet—400 square feet for one person, 750 for two, 1,000 for three, and so on (American Public Health Association, 1950). A standard of square feet may be suitable for builders and housing inspectors, for whom it is intended, but presents difficulties for enumeration or research. An easier standard to use counts the number of people per room in a housing unit. One person or less per room is considered adequate. Earlier standards counted 1.5 or 2 persons per room as adequate. A similar standard relates the number of people to the number of bedrooms—one bedroom for two people, two for three or four people, and so on. Number of people, number of bedrooms, and total space required may be combined into a more complicated formula. Thus, three people in two bedrooms require about 554 square feet (International Union of Family Organizations, 1957). There has been some interest, finally, in developing definitions more descriptive of family functioning. "Use crowding" describes the situation in which a room designated for one function (living room) is used also for a different function (bedroom (Chapin, 1961). Though such a definition has not been greatly elaborated, it holds the promise of taking into account both space and family needs at the same time. A numerical space measure, on the other hand, assumes that all families carry on more or less the same activities in the same ways.

Psychological Effects of Crowding.—It has already been noted that crowding, along with other physical and social factors, bears a relationship to stress and self-perception. Plant (1930, pp. 850–854) identified four other psychological consequences of crowding. "The first is the challenge to the sense of individuality. . . ." Because he is so rarely alone, the child fails to learn to look to himself for the real satisfactions of life. "The second is the challenge to the child's illusions about other people. . . ." Brought into unavoidable contact with adult weakness and greed, children find it difficult to build up identifications with hero-parents or other ideals. "The third is the challenge to any illusions about sex." Crowding makes "the physical aspect of the sexual life primary instead of realizing it as largely the symbol of idiomatic personal relationships." Finally, he noted "the challenge to an objective study of the world or its problems. [Crowded children] are so much *in* life that they can rarely look *at* it." Plant writes out of his experience with children, but the analysis applies to adults as well.

These are clinical conclusions, undemonstrated and indeed untested. If they are accurate, what would one expect of the adult who is a product of crowded housing? He should tend to be gregarious, to look outside himself for stimulation, and to be comparatively uninterested in solitary pursuits. He is likely to be cynical about people, not to say organizations and governments. Sexual expression should be regarded as a physical matter, rather than an element of a relationship. He should feel unable to understand clearly the events that move him, let alone feel able to take hold of and move events. Such a description is consistent with the findings of studies of slum inhabitants, as well as with the broader descriptions of lower class culture. Obviously, we do not conclude that crowding is the single or the major element that produces a "culture of poverty." More likely, the personality of the slum dweller is "overdetermined." That is, crowding keys in with other deprivations, each reinforcing the other, to shape the slum dweller.

One insight that is somewhat similar to Plant's *has* been tested. It is suggested that if male children sleep with their mothers for a year or more, drastic measures must be provided at adolescence to break the mother-son bond. Analysis of 56 societies confirms that such a sleeping arrangement tends to be followed by rituals that enforce separation. Our own society does not enforce separation except, perhaps, in requiring military service—and that rather late. It is suggested that the consequences, where a strong relationship with the mother has not been interrupted, are delinquency or open rebellion against paternal authority (Whiting, Kluck-

hohn, & Anthony, 1958). The relevance of this analysis lies in the likelihood that where there is crowding, such a sleeping arrangement will persist.

Something more may be said about the effects of crowding on sexual behavior. Bingham Dai (1949, p. 446) writes:

> As a slum child I had frequent clandestine sex experiences. No attempt was made to hide the facts from me. People laughed at small children's acts toward sex expression.

A number of accounts, usually at secondhand, tend to link seeing and doing rather simply together. For example, youths in the "pilot area" of Baltimore, though they responded to community rehabilitation efforts, showed least change in their sexual behavior. Probation officers and recreation leaders felt that the poor example set by adults was responsible (Millspaugh & Breckenfeld, 1958). However, the material that is available suggests a different sequence.

Having reviewed the literature of lower class sexual behavior, Lee Rainwater (1961, p. 5) writes:

> The sexual stimulation that comes in all of these cultures [Mexico, Puerto Rico, England, the United States] from the close living together of children and adults is apparently systematically repressed as the child grows older. The sexual interests stimulated by these and other experiences are deflected for the boys onto objects defined as legitimate marks (loose women, careless girls, prostitutes, etc.) and for the girls simply pushed out of awareness with a kind of hysterical defense (hysterical because of the fact that later women seem to protest their ignorance too much).

How is it, then, that many poor youngsters do have sex relations and that they show high rates of venereal disease and illegitimacy? Why, in particular, would girls, in having relations, permit themselves to be defined as loose? Conceivably, in the hope of getting a husband where husbands are comparatively unavailable. Conceivably, for favors and payment. And conceivably, for an appearance of regard which comes particularly hard to the girl who does not value herself very highly. Moreover, it has been noted from time to time that where genuine opportunity is not or does not seem to be available, energy is "diverted to sex, recreation, and gambling" (Davis, 1946). In effect, then, we see crowding as providing a high degree of sexual stimulation which may lead, for some girls, to expression after a tortuous course through repression, boredom, and discouragement. It is not so appealing a picture as the simpler one. As for youngsters who do not react in this way, some will reject sexuality categorically, defending themselves from one problem with another.

In the sense in which we have been discussing crowding, it is almost purely a lower class phenomenon. Yet there is a serious issue whether it is middle-class city planners or lower class slum dwellers who feel strongly about crowding. The issue is raised particularly at the level of public policies concerning forced relocation. On one hand, there has been a series of studies of the effect of crowding that demonstrate its undesirable consequences. Some of these studies, at least, leave the impression that the researcher himself placed a sufficiently high value on solitude to influence his conclusions (Chapin, 1951; Chapin, 1961). On the other hand, there are studies that suggest that other, conflicting values are more important to lower class families than the privacy that adequate space permits. For example, in a new Chilean housing project residents moved furniture from their living rooms into the hall so they could be together, as was their custom. Again, though some people may wish to have privacy, others may feel frightened when they cannot see and hear their neighbors (Fried, 1961).

It does not appear impossible to reconcile the two points of view. For one thing, privacy is not the opposite of crowding, though it is sometimes treated as if it were. It is hard to be private while crowded, but the Chileans, for example, were convivial even though they had more than adequate space. Further, there does not appear to be a genuine difference of opinion whether poor people wish to live "seven deep." The differences are rather these: If space of minimum adequacy is provided, will working-class and middle-class people have similar desire for *additional* space (Rosow, 1961)? This question is susceptible of research and has hardly been resolved. Poor families express much more modest desires about space, as about everything else. We have already indicated, however, that such expressions are colored by what a family has and what seems practical.

The second real difference is this: Are there poor people who wish to yield, for the adequate space they would presumably like, the familiar secure neighborhood that may be crucially important (Gans, 1959)? This question seems less likely to be resolved by research. The problem is, in a sense, in motion. If crowding leads to a preference for being with people, as Plant suggests, then the provision of adequate space will be followed by the need for it. There is an interesting example of this transition in an English study of families rehoused from 19th-century dwellings to a housing estate (Hole, 1959). They had lived long in densely populated housing, with the closeness and warmth that are characteristic of some slums. Upon moving, the families reported a decrease in tension, particularly between fathers and daughters, as privacy became more readily available. No one would any longer sleep in the living room. On the other hand, some unnecessary sharing of bedrooms persisted during the year of the study; homework and other tasks were done in company, by choice. One perceives, all intermixed, the families' interest in changing, the strain in changing, and the limiting conditions that old and new structures place upon their living patterns.

It is not only attitudes about space that are in transition; the whole value system of a poor family may be in motion. While some families would cast their lot with familiarity, others—depending on age, family situation, and so forth—would plump for improved housing. (We should tag them "upwardly mobile" and feel that we understand them.) Thus, a categorical choice between space and familiarity may elude us. Yet it becomes clear that one cannot assume that all families wish or should wish to move. This is in fact the policy issue at which the argument is usually aimed: Renewal and relocation policies need to take account of the families who do not wish to move.

Other Effects of Crowding and Layout.— We have noted the effect of housing on health. It is appropriate to add, in speaking of direct physical effects of housing, that fatigue and too little sleep may be consequences of seriously inadequate housing. The point is frequently made that crowding leads to irritations and interruptions. Reviewing cases, Dr. Lemkau concludes that these in turn "lead to unproductive expenditure of energy which in turn ends in overfatigue . . ." (American Public Health Association, 1950, p. 1). A study of working-class Negroes in Chicago in 1945 revealed that most of them slept less than 5 hours a night. The study ascribes this finding simply to lack of space for beds (Davis, 1946). It is hardly necessary to point out the relationship of rest to health.

We have dealt so far almost exclusively with the effects of crowding on personal feelings and behavior. We need also to take account of family activities, particularly the function of child rearing. The effect of crowding on intrafamily friction is observed in various connections. For example, one reason that suburban families gain in morale is that, with more space, family members no longer get in each other's way (Gans, 1961). A small kitchen gives difficulty to the housewife trying to prepare food and cope with children or other adults at the same time (Hall, 1961).

One result of seriously inadequate space appears very often to be that family members spend their time out of doors. An illustration was observed in families moving to small apartments in Vienna, who began to seek outside recreation they had not used before. When recreation was not available, families showed aggravation of any predisposition to neurotic behavior (Strotzka, 1961). The tendency to spend time outside the home may be a particularly serious matter in relation to children. It has been observed that they do not study (Jackson,

1955); more than that, they are not within reach of parental control. Study of low-income families in the District of Columbia suggests strikingly early "cutoff points" in parental will and ability to control children. Children do, indeed, seem to seize control —some as early as at the age of six (Lewis, 1961; Riemer, 1943). One can hardly overlook the relevance of such a pattern to the fact that children cannot reasonably be kept in the house. Inside the house, and at an earlier point in the child's life, another kind of problem exists. If there is an arrangement for him to keep a certain number of things, to set up projects, and so forth, the more or less natural course is to protect the child from adults, and vice versa. If space does not permit such an arrangement, a wholly different problem arises. One study concluded that the problem arises for most families with two children in two-bedroom apartments. The inevitable consequence is a certain amount of tension, more for the "permissive" than the "traditional" families (Blood, 1952).

In discussing the influence of crowding upon family relationships, it is well to bear in mind that those who are crowded together may not be only the husband and wife and their children. The group frequently includes other relatives or nonrelatives. There was a good deal of concern about doubled-up families following World War II, as it was felt that the scarcity of housing forced an undesirable situation upon them (American Public Health Association, 1950). With housing now more plentiful, it may be supposed that larger family groups live together out of choice. We shall see, in discussing the strategies that the poor use to secure housing, that doubling up is not only a matter of choice.

It should be clear that the arrangement of space, as well as the amount of space, may be influencing behavior. Where space is grossly inadequate, it is difficult to see the effects of another variable. Where the basic amount of space is adequate, however, such questions arise as the effect of devoting increased proportions of the cost of a house to appliances rather than space and the effect of one-story compared with two-story houses. (These particular questions were listed by Catherine Bauer in 1952, and remain quite untouched a decade later.)

Such study as has been done of the effects of internal design has chiefly sought to find the preferences of families. (Preferences, like satisfaction, may be difficult to interpret.) Thus, one of the earliest studies (National Housing Agency, 1945) established that, if the dining room has to be eliminated for reasons of economy, low-income families prefer the kitchen to the living room for eating. An English study has found it useful to observe family preferences, as well as to ask questions about them. It finds the kitchen to be especially important to family life: half the housewives had someone with them while preparing meals. Whether families eat in a kitchen or living room, this study finds, is strongly dependent on personal preference (Allen, 1955). The choice of illustrations about eating and the kitchen is not accidental; these are the functions that have interested researchers. Working-class women also view the kitchen as the most important room in the house (Rainwater & Handel, 1961).

In any case, preferences are hardly a satisfactory indication that housing has an effect upon attitudes and behavior. "There is little evidence," Rosow (1961) writes, "that satisfaction with new housing is directly related to liveability resulting *from design per se*, except when there is a significant improvement in housing, especially where people come from substandard housing, or occupants are particularly conscious of housing in highly literate, sophisticated terms." On the other hand, students such as Svend Riemer (1943, 1947) have supposed that internal design has an important effect upon patterns of family living.[2] In fact, there is little evidence either way. It is unfortu-

nate that these factors have received so little research attention. Architects and builders are left to rely almost entirely upon tradition and intuition.

NEIGHBORHOOD EFFECTS

Social and Family Relationships.—Having complained about the lack of research into the human effects of internal arrangement of space, fair play compels a balancing acknowledgment. The effects of place and neighborhood upon social and family relationships have occupied one of the main streams of social science research. Occasionally it is rewarding to wonder what moves research in one direction more than another. Surely, we live in a time when relationships occupy the center of our stage. The building of entire communities at once, a comparatively recent development, focuses attention on a natural laboratory for observing interaction. By contrast, the natural laboratory that is *inside* the house or apartment escapes attention. Further, the data that have become available represent a convergence of several rather different developments: small group research; research into class, particularly working class, patterns; the simultaneous flowering of interest and disenchantment (if disenchantment can flower) in the suburban rearrangement; and concern (irritation? anger? guilt?) at the slum dwellers who conduct a characteristically unconcerted stay-in strike against urban renewal. One suspects, too, that some sociologists may be charmed by a quasi-physical scientific relationship between human elements and the compounds they form.

Observation of planned or large-scale housing development appears to have established that "those people who reside closest to each other in terms of distance, physical orientation, or accessibility tend to become friends or form closely knit social units" (Festinger, Schachter, & Back, 1950; Form, 1951; Whyte, 1956). An analogy to physics leads us to Boyle's law of social interaction: The physical space that neighbors occupy is inversely proportional to the likelihood of interaction. In the planned, fairly homogeneous communities that have

[2] There have been some quite distinguished supposers: Winston Churchill said that "we shape our buildings and afterwards our buildings shape us" (Merton, 1948, p. 204). Said Queen Juliana, "There is absolutely no point in letting the world be run by nervous wrecks. Everybody should try to find a spot to be alone to concentrate and think of everything an adult and responsible person should think about. The result might be astonishing" (Pond, 1957, p. 155).

been studied, social interaction tends to be high. Because these studies have been done in young communities, it is uncertain whether the influence of physical proximity remains significant over a period of time. Longer range observations hint that, as the community ages, friendships tend to form more around formal organization and occupation and less in response to simple proximity. Two phases of reaction of a new population have been distinguished: Phase I —eager interaction and mutual help, and Phase II—selective, restrictive interaction and withdrawal (Mogey, 1956). A second qualification of the law of social interaction is: Families may move to suburban communities because they want to socialize. That they do socialize, then, can hardly be attributed to the physical nature of the suburbs. Gans (1961) has offered a third qualification. He points to the substantial social and economic homogeneity of the communities that have been studied. Since the families' behavior patterns, values, and interests are alike, they naturally tend to form friendships with one another. Homogeneity, he argues, is more significant in creating a large number of friendships than is proximity. Even within homogeneous groups, however, physical placement influences friendships.

Whether one evaluates physical proximity as crucial or secondary, it seems clear that it has an influence on social relationships. One detects that this conclusion leaves officials and builders with an unwelcome sense of importance. They are called upon to exercise judgment, but what sort of judgment? How much social interaction is desirable? It has been pointed out that if people are close together, enmities may be increased as well as friendships (Wallace, 1956). They may join community organizations out of displeasure with their neighbors as well as pleasure (International Research Associates, 1959). Moreover, neighborhood friendships may carry a family along in a pattern not their own and not quite satisfying. Describing the cost of "happiness," Whyte (1956, p. 365) writes:

Suburban families ". . . sense that by their immersion in the group they are frustrating other urges, yet they feel that responding to the group is a moral duty —and so they continue, hesitant and unsure, imprisoned in brotherhood."

In response to this dilemma, there has been increasing emphasis on planning blocks and neighborhoods so that families are left free to choose whether or not they wish to socialize, and how.

The evidence we have been discussing cuts across socioeconomic class, and it treats families at or near the point of their arrival in the community. There have been a number of observations of working-class families after the fact, so to speak. That is, the families are observed in the neighborhoods in which they have lived for some time, neighborhoods they have formed and of which they are a product. This material suggests that it is not only social interaction that is influenced by a family's location but the nature of family relationships as well. Moreover, social and family relationships flow together; change in one changes the other. It is important to bear in mind that these studies generally describe moderately deteriorated neighborhoods with fair proportions of stable families. The social networks of the more deteriorated, disorganized neighborhoods in the United States have not been described as carefully.

In the neighborhoods that have been described, families tend to be centered around the mother—one sees references to the "matriarchy of the slums" (Mogey, 1955). The father is engaged at work and socially with other men. Family membership is concentrated in the locality; the most active ties are with other members of the family. It appears that it is the closest relatives of the parents, rather than more distant ones, who are significant. Proximity makes for frequent contacts with relatives and other neighbors, casually in passing and less casually on the sidewalk or in the corner tavern. Neighbors tend perforce to be deeply involved in one another's family life. There is considerable closeness to a group of people, but comparatively little singling out of intimate friends in the middle-class manner. There is considerable attachment to the place in itself. Relationships are identified with locality and it is difficult to conceive them separately. Two characteristics of working-class areas appear to be unique:

. . . the interweaving and overlap of many different types of interpersonal contacts and role relationships, and . . . the organization and concrete manifestation of these relationships within a common, relatively bounded spatial region (Fried & Gleicher, 1961).

Researchers report, occasionally with some warmth of their own, that the mood of these neighborhoods is one of warmth, of security, and of identity (Campleman, 1951; Fried & Lindemann, 1961; Fried & Gleicher, 1961; Gans, 1959; Hole, 1959; Mogey, 1955; Mogey, 1956; Michel, 1960; Young & Willmott, 1957).

It is evident that, if they were moved, many of these families would find it difficult to maintain their patterns of relationship. The impact of one change must somehow be reflected: As locality and the extended family are no longer coterminous, it is no longer possible to be neighborhood-centered and extended-family-centered at once. A complex series of adjustments that depends on the precise circumstances gets under way. For example, a group of relocated old people faced the problem of finding meaningful activity and keeping in touch with their children. The children undertook to come to the old people, shifting to weekend visits from the more casual daily contact that had been typical. For weekday activity, the old men and women turned to other old people in their immediate neighborhood (Frieden, 1960). Study in France suggests that old people living in a crowded, deteriorated neighborhood develop with those who happen to be neighbors ties that "rapidly become effective and full substitutes for kinship relationships" (Michel, 1960). The development of this pattern, though it was not customary for them, suggests a highly flexible patterning of family and neighborly relationships dependent upon the neighborhood.

Younger family groups who move may develop a family-centered society in the place of the neighborhood-centered society

they have known. The change is not only expressed in the degree of the contact with one person or another but, as one might expect, in the kind of contact. There is a shift from spending time with collateral relatives to husband and wife or children. Marital disagreement diminishes, and sharing of household chores increases. Less contact with distant relatives is accompanied by more contact with neighbors (Mogey, 1956). There may be a relatively easy or eager shift in pattern, and gains may be perceived. "There is a tendency for the conjugal type of family to discover itself and for the obligations of kinship to be relaxed" (Mogey, 1955, p. 128). Contacts with relatives, though less frequent, may be more satisfactory because there is more to talk about and less interruption (Hole, 1959).

On the other hand, it has been pointed out that it is not only distance from relatives and friends that is a new factor to families that move, but "the lack of both an ideology and of a physical framework in which suitable fresh relationships could develop" (Hole, 1959, p. 171). There may be unfamiliarity with telephones, and other substitutes for face-to-face contact. The concepts of friendly but limited intercourse with neighbors and of formal organizations may come slowly, and with strain, to families who have not known them. It somewhat simplifies the problem to view it as one of establishing in a new community the relationships that were possible in the former one, if that were possible. For some of the families, the meaning of the move includes a wish or readiness to exchange old patterns for new ones. Other families, as we have noted, cannot navigate the change or resent it.

Even for young families, the shift from neighborhood-centered to family-centered activity is only one possible sequence. A move to fairly dense, centrally located new housing, may not produce as much alteration. For example, a Baltimore study of rehoused families finds them more proud of and involved in their new neighborhoods than the families who remained in poor housing (Wilner & Walkley, 1962; Wilner, Walkley, Pinkerton, & Tayback, 1962). We must also note explicitly that some part of the effect of a neighborhood on families is an effect of demographic selectivity. A suburban neighborhood, currently at least, draws a high percentage of families with young children. They will be interested in the PTA and school taxes. High rates of membership in certain kinds of organizations and interest in local political affairs may seem to be a response to neighborhood. It is also, of course, a response to the stage of the family cycle. So, too, it has been noted that slum neighborhoods are hospitable to those who seek anonymity because others with the same aim are already there.

REFERENCES:

Allen, P. Meals and the kitchen. *Housing Centre Review*, 1955, **5**, 14–17.

American Public Health Association, Committee on the Hygiene of Housing. *Planning the home for occupancy*. Chicago, Ill.: Public Administration Service, 1950.

Back, K. *Slums, projects and people: Social psychological problems of relocation in Puerto Rico*. Durham, N.C.: Duke University Press, 1962.

Bauer, C. *Social questions in housing and town planning*. London: University of London Press, 1952. Also appears in C. Bauer, Social questions in housing and community planning. *Journal of Social Issues*, 1951, **7** (1) & (2), 1–34.

Berle, B. *80 Puerto Rican families in New York City*. New York: Columbia University Press, 1958.

Blood, R. *Developmental and traditional child rearing philosophies and their family situational consequences*. Doctoral thesis, University of North Carolina, Chapel Hill, 1952.

Campleman, G. Some sociological aspects of mixed-class neighborhood planning. *The Sociological Review*, 1951, **43**, 191–200.

Cassel, J., Patrick, R., & Jenkins, D. Epidemiological analysis of the health implications of culture change: A conceptual model. *Annals of the New York Academy of Sciences*, 1960, **84**, 938–949.

Chapin, F. *Experimental designs in sociological research*. (Revised Ed.) New York: Harper & Bros., 1955.

Chapin, F. Some housing factors related to mental hygiene. *American Journal of Public Health*, 1951, **41** (7), 839–845.

Chapin, F. The effects of slum clearance and rehousing on family and community relationships in Minneapolis. *American Journal of Sociology*, 1938, **43** (5), 744–763.

Chapin, F. The relationship of housing to mental health. Working paper for the Expert Committee on the Public Health Aspects of Housing of the World Health Organization, June 1961, mimeographed.

Cottam, H. Cited in F. Chapin, Some housing factors related to mental hygiene. *American Journal of Public Health*, 1951, **41** (7), 841.

Dai, B. Some problems of personality development among Negro children. In C. Kluckhohn & H. Murray (Eds.), *Personality in nature, society and culture*. New York: Alfred A. Knopf, 1949. Pp. 437–458.

Davis, A. Motivation of the underprivileged worker. In W. Whyte (Ed.), *Industry and society*. New York: McGraw-Hill, 1946. Pp. 84–106.

Dean, J. The ghosts of home ownership. *Journal of Social Issues*, 1951, **7** (1) & (2), 59–68.

Faris, R. Cited in F. Chapin, Some housing factors related to mental hygiene. *American Journal of Public Health*, 1951, **41** (7), 841.

Ferguson, T., & Pettigrew, M. A study of 718 slum families rehoused for upwards of ten years. *Glasgow Medical Journal*, 1954, **35**, 183–201.

Festinger, L., Schachter, S., & Back, K. *Social pressures in informal groups*. New York: Harper & Bros., 1950.

Form, W. Stratification in low and middle income housing areas. *Journal of Social Issues*, 1951, **7** (1) & (2), 109–131.

Fried, M. Some implications of housing variables for mental health, a reply to Professor F. Stuart Chapin. *Memorandum A4 of the West End Research Project of the Center for Community Studies*, Department of Psychiatry, Massachusetts General Hospital and the Harvard Medical School, Jan. 5, 1961.

Fried, M., & Gleicher, P. Some sources of residential satisfaction in the urban slum. *Journal of the American Institute of Planners*, 1961, **27** (4), 305–315.

Fried, M., & Lindemann, E. Sociocultural factors in mental health and illness. *American Journal of Orthopsychiatry*, 1961, **31** (1), 87–101.

Frieden, E. Social differences and their consequences for housing the aged. *Journal of the American Institute of Planners*, 1960, **26** (2), 119–124.

Gans, H. Planning and social life: Friendship and neighborhood relations in suburban communities. *Journal of the American Institute of Planners*, 1961, **27** (2), 134–140.

Gans, H. The effect of a community upon its residents: Some considerations for sociological theory and planning policies. Presented to the American Sociological Association, St. Louis, Mo., Sept. 1, 1961.

Gans, H. The human implications of current redevelopment and relocation planning. *Journal of the American Institute of Planners*, 1959, **25** (1), 15–25.

Hall, E. The language of space. *Journal of the American Institute of Architects*, 1961, **35** (2), 71–74.

Hart, M. *Act one*. New York: Random House, 1959.

Hole, V. Social effects of planned rehousing. *The Town Planning Review*, 1959, **30** (2), 161–173.

Hudson Guild Neighborhood House and New York University Center for Human Relations and Community Studies. *Human relations in Chelsea*, 1960. Report of the Chelsea Housing and Human Relations Cooperative Project.

International Research Associates, Inc. *The April 1958 Benchmark Survey: Some implications for policy.* Prepared for Chelsea Closed Circuit Television Project, Feb. 25, 1959, New York City.

International Union of Family Organizations. *Minimum habitable surfaces.* Cologne: Family Housing Commission, 1957.

Jackson, W. Housing and pupil growth and development. *The Journal of Educational Sociology*, 1955, **28** (9), 370–380.

Kennedy, R. Sociopsychological problems of housing design. In L. Festinger, S. Schachter, & K. Back (Eds.), *Social pressures in informal groups.* New York: Harper & Bros., 1950. Pp. 202–220.

Kluckhohn, F., & Spiegel, J. Integration and conflict in family behavior. *Report No. 27*, Group for the Advancement of Psychiatry, Topeka, Kans., August 1954.

Lemkau, P. *Mental hygiene in public health.* (2nd ed.) New York: McGraw-Hill, 1955.

Lewis, H. Child rearing among low income families. Address to the Washington Center for Metropolitan Studies, June 8, 1961, processed.

Lewis, H. Child rearing practices among low income families in the District of Columbia. Presented at the National Conference on Social Welfare, Minneapolis, Minn., May 16, 1961, mimeographed.

Merton, R. The social psychology of housing. In W. Dennis et al., (Eds.), *Current trends in social psychology.* Pittsburgh: University of Pittsburgh Press, 1948. Pp. 163–217.

Michel, A. Kinship relations and relationships of proximity in French working-class households. In N. Bell & E. Vogel (Eds.), *A modern introduction to the family.* Glencoe, Ill.: The Free Press, 1960. Pp. 287–294.

Millspaugh, M. & Breckenfeld, G. In M. Colean (Ed.), *The human side of urban renewal.* Baltimore: Fight Blight, Inc., 1958.

Mogey, J. Changes in family life experienced by English workers moving from slums to housing estates. *Marriage and Family Living*, 1955, **17** (2), 123–128.

Mogey, J. *Family & neighborhood.* New York: Oxford University Press, 1956.

Mogey, J., & Morris, R. An analysis of satisfaction. 1960, typescript.

Mumford, L. *The city in history.* New York: Harcourt Brace, 1961.

National Housing Agency. *The liveability problems of 1,000 families.* Washington, D.C., October 1945.

New York Academy of Medicine. Report of the Subcommittee on Housing of the Committee on Public Health Relations. *Bulletin of the New York Academy of Medicine*, June 1954.

Plant, J. Some psychiatric aspects of crowded living conditions. *American Journal of Psychiatry*, 1930, **9** (5), 849–860.

Pond, A. The influence of housing on health. *Marriage and Family Living*, 1957, **19** (2), 154–159.

Rainwater, L. Marital sexuality and the culture of poverty. An expanded version of a paper read at the Plenary Session on Sex and Culture of the 60th Annual Meeting of the American Anthropological Association, Philadelphia, 1961, mimeographed.

Rainwater, L., & Handel, G. *Status of the working class in changing American society.* Chicago: Social Research, Inc., 1961.

Riemer, S. Architecture for family living. *Journal of Social Issues*, 1951, **7** (1) & (2), 140–151.

Riemer, S. Maladjustment to the family home. *American Sociological Review*, 1945, **10** (5), 642–648.

Riemer, S. Sociological perspective in home planning. *American Sociological Review*, 1947, **12** (2), 155–159.

Riemer, S. Sociological theory of home adjustment. *American Sociological Review*, 1943, **8** (3), 272–278.

Rohrer, J., Edmonson, M., Lief, H., Thompson, D., & Thompson, W. *The eighth generation.* New York: Harper & Bros., 1960.

Rosow, I. The social effects of the physical environment. *Journal of the American Institute of Planners*, 1961, **32** (2), 127–133.

Rossi, P. *Why families move.* Glencoe, Ill.: The Free Press, 1955.

Rubin, M., Orzack, L., & Tomlinson, R. Resident responses to planned neighborhood redevelopment. In M. Sussman (Ed.), *Community structure and analysis.* New York: Thomas Y. Crowell Co., 1959. Pp. 208–234.

Sarchett, B. Cited by M. Millspaugh & G. Breckenfeld. In M. Colean (Ed.), *The human side of urban renewal.* Baltimore: Fight Blight, Inc., 1958. P. 111.

Searles, H. *The nonhuman environment in normal development and in schizophrenia.* New York: International Universities Press, 1960.

Strotzka, H. Cited in F. Chapin, The relationship of housing to mental health. *Working paper 3A* for the Expert Committee on the Public Health Aspects of Housing of the World Health Organization. Meeting in Geneva, June 19–26, 1961. P. 7.

Wallace, A. Planned privacy: What's its importance for the neighborhood? *Journal of Housing*, 1956, **13** (1), 13–14.

Whiting, J., Kluckhohn, R., & Anthony, A. The function of male initiation ceremonies at puberty. In E. Maccoby, T. Newcomb, & E. Hartley (Eds.), *Readings in social psychology.* New York: Holt, 1958. Pp. 359–370.

Whyte, W. *The organization man.* New York: Simon and Schuster, 1956.

Wilner, D., Walkley, R., Pinkerton, T. & Tayback, M. *The housing environment and family life.* Ch. 17, Summary and conclusions. July 1960, processed.

Wilner, D., & Walkley, R. The effects of housing on health, social adjustment and school performance. March 23, 1962. Presented at the 39th Annual Meeting of the American Orthopsychiatric Association, Los Angeles, Calif.

Wilner, D., Walkley, R., & Cook, S. *Human relations in interracial housing.* Minneapolis: University of Minnesota Press, 1955.

Wilner, D., Walkley, R., & Tayback, M. How does the quality of housing affect health and family adjustment? *American Journal of Public Health,* 1956, **46** (6), 736–744.

Wilner, D., Walkley, R., Pinkerton, T., & Tayback, M. *The housing environment and family life: A longitudinal study of the effects of housing on morbidity and mental health.* Baltimore: The Johns Hopkins University Press, 1962.

Woodbury, C. (Ed.) *The future of cities and urban redevelopment.* Chicago: University of Chicago Press, 1953.

Young, M., & Willmott, P. *Family and kinship in East London.* Glencoe, Ill.: The Free Press, 1957.

35 Some Sources of Residential Satisfaction in an Urban Slum[1]

Marc Fried and Peggy Gleicher

The gradual deterioration of older urban dwellings and the belief that such areas provide a locus for considerable social pathology have stimulated concern with altering the physical habitat of the slum. Yet the technical difficulties, the practical inadequacies, and the moral problems of such planned revisions of the human environment are also forcing themselves upon our attention most strikingly (see Gans, 1959). While a full evaluation of the advantages and disadvantages of urban renewal must await studies which derive from various disciplines, there is little likelihood that the vast sums currently available will be withheld until there is a more systematic basis for rational decisions. Thus it is of the utmost importance that we discuss all aspects of the issue as

Reproduced by permission of the *Journal of the American Institute of Planners* (November 1961, Volume XXVII, No. 4), and the authors.

[1] This report is part of a study entitled "Relocation and Mental Health: Adaptation Under Stress," conducted by the Center for Community Studies in the Department of Psychiatry of the Massachusetts General Hospital and the Harvard Medical School. The research is supported by the National Institute of Mental Health, Grant No. 3M 9137-C3. We are grateful to Erich Lindemann, the Principal Investigator, and to Leonard Duhl of the Professional Services Branch, NIMH, for their continued help and encouragement. Edward Ryan has contributed in many ways to the final formulations of this paper, and Chester Hartman and Joan Levin have given helpful criticism and advice.

thoroughly as possible and make available even the more fragmentary findings which begin to clarify the many unsolved problems.

Since the most common foci of urban renewal are areas which have been designated as slums, it is particularly important to obtain a clearer picture of so-called slum areas and their populations. Slum areas undoubtedly show much variation, both variation from one slum to another and heterogeneity within urban slum areas. However, certain consistencies from one slum area to another have begun to show up in the growing body of literature. It is quite notable that the available systematic studies of slum areas indicate a very broad working-class composition in slums, ranging from highly skilled workers to the nonworking and sporadically working members of the "working" class. Moreover, even in our worst residential slums it is likely that only a minority of the inhabitants (although sometimes a fairly large and visible minority) are afflicted with one or another form of social pathology. Certainly the idea that social pathology in any form is decreased by slum clearance finds little support in the available data. The belief that poverty, delinquency, prostitution, and alcoholism magically inhere in the buildings of slums and will die with the demolition of the slum has a curious persistence but can hardly provide adequate justification for the vast enterprise of renewal planning.

In a larger social sense, beyond the political and economic issues involved, planning for urban renewal has important human objectives. Through such planning we wish to make available to a larger proportion of the population some of the advantages of modern urban facilities, ranging from better plumbing and decreased fire hazards to improved utilization of local space and better neighborhood resources. These values are all on the side of the greater good for the greatest number. Yet it is all too apparent that we know little enough about the meaning and consequences of differences in physical environment either generally or for specific groups. Urban renewal may lead, directly and indirectly, to improved housing for slum residents. But we cannot evaluate the larger effects of relocation or its appropriateness without a more basic understanding than we now have of the meaning of the slum's physical and social environment. This report is an initial essay toward understanding the issue. We shall consider some of the factors that give meaning to the residential environment of the slum dweller. Although the meaning of the environment to the resident of a slum touches only one part of the larger problem, it is critical that we understand this if we are to achieve a more effectively planned and designed urban environment.

I. THE SIGNIFICANCE OF THE SLUM ENVIRONMENT

People do not like to be dispossessed from their dwellings, and every renewal project that involves relocation can anticipate considerable resistance, despite the best efforts to insure community support. It is never quite clear whether most people object mainly to being forced to do something they have not voluntarily elected to do; or whether they simply object to relocation, voluntary or involuntary. There is, of course, considerable evidence for the commitment of slum residents to their habitat. Why this should be so is less clear and quite incomprehensible in the face of all middle-class residential values. In order to evaluate the issue more closely we shall consider the problem of the meaning and functional significance of residence in a slum area. Although we are primarily concerned with a few broadly applicable generalizations, a complete analysis will take better account of the diversities in the composition of slum populations.

The fact that more than half the respondents in our sample[2] have a long-standing experience of familiarity with the area in which they lived before relocation suggests a very basic residential stability. Fifty-five percent of the sample first moved to or were born in the West End approximately 20 years ago or more. Almost one-fourth of the entire sample was born in the West End. Not only is there marked residential stability within the larger area of the West End, but the total rate of movement from one dwelling unit to another has been exceedingly low. Table 35-1 gives the distribution of movement from one dwelling unit to another within the ten years prior to the interview. It is readily evident that the largest proportion of the sample has made very few moves indeed. In fact, a disproportionate share of the frequent moves is made by a small group of relatively high-status people, largely professional and semi-professional people who were living in the West End only temporarily. Regardless of which criterion we use, these data indicate that we cannot readily accept those impressions of a slum which suggest a highly transient population. An extremely large proportion shows unusual residential stability, and this is quite evenly distributed among the several levels of working-class occupational groups.

The Slum Environment as Home

What are the sources of this residential stability? Undoubtedly they are many and variable, and we could not hope to extricate the precise contribution of each factor. Rents were certainly low. If we add individually expended heating costs to the rental figures reported we find that 25 percent were paying $34 a month or less, and 85 percent paying $54 a month or less. But though this

[2] These data are based on a probability sample of residents from the West End of Boston interviewed during 1958–1959. The sampling criteria included only households in which there was a female household member between the age of 20 and 65. The present analysis is based on the pre-relocation data from the female respondents. Less systematic pre-relocation data on the husbands are also available, as well as systematic post-relocation data for both wives and husbands and women without husbands.

Table 35-1 Number of Moves in Previous Ten Years

Moves	Number	Percent
Totals	473	100
None	162	34
One	146	31
Two	73	15
Three or more	86	19
No answer	6	1

undoubtedly played a role as a background factor, it can hardly account for the larger findings. Low rental costs are rarely mentioned in discussing aspects of the West End or of the apartments that were sources of satisfaction. And references to the low West End rents are infrequent in discussing the sources of difficulty which people expected in the course of moving. In giving reasons for having moved to the last apartment they occupied before relocation, only 12 percent gave any type of economic reason (including decreased transportation costs as well as low rents). Thus, regardless of the practical importance that low rents must have had for a relatively low income population, they were not among the most salient aspects of the perceived issues in living in the West End.

On the other hand, there is considerable evidence to indicate that living in the West End had particular meaning for a vast majority of West End residents. Table 35-2 shows the distribution in response to the question, "How do you feel about living in the West End?", clearly indicating how the West End was a focus for very positive sentiments.

That the majority of West Enders do not remain in or come back to the West End simply because it is practical (inexpensive, close to facilities) is further documented by the responses to the question, "Which neighborhood, this one or any other place, do you think of as your real home, that is where you feel you really belong?" It is quite striking that fully 71 percent of the people named the West End as their real home, only slightly less than the proportion who specify liking the West End or liking it very much. Although there is a strong relationship between liking the West End and viewing it as home, 14 percent of those who view the West End as home have moderately or markedly negative feelings about the area. On the other hand, 50 percent of those who do not regard the West End as home have moderately or markedly positive feelings about the area. Thus, liking the West End is not contingent on experiencing the area as that place in which one most belongs. However, the responses to this item give us an even more basic and global sense of the meaning the West End had for a very large proportion of its inhabitants.

These responses merely summarize a group of sentiments that pervade the interviews, and they form the essential context for understanding more discrete meanings and functions of the area. There are clearly differences in the details, but the common core lies in a widespread feeling of belonging someplace, of being "at home" in a region that extends out from but well beyond the dwelling unit. Nor is this only because of familiarity, since a very large proportion of the more recent residents (64 percent of those who moved into the West End during 1950 or after) also showed clearly positive feelings about the area. And 39 percent of those who moved in during 1950 or after regard the West End as their real home.[3]

Types of Residential "Belonging"

Finer distinctions in the quality and substance of positive feelings about the West End reveal a number of variations. In categorizing the qualitative aspects of responses to two questions which were analyzed to-

Table 35-2 Feelings about the West End

Feelings	Number	Percent	
Totals	473	100	
Like very well	174	37	75
Like	183	38	
Mixed like-dislike	47	10	14
Indifferent	18	4	
Dislike	25	5	10
Dislike very much	23	5	
No answer	3	1	

[3] It is possible, of course, that we have obtained an exaggerated report of positive feelings about the area because of the threat of relocation. Not only does the consistency of the replies and their internal relationships lead us to believe that this has not caused a major shift in response, but, bearing in mind the relative lack of verbal facility of many of the respondents and their frequent tendencies to give brief replies, we suspect that the interview data often lead to underestimating the strength of sentiment.

gether ("How do you feel about living in the West End?" and "What will you miss most about the West End?"), we distinguished three broad differences of emphasis among the positive replies. The three large categories are: (1) *integral belonging*: sense of *exclusive* commitment, taking West End for granted as home, thorough familiarity and security; (2) *global commitment*: sense of profound gratification (rather than familiarity), pleasure in West End and enjoyment; and (3) *discrete satisfaction*: specific satisfying or pleasurable opportunities or atmosphere involving no special commitment to *this* place.

Only a small proportion (13 percent) express their positive feelings in terms of logically irreplaceable ties to people and places. They do so in often stark and fundamental ways: this is my home; it's all I know; everyone I know is here; I won't leave. A larger group (38 percent) are less embedded and take the West End less for granted but, nonetheless, express an all-encompassing involvement with the area which few areas are likely to provide them again. Their replies point up a less global but poignant sense of loss: it's one big happy family; I'll be sad; we were happy here; it's so friendly; it's handy to everything and everyone is congenial and friendly. The largest group (40 percent) are yet further removed from a total commitment but, in spite of the focused and discrete nature of their satisfaction with the interpersonal atmosphere or the convenience of the area, remain largely positive in feeling.

Differences in Foci of Positive Feelings

Thus, there is considerable variability in the depth and type of feeling implied by liking the West End; and the West End as home had different connotations for different people. For a large group, the West End as home seems to have implied a comfortable and satisfying base for moving out into the world and back. Among this group, in fact, the largest proportion were more concerned with accessibility to other places than with the locality itself. But for more than half the people, their West End homes formed a far more central feature of their total life space.

There is a difference within this larger group between a small number for whom the West End seems to have been the place *to* which they belonged and a larger number for whom it seems rather to have been the place *in* which they belonged. But for the larger group as a whole the West End occupied a unique status, beyond any of the specific attributes one could list and point to concretely. This sense of uniqueness, of home, was not simply a function of social relationships, for the place in itself was the object of strong positive feelings. Most people (42 percent) specify both people and places or offer a global, encompassing reason for their positive feelings. But almost an equally small proportion (13 percent and 10 percent, respectively) select out people or places as the primary objects of positive experience.

With respect to the discrete foci for positive feelings, similar conclusions can be drawn from another question: "Which places do you mostly expect to miss when you leave the West End?" In spite of the place-orientation of the question, 16 percent specify some aspect of interpersonal loss as the most prominent issue. But 40 percent expect to miss one of the places which is completely identified with the area or, minimally, carries a specific local identity. The sense of the West End as a local region, as an area with a spatial identity going beyond (although it may include) the social relationships involved, is a common perception. In response to the question: "Do you think of your home in the West End as part of a local neighborhood?"[4] 81 percent replied affirmatively. It is this sense of localism as a basic feature of lower-class life and the functional significance of local interpersonal relationships and of local places which have been stressed by a number of studies of the working class (see Hoggart, 1857; Young & Willmott, 1957) and are documented by many aspects of our data.

---

[4] This question is from the interview designed by Leo Srole and his associates for the Yorkville study in New York.

In summary, then, we observe that a number of factors contribute to the special importance that the West End seemed to bear for the large majority of its inhabitants.

1. Residence in the West End was highly stable, with relatively little movement from one dwelling unit to another and with minimal transience into and out of the area. Although residential stability is a fact of importance in itself, it does not wholly account for commitment to the area.

2. For the great majority of the people, the local area was a focus for strongly positive sentiments and was perceived, probably in its multiple meanings, as home. The critical significance of belonging in or to an area has been one of the most consistent findings in working-class communities both in the United States and in England.

3. The importance of localism in the West End, as well as in other working-class areas, can hardly be emphasized enough. This sense of a local spatial identity includes both local social relationships and local places. Although oriented around a common conception of the area as "home," there are a number of specific factors dominating the concrete meaning of the area for different people.

We now turn to a closer consideration of two of these sets of factors: first, the interpersonal networks within which people functioned and, in the subsequent section, the general spatial organization of behavior.

II. SOCIAL RELATIONSHIPS IN PHYSICAL SPACE

Social relationships and interpersonal ties are not as frequently isolated for special attention in discussing the meaning of the West End as we might have expected. Despite this relative lack of exclusive salience, there is abundant evidence that patterns of social interaction were of great importance in the West End. Certainly for a great number of people, local space, whatever its independent significance, served as a locus for social relationships in much the same way as in other working-class slum areas (for

example, Gans, 1962; Mogey, 1956; Kerr, 1958). In this respect, the urban slum community also has much in common with the communities so frequently observed in folk cultures. Quite consistently, we find a strong association between positive feelings about the West End and either extensive social relationships or positive feelings about other people in the West End.[5] The availability of such interpersonal ties seems to have considerable influence on feelings about the area, but the absence of these ties does not preclude a strongly positive feeling about the West End. That is, despite the prominence of this pattern, there seem to be alternative sources of satisfaction with the area for a minority of the people.

The Place of Kinship Ties

Following some of the earlier studies of membership in formal organizations, which indicated that such organizational ties were infrequent in the working class, increasing attention has been given to the importance of kinship ties in lower-class groups (see Dotson, 1951). Despite the paucity of comparative studies, most of the investigations of working-class life have stressed the great importance of the extended-kinship group. But the extended-kinship group, consisting of relationships beyond the immediate family, does not seem to be a primary source of the closest interpersonal ties. Rather, the core of the most active kinship ties seems to be composed of nuclear relatives (parents, siblings, and children) of both spouses. Our data show that the more extensive these available kinship ties are within the local area, the greater the proportion who show strong positive feeling toward the West End. These data are given in Table 35-3 and show a quite overwhelming and consistent trend in this direction. Other relationships point to the same observation: the more frequent the contact with siblings or the

[5] These associations between feelings about the West End and interpersonal variables include interpersonal relationships outside the West End as well. Thus there is the possibility that an interrelated personality variable may be involved. We shall pursue this in subsequent studies.

Table 35-3 Extensiveness of Kin in West End by Feelings about West End

Extensiveness of kin in West End	Number of respondents	Feelings about West End (percent)			
		Totals	Strongly positive	Positive	Mixed negative
None	193	100	29	46	25
Few	150	100	37	38	25
Some	67	100	45	31	24
Many	52	100	58	27	15

Table 35-4 Preference for Relatives or Friends by Feelings about West End

Preference for relatives or friends	Number of respondents	Feelings about West End (percent)			
		Totals	Strongly positive	Positive	Mixed negative
Relatives preferred	232	100	39	39	22
Mixed preferences	81	100	35	32	33
Friends preferred	148	100	36	42	22

more frequent the contact with parents or the greater the desire to move near relatives, the greater the proportion who like the West End very well.

The Importance of the Neighbor Relationship

Important as concrete kinship ties were, however, it is easy to overestimate their significance and the relevance of kinship contacts for positive feelings about the residential area. Studies of the lower class have often neglected the importance of other interpersonal patterns in their concentration on kinship. Not only are other social relationships of considerable significance, but they also seem to influence feelings about the area. The similar effects of both sets of relationships is evident in Table 35-4, which presents the association between feelings about the West End and the personal importance of relatives versus friends.[6] A greater proportion (50 percent) have a strong preference for relatives, but a large group (31 percent) indicates a strong preferential

orientation to friends. More relevant to our immediate purpose, there is little difference among the three preference groups in the proportions who have strong positive feelings about the West End.

In view of the consistency in the relations between a wide variety of interpersonal variables and feelings about the West End, it seems likely that there are alternative paths to close interpersonal ties of which kinship is only one specific form.[7] In fact, the single most powerful relation between feelings about the West End and an interpersonal variable is provided by feelings about West End neighbors (Table 35-5). Although the neighbor relationship may subsume kinship ties (i.e., when the neighbors are kin), the association between feelings about neighbors and feelings about the West End is stronger than the association between feelings about the West End and any of the kinship variables. Beyond this fact, the frequent references to neighbors and the stress on *local* friendships lead us

[6] The "Preference for Relatives or Friends" item is based on four separate questions presenting a specific situation and asking if the respondent would prefer to be associated with a relative or friend in each situation.

[7] We do not mean to imply that this exhausts the special importance of kinship in the larger social structure. There is also evidence to suggest that some of the basic patterns of the kinship relationship have influenced the form of interpersonal ties more generally in the urban working class (see Fried and Linemann, 1961).

Table 35-5 Closeness to Neighbors by Feelings about West End

Closeness to neighbors	Number of respondents	Feelings about West End (percent)			
		Totals	Strongly positive	Positive	Mixed negative
Very positive	78	100	63	28	9
Positive	265	100	37	42	21
Negative	117	100	20	39	41

to suggest that the neighbor relationship was one of the most important ties in the West End. And, whether based on prior kinship affiliation or not, it formed one of the critical links between the individual (or family) and the larger area and community.

Localism in Close Interpersonal Ties

Since the quality of feeling about the West End is associated with so wide a diversity of interpersonal relationships, it is not surprising that the majority of people maintained their closest ties with West Enders. The distribution of relationships which were based in the West End or outside the West End are given in Table 35-6. The striking proportion whose closest ties are all or mostly from the West End is clearly evident. As we would expect on the basis of the previous results, the more exclusively a person's closest relationships are based in the West End, the greater the likelihood that he will have strong positive feelings about the West End.

A few significant factors stand out clearly from this analysis.

Table 35-6 West End Dwelling of Five Closest Persons

Five closest persons	Number	Percent	
Totals	473	100	
All West End	201	42	60
Mostly West End	85	18	
Equally West End and outside	13	3	
Mostly outside West End	70	15	25
All outside West End	46	10	
Unspecified	58	12	

1. Although the kinship relationship was of considerable importance in the West End, as in other working-class communities, there were a number of alternative sources of locally based interpersonal ties. Among these, we suggest that the neighbor relationship is of particular importance, both in its own right and in its effect on more general feelings about the area.

2. There is considerable generality to the observation that the greater one's interpersonal commitments in the area, in the form of close contact or strongly positive feelings, the greater the likelihood of highly positive feelings about the area as a whole. This observation holds for all the forms of interpersonal relationship studied.

What is perhaps most striking about the social patterns of the West End is the extent to which all the various forms of interpersonal ties were localized within the residential area. Local physical space seems to have provided a framework within which some of the most important social relationships were embedded. As in many a folk community (see Goodenough, 1951), there was considerable overlap in the kinds of ties which obtained: kin were often neighbors; there were many interrelated friendship networks; mutual help in household activities was both possible and frequent; many of these relationships had a long and continuous history; and the various ties often became further intertwined through many activities within a common community.

The street itself, favorite recreation areas, local bars, and the settlement houses in the area all served as points of contact for overlapping social networks. Thus the most unique features of this working-class area (although common to many other working-class areas) were: (a) the interweaving and overlap of many different types of inter-personal contacts and role relationships, and (b) the organization and concrete mani-festation of these relationships within a common, relatively bounded spatial region. It is these characteristics which seem to have given a special character and meaning both to the quality of interpersonal relation-ships and to the area within which these relationships were experienced.

We have repeatedly stressed the observa-tion that, granting the importance of local social relationships, the meaning of "local-ism" in the West End included places as well as people. It is difficult to document the independent significance of either of these factors, but the importance of the physical space of the West End and the spe-cial use of the area are evident in many ways. Previously we indicated the impor-tance of physical areas and places as sources of satisfaction in the West End. We now wish to consider more systematically the way in which the physical space of the area is subjectively organized by a large propor-tion of the population. In understanding the importance of such subjective spatial or-ganization in addition to the significance of local social relationships, we can more ade-quately appreciate the enormous and mul-tiply derived meaning that a residential area may have for people.

III. SUBJECTIVE SPATIAL ORGANIZATION

There is only a fragmentary literature on the psychological, social, or cultural implications of spatial behavior and spatial imagery. The orientation of the behavioral sciences to the history, structure, and dynamics of social relationships has tended to obscure the po-tential significance of the nonhuman en-vironment generally and, more specifically, that aspect of the nonhuman environment which we may designate as significant space. Although there have been a number of important contributions to this problem, we are far from any systematic understanding of the phenomena. We do not propose to discuss the problems or concepts, but only to start with a few very primitive considera-tions and to observe the working-class rela-tionship to space in several respects. We are primarily concerned with the way in which space is organized or structured in defining the usable environment and in providing restrictions to or freedom for mobility in space.[8] In this way we may hope to see more broadly the constellation of forces which serve to invest the residential en-vironment of the working class with such intense personal meaning.

Spatial Usage Patterns in the Middle Class

There are undoubtedly many differences among people in the way space is organized, according to personality type, physiological disposition, environmental actualities, social roles, and cultural experience. We wish to focus only on some of those differences which, at the extremes, distinguish the work-ing class quite sharply from higher-status groups. Although we do not have compara-tive data, we suggest that in the urban middle class (most notably among rela-tively high-status professional and business groups) space is characteristically used in a highly *selective* way. The boundary be-tween the dwelling unit and the immediate environs is quite sharp and minimally per-meable. It is, of course, possible to go into and out of the dwelling unit through chan-nels which are specifically designated for this purpose. But walls are clear-cut bar-riers between the inside of the dwelling unit and the outer world. And even windows are seldom used for any interchange between the inner world of the dwelling unit and the outside environment (except for sunlight and air). Most of us take this so much for granted that we never question it, let alone take account of it for analytic purposes. It is the value of the "privacy of the home." The dwelling unit may extend into a zone of lawn or garden which we tend and for which we pay taxes. But, apart from this,

[8] We shall not touch on a related problem of considerable interest, the basic modes of con-ceiving or experiencing space in general. We assume a close relation between general con-ceptions of space and ways of using spatial aspects of specific parts of the environment, but an analysis of this problem is beyond the scope of the present discussion.

the space outside the dwelling unit is barely "ours."

As soon as we are in the apartment hallway or on the street, we are on a wholly *public* way, a path to or from someplace rather than on a bounded space defined by a subjective sense of belonging.[9] Beyond this is a highly individualized world, with many common properties but great variability in usage and subjective meaning. Distances are very readily transgressed; friends are dispersed in many directions; preferred places are frequently quite idiosyncratic. Thus there are few physical areas which have regular (certainly not daily) widespread common usage and meaning. And contiguity between the dwelling unit and other significant spaces is relatively unimportant. It is primarily the channels and pathways between individualized significant spaces which are important, familiar, and common to many people. This orientation to the use of space is the very antithesis of that localism so widely found in the working class.

The Territorial Sense in the Working Class

Localism captures only a gross orientation toward the social use of an area of physical space and does not sufficiently emphasize its detailed organization. Certainly, most middle-class observers are overwhelmed at the degree to which the residents of any working-class district and, most particularly, the residents of slums are "at home" in the street. But it is not only the frequency of using the street and treating the street outside the house as a place, and not simply as a path, which points up the high degree of permeability of the boundary between the dwelling unit and the immediate environing area. It is also the use of all channels between dwelling unit and environment as a bridge between inside and outside: open windows, closed windows, hallways, even walls and floors serve this purpose. Frequently, even the sense of adjacent human beings carried by noises and smells provides a sense of comfort. As Edward Ryan points out:[10]

> Social life has an almost uninterrupted flow between apartment and street: children are sent into the street to play, women lean out the windows to watch and take part in street activity, women go "out on the street" to talk with friends, men and boys meet on the corners at night, and families sit on the steps and talk with their neighbors at night when the weather is warm.

It is not surprising, therefore, that there is considerable agreement between the way people feel about their apartments and the way they feel about the West End in general (Table 35-7). Without attempting to assign priority to feelings about the apartment or to feelings about the West End, it seems likely that physical barriers which are experienced as easily permeable allow for a ready generalization of positive or negative feelings in either direction.

We would like to call this way of structuring the physical space around the actual residential unit a *territorial* space, in contrast to the selective space of the middle class. It is territorial in the sense that physical space is largely defined in terms of relatively bounded regions to which one has freedom or restriction of access, and it does not emphasize the path function of physical space in allowing or encouraging movements to or

[9] The comment of one reader to an early draft of this paper is worth quoting, since it leads into a fascinating series of related problems. With respect to this passage, Chester Hartman notes: "We tend to think of this other space as anonymous and public (in the sense of belonging to everyone, i.e., no one) when it does not specifically belong to us. The lower-class person is not nearly so alienated from what he does not own." To what extent is there a relationship between a traditional expectation (even if occasionally belied by reality) that only *other* people own real property, that one is essentially part of a "propertyless class" and a willingness to treat any property as common? And does this provide a framework for the close relationship between knowing and belonging in the working class in contrast to the middle-class relationship between owning and belonging? Does the middle-class acceptance of legal property rights provide a context in which one can *only* belong if one owns? From a larger psychological view, these questions are relevant not merely to physical space and physical objects but to social relationships as well.

[10] This comment is a fragment from a report on ethnographic observations made in the area.

Table 35-7 Feelings about the Apartment by Feelings about West End

Feelings about apartment	Number of respondents	Feelings about West End (percent)			
		Totals	Like very well	Like	Mixed-dislike
Like	367	100	43	40	17
Mixed-indifferent	41	100	20	42	39
Dislike	60	100	12	30	58

from other places.[11] There is also evidence, some of which has been presented in an earlier section, that it is territorial in a more profound sense: that individuals feel different spatial regions belong to or do not belong to them and, correspondingly, feel that they belong to (or in) specific spatial regions or do not belong.[12]

Spatial Boundaries in the Local Area

In all the previous discussion, the West End has been treated as a whole. People in the area did, in fact, frequently speak of the area as a whole, as if it were an entity. However, it is clear that the area was differently bounded for different people. Considering only the gross distinction between

[11] These formulations refer to modal patterns and do not apply to the total population. Twenty-six percent do select out the "accessibility" of the area, namely a path function. The class difference, however, is quite striking since 67 percent of the highest-status group give this response, but only 19 percent of the lowest-status group and between 28 percent and 31 percent of the middle- (but still low-status) groups select out various types of "accessibility."

[12] Without attempting, in this report, a "depth" psychological analysis of typical patterns of working-class behaviors, we should note the focal importance of being accepted or rejected, of belonging or being an "outsider." Preliminary evidence from the post-relocation interviews reveals this in the frequent references to being unable to obtain an apartment because "they didn't want us" or that the landlord "treated us like dirt." It also emerges in the frequently very acute sensitivity to gross social-class differences, and a sharp sense of not belonging or not fitting in with people of higher status. Clarification of this and related problems seems essential for understanding the psychological and social consequences of social-class distinctions and has considerable implication for urban residential planning generally and urban renewal specifically.

circumscribing the neighborhood as a very small, localized space in contrast to an expansive conception of the neighborhood to include most of the area, we find that the sample is about equally split (Table 35-8). It is apparent, therefore, that the territorial zone may include a very small or a very large part of the entire West End, and for quite a large proportion it is the former. For these people, at least, the boundary between dwelling unit and street may be highly permeable; but this freedom of subjective access does not seem to extend very far beyond the area immediately adjacent to the dwelling unit. It is also surprising how little this subjective sense of neighborhood size is affected by the extensiveness of West End kin or of West End friends. This fact tends to support the view that there is some degree of independence between social relationships and spatial orientations in the area.[13]

Thus, we may say that for almost half the people, there is a subjective barrier surrounding the immediately local area. For this large group, the barrier seems to define the zone of greatest personal significance or comfort from the larger area of the West End. However, it is clearly not an impermeable barrier. Not only does a large proportion of the sample fail to designate this boundary, but even for those who do perceive this distinction, there is frequently a

[13] The social-class patterning is also of interest. Using the occupation of the head of household as the class criterion, there is almost no difference among the three working-class status levels in the area included as a neighborhood (the percentages who say "much or all of the area" for these three groups are, respectively, 51 percent, 46 percent, and 48 percent). But only 38 percent of the high-status group include much or all of the West End in their subjective neighborhood.

Table 35-8 Area of West End "Neighborhood"

Neighborhood	Number	Percent
Totals	473	100
Much of West End: all of area, West End specified, most of area, large area specified	191	40
Part of West End: one or two streets or less, a small area, a store	207	44
People, not area: the people around	17	4
Not codeable	58	12

Table 35-9 Area of West End Known Well

Area	Number	Percent
Totals	473	100
Just own block	27	6 ⎫ 20
A few blocks	65	14 ⎭
Large part	66	14 ⎫ 64
Most of it	237	50 ⎭
Uncodeable	78	16

sense of familiarity with the area beyond.[14] Thus, when we use a less severe criterion of boundedness than the local "neighborhood" and ask people how much of the West End they know well, we find that a very large proportion indeed indicate their familiarity with a large part or most of the area (Table 35-9). Although almost half the people consider "home ground" to include only a relatively small local region, the vast majority is easily familiar with a greater part of the West End. The local boundaries within the West End were, thus, boundaries of a semipermeable nature although differently experienced by different people.

[14] Of those who include only part of the West End in their designation of their neighborhood, 68 percent indicate they know a large part or most of the West End well. Naturally, an even higher percentage (87 percent) of those who include much or all of the West End in their neighborhood are similarly familiar with a large part or all of the area.

The Inner-Outer Boundary

These distinctions in the permeability of the boundaries between dwelling unit and street and across various spaces within the larger local region are brought even more sharply into focus when we consider the boundary surrounding the West End as a whole. The large majority may have been easily familiar with most or all of the West End. But it is impressive how frequently such familiarity seems to stop at the boundaries of the West End. In comparison with the previous data, Table 35-10 demonstrates the very sharp delineation of the inner space of the West End from the outer space surrounding the West End. The former is generally well explored and essentially familiar, even though it may not be considered the area of commitment. The latter is either relatively unknown by many people or, if known, it is categorized in a completely different way. A relatively large proportion are familiar with the immediately adjacent areas which are directly or almost directly contiguous with the West End (and are often viewed as extensions of the West End), but only slightly more than a quarter (26 percent) report familiarity with any other parts of the Boston area. Thus there seems to be a widely experienced subjective boundary surrounding the larger local area and some of its immediate extensions which is virtually impermeable. It is difficult to believe that people literally do not move out

Table 35-10 Familiar Areas of Boston

Area	Number	Percent
Totals	473	101
West End only: no other area, none	141	30
Adjacent area: North End, esplanade	216	46
Contiguous areas: East Boston, Cambridge	98	21
Nearby areas: Revere, Malden, Brookline	12	3
Metropolitan Boston, beyond "nearby" areas	1	0
Outside Boston area	3	1
No answer	2	0

of this zone for various activities. Yet, if they do, it apparently does not serve to diminish the psychological (and undoubtedly social) importance of the boundary.[15]

These data provide considerable evidence to support, if they do not thoroughly validate, the view that the working class commonly organizes physical space in terms of a series of boundaries. Although we do not mean to imply any sense of a series of concentric boundaries or to suggest that distance alone is the critical dimension, there seems to be a general tendency for the permeability of these boundaries to decrease with increasing distance from the dwelling unit. Significant space is thus subjectively defined as a series of contiguous regions with the dwelling unit and its immediately surrounding local area as the central region. We have referred to this way of organizing physical space as *territorial* to distinguish it from the more highly *selective* and individualized use of space which seems to characterize the middle class. And we suggest that it is the territorial conception and manner of using physical space which provides one of the bases for the kind of localism which is so widely found in working-class areas.

In conjunction with the emphasis upon local social relationships, this conception and use of local physical space gives particular force to the feeling of commitment to, and the sense of belonging in, the residential area. It is clearly not just the dwelling unit that is significant but a larger local region that partakes of these powerful feelings of involvement and identity. It is not surprising, therefore, that "home" is not merely an apartment or a house but a local area in which some of the most meaningful aspects of life are experienced.

IV. CONCLUSIONS

The aims of urban renewal and the sources of pressure for renewal are manifold: among the objectives we may include more rational

---

[15] We do not have data on the actual frequency of use of the various areas outside the West End. Thus we cannot deal with the problem of the sense of familiarity in relation to actual usage patterns.

and efficient use of land, the elimination of dilapidated buildings, increase in the municipal tax base, and the improvement of living conditions for slum dwellers. Although the social benefit to the slum dweller has received maximum public attention, it is always unclear how the life situation (or even the housing situation) of the working-class resident of a slum is supposed to be improved by slum clearance or even slum improvement. Public housing has not proved to be an adequate answer to this problem for many reasons. Yet public housing is the only feature of renewal programs that has even attempted to deal seriously with this issue.

In recent years, a number of reports have suggested that concern about slum conditions has been used to maneuver public opinion in order to justify use of eminent domain powers and demolition, largely for the benefit of middle- and upper-status groups. Although we cannot evaluate this political and economic issue, we do hope to understand the ways in which dislocation from a slum and relocation to new residential areas has, in fact, benefited or damaged the working-class residents involved. It is all too apparent, however, that the currently available data are inadequate for clarifying some of the most critical issues concerning the effects of residential relocation upon the subject populations.

We know very little about slums and the personal and social consequences of living in a slum. We know even less about the effects of forced dislocation from residential areas on people in general and on working-class people specifically. But rational urban planning which, under these circumstances, becomes urban *social* planning, requires considerable knowledge and understanding of people and places affected by the plans. It is incumbent upon us to know both what is wrong with the slum and with slum life and what is right about slums and living in slums. It is essentially this question, formulated as the meaning and consequences of living in a slum, that has motivated our inquiry into the sources of residential satisfaction in an urban slum. In turn, this study provides one of the bases for understanding the ways in which dislocation and relocation affect the patterns of personal and social adaptation of former residents of a slum.

In studying the reasons for satisfaction that the majority of slum residents experience, two major components have emerged. On the one hand, the residential area is the region in which a vast and interlocking set of social networks is localized. And, on the other, the physical area has considerable meaning as an extension of home, in which various parts are delineated and structured on the basis of a sense of belonging. These two components provide the context in which the residential area may so easily be invested with considerable, multiply determined meaning. Certainly, there are variations both in the importance of various factors for different people and in the total sense which people have of the local area. But the greatest proportion of this working-class group (like other working-class slum residents who have been described) shows a fairly common experience and usage of the residential area. This common experience and usage is dominated by a conception of the local area beyond the dwelling unit as an integral part of home. This view of an area as home and the significance of local people and local places are so profoundly at variance with typical middle-class orientations that it is difficult to appreciate the intensity of meaning, the basic sense of identity involved in living in the particular area. Yet it seems to form the core of the extensive social integration that characterizes this (and other) working-class slum populations.

These observations lead us to question the extent to which, through urban renewal, we relieve a situation of stress or create further damage. If the local spatial area and an orientation toward localism provide the core of social organization and integration for a large proportion of the working class, and if, as current behavioral theories would suggest, social organization and integration are primary factors in providing a base for effective social functioning, what are the consequences of dislocating people from their local areas? Or, assuming that the potentialities of people for adaptation to crisis are great, what deeper damage occurs in the process? And, if there are deleterious effects,

are these widespread or do they selectively affect certain predictable parts of the population? We emphasize the negative possibilities because these are closest to the expectations of the population involved and because, so frequently in the past, vague positive effects on slum populations have been arbitrarily assumed. But it is clear that, in lieu of or along with negative consequences, there may be considerable social benefit.

The potential social benefits also require careful, systematic evaluation, since they may manifest themselves in various and sometimes subtle ways. Through a variety of direct and intervening factors, the forced residential shift may lead to changes in orientations toward work, leading to increased satisfaction in the occupational sphere; or, changes may occur in the marital and total familial relationship to compensate for decreased kinship and friendship contacts and, in turn, lead to an alternative (and culturally more syntonic) form of interpersonal satisfaction; or, there may be either widespread or selective decreases in problems such as delinquency, mental illness, and physical malfunctioning.

A realistic understanding of the effects, beneficial and/or deleterious, of dislocation and relocation from an urban slum clearly requires further study and analysis. Our consideration of some of the factors involved in working-class residential satisfaction in the slum provides one basis for evaluating the significance of the changes that take place with a transition to a new geographic and social environment. Only the careful comparison of pre-relocation and post-relocation data can begin to answer these more fundamental questions and, in this way, provide a sound basis for planning urban social change.

REFERENCES:

Dotson, F. Patterns of voluntary association among urban working class families. *American Sociological Review*, 1951, **25**, 687–693.
Fried, M., & Lindemann, E. Sociocultural factors in mental health and illness. *American Journal of Orthopsychiatry*, 1961, **31**, 87–101.
Gans, H. The human implications of current redevelopment and relocation planning.

Journal of the American Institute of Planners, 1959, **25**, 15–25.

Gans, H. *The urban villagers.* Glencoe, Ill.: The Free Press, 1962.

Goodenough, W. *Property, kin, and community on Truk.* New Haven, Conn.: Yale University Publications in Anthropology, 1951.

Hoggart, R. *The uses of literacy.* London: Chatto & Windus, 1857.

Kerr, M. *People of Ship Street.* London: Routledge & Kegan Paul, 1958.

Mogey, J. M. *Family and neighbourhood.* London: Oxford University Press, 1956.

Young, M., & Willmott, P *Family and kinship in East London.* Glencoe, Ill.: The Free Press, 1957.

36 A Poor Family Moves to a Housing Project

Oscar Lewis

The social worker told me it would be a good idea to get the children out of La Esmeralda because there's so much delinquency there. Moving here to the housing project was practically her idea; she insisted and insisted. Finally one day she came to me and said, "Tomorrow you have to move to the *caserío* in Villa Hermosa." I didn't want to upset her because she's been good to me, so I said *O.K.*

You should have seen this place when I moved in. It was spilling over with garbage and smelling of shit, pure shit. Imagine, when the social worker opened the door that first day, a breeze happened to blow her way. She stepped back and said, "Wait, I can't go in. This is barbarous." I had to go outside with her. I tell you, the people who lived here before me were dirtier than the dirtiest pigs. When I moved out of my little room in La Esmeralda, I scrubbed it so clean you could have eaten off the floor. Whoever moved in could see that a decent person had lived there. And then I came here and found this pigsty, and the place looked so big I felt too little and weak to get it clean. So, fool that I am, instead of

Condensed from *La Vida,* by Oscar Lewis. © Copyright 1965, 1966 by Oscar Lewis. Reprinted by permission of Random House, Inc., and the author.

sending out for a mop and getting right down to work, I just stood in a corner and cried. I locked the door and stayed in all day, weeping. I cried floods.

And this place isn't like La Esmeralda, you know, where there's so much liveliness and noise and something is always going on. Here you never see any movement on the street, not one little domino or card game or anything. The place is dead. People act as if they're angry or in mourning. Either they don't know how to live or they're afraid to. And yet it's full of shameless good-for-nothings. It's true what the proverb says, "May God deliver me from quiet places; I can defend myself in the wild ones."

Everything was so strange to me when I first moved here that I was scared to death. I hated to go out because it's hard to find your way back to this place even if you know the address. The first couple of times I got lost and I didn't dare ask anybody the way for fear they would fall on me and beat me. If anyone knocked on my door I thought four times before deciding to open it. Then when I did, I took a knife along. But I'm not like that any more. I've made my decision: if someone wants to kill me, let him. I can't live shut in like that. And if anybody interferes with me it will be the worse for them. I have a couple of tricks up my sleeve and can really fuck things up for anybody when I want to.

After a few days I finally started cleaning up the place. I scrubbed the floors and put everything in order. I even painted the whole apartment, although I had to fight tooth and nail with the man in charge of the buildings in order to get the paint. That old man wanted to get something from me in return, but I wouldn't give it to him. I never have been attracted to old men.

The apartment is a good one. I have a living room, bedroom, kitchen, porch and my own private bathroom. That's something I never had in La Esmeralda. I clean it every morning and when the children use it I go and pull the chain right away.

I never had a kitchen sink in La Esmeralda either, and here I have a brand-new one. It's easy to wash the dishes in these double sinks because they're so wide and comfortable. The only trouble is the water, because sometimes it goes off, and the electricity too—three times since I've been here.

I still don't have an icebox or refrigerator, but the stove here is the first electric one I've ever had in my life. I didn't know how to light it the day I moved in. I tried everything I could think of, backward and forward. Luckily, the social worker came in and she turned it on for me, but even so I didn't learn and Nanda had to show me again that afternoon. She has worked for rich people so long that she knows all those things. I really miss my own little kerosene stove, but Nanda wanted it, so what could I do? She's my *mamá*, and if she hankered after a star I would climb up to Heaven to get it for her if I could.

The main advantage of the electric stove is that when I have a lot of work to do and it gets to be ten or eleven o'clock, I just turn on the stove and have lunch ready in no time. In La Esmeralda I had to wait for the kerosene to light up well before I could even start to cook. And this stove doesn't smoke and leave soot all over the place, either. Still, if the power fails again or is cut off because I don't pay my bill, the kids will just have to go hungry. I won't even be able to heat a cup of milk for them. In La Esmeralda, whenever I didn't have a quarter to buy a full gallon of kerosene, I got ten cents' worth. But who's going to sell you five or ten cents' worth of electricity?

I haven't seen any rats here, just one tiny little mouse. There's no lack of company anywhere, I guess; rats in La Esmeralda and lots of little cockroaches here.

This apartment is so big that I don't have to knock myself out keeping it in order. And there's plenty of room for my junk. I even have closets here, and lots of shelves. I have so many shelves and so few dishes that I have to put a dish here and a dish there just to keep each shelf from being completely empty. All the counters and things are no use at all to me, because I just cook a bit of oatmeal for the children and let them sit anywhere to eat it since I have no dishes with which to set a table. Half of my plates broke on the way from La Esmeralda. I guess they wanted to stay back there where they weren't so lonely.

Here even my saints cry! They look so sad. They think I am punishing them. This house is so big I had to separate the saints and hang them up in different places just to cover the empty walls. In La Esmeralda I kept them all together to form a little altar, and I lit candles for them. They helped me there but here I ask until I'm tired of asking and they don't help me at all. They are punishing me.

In La Esmeralda I never seemed to need as many things as here. I think it is because we all had about the same, so we didn't need any more. But here, when you go to other people's apartments and see all their things! It's not that I'm jealous. God forbid! I don't want anyone to have less than they have. It's only that I would like to have things of my own too.

What does bother me is the way people here come into my apartment and furnish the place with their mouths. They start saying, "Oh, here's where the set of furniture should go; you need a TV in that corner, and this one is just right for a record player." And so on. I bite my tongue to keep from swearing at them because, damn it, I have good taste too. I know a TV set would look fine in that corner, but if I don't have the money to buy one, how can I put it there? That's what I like about La Esmeralda—if people there could help someone, they did; if not, they kept their mouths shut.

I really would like a TV, though, because they don't have public sets here, the way they do in La Esmeralda. I filled in some blanks for that program, *Queen for a Day*, to see if I can get one as a gift. Even if you aren't chosen Queen, those people give you what you ask for. It was Fernanda's idea, and she's so lucky that maybe I will get it. If I do, then at least I could spend the holidays looking at TV. And the children might stay home instead of wandering around the neighborhood so much.

The traffic here really scares me. That's the main reason I don't like this place. Cars scud by like clouds in a high wind, and I'm telling you, I'm always afraid a car will hit the children. If something should happen to my little penguins I'd go mad, I swear I would. Here there is plenty of room to run around indoors, but my kids are little devils, and when I bring them in through the front door, they slip out again by climbing over the porch railing. Back in La Esmeralda, where our house was so small, they had to play out in the street whenever people came over, but there were no cars to worry about.

Maybe I was better off in La Esmeralda. You certainly have to pay for the comforts you have here! Listen, I'm jittery, really nervous, because if you fail to pay the rent even once here, the following month you're thrown out. I hardly ever got behind on my payments in La Esmeralda, but if I did, I knew that they wouldn't put me out on the street. It's true that my rent is only six-fifty a month here while I paid eight dollars in La Esmeralda, but there I didn't have a water bill and I paid only one-fifty a month for electricity. Here I have already had to pay three-fifty for electricity, and if I use more than the minimum they allow for water I'll have to pay for that too. And I do so much washing!

It's a fact that as long as I lived in La Esmeralda I could always scare up some money, but here I'm always broke. I've gone for as long as two days without eating here. I don't play the races any more. I can't afford to. And I can't sell *bolita* numbers here because several cops live in this *caserío* and the place is full of detectives. Only the other day I almost sold a number to one of them, but luckily I was warned in time. I don't want to be arrested for anything in the world, not because I'm scared of being in jail but because of the children.

Since I can't sell numbers here, I sell Avon cosmetics. I like the pretty sets of china they give away and I'm trying to sell a lot so that they'll give me one. But there's hardly any profit in it for me.

In La Esmeralda I could get an old man now and then to give me five dollars for sleeping with him. But here I haven't found anything like that at all. The truth is, if a man comes here and tries to strike up a conversation I usually slam the door in his face. So, well, I have this beautiful, clean apartment, but what good does it do me? Where am I to get money? I can't dig for it.

In La Esmeralda we used to buy things cheap from thieves. They stole from people who lived far away, in Santurce or Río Piedras, and then they came to La Esmeralda through one of the side entrances to sell. And who the hell is going to go looking for his things down there? Not a chance! You hardly ever saw a rich person in La Esmeralda. We didn't like them and we scared them off. But so far as I can tell, these dopes around here always steal from the *blanquitos*, the rich people, nearby. Suppose one of them took it into his head to take a look around here for his missing things? What then?

Since I've been living here I'm worse off than I have ever been before, because now I realize all the things I lack, and besides, there are so many rich people around, who always want everything for themselves. In La Esmeralda you can bum a nickel from anyone. But with these people, the more they have, the more they want. It's everything for themselves. If you ask them for work, they'll find something for you to do fast enough, but when it's time to pay, you'd think it hurt them to pull a dollar out of their pocket.

I buy most of my food at the Villa Hermosa Grocery. It's a long way from here and I have to walk it on foot every time I need something. It's a supermarket, so they don't give credit, but everything is cheaper there, much cheaper. A can of tomato sauce costs seven cents there and ten cents in La Esmeralda. Ten pounds of rice cost a dollar and a quarter in La Esmeralda and ninety-nine cents here. The small bottles of King Pine that cost fifteen cents each in La Esmeralda are two for a quarter here.

Sometimes I want to go back to La Esmeralda to live and other times I don't. It's not that I miss my family so much. On the contrary, relatives can be very bothersome. But you do need them in case you get sick because then you can dump the children on them. Sometimes I cry for loneliness here. Sometimes I'm bored to death. There's more neighborliness in La Esmeralda. I was used to having good friends stop by my house all the time. I haven't seen much of this neighborhood because I never go out. There's a Catholic church near by but I've never been there. And I haven't been to the movies once since I've been living here. In La Esmeralda I used to go now and then.

And in La Esmeralda, when nothing else was going on, you could at least hear the sea.

37 Urban Neighbourhood as a Socio-Spatial Schema

Terence Lee

The definition and analysis of neighbourhood has been an intractable problem in sociological theory since the 1920's, and in the post-war years its role in housing development has been a lively issue among planners and architects.

Neighbourhood as a Theoretical Concept

The major difficulty for the social scientist seems to be the elusiveness of neighbourhood. He cannot capture it whole in the net of a single concept. If he isolates it as a piece of territory, he often finds little or no correspondence with human behaviour; if he concentrates instead on social relationships he finds that these do not synchronize with geography. Yet he persists in thinking that the two components are somehow crucially interdependent.

The first empirical approach to urban sub-areas can be traced to Park (1915) and the Chicago School of the following two decades, particularly E. W. Burgess, R. D. McKenzie and J. A. Quinn. By plotting indices of the physical features of the city and also of such correlated behaviour as delinquency, mental disorder and racial composition, they delineated "natural areas." It was from this era that Burgess's well-known concentric zonal hypothesis originated. This method has continued to characterize human ecology and urban geography, though of course with increasing quantitative sophistication [see Hauser & Schnore (1965) for excellent critical reviews].

Although it is assumed that residence in such areas is accompanied by at least a rudimentary sense of self-consciousness, no

From *Human Relations*, 1968, **21**, 241–268. Reprinted by permission of the author and publisher.

measurement of this is included in the method, and it is reasonable to expect that since behaviour changes much more rapidly than the physical environment, the method may sometimes be misleading. There may also be subdivisions that are of great social importance but which are not sensitive to the physical measures employed.

A number of planning surveys were conducted in Britain during the post-war years, encouraged by the formalization of planning machinery and by the statutory requirement to prepare city development plans. Although deriving much of their methodology from the ecologists, these did try to come to terms with the awkward duality of physical and social. Lock's (1948) survey of the Hartlepools, for example, included the following definition of neighbourhood:

> . . . an *area* in which people can reach within easy walking distance (ten or fifteen minutes) those institutions which serve the local community and so foster a neighbourly *social* life.

The most explicit example of this approach, perhaps, has been that of Glass (1948), who proposed two distinct definitions:

> (a) an area delimited by virtue of the special physical characteristics of the area and the specific social characteristics of its inhabitants, and
> (b) a territorial group, the members of which meet on a common ground within their own area for primary social contacts.

The existence of (a), i.e. the physical areas, was confirmed, but when the catchment areas for schools, youth and adult clubs, post offices, grocery and green-grocery stores were plotted to define (b), they showed almost no coincidence. The investigation has been criticized on the ground that no direct measures of the residents' consciousness of the neighbourhood or of their social relationships were taken.

In a sense, Glass implicitly offered a third concept by tentatively predicting a correspondence between the physical and the social areas, which would have given a clear lead both to theory and practice, but this did not materialize from the observations.

If we shift ground to those who have assumed that neighbourhood is mainly a social group, we find a corresponding neglect of the physical component. Cooley (1909) was perhaps the first to express clearly the primary group concept of neighbourhood. Characteristically, it would contain fifty or sixty adults in face-to-face interaction practising mutual aid (particularly in emergency) and maintaining social control to preserve a set of norms.

Later workers in this tradition have made applied rather than theoretical contributions, by emphasizing the decline of the primary group neighbourhood as a consequence of urbanization (Roper-Power, 1937). McClenahan (1929, 1945) has gone further in suggesting from a study of a Los Angeles suburb that a new concept of primary group *without territorial attachment* is needed, *the communality*. This was to cover the highly mobile resident with friends and special interest groups scattered throughout the city.

Riemer's (1951) *contact clusters* in various parts of the city are a similar concept, in so far as they apply to friendships. Sweetzer (1941, 1942) also concentrated on social relationships, asking subjects to nominate associates and acquaintances and confirming the existence of "personal neighbourhoods," which were judged to be ". . . spatially discontinuous and compositionally unique."

At this point it is perhaps tempting to join Mann (1965), who concludes that:

> Attempts to define the boundaries of the physical neighbourhoods may be sterile in that they bear so little relation to social relationships. It is more useful to consider the social relationships themselves rather than to worry about where neighbourhoods begin and end.

There are three reasons why this conclusion is hard to accept:

(a) There is widely accepted meaning in such statements as ". . . they have bought a house in a nice neighbourhood."

(b) Because almost every investigator who has made his main approach through social relationships has built in some implicit restriction, however vague, of physical location, and this should be made explicit.

(c) A planner may not expect to create a neighbourhood, but he does expect to design its environmental component, to know, in fact, where it might "begin and end."

Finally, if neither social nor physical are dispensable, but yet cannot be shown to be aspects of a single phenomenon, a possible alternative is to define two separate concepts and to defer the formulation of a set of generalizations which relate them.

Morris & Mogey (1965), in their study of Berinsfield, for example, renounce the quest for a unified concept, because "social and physical groupings do not often coincide in an urbanized society." Instead they postulate: (i) physical units: sets of people who share a territorial bond, (ii) neighbourhoods: close co-residents with whom there is regular interaction, i.e., a social network rather than a group, and (iii) residential groups, when the population of a physical unit is also a distinct social group, i.e., when the networks of neighbours coincide.

This approach has the virtue of comprehensiveness, but it retains certain limitations. The first is that it makes no provision for the condition where many residents each have a social network, but these do *not* coincide. The second is that the superimposition of a network of acquaintanceship on a physical frame neglects the many other forms of interaction (social control of amenities, dustbins, children, noise, etc.) which characterize the urban scene.

The last objection cannot be levelled at Greer's definition of neighbourhood as a ". . . precipitate of interacting households . . . which produces, at the least, some order among the small enclave of residents." This would be wholly admirable, except that, again, the limits of the precipitate and indeed its presence, often cannot be specified although all the elements seem to be undergoing the chemical reaction.

Neighbourhood as a Planning Principle

The idea of the neighbourhood unit emerged as a planning principle in reaction to the drab uniformity of uncontrolled mass housing. As a principle it is not rigidly defined. A socio-economically balanced population of about 10,000 is given a distinct identity by emphasizing boundaries with flanking main road, green belts, etc. A school, community centre and shopping precinct form a focus at the centre of a radial network of residential roads, many of the houses are "path-access," and industrial units are sited as near as possible. The aims are aesthetic, economic, but most important, social, i.e. to create a "sense of community."

The neighbourhood unit has a long history with a flavour of genuine social idealism and three main roots. The most important of these was the Garden City movement, but there were also the Community Centre movement and the University Settlements. The first clear formulation is attributed to Perry (1929) and the principle was espoused during the 1930's by such leading architectural thinkers as Lewis Mumford, Clarence Stein, Walter Gropius and Frank Lloyd Wright. Several projects were successfully realized in this period (notably Wythenshawe in Britain and Radburn in the U.S.A.), but it was not until the surge of reconstruction and new development in post-war Britain that it gained near prominence. The Dudley Report (Design of Dwellings 1944) gave official blessing to the principle and the Town and Country Planning (1947) Act authorized the government to build New Towns, ". . . to consist of integrated neighbourhoods." Although rarely implemented in its ideal form, large numbers of neighbourhood units were built in the next twenty years and it became the established model for urban residential development.

There has been a dissenting minority. Their view is that decentralization and local grouping is outmoded, that "village green planning" is misplaced bucolic nostalgia (Isaacs, 1948; Dewey, 1950; Churchill, 1948). Sociologists have pointed out that the modern city dweller is highly mobile and prefers anonymity (Wirth, 1938; Meyer, 1951); his behaviour is no longer rooted in local territory but diffused throughout the city; it is based on shared interests and not on local affiliation (McClenahan, 1945; Riemer, 1951).

The issue has been pervaded by the classical sociological theme of anomie or desocialization, without, perhaps, due acknowledgement of the *relative* nature of this process. There is certainly widespread evidence that neighbourhood as a primary group is now rare, but this has been uncritically taken to mean that behaviour is randomly distributed in residential space. In recent years, a number of empirical and quantitative urban studies have begun a reversal of this traditional thinking by demonstrating that a substantial proportion of behaviour is still locally oriented (Foley, 1950; Smith, Form & Stone, 1954; Axelrod, 1956; Williams, 1958; Wilmott & Young, 1960; Gans, 1967).

In spite of this, or perhaps because there is a lag between sociological research and planning practice, or, more likely, because the theory is still confused, planners have become disenchanted and there is much less evidence of neighbourhood planning in the more recently developed New Towns. Ritter (1964), however, claims that it has not had a reasonable test because ". . . planning has ignored vital functions." There is certainly no published evidence available which compares the neighbourhood unit with alternative forms of development, or indeed, which identifies its "vital functions."

OUTLINE OF THE PRESENT INVESTIGATION

The argument of this paper, based on a research sample representative of the whole of a small provincial city, is that the duality of physical and social neighbourhoods can be joined only by a *phenomenological* approach. The research method is inductive, i.e., housewives were asked to draw a map of their own neighbourhood and to describe in detail their behaviour in the immediate environment. The "schema" is then proposed to conceptualize the mental representation of physical-social space. It is shown that the size and composition of schemata are a function both of the physical environment and of characteristics of the person.

The relevance of this to urban planning is demonstrated through the development of an index called the "neighbourhood quotient" (Nh.Q.). Neighbourhood quotients are schemata expressed as ratios of the physical properties of the presented environment. Evidence is adduced that they represent not only a cognitive but also a social orientation, along a continuum from low to high involvement.

The calculation of variation in Nh.Q.s for any given aggregate of subjects is taken, obversely, as a measure of *consentaneity*— a concept that implies agreement and interdependence, but not necessarily in reciprocal systems.

The possible implications for the neighbourhood unit principle are considered in terms of the following questions:

(i) What is the size and composition of the physical areas corresponding to neighbourhood schemata?

(ii) How do the manipulable physical variables of the urban environment influence schemata, e.g. density?

(iii) To what extent is the immediate locality used by city dwellers?

(iv) What is the effect of subject variables: social class, age, length of residence, location of husband's work, native status, car ownership, family size, type of house?

(v) Is high mean involvement (Nh.Q.) related to shared norms about physical boundaries?

(vi) Is it related to heterogeneity of social class?

METHOD

The Sample

The study was carried out in the city of Cambridge.

Full details of the sampling procedure are given in Lee (1954), but briefly, a representative 19 of the 35 residential polling districts were sampled from the electoral roll by households, with a basic interval of 40. In each case, the housewife was interviewed. Notwithstanding repeated callbacks, 8 were unobtainable and there were 8 refusals. The final sample was 219.

Since much of theorizing in urban sociology has been concerned with the variables of city size, density, and stage of industrialization, it is necessary to place Cambridge in this context with a brief description.

Up to 1914, the city was a university and market town and an important railway centre but not much else. Since that time

there has been a rapid growth in light manufacturing, the prosperity of surrounding agriculture has increased and it has become a regional centre for commerce and government. Less than 6 percent of the working population is now employed by the University. The manufacture of radios, food and drink, tobacco and scientific instruments is higher than the national average; personal service is only very slightly higher.

The population of urban Cambridge at the time of the investigation was approximately 104,000 (Cambridge, M.B. 86,000) and gross density 8.9 persons per acre. The latter is about the same as Southport, and somewhat lower than Oxford, Bath, Ipswich and Norwich. There has been little central redevelopment and ribbon extension to adjoining villages has spread the city so that one traverse extends more than 8 miles from north to south. Industry is scattered. Although the gross density is low, there are considerable variations in net density and apart, of course, from the University area, the architecture is undistinguished if not drab.

The sample was drawn to represent the residential areas, where there is nothing to suggest that the ordinary everyday behaviour in the locality would be different from that in other conurbations of about the same size.

The Interview

This was open-ended and intensive. It took place usually in the house but sometimes on the doorstep and lasted from 40 to 60 minutes. The form of the interview comprised particular points on which elucidation was systematically sought, rather than a rigid schedule of pre-set questions. The topics were ones which the subjects could discuss easily, freely and in many cases eagerly. Inevitably, much of the respondent material appears in the analysis that is to follow only in the form of simple ratings, but each of these represents the distillation of considerable information. Every interview was conducted by the writer, accompanied by his wife. This joint approach was undoubtedly helpful in disarming suspicion and had the additional advantage that all the data could be recorded on the spot, some of it verbatim, without any break in conversation. Standardized recording forms were used, partially pre-coded, the information being transferred later to a coding form for punched card analysis.

The main section was concerned with social behaviour, and in particular with the number and whereabouts of friends and acquaintances. After careful enquiry, these were separately assessed as many, few or none, (a) within a radius of half a mile, and (b) elsewhere within the city. Questions were also asked about the number of memberships of clubs and similar formal organizations and these were classified by their location into *local* (see below), *non-local* and *central area*. The frequency of attendance was also discussed, but this was mainly to confirm that an active role had been taken up and the information was not used subsequently. Other questions in this section dealt with shopping behaviour.

Another section was composed of "background" questions: e.g., length of residence; previous residence; husband's occupation and place of work; number and age of children, etc. A third section was devoted to attitudes—satisfaction with the city, the locality and the house; convenience; ideal choice of locality, etc. No quantitative analysis was made of this material because it was felt, in retrospect, to be often ambiguous both in question and answer.

It should be noted that nothing was said at this phase of the interview about *neighbourhood*. The questions were based, where necessary, on the half-mile radius *locality*. This precaution was taken to avoid contamination of the primary datum of the study, the neighbourhood map. The replies to questions were often phrased in neighbourhood terms, but no elaboration of the concept was sought until later.

The Neighbourhood Map

This method of measurement was developed during a pilot study, when, tentatively at first, a map was produced to help subjects in the description of their neighbourhoods. In its final form, each subject was given a unique foolscap-size section covering about two and a half square miles from the Ordnance Survey 6″/mile sheet. This is large enough for buildings and street names to be clearly visible. Each subject's house was approximately in the center and marked with a large cross. The instructions, printed on the sheet and given verbally, were:

> *Please draw a line round the part which you consider acts as your neighbourhood or district.*

From the interview sample of 219, a total of 165 drew a neighbourhood map. Twenty-four said they could not do so because their neighbourhood was "too vague"; 14 lacked the necessary sophistication to orient themselves to a map, even with help; and a further 16 gave the impression that their willingness to co-operate was approaching its limit.

A check was made against the possibility that the size of neighbourhood maps was influenced by the dimensions of the total section presented. For approximately half of the sample, the rectangular sections were made in the vertical plane, and for the other half, in the horizontal. No corresponding differences were evident in the neighbourhood maps.

Land Use Survey

A detailed analysis of the physical composition of the neighbourhoods was made with the help of a Land Use Survey of the city, kindly loaned by the County Planning Office. This specified, on a separate punched card, the nature, condition and use of each building and made it possible to derive exact and detailed counts for the 165 areas. The categories of use were later simplified to three main groups:

1. *Dwelling Units*: hereafter called "houses" for brevity
2. *Shops*: food and all other combined
3. *Social Amenity Buildings*: churches, schools, public houses, clubs, and other "places of assembly."

The Locality

In order to investigate the effect of differing physical environments upon the neighbourhood, the content of a locality, a half-mile radius from the subject's house, was analysed in the same way from the Land Use

Survey. The locality is a unique area for each household by means of which it was possible to compare the composition of the "presented" environment with the "accepted" neighbourhood.

A correction to the count was applied for some localities where part of the area was made inaccessible by a physical barrier such as a river or a railway. Only those streets which could be reached by travelling (via a bridge) for five-eighths of a mile from the home were included.

The Restriction to Housewives

It is a limitation of the investigation that it was, of necessity, restricted to housewives. Although the neighbourhood is often common to a family, it was clear in some cases that the interest and activities of husband and wife in relation to the local environment were so different that the husband would doubtless have drawn a different map. The same could certainly be said of children, but these within-family differences were regretfully regarded as beyond the scope of the present study. It might be added, in mitigation, that critical planning decisions about neighbourhood have to be based on housewives. Urban mobility is bimodal and the housewife is sufficiently important for planning to be adjusted to her mode.

RESULTS

The Neighbourhood Schema

In view of the uncertainty among planners and sociologists as to whether or not the neighbourhood is an extant phenomenon of urban life, perhaps the most significant result of the present study is that the method it employed was *possible*. Seventy-five percent of the sample had a sufficiently salient mental organization of the space and people around about them to communicate a decided impression of it to an unexpected caller. Of the remaining 25 percent, some would clearly have been able to do so if they had been resident longer.

However, the conventional concepts of neighbourhood as either a *collectively acknowledged* geographical area with definable boundaries, or as an interacting social group, were both found to be inappropriate.

It was found that people perceive, organize and react to their physical and social environment differently from their neighbours. Each person's constellation of experience and action is apparently unique, although there is some evidence of norm-formation. Repeated transaction with people and places in the urban environment leads, by a process of differentiation, to the separation of an organized socio-spatial whole. The process is probably bi-directional— expanding outwards from the home and contracting inwards from the total city. We locate shops, cinemas, churches, parks and phone boxes; we learn the whereabouts of people who will cater to our specific needs —grocers, taxi-drivers, policemen and plumbers; and those who will give us the more general satisfactions of acquaintance and friendship. The roads and pathways which link them serve as a framework. People, buildings and space are articulated into a *figure* which is well-defined and stands out from the *ground*, which is vague and formless. The figure has boundaries and the space within is continuous; it appears "different" from the remainder; it has familiarity and "meaning." It is a representation in which the objects and people have affective as well as locational coding.

There may be an imperfect correspondence between the proportions and composition of the neighbourhood and the physical actuality. We are often surprised to find that subjectively short distances are objectively long, and the reverse; or that something we thought to be in one direction is discovered in another. When we return from a long holiday we are surprised to find that our locality does not match the neighbourhood "model" we have been carrying in our head. While we were away, interpolated material has modified the memory, but as the renewed sense impressions are assimilated, the strangeness begins to disappear.

It might be argued that the subjects were not possessed of such a personal constellation until the investigator "put it into their heads." There are several answers to this. The first is that in the pilot stage, we called at a variety of houses and encouraged families to talk freely about their experiences in "this neighbourhood," unwittingly adopting the common concept of a distinguishable physical area. It was these early interviews that forced the adoption of a phenomenological, socio-spatial concept as the only one that could contain the otherwise perplexing data. Secondly, the same method has since been used by student interviewers in an Edinburgh housing estate and in Corby New Town with similar results.

A third answer may seem like wisdom after the event, but the results might well have been predicted from experimental psychology. The neighbourhood map epitomizes the organized, contoured, unique, multi-dimensional, dynamic yet stable nature of human perception. We are so accustomed to the responses to simple laboratory stimuli in the study of perception that reaction to a complex field stimulus may seem at first unfamiliar. This begs the larger question whether the neighbourhood map is in fact anything more than a cognitive organization (if such an organization can exist in isolation from action) but this will be considered shortly.

It must be remembered that all the usual limitations which bedevil the communication of subjective phenomena were present, and that a neighbourhood map is only a thin reflection of the rich mental organization that it represents. For example, although all the maps are outlined by a single line, this had to serve for all degrees of definition. From remarks like: "When I get off the bus and cross over Chesterton Road I feel I am home in my own neighbourhood," it was clear that most boundaries were fairly distinct subjective experiences, but in other cases they were blurred, or consciously recognized as smooth gradients.

"I can't properly say when I've gone out of our part, it seems to gradually dawn on you as you walk up Mill Road that you're leaving it, like."

None the less, the space within was continuous and it is the characteristics of continuity and contour, figure and ground, which give the experience of "wholeness" which the neighbourhood undoubtedly possessed for many people.

The concept which seems most apposite is a venerable one in psychology—the *schema*. This was first used by Sir Henry Head, nearly forty years ago, to describe the mental organization which is continuously being constructed to tell us where our limbs are; an ideational spatial framework built up of past movements and perceptions and serving as a basis for future ones. Bartlett (1932) developed the concept in relation to perception, memory, and skill, and Piaget has also employed it, but so far it has not been used to describe the representation of a spatial framework much beyond the reach of the limbs, although Wolters (1936) perceived its possibilities for social psychology. The particular value of this concept to neighbourhood research is that it can be used to imply a *synthesis* of physical objects, social relationships, and space. Either one or the other of these were variously emphasized in the interviews and, indeed, can be discussed and analysed separately, up to a point. But then it appears that the space is affected by what fills it, the social relationships are influenced by the space, and the physical objects are closely identified with the people who live in them or make use of them. This complex interdependence results in a mental organization that functions as a unit, concerned with behaviour in one part of the surrounding environment. It can best be described as a socio-spatial schema.

It is important to emphasize that Bartlett's main extrapolation of Head's thinking was to represent the schema as not only sensory, or cognitive, but as *dispositional*— and this is essential to its use in the present context.

A Typology of Neighbourhood Schemata

The use of a typology is fraught with danger. It has great value for conveying a general impression, but its deceptive facility in use tends to conceal the fact that it is the least efficient way we have of handling psychological data. In particular, it should be stressed that none of the three types to be outlined is mutually exclusive; they are formed by the interaction of a number of correlated continuous variables.

(i) The Social Acquaintance Neighbour-hood. The boundaries of this first type are set by social interaction, but its understanding depends heavily on the distinction between "knowing" or "being acquainted" with people and "being friends" with them. The schema includes a small physical area, perhaps half a dozen streets containing only houses, apart from the few corner shops and pubs that inevitably go with them. Sheer propinquity produces a state of affairs in which the family knows everyone else but in which they disclaim even the casual acquaintanceship interaction which they patently have. They say that they "keep themselves to themselves"; "don't mix in with 'em"; "don't go out to quarrel." They form few, if any, friendships. Their main involvement, their support in times of trouble, their source of security and of social control —is their kin. When, as is usually the case in Cambridge, their extended family is scattered quite widely throughout the city, the low commitment to the locality becomes particularly evident. Sometimes, it is obvious that the immediate, rather than the extended family is serving as the only effective unit and this is especially liable to happen if the housewife goes out to work or is preoccupied with "lets."

Several of the housewives with this kind of schema put the matter clearly when they said, for example, "we're both big families and have no need of friends," or "there are enough of us, we don't need to bother ourselves with neighbours."

In Cambridge, this kind of schema was found not only in the old congested artisan cottage localities, but also in the municipal estates and in the slightly higher status terraces of small Victorian villas. In fact, it would be difficult to investigate if it were not regarded as a characteristic of *people* rather than of localities.

(ii) The Homogeneous Neighbourhood. An important principle, emerging most clearly in the neighbourhoods of lower-middle-class and upper-working-class families, is homogeneity. "People like us"; "our sort"; a principle whose application is quickly followed by an assurance that no snobbishness is intended. The level of social interaction is relatively low and cognitive factors play a large part. A more accurate reflection of the schema would be not "people like us," but, "people who live in houses like ours."

Homogeneity is an inevitable characteristic of the social acquaintance neighbourhood also, but there it is not the basis for delineation. In the homogeneous type the boundaries are set by a gradient in the size, price or condition of the houses and the kind of people who live in them.

After the first year or two, the family forms some friendships in nearby streets, developing slowly out of a rather larger number of acquaintances. There is some visiting within houses (restricted to a selected few) but more commonly wives go out together, shopping or to the pictures. The most pervading social relationship, however, is one of "mutual awareness," a largely cognitive interaction which none the less has an important place in the neighbourhood schema and which probably exerts social control although no overt interaction takes place.

(iii) The Unit Neighbourhood. The third type fits quite closely the planners' conception of a neighbourhood unit. It is generally larger than the others in its physical aspects, covers a wider area, and contains a balanced range of amenities: shops, schools, churches, clubs, etc. In its social aspects, what is often an appreciable number of friends are scattered over a wider area with far less dependence upon the immediately adjacent streets. The area contains many acquaintances also, but these are scattered and the spaces in between are filled with relationships of mutual awareness. The unit type tends to be heterogeneous in the composition of its population and the kind of houses they live in.

The Physical Dimensions of Schemata

Frequency distributions for four of the physical dimensions of neighbourhood maps— area, number of houses, number of shops and number of amenity buildings—are shown in Figure 37-1. The distribution of these measures for the localities are also superimposed. It will be seen that all neighbour-

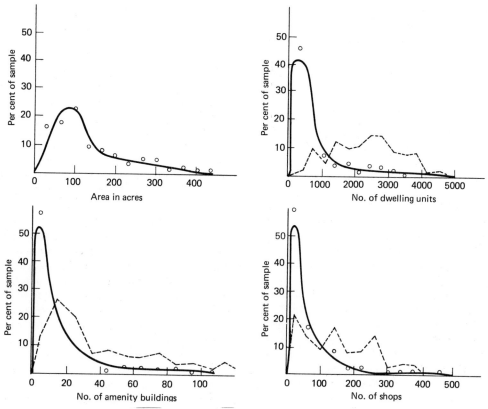

Figure 37–1. Distributions of the physical content of neighbourhood maps and of localities (dotted lines).

hood schemata refer to an area substantially less than the half-mile radius. In all four measures there is a very marked positive skewness, enough, indeed, to invite comparison with the J-shaped curves which have been found to characterize behaviour in social situations where there are strong pressures to conformity. It is doubtful if this is the explanation in the present case, since there is very little *public* awareness of, or commitment to, neighbourhood schemata. A more apt analogy would be with the memory span. It is suggested that although there are wide individual differences in the urban socio-spatial area that is perceived as an organized whole, there is a limit to the span, beyond which only a relatively small proportion of the population extend. It should be noted, however, that this span is different for each of the physical features, or expressed another way, the composition of neighbourhoods is selective and not

merely a random slice from the environment. This can be seen from the overlap between the two distributions. On average, about 30 percent of the houses presented in the localities are included in the neighbourhoods but for shops and amenity buildings the percentages are more like 50 percent and 60 percent respectively.

The relevance of these sample dimensions to planning will be discussed later.

The Neighbourhood Map and Social Behaviour—A Validation

If the neighbourhood map is more than a cognitive phenomenon, if it also represents a social space, an individual-behavioural space as distinct from a conventionally prescribed one, then its physical dimensions and pattern should correlate with measures of behaviour.

The simplest form of this hypothesis is

that a relationship exists between physical span and social participation. All four of the physical variables already mentioned, i.e. area, number of houses, shops, and amenity buildings circumscribed by the map were compared with three behavioural criteria.

For the two criteria of friends in the locality and the local club memberships, all eight relationships are positive and significant (*Appendix*). A third criterion is the use of local shops, but here the relationship, though positive, is not significant. A much more demanding expression of the hypothesis is that the physical composition or pattern of the schema is related to corresponding differences in social behaviour. This asks, in effect, for quantitative confirmation of the typology of schemata outlined earlier.

The ratio of houses to shops for each map was computed and related to the local-friendship rating. The results are significant and are shown in the *Appendix*. Similar results were found for a house/amenity-building ratio. The implication is that the more heterogeneous the physical content of neighbourhood, the more socially involved will the subject be. This is not merely a restatement of the relationship between size and local friends because although both of the ratios are a function of density, density and size are not related and in any case, the relationship still appears with size held constant.

It is a pity that there is no feasible measure of heterogeneity of housing type that could be used to supplement the present argument. The homogeneous neighbourhood

can be physically distinguished from the smaller social acquaintance one only by its size, although it is clearly distinguishable from the unit type by its lack of amenities.

In order to show more clearly the relationship between physical pattern and social participation, approximate "cut-off" points were established on a bivariate frequency distribution of number of houses and the house/shop ratio, to give a classification that would maximally discriminate on the local-friendship rating. It will be seen from Table 37-1 that the results largely confirm the descriptive typology. It becomes, however, increasingly difficult to think in anything but continuous variables. A physically small neighbourhood schema is not always a socially impoverished one. If it includes the physical features of a high proportion of shops and amenities, it acquires the social character of a small unit schema; again, physically, there is no clear division between the small homogeneous schema and the large social acquaintance one if the latter is low in shops and amenities. Clearly, some compound of continuous variables would be the best yard-stick of individual differences in neighbourhood, but, paradoxically, the problem of developing such a measure must be deferred until some of the causes of variation in schemata have been determined.

The Influence of the Physical Environment on Schemata

In one sense it is obvious that the neighbourhood schema is influenced by the physical environment, because it represents a part

Table 37-1 Approximate Cut-offs for Types of Neighborhood

| Neighbourhood Type | Cut-offs | | Subjects' no. of local friends | | | Total |
	No. of Houses	House/ Shop Ratio	Many	Few	None	
Social Acquaintance	0–400	40:1+	0	11(50%)	11(50%)	22(100%)
Homogeneous	400–1000	40:1+	3(14%)	11(50%)	8(36%)	22(100%)
Unit:						
Small	0–400	−40:1	5(22%)	11(50%)	6(28%)	22(100%)
Medium	400–1000	−40:1	12(19%)	42(66%)	9(15%)	63(100%)
Large	1000+	−40:1	11(31%)	19(53%)	6(16%)	36(100%)
Total			31	94	40	165

of it. However, it has been shown to be a unique and selective part and it is therefore necessary to ask whether the selection varies in different parts of the city, as a function, for example, of housing density. In the present investigation this question resolves itself into one of correlation between the characteristics of localities and of schemata, the latter including its social-behavioural features.

The Effect of Housing Density

It was found that housing density, which varies in the sample over a very wide range, has no effect on the area of schemata (Figure 37-2). This implies that size in this sense has been determined by delineating a territory and not a population aggregate. The finding is supported by the absence of any relationship between housing density and local friendships. Even the most sparsely populated residential suburbs apparently provide enough neighbours for every resident to make her optimum number of friends. The level of each one's social interaction is presumably set by herself rather than by the density or proximity of potential friends.

If area is constant, the number of houses within the schemata would be expected to increase proportionately with the locality,

and a very close fit to a linear regression line was in fact found.

The Level of Provision and Siting of Shops

The regression of neighbourhood shops upon locality shops is also linear. In areas of high density there are, of course, very large increases in the gross number of shops which neighbourhoods contain, but the proportion of those "accepted" in neighbourhoods to those "presented" in localities remains approximately stable.

Although it was noted that wide differences in housing density do not affect the number of local friendships formed, variations in the density of shops and of amenity buildings (see below) *do* have their effects on the corresponding behaviour.

In the case of shopping the influence is slight, because the large majority use shops in their locality, whatever they consist of, for their regular food supplies. It is interesting, however, that such effect as there is occurs at a threshold. In localities with fewer than 80 shops, 69 percent of residents use them; with more than 80 shops, the percentage moves sharply to 80 percent but then remains stable over the whole range of provision up to 400 shops per locality.

There is another effect which relates, not

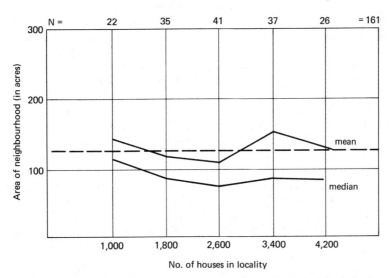

Figure 37–2. Relationships between the area of neighbourhood maps and the housing density of localities. (Four cases outside limits of grouping are excluded.)

to the number of shops, but to their *position* in relation to the home. It was found that housewives prefer to use not-too-distant shops in the direction of the town centre instead of ones which, though nearer, are in the opposite direction. These data confirm what has been named "Brennan's Law" and they have been reported in more detail elsewhere (Lee, 1962). Theoretically, they imply that distances in the subjective schema may be consistently biased from "reality."

The Level of Provision and Siting of Amenity Buildings

Amenity buildings (i.e. clubs, recreation rooms, church halls, public houses, etc.) in the schemata also increase linearly with the number in the locality. However, as with shops, there is a positively accelerating increase as housing density rises. Where there are 1,500 houses per locality, there is one amenity building per 150 houses; at 3,000 density there is one per 100; at 4,000 density there is one per 37 houses. This does not include the very heavy concentration in the city centre.

This gradient is so steep that it is necessary to ask who uses the extra provision per household in the more densely populous areas? One possibility is that it is used by an influx of people from areas less well-endowed. This would be supported by the commonly-held assumption that membership in formal organizations is optimally obtainable by all who want it (with the possible exception of those in new, outlying housing estates) in the modern city. The residents, it is claimed, use their high mobility to exercise freedom of choice over a wide area. An alternative hypothesis is that the tendency for each resident to "join" is actually influenced by the number of buildings relative to the population that is provided for the purpose in the immediate locality.

Data from the present investigation strongly supports the second of these hypotheses. There is an increase in the ratio of "joiners" to "non-joiners" that is directly proportional to the absolute number of amenity buildings in the locality and which

shows no evidence of saturation over a range of provision extending as high as 65 amenity buildings per locality. Further analysis has shown that this is unlikely to be a secondary effect of social class or of several other concomitant variables that were analysed. It is not, of course, the mere proliferation of buildings that is responsible, but the fact that an increasing number implies a smaller average distance to the nearest one (probably the main influence) and a wider variety of choice for each consumer (Lee, 1963).

It will be seen that although the locality does not affect the area of neighbourhoods or the making of local friends (these differences must be attributed to subject variables), it is apparently capable of determining not only the physical pattern of the schema but also the social behaviour of joining local clubs and, to a lesser extent, of using local shops. This does not exclude the possibility that these may also be influenced by subject variables, but to explore this it is necessary to hold constant the environmental differences.

The Extent of Locality Based Behaviour

Hitherto, we have been concerned largely with the effects of variations in locality upon neighbourhood schemata and behaviour. However, in considering whether planners should subdivide cities into smaller units, it is also relevant to assess the relative distribution of behaviour as between the locality and the remainder of the city.

Seventy-three percent of the sample have local friends, but only 60 percent have friends in other parts of the city. More than half of all friends are made in the locality although this contains, on average, less than 2 percent of the population. Thus, there is strong confirmation that propinquity on this scale influences friendship although it was found to be unrelated on the within-locality scale.

Turning to club memberships, of those who had formed at least one, 59 percent had done so within the locality although this contained only a small fraction of the city's amenity buildings. For shopping, 76 percent of the sample regularly use local food shops. The median length of residence is 14 years and 14 percent have remained in the same house for more than 30 years. Other city dwellers may be more highly mobile than the present sample indicates, but this aspect of urban living may well have been exaggerated both for Britain and the U.S.A. because high mobility is part of our middle class value-system.

THE NEIGHBOURHOOD QUOTIENT—A SCALE

The neighbourhood schema is a precipitate of experiences in the present urban environment, in past ones, and probably in many other spatial contexts. Once we have lived in a spatial framework, we develop a more or less enduring predisposition to react to future spaces in a way that reflects this experience. The same learning occurs in social situations and in the several socio-spatial frameworks of which we have experience—the body, the home, street, neighbourhood, city, country, etc. Qualitative evidence from the interviews suggested strongly that people have different attitudes to the urban locality—attitudes that, when expressed in the same environment, lead to the formation of different neighbourhood schemata. What is indicated is an intervening variable, itself determined by subject variables such as social class, age, etc. The main dimension of the differences is from zero to full *participation* or *involvement* in, or *incorporation* of, the physical and social environment that surrounds the home.

The difficulty of assessing it is that the neighbourhood schema is the result both of the attitude and of the physical constraints of the locality in which the subject happens to be set. An approximate solution is possible, however, because of the consistency of the latter relationship. It is possible to partial out the effect of differences in physical environment by expressing the schema as a *ratio* of the locality. This is analogous to the construction of a scale of intelligence which expresses mental age as a ratio of chronological age.

Such an approach sacrifices some of the fascinating idiosyncrasy of urban living, but this is a price that must usually be paid for dependable generalizations.

The steps followed in the construction of the scale are illustrated in Figure 37-3. There is a linear relationship between three of the dimensions of neighbourhood maps and of localities; the number of *houses*, of *shops* and of *amenity buildings*. These were expressed in ratio form, i.e. number included in neighbourhood/number presented in locality. The three resulting ratio scores were found to be independent of density. The *area* of maps is a fourth score which can be used in the raw form. Each of these four sub-scales is related to the behavioural criteria, as will be seen from Table 37-2. Since the sub-scales are not normally distributed, these differences were tested using distribution-free statistics and the results of Chi-square tests are given in the Table. Rank r's with joining behaviour are also shown. In this comparison, since behaviour increases with provision, it was necessary to express membership as a ratio of possible memberships.

It is clear that the separate sub-scales are related to behaviour, but it has been shown already that it is not only the size but the *pattern* of schemata that is pertinent to social participation. Instead of a simple summation, then, the four scores were weighted to give a combined, single score with maximum discrimination of the main behavioural criterion—the number of local friends.

The statistic used was the Discriminant Function and the constants are shown in Figure 37-3. The test of significance (Barnard, 1935) shows whether any pair of samples from the triad "many," "few" or "no" local friends may be expected to derive from a common population. This hypothesis was rejected for all pairs at the one percent level. The final scale was skewed and it was therefore normalized by conversion to a T scale with a mean of 50 and standard deviation of 10. In this form it is conveniently referred to as the Neighbourhood Quotient and abbreviated to Nh.Q.

A summary of the evidence that Nh.Q. is

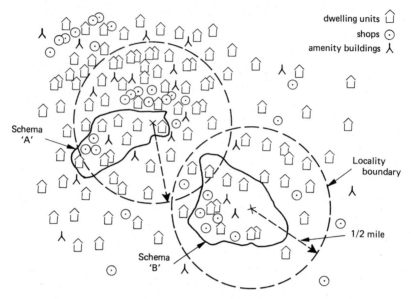

Figure 37–3. Illustrative calculations; an average Nh.Q. subject from a high-density locality (A) and a high Nh.Q. subject from a low-density locality (B).

	Schema A					Schema B				
	No. in Schema	No. in Lo-cality	Ratio	× D.F. Con-stant	=	No. in Schema	No. in Lo-cality	Ratio	× D.F. Con-stant	=
Area*	.034	—	—	1.16	.395	.52	—	—	1.16	.604
Houses	8	42	.19	−1.000	−.190	8	20	.40	−1.000	−.400
Shops	3	13	.23	.639	.148	5	7	.71	.639	.454
Amenity	1	9	.11	1.387	.154	2	3	.66	1.387	.915
Total					.507					1.573
	Converted to T scale, Nh.Q. = 52					Converted to T scale, Nh.Q. = 69				

(* Area in sq. inches/100 from 6″ Ordnance Survey)

related to social behaviour will be found in Table 37-2.

SUBJECT VARIABLES AND NH.Q.

Social Class

Subjects were divided at the time of interview into four socio-economic groups. The assessment was made from occupation, income and the usual indices of cultural interest. Roughly, the four classes correspond occupationally to professional/managerial; clerical/supervisory; skilled/manual; and unskilled workers.

The distribution and mean scores for each group on the Nh.Q. scale are shown in Figure 37-4. There are certainly differences associated with social class, and those between I and II, III and IV, and I and IV are significant where p < .05. Second-order breakdown showed that these differences were not due to length of residence, which varies appreciably by social class. On the other hand, when a heterogeneous sample of this kind is considered, it becomes apparent from the distributions that although particular kinds of neighbourhood attitude might be said to characterize social classes— it can be put no more strongly than this. As was made clear in outlining a typology of neighbourhood, most types of schemata are

Table 37-2 Tests of the Hypothesis that Ratio Sub-scales and Nh.Q. are related to Social Behaviour

Ratio Sub-Scales	No. of local friends			No. of local memberships as percent amenity buildings (N = 41)	
	D.f.	Chi-square	p<	Spearman's rho	p<
Area	6	27.14	.001	.55	.01
Houses	4	12.70	.02	.62	.01
Shops	6	29.17	.0001	.52	.01
Amenity buildings	6	21.40	.01	.53	.01
Nh.Q. scale	Product moment			Product moment	
	$r = .359$		.01	$r = .70$	.01
	Biserial			The Nh.Q. scale is related to use of	
	$r = .366$			local shops;	
				Chi-square = 4.80; 1 d.f.; $p < .05$	

to be found in each social class, though in different proportions.

A reminder should be given that, in considering the Nh.Q., we have partialled out those aspects arising from the disparate physical environments, which otherwise give a pronounced appearance of difference to the *schemata* of different social classes.

Length of Residence

We would expect that both the cognitive and social aspects of neighbourhood would widen and deepen with the passage of time and that this would be reflected in the Nh.Q. scale. When the scale was plotted against years of residence, a positive relationship was shown, but only for the period above five years, which included 75 percent of the sample ($r = .238$; $p < .01$).

It was thought at first that this must be due to a tendency, already referred to, for some new residents to draw a large "contracting" map before they had any genuine orientation or involvement. This explanation was discarded when analysis showed that a parallel effect occurred in the behavioural data, both for number of local friends and

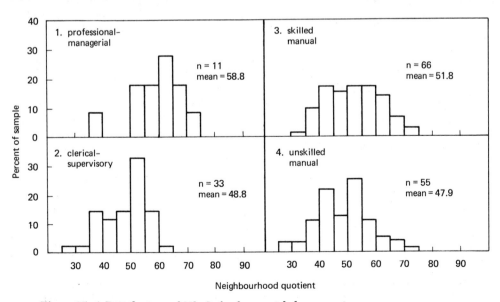

Figure 37–4. Distributions of Nh.Q. for four social class groupings.

for joining behaviour. However, for these two variables, data are available for the total sample of 219, as distinct from the map-drawing sample, and when these are plotted, the reversal disappears, although there is still no positive relationship between years of residence and involvement over the first few years.

The reason for the difference between the two samples may be that the map-drawing one, in addition to under-representing people with short terms of residence (for whom it was too early to formulate a schema) did so selectively, i.e. it *included* those who were sociable enough to have made friends quickly. For the total sample, using the criterion membership/non-membership, the relationship with years of residence is significant (Chi-square = 10.51; 3 d.f.; p < .02) as is also the number of local friends with years of residence (Chi-square = 18.18; 6 d.f.; p < .01).

What conclusions can be drawn? It appears that newcomers to a locality become involved, up to a given low level, quite quickly. Thereafter, they remain more or less static for about five years, after which their involvement begins to increase steadily. An important implication is that some of the gloomy prognostications about "lack of community spirit" in post-war housing estates may simply be premature.

Age

This is a convenient point at which to consider age, for this variable is obviously associated with length of residence. When considered alone, age is not correlated with the Nh.Q. scale. When length of residence is taken into consideration the picture changes slightly and is more in accord with expectation.

Only that part of the sample with six or more years of residence (N = 125) was considered. The distribution of years of residence is skewed, and was therefore converted to a T scale. When this was correlated with age, r was found to be .363. r between years of residence and the Nh.Q. scale was .238 and between age and the Nh.Q. scale, .002. The partial r between

years of residence and the Nh.Q. scale, with age held constant, remained at .238 and this is significant at the one percent level. The partial r between age and the Nh.Q. scale, with years of residence held constant, is −.100. This is a small and non-significant relationship but in the expected direction.

People have higher Nh.Q. scores as a function of years of residence and this is associated with age, but if older people have lived in a locality for the same period as young people they are likely to have a slightly lower Nh.Q. score. It should be noted that both age and length of residence are related to stage of family.

The Location of Husband's Work

It has been suggested by Brennan (1948), Madge (1950) and others, that families are likely to be more involved in neighbourhood life if the wage-earner is actually working in the locality. It has been one of the themes of those who advocate the neighbourhood unit principle that it would re-unite the unnatural division between work and living that has prevailed since the Industrial Revolution.

Details of the husband's place of work were collected from 154 of the map sample. Of these, 24 were spinsters, widows or the wives of retired men. Mean Nh.Q. scores were computed for four groups, representing various degrees of dispersal from the home. Twenty cases of peripatetic occupations were excluded. Since we have already pointed out that there are differences in the neighbourhoods of social classes, and since social class is systematically related to work-location, it was necessary in testing this hypothesis to break down the data into separate social class groupings. The results of the analysis are shown in Table 37-3. It will be seen that the hypothesis is confirmed for all classes except II. F for social class = 3.24; p < .05. F for work location = 4.17; p < .05.

Further tests of the hypothesis were made with the behavioural data. Chi-squared tests showed that the relationship between work location and number of friends and between work location and joining behaviour were

Table 37-3 Nh.Q., Location of Husband's Work, and Social Class

Source of Variation	Sums of squares	d.f.	Estimate of variation	F
Work Location*	394	1	394	4.17†
Social Class	918	3	306	3.24†
Interaction	172	3	57.30	.60
Within Sets	9633	102	94.44	
Total	11117	109		

* "Within ½ mile" combined with "same side" v. "city centre" combined with "cross city."
† $p < .05$.

both positive and significant. For the former, Chi-square = 6.82; 2 d.f.; $p < .05$. For the latter, Chi-square = 7.15; 1 d.f.; $p < .01$.

Natives and Immigrants

When considering the effects of being a native of the city, there are two related aspects. The first is that there may be differences in neighbourhood orientation as part of the distinctive culture of a city or region. The second is that natives have local kin and are therefore less dependent on neighbours. Either or both could explain the not uncommon assertion by immigrants that Cambridge people are unfriendly and aloof, but the second aspect is probably most important.

Natives, in many cases, form small social-acquaintance schemata and this may explain the relatively small effects of time on the Nh.Q., for the natives are the ones with long periods of residence. The mean Nh.Q. is lowest when both husband and wife are natives, next when the wife is a native, then when the husband only is a native and *highest* when neither are natives. When the latter group are compared with the rest of the sample the difference is significant (Chi-square = 4.64: 1 d.f.; $p < .05$).

Type of House, Number of Children and Car Ownership

Subjects living in detached houses have the highest average Nh.Q., followed by terraced and then by semi-detached houses. Any ecological effects on social interaction are likely to be overlaid in this relationship by social class differences, but it is interesting that when considering simply the number of local friends, subjects living in terraced houses have most, followed by detached houses and then semi-detached. This difference is significant (Chi-square = 17.64; 4 d.f.; $p < .01$).

Both the number of children in the family and the ownership of a car show a slight positive relationship to the Nh.Q. scale, but neither of them reach conventional levels of significance.

COLLECTIVE ASPECTS OF NEIGHBOURHOOD

Hitherto, neighbourhood has been considered as an individual phenomenon, but there is obviously a sense in which it has collective expression. Although there is diversity there is also uniformity and the relations between overlapping individual neighbourhoods need to be conceptualized and measured.

Do they constitute, for example, a social group? Even if we take the minimal definition—a number of people who interact with each other more than with others—the answer is no. Ecologically-based interaction certainly occurs but not in very clearly defined systems. A may interact with B, but although B interacts with A to some extent, she interacts even more with C; A and C do not interact at all, covertly or otherwise, and could not be said to be in a social group with each other. The multiplication of such instances leads to the conclusion that although there may be gradients and foci of interaction, there are no definitive boundaries that are collectively acknowledged and it would be procrustean to impose them. This is not to deny that social groups in the normally accepted sense sometimes occur in cities—only that this concept does not fit the general case.

Is it perhaps a "social field" in the Lewinian sense? If a social field is a life space which includes social objects, then the analogy is closer to the individual socio-spatial schema and we are no further forward with the collective aspect. But the implication is that "social fields" are in some way compounded from individual life spaces. This would be the necessary step, but as Argyle (1957, p. 91) has pointed out, no one has yet shown how this step might be taken.

Nor is collective neighbourhood a *reference group*, for it is not formulated as an entity by any of the residents. It could be argued that the neighbourhood schema itself, in its social aspect, has reference group properties—but not any particular aggregate of schemata.

To call it a *network* (Bott, 1955) would be a better fit in some respects, for it allows us to conceive of chains of influence instead of the planetary systems implied by the concept of social group. The shortcoming would seem to be that although it deals adequately with the social aspects of neighbourhood, i.e. with who interacts with whom, it does not take account of the way in which these relationships are rooted in a physical environment or of the pervading "mutual awareness" that is so important a form of urban social interaction.

It is, in fact, the physical/spatial referent for the social relationships which is prominent in neighbourhood, and we strongly suspect that this aspect is relevant in many more social situations than is commonly supposed; not only in communities for living, but in industry and education for example. The concept of the social group is probably a dangerous one, because it leads us into a language and a methodology which distinguishes "groups" and "not groups"— when we should be concentrating on the process of *grouping*, which is often too fluid a process to be encapsulated in the noun form. It is like trying to divide "walking" into "walks"; "talking" into "talks." The subdivision can sometimes be made—but not with the most characteristic or even with the majority of the products.

This argument cannot be developed here, but it led to the measurement of the *consentaneity* of schemata, a concept that implies agreement and interdependence but not necessarily in reciprocal systems. Consentaneity is a matter of degree, measurable statistically from the schemata formed by a set of individuals in relation to a given physical space, at a given point in time or in a given stimulus situation. For any given aggregate of people selected on some independent practical or theoretical criterion, the mean of their Nh.Q.s serves as a measure of the level of their social participation and the variance as a measure of their consentaneity.

This implies, conversely, that a sample for which either of these statistics differs significantly from another sample, has been subject to some socio-physical influence in the formation of schemata. It implies, further, that it would be possible to separate samples which show a *maximum* difference in level or consentaneity, but that this would always be a relative distinction.

It should be noted that in using the Nh.Q. in measures of variance, we are taking into account more than spatial coincidence of schemata—we are considering a general orientation to the physical and social environment, for which spatial coincidence is a sufficient but not necessary condition.

The first hypothesis to be tested, using this conceptual approach, was the null hypothesis of a random distribution of Nh.Q. scores. The aggregates chosen were polling districts. These could not be expected to yield optimum consentaneity, but they had the advantage of being independently determined.

Analysis of variance was applied to the Nh.Q. scores in 19 polling districts, separating within from between variance. The F ratio of 1.94 is significant where $p < .05$. This could be due to differences between means or between variances. Separate F tests showed differences between variances. Eight polling districts with low variance were separated from eleven with high variance. Analysis of variance applied to the former group gave $F = 3.30$ ($p < .01$), which indicates differences in means.

Although this demonstrated the existence of consentaneity, it did not optimize it. One characteristic of the polling district group-ings was that their variance was correlated with distance from town centre. The latter was computed by taking the mean of each subject's distances. These were then ranked and found to correlate with the ranked variance of Nh.Q. for subjects in each poll-ing district (rho = .64; p < .01). It was important to know whether this was an artefact of these particular groupings, or a general effect.

Neighbourhood Grouping

Fifteen, more optimum, groupings were separated. This was done at first by inspec-tion, and then by transferring marginal sub-jects by the principle of least squares. The areas are reproduced in Lee (1954). The rho between distance from city centre and consentaneity, referred to above, was now small and non-significant.

Some rank correlations which confirm the validity of the procedure may be quoted. The mean Nh.Q. for the groupings is related to the mean number of friends (rho = .54) and the proportion of joiners to non-joiners (rho = .47). Median years of residence is associated with higher consentaneity (rho = .38 with Nh.Q. variance) and with num-ber of friends (rho = .46).

It has often been claimed for the neigh-bourhood unit principle that its clearly de-fined boundaries will create a "sense of belonging." This is similar to saying that where there is high consentaneity, there will be high involvement or participation also. A test of this hypothesis is complicated by the fact that variance normally increases proportionally with mean, so that a baseline positive correlation, upon which other influ-ences would be superimposed, is to be ex-pected. In the present case, comparing Nh.Q. median with the Nh.Q. variance for the 15 groupings, rho has a *negative* value of −.24, which appears to argue strongly in favour of the hypothesis, but which can-not be tested in the usual way against a baseline of zero. If the coefficient of varia-tion is used as a measure of variance, we theoretically correct for the unequal means, and this gives rho = −.30. The use of this coefficient is somewhat questionable, it

should be pointed out, with a scale that is not equal-interval.

Another problem of some importance to the neighbourhood unit principle is whether heterogeneity of population will produce more, or less, participation. Three variables may be mentioned here: age, years of resi-dence, and social class, variance being com-puted for each variable for the groupings (n = 15) and the resulting values ranked. Age and years of residence show no effect, but variance of social class, the one nor-mally considered in this context, is related to the median Nh.Q. (rho = .55; p < .05). The more heterogeneous the grouping, it seems, the higher the level of participation. This is confirmation at the collective level of an effect which has already been demon-strated for individual schemata by the evi-dence that unit type schemata include more friends.

CONCLUSIONS AND IMPLICATIONS FOR PLANNING

Neighbourhood, it seems, remains a highly salient phenomenon of urban living. People move about the local urban environment to satisfy a wide range of needs with minimum effort. The continual locational coding that arises from this activity precipitates in the form of a socio-spatial schema which, in turn, governs future navigation and move-ment. Each schema is unique, but is related in lawful ways to the physical environment and to the personality of its possessor.

Consentaneity of schemata occurs in vary-ing degrees and its measurement provides a means of predicting behaviour for a given aggregate of people with a territorial base.

More friendships, club memberships and shopping links are formed in the locality than elsewhere and their number is corre-lated with the physical span of schemata. The latter, however, remains constant under wide variation in density, although the com-position of schemata changes as the ratio of local shops and amenity buildings to houses is increased. Such increases do not affect friendships but yield substantial changes in club memberships and slight changes in local shopping.

If the dimensions of neighbourhood schemata are expressed as ratios of the locality in which they occur, a measure of individual involvement in the urban social/physical milieu is derived (Nh.Q.) which is valid by comparison with behavioural criteria. The Nh.Q. varies with social class, age, length of residence, native status, type of house and husband's work-location.

The absence of relationship between number of friends and density removes any force from the argument that people in a given locality should be pre-selected for similarity in social class or other ways so that they can make friends easily. The number of "similar" people will normally be adequate even in a mixed community and the latter has the advantage of providing a variety of people to fit community roles and to enhance "mutual awareness." It is also found that social heterogeneity is positively related to consentaneity of Nh.Q. and again, physical heterogeneity (i.e. the inclusion of shops and amenity buildings in the schema) to social participation.

This evidence all points to the conclusion that planning should be directed towards heterogeneous physical and social layouts, deliberately emphasizing the local (and therefore most effortless) satisfaction of needs.

It could be argued that nothing would be gained from subdividing the physical environment into separate units, because each resident's orientation is unique. On the other hand, the schemata show some concordance on the prominent boundaries, and this would probably be closer if the boundaries were accentuated, if the areas they circumscribed were more equivalent in size to the average schema and if the residents moved simultaneously into a locality. Boundaries could be emphasized by more use of path-access housing, so that traffic roads, as well as open spaces, etc. could be used to delineate sub-units. Ritter (1964) has shown that path-access housing is associated with higher social participation on a number of criteria. The finding from the present study that terrace-housing residents have more local friends is also relevant.

In any case, there are undoubtedly good economic and engineering reasons why urban space should be differentiated, and one oft-quoted consideration is that a population of 5,000 is appropriate for a primary school, which should have traffic-free access.

If the case for subdivision is conceded, the next question becomes one of size. Neighbourhood unit dimensions have invariably been quoted in terms of population, but it has been shown that this is not critical and area is the more appropriate measure. A sub-unit of 75 acres would correspond to the mode of the present sample, and would have the advantage that two units would contain the majority of schemata. It is not suggested that schema boundaries would coincide with physical ones, but it would become more probable on this scale.

By the recommended gross density standards of 35 persons per acre which prevailed in the post-war years (Housing Manual, 1949), this area would accommodate only 2,600 people, but recent planning policy has moved in favour of high density development, up to figures as high as 100 persons per acre, as, for example, in Cumbernauld New Town. Seventy-five acres could now therefore contain a population of 5,000 to 7,500 and this would be sufficient to support a good range of shops and amenity buildings. These would be in close proximity, a fact that the present study shows to be critical in maximizing their use by local residents. Shops should be positioned off-centre, towards the down-town edge of the unit, or some residents may gravitate to their subjectively "nearer" centre in the adjacent unit. If the wage earner works near to his home, the family has a higher involvement in the locality, and this would argue for some spread of industry throughout the city, instead of in one "industrial estate" complex. Finally, length of residence is positively related to the Nh.Q. and so continuity (usually a matter for the housing manager but one which the planner can also facilitate by providing for changing family stages) is desirable. The rise in Nh.Q. does not take place for some years, however, and the planner should not be discouraged by the slowness of social integration in our culture into thinking his design is a failure.

The role of the planner in modern society is equivocal. He is employed to fashion the environment of the future, and in this he idealistically includes the creation of *communities*. However, some critics feel that he *cannot* and others that he *should not* attempt to determine human behaviour:

> Provide plenty of housing so that there is choice, and plenty of work so that choice may be exercised, put the housing and the work in a physical environment that is open, pleasant, healthful and safe, and I don't give a damn about the specific pattern, because people can work out their own groupings. Planning is not a cure-all, nor are the planners omniscient (H. S. Churchill, 1948).

The writer's view is that social planning, like anticipation in the individual, is inevitable in a complex society that values order. Also there is accumulating research evidence that behaviour and environment are interdependent, which implies that the planners' manipulations *can* influence behaviour. If the flavour of oligarchy in such assumptions is unpalatable, that is no reason to question their validity. However, much of the emotiveness of the free will–determinism issue can surely be dispelled if it is acknowledged that the planner is acting, not to express his own whims, but to realize the values of the society of which he is a duly accredited agent. He is an innovator of means and not of ends. If his means are unsuccessful or his objectives unacceptable, his actions will be negatively reinforced by ordinary people. What he most lacks at present is the ability to predict the consequences of his decisions for human behaviour.

REFERENCES:

Argyle, M. *The scientific study of social behaviour*. London: Methuen, 1957.

Axelrod, M. Urban structure and social participation. *American Sociological Review*, 1956, 21, 13–18.

Barnard, M. M. The secular variations of skull characters in four series of Egyptian skulls. *Annals of Eugenics*, 1935, 6, 352–371.

Barlett, F. C. *Remembering*. Cambridge: Cambridge University Press, 1932.

Bott, E. Urban families: Conjugal roles and social networks. *Human Relations*, 1955, 8, 345–384.

Brennan, T. *Midland city*. London: Dobson, 1948.

Churchill, H. S. An open letter to Mr. Isaacs. *Journal of the American Institute of Planners*, 1948, 14, 40–43.

Cooley, C. H. *Social organisation: A study of the larger mind*. New York: Scribners, 1909.

Design of dwellings. London: H. M. Stationery Office, 1944.

Dewey, R. The neighborhood, urban ecology and city planners. *American Sociological Review*, 1950, 15, 502–507.

Foley, D. L. The use of local facilities in a metropolis. *American Journal of Sociology*, 1950, 56, 238–246.

Gans, H. J. *The Levittowners: Ways of life and politics in a new suburban community*. London: Allen Lane, 1967.

Glass, R. *The social background of a plan: A study of Middlesbrough*. London: Routledge & Kegan Paul, 1948.

Hauser, P. M., & Schnore, L. F. *The study of urbanisation*. New York: Wiley, 1965.

Housing manual. London: H. M. Stationery Office, 1949.

Isaacs, R. R. The neighbourhood theory; An analysis of its adequacy. *Journal of the American Institute of Planners*, 1948, 14, 15–23.

Lee, T. R. *A study of urban neighbourhood*. Unpublished Ph.D. dissertation. University of Cambridge, 1954.

Lee, T. R. "Brennan's Law" of shopping behavior. *Psychological Report*, 1962, 11, 662.

Lee, T. R. The optimum provision and siting of social clubs. *Durham Research Review*, 1963, 4, 53–61.

Lock, Max. *The Hartlepools: A survey and plan*. London: Dobson, 1948.

Madge, C. Planning for people. *Town Planning Review*, 1950, 21, 131–144.

Mann, P. H. *An approach to urban sociology*. London: Routledge & Kegan Paul, 1965.

McClenahan, B. A. *The changing urban neighbourhood*. Los Angeles: University of Southern California, 1929.

McClenahan, B. A. The Communality: The urban substitute for the traditional community. *Sociology and Social Research*, 1945, 30, 264–274.

Meyer, J. The stranger and the city. *American Journal of Sociology*, 1951, 56, 476–483.

Morris, R. N., & Mogey, J. *The sociology of housing*. London: Routledge & Kegan Paul, 1965.

Park, Robert E. The city: Suggestions for the investigation of human behaviour in the city environment. *American Journal of Sociology*, 1915, 10, 577–612.

Perry, C. A. The neighbourhood unit. *Regional Plan of New York and its Environs*, 1929, 7, 22–140.

Riemer, S. Villagers in metropolis. *British Journal of Sociology*, 1951, 2, 31–43.

Ritter, P. *Planning for man and motor*. London: Pergamon, 1964.

Roper-Power, E. R. The social structure of an English County town. *Sociological Review*, 1937, 29, 391.

Smith, J., Form, W. H., & Stone, G. P. Local intimacy in a middle-sized city. *American Journal of Sociology*, 1954, 60, 276–284.

Sweetzer, F. L., Jr. *Neighbourhood acquaintance and association, a study of personal neighbourhoods.* Unpublished Ph.D. dissertation. New York: Columbia University, 1941.

Sweetzer, F. L., Jr. A new emphasis for neighbourhood research. *American Sociological Review,* 1942, **7,** 525–533.

Williams, J. H. Close friendship relations of housewives residing in an urban community. *Social Forces,* 1958, **36,** 358–362.

Willmott, P., & Young, M. *Family and class in a London suburb.* London: Routledge & Kegan Paul, 1960.

Wirth, L. Urbanism as a way of life. *American Journal of Sociology,* 1938, **44,** 1–24.

Wolters, A. W. P. The patterns of experience. *Report of the British Association for the Advancement of Science,* 1936, 181–188.

APPENDIX

Relations between Neighbourhood Map Dimensions and Behavioural Criteria

Map dimensions	Local friends			Local memberships		
	D.f.	Chi-square	p<	D.f.	Chi-square	p<
Area	6	27.14	.001	3	9.84	.02
No. of houses	4	12.14	.02	3	12.14	.01
No. of shops	4	11.39	.05	4	9.71	.05
No. of amenity buildings	2	6.19	.05	3	13.72	.01

Ratio of Houses: Shops in Neighbourhood Map and No. of Local Friends

Ratio of houses/shops	No. of local friends			
	Many	Few	None	Total
40:1+	3	22	19	44
20:1–39:1	14	26	6	46
0–19:1	14	46	15	75
Totals	31	94	40	165

Chi-square = 16.753; 4 d.f.; p < .01.

38 The Outdoor Play of Children Living in Flats: An Enquiry into the Use of Courtyards as Playgrounds

L. E. White

BACKGROUND TO THE ENQUIRY —PHYSICAL LOCATION AND SOCIAL BACKGROUND

The area covered by this enquiry is part of a small triangle of territory between Camberwell Road, Camberwell New Road and Wyndham Road, within five minutes' walk

From Leo Kuper (Ed.), *Living in Towns.* London: The Cresset Press, 1953, pp. 235–258. Reprinted by permission of the author and publisher.

from Chamberwell Green in South London (see Figure 38-1). At one time this triangle comprised entirely slum property including a number of streets of somewhat notorious character. Now these have gone, replaced mainly by the massive four-storey tenement blocks of the London County Council Comber Estate built between 1927 and 1932. The few remaining streets of old two-storey houses suffered heavy damage from bombs and there are therefore several bomb-sites and a number of badly damaged houses— both important factors in the play activities of city children today. At one corner of the Comber Estate, a new five-storey block of flats was completed by the L.C.C. in June 1949 on a bomb-site adjacent to two of the old four-storey tenement blocks. These three together form a unit slightly separated from the rest of the estate, and between them, in the shadow of the tall blocks, lie the courtyards which are the subject of our enquiry. Their location and layout in relation to the rest of the neighbourhood will be seen in the accompanying diagram.

The first impression of the neighbourhood as a whole is the preponderance of four-storey buildings sited closely together shutting out the sky, and the lack of open spaces other than the few bomb-sites. No separate figures are available for so small an area, as to density and structure of population, but from the two facts just given, it may with reasonable certainty be assumed that the density is in fact very high and comprises a relatively large proportion of children.

As street activities are important in areas deficient in playgrounds, it is important to note that the triangle as a whole is an island of comparative safety (no real traffic routes intersect it) surrounded by two swift-flowing streams of highly dangerous traffic, and bounded on the third side by the smaller

and less hazardous stream of a secondary traffic route. The limited survey area is the safest part of all, containing no streets, and flanked only by two lightly used service roads.

SOCIAL CHARACTERISTICS

The neighbourhood as a whole is dominated by the huge slum-clearance area of the L.C.C. Comber Estate. This is wholly working class in character. There are still left a few pockets of decaying slum property, one block of private flats of substantial nature dating from the Edwardian era, and surprisingly, one small and incongruous block of comparatively high-class private flats completed only last year. The three L.C.C. blocks which are the subject of our enquiry present interesting social contrasts, for the two old blocks, Moffatt House and Grenfell House, date from the slum clearance era, whilst the new block, Laing House, contains

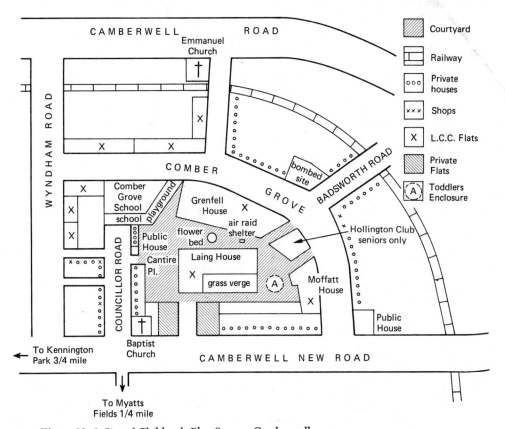

Figure 38–1. Site of Children's Play Survey, Camberwell.

a very much more mixed population, although it too is predominantly working class in character. Inevitably the tenants of these old blocks so lacking in modern amenities look somewhat enviously at the glistening new block towering above them with its electric passenger lifts (source of much juvenile curiosity and enjoyment!), its small private balconies and the rumoured luxuries of its internal fittings. This social cleavage, although not perhaps serious, does have some effect on the freedom of children's play, as we shall see later.

METHOD: HOW THE ENQUIRY WAS CONDUCTED—ITS OPPORTUNITIES AND LIMITATIONS

In June 1949 I came to occupy a flat on the ground floor of this new block overlooking the courtyard and playing space. At that time I was Warden of the Camberwell Junk Playground half a mile away, and in my odd moments of leisure it was of profound interest to compare and contrast the behaviour, attitudes and play of the children in these tidy courtyards, with those of similar Camberwell children at the Junk Playground. Later when I resumed my previous work as a writer, my desk looked out on to these same courtyards, affording unique opportunity to study unobtrusively the ways of the children at play there.

The method adopted was to make regular daily observations to obtain data covering the widest possible range of conditions. These observations cover varying times— morning, afternoon and evening, weekdays, Saturdays and Sundays, holidays and term time, and—since weather is such a determinant factor in outdoor play—a range of climatic conditions varying from the driving sleet of a winter's afternoon to the warm sunshine of a spring day. Unhappily—and here is the first limitation of the enquiry— I moved from this address with its unique vantage point in early March, so that the enquiry had to be limited to winter and spring activities. This accounts for the absence of information on such seasonal games as tops, hoops, hopscotch and marbles.

The second difficulty or limitation arose from the actual method of recording. The mere counting of numbers of children engaged quite freely in a variety of spontaneous activities cannot be very satisfactory. Children's play is never static; groups form and reform almost kaleidoscopically as children detach themselves from their previous groups and start some new activity. As some endeavour was made to differentiate between age groups, and as particular emphasis was laid on recording the almost hidden activities of small groups in odd corners in porches and the entrances to the common staircases, it will be realised that some margin must be allowed for mathematical inaccuracies, e.g. counting the same child twice in swiftly changing groups or errors in allocating to the correct age group. (These would in any case be *apparent* ages.) For this reason it will be clear that the statistical evidence must be treated with some reserve, and greater importance should be attached to the nature of activities than to the number of children actually engaged in them at any one moment.

THE STANDPOINT FROM WHICH THE ENQUIRY WAS MADE

At the time of the enquiry my status was not that of social worker living in the block of flats, but merely that of an ordinary tenant, a relationship I was careful to preserve. This had both advantages and disadvantages. It precluded for instance any questionnaire to parents or the door-to-door enquiries of either a general or sample survey. But the informal neighbourly relationship and the exigencies of daily living in the flats opened the way to many invaluable conversations and the volunteering of a great deal of interesting information by the children. Moreover, my wife was able, in discussion and casual conversations with the mothers on balconies and in the communal drying rooms, to fill in many of the gaps in our knowledge as to the views of parents.

AGE GROUPINGS

The age limits selected were from 2–15, divided into two groups, 2–5's—the nursery school age—and 5–15. Further statistical sub-division proved impracticable, although of course the observations took account of the vastly differing activities of younger and older children. The activities of the older adolescents were considered to lie outside the scope of the enquiry, except where they impinged on the play of the younger children.

THE EFFECT OF L.C.C. RULES ON PLAY IN THE COURTYARDS

It is obvious that these will be a determining factor in the use of the courtyards as playgrounds. Since it is not the practice of the L.C.C. to make some of these rules widely known, a certain amount of confusion exists, and in practice the matter is left largely to the discretion of the resident caretaker in the block and the good sense of the tenants. This question is, however, one of great difficulty as there is a fundamental clash of interest between the needs of the children for playing space and the desire of the tenants—particularly those on the ground floor, in immediate proximity to where the children play—for some measure of privacy and quiet. For it must be remembered that with the design of block dwelling in general use in this country, with its ground-floor doors opening direct on to the asphalt courtyard, the ground-floor tenants are in effect living, for a large part of the time, in a children's playground. This is even more apparent in summer-time with windows wide open. Residents on upper floors are less affected, although there is a tendency for the tall buildings and high walls to act as a sounding board and to magnify and echo every joyful shout and scream from the children at play. This defect incidentally is even more apparent when the blocks are built on the now discredited "hollow square" design.

It is significant that even the long list of rules and conditions of tenancy in every tenant's rent book, is strangely silent on the use of courtyards as playgrounds. The only rule with any bearing on the matter is the very general one which states:

The tenant shall be responsible for the orderly conduct of his children on any part of the estate, for any nuisance or

annoyance they may cause to other tenants or to members of the public; for any damage to or defacement of any building, wall, fence, gate or any other property of the council, and shall repay to the council the cost of making good any such damage or defacement. The tenant shall replace or repay to the council the cost of replacing windows broken in the premises during the tenancy.

By implication, rather than expressly, these two rules place some limitation on ball games. It is not, however, the Council's practice to charge ground-floor tenants with the replacement of windows broken from outside by balls or other missiles—a tacit admission that ball games will in fact be played.

Another rule, posted in the courtyards, prohibits cycling. This does not of course forbid the use of children's tricycles or miniature bicycles—but the dividing line between this and cycling is not always clear and is in practice governed more by the application of another unwritten rule, that children over 14 shall not play in the courtyards. (It is not clear whether the raising of the school-leaving age to 15 has resulted in an automatic raising of the play limit too.) Play by outsiders is discouraged although they generally go unnoticed until they engage in some form of anti-social activity or come into conflict with the children who inhabit the particular block.

The basic principle underlying all these unwritten rules is a wise recognition of the fact that no concessions made to the children can really compensate for the fact that playing facilities in block dwelling areas are sadly deficient, and that almost any activity should therefore be permitted up to the point where it becomes a nuisance and a serious infringement on the rights and convenience of ground-floor and other tenants.

The lack of explicit ruling on the use of the courtyards led in this case to extraordinary misunderstandings and confusion. The small asphalt area marked "A" on Figure 38-1, was surrounded by a low iron railing 3 feet high. At first no one knew the purpose of this enclosure, though rumour had it that it was to be a "fitted playground." Although not particularly suited to ball games because of its inadequate boundaries, it did in fact become almost exclusively a football pitch, for which purpose, as the table will show, it was in almost constant use by the older boys and adolescents. My surprise therefore was considerable when I learned from a friendly L.C.C. official with a wide practical experience of the problems of supervision of block dwelling estates, that this was actually the "toddler's enclosure"! As it had even taken me a considerable time to elucidate the mystery of this playing area, it is hardly surprising that the wrong children played there. In any case it would be very difficult to imagine any area less suitable or less attractive to toddlers than this barren and featureless asphalt enclosure. It may be wondered how such an extraordinary misunderstanding could persist, but it must be remembered that there was no Tenants' Club or similar organisation, nor indeed any place where tenants might meet or come together for any purpose whatsoever, and there was therefore no way in which a community problem of this kind could be discussed. It will be readily appreciated that this fundamental weakness—the inability of tenants to meet together—was a main cause of the lack of co-operation between the tenants themselves in the solution of community problems such as those under review in this paper, and a contributory cause to their failure to co-operate with the housing authority in these matters. It is true that suggestions could be made to the resident caretaker or to the rent collector who called weekly. There is evidence that this was occasionally done, but none that it ever achieved any useful purpose, despite the fact that both these officials were sympathetic, intelligent and conscientious and had a considerable practical knowledge of the community problems involved.

There is little doubt that this element of uncertainty as to what they might and might not do was highly detrimental to the childrens' sense of security in their play, as they were doomed to spend a great deal of their time being driven from one "illegal" activity to another, harassed by parents, other adults, and various officials ordering them to cease doing many of the things they most enjoyed doing. From the youngest to the oldest they were exposed to constant repressions and frustrations and the working of a system which was inconsistent and capricious. This instability and insecurity—in such marked contrast with the security, consistency and justice they would find in their games at school, play centre or children's club—may have accounted to some extent for their marked hostility to any adult authority which checked them in their games and play in the open.

ALTERNATIVE ACTIVITIES FOR CHILDREN IN THE NEIGHBOURHOOD

It may be well to consider first the indoor "counter-attractions" as these have a considerable bearing on children's outdoor play, although no doubt it will be agreed that no indoor facilities, however attractive, can compensate for the lack of outdoor play. It will be obvious that the very nature of life in flats with its cramping restrictions on children's play (both for lack of space and the need not to offend neighbours), lays additional stress on the necessity for good outdoor opportunities for play and exercise.

INDOOR ACTIVITIES

(a) Playing at Home.—It is a well-known fact that children in working-class flats do not play much indoors. Even while the weather is inclement they prefer to play on the common staircases and landings or in the entrance porch at the foot of the stairs. At home rooms are small and often crowded, whilst harrassed mothers dislike having the children continually under their feet and so like to send them out to play. One little problem boy used to ask to come into our flat because he was not wanted at home. And since sound-proofing even in the latest blocks of flats is far from perfect, there is constant worry that the children's play will annoy the neighbours below or even above.

(b) Children's Organisations.—In these the neighbourhood abounds. Organisations with children's activities include: The London

County Council Play Centre (open every night from 5–7) in Comber Grove School adjacent to the flats; Baptist Church (100 yards away) with its Boys Brigade, Lifeboys, Sunday School and Clubs; Parish Church with Sunday School and Choir (200 yards away); Free Salvationist Mission (300 yards away); Hollington Club (¼ mile away); Cambridge House, with its well-established Junior Clubs, lies just outside the triangle. Numbers and influence are difficult to estimate. The Play Centre keeps no register of individual members but the Supervisor thought that a number of children from our three blocks attended and my own observation confirmed this. With such an unusual choice it is hardly surprising that there is a great deal of interchange and duplication of membership, and particularly with the youngest age group a considerable floating population. Most of the children questioned seemed to have belonged to one or more of these organisations at some time or other.

(c) Commercial and Provided Entertainment.—Again the area abounds in such provision. There are two cinemas within 200 yards and two others within ¼-mile radius, also the Camberwell Palace (Variety Theatre). Two of the cinemas have Saturday morning Cinema Clubs. Membership and attendance at these was practically universal amongst our children. There is no fun fair or amusement arcade.

OPEN AIR ACTIVITY (OTHER THAN THE COURTYARDS)

Here the provision is much less lavish.

There is no formal playground in the neighbourhood, but Myatts' Fields is only just over a ¼ mile distant. Unfortunately it is cut off from these flats by an extremely dangerous main road and is therefore virtually inaccessible to the younger children. This is a great pity as it is a beautiful little park with a well-equipped children's corner with swings, roundabouts, giant stride, sandpit, netball court. The park is too small for football pitches, but football is played informally on one of the two grassy areas. Excellent children's entertainments are ar-ranged in the holidays and summer months and there is a well-frequented refreshment hut.

Kennington Park is more popular with our children although it is ¾ mile distant. No main roads have to be crossed but there are some dangerous secondary routes to traverse and some busy traffic intersections. It is one of the best equipped playgrounds in South London, with all the facilities detailed above plus a paddling pool, floodlit football pitches (boys' size, rubble surface). In the holidays it is popular with our children, some of whom take a sandwich lunch and stay there all day. Valuable as these two parks are to our children their use is limited. They are too inaccessible for casual play and visits to them are more in the nature of premeditated and organised expeditions. This is even more true of the slightly more distant Ruskin Park (Denmark Hill), which they can reach quite cheaply by tram or bus.

Some of the children's organisations listed in (*b*) have sporadic open air activities, e.g. Club football teams (greatly handicapped by the lack of pitches); Boys' Brigade Camps, and Sunday School outings and expeditions. The Play Centre, which is open every day from 5–7 in term time, runs a football team which has organised expeditions to the floodlit playground at Kennington Park. An increasing number of children go to summer camps and holidays arranged through the schools, children's organisations and voluntary bodies such as the Children's Country Holiday Fund, but it was considered that these lay outside the scope of the present study, as do the present proposals for meeting the shortage of playing fields by taking children from the inner London areas to playing-fields in the outer ring for a weekly games and open-air day.

CHILDREN'S ACTIVITIES IN THE COURTYARDS

From the 28th December to 14th February the record of observations was kept in the form of a daily log; in the latter half of February rather fuller notes in the form of a diary were kept. The general trends or tendencies observable therein may briefly be summarised as follows. There is comparatively little variety or imagination in the general pattern of play which tends to be very stereotyped. Two games—"gang" games in their many varieties, such as "robbers and coppers," "cowboys and Indians," "prisoner and base," and football, completely dominate the scene. Apart from an occasional change of weapon—bows and arrows for Sten guns—or dressing up with feathers for "cowboys and Indians"—very little originality is displayed. The gang games are played by both sexes and by all ages from 4–14, although boys of 6–12 predominate. Football is normally an exclusively male preserve, although the log records one girl footballer of sufficient prowess to be allowed to play with the boys. Football appears to be a dominant male interest from 8 years onwards.

The second generalisation is that the boys always outnumber the girls, often by as many as two to one. Reasons are varied; they are in part due to the physical nature of the yards which encourage games requiring space and movement such as the two already mentioned, whilst the generally barren and unimaginative nature of the yards does not lend itself so well to smaller-scale games of imagination popular with the girls. It is also probable that the girls have more domestic duties in the home. They are frequently to be observed laden with shopping baskets. They are certainly much in evidence escorting younger brothers and sisters. Weather, too, may have some influence, as the disparity between the sexes was less evident during a preliminary census taken last summer before the enquiry officially began.

Some of the girls missing from the yards would be found up on the balconies, either near their own front doors or occasionally grouped on the stairs, playing mothers and fathers or school. Frequently one has to step over such games when visiting other flats. The boys only seem to join in for exceptional reasons, e.g. when they are forbidden to go right down to the yard to play.

The extraordinary predominance of gang games over all other forms of activity is not easy to explain. A few of the special devotees appeared to play practically no other games at all. Their gang games were played with such monotonous regularity that the observer might have come to accept this as the norm for all English children. But this is not in fact true, as observations (both previous and subsequent to the enquiry) with two other groups of children—one at the Junk Playground and another on a new housing estate in the country just outside London—confirmed.

If this type of playground is less suitable for girls than boys, it would appear to be least suitable of all for little children. Not only is the toddler lost in the immensity of the great blocks and the wide unyielding asphalt courtyards, but there is so little opportunity for him to exercise his imagination. There are so few intimate little corners where he can hide himself away or create his tiny world of fantasy: no earth in which to dig, nothing on which to climb, no materials to pile up and knock down, no lessons to be learned in balance, few places in which to seek adventure, and little to stimulate the childish imagination. There are therefore only two main activities in which the 2–5's engage—running, with or without a ball, and cycling round on their little tricycles in great arcs and circles about the empty yards in the mornings and afternoons. On the credit side it is true that they have more than ample room for movement and then can enjoy a measure of safety unknown to dwellers in the conventional street. For this reason, mothers will allow even very young children to play unattended. From conversations with them, it is clear that this point of safety is appreciated by many mothers. On the other hand a considerable proportion of the more careful mothers are very anxious when their youngest children are out of sight in the yards down below. Rarely if ever can mothers be seen playing with their tiny children. There are no seats or other inducements for them to come down and watch them play. Hence the inevitable stance on the balcony, and the apprehensive and often strident shout so different from the intimate tones associated with motherhood.

Although the toddlers appear to be most handicapped by the nature of the yards, there is little doubt that the older children also suffer from the fact that the courtyards lack four of the great essentials to children's play:

(a) Something on which to climb (hence the popularity of illegal fence climbing).

(b) Opportunities for secrecy (e.g. sheds, caves, hidden corners in woods. Hence the appeal of porches, and the corners near the dust-chutes).

(c) Water and plastic materials such as mud and sand.

(d) Mystery (like dark woods) and beauty to stimulate the imagination.

In view of the apparent unattractiveness of the yards for play, it is at first sight a little surprising that more use was not made by the children of the bomb-sites and bombed houses. But the latter were fairly effectively boarded up and decorated with warnings about police action. They were nevertheless occasionally used by the more adventurous for gang headquarters and similar purposes. They were also an ever-useful source of supply for the youthful firewood syndicates which hawked their ill-gotten timber around the blocks. The bomb-sites were singularly dull and uninteresting, lacking the usual allurements to the venturesome child. A mere litter of tin cans and small brickbats, they were too rough for ball games and too smooth, unexciting and lacking in suitable materials to encourage any building or other constructive activities.

Returning to the courtyards, the records indicate the great popularity of wheeled toys of every description, ranging from home-made scooters and orange-boxes on skates to the most elaborate and expensive model racing cars and miniature cycles. Here again it would appear that the physical nature and construction of the yards with their large areas of smooth safe asphalt, are at least partly responsible for this emphasis.

The use of porches (the covered entrance at the foot of the common stairs) will have been noted in the log and diary. But it is very doubtful if this very important feature of block dwellings is sufficiently realised by architects and housing authorities. In wet or cold weather they often become unofficial "club-rooms": sometimes the children sit on the stairs reading comics; at other times the porch becomes a stage, and, with the staircase and handrail offering some scope for scenery and "decor," quite elaborate plays, pantomimes, concerts and dancing displays are given. Cigarette cards seem more popular here than marbles. Cards are sometimes played but gambling games seem comparatively rare (although common on other block housing estates). This may be due to the lack of privacy. Laing House (the new block) has two porches. In each case the ground-floor entrance to the electric passenger lift is in the porch, and as the front door of my flat was also adjacent, I was in a specially favourable position to observe the uses of this unofficial "club-room." Its magnetic attraction for the children arose from the fact that it was the largest covered and sheltered space to which they had access. (The resident caretaker, a very conscientious man, lived in the flat similar to mine at the foot of the other staircase.) Above all it housed the ever-popular electric lift. This porch was popular not only with the children from Laing House, but it attracted those from Grenfell and Moffatt Houses also, thus helping to break down the social cleavage between the two groups.

Naturally the incursion of these visitors was not welcomed by all the residents of the new block; the "superior" parents were particularly resentful. It was also noticeable that in the frequent quarrels which arose among the children, there was a tendency for the warring factions to align themselves on the basis of territorial residence. On such occasions the porch might become a base camp to be defended from the warlike depredations of opposing rival blocks. Another attraction of our porch was that it was so much lighter and cleaner than the rather dark and dismal arches of the older buildings; its bright clean tiles and gay colour scheme apparently appealed to the children. Had they been allowed to play there freely, its use would have been much greater, but owing to the lack of soundproofing between our flat and the porch, there were many times when the children had to be discouraged and driven away. (Obviously this use of the porch had not been envisaged by the architect!) At times this became a really heavy responsibility for the caretaker. It was clear that there was a very great need for some covered space or shelter. A suggestion was made that a disused air-raid shelter in the yard should be used as a club-room or playroom, and a young man, son of a tenant in one of the older blocks, offered to run it. Funds were raised by collections in the buildings, but the L.C.C. did not see their way to accede to this request. There may have been technical difficulties to prevent the use of this shelter, but it was perhaps unfortunate that this, the only spontaneous effort on the part of the tenants to solve a serious community problem, was rejected. It must be admitted, however, that the problems of supervision and responsibility for children's activities are very onerous. There seems little doubt that the decision of the authorities would have been different had there been a tenants' committee to assume responsibility, but here there is evidence of a vicious circle to be broken: the very existence of such a committee would presuppose the use of the shelter for its meetings, there being no other community room available.

As might be expected, the lifts provided a special problem, particularly the one in our wing, remote from the watchful caretaker's eye. It should be explained that these lifts are of an extremely ingenious fully automatic type, offering almost infinite scope for experiment and play. The call-button brought the lift, its coming heralded by a flashing green light indicator. The door opened without human agency, and after an interval of seconds, allowing time for the passengers to embark, the door closed itself just as mysteriously. It had a pneumatic rubber edge similar to those in Underground trains, and in the event of it closing too quickly, a smart tap would cause the door to open again mysteriously and the process could then begin all over again. Although the almost bewildering array of switches for the five floors, stop, and alarm, were placed high up out of the reach of the smaller children, they could always become passengers by holding each other up to press the forbidden switches. The lifts were practically foolproof, except that when all the switches were pressed simultaneously the fuses would sometimes blow, and the

trapped miscreants would then have to press the break-down bell and await rescue and the parental wrath to come. Another favourite game was the despatch of the empty lift from one floor to another, its interception at various points en route, or the trick of attracting the lift just as some adult passenger was waiting to use it. It is hardly surprising that a toy of such fascination should attract children from near and far. The surprising thing is that in time the novelty wore off, and except for occasional joyriding or evening skylarking mainly by adolescents, the lifts, with comparatively few breakdowns, in time fulfilled their proper purpose.

The enquiry took place at a time of the year when the evenings were dark; thus evening activities were limited to the ever-popular gang games, hide and seek, tracking and stalking round the houses. Naturally it was not easy to make accurate observations of activities which depended to some extent on the friendly cloak of darkness, but there was usually plenty of aural evidence. On most nights the tumult and shouting died away soon after 8 p.m., except on Saturday nights when the games went on longer. Except for a handful of rather neglected children, there was little evidence of really late hours during the winter season. Naturally the unofficial "club-rooms"—the porches and common staircases —were used constantly in the earlier part of the evening as they were light and comparatively warm.

Relationships between boys and girls seemed fairly normal and require no special comment, except perhaps to say that games involving the sex element—"kiss and kick" and its variants—seemed rather rarer than usual.

In view of the popularity of the flood-lit playgrounds with which the L.C.C. have been experimenting, it is surprising that little use was made in the evenings of those portions of the yards illuminated quite brightly by the powerful electric lamps on the walls of the new block. Only occasionally was advantage taken of this new development.

Games such as hop-scotch requiring extensive chalking of the ground are usually popular in the yards of block dwellings, but here for some reason they were almost completely absent. This may have been due to the roughness of the new asphalt, but it was more likely that our efficient caretaker disliked having his well-swept yards thus disfigured.

Although the surrounding wall was very high, 10 feet, and surmounted by a further 6 feet of wire netting, thus affording considerable scope for wall games with various types of ball and improvised courts, the children displayed no ingenuity in working out such games for themselves. The only use to which the walls were put was as goals or as cricket back-stops. On one occasion improvised open-air "table tennis" of quite remarkable standard was played by some 14-year-old boys, over the low fence of the "toddlers' enclosure."

GARDENS, TREES AND ORNAMENTAL SHRUBBERIES

As will be seen from the plan, the yard on one side of the new block was flanked by a flower bed, and also contained a small triangular garden and ornamental shrubbery, both separated from the yard by a low brick wall and iron rail. The children were kept off by the watchfulness of the caretaker. During the period of the survey, both bed and garden were planted with young trees, shrubs and plants. Although a few of these were stolen soon afterwards, on the whole the gardens appeared to be surviving well, and it looked as though the experiment of having only a low fence might be successful. Some of the children were noticeably careful when retrieving lost balls. The yards of the two old buildings contained several fine plane and mulberry trees. Round their roots lay a few inches of blackened earth in which the tiny children, left to themselves, would sometimes dig and scratch. On the other side of the new building lay a considerable rectangle of rough grass which was prepared and turfed as a lawn during the period of the enquiry. It too was protected only by a low fence, and in its rougher state, littered with the remains of recent building operations, it had an irresistible attraction for the children, particularly the little ones, who loved to play with the sand and dry earth. During the building opera-

tions, as soon as the workmen left in the evenings, the children of the neighbourhood swooped down and took possession of this "unofficial Junk Playground." Later on, as it lay right under the windows of the caretaker's flat, it was easy to defend against all comers. When it finally became a smooth green lawn, the only child trespassers were those who came to retrieve lost balls. The decision to preserve such greens for show rather than use is an inevitable one in all areas of high density housing where the choice must always lie between green grass to look at, or bare mud on which to walk. These green lawns also provide the only possible privacy for ground-floor tenants whose living-rooms face pleasantly on to them; they are real oases in the barren deserts of asphalt.

VIEWS AND OPINIONS OF PARENTS AND OTHER ADULTS

As already indicated, no general or sample survey of such opinion was possible, for the reasons outlined in the introduction. But the general consensus of parental opinion may be summarised as follows: A minority —those who felt themselves superior (found mostly in the new block)—were frankly worried that there was no way of preventing their children from mixing and playing with those they felt were "the roughs." This is understandable as some of the children from the older buildings were, judged by normal standards of today, uncouth, quarrelsome and foul-mouthed. Such parents felt acutely the lack of private gardens and raised the question on a number of occasions by asking for the new block to be fenced off. The desire for a garden was not, however, confined to this minority. It was a very general and often expressed feeling. There was genuine relief at the safety of the yards from traffic dangers, tempered, however, by a vague and not easily defined feeling that somehow the yards were not adequate for the children's real needs. This feeling became vocal when some child, not necessarily their own, was in trouble for antisocial action of some kind. "Poor little b's, you can't blame 'em—this is no proper place for kids," was a typical comment at such times. In some cases this may have been mere excuse for lack of parental control and supervision, but in other cases it appeared to be based on intelligent observation and an instinctive understanding of the real needs of children.

Since the flats and their yards seem to provide such an outstandingly unsuitable environment for very young children of the nursery age, it is perhaps unfortunate that only one out of the 39 children of this age was able to attend the local Day Nursery. This was because the nursery had a long waiting list and could only take special priority cases.

Opinions of adults without children varied very much according to the floor on which they lived—the nearer they were to the ground floor, the less their enthusiasm for the yards as playgrounds.

In the same way, the opinions of officials vary to some extent according to their proximity to the problem. With a few notable exceptions it will be obvious that the higher officials, planners, architects and committee members do not themselves live in the conditions for which they must legislate and plan. Some of them, however, have had long and wide practical experience of many of the problems involved, and with deep insight and understanding have done all in their power to solve them. For them the tragedy is that many of the problems discussed in this study are incapable of solution within the framework of present planning policy, with its emphasis, particularly in London, on high density housing in flats.

This enquiry also suggests that there is still too little opportunity for the expression of consumer-opinion and co-operation on such practical matters as these.

CONCLUSIONS AND RECOMMENDATIONS

The results of this enquiry, however incomplete and imperfect, suggest certain inescapable conclusions and lead to a number of recommendations. Briefly they may be summarised as follows: The problem is one of great and increasing importance, since the London plans alone assume that something like 80% of the County of London population will be rehoused in flats. Many

authorities assert that the major criticism against flats is that they provide an unsatisfactory biological background for family life and the upbringing of children, denying to them the essentials of space, creative activity, freedom to play, and contact with living and growing things. However, since the present plans for London and other great cities provide no alternative for a considerable proportion of their population, there is the strongest argument for giving this problem urgent consideration, in order to make the best of what can never be an entirely satisfactory situation.

In some existing block dwelling estates such as the one under review here, density of development and lack of space precludes any radical improvement, but even here some more intelligent and imaginative use of the limited space might be made. In new block dwelling projects and those further out from the crowded central areas, greater improvements could be made. Wherever extensive block dwelling schemes are taking place, it seems essential that some co-ordinated plan for children's play and outdoor recreation should be outlined in advance, then developed in greater detail by co-operation between the residents of the neighbourhood, local voluntary organisations, and the various authorities concerned. This might be one of the important functions of a neighbourhood organisation such as a community association.

Schemes either creating new amenities or improving existing ones, seem largely dependent on some form of neighbourly co-operation. This survey instances only one of many promising schemes which have failed to materialise for lack of this essential tenant co-operation. It must be clear, however, that the onus in the first place must lie with the authority to provide some place, however simple, where tenants may meet to plan amongst other things, for their children's welfare.

In the actual planning of new schemes or improvements to those already existing, the primary need is not money, but imagination. It is a strange irony that the same authority which may plan with real insight the equipment of Day Nurseries and Infant Schools can fail so surprisingly to bring the same imagination to bear on the design and equipment of playing space in block dwellings.

Having regard to existing facilities, or those planned for the immediate neighbourhood, it is suggested that block dwelling playgrounds (or the yards of such flats where no separate playground is possible in the near vicinity) should contain the following basic and essential elements. In a study of this nature it is not possible to lay down plans, sizes and standards, but rather to indicate certain principles which should be observed. From this study of children at play in all their joys and happiness as well as their frustrations and frequent anti-social behaviour, it is suggested that the lay-out and equipment of the block-dwelling playground should include the following essential elements, proportionate and related to the needs and existing facilities of the neighbourhood:

(*a*) Retention of the present wide asphalt spaces, so admirable for running, general play, and all wheeled toys (bicycles, tricycles, cars, scooters, skates, etc.). In view of the great popularity of the latter in existing playgrounds, valuable instruction and training in safety first principles might be linked with play, by the laying out of simple miniature cross-roads, junctions etc., with appropriate signs.[1] Schools, police and youth organisations might well co-operate in occasional safety first campaigns.

(*b*) A small ball-games area with protective netting, as far from windows as possible, thus providing for football, netball, cricket and other ball games. Use of walls with marked courts would provide interesting alternative games. Concrete table tennis tables, which have proved popular in American housing schemes, should also be considered.

(*c*) Since existing courtyards are so unsuitable for little children, the "toddlers' enclosure" should include a small sandpit, a splash pool surrounded by a few mounds, a few trees and seats for mothers. Plans and pictures of such a unit will be found in Housing and Recreation published in 1939 by the Federal Works Agency of the U.S.

Housing Authority. The estimated cost at that time of the splash pool was as low as $300–400. Two criticisms are likely to be raised—supervision and maintenance. The first is of course linked with the fundamental problem of so many housing estate amenities—tenant and parent co-operation and organisation. The seats where mothers may sit and watch their children at play should go far to solve this first problem— despite the reluctance sometimes shown by working-class parents to accept responsibility for other peoples' children. On the score of maintenance, it may be argued that both sand-pit and pool are impracticable as they would soon become receptacles for broken glass, etc. In answer to this it may well be that some of the time and energies which the caretakers have to expend at present in the negative and unprofitable tasks of policing the yards and stopping the children from doing many of the things they would like to do, could more usefully and constructively be employed in keeping a friendly eye on this type of equipment and ensuring its safety.

(*d*) Whilst some of the simple and cheaper traditional apparatus such as swings, and see-saws and chutes should be retained, the provision of the more elaborate apparatus should be abandoned. At this stage of our knowledge and experience, the setting up of Junk Playgrounds on any considerable scale seems impracticable. But the application of certain of the principles of the Junk Playground might well be considered, and in place of some of the traditional apparatus now fitted, it is suggested that a small rough area of earth (not asphalt) might be enclosed and supplied with old bricks and a few planks, which the children's imagination and creative activity will soon transform into houses, caves and wigwams and gardens.

(*e*) Ideally such a playground should be related to a children's club-room, workshop or playroom on the ground floor of the block of flats. The use of ground floor space in the building for this and similar non-residential purposes appears to offer the only effective answer to the problem of noise and lack of privacy for ground floor tenants (except where small private gardens can be provided, for instance for old people need-

---

[1] It is important that these should not be permanent or the children may only learn to disregard them.

ing ground floor accommodation; see Stein, 1949).

(f) In order to solve the problem of the porches and to meet some of the unanswered needs of the girls, the play area should include a small simple shelter or covered space incorporating a low platform capable of being used as an informal stage, so designed that it can be used by limited numbers in bad weather or for bigger open-air audiences.

To sum up, the suggestions and recommendations outlined above require neither the use of an impracticable amount of space, nor the lavish expenditure of money or materials. They require intelligent planning and use of all the available space and the expenditure of a great deal of imagination. But they might go far to turn these barren areas, at present so unattractive and so unsuitable for children in many important ways, into real playgrounds where they would play happily and constructively, and where delinquency and vandalism—so often the products of childish boredom—would not so easily find a place.

REFERENCE:

Stein, C. Towards new towns for America, Section V—Hillside Homes. *Town Planning Review*, 1949, **20**, No. 3.

39 The Uses of Sidewalks: Assimilating Children

Jane Jacobs

Children in cities need a variety of places in which to play and to learn. They need, among other things, opportunities for all kinds of sports and exercise and physical skills—more opportunities, more easily obtained, than they now enjoy in most cases. However, at the same time, they need an

unspecialized outdoor home base from which to play, to hang around in, and to help form their notions of the world.

It is this form of unspecialized play that the sidewalks serve—and that lively city sidewalks can serve splendidly. When this home-base play is transferred to playgrounds and parks it is not only provided for unsafely, but paid personnel, equipment and space are frittered away that could be devoted instead to more ice-skating rinks, swimming pools, boat ponds and other various and specific outdoor uses. Poor, generalized play use eats up substance that could instead be used for good specialized play.

To waste the normal presence of adults on lively sidewalks and to bank instead (however idealistically) on hiring substitutes for them, is frivolous in the extreme. It is frivolous not only socially but also economically, because cities have desperate shortages of money and of personnel for more interesting uses of the outdoors than playgrounds—and of money and personnel for other aspects of children's lives. For example, city school systems today typically have between thirty and forty children in their classes—sometimes more—and these include children with all manner of problems too, from ignorance of English to bad emotional upsets. City schools need something approaching a 50-percent increase in teachers to handle severe problems and also reduce normal class sizes to a figure permitting better education. New York's city-run hospitals in 1959 had 58 percent of their professional nursing positions unfilled, and in many another city the shortage of nurses has become alarming. Libraries, and often museums, curtail their hours, and notably the hours of their children's sections. Funds are lacking for the increased numbers of settlement houses drastically needed in the new slums and new projects of cities. Even the existing settlement houses lack funds for needed expansions and changes in their programs, in short for more staff. Requirements like these should have high priority on public and philanthropic funds—not only on funds at the present dismally inadequate levels, but on funds greatly increased.

The people of cities who have other jobs

and duties, and who lack, too, the training needed, cannot volunteer as teachers or registered nurses or librarians or museum guards or social workers. But at least they can, and on lively diversified sidewalks they do, supervise the incidental play of children and assimilate the children into city society. They do it *in the course of carrying on their other pursuits.*

Planners do not seem to realize how high a ratio of adults is needed to rear children at incidental play. Nor do they seem to understand that spaces and equipment do not rear children. These can be useful adjuncts, but only people rear children and assimilate them into civilized society.

It is folly to build cities in a way that wastes this normal, casual manpower for child rearing and either leaves this essential job too much undone—with terrible consequences—or makes it necessary to hire substitutes. The myth that playgrounds and grass and hired guards or supervisors are innately wholesome for children and that city streets, filled with ordinary people, are innately evil for children, boils down to a deep contempt for ordinary people.

In real life, only from the ordinary adults of the city sidewalks do children learn—if they learn it at all—the first fundamental of successful city life: People must take a modicum of public responsibility for each other even if they have no ties to each other. This is a lesson nobody learns by being told. It is learned from the experience of having *other people without ties of kinship or close friendship or formal responsibility to you* take a modicum of public responsibility for you. When Mr. Lacey, the locksmith, bawls out one of my sons for running into the street, and then later reports the transgression to my husband as he passes the locksmith shop, my son gets more than an overt lesson in safety and obedience. He also gets, indirectly, the lesson that Mr. Lacey, with whom we have no ties other than street propinquity, feels responsible for him to a degree. The boy who went unrescued in the elevator in the "togetherness"-or-nothing project learns opposite lessons from his experiences. So do the project children who squirt water into house windows and on passers-by, and go unrebuked because they

are anonymous children in anonymous grounds.

The lesson that city dwellers have to take responsibility for what goes on in city streets is taught again and again to children on sidewalks which enjoy a local public life. They can absorb it astonishingly early. They show they have absorbed it by taking it for granted that they, too, are part of the management. They volunteer (before they are asked) directions to people who are lost; they tell a man he will get a ticket if he parks where he thinks he is going to park; they offer unsolicited advice to the building superintendent to use rock salt instead of a chopper to attack the ice. The presence or absence of this kind of street bossiness in city children is a fairly good tip-off to the presence or absence of responsible adult behavior toward the sidewalk and the children who use it. The children are imitating adult attitudes. This has nothing to do with income. Some of the poorest parts of cities do the best by their children in this respect. And some do the worst.

This is instruction in city living that people hired to look after children cannot teach, because the essence of this responsibility is that you do it without being hired. It is a lesson that parents, by themselves, are powerless to teach. If parents take minor public responsibility for strangers or neighbors in a society where nobody else does, this simply means that the parents are embarrassingly different and meddlesome, not that this is the proper way to behave. Such instruction must come from society itself, and in cities, if it comes, it comes almost entirely during the time children spend at incidental play on the sidewalks.

Play on lively, diversified sidewalks differs from virtually all other daily incidental play offered American children today: It is play not conducted in a matriarchy.

Most city architectural designers and planners are men. Curiously, they design and plan to exclude men as part of normal, daytime life wherever people live. In planning residential life, they aim at filling the presumed daily needs of impossibly vacuous housewives and preschool tots. They plan, in short, strictly for matriarchal societies.

The ideal of a matriarchy inevitably accompanies all planning in which residences are isolated from other parts of life. It accompanies all planning for children in which their incidental play is set apart in its own preserves. Whatever adult society does accompany the daily life of children affected by such planning has to be a matriarchy. Chatham Village, that Pittsburgh model of Garden City life, is as thoroughly matriarchal in conception and in operation as the newest dormitory suburb. All housing projects are.

Placing work and commerce *near* residences, but buffering it off, in the tradition set by Garden City theory, is fully as matriarchal an arrangement as if the residences were miles away from work and from men. Men are not an abstraction. They are either around, in person, or they are not. Working places and commerce must be mingled right in with residences if men, like the men who work on or near Hudson Street, for example, are to be around city children in daily life—men who are part of normal daily life, as opposed to men who put in an occasional playground appearance while they substitute for women or imitate the occupations of women.

The opportunity (in modern life it has become a privilege) of playing and growing up in a daily world composed of both men and women is possible and usual for children who play on lively, diversified city sidewalks. I cannot understand why this arrangement should be discouraged by planning and by zoning. It ought, instead, to be abetted by examining the conditions that stimulate minglings and mixtures of work and commerce with residences, a subject taken up later in this book.

The fascination of street life for city children has long been noted by recreation experts, usually with disapproval. Back in 1928, the Regional Plan Association of New York, in a report which remains to this day the most exhaustive American study of big-city recreation, had this to say:

Careful checking within a radius of ¼ mile of playgrounds under a wide range of conditions in many cities shows that about ⅐ of the child population from 5 to 15 years of age may be found on these grounds . . . The lure of the street is a strong competitor . . . It must be a well administered playground to compete successfully with the city streets, teeming with life and adventure. The ability to make the playground activity so compellingly attractive as to draw the children from the streets and hold their interest from day to day is a rare faculty in play leadership, combining personality and technical skill of a high order.

The same report then deplores the stubborn tendency of children to "fool around" instead of playing "recognized games." (Recognized by whom?) This yearning for the Organization Child on the part of those who would incarcerate incidental play, and children's stubborn preference for fooling around on city streets, teeming with life and adventure, are both as characteristic today as they were in 1928.

"I know Greenwich Village like my hand," brags my younger son, taking me to see a "secret passage" he has discovered under a street, down one subway stair and up another, and a secret hiding place some nine inches wide between two buildings, where he secretes treasures that people have put out for the sanitation truck collections along his morning route to school and that he can thus save and retrieve on his return from school. (I had such a hiding place, for the same purpose, at his age, but mine was a crack in a cliff on my way to school instead of a crack between two buildings, and he finds stranger and richer treasures.)

Why do children so frequently find that roaming the lively city sidewalks is more interesting than back yards or playgrounds? Because the sidewalks are more interesting. It is just as sensible to ask: Why do adults find lively streets more interesting than playgrounds?

The wonderful convenience of city sidewalks is an important asset to children too. Children are at the mercy of convenience more than anyone else, except the aged. A great part of children's outdoor play, especially after they start school, and after they also find a certain number of organized activities (sports, arts, handcrafts or whatever else their interests and the local opportunities provide), occurs at incidental times and must be sandwiched in. A lot of outdoor life for children adds up from bits. It happens in a small leftover interval after lunch. It happens after school while children may be pondering what to do and wondering who will turn up. It happens while they are waiting to be called for their suppers. It happens in brief intervals between supper and homework, or homework and bed.

During such times children have, and use, all manner of ways to exercise and amuse themselves. They slop in puddles, write with chalk, jump rope, roller skate, shoot marbles, trot out their possessions, converse, trade cards, play stoop ball, walk stilts, decorate soap-box scooters, dismember old baby carriages, climb on railings, run up and down. It is not in the nature of things to make a big deal out of such activities. It is not in the nature of things to go somewhere formally to do them by plan, officially. Part of their charm is the accompanying sense of freedom to roam up and down the sidewalks, a different matter from being boxed into a preserve. If it is impossible to do such things both incidentally and conveniently, they are seldom done.

As children get older, this incidental outdoor activity—say, while waiting to be called to eat—becomes less bumptious physically and entails more loitering with others, sizing people up, flirting, talking, pushing, shoving and horseplay. Adolescents are always being criticized for this kind of loitering, but they can hardly grow up without it. The trouble comes when it is done not within society, but as a form of outlaw life.

The requisite for any of these varieties of incidental play is not pretentious equipment of any sort, but rather space at an immediately convenient and interesting place. The play gets crowded out if sidewalks are too narrow relative to the total demands put on them. It is especially crowded out if the sidewalks also lack minor irregularities in building line. An immense amount of both loitering and play goes on in shallow sidewalk niches out of the line of moving pedestrian feet.

There is no point in planning for play on sidewalks unless the sidewalks are used for a wide variety of other purposes and by a wide variety of other people too. These uses need each other, for proper surveillance, for a public life of some vitality, and for general interest. If sidewalks on a lively street are sufficiently wide, play flourishes mightily right along with other uses. If the sidewalks are skimped, rope jumping is the first play casualty. Roller skating, tricycle and bicycle riding are the next casualties. The narrower the sidewalks, the more sedentary incidental play becomes. The more frequent too become sporadic forays by children into the vehicular roadways.

Sidewalks thirty or thirty-five feet wide can accommodate virtually any demand of incidental play put upon them—along with trees to shade the activities, and sufficient space for pedestrian circulation and adult public sidewalk life and loitering. Few sidewalks of this luxurious width can be found. Sidewalk width is invariably sacrificed for vehicular width, partly because city sidewalks are conventionally considered to be purely space for pedestrian travel and access to buildings, and go unrecognized and unrespected as the uniquely vital and irreplaceable organs of city safety, public life and child rearing that they are.

Twenty-foot sidewalks, which usually preclude rope jumping but can feasibly permit roller skating and the use of other wheeled toys, can still be found, although the street wideners erode them year by year (often in the belief that shunned malls and "promenades" are a constructive substitute). The livelier and more popular a sidewalk, and the greater the number and variety of its users, the greater the total width needed for it to serve its purposes pleasantly.

But even when proper space is lacking, convenience of location and the interest of the streets are both so important to children—and good surveillance so important to their parents—that children will and do adapt to skimpy sidewalk space. This does not mean we do right in taking unscrupulous advantage of their adaptability. In fact, we wrong both them and cities.

Some city sidewalks are undoubtedly evil places for rearing children. They are evil for anybody. In such neighborhoods we need to foster the qualities and facilities that make for safety, vitality and stability in city streets. This is a complex problem; it is a central problem of planning for cities. In defective city neighborhoods, shooing the children into parks and playgrounds is worse than useless, either as a solution to the streets' problems or as a solution for the children.

The whole idea of doing away with city streets, insofar as that is possible, and downgrading and minimizing their social and their economic part in city life is the most mischievous and destructive idea in orthodox city planning. That it is so often done in the name of vaporous fantasies about city child care is as bitter as irony can get.

40 The Physical Setting and its Influence on Learning

Elizabeth Richardson

1. THE CLASSROOM LAY-OUT AND ITS EFFECT ON LEARNING

The traditional image of the teacher dies hard. Certainly to most members of the public, and probably to most of his pupils, he figures as the person who should be the focus of all eyes, the central authority who tends either to be asking all the questions or supplying all the answers, the presiding adult through whom all communication must go. Is it the conventional arrangement of desks in straight lines that is responsible for the persistence of this image? Or is the teacher image responsible for perpetuating the desk arrangement? It is hard to say. The pattern has simply become familiar. Many teachers would feel lost without it; and the very pupils who most resent being penned in desks might resist most stubbornly any attempt on the part of a newcomer to change the convention.

Some years ago I heard a young American high-school teacher describing how she and

From *The Environment of Learning*. New York: Weybright and Talley (London: Thomas Nelson & Sons, Ltd.), 1967, Ch. 5. Reprinted by permission of the author and publishers.

her classmates in a twelfth-grade class (comparable to an English sixth form) set their faces against a young history teacher who tried to base his teaching on project work and arranged his classroom to facilitate group planning and discussion. So successful was their opposition that he soon felt himself obliged to admit defeat and resume the spoon-feeding to which they had been accustomed. On another occasion an English teacher recalled to me her experiences as a staff member in one of the Cambridge Village Colleges, during the war, where, among other innovations, an English room had been set up like a university seminar room: desks had been dispensed with entirely, and the chairs provided had extended left arm-rests to accommodate books and papers. Far from responding with pleasure to this unschool-like atmosphere, far from seeing the new-style chairs as symbols of their near-adult status, the pupils (who were in their mid-teens) saw them as objectionable and menacing, and complained openly, at first, that they did not like the room. To take a third example: a student who was doing her term's teaching practice in a small country grammar school was given permission to take a small fourth-year group into the sixth-form room in the new wing for a series of discussion lessons on twentieth-century war poetry. The room was attractively decorated and had been furnished with comfortable fireside chairs. The sixth form were delighted with it and proud of the status it conferred on them as near-adults, with something like a common-room of their own. But the fourth-form boys and girls who were allowed to borrow it, far from feeling relaxed and free to talk more spontaneously and naturally as the teacher had hoped they would, were for the first two or three periods very shy and ill at ease. It turned out that they had to *learn* to accept comfortable and grown-up-looking surroundings and to rise to the demands of a more adult relationship with a teacher.

How can we prevent the familiar visual image of the classroom from becoming so set in the pupil's mind that any departure from it will constitute a threat? Why, after all, should it be assumed that an arrangement of desks that is appropriate for the work going on in one room is equally appropriate for the work going on next door? Must all classrooms look exactly alike?

Consider how the variety of activity patterns in five first-year or second-year classes might be expressed visually in the arrangement of the classroom furniture. In Room 1, where a test is going on, the traditional arrangement of rows of desks will obviously be appropriate. In Room 2, however, where a class is working in groups, the desks have been pushed together in fours to make little tables, at which the children are seated face to face so that they can communicate with the minimum of noise and difficulty. In Room 3, a panel is presenting a prepared reading from a novel. Six members of the class are seated at the teacher's table as a platform party, while the others are sitting on chairs in a double or treble semi-circle, the desks being temporarily stacked round the walls. In Room 4, the desks have been arranged in a large, hollow rectangle, and the whole class is seated at this in council formation. One of the pupils acts as chairman, sitting at the middle of the top table, with a pupil secretary on his right; his job is to help the class arrive at certain decisions concerning the allocation of tasks for a history project. In Room 5, a French lesson is under way. The chairs have been set out in lines, two down each side of the room facing inwards; the teacher is working from the back of the room with a projector and a tape recorder; the screen is at the front and there is plenty of space down the middle of the room. The children are seated so that they can easily look either at him or at the screen. Later in the lesson he will be calling members of the class out into the space near the front to carry out various actions in relation to each other and to him.[1]

Each of these arrangements presupposes a different kind of communication to be at the heart of the lesson. Moreover, in each the role played by the teacher is different. The teacher in the first is simply an invigilator. In the second there is no one leader, though the teacher is available to give help or advice to any group needing it. In the third room one group is responsible for communicating something of interest to the rest of the class, and the teacher is really part of this group's audience and, in fact, sits with the audience. In the fourth room the teacher is a committee member, working under the chairmanship of one of the pupils, though recognized as a member with special skills and knowledge of resources and with a special teaching role in the group. In the fifth room the teacher is himself communicating some new information to the class, helping them to increase their skill in a foreign language and using mechanical aids that will enable them to judge their own achievements objectively.

It is obvious that the actual process of communication between pupils, as well as from pupils to teacher, will be affected in some way by the physical arrangements in these different rooms. What, then, are the actual day-to-day effects of the conventional arrangement of desks on the children who occupy them? Being entirely teacher-centered, this arrangement impedes natural communication between pupils in different parts of the room. It almost encourages shy children to be inarticulate and to rely on the teacher to be their interpreter. The girl who answers a question or offers a comment from the front of the room may be quite inaudible to those sitting behind her, and she will certainly be unable to see their reaction to what she says. The boy who speaks from a seat near the back will probably be heard by the rest of the class, since he will have to use more volume in order to be heard by the teacher; but he will be little better informed than the girl at the front about the reactions of his fellow-pupils, since he will be looking, for the most part, at the backs of their heads. Some children enter cheerfully into the competition to secure the teacher's attention and approval. Others find the whole situation threatening and become intellectually crippled by it. Others, of course, prefer to form their own systems of communication in their own part of the classroom.

How many children are prevented from playing a full part in the classroom by sheer mistrust of their own verbal skill in these

[1] As recommended in C.R.E.D.I.F. (1958) *Voix et Images*, Paris: Didier, p. xxx.

difficult circumstances? Even as adults, most of us experience these feelings from time to time, when we hesitate to enter a discussion following a public lecture or to express our views at a meeting. Now, an adult discussion can be facilitated to a remarkable degree by the simple expedient of rearranging the lecture room so that the usual rows of chairs facing the speaker give way to some kind of semi-circular or horseshoe formation, which enables members of the audience to face one another as well as the speaker. Yet the school classroom, in which most teachers are trying to encourage the articulate exchange of knowledge and ideas, clings to a physical arrangement that inhibits it.

Admittedly, rapid re-organization of a room is possible only if the desks are light, flat-topped and stackable. Admittedly, teachers have to work with the furniture they happen to have: and in some of the older schools they and their pupils are still having to struggle with old battered-looking desks, perhaps heavy with ironmongery, perhaps fastened permanently to benches, frequently cursed with sloping lids, and almost invariably so clumsy that children cannot easily move them from one part of the room to another. Even in the old buildings, however, rooms can sometimes be used to better advantage than they are. And in the new ones, where desks are a great deal more portable, the traditional arrangement in straight rows facing the teacher's table has changed scarcely at all. Sometimes the regrouping of a class does not call for any shifting of furniture, but merely for a slightly unusual use of the furniture as it stands. Opportunities can easily be missed, especially in a situation that does not at first sight look very promising.

In the examples that follow, we see a number of young teachers, engaged in a term of school practice, a little unsure of their right to do anything unexpected with furniture and anxious to conform to what is expected of them as students in training rather than as fully-fledged staff members. Sometimes, perhaps because of the uncertainty about their status, they fail to see how a class can be redistributed in a room or how a room intended for one kind of lesson can be adapted for another. Occasionally they do something that looks un-

orthodox and find that the action has surprisingly welcome results.

On one occasion I see a lower-sixth-form class taken by an English specialist in a rather large needlework room. Eight girls are assembled for a lesson on Sheridan's play *The Rivals*. Miss N., as any of us might have done, seats herself at the rather high teacher's desk, itself elevated on a platform. The girls are distributed between three of the six long heavy work tables, each of which has a sewing machine fixed to one end of it. Three girls are sitting at the second front table on the left, three at the second front one on the right, and the other two at the table behind that. It seems hardly possible for nine more or less adult people to be seated more awkwardly for any kind of discussion. Miss N. has to look from side to side as though she were umpiring a tennis match, and she can hardly avoid taking upon herself the task of asking all the questions and making all the decisions. After a recapitulation of events, the scene is staged in a narrow space between the side of one long table and the platform on which the teacher's desk stands. One of the girls has it in her to give a very spirited performance and obviously enjoys her role; but as she has had no chance to plan her entrance or any of her moves with the others, she can do little with the part except use her voice as effectively as possible.

Throughout this lesson the girls, who are all about sixteen to seventeen, show no overt reaction either to being kept at arm's length during the preliminary discussion or to being given so little say in how the acting itself should be tackled. Indeed, it is fair to say that since they have chosen to sit spread out in this way, they have apparently wished to keep the teacher at arm's length and to avoid energetic cooperation with each other. Yet, as I watch them, I have the impression that they are feeling slightly frustrated without quite knowing why. I find myself regrouping them in imagination. I see the eight girls, with Miss N., sitting close together at one of those long tables, facing each other across the length and breadth of it, and planning vigorously, as a production group, how this scene can be staged, how the available space and furniture in the room can best be used, which member of the group should be given this role and which that, who should be the producer once the scene gets under way, and so on. When, at the end of the lesson, I ask one of the girls who has taken no part whether she thinks such a piece of production work could have been tackled by the group, she looks slightly surprised, considers for a moment and says: "Well, I've never thought about it. I don't know. Perhaps we could."

Occasionally a teacher will find himself faced with what looks like a difficult room to teach in, only to find that the very unusualness of the physical setting helps to turn a school-ridden class into a stimulating and quite adult seminar. An English specialist who had had great difficulty in getting her sixth form to talk about poetry when they were in an ordinary classroom, found that they were much easier to teach when they had to have their lesson in a library, where she and they sat round a table naturally as adults. Yet her earlier attempt to reduce the distance between herself and them by sitting on a desk with her feet on a chair had only increased the distance and had had no effect whatever on the quality of the discussion. Again, a man teaching in a boys' school, who had a sixth-form group twice a week for English, found that the lesson when they met in the dining-room, and sat round on benches in a rough oval between two of the tables, was far more lively and productive of ideas than the lesson for which a classroom was available.

This kind of improvisation is comparatively easy with a group of a dozen or so sixth-formers. But what happens when a middle-school class of more than thirty children are deprived of their usual classroom and have to move to a library, or to the dining-room or to a science laboratory? It was hardly surprising, perhaps, that Miss O. was filled with apprehension when she found that she had to take a current-affairs lesson in the junior library, where her thirty pupils would be sitting at small tables in groups of five or six; and that Mr. P., a classics specialist, went to pieces when he unexpectedly had to teach his third form in a biology laboratory.

Both these teachers, presented with an unfamiliar and apparently threatening room, reacted, as many of us would have done, by trying to make it approximate as closely as possible to the conventional classroom to which they were accustomed. The current-affairs lesson could have been handled in such a way as to turn the grouping at the small tables into an advantage; but for this to have happened Miss O. would have had to realize that some division of responsibility between these groups was necessary, and—more important—to have had faith in the ability of each group to take on a limited task for the lesson and report its achievement to the other groups at the end. Instead of this she struggled to conduct the kind of lesson she had planned for a formal classroom, and had to use up a good deal of energy in forestalling conversation between the children sitting together in such close proximity at the various tables.

Mr. P.—the classics specialist in the biology laboratory—faced a much greater difficulty. He too reacted by trying to do in this room what he would have done in an ordinary classroom. So, not unnaturally, he took up his position behind the master's demonstration bench, thereby robbing himself of all flexibility of movement. The boys, also not unnaturally, sat at the work benches in such a way that about a third of the class had their backs to Mr. P. As the lesson went on, they became more and more hostile to him and he gradually lost control, reciprocating their hostility. In this very awkward situation he might have fared much better if he could have improvised a completely unexpected seating arrangement, perhaps collecting all the boys in a wide circle on stools round two of the benches, sitting on a stool at one end of one of them himself, and relying on informality and closeness rather than on formality and separation. By this means he would have emphasized the unusualness of the situation, somehow turning it into something rather pleasant, and drawing his class into a kind of cheerful conspiracy with himself to defeat the feelings of discomfort and deprivation into which their loss of a classroom had temporarily plunged them.

Even given a group small enough to be handled in tutorial fashion, young teachers rarely think of the shape the group makes as it distributes itself about the room. In this situation the problem is one of compression rather than of expansion. The smaller the group the more intimate it can be; the seating should emphasize this difference in the relationship between the members, and it should enhance the possibility of seminar-like methods of work.

On one occasion I found myself in a large airy classroom in a new comprehensive school, watching a modern linguist (Miss Q.) teaching a group of nine rather backward fourth-formers who were making a serious, if belated, attempt to study French. They worked with her for five periods a week, moving about from one free classroom to another. In the particular room in which I saw them, the desks were so arranged that in a large class about half the pupils would have been sitting along three sides of the room, facing the centre, and the rest would have been in rows across the middle. The six girls in this small group had chosen to sit along the window wall, at right angles to the teacher's table, and the three boys were sitting across the room in the second row from the front. Miss Q. therefore found herself in a very curious position in relation to her class, just off the corner of the angle formed by the girls' axis along the window and the boys' axis across the front. The effect of this formation as the lesson proceeded was significant: Miss Q., quite unconsciously, gave the boys more and more of her attention; towards the end of the lesson, the girl at the far end of the girls' axis was beginning to look lost and rather neglected, though she was not inattentive; and the only girls who seemed to get any share of Miss Q.'s attention were the two at her end of the axis, sitting almost level with the boys. Miss Q. was astonished, later, that it had not occurred to her to find a more satisfactory seating arrangement for this rather intimate and earnest little group. She realized, on reflection, that during their wanderings from room to room neither she nor the pupils had ever really paused to consider what might be the most effective way for ten people to sit down and work together.

Such failure to notice the effect of physical grouping on communication and even on the emotional climate of a lesson is not uncommon. I find in my notes, jotted down during students' lessons from time to time, a diagram of a class of fifteen fifth-form pupils, also studying French, scattered to the extremities of a fairly large classroom, presumably occupying the places they would normally have occupied when the whole class was present, and with similarly disastrous effects on the lines of communication.

The problem is, of course, more complex than it looks. Like the girls in the needlework room, these boys were in a sense wishing to keep the teacher at arm's length. And if he had proposed that they should leave their own desks to form a closer group it is more than likely that his request would have aroused immediate resentment, even though the reorganization would ultimately have made for pleasanter and more efficient working conditions. Once again, we are back to the problem of ambivalence which was discussed in the first chapter. The wish to be close to the teacher and to work cooperatively with him is in conflict with the wish to draw away from him and so avoid sharing the responsibility for the carrying out of the task.

There is also another kind of conflict, which, as we have already seen, is always present to some extent in a group—the conflict between the conscious, sophisticated aims of the individual and the unspoken, primitive aims of the group. The fifth formers in this classroom, with an important examination ahead, did not, presumably, want to waste their time. Each must have wanted the best possible working conditions with this teacher; as individuals they must have been well aware of the absurdity of remaining scattered all over the room as they were. Yet the group contrived to keep them in these positions and even prevented the teacher from taking any action to improve the situation.

Sometimes it is one individual pupil who, in the end, suffers from an inefficient classroom grouping. In another lesson, this time with twelve members of a fourth-form class, Miss R. is working orally through a French prose, writing certain phrases on the board. For the most part she is encouraging them to regard this as a trial run through a task which they will be tackling independently for themselves for homework. These pupils are not too widely scattered, and up the middle of the room from front to back, there is a block of desks in threes, which makes for a fairly close concentration in one part of the room. But one member of the group, who is isolated at the back of the room, sits rather huddled over her desk, and although she raises her hand quite often in the first half of the lesson, she gradually gives up signalling her willingness to answer questions as time goes on, feeling apparently that the teacher has forgotten her. The fact is that from the position that Miss R. occupies for most of the lesson this girl can hardly be seen at all, though I, from my seat at the desk level with hers on the far side of the room, am well placed to watch her reactions and the fall in the barometer of her attentiveness. Towards the end of the period a chance move by Miss R. in the direction of the windows brings this girl suddenly into view, and she at last gets her chance to take some part in the lesson.

Interestingly enough, what inexperienced teachers are most often told is that they ought to bring their pupils near the front of the classroom in the interest of control and discipline. This implies that the rearrangement is to be made primarily for the benefit of the teacher; and of course with some classes the need for control will be the most crying need. The notion that a different kind of grouping, even with a well-behaved class, might in fact be pleasanter for the pupils, or that the teacher is seeking a physical grouping in which his own position can be less dominating rather than more so, is seldom given the prominence that it merits.

Merely bringing the group to the front of the room is not really the most important part of the operation. Nor does it necessarily, of itself, solve disciplinary problems if they exist. Another modern linguist, Miss S., trying to conduct oral work with a particularly restless group of eight first-year children, brings them, sensibly enough, to the front of the room, but finds herself with a row of meek little girls in front of her table, flanked on both sides by two pairs of boisterous little boys, who successfully engage most of her attention simply by demanding it noisily, first from one end of the row and then from the other. In fact, the pair of boys on the left are sitting just behind the girls, while the pair on the right are sitting just in front of the girls. Thus the situation is made even more difficult by the fact that the class, small as it is, is really operating as three sub-groups (the docile quartet and the two noisy pairs) so that Miss S. never has a unified group working with her. This she might have had if she had brought the children together into a semicircle, or even seated them with her at her own table.

As with younger classes, a changed use of furniture may even help to solve a disciplinary problem with truculent older pupils. This kind of problem is, of course, extremely unlikely to arise in any sixth-form group; but it can very easily arise with day-release classes in technical colleges, where groups of young people in their late teens may react violently against the all too familiar classroom situation that they thought to have left behind when they left school at the age of fifteen. One teacher who was doing a term's practice at a technical college encountered such a group and handled the difficulty in rather an unusual way.

The group consisted of about a dozen young men of about seventeen or eighteen. Their attitude was uncooperative, to say the least: they were noisy and outspoken; and two of them were hostile to the point of rudeness. They were being taught in a small room crowded with desks which could not possibly be moved into any new formation. Accordingly Mr. T. obtained permission to move his class into a small staff common room near-by which was not, as it happened, needed by any of his colleagues during that period, and in which there were two fairly large tables. He seated his students round these tables in such a way that the two most difficult members were separated. He himself hovered between the two tables trying to keep some control over the discussion without exerting the sort of school-room authority that would only have increased the hostility between certain individuals and himself. The most significant thing that happened was that the students themselves began to take over the two most difficult members—as they would never have been able to do in the old classroom. By moving the class into a different physical setting, Mr. T. had, first, given them more comfortable working conditions; but, more important still, he had shifted the emphasis from the teacher–class conflict to the conflict within the group. Thus the behaviour problem became the group's responsibility; and in deciding how to deal with this, the group had to decide whether they were really in that college to learn and grow or to waste time and deteriorate. The move out of a room that looked like a school classroom into a room that looked like an adult common room may well have had some effect also on the decision they made.

2. RITUAL AND SYMBOLISM

There seems to be little doubt that furniture has symbolic significance as well as functional significance for pupils of all ages. Desks and tables, chairs normally occupied by teachers, chairs normally occupied by pupils—all these stand for certain kinds of ritual and for certain expectations about roles and relationships in schools. Some of these rituals are sophisticated, others are primitive; some facilitate adult behaviour, others perpetuate childish behaviour.

Compare, for example, two school dining rooms, both in secondary schools. One has a high table where the staff eat and two rows of long refectory tables, where the pupils eat; the other has a network of octagonal tables, of which two or three, not easily identifiable, happen to be staff tables. Each of these dining rooms has its rituals. In the first, the ritual may involve frequent orders and reprimands from the high table, echoed by similar orders and reprimands from the heads of the tables on the floor; the majority are expected to obey the instructions of the few; the noise is usually unbearable. In the second dining room, no one appears to be giving any orders; the eight people at each table appear to be jointly responsible for fetching, serving and clearing away the meal, and to have some well-understood routine for dealing with these tasks; the noise is surprisingly low

for the number of people in the hall. There is no need to say which of these is the more adult situation, though there is no difference between the numbers of people eating at the same time in the two dining rooms.

Again, the ritual in a classroom at nine o'clock may suggest a benevolent autocracy or a genuine pupil–teacher relationship. Recently I talked to a man who was teaching in a school where a twenty-minute form period was allowed at the beginning of every school day. The conventional image of this form period suggests a form master spending most of his time, if not all of it, sitting at his table, doing the routine tasks of form administration and talking across the table, if time allows, to the class as a whole. This teacher, on the contrary, had been making a point of keeping right away from his own table during those twenty-minute form periods. The boys had their own arrangements for marking the register and collecting the dinner money, doubtless using his table for the purpose. He, meanwhile, would sit in a different part of the room every day, talking with a little group of boys about any subject that happened to be in people's minds, and in this way getting to know his boys as individuals, and also getting to know something about the groups within his class.

Another ritual, described to me by a history master in a boys' public school, had a more direct bearing on classwork. Mr. U. told me how he had deliberately used a certain ritual with chairs to symbolize two rather different roles in relation to the same sixth-form group. This was a school which recognized the near-adult status of its older pupils by providing for them a room quite unlike the conventional classroom and furnished with a large table instead of desks. It happened in one year that Mr. U. had a sixth-form group both for "A" level history and for current affairs, and that quite a number of boys were in both classes. In his history periods, which might have been described as directed seminars, he would sit at one end of the table and lead the discussion fairly strenuously. But in the current-affairs periods, which took the form of free discussion on agreed topics, he would sit half-way down one side of the table, and would expect more of the leadership to come from the boys. The boys who attended both these classes easily learned to associate the two chairs he occupied with the two somewhat different roles that he carried. As it turned out, they were also able to react spontaneously, and quite appropriately, to a sudden change of role in one of these situations.

About half-way through the spring term, Mr. U. handed over his current-affairs period to a student who was doing his teaching practice in the school and who had been observing this class for some weeks. As an observer the student, too, had sat at the table—on the opposite side to Mr. U., near one corner. When the day came for the student to take over, nothing had actually been said about where he should sit; yet, without any pre-planning, Mr. U. went over to the seat which had hitherto been occupied by the student, and the student, coming in a minute or two later, went equally naturally to the seat hitherto occupied by Mr. U. The boys immediately accepted the student in the role of staff member, and only about half-way through the lesson realized that Mr. U. was sitting at the table, quietly observing what was going on, as, up to that day, the student had been in the habit of doing.

By ritualizing the use of these three positions at the table, this teacher had evidently been able to establish a pattern within which behaviour could be flexible because the important roles were clearly understood. He had also made it possible for a student to take over his role in his presence, without having to offer any elaborate explanations which might have weakened the student's position by emphasizing his junior status. The boys were thus able to respond to the student quite naturally, when the master and the student changed roles.

It is not children only who read such meanings into the way we use furniture to express certain kinds of relationship. The parent in the headmaster's study feels the nature of the interview to be different according to whether he speaks to her from behind his desk or comes over to her side of the room and sits in an arm-chair similar to the one that she occupies. The student

in the tutor's room feels the nature of his essay tutorial to be different according to whether the tutor remains at his desk or moves away from it to a chair more like the one he offers the student. The role of the seminar leader is seen to be more dictatorial if he conducts the discussion from a special staff member's chair and less dictatorial if he sits on the same kind of chair as all the other members of the group. On the other hand, a student who is reading a paper to the seminar may feel more confident if he is given the privilege of sitting in a more important-looking chair than anyone else on this occasion. Another may feel this distinction to be threatening rather than supporting and may prefer to sit like the others.

Now however such children may at first dislike and even oppose modifications to the "normal" use of furniture when these are carried out by their teachers, they make use of symbolic and ritualistic innovations themselves when they wish to communicate with their teachers on an emotional level. The novelist G. W. Target describes a particularly violent form of this kind of reaction in *The Teachers* (1960), where one class expresses its disapproval and disgust against its form master by wrecking the classroom in the most sadistic and objectionable way it can devise. Although no individual or sub-group within the class admits responsibility for the outrage, the message to the master concerned is clear and unequivocal and leads to a considerable amount of heart-searching in the staff group as a whole. This, of course, is a fictitious example. But it has its counterpart in acts of aggression against youth-club premises and, occasionally, against school premises. These attacks are often unrelated to any thefts or self-gain, and appear to be directed more against society, or schools, or teachers in general than against any one person in particular. During the war I myself taught in a school that was burgled one night by a group of boys who, as far as was known, had no connection with the school at all. Apart from a few pencils, nothing was stolen, but drawers and cupboards in the headmaster's room were rifled, papers and other objects being left scattered all over the room; the housekeeper found that her white overall had been ruined by an ink drawing down the back and a ludicrous inscribed message from "the Saint"; and a pair of shoes that a member of the staff had left in the cloakroom has been filled up with Harpic and water and made completely unwearable. A meaningless series of pranks, apparently. Yet the gesture must have had some meaning to those who made it.

When these hostile acts are committed openly in the school classroom by children who, at other times, show considerable benevolence towards their teachers, it is important that the adult should try to understand the feelings that give rise to them—perhaps even to tolerate some acting out of such feelings. In the formally structured classroom accommodation of our times, the obvious item of furniture to be used by children in this way is the blackboard. For example, a group of third-year boys and girls expressed, in an ambiguous message on the blackboard, their confused and highly ambivalent feelings towards their geography master. A first-year boy expressed similarly ambivalent feelings on behalf of his class by writing "ABK is mad" first on the blackboard and then on the dusty corridor window.

Now what most of us are tempted to do in moments of crisis like this is to concentrate our attention on the individual whom we know or suspect to have inscribed the message on the board. But here again we may be dealing with a group phenomenon; and it may be that the problem should be discussed at the group level rather than at the individual level. If the action of the one boy is tolerated by the other twenty-nine, it becomes to some extent a public statement. It therefore represents some feeling that is shared and cannot be attributed only to the child who has dared to give symbolic expression to it.

My own memories go back to an even more disturbing occasion when, as a young and still far too shockable teacher, I was subjected to a test-out by a bright, rebellious fourth form in a boys' school during the war. This incident probably left me a good deal more shaken than the "mad" teacher quoted above. I arrived in the classroom one day to find on the blackboard a large, crude drawing of a naked male figure. In

the general scuffle that greeted my entrance, it seemed to me that one boy only—a boy I particularly disliked—had been out of his place.

If I had been a man, it is probable that the figure on the blackboard would have been female. And we have to recognize that a test-out of this kind will take different forms according to whether the teacher is a man or a woman, whether the class is co-educational or single-sex, and if the latter, whether boys or girls. What, in principle, does the teacher do, faced with this kind of demonstration? Does he express anger, or shock, or pain, and embark on a futile attempt to discover which member of the form is responsible for the drawing? Does he pretend not to notice it or have it rubbed off the board as casually as if it were merely a diagram left up from the previous lesson? Or does he abandon his prepared lesson and try, quietly, and without embarrassment or rancour, to get the class to talk about the feelings or preoccupations or anxieties that give rise to such a demonstration of hostility against an adult?

I wish I could say that I, in my wisdom, had been able to take the third course on that occasion, or even that I had had the presence of mind to take the second. But I have to admit that my reaction was more like the first. I got through the lesson somehow, and in time this class and I did manage to establish a good working relationship. But I believe now that we could have done so a great deal sooner if I had been mature enough to see behind the action of that one boy (whichever member of the form it was) to the more important message the whole group needed me to receive. I believe now that the real protest was against my failure to treat them as adults at a time when a woman who was prepared to make them feel like men could have achieved a great deal with them. If, instead of reacting with panic and anger, I had been able to make them talk openly about the feelings that lay behind this incident—meeting their immaturity with maturity, to use Dr Winnicott's phrase (1962)—we might have achieved a more genuine understanding instead of the uneasy armed neutrality that was the immediate sequel to it.

It is rare, in fact, for a whole class to act

out feelings of this kind against a teacher. More often one member is left to express the feelings that all, to some extent, share. On the whole, children accept the teacher's rituals fairly unquestioningly. They obligingly write only the expected words or drawings on the board, and they preserve the normal arrangement of the furniture. In fact, as we have seen, attempts on the part of a teacher to change the conventional arrangement of desks in rows facing the front of the classroom are likely to be met with stubborn resistance. Yet in moments of rebellion or strong hostility, a class (or an individual representing the class) will very often express defiance by breaking some established ritual over the use of furniture.

One example of this is the bizarre situation, perhaps subconsciously dreaded by every teacher, of the class which has turned all the desks round so that they face the back of the room. In fact this situation has been known to occur outside the more hilarious works of fiction about the secondary modern schools; and when it does occur it may be far from hilarious for either the teacher or the class. If the teacher perceives this as a light-hearted joke of the April-Fools'-Day order, the most appropriate action may be simply to prick the bubble by walking to the back of the room and conducting the lesson from there—thus replying with a counter-joke. But if the episode occurs as part of a gradually deteriorating situation between the teacher and the class, it is probable that the feelings expressed by it go very deep; and what the class really needs from the teacher is time to work through the conflicts that are being dramatised. Mere disciplinary action may restore the desks and chairs to their normal positions without touching the underlying causes of the rebellion.

When this kind of impasse is reached in a classroom it may appear that survival depends on quick action by the teacher, summary punishment of the ringleaders and prompt restoration of the usual visual pattern of the classroom. Yet this sequence of events, though restoring the *status quo*, may conceal for ever the real or imaginary grievance that is blocking communication between teacher and class. More important

still, the positive elements in the relationship may never have the chance to reaffirm their existence in a spontaneous way. The official action drives the wedge more firmly in, where a pause might have enabled the class members themselves to loosen it.

3. MEMORIES AND ANTICIPATIONS

We have been thinking about the conscious and unconscious uses to which teachers and children put their school furniture. What of the effects of the buildings themselves—their oldness or newness, their datedness or modernity—on learning processes and on the relationships within the school?

The inequalities between schools—simply in terms of buildings and furniture—are enormous. And in looking at buildings and furniture we are looking at more than expenditure or at the gaiety and comfort that money can buy: we are facing inequalities in the kind of educational experiences that are possible for the pupils and their teachers. Schools, of course, are far more than bricks and mortar, or steel and concrete, and we all know that there are many teachers working in cheerless old buildings who are creating for their pupils a concept of education that is very different from that suggested by the school architecture of the last century. And so a child who has learned to love an apparently dreary old building may not, at first, find much compensation for his sense of loss even in a cheerful new building. It is not the surrounding fabric that determines the culture of a school, but the people living in it.

At any time of transition a child is being pulled both forwards and backwards. For the great majority, of course, the most dramatic transfer occurs at the age of eleven, when they move from primary to secondary school. And it is important to realize that a child's feelings about this change are going to be determined as much by what he leaves behind in the old building as by what he finds in the new one. He may have come from a shabby, badly furnished building in the centre of the city, or from a new, well-equipped building on the outskirts.

A moment's reflection is enough to remind us, then, how different in quality these acts of transition must be for the thirty to forty members of any class of eleven-year-olds. Simply to say that all these children are undergoing a move from a primary school to a secondary school is saying nothing at all about the realities of their various experiences. What looks new and exciting to one child may look intolerably dreary to another. What this girl sees as a prison, that one may see as a haven of peace. To one boy, remembering the clump of trees and the slope of grass he could see from his last classroom window, this famous old grammar school may look as dark and sombre as the heavy desk he is sitting at; to the boy next to him, sharing this desk, the situation looks quite different, for he knows that there are playing fields near-by, even if he cannot see them at present, whereas the school from which he has come had nothing but a small, enclosed asphalt yard. To the boys sitting in front, the cumbersome desk is in itself something to wonder at, since they have come from a school where classrooms were furnished with light tables, which could be put together in several ways or could be moved away or stacked against the wall when space was needed for acting, or singing or painting at easels.

And so we could go on. For although these examples are imaginary, they represent aspects of reality and verbalize a few of many possible combinations of past and present experience. In fact, coming to a new school is rather like learning a new language. The difficulties encountered in the new language arise out of the habits formed in speaking the native language: what is difficult for a German learning English may not be difficult for a Spaniard. And so it is with a child learning the language of a new school: he comes to it with habits of thinking and feeling already learned in another school.

In these days of fairly rapid building programmes, it not infrequently happens that a whole school has to move from an old building to a new one. Such a school may be an object of envy to neighbouring schools that see no prospect of escape from shabby old premises. Yet to the staff and children who are involved in such a move, the experience is unlikely to be wholly pleasant. A visitor may expect to find, in the new building, a mood of elation. What he may find, however, is a mood of depression and disappointment, accompanied by a good deal of nostalgia for the (now) loved old building. Complaints about the new one may be legion. The position of the headmaster's room and the office, the narrowness of the staircase, the inadequacy of the locker space, the mistakes in the design of the apparently splendid stage—all these may excite loud comment. Little or nothing may be said about the lightness and airiness of the classrooms, the extended laboratory and gymnasium accommodation, the pleasant views from the windows, the more spacious and attractive hall. And there may even be some envy of the school that has now taken over the old building. Why should this be? What are the new buildings, so often described as "luxury palaces" by the public, really like compared with the old ones that they are gradually superseding?

Certainly there has been some change in the design of certain rooms—a move away from the old idea of central supervision and towards the idea of group autonomy. Libraries now may incorporate alcoves or private bays, where pupils can sit and work without feeling that they are constantly under the eye of the teacher. The domestic science room has its flat, in which small groups of girls (four or six at a time) can spend a morning, perhaps a full day, perhaps even a week, doing the cleaning, the washing and ironing, the planning, cooking and serving of meals, as these tasks would be done in a well-organized home. Science laboratories suggest less emphasis on demonstration by the teacher and more on experimenting by the pupils. The school hall may be designed so that one end of it can be partitioned off as a drama room, with different floor levels or movable rostra that enable children to work separately in small groups or together in large groups or to perform scenes to one another, either in an arena-type stage or on a raised stage.

On the other hand, the changes are not always for the better. The hall may be open on to a corridor at one side, so that a drama class is constantly subject to the feeling of being overlooked, perhaps disapprovingly, by passers-by. Classrooms in the newest buildings have become more standardized, if anything, as have corridors and staircases. Part of the charm of the better old buildings—the ones that have some of the pleasant characteristics of a rambling old private house—is that nearly every room has its own special size and shape and character. In the old school building that we have left behind, "Room 8" may have suggested a particular place with a distinctive individuality, rather than a mere number on one of a series of identical doors leading into identical square boxes as it does here in the new building.

We still await the real revolution in school architecture, the kind of revolution that has been foreshadowed in the Newsom Report (1963, Ch. 11). We need far greater variety in the size and equipment of rooms than we are yet getting even in the newest schools. The concept of the standard classroom is out of date. We need buildings that include small tutorial and seminar rooms with appropriate furniture for work based on discussion and enquiry, along with a variety of workshops and rooms specially designed for activities such as music, film, language work with audio-visual aids and projects that cut across different subjects in the social studies fields. New buildings, as the Newsom Committee pointed out, are still being designed to express current practice, whereas they ought to be designed to meet the teaching needs of the future.

And so it is perhaps not surprising to find that a new building may arouse mixed feelings in those who move into it from a familiar old building. It will have some obvious advantages; but it may prove less radically "different" as a setting for work than it seemed to give promise of being, and so may fail to satisfy the expectations of its incoming teachers and pupils. Part of this sense of let-down, then, springs from a real sense that the new is not unreservedly an improvement on the old. At the same time, there may be an unacknowledged emotional problem too—one that is familiar to sociologists who have studied the effects of the transportation of families from condemned living quarters to new housing estates. It is not only old inconveniences and discomforts that are lost, but also old patterns of life and ways of thinking and feeling. The community seeks to rediscover its old way of life in quite new and unfamiliar premises, but some things do not fit any more. The old time-table seems unmanageable now that the physical shape of the school is different. Distances from one part of the school to another may be greater. The desks, perhaps, no longer contain books, and so the children have to remember to bring into the classroom all the books and equipment they need for a lesson, and as they frequently forget, new causes of friction suddenly come into existence. The school hall seems to call for a slightly different kind of assembly, the science laboratories for different kinds of science lessons, the new gymnasium for some changes in the planning of P.E. work.

The problem of making an old building a tolerable setting for school work demands powers of improvisation and adaptation. Teachers who are creating a happy and vigorous community in a grey old Victorian building are conscious daily that they are working against heavy odds and can measure their success against the physical disadvantages of the premises in which they work. Faced with a new building—even one that has glaring faults—they can no longer say: "We are achieving this and this and this in spite of this old building!" They now have to say: "Our new building offers us chances, at least in some areas of school life, to teach more flexibly; will we be able to use these opportunities, or will we be content to go on working in the old way, as if we were still struggling under the same disadvantages?"

REFERENCES:

C.R.E.D.I.F. *Voix et images*. Paris: Didier, 1958. P. xxx.
Newsom Report, Building for the future in *Half our future*. London: H.M.S.O., 1963, Ch. 11.
Target, G. W. *The teachers*. Harmondsworth: Penguin Books, 1960.
Winnicott, D. W. Adolescence. *New Era*, October 1962, **43**.

41 *Excerpts from* Faces in the Water[1]

Janet Frame

CLIFFHAVEN

It is said that when a prisoner is condemned to die all clocks in the neighborhood of the death cell are stopped; as if the removal of the clock will cut off the flow of time and maroon the prisoner on a coast of time-lessness where the moments, like breakers, rise and surge near but never touch the shore.

But no death of an oceanographer ever stopped the sea flowing; and a condition of sea is its meeting with the land. And in the death cell time flows in as if all the cuckoo clocks grandfather clocks alarm clocks were striking simultaneously in the ears of the prisoner.

Again and again when I think of Cliff-haven I play the time game, as if I have been condemned to die and the signals have been removed yet I hear them striking in my ears, warning me that nine o'clock, the time of treatment, is approaching and that I must find myself a pair of woolen socks in order that I shall not die. Or it is eleven o'clock and treatment is over and it is the early hours or years of my dream when I was not yet sitting in rainbow puddles in Ward Two Yard or tramping the shorn park inside the tall picket fence with its rusty nails sprouting from the top, their points to the sky.

Eleven o'clock. I remember eleven o'clock,

[1] Two different psychiatric hospitals, Cliffhaven and Treecroft, are described in Janet Frame's novel *Faces in the Water*. The protagonist of the narrative, Estina Mavet, first went to Cliffhaven, only to return there after a period of hospitalization in Treecroft. She was confined to a few wards in each hospital. The work provides a moving patient's-view of all aspects of an institution.

the pleasant agony of trying to decide when plump pale-faced Mrs. Pilling ready with the laundry basket with the cheese-smelling tablecloth inside would ask me, "Will you come for the bread with me?"

And at the same time anxious Mrs. Everett who was detained in hospital, as they say, "at the sovereign's pleasure" would appear with an empty milk jug and ask "Will you come with me to collect the cream for the specials?"

The prospect of two journeys at the same time beyond the locked doors was so full of delight that I dallied to savor the pleasure and to hold a debate with myself on the merits of bakery and separator room. Bread or cream? The bakery with Andy shoveling the trays of loaves like yeasted molars into the yawning oven, slicing our ward bread and trying to sing above the slicer a duet for baker and bread machine with incidental crusts, or perhaps inviting me into the back room to give me a pastry left over from the Superintendent's party, or an advance chunk of the currant-filled Sunday Borstal cake.

Or the walk up the hill to the farm, past the deserted dung-smelling cowsheds into the separator room where Ted had arranged the cream cans in order of importance the way we used as children to arrange cups— first in the class, second in the class, and so on, when we played school with them.

First, the Superintendent's can, well polished with no dents and no ridge of old cream inside the shoulders. Next, the can for the doctors, also cleaned. Then for the Chief Clerk the farm manager and his family the engineer matrons and head attendant the attendants and nurses. Finally, the special patients who were too frail or suffered from tuberculosis and whose names appeared on a list pinned to the dining room wall. From a ward of one hundred women only ten or fifteen could be "special" enough to have cream. I remember my amazement and gratitude when for some weeks my name appeared on the list of "specials" and I sat smugly at dinner while the nurse poured cream on my tapioca or rice or farina or bread pudding (Mondays) or (Thursdays in season) baked apple.

You know that I have been pretending;

you know that it is eleven o'clock and I am not allowed to go for the bread or up the hill past the poplar trees and the broom bushes and the wattle to fetch the cream; that I am hiding in the linen cupboard, sitting on an apple box of firewood and crying and afraid to be seen crying in case I am written up for E.S.T. The linen cupboard is my favorite hiding place. It is scrubbed every morning by the T.B. nurse and the floor looks like the deck of a ship. From here I listen to Margaret who has T.B. and whose hoarse whisper tells continually of the First World War. She pleads with anyone who passes in the corridor to help her to evict the enemy from her room. She has lived for many years in this room, seeing the sun only for a few hours on a summer afternoon when shafts of light maneuver their way through the rusted wire netting of the window to shine and set the motes dancing on the wall. Sometimes on an afternoon walk with the nurse you can see Margaret standing in the sunlit corner of her room; the sun seems to shine through her as if the texture of her bones were gossamer. Her face is without color, even without the two familiar fever spots on her cheeks, and her body is like a skeleton. Looking at her you think, She is dying. Yet she goes on living, year after year, while other consumptives more robust on appearance—Effie, Jane, die and their bodies are hastily and antiseptically dispatched to the mortuary which is at the back of the laundry, facing the greenhouse, surrounded by rows of flowers and vegetables, the hardy plants outside and, inside, the sensitive begonias in pots used for surrounding the piano when the blind man from the city comes to play.

The mortuary is faceless.

If it were built in proportion, to really house the dead, its size would swallow the greenhouse and the laundry and the boiler house and the Big Kitchen, perhaps the entire hospital. But it is small, unobtrusive, and begs that patients conform to the rule of loneliness by dying one at a time.

In spite of the scrubbed appearance of the linen cupboard the smell pervading it is of floor polish boot polish (from the little-used caked tins of black and brown kept inside the large dented biscuit tin which bears on its lid the earnest profile of George the Sixth); wet-stained chipped wood whose smell leaves a parched blocked taste in the mouth; clinging wet linen; and the muffled ironed smell of fresh linen on the shelves labeled Drawers Chemises Nightgowns Sheets Counterpanes (with their scrolled patriotic design *Ake Ake*, Onward Onward). Here are kept the T.B. masks and dishes and the cardboard sputum boxes as they are procured, unfolded, from the stores. The T.B.'s, as part of their realistic occupational therapy, spend some of their time folding the boxes tucking in the flaps setting them upright with the ounces clearly marked on the side; like a kindergarten class engaged in constructing do-it-yourself coffins. Here are the cut-down kerosene tins where the used T.B. dishes are put to be boiled, for there is yet no sterilizer for them, on the open fire in the dining room.

This process is supervised by Mrs. Everett and Mrs. Pilling who share control of kitchen affairs and are responsible for the fire. It is Mrs. Pilling (the most trusted patient in the ward) who also arranges the making of toast over the open fire in the morning, the collecting of bread and cream, the carrying out to the side door of the full pig-tin ready for the golden-haired pig-boy to pick up on his way to the farm driving the leisurely old cart horse. When the tin has been loaded on the back he rummages through the food, bypassing the cold skilly bog of leftover porridge and reaching for the more appetizing dainties of discarded toast and sodden pieces of currant bun, all of which he stuffs hungrily in his mouth and, chewing contentedly, climbs again to the front of the cart and with a tug of the reins and a "Gee-up" sets the morose but patient horse on his way. Mrs. Pilling in her undemonstrative silent manner has an understanding with the pig-boy and though she recoils from his habits she has a stolid tolerance and respect for other people's peculiarities and is inclined to act out of character herself in order to preserve someone else's individuality.

She sometimes leaves a slice of staff cake on the pig-tin. It seems that she has no husband no children no relatives. She never has visitors. She never speaks of her personal concerns; one is seldom aware that she has any. She has lived for many years in the hospital and has a small room at the end of the T.B. corridor; one is surprised on passing it to notice that it has a cosy appearance as far as that is possible in a room in a mental hospital. She is allowed to keep her overcoat. It hangs behind the door. There is a feminine smell of powder and clothes. At one time someone must have given her a potted plant; it now stands on a chair in one corner, and an old calendar of five years ago, presumably kept for its old-fashioned English country scene, hangs over the hole in the center of the door so that the nurses may not peep in at her in the night. She is allowed that privacy.

Her sobriety, her apparent acceptance of a way of life that will continue until she dies—these frighten me. She seems like someone who could set up camp in a grave-yard and continue to boil the billy, eat and sleep soundly and perhaps spend the day polishing the tombstones or weeding the graves. One watches her for a ripple of herself as one watches an eternally calm lake for evidence of the rumored creature inhabiting perhaps "deeper than ever plummet sounded." One needs a machine like a bathysphere to find Mrs. Pilling. A bathysphere of fear? Of love?

In the beginning and the end her life is bread cream building the dining room fire; making sure with Mrs. Everett, who also has a passion for polishing, that the copper tea-urn is given its daily shine; setting out the Private Cupboard food. Fruit sweets cakes biscuits brought by visitors and not eaten during the Saturday and Sunday visiting hours are taken from the patients and locked in the Private Cupboard and at tea-time, depending on how much food has been stored for you, you find beside your place at the table a dish with your name on it containing perhaps two or three wrapped chocolates an orange an apple. Sometimes, because I seldom have visitors, I contrive to help Mrs. Pilling and the nurse and wait greedily for the expected moment when the nurse arranging on a plate a glittering still life of chocolates says suddenly, "Here, have one."

I protest, "Oh no. They do not belong to me."

The nurse answers according to plan, "No, this patient has bags and bags of food; it's going to waste."

Guiltily I seize the chocolate unwrap it slowly smoothe the wrinkles from the silver paper take a small bite testing for hardness then, like a thief, like the cunning scrounger that I am, I eat it. In the same way after visitors leave and the patients depressed and agitated talking about husband home children are wandering around clutching their only visible and palpable remnants of visiting hour, their small collection of biscuits sweets fruit, then I, with nothing in my hand and trying calmly to answer the question "Who came to see you?" will "happen" to appear in the most crowded corner of the dayroom where I know I will be offered an orange or a peppermint or a biscuit.

"You should keep them for yourself," I protest, greedily holding out my hand.

There is no past present or future. Using tenses to divide time is like making chalk marks on water. I do not know if my experiences at Cliffhaven happened years ago, are happening now, or lie in wait for me in what is called the future.

I know that the linen room was very often my sanctuary. I looked through its little dusty window upon the lower park and the lawns and trees and the distant blue strip of sea like sticky paper pasted edge to edge with the sky. I wept and wondered and dreamed the abiding dream of most mental patients—The World, Outside, Freedom; and foretasted too vividly the occasions I most feared—electric shock treatment, being shut in a single room at night, being sent to Ward Two, the disturbed ward. I dreamed of the world because it seemed the accepted thing to do, because I could not bear to face the thought that not all prisoners dream of freedom; the prospect of the world terrified me: a morass of despair violence death with a thin layer of glass spread upon the surface where Love, a tiny crab with pincers and rainbow shell, walked delicately ever sideways but getting nowhere, while the sun—like one of those woolly balls we made at occupational therapy by winding orange wool on a circle of cardboard—rose higher in the sky its tassels dropping with flame threatening every moment to melt the precarious highway of glass. And the people: giant patchworks of color with limbs missing and parts of their mind snipped off to fit them into the outline of the free pattern.

I could not find my way from the dream; I had no means to escape from it; I was like a surgeon who at the moment of a delicate operation finds that his tray of instruments has been stolen, or, worse, twisted into unfamiliar shapes so that only he can realize their unfamiliarity while the team around the table, suspecting nothing, wait for him to make the first incision. How can he explain to them what they cannot understand because it is visible only to him? Dutifully I thought of The World, because I was beyond it—who else will dream of it with longing? And at times I murmured the token phrase to the doctor, "When can I go home?" knowing that home was the place where I least desired to be. There they would watch me for signs of abnormality, like ferrets around a rabbit burrow waiting for the rabbit to appear.

I feared the prospect of a single room. Although all the small rooms were "single" rooms the use of the phrase *single room* served to make a threat more terrifying. During my stay in Ward Four I slept first in the Observation Dormitory and later in the dormitory "down the other end" where the beds had floral bedspreads and where, because of the lack of space, there was an overflow of beds into the corridor. I liked the observation dormitory at night with the night nurse sitting in the armchair brought in from the mess-room, knitting an endless number of cardigans and poring over pullout pattern supplements in the women's magazines, and snatching a quick nap with her feet up on the fireguard and the fire pleasantly warming her bottom. I liked the ritual of going to bed, with the faithful Mrs. Pilling sending in a tray of hot milk drinks, and one of the patients marching in balancing like a waitress a high pile of dun-colored chambers. I liked the beds side by side and the reassurance of other people's

soft breathing mingled with the irritation of their snoring and their secret conversations and the tinkle-tinkle and warm smell like a cow byre when they used their chambers in the night. I dreaded that one day Matron Glass hearing that I had been "difficult" or "uncooperative" would address me sharply, "Right. Single room for you, my lady."

Hearing other people threatened so often made me more afraid, and seeing that a patient, in the act of being taken to a single room, always struggled and screamed, made me morbidly curious about what the room contained that, overnight, it could change people who screamed and disobeyed into people who sat, withdrawn, and obeyed listlessly when ordered Dayroom, Dining room, Bed. Yet not all people changed; and those who did not respond to the four-square shuttered influence of the room, who could not be taught what Matron Glass or Sister Honey decreed to be "a lesson," were removed to Ward Two.

And Ward Two was my fear. They sent you there if you were "uncooperative" or if persistent doses of E.S.T. did not produce in you an improvement which was judged largely by your submission and prompt obedience to orders—Dayroom Ladies, Rise Ladies, Bed Ladies.

You learned with earnest dedication to "fit in"; you learned not to cry in company but to smile and pronounce yourself pleased, and to ask from time to time if you could go home, as proof that you were getting better and therefore in no need of being smuggled in the night to Ward Two. You learned the chores, to make your bed with the government motto facing the correct way and the corners of the counterpane neatly angled; to "rub up" the dormitory and the corridor, working the heavy bumper on the piece of torn blanket smeared with skittery yellow polish that distributed its energetic soaking smell from the first day it was fetched with the weekly stores in the basket beside the tins of jam jars of vinegar and the huge blocks of cheese and butter which Mrs. Pilling and Mrs. Everett quarried with a knife specially unlocked from the knife box. You learned the routine, that it "was so," that bath night was Wednesday, but that those who could be trusted to wash further than their wrists were allowed to bathe any night in the large bathroom where the roof soared like in a railway station and three deep tubs lay side by side each with its locked box containing the taps. In small print so that one might mistake it for a railway timetable the list of bathing rules was pasted on the wall. It was an old list, issued at the beginning of the century, and contained fourteen rules which stated, for example, that no patient might take a bath unless an attendant were present, that six inches only of water should be run into the bath, the cold water first, that no brush of any kind should be employed in bathing a patient. . . . So we bathed, one in each bath, without screens, gazing curiously at one another's bodies, at the pendulous bellies and tired breasts, the faded wisps of body hair, the unwieldy and the supple shapes that form to women the nagging and perpetual "withness" of their flesh.

TREECROFT

So I went up north to a land of palm trees and mangroves like malignant growths in the mud-filled throats of the bays, and orange trees with their leaves accepting darkly and seriously, in their own house as it were, the unwarranted globular outbursts of winter flame; and the sky faultless and remote. This was "up north." I stayed for a few weeks with my sister. Have you ever been a spinster living in a small house with your sister and her husband and their new first child? Watching them rub noses and pinch and tickle and in the night, when you lie on the coffin-narrow camp cot that would not hold two people anyway, listening to them because you cannot help it?

I did not know my own identity. I was burgled of body and hung in the sky like a woman of straw. The day seemed palpable about me yet receded when I moved to touch it, for fear that I might contaminate it. I nagged at the sky. It grew protective porcelain filling of cloud. I was not a mosquito nor a cricket nor a bamboo tree, therefore I found myself, when it was full summer, lying in a gaily quilted bed in a spotless room called an observation dormitory

in Ward Seven of Treecroft Mental Hospital, up north. The room overlooked a garden of blown roses and orange-centered arum lilies that grow wild, surrounding a sun-dried lawn with a weeping willow tree in the center. Although there was no creek or river the weeping willow tree surely grew there, no doubt with the faithful reckoning that keeps some people and trees alive, waiting for the secret provision. Around the garden stood a high wall disguised and made more seemly by its dress of slow-burning ivy. I noticed that the windows of the dormitory opened casement style so that one would not have guessed they were fixed to open a limited distance; I could not see upon them the crudely nailed boards which were a feature of Cliffhaven windows. The dormitory felt cool and shaded; I could see, outside, people in sun frocks walking to and fro or sitting down in the shade of the weeping willow. The air was peaceful. There were no screams protests moanings; no sound of scuffles as a patient was forcibly persuaded to obey orders. For the people *were* patients. And it was a hospital.

Wasn't it?

I thought yes certainly it is a hospital; I had heard them say Treecroft Mental Hospital where the murderers go, this way driver.

In the bed opposite me was a woman sitting up talking to anyone who might be listening.

"I am Mrs. Ogden," she said.

Her dresses had been marked, her shoes, her nighties, and in the rush of admission they had forgotten to mark her, therefore she was telling people her name, indelibly, like the ink on the tape.

"I am Mrs. Ogden."

Her face had the damply absorbent pallor, her mouth the moistness with the corners drawn in, that I had seen on the consumptives at Cliffhaven. She talked breathlessly, incessantly, full of the excitement of her operation in the city where she had had a number of ribs removed. She displayed the scars. She recounted the occasion. She explained esoteric phrases of life in a general hospital.

"I was 'on hours,' " she said blissfully. "Do you know what that means? It means you are allowed up each day for so many hours. We sat around in ward chairs, in our dressing gowns. There was thunder and lightning twice and rain for a week and the rest sun. On the terrace. It's 'way out of town really. People call me Betty."

Although I could not communicate with her because I was speechless I lay in my bed, staring at her, and trying to warn her of the veneer of peace and pleasantness, the brightness of the bedspreads and the sun-frocked people outside; I tried to say beware the room is laid with traps and hung with hooks. For there was growing in my mind a dread which was not diminished but increased by the sight of the garden, the weeping willow the apparently contented patients roving freely across the sun-baked lawn. I marveled that Mrs. Ogden seemed so untroubled. How could she not know about the danger? Why did she not beware, surround herself with all possible safety measures, move lower down in her bed and draw the bedclothes up for protection?

I lay and watched the dark dread growing like one of those fairy-tale plants whose existence depends upon their lack of discipline, their uncontrolled urge to grow through and across and into and beyond until they reach the sky and block the sun. My fear crept beyond myself and into the tranquil dormitory, and turned upon me, like a child upon its parent, threatening me.

I watched the ward sister, Sister Creed, going her rounds with the doctor, speaking softly and calmly and smiling at Mrs. Ogden and myself, the only one in bed, as a genteel hostess might welcome her guests for the week end. But as they passed nearer and walked in full view through the open door into the garden I noticed, with a feeling of alarm, that both the doctor and Sister Creed were limping. Surely it was more than coincidence! I was filled with the superstitious fear that besets primitive people and children and makes them invoke gods and repeat rhymes when faced with deformities. I was reminded of a woman we used to call the Late Lady. We used to meet her on the way to school if we were in danger of being late. "The Late Lady," we would whisper with horror in our voices and with our hearts beating fast, and with the stitch in our sides we would run for dear life to get out of sight of the limping lady and to get to school in time for the march in.

Further, the sight of the Treecroft matron convinced me that my fears were not groundless, and at first I thought that Matron Glass had followed me up from the south and adopted the identity of Matron Borough; even their bodies were the same, huge, encased in the white uniform through which you could see the marks, like bars, of their corset. Matron Borough's voice was deep and admonishing and when she looked at Mrs. Ogden and myself her expression told us that our lying in bed, putting into disarray the stiff sheets spotless from the hospital laundry, and interfering with the peaceful effect created by the rows of spruce unoccupied beds their quilts flipped exactly their castors turned at the right angle, was an affront to Ward Seven and the sooner we were "up out of that" the better.

I dreaded the moment when I should have to get dressed and stand upright buffeted by the waves in the mid-ocean of the room; and test the reality of the peace and contentment that I had observed from my bed. I could not explain my fear. What if Ward Seven were but a subaqueous condition of the mind which gave the fearful shapes drowned there a rhythmic distortion of peace; and what if, upon my getting up from my bed, the perspective was suddenly altered, or I was led into a trap where a fire burning in the walls had dried up the water and destroyed the peace by exposing in harsh daylight the submerged shapes in all their terror? How could I know?

The rule was to stay in bed for two days; I was grateful. I lay and let the doctor examine me, with the dormitory nurse modestly arranging the blankets. I made a fist, followed Dr. Tall's finger, pressed his hands away, felt the pin prick, breathed, said ninety-nine, had my knee tapped and the sole of my foot scraped. I did not ask the doctor to explain Sister Greed's limp or the startling resemblance between Matron Borough and Matron Glass of Cliffhaven; or to tell me the meaning of the weeping willow tree, the message of the mosquitoes, the bamboo, the telephoning crickets, mason flies, huhu bugs, ants that stopped in their tracks and wept if they lost their way; the great clifflike rents in the earth; the aluminium rain boiling upon the earth.

Dr. Tall was a late afternoon shadow, neat, in a white coat, with gold planted between his two front teeth; a flashy loot to which his tongue kept returning as if to make sure of its safety, or perhaps to work it loose and get rid of it like an overexposed bad habit that has lost its original delight and value.

"Do you know where you are?"

I was tempted at first to question that I was lying in Ward Seven of Treecroft Mental Hospital. Treecroft. It made me think that perhaps I had been admitted to a dovecote. But I was speechless and only stared at Dr. Tall's gold tooth. "We'll give her E.S.T. tomorrow," he told Sister Creed.

I could not absorb any more fearful possibilities; I was so tired; if it rained, the harp hanging on the willow tree would get wet, and still I did not care. Mrs. Ogden was coughing, reaching for her sputum box and carefully measuring what she spat into it. She was flushed as if she had been making love to something or somebody that no one else could see, and she drew her breath excitedly when she saw the nurse approaching with chart and thermometer.

"It's up," she said triumphantly, as if she had won an argument with the invisible presence that seemed to attend her.

The next morning I was led with other patients in my nightgown and dressing gown into the garden and across to another ward which also opened upon the garden. I was put to bed in a room in a corridor of single rooms and told to lie there quietly and wait. I lay, tracing the pattern of the red mat on the floor, and thinking that at Cliffhaven I had never seen mats on the floors of rooms, and drowsily wondering what was going to happen to me, as if I were a threatened character in an episode of a not very gripping serial. Suddenly I heard the familiar calamitous despairing cry of a patient undergoing E.S.T., and snorting noises in the room next door, and the sound of something being wheeled along the corridor to my room.

The door opened. A strange doctor stood there with an E.S.T. machine on a trolley. He gave me a quick evil glance, approached my bed, thrust the headphones over my temples, and suddenly I was unconscious, contending alone with nightmares of grief and despair. When I woke I was led back through the garden, past the weeping willow and the empty bird bath where a few sparrows flipped themselves with dust, to peaceful Ward Seven, so peaceful that I might have wondered if the screams and the creeping machine really existed, had I not retained in my memory, as if it had entered almost without my permission, the peculiar smell of the other ward, a kind of ward body odor of polish and urine blended, in the manner of tobacco or herbs, to a compression of desolation and exuded now strongly now faintly as it was whittled, deliberately or casually, by the hanging-around corner-leaning presence that one may call Time.

In a few days I was up and dressed wandering around the ward and sitting in the garden under the willow tree and learning, as I tried to forget my still-growing disquiet and dread and the haunting smell of the other ward, as I became to all appearances one of the gentle contented patients of Ward Seven, that the E.S.T. which happened three times a week, and the succession of screams heard as the machine advanced along the corridor, were a nightmare that one suffered for one's own "good." "For your own good" is a persuasive argument that will eventually make man agree to his own destruction. I tried to reassure myself by remembering that in Ward Seven the "new" attitude ("mental patients are people like you and me") seemed to predominate the bright counterpanes, pastel-shaded walls supposed to soothe, a few abstract paintings hanging paint-in-cheek in the sitting room; tables for four in the dining room, gay with checked cloths; everything to keep up the pretense that Treecroft was a hotel, not a mental hospital, and anyway the words *mental hospital* were now frowned upon; the proper designation was now *psychiatric unit*.

The kindly Sister Creed dined with us. We had cream on our pudding, bacon and eggs for breakfast, all cooked in the ward kitchen by Hillsie, Mrs. Hill, another of the faithful long-term patients whose life is to serve. She worked from morning till late at night, though her face was always pale, her eyes cavernous and dark, and her ankles swelled at night.

"Look at my ankles," she would say.

Someone would remark, "Hillsie, you shouldn't work so hard."

"No, perhaps I shouldn't," was the answer.

But the next morning she would be up early and in the kitchen preparing breakfast, looking after the nurses with surprise cups of tea ("Hillsie, you're an angel"), scrubbing polishing. On Sundays, her only day off, when she stayed in bed all day, people would ask, with a trace of panic and irritation, "Where's Hillsie?" And on that day nothing seemed to go right, food was burnt and shriveled, utensils were lost, nobody knew where to look or how to set about doing things and Hillsie was being continually interrupted in her rest by people going to her room and demanding to know where and why and how. Hillsie's room, like Mrs. Pilling's, was decorated with pictures and calendars. She had roses from the garden in a bowl on her dressing table and a photograph of her son in his sailor's uniform, a pale handsome lad like his mother. She had been taken to Treecroft when he was born and in those days there had been no treatment for her.

On visiting days almost everyone had a visitor. An aunt decided to "adopt" me and visit me each week making a long journey by tram from the outskirts of the city. She was a middle-aged woman who had unconsciously or deliberately followed the current fashion advice that pink and gray are "right" colors for middle-aged people. She wore pink blouses and gray suits and floating chiffon scarves. Her complexion was a tinted map of red patches and vein tributaries; her eyes were vague, the whites curdled with pink like blood-specked white of egg. She was all kindness, with an intuitive knowledge of how to be a good hospital visitor— to bring comforting things to eat and after the first rather embarrassed "How are you?" which did not demand a detailed reply, sit dreamily in the garden, quiet composed

uninquisitive, offering at intervals peppermint creams and fancy cakes. She expressed delight at the hospital, at the kindness of the staff, the cheerfulness of the ward, and the fact that the patients "seemed to have nothing wrong with them." One could hear other visitors making similar remarks.

"You're lucky to be here, with everybody so good. It looks to me like an expensive hotel. I think I'll have a nervous breakdown myself some time. I'm only joking of course. I know what you've been through."

Most of the patients in Ward Seven liked to talk with their visitors about their "nervous breakdown," the plan of it, and details of it, as if it were a piece of property they had unexpectedly acquired. They liked to tell those nearest to them what they had "been through." And their visitors comforted them by saying, truthfully, "You'll be home soon; another few weeks and you'll be home."

And many patients did go home. There were farewells and thank yous, addresses exchanged, and promises to write, and promises to spread the news that mental hospitals were certainly not what people seemed to think, that the letters full of shocking details that appeared in the newspapers were the work of cranks and liars.

For had not the patients of Ward Seven seen for themselves the modern conditions? —that patients were regarded as human beings and cared for with kindness? Certainly shock treatment was unpleasant but after all it was for people's own good wasn't it; besides, it was held in another ward, and you were so dopey going and coming that you didn't remember much anyway. The point was that you were better and going home and you wouldn't be afraid if at any other time you had to return to Treecroft hospital.

And one day Dr. Tall said to me, too, "We'll soon have you fit and well." We saw little of him; he was always busy and only rarely found time to say "What are you knitting?" "You're doing nicely." "Hot today isn't it?" and other stagnant phrases. He cared for, or tried to care for, at least one thousand women.

I didn't feel ill; but I was afraid. Dr. Tall limped. Sister Creed limped. Matron

Borough's butcher-like face swelled before me in a threatening manner. Yet I went obediently to the other ward, known as Ward Four-Five-and-One, for E.S.T. and tried to suppress the disquiet which amounted to panic at the distinctive ward smell, and at the very name of the ward—*Four-Five-and-One*—a sinister code no doubt; and at the sight of the ward's T.B. wing which opened off the kitchen and had a shacklike appearance with its bare wooden floors and corrugated iron roof which must have given the rooms an unbearable intensity of heat from the daylong sun, thudding like a headache in the sky. The bare floors, contrasting with the dignity and brightness of Ward Seven, depressed me, and I tried to forget them and I felt the necessity of not believing in their existence. In my mind I dare not contain an image of both Ward Seven and the Four-Five-and-One T.B. wing.

I returned with almost hysterical pleasure from the smell of desolation and the sight of the stark makeshift ward, to the supposed reality of Ward Seven and Betty Ogden's confident chatter and the fretful languor of the women gently describing their homes, their families, their symptoms, and the pleasant conditions they found in hospital. But I felt increasingly like a guest who is given every hospitality in a country mansion yet who finds in unexpected moments a trace of a mysterious presence; sliding panels; secret tappings; and at last surprises the host and hostess in clandestine conversations and plottings with mention of poison, torture, death. Or was I inhabiting, as it were, as guest for the week end, my own mind, and becoming more and more perturbed by its manifestation of evil?

But suddenly one evening there was a quarrel in the bathroom between Elizabeth and Mrs. Dean.

"I'm having first bath."

"No. I'm having first bath."

A mere quarrel about a bath, you will say. What is important in that, or unusual or terrifying? Few people quarreled in Ward Seven; a patient who became "uncooperative" in this respect was speedily transferred to what was called vaguely "another ward." Perhaps the argument might have died or

been solved peaceably had not Matron Borough on her evening round, overheard, and opening the door of the bathroom inquired in a shocked voice, "What on earth is going on?" and stood with her fierce gaze on the half-dressed Mrs. Dean, a middle-aged woman suffering from the fact of middle age, her mind out of step with her body, nervous, worried about her appearance and her accumulation of fat and trying to tear down the signpost held before her by her age. Matron Borough's glance sent her into a fury. She began to call Matron names, to swear at her.

"You big fat bloody bullock don't you stare at me."

Matron's face and neck reddened; she too was sensitive about her appearance.

"Out of here," she said. "You ought to be ashamed of yourself. Pull yourself together. There's no excuse for your behavior."

Mrs. Dean refused to leave the bathroom. Elizabeth was standing by, subdued, a picture of cooperation.

"Right," snapped Matron, beckoning to a nurse; and moving towards the door in the bathroom which was always kept locked and which I had never seen used, Matron Borough opened it, and with the three other nurses who had arrived, dragged the struggling Mrs. Dean through the door.

She never returned to the ward.

I brooded upon this mysterious disappearance. Where had she gone? To "another ward"?

Then one day, in recognition of the fact that I was getting well and would soon be allowed out, a nurse asked me to accompany her to the "big kitchen" to return the porridge can—the porridge was the only food not cooked by Hillsie. I had never seen beyond the Ward Seven garden, and I gazed about me, asking questions, and expressing surprise that the hospital was such an extensive place. Seen from the outside, from beyond the genteel front entrance where it looked like an ivy-covered mansion, it was a number of sprawling dilapidated buildings; the big kitchen squat and dirty in appearance stood opposite a ward that seemed in such a state of decay that I asked its name.

"What's that place?"

"Oh that? Lawn Lodge."

We entered the poorly lit poorly ventilated kitchen, and were immediately surrounded by the smell of boiled cabbage. We passed a vat which bubbled with greasy meat, and another where a thick mess of farina was cooking, watched over by a hairy-chested man in an open-necked check shirt. He suddenly thrust his hairy arm into the vat of farina and began stirring vigorously. I was amazed, and impressed, and eager to get back to reassure myself that our ward meals were cooked by Hillsie, indeed that Ward Seven was still in existence. Returning past the conglomeration of old buildings which seemed unreal in their lack of relationship to our bright admission ward, we met two attendants carrying out the back way from Four-Five-and-One, a corpse, bloated-looking under its canvas.

"That's Mrs. Dean," the nurse said indiscreetly. "She died."

I was glad to return to Ward Seven and try to convince myself that the garden, the lawn, the weeping willow, the windows and doors wide open, were not a dream, and that Treecroft, even if some of its buildings appeared antiquated, was a hospital with a modern attitude to mental illness. But I was attacked increasingly by disquiet; I had seen, as it were, the sliding panels, overheard the sinister conversation.

CLIFFHAVEN: READMISSION

So I went to join the strange people whom I had seen before on my previous stay at Cliffhaven; and on that first day among them, when I climbed the park fence and returned to Ward Four, I was greeted with "Pull yourself together. You've been in places like that before. Don't pretend you're not used to them." And I was marched back by the Matron herself who reiterated, when handing me over to Sister Bridge. "She's used to these wards. She needs to be taught a lesson."

Part of Ward Two was a new building made to replace the old refractory ward which had been burned, with thirty-seven patients, a year before I first came to Cliffhaven. The old Brick Building was still used as the sleeping quarters, accommodating the sixty-seven women of the ward.

In Ward Two the "new" attitude was made easier to put into practice by the modern living quarters which consisted of a dining room, a "dirty" dayroom where the continually ill patients were locked and where those with intermittent attacks were kept as long as their attacks lasted; a "clean" dayroom, its walls hung with sea- and mountainscapes, its furniture new and bright (as was the furniture in the "dirty" dayroom), its wall of windows giving an occasional view of people passing and little dogs trotting and trees changing color with the seasons, so that one did not have the feeling of being immured and left to rot in an abandoned dwelling. The rest of the building consisted of a bathroom with three baths, two sets of lavatories, one doorless, the other with the doors three-quarter-length, staff office, clinic, clothing cupboard and cloakroom, and storeroom, dining room and pantry. Doors led from the ward to the yard and across the road to the park, and through the yard to the Brick Building with its locked single rooms, dirty dormitories, and upstairs open dormitories. The hospital had learned the lesson of the fire. Under Dr. Portman, sprinkler systems had been installed in all the buildings and existing fire escapes straightened and new ones built for all the upper floors.

There were no people in strait jackets in Ward Two. Cynics used to say there was no need for them as the worst patients had perished in the fire; yet the more experience one had of Ward Two the more one realized that, in any case, strait jackets were treatments, or restraining processes of the past. Whereas in Treecroft the best-cooked meals (and the most plentiful), the gayest pictures, the brightest bedspreads were to be found in Ward Seven where the so-called "sensible" patients lived, in Cliffhaven the brightest ward was Ward Two—that is, in terms of purely chromatic dispersion! And let no one imagine that the framed and glassed landscapes on the walls suffered from the attacks of the disturbed patients. Although the surroundings were not openly studied or even admired by the patients, they were not abused. Windows might be broken in the course of a day yet the pictures remained untouched and the flowers stayed in their vases. It seemed that the more articulate members of the ward exuded a fertile pride that spread and flourished silently even in the midst of what one might have called the desert of the most withdrawn patients.

Cake for tea; chocolate cake, pink-iced cake, madeira-cake; and if there was not enough for all it was not, as might be supposed, the more "sensible" patients who benefited on the grounds of their being able to "appreciate" what they were given, but those from the dirty dayroom who had their meals in the first sitting—that is as far as any of them sat and did not stand and grab; the demented ones who spent the sunny days lying like animals shamming death in the face of great danger, or running and raging and skipping in the park or the yard. They went to bed at four o'clock in the afternoon. We used to see them rushing past the door of the clean dayroom in their dirty striped smocks, clutching their remnants of snacks—slices of rainbow sponge or fruit cake.

Sister Bridge cared for them. She told me once, in a moment of confidence which she always regretted and which caused her to show to me the kind of antagonism often felt towards those who share the secrets of our real or imagined frailties, that she had begun nursing as a timid young girl in the days when, as a matter of course, all disturbed patients wore locked boots and strait jackets; and that, after her first day on duty, she cried most of the night and resolved, though she never kept her resolution, to submit her resignation and leave the appalling place and become a nurse in a general hospital where the patients were not shamed and abused because of their illness and where you could at least see what was wrong with them and prepare a neat dressing with ointment and clean white bandages to soothe and heal, and with no difficulty keep the patient quietly trapped in bed. But here at Cliffhaven or any mental hospital you had to provide your own bandages from within yourself to bind wounds that could not be seen or measured, and at the same time it seemed you had to forget

that the patients were people, for there were so many of them and there was so much to do. The remedy was to shout and hit and herd.

Sister Bridge was now thirty-six and married to one of the attendants. Her appearance—that of a female butcher, red haired, freckle faced, fat, blowsy—was so much like that of other domineering, insensitive mental nurses that it seemed to have sought her out and attached itself to her as a camouflage in order to protect her and give her prestige among her species and safeguard her own sensitivity. She had known many of the patients for years and was loved and trusted by them and her attitude was usually one of happy sarcasm where words which came from her as sarcasm and mockery, a habit which she had perhaps acquired when learning to impress and obey the dictatorial matron of years ago, seemed in the air to undergo a transformation, to be fused with her abundance of vitality and sympathy so that they arrived without seeming to hurt. She was like a conjuror who, in mid-air, changes the fire he has breathed to wine. The patients would smile delightedly at whatever Sister Bridge said to them. Sometimes I wondered if perhaps she had not actually discarded words as a means of communication and was putting her meaning across in some other way while shouting (she usually shouted) the sort of near-abuse that one hears spoken every day by mental nurses to their patients.

Unfortunately I observed Sister Bridge too closely. This unself-conscious giving of herself to those in her care was a marvel worth watching, and it caused me great sadness when, one day, as I was standing quietly by, she noticed me and knew immediately that I had been marveling at her almost telepathic sympathy with the patients. She blushed, as if with shame, and turned angrily to me.

"Oh," she said sarcastically, "so we're observing are we? You're studying me are you, Miss Know-all? Am I doing something wrong perhaps?"

"It's not that," I said. "It's not that." And I was silent.

From then on Sister Bridge showed her resentment towards me and seized every opportunity to hurt me. By an unintentional glance I had surprised her into surprising herself into an uncomfortable consciousness that seemed to amount to fear.

Her delight now was to make me suffer and her motive was reinforced by the matron's words, "She needs to be taught a lesson."

42 Space as Experienced: Therapeutic Implications[1]

P. Sivadon

The purpose of this essay is to seek a theoretical justification for empirically tested therapeutic techniques.

Psychotherapy in its traditional aspects soon discovers the limitations of its applicability. It must modify its techniques when it deals no longer with neurotics, but with psychotics or mental defectives. In so doing, it approximates the methods used in child psychiatry: manipulation of objects, body relationships with the therapist, projection into space in a symbolic and concrete way of conflictual situations.

The question can be raised as to whether —and to what extent—the methods known as occupational therapy and physiotherapy are not of this general type and whether, more generally speaking, the patients' relation to space does not constitute a choice therapeutic approach that deserves to be developed in a variety of ways.

Psychotherapy for adults is concerned almost exclusively with the temporal dimension of personality. Its aim is to reconcile the patient with his past, but it is clear that to the extent that it succeeds in doing so, the result is an enlargement not only of the subject's temporal horizon but also of his present behavioral space. This is to be ex-

From *L'Evolution Psychiatrique*, 1965, No. 3, pp. 477–498. Reprinted by permission of the author and publisher. Translated by Dr. Rosette Avigdor-Coryell.

[1] Lecture given at "L'Evolution Psychiatrique," November 24, 1964.

pected since the spatial and temporal axes of personality are closely related. Why not then utilize this spatial dimension of personality in a therapeutic plan in which the temporal aspects would retain their proper place?

Since the aim of every therapy is to help the organism master any heterogeneous elements that threaten his unity, why not try to reduce the heterogeneous elements to a form and dimension that best permits this mastery? Wouldn't space as it is experienced be basic, simpler, and more easily mastered than time as it is experienced? Is it not easier to remove oneself from an object located in space—whatever its symbolic charge—than from a memory, and to regulate and measure this distance?

In the first part of this essay, an attempt will be made to show that the relation to space is more basic, simpler, and easier to handle than the time relation. In order to do so, the evidence will be based on the data of genetic psychology. A literary reference, space as experienced in Proust, will introduce the idea that, if time seems to correspond to an internalization of space relations, that is, of movements, the problems of the time organization of personality could be expressed in terms of space. This reduction to spatial terms offers the advantage of easier therapeutic manipulation: it corresponds to a regressive movement, makes it possible to regulate the relations of distance and dimension, and confronts the organism with its problem in an analogous form facilitating mastery or at least desensitization. This in essence is the picture of the techniques of physical reeducation of the mental functions, that we have been using empirically for nearly twenty years.

In the second part, the evidence will be based on the data of animal ethology and on some observations made in an asylum environment. We will stress the importance of the spatial framework which conditions the relations of distance and position of human beings, one to the other, and is likely to create a feeling of security or insecurity, depending on its form and dimension. From this come various medical and particularly architectural applications. This will lead to certain considerations about the therapeutic use of the division and organization of space in a hospital environment and to remarks concerning the possible applications of these data to urban planning from a mental hygiene point of view.

I. SPACE RELATIONS AND TIME RELATIONS

Precedence of the Spatial over the Temporal

The dynamics of personality can be described, in an extremely simplified way, as the totality of processes through which the organism experiences the meaning of its relationship to the world, and organizes the situation so as to preserve best its own constancy, while adjusting to the demands of the environment. Each moment of this evolution involves the integration of the subject's tendencies with his image of his relation to the outside world. Personality is thus enriched by a process of internalization of successive situations. In the case of the adult, it is an individual history which is constantly confronted with a new situation composed of collective images, the product of a certain culture, and therefore of a social history. This is why the historic, and therefore the temporal, aspect of the personality seems most important.

But if, by an effort of phenomenological reduction in Husserl's sense, we manage to return to this "world before knowledge" which is certainly that of the child and of the animal, and seems also to be that in which the mentally sick and regressed individual lives, it becomes clear that the "situation" is no longer the encounter between an individual history and a social history, but simply of a living organism and a world which derives its meaning from essentially spatial relationships rather than cultural layers.

The child's first fear reaction, his tonic reflex to a fall, is directly related to a sense of spatial confusion. Only much later does his temporal anxiety appear due either to delay or the child's lack of recognition.

It is as if the spatial situations, by their constantly renewed internalization, build personality in its temporal aspects. As the personality is enriched, it becomes increasingly capable of integrating a wider and wider space to the extent that it can display a harmoniously organized history consisting of a well-assimilated past, and of a plan firmly anchored in the future.

Bergson (1908, p. 68), whose distinction between pure duration and time is well known, assumed that the latter is taken in the sense of an environment in which one discriminates and counts, and is nothing more than space. This view could be confirmed mainly by the fact that in order to describe the sense the reflexive consciousness has of time and even of succession, one must borrow from the concepts of space.

It would be spurious to try to establish an absolute hierarchy between space and time. Once constituted, they are so closely correlated to each other that they can no longer be disassociated. Modern physics has synthesized them into a single concept: space-time. What actually unifies them is movement.

Descartes and Malebranche considered movement and extension as "clear and distinct" ideas, but not duration. Psychological research shows that what is experienced first is the object detaching itself from cosmic space. According to Gesell, "from the day of its birth, the baby can, with a single open eye, fixate an object which is moved towards him." By the end of the second month, he can coordinate the behavior of his two eyes in order to explore his surroundings with a circular look: ". . . the conquest of space is well under way." "Having cleared a path with his agile eyes, he must now make use of his hands to penetrate the disturbing world of space."

Gesell has observed that if the baby has the sense of passing time, it is because his expectation of already known situations, and therefore of recurring anterior space relations, enables the child to identify time. Temporal concepts evolve almost parallel to those of space, and this is why one can be so easily converted into the other. Gesell thinks, however, that the concept of time is more abstract than that of space. And in his developmental gradients, he observed that the knowledge of space slightly precedes that of time. At the age of one, the child is able to express his desire to be put down or taken into his mother's arms. He plays peek-a-boo. At 18 months, he runs toward the adult and knows how to find his way. Only at the age of 21 months does he react to the arrival of his father as a signal for dinner and is able to sit down at the table and wait for his food. At the age of seven, he is aware of the existence of other places than "here," and at eight takes an interest in foreign countries. But at this age he is still unaware of historic time, which he will not grasp until about the age of ten.

Wallon (1947) emphasizes that, among the early differentiations, place relations are the first to emerge from experience. First occurring is the reduction of sensorial, postural, prehensive, and locomotor space into a single one which becomes simultaneously detached from the gestures or from the objects which are the manifestations of these spaces. The location and the object are not at first differentiated from each other: "thing and position remain confused." "Space is in things rather than things in space." The same is true of causality, which is sometimes reduced to relations of position. Cause and place remain confused.

It is only when the object becomes detached from the surrounding space, in other words, when it remains identical while changing place, and can also be conceptualized, and therefore imagined and expected, that time makes its appearance.

Piaget (1948, 1964) draws a distinction between sensory-motor space, which is constructed in the first years of life, and representative space. The former is related to the progress of perception, and motor behavior plays an important role until the simultaneous appearance of language and representation in images (i.e., the symbolic function in general). Representative space, strangely enough—while benefiting, in a sense, from the acquisition of perception and motor behavior—develops from nothing, from the most elementary insights. For Piaget and Inhelder, the most elementary relations are those of proximity, of separation, of order and spatial sequence, of surrounding or enveloping, of continuity. This constitutes the period up to three or four

months. In the second period (4–5 months to 10–12 months) the manipulation of objects leads to concepts of objects, to the constancy of the object and its dimensions and, through the coordination of various points of view, to perspective. Only in the third period do the relations of objects to one another emerge: successive positions, changes of place, relation of the container to the content, etc. And it may be assumed that it is only when order and succession, after being internalized, can be represented, that the concept of temporal sequence makes its appearance.

Schematically, the successive stages of personality's acquisitions could be described in the following way: extension, movement, duration, represented space, and represented time. Each stage assumes the preceding, and emerges from them by a process of differentiation, without destroying them.

Movement presupposes extension just as duration presupposes movement. Next develops the representation of space with the help of movement and duration, the movement of the stars (rising and setting), of bodies (near at hand, a hundred feet away). Last emerges the concept of social time, which derives from the relation of a constant movement to a definite space (the hand on the clock).

Disintegration of Personality and Spatial Regression

While personality develops in the form of a temporal continuum resulting from the internalization of previously experienced situations, disintegrations result, first of all, in a loss of temporal references before the spatial references are affected. Experiences of prolonged isolation always confirm this initial disintegration of the concept of time. One step further and the spatial references disappear; however, when a personality strives to restructure itself again, it primarily uses these references.

In pathological disintegration such as psychoses, what had been internalized is now externalized. "Reflection"—the dialogue with the "internalized other"—becomes a dialogue with an "externalized imaginary other." Even in the normal subject, in a state of autistic regression, we find the phenomenon of "talking-to-oneself," where the inner partner is imagined as external.

In these cases it appears as if the disintegrating personality, a temporal structure, being unable to contain all its components, allows the most heterogeneous elements to escape into space. Hallucination and passivity phenomena probably represent the residual and, in a sense, the failure, of the organism's attempt to externalize its problems in order to better control them.

An analogous mechanism can be observed in neurosis. Anxiety—experienced temporally as an anticipated misfortune—becomes a phobia in order to be experienced spatially, and space phobias, in a more or less disguised form, are its most frequent manifestations.

Spatial Usage and Analogical Reduction

The spatial reduction of situations in an analogical form in order to manipulate and assimilate them is a technique used by everyone. Drawing a blueprint, writing a program means reducing to manageable dimensions the complexities of temporal development of successive actions so that they may be inspected with a single look.

In our view, spatial usage and analogical reduction constitute frequent defenses of the personality against anxiety, and they also are found in the failure of these defenses (e.g., phobias, hallucinations, etc.). Spatial usage then might justifiably be used as a therapeutic method.

Empirically, people have always tended to "forget themselves" by changing their spatial environment, and also by investing their anxiety in creative activity. This is the meaning of therapy through artistic expression and through work. It is a question of transforming one's relation with objects and people by manipulating or transforming the objects in such a way as to express the subject's problem in an analogical form communicable to others.

The object becomes a symbolic mediator. For the creator, it represents anxiety itself from which he has been freed; for the others, it evokes, on a symbolic plane, an analogous, though attenuated feeling. Thus the intermediary object behaves like an absorbent screen that retains the anxiety and lets filter through the symbol, the vehicle of communication. By means of a similar approach, an attempt can be made to reduce to spatial terms the problem of restoring the autonomy for some very regressed patients.

A dual tendency orients the behavior of every human being: to evolve towards a greater degree of autonomy, thus a greater distance from the mother and her substitutes, and to maintain the conditions of its security, which implies proximity and dependence. This involves a proximity-distance dialectic, therefore a problem that can be formulated in spatial terms. A certain degree of proximity, through the security it brings, makes possible the internalization of a situation, or, in other words, of a certain type of relation. This internalization is conducive to autonomy, leading to greater distance, which —owing to the accompanying security— brakes the development of this very autonomy. The cybernetic pattern of regulation by negative retroaction can be perceived in this process. The problem, of course, is not so simple. Specifically, proximity causes security only to the extent that it creates dependence, which, in its turn, causes insecurity. Conversely, independence, while it causes insecurity because it implies distance, is a factor of freedom and self-assertion which causes security.

It is nevertheless true that, by reducing the most complex situations to a simplified analogical model of spatial relations, it is possible to restore the patient's capacity for autonomy.

It was from this first viewpoint that, for the past fifteen years with my team at Ville-Evrard, then at La Verrière, we have been developing simple techniques, of which I shall give only a few examples (Sivadon, 1965).

In view of the fact that certain markedly regressed schizophrenic patients would emerge from their catatonia and could make a few movements when held by the hand, only to relapse into frozen immobility when released, exercises consisting of round-dances and "farandoles" were organized: holding, then releasing the hands, with the aid of motor rhythm, possibly reinforced by musical rhythm. The exploration of space (the learning of distance) was facilitated through the contact of bodily proximity. The method of general massage facilitates, in another way, the combination of an interpersonal relation accomplished by securing bodily contact, mediated, however, by a technique which, by acting as a screen, prevents massive transference. This bodily contact is security inducing because it occurs through a form of treatment which is generally known as beneficial, and not because it takes place with a particular therapist. Moreover, the technique is repeated while the masseur changes.

At even more regressive levels, the re-education of the sense of distance is carried out in a small swimming pool. Here the patient, immersed in a liquid environment which brings him back to the stage of "aquatic endoparasite" (Férenczi), learns to move around, to approach and go away from the instructor. Afterwards, a hose-shower establishes another type of relation through water, which can take a wide variety of forms.

In other exercises—this time in the open air—the patient learns to exchange an object with his instructor, then with other patients, at greater and greater distances. The object in question is a big ball whose form, according to Jung, expresses the total human being, and also perhaps recalls the maternal breast.

Such exercises, continued for a long time, help enable the personality to resume its development and can mark the beginning of remarkable transformations, and even cures. The examples given here are chosen from a wide variety of methods of the same type, whose aim is to teach the subject to reorganize his space and thereby to reorganize his personal history. He becomes reconciled to his past as he familiarizes himself with a present which is more completely immersed in space. While under the influence of psychotherapy a history may fall into order and, as a by-product, spatial relations may be broadened. Personal problems may also often reappear as the subject learns to appreciate distance, and further

spatial progress is possible only when these problems have been made explicit, if not actually resolved.

This is the first way of utilizing space in therapy, the proximity-distance dialectic corresponding to that of security-autonomy.

The various exercises by which the subject learns to maintain contact with others through a mediating object will next be accompanied by relations established through gesture and movement. The individual learns to "see himself as others see him" when he sees another person going through the same motions as himself. The learning of this basic step in the construction of the personality, in which the self-image, as it is seen through the eyes of others, coincides with that which emerges from a postural pattern, is mainly spatial: it is achieved through exercises involving distance, group complexity, the presence or absence of a mirror.

II. BEHAVIORAL SPACE: ITS STRUCTURE

"Proxemics" and Territory

The second aspect of the interpersonal spatial relation is the meaning that everyone attaches to the position of his own body in its relation to others. This is the "silent language," to borrow the phrase of Edward T. Hall (1959), an American anthropologist, who developed the study of this subject under the name of "proxemics." Proxemics is the study of man's spatial relations. Starting from the observation of cultural differences in the utilization of space, Hall sought the human constants underlying them, and he was soon led to compare these constants with those of animal behavior.

In a very general way, all higher living beings, practically all the vertebrates, exhibit a double need, analogous and related to the need to eat and reproduce: the need to maintain a territory, and to keep some distance from other beings.

The territorial instinct of animals is now being quite extensively studied. But only in the past fifty years, following the work of Howard on "territory in the life of birds," has this study been undertaken systematically. The animal takes over a territory, temporarily or permanently, at the very least for the purpose of guaranteeing his reproduction and the raising of his offspring. He marks its limits and defends it from intrusion by relevant attitudes and behavior. Social reflexes in general enable congeners to establish good neighborly relations: a stranger of the same species does not enter another's territory unless invited and leaves when he is given the sign. But with respect to the attacking and predatory animal, the territory has a different meaning: it is the area of reference which makes it possible to measure its progress and speed, to calculate the chances of a counterattack, and to ensure the best conditions of flight. Here such factors as the dimension, form, and lay of the territory play a role, the latter being secure or insecure depending on its familiarity and conformity to certain criteria. These criteria are mainly the following:

The dimensions must make it possible to keep an easy watch on the boundaries, which implies that a part of the outer limits be protected by natural or artificial obstacles; it is impossible to keep watch on all sides at once. The dimensions and form must be such as to permit an exact estimate of the moves of an intruder; they therefore vary according to the size of the species. For land creatures, the rectangular form is most conducive to the detection of movement. On the other hand, diamond-shapes are acceptable only when they are very familiar. If this is not the case, they act like the distorted rooms of Ames, which are perceived as normal, while their content is perceived as distorted.

Last but not least, the territory must be laid out in such a way as to give its owner an advantageous position with respect to his attacker and, above all, possibilities of withdrawal and flight.

Hediger, who has extensively studied wild animals in captivity, observed that restriction of an animal's space induces a state of stupidity. For some, the territory is of such importance that when they are deprived of it they no longer reproduce, and sometimes no longer eat, and therefore die. Among the higher anthropoids closest to man, gorillas, the situation of impasse—

that is, the impossibility of either flight or attack—results in individual or collective suicidal behavior (murdering females and children before jumping to their own death). Hediger has observed that the stereotyped motor behavior was a quasi-experimental product of captivity. Racamier mentioned these facts, stressing the role played by material and affect isolation in the origin of incontinence and coprophagy, behavior patterns also observed among captive chimpanzees. Racamier stresses the importance of the meaning of space: "stereotyped activity takes place in schizophrenics when they are in a spatial environment which at one and the same time induces action and makes that action impossible." And he mentions the interminable pacings along sidewalks or around living rooms. "It is as if they were waiting for a train that never arrives" (Racamier, 1957, pp. 47–91).

The need for personal territory appears in the child around the age of seven, according to Gesell. The absence of territory caused by limited space and overcrowding leads to regression. Kurt Lewin has already noted that a change of environment sometimes brings on enuresis. But it was Woodbury who, in a symposium at Chestnut Lodge in 1958, reported the most suggestive facts. In a large overcrowded and rather neglected ward of Saint Elizabeth's Hospital in Washington, space had become a genuine value because of its scarcity. The dominant patient, the alpha, had full control of the hall, while those who came after him in the hierarchical order had access only to limited space. Nobody could intrude on the territory of a person more powerful than himself. At the bottom of the ladder, the omega had the use of nothing more than the bench on which he slept. He could not even go to spit in the drain located in the middle of the hall, and had no right to use the toilets. His incontinence was more the result of his social status than of his psychosis. As soon as they were given access to a decent amount of space, 50 percent of these patients ceased to be incontinent.

Searles, in a study of disturbances in space perception of mental patients, observed that some come to the point not only of losing awareness of the limits of their own bodies—

a well-known phenomenon—but of confusing them with the limits of the room.

All this merely confirms, for those accustomed to handling large concentrations of patients, what the early alienists already knew: the dangers of overcrowding, of changing the physical setting during confinement, of a restrictive environment. And we shall see later what use can be made of these concepts in the construction and arrangement of a hospital.

But let us return to the other aspect of interpersonal relations, to the "silent language" involving position and distance of one human body from another. Needless to say, verbal language merely borrows this silent language to express social positions and distances: superior and inferior, near and far, the right and left of the hostess, and the head of the table. All the rites of protocol and most of the rules of politeness (giving one's place, keeping one's distance, etc.), correspond to the art of situating oneself and situating others in relation to oneself. It is an art which has its own complexities: to be first, to go ahead, also means to put oneself at the mercy of those who are behind. If the young captains show the way, the old generals, the princes and kings arrive last. And we find these special hierarchies reflected in temporal behavior: if the future belongs to those who rise early, the present is controlled by those who go to bed late. The proof of this is provided by the way the strata of the social hierarchy succeed each other at various hours of the day in the subway.

The space which separates individuals is particularly significant. It may have a regulation aspect (an officer is saluted at six feet), but it always has a cultural aspect. The anthropologists have observed important differences among the various regions of the world. The Americans, for example, find that the Latins come too close to speak, and tend to move a comfortable distance away, but they feel then that others consider them cold. On the other hand, accustomed as they are to close neighborly relations, they are surprised, when in England, to find no particular emotional warmth in the people living near them. But despite these cultural differences, interpersonal distances

answer a deep biological need. The ethologists distinguish a flight distance, a social distance, and a personal distance. The flight distance, or critical distance, is that at which an animal reacts by flight to the approach of an assumed enemy. This distance, like the territory's dimension, varies with the size of the animal and with its capacity for flight or attack. An antelope flees at 500 meters, while a lizard can be approached as close as 2 meters. Racamier, in the work cited above, stresses the importance of this concept of critical distance in the relationship with schizophrenics. Beyond this distance, a person is simply not perceived, while within it he is perceived as either dangerous or secure. It is at this critical distance that flight or aggressive behavior is most likely. With animals as with man, it is possible to come within the critical distance by indicating submission: the animal sticks out his neck as if to have it cut, the supplicant prostrates himself at the feet of the victor, or bares his breast showing his empty, unarmed hands. In this way any aggressive instinct is stifled. The bear hunters of Anatolia use the following stratagem: a young hunter slowly enters the bear's cave nude and, of course, unarmed. He goes and snuggles up to the animal, placing himself at its mercy. Thus morally disarmed, the bear lets itself be led quietly to the exit.

Bodily distance is constantly used in the doctor-patient relationship, although it has seldom been studied in an objective way. This is all the more surprising in view of the fact that nothing is more easily objectifiable than spatial dimensions. The place of the psychoanalyst behind the patient's couch puts him in a definite hierarchical position: he is the one who sees without being "seen seeing."

A survey of a number of American psychiatrists showed that they were all perfectly aware of the importance of spatial relations in the doctor-patient relationship. An executive desk separating the doctor and his patient obviously provides only superficial human contact.

The therapist needs clinical sense to determine the distance he should put between himself and his patients. Sullivan was in the habit of sitting at a 45° angle from his patients, having noted that schizophrenics can hardly bear being looked at straight in the face. And de Clerambault observed that when their eyes had been looked into closely in a routine neurological examination, they would frequently stick out their tongues aggressively as soon as the doctor moved away.

Architecture and Psychiatric Therapy

In collaboration with two Englishmen, a psychiatrist, A. Baker, and an architect, L. Davies, I was able to devote two months in 1956 to the study of this problem for the World Health Organization (Baker, Davies, & Sivadon, 1960).

We rediscovered and developed the concepts already studied by the rare psychiatrists who have dealt with this aspect of the problem: security or insecurity-inducing spaces, which Vincent Kling calls "happy spaces" and "sinister spaces," and Osmond, "sociopetal" and "sociofugal."

We also rediscovered the notion that the structure of space is related to the structure of behavior. Whether in the "bororo" villages described by Lévi-Strauss or in modern institutions, functions are located in space in a meaningful way. The center has more value than the periphery: it is more inducive to security because it facilitates the use of the surrounding space. The experiments of Calhoun on rats show that if cages are lined up in rows of four and communicate with each other, the two in the middle are preferred: they have an opening on each side rather than just one. When the violent ward is located on the periphery of a hospital, it is clear that it does not get much consideration.

Since the work of Faris and Dunham on the distribution of mental patients in the cities, we know that the least organized peripheral areas have the highest proportion of mentally unbalanced inhabitants. The work of Strotska in Vienna, and of Chombard de Lauwe in France, confirm the relation between behavior disorders and poor distribution of space. But it is impossible to say with absolute certainty if unorganized spaces simply attract deviants or if they are pathogenic in themselves. This correlation probably derives from multiple causes. However that may be, it seems strange that so little thought has been given to the use of these concepts to reorient the behavior of mental patients and, if possible, render it normal. Aside from the WHO pamphlet nothing on this subject is to be found in the literature except a series of articles by Osmond and Izumi.

These latter stress the fact that most of the asylum buildings are antitherapeutic. They suggest designs involving spaces of different dimensions, ranging from the individual room, through quarters facilitating interrelations in small groups, to large meeting halls. Very logically, they place the individual rooms along the rays of a circle that surrounds a series of larger rooms intended for small groups. These rooms, in their turn, encircle a larger meeting hall. In the center of this radial system is the hospital staff. The disadvantage of this system, which has been used again by the architect who designed the French Radio and Television building, results from the fact that it creates strongly insecure spaces because of the almost total absence of perpendicular axes, helpful in orientation, and the existence of long, circular corridors making any visual survey impossible. You do not know where you are at any moment, or what may happen next. In the course of our research work with Baker and Davies, we had access to another field of experiment, the Palais des Nations in Geneva. It had become clear to us that a corridor longer than 40 meters, even if well lit, was anxiety producing if it had no shelters or, better yet, side exits. The Palais des Nations in Geneva, with endless series of offices along interminable corridors, has at least the advantage of rectangular forms and a few turns. By getting lost voluntarily in the corridors of the Radio House, I tried recently to recapture the anxiety of being disoriented. I quickly succeeded, and was by no means surprised to learn that states of depression were abnormally frequent among the personnel. The usual answer of the architects is that it is only a question of habit. This is partly true: the normal man can get accustomed to anything, but at the price of unconscious suffering. As for the mental patient, with his weakened adjustment ability, he reverts to the biological needs which are common to all the anthropoids: a territory inducing security through its form and dimensions. These demands are built into the structure of our body and correspond to thousand-year-old ancestral instincts. It is doubtful if, on the individual level, habituation can counteract the suffering caused by a space that induces insecurity.

The various architectural arrangements at the Marcel Rivière Institute at La Verrière were worked out on my advice so as to take into account the various aspects of space, its functional structure, its form and dimensions.

The general structure involves five main functional groups distributed in such a way as to make their differentiation very obvious: a Medical Center, a Social Center, and three Villages, each including three or four cottages (a total of ten). Two other units, smaller in size, are attached to the Medical Center and intended for therapy involving special technical difficulties. In these units, which can accommodate a maximum of 15 patients each, 9 rooms are located on the ground floor next to a meeting hall; the 6 rooms on the first floor surround a common space. Two of these six rooms are so designed that the amount of space available to the patient can be adjusted by means of a large sliding door. An adjoining courtyard, intended for badly disturbed patients, is located on the second floor terrace, thus replacing the traditional "snake pit" by an overhanging position which induces security by enhancing the patient's value, and enables him, by taking some risk, to escape from an enemy, if necessary. Each of the residential cottages includes 30 individual rooms. Various architectural arrangements divide them into smaller units including living rooms which can be used for small group meetings. Half-floors are created through an artificial relief that makes differentiation possible on the vertical as well as horizontal plane. All the lines are rectangular, the hallways are relatively wide

and not very deep; the exits are double so as to avoid, at all times, any feelings of captivity or, especially, of being caught in an impasse.

The cottages are grouped together in villages. In one of them, the units are arranged to form an inner space in an attempt to create a typical security-inducing territory: the patient, protected on three sides by buildings, can go up on a slightly elevated terrace and overlook the entrance to the territory as well as all the movements taking place within it. The other villages have similar arrangements but are less well protected.

The Social Center, with its common dining room, its bar, its library, its theater, has a semicircular shape. It is a pole of attraction. But there one meets the crowd in a more complex architectural structure, and spatial obstacles must be surmounted to reach it. Coming from the first two villages, a vast empty space must be crossed by paths arranged, not in rectangles, but in semidiamond shapes. We know that this arrangement, which the child learns to recognize only a year or two after the square and the triangle, does not facilitate orientation. It is anxiety generating and "sociofugal." Coming from the third village, it is necessary to cross under an arch and through a pass, which, as we know, also creates a sense of insecurity.

Thus two poles of attraction guide the behavior of the patient: A village where he feels secure and fulfills his need for dependency; a social center where he finds satisfaction for his stomach and his mind, but in an environment where he is exposed to the danger of encounters. And between these two poles—both attractive for opposite reasons—is an insecurity-inducing spatial obstacle.

This is but one example among many bipolar structures which aim to orient the patient's behavior toward a succession of regressive and progressive attitudes, of situations of dependence and autonomy, to plunge it into the proximity-distance dialectic which represents the spatial aspect of personality's progress. Will we succeed? The future alone will tell. The inhabitants of the institute already exhibit a feeling of spatial ease, enabling us to consider it an architectural success. But to what extent is this due to the artistic talent of the architect, and to what extent to the spatiodynamic conception that inspired the overall design?

We should not fail to relate this attempt at hospital therapy to the attempts of the urban planners who are taking "psychological factors" increasingly into account. Everyone has his opinion on these matters: some advocate small homes, traditional streets, closed yards, and others vertical structures, big open spaces, linear cities. Careful observation of the achievements and the writings of urban planners often leads one to suspect that, whatever the rationalizations they offer, their choices derive from their personal tastes, or more accurately, distastes. They all exhibit some of the characteristics of space phobia. Some are at ease only in strictly limited enclosures, others dream only of vast horizons.

Bachelard points out that the home represents the human body. It also serves as its shell. And we have seen that some patients confuse the limits of their body with those of the room in which they are confined.

All this shows the vital importance of architecture and urbanism for mental health. At a time when, under the impact of the population explosion, new cities are arising everywhere, psychologists should take an active part in this effort of reflection and elaboration concerning the structure of this part of themselves, of this shell which men build.

We have dealt with the heterogeneous aspects of our problem so that, by bringing together many varied facts, it would be possible to derive a concept general enough to clarify and enrich therapeutic techniques still in a rudimentary stage. This concept involves a hypothesis and a thesis.

The hypothesis defines the aspects of personality with which we are concerned. The mental functions correspond to the image the organism has of its relation to the world, and to the behavior by which it reacts to that image. This image and this behavior are linked to the spatial-temporal setting in which the organism is located. Personality is constituted by the internalization of the organism's successive relations with its environment in terms of its history and its future plans, in other words, the integration of its spatial and temporal experience. The disintegration of personality is expressed by the externalization of what had been internalized.

The thesis advocated here can be summarized as follows: of the two relational aspects, temporal and spatial, whose integration constitutes personality, the latter seems to be genetically the earlier, and therefore the simpler and stronger, the more easily concretized and directly accessible. The spatial *experience* and the *image* of the present relation to objects and persons— therefore the immediate behavior—can be partly modified, at the will of the therapist, through the *objective arrangement* of this space and of these relations. Here is a mode of approach to personality, whose therapeutic application has remained fragmentary until now that is empirical and generally underestimated, but that, in our opinion, deserves to be further developed.

SUMMARY

Personality can be viewed as a continuous process of integration of an individual history with situations constituted by the meeting in space of the organism with objects and persons.

Spatial relations of the organism constitute the most elementary and the simplest of the situations whose internalization and integration constitute the temporal aspect of personality.

Most psychotherapists deal with this temporal aspect; the problem is to reconcile man to his past and enable him to insert himself into the future. But as success is achieved, the first gain obtained is an enlargement of the patient's behavioral space. We may then conclude that approaching personality on the spatial plane would also facilitate its temporal reconstruction. This is the aim of various techniques which have long been applied empirically—physical therapy and occupational therapy. They achieve the analogical reduction of situations having similar structures (relations to persons and objects)—now relieved of their pathogenic emotional charge.

It is possible, moreover, to use the spatial setting to favor feelings of security or insecurity which, set off against each other, make it possible to create artificially controlled situations for therapeutic purposes. These concepts have been applied by the author to hospital architecture at the Marcel Rivière Institute.

The same concepts, based on research in genetic psychology, ethology, and social psychology can also be applied to the mental hygiene of urbanism.

REFERENCES:

Baker, A., Davies, L., & Sivadon, P. *Services psychiatriques et architecture.* WHO, Cahiers de Sante Publique, No. 1, 1960.
Bergson, H. *Essai sur les données immédiates de la conscience.* 1908.
Hall, E. T. *The silent language.* New York: Doubleday, 1959.
Piaget, J., & Inhelder, B. *La representation de l'espace chez l'enfant.* Paris: Presses Universitaires de France, 1948.
Piaget, J., and associates. *L'épistemologie de l'espace.* Paris: Presses Universitaires de France, 1964.
Racamier, P. C. Introduction a une sociopathologie des schizophrenes hospitalisés. *L'Evolution Psychiatrique,* 1957, **1,** 47–91.
Sivadon, P., & Gantheret, F. *La réeducation corporelle des fonctions mentales.* Paris: Editions Sociales Françaises, 1965.
Wallon, H. *Origines de la pensée chez l'enfant* (2nd ed.). Paris: Presses Universitaires de France, 1947, 2 vols.

43 The Environmental Psychology of the Psychiatric Ward

William H. Ittelson, Harold M. Proshansky, and Leanne G. Rivlin

The significance of the environment for the life of man has become obvious. No longer is it something to be conquered; it is something to be lived with. And it is becoming an increasingly unpleasant companion—aesthetically, as seen in urban and rural landscapes; functionally, as in the urban transport systems; biologically, as in air and water pollution; ecologically, as in the population explosion; and behaviorally, as in the plight of the culturally deprived. To deplore environmental deterioration in these instances and many others has become commonplace. At the same time, a body of environmental sciences is steadily though belatedly developing, and its goals are the classic goals of all science: to understand and control the phenomena with which it is concerned.

Environmental psychology is one of the most recently developed areas of study. It shares with other environmental sciences the characteristic of growing out of pressing social needs, but perhaps more than some of the other sciences, it finds that solving its "applied" problems requires basic knowledge that is not yet available. Traditionally, psychology has treated the physical environment as either the source of physical stimuli to which an organism responds or as an object to be perceived or cognized. Rarely has it been treated as an inextricable part of the life processes of the organisms studied. Environmental psychology thus finds much that is useful in the body of scientific psychological knowledge but little that can be immediately applied to environmental problems.

The research on the psychiatric ward reported here is representative of the direction work in environmental psychology has been forced to take. These investigations try to contribute to an immediate need—to increase the therapeutic effectiveness of psychiatric facilities through appropriate design—and thereby to provide a more basic understanding of man's relationships to his immediate physical surroundings. The psychiatric ward offers the advantage of a relatively clearly delineated physical and social system. On the other hand, there are obvious dangers in generalizing from the ward to other situations. These considerations make it useful for us to look briefly at the settings for these studies before turning to the studies themselves.

The psychiatric ward as we know it today has its ancestors in antiquity, but its immediate predecessors can probably be traced back no more than two hundred years. Its history, which we shall not examine here, does not reveal a steady evolution from some primitive form to a contemporary, more complex and more adequate end product. Quite the contrary. It is a story of fits and starts, of blind alleys, and of full circles. We can reasonably assume that today's psychiatric wards are also transient forms, and this assumption is supported by evidence from new approaches to the treatment of mental illness.

Most psychiatric wards today are found in psychiatric hospitals ranging in size from small, 20- to 30-bed private hospitals to mammoth state institutions with 10,000 or more beds. Such hospitals are located in all possible settings from central urban to remote rural. They account for the great majority of psychiatric beds in the United States.

Most of the remaining psychiatric beds are found in the psychiatric wards of general hospitals. These hospitals treat all types of illness, and the psychiatric service is coming to be recognized as one of their necessary components. General hospitals tend to be located in urban centers. They emphasize short-term, active treatment of psychiatric problems, and they are rapidly becoming the place at which initial psychiatric treatment is received. Some of them also serve as community mental health centers that, together with other such centers, may reduce the need for long-range, custodial mental hospitals. Our studies covered psychiatric wards in two general hospitals and wards in a state mental hospital.

Although all psychiatric wards treat mental illness, we quickly learned that they serve other functions and that the totality of such functions varies widely. We have found it useful to distinguish between functions that arise from the intrinsic nature of the hospital and extrinsic goals or functions that are imposed on it through its position in the community. Without attempting to catalogue these functions, we can sample some of those that have been compelling in the construction and operation of the hospitals we have studied.

Certain extrinsic functions are quite formally and explicitly stated and openly enforced by the community. Cost control in construction is perhaps the most obvious example, but there are also zoning regulations and building codes. Many other extrinsic goals are vague and informally enforced; they may even be unrecognized until research discloses them. The removal of socially undesirable people from the community for longer or shorter periods of time is rarely, if ever, an explicitly stated function of the hospital. But in many cases this has most assuredly been a de facto function the community has imposed upon the hospital. Psychiatric treatment has been shown on occasion to be used as a punitive measure, and the social class determinants of who goes to what hospital and receives what kind of treatment have been well documented. A different kind of informal, extrinsic function of the hospital is its role as a community status symbol. Still another is seen in its complex economic relationship with the community.

The intrinsic goals of the hospital are more likely to be formally and explicitly stated. The care and treatment of patients, the conduct of medical research, and the training of medical personnel are patent examples. Other intrinsic functions, however, are not so formally stated nor so easily recognized. For example, every hospital has a complex system of interlocking, status-related hierarchical relationships among its personnel. The maintenance of these relationships cannot be overlooked as an important intrinsic, though seldom explicitly stated, function of the hospital. All of these considerations, extrinsic and intrinsic, explicit and implicit, have played a role at one time or another in determining the nature of the facilities, the personnel, the treatments, and the patients encountered in the psychiatric wards we have studied.

Just as psychiatric wards are found in various locations and serve diverse functions, they also come in many different sizes and shapes. In size they range from 18 or fewer patients to 40 or more on the ward. They may be segregated as to sex or mixed. All patients may occupy private rooms, all may be housed in a large dormitory, or there may be a combination of room arrangements. Most psychiatric wards seem to share at least one feature in common, however:

they typically have too many patients and too few staff. They also have a number of physical features in common. Most provide facilities for sleeping, for socializing, for personal hygiene, for eating, for therapeutic activities, and for medical treatment. They also typically have security features of one sort or another on the basis of the stated assumption that psychiatric patients need to be protected from themselves and the unstated assumption that the community needs to be protected from the patients. Perhaps the most common security feature is controlled access to the ward, usually by means of a door that may be locked or open. In either event the door, in most psychiatric wards although not in some of recent design, constitutes a real barrier. When entering through it there is a strong sense of passing into the world of the psychiatric patient, and when leaving through this door, there is the corresponding sense of leaving this special environment and returning to the "real world."

In addition to these common features, the psychiatric wards we studied have distinct characteristics and features that must be recognized for an understanding of the behaviors seen on them. They are located in three large metropolitan hospitals. Two are general hospitals, each with a relatively small psychiatric service: one hospital has two wards, one male, one female, with a total population of approximately 40 to 50 patients, and the other has four wards with a total population of about 90 patients. The third hospital is a large, state-supported, psychiatric institution housing almost a thousand patients in two modern, high-rise buildings.

These three psychiatric services present an interesting pattern of similarities and contrasts. All three are affiliated as teaching hospitals with medical schools. All are run by dedicated men and women who are thoroughly trained and well schooled in the latest psychiatric developments. All operate under approximately the same treatment philosophy, which, briefly, is aimed at returning the patient as quickly as possible to his customary environment through the use of all available psychiatric and psychological techniques. While all three hospitals seek to move patients out of the hospital environment rapidly, the psychiatric services in the general hospitals concentrate on short-term, intensive, active treatment of acute mental breakdown while the state hospital accommodates long-term, chronic patients as well.

A look at the differences between the hospitals reveals marked contrasts, and it is for this very reason of their contrasting physical environments within a context of similar treatment philosophies that we chose these three institutions. One of the general hospitals is a city hospital offering medical care principally to people who are unable to pay more than a small fraction of the cost. The patient population is largely from the lower socioeconomic groups and ethnically mixed. The psychiatric wards are former medical wards that have been more or less crudely converted to psychiatric uses. Basically they maintain the medical ward structure, but many amenities and conveniences of living have been removed for security reasons.

The immediate impression as one walks into one of these wards is of lights and sounds reflecting from the hard tile walls of a long corridor; of too many people doing too many things too rapidly in too small a space; of an appalling lack of privacy as every bedroom holds either three or six beds and is completely exposed to the corridor. And yet, in spite of, or perhaps because of, the noise and the excitement and the continuing movement of too many people, one has the impression that this is an active place in which things are being done and that it is earnestly dedicated to the well-being of its patients.

The state hospital is a large psychiatric institution with predominantly voluntary admissions. Although it aims to minimize length of hospitalization, its facilities are limited and its patients receive relatively little individual treatment. This hospital is distinguished, however, by its innovative and experimental approach to mental illness within the limitations of its status as a state institution. Patients pay for their hospitalization according to their means. They are drawn from community mental health centers in three different areas of the city and are separated within the hospital according to the location of their residence. In this way there is continuity of treatment from neighborhood to hospital. Of the three areas which feed into the hospital, one is middle income, one is lower income, and one is mixed middle and lower.

The two wards we observed housed the latter two income groups. The important distinctions between the wards, however, reflect differential administrative policies rather than patient differences. Both wards had a small number of patients in private rooms and the rest in 20-bed wards or in 3- to 6-bed rooms. Privacy was difficult to achieve because all rooms had some type of window facing onto the corridors. The number of single rooms is rapidly declining as the demand for medical office space increases.

Although the wards were structurally almost identical, "Ward A" was bright, clean, and efficient looking, and "Ward B" had an air of darkness and neglect that, since the time of the study, has been dramatically changed. Ward A housed approximately 23 female patients who had a voice in ward policy and who worked together with the staff to decorate and brighten their sparsely furnished ward. At that time on Ward B, however, relatively few attempts had been made to alter the barren institutional look, and the activities of the approximately 24 female and 4 male patients generally appeared to be less cohesive and less goal-directed.

It is a long journey in every sense of the word to our third hospital, a private institution. Although it has some indigent patients, this hospital caters primarily to those who can and do pay a considerable sum for the services of what has come to be known as one of the best small psychiatric units in its part of the country. Stillness, security, and efficiency are the immediate impressions as one walks onto a ward. The subdued lighting, pastel walls, and attractive furnishings reflect the rational planning of a carefully conceived design. Few people are in evidence, and they seem to know where they are going and what they are doing. An occasional open door reveals neat one- and two-occupancy rooms, and a nicely furnished dayroom completes the impression that one has perhaps lost one's way and walked into a rather comfortable family hotel. One feels that whatever has to be done will be done neatly, quietly, and efficiently by people who clearly know how to do it.

Among the patients, one finds a corresponding pattern of similarities and differences. Medically, patients in the private and city hospitals are quite similar in terms of diagnoses, severity of illness, types of treatment, previous medical histories, age and sex, and other relevant characteristics. Patients in the state hospital tend to be more severely ill and to have had more extensive previous psychiatric treatment. In the social and related experiential backgrounds of patients, however, important differences emerge among the hospitals.

As has already been suggested, the patients in the city hospital are drawn primarily from the depths or fringes of poverty. They are mixed ethnically, approximately one-third white, one-third Puerto Rican, and one-third Negro. All are given free or low cost medical care at the expense of the city. In contrast, the patients in the private hospital are predominantly white and, except for a few "city patients," are drawn primarily from the middle class or above. The state hospital, with its policy of drawing from and separating three distinct neighborhood populations, falls somewhere between the other two. One of the wards we studied paralleled the ethnic distribution of the municipal hospital, while the other had a predominantly white population. In brief, the patients in the three hospitals are grouped in ways that represent the two societies into which the city is divided.

Without pausing to consider the social and ethical implications of this fact, we can speculate that the two groups may show different patterns in their use of the facilities of the ward. Among the vast differences in way of life that separate them, two might be expected to have a direct influence on their responses to the ward: experience in other psychiatric settings, and home surroundings.

In the private and city hospitals during

the course of our studies, approximately half of the patients were new admissions and half had previous psychiatric hospitalization. In the state hospital, close to 90 percent had previous hospitalization. Most patients thus enter these hospitals with a clear idea, gained from previous experiences, of what to expect and how to behave. Where they acquired this knowledge is suggested by Table 43-1, which represents a single 100 percent sample of the particular wards studied. Of the patients at the private hospital, 22 (47 percent) had a total of 25 previous hospitalizations in 11 different hospitals. At the city hospital, 9 patients (43 percent) had a total of 16 previous admissions in 9 different hospitals. In the state hospital, 34 patients (85 percent) had a total of 97 previous admissions in 25 different hospitals. Except for the fact that two of the hospitals operated as major emergency-intake hospitals,

Table 43-1 Previous Psychiatric Hospitalizations[a]

	PRIVATE	CITY	STATE
Number of patients	47	21	40
Number with previous hospitalizations	22	9	34
Total number of previous hospitalizations	25	16	97
Total number of hospitals	11	9	25
Previous hospitalizations in private hospitals			
PRIVATE	5	1	1
Other private hospitals	10	1	9
Previous hospitalizations in public hospitals			
CITY	0	4	0
STATE	0	0	12
Two municipal emergency intake hospitals	10	4	10
Other public hospitals	0	6	65

[a] Data refer to a single, 100 percent sample of two wards in the private and state hospitals and one ward in the city hospital. Twelve unusable responses are not included.

there is almost a complete separation between the two groups of patients. None of the private patients had been in the city or state hospitals or in the other public institutions represented there. Similarly, among the city and state patients, only two had previously been to the private hospital, and all private hospitals in the sample accounted for only 10 percent of their previous hospitalizations. Thus, in terms of hospitals there is virtually no overlap between the two groups of patients. The two societies are as effectively separated in medical care as in other aspects of living.

The contrast in home environments is equally striking, as seen in Table 43-2, which compares private and city patients (no comparable data are available for state patients). Of those who gave usable responses, approximately one-third of the private patients and none of those from the city hospital lived in apartments with at least two rooms per person or in private homes. In contrast, one-third of the city patients and only a single one from the private hospital were homeless or lived in rooming houses. These figures, of course, show only quantitative differences between the home settings of the two groups.

These were the three settings in which we posed for ourselves the task of evaluating the effect of physical surroundings on the behavior of patients on a ward. It is quite clear that the three hospitals offer such a complex pattern of similarities and differ-

Table 43-2 Descriptions of Patients' Homes[a]

	PRIVATE	CITY
Homeless	0	1
Rooming house	1	5
Apartment		
Fewer than 2 rooms per person	22	12
More than 2 rooms per person	9	0
Private house	2	0
Religious order	4	0
No classifiable response	9	3

[a] Data refer to a single, 100 percent sample of two wards in the private hospital and one ward in the city hospital.

ences that an attempt to attribute observed differences in behavior to architectural features or to any other single factor would be open to question and therefore was not our primary intent. Rather, the studies reported here are aimed at isolating consistent patterns in the utilization of space and, if possible, at taking a step toward developing general principles applicable to a variety of settings. Three contrasting hospitals were used, therefore, not primarily for the purpose of making comparisons, but rather to make more likely the discovery of patterns of behavior that could be checked across very different psychiatric ward settings.

METHODOLOGY

The problem of studying behavior as it relates directly to physical surroundings required the development of a new technique that we have called *behavioral mapping*. Because this procedure is described in detail in Part Six, it is only briefly outlined here. Observers record, for each of various predetermined physical locations on the ward, the number and description of the participants engaging in each of a set of observational categories of behavior. The participants are identified as male or female patients, staff, or visitors. The observational categories were derived from a pilot study in which a large sample of behaviors on the ward were observed and recorded. The behavioral maps presented here show only the behavior of patients assigned to the ward while they are on the ward. Maps showing the behavior of staff or of patients visiting from other wards are of interest but are not included here. Data are recorded on forms that permit their rapid collection by experienced observers. This technique, coupled with the use of a sufficient number of observers, permits almost instantaneous observation of all areas on the ward. All the findings reported here are based on such observations made on a time-sampling basis. Typically, observations were made every 15 minutes throughout the active periods of the day—that is, the morning hours following breakfast and before lunch; the afternoon hours following lunch and before dinner; and the evening hours following dinner

and before bedtime. In all, 9 hours per day are represented by observations at 15-minute intervals for a total of 36 separate observations of each area on each ward for each day.

Wards in the private and city hospitals were observed and mapped twice, but one mapping was completed for the state hospital. In the private hospital the first mapping was the more intensive; it covered two wards for six days a week during three weeks. The second mapping was done almost three years later; it was aimed at determining the stability of the patterns observed in the first mapping and covered only one ward for two days. The hospital made some changes in administrative and medical policies during this period, including an extension of a modified open-door policy to all floors, and a greater tendency to mix types of patients on each ward.

The two mappings of the city hospital were limited to the female ward and were separated by an interval of two months; both were equally extensive. In the interim between them, two significant changes occurred that might be expected to influence behavior. One of these was unexpected and unplanned by the experimenters. Although the adjacent male ward had been operating at approximately two-thirds of its capacity, or 16 patients, in the period between mappings it was increased to full capacity, or 24 patients. Since patients moved freely between the two wards during the periods of the day when we mapped behavior, the change in the census of the two wards from 16 men and 25 women in the first mapping to 24 men and 24 women in the second mapping might be expected to influence behavior on the female ward. In analyzing the data, we tried to determine which changes could reasonably be attributed to the change in the census of the male ward.

The second change that occurred between the two mappings was planned and carried out by the experimenters for the precise purpose of attempting to influence behavior. Two areas on the ward—a dayroom and a solarium—in addition to the corridor, are open to all patients and visitors. Earlier mappings had shown that the solarium was seldom used, and we hypothesized that the causes were its location at the far end of the corridor and the inadequate and uncomfortable facilities it offered. We subsequently decided to study the effect on the use of the solarium of providing comfortable, attractive, and carefully laid out seating arrangements. Adequate seats were placed in front of the television set, two easy chairs were added in a remote corner of the room, and a table, couches, and easy chairs that were conducive to group conversations were placed in another corner. These furnishings were introduced immediately after the first mapping, and the second mapping was conducted after a period of time judged sufficient to allow the establishment of enduring patterns of use.

In the state hospital, the two wards previously described were observed simultaneously and only once. These wards were mapped over a period of several weeks for a total of 12 complete days in such a way that two simultaneous maps of two full weeks (excluding Sunday) were obtained.

The behavioral maps provided by these various sets of observations are given in the form of tables in which the vertical columns represent behavior categories and the horizontal rows represent areas of the ward. Each figure in a table, unless otherwise noted, is the percentage of patients assigned to that ward observed in the particular location performing the particular behavior. As shown in more detail in Part Six, the fairly large number of observational categories can be divided into smaller numbers of analytical categories. In general, the tables provided here represent either six categories—traffic, visiting, other social, mixed active, isolated active, and isolated passive behavior—or

the combined categories (excluding traffic)—isolated passive, total active, and total social behavior. The most stringently defined category is isolated passive behavior, which includes, unless specifically noted otherwise, only the observational categories of lying in bed, either asleep or awake, and sitting, either asleep or doing nothing. This very restricted range of behaviors sometimes occupies a large percentage of a patient's time.

RESULTS

Private Hospital: A Typical Ward

The behavioral map of an average ward in the private hospital is given in Table 43-3. It is a hypothetical ward, since it represents overall averages of all data from the initial mapping of two wards. It represents what we have come to recognize as a fairly typical distribution of behaviors on a ward in this hospital. Roughly speaking, one-third of the patients are off the ward. The reader should understand that the figures in the table are percentages of the total patients assigned to the ward, although the activities of only the patients remaining on the ward are given.

Total activity is fairly evenly divided among the five major categories; social activity is highest, but the ratio of highest to lowest is less than 2 to 1. When we look at the bedrooms and the public rooms separately, however, we see that the behaviors are much less evenly distributed. In the bedrooms, the range is from less than 1 percent for mixed active behavior to more than 10 percent for isolated passive. In the public rooms, isolated passive is lowest (2.6 percent) and social is highest (14.3 percent).

Table 43-3 Distribution of Activities on an Average Ward of the Private Hospital[a]

	Traffic	Visiting	Social	Mixed Active	Isolated Active	Isolated Passive	Total
Bedrooms	0.1	3.2	3.9	0.8	5.7	10.4	24.1
Public rooms	2.7	6.5	14.3	9.4	4.6	2.6	40.1
Total	2.8	9.7	18.2	10.2	10.3	13.0	64.2

[a] Unless otherwise indicated in this and subsequent tables, the numbers represent the percent of patients assigned to the ward engaged in each activity; the times of observations were 9:30 A.M.–12:30 P.M.; 1:30–4:30 P.M.; 6–9 P.M.

Private Hospital: Comparison between Two Wards

Separate maps for the total activity on each ward are given in Table 43-4. The distribution of behaviors in the two wards is virtually identical. On the basis of this finding, we will combine data from the two wards for the analysis of all subsequent findings.

It is interesting to note, however, that the wards were different in many respects. They were defined differently by the hospital: one was an admissions ward for incoming patients, while the other was a recuperative ward for patients who generally had spent more time in the hospital and who usually came there from admissions wards. Recuperative ward patients were more accustomed to hospital routine. Admission to the recuperative ward indicated positive progress toward discharge. On the admissions ward the ratio of females to males was much higher, the mean age was lower, and the age range of males was much less evenly distributed. In addition, there were administrative differences between the wards. The admissions ward had a larger staff with more assistance from student nurses and aides; patients on it were given more attention and more encouragement to leave the ward and engage in therapeutic activities.

Private Hospital: Comparison of Days of the Week

Total activity by days of the week for the combined wards is shown in Table 43-5. The distribution is remarkably constant over the five weekdays, during which behavior in each category, except visiting, varies less than ±3 percent from its mean value. The high figures for visiting on Tuesday and Thursday reflect the hospital's designation of these days as visiting days. Saturday is an atypical day in that more than 50 percent of the patients are off the ward (a large number of weekend passes are given). The patients remaining distribute their activities rather differently than on other days. Visiting is the highest single category, although the distribution over the entire range of behavior is remarkably flat; the spread from highest to lowest is only 3 percent on Saturday, compared to a mean spread for the other days of 13 percent.

Private Hospital: Time of Day Comparisons

The distribution of activities by time of day (morning, afternoon, and evening), shown in Table 43-6, reveals several interesting patterns. Looking first at the total activity, while there are differences between morning

Table 43-4 Distribution of Activities on Two Wards of the Private Hospital

	Traffic	Visiting	Social	Mixed Active	Isolated Active	Isolated Passive	Total
Ward 1	2.5	8.0	17.9	11.0	10.6	12.6	62.6
Ward 2	3.1	11.4	18.5	9.4	10.0	13.4	65.8

Table 43-5 Distribution of Activities by Days of the Week—Private Hospital: Average of Two Wards

	Traffic	Visiting	Social	Mixed Active	Isolated Active	Isolated Passive	Total
Monday	3.2	3.4	20.6	11.2	10.1	14.0	62.5
Tuesday	3.2	15.2	18.4	8.0	11.0	13.4	69.2
Wednesday	3.2	7.8	21.6	11.2	10.4	14.4	68.6
Thursday	2.2	13.2	20.0	12.2	8.4	12.8	68.8
Friday	3.4	8.0	20.2	9.8	14.0	12.0	67.4
Saturday	1.8	11.0	8.4	8.8	8.0	10.2	48.2

Table 43-6 Distribution of Activities by Time of Day—Private Hospital: Average Ward

	Traffic	Visiting	Social	Mixed Active	Isolated Active	Isolated Passive	Total
Bedrooms							
Morning	0.1	1.5	3.3	0.6	6.9	8.4	20.7
Afternoon	0.2	3.3	3.6	0.6	5.4	13.5	26.4
Evening	0.0	5.0	4.8	1.0	4.9	8.7	24.5
Public rooms							
Morning	2.7	5.4	18.9	9.0	6.0	3.6	45.9
Afternoon	2.4	3.9	9.6	4.2	2.4	6.0	28.2
Evening	3.2	10.4	14.5	13.1	3.7	2.0	46.9
Total							
Morning	2.8	6.9	22.2	9.6	12.9	12.0	66.6
Afternoon	2.6	7.2	13.2	4.8	7.8	19.5	54.6
Evening	3.2	15.4	19.3	14.1	8.6	10.7	71.3

and evening (principally, visiting is particularly high in the evening), it is clear that the afternoon is atypical. More than two-thirds of the patients remain on the ward in the morning and evening, but this figure drops to about one-half in the afternoon. The expectation would be that all categories of behavior are correspondingly lower in the afternoon, and this is true, except for visiting, which is fractionally higher in the morning than in the afternoon, and isolated passive behavior, which dramatically almost doubles in the afternoon. While there are fewer patients on the ward in the afternoon, more of them, not just proportionally but in actual numbers, engage in isolated passive behavior.

Examination of the breakdown of activities between bedrooms and public rooms shows that the major change in the afternoon occurs principally in the public rooms, where total activity drops from 46 percent in the morning and evening to 28 percent in the afternoon. At the same time, isolated passive behavior increases in absolute amount as well as relatively in the public rooms, rising from least popular status in morning and evening to second most popular in the afternoon. The bedrooms show a related, though not so marked, change in the afternoon, when the largest number of patients are found in the bedrooms. Isolated passive behavior, always the most popular in bedrooms, rises disproportionately in the afternoon.

Private Hospital: Male-Female Comparisons

The overall distribution of activity is quite similar for men and women, as shown in Table 43-7, but there are some differences in the way their activities are divided between bedrooms and public rooms. In par-

Table 43-7 Distribution of Activities for Male and Female Patients—Private Hospital: Average Ward

	Traffic	Visiting	Social	Mixed Active	Isolated Active	Isolated Passive	Total
Bedrooms							
Male	0.2	2.3	3.4	0.8	4.3	8.9	19.9
Female	0.3	3.8	4.1	0.8	6.6	10.7	26.3
Public rooms							
Male	3.4	5.7	16.7	8.2	5.6	3.1	42.7
Female	2.2	7.2	12.5	10.6	4.1	2.9	39.5
Total							
Male	3.6	8.0	20.1	9.0	9.9	12.0	62.6
Female	2.5	11.0	16.6	11.4	10.7	13.6	65.8

ticular, women spend somewhat more time in their bedrooms than men, although an analysis by bedroom size shows that this difference is contributed entirely by women in single rooms. The most striking conclusion from Table 43-7, however, is that men and women do very much the same things on the ward.

Private Hospital: Comparison of Two Separate Mappings

It will be recalled that one of the wards in the private hospital was mapped again after a period of three years. Although the second mapping was less extensive, it was sufficient to provide a reliable picture of activities on the ward. Some changes in hospital administration and medical policies had occurred, but the characteristics of the patients in the two samples in terms of age, sex, and diagnosis are remarkably similar. There was a general impression shared by the staff and observers that the patients in the second mapping were somewhat sicker than those in the first. This assessment probably offers a correct picture of the differences between the two situations, and is very likely a result of the policy of mixing all types of patients on each floor.

The distributions of total activity in the two mappings, as given in Table 43-8, are similar; the mean values in each case differ no more than ±3 percent from the two extremes. The differences for the most part are consistent with the impression of greater sickness in the second mapping: more pa-

tients stay on the ward; there is more isolated passive behavior and less social behavior.

Bedroom activities remain almost exactly the same in the second mapping as in the first; indeed, the differences between the two mappings are attributable almost entirely to behavior in the public rooms. The larger number of patients who remained on the ward stayed in the public rooms, and they exhibited a general trend toward individual and away from social behavior. The most dramatic change is the almost 7 percent increase in mixed active behavior, which in this case was almost exclusively an increase in television watching.

City Hospital: A Typical Ward

Two mappings, two months apart, were made of the female ward studied in the city hospital. As we indicated earlier, the interval between mappings brought changes in both hospital policy and ward structure. The specific influence of these changes will be discussed later. At this point, however, we are interested only in the general distribution of activities, as revealed in Table 43-9. The number of patients remaining on the ward dropped from the first to the second mapping by 11 percent, and this drop is represented almost entirely by a decrease in social behavior of about 9 percent. Other categories remain constant, drop 1 or 2 percent, or in the case of isolated passive, increase by approximately 4 percent. The change from the first to the

Table 43-8 Distribution of Activities in Two Separate Mappings of Private Hospital

	Traffic	Visiting	Social	Mixed Active	Isolated Active	Isolated Passive	Total
Bedrooms							
Map No. 1	0.1	3.2	3.9	0.8	5.7	10.4	24.1
Map No. 2	1.0	3.7	2.0	0.1	5.3	12.7	24.8
Mean	0.5	3.5	3.0	0.4	5.5	11.6	24.5
Public rooms							
Map No. 1	2.7	6.5	14.3	9.4	4.6	2.6	40.1
Map No. 2	3.5	3.7	10.9	16.1	7.3	6.3	47.8
Mean	3.1	5.1	12.6	12.7	6.0	4.5	44.0
Total							
Map No. 1	2.8	9.7	18.2	10.2	10.3	13.0	64.2
Map No. 2	4.5	7.4	12.9	16.2	12.6	19.0	72.6
Mean	3.7	8.6	15.6	13.3	11.5	16.1	68.8

Table 43-9 Distribution of Activities in Two Separate Mappings of City Hospital

	Traffic	Visiting	Social	Mixed Active	Isolated Active	Isolated Passive	Total
Bedrooms							
Map No. 1	0.0	0.0	5.0	0.0	4.5	16.6	26.1
Map No. 2	0.0	0.9	1.5	0.0	3.2	23.7	29.3
Mean	0.0	0.5	3.3	0.0	3.9	20.2	27.9
Public rooms							
Map No. 1	3.7	4.0	16.2	8.8	4.1	14.1	50.9
Map No. 2	2.3	2.2	11.0	6.4	5.5	10.8	38.2
Mean	3.0	3.1	13.6	7.6	4.8	12.5	44.6
Total							
Map No. 1	3.7	4.0	21.2	8.8	8.6	30.7	78.5
Map No. 2	2.3	3.1	12.5	6.4	8.7	34.5	67.5
Mean	3.0	3.6	16.9	7.6	8.7	32.7	72.5

second mapping is reflected in both bedrooms and public rooms, in the former primarily by an increase in isolated passive behavior and in the latter by a decrease in total activity with corresponding decreases in all categories except isolated active behavior, which shows a slight rise.

State Hospital: Comparison of Two Wards

The distributions of behavior in two wards of the state hospital are shown in Table 43-10. In this table the "visiting" category has been combined with the "social," since visiting accounted for less than 2 percent of the total activity. The observers had the impression, however, that visiting was somewhat more frequent than this rate would indicate, but that it occurred primarily off the ward.

The two wards differ quite markedly in

a number of ways; most obviously, more patients are off Ward A than Ward B. This difference is attributable entirely to the reduced use of the bedrooms on Ward A, and in the bedrooms, it is reflected only in a reduction of the level of isolated passive behavior. These differences are perhaps related to some explicit policy differences between the two wards—differences that were in fact voted upon by the patients. On Ward A more off-ward activities were scheduled and more passes to leave the ward were issued. Use of the bedrooms was discouraged and TV-watching was limited to certain times. It seems reasonable to assume that these policies were intended to produce a more active, more social ward. In fact each difference in policy between the two wards is related to a corresponding behavioral difference, as seen in Table 43-10. On Ward A, more patients are off the ward and both bedroom use and mixed active

Table 43-10 Distribution of Activities on Two Wards of the State Hospital

	Traffic	Social	Mixed Active	Isolated Active	Isolated Passive	Total
Bedrooms						
Ward A	0.6	1.6	2.2	2.2	9.6	16.2
Ward B	0.9	1.3	2.3	2.4	21.3	28.2
Public rooms						
Ward A	5.3	12.4	6.2	3.8	8.7	36.4
Ward B	5.9	9.1	9.9	3.7	7.7	36.3
Total						
Ward A	5.9	14.0	8.4	6.0	18.3	52.6
Ward B	6.8	10.4	12.2	6.1	29.0	64.5

behavior, including TV-watching, are reduced. Whether the policies caused these differences, and more importantly whether they actually produced more social and active behavior cannot be directly answered, but answers can be inferred from the data.

At first glance, Table 43-10 would seem to indicate success in "activating" Ward A. The number of patients in the bedrooms is sharply reduced (57 percent of Ward B). Furthermore, while on Ward B total behavior, exclusive of traffic, is evenly divided between isolated passive and all others, on Ward A active behaviors are 50 percent more frequent than isolated passive. Clearly Ward A is more active than Ward B. But the absolute amount of combined social and active behavior on the two wards is identical; the difference between them is entirely attributable to the reduced occupancy of the bedrooms and the resulting reduction in isolated passive behavior in the bedrooms on Ward A. It is possible, though not probable, that these patients simply engaged in the same isolated passive behavior off the wards that they would have carried out in the bedrooms had they been permitted. The observers had the impression that this was not the case, but final assessment of the efficacy of Ward A policies clearly depends on knowledge of the patients' behavior off the ward, which is not provided by our data.

That the policy differences were responsible for the behavioral differences can more definitely be inferred from Table 43-10. The policy was to reduce the number of patients in the bedrooms and to increase the number off the ward, and the data show exactly these effects. The presumption that these

effects were a result of the policies is supported by Table 43-11, which compares the two wards for three different times of day. The differences between the wards are accentuated in the morning and the afternoon, when policy differences were strictly enforced, and almost wiped out in the evening, when policy differences were relatively unenforced.

Comparisons of the Three Hospitals

Tables 43-8, 43-9, and 43-10 reveal detailed patterns of similarity and difference among the three hospitals. The major comparisons are more clearly seen in Table 43-12, in which the observed behaviors are combined under the three major categories: total social, total active, and isolated passive.

Looking first at the total activities in the three hospitals, the private hospital shows a pattern that is qualitatively different from the others. Social and active behaviors there are virtually identical and markedly greater than isolated passive. In contrast, both of the other hospitals show more isolated passive than other behavior, although in Ward A of the state hospital this difference is minimal. In general, the private hospital shows higher levels of social and active and lower levels of isolated passive than do the public hospitals, and the state hospital is especially low in social behavior.

The bedrooms do not show any striking qualitative differences among the hospitals. In all cases behavior in the bedrooms is predominantly isolated passive. There are quantitative differences, however. Slightly less than 50 percent of the bedroom activity

Table 43-11 Distribution of Activities on Two Wards by Time of Day—State Hospital

	Traffic	Social	Mixed Active	Isolated Active	Isolated Passive	Total
Morning						
Ward A	7.8	16.1	7.4	5.7	13.3	50.3
Ward B	7.6	11.0	9.0	7.5	25.4	60.5
Afternoon						
Ward A	5.1	14.5	6.7	5.3	16.2	47.8
Ward B	6.7	11.3	11.9	5.0	29.9	64.8
Evening						
Ward A	4.8	11.6	11.1	6.9	25.3	59.7
Ward B	6.0	8.4	15.6	5.5	31.4	66.9

Table 43-12 The Distribution of Activities in Three Hospitals

	Total Social	Total Active	Isolated Passive	Total on ward including traffic
Bedrooms				
Private	6.5	5.9	11.6	24.5
City	3.8	3.9	20.2	27.9
State A	1.6	4.4	9.6	16.2
State B	1.3	4.7	21.3	28.2
Public rooms				
Private	17.7	18.7	4.5	44.0
City	16.7	12.4	12.5	44.6
State A	12.4	10.0	8.7	36.4
State B	9.1	13.6	7.7	36.3
Total				
Private	24.2	24.6	16.1	68.5
City	20.5	16.3	32.7	72.5
State A	14.0	14.4	18.3	52.6
State B	10.4	18.3	29.0	64.5

in the private hospital is isolated passive compared to 60 to 75 percent in the others, although the absolute level of isolated passive in Ward A bedrooms of the state hospital is lower than in the private hospital bedrooms. One other interesting quantitative comparison is the low level of social activity in the city hospital bedrooms and its virtual absence in the state hospital bedrooms, as compared with bedrooms of the private hospital.

The public rooms in the private hospital show a very low level of isolated passive behavior; 83 percent of the activity in these rooms is approximately evenly divided between social and mixed active behaviors. In contrast, neither of the other hospitals exhibit a comparable dip in isolated passive behavior, and the activity in the public rooms of both is much more evenly distributed over the three behavior categories.

There are also consistent differences in the level of each activity across hospitals. Social activity is highest in the private hospital, very closely followed by the city hospital; it drops sharply in the state hospital. Active behavior also is highest in the private hospital, but it drops to a more or less constant lower level in the other two. In contrast, as we pointed out earlier, isolated passive behavior is lower in the private hospital and markedly higher in the others, although for Ward A of the state hospital

this trend is almost eliminated by the reduction in bedroom use.

Some interesting and important differences in the distribution of activities are thus revealed by the comparisons given in Table 43-12. It is interesting to speculate upon the origins of these differences, and it is relevant to ask in the context of the present studies whether the differences can in any way be attributed to the architectural design of the wards or whether they more probably are due to other factors. If we look at the public rooms first, we are inclined to attribute differences to other factors. Wards in all hospitals have public rooms that serve more or less equivalent functions. Each has a corridor; each has a dayroom; and each has an additional multipurpose public room. They do of course differ in design and decor, but they have roughly equivalent facilities. Nevertheless, as we have seen, there are important differences among hospitals in the ways the public rooms are used. It is difficult to believe that these differences are entirely due to differences in design, however. The most reasonable assumption at this point is that they are due, not to design factors, but rather to other differences among the hospitals.

The situation with respect to bedrooms is more difficult, since there are considerably greater design differences in bedrooms than in public rooms in the three hospitals. In particular, the private hospital has 1-, 2-, and 4-bed rooms, the city hospital has 3- and 6-bed rooms, and the state hospital has 1-, 3-, 6-, 8-, and 12-bed rooms, the latter two representing the number of beds occupied in large rooms holding twenty beds. An understanding of the activities in the bedrooms of the hospitals requires an analysis of the influence, if any, of the number of patients assigned to a room. Table 43-13 shows, of the total activities going on in bedrooms of a given size, the percentage that is devoted to each of the three major behavior categories. This table gives data for women only, since two of the wards studied were occupied only by women and one was predominantly women. Comparable data for male patients are not available, although a separate analysis of men and women in 1- and 2-bed rooms in the private hospital shows little difference in the distribution of activities.

Table 43-13 shows some marked and interesting trends. The proportion of isolated passive behavior clearly rises regularly with the size of the bedroom in each of the hospitals separately, with one minor reversal (Ward B, state hospital). The combined data for all hospitals show a rank-order correlation between bedroom size and proportion of isolated passive behavior of 0.60 and, for the private and city hospitals combined, of 1.00. Almost exactly the opposite

trend is seen for the total social category, which decreases regularly with bedroom size in the private and city hospitals and shows no trend either way in Ward B of the state hospital. In the case of Ward A, social behavior decreases markedly in the 12-bed room. The rank correlation of bedroom size and social activity is -1.00 for the private and city hospitals combined and -0.62 for all hospitals combined. Total active behavior shows no consistent relationship to room size.

The amount of use of the bedrooms, given in Table 43-14, shows, as expected, that the mean number of patients using the bedrooms increases regularly with the number of patients assigned to the rooms. This is true for each hospital separately and, with one reversal, for all hospitals combined, which show a rank-order correlation between bedroom size and mean number of occupants of 0.96. The rate of use of the bedrooms, however, does not show any consistent relationship to room size. That is, no one size bedroom seems to draw a proportionately higher percentage of its occupants than any other. Except for the underused rooms in Ward A of the state hospital, all bedrooms are occupied, on the average, by ⅕ to ⅓ of the patients assigned to them.

If we turn our attention only to bedrooms which are occupied, the mean number of patients in an occupied room increases regu-

Table 43-13 Distribution of Activities in Bedrooms as a Function of Bedroom Size (Females Only)[a]

Bedroom Size	Total Social				Total Active				Isolated Passive			
	Private	City	State A	State B	Private	City	State A	State B	Private	City	State A	State B
1 Bed	30		10	6	29		36	20	39		53	73
2 Beds	22				31				45			
3 Beds		17	14			14	25			67	60	
4 Beds	14				15				70			
6 Beds		12		6		14		16		73		77
8 Beds (in 20-bed ward)				8				19				71
12 beds (in 20-bed ward)			5				29				64	

[a] Numbers represent the percent of total behavior in each bedroom, for each hospital, traffic excluded. A blank cell indicates that no bedroom of that size existed on the ward.

Table 43-14 Use of Bedroom as a Function of Bedroom Size

Bedroom Size	All Bedrooms								Occupied Bedrooms			
	Mean number of patients in bedrooms				% of patients assigned to each bedroom				Mean number of patients in occupied bedrooms			
			State				State				State	
	Private	City	A	B	Private	City	A	B	Private	City	A	B
1 Bed	0.33		0.12	0.25	0.33		0.12	0.25	1.08		1.03	1.02
2 Beds	0.44				0.22				1.19			
3 Beds		0.54	0.65			0.18	0.22			1.17	1.43	
4 Beds	0.81				0.20				1.46			
6 Beds		1.92		1.58		0.34		0.27		2.32		1.89
8 Beds in (20-bed room)				2.63				0.33				>3
12 beds in (20-bed room)			1.46				0.12				>2	

larly with room size also. However, the actual number of patients in each room is remarkably low. It is only in bedrooms with six or more patients that the probability of finding more than one patient in an occupied room is greater than the probability of finding only one. For all smaller occupied rooms, the most probable number of patients in an occupied room is one. Combining Tables 43-13 and 43-14, we can compare the number of patients in the bedrooms with the distribution of activities in these rooms. Table 43-15 shows that, in all three hospitals combined, the mean number of patients in 1-, 2-, and 3-bed rooms is 1.2, and in 4-, 6-, 8-, and 12-bed rooms it is more than 2.1. This increase in room occupants is accompanied by a decrease in social activity from 17 percent to 9 percent and a rise in isolated passive behavior from 56 percent to 71 percent.

The overall effect of bedroom size, then, is quite clear. For all bedrooms isolated passive is the most frequent behavior, although in the single rooms of the private hospital this difference almost disappears. Furthermore, as the number of patients in the room increases, isolated passive behavior assumes an increasingly large proportion of the total activity in the bedroom, while the other categories, especially social, correspondingly decrease. Table 43-15 can be thought of as contrasting two hypothetical hospitals, one with only 1-, 2-, and 3-bed rooms and the other with only 4- to 12-bed rooms. In the first hospital, 56 percent of the bedroom activity is isolated passive and in the second 71 percent is isolated passive. This results, on the basis of the average amount of use of the bedrooms, in a difference of approximately 6 percent in the total isolated passive behavior on the ward. If we add to this an equivalent difference of 6 percent on hypothetical policy differences between the wards, we would expect either a 12 percent difference in total isolated passive

Table 43-15 Distribution of Activities as a Function of Number of Patients in Occupied Bedrooms (three hospitals combined)

Number of patients assigned to bedroom	Number of patients in occupied bedrooms	% of activity in bedrooms devoted to each category of behavior (mean of means)		
		Total Social	Total Active	Isolated Passive
1, 2, 3	1.2	17	25	56
4, 6, 8, 12	>2.1	9	19	71

behavior, or no difference, depending on the direction of the policy differences.

If this reasoning is correct, it becomes interesting to compare the proportion of isolated passive behavior in the private hospital (in which most patients were in 1- and 2-bed rooms) with that of the city and state hospitals (in which most patients were in larger rooms). In the city hospital 16 percent, and in Ward B of the state hospital 13 percent, more patients were engaged in isolated passive behavior than in the private hospital. On Ward A only 2 percent more engaged in isolated passive behavior.

It becomes at least reasonable, therefore, to suggest that the differences in total isolated passive behavior observed in the wards we studied are due to a combination of factors. Roughly one-half of the differences can be attributed to the architectural design of the hospital—in particular, the distribution of patients in the bedrooms—and the other half to some nonstructural differences either in administration, in types of patients, or in other factors. We have already, for example, commented on the policy differences between Wards A and B.

City Hospital: The Effect of Change in Solarium Furnishings

As reported earlier, the female ward of the city hospital was mapped a second time after an interval of two months. In the intervening period, two major changes took place —one change planned by the experimenters and one unpredicted change in hospital policy. Each produced effects on the ward that can be examined separately.

The change in hospital policy resulted in an increased census in the adjacent male ward. Although it was occupied by only 16 patients during the initial mapping of the female ward, by the second mapping the male ward had 24 patients. The census for the female ward was 25 for the first mapping and 24 for the second. The general effect of the increased male census was to increase the level of activity on both wards and, in particular, to increase the amount of visiting between the two wards by an amount considerably in excess of the increase in the census. In the second mapping,

three times as many male patients visited the female ward as were found there during the initial mapping. Similarly, the percentage of patients off the female ward rose from 21.5 percent to 32.5 percent. This increase presumably represented female patients who were visiting on the male ward.

If we look at the distribution of activity on the ward in Table 43-9, we see that the drop in the number of women on the ward is almost entirely accounted for by a corresponding drop in the level of social activity. This finding seems reasonable, if we assume that the women who went to the men's ward are likely to be those more interested in social activities. Except for the increased number of patients off the ward and the decreased general level of social activity on the ward, the distributions of activities in the two mappings are virtually identical.

The distribution of activities in the public rooms on the ward changed in important ways from the initial to the second mapping, and it seems most reasonable to attribute these changes to the alterations made in the furnishings of the solarium. The most notable difference is that the solarium's share of total activity occurring in all public rooms increased from 25 percent to 42 percent, while the percentage of activities occurring in the dayroom dropped from 48 to 41 and in the corridor from 27 to 17 percent. After the change, the solarium was clearly more popular with the patients, relative to the other public areas, than it had been before.

An examination of the distribution of the various categories of behavior among the public areas shows that the increased popularity of the solarium was reflected in an increase in its share of all three. Table 43-16 shows that before the change the solarium's share of total social behavior in all public areas was 15 percent. It increased to 27 percent after the change, and the proportion of social behavior occurring in the dayroom and corridor decreased. Similarly, before the change the solarium had 33 percent of all active behavior in public areas, but it had 55 percent after the change. This increase is largely accounted for by a drop of from 28 to 11 percent in the dayroom's share of active behavior; in the corridor,

Table 43-16 Distribution of Activities among Public Rooms in City Hospital before and after Changes in Solarium[a]

	Solar-ium	Day-room	Cor-ridor
Total social behavior			
Before	15	68	17
After	27	61	12
Total active behavior			
Before	33	28	39
After	55	11	34
Isolated passive behavior			
Before	32	36	32
After	49	46	5
Total behavior (without traffic)			
Before	25	48	27
After	42	41	17

[a] Numbers represent the percent of total activity in all public rooms for each activity category.

Table 43-17 Distribution of Activities within Public Rooms of City Hospital before and after Changes in Solarium[a]

	Total Social	Total Active	Isolated Passive
Solarium			
Before	28	32	40
After	24	40	36
Dayroom			
Before	63	14	23
After	56	8	36
Corridor			
Before	28	35	37
After	28	63	9
All public rooms			
Before	45	24	31
After	38	31	31

[a] Numbers represent the percent of total activity within each room.

active behavior dropped only from 39 to 34 percent. The distribution of isolated passive behavior showed the most marked shift; it increased in both the solarium and the dayroom but almost disappeared from the corridor, where it dropped from 32 to 5 percent. It is clear that what occurred was not merely an increase in the solarium's share of behavior with proportional drops in the other public areas, but rather a marked alteration of the entire patterning of activities among the public areas.

The distribution of activities within each public area also changed from the initial to the second mapping, as is seen in Table 43-17. All public rooms combined showed a small increase in the proportion of active behavior, from 24 to 31 percent, and a corresponding drop in social behavior from 45 to 38 percent; isolated passive behavior remained constant at 31 percent. Within each individual public area quite different changes took place, however. The distribution of activities in the solarium remained most constant, the largest shift was an increase of active behavior from 32 to 40 percent. The major changes took place in the other areas. In the dayroom the proportion of isolated passive behavior rose from 23 to 36 percent, and there were attendant drops in the other categories. In the corridor the effect was the opposite: isolated passive

behavior dropped from 37 to 9 percent, while social behavior remained constant and active behavior rose from 35 to 63 percent. Clearly, the changes introduced in the solarium had their most marked effect on the distribution of behavior within the other public areas.

DISCUSSION

It is clear from these results that certain regularities in the data permit us to make some empirical generalizations that, though necessarily tentative, may have some value. The first of these empirical generalizations has to do with the distribution of activities in space, and the second, with the stability of this distribution.

Peaking and *dipping* have proved to be useful terms for describing patterns of activities that are characteristic of those found on the ward. *Peaking* is a marked predominance of a particular category of behavior in a particular location, and *dipping* is a pronounced scarcity of an activity. We can arbitrarily define a peak as a level of an activity that exceeds the level of the next most popular activity by at least 50 percent and a dip as a level of an activity that is no greater than 50 percent of the activity next highest in popularity. These terms will prove useful in characterizing the qualitative nature of the distribution of activities in particular situations and in distinguishing one distribution from another. It should be noted that traffic, which consistently runs between 2 and 4 percent of the total activity on all wards studied, is omitted from these general descriptions.

Looking at the three hospitals in relation to each other, certain differences become apparent. They are best summarized in Table 43-12. In the private hospital, the total activity on the ward shows a remarkable evenness of distribution over the three summary categories. In contrast, in the city hospital, there is peaking of isolated passive behavior. At the same time, although it is not explicitly shown in Table 43-12, there is a marked dipping of visiting. An absence of visitors and a tendency to do nothing are the characteristics, then, that distinguish the city hospital from the private hospital.

The state hospital shows a somewhat more varied picture. First, it will be remembered that visiting was virtually nonexistent on the ward; in this respect, both state wards resemble the city hospital and differ from the private. Also like the city hospital, Ward B shows peaking of isolated passive behavior, but it approaches a dip in social behavior and in this way differs from all other wards studied. Ward A shows a very even distribution over the three categories and in this respect resembles the private hospital. In the private hospital, however, the level of isolated passive behavior is approximately two-thirds that of the other categories, while in Ward A isolated passive is about 25 percent greater than the others. Even Ward A, therefore, tends to favor isolated passive behavior, when it is compared to the private hospital.

Bedrooms and public rooms considered separately differ from these overall patterns. All bedrooms of all hospitals, with the exception of the single rooms in the private hospital, show peaking of isolated passive behavior. Bedrooms in the private and city hospitals show even distribution of the other two major categories, but bedrooms of the state hospital show a dip in social behavior. Differences between hospitals and between bedroom sizes within this overall pattern are quantitative—they show in the magni-

tude of the peaks and dips rather than in the qualitative nature of the distribution. The public rooms show a different pattern. In the city and state hospitals, the distribution of activities is even over all three categories (although there is some tendency toward peaking of active behavior in Ward B), but in sharp contrast, those in the private hospital show marked dipping of isolated passive behavior.

We can, then, briefly describe the distribution of activities in the wards we have studied in the following way: in the bedrooms, marked peaking of isolated passive behavior, except in the single rooms of the private hospital, and dipping of social behavior in the state hospital; in the public rooms, even distribution in the city and state hospitals and marked dipping of isolated passive behavior in the private hospital; and finally, for total activity, even distribution in the private hospital and peaking of isolated passive in the city and state hospitals. Within these major generalizations are many subdistributions that are characteristic of particular situations within each institution.

Once we identify characteristic distributions of activities, the question of their stability necessarily arises. To what extent do these patterns persist over time and circumstances? As we have seen in the Results section, our wards have been mapped over intervals as short as a time of day and a day of the week and as long as several months and even several years. The overall picture shows remarkable stability. Both mappings of the private hospital, which were separated by almost three years, show the qualitative distributions described above, though with quantitative fluctuations. The overall distribution is even in both mappings. The bedrooms in both mappings show the characteristic peak of isolated passive, and the public rooms show in both cases the characteristic dip of isolated passive. Similarly, in both mappings of the city hospital, the bedrooms show the marked peaking of isolated passive behavior, and the public rooms an even distribution, in spite of considerable changes in hospital policy during the intervening time. The only difference between the first and second mappings of the city hospital occurs in the single category of total overall social behavior in the first mapping. Here the uncharacteristically high figure has already been accounted for in terms of hospital policy. With this one exception, the two maps of activity are also virtually identical. Both hospitals thus show a very high degree of stability, both within themselves and in relation to each other over fairly long periods of time. No comparable data are available for the state hospital.

When we look at shorter time intervals, there is a fluctuation within the patterns. We have already seen that the patterns for nonvisiting days are identical with each other, but different from those on visiting days. Weekday patterns in general also differ somewhat from weekend patterns. These differences all reflect objective considerations and thus lend further credence to the evidence that patterns of behavior on the ward are indeed rather stable.

Patterns over the course of one day, however, do not exhibit the stability shown over longer periods of time. We have seen that characteristic distributions of activity differ in the morning, afternoon, and evening and from hospital to hospital. One must say, therefore, that the distribution of behavior on the ward is unstable over the course of the day. Changes over the course of the day are not evenly distributed over all categories, so that some forms of behavior show remarkable constancy within the generally fluctuating pattern.

This emphasis on stability, however, must not be allowed to overshadow the large and important changes that occur constantly on the wards we have studied. In a very real sense, change is the order of the day. This is most dramatically illustrated by the changes in the city hospital over the course of the two months between our mappings. We have already seen that a combination of design changes on the ward and policy changes made off the ward produced marked alterations in the patterns of the use of space both on the ward and off. We have also seen that a design change in one area of the ward affected the distribution of behavior in all parts of the ward. Less dramatic but still interesting changes were brought about over a period of years in the private hospital, presumably as a consequence of rather subtle changes in the patient population and other changes in administrative policy with respect to the assignment of patients to the four floors.

It is clear that change can be brought about from a variety of directions. Changes in the individuals on the ward, both patients and staff, can result in different patterns of behavior and different uses of the various spaces and facilities. Quite clearly, changes in administrative policy can have a major impact on the way the ward is utilized, as we have seen in some detail in comparing Wards A and B of the state hospital. Finally, changes in the physical design of the ward can bring about major changes in the kinds of behaviors taking place on the ward as well as in the distribution of these behaviors within the various areas of the ward. We cannot avoid noting that these findings have implications for planning changes in the hospitals. Since change can be brought about from many directions, it would seem most appropriate, in each case, to determine the best and most appropriate mode for introducing a desired change. Informal observation of the hospitals has produced examples in which change was attempted through alterations in physical design that might much more readily have been accomplished through administrative changes, and, conversely, other examples in which administrative attempts to improve the wards were negated by the physical facilities. Our own attempts to introduce changes through minor alterations of physical design illustrate the complexity of the problem and the need for careful study of the process involved in introducing planned modifications.

The study of change on the ward provides some insight into the factors that produce the rather stable patterns of behavior that seem to be characteristic of the facilities we have studied. People, policies, and partitions—it is tempting to say that these are the three great determinants of behavior on the ward. Who is on the ward? Under what set of guiding principles do they operate? And within what physical constraints and opportunities? We have looked at each of these questions in varying detail, although we have not exhausted them. The diverse backgrounds and experiences of the patients in the three hospitals may account for some of the differences in the use of space, but the possible contribution of individual differences and personal styles in relation to the physical world remains to be studied.

We have seen that administrative policy exerts its influence in many specific ways. Visiting is allowed only on Tuesday and Thursday. Visiting in the city hospital is not allowed in the bedrooms. Use of bedrooms is sharply curtailed. The census on an adjoining ward is changed. Each of these administrative decisions and others affect the distribution of activities on the ward. Our studies have only hinted at the effect of more basic kinds of policy decisions involving such issues as patient-to-staff ratios, staff salaries, and approaches toward treatment. We can only speculate that considerations of this sort may underlie in part the differences among our three hospitals. The role of the physical facilities and their design is clearly indicated, most notably in the bedrooms and in the planned changes in the solarium of the city hospital, but also, by implication, throughout many of the findings concerning the patterning of activities in the various areas of the ward. People, policies, and partitions clearly do affect patterns of behavior. At the same time, however, it would probably be a gross oversimplification to think of them as three sets of "independent variables," which, when manipulated properly, produce a given set of activities on the ward.

The complex pattern of causal relationships on the ward can perhaps be made clear by a brief examination of some of the factors involved in determining a patient's choice of a particular behavior on the ward. Some indication of the range of choice open to a patient in a given location on the ward can be suggested by the pattern of activities characteristic of that location. Where marked peaking occurs, we can assume that the participants exercise very little choice in their activities and, for reasons that may not be at all clear, are constrained to act in

a particular way. Similarly, in areas characterized by a marked dip in a particular behavior, the participants are constrained to avoid that activity, so that their range of choice is again limited. The widest range of individual choice can be assumed to occur in situations where the entire range of possible behaviors is evenly represented.

The way the patients use their bedrooms, when looked at in light of these assumptions, proves especially interesting. The number of patients using a bedroom at any given time increases more or less proportionately with the number assigned to the room. It is only in six-bed and larger rooms, however, that more than one patient is likely to occupy the room at a given time. In smaller rooms, the most probable number of occupants is one. Insofar as possible, the patients seem to treat all bedrooms, regardless of size, as if they were single rooms. Their remarkable success in achieving this goal suggests a tacit arrangement among them to leave each other alone in the bedrooms. Whether this represents a mutual respect for each other's privacy, the dominance of one patient, who stakes out the room as his territory, or some other social process cannot be determined from our data.

A look at the distribution of activities within the room reveals differences between the one-, two-, and three-bed rooms and the larger rooms. In small rooms, the activities are more evenly distributed over the range of possible activities, although social activity is relatively more frequent and isolated passive relatively less frequent. The patient in the smaller room seems to experience the entire range of possible behaviors as open to him, to feel free to choose from the whole range of options, and in fact to choose more or less equally from among all possibilities. This is most dramatically shown in the single rooms of the private hospital, where behavior is equally distributed over all possible behaviors.

In contrast, the patient in the larger rooms is far more likely to be engaged in isolated passive behavior than in anything else; he spends from two-thirds to three-fourths of this time in his room lying on his bed, either asleep or awake. He seems to see the range of options from which he can choose as severely limited and to be constrained to choose isolated passive behavior over any other. The small room thus appears to provide the patient with wide freedom of choice in what he does in his room, while the large, multiple-occupancy room limits freedom of choice and almost forces him into isolated passive behavior.

These patterns of activity in one-, two-, and three-bed rooms, as opposed to larger rooms, together with the data on occupancy rates, suggest the need for a reconsideration of the concept of privacy in the psychiatric ward. Privacy has most generally been looked upon as the physical isolation of one individual from others. There is a wide range of individual, cultural, and situational differences, however, in the activities that can be carried out in the presence of others and those that can be done only "in private." These diverse conditions can be conceptualized in a single framework by recognizing that there are functional equivalents of privacy that do not necessarily involve physical separation. In this context, the pattern of activity in the bedrooms would suggest that the functional meaning of privacy is not "being alone," but rather having the widest range of personal choice. The small room (ideally, from our data, the single room) provides this range of options, of which being alone is only one.

The sense of privacy experienced by a particular patient, therefore, is a complex product of many interrelated factors. The individual's own definition of what behaviors are allowable in a particular situation is itself a product of individual and cultural history. This personal definition of available options is directly confronted by formally and informally communicated rules and norms, as well as by the immediate response of others to his behavior. All of this operates in a context of environmental constraints, which themselves are a complex product of the physical facilities and the rules for their use. The precious personal sense of privacy thus both defines and is defined by the perceived range of choices open to the individual in a continually varying feedback process.

44 The Sociology of Time and Space in an Obstetrical Hospital

William R. Rosengren and Spencer DeVault

Duncan and Schnore (1959) recently argued that studies of social organization seem increasingly to stem from either a cultural or a behavioral perspective, with a corresponding dearth of investigations from a distinctly ecological or morphological point of view. This trend appears to be true not only of studies of the organization of communities but of investigations of particular social establishments as well. In this sense, therefore, there are numerous reports of the behavioral and cultural aspects of general and mental hospitals, of various industrial organizations, of government agencies, and so forth. Furthermore, sociological studies of the organization of social establishments seem increasingly to focus upon informal patterns of behavior in so far as clique structures, differences in channels of communications, incongruous and unmet role expectancies, and differences in values and meanings converge or fail to converge with the officially prescribed goals and procedures of the establishment. This suggests that in many ways the "cultural" and "behavioral" perspectives typically are joined to form an interpersonal model from which the analysis of organizational activity then proceeds. Implied here is that investigators are forced to choose between *either* an ecological *or* a culture-behavior approach to social organization.

In his discussion of cultural ecology, Steward (1955) eschews such an "either-or" point of view. He suggests that although the cultural system may in many ways affect the manner in which the ecological environment acquires meaning and is put to use, the

Reprinted with permission of The Macmillan Company from *The Hospital in Modern Society* edited by Eliot Freidson. © The Free Press of Glencoe, a Division of the Macmillan Company, 1963.

environment does itself limit the uses to which it can be put. Just as a "rice culture" is not feasible in a geography of timberline, so too one might suspect that norms of subordination-superordination are contingent upon compatible physical settings.

We suggest, then, three possible general models for the analysis of either a community or a social establishment. A model in which: (1) the ecological or physical setting is regarded as the prime factor in the social behavior taking place in it; (2) the behavior system of a community or an organization manipulates the environment to conform to the norms of the participants; (3) the normative patterns are only compatible with—limiting and limited by—the facts of the physical setting. In other words, in model (1) persons are "used" by the setting; in (2) the environment is "used" by the persons acting in it; in (3) neither personal conduct is changed substantially because of the setting, nor is the setting and its existing limits circumvented to any great extent by the participants. Rather, each exists in a condition of unstable equilibrium or minimal accommodation. In urban ecology, for example, luxury apartments (and their attendant way of life) are seldom found in the light-industry region of the city. Also, the persons involved in such a way of life often do not wish to live there. Similarly, the suburbs are seldom dominated by steel mills, and industrialists often do not want to set up factories in such an environment. In both instances, therefore, not only is the way of life dependent upon the ecology of the place but the stability of the ecological pattern is dependent upon the presence of a compatible way of life as well. Each adapts to, and is adapted by, the other. In yet another sense, however, certain places are less clearly defined in their relation to ecological and normative compatibility. We might refer to the "rurban fringe" in which we sometimes find a condition of accommodation between urbanism and ruralism as ways of life. Here the relations between the ecology and the social organization are less precise. Neither the environment fully articulates the normative system, nor does the normative system fully adapt the environment. We may look here for a condi-

tion of unstable equilibrium inasmuch as the culture-behavioral system exists within the context of a relatively unfriendly ecological setting, and under which the environment is continually being insulted by the normative pattern.

By way of introduction, we persist in our conviction that one need not make a choice between *either* an ecological approach *or* a behavioral approach. Rather, we think that observations might best proceed jointly from three perspectives: the possible independence of the ecological complex, the possible independence of the normative system, and the possibility of a state of unstable adjustment between the two. The last, we suggest, is a major contributing factor to the emergence of "informal organization" and "patterned deviations" in social establishments as well as in communities.

The term "ecology" has thus far remained undefined. Hawley (1950) regards ecology as "the study of the morphology of collective life in both its static and dynamic aspects" —an approach that points to the basic and cogent nature of viewing social behavior in terms of both spatial and temporal dimensions. From such a perspective a few studies have emerged showing a concern with ecological processes in organizational life. Rose Laub Coser (1958), for example, studied spatial patterns in relation to decision-making processes in two wards of a general hospital. Freidson (1960) has discussed the location of patients in different referral systems in relation to practitioner controls. Wilson (1954) has illustrated the importance of tempo and timing in the organization of the surgical team, and Mack (1954) has pointed out that the patterns of ethnic segregation characteristic of the larger community tended to be duplicated within a specific industrial establishment. As we have suggested, none the less, the study of social establishments has focused more upon the adaptation of the environment to the norms shared by the participants than upon mutual interactions.

Our purpose is to describe some aspects of the social organization of an obstetrical hospital from an ecological viewpoint rather than from an interpersonal model. More specifically, our aim is to suggest the ways in which both the cultural and the behavioral processes in one social establishment seem to be, in part at least, functionally associated with its social morphology.

THE HOSPITAL SETTING

The observations that formed the basis for this essay were made in a large lying-in hospital in an eastern metropolitan area. In addition to providing obstetrical services for the patients of privately practicing obstetricians, the hospital also has an active clinic service with its own staff. In 1958 the hospital ranked fifth in the nation for the number of deliveries that took place in it— more than 8,000. As might well be expected, the clinic service clientele is drawn mainly from the lower socioeconomic groups in the community, with an overrepresentation of ethnically distinct persons—chiefly Italian and Portuguese. Prenatal care of the clinic patients takes place in the hospital. The private patients are seen in the obstetricians' offices in the city, but both clinic and private patients share a common delivery service.

In a four-month period we spent some 150 hours observing in this delivery service. This was done in connection with two independent studies of social psychological factors in pregnancy.[1] We had numerous contacts with the interns and residents in the service for more than a year before we began to make our observations. As a result of these earlier meetings, an adequate rapport seemed to exist. Our procedures were simple. On the days (or nights) on which we came to the hospital, we were provided with a room in the residents' quarters, and supplied with hospital uniforms, caps, masks, and insulated shoes. We then observed all the activities of the service, talked informally with the staff during coffee breaks, while relaxing in the lounges, and

in the work situations. During the first two or three evenings, the most pronounced obstacle to both accurate observation and acceptance by the personnel was the fact that from their point of view we had neither legitimate status nor meaningful roles in the hospital. Simply, people wondered what we were doing there and how they should relate themselves to us. Initially, many of the personnel—particularly the staff nurses— seemed to think that we were new externs (medical students). And perhaps because of this we were occasionally called upon by the nurses to assist in a subordinate fashion with some of the minor tasks preparatory to delivery. Others seemed to feel that we were "inspectors" from the National Institute of Neurological Diseases and Blindness.[2] For ourselves, we remained mum on the issue. The first definition of us by the staff gave us meaningful roles but no status. The second gave us legitimate status but no meaningful role. As observers, therefore, we were caught up in an almost ideal contradiction of status and role. The dilemma was gradually resolved: First we were given a kind of status, primarily by being allowed to observe high-status private obstetricians and their patients. We were then provided with a meaningful role, from the point of view of the obstetrical team, by helping them with some of the observations and recordings required by the National Collaborative Study, which the team members found burdensome to do themselves.

All our observations were independently recorded when time permitted, with both of us working from a general outline of factors for which to search. We both recorded the typical field-note type of material, and we compared them after each observational experience. Our original purpose was not that of posing questions about the social organization of the delivery service. As time went on, however, we were increasingly impressed that the behavior of the

[1] One is a study entitled "Socio-Cultural Factors Affecting the Behavior of Expectant Mothers," under a grant from the Association for the Aid of Crippled Children, New York. The other is entitled "A Psychological Study of Emotional Factors in Pregnancy," under a grant from the U.S. Public Health Service. It is under the direction of Dr. Anthony Davids of Brown University and the E. P. Bradley Hospital.

[2] The hospital in which these observations were made is one of sixteen throughout the country that are participating in a long-range medical investigation of birth defects. Part of the research procedure involves maintaining detailed accounts of each delivery as it takes place. We helped in the completion of these records.

personnel seemed to differ markedly, depending upon where it took place and in what sequence. Although we did not set out to make an informal study of the social morphology of the obstetrical hospital, we were eventually convinced that the ecological organization we observed was intimately in exchange with many of the salient social processes of the hospital. For example, the structures of both time and space appeared more and more to serve to delineate status and define roles. Whereas most studies of medical settings persist at the level of status and role, we became more interested in the relations between status and role and the morphological structures that underlay the conduct we observed. We found it improper, for example, to speak only of the "doctor-nurse" relationship without specifying where those two persons interacted and when. Inadvertently, as it were, the notion of the importance of the physical setting was in some sense thrust upon us. We began, therefore, to focus what we saw and heard more specifically in terms of time and space associations.

SPATIAL AND TEMPORAL ASPECTS

Following these initial leads, we found it useful to consider our experiences under these general rubrics:

1. The *spatial* distribution of activities in the delivery service in so far as certain regions appeared to be set aside for particular modes of behavior and attitudes—staff to staff and staff to patients. That is, it became increasingly clear that both attitudes and overt behavior of the several functionaries in the service—patients, nurses, and doctors—varied, depending upon the particular place in which they might be found.

2. The *segregation* of behaviors, one from the other, in so far as persons occupying the same status appeared to behave differently in different places, depending upon the ecological factors involved in each place —its position in temporal sequences, its physical symbols, and the ways in which each place was physically separated from other places. In other words, the differences in behavior that were noted to be dependent upon particular areas were not fully a func-

tion of purposive choice on the part of either the personnel or the patients, but they were both sanctioned by the normative system and elicited by the nature of the physical settings themselves. In addition, what was actually at stake here was the association between the morphology of the service and the patterning of status relationships among the personnel.

3. The *rhythm* of activities—the periodicity with which events took place to the extent that the behavior of the personnel was organized and patterned in terms of regularities of occurrence.

4. The *tempo of activities*—the number of events, both social and physiological, that occurred within any given unit of time. Important here is the fact that the temporal organization of the hospital was, in part, a function of the continual imperfect balance between the physiological and functional organization of activities.

5. The *timing* of activities—the coordination of separate and diverse pulsations— both physiological and functional—in so far as different rhythms and tempos were taking place at the same time. It was by means of timing sequences, therefore, that temporal organization could actually take place.[3]

Although these were the main ecological factors guiding our observations, their importance is not that they constituted a kind of taxonomy, but rather that they provided a kind of base line from which to look for interrelationships.

Distribution and Segregation of Activities: Barriers and Atmospheres

The obstetrical service is schematically represented in Figure 44-1. The two places of greatest spatial segregation are the clinic examination rooms and the delivery service itself. The clinic is located in a wing completely separate from the delivery service. Thus, the patient has no contact with the delivery service until the day of delivery arrives, except in the case of some private patients who are given a "tour" of the service during their prenatal care. For most patients,

[3] These conceptions of ecological processes are from Hawley (1950).

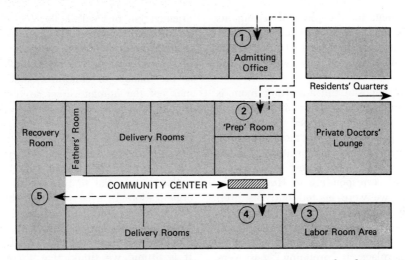

Figure 44–1. Map of the obstetrical service. Arrows indicate route taken by patients.

however, the transition from the prenatal area to that of the delivery service represents—both spatially and symbolically—their retirement from one world and their entrance into a totally new and different world, with a corresponding spatially enforced change in self-image.

More than that, each region in the service is itself set apart in several ways from the others. This segregation appears to be accomplished not only by space but also by rules of dress, of expected behavior, and of decorum—all of which serve to indicate the dissimilarity of each place, as well as to present an image of the place that might cast both patients and staff into desired roles with respect to one another.

First, the residents' quarters are separated from the other parts of the service by a long corridor and heavy doors. The general atmosphere here is not unlike that of a modern motel—comfortable but austere and suggestive of the fact that people never really settle down here, as indeed the residents do not. This region is the temporary retreat for the residents and interns, but allows little means by which those who have gone before may be remembered by those currently in residence. By the very spatial location and physical trappings of the place, the occupants are in some sense depersonalized, and this fact is generally in keeping with both the residents' comparatively low status and the rather diffuse roles that they

enact. In large part, the residents' quarters serve, in Goffman's (1959) terms, as their backstage area—a notion to which we shall return. And it is backstage to the extent that it is here the interns and residents may enact among their own kind the informal roles that attach to their formal status as hospital staff members. As a backstage area it is less than complete because the lounge area is bordered on one side by a small laboratory and on the other by a library. These rooms serve to remind the residents that they are in the hospital chiefly as the occupants of a formal work-role and not really as persons. Moreover, there is a rather massive "scoreboard" on which is noted essential information about deliveries taking place in the service during the past twenty-four hours. Thus tempo, timing, and rhythm also invade the residents' backstage area to reassert the *raison d'être* for their presence at the hospital and to modulate the effect of the spatial segregation of the quarters.

The admitting office is just beyond the residents' quarters. Significantly, perhaps, here there are no barriers of any kind—not even doors—almost as a symbol of welcome to the incoming patient. A mood of friendly casualness characterizes the behavior of the admitting room staff, and it is here where the staff is most casual in regard to decorum in both attitudes and dress. This is consistent with the function of the admitting office as the intermediary stage in the hospitalization of the patient, for the physical setting, its spatial location, and the behavior of personnel in it serve as a gradual introduction of the patient to the new world of the service.

Directly opposite the admitting room is the preparation or "prep" room where the incoming patient is stripped of her self-image as "person," and cast most effectively and promptly into her new status of "medical phenomenon." Of interest to us as observers and corresponding to Hughes's observation,[4] we were invited into the prep room only when it was occupied by an unmarried, lower-class Negro prostitute. Until that time we were told almost nothing of what took place in "prepping," nor were we told the names of those who worked there or their occupational status. Segregation of the prep room was accomplished not only by physical and symbolic barriers but also by an atmosphere of anonymity exceeded nowhere else in the service.

This aura of *mystique* surrounding the prep room does not seem to conform to the popular image of childbirth. Ordinarily modern hospital childbirth calls forth an image of immaculate lying-in rooms, urgently attentive doctors and nurses, the drama of birth, and subsequent visits by a proud father, friends, and relatives. The total reality is, of course, considerably more mundane. The organizational stages of delivery involve situations and tasks that must be performed and that do not conform to the common image. Indeed, every social establishment is faced with the need to accomplish certain tasks and to fulfill certain functions that are at odds with, inconsistent with, or otherwise in greater or lesser conflict with both the ultimate goals of the establishment and its own image and ideology. And it may well not be unique to this one obstetrical hospital that the distribution of such "deviant" functions occurs in the context not only of the status system of the

organization but within the ecological system as well. It is true, in any event, that it is in keeping with the professional image of the modern obstetrical hospital, as well as the folklore of childbirth, that the "climax" of the human career in the hospital should take place in the delivery room in which the miraculous and often dramatic birth takes place. But it is equally obvious that much else takes place—both before and after this single climax time and place—that is essential to the operation of the organization. In a larger sense, these other activities—prepping, labor, and recovery in particular—are the deviant but necessary functions of this particular establishment. It is fitting, we think, that these deviant activities should be accomplished in regions segregated both physically and symbolically from the rest of the service and that the overseers of these activities should be the lower-status personnel—nurses and student nurses in particular.

In the area of the labor rooms, one is isolated from the nurses in charge, and from the patients, by a sturdy shoulder-high and seemingly nonfunctional barricade. This not only segregates the patients from those who pass by but also symbolically segregates the attending nurses from others in the hospital. Perhaps implicit in this mode of segregation is the notion that the nurses are definitely "in charge" and that others in service have no authority beyond that point. Moreover, the area of the labor rooms in some sense corresponds to the residents' quarters in so far as it serves as the nurses' backstage area. Also, the physical barrier—serving to maintain status differences—seemed to us to be reinforced symbolically by the dim lighting and drab decor of the interior of the labor rooms. The staff was in agreement that the patients seemed to "behave better" while in labor under the quieting effect of the gray decor of the rooms. At the same time, here the nurse was most likely to conduct herself with most confidence in the role of the nurse in the presence of other personnel, and perhaps least like a nurse when interacting only with other nurses. From a slightly different perspective, both the physical and the symbolic segregation of the labor rooms may be understood to be a function of labor as a

---

[4] During an informal colloquium at the Department of Sociology and Anthropology at Brown University in December, 1957, Professor Hughes pointed out that the extent of both physical and symbolic "closeness" between staff and patients was related to the social status of the patient.

kind of "deviant" activity in the service. That is, there is none of the "highlighting" of the place or of the patients here to suggest that what takes place in the region is actually germane to the entire process.

Thus far we have discussed some of the regions of the service in terms of spatial and segregational aspects as if they had distinct boundaries. Of course, this is not true; if it were, it would suggest that moods, attitudes, and behaviors had discrete boundaries as well. It is more proper to speak of the overlapping of regional boundaries—a frame of reference that may account for the periodic times and occasional places where the behavior patterns among the staff are less clear and distinct than they are when one is observing well within a bounded area. This overlapping of boundaries could be seen most clearly in the hallways, where the regions of the labor rooms, the doctors' lounge, and the delivery rooms converge. For this area was ambiguous not only as to its spatial relationship to the several other distinct regions of which we have talked, but also with regard to the relationships between the functionaries in the service who interacted there. Doctors and nurses appeared to know quite clearly what the appropriate modes of interaction were between them when they were within one of the distinct regions, but this was less true in overlapping areas. The formalized aspects of doctor-nurse interaction seemed to break down here, and those persons tended to interact in a more spontaneous and less formalized fashion.

On one occasion, for example, an attending nurse rushed into this "interstitial" area, announced to a private obstetrician that a patient who had recently been ordered to the delivery room by the doctor should not have been so ordered, and insisted that the doctor return the patient to the labor room. A heated discussion ensued between the nurse and the doctor, and the outcome was that the patient was returned to the labor room. The tenor of the encounter was not that of a subordinate-superordinate relation, but rather that of a dispute between professional equals with a disregard for the possible impact the exchange might have upon the surrounding audience. The stresses and

conflicts among and between the doctors and nurses that were less manifest within a specific region became considerably more apparent in such "interstitial" areas. Whereas each particular functionary group in the service had, to a greater or lesser extent, its own backstage region, areas of overlap between distinct regions served more as the backstage place for interaction between functionaries.

The administrative nurses hold forth in the area of the delivery rooms. At this point —which is really the "community center" and the point of both physiological and social climax—we found it interesting to note that the projected image of the hospital and, consequently, the expected roles and attitudes of both staff and patient are cast most effectively by symbols—uniforms, stainless steel, medicines with their odors, brilliant lighting, and so forth.

The operating arena is just beyond the delivery room; it is segregated from the rest of the service by a wide red line painted wall to wall and ceiling to floor. No one without surgical cap, face mask, and insulated shoes is allowed beyond that point. During our first conducted tour of the service we entered that region without the required accoutrements—perhaps because we were not yet really considered a "part" of the scene.

Farther along this corridor, and perhaps significantly farthest from the community center, is the recovery room. This is a large, dimly lit room attended by one nurse. The functions here are also of the "deviant" variety. The mother is relegated here after delivery of the child, while the newborn is retained in the community center where much attention is paid to it by high-status personnel—obstetricians and pediatricians. This spatial indication of the importance of the child is reinforced by timing sequences, and the value placed on the child may, in fact, account for the emphasis that is placed upon administering anesthesia. Without anesthesia the patient may become troublesome to the obstetrical team, and their reassuring and comforting gestures toward the patient often give way to irritability.

A further mode of segregation indicative of status differences seemed to relate to having delivery-room doors open or closed. Never in our experience was a delivery-room door closed when a clinic patient was there, but this frequently happened with private patients, thus limiting access to the place of climax.

The "fathers' room" is adjacent to the recovery room—unattended and suggestive that the father is regarded as the least important person in the process. By its sparseness of furnishing, its physical isolation, and its small size, this room seemed to communicate symbolically the idea that the fathers are unnecessary and functionally peripheral.

The lounge for the private obstetricians is immediately adjacent to the labor rooms and near the center of communication. It is segregated from the rest of the service both by soundproofing and by doors without windows. The lounge is tastefully and discreetly decorated and suggests many personal touches left by some of the private obstetricians. The anonymity of the residents' quarters is absent, and in further contrast the work-role symbols of library, laboratory, and scoreboard are absent. Lastly, and consistent with the comparative high status of the private doctors, this lounge permits the doctors to come and go with little chance of being observed by others in the service. The interns and externs from the clinic service are free to use the private lounge whenever they desire, but they seldom do so unless they are called "to scrub" with a private obstetrician. Implied here is the question of relations between normative and ecological systems. One might say that the failure of the interns to use the lounge is a function of the understood status differences between themselves and the "pros." On the other hand, such a pattern may be a function of the spatial and symbolic separation of the lounge from other parts of the service. More likely, perhaps, it is a mutual effect of both, inasmuch as the interns use it under certain specified conditions and not under others.

In general, it would appear that the behavior in each of the several regions in the service is at least partially a function of the kinds of spatial, symbolic, and physical segregation that set each region apart from others. Each functionary in the establish-

ment has, to a greater or lesser degree, an area of "front-staging" and "back-staging." But the extent of available backstage area appears to be related to status. The higher the status of the personnel (the private doctors), the greater is the availability of a "pure" backstage area; the lower the status (the student nurses), the least available is the backstage region. Although the spatial distribution and segregation do not actually determine the formal and informal status systems in the service, they do lend a distinctive idiom to relationships among the staff and to their demeanor toward the patients.

In terms of spatial patterns, it would appear that the extent of spatial segregation relates to the value placed upon the activities in the region relative to the "business" or "goals" of the establishment. That is, those areas that are most dispensable with regard to the delivery of babies are those that are spatially most apart from the community center. Physical segregation, on the other hand, seemed to be most related to status differences among the staff members—doors, walls, counters, and the like. Finally, symbolic forms of segregation between regions appeared to us to be most related to the communication of organizationally appropriate attitudes and values—colors, odors, lighting, signs, and so forth. Whereas physical segregation served in some sense to declare gradations in status, symbolic forms of segregation appeared more to articulate roles. Such associations may appear quite clear in most instances, but they are less clear in others. This is consistent with our earlier position that mutually interdependent contingencies exist between the dominance of ecology on the one hand, and the dominance of the behavior norms on the other.

For example, the relation of status to anonymity is exemplified by the fact that the staff, when talking among themselves about patients, most often refer to the clinic patients by name. With the private patients, however, a perhaps implicit shield of anonymity is erected, for they are referred to by room number.

From a similar perspective, differential behavior of the nurses toward the doctors, interns, and student externs was noted by place—generally depending upon whether the patient could hear what was being said. In the presence of the wakeful patient, the nurses tended to refer to the student externs respectfully as "Dr." even though they do not hold the M.D. degree. This form of address functions not only to maintain patient confidence in those who are caring for her but also to maintain the self-image of the nurse as one who "takes orders only from superiors." In the delivery room, with the patient under anesthesia, the demeanor of the nurses toward the younger interns and externs frequently changed to giving orders and calling by last name only.

Differential expression of humor seemed also to be graded by status. The doctor heading the obstetrical team expressed the greatest amount of tension release through humor, going gradually down to the student nurses who were the most sober and serious members of the team. In some sense, therefore, the higher-status personnel could "backstage" in regions where low-status personnel could not. This seemed to be less true, however, with patients of extremely low social status. Here the expression of humor was more often diffused through the entire team.

Rhythm: The Contingent Nature of the Role of the Patient

An important factor in establishing rhythmic patterns of behavior in the hospital is the fact that the patient is potentially both "ill" and "not ill." Pregnancy does not necessarily entail abnormal complications, but that possibility always exists. Because of this the demeanor of the doctors and nurses takes on a studied casualness about childbirth— but always with a watchful eye toward unforeseen difficulties. This was most pronounced when the team included student externs. The students were always more oriented toward complications and pathology in labor and delivery than were the resident doctors. As a consequence, perhaps, a modulated kind of crisis seemed always to exist on the service. In cases where no complications were medically indicated, an atmosphere of general apprehension pervaded the team—particularly during delivery. In cases

with possible imminent complications, the members of the team seemed to be considerably more at ease, tension lessened, and they appeared more able to set about their tasks in a more relaxed and workmanlike fashion. To the students, the latter situations were those in which they were actually "learning something."

As in most hospitals, the nurses and doctors refer to the complaining and excitable patients as "crocks." This most frequently meant that the patient was demanding too much sedation while in labor. The term "crock" was often applied by the residents to the patients of private obstetricians, but it was also used to refer to clinic patients under their care as well. The clinic-patient "crock" was regarded as a drug addict. The private-patient "crock," on the other hand, was usually regarded as having been "pampered." In terms of rhythm, however, the clinic crock is simply disturbing the usual periodicity with which medication is ordinarily offered—she is upsetting the rhythmic expectations to which the team members have become accustomed. The disturbance of rhythm by the private-patient crock, however, relates to other rhythms in the social morphology of the service. In such cases, the residents are usually reluctant to administer medication over and beyond what the private doctor might have ordered —a case not only of status differences but of the sacredness of private clientele as well. Thus, the "crock" label was most frequently applied to private patients during the late evening and nighttime hours when the private obstetrician was least likely to be on the service to minister to his complaining lady. The former, then, related to the rhythm of medication, while the latter was associated with the work rhythms of the establishment.

Tempo: Conceptions of the "Normal" in the Hospital

The number of deliveries taking place in a given period of time particularly relates to the tempo of the service. In the clinic service, the number of births in a twenty-four-hour period may range from as few as one or two to as many as fifteen or twenty. This lack of a natural tempo seemed to be handled in a number of ways in order to impose a "functional" tempo where a "physiological" tempo did not exist. For example, when deliveries were occurring at a naturally slow pace, the residents showed much anxiety and concern over the one or two women who might have been holding up the tempo of events in labor—constantly checking and rechecking for signs of change. Similarly, in the delivery room itself, there seemed to be an attempt to impose a tempo —to adhere to a pace of scrubbing, of administering anesthesia, and so forth. There was also an emphasis upon keeping track of the length of time involved in each delivery. In terms of tempo, the unusually prolonged delivery was as upsetting to the team as was an unusually rapid delivery—even though both might be equally normal or abnormal from a medical point of view. As one resident put it, "Our [the residents'] average length of delivery is about 50 minutes, and the Pros [the private doctors] is about 40 minutes." Thus, the "correct" tempo becomes a matter of status competition and a measure of professional adeptness. The use of forceps is also a means by which the tempo is maintained in the delivery room, and they are so often used that the procedure is regarded as normal.

The student externs showed particular reluctance about admitting patients to the service because of the possibility that the patient might be in "false labor." This would upset both the rhythm and the tempo. It may not be unrelated to the fact that such a "mistake" on the part of low-status personnel is much more crucial than a similar mistake on the part of higher-status personnel. In addition, the potential high tempo for the obstetrician is necessarily limited; he can be in attendance for just one case at a time. When the physiological tempo begins to outrun the functional tempo, the margin of safety can be partially maintained by the anesthetist, who can hurry cases along or delay them, depending upon the kind and amount of anesthesia he administers. As one anesthetist joyously announced one night when the physiological tempo was very high, "I've got five going [ready for delivery but delayed] at once now."

Timing: Expectations of the Normal Course of Events

In the naturally expected sequences of events, it is of interest to note how the coming together of the team members for delivery differs from the situation in the regular surgical setting. Ordinarily the high-status personnel—the surgeons—arrive last (Wilson, 1954). In the obstetrical service, however, it is difficult to know whether the patient can actually wait for the doctor. Frequently, therefore, the doctors arrive on the scene before the subordinates do, and not infrequently before the patient herself. This disturbance in timing usually leaves the doctors either making "busy-work" with the administrative nurses or leaving the region to check another patient in labor whom minutes before they may have referred to as a "crock."

The normal circuit: admitting office, to prep room, to labor room, to delivery room, to recovery room, and finally to the lying-in room is adhered to scrupulously. The physiological tempo would often indicate that at least one or more rooms might better be forgotten, but the patient must adhere to this timing of movements from region to region, even if it means at a fast trot.

Timing may also be disturbed if key personnel happen to be absent from one of the places in the timing sequence. One evening, for example, a man rushed into the service claiming that his wife was about to have her child and that no one was in the admitting office. The doctors' advice—in all candor and sincerity—was that she was probably in false labor, and they encouraged the man to return to the admitting room. In a second instance, a woman who had previously given birth to seven children appeared in the last stages of labor. There was not enough time to administer the usual anesthesia, even though it seemed obvious that she could bear her child easily without it. The obstetrical team, however, was in a state of much agitation until the baby suddenly appeared. These inroads upon the timing of events are highly disturbing to the service personnel. And, in general, it may be said that there appeared to be a kind of gradient of the temporal organization of the hospital, with the greater emphasis upon rhythm, tempo, and timing, the closer one got to the community center.

A Substantive Example:
The Ecology of Pain

Thus far, we have discussed the social morphology of the obstetrical service strictly from the view of the flow of work in both time and space, threading into our discussion appropriate substantive examples. To express more fully the interrelationships between time, space, and social behavior, we turn now to a specific substantive area: the ways in which the hospital is organized to define, legitimatize, sanction, and handle the expression of pain by patients.

As Parsons (1953) has pointed out in his theoretical analysis of the doctor-patient relationship, a requisite for the maintenance of the professional self-image and, therefore, professional behavior toward patients, is the maintenance of an affectively neutral orientation toward the patient. The patient must be regarded as a clinical phenomenon rather than as a person in order for the doctor to behave as doctor. It may well be that an important function of the "prepping" process in the flow of work is to reassert both the clinical nature of the patient and the professional self-images of the personnel. Certainly the expression of pain by a patient as well as the recognition of painfulness, as such, by the doctor is a salient means by which the affectively neutral orientation may be changed to that of an emotionally involved or affective orientation. Such a contingency is handled in a variety of ways.

There are, first of all, certain places in the service where pain is legitimatized and defined as such, and others in which it is not. By and large, pain is not sanctioned in any place other than the delivery room, for it is only here that the hospital provides the means to handle pain in an affectively neutral fashion—namely, anesthesia. The acceptance or sanctioning of pain in any other regions—the admitting room, the prep room, and even the labor rooms—would necessitate a more personalized orientation toward the patient by the staff, rather than the technical, mechanical, and personally neutral means that are so characteristic of the delivery room. This is not to say that women are in pain only in the delivery room, but merely that it is neither accepted nor dealt with as such by the staff—particularly high-status staff. And not only does the staff segregate pain in this spatial sense, but this meaning appears to be shared by the patients as well—many patients seem a bit apologetic about having pain when in these other regions. In places not sanctioning pain, when the patient's discomfort intrudes itself upon the staff, various means are employed to cope with it in an affectively neutral fashion. In the prep room it is handled by the use of humor and comparatively low-status personnel; in the labor room, not only by the more intimate contact taking place between patient and low-status personnel but also by defining the phenomenon as something other than pain—complaining, pampering, nervousness, or what have you; and in the recovery room by its spatial and symbolic segregation as well as by defining it as unconscious behavior of one who is still under the effects of anesthesia.

The symbolism of lighting, individual segregation of patients, and perhaps even the mood and attitudes of the nurses on duty, serve to minimize the patient's attempts to legitimatize her discomfort as genuine pain. Spatially there appeared to be a kind of gradient as to the legitimation of pain, with the greater sanctioning of pain found the closer the "place" is to the delivery rooms, and a corresponding decrease as one moves away from the community center. Significantly, it is in this "climax" region of the delivery room, where pain is most fully sanctioned and accepted by the staff, that the affectively neutral orientation is most likely to break down. For here—perhaps for the first time—the entire obstetrical team is confronted, and at close quarters, with the patient and her discomfort. She is highlighted not only in a physical and interactional sense but in an organizational sense as well. An important relation between status and "place" is clearly evident here because the anesthetist has no part to play in the labor room, even though the manifestation of pain there may actually be as great as, or even greater than, that shown in the delivery room. Once pain is accepted as such—in the delivery room—there is then a special functionary to handle it in an affectively neutral fashion: the anesthetist. Pain is not only sanctioned in the delivery room; it is expected, too. If there is no pain, this would mean that the anesthetist, who occupies a position of considerable prestige, would be superfluous. Moreover, the legitimation of pain is also organized temporally. There are patterns according to which pain is sanctioned and expected—only so often and for only so long. To show pain either too frequently or too infrequently or, indeed, not at all, is disrupting to the obstetrical team.

On one occasion, for example, the team was preparing for the delivery of a patient, a mother of several children. The chief resident was heading the team and he was assisted by an intern, a staff nurse, and a student nurse. The anesthetist, of course, was on the service should he be needed. All phases of the preparatory stage were going according to schedule until the staff nurse attempted to administer anesthesia by means of a nose mask. Apparently for technical reasons, the apparatus failed to operate. There are three masks in each delivery room —each containing a different form of anesthesia—and the nurse tried the other two; neither one worked. Although the patient did not appear to be suffering undue pain, with each failure of the apparatus the team members—particularly the chief resident—became increasingly agitated, excited, and alarmed. This pattern of deprofessionalization of the doctor continued until he excitedly hurried from the room in search of the anesthetist who hopefully could somehow handle the situation. What was apparently happening in this instance, and according to our frame of reference, was first that pain was sanctioned and accepted as such by the physician in the delivery room —it was expected as well. Second, the delivery room was the place where the hospital was organized to maintain affective neutrality in the face of pain by means of the anesthesia apparatus. When this apparatus did not function properly, an important mechanism by which affective neutrality is maintained broke down. With it the affec-

tive neutrality of the obstetrical team also broke down.

Some Implications for the Study of Social Establishments

We said at the outset that three possible approaches to the relations between the ecological setting and the normative system would be pursued. First was that which regarded the ecological system as dominant and determining the nature of the normative patterns between the participants. Second was that which viewed the normative patterns as determinants of the uses to which the ecological system would be put. Third was that in which a condition of unstable accommodation existed between the "givens" of the physical setting and the requirements of the normative system. We shall now consider our observations in the light of these perspectives.

The first approach would suggest that the patterns of normative behavior we observed would have been dramatically different in the context of a different physical setting. For example, would the relatively blasé attitudes toward the period of postpartum recovery have persisted without the presence of a defined place in which such attitudes might be elicited and distinguished (the recovery room)? Or would the demeanor of the interns vis-à-vis the privately practicing "pros" have been what it was without the spatial segregation of the residents' quarters and the physical and symbolic segregation of the private lounge? In all candor we must confess that, on the basis of a field study of this type, such questions cannot easily be answered with any degree of confidence. It was impossible, in the context of our observations, to manipulate such "givens" and then to derive indicators of their relative importance. We suspect, however, that the dominance of the ecological setting, through spatial segregation, symbolic segregation, and temporal organization, might qualify normative patterns, the forms in which they might be expressed, and their relative importance in the conduct of the participants. Although a pattern of subordination-superordination is commonly found in relations between doctors, interns, and nurses, it would have greater or lesser saliency depending upon the time and space structures of the environment.

A further aspect of the dominance of ecology is related to the association between status and place and what Hughes has referred to as professional mistakes (Hughes, 1958). In large part, the lower the status of the functionary (nurse, intern, or student nurse), the less is the likelihood that he will risk the possibility of committing either an interpersonal or a technical mistake. The reverse seems to be true of high-status personnel. The physician in the delivery room need not fear such errors—his status is sufficiently high that he may correct it—or not correct it—without loss of the esteem of the team. The staff nurse may sometimes point out a mistake to the doctor, but ordinarily in only indirect ways—by mood, attitude, and other forms of nonverbal communication. Her danger lies not in failing to point out a mistake but in pointing it out incorrectly. The student nurse is seldom to be found either making a mistake or pointing out the errors of others. However, in the interstitial areas of the service—the hallways, the community center, and even in the cafeteria—normative taboos against pointing out errors made by high-status personnel are less in evidence. Here the doctor, nurse, intern, and student nurse may be found speaking together in the most candid fashion. In the interstitial areas the most blunt questions can be asked without prestige and esteem becoming serious considerations. In Homans' (1961) terms, the behavior of the participants is contingent upon the interpersonal costs involved in relation to the interpersonal profits. The ecological system is crucial in so far as both the costs and the returns are highly associated with where the behavior takes place. For the nurses, the cost of risking an error in the delivery room is quite high—with the potential returns at a minimum. In the interstitial areas, on the other hand, costs are reduced and potential returns are increased.

Our second approach—that which views the normative system as dominant—raises different questions: Would the patterns of behavior that we observed have remained substantially the same in the context of a thoroughly different physical setting? Per-haps most crucial in the normative system between functionaries are the clients—the patients. It would appear that in some sense the ecological structures seemed to be least salient when there was no significant audience before which the participants acted. This raises the question whether the pattern of subordination-superordination between doctors and nurses is strictly a consequence of the "shoulder-high" barrier in front of the labor rooms, or whether the counter comes to have symbolic meaning only in relation to an already existing pattern of professional prerogatives. We would suppose that the "physical barrier" of the counter would tend to have less significance in the relations between doctors and nurses if the labor rooms were empty of patients. By and large, it would seem that the posture the functionaries took toward each other in the clearly defined places of the service was contingent upon the presence of the patient, who always stood in need of having her role articulated for her by others in the establishment. One might say, then, that where there are lacunae in the behavioral expectations among persons acting in a physical setting, the physical setting itself—spatially and symbolically—will provide symbolic cues to fill such lacunae. On the other hand, where the physical setting itself is less than complete in boundaries and barriers, the normative system will define such barriers to conform with itself.

Often, however, neither the physical setting nor the normative system is fully adapted one to the other. This is the third approach, in which a condition of unstable equilibrium exists between the normative system and the ecology. This may well be the most typical condition not only in our single hospital but in most social establishments. This is merely to say that there is no such thing as a "social psychology of architecture."

There are, then, numerous contingencies in the tasks that occur in the hospital in which the normative system is endangered by events that might take place in certain places, and certain aspects of the physical setting that lend a kind of ludicrousness to some aspects of the normative system. It is in the light of such contingencies that interstitial areas become places where the normative system changes, to some extent, and the dominance of "place" becomes less pronounced. The hallways, the community center, and the like appear to be ill-defined areas in which incongruities between the physical setting and the normative system are resolved. It is here that informal social organization becomes most apparent, where candor between doctors, interns, and nurses is expressed most fully. These contingency situations also appear to arise in the face of crises—the breakdown of technical equipment, the deviation of a patient from the normally expected series of physiological stages, and the like. Such crisis situations are seldom fully resolved within the confines of a clearly defined ecological area in the service, perhaps because their resolution would alter the normative patterns regarded as appropriate for that *place*. Rather, resolution of crises is more often found in the interstitial areas where roles may be transcended, where the usual rights and obligations of status need not be adhered to, and where esteem and prestige are less at stake. In short, it is here where the costs of "mistakes" are decreased. Moreover, in the interstitial areas communication between the functionaries is less stereotyped and more spontaneous. There, the resolution of a problem can be of more significance than the distribution of roles among the members of the obstetrical team because both normative and ecological systems are ill-defined and emergent.

In general, it appeared to us that both the spatial and the temporal organization of the service seemed to be geared to cast the incoming patient into a role and mood that would allow the personnel of the service to behave in the ways which they had learned to expect that they should. The staff members themselves—residents, interns, and so on—seemed to be subject to the same proscriptions that stemmed from the morphology of the hospital. In the case of both staff and patients this process was accomplished apparently less by verbal instruction, or even by informal socialization processes, than by the erection of both physical and symbolic barriers to the undesired behaviors and attitudes.

It is perhaps gratuitous to point out that all social establishments, as well as commu-

nities, are organized within and around distinctive physical settings. These physical settings may be considered as consisting of many interrelated parts spatially separate from each other. None the less, the basis of social organization and social establishments consists of the integration of those parts into time and space. We suggest that the behaviors that might otherwise legitimately be viewed from a cultural-behavioral perspective are importantly related to the spatial and temporal aspects of the hospital. Although many social psychologists may tend to be particularly enamored of an approach that focuses exclusively upon the normative system, we might well profit by becoming increasingly sensitive to the major role played by ecological factors.[5]

It would be audacious not to make a necessary caveat at this point. Our observations stemmed from experiences in a single setting. It is not possible to assert certitude as to the validity and reliability of these observations and remarks, or to suggest generalizability to other social establishments—particularly hospitals. We suspect that the ecological structure of this one hospital is in many ways unique. Very likely the normative patterns among the staff are in many ways unlike those found in other settings. Our purpose has been to suggest an approach and a perspective that may have future meaning for the study not only of social establishments but of communities as well. The rigid "either-or" choice between a morphological approach on the one hand, and a "culture-behavior" approach on the other, appears to us to be unduly constraining.

REFERENCES:

Coser, R. L. Authority and decision-making in a hospital. *American Sociological Review,* 1958, **23,** 56–63.

Duncan, O. D. & Schnore, L. Cultural, behavioral and ecological perspectives in the study of social organization. *American Journal of Sociology,* 1959, **65,** 132–146.

Freidson, E. Client control and medical practice. *American Journal of Sociology,* 1960, **65,** 374–382.

Goffman, E. *The presentation of self in every-*

[5] Studies from a nonecological perspective stemming from this same research are found in W. R. Rosengren (1961a, 1961b, 1962).

day life. New York: Doubleday Anchor, 1959.

Hawley, A. H. *Human ecology: A theory of community structure.* New York: Ronald Press, 1950.

Homans, G. C. *Social behavior: Its elementary forms.* New York: Harcourt, Brace and World, 1961.

Hughes, E. C. *Men and their work.* Chicago: University of Chicago Press, 1958.

Mack, R. W. Ecological patterns in an industrial shop. *Social Forces,* 1954, **32,** 351–356.

Parsons, T. *The social system.* New York: The Free Press, 1953.

Rosengren, W. R. Social sources of pregnancy as illness or disease. *Social Forces,* 1961a, **39,** 260–267.

Rosengren, W. R. Social-psychological aspects of delivery room difficulties. *Journal of Nervous and Mental Disease,* 1961b, **132,** 515–521.

Rosengren, W. R. Social instability and attitudes toward pregnancy as a social role. *Social Problems,* 1962, **9,** 371–378.

Steward, J. *Theory of culture change: The methodology of multilinear evolution.* Urbana: University of Illinois Press, 1955.

Wilson, R. N. Teamwork in the operating room. *Human Organization,* 1954, **12,** 9–14.

45 The Prisoner's Status as Conveyed by the Environment

Gresham Sykes

It is sometimes claimed that many criminals are so alienated from conforming society and so identified with a criminal subculture that the moral condemnation, rejection, or disapproval of legitimate society does not touch them; they are, it is said, indifferent to the penal sanctions of the free community, at least as far as the moral stigma of being defined as a criminal is concerned. Possibly this is true for a small number of offenders such as the professional thief described by Sutherland (1937) or the psychopathic personality delineated by William and Joan McCord (1956). For the great majority of criminals in prison, however, the evidence suggests that neither alienation from the ranks of the law-abiding nor involvement in a system of criminal value is sufficient to eliminate the threat to the

Reprinted by permission of Princeton University Press and the author from *The Society of Captives: A Study of a Maximum Security Prison,* by Gresham M. Sykes (1958).

prisoner's ego posed by society's rejection (see Reckless, 1955, pp. 428–429). The signs pointing to the prisoner's degradation are many—the anonymity of a uniform and a number rather than a name, the shaven head, the insistence on gestures of respect and subordination when addressing officials, and so on. The prisoner is never allowed to forget that, by committing a crime, he has foregone his claim to the status of a full-fledged, *trusted* member of society. The status lost by the prisoner is, in fact, similar to what Marshall has called the status of citizenship—that basic acceptance of the individual as a functioning member of the society in which he lives (see Marshall, 1950). It is true that in the past the imprisoned criminal literally suffered civil death and that although the doctrines of attainder and corruption of blood were largely abandoned in the 18th and 19th centuries, the inmate is still stripped of many of his civil rights, such as the right to vote, to hold office, to sue in court, and so on (Tappan, 1954). But as important as the loss of these civil rights may be, the loss of that more diffuse status which defines the individual as someone to be trusted or as morally acceptable is the loss which hurts most.

In short, the wall which seals off the criminal, the contaminated man, is a constant threat to the prisoner's self-conception and the threat is continually repeated in the many daily reminders that he must be kept apart from "decent" men. Somehow this rejection or degradation by the free community must be warded off, turned aside, rendered harmless. Somehow the imprisoned criminal must find a device for rejecting his rejectors, if he is to endure psychologically (see McCorkle and Korn, 1954).

There are admittedly many problems in attempting to compare the standard of living existing in the free community and the standard of living which is supposed to be the lot of the inmate in prison. How, for example, do we interpret the fact that a covering for the floor of a cell usually consists of a scrap from a discarded blanket and that even this possession is forbidden by the prison authorities? What meaning do we attach to the fact that no inmate owns a common piece of furniture, such as a chair, but only a homemade stool? What is the value of a suit of clothing which is also a convict's uniform with a stripe and a stenciled number? The answers are far from simple although there are a number of prison officials who will argue that some inmates are better off in prison, in strictly material terms, than they could ever hope to be in the rough-and-tumble economic life of the free community. Possibly this is so, but at least it has never been claimed by the inmates that the goods and services provided the prisoner are equal to or better than the goods and services which the prisoner could obtain if he were left to his own devices outside the walls. The average inmate finds himself in a harshly Spartan environment which he defines as painfully depriving.

Now it is true that the prisoner's basic material needs are met—in the sense that he does not go hungry, cold, or wet. He receives adequate medical care and he has the opportunity for exercise. But a standard of living constructed in terms of so many calories per day, so many hours of recreation, so many cubic yards of space per individual, and so on, misses the central point when we are discussing the individual's feeling of deprivation, however useful it may be in setting minimum levels of consumption for the maintenance of health. A standard of living can be hopelessly inadequate, from the individual's viewpoint, because it bores him to death or fails to provide those subtle symbolic overtones which we invest in the world of possessions. And this is the core of the prisoner's problem in the area of goods and services. He wants— or needs, if you will—not just the so-called necessities of life but also the amenities: cigarettes and liquor as well as calories, interesting foods as well as sheer bulk, individual clothing as well as adequate clothing, individual furnishings for his living quarters as well as shelter, privacy as well as space. The "rightfulness" of the prisoner's feeling of deprivation can be questioned. And the objective reality of the prisoner's deprivation —in the sense that he has actually suffered a fall from his economic position in the free community—can be viewed with skepticism, as we have indicated above. But these criticisms are irrelevant to the significant issue,

namely that legitimately or illegitimately, rationally or irrationally, the inmate population defines its present material impoverishment as a painful loss.

Now in modern Western culture, material possessions are so large a part of the individual's conception of himself that to be stripped of them is to be attacked at the deepest layers of personality. This is particularly true when poverty cannot be excused as a blind stroke of fate or a universal calamity. Poverty due to one's own mistakes or misdeeds represents an indictment against one's basic value or personal worth and there are few men who can philosophically bear the want caused by their own actions. It is true some prisoners in the New Jersey State Prison attempt to interpret their low position in the scale of goods and services as an effort by the State to exploit them economically. Thus, in the eyes of some inmates, the prisoner is poor not because of an offense which he has committed in the past but because the State is a tyrant which uses its captive criminals as slave labor under the hypocritical guise of reformation. Penology, it is said, is a racket. Their poverty, then, is not punishment as we have used the word before, i.e. the just consequence of criminal behavior; rather, it is an unjust hurt or pain inflicted without legitimate cause. This attitude, however, does not appear to be particularly widespread in the inmate population and the great majority of prisoners must face their privation without the aid of the wronged man's sense of injustice. Furthermore, most prisoners are unable to fortify themselves in their low level of material existence by seeing it as a means to some high or worthy end. They are unable to attach any significant meaning to their need to make it more bearable, such as present pleasures foregone for pleasures in the future, self-sacrifice in the interests of the community, or material asceticism for the purpose of spiritual salvation.

The inmate, then, sees himself as having been made poor by reason of his own acts and without the rationale of compensating benefits. The failure is *his* failure in a world where control and possession of the material environment are commonly taken as sure indicators of a man's worth. It is true that our society, as materialistic as it may be, does not rely exclusively on goods and services as a criterion of an individual's value; and the inmate population defends itself by stressing alternative or supplementary measures of merit. But impoverishment remains as one of the most bitter attacks on the individual's self-image that our society has to offer and the prisoner cannot ignore the implications of his straitened circumstances. Whatever the discomforts and irritations of the prisoner's Spartan existence may be, he must carry the additional burden of social definitions which equate his material deprivation with personal inadequacy.

REFERENCES:

Marshall, T. H. *Citizenship and social class.* Cambridge, England: The Cambridge University Press, 1950.

McCord, W., & McCord, J. *Psychopathy and delinquency.* New York: Grune and Stratton, 1956.

McCorkle, L. W., & Korn, R. R. Resocialization within walls. *The Annals of the American Academy of Political and Social Science,* 1954, **293**, 88–98.

Reckless, W. C. *The crime problem.* New York: Appleton-Century-Crofts, 1955.

Sutherland, E. H. *The professional thief.* Chicago: University of Chicago Press, 1937.

Tappan, P. W. The legal rights of prisoners. *The Annals of the American Academy of Political and Social Science,* 1954, **293**, 99–111.

46 Architectural Factors in Isolation Promotion in Prisons

Daniel Glaser

Certainly one major determinant of inmate isolation from other inmates is the physical arrangement of prison housing units. Our data on self-isolation of older inmates, and pursuit of close friendships by younger inmates, are relevant here. They suggest that dormitories, honor units, and other inmate

From *The Effectiveness of a Prison and Parole System* by Daniel Glaser, copyright © 1964, by The Bobbs-Merrill Company, Inc., and reprinted by permission of the publishers.

housing which facilitate inter-inmate socialization do not promote the spread of criminal attitudes as much among older inmates as among younger ones. This conclusion contradicts prevailing practice in prison and training-school architecture, where dormitories predominate in juvenile and youth institutions, with no privacy possible for an inmate, and are decreasingly used as the average age of institution population increases.

Single rooms or cells seem preferable to dormitories as housing for all inmates, to permit privacy and to reduce the competition of inmate influences with other influences (staff, correspondents, studies, etc.). Presumably inmate criminogenic influences are most effective during the unprogrammed parts of the inmate's day, when he has free time, as opposed to the periods of organized work, study, or recreation activity. Accordingly, effective strategy would appear to be to maximize privacy during periods when activities are not directed by the organized institution program.

Prisons vary greatly in the extent to which inmates are allowed to leave and enter rooms or cells freely to visit each other, when not in programmed activities, or to use dayrooms or other group facilities. This variation may be a function of construction and of custodial as well as treatment considerations. In the typical large inside cellblock of most state prisons, unrestricted freedom of movement to and from all cells generally is out of the question from a custodial viewpoint, in addition to its antirehabilitative significance in preventing privacy. Treatment interests in facilitating certain inter-inmate communication and impeding other inmate contacts suggest the need for compartmentalization of large residential structures into smaller units, with considerable freedom of interaction within units.

Compartmentalization probably has been most developed in the newer California prisons, which include separate dining halls and recreation facilities for each major residential unit. In such structures, placing inmates in different units separates them more completely than usually can be done in a single prison without extreme restriction of freedom.

Procurement of quiet and privacy, when desired, may become more difficult for an inmate in a small unit because of the greater intimacy of the group there and their mutual involvement in group programs. Possibly the staff can facilitate privacy when inmates desire it by an effort to keep unstructured activities of two or more inmates in day-rooms or other public areas. Perhaps an ideal solution involves single-room housing for inmates, away from the dayroom area, with a means by which inmates can lock their rooms even though custodians also have master keys for opening and locking any rooms, and the custodians also can view and audit inmate activity without opening the door. This has been instituted in prison construction at the Federal Correctional Institution at Seagoville, Texas, at the California Men's Colony at Los Padres, near San Luis Obispo, and in part of California's Soledad prison. In these prisons, inmates are issued keys with which they can lock their separate cells or rooms. These institutions all have a surprisingly large variety of penitentiary-type inmates.

The California "isolation promotion" cells, for which the inmates carry their own keys, are designed in a rather interesting manner for single occupancy. These designs, officials advised me, were deliberately intended to make it difficult for a later administration to house more than one inmate in the cell, as an alternative to constructing additional housing units, if the prisons become over-crowded. The cells in the "North Facility" at Soledad are square, with the prisoner's cot fitting only against the wall which has a window (plumbing and the door prevent use of the other sides for the cot). Therefore, replacing the single cot by a double-deck cot would mean blocking the window.

The California Men's Colony cells have vertically zig-zagged walls on one side of each cell, designed to place the two levels of a double-deck bed in different cells; one cell has only the upper deck and the adjacent cell has only the lower deck. With this "over-and-under" design there is insufficient floor space left to place a second cot in any cell. Such cells also are used as an isolation promotion device at the Reception Center

for new prisoners at Chino, where the newly received inmates, of course, are not given their own keys. This "over-and-under" design permits construction of four single cells in the floor space normally used for three, so it has economy appeal as well as isolation promotion advantages, but it is not as economical as would be the abandonment of privacy facilitation by construction of cells housing two or more inmates, or by dormitory construction.[1]

The foregoing analysis of isolation promotion policies may be summarized in a few simple propositions:

Promoting the isolation of inmates from each other fosters rehabilitation where the techniques for promoting isolation consist of:

a. Providing physical arrangements of inmate housing which facilitate an inmate's achievement of privacy when he desires it

b. Separating inmates considered criminogenic influences on each other

c. Encouraging staff-desired patterns of inmate discrimination in choice of prisoner associates.

ISOLATION PROMOTION AND CUSTODY GRADING

Table 46-1 contrasts the activities of men who were in single rooms, crowded dormitories, and uncrowded dormitories. Crowdedness here is defined arbitrarily as under 70 square feet per man. Excluded are cells with two or more inmates. It will be seen that the differences in activity associated with these types of housing vary consider-

[1] California and U. S. Bureau of Prisons architects have had divergent evaluations of this over-and-under cell design. Federal objections were on aesthetic grounds, and also involved some questioning of California's economy and space justifications for this design. However, California, after initial experience with these cells at Chino, has built all 1600 cells of the new Men's Colony structures in this over-and-under design, using a steel zig-zag wall between cells, and solid masonry end walls. California officials expressed great satisfaction with this design when I visited in 1961. See: U. S. Bureau of Prisons, p. 16.

Table 46-1 Average Hours per Day at Various Activities by Type of Housing Unit, Weekdays Only[a]

Institution and housing[b]	Activity						No. of cases
	Work	Just talk with inmates	Play	Read	Eat	Sleep	
Leavenworth							
A. Single cell	6.7	1.0	1.6	2.6	2.6	8.8	42
B. Crowded dormitory	6.7	0.6	2.9	1.9	2.5	8.6	36
C. Uncrowded dormitory	6.0	0.8	3.6	1.1	1.8	9.3	8
Terre Haute							
A. Single cell	5.0	0.5	3.8	1.6	2.6	9.2	61
B. Crowded dormitory	5.5	0.8	3.7	1.3	2.5	9.1	66
C. Uncrowded dormitory	5.0	0.6	3.6	2.4	3.0	9.1	5
Milan							
A. Single cell	6.3	0.4	2.3	2.4	2.3	8.8	24
B. Crowded dormitory	5.0	0.5	3.2	1.7	1.9	9.2	94
C. Uncrowded dormitory	5.0	0.6	3.6	1.8	2.0	8.8	24
Chillicothe							
A. Single cell	4.0	0.8	2.8	2.3	2.6	9.3	18
B. Crowded dormitory	6.0	0.9	2.0	1.5	2.4	9.4	30
C. Uncrowded dormitory	5.6	0.7	3.1	1.1	2.4	9.2	87
Ashland							
A. Single cell	5.8	1.5	3.0	0.8	2.3	8.9	26
B. Crowded dormitory	6.6	0.9	2.9	0.7	2.3	9.0	31
C. Uncrowded dormitory	6.5	1.3	2.5	1.4	2.2	8.9	60
All institutions							
A. Single cell	5.6	0.8	2.8	1.9	2.5	9.0	171
B. Crowded dormitory	5.9	0.7	3.1	1.5	2.2	9.1	257
C. Uncrowded dormitory	5.8	0.8	3.0	1.3	2.2	9.0	184

[a] Prison Panel Study; all but first-week interviews.
[b] Housing Code: A. Man alone in cell; B. Crowded dormitory: under 70 square feet per man; C. Uncrowded dormitory: 70 or more square feet per man.

ably from one institution to the next; every conclusion which one may make from the "All Institutions" section is contradicted by at least one of the sections which represents a single institution. This inconsistency in the results suggests that other factors must affect inmate activity more than it is affected by the attributes of residence dealt with in Table 46-1. Ideal research on the effects of housing would require random assignment of two or more samples of inmates with a given program to different types of housing. Nevertheless, some trends in Table 46-1 are of interest.

The most consistent of the imperfect relationships evident in Table 46-1 is that of more reading in single cells, as compared with dormitories, and also that men in single cells spent more time eating than did men in dormitories. One would expect a single cell to be conducive to reading, of course, and we presume it also is associated with more time at eating because eating represents an escape from the isolation of the cell. We expected less play in the cells than in the dormitories, but this occurs only at Leavenworth and Milan, where those in the cells happen to put in more hours at work than do those in the dormitories. Incidentally, the "sleep" tabulation in our tables is a midnight-to-midnight total which includes daytime naps in addition to sleeping at night. It might be mentioned also that in 1960–62 the Terre Haute work hours were increased to about eight through more than doubling inmates permitted to work outside the prison, eliminating general service labor crew assignments, and keeping many work assignments less heavily manned than previously.

We also compared detailed play activities in various institutions and types of housing, but found differences only in the three institutions for adults (Leavenworth, Terre Haute, and Milan). There the inmates in cells spent less time in listening to radio or watching television and more time at physical culture and at art than inmates in dormitories.

At Chillicothe Reformatory our researcher noted the specific dormitory designation on his interview forms in order to procure square feet data later. This permitted us to analyze the relationship of inmate activity not only as first planned, to the physical attributes of the housing, but also to the custody grading system's progressive reduction of surveillance. This also provides an illustration of extreme development in an honor stratification system in inmate housing.

There were six dormitory structures through which inmates were transferred at Chillicothe as their behavior warranted. At the time of our research an inmate remained at least thirty days in one unit before being eligible for transfer to a more favorably graded unit. Relevant policies and physical conditions at the time of our interviews, in 1959, are described below, with the dormitories arranged in order of increasing honorific status in the custody grading system:

> F-DORMITORY: This is a three-story structure, each floor consisting of a 6500-square-foot room with 88 to 100 steel cots on either side of a small central recreation area and officer's glass-walled office. There is a small separate locker for each man by his cot, and welded to the cot, beneath the spring, is a small drawer for which the inmate receives a key lock and may purchase a combination lock. Each floor has a washroom and television set. This is the first dormitory in which inmates are placed when they are permitted to advance out of the cell-houses (which also are graded). Men in this dormitory are required to be in their beds from 10 P.M. to 6:50 A.M. (8 hours, 50 minutes). An officer always is present on each floor.

> A-DORMITORY: This is physically like F-Dormitory except that it has only two

floors. Inmates are moved here when their behavior earns them movement out of F-Dormitory in the direction of more "honor" and lower custody. Men in this dormitory are required to be in their beds from 10 P.M. to 6:30 A.M. (8 hours, 30 minutes). An officer always is present on each floor, but one leaves occasionally when also supervising B-Dormitory.

> C-DORMITORY: Physically identical with A-Dormitory, and scheduled and staffed like A-Dormitory, this unit is one step higher on the "honor" scale, so inmates may move here from A-Dormitory.

> D-DORMITORY: Physically this is not the kind of structure usually connoted by the term "dormitory," since inmate housing consists of 150 separate one-man rooms, the doors of which are never locked. Each room has 50 square feet of floor space. The men in this unit are to be in their rooms from 10 P.M. to 6:30 A.M. on Sunday through Thursday nights (8 hours, 30 minutes), and from 11 P.M. to 7:30 A.M. on Friday and Saturday nights. This is the highest-grade dormitory to which men can be advanced who are classified for "medium custody," so those who, at release, will be wanted by another law-enforcement agency on a serious charge are not likely to be moved beyond this unit regardless of how well they behave. It is a semi-honor unit in that, although an officer is always at the door, the men are not as continuously under his surveillance as in lower-grade dormitories.

> B-DORMITORY: This also houses men in separate rooms, the doors of which are never locked. There are 123 rooms, each of 50 square feet. Men are to be in their rooms from 10 P.M. to 6:15 A.M. on Sunday through Thursday nights (8 hours, 15 minutes), but on weekends they may be out of their rooms until 11 P.M. Men in this dormitory include those classified in a special category not standard in federal prisons, called "Medium Out" custody, who are medium-custody inmates but work outside the prison fence, always under the surveillance of an officer. It is an honor unit in that at times, when most of the men are out at work, it may be supervised only by an officer of adjacent A-Dormitory, who mostly locks and un-

locks the B-Dormitory entrance to let men in and out.

G-DORMITORY: This unit is a true "honor" unit in that officers are not routinely present there at any time, although it is checked at night, when there is a count, and rooms are periodically inspected to observe housekeeping. This dormitory provides a separate room for each inmate, 75 square feet in area, with the doors never locked. It has bed capacity for only 51 inmates, but this includes a few new transfers there who sleep in a large room until a single-room vacancy occurs. All men quartered here are classified "minimum custody," and the outside door to this dormitory is never locked. Men in this unit can go to the dining room at any time in which meals are being served, rather than in a limited period, as is the case with the other housing units even under continuous feeding. The men are expected to be in their own rooms no later than 11 P.M. Sunday through Thursday night, and they arise at 6:45 A.M. (7 hours, 45 minutes). On Friday and Saturday night, and on some holidays, they need not retire to their rooms until midnight. It also is noteworthy that they may have the light on in their room at any time. The elected inmate advisory council member there has an office and has some authority in coordinating housekeeping and in selecting television programs.

The behavior distinguishing inmates interviewed from each of these dormitories at Chillicothe is summarized in Table 46-2. Here, for the first time in the application of our daily activity data to analysis of the effects of housing, marked and interesting relationships were indicated, despite a relatively small number of cases for some units. It will be noted that work increased and play decreased as one moved up the grading system, until the honor units. Here a sharp reversal of trend occurred, with work decreasing and play increasing. Also, the type of play changed, to consist more of card-playing in both honor dormitories. A similar curve was found in the talk topics distribution, in that prison-life topics continually decrease as one progresses up the custody-grading hierarchy until the honor

units, at which point there suddenly is peak concern with prison-life matters.

The foregoing suggests an increasing orientation to self-improvement and preparation for postrelease life in the beginning stages of the custody-grading system, but a replacement of this in the honor units by what Clemmer seemed to have in mind by the term "prisonization." In the honor units, although nearer to release, the men seem more concerned simply with maximizing their pleasure in prison. Like the proverbial mice when the cat is away, the inmates in groups completely free of the surveillance of officers seemed to follow the behavior dictated by their most pleasure-oriented members. We heard repeated inmate reports of large-scale gambling in G-Dormitory while our research was under way. Organized cliques of inmates set up the games, posted lookouts for officers, recruited participants with high commissary resources to wager, and promoted election of the inmate council representatives most tolerant of this activity. Other residents of the dormitory, mostly the rural ones according to our informants, opposed these game operators, but collaborated in smuggling coffee into the dormitory for late television-watching parties and other diversions.

Although the number of cases covered in Table 46-2 is small, the pattern is consistent enough on markedly different items to warrant considerable confidence. One should note especially that the behavior trends continue to be away from the honor-unit pattern even in C- and D-Dormitories, where the proportion of inmates near release is increasing; therefore, the high proportion near release does not seem sufficient to account for the change of behavior in the honor units.

We also procured completely independent and large-scale information with which to check on this picture of the constructive and unconstructive behavior in honor and nonhonor units at Chillicothe. We made an analysis of 1136 correspondence-course records at that institution, primarily to investigate certain aspects of course administration not connected with the study of the effects of housing. However, the housing unit of the student was entered in these records, permitting an analysis which is summarized in the following paragraph from a report submitted to the Bureau of Prisons in August 1959:

> At Chillicothe, 26 percent of enrollments occur when inmates are quartered in the Admission and Orientation unit, but only 13 percent of course completions occur there. Only 6 percent of both completions and enrollments occur in the cellhouses. F-Dormitory, the first unit to which inmates move when promoted from the cellhouses, has 19 percent of both enrollments and completions, and A-Dormitory has 21 percent of enrollments and 23 percent of completions. The next higher units in the honorific hierarchy, C- and D-Dormitories, have respectively, 12 and 10 percent of enrollments and 19 and 14 percent of completions. When we get to highest honor ranking, we find only 5 percent of enrollments and 6 percent of completions in B-Dormitory, which houses about 9 per-

Table 46-2 Average Utilization of the Day by Prisoners in Dormitories of Different Custody Grading, at Chillicothe Federal Reformatory, for Weekdays Only[a]

	F-DORM 1st Dorm	A-DORM 2nd Dorm	C-DORM 3rd Dorm	D-DORM Semi-Honor	B-DORM Honor	G-DORM Top Honor
Type of activity						
Work	5.6 hrs.	5.9 hrs.	6.2 hrs.	6.9 hrs.	5.0 hrs.	4.3 hrs.
"Just talk" with inmates	0.5 hrs.	0.5 hrs.	0.7 hrs.	0.3 hrs.	1.1 hrs.	0.6 hrs.
Play	3.0 hrs.	2.7 hrs.	2.1 hrs.	1.9 hrs.	3.7 hrs.	4.6 hrs.
Read	0.8 hrs.	1.4 hrs.	1.2 hrs.	1.2 hrs.	1.2 hrs.	0.2 hrs.
Write	0.6 hrs.	0.5 hrs.	0.5 hrs.	0.4 hrs.	0.5 hrs.	0.5 hrs.
Eat	2.2 hrs.	2.3 hrs.	2.2 hrs.	2.6 hrs.	2.3 hrs.	2.9 hrs.
Sleep	9.4 hrs.	8.9 hrs.	9.5 hrs.	8.9 hrs.	9.0 hrs.	9.5 hrs.
Other	1.8 hrs.	1.7 hrs.	1.4 hrs.	1.3 hrs.	1.0 hrs.	0.7 hrs.
Percent of play at various	All play	All play	All play	All play	All play	All play
types of play	3.0 hrs.	2.7 hrs.	2.1 hrs.	1.9 hrs.	3.7 hrs.	4.6 hrs.
Cards	7%	4%	11%	8%	24%	20%
Radio and TV	28%	46%	58%	50%	41%	60%
Weight lifting, boxing, wrestling	18%	8%			6%	10%
Other sports	19%	15%	11%	17%	12%	10%
Art	5%	12%				
Checkers, chess, etc.	5%	8%				
Yard, unspecified	18%	8%	21%	17%	12%	
Other				8%	6%	
Talk topics frequency						
Sentences	1%	2%	1%		1%	
Paroles	2%	4%	7%	4%	11%	15%
Work assignment	24%	25%	17%	27%	23%	17%
Studies	3%	5%	9%	7%	4%	
Play and hobby activities	16%	9%	5%	4%	16%	15%
Punishment	1%	1%	2%			2%
Food and comfort	5%	4%	4%	7%	7%	4%
Correspondence and visits	1%	2%				
About inmate acts and traits	5%	5%	5%	2%	4%	4%
About staff acts and traits	3%	1%	3%	2%	3%	6%
Other prison-life topics		1%	1%	1%	2%	2%
Total prison-life topics	62%	56%	54%	53%	70%	64%

Table 42-2 (*continued*)

	F-DORM 1st Dorm	A-DORM 2nd Dorm	C-DORM 3rd Dorm	D-DORM Semi-Honor	B-DORM Honor	G-DORM Top Honor
Sports	8%	10%	3%	6%	5%	5%
Work or trade on past jobs			3%	2%		
Work or business plans	1%	3%	6%	4%	2%	
Fun we used to have	2%	1%	2%	1%		
Crime	1%			3%		1%
Women, sex, dirty jokes	5%	6%	4%	9%		
Family and home	1%	4%	3%	3%		
Mechanics and science	1%	1%	2%	3%	1%	
Religion		1%				
News, politics, war		2%	6%	2%	2%	
Weather and small talk	18%	16%	18%	14%	14%	30%
All other talk	2%	1%	1%	2%	4%	
Total non-prison topics	38%	44%	46%	47%	30%	36%

	Number of cases, by interview					
Fourth month	18	4				
Sixth month	10	13	9	3		
Midterm	9	3	2	5	6	2
Near release	7	3	9	3	7	4
All interviews	44	23	20	11	13	6

a Prison panel study; all except first-week interviews.

cent of the inmate population, and absolutely no participation in correspondence courses by the 4 percent of the inmate population in the most honored unit, the inmate-run G-Dormitory.

The fact that honor dormitories had more prisoners nearing their date of release than did other housing units undoubtedly accounts, in part, for their low rate of participation in education. Our data on education as well as on other activity suggest that there is a general relaxation of behavior expectations from inmates as they approach return to the free community. Prison personnel often talk of once diligent inmates "coasting" as their parole date approaches.

HONOR UNITS AND REHABILITATION

The conclusion on the effects of housing policy which the foregoing, and other data, repeatedly suggest is that the "honor" units

may often contribute more to the comfort of both the inmates and staff than to the reformation of the inmates. One would expect extreme honor programs to be corrupted most frequently by youthful prisoners; with these inmates, group pressures for conformity to the most delinquent behavior suggested are likely to be greatest, and are most readily enforced by violence if there is no surveillance. Our data suggest that one cannot equate staff permissiveness with rehabilitative treatment; where staff permissiveness includes nonsurveillance, it may simply create a power vacuum which the more prisonized components of the inmate population will fill. Inmate surveillance replaces staff surveillance, and inmate life may become less permissive in terms of the freedom available to choose between alternate modes of behavior. Certainly reduction of formal surveillance is appropriate in the development of inmate responsibility, but the complete elimination of inmate-staff contact in quarters arbitrarily impedes informal surveillance by staff and blocks the development of reformative personal relationships between staff and inmates.

The arguments for permissiveness from the standpoint of intense milieu psychotherapy do not apply to the reformatory honors dormitory. The permissive group-psychotherapeutic institutions have about a one-to-one staff-inmate ratio. They favor continuous staff observation of inmate interaction in order to learn from it, and also, to some extent, to manipulate it. The honors-dormitory situation in the reformatory, on the other hand, permits a prolonged and complete daily escape from staff observation and from staff communication and manipulation. The opportunity to manipulate inmates then may fall more exclusively than ever into the hands of those inmates in the dormitory most opposed to staff-promoted values.

Possibly what is confounded in the non-surveillance "honor" conception is the difference between permissiveness in the psychotherapeutic sense of a situation encouraging the spontaneous expression of impulses, and freedom in its most sophisticated political sense, as a condition where there is widespread individual responsibility rather than dependence on authoritarian direction. It is freedom in the latter sense that is involved in what is described later in this chapter as the strategy of group responsibility, which may be highly rehabilitative. This type of freedom need not mean absence from staff observation, but more emphasis on the staff as assisting and coaching rather than as driving the men in their work.

I encountered in some federal prisons other objections by some senior officials to as fine a stratification of housing units by behavior requirements as that in Chillicothe and in certain other federal prisons. These men argued that having many units through which individuals must progress tends to create in some of the low-rated housing units concentrations of inmates who create an antirehabilitative climate that impedes the progress of other inmates. These units are a sort of "bottleneck" to movement through the many strata. The opposite approach in custody grading involves what

has been called "balance," or the distribution of many types of inmates in housing and work units, so that there is nowhere a concentration of inmates who might dominate the situation reinforcing each other in antirehabilitative attitudes.

Although the limitations of our data on the effects of custody grading make our conclusions on it more tentative and hypothetical than most of our other research findings, further test of the custody-grading conclusions may be facilitated by stating them formally, as follows:

Custody-grading systems foster rehabilitation by providing effective incentives to self-improvement activity, and to inmate discrimination in choice of associates, but they impede rehabilitation:

a. if the rewards for conformity to prison regulations include such reduction of inmate-staff contacts in quarters as to facilitate domination by inmate elements there who seek hedonistic escape from the effort of rehabilitation

b. if they provide freedom without effectively imposing responsibility

c. if one of their consequences is such concentration of antirehabilitative inmates in certain units that they dominate other inmates there and seriously impede their reformation, particularly in a unit through which most inmates are expected to pass in their progression up a custody-graded hierarchy of units.

A check on the consequences of custodial grading systems should be a routine part of prison-records analysis. It should compare the records of men during the months preceding their entrance into an honor unit with their records thereafter. For these comparisons, a variety of objective indexes of rehabilitative progress might well be tabulated, including educational advancement, work ratings, letter writing, and other variables. Patterns of change in performance with change in housing, using several independent performance indexes, would be most convincing. However, evaluating men in different housing according to their official infraction record would be rather pointless if the honor units permit and promote the commission of infractions without staff knowledge.

REFERENCE:

U. S. Bureau of Prisons. *Recent prison construction, 1950–60.* Washington: U. S. Dept. of Justice, 1960.

47 Office Design: A Study of Environment

Peter Manning

INTRODUCTION

Building in 1965 is a matter of considerable political importance receiving governmental attention on a scale previously unknown. But current interest resides largely in the ways and means of construction, especially in speed and quantity; whether what is being built is what is really needed is rarely questioned. Although environment is a word often heard when the design of modern buildings is being discussed, it tends to be employed loosely and imprecisely. Sometimes it is seen as a side-effect of design. It is rarely treated (as it is in this study) as the essential basis. Yet environment is the essence of architecture.

An ordered assembly of existing knowledge of environment in relation to building design does not exist, for studies have largely consisted of separate and unrelated investigations—for example, of lighting, heating or acoustics. This has been convenient for the understanding of individual topics but not very helpful to the understanding of the whole, for the parameters interact. The Pilkington Research Unit has been established with the express long-term aim of

From *Office Design: A Study of Environment.* Liverpool, Eng.: The Pilkington Research Unit, 1965. Reprinted by permission of the author and the publisher. Dr. B. W. P. Wells served as psychologist on the Pilkington Research Unit staff.

making scientific studies of the "total environment." Studies of the individual environmental factors and their interaction with one another, at both physical and subjective levels, are fundamental to the development of architecture.

The Unit's aim being long term, simpler objectives are necessary for the short-term stages of the study. This exploratory investigation has been centred on the design of offices because such a method of study has enabled many aspects of environment to be studied in relation to a building type which needs some fresh thought. The members of the Unit have been working to a common purpose but they have been individually responsible for those aspects of the study for which their qualifications best fit them. This report is an attempt to draw together the work of the Unit as a whole and also to present a unified picture of environment in the context of office design.

Several surveys of environment in offices have been conducted in recent years by administrators, public health inspectors, medical officers and others. Each one of the published reports has some interest, but by demonstrating that it is impossible for individuals or groups of laymen to possess all the necessary skills and experience to appraise the many aspects of an environment, they reinforce the need for a multi-disciplinary approach.

THE BUILDING ENVIRONMENT

The ramifications of building environment are endless. Conditions within a building are dependent on the surroundings, circumstances and climate outside. The form and relationship of building groups (e.g., town centres) influences the design of individual buildings. Building owners' and architects' ideas about people's social and psychological needs will form a basis for fundamental policy decisions about a building's form, although there will be little or no evidence to substantiate them.

An example of this is the argument that, in terms of spatial layouts and environmental conditions, a building should be stimulating, for in that way it can optimally achieve its practical ends:

Normal consciousness, perception and thought can be maintained only in a constantly changing environment; when there is no change a state of "sensory deprivation" occurs. Experiment has shown that a homogeneous and unvarying environment produces boredom, restlessness, lack of concentration and reduction in intelligence.

This is the psychological basis for deliberately creating varying conditions in buildings. Office blocks in which each floor has the same layout, colour, materials and climate are just asking for trouble. . . . The sort of variation that we often demand instinctively on aesthetic grounds, has a sound physiological and psychological basis. A change in environment stimulates our built-in devices to perceive and respond rapidly to significant events and efficiency is thereby increased. It is worth paying for variety (Noble, 1963).

This argument, which is heard at many conferences and put forward by many architects when referring to open plan offices, seems to arise from a misunderstanding of what constitutes sensory deprivation. The existence of a book with that title (Soloman, 1961) is well known to architects, but few have read it and understand that the effects described are the result of fairly gross sensory deprivation in the sense usually meant by psychologists. It is true, though, that some office environments are very dull and lack stimulus. Whether this has any implication for efficiency, what the optimal limits of environmental stimulation are, and how they are to be attained, are all questions yet to be answered. It is perhaps, therefore, premature to state that "it is worth paying for variety." Yet if building environments have a major influence, good or bad, upon people's mental state, as well as upon their physical comfort and, possibly, health, then this is not something which should be left to chance, nor to inexpert investigation. There exists a clear need for research which will establish the facts.

One problem which has to be recognised in any such research is that people are not necessarily the best judges of what they need; they have a tendency to state a preference for the conditions with which they are most familiar. Furthermore, it is dangerous to generalise from one case to another without examining the differences between sub-samples of a population. This study has demonstrated that office staff responses to an environment are likely to differ according to the respondents' age, sex, status, and experience of working in other buildings. Some recent official studies of office conditions may be suspect because this matter, so far as can be seen, was not taken into account.

Although their effect has to be seen in its totality, the major components of an environment have, unavoidably, to be considered separately.

Space

Today's typical office building has a linear plan-form with a building width of around 35 to 50 ft which consists, internally, of a central corridor with shallow offices on either side. The only substantial points of difference with many office buildings of the immediate prewar period are external cladding and fluorescent lighting systems.

The most likely explanation for the continuation of this type of design is habit; a prolongation, possibly, of the traditional search for daylight. The feasibility of natural lighting in city centres is rarely questioned, even for first floor offices in densely built-up and overshadowed areas, and there is still a widespread belief that bylaws dictate a minimum window-to-floor-area ratio. The virtue of large windows has been part of the philosophy of the "modern movement" in architecture for so long that it would be surprising if both architects and local authority planning officers had not been moulded to uncritical acceptance of the daylight "slab."

Yet another possible explanation can be attributed to the general preference for (or at least expectation of) small-sized office spaces which is found in large organisations as well as small. However, an important consequence of departing from linear plan-forms and adopting deep buildings is the probable need for very large clerical areas (i.e., open planning) so that people's view of daylight and the world outside the building shall not be obstructed by partition walls.

An examination of the attitudes towards small and large general office areas held by the three main hierarchical sub-groups of managers, supervisors and clerks showed that only managers were able to cite substantial advantages for the large spaces. Other users expressed a clear preference for smaller areas. Supervisors were the group most averse to large offices, their reasons mainly being in terms of "keeping track of staff" and creating "esprit de corps." The clerks who least liked large offices were not the ones who worked in such spaces but the occupants of smaller, partitioned areas. This suggests that people may be more prepared to accept some (perhaps unusual) environmental features if they have already acquired some experience of them.

Sociometric studies have indicated some possible consequences for management of the choice between large and small workspaces: small office areas containing single working units may help to generate within them small competitive teams whose immediate loyalties are to themselves, whereas large areas may produce a more generally collaborative whole. If this should be confirmed, the implication is that, where the performance of the work will be assisted by inter-group rivalries, small working areas should be provided. On the other hand, where work demands the co-operative efforts of many, the large areas may be found more effective. But whatever the relation between space-size and group cohesiveness or loyalties, buildings can only be designed to be most efficient and satisfactory in use if the operational consequences of the design decisions are understood.

Light

Historically, the purpose of windows was to provide light. It is now possible to do this more consistently and more reliably (perhaps, therefore, less interestingly) by electricity. Office workers are likely to say that they would rather work in daylight than electric light, and their belief in the importance of daylighting is shared by both physicians and architects. No objective support for this belief is known to exist, and an assessment of what constitutes a subjectively acceptable visual environment showed that in conditions where permanent artificial lighting and an unobstructed view of windows exists, people working substantially in artificial light tend to grossly over-estimate the proportion of daylight to artificial light on the working plane. The probabilities are that windows are really valued for their view of the exterior and that in the second half of the twentieth century this is their important function. The study suggests that daylighting provisions might more reasonably be made in terms of meeting subjective needs than of attaining arbitrary physical levels.

Modern technology is influencing the function of windows in other ways. An increase in the volume of traffic in city centres has created the problem of external traffic noise which is transmitted through the external fabric to the interior of the buildings, most of it going through the windows. Windows are usually kept shut in order to limit the annoyance, but this affects their performance as ventilators. In many modern buildings the size of windows has created a problem of solar radiation gains and the consequent likelihood of the interiors becoming too hot. Windows occupy a central position in a study of building environment; the problem of their design is to reconcile the conflicting requirements which are made upon them.

Thermal Conditions

Heating installations in modern office buildings are normally capable of providing comfortably warm conditions in the most severe winter. Nowadays office staff are likely to prefer a fairly high air temperature, in the region of 70 to 72°F. This is often provided but ventilation is rarely efficient and sensations of draughts, whether caused by movement of air or radiation from the body to cold surfaces like windows, are commonly experienced.

In some recent British owner-occupied office buildings a better control of the thermal environment has been obtained by the installation of complete airconditioning systems. These can remove unwanted heat gains from solar radiation and mechanical and electrical equipment, and control ventilation rates, air temperatures and relative humidities. An airconditioning plant will also eliminate the ingress of atmospheric pollution and, by permitting fixed windows, reduce the transmission of external noise.

Noise

Noise is perhaps the major environmental problem of offices in city centres. It is commonly believed that large general clerical areas present special difficulties in the control of internal noise but surveys have shown that this is not necessarily true. Although it is impossible to make unequivocal comparisons with smaller offices or with other buildings, the sound levels registered in one building in large open offices whose area is of the order of 35,000 sq.ft rarely exceeded 55 dBA. This was only slightly higher (and sometimes lower) than the sound levels recorded in smaller office areas in the same building and in offices of 20 to 40 people elsewhere. Much can be done to reduce the problem with suitable acoustic treatment of the ceiling and floor surfaces. Nonmetallic waste bins and chairs with rubber-tipped feet will limit the amount of noise created within the office, and it has a better chance of being absorbed if the space is large, e.g., upwards of 50 ft wide.

A substantial reduction of window areas, the use of double glazing, the elimination of opening lights and the use of heavy forms of construction in preference to light ones, such as curtain walling, will reduce the effects of street noise. But the only way in which the problem will be really solved will be by re-locating offices in quiet zones or, in the long term, by new town planning policies.

THE ENVIRONMENTAL DESIGN PROCESS

The creation of the total environment has traditionally been the architect's job but it is now such a complex task that, in the most enlightened offices, multi-disciplinary design teams are found to be necessary.

Decisions which affect the office environment are seldom based upon research findings. This could scarcely be otherwise for there have been few user-requirement studies in buildings. Such topics as lighting and ventilation and heating have been studied in great detail by psychologists, physiologists and other specialists, but their influence has been less than might be expected. Environmental design has tended to mean the adaptation of a given constructional design by the piecemeal addition of lights, heaters, blinds, ventilators, and other fittings. There has been no serious movement to design commercial buildings around the functions they are meant to serve.

Environmental design is so complicated that it is not surprising that designers sometimes succeed in manufacturing their own problems. For obvious reasons a wholly intuitive approach cannot be very successful, yet this is the main basis of current practice, as, for the moment, it must be. Not only is there little positive design guidance available but the building educational system has been such that there are few designers who could or would use it if there were more. The provisions of recent office legislation are rudimentary, and offer no help; it is safe to say that the standards which have been established so far will be exceeded by a comfortable margin in all new office buildings. And the history of environmental legislation (consider, for example, the Factories Act) does not suggest that regulations, when they are made, will be unduly restrictive.

The design of office space is unlikely, in the immediate future, to change from being a matter of arbitrary decision and personal hunch. Because of the nature of their training most architects already qualified will continue to take a fragmented view of the design team's responsibilities in this particular sector. They will regard it as their task to deal with some parts of the problem and they will leave other parts to their specialist consultants. The consultants are likely to display a lack of interest in the total environment and they may interpret their responsibilities narrowly: concerning themselves solely with, say, the electric lighting design, or the thermal environment. Some matters will probably be taken for granted, including the place and function of windows, which, in all probability, will be designed for their effect upon the external elevations. The social consequences of design of office space will not be questioned, for it is probable that none will be expected. A change of attitude will only occur slowly, and must eventually be brought about by changes in architectural education. But it is not surprising that practising architects simplify their design process, even if it means curtailing consideration of important matters, for where environmental design procedures have been evolved they are often complicated, time-consuming and suspect.

There should be no doubt about the low efficiency of present design procedures and current attitudes to office environment: the results can be seen in that part of the approved 120 million or so square feet of post-war office space already constructed. It is fair to ask how many office buildings really are functionally efficient, and provide pleasant working conditions; how many really integrated examples of commercial architecture are to be seen, and how many buildings still look well after only a few years' use. The fault is not the architect's alone, for when he designs the buildings, the users are frequently unknown, and offices are sometimes badly mis-used (see, for example, Casson, 1964). Moreover, there is quite inadequate feedback of information to the architect about the performance of his buildings.

There is need for new thought about the requirements of office space, not least from building owners and users. Owners will need to take a more prominent part in preparing the brief than they do now, for, after all, they know best the use to which the building will be put. Unfortunately, a serious problem of understanding and communication is all too common. Langdon (1963) has described this as happening in acute form in mechanised offices: the client is insufficiently analytical in preparing a detailed brief and the architect is too unfamiliar with the requirements to complete it himself.

Flexibility (or Adaptability)

The likelihood of change in office work and in the use of office space has become so great that it is now usual for a measure of "flexibility" to be built into a new office build-ing. The use of modules is convenient for construction at least as much as for adaptability in use. Increasing use of industrial methods of building will inevitably result in even greater use of dimensional standardisation. Demountable partitions are used extensively to meet present needs for both private offices and flexibility. Their functional requirements of lightness and sound insulation are in obvious conflict; in practice it is both difficult and expensive to achieve any useful sound insulation from demountable partitions in combination with suspended ceilings. It is possible that such problems in the use of partitions will be resolved by their omission.

A TREND TO OPEN PLANNING IN OWNER-OCCUPIED OFFICES

In most commercial establishments O and M departments seem to occupy a relatively lowly position, being more concerned with method than organisation, so an impression acquired during this study that the building requirements of office functions have not been appraised very critically is probably true. This helps to explain the lack of any clear and positive directions in the planning of office spaces by commercial organisations. Taken together, the likelihood of increasing needs for flexibility and for inter-office communication, the use of mechanical or electronic procedures, and the findings that the lighting requirements of clerks can, in suitable circumstances, be adequately met by well designed artificial lighting, suggest the suitability for more widespread use of deep, artificially lit office buildings. These will need to contain open-planned office space, with a minimum of partitions and a maximum size of window, so that staff working in the interior of the space have an adequate view to the outside world.

The choice between slab or block design is, however, one which in general can only be made by owner-occupiers: deep buildings are unlikely to be suitable for letting, unless it can be expected that the unit of letting will be a whole floor. Office layouts approximating to this form have often been used for junior staff employed on routine work and they are also quite common for highly-paid professional and technical staff in drawing offices. But they are rarely used for junior and middle grades of clerical office management in this country, although the practice is common in the United States. Indeed, the most senior executives of some firms in that country work in shared offices for the express purpose of achieving better communications and rapid decision-making. From this point of view, private rooms for any staff are less efficient than open offices just because they restrict opportunities for direct and informal communication. They are also more expensive in both spatial and economic terms.

It is possible, then, that an important trend in the design of owner-occupied office buildings will be towards deep, open-planned space, for this is certainly the most flexible arrangement. Full airconditioning is likely to become more necessary and therefore more common.

THE LESSONS OF THE PROJECT FOR FURTHER ENVIRONMENTAL RESEARCH

This office building research project has been a first experiment in the working of a particular type of multi-disciplinary research team and, for at least half the members of the team, an introduction to architecture and building problems. This report must necessarily be regarded as an interim statement, constituting a starting point for further studies. Besides reviewing much work already published, the team has explored several new fields. Inevitably, a great deal has been left outstanding. The most important points of office design needing further attention are first: an examination of sizes of office occupancy, and second: studies of the nature of office work as it affects the need for office space.

The study has shown that the working environments which architects create will influence human behaviour in many ways, and the value of psychological investigations of building design problems has been demonstrated. There are a number of questions of particular psychological importance which need further work to develop the line of investigation which has been opened up, notably, perhaps, the degree to which one environmental factor affects the subjective

experience of another. There is much anecdotal, and little experimental, evidence in this field, yet it is likely to be at the very root of an understanding of the total environment.

The use of a "building type study" as the basis for research into the total environment has, on the whole, been successful, for it permits examination of all or most of the environmental factors. But it has the disadvantage that it becomes difficult to separate what unavoidably become the two objects of the work, i.e., the environmental aims of the long-term research programme and the building-type problems thrown up by the immediate investigations. The Unit already has two building-type projects running simultaneously; it now seems advisable to change one of these to an expressly environmental project. A single-parameter study would be a retrogressive step; what is wanted, perhaps, is a multi-building-type study. One possibility is a consideration of the "windowless" environments which are increasingly being provided in such a variety of buildings as department stores, underground railways, photographic laboratories, race-track-plan hospitals, factories and, perhaps, even space-craft and submarines.

Finally, a necessary task which remains for the future is the establishment of a means to evaluate and compare total environments. It is already abundantly clear that it will be difficult to devise a method which can secure general acceptance: the number of thermal comfort scales in use, for example, indicates the problems of weighting the components of even a simple index.

At the time of writing, "environment" is a word in popular use, especially in connection with architecture, but it tends to have different meanings and implications for different people. In this report it is taken to be the sum of the physical and emotional sensations experienced by people within buildings and arising out of their use of those buildings. These sensations include bodily comfort, aesthetic sensibilities and social relationships; they may originate in the external climate, the location and the social milieu, but they are influenced and modified by the building's design.

The *long-term* aim of the research is the

academic development of an understanding of this "total environment." A building type is a convenient base for such studies because it provides real situations in which many of the component environmental factors are acting together.

The choice of offices as such a base was made for a number of reasons. This building type seemed to be a natural progression from factories because it was another workplace, with related functions and similar purposes. The annual capital investment was unknown (there are no central agencies maintaining records) but was believed to be high. No current research into this building type was known apart from a user-satisfaction survey by the Central Office of Information (see Langdon and Keighley, 1964) and a study of the design of space for automatic data processing by the Building Research Station (Langdon, 1963). It was considered more worth-while to investigate building types where the gap between knowledge available and knowledge applied to design was not very wide; contemporary practice in office design did not lag significantly behind existing knowledge, indicating a need for some new thought. Many buildings were available for study, there seemed no necessity for the Unit to obtain staff with specialised knowledge of the building type and opportunities for studying environment were plentiful.

The form of the office project has been as follows (for a detailed description see Manning, 1964):

(i) A series of background studies to compile a bibliography and define the characteristics, population and distribution of post-war office buildings (Taylor, 1962).

(ii) Preliminary visits to a representative sample of buildings in Liverpool, Manchester and elsewhere.

(iii) A series of detailed investigations of environmental conditions and other matters. Physical conditions were examined in a sample of nine buildings. Psychological studies of clerical staffs' attitudes towards their physical and social environment were made in the new headquarters office building of the Cooperative Insurance Society (the CIS) in Manchester, which houses more than 2,500 staff.

(iv) Individual reports by the four research staff:

(a) a general survey by the architect of the literature relating to office design and environment

(b) an account by the geographer of the general characteristics, population and location of post-war office buildings in England and Wales

(c) a report by the physicist upon the results of surveys in offices of thermal conditions in winter and summer, noise, and lighting

(d) a report by the psychologist upon the response of the CIS staff to their working environment and its implications for office design (Wells, 1964).

These four separate reports have been combined together to form this present "multidisciplinary" report. Although an environment is experienced as a whole, with all the different stimuli acting simultaneously, this report has necessarily to deal with the more obviously important components in isolation.

THE PILKINGTON RESEARCH UNIT'S PRELIMINARY SURVEY OF OFFICES

The Unit's preliminary visits were to 21 buildings in the north-west of England which were representative of "large," "medium" and "small" office buildings (Taylor, 1962). A total of 37 businesses occupying space within these buildings was visited. The sample included different departments of central and local government, representative professions, public corporations, insurance, shipping, industry, chain stores and the building industry (Table 47-1). The areas of office space in individual occupation ranged upwards from 200 to several hundred thousand square feet.

Use of Space

Most office space was used as a combination of open offices together with a number of small rooms accommodating one or two people. It was noticeable, however, that the larger the organisation and its floor space, the more marked was the tendency for bigger and more open offices to be used. At the

Table 47-1 Analysis by Standard Industrial Classification of business interest of 37 firms visited during preliminary stage of project

SIC Order		No. of firms
I	Agriculture, Forestry, Fishing	1
IV	Chemicals and Allied Industries	1
VI	Engineering and Electrical Goods	1
X	Textiles	1
XV	Paper, Printing and Publishing	1
XVII	Construction	1
XIX	Transport and Communication	5
XX	Distributive Trades	6
XXI	Insurance, Banking and Finance	7
XXII	Professional and Scientific Services	2
XXIII	Miscellaneous Services	4
XXIV	Public Administration and Defence	7
	Total no. of businesses	37

Note. Unless a firm was known to be a wholesaler or factor without manufacturing capacity, the classification was by SIC Order of the original producer.

other extreme, small organisations employing total office staffs of six or seven might accommodate them in three, four or five separate rooms.

Original planning decisions may exert a great deal of influence upon the way in which open office space is used. A number of buildings, for example, had been designed as long blocks or wings, with a total width of 40 to 50 feet. The office space in these was usually served by a central corridor and the depth of the room from the windows was a maximum of about 25 ft and frequently less than 20 ft. It was rare to see such offices more than 100 ft or so long. Small private offices partitioned off from large open offices were usually arranged on the building perimeter, i.e., by the windows. Areas of usable office space (i.e., in the case of tenants, rented area) varied from 61 to 182 sq.ft per person.

User Requirements of Office Space

Each occupier was asked whether his firm's work made any special requirements of the office space. The main need was for general-purpose space and there was little demand for special provision for excessively large or heavy or noisy equipment or individual procedures.

The office managements were also asked what they considered to be important factors in the design of office space. Most firms said they had been looking for good working conditions. This sometimes meant low levels of noise but more often good lighting (by which they intended daylighting). The need for space which would be readily adaptable to new layouts was mentioned; one firm chose their present offices because the standards of finishes and fittings in that building were reasonably good, while in alternative buildings they were "cheap and nasty."

Spatial Standards

Only a few large firms had an established policy for determining their office standards. Where such standards had been fixed the minimum area was of the order of 60 sq.ft per person. A feeling was often expressed that the heights of office spaces were inadequate nowadays: for example, 9 ft was sometimes held to be too low. The structural design of floors often dictated the layout of an office because of the need to locate banks of filing cabinets over beams.

Lighting

Almost all managements assumed that good daylight was an essential requirement for their offices, but few appeared to be very critical of the widely varying standards they had. In broad terms, there seemed to be three types of plan arrangement of general office space in relation to lighting:

(i) Long narrow rooms with windows on one side and a typical maximum depth of 3 desks arranged at right angles to the windows

(ii) Large open areas with moderate to good electric lighting; people not on the perimeter were working partly or mainly by electric light, but they had some sort of a view to the outside

(iii) Badly shaped spaces and ill-designed lighting installations; people were working in poor daylight conditions or with inadequate electric light, sometimes without a view outside.

It is obvious that some electric light will always be used during office working hours in categories (ii) and (iii). Offices with the arrangements described in category (i) normally expect to work without electric light (especially during the summer months) although, in practice, it was not unusual to find that electric lights were being used. But this could be due to a number of factors, including window design, weather condition and time of year. Many offices in city centres, particularly those on lower floors, are seriously overshadowed, so that any daylight received at points more than two or three feet from the window is indirect, being reflected from buildings opposite.

In some large organisations it seems to be tacitly accepted that clerical staff should not work except in daylight (i.e., within about 10 to 15 ft of a window) and it seems likely that this attitude influences the design of the buildings which these organisations rent or build. Several post-war buildings contained internal light wells which were lined with white or glazed bricks which had become dirty and were patterned with drain pipes. Invariably they looked depressingly dingy, yet the managements seemed certain that although their staffs would prefer an external wall to an area wall, the area was acceptable in a way that total reliance upon electric light would not have been.

On the whole, people appeared to like working fairly high up in buildings (e.g., 8 to 10 storeys high or higher) because of the better opportunity for daylight and a view, and of being away from street noises. Venetian blinds, sun blinds or curtains were usually fixed after the building contract had been completed and when their necessity had become apparent. In the upper floors of the very high buildings the view from the working position was onto very bright sky. The views from the lower floors were more likely to be of other buildings.

A majority of the offices used tubular fluorescent lighting.

Heating and Ventilation

The principal difficulties concerned with heating and ventilation in offices seemed to arise from the different thermal requirements of different individuals. Differences of attitude to the thermal environment between men and women, and young and old may be expected, but people of the same age and sex, working together, may complain of completely different conditions (e.g., draughts and stuffy atmospheres) at the same time. Of all the environmental problems this seems to be the one of which office managers are most aware and which they find most intractable. The problem may at times be extreme. To avoid disputes as to whether windows should be open or closed, one manager had instructed his porter to go round the building opening all windows for five minutes in each hour. This building received more fresh air than most, for, typically, the offices which were visited during the period July to November had almost all their windows shut tight.

Practically all of the offices which were visited were heated by radiators placed under the windows. Where private offices were partitioned off from an open space it was not unusual for thermal conditions in the small rooms and the main spaces to be quite noticeably different. On several occasions office managements mentioned the need for heating systems to be subject to greater and more local control. In a number of buildings noticeable differences in air temperature were reported to occur between the upper and lower floors (the upper floors being the colder ones) and between rooms on the north and south sides.

Thermal Conditions in Summer

Several firms reported uncomfortably hot conditions during summer, but the principal form of discomfort during this time of the year seemed to be caused by glare. It was, however, difficult to assess the importance of this issue for response may be largely dependent upon recent conditions and the summer of 1962 (when these preliminary visits were made) was not a noticeably hot one.

Noise

Where offices are sited fronting onto busy main shopping streets or traffic routes, disturbance from outside noise can be substantial. The noise level can be reduced by closing all windows but this presents the office workers with a choice of reducing the noise level and having to suffer a stuffy atmosphere, or of ventilating their rooms and accepting the noise. The usual course is to keep windows closed. Some of the offices in the sample which were located in shopping areas had to contend with canned music from the shops beneath.

Internal noises seemed to be relatively unimportant, even in large open offices, although one organisation explained its use of small rooms on the grounds that they limited the number of people distracted by telephone calls. In small offices shared by an executive and his secretary the typewriter could not be used during a conversation on a telephone or with a visitor. Most large office organisations had machine sections, but these were usually partitioned off from normal clerical offices.

Construction work was a common cause of complaints of noise, particularly in the early days of a building's life when some parts were undergoing preparations for a new tenancy, and the noise created—especially that transmitted through the structure—annoyed tenants already established. Heavy footfalls from public corridors and even from floors above were often audible.

In most private offices where an adequate degree of privacy was considered necessary, the requirements were met, but in some small offices it was often possible to be aware of telephone conversations in adjoining rooms.

A CASE STUDY OF THE CIS BUILDING IN MANCHESTER

The Pilkington Research Unit's long-term aim is the development of an environmental discipline in which the components are studied as a whole. This section consists of a case study of the total environment in Britain's tallest office building: the headquarters of the Co-operative Insurance Society Limited in Manchester, which was completed in 1962.[1] The building consists of an extensive podium which is about

175 ft by 250 ft and contains the ground to fourth floors. A tower containing twenty-one further floors rises above. The staff number about 2,500.

The Unit's research interest in the building developed from a letter received from the General Manager of the CIS (Dinnage, 1962), who said that he had read of the office-building project in *The Guardian* (Anon., 1963) and would be glad to offer facilities for study. These were readily accepted, for not only was the building probably the most advanced of its kind in the country, but the physical and human problems of populating it with a large staff which had previously worked in a variety of conventional and much smaller office buildings presented an unusual opportunity to study the human aspects of a modern environment.[2]

An environment results from the satisfaction of a functional need for space. At its simplest, the requirement may be entirely utilitarian; in a more complex form, there may be substantial overtones of a subjective type, e.g., "the projection of the company image." But with all design—even of utility buildings—decisions have to be made which involve the expression of subjective preferences. Translated into a building these decisions have a permanent effect upon people's behaviour and comfort. In this chapter an attempt will be made to describe how the environment of the CIS was created, how the decisions were made, what sort of environment has resulted, and how the occupants have reacted to it.

THE APPOINTMENT OF THE DESIGN TEAM

At an early stage in the Company's consideration of its new building, Mr G. S. Hay, Chief Architect to the CWS in Manchester, had been appointed architect for the development; subsequently Mr Gordon Tait of London was invited to act as Associate with Mr Hay. The joint architects then advised on the appointments of consulting structural, electrical and mechanical engi-

---

[1] For an account of the early studies (particularly the psychological investigations) in this building see Wells (1963), and Wells, in this section. For a short reappraisal of the CIS environment after its first 18 months in use see Manning & Wells (1964).

[2] The building has been described and illustrated in many technical journals. See, for example, Scott (1963).

neers. According to the General Manager, it had always been considered possible that the building would be fully air-conditioned, and the consultant mechanical engineer was therefore asked, soon after his appointment, to investigate the financial implications of such a decision.

A party consisting of a CIS director, the Investments Secretary, and two architects and the mechanical engineer made a visit to North America to study the design of tall office buildings, and the problems of heating, ventilating and airconditioning, and vertical movement of staff mail and documents.

This visit appears to have had a major influence upon the building's design. On the deputation's return the architects were asked to prepare a scheme for a single large block of between 20 and 25 storeys, to proceed on the assumption that curtain walling would be used, and, providing the cost was not prohibitive, to employ full airconditioning. A previous intention of adopting open-planned offices was confirmed. The architects and probably the other members of the party, too, had obviously been greatly influenced by the work of the American architects Skidmore, Owings and Merrill, especially, perhaps, by their administrative building for the Inland Steel Company in Chicago.

Later, a third firm of architects and interior design consultants (Design Research Unit) was appointed to take responsibility for the interior decor and furniture. The largest part of their interior design work is to be seen in the entrance hall, dining rooms, and in the executive suite, but they were also responsible for the partitions, furniture and colour schemes in the general office areas.

THE REASONS AND POLICIES UNDERLYING CERTAIN IMPORTANT FEATURES OF THE DESIGN

The building has two features which make it somewhat remarkable. In the first place it is unusually tall; and, secondly, the interior was conceived as an example of "open planning."

The principles for design proposed by the project steering committee were threefold:

(i) The building should add to the prestige of the Society and the Co-operative movement

(ii) It should improve the appearance of the City of Manchester

(iii) It should provide first-class accommodation for staff, with a view to attracting new and retaining existing staff (Dinnage, 1961).

The General Manager has said, "If I may use a rather hackneyed phrase, we wanted to impress an 'image' on the people of Manchester and elsewhere of the strength and size of the CIS through the medium of a modern office building. Very few people see our balance sheet or read our chairman's report but this new building will be a constant reminder that the CIS is a large and first-class insurance office. We have already made use of the model in our advertising material and hope to extend this when the building is completed. We believe that these new premises will have an impact upon our staff, including the senior staff, by giving them a feeling of pride."

One of the reasons for the original decision to use open planning was said to be that there is a work-flow in insurance just like that of industry. Examples were given of the processing of a new policy and the settling of a claim, where many departments would be concerned. The need for flexibility in both work-flow and departmental size, because of changes of work method and increasing mechanisation, was underlined. In fact, in many cases the policy does not seem to have been followed consistently and a substantial amount of partitioning has been used. The reasons for enclosing areas and separating departments have been sought, for this action was in direct contradiction to the stated policy of open planning. In the course of the project it seemed virtually impossible to determine a particular reason why this was done or who was mainly responsible. The management, however, do not necessarily endorse those impressions of their partitioning policy formed by the Unit and reported in this and the two succeeding paragraphs.

A number of explanations has been given. One senior executive said that he had tried to imagine how youngsters and nervous people would feel when walking across one of the podium floors, each of which contains approximately 35,000 sq.ft of office space exclusive of service areas. He had felt that the open spaces and great numbers of people might result in unpleasant self-consciousness, and therefore decided to include a certain amount of partitioning to break-up these very large areas. Thereafter, partitioning had just crept into the plans of the tower floors.[3]

It is possible that the original conception of open planning was not strongly held, or that the custom of physically separating departments was too strong. It seems more likely, however, that many departmental managers had been vociferous—and successful—in their demands for partitioning around their departments. Some small areas within departments are enclosed by partitions. An explanation for this was given in terms of supervisor needs: a supervisor could do his job more easily if he could clearly see where his responsibilities ended. Asked whether supervisors would be able to supervise more efficiently if their sections were screened off and separated from other staff, a respondent replied that he could not think of any reason why this should be the case, but that supervisors preferred to be screened off from one another.[4]

The practice in the old office buildings, by which chief clerks had raised platforms approximately 10 ft square in size which were screened but not separated-off as offices has been carried over to the new building, where they have an area 2 × 2

modules in size (approximately 100 sq.ft) raised above the floor to a height of approximately 10 inches and surrounded on three sides by glass screens. The reasons given for the platform are better provision for the supervision of staff, a degree of privacy behind which clerks can be interviewed and a status symbol and prop to the authority of the chief clerks. In fact, as chief clerks are placed on the perimeter of the building so that they can face inwards towards the staff, some of them have difficulty in supervising because of the reflections on the glass of their partitions from the windows behind them. They can be easily seen but cannot easily see!

Totally enclosed private offices were not envisaged at all in the early stages of planning but the strong objections put forward by the senior employees brought about a change in policy.[5] The system of private offices was simplified by having only two sizes, their allocation depending upon seniority, and available only to employees with the rank of "official" (i.e., executive). They are constructed of floor-to-ceiling partitioning which follows the line of the modules forming the planning grid for the office space. A clear criterion of the size of a private office derives from the company's rating of seniority. The rank of "senior official" entitles the holder to a 3 × 3 module (approximately 240 sq.ft) office; the rank of "official" entitles its holder to a 3 × 2 module (approximately 160 sq.ft) office. The criterion is a clearly understood one, and has the rationale that senior officials are more frequently liable to hold conferences and receive visitors in their offices. The occupants of the 3 × 2 module office were given the choice of three complete decors but were not able to take part of one and part of another. Senior officials had a greater range of choice.

There were certain eating distinctions in the old premises: a staff dining room for the rank and file employees, a dining room for chief clerks and junior officials, and a separate dining room for senior officials.

---

[3] On seeing the draft of this section, the management stated that partitions have only been provided in the following cases:

   i. private offices for officials, which were always intended
   ii. divisions between quite separate departments
   iii. cloakrooms
   iv. storerooms
   v. interview rooms
   vi. where isolation was justified on grounds of noise

The management also states that *no* partitioning has been introduced "to break up large areas"; no partitioning has "just crept into the plan."

[4] The management emphasises that all supervisors do *not* have separately screened sections.

[5] The management has explained that the occupants of the private offices had some influence upon the decision to change from partial screening to full-height screening.

The new arrangement consists of three restaurants on the twenty-fourth floor and a cafeteria in the basement. Of the restaurants, one is for visitors, one for all grades of officials and another for chief clerks. Junior officials and chief clerks have now moved apart; as one chief clerk described it, into officers' and sergeants' messes. Rank-and-file members of the staff eat in the basement cafeteria. It seems unfortunate that there should be a physical separation of twenty-odd floors between the two sets of dining services, for not only must this be an uneconomical arrangement, but it introduces the possibility of the creation of a substantial psychological gulf between management and workers.

THE PHYSICAL ENVIRONMENT

Spatial

The use of a plan-module for the office space has already been mentioned; its dimension is 5ft 2in. in both directions, determined, so far as can be seen, quite arbitrarily. It consists of a square of twenty-five 1 ft square floor tiles bounded by a 2 inch wide strip. The ceiling has the same overall pattern of 5ft 2in. squares, but it has a marked directional character, for the finish consists of ribbed metal pans with a recessed 5 ft by 1 ft light fitting in the centre.

The total area of *office* space (i.e., excluding lavatories, lifts, stairs, etc.) on one of the podium floors is about 35,000 sq.ft; on one of the tower floors about 7,500 sq.ft. Gross areas per clerk (i.e., including circulation, coat hanging space, etc.) vary from about 77 sq.ft in the more densely occupied podium floors to 83 sq.ft and upwards in the tower block. Net areas per clerk (i.e., the actual desk and chair space and immediate circulation) range upwards from about 45 sq.ft.

Visual

The outer walls of the CIS are clad with an elegantly detailed system of curtain walling. Glazing extends from the top of the perimeter heater outlet (which is only 9 inches high) to the ceiling, and there are no opening lights. Although the "window"

area is so extensive, it could not be sufficient to provide an adequate amount of daylight for working in the inner areas of either podium or tower. This was clearly recognised at the design stage by both architects and owners and the electric lighting installation is used constantly and without restraint. The windows in the tower provide magnificent views and adjustable vertical white blinds, which are both attractive and efficient, are used to provide protection from sun or sky glare.

Levels of daylight in this building have not been measured, for they would be largely meaningless. Most, if not all, of the 19 tower office floors receive daylight from a virtually unobstructed sky, but much of the podium, in which rather more than half the total number of staff work, is obstructed by nearby buildings.

The electric lighting installation consists of one 5ft 65 watt "warm daylight" fluorescent tube per 5ft 2in. square module mounted within a fitting whose plastic louvred under-surface is flush with the ceiling. Measurements of the illumination at night have shown the typical range of illumination on the working surface of desks to be between 24 and 30 lm./sq.ft with a mean of 28 lm./sq.ft. The ratio of minimum to maximum illumination is 0.8, so that both the value of the illumination and its consistency are high—though the working illumination is not so high as the value of 36 lm./sq.ft which was intended. It has only been possible to estimate the glare index; it seems, however, that the value achieved is lower (i.e., better) than the recommended 19.

The reflectivities of the ceiling and desk tops are fairly high (75 and 32 percent respectively) but the floor is very dark (8 percent) and because so little light is reflected back to the ceiling, this surface appears dark too and, especially in some areas of the podium, gives a rather gloomy impression of the interior.

Thermal

The design criteria for the heating, ventilation and airconditioning of the office areas were (Anon., 1962):

Winter 70°F air temperature
Summer 75°F air temperature
Relative humidity 50 percent at all seasons
Fresh air changes per hour 2.0 to 3.9 (a minimum of 3.1 in the podium)

Surveys of the thermal conditions in this building were made during both winter and summer.

There were two surveys of *winter thermal conditions*. One was in January 1963, during a period of continuous frost. On this occasion, a number of measurements were taken on the eighth floor, which is completely open and without any private offices, over a period of 2 days. The number of occupants at the time of the survey was about seventy-five. The arrangement of the desks was such that no person was seated nearer than 4 ft to the perimeter heating and airconditioning units. The globe thermometers which marked the measuring stations were distributed over the occupied area, none being nearer to the windows than 4 ft.

During the two mornings of the survey external conditions were very similar, as indeed they were inside the building. There was a slow rise in the mean globe temperature on both days and, as might be expected for periods without direct sunshine, the maximum globe temperature was recorded at a station near the centre of the room, the minimum on the northern side of the building. During the afternoon, and due to some sunshine, globe temperatures at two positions on the south-western face of the building increased to above 75°F. It was found that:

(i) The relative humidities were all well within the range 30 to 70 percent.

(ii) The rate of air movement seldom rose above what is considered to be the upper limit for the comfort of people doing sedentary work. Values of 40 ft/min. or above were recorded for only 6 percent of the total readings, and none were above 43 ft/min. The average values of air movement were about 23 ft/min.

(iii) The mean globe temperatures varied throughout the two days by about 2 deg F; the variations of the globe temperatures at individual positions were similar to the variations of the means except when the sun shone brightly. Horizontal temperature gradients were small except during periods of bright sunshine.

(iv) In contrast with the results of some other surveys (Black, 1954), air temperatures in this office (mean values of between 73 and 74°F) were high.

(v) Equivalent temperatures were generally within the range reported as being suitable for normally clothed sedentary adults, of 66 to 72°F (Billington, 1953). The upper limits of the comfort ranges were exceeded for short periods only when there was direct sunshine, and this could have been avoided if the venetian blinds had been drawn more often.

(vi) The vertical temperature gradients were small, none exceeding 3°F between floor and ceiling.

Similar surveys of *summer thermal conditions* were made, again on the eighth floor, during the period 11th to 13th June 1963. A maximum shade air temperature of 80°F was recorded at the nearby meteorological station on June 11th; maximum CET inside the building at positions not in direct sunshine was as high as 72°F. Globe temperatures of over 80°F were recorded at only two positions. These occurred between 1300 and 1420 hours at a position near the southern corner and, after 1600 hours, at a position on the western corner where, because the blinds had not been drawn, the sun had shone directly onto the globe thermometers.

The next day was not quite so hot nor was the sunshine so prolonged, but external air temperatures were above 70°F for the greater part of the working day. The mean globe temperatures varied between 74.0 and 75.2°F; the highest reading was 80°F.

On the 13th June there was an abrupt change for the worse in the weather, but globe temperatures were only a few degrees lower than on the previous days. Air temperatures varied between 73°F on the 11th to 70°F on the 13th. Relative humidity was stable at 50 to 60 percent. The rate of air movement varied between 12 and 40 feet per minute with an average of 23 ft/min.

Aural

Measurements of noise level were made on the ground, second, fourth, eighth, and twenty-third floors, and included four large general offices, two machine rooms, a conference room, a private office and the staff cafeteria. The noise in the occupied general offices originated mainly within the rooms. In the large general offices on the second floor, i.e., the largest and most open space in the whole building, the noise levels complied with Beranek's criteria and the highest reading was only 2dBA above the Wilson Committee's recommendation (Committee on the Problem of Noise, 1963) of 55 dBA. Although the noise levels in the machine rooms exceeded Beranek's criteria, and were of the order of 75 dBA, they were not unreasonably high by comparison with similar measurements in machine rooms in other buildings.

In private offices, conversation and movement could be heard from the adjoining working areas.

PRELIMINARY INTERVIEWS WITH THE STAFF

An important requirement of a study of office environment is a specification of those features in a building which are influential in determining a person's subjective reactions to his workplace. In order to obtain this representatives of the rank-and-file clerical workers were interviewed, and their views on any aspect of the environment that they felt to be important to them were sought. The interviews were completely free-ranging, though the experimenter made sure that a number of specific topics were introduced.

Eight discussions were held, on each occasion with groups of six plus the interviewer. The composition of the different groups varied considerably in respect to age, sex, occupation and status, but the composition of a particular discussion group was usually fairly homogeneous. The participants were always drawn from the same department so that the members of a group should have points of common reference and be more at ease in familiar company. The age range was from fifteen years old (female juniors) to elderly (male section clerks).

The experimenter played the dual role of instigator and chairman. A number of general questions about the new environment were put to each group but the direction of the discussion was allowed to follow the interests of the participants and was not redirected unless the discussion became irrelevant or a mere catalogue of complaints.

What was being sought from the meetings was not an appraisal of the building but an estimate of the features that were subjectively of greatest importance, for the interviews were to act as a guide to the questions later to be asked in questionnaires. Obvious features such as heating, lighting and ventilation were raised, together with more general questions about liking the new building. The following is a summary of the sort of attitudes commonly expressed and the quotations, where used, have been selected because they were typical.

Because the interviewer had to start the discussion, a number of specific questions was asked about the airconditioning induction units which, to the staff, represent the heating installation. The first transcription comes from a single interview with a group of typists. It was typical of the response to the system in the early days of occupation when teething troubles were being sorted out, and it also suggests that position in the room was an important variable, a view supported by other testimony.

(*Interviewer*): "*What about the air-conditioner: do you find it to your liking?*"

"No, we don't." (loud agreement)

"I've got cramp up my arm and up my back."

"It isn't constant: you perhaps go in in the morning and it's really warm, so off comes your cardigan and you're really warm. You've been in about an hour or so and then it goes cold and you start getting a terrible draught on your feet, and this week we've noticed it as though it's going up to the ceiling and then hitting you on the back of the neck."

(*Interviewer, to girl who had not agreed with others about draughts*): "*How about you, do you get draughts?*"

"I don't know, and yet the girls on the next row of desks say they do. We don't notice it much where I am."

Also germane to the discussion of the air-conditioning system were questions of stuffiness and odours. Odours did not seem to present much of a problem, but the number of reports of stuffiness raised the question whether this might be due to the individual's working position on a floor, or the density of occupation of that floor.

The cleanliness of the new building was a question which was also relevant as the building is effectively sealed and the entire intake of air is filtered before being circulated. A girl commented: "Here you keep nice and clean, whereas before you were never clean. Your underclothes were filthy, and your body was filthy with the dirt you were kicking up, but here the atmosphere is very, very clean." Irritation with the noise made by the ventilating system was sometimes mentioned, as was the noise of the mechanical document conveyor, but most people commented on the comparative quiet of the new building. This was perhaps not surprising as the former head office stood beside a main line railway station.

Floor treatment was a topic in which almost no one was interested (possibly because it is a good surface) and, in itself, provoked no comment. There was a number of complaints from women that they were being made to wear flat heels so that they did not damage it. The senior management, however, has disclaimed any knowledge of such a directive and pointed out that only negligible damage to the office floors has occurred, although stiletto heels are now freely worn.

Ceiling height was treated more seriously. It emerged many times that those who found it too low were those who either sat in the middle of the room or who sat facing inwards. Many used the epithets "oppressive" or "depressing" to describe the effect of a low ceiling.

The colour scheme was a topic which provoked a good deal of discussion and disagreement. It was not possible to form any general impression as the range of agreement and disagreement was very great and

did not appear to be associated with age, sex, place where the respondent worked, or indeed anything else.

Lighting, both daylight and electric, is one of the most important components of the internal environment. Yet, surprisingly, it was not a topic which created much comment or feeling. The following was typical of many discussions:

(Interviewer): "What about the lighting; is this adequate?"
"Oh, the lighting doesn't bother me personally."
"I like the way it's covered up—you don't get the glare from it."
(Interviewer): "Oh, I see, you're talking about the fluorescent lights; I was thinking about the illumination in general."
"Oh, I think it's quite light enough."
"I've got no complaints about the lighting."
(Interviewer): "What about glare from the windows?"
"No, no we don't get any of that."
"We haven't had anything like that."
"The only thing is on the other side of the building; if it's sunny, you get the sun. But then, of course, you've got the venetian blinds and you can just adjust them to keep the light off your face without making it dark."

However, a view through the windows was felt to be of great importance; not necessarily a pleasant view but merely the opportunity to see out. The following arose when the colour scheme (not the fenestration) was under discussion:

"The windows here are marvellous because, before, we were caged in by bars and windows that you couldn't look out of at all. So the windows, lighting and pleasant surroundings here are a great boon."
"Well, in the room we were in before it was just four walls with windows up in the roof."
"You didn't know what it was doing outside unless it was brilliant sunshine beating down on the back of your neck (laughter). But apart from that you didn't know what the weather was like; whether it was rainy or foggy, or quite nice. Really you had no idea."

The feeling that it was important to be able to see what was going on outside was very widely held. The opposite view was never strenuously put in discussion, although a small proportion of people felt that it was a question of very little consequence.

Of the specific features discussed, the one which occupied the greatest amount of time was the lavatory facilities. Men were much less interested in the toilet accommodation than women, but nevertheless they rated them high on their list of priorities of office design. A number of specific criticisms were made of the new lavatories (even though they are of a standard very much higher than is usual), mainly in terms of overcrowding, overheating, wash basin design, and the lack of space for standing handbags. The men's concern was more in terms of privacy, cleanliness, and number of fittings. By contrast, the emphasis of the women's interest was on the attractiveness of the toilets. One girl commented about the lavatories in the previous office:

"It was a horrible place and made you feel contaminated by going in there, and it was very gloomy and depressing."

Other typical comments were: "Nice toilets seem to add to your personal comfort somehow," and, "It plays a big part in your working day."

Toilets are also places which women connect with their personal attractiveness, places to appraise themselves in a mirror and to make-up. They stressed the need for nice colours and elegant fittings and felt that these spaces should be at least as well appointed as the rest of the building.[6]

Apart from the discussion of the physical characteristics of the building, a good deal of time was devoted to intangibles, like the effects of the new building on such matters as personal relationships, work attitudes, and morale. Such discussions largely arose from the probing of attitudes to the building in general, to tower block design, and to the open planning of the interior.

A large proportion of those people interviewed were proud of working in this tall and very impressive building. One clerk expressed it this way:

"I feel very different when anybody says to me, 'Where do you work?' and I say 'at the CIS' and they say 'Oh, that big place.' You feel different."

"I don't know. You don't feel as if you're someone but you see they seem interested. I don't know, you just feel different with working somewhere different. . . . I don't know what it is, but I think most of us feel that way."

Although no one confessed to being personally afraid of the height, many people commented that there were plenty of others (always supposed to be female) who were. Several people said that they would be very unhappy if the horizontal members of the windows were not there.

The discussion of the new building often led to considerable talk about staff/management relations. Many people felt that these had suffered with the move into the new building. There was a feeling that the rank and file were being regimented. "It's more like the army now," and, "There are too many regulations; it was very easygoing before."

This appeared to be due, in part, to the management's and supervisors' zeal to keep everything crisp and tidy; to ban any personal effects, and to insist on desks being tidied every night. The new, more autocratic form of supervision was regarded as being a consequence of the large offices, which, it was felt, foster a passion for symmetrical layouts and obsessional tidiness. Section clerks, used to more autonomy and privacy, commented on the question whether they would rather have partitioning between sections:

"Oh, yes, partitioning is important. It's very distracting having other sections around you, maybe having discussions or something."

"Say something has gone wrong on your section, you can't tell your people off in private without every other section knowing about it."

---

[6] It is interesting to note that the standard of care taken by employees in the toilets has improved out of all recognition. A 5 PM inspection of all male and female toilets showed them to be immaculate; this was certainly not the experience in the old buildings. It seems, therefore, that the provision of high amenity levels has resulted in much better behaviour and treatment of the property.

(Interviewer): *"Do you find it easier or more difficult to supervise what's going on?"*

"Well, I don't say it's more awkward but, if something goes wrong, they've all got to know."

Typical comments from rank-and-file clerical workers were: "You feel guilty when you get up," and, "You feel self-conscious if you have to walk across the room to the front of one of the cabinets. You walk back across the room again and you feel—I don't suppose you are—but you feel that you're being watched." Perhaps most commonly of all though: "You feel they've got you where they can keep an eye on you." At a more general level, many people felt that they would prefer to work in a smaller group: "You get a more friendly atmosphere in a small place."

There was a great deal of indirect criticism of the new building in people saying that they had been much happier in the previous office, despite the poorer physical conditions.[7]

These comments, of course, are no more than impressionistic, and it must be emphasised, were obtained soon after the move into the new building and at a time when many of the staff may have been feeling uprooted from a way of life to which they had grown accustomed. They do, however, provide an overall view of the attitudes of

[7] These comments stimulated an interesting remark from the management, which is reproduced: "This is a strange reaction and, in my experience, true but possibly transitional. I have concluded that the more perfect one makes the environmental conditions the more the occupants will complain about deviations from the ideal. An example of this occurs during hot weather conditions when the occupants readily complain if the temperature inside the building reaches 74°F when a telephone call to neighbouring non-airconditioned buildings shows that temperatures of 80°F are being suffered without complaint. The simile of spoiled children comes to mind and if the criterion is a happy atmosphere and not an efficient and healthy one then the C.I.S. building may not be the right answer. For this reason social amenities become very important. Nothing has been said of our social amenities in the report, and it may be that they are an essential integral part in modern design to counteract the 'regimentation,' the 'regulations' and the 'coldness' referred to in the report."

the staff towards their management and their new building, at that time. The questions were not always the same, and the emphasis of interest varied with every group. Their value was not intrinsic, but consisted rather in providing an exploratory and descriptive background to a more comprehensive study. The impressions gained from them were subsequently used in the planning of questionnaires and more systematic surveys, experiments, and programmes of interviewing.

THE QUESTIONNAIRE SURVEYS OF ENVIRONMENTAL CONDITIONS

The First Questionnaire

Having learnt, from interviews, something of the staff's response to their building, the next step was to examine these attitudes in a more specific way and on a larger scale. The method adopted was to circulate a questionnaire to all the 2,500 employees, the replies to which were then analysed statistically.

Perhaps the first thing a building owner and architect would want to know from such an enquiry is whether a building had been produced which was satisfactory for the greatest number of people. The best indication of this is provided by the response to one of the groups of questions: more than 80 percent found their work no less enjoyable in the new building than it had been in the old and three-quarters of these actually stated that their work had become *more* enjoyable. 73 percent of the staff said that their personal relationships with their colleagues were either unaffected or even more friendly than previously (the remaining 27 percent found their personal relationships less friendly). Only a small number disliked working in a tall office block; 75 percent preferred the new building to the old. Taking the building as a whole, there is little doubt, then, that it is well-liked by its occupants.

The teething troubles with the airconditioning system have already been mentioned; the first questionnaire showed that the uncomfortable thermal conditions which were experienced in the early days of the building's occupation weighed very heavily with the staff. Lifts, too, were initially troublesome, and a majority of the users were critical of their functioning. Nearly 40 percent of the staff considered that the toilet accommodation was inadequate in some degree.

In spite of the impressions given by the interviews, the ceiling height was generally approved, and over 80 percent found the electric lighting satisfactory. Very few people were aware of any glare from the windows. 65 percent never found their office distractingly noisy. The colour scheme, however, came in for a great deal of criticism; it was the characteristic of the environment which the greatest number of occupants felt might be improved.

Asked to check a list of words they considered descriptive of their building, the majority of the staff expressed themselves in terms which were, no doubt, the guiding aims of both owners and architects: modern, light, comfortable, pleasant, friendly and efficient.

There was no significant change, for better or worse, in the number of people suffering from headaches or eyestrain. A question was asked about attitudes to the new staggered working hours which were made necessary in order to relieve the load of a concentration of staff on both the lift service and public transport system. The psychological interest of the question lay in whether the move into the new building had created any substantial measure of discontent and, if it had, whether it was influencing people's general satisfaction with the new building. In fact, less than one-fifth expressed any sort of disapproval.

The remaining questions differed from the others in that they did not call for a direct assessment of the actual environment, but instead were concerned with the individual's assessment of the ideal environment. Asked whether they felt it important to be able to see out of the office, even if there was plenty of electric light to see by, the response was overwhelmingly that it *was* important. Another question asked whether it was as good for the eyes to work

by electric light as by daylight: consistently, the great majority felt it was better for their eyes to have daylight to work by. It must, however, be noted that though these questions are complementary in some respects, the underlying attitudes and beliefs upon which they depend may be very different.

A final question asked in what sort of office the respondent would prefer to work, and offered three alternatives. 28 percent opted for a large open one, 45 percent for a smaller partitioned area, and the remainder stated that they had no preference. The result is interesting, for the conception of the building is basically an open plan. The fact that nearly half the staff said they preferred a smaller partitioned area, must constitute an implicit criticism of the type of accommodation provided.

Summarising the findings of a broad analysis of the first questionnaire, it was found that the building was generally regarded with favour by the majority of occupants, in spite of strong criticism of a number of features, notably the lift service and the airconditioning (both of which have been improved since) and the colour schemes.

Without going into a detailed analysis of the answers to the questions it is possible to make some general comments about the pattern of the results. The position or aspect of the building at which the individual works did not seem to have a very great influence upon the way he responded to his environment. It may be, of course, that there were marked differences in particular cases, but it did not seem that this variable had much general influence. There was a significant difference in the answers of men and women to nearly all the questions, and this is a finding of considerable importance.

The influence of floor was very marked indeed. It was not surprising to find that the ground and first to fourth floors in the podium produced consistently significant results. This might have been predicted from the obvious physical differences between them and the tower floors, although it would be hard to specify *a priori* (or from the physical measurements which have been made) the causes of such marked differences. Significant differences between most of the floors were found to exist but most such differences are explicable in terms of their manner of use and type of staff. For example, some floors are predominantly typing pools or machine rooms, others house such specialists as solicitors in private offices.

The younger workers have a different view of their surroundings from their elders, and this is not surprising, particularly as the building is so much a product of contemporary thought. It would be interesting to trace further the direction of their opinion and see whether they are the most satisfied or the hardest critics of the design. This is something which is not easy to guess for it depends upon their expectations and these, presumably, are less influenced by experience than those of the older groups.

Of the male grades only the officials stand out. The reasons may be in terms of their general level of satisfaction with the amenities they and their departments enjoy, or it may reflect vested interest: many officials were personally involved with some stages of the planning and layout and they were all given private offices with a choice of carpet and colour schemes. Their physical conditions are, therefore, completely different from those of all other staff. Finally, the very fact of being in a small office implies a different experience of the airconditioning unit which was the source of much general criticism.

The Second Questionnaire

The first questionnaire enquiring into staff reactions to the physical environment was circulated in October 1962, shortly after the move into the new building. A follow-up questionnaire to a sample of the total staff was circulated in August 1963, with the object of seeing what changes in attitude had occurred in the intervening ten months.

A comparison of the answers showed that, in most ways, the building had decreased as a subject of interest. The one significant change was in the staff's attitude to the thermal environment. Temperatures were more steady and fewer people reported unpleasant draughts, but there were more complaints of uncomfortably high tempera-

tures and the air was thought to be less fresh.[8]

Some change of feeling could be expected for, at the time the building was occupied (and the first questionnaire circulated) it was generally agreed that the airconditioning system was working at well below its operational standard. However, it is clear that the changes in opinion were by no means entirely favourable.

OVERALL ASSESSMENT OF THE ENVIRONMENT

A judgment of the success or failure of the total environment within a building necessarily takes account of all the contributors: owners, users, design team, constructors, maintenance staff—and of all the contributory factors: economic, physical, social, and psychological. At present there is no way of attaching a meaningful weighting to any of these and appraisals of the total environment can only be made on an individual basis and by comparison with other buildings. No criteria exist.

This is undoubtedly the finest office environment in which the Pilkington Research Unit has worked. It is the most thoughtful, and of all the buildings in the Survey Sample it is the best designed, best detailed, and best built. It is among the best kept, but certainly the most expensive. The CIS building is a major advance on the "routine" office block and, without doubt, among the two or three most beautiful office buildings in the country.

As a functional working tool it is almost certainly satisfactory, but it has an additional business justification, for it is the outward and visible sign of an active and determined company: forward looking, adventurous and successful.

The building provides an excellent physical environment for the staff, incomparably better than the conditions which existed in

---

[8] The management comments that it has agreed with the workers' union (the Guild of Insurance Officials) that the average temperature maintained within the building should be 72°F, and that this caters to the majority of the staff, who are lightly clad females. As a result, many males "mildly complain" of the heat.

their former building. Whether it provides a better *social* environment is more open to doubt, but only because this is not a fixed thing, and there are as yet no means of measuring it with the degree of accuracy which can be applied to space, light, heat and sound. The Unit's general impression is that, on the whole, and now that the management's initial zeal for order and discipline has relaxed, the building is a considerable success. It has attracted many more applicants for employment with the Society, and is something of which the majority of the staff are proud.

REFERENCES:

Anon. Air conditioning for the Co-operative Insurance Building, Manchester. *Heating,* September 1962.

Anon. Research unit's inquiry into office design. *The Guardian,* July 1963.

Billington, N. S. Comfort at work. *Journal of the Institute of Heating and Ventilating Engineers,* 1953, **21,** 141–144.

Black, F. W. Desirable temperatures in offices: A study of occupant reaction to the heating provided. *Journal of the Institute of Heating and Ventilating Engineers,* November 1954.

Casson, H. The executive slum. *Sunday Times* colour magazine, January 1964.

Committee on the Problem of Noise. Noise: Final report. Cmnd 2056, *HMSO,* July 1963.

Dinnage, R. Design policy for corporate buying. Paper by the General Manager of the CIS to the International Design Congress, 1961.

Dinnage, R. Co-operative Insurance Society Ltd.: Letter to P. Manning, July 1962.

Langdon, F. J. The design of mechanised offices. *Architects' Journal,* May 1963.

Langdon, F. J., & Keighley, E. C. User research in office design. *Architects' Journal,* February 1964.

Manning, P. The organisation of a programme of research. *Architects' Journal,* December 1964.

Manning, P., & Wells, B. CIS: Re-appraisal of an environment. *Interior Design,* July/August 1964.

Noble, J. The how and why of behaviour: Social psychology for the architect. *Architects' Journal,* March 1963.

Scott, K. N. Manchester's skyscraper. *Architectural Building News,* January 1963.

Soloman, P. (Ed.). *Sensory deprivation.* Cambridge, Mass.: Harvard University Press, 1961.

Taylor, S. Post war office building: A survey. *Architects' Journal,* December 1962.

Wells, B. Psychology in the office. *The Guardian,* October 1963.

Wells, B. W. P. *Office design and the office worker.* Ph.D. thesis, University of Liverpool, 1964.

48 Individual Differences in Environmental Response

Brian Wells

Anyone having much to do with user requirement studies will sooner or later be brought up against the problem of what constitutes a significant minority dissent to a majority response. The mathematical solution would tell one whether the dissenters were statistically significant, yet if only one person dissents, and if his reaction is such as to cause him intense unhappiness or even to quit his job or house, that might perhaps be regarded as being more serious than that a significant statistical minority had mild cause for complaint. Optimisation may call for any amount of balancing of quantitative and qualitative reactions, but individuals vary tremendously, and the best and most humane solutions will be achieved by those who know most about the causes of individual differences, and are least easily seduced by the tyranny of averages. The purpose of this contribution is then simply to look at how some individual differences occur in the architectural setting, and the procedures used in order to trace them. What follows is not meant to be a weighty scientific contribution, rather an introduction to the method of approach and a sample of results of significance to further user requirement studies.

The conduct and interpretation of a user satisfaction study is a little more devious than the questioning itself might suggest, and I should like to illustrate this, and the nature of individual differences, by reference to a study made recently together with colleagues in Liverpool University's Pilkington Research Unit in a large modern office block. The building chosen was a very new one, occupied only weeks before this study

From *Arena, Architectural Association Journal,* 1967, **82,** 167–171. Reprinted by permission of Dr. Brian Wells and The Architectural Association.

was made, and comprised a very deep podium floor upon which was set a twenty-storey tower. All the people working in it were employees of the same insurance company and had previously been housed in a number of different and rather decrepit office buildings. The survey was made by means of a questionnaire aimed at establishing subjective reactions to a very carefully planned and controlled total environment. The purpose was not to develop existing lines of research but was meant rather to be exploratory and heuristic, probing the personal and physical determinants of the responses. This is also a useful method for locating specific problems for later detailed study (Wells, 1965, a, b).

CHOOSING A SAMPLE

Sampling always presents difficulties in questionnaire surveys, especially if one is later to claim a wide generality for the findings. In the present case the population from which the sample was drawn was, of course, clerical occupations in general. However, because of the great differences existing within this total population from say solicitors clerks at one extreme to tally clerks at the other, the definition of the population had to be made more specific. Fortunately, insurance companies are part of the more limited population of semi-professional clerical occupations of banking, insurance and civil servants which are normally grouped together because of the broad equivalence of their educational requirements, demands of the job, rates of pay and conditions of service. Each contains sub-groups of skilled, semi-skilled and unskilled clerical workers and also typists, secretaries and machine operators. The population then, though exclusive at its lower extremes, tends also to include a cross-section of clerical employees in general, though one might expect that the representation of each of these groups would be different from that in the general clerical population.

The sample taken for this study was the total clerical staff of the company, some 2,500 persons. The sex composition was in the ratio of one man to two women, which was shown in the 1951 census to be true for clerical workers in general (Mann, 1962).

The idea of drawing a smaller sample from within the building, say one in ten, was rejected because it was estimated that, in order to get large enough samples for the sub-analyses that were projected, the original population size would have to be substantial. The proposed analysis involved study of the influence both of physical variables, like the floor on which the respondent worked or the position on that floor, and of personal variables like age and sex.

Clearly, any research making the assumption that age, sex, level of employment, previous experience, and the other host of personal variables so influential in everyday life, may be disregarded, is liable to run into serious error. This will be especially true where these variables are unevenly distributed throughout the population being studied, and are not therefore self-cancelling as, for example, unevenly balanced proportions of age, grade and sex groups.

As an alternative to studying a single company, the possibility of random sampling either from the broadest clerical population or from the more limited one of banking, insurance, and civil service, was entertained but rejected on two counts. Firstly, each individual building would contain workers who had not themselves been drawn together on any random basis, and secondly there would be an almost infinite variation in the actual physical environment of these smaller groups. In any case, the number of samples drawn on this basis would have to be impossibly large. The alternative would be an attempt at the definition of representative sub-groups of the population, and a sample drawn on a stratification basis. However, the limitations of time and money made both of these approaches impractical. It was therefore decided to proceed with a study within a single organisation where the composition of the staff, and the physical environment, were more homogeneous than one could otherwise expect. On this basis a sample was drawn which offers many clear advantages for studying individual differences of subjective reaction.

A final reason for selecting one single company and building as a satisfactory sample for such a study was because conditions were, physically speaking, substantially uniform throughout the building and this is a necessary condition for disentangling the relative importance of the array of physical and personal variables that influence the way in which the environment is experienced.

GUIDING AIMS

As stated above the study was basically heuristic but observation and interviews with groups of clerical workers had fostered the belief that a study of subjective response could not be conducted by a method which did not take individual variables into account. It is quite obvious that immediate physical differences in the environment influence subjective reactions to the conditions, but it also seemed likely that personal factors such as age, sex, or type of conditions from which the respondent had come prior to experiencing the new environment, might be similarly influential. Differences could also be expected to arise from physiological considerations, habits of dress, and organisational changes. The causal links were not individually predicted but were to be traced in the analysis. A complex pattern of interaction between the physical and personal variables was also expected to be apparent from the response patterns though no particular effects were predicted.

CONSTRUCTION OF THE QUESTIONNAIRE

The first step in the construction of a questionnaire must, of course, be to decide on the information to be gathered. In general terms this was quite straightforward. Common sense had suggested that there was sufficient variation in the physical environment of the building to produce a range of replies to any general questions about the environment, and a series of interviews with staff had already suggested that differences in age, sex and status were also likely to be potent factors in determining the way in which the environment was experienced. It was therefore a matter of producing questions covering details of personal history and the range of environmental experience.

The first group of questions in any such questionnaire presents no difficulties whatever. These are the facts about the respondent—age, sex, grade, previous workplace and current working position within the building. The second group depends upon the experience of the investigator to cover the effective range of questions about the physical working environment. In this instance the experience was derived from the field survey of post-war office accommodation in which the investigator had participated but more particularly from the interviews referred to above. Based on these interviews a note was made of all the topics discussed which bore on the physical environment, or on their direct consequences to convenience or work satisfaction, and questions were framed for each of them. The use of descriptive terms was also noted and used in check-lists and in framing the questions. A more complex but not insuperable problem was to establish the exact physical location of each respondent. One needed to know, for example, whether the respondent was on a podium or a tower floor, which face of the building he worked on, and his actual distance from the windows, and thus from the heating and ventilating outlet ducts around the perimeter. This precise information was needed as the subjective reactions were to be correlated with extensive physical measurements made at the same time as the questionnaire survey.

Having established that the instrument covered the desired range of topics, it then remained to establish the form of the questioning: whether it was to be explicit and direct, or whether it should be indirect in order that attitudes and opinions could later be inferred. The first method may be termed empirical, whereas the latter is the method of attitude scaling. Which one is chosen will depend upon the affective quality of the material and the ends to which the data are to be put.

The construction of an attitude scale is called for where the objective is to measure "the degree of positive or negative effect associated with some psychological object" (Thurstone, 1946). Such techniques demand that the instrument should manifest the properties of reliability and validity. Neither of these properties were planned to be intrinsic to the instrument under construction. Reliability of data requires that the results should be essentially repeatable, but in the case of collecting information about an event which was unique and unrepeatable (i.e. the first impressions of a totally new environment, or even a moment in a changing environment), such a criterion could not reasonably be demanded. However, though it was found from a later follow-up study that the instrument was indeed reliable, and that the results were repeatable after a period of almost a year, this was not a necessary condition for the questionnaire's construction.

Validity is another criterion demanded of an attitude scale. In other words, it must be independently demonstrated that the attitudes claimed to be measured by the instrument are indeed measured by it, and that the points on the scale correspond to strengths of the attitude measured by some other means. If this cannot be shown to be so, then the data must depend upon face validity, that is, upon common sense inferences about what is being measured and the relative strength of the points on the scale. In this type of survey where most of the questions demand information about subjective experience which is otherwise virtually unverifiable one does rather have to depend upon face validity. It is, however, worth pointing out that in the case being described where the information was collected in such a way that the respondent was certain of complete anonymity, and where the effective tone of the questions themselves was fairly or completely neutral, there is no reason why the face validity of the replies should be seriously questioned. More interesting is the pattern of the replies, and whether significant differences in reply pattern occur as a result of either physical working conditions or personal variables.

In view of the preceding considerations, the method finally chosen for the construction of the questionnaire was the empirical one of direct questioning. The technical process of devising it then began; a full account of the necessary steps being given in Appendix C of *Research Methods in Social Relations*, Selltiz, Jahoda, Deutsch and Cook (1959). This offers a virtual checklist of the requirements and dangers involved. The draft stage was not passed until it had been established that all the questions so far prepared were necessary, that the answers called for were within the range of the respondent's experience, and the questions were framed so that they were neither too general nor too concrete. Care was taken that questions biased in one direction were balanced by others, and that unwarranted assumptions were not built into the questions themselves. The wording of the questions was thoroughly checked to ensure that they were clear, direct, and unambiguous, and that they expressed all of the alternatives with respect to the question.

The penultimate stage in questionnaire construction is the placing of the questions in a suitable psychological order. To do this it is necessary to lead the respondent into the questionnaire gently, to open with simple and direct questions about pedestrian topics, and then to move on to the ones requiring thought and judgment. In the present case this was naturally accomplished with the first five questions being on matters of fact about the respondent. The subsequent order of questions is a matter of personal judgment: a compromise between putting all the related questions together and randomising them. On the one hand, it is desirable to separate related questions so that the respondent would not be compelled to reply to them all in a similar way because of their closeness making any apparent contradictions obvious. Also, grouping might result in stereotyped replies deriving from an attitude to a particular general topic, rather than a consideration of each question separately. On the other hand, complete randomisation would lead to an unnaturalness and incoherence of the questionnaire which might raise reasonable suspicions in the mind of the respondent that he was being used as an experimental subject, rather than a source of information. The final form of any questionnaire must be the individual's interpretation of what represents the best optimisation of these opposing considerations.

Having obtained the draft form of the questionnaire, the final step was to pretest it. This was done by submitting copies to colleagues, clerks, and typists for their comments and, in the case of clerks and typists, asking them to complete the form as far as was possible in order to make sure that the questions and instructions were clearly understood and unequivocally interpreted. Faults and omissions were corrected at this stage and a final document and covering letter encouraging cooperation and stressing confidentiality were produced.

ANALYSIS OF THE DATA

Large scale surveys usually depend upon mechanical aids for analysis and this present one was no exception. Once the data had been coded they were transferred onto punched cards and firstly sorted for total response to each question of the questionnaire; and then the replies were cross-tabulated against those variables which, it was hypothesised, would be influential in determining an individual's response to his environment. The personal variables related to the respondent were his previous workplace, age, sex and occupational grade. The variables concerning physical differences in environment had to be limited to floor, and to whether the respondent worked on the north, south, east or west of the building, or whether he worked in the perimeter strip around the building or deeper in the interior. Actually the categorisation of personal and physical variables is not exclusive in all cases. For example, a senior executive has a very different physical environment from that of a pool typist, as well as there being personal differences like sex and age. The purpose of the study amounts therefore to an examination of the interaction of these factors, and the tracing of causal links. In fact, it transpired that it was not possible to make any correlational comparisons of response with the instrument measurements of temperature, air movement and humidity, which had been made by colleagues. This was due to the very small differences recorded between floors and zones, and even the recorded differences were not constant and were of an even smaller order than the variations recorded during the course of a day, or between days, at any one point. It was found by the physicist colleague responsible for the instrumentation, that no significant differences existed between the physical characteristics of the zones (it was at that time late autumn and dull, cloudy weather), and that the floors and zones could be regarded as substantially uniform. An analysis of the differences in responses made by people on different floors and on different orientations and different parts of the building was made but it was found that most of the significant differences could be explained on a straight sampling basis (e.g. floor x being exclusively a typing pool), and so a discussion of the influence of physical conditions may very reasonably be left aside in favour of the more potent personal variables.

The method of analysis chosen, the cross-tabulation and chi-squared analysis of eight main variables (male and female grades being treated separately) involving as it did seventy-three sub-groups and the replies to twenty-eight questions, naturally involved a tremendous amount of computation. A programme for the calculation of chi-square was therefore written and the data processed by computer. Without going into the details of the results, the following examples may be taken as showing the trend of the findings.

INFLUENCE OF PERSONAL VARIABLES ON RESPONSE PATTERN

The most striking thing about the results was the high proportion of cases in which there was a significant degree of heterogeneity of response on the variables chosen for study. Two thirds of analyses showed significant differences between the people comprising the various sub-groups of age, sex, grade, etc. The importance of this type of break-down is that it goes beyond simple tabulations and the numerically average response of an amorphous group of people to give clues as to the influences which determine the way in which the environment is experienced. It is also a way of studying the reactions of numerical minorities whose point of view is often lost in averages. More important, it provides a large number of facts from which many new hypotheses may be generated. These combined with the experimental findings of social and industrial psychology, can then be used to establish tentative hypotheses about the influence of the building environment and the way in which it is perceived. This is the main advantage of having such a diversity of facts about a single group of people in a single building at a given period of time, though further studies will be needed to establish the generality of such findings.

Looking more closely at the variability existing within the sub-groups, it emerges that some sub-groups are far more often significantly at variance with the overall distribution of responses than others.

THE INFLUENCE OF PREVIOUS WORKPLACE

For example, the place in which a person last worked appears to have a considerable influence in shaping attitudes to a new workplace. The premises forming the sub-groups of this analysis had, in fact, very different characteristics but they did have in common the fact that they were all very old buildings. It was anticipated that the manner of reply would depend upon the standards and expectations derived from the conditions under which the respondent had until so recently been working.

Only one question included in the analysis produced a result where the employees from different buildings did not differ significantly in their appraisal of the new environment, and this was one dealing with basic attitudes to the health aspects of artificial lighting, which was irrelevant to this type of analysis and which had been included inadvertently. It was, however, useful to have this one question because, in view of the solid differences existing on all other questions, the

doubt might have remained as to whether there were unsuspected differences between the staffs of these offices which might have accounted for the results.

The details of the questions are not really important. It is sufficient to say that they covered the whole range of physical conditions from heating and ventilation to colour schemes, and from lifts to social relations, but it is interesting to speculate why such pronounced variability of response should occur. The point has already been made that reference standards might be expected to differ as a result of different experience, but it would be difficult to predict any specific effects. The investigator visited each of the nine premises occupied by the company prior to its move into the new building, but the description of environmental differences defies any attempt. There were very marked differences between say the original head office building which had that sort of head office air, and some of the smaller ones which were more like provincial branches. Another building was a complete contrast to either of these. It was housed in a converted mill with roof lighting and virtually no side windows, and still conveyed the impression of a factory. It is interesting to note that the staff of this last office were significantly at variance with the staffs from other premises on the greatest number of occasions on which they were compared.

Conversely, there was one condition which was exactly the same at each of the old premises, but which was changed in the new. This was the matter of working hours. In reply to the question dealing with the liking of the new hours, there were, of course, highly significant differences in the responses.

The differences between conditions in the old offices were due to more than differences in the physical environment. There were also obvious differences in the stringency and form of supervision and in the quality of the social interactions within the office. Managers had become relatively autonomous and arranged their departments differently. Very different atmospheres prevailed, some strict and others permissive. Such differences did not, of course, disappear entirely in the new premises; departments moved bodily on to floors or groups of floors and thus retained much of their separate nature. This fact also probably accounts for many of the differences in response patterns which were found in the survey to exist between floors.

STATUS DIFFERENCES BETWEEN MEN

The influence of male grade as a variable influencing response pattern was one of the least pronounced though by no means insignificant. One of the more interesting questions was that dealing with preferred office size where the distribution of replies showed that the two most junior grades chose the large open office more frequently and the smaller partitioned area less frequently than they would have been expected to do from the overall distribution of replies. By contrast the executives and supervisory grades both opted relatively more frequently for the smaller partitioned areas rather than for the open offices. It seems that each group chose on the basis of their personal needs or expectations. One can see that the executive would be likely to choose as he did since the small private office is the accepted practice. The reasons why different occupational levels should differ in their beliefs about optimal office size was a topic later dealt with in detail (Manning, 1965).

STATUS AND OCCUPATION DIFFERENCES BETWEEN WOMEN

The influence of status and actual job proved, in the case of women, to affect response to environmental conditions very much more than was the case with men. In fact, there were significant differences between the sub-groups in 70 percent of all the cases tested.

In reply to the question asking respondents to record their preference for type of office under one of the three categories—"A large open one," "A smaller partitioned area," and "No preference"—it was interesting to note that the typists expressed their preferences in a similar way to the rest of the clerical employees. Machine operators,

on the other hand, made significantly more choices of a large open area. Two possible explanations suggest themselves: in the first place these particular typists had only recently been placed in very large pools, whereas the machine operators were used to the larger areas. This would be the simple case of preferring what one knows best. The second explanation is in terms of actual differences between the two groups. It may be that typists and machine operators self-select themselves for their occupations on different criteria. For although the demands of the jobs may be generally somewhat similar, nevertheless the former tends to be regarded as a clerical occupation proper, the latter as a quasi-industrial occupation. Consequently one would not be surprised to find fundamental differences in the attitudes, preferences and expectations of the two groups. Indeed this certainly appears to be the case as the machine operators' response patterns were significantly different from the remaining female groups in 63 percent of all cases. In fact, the typists formed the next most heterogeneous sub-group of all the female grades, though differing in only one third of cases.

It is interesting to compare these findings with those of Langdon and Keighley (1964), who found that:

> Studies of drawing offices, of automatic data processing offices and, most recently, of large samples of clerical offices have revealed the tendency for the order of user satisfaction with different aspects of the environment to remain fixed, so forming a list of design priorities. Despite wide differences in the type and function of the offices, with their attendant variations in functional requirements, users show broadly similar patterns of response in assessing both the quality and relative importance of various environmental features.

The findings of this study were therefore quite different from those of Langdon and Keighley, and it seems clear that further research on this topic should be done, as the matter is one which affects sampling procedures and the generality of the results of any further user requirement studies.

SEX DIFFERENCES

Sex proved to be a variable which also produced considerable differences in the response to environmental conditions, significant differences occurring between the sexes in 82 percent of the replies to the questionnaire. Some of these, such as the questions concerned with the thermal environment, are perhaps not too unexpected because of the actual physiological differences between men and women, and the differences in their manner of dress. Bruce (1960) has cited the evidence of research by Hardy and Du Bois (1940) and Inouye *et al.* (1953) to show that the thermo-regulatory mechanisms of women differ from those of men. Better metabolic adjustments and greater variability of tissue conductance result in the physiological superiority of women's total thermo-regulatory adjustments.

However, clothing is also an important factor in the comfort experienced at various temperatures. As Bedford (1964) has pointed out, the thermal efficiency of clothing will differ with the insulating value of the material, and with the amount of body surface covered. There is no doubt that there are generally substantial differences between men's and women's clothing, both in terms of the fabrics used and the amount of body surface covered. In an experiment by Yaglou and Messer (1941) the influence of the different types of clothing of the two sexes was shown to be related to their differences in preferred temperatures. For the purpose of the experiment a group of men and women were dressed in clothes of the opposite sex and then in clothes of their own sex. Body temperatures and comfort assessments were recorded and it was found that, contrary to the usual case where women prefer higher room temperatures, when both sexes were dressed in similar types of clothing temperatures required for optimal comfort were virtually the same. It was therefore concluded that the reasons for differences in warmth standards for men and women were almost entirely due to differences in clothing. But, whatever the relative importance of physiological mecha-

nisms and dress habits may be, substantial differences between men and women were recorded on each of the five items dealing with thermal environment.

Other questions in the questionnaire, like the one dealing with changes in personal relationships, may also be due to objective differences in the experience of the sexes. In this case a policy of centralising pools and withdrawing typists and secretaries from departments was instituted at the time of the move, and so the answers might be interpreted as referring to matters of fact.

Finally, differences in the pattern of responses analysed by sex may also be related to other variables, especially age. It was broadly the policy of this company to recruit young men for a professional career and young women on the assumption that they would leave to get married by their early twenties. This is a fair generalisation of what happens. Consequently the average age of the females tends to be somewhat lower than that of the men. One would expect the same to be true of any large organisation. If age group is a significant variable determining response to environmental conditions, then it is reasonable to suppose that it would also be a contributory factor in an analysis by sex.

AGE GROUP

It was remarked in connection with the observed sex differences that differences in average age might influence the results. Conversely, age groups will also tend to be influenced by considerations of sex composition. There are, however, a number of other related factors which might also be expected to influence the way in which the physical and psychological environment is experienced. For example, Weston (1949) draws attention to the relationship between demands for higher levels of illumination and advancing age, citing evidence of reduced accommodative power, increased light absorption in the ocular media, and perhaps even reduced efficiency of the central components of the visual system. In reply to a question dealing with the comfort of the illumination in terms of brightness, it appeared from the cross-tabulation with the age variable that the results would support Weston's contention. It was indeed the two youngest groups (from ages 15 to 24) who rated significantly above the average the working illumination as being too bright, and the other older groups who rated it below the average. However, as both groups predominantly rated the lighting as comfortable, the conclusion was that the level of lighting provided in that instance, though generally very good, was rather more satisfactory for the older workers than the younger.

Heating is another factor in which one might anticipate differences in the comfort assessments of different age groups. Increasing age results in a steep decline in basal metabolism (Yaglou 1924, p. 365) and the older worker is therefore more prone to feeling cold. However, in reply to a question which asked for a statement of how often the respondent felt uncomfortably cold whilst working, the responses of older workers were not distinguishable from those of the younger, except for the very youngest group who were predominantly young girls. Similarly in the case of a question concerning the incidence of feeling uncomfortably hot, the youngest group of workers, the 15- to 19-year-old group, reported a significantly higher incidence of heat discomfort, as one might predict from their metabolic rate. No doubt these findings also reflect the sex composition of the different age groups, and also differences in mode of dress.

Increasing age also usually brings decreasing sensitivity of hearing, so one might expect that distractions due to environmental noise would be less frequent in the older worker and relatively more frequent amongst the young with their acute sense of hearing. In reply to a question which asked the respondent whether he felt the work place to be distractingly noisy, it was indeed the younger group (15 to 24) who differed significantly from the other sub-groups in the direction of more reports of distracting noise in the office. In fact, over-all analysis of results showed that it was the youngest age group which is most frequently at variance with the other age groups, this being true of 72 percent of all cases. So it appears

that the age of the office worker, whether young or old, is an important variable in determining his subjective reactions to the environment.

CONCLUSION

Writing a conclusion to a piece such as this, comprising as it does neither a complete do-it-yourself consumer research kit, nor a systematic analysis of findings, is less than easy. By attempting to contain two rather divergent aims under a single rubric one has, of course, to pay certain penalties. But, by way of justifying the attempt, one hopes that the effect will be to stimulate the reader in theory, design practice, and practical investigation.

At the theoretical level one is interested in producing a comprehensive account of the nature, and interactions, of those personal and group differences which govern the response to given environmental conditions. Doing this, as the results of this brief article will have shown, should make us more cautious about accepting existing studies, and the recommendations based on them, which have not taken personal variables into account. A greater interest both in sampling for user studies, and in interpreting their results, is therefore indicated.

Having established a more refined model of user requirements, it may then prove practical, in some cases at least, to optimise environmental conditions by empirically determined differential provisions, rather than by aiming at broad compromises. However, where compromise decisions do have to be taken, it is surely best that they should be taken on the basis of a maximal knowledge of both the quantitative and qualitative aspects of differing user requirements.

But perhaps the most important reason for presenting a fairly detailed account of this case study procedure is that it may stimulate students of architecture to undertake studies of this sort for themselves. There is no mystique about such work; a good deal of effort, background reading, and subtlety is needed, but the procedure should be within the range of the average student doing extended project or thesis work. User satisfaction studies are fascinating to do, especially if one keeps the range of topics to be investigated well under control, and they offer the student an opportunity to come to closer terms with an important aspect of his profession in a way which he may never be able to do again once he enters practice.

REFERENCES:

Bedford, T. *Basic principles of ventilation and heating* (2nd ed.). London: Lewis, 1964.

Bruce, W. *Man and his thermal environment.* Tech. Paper No. 84 of the Division of Building Research (NRCSS14). Ottawa, Canada: National Research Council, 1960.

Hardy, J. D., & Dubois, E. A. S. Differences between men and women in their response to heat and cold. *Proceedings of the National Academy of Sciences,* 1940, **26**, 389.

Inouye, T., Hick, S. H., Keeton, L., Lisch, L., & Glickman, N. A comparison of physiological adjustments of clothed women and men to sudden changes in environment. *ASHVE Journal.* Soc. D. of HPAC 25, 1953, **5**, 125.

Langdon, F. J., & Keighley, E. C. User research in office design. *Architects Journal,* Feb. 5, 1964.

Mann, D. S. C. *Better offices.* London: Institute of Directors Publication, 1962.

Manning, P. (Ed.). *Office design: A study of environment.* University of Liverpool: Dept. Building Sci., 1965.

Selltiz, C., Jahoda, M., Deutsch, M., & Cook, S. W. *Research methods in social relations.* London: Methuen, 1959.

Thurstone, L. L. Comment. *American Journal of Sociology,* 1946, **52**, 39–50.

Wells, B. W. P. Subjective responses to the lighting installation in a modern office building and their design implications. *Building Science,* 1965a, **1**, (1), 57–68.

Wells, B. W. P. The psycho-social influence of building environment: Sociometric findings in large and small office spaces. *Building Science,* 1965b, **1**, (2), 153–165.

Weston, H. C. *Sight, light and efficiency.* London: Lewis, 1949.

Yaglou, C. P. The heat given up by the human body and its effect on heating and ventilating. *Transactions of the American Society of Heating and Ventilation Engineers,* 1924.

Yaglou, C. P., & Messer, A. The importance of clothing in air conditioning. *Journal of the American Medical Association,* 1941, **117**, 1261–1262.

PART FIVE
Environmental Planning

The inclusion of a section on environmental planning in a volume concerned with the relatively new area of environmental psychology might be considered premature and a bit presumptuous. In the introduction to this book, we indicated that the task of the environmental sciences was to increase the ability to predict and control the consequences of man's environmental manipulations and to increase understanding of the consequences of environmental change. The function of Part Five is to set some limits to the contribution of environmental psychology to the planning process and to review some of the problems and ideas of designers as they concern a psychological approach to the study of planning.

In spite of the fact that theory is just developing and empirical studies in the field are very limited, the examination of a number of issues related to planning can broaden the view of the environmental psychologist. First, it is clear that the assumptions underlying planning are most difficult to define and that its consequences have rarely been systematically evaluated. The pressures to construct tend to force city planners, landscape architects, and general architects alike to the rapid completion of a product, but seldom is there an explicit declaration of the varied goals of the plan, and even less often an opportunity to evaluate the goals in the light of the management, administration, and use of the finished product. From a practical standpoint, checking back on a completed construction might be a great luxury, but planners are becoming increasingly aware of the need to include a broad evaluation stage in their work. For the purpose of evaluation, clear goals are essential, but defining meaningful goals is complex. The purely physical objectives might be construed as relatively simple to outline, with sound construction at the base. It is apparent, however, that successful planning involves more than a building that does not topple or one that is pleasing from aesthetic standards alone. The use of the building or park or city must ultimately determine its success, even from a physical standpoint, and use involves social and psychological factors in the context of an economic reality. Thus, the planner facing the task of designing an environment must combine his own special skills with a vast knowledge of what people need in space, how they tend to use space, the social context of this use, and the economics of spatial usage. Whether he is aware of it or not, he is actually designing the physical matrix in which a social system will operate, with tremendous potential impact on the occupants, both as they use the construction and as they move into other spheres of their lives. A construction sets the framework for a complex and far-reaching series of relationships and attitudes, all of which must affect both intra- and extramural behavior. In this sense the planner is actually an agent of social influence and control. The strong effect of a building on behavior has been recognized by many, most notably by Winston Churchill, whose comments on the rebuilding of the House of Commons were cited earlier in this volume.

We might ask what can be expected from the planning process. It is obvious that physical goals alone are inadequate. Environmental planning is no longer exclusively a product of the architect's drafting table, but rather a complex series of steps beginning with a budget and ending with the manipulation of space, building materials, and landscape—ideally to meet the functional as well as the aesthetic needs of the potential occupants. For years planners have operated on the basis of implicit notions of people's needs, and to a considerable degree their vast experience provided reasonable cues for each successive task. However, the tremendous increases in population and the great pressures to build make it necessary for the planner to have more systematic cues. What this volume suggests is that the process of planning is an interdisciplinary task and that the greater the use of multiple skills, the greater the possibility of an effectively designed environment. Many disciplines are involved, but here we are especially hopeful for the contribution of the social sciences. Planners can offer a special perception of the world to the behavioral scientist, and the behavioral scientist can offer empirical work on the senses, the emotions, aesthetic values, and interpersonal behavior—all of which affect the individual's use of space. This reciprocal relationship can facilitate the evaluation phase, in which the management of the construction is considered in addition to the occupants' use of it. The evaluation would also include an alteration period that would enable planners to make modifications in the structure or changes in the management of the structure. Freedom to make changes after the nominal completion of a plan seems essential; it is in no way a rejection of the original ideas. An evaluation can be expected to uncover new, and sometimes unexpected, functional as well as aesthetic criteria of design. These can be incorporated into a modification phase in the building and can also act as guideposts for future construction.

Planning can be expected to avoid problems rather than solve them, first by applying existing knowledge in designing a given environment, and second by anticipating future needs and conditions. Too little is known for the planner to presume to solve all problems, but enough evidence is available to permit him to circumvent many problems of the past. For example, the "ideal" or optimally functional school, or hospital, or office building, or city cannot be fully conceptualized at present and may never be approached. In fact, it is most difficult to translate multiple behavioral goals into architectural terms, for these goals are often contradictory or mutually exclusive; in such cases, the "ideal" is a compromise between conflicting goals. But the planning process might aim to avoid creating poor traffic lanes, it could avoid air-polluting garbage disposal, and it could provide flexibility in room construction on the basis of past lessons learned. By examining many details of the building process, planning can begin to accumulate evidence that will eventually provide systematic cues to avoiding problems. Whether the process of accumulating and applying this information is done by electronic computer techniques or by more traditional methods, it would reduce much of the waste of repeating past errors. An example can be seen in the design of psychiatric hospital facilities. Although planners may not be able to describe all the details of the therapeutically ideal hospital, and even though there is disagreement over what constitutes an ideal form of therapy, many construction pitfalls can be avoided. Social rooms can be placed where their use would be encouraged. Bedrooms can be designed to enhance the patient's sense of dignity, and the patient's confusion can be reduced by a clear and unambiguous design throughout the hospital. Simple as they seem, these construction details are frequently lacking in existing psychiatric structures.

Planning must anticipate future needs, not just meet present ones. The time context of planning is such that the needs to be met are not those existing when the plans are drawn, but rather those contemporary with the finished construction and those extending to the future use of the finished product. Projection into the future is at the heart of the planning process, yet it is the characteristic most difficult to include. Many structures are obsolete when they are designed. The anticipation of future needs is complicated by the difficulty in clearly defining goals in advance, as well as by the tendency of goals to change. Limited by a fixed budget, the planner often must operate with partial blindfolds. Some aspects of building that can be anticipated—for example, the increasing rate of population growth and the shifts in population—are often ignored as highways are inadequately built and schools and hospitals are unable to meet the demand for space. In our own work in psychiatric hospitals, we have repeatedly found wards increasing their capacity by pushing beds into rooms as long as there was floor space. This was done despite the fact that other services and facilities in the hospital were designed for much more limited numbers.

Even when goals are set forth in advance, the pressures of the present moment often take precedence. For example, in one hospital the original plans of the architect and administration clearly indicated that the patients would be assigned to single rooms, double rooms, or wards on the basis of therapeutic needs. In actual fact, the assignment procedure had to become more arbitrary, as the pressure to admit increased numbers of patients resulted in the conversion of many of the single rooms into multiple units. In addition, the fact that the wards were almost always filled to capacity reduced flexibility in the assignment of beds. Thus, the original intentions of the planners were negated by administrative decisions, but also by the failure to provide space for the beds that were needed as the patient load increased.

The economic pressures of the moment often lead to short-term economies that are false economies from a long-term view. A tightly constructed building with little opportunities for additions, alterations, or modification of existing structure must be obsolete before it is occupied. These are the concerns of planners today. The search is for appropriate avenues to flexibility in design and for meaningful application of the vast body of information now available. These issues are reflected in many of the papers in this section.

Some apparent cues to designing for future needs obviously rest in a knowledge of these needs. As already indicated, our conviction is that the behavioral sciences could have a role in planning, but part of the problem seems to be to translate relevant work in behavioral science into planning terms. The other part is clearly the limitations of the data of the social sciences. The confrontation of different disciplines involves a period of groping for a clear means of communicating, and the work of architectural psychology and environmental psychology is a reflection of the growing capacity for interchange between the designers and the behavioral sciences. What kind of planning is involved? It varies from site planning to city planning, from the design of a house or a kitchen to the design of parks, playgrounds, schools, and other institutions. Each construction has its own set of problems and there is no quick and easy solution, but the data of the behavioral sciences can give some ideas regarding the motivation and potential behavior of the occupants, which should have some value in long-range planning.

There is a fine balance between maintaining the natural surroundings and meeting the urgent and immediate needs of people. It is hoped that the art of planning, joined with the environmental sciences, can approach this equilibrium.

49 The Concept of Environmental Management

Serge Boutourline

The dominant situation of modern life is individuals living in a setting which was not built for them. This situation is so widespread that we have already forgotten the specialized designations of the immediate past. Few now reading this sentence will be doing so while sitting in a reading chair; fewer still in a reading room. The operational problems of voyagers in the Time Tunnel or the group of middle-class Americans stranded on Gilligan's Island and Lost in Space are similar to the environmental problems facing the present day city dweller.

From *Dot Zero IV*, September 1967, Copyright 1967. Reprinted by permission of the author and publisher.

James Bond, Derrick Flint, Maxwell Smart and Modesty Blaise have shown us how an individual moving through a changing, not-designed-for-them, unpredictable and often hostile environment, can maintain himself in emotional and physical security. They rarely get hurt or lose their cool. These folk heroes are actually introducing millions of modern people to modern techniques of environmental control. Bond and his adversaries do not lament that at some earlier time a designer did not predict their presence in a particular place and make over that spot to insure their well-being. They accept that such a prediction would be difficult if not impossible, given their unique interests and the rate of change which exists in environmental systems. Their problem is to accomplish their missions within such a pre-existing, changing system. They do this by moving strategically through a system so that their immediate environment is the desired one. They also make minor interventions in existing environmental systems so that these systems operate quite differently. Or they carry elements of their own environment—such as miniature two-way radios or oxygen tanks—with them.

Marshall McLuhan has presented a powerful argument that the flux of environmental change we all are experiencing is likely to continue indefinitely. His contribution has been to present us with a more acceptable stance in the world of change. McLuhan suggests that we can act within the flux of change with some semblance of control and real choice rather than having to stumble constantly from one adjustment to another. While there are many interpretations about what McLuhan's theories actually are, it is more significant that few question McLuhan's basic position: that change is here to stay and that it is, in principle, possible for man to act purposefully and creatively within the changing world over which he has little control. By analogy his position is this: you may not be able to control the waves of the sea, yet this does not prevent you from surfing in your own style nor does it prevent you from going to the beach on a quiet day when you can also choose to swim rather than surf.

This changing world has challenged the ability of the design community to control the environment through their performance of traditional design services. First it was realized that individual objects function differently in different physical surroundings. Whether a reading lamp is bright enough is as dependent upon its placement in a room as it is upon the brightness of the bulb it uses. Considerations of this sort have led to a turning away from the design of objects as an adequate definition of the task of the industrial designer. The design of the total environment is currently thought to be a more adequate goal. Environmental design means designing objects systematically so that the designer controls the process of assembling and arranging all the objects in a given system, rather than designing objects individually. The concept of environmental design assumes that if a system were designed at one time and if researchers

were able to provide for designers a knowledge of the effect of the physical environment on people, then it would be possible to design essentially optimum human environments by eliminating the problems encountered by designing objects independent of their physical and use content.

But the concept of environmental design as understood here has grave limitations. Design proceeds over time, not all at once, with many decisions made early in time which act to work against objectives which are later found to be desirable. Designers are very rarely the only ones making decisions, and group decision-making is more often a political negotiation process than a rational one. Designers, furthermore, will always discover that research findings are unable to reduce most of the uncertainties which they bring to a design decision, because decision mainly concerns itself with a broad range of variables while psychological research, and research generally, concerns itself with very narrow dimensions.

But these considerations are of minor importance, for it is still possible to think of designing systems of objects within the context of making subjective probability judgments and an iterative rather than an all-at-once concept of a design system. The far more important fact is that in today's world we can predict much less about ultimate users, their patterns of behavior and their value systems. The key fact facing designers today is that behavior patterns are not stable and values change. The claim to have designed an environment for people thus just raises more critical questions: What people when? What specific mixes of activities at what time? What will the value system of users be when they actually use the system? In fact it can be seen that the problem of environmental design is as operationally alienated from the context as is the problem of product design.

It is evident that extending our framework of analysis from single objects to complete systems of objects does not really substantially extend our ability to have designed the experience of users much more than singly designing individual objects. These statements should not be interpreted as a denial of the value of either product design or environmental system design, but as a statement of the fact that today designers can know increasingly less about the future users of their products. Designers have failed to see the real nature of the change technology has brought about, and continue to insist that the need is for new techniques of making design decisions instead of for exploring new roles which designers can usefully play in modern society. The concept of the real time designer, a man who helps existing, ongoing organizations to maximize the utilization of their existing environments, which we shall discuss here, is such a role, and it is this function that we shall call environmental management.

The idea most central to environmental management is the definition of environment. Most definitions of environment refer to a particular physical place. Other definitions, particularly those used in the social sciences, refer only to the people in a place. Still other, more sophisticated definitions include the many people in a place as part of an object-people system.

The problem with all such definitions is that people never physically experience a total place all at once. Physically, people experience only a single location of physical space at one time. The environment at that location is unique; no other location in the room has quite the same configuration of signals, or physical events, reaching it.

Because of the changing character of most spaces, the set of signals reaching a particular location changes over time. Given a particular clock time, it would be very unlikely that exactly the same set of signals would reach any given room location again. This is true of even seemingly uneventful places such as, for instance, a particular spot in an empty courtyard. It is, of course, especially true if the place contains more than one person or if the environment contains a device such as a TV set, radio or telephone. Such devices permit people and things from literally all over the world to generate unique patterns of signals in a given place. The idea of a fixed "environment" is a concept hard to apply to most natural settings and especially to modern, man-made settings. Fixed environments ex-

ist for unobservant people or for people who have chosen to define environment as those features of a place which are unchanging.

The definition of environment being developed here can be stated more formally. Environment is a specific set of measurable physical phenomena existing during a specified period of time at a specified location point. These physical events may be light rays, sound vibrations, chemical particles in the air, measured pressure, measured temperature or any of a number of physical events which are measurable. A room can be thought to be a three-dimensional grid consisting of a finite set of points, each with its own unique inventory of physical events which change over time.

This definition of environment does not depend upon a perceiving person in a space. Using this definition, we could describe a place no person has ever been. The specific set of measurable physical events which we would pick would depend upon our specific reasons for wanting to describe an environment. If one wanted to decide where to place a spotlight, one might think only in terms of the structure of light rays existing at a set of points in a room. If one wanted to decide where to place a computer, one might think only of the strength and direction of magnetic fields at that same set of points.

Once one has shifted to this definition of environment then the possibility of environmental management becomes considerably easier to grasp. If an exhibit manager moves a spotlight in an open room, then every point in that room will experience an altered structure of light rays. This, in itself, would not be significant if people did not respond to sets of events rather than to isolated events. Thus, the ability to introduce what may seem to be relatively minor changes in existing environmental systems can change the meaning of the entire environment for people. One of the central activities of environmental management is to introduce such changes so that people will have experiences which are more valuable for them.

So far we have been describing environment apart from the existence of an actual person. People do not, as a rule, stand still for any length of time in normal spaces.

Given any substantial time period, say five minutes, people can, and often do, move a considerable amount. Walking in a city or an exhibition, one can travel as far as a quarter of a mile in this time. A great many different environments are experienced during such movement. The average person's day is such a flow of events and is not the experiencing of the single static perspective of the still camera. Given any period of time in an individual's life, his environment can be described in terms of sequence of exposure to such physical experiences. This sequence of events is human environment. It is this definition of environment that the environmental manager will find most useful for decision making.

If a person's behavior is altered in a given space (if his speed of movement changes; if he stops where he did not stop before or if he alters his path through the space), then the flow of events to which he will be physically exposed will alter. In this sense each person continuously controls his environments by behaving in settings which are not in themselves changed by him. One can create a slow-moving environment by walking slowly. The first technique of environmental management is obviously an individually controlled process.

Making minor interventions in existing physical systems is a second environmental management activity conducted by all people. When we move into an office, even for a short time, we may order walls knocked down, new lighting installed and new seating. Even more frequently we turn lights on and off, move furniture, open and close doors and make a variety of minor interventions in spaces as we find them. We make such decisions frequently as an inherent part of living in the modern world. A major aim of environmental management theory and education is to improve the effectiveness of such decisions.

What makes an environmental action "management" rather than "design" depends on when the decision is made and how long its outcome is expected to endure. Using this definition, one sees that environmental management decisions are made by a broad group of professionals other than ultimate individual users. The person who raises and dims the lights in a restaurant is making an environmental management decision as is the person raising and lowering the volume control of the music system in the same room. The number of people in the room, the amount and kind of noise they are making and even the time of day influence these decisions. The placement of policemen on subway trains in New York City was an environmental management decision. Doing so markedly changed the range of physical actions that occurred in an otherwise unchanged behavior setting.

The museum director who advertises a particular part of his museum is also making an environmental management decision. By giving visitors certain expectations he is changing their behavior in an otherwise unchanging setting. By going to a different place in the museum, each visitor will physically experience a different environment. The museum director has physically changed the "museum" to which visitors will be exposed without changing any of the exhibit hardware.

Such decisions affect individual human environments but are not under the direct control of the people affected. They are reversible, affect the immediate environment of a specific population of users within a short time of taking action, and are made within the context of preexisting, ongoing social-physical systems. The analytical and conceptual tools required for these decisions are, moreover, similar. What these decisions are about is the total experiences of a set of people and the different values such experiences might have, given various alternative interventions.

A great many occupations and professions are involved in making environmental management decisions on a daily basis. All occupations performing a direct service to people are making environmental management decisions. In addition there is a broad group of people that Dr. William Ittelson of Brooklyn College refers to as "space managers." Restaurant managers, hotel managers, exhibition space managers and even office managers are examples. Those familiar with the recent work of Thomas Hoving of the New York Parks Department are aware of the extent to which people's experiences in a given space—for example, Central Park in New York—can be changed by making effective environmental management decisions and successfully implementing these decisions.

What the environmental manager lacks in power to make changes, he makes up for by a greater knowledge of the probable value, to him and to others, of his actions. Even the preexistence of a given physical system works in his favor. Unlike the designer, who often must make decisions about components without knowing the nature of the whole system or its exact functions, the environmental manager knows most of the components in the system, how they work together, the specific users and their specific activities. For this reason the few decisions he makes to intervene within this system can have great value.

Let us turn now to the exhibit space manager so that we can focus on some of the decisions which are open to him. Our aim will not be so much to examine his decision-making process as to illustrate the type of decisions he faces and the kinds of situations within which these decisions occur.

After the first day a new exhibit had been opened to the public, the exhibit manager noticed that, contrary to the expectations of the designer, people were turning left rather than right as they came into the exhibit room. Thus, visitors were seeing the final panels of the exhibition first and seeing the introductory panels last. The manager estimated that less than 5 percent of visitors were experiencing the sequence of events expected by the exhibit designer and the sponsors of the exhibit. The manager wondered if he should take action to reverse the flow of traffic, change the physical order of the panel or do nothing.

An exhibit space in an industrial trade show included one exhibit consisting principally of a 16mm sound film which was shown to visitors by a rear screen projection. When only a few people were in the space (which was 8 out of the 12 hours a day), a volume-control setting of 1 on the sound-system volume control was sufficient to provide an audible intelligible signal to those standing in front of the exhibit screen. The exhibit manager noticed that during the four hours of the day when there was a crowd (during which 75 percent of the daily attendance came to the exhibit), the normal volume-control setting did not permit the sound to be heard above the noise of the crowd. One afternoon he tried changing the volume-control settings and found that an optimum setting during crowded times was somewhere between 4 and 7, depending upon the number of people in the room at the time. In thinking about the problem, the manager estimated that over 4,000 people a day were in the exhibit room, of which 2,000 stayed to see all or part of the film. This meant that only 50 percent were getting the message for which the sponsor had spent $20,000 (for the film).

An exhibit was delivered to a medical exhibition. The first day that it was on the floor the exhibit manager noticed that one person standing in front of the exhibit was sufficient to obliterate the view of the exhibit from all passers-by. While an average of over 450 people an hour were indeed passing by this exhibit, the exhibit manager estimated that no more than 50 persons per hour actually got a view of the exhibit. He wondered whether he should take remedial actions, such as raising the exhibit so that it would not be concealed by the body of a single visitor or preventing anyone from stopping at the exhibit by putting it in a narrow aisle. In any case he felt that the client corporation was not meeting its exposure objectives, and it occurred to him that there was some obligation on his part to let them know since they had been told that several hundred people an hour would see this exhibit.

A small art museum specializing in modern art was requested by a local high school group to make its main exhibition space available for a rock 'n' roll dance. The museum director had wanted to attract more younger people to his museum and wondered if this request for space, though quite unusual, should be granted.

In all the above cases the exhibit space manager could complain that if a designer had at a previous time made a different decision, then the exhibit manager would not be faced with a particular problem or, on the contrary, could claim that any decision he might make would conflict with the designer's original intentions. These positions are often in fact taken and usually can only be regarded as absolution of a manager from the responsibility of managing. Attitudes of this kind have often reduced the exhibit manager to a caretaker role rather than a position of positive force which maximizes the value of the exhibition under his control.

Yet environmental management decisions can have great value, and making them can be a stimulating and rewarding activity. This viewpoint is really an attitude as to how much can be done to change human environment once a system of objects has been designed and constructed. Until designers realize that environmental management is possible and valuable, they will continue to see their designs mismanaged and poorly presented by caretaker managers dedicated to a static conception of environment. And until the clients of designers see the essential need for environmental management in their own operations, such clients will be disappointed in the failure of designers to design adequately for unforeseeable circumstances, thus discrediting the meaningful contributions that designers can make in a rapidly changing world.

50 Planning and Social Life: Friendship and Neighbor Relations in Suburban Communities[1]

Herbert J. Gans

Studies of wartime housing projects and postwar suburban subdivisions have shown that the residents of these developments do a considerable amount of visiting with the

Reprinted by permission of the *Journal of the American Institute of Planners* (1961, Volume XXVIII, No. 7) and the author.

[1] I am indebted to Paul Davidoff, John W. Dyckman, Lewis Mumford, Janet and Tom Reiner, Melvin M. Webber, and William L. C. Wheaton for helpful critiques of earlier versions of this paper.

nearest neighbors, and may select their friends from among them. Social relationships appear to be influenced and explained by *propinquity* (see Merton, 1947; Caplow & Foreman, 1950; Festinger, Schachter & Back, 1950; Festinger, 1951; Kuper, 1953; Whyte, 1953, 1957; Rosow, 1961).[2] As a result, they are affected by the site plan and the architectural design, which determine how near people will live to each other. In fact, Festinger, Schachter and Back (1950) have suggested that:

The architect who builds a house or designs a site plan, who decides where the roads will and will not go, and who decides which directions the houses will face and how close together they will be, also is, to a large extent, deciding the pattern of social life among the people who will live in those houses.

Conversely, other studies of social life have shown that people tend to choose friends on the basis of similarities in backgrounds, such as age and socio-economic level; values, such as those with respect to privacy or child rearing; and interests, such as leisure activity preferences (see, e.g., Lazarsfeld and Merton, 1954). These findings suggest that social relationships are influenced and explained by people's *homogeneity* with respect to a variety of *characteristics*, although it is not yet known exactly what combination of characteristics must be shared for different social relationships. This explanation would imply that the planner affects social life not through the site plan but through decisions about lot size or facility standards that help to determine, directly or indirectly, whether the population of an area will be homogeneous or heterogeneous with respect to the characteristics that determine social relationships.[3]

[2] The discussion that follows draws on these studies and on my own research and observations in two suburban communities, Park Forest, Illinois, and Levittown, New Jersey.

[3] Hereafter, when I describe a population as homogeneous or heterogeneous, I always mean with respect to the characteristics that are relevant to the particular aspect of social life under discussion, although for stylistic reasons, the qualifying phrase is usually left out.

The two explanations raise a number of issues for planning:

1. Whether or not the planner has the power to influence patterns of social life.

2. Whether or not he should exert this power.

3. Whether some patterns of social life are more desirable than others, and should, therefore, be sought as planning goals. For example, should people be encouraged to find their friends among neighbors, or throughout, or outside their residential area? Should they be politely distant or friendly with neighbors?

If propinquity is most important in determining friendship formation and neighbor relations, the ideal patterns—if such exist—would have to be implemented through the site plan. If homogeneity of characteristics is most important, the planner must decide whether to advocate homogeneous residential areas, if he wishes to encourage friendliness and friendship among neighbors; and heterogeneous ones, if he wishes to encourage more distant neighbor relations and spatially dispersed friendship.

Although the available research does not yet permit a final explanation of the patterns of social life, a preliminary conclusion can be suggested. This permits us to discuss the implications for planning theory and practice.

PROPINQUITY, HOMOGENEITY, AND FRIENDSHIP

The existing studies suggest that the two explanations are related, but that homogeneity of characteristics is more important than propinquity. Although propinquity initiates many social relationships and maintains less intensive ones, such as "being neighborly," it is not sufficient by itself to create intensive relationships. Friendship requires homogeneity.

Propinquity leads to visual contact between neighbors and is likely to produce face-to-face social contact. This is true only if the distance between neighbors is small enough to encourage one or the other to transform the visual contact into a social one.[4] Thus, physical distance between neighbors is important. So is the relationship of the dwellings—especially their front and rear doors—and the circulation system. For example, if doors of adjacent houses face each other or if residents must share driveways, visual contact is inevitable.

The opportunity for visual and social contact is greater at high densities than at low ones, but only if neighbors are adjacent horizontally. In apartment buildings, residents who share a common hallway will meet, but those who live on different floors are less likely to do so, because there is little occasion for visual contact (see Festinger, Schachter & Back, 1950; Wallace, 1952). Consequently, propinquity operates most efficiently in single-family and row-house areas, especially if these are laid out as courts, narrow loops, or cul-de-sacs.

Initial social contacts can develop into relationships of varying intensity, from polite chats about the weather to close friendship. (Negative relationships, varying from avoidance to open enmity are also possible.) Propinquity not only initiates relationships, but it also plays an important role in maintaining the less intensive ones, for the mere fact of living together encourages neighbors to make sure that the relationship between them remains positive. Propinquity cannot determine the intensity of the relationship, however; this is a function of the characteristics of the people involved. If neighbors are homogeneous and feel themselves to be compatible, there is some likelihood that the relationship will be more intensive than an exchange of greetings. If neighbors are

---

[4] If the physical distance is negligible, as between next door neighbors, social contact is likely to take place quickly. When neighbors are not immediately adjacent, however, one or the other must take the initiative, and this requires either some visible sign of a shared background characteristic, or interest, or the willingness to be socially aggressive. This is not as prevalent as sometimes imagined. Although the new suburbs are often thought to exhibit an inordinate amount of intrablock visiting, I found that on the block on which I lived in Levittown, New Jersey, some of the men who lived three to five houses away from each other did not meet for over a year after initial occupancy. The wives met more quickly, of course.

heterogeneous, the relationship is not likely to be intensive, regardless of the degree of propinquity. *Propinquity may thus be the initial cause of an intensive positive relationship, but it cannot be the final or sufficient cause.*

This is best illustrated in a newly settled subdivision. When people first move in, they do not know each other, or anything about each other, except that they have all chosen to live in this community—and can probably afford to do so.[5] As a result, they will begin to make social contacts based purely on propinquity, and because they share the characteristics of being strangers and pioneers, they will do so with almost every neighbor within physical and functional distance. As these social contacts continue, participants begin to discover each other's backgrounds, values, and interests, so that similarities and differences become apparent. Homogeneous neighbors may become friends, whereas heterogeneous ones soon reduce the amount of visiting, and eventually limit themselves to being neighborly. (This process is usually completed after about three months of social contact, especially if people have occupied their homes in spring or summer, when climate and garden chores lead to early visual contact.) The resulting pattern of social relationships cannot be explained by propinquity alone. An analysis of the characteristics of the people will show that homogeneity and heterogeneity explain the existence *and the absence* of social relationships more adequately than does the site plan or the architectural design. Needless to say, the initial social pattern is not immutable; it is changed by population turnover and by a gradual tendency to find other friends outside the immediate area (see Form, 1951).

If neighbors are compatible, however, they may not look elsewhere for companion-

ship, so that propinquity—as well as the migration patterns and housing market conditions which bring homogeneous people together—plays an important role. Most of the communities studied so far have been settled by homogeneous populations. For example, Festinger, Schachter, and Back (1950) studied two student housing projects whose residents were of similar age, marital status, and economic level. Moreover, they were all sharing a common educational experience and had little time for entertaining. Under these conditions, the importance of propinquity in explaining visiting patterns and friendship is not surprising. The fact that they were impermanent residents is also relevant, although if a considerable degree of homogeneity exists among more permanent residents, similar patterns develop.

PROPINQUITY, HOMOGENEITY, AND NEIGHBOR RELATIONS

Although propinquity brings neighbors into social contact, a certain degree of homogeneity is required to maintain this contact on a positive basis. If neighbors are too diverse, differences of behavior or attitude may develop which can lead to coolness or even conflict. For example, when children who are being reared by different methods come into conflict, disciplinary measures by their parents will reveal differences in ways of rewarding and punishing. If one child is punished for a digression and his playmate is not, misunderstandings and arguments can develop between the parents. Differences about house and yard maintenance, or about political issues can have similar consequences.

The need for homogeneity is probably greatest among neighbors with children of equal age and among immediately adjacent neighbors. Children, especially young ones, choose playmates on a purely propinquitous basis. Thus, positive relations among neighbors with children of similar age are best maintained if the neighbors are comparatively homogeneous with respect to child-rearing methods. Immediately adjacent neighbors are likely to have frequent visual

[5] Home buyers do not, however, move into a new area without some assurance that neighbors are likely to be compatible. They derive this assurance from the house price (which bears some correlation to purchasers' income level), from the kinds of people whom they see inspecting the model homes, and from the previous class and ethnic image of the area within which the subdivision is located.

contact, and if there is to be social contact, they must be relatively compatible. Some people minimize social contact with immediately adjacent neighbors on principle, in order to prevent possible differences from creating disagreement. Since such neighbors live in involuntary propinquity, conflict might result in permanently impaired relationships which might force one or the other to move out.

Generally speaking, conflicts between neighbors seem to be rare. In the new suburbs, current building and marketing practices combine to bring together people of relatively similar age and income, thus creating sufficient homogeneity to enable strangers to live together peaceably. In the communities which I have studied, many people say that they have never had such friendly neighbors. Where chance assembles a group of heterogeneous neighbors, unwritten and often unrecognized pacts are developed which bring standards of house and yard maintenance into alignment and which eliminate from the conversation topics that might result in conflict.

THE MEANING OF HOMOGENEITY

I have been stressing the importance of resident characteristics without defining the terms homogeneity and heterogeneity. This omission has been intentional, for little is known about what characteristics must be shared before people feel themselves to be compatible with others. We do not know for certain if they must have common backgrounds, or similar interests, or shared values—or combinations of these. Nor do we know precisely which background characteristics, behavior patterns, and interests are most and least important, or about what issues values must be shared. Also, we do not know what similarities are needed for relationships of different intensities or, for any given characteristics, how large a difference can exist before incompatibility sets in. For example, it is known that income differences can create incompatibility between neighbors, but it is not known how large these differences must become before incompatibility is felt.

Demographers may conclude that one community is more homogeneous than an-

other with respect to such characteristics as age or income, but this information is too general and superficial to predict the pattern of social life. Social relationships are not based on census data, but on subjectively experienced definitions of homogeneity and heterogeneity which terminate in judgments of compatibility or incompatibility. These definitions and judgments have received little study.

Sociologists generally agree that behavior patterns, values, and interests—what people think and do—are more important criteria for homogeneity than background factors (see Lazarsfeld & Merton, 1954). My observations suggest that in the new suburbs, values with respect to child rearing, leisure-time interests, taste level, general cultural preferences, and temperament seem to be most important in judging compatibility or incompatibility.

Such interests and values *do* reflect differences in background characteristics, since a person's beliefs and actions are shaped in part by his age, income, occupation, and the like. These characteristics can, therefore, be used as clues to understanding the pattern of social relationships. *Life-cycle stage* (which summarizes such characteristics as age of adults, marital status, and age of children) and *class* (especially income and education) are probably the two most significant characteristics. Education is especially important, because it affects occupational choice, child-rearing patterns, leisure-time preferences, and taste level. *Race* is also an important criterion, primarily because it is a highly visible—although not necessarily accurate—symbol of class position.[6]

Background characteristics provide crude measures that explain only in part the actual evaluations and choices made by neighbors on a block. Until these evaluations themselves are studied—and then related to background data—it is impossible to define homogeneity or heterogeneity operationally.

[6] Studies (Deutsch & Collins, 1951; Greer & Greer, 1960) suggest that where people are relatively homogeneous in class and age, race differences are no obstacle to social relationships, and race is no longer a criterion of heterogeneity. This is especially true in middle-class residential areas occupied by professional people.

Since considerable criticism has been leveled at the new suburbs for being overly homogeneous—at least by demographic criteria—such research is of considerable importance for the planner's evaluation of these communities and for the planning of future residential areas.

VARIATIONS IN HOMOGENEITY

The degree of population homogeneity varies from suburb to suburb. Moreover, since residents usually become neighbors by a fairly random process—for example, by signing deeds at the same time—many combinations of homogeneity and heterogeneity can be found among the blocks of a single subdivision.[7] In some blocks, neighbors are so compatible that they spend a significant amount of their free time with each other and even set up informal clubs to cement the pattern. In other blocks, circumstances bring together very diverse people, and relationships between them may be only polite, or even cool.

Whyte's studies (1957) in Park Forest led him to attribute these variations to site planning features. He found that the small "courts" were friendly and happy; the larger ones, less friendly and sometimes unhappy. He also found that the residents of the smaller courts were so busy exchanging visits that, unlike those of the larger ones, they did not become active in the wider community. My observations in Park Forest and in Levittown, New Jersey, suggest, however, that homogeneity and heterogeneity explain these phenomena more effectively.[8] When neighbors are especially homogeneous, blocks can become friendly, regardless of their size, although the larger

blocks usually divide themselves into several social groupings. Block size is significant only insofar as a small block may *feel* itself to be more cohesive because all sociability takes place within one group. In the larger blocks, the fact that there are several groups prevents such a feeling, even though each of the groups may be as friendly as the one in the smaller block.

Community participation patterns can be explained in a similar fashion. If the block population is heterogeneous, and residents must look elsewhere for friends, they inevitably turn to community-wide clubs, church organizations, and even civic groups in order to meet compatible people. If participation in these organizations is based solely on the need to find friends, however, it is likely to be minimal, and may even cease, once friendships are established. This type of membership differs considerably from civic or organizational participation proper. The distinction between the two types is important. Whyte recommends that site planners encourage participation by making blocks large enough to discourage excessive on-the-block social life. While this might increase the first type of participation, it cannot affect the second type. People who are inclined to be really active in community-wide organizations are a self-selected minority who will desert the social life of the block, regardless of the block's layout or of the neighbors' compatibility. They are usually attracted to community participation by pressing community problems and by interest, ambition, or the hope of personal gain. Site planning techniques cannot bring about their participation.

THE ROLE OF PROPINQUITY

Given the importance of homogeneity in social relationships, what role remains for propinquity? Since propinquity results in visual contact, whether voluntary, or involuntary, it produces social contact among neighbors, although homogeneity will determine how intensive the relationships will be and whether they will be positive or not. Propinquity also supports relationships based on homogeneity by making frequent contact convenient. Finally, among people who are comparatively homogeneous and move into

---

[7] This is true of the larger subdivisions. Smaller ones are sometimes not settled randomly, but are occupied by groups, for example related households or members of an ethnic group moving *en masse* from another area.

[8] These comments are based on observations, however, rather than on systematic studies. Macris (1958) studied visiting patterns in Park Forest in 1957 and found considerably less intrablock visiting than did Whyte (1957). He also found that there was almost no visiting at all between tenants and homeowners, even though they were living in physical propinquity in the area he studied. This suggests the importance of neighbor homogeneity.

an area as strangers, propinquity may determine friendship formation among neighbors.

In addition, some types of people gravitate to propinquitous relationships more than others. Age is an important factor. As already noted, children choose their playmates strictly on a propinquitous basis, though decreasingly so as they get older. This is why parents who want their young children to associate with playmates of similar status and cultural background must move to areas where such playmates are close at hand.

Among adults, the importance of propinquity seems to vary with sex and class. Women generally find their female friends nearby, especially if they are mothers and are restricted in their movements. In fact, young mothers must usually be able to find compatible people—and therefore, homogeneous neighbors—within a relatively small radius. Should they fail to do so, they may become the unhappy isolated suburban housewives about whom so much has been written. My observations suggest that most women are able to find the female companionship they seek, however. In addition, the increase in two-car families and women's greater willingness to drive are gradually reducing the traditional immobility of the housewife.

The relationship between propinquity and class has received little study. Generally speaking, the "higher" the class, the greater the physical mobility for visiting and entertaining. Thus, working-class people seem to be least mobile and most likely to pick their friends on a propinquitous basis. However, since they visit primarily with relatives, they may travel considerable distances if relatives are not available nearby (Young & Willmott, 1957). Upper-middle-class people seem to go farther afield for their social life than do lower-middle-class ones, in part because they may have specialized interests which are hard to satisfy on the block.

Propinquity is also more important for some types of social activities than others. In America, and probably everywhere in the Western world, adolescents and adults socialize either in peer groups—people of similar age and sex—or in sets of couples. Peer groups are more likely to form on the basis of propinquity. For example, the members of that well-known suburban peer group, the women's "coffee klatsch," are usually recruited in the immediate vicinity. Since the participants indulge primarily in shop talk—children, husbands, and home —the fact that they are all wives and mothers provides sufficient homogeneity to allow propinquity to function.[9] For couples, homogeneity is a more urgent requirement than propinquity, since the two people in a couple must accept both members of all other couples. The amount of compatibility that is required probably cannot be satisfied so easily among the supply of neighbors within propinquitous distance.

The role of propinquity also varies with the size of the group, and with the activities pursued. The larger the group, the less intensive are the relationships between participants, and the less homogeneity is required. If the group meets for a specific activity, such as to celebrate a major holiday or to play cards, the behavior that takes place is sufficiently specialized and habitual that the participants' other characteristics are less relevant. If the group meets for conversation, more homogeneity of values and interests is required.[10]

LIMITATIONS OF THESE OBSERVATIONS

The foregoing comments are based largely on observations and studies in new suburban communities. Little is known about the role of propinquity and homogeneity in established communities, although there is no reason to expect any major differences (see Rosow, 1961, p. 131). Whatever differences exist are probably due to the reduction of much of the initial homogeneity in estab-

[9] There must, however, be general agreement about methods of housekeeping, getting along with husbands, and child rearing. Since these methods vary with education and socio-economic level, some homogeneity of class is necessary even for the coffee klatsch.

[10] The kinds of gatherings which Whyte (1957) studied so ingeniously in Park Forest were mainly those of peer groups indulging in single-purpose activities. This may explain why he found propinquity to be so important.

lished communities through population turnover. The same process is likely to take place in new communities. Moveouts create a gap in established social groupings. Newcomers may be able to fill this gap—provided they are not too different from those they have replaced. Even so, it is hard for a newcomer to break into an established coffee klatsch or card party, and only people with a little extra social aggressiveness are likely to do so. In addition, there is the previously noted tendency of the original residents to find new friends outside the immediate area and to spend less time with neighbors. As a result of these processes, patterns of social life in new communities will eventually resemble those in established areas.

Most of my observations are at present only hypotheses that need to be tested by more systematic research. Two types of studies are especially important. The first should investigate the influence of resident characteristics by analyzing the existence of propinquitous relationships among a variety of blocks, all similar in site plan and architectural design but differing in the degree of homogeneity among neighbors. The second study should analyze the impact of site plans and housing design on propinquity, by studying subdivisions which differ in physical layout but are occupied by similar kinds of residents.

CONCLUSIONS

At the beginning of this paper, I raised three questions: whether the planner had the power to influence patterns of social life; whether he ought to use this power; and if so, whether ideal patterns existed which should be advocated as planning goals. These questions can now be answered in a preliminary fashion.

The planner has only limited influence over social relationships. Although the site planner can create propinquity, he can only determine which houses are to be adjacent. He can thus affect visual contact and initial social contacts among their occupants, but he cannot determine the intensity or quality of the relationships. This depends on the characteristics of the people involved.

The characteristics of the residents can be affected to some small degree by subdivision regulations, lot-size provisions, facility standards, or by any other planning tools which determine the uniformity of the housing to be built and the facilities to be provided—and can therefore affect the degree of homogeneity or heterogeneity among the eventual occupants. The planner has considerably less influence, however, than the private and public agencies which combine to finance, build, and market houses. These in turn respond to housing demand—and to the fact that most buyers are willing to accept similarity in house type and want a fair degree of homogeneity in their neighbors.

Consequently, within the context of present planning powers and practices, the planner's influence on social relationships is not very great. Whether or not it should be greater can only be decided on the basis of value judgments about patterns of social life.

Needless to say, a wide variety of value judgments can be formulated. My own judgment is that no one ideal pattern of social life can be—or should be—prescribed, but that opportunity for choice should be available both with respect to neighbor relations and friendship formation.

Neighbor relations should be positive; no benefits, but many social and emotional costs, result from life in an atmosphere of mutual dislike or coolness. Beyond this point, however, the intensity of relationships should not be a subject for planning values. Whether neighbors become friends, whether they remain friendly, or whether they are only polite to each other should be left up to the people who come to live together. Each type of relationship has its pros and cons, but none is so much more desirable than another that it should be advocated by the planner.

Friendship formation is a highly personal process, and it would be wrong for anyone to presume to plan another person's friendships. Moreover, one pattern of friendship does not seem to me to be preferable to any other. Finding one's friends on the block is convenient, although propinquity may encourage so much social contact that no time is left for friends who live farther away. Also, propinquity may make life on the block difficult if the relationship should cease to be friendly. Dispersal of friendship over a larger residential area may help people to know their community a little better, but unless they are already interested in gathering and using such knowledge, this is not likely to make much difference to them, or to the community.

Prescribing the opportunity for choice requires also that no one should be forced into any social relationship not of his own choosing. For example, no site plan should so isolate blocks from one another that residents must find it too difficult to maintain social contacts outside the block. Likewise, no residential area should be so heterogeneous in its population make-up that it prevents anyone from finding friends within the area; nor should it be so homogeneous that residents socialize only on their own block.

IMPLICATIONS FOR PLANNING PRACTICE

Detailed implications cannot be spelled out until considerably more data are available on the relative roles of propinquity and homogeneity. Some guides can be suggested, however.

The site planner should not deliberately try to create a specific social pattern, but he should aim to provide maximum choice. If possible, the site plan should contain a variety of house-to-house relationships, so that residents who desire a large number of visual and social contacts and those who prefer relative isolation can both be satisfied. If density requirements permit, however, the site planner should not locate dwelling units within such close physical and functional distance to each other that the occupants are constantly thrown together and forced into social contact. In areas of single-family houses, the planner should avoid narrow courts. In row-house developments, soundproof party walls are necessary. In addition, some type of separation between houses should be provided to shield front and rear doors from those of adjacent houses. Since Americans seem to dislike complete and permanent separation from neighbors,

however, something less irrevocable than a solid wall is desirable.

Blocks and courts should be so laid out that they do not become prisons. At the same time, however, they should not be spread out in such a fashion that all visual and social contact between neighbors is prevented. This is a problem in areas of very low density, where lots are so large that neighbors have difficulty in meeting each other.[11]

If and when sufficient research has been done to establish the relationship between site planning and social life on a sounder empirical basis, the concept of voluntary resident placement should be explored. Thus, if the studies indicate that some locations in a site plan will inevitably result in greater social contact than others, potential occupants should be informed, so that they can take this fact into account in choosing their houses.

Since homogeneity is an important determinant of social relationships, some degree of homogeneity on the block would seem to be desirable. This would encourage positive relationships among neighbors and would allow those who want to find friends in the immediate vicinity to do so without impairing the ability of others to seek friends on the outside. If blocks are too homogeneous, however, those people who differ from the majority are likely to be considered deviants, and may be exposed to social pressure to conform or sentenced to virtual isolation. Conversely, heterogeneous blocks would produce cool and possibly negative relations among neighbors and would eliminate the chance to make friends on the block.

The proper solution is a moderate degree of homogeneity, although at this point no one knows how to define this degree operationally or how to develop planning guides for it. Moreover, the planner lacks the power to implement such guides. *My observations*

---

[11] Erich Lindemann (in a personal conversation) has reported that this resulted in an upper-income community which he and his associates have studied. The large lots which satisfy the status needs of their owners also create loneliness for women who have no social contacts in the larger community.

suggest that, by and large, the present crop of suburban communities provides the degree of homogeneity described here. Consequently, the planner need not worry about his inability to intervene.

My proposals in behalf of residential homogeneity are based on the value judgments defended here and apply only to one phase of residential life. Planners have long debated whether residential areas should be homogeneous or heterogeneous. Some planners, who give higher priority to other planning values, and are more concerned with other phases of residential life, have advocated balanced communities, with heterogeneous populations.

REFERENCES:

Caplow, T., & Foreman, R. Neighborhood interaction in a homogeneous community. *American Sociological Review,* 1950, **15,** 357–366.

Deutsch, M., & Collins, M. *Interracial housing.* Minneapolis: University of Minnesota Press, 1951.

Festinger, L., Schachter, S., & Back, K. *Social pressures in informal groups.* New York: Harper & Bros., 1950.

Festinger, L. Architecture and group membership. *Journal of Social Issues,* 1951, **7,** 152–163.

Form, W. Stratification in low and middle income housing areas. *Journal of Social Issues,* 1951, **7,** 116–117.

Greer, E., & Greer, G. *Privately developed interracial housing.* Berkeley: University of California Press, 1960.

Kuper, L. Blueprint for living together. In L. Kuper (Ed.), *Living in towns.* London: Cresset Press, 1953, 1–202.

Lazarsfeld, P., & Merton, R. Friendship as a social process: A substantive and methodological analysis (Part I: Substantive analysis, by R. Merton), in M. Berger, T. Abel, & C. Page (Eds.), *Freedom and control in modern society.* New York: Van Nostrand, 1954, 21–37.

Macris, D. *Social relationships among residents of various house types in a planned community.* Unpublished master's thesis, University of Illinois, 1958.

Merton, R. The social psychology of housing. In W. Dennis (Ed.), *Current trends in social psychology.* Pittsburgh: University of Pittsburgh Press, 1947, 163–217.

Rosow, I. The social effects of the physical environment. *Journal of the American Institute of Planners,* 1961, **27,** 127–133.

Wallace, A. *Housing and social structure.* Philadelphia: Philadelphia Housing Authority, 1952.

Whyte, W. H., Jr. How the new suburbia socializes. *Fortune,* August 1953, 120–122, 186–190.

Whyte, W. H., Jr. *The organization man.* New York: Simon and Schuster, 1957.

Young, M., & Willmott, P. *Family and kinship in East London.* London: Routledge and Kegan Paul, 1957.

51 Site Planning and Social Behavior[1]

Robert Gutman

With the United States about to enter a period during which two million housing units will be constructed annually (Meyerson, Terrett, and Wheaton, 1962), it is inevitable that there should be increasing interest in the impact of housing on individual behavior and social organization. Put very simply, the issue which is being raised by architects, planners, banks and mortgage companies, local officials, zoning boards and consumers of housing is this: does the style and character of housing make a difference for the lives of its occupants? In this paper, I wish to comment on the present state of social science knowledge with respect to one aspect of this subject, namely the site plan or spatial arrangement of dwelling units. How does the spatial arrangement influence residents of a site? I propose to summarize existing research on the question to the extent the task can be accomplished in a short paper, which necessarily means that many of my statements will be all too brief and my review will be highly selective. The review will be presented through the artifice of providing answers to four specific questions: what is the general nature of the

From *The Journal of Social Issues,* 1966, **22,** 103–115. Reprinted by permission of the author and the publisher.

[1] I am grateful to the Urban Studies Center at Rutgers, and its Director, Professor John E. Bebout, for continuing support of my investigations. The Institute of Urban and Regional Development of the University of California, Berkeley, and its Director, Dr. William L. C. Wheaton, provided me with an opportunity to learn more about the problems of site planning. I also want to thank Miss Dorothy Whiteman, Assistant to the Director of the Bureau of Urban Research, Princeton University, for bibliographical advice.

phenomenon under consideration; what is meant by the site plan; what is the process through which site plans influence behavior; and what kinds of behavior conceivably can be influenced by a site plan?[2] To the reader who may wonder why I choose to consider the site plan instead of some other dimension of the housing environment, I should point out that the behavioral implications of the site plan have been widely commented on by architects and city planners, i.e., the professional groups which in our society have primary responsibility for the design of housing; and that this dimension of housing has been more persistently and more carefully examined by sociologists and social psychologists than almost any other aspect of the general subject.

1. What general perspective is appropriate to understanding the relationship between site planning and individual behavior and social organization?

This question is worth raising for two reasons. In the first place, as the inclusion of a paper on site planning in this symposium implies, there is something special about the site plan which distinguishes it from other phenomena whose relation to behavior usually is studied by the behavioral sciences. This special feature is the spatial quality of the site plan which moves it out of the ontological category of social facts, and into the realm of non-social facts. When social scientists raise questions about the sources of social action, they seek an explanation in terms of other social variables, or through psychological facts,[3] but this description obviously is not true of research concerned with the social effects of the site plan.

The second justification for emphasizing the question is that most of the literature

on site planning has been written by professional architects and planners; and both groups ordinarily do not concern themselves with the distinction between the site plan as a physical variable and the activities, or social and psychological variables, which represent the complex human responses to the spatial features of a site. It is common practice, for example, for architects to label particular spaces in their drawings with words like "park," "sidewalk," "play area," and so on. However, from the perspective of trying to understand the influence on behavior of site plans, it seems more reasonable to define these areas according to their purely physical or spatial properties. Thus, parks, walks and play areas would be regarded as congeries of materials and shapes, including cement, steel, wood and grass; or as systems of green areas, pavement and benches. Then it would be easier to make it clear that we are dealing with an empirical question to be answered through observation; when we inquire if the shapes and material systems acquire the social uses intended by the designers; whether, say, the grassy space really does become a play area for children, or whether oldsters do sit on the benches. The distinction is of more than academic significance, since the history of contemporary building is full of examples of areas set aside for parks which never have been used for this purpose. The children who were supposed to play in the grassy space can be found tumbling in the adjoining sandlot; instead of sunning themselves on the benches, the men are gossiping and drinking at the saloon around the corner (Willmott, 1964).

The general perspective which must govern site planning research and theory grows out of this distinction between the non-social and social aspects of the site plan. The perspective prescribes that research and theory should result in a series of statements which help us to understand how a physical fact is capable of exerting its influence on social facts.

2. What is a site plan?

In order to conduct a research on site planning, a more precise description of its

---

[2] I have discussed these questions more fully, elsewhere (Gutman, 1964). Other discussions of the literature can be found in Heyman (1964) and Architectural Research Lab. (1965).

[3] There are numerous ways in which social scientists express the distinction between the social and non-social environment in their discussions of social theory (Gutman, 1949). I have commented on these expressions in another paper (Gutman, 1963).

nature is required than is revealed by the statement that it is a phenomenon defined by its physical properties. A typology is needed which classifies those features of the site which are especially relevant for discovering the impact of the plan on social action. With this typology in hand, it should be a relatively easy task to then develop operational definitions of site plans.[4] The operational definitions will presumably point to facts that can be measured with the instruments available to surveyors, engineers and others who regularly quantify spatial features of the landscape.

Unfortunately, the existing literature on site planning does not offer an adequate typology of features which are relevant to behavioral studies. In part, the deficiency reflects the dependence of site planning research on the design tradition, which has led architects and planners to formulate and evaluate plans according to other criteria than their possible impact on social action. In schools of architecture, for instance, students are taught to look at site plans from the point of view of the geometrical principles which govern spatial forms; to consider their efficiency in controlling the effects of climate, sunlight and wind, underground water and soil composition; and to keep in mind whether or not the plans conform to local building and housing codes, and zoning ordinances (Lynch, 1962). This training results in an intellectual orientation which then classifies site plans in terms of the organization of spaces described by means of the location of planes, solids and voids; or a different but still related orientation which emphasizes gross physical details including street patterns, type of housing and the proportion of the total area of the site allocated to these and other details (Gutman, 1964). Although designers will argue that these distinctions among plans have implications for the way in which their residents and users behave, most efforts by social scientists to forecast behavior patterns given a knowledge of these

site plan characteristics have not been successful.

Recently, some planners, particularly those influenced by the writings of Kevin Lynch, have paid attention to the images which urban forms create in the eyes of their beholders. Lynch and his students are concerned with the effect of these images on the attitudes of residents to their spatial environments. Most of their work still is focused on the methodological issues which emerge in the course of trying to investigate the sources of these attitudes (Lynch, 1960).

When we recall that empirical studies of site planning are oriented specifically to its influence on behavior, the continued absence of a typology must be taken as evidence of the difficulty of developing appropriate conceptualizations of the physical features of a site, and also as a sign of the still infant state of the science of site planning. Ideas which can contribute the rudiments of a typology exist in the form of insights, passing comments and limited hypotheses, but do not meet the standards of systematization needed to compose a typology. Gans (1961), whose studies represent the most careful investigation of the problem, emphasizes the role of *propinquity*, or the distance between dwelling units, as a factor leading to residential sociability. The interest in propinquity suggests concern for the proper level of analysis, since it focuses on the physical properties of the site considered separately from the social activities which may occur on it, and furthermore, expresses this interest in terms of an abstract concept which is redolent with meaning for behavior. However, one weakness of Gans' analysis is that he does not go on to consider other abstract elements which may be relevant, although he recognizes that the concept of propinquity is related to two features of a site conceived at a still higher level of abstraction: physical distance and functional distance.

Physical distance is the distance between the portals of two dwelling units on a line connecting the units, as they ordinarily are shown in a two-dimensional plan; functional distance is the distance which must actually be traversed in getting from one

---

[4] The nature and significance of typological analysis is discussed in Barton (1955). For an example of the manner in which typological analysis can be used to criticize social theory see Gutman and Wrong (1961).

portal to another after the building is constructed. It is another sign of the incompleteness of site planning theory that Festinger, who first made use of the distinction between the two kinds of distance, also did not consider other dimensions of the site plan. The omission is particularly troublesome for understanding the sociometric patterns which emerged in his study of the M.I.T. graduate student housing project known as Westgate (Festinger, Schachter and Back, 1950). The site included both fully detached and semi-detached dwelling units, which in the analysis of residential interaction were then treated as equivalent units on the grounds that the functional distance between the portals was not affected by whether they were entries to free-standing units or to adjoining units. No attention whatever was paid to the fact that occupants of the semi-detached units shared a party wall; yet one of the most interesting findings from other studies is that the party wall is largely responsible for public dissatisfaction with town house and row house settlements (Kuper, 1953).

Other examples from the social science literature could be given, but the point is probably clear: on the important question of developing a typology of site plan features, we find that the existing studies do not specify the full range of relevant features; and that even when a range is indicated, the studies do not provide the data for the composition of an exhaustive typology. The lack of an adequate typology is distressing not only for the reasons already mentioned. Up to now, the site plans chosen for study have been selected *ad hoc*, usually in response to immediate concerns of private or public agencies charged with formulating or evaluating a housing policy. One way around this situation in the future would be to make decisions about the sites to be studied in terms of what social scientists and planners together believe are the crucial differences among site plans. But it is extremely difficult to develop a design for a comparative study, without a useful typology of the attributes of the independent variable whose effects are being investigated.

3. *What is the process through which site plans can influence behavior?*

The inhabitants of a plan area breathe, see, eat, excrete and move about. A primitive level of these activities is required for human survival; and, of course, functioning at higher levels must be sustained if the residents are to participate in a complex, modern society. The amenities available at the site, in the form of facilities which enhance air circulation, illumination, temperature control, sanitation and accessibility to consumer and recreational facilities, will contribute to survival. Since survival is rarely the problem now, given the superior standards for housing which prevail in industrial societies, the quality of amenities is more likely to be relevant to the individual's social effectiveness in the family and the work group. The residents of housing developments are social animals, too, who require the support of others for their own mental well-being and for the initiation and maintenance of the cooperative organized activities upon which group life and the survival of society itself ultimately depend. To establish and carry out these activities the occupants of plan areas must be able to communicate with their neighbors and with other persons and families living nearby. Social communication relies upon the use of the senses, the human faculties of receiving mental impressions through the bodily organs and through the awareness of changes in bodily states. Site plans acquire some of their significance from their capacity to facilitate or thwart the use of the senses; in other words, through their power to regulate the communication process among the residents and other users of a plan area.

The inhabitants of a spatial environment also possess an intricate psychic structure, whose functions are involved in their response to the site plan. One such function is that aspect of man's perceptual apparatus which enables him to see and visualize individual artifacts and then to organize them into spatial forms. Architects and planners continue to give primary attention to the play of this apparatus, making use of established conventions for creating optical illusions (Gropius, 1962). Another function is the human capacity to endow objects with symbolic meaning. Open sites, for example, with good and mature trees, large and green lawns, including sidewalks, cul-de-sac streets and private community facilities are taken as a sign that their inhabitants are families of status and wealth. These and similar meaning associated with site plan features are sufficiently well established so that sociologists can make use of spatial and ecological factors to measure socio-economic status. Spatial artifacts in turn become reflexively significant for the individuals who occupy, use and possess them. Thus houses and sites that represent a style of life consistent with a woman's imagined social rank have a positive impact on her ability to adapt to the experience of moving from one settlement to another (Foote, 1960). Sites whose spatial arrangements signify downward mobility are a source of frustration and reduce the capacity for successful adaptation, even when the new house offers amenities not available in the former dwelling (Gutman, 1963). Sites and urban locations which have acquired a negative symbolic meaning produce psychological responses which have been likened to the grief reaction found among persons who have recently experienced the death of a beloved member of the family (Fried, 1963).

There are, then, at least four pathways through which the site plan can be linked with behavior; and each of these linkages is based on some capacity, faculty or trait of human nature which enables physical artifacts to exert an influence over man. However, empirical studies of site planning have not exhibited an equal amount of interest in each of the four. The older city planning tradition, going back to the housing studies conducted by social reformers around the turn of the present century, was concerned principally with the provision of adequate amenities, particularly fresh air, heat, illumination and sanitation. Making use of the primitive but nevertheless adequate survey procedures of the era, they demonstrated that slums and tenement housing produced high rates of morbidity and mortality (Schorr, 1963). The general level of housing amenities in this country is now sufficiently good, and the conclusions of earlier studies have been accepted so fully, that investigations to demonstrate the consequences of amenity deprivation are superfluous and appear infrequently. Studies of the influence of site plan esthetics always have been rare, even while the designers of sites continue to found their solutions on an endless variety of unproven, speculative assumptions concerning their behavioral significance. Sociologists and students of psychological process, particularly those with a psychoanalytic orientation, have speculated about the ways in which objects acquire symbolic meaning (Schilder, 1935; Searles, 1960), and these speculations constitute the theoretical foundation for the numerous empirical studies of the adaptation to new settlements, some of which are referred to above.

The dominant research activity of the last two decades has been conceived in terms of the influence which the site plan exerts through its regulation of the communication process. In this tradition, it is assumed the physical features of the plan establish a specific network through which residents and other users exchange messages. Certain avenues of contact between persons are opened up and others are sealed off; some persons are available to receive messages while there are barriers to exchanging messages with others. Studies which employ this conceptual framework have paid particular attention to the role of visual communication and sound communication. Visual communication is defined operationally to mean the sight of one resident in a housing area by another. Successive observations in American suburbs report that it is this form of communication which lays the foundation for initial interpersonal contact among the inhabitants of a site (Gans, 1961). The kind of sound communication studied is speaking or shouting, or the noise of mechanical equipment, including automobiles, lawn-mowers, and interior plumbing. The problem of noise looms largest in row houses, and town house settlements, and in other types of communities made up of multi-family dwellings. The presence of party-wall construction combined with the difficulty of building effective insulation at reasonable cost are the major sources for the disturbance (Kuper, 1953). In multi-family dwellings, noise is often the principal evidence of the life of neighbors, particularly during the early stages of residence. When not accompanied by more civilized forms of communication and contact, equipment noises or the sound of anonymous and inarticulate voices account for the irritation and dissatisfaction reported by occupants of this type of housing. The relative insignificance of noise in the communication process among inhabitants of suburbs testifies to the role of the site plan. Although the decibel level of, say, a lawn-mower, is higher than the sound of a toilet flush, the separation of houses and the opportunity for visual communication to influence the growth of social relations, modifies the negative effects that otherwise might result.

4. What kinds of behavior conceivably are influenced by the site plan?

In view of the tendency of designers to make imperious claims about the impact of the site plan, and the availability of four distinct channels through which the site plan can work, it is hardly surprising to discover that innumerable forms of behavior and various types of social actions have been regarded as the consequence of site plans. If we look mainly at empirical studies, however, and keep in mind that most of them have regarded the plan as a communication network or as a social symbol, then it can be said that four types of behavior have been the principal subject of investigation. The four are: group life and social organization of the site; the relation of the site plan community to the larger settlement in which it is located; family organization and household life; and the mental health of individual residents. These emphases are characteristic of European, particularly British studies, as well as of research in the United States (Mann, 1965). In general they reflect the fascination of contemporary sociology and social psychology with the role of primary group relations and communality in

societies troubled by problems of malintegration, social disorganization, impersonality and the other structural disturbances of a modern, urban, industrial and bureaucratic society.

Studies of group life have been interested in the intensity of social relations among residents and in their extensity, or the proportion of residents who are involved in relations of stated intensity (Caplow, Stryker and Wallace, 1964). Investigations of intensity usually employ a scale of neighboring, with low intensity defined as the ability to name other residents, and with high intensity measured by the frequency with which neighbors share personal intimacies and confidences (Fava, 1958). Research on extensity typically considers the proportion of site plan residents who are chosen as friends and the proportion who depend on persons outside the plan area for social and emotional satisfaction.

A good deal of work on neighboring has been published and substantial agreement has been reached on several basic generalizations, such as the conclusion already mentioned that site plan features are more influential during the early stages of residence; or the generalization that the simple interaction among persons thrown together by accidents of propinquity is converted into more enduring ties only when the parties to the relationship are socially homogeneous. An example of an issue which still is unresolved is the meaning of "homogeneity" in this context. If the relationship is to survive, must the residents be similar in social background, values and attitudes, interests, or in only some of these factors (Gans, 1961)? For example, is it more significant for the maintenance of neighborly relations that residents agree about child-rearing practices than about political affiliations? Is a resident's attitude toward his neighbor influenced more by the other's conversational topics or by his preferred leisure-time and recreational activities (Gutman, 1964)?

In studying the relations of residents to the surrounding town, behavioral research has investigated their knowledge of municipal affairs, their use of shopping and recreational facilities outside the site, and their degree of involvements in voluntary associations and local politics. The concern displayed in these subjects is the direct heritage of the city planning tradition known as "neighborhood theory," which believed that the formation of small residential communities within larger urban complexes would foster grass roots democracy (Isaacs, 1948). Unfortunately, the literature suggests that the connection between spatial planning and politics is a good deal more complicated than Perry (1929), Stein (1957), and other exponents of neighborhood planning apparently realized. For instance, Festinger's work confirms the obvious point that the information relevant to the immediate needs of a residential group will be communicated to members more readily than news of other matters, but adds the more interesting finding that only rarely are problems of the larger political unit regarded as relevant to the residential group (Festinger, Schachter, and Back, 1950, Chap. 7).

Other errors in the assumptions of neighborhood theory are revealed by investigations which indicate that participation in the affairs of the wider community can be fully accounted for by the social and personal characteristics of the membership of different residential groups, without regard for the spatial features of the sites in which these groups are situated (Greer, 1960). Of course, if shops and parks are located within the plan areas, residents will tend to use them in the manner Stein (1957) anticipated when he included these facilities in his designs for housing development in New York, Fairlawn, Pittsburgh and Los Angeles. However, it does not follow that if community facilities are lacking, that then the residential group will not be cohesive. On the contrary, the literature indicates that when dwelling units are far from grocery stores, then their occupants are more likely to borrow food and kitchen supplies from each other; while the absence of a nursery school near the site leads the residents to turn to neighbors for help in caring for infants and young children (Kuper, 1953).

On the matter of the relation of the site plan to family life, White (1957) reports

that there is "little evidence on the basis of controlled investigations, that the dissatisfactions and conflicts of individual family members can be modified or ameliorated by the residential environment." My guess is that this conclusion will continue to be validated, as it applies to the relation between site planning and the emotional overtones of family interaction but that the site plan may have implications for the allocation of tasks within the family system. Unfortunately, there is still little information about the manner in which the organization of residential space affects, say, the amount of time a father spends maintaining the home or the proportion of her daily routine the wife and mother devotes to household chores. One wonders why these subjects have not received more attention. Is it because consideration of them necessarily demands that we think about the site plan as an amenity, and the level of amenities is no longer a problem in the suburban populations whose site planning behavior has been studied most intensively?

Studies of the influence of site planning on mental health typically pay special attention to the role of community identification in personality integration. The conceptualization of mental health phenomena in these terms (Fried & Gleicher, 1961) again illustrates the desire of researchers to look upon the site plan as a communication network or a social symbol. The emphasis is not unwarranted, in view of the studies mentioned earlier which testify to the deep sentimental attachments which residents develop with urban areas. However, these studies fail to reveal whether the devotion to "place," the "need for roots," and the "sense of belonging" to a particular community are essential conditions for personality integration. Numerous psychiatrists will argue in the affirmative (Wheelis, 1958) and there are research findings of a general nature to support their position, including Goffman's studies (1959) of the importance of familiar spatial environments in the presentation of the self. But there is also the argument of Webber (1963) and Meier (1962), that some of the personality-forming and self-maintaining functions performed by physical proximity in previous historical eras now can be served equally well by technologies which offer opportunities for communication to persons scattered widely through the urban landscape.

Taken altogether, empirical studies do not make a very compelling case for the argument that the site plan is an important influence on individual behavior and collective social action. This raises certain issues about the fundamental character of the research which, even though there is no space here to discuss them fully, do require comment. Keeping these issues in mind helps, I think, to avoid a pessimism which might confirm social scientists in their original prejudice that the non-social environment is of little consequence for behavior.

In the first place, it should be remembered that site plans, like other physical and biological conditions to which human life responds, are significant in the sense that without them obviously there would be no human society as we know it. The question to be attended to, therefore, is not the importance of the existence of the spatial environment, but rather whether *differences* in site plan features result in corresponding differences in behavior. In response to the question phrased in this fashion, I believe we have to admit that the site plans investigated by empirical research do not include a wide enough range of variations to enable us really to deal with the issue intelligently. Most site plan studies have looked at spatial environments all of which can be broadly characterized as suburban. Social scientists have not studied, largely because they do not exist, urban forms that would represent a radical departure from contemporary modes of spatial organization. Consequently, it may be argued that the ultimate test of the general question under discussion can be made only after we have built an urban region with the form and scale say, of a Ville Radieuse (Boesiger and Girsberger, 1960).

A second point goes along with the claim that research has not comprehended the critical range of organizational alternatives implicit in the site planning concept. Can it not be said with some justification that the behavior patterns examined fail to represent many of the effects attributed to site plans which are most relevant to the problems of urban planning in modern society? In its fascination with the impact of the site plan on communality and mental health, research has largely ignored the seemingly more prosaic questions of the impact of site planning on the future availability of urban land, on circulation problems and movement systems, on the development of urban technologies, and the over-all integration of regional social systems. The ways in which present standards of site planning influence these phenomena may not have an immediate, direct and catastrophic effect on individual functioning or group life within the plan area. Nevertheless, since the efficiency of the technological base for inhabiting and utilizing the earth's surface is the fundamental substratum on which the operation of modern society depends, over the long-run the relation of individual site plans to the general organization of the environment may be tremendously significant for the human capacity to adapt to urban conditions.

Thirdly, those who would quickly dismiss the significance of physical facts for behavior on the basis of available findings, ought to consider that this conclusion may reflect the excessive attention given to the site plan as a communication network. If we look at research conducted from the perspective of other definitions, the results are more encouraging. Many of these have been mentioned in passing, including the studies which document the influence of tenement sites on morbidity and mortality; and studies which reveal the social and psychic costs accruing from the removal of residents to new environments which lack established sentimental associations. Perhaps similar affirmative indications will be developed when the social sciences learn how to translate architectural theories into terms which can be tested with empirical techniques.

These caveats may help us to understand why site planning research continues to be a vital field of endeavor at the present time: intuitively, people who work with site plans, and all of us who live in sites, sense that the behavioral sciences up to now have failed to articulate properly the problems which are of ultimate concern. Well over one million new dwelling units will be built this year, and the number of housing starts presumably will exceed twice that number a decade hence. It has been estimated that in the next forty years, this nation will have constructed as many new dwelling units as were built in the previous two centuries of United States history. It is difficult to accept the conclusion, that it makes no difference how these houses are built, where they are located, and how they are arranged in space. Surely, there must be better and worse methods of planning a site, and hopefully the social sciences will be able to guide us in deciding what these methods are.

REFERENCES:

Architectural Research Laboratory, School of Architecture, University of Michigan, SER 1: Environmental abstracts. Ann Arbor: School Environments Research Project, 1965.

Barton, A. The concept of property-space in social research. In P. Lazarsfeld & M. Rosenberg (Eds.), The language of social research. New York: The Free Press, 1955, 40–53.

Boesiger, W., & Girsberger, H. Le Corbusier, 1910–1960. New York: George Wittenborn, 1960, 288 ff.

Caplow, T., Stryker, S., & Wallace, S. E. The urban ambience. Totowa, N.J.: The Bedminster Press, 1964.

Fava, S. F. Contrasts in neighboring: New York city and a suburban community. In W. Dobriner (Ed.), The suburban community. New York: G. P. Putnam, 1958, 122–131.

Festinger, L., Schachter, S., & Back, K. Social pressures in informal groups. New York: Harper and Bros., 1950.

Foote, N., et al. Housing choices and housing constraints. New York: McGraw-Hill, 1960.

Fried, M. Grieving for a lost home. In L. Duhl (Ed.), The urban condition. New York: Basic Books, 1963, 151–171.

Fried, M., & Gleicher, P. Some sources of residential satisfaction in an urban slum. Journal of the American Institute of Planners, 1961, 27, 305–315.

Gans, H. J. Planning and social life. Journal of the American Institute of Planners, 1961, 27, 134–140. The balanced community, ibid., 1961, 176–184.

Goffman, E. The presentation of self in everyday life. Garden City, N.Y.: Doubleday, 1959.

Greer, S. The social structure and political process of suburbia. American Sociological Review, 1960, 25, 514–526.

Gropius, W. Scope of total architecture. New York: Collier Books, 1962.

Gutman, R. A sociologist looks at housing. Address to the Seminar for Housing Internes, Housing and Home Finance Agency, Washington, D.C., November, 1963a. Copies available from the Urban Studies Center, New Brunswick, New Jersey.

Gutman, R. Population mobility in the American middle class. In L. Duhl (Ed.), The urban condition. New York: Basic Books, 1963b, 172–183.

Gutman, R. Notes for a science of culture. Dartmouth Quarterly, 1949, 4.

Gutman, R. Site planning and social organization: A research proposal. Berkeley: Institute of Urban and Regional Development, 1964. (Mimeo)

Gutman, R., & Wrong, D. H. David Riesman's typology of character. In S. M. Lipset and L. Lowenthal (Eds.), Culture and social character. New York: The Free Press, 1961, 295–315.

Heyman, M. Space and behavior. Landscape, 1964, 13, 4–10.

Isaacs, R. The neighborhood theory. Journal of the American Institute of Planners, 1948, 14, 13–22.

Kuper, L. Living in towns. London: Cresset Press, 1953.

Lynch, K. Site planning. Cambridge, Mass.: M.I.T. Press, 1962.

Lynch, K. The image of the city. Cambridge, Mass.: M.I.T. Press, 1960.

Mann, P. H. An approach to urban sociology. London: Routledge and Kegan Paul, 1965.

Meier, R. A communications theory of urban growth. Cambridge, Mass.: M.I.T. Press, 1962.

Meyerson, M., Terrett, B., & Wheaton, W. L .C. Housing, people, and cities. New York: McGraw-Hill, 1962.

Perry, C. The neighborhood unit. New York: Regional Plan of New York and Its Environs, 1929.

Schilder, P. The image and appearance of the human body. London: Kegan Paul, French and Trubner and Co., 1935.

Schorr, A. L. Slums and social insecurity. U.S. Department of Health, Education and Welfare, Social Security Administration, Division of Statistics, Research Report No. 1, Washington 25, D.C., 1963.

Searles, H. F. The non-human environment in normal development and in schizophrenia. New York: International Universities Press, 1960.

Stein, C. Toward new towns for America. New York: Reinhold, 1957.

Webber, M. Order in diversity: community without propinquity. In L. Wingo (Ed.), Cities and space. Baltimore: The Johns Hopkins University Press, 1963, 23–56.

Whellis, A. The quest for identity. New York: W. W. Norton, 1958.

White, R. A study of the relationship between mental health and residential environment. Master's thesis prepared for the Department of City and Regional Planning, M.I.T., Cambridge, Mass., 1957.

Willmott, P. East Kilbride and Stevenage: Some social characteristics of a Scottish and an English new town. The Town Planning Review, 1964, 43, 307–316.

52 The City of the Mind

Stephen Carr

When I think of the state of city design today I am reminded of that stage in the development of a child—which we all know so well—when he begins to ask "why?" For we city planners and designers are now beginning to seriously question the simple concepts of our conventional wisdom. We are struggling to emerge from a state of naive acceptance of "common knowledge" to the next stage of development in which we can begin to understand and thus to master our environment. If this seems a strange parallel, let me pursue it a bit.

In the process of intellectual development the child must create a stable and meaningful environment from the "blooming, buzzing confusion" of disconnected events that constitute the infant's world. He can only gradually free himself from his early bondage to the continuously changing vivid qualities of his surroundings: the particular shapes or textures or sounds of things. He does this by building up a model of the world by which he conserves his past experience, simplifies and connects it, and relates it to new experience. This model represents past experience in several ways: as learned sequences of action, in the form of visual imagery, and most powerfully in terms of language. It is largely by means of language that we progress from the distractible, novelty-bound state of early childhood to the relatively coherent and competent state of adulthood (Bruner, Olver, Greenfield, et al., 1966; Brown, 1958; Vygotsky, 1962; Whorf, 1956).

For this gain in economy and control, however, we pay the price of a loss in our sense of the unique reality of direct experience and become victims of conventionality.

From *Environment for Man: The Next Fifty Years*. W. R. Ewald, Jr. (Ed.), Bloomington, Indiana: Indiana University Press, 1967. Reprinted by permission of the author and publisher.

We learn to use the traditional images and concepts of our society, its conventional wisdom, to organize our experience. In this process of "acculturation," society substitutes cultural bondage for the earlier bondage to continuously varying sense impressions. In time, we usually become "well adjusted" to existing conditions by means of these cultural norms. However, at some time rather early in this process the young child, perhaps sensing that there may be a way to escape this bondage too, begins to ask "why?"

We city planners and designers have been confronting the real blooming, buzzing confusion of our megalopolitan urban environment with the concepts of our conventional wisdom. We have a modest but growing vocabulary of techniques by means of which we represent and organize our world, whether in the form of land use maps or of verbal jargon. We know a "mixed use" when we see one. We have a few simple concepts like accessibility and dominance for relating the parts of a city. We know a few techniques for manipulating the urban environment and we once had a rather clear set of limitations on what it was our task to manipulate (Lynch & Rodwin, 1958). Yet we have finally reached the "why" stage, or so it would seem from the controversies of these last few years.

When a young child begins to ask why, we recognize that it is a critical moment in his life. He has now begun to question the simple commonplaces and seeming regularities of the limited world which had heretofore organized his short-sighted, day-by-day activities. He has become, one might say, a budding scientist and is therefore in need of very careful cultivation. At this stage he can be instructed in the acceptance of authority and conventional wisdom or he can be encouraged to form his own hypotheses about the way things are and to set out to gather the evidence necessary to test them.

We are embarking on a quest for the "good" day in an "optimum" environment. We ask why we should be concerned with the form of the environment and how city form might contribute to the quality of life.

To be sure, we lack much relevant knowledge, but worse than that we lack a way of getting beyond our current conceptualizations of city form and its functions. Indeed, the most perplexing problem we face in attempting to improve the relationship of people with their urban environment is the persistence of conventional images and models of conceiving the city in the face of changing urban realities and human purposes.

We may surmise that the same dilemma faces ordinary city dwellers. For in a very real sense the city is what people think it is. The city that we know personally—the city of the mind—largely determines the world in which we have our life's experience and through which we strive to gain many of our daily satisfactions. The child's early model of his small world grows eventually to influence the form of all his interactions with the environment.

It is really the form in which people interact with the environment that should concern us as planners. But the interaction of people with their environment is a two-way process, shaped both by the form of the environment and by the psychological characteristics of people. As city planners and designers we have studied city form but have given very little study to the human half of the equation. It is time to try to understand something of this "city of the mind." For it is from such understanding, however limited at first, that we can most effectively develop new hypotheses about what would constitute a good city form. By shifting our perspective we may hope to get beyond our traditional approaches to design and, on the basis of our new hypotheses, to be able to propose more meaningful criteria and standards for city form and to invent new forms. Beyond that we will need to establish more constructive relationships with the people for whom we wish to design. For only their responses to our innovations can provide the test of potential effectiveness that we need. In the process we can hope to broaden their perspective as well, so that a better shape for the future metropolis might begin to emerge, both in the minds of people and as a concrete reality.

THE HUMAN USES OF ENVIRONMENTS

You are well aware that planners are only human, but consider the news that all human beings are planners. What I mean by this is nothing mysterious, merely that most, perhaps all, of our interactions with the environment are intelligent ones. Notice I do not say rational or even conscious but rather "intelligent": guided by intelligence, by some mental plan or strategy, whether innate, learned to the point of habit, carefully worked out in advance, or invented on the spot. Each of these plans is intended to satisfy certain identifiable needs or to accomplish particular objectives (see Miller, Galanter & Pribram, 1960).

Since we are concerned with urban behavior, we need to know how the form of the city may facilitate or inhibit effective "planfulness." Take an example: Mrs. Jones' husband has just been transferred by his company, General Monopoly Incorporated, to Fringeville, where the family can expect to remain for 4.8 years. Mrs. Jones has a pressing need: she must adapt to Fringeville and if possible she must make it her own place. She will need to discover whether Fringeville is pleasant, to find her way to the shopping center and learn how to get to the grammar school, and to see what is required in the way of status symbols to bring the Jones' split-level ranch house up to the local standard. Beyond such utilitarian problems, Mrs. Jones will be trying to discover whether the form of Fringeville offers qualities to which she can come to attach deeper, more personal values and meanings. To accomplish all these purposes, Mrs. Jones will need to develop and carry out appropriate plans for exploring the new environment and acquiring the information she needs.

For each of these purposes and plans the particular form of Fringeville may make Mrs. Jones' life easier and more satisfying or more difficult. The information she needs may not be organized and made visible or the qualities she seeks may be lacking. The pleasant areas of town may be hidden behind the crass facades of shabby main streets. The street patterns may be too complicated, making it difficult to find important destinations and hard to remember how to get there again once they are found. Or the available environmental means for expressing oneself may be so limited as to obscure meaningful differences among people. Even more likely, Fringeville may fail to provide any places to which Mrs. Jones can assign deeper meaning and significance. To be sure, even in the worst case Mrs. Jones will learn enough about Fringeville to serve her allotted 4.8 years there, but not without disappointments, frustration, and psychological strain. And as we all know, Mrs. Jones and Fringeville are not isolated cases in our urban society.

In cities, all of our daily activities and many of our satisfactions in life are dependent in some way on the form of our interaction with a man-made world. This built environment, among other things, reflects public purpose in its form, no matter how limited or misguided that purpose. I have suggested that we need to understand the nature of urban man's interaction with his environment in order to control it to better effect. Some relevant knowledge already exists. It comes mainly from experimental psychology but in part from our own primitive investigations. As we have seen, to pull scattered information together it is essential to have a model, a conceptual framework. Such a model must deal with those psychological characteristics of people which are relevant to their interaction with the urban environment. Linked to this is the question of which properties of the environment are most important in supporting or constraining the various forms of interaction.

I have found that the most fruitful way to organize my own thinking about these matters is in terms of phases of the man-environment interaction process. Any interaction with the environment can be subdivided into the following phases: (1) A *directive phase* in which some one of our many needs and purposes becomes sufficiently predominant to direct us to prepare to change our course of action. (2) An *intelligence phase* in which we search for new relevant information from the environment and organize it to be retained, usually in the form of memory representations. (3) A *planning phase* in which appropriate information is retrieved from such representations, or from other sources, and transformed to be used in the generation, evaluation, and selection of sets of possible actions. (4) An *action phase* in which the plan or set of plans judged most appropriate to our purposes is executed in a particular environmental context. (5) A *review phase* in which the effectiveness of the particular course of action is assessed in order to correct further action and to assign value and meaning to the experience.

Notice that this formulation can apply to any level of planful interaction with the environment from personal planning through city planning to national planning. A course of action at any level need not explicitly involve all of these phases, but they are always implied. Routine habitual actions may require little articulation of need or purpose, gathering of new information, planning or review. Certainly the process is not always a conscious one. Sometimes it is only barely under control, as when we are caught in a stream of traffic, or are coerced to carry out plans relating to others' purposes but not our own.

Notice also that the phases of planful interaction are intentionally indifferent to the question of which dimensions of the environment happen to interest us.[1] The

---

[1] It is true that city planners by tradition and the present definition of their role manipulate mainly spatial variables. Lately, however, we have begun to broaden our scope to include some temporal dimensions, to attempt to design processes of change rather than final forms. More recently still we have been urged to operate directly on the social structure through the design of social action programs. Whether or not we are presently competent to assume such broadened responsibilities, there is little doubt that they are being thrust upon us by the pressure of events. In the continuing reassessment of our role, however, controversies between "physical" and "social" planners will probably be resolved. This will happen as we come to realize that what city planners and designers are really doing is helping to shape the *form of interaction* of people and environments. Such interaction, while socially conditioned, is also and always affected by the particular setting in space and time.

form of man's interaction with his built environment is determined by the social, spatial, and temporal structure of each environmental situation into which he enters (consider, for example, the first night of a long prison term), and also by the psychological characteristics of the individual. There seem to be general rules or strategies by which people deal with the environment which come into play in each phase of the interaction process. There are also characteristic group and individual differences both in psychological structure and in the purposes, knowledge, and plans which determine specific interactions. Here we can describe only what seem to be some of the most fundamental common psychological characteristics of people which might serve as a beginning in understanding the demands upon the form of the environment. Later, we will turn to the difficult question of how we might learn to take proper account of differences among people.

The Directive Phase: Needs and Purposes of Interaction

The determination of people's environmental needs and desires as a basis for the objectives of public policy is not a simple matter. The various lists of supposedly basic human needs are of very little help (see Dewey, 1963; Murray et al., 1938). We can state minimum subsistence requirements for food or shelter, although our ability to prescribe tapers off rapidly as we leave the extremes. We can state some tentative standards for satisfactory air and water or light and noise levels, although man's physiological and psychological adaptability make even this difficult (see Dubos, 1965, Ch. 10). At best we can assert that it is not necessary to force people to adapt to obviously bad conditions and try to establish pleasanter levels of adaptation (see Carson, 1965, pp. 13–52). But even such a limited attempt at environmental standards is further complicated by the fact that pleasant levels of adaptation are determined in large part by the purposes of interaction. We can adapt to much higher noise levels if we are not trying to talk to someone.

Beyond such simple needs, we soon encounter the problems of individual and group differences, real but often unrecognized. Moreover, there is the knottier problem of how to legitimately raise people's levels of aspiration, how to help them realize what they might want if they were more fully aware of themselves and their needs.

Urban behavior is motivated by a tremendous variety of similar but basically unique needs, desires, and purposes. The potential expression of this diversity is, as we have seen, radically constrained by the limitations of a common language and set of cultural norms. It is further constrained by the limitations of the existing urban form. Imagine the richness of personal adaptation of the environment that would result if each family had the opportunity and the skill to select the site for their own dwelling and to design it—with whatever degree of professional assistance they desired—for themselves. The statistical trends of urban life, which we follow so assiduously and often take as an indication of "what people want," are at least as much a result of what is available for their choice as of what they might want.

The planner or designer, with his personal vision of a better world so different from present reality, often concludes that people's desires are apparently misguided and that their level of aspiration is too low. But we must also remember that people need what they want, even though as "impartial" observers we may feel that what they want is not always best for them. It has been a persistent technocratic ideal to imagine that the professional's special role is to determine people's needs, apart from their desires, to satisfy those "real needs" and then to wait for them to change their ways and express their gratitude. It is of course possible to change people's desires, at least superficially, by means of advertising and more profoundly through education (see Reeves, 1961). Undoubtedly, the gradual and largely uncontrolled changes in the environment, especially in our technology, do alter people's wants in time (see McLuhan, 1964). We are generally agreed that we should attempt to change people's perceptions of the possible, and thus their desires, through education and exposure to wider environmental choices. We are just beginning to learn how city form itself educates, how it may help to broaden the individual's conception of the possible and thus raise his level of aspiration (see Dyckman, 1961). But that is quite another matter from imposing unwanted environments on people out of some higher conception of their needs which they do not share.

With all that, there may still be some fundamental psychological needs which, if understood, can determine performance standards for city form. These are the complementary needs for comprehension and for novelty, and there is a fair amount of evidence supporting their universality (see Berlyne, 1960, Chs. 2 & 8; Fiske & Maddi, 1961, pp. 380–401; Fowler, 1965; White, 1963, 1959). They are complementary because they call on the one hand for sufficient order in the environment to facilitate comprehension and on the other for sufficient complexity and change to stimulate curiosity and exploration (see McMahon, 1966). In order to understand these requirements, however, we must first consider further how people operate in the environment.

The Intelligence Phase: Perceiving and Remembering the Environment

The environment is a bigger book than we can read. It contains far more potential information at any moment than we have the cognitive capacity to deal with. Because of our limitations, we are by nature selective (see Miller, 1956). Norbert Wiener (1964) remarked that the environment might best be conceived as a myriad of To Whom It May Concern messages, thus putting emphasis on the necessity for selection. The counterpart of that statement might be that each of us is able to decide remarkably well which messages concern him and to ignore the rest. If this were not the case, we would fall into a state of confusion and paralysis from information overload—as sometimes happens, I am told, to unwary city planners. What is the secret of our selective powers?

We must understand, first of all, that perceiving and knowing are related processes. We begin by taking in an enormous amount of information through our eyes, ears, and other sense organs, most of which at any moment is irrelevant to our concerns. In order to put this information to effective use, to make something meaningful out of it, we must both condense it and relate it to the rest of our experience, past, present, and future. We have a number of more or less automatic mechanisms which sort and discard much information in accordance with an apparently fundamental human plan to seek and find simple features and objects whenever possible (see Gregory, 1966). And what is simple in our experience is a question both of form and of familiarity. Thus we find again that by a kind of conventionality, by being most receptive to the recurrent regularities of our experience, we are able to select from the flood of incoming sense data that which most simplifies our lives. And of course we lose detail in the process (see Attneave, 1954).

However, there are some details we cannot afford to lose. We strive to be ready to see those features of the environment which relate to our current needs and purposes, whatever their unfamiliarity. Even in a strange city we must be able to locate a restaurant efficiently when we are hungry. We must also be ready at all times to perceive at least some kinds of novelty, for what is unfamiliar may be dangerous. And we must be maximally receptive to other potential danger signals such as rapid motion or flashing lights. Moreover, sense data sometimes come in too rapidly, conflict or are incomplete, so that we have difficulty in formulating a satisfactory hypothesis about what is really "out there" (see Bruner, 1957). For all these reasons our elegant plan for organizing our perceptual experience by simple forms and nameable objects is often thwarted, especially in a fast-moving complicated environment such as the city. We may find ourselves confused, temporarily disoriented, straining to narrow even further those signals from the environment to which we will respond. Fortunately for us we can, within broad limits, make such an adaptation but we often do it at the cost of missing half our potential experience. We discover our loss when we return from a hectic trip abroad and suddenly see in our color slides hints of the richness we missed.

By analyzing how such perceptual selection operates in various types of environment and under varying conditions of planfulness and need, we can begin to understand one important human function of environmental form. Whatever the information we seek, our ability to achieve it is affected by the form of the environment, but people with different levels of familiarity with the same environment and carrying out different specific plans will attend to different features of that environment. An awareness of such diversity may make the designer's task more difficult but it may also make his designs more relevant to human use. In any case, in each specific environment only a few predominant types of plan are being executed, so the problem may be less serious than it at first appears. It should be possible to determine what those plans are and to direct design attention to the relevant features. Some designers attempt to do this in a rough intuitive way, but a radical improvement in our ability to create relevant forms can be achieved through research. We need only observe and question the users of various environments.

The form of the environment influences not only our ability to achieve new information but also how we organize our experience in memory. Remembering continues the process of simplification. The task of memory is to represent an experience in a form which can be retained in the brain unused for an indefinite period and then located at an appropriate later time. As in any filing system, the need to retrieve information requires that we store it in as efficient a way as possible. This filing task occupies much of experience and we have typical strategies for accomplishing it economically under varying conditions. Thus, while we may retain literal images of some significant events or places, we normally use a few key perceptual features to classify each unique experience under some simple, usually verbal, category (see Bruner, Goodnow, & Austin, 1956, Chs. 1 & 2). By that token the experience is not only simplified and condensed but is also automatically related to other similar past experience. Thus, while we may also have a visual image of it, we are likely to represent a

street in memory as "a high-class shopping street" with certain named stores, since that is the most effective way of relating it to our other knowledge of the city and thereby make our memory of it more accessible for future use. Within a common culture the attributes used in achieving such categories as "high-class shopping street" are likely to be quite similar and predictable. The city designer needs to discover what these critical features of the city are.

There are some essential features of the urban environment which cannot easily be translated into words, however. Perhaps the most important is the visible form of its spatial pattern. About ten years ago, Kevin Lynch (1962) began to investigate how the form of the city affected people's ability to represent it to themselves in some coherent way. Since *The Image of the City* there have been a handful of other studies which have attempted to extend his work or to repeat it in other contexts (Gulick, 1963; de Jong, 1962). By now, the evidence seems to be that some of the variables mentioned by Lynch besides clarity, simplicity, and dominance of visible form are more significant in determining the memorability of a city element than they at first seemed to be. On the basis of current evidence, the relative social values which districts, streets, or buildings symbolize and the simple exposure of these elements to the public eye would appear to be at least as important as their visible form. Indeed, when we understand how memory works to organize experience on the basis of its significance to us—in part a question of perceived value and in part of it familiarity or recurrence in our lives—it would be surprising if social value and exposure were not crucial variables.

The relative visual and social dominance of various elements, while important, gives little indication of how people structure their representations of the city. Evidence on the structuring of spatial images of cities is still scarce. What there is indicates that here too we try to simplify and organize. As there are three basic human modes of representing the environment through actions, images, and words, there would seem to be three basic types of structuring subjective city models, the use of which varies in part with the form of the city and in part with our familiarity with it. Thus we may structure our memories of the city in terms of familiar sequences of visual images, in the form of extended spatial images of important areas, or schematically, as a simple over-all diagram, easily describable in words.[2] The particular spatial form of a city can facilitate or inhibit the development of such structuring.

The function of an extensive, well-organized, economical, and *accurate* representation of the city is to facilitate planful action. As urban activities become dispersed we have an increasing need to get around in our environment without strain. We need to find many places of interest and thus to be able to execute more types of plans more easily. We already know some techniques for making city form more legible and we are gradually learning how to facilitate more effective structuring. But it is critical now to learn more about the intelligence phase,

[2] Interview investigations which I have carried out in Rome indicate that perhaps most frequently people remember the city as sequences of images along main routes through it. This is the image of the habitual automobilist, the young resident who has not yet built up his familiarity with whole areas of the city, or the newcomer unaided by a map. Although these sequential images may be linked together at key intersections, the over-all image which results is typically a rather distorted and often disorganized picture of the whole, with many significant gaps between routes. Beyond this, people may build up rather accurate spatial images of the extended areas of cities with which they are most familiar, their own neighborhood or the central areas of cities such as Lynch studied. These images are typically built up by the detailed interlocking of sequences—whether automobile or pedestrian. This tends to be a self-correcting process but may nevertheless produce significant distortions depending on the degree of ambiguity in the form. Finally we attempt, where the form allows it, to achieve very simple, diagrammatic representations, somewhere between a simplified map and a verbal description. Some patterns, of course, make such representation easy, as when we realize that Manhattan is an oblong gridiron "with its long, wide, named streets far apart and running north-south and its short, narrow, numbered streets close together and running east-west." When the pattern is complex or we are dealing with the whole city, such a simplified diagram may be achieved only by long familiarity, if ever.

especially about how information on nonvisible activities or social values is integrated with visual-spatial representations—how our concepts about the city relate to our pictures of it (see Strauss, 1961).

The Planning Phase: Using Our Model

Acquiring and retaining knowledge about the environment is not the same as putting it to effective use. To make a plan is to transform information in such a way as to generate a course of action different from that in which the information was originally gained. We may know what the river is like, but we cannot step twice into the same river in the same way. We must integrate information gained from past experience with information gained from other sources, including feedback from on-going activity. And we must integrate new plans with plans already in the process of being executed, with overriding life plans and with the plans of other people (see Miller, Galanter, & Pribram, 1960, Ch. 7). What most concerns us in all this psychological complexity is the influence of the form of the environment on the effectiveness of planning.

We have seen that the extensiveness and accuracy of our model of a city is affected by its form. The extensiveness and accuracy of this model determine our ability to predict the outcome of alternative courses of action in making our plans. Further, city form, through the model, affects accurate remembering, which is essential to effective planning. For example, the perceptual characteristics of environments may be ambiguous or mixed in incongruous ways so that they cannot be easily related to our verbal concepts and to social values. Thus what appears to be a "slum" may turn out to be a haven for struggling writers and painters, or a "residential street" may really be lined with institutions and professional offices. Such ambiguity or incongruity, while sometimes desirable for other reasons, inhibits accurate remembering. For remembering is a process of reconstruction in which we typically begin by recalling what we believe to be the most characteristic features and concepts and proceed to fill in the picture in whatever way is most consistent with these general features (see Hunter, 1964; Bartlett, 1932).

On the other hand, environmental form can facilitate planning by making it less necessary to specify a plan in detail. The metropolitan world presently in the making is one in which it is becoming increasingly necessary to plan out our daily activities carefully. As functions separate and disperse, for example from town centers to spatially separate highway-oriented locations, we need more elaborate plans, more time and more patience to carry out our weekly round of activities. That the housewife has become a chauffeur is well known, but she is also becoming a dispatcher. As cities approach a formal state in which nothing is on the way to anything else, we also become unable to execute "spontaneous" plans, whether it be to stop off for a refreshing interlude in a bar or in a park or to make a needed but unplanned purchase. Areas of mixed use and character, if not so mixed as to be confusing or difficult to remember, clearly make planning easier by requiring less of it in advance.

Further influences of environmental form on our ability to formulate effective plans could readily be determined. All that is required is to set people from different environments problems to solve using their knowledge of those environments. The Lynch interview techniques, while developed for somewhat different purposes, are a model for this kind of research. Special purpose maps or trip descriptions showing how various types of activities would be carried out would give much information about the human uses of cities and also about the failures of city form. And such information would not be of merely theoretical interest. It would be directly useful in design.

The Action Phase: Supports and Constraints in the Environment

It is when we carry out our plans in real environmental situations that the consequences of form are most directly experienced. The form of the environment provides support for certain actions and constrains others. The significance of environmental form for human action, however, is as much a function of how people perceive supports and constraints as it is of the physical form itself (see Allport, 1955, Ch. 6; Chein, 1954). No matter how skillful we become at measuring various end effects of environmental form, if we wish to understand the process of interaction of which such effects are the products, we must turn again to the city of the mind.

The environment is a potential field of human action but it does not become effective until we perceive what actions are possible and carry them out. Thus, if we plan to build a branch library in a neighborhood without one, what matters is that there are people in that neighborhood who would feel a need to use a library, who would perceive this particular library as one usable by them, and who would in fact have the time and ability to do so. Jane Jacobs (1961) has pointed out that planned environments, such as playgrounds in slum areas, sometimes fail to become effective ones. The local residents may feel that it is an imposition, not needed in comparison with other more pressing needs, may not perceive it as a safe place to go, and may have insufficient time or be unable to supervise children who might use it. In any case, a different unplanned use may be perceived and the playground may become a battlefield for gang warfare.

The whole environmental field may be thought of as being subdivided into regions or settings for action, each of which determines, to varying degrees, the behavior which occurs within it (see Tolman, 1951; Barker & Wright, 1955; Goffman, 1959, Ch. 3; Goffman, 1963, Ch. 9; Hall, 1966, Ch. 9). We might say that although people have plans, the environment has "programs" built in which tend to coerce particular actions within a generally planful personal course of action. As we enter each setting, for example a traffic interchange or a shopping street, we must adapt our actions to the existing pattern of activity in the setting. Such action settings have both functional-physical dimensions and social-symbolic dimensions and they have a typical temporal scheduling of cycles of activity (see Hackett, 1964). Environmental designers are used to thinking of their world as a nesting hierarchy of such interconnected settings beginning with a single room and running through neighborhoods and communities up to the scale of the metropolis.

We city planners have recently been scolded, with some justification, for conceiving of cities in an exclusively place-conscious fashion in the age of electronic communications (Webber, 1964, pp. 79–153). There is no doubt that the boundaries between settings are increasingly permeable to interchanges of both communications and people. However, a basic characteristic of such settings is that they have a form—an ordered internal arrangement in time and space tending to determine human actions within them —which persists independently of particular actors. Our propensity to conceive of the environment in terms of such settings or regions is deeply rooted and justified; that they are becoming more interdependent does not make their real human functions less important.

By saying that, I do not mean to imply that all the functions of urban activity settings are well understood. Their economic and political functions are better understood than their social functions; their aggregate social functions are better understood than their specific psychological and behavioral functions. The effects of particular attributes of these settings, such as size or density, even though they have received some study, remain ambiguous (see Barker & Gump, 1964). For although the size of a community tends to be associated with desirable goods such as political power or choice, these depend on such factors as the degree of homogeneity or diversity within the community as well as on the particular structure of relationships that exists. Moreover, the achievement of power and diversity does not in itself indicate the degree of individual participation in these goods. The same may be said for the human effects of density— for density cannot be separated from other variables operating in the dense region, as we find even with the rats which some writers are so fond of comparing to people in slums (Duhl, 1963, pp. 33–44; Hall,

1966, Ch. 13). And so it goes with any single variable which we try to isolate from the multidimensional environment.

If we are concerned, as city designers, with predicting the more important effects of environmental form, it is likely that we will get much further, at least initially, by conceiving of the environment in terms of these multidimensional action settings and the relationships among them than we will by attempting to isolate single variables. For as we move from setting to setting, carrying out a plan of activity, so many variables change that it would be all but impossible to keep analytical track of them. By dealing with these settings we will be operating on units which have a relatively clear relationship to psychological and behavioral realities. They are the real units to which individuals must adapt their actions.

The Review Phase: The Meaning and Value of Environments

What can be said about how interaction with the environment produces meaning and value? I have suggested that the meaning and value of environments arise from a review function in which we assess the consequences of a course of action. But you will recall that I also began by asserting that the concepts by which we organize experience are imposed upon us by our culture and language. The explanation of meaning and value, then, must be in the nature of the relationship between conventional wisdom and personal experience (see Lowenthal, 1961; Osgood, Suci, & Tannebaum, 1957).

In simplest terms, meaning arises when we fill out the skeleton of culturally acquired concepts with the flesh and blood of significance derived from direct experience. Meaning is the increment to knowledge resulting from action—the subtle change in the shading of our environmental image produced by each unique experience of the environment. Each different house that we experience, provided we are attending to the experience, adds in some way to the meaning of "house." The amount it adds depends on the degree of its novelty and the state of our openness to new experience. That meaning arises from review simply means that in each meaningful experience there is an *effort* required to match new experience to existing categories (Bartlett, 1932).

Similarly with value. In the normally developing individual, culturally derived values are continually tested against personal experience. By reviewing these tests we begin to create a personal system of values associated with various regions of the environmental field. These personalized values are closely linked with environmental meanings (see Morris, 1964).

Because we begin with a more or less common set of concepts and share many experiences with other people, especially with those of our class and local environment, many personal meanings and values are shared. We can therefore distinguish various realms of environmental meaning and value ranging from settings which may be personally meaningful and valuable for the great majority of citizens, for instance the Boston Common, to those which have meaning and value only to single individuals (see Firey, 1945; 1947).

Environmental meanings and values can also be differentiated by type and by mode of communication. In simplest terms there are functional, social, and esthetic meanings and values. Functional meanings are often expressed rather directly by visible forms or have a learned correlation with forms, which almost amounts to the same thing. Sizes and shapes of buildings and spaces and locational patterns may be immediately revealing to anyone familiar with the culture. And often, function is expressed explicitly by means of signs. Social meanings and values are seldom immediately apparent from the form and frequently lack even a conventional relationship to form. While obelisks typically mark a historic figure or event and domes are usually associated with public buildings, many parts of the environment with no particular distinguishing features may have historic or other social meaning and value. Social significance, usually as widely known to the residents of a place as functional significance, may be difficult to determine from the outside, except long familiarity, or more objectively, by survey-

ing the local residents and noting frequency of agreement.

Esthetic significance is an environmental quality about which there would likely be less agreement. Psychology has little to offer beyond psychoanalytic speculations and endless experiments on people's preferences for this or that type of visual pattern (see Ehrenzweig, 1953; Valentine, 1962; Gombrich, 1962). There is even considerable disagreement as to what constitutes an esthetic experience. My own preference is for a definition by Albert Guérard (1954) which states that: "Art is the quest of pleasure through the conscious expression of emotion." I like it because it applies equally to the creation or appreciation of art, because it asserts that art is an active, never a passive, state, because it does not quibble about pleasure as the end of art, or about the necessity of consciousness, communication with a public, and emotion. If you disagree with this definition, no matter; I do not urge it upon you.

By agreeing with Guérard that the essence of art is "the quest for pleasure in conscious expression of emotion," I do not wish to exclude its other functions. Art, like science, can connect realms of experience previously separate in our minds and it has a special means for doing so: the metaphor (see Bruner, 1962). Thus, the form of a house can represent the myriad forms of human sheltering: womb, cave, tent, tower, castle, palace. How much more could the form of the city represent the richness of the world if we could master its metaphoric possibilities! While it has been suggested that art, which is after all a cognitive activity, will be found to conform to rules like those guiding other cognitive processes, we cannot write these rules of metaphor as yet.

Whatever our abilities as designers, city form becomes art willy-nilly. Pop Art shows us how to create our own "art" merely by observing the present environment. If such an inversion of value brings pleasure to some, it is not to be despised. By increasing the opportunities for sensuous involvement with the environment we can increase the chances for art, whether created by an "artist"-planner or by a "nonartist"-observer or both. Thus a city form which facilitates our more utilitarian activities can increase the possibilities for pleasurable city watching. For we need not always be bound by utilitarian concerns. We can learn, or relearn, to see the environment in its sensory richness, to see the abstract patterns of light and color, texture and movement where normally appear the useful objects of our daily lives. Such perception, while not the highest form of art, brings a kind of immediate childlike delight in the sights and sounds of the world. It is the sensuous foundation on which art, with its layers of cultural meaning, is built. Environments which are sufficiently orderly or sufficiently well known free us for this kind of perceiving, provided that the sensuous form is rich enough to reward our attention to it.

Perceiving and representing the environment, acting in it, and reviewing the consequences are the processes by which we create our personal city of the mind—our own "life space," as it has been called. The form of the environment can help to make that space narrow and confined or broad and open, constantly growing. By organizing the environment properly we can make ordinary city-using tasks simpler to accomplish. We can increase the scope of possible actions for any individual as well as his sense of competence in carrying them out. And we can increase his experience of meaning and esthetic pleasure.

One general question to be asked of environmental form, then, is whether it provides the required settings to support the socially desirable planful behavior of its residents and to bring increased meaning and pleasure to their lives. In other words, can the residents adapt the environment, by their pattern of interaction within the settings provided, to create a satisfying "life space"? Marc Fried's (1963) now famous study of the interaction of a working-class community with its local environment in Boston's now infamous West End is a case in point. Fried found what he called a "sense of spatial identity," related to feelings of social group identity, in the attitudes of local people toward their environment and the places within it. He contrasted this feeling of identity or attachment to the settings of

a particular territory with the typically selective and individualized middle-class use of space. From his finding that some 46 percent of these people suffered some form of prolonged and "rather severe grief" upon being dislocated from their extended home, one might argue that the West Enders were too narrowly adapted at the cost of adaptability (see Rainwater, 1966); yet why not simply conclude that they suffered a real loss? For here may be a rather clear example of a relationship between the life image and satisfaction of a group of people and the form of their environment.

Taken in the context of knowledge that I have been describing, this study and others like it would seem to suggest, and here I will speculate, that under optimum conditions man's interaction with his environment is a kind of spiraling process of development. Having certain needs and purposes in mind, we interact in some way with a specific environment. This interaction, when successful, has adaptive value, either by increasing our adaptation to the environment or vice versa. By such adaptive interaction we gain in competence, we improve our image of the environment and our skill in manipulating it to our purposes. Increased competence, providing that we have a sense that the general environment is open and responsive, leads to the formulation and execution of plans of action directed toward satisfying new, more challenging needs, and so on. This, it seems to me, is the most useful of the many meanings of "mental health" (see Jahoda, 1958, Ch. 3). At any point in this process, however, we may come up against a dead end, either because the strains of adapting to a particular environment are so severe as to have crippled us or because we sense that the general environment beyond our haven is hostile or both. Thus the industry and positive striving reported to exist in many of the shanty-towns of Latin America can be contrasted with the despair and frustration of a Watts.

This perspective may help to interpret other findings on the psychological and social effects of environmental form. For instance, the much discussed relationship between friendship and proximity in homogeneous impermanent communities may be seen as an early stage of this adaptive process (see Festinger, 1951). As confidence and competence increase in a new environment, friendships probably become more selective and less determined by spatial form. A higher state of development is always marked by an increasingly selective and creative use of the total environment. As we consider more developed states we necessarily change our focus from environmental determinants of behavior to qualities affecting the personal meaning and value of environments.

SOME CRITERIA FOR ENVIRONMENTAL FORM

Given the current limited state of our knowledge about the relationship between the city of the mind and the city "out there," what criteria for environmental form can reasonably be deduced? In very general terms, we might conclude that a good environment should at the least support socially desirable planful behavior and facilitate man's effort after meaning. However, such statements are not much help to the hard pressed city planner or designer. Much more research is needed of course, but even without it a number of still general but somewhat more operational criteria are suggested by what is known. Before stating these, I must stress that such criteria must be more in the nature of hypotheses than design tools at the moment. They are deductively derived and projected from present knowledge, testable but untested, capable of being made operational but not yet made so, and certainly incomplete. Further, since they are not applied to a specific case, they are unweighted and no attempt has been made to eliminate possible conflicts between them. They are, in short, very much like the other criteria we use in city planning. While some speculation is unavoidable, I will list only those criteria which seem to me to be rather well supported by current knowledge:

1. *Increase the exposure of people to a variety of environmental settings and potential interactions.* This will of course provide choice and allow for individual differences, but it should also have important effects on increasing people's sense of the possible and level of aspiration. For this reason it may be especially important for children. It can be accomplished by increasing the real variety of action settings, linked together in space and accessible within some limited time, or by increasing the mobility of people. When applied to the settings of daily activities or the routes of typical trips, increasing accessible variety means a reduction in the need for detailed planning of daily activities and increasing personal efficiency. What constitutes accessible variety depends in part on particular publics: a great variety of high-priced, upper-class stores nearby will offer few benefits to a population of poor Negroes. Finally, exposure to new or different environmental types can be accomplished by various special aids such as field trips or presentations by television or other media, with the implications for the quality of life made concrete.

2. *Stimulate and facilitate exploration of the environment.* While exposure may be helpful in this it does not by itself guarantee that seen environments will be explored. What is apparently required is the right level (not yet established) of novelty and complexity to stimulate curiosity plus sufficient openness and connectedness to allow easy access to new settings and experiences. Exploration can satisfy what may be a basic human need for new experience. By increasing individual interaction with novel and complex environments it leads to growth both by broadening the individual's categories and concepts about the world and by increasing his sense of competence and capacity to formulate and execute new plans. Increases in the rate and scope of interaction can also be accomplished by means of special enrichment programs and techniques, but these are clearly more artificial and may be less effective than if the environment itself facilitates exploration.

3. *Increase the perceptual accessibility of city form.* We can make environmental elements and settings easier to recognize, identify, and remember by making sure that those few form attributes which are critical in recognition are most visible, as well as by simplifying and clarifying visual shape. Simplification of shape is easiest to

accomplish at the moment because more is known about it. We may have a good intuitive sense of which attributes are critical in identification, mainly by attending to tradition and stereotypes, but not much is objectively known as yet. And of course the identity of some settings, such as slums, should probably not be clarified as such. Further, by decreasing ambiguity and incongruity in city form we tend to increase conventionality and reduce novelty and complexity. Thus this criterion might best be stated as a constraint on the facilitation of exploration or vice versa. Either way, there is a delicate balance to be drawn in design.

4. *Structure city form to facilitate the various modes of structuring mental representations.* This would require attention to sequential, areal, and schematic structures. By facilitating various modes of structuring we can make city form comprehensible to more types of people. Clearly some parts of the city such as commercial centers should facilitate all three types of structuring. In general, however, sequential structuring is most appropriate for habitual trips and the extended spatial structuring of an area where there is a concentration of heavily frequented action settings. Simplified schematic structuring may be most appropriate over large sectors of the city to facilitate fitting together sequences and limited spatial images.

A further help in structuring and in comprehension would be to increase the number and variety of available information aids and their correlation with city form. This may seem trivial but could be very important in facilitating more effective planning. In some European cities telephone books contain maps which indicate both street names and how the numbers run, a great aid in locating places. Information boards could be placed at strategic points, preprogrammed to light up the quickest or the most scenic route to any destination. Much could also be done to aid more important, longer-range planning. For example, detailed and generally accessible information on the real estate market in various parts of the city would greatly aid in house hunting.

5. *Enhance the unique qualities of en-*vironmental settings. By emphasizing the special character of places we can encourage the formation of individual or small-group attachments and meanings. It is also a way of increasing variety and novelty. It may act as a further constraint on the conventional aspects of perceptual accessibility or it may in many cases be more highly valued than ease of recognition.

6. *Increase the relative exposure of city elements and settings of highest common significance, both functional and social.* This will increase the amount of real experience of these settings and thus increase the realization of their personal meaning and value for more individuals. It will also tend to reinforce their common significance, adding to group solidarity and perhaps impeding desirable changes or shifts in value. The need for continuity in change is doubtless real but indeterminate for the moment.

7. *Increase the plasticity and manipulability of city form to the actions of small groups and individuals.* This may be one of the most effective means for increasing the personal meaning and value of the environment as well as for increasing people's sense of competence and effectiveness. It should also increase variety and the uniqueness of places. The relatively greater degree of plasticity offered by the single-family house with its private manipulable yard has undoubtedly increased the individual meaning and value of the environment, although there are system constraints on the expression of uniqueness.

8. *Facilitate a rhythm of behavioral and perceptual constraint and release in the organization of environmental settings.* This would increase the opportunities for contrast, comparison, and the formation of new mental connections between objects and events. It would also increase the freedom of action of the individual as he moves through the environment, executing his plans. It could be accomplished by the provision of alternative routes to the same destination, contrasting in type and character, or by juxtaposing quiet places to busy ones. It requires attention to the scheduling of events within settings to enhance temporal rhythms as well as spatial ones.

9. *Adapt the form of environmental set-*

tings to facilitate the predominant plans being executed within them. This is obviously a catch-all, but an important one. To make it operational requires that we discover what plans are actually being carried out within various typical settings and develop client-centered techniques for establishing their relative importance. I would include here such physiological requirements as microclimate, light and noise levels since they are in general relative to the types of plans being carried out. Without being able to propose specific criteria in the abstract, I could suggest, for example, that in "general purpose" environments such as town centers, settings should be structured on several levels to facilitate the execution of several types of plans (utilitarian to pleasure-seeking) without conflict.

Although these criteria do not include all the performance characteristics that city form must satisfy, I believe that they may be some of the most useful and important for design. They can be tested both by attempting to apply them to design and by further research. We should proceed on both fronts at once.

If such criteria were developed into a consistent, weighted, operational set and imaginatively used in design, what would the resulting city form be like? At MIT, under the general direction of Kevin Lynch, we have been working to develop the implications of similar criteria for city form (Lynch, 1965). Although we have made some progress, inventing the future metropolis (as Britton Harris recently put it) is a demanding task. To develop my own ideas, based on these criteria, is worthy of another separate effort. But, although such utopian design research is much needed, significant advances could be made now in the practice of city design.

TAILORING THE FORM OF THE FUTURE METROPOLIS TO ITS USERS

The most fundamental problem for the practice of city design today is not the expansion and refinement of a set of performance criteria, or even the invention of new forms,

as important as these may be. It is rather the identification, development, and meaningful collaboration with a client, or set of clients. Most city design is done today in a way not far different from the way it was done in the Renaissance. There is a patron, usually a director of planning or redevelopment, with some power to change the form of sections of the city. There is also the currently favored "urban designer," often not a planner and often brought in specially for the job. The amount of contact between this designer and the users of the environment is usually nil (see Montgomery, 1965). Since the shape of the environment will have a real effect on people's lives, as we have seen, this should not be a tolerable situation. Nor can we delude ourselves that the citizen groups, planning boards, and elected officials who will influence and make final decisions are truly representative of these users.

To say that the city designer should be a servant of the people is a proposition that we can all accept in the abstract. It means in practice that he will often need to become their advocate. But to be an effective advocate he will need to know as much about them as possible, as well as being an expert at his trade of relating their needs and purposes to proposals for city form. All of the existing political mechanisms plus others that have hardly been tried or are not yet developed will need to be employed for identifying the real clients of design and for establishing meaningful communication with them. The designer cannot be expected to be an expert in the development of these various kinds of knowledge, whether by anthropological field methods, attitude surveys, observation of behavior, or whatever. He can and should be involved with deciding what knowledge is to be sought and with interpreting the results.

His basic role, however, which only he can perform, is the development, evaluation, elaboration, and presentation of form alternatives which clearly relate to the needs, purposes, and values which have been identified. He must be centrally involved in establishing a process whereby new alternative forms for the city are presented to the relevant publics by various methods, their reactions assessed, revisions made, followed by new presentations, and so on. Only in this way can city form become truly a joint product of designer and the people who will use it. If in the process, the designer loses some of his cherished artistic license, it will be a small price to pay for better cities.

The city which emerges from this process will not be a unified total work of art. Rather it will be many cities in one—perhaps not all things to all men, but at least reflecting the true diversity of social groups, functions, and unique environmental settings of our urban world. To be sure, there are many economic and social barriers on the way to such an achievement. But we are now in the midst of a revolution to increase the participation of people in shaping the social, economic, and urban forms which in turn determine the quality of their lives. We city planners and designers by the traditions of our profession and the solemnity of our avowals that "the city is the people" must be with such a revolution.

And of course there is no end to it—no achievable "good" day in an "optimum" city which will suddenly put a happy ending to our dissatisfactions. For the specific needs, purposes, and desires which guide our striving are in constant flux as the conditions of our society change. That the future is uncertain and utopia unreachable, however, is no reason not to work for better days in better cities.

REFERENCES:

Allport, F. H. *Theories of perception and the concept of structure.* New York: John Wiley, 1955.

Attneave, F. Some informational aspects of visual perception. *Psychological Review,* 1954, **61,** 183–193.

Barker, R. G., & Gump, P. V. *Big school, small school.* Stanford, Calif.: Stanford University Press, 1964.

Barker, R. G., & Wright, H. F. *Midwest and its children.* New York: Harper & Row, 1955.

Bartlett, F. C. *Remembering.* Cambridge, Eng.: Cambridge University Press, 1932.

Berlyne, D. E. *Conflict arousal and curiosity.* New York: McGraw-Hill, 1960.

Brown, R. W. *Words and things.* New York: The Free Press, 1958.

Bruner, J. S. On perceptual readiness. *Psychological Review,* 1957, **64,** 123–152.

Bruner, J. S. Art as a mode of knowing. In *On knowing.* Cambridge, Mass.: Harvard University Press, 1962.

Bruner, J. S., Goodnow, J. J., & Austin, G. A. *A study of thinking.* New York: John Wiley, 1956.

Bruner, J. S., Olver, R. R., Greenfield, P. M., et al. *Studies in cognitive growth.* New York: John Wiley, 1966.

Carson, D. H. The interactions of man and his environment. In SER-2, *School environments research: environmental evaluations.* Ann Arbor, Mich.: University of Michigan Press, 1965.

Chein, I. The environment as a determinant of behavior. *Journal of Social Psychology,* 1954, **39,** 115–127.

De Jong, D. Images of urban areas. *Journal of the American Institute of Planners,* 1962, **28,** 266–276.

Dewey, R. Needs and desires of the urbanite. In C. Woodbury (Ed.), *The future of cities and urban redevelopment.* Chicago: University of Chicago Press, 1963.

Dubos, R. *Man adapting.* New Haven: Yale University Press, 1965.

Duhl, L. J. (Ed.) *The urban condition: People and policy in the metropolis.* New York: Basic Books, 1963.

Dyckman, J. The changing uses of the city. *Daedalus,* 1961, **90,** 111–131.

Ehrenzweig, A. *The psychoanalysis of artistic vision and hearing.* New York: Julian Press, 1953.

Festinger, L. Architecture and group membership. *Journal of Social Issues,* 1951, **7,** 152–163.

Firey, W. Sentiment and symbolism as ecological variables. *American Sociological Review,* 1945, **10,** 140–148.

Firey, W. *Land use in Central Boston.* Cambridge, Mass.: Harvard University Press, 1947.

Fiske, D., & Maddi, S. *Functions of varied experience.* Homewood, Ill.: Dorsey Press, 1961.

Fowler, H. *Curiosity and exploratory behavior.* New York: Macmillan, 1965.

Fried, M. Grieving for a lost home. In L. J. Duhl (Ed.), *The urban condition: People and policy in the metropolis.* New York: Basic Books, 1963.

Goffman, E. *The presentation of self in everyday life.* Garden City, N.Y.: Doubleday, 1959.

Goffman, E. *Behavior in public places.* New York: The Free Press, 1963.

Gombrich, E. H. *Art and illusion.* New York: Pantheon Books, 1962.

Gregory, R. L. *Eye and brain.* New York: McGraw-Hill, 1966.

Guérard, A. L. *Bottle in the sea,* part II. Cambridge, Mass.: Harvard University Press, 1954.

Gulick, J. Images of an Arab city. *Journal of the American Institute of Planners,* 1963, **29,** 179–197.

Hackett, C. S. In F. S. C. Northrop & H. H. Livingston (Eds.), *Cross-cultural understanding.* New York: Harper & Row, 1964.

Hall, E. T. *The hidden dimension.* Garden City, N.Y.: Doubleday, 1966.

Hunter, I. M. L. *Memory: Facts and fallacies,* (Rev. ed.) Baltimore: Penguin Books, 1964.

Jacobs, J. *The death and life of great American cities.* New York: Random House, 1961.

Jahoda, M. *Current concepts of positive mental health.* New York: Basic Books, 1958.

Lowenthal, D. Geography, experience and imagination: Toward a geographical epistemology. *Annals of the Association of American Geographers,* 1961, **51**, 241–260.

Lynch, K. *The image of the city.* Cambridge, Mass.: MIT Press, 1962.

Lynch, K. The city as environment. *Scientific American,* 1965, **213**, 209–219.

Lynch, K., & Rodwin, L. A theory of urban form. *Journal of the American Institute of Planners,* 1958, **24**, 201–214.

McLuhan, M. *Understanding media.* New York: McGraw-Hill, 1964.

McMahon, M. L. The relationship between environmental setting and curiosity in children. Unpubl. Master's thesis. MIT: Department of City and Regional Planning, 1966.

Miller, G. A. The magical number seven plus or minus two: Some limits in our capacity for processing information. *Psychological Review,* 1956, **63**, 81–97.

Miller, G. A., Galanter, E., & Pribram, K. H. *Plans and the structure of behavior.* New York: Henry Holt, 1960.

Montgomery, R. Improving the design process in urban renewal. *Journal of the American Institute of Planners,* 1965, **31**, 21–30.

Morris, C. *Significance and signification.* Cambridge, Mass.: MIT Press, 1964.

Murray, H., et al. *Explorations in personality.* New York: Oxford University Press, 1938.

Osgood, C. E., Suci, G. J., & Tannebaum, P. H. *The measurement of meaning.* Urbana, Ill.: University of Illinois Press, 1957.

Rainwater, L. Fear and house as haven in the lower class. *Journal of the American Institute of Planners,* 1966, **32**, 23–30.

Reeves, R. *Reality in advertising.* New York: Knopf, 1961.

Strauss, A. *Images of the American city.* New York: The Free Press, 1961.

Tolman, E. The model. In T. Parsons & E. A. Shils (Eds.), *Toward a general theory of action.* Cambridge: Harvard University Press, 1951.

Valentine, W. L. *The experimental psychology of beauty.* London: Methuen, 1962.

Vygotsky, L. S. *Thought and language.* Cambridge, Mass.: MIT Press, 1962.

Webber, M. M. *Exploration into urban structure.* Philadelphia: University of Pennsylvania Press, 1964.

White, R. W. Motivation reconsidered: The concept of competence. *Psychological Review,* 1959, **66**, 297–333.

White, R. W. Ego and reality in psychoanalytic theory. *Psychological Issues,* 1963, 3, No. 11.

Whorf, B. L. *Language, thought and reality.* New York: The Technology Press and John Wiley, 1956.

Wiener, N. *The human use of human beings.* Boston: Houghton Mifflin, 1964.

53 Order in Diversity: Community Without Propinquity

Melvin M. Webber

The spatial patterns of American urban settlements are going to be considerably more dispersed, varied, and space-consuming than they ever were in the past—whatever metropolitan planners or anyone else may try to do about it. It is quite likely that most of the professional commentators will look upon this development with considerable disfavor, since these patterns will differ so markedly from our ideological precepts. But disparate spatial dispersion seems to be a built-in feature of the future—the complement of the increasing diversity that is coming to mark the processes of the nation's economy, its politics, and its social life. In addition, it seems to be the counterpart of a chain of technological developments that permit spatial separation of closely related people.

At this stage in the development of our thinking, students of the city are still unable to agree even on the nature of the phenomena they are dealing with. But it should surprise no one. For the plain fact of the matter is that, now, when the last rural threads of American society are being woven into the national urban fabric, the idea of city is becoming indistinguishable from the idea of society. If we lack consensus on an organizing conceptual structure of the city, it is mainly because we lack such a structure for society as a whole. The burden, then, rests upon all the arts, the humanities, and the sciences; and the task grows increasingly difficult as the complexity of contemporary society itself increases and as rapidly accumulating knowledge deprives us of what we had thought to be stable pillars of understanding.

From *Cities and Space: The Future Use of Urban Land,* edited by L. Wingo, Jr., published by The Johns Hopkins Press for Resources for the Future, Inc., 1963. Reprinted by permission of the author and publisher.

In previous eras, when the goals, the beliefs, the behavior, and the roles of city folk were clearly distinguishable from those of their rural brethren, and when urban settlements were spatially discrete and physically bounded, schoolboy common sense was sufficient to identify the marks of "urbanness." Now all Americans are coming to share very similar cultural traits; the physical boundaries of settlements are disappearing; and the networks of interdependence among various groups are becoming functionally intricate and spatially widespread. With it all, the old symbols of order are giving way to the signs of newly emerging systems of organization that, in turn, are sapping the usefulness of our established concepts of order.

Especially during the last fifteen years, the rapid expansion of the large metropolitan settlements has been paralleled by a rising flood of commentary, reporting and evaluating this remarkable event; and we have developed a new language for dealing with it. Although the scholarly contributions to this new literature tend to be appropriately restrained and the journalistic and polemic contributions characteristically vituperative, the emerging patterns of settlement are typically greeted by both with disapproval if not frantic dismay. By now almost everyone knows that the low-density developments on the growing edge of the metropolis are a form of "cancerous growth," scornfully dubbed with the most denunciatory of our new lexicon's titles, "urban sprawl," "scatteration," "subtopia," and now "slurbs"—a pattern of development that "threatens our national heritage of open space" while "decaying blight rots out the city's heart" and a "demonic addiction to automobiles" threatens to "choke the life out of our cities." Clearly, "our most cherished values" are imperiled by what is synoptically termed "urban chaos." However, such analysis by cliché is likely to be helpful only as incitement to action; and action guided by obsolescent truths is likely to be effective only as reaffirmation of ideology.

We have often erred, I believe, in taking the visual symbols of urbanization to be marks of the important qualities of urban society; we have compared these symbols with our ideological precepts of order and found that they do not conform; and so we have mistaken for "urban chaos" what is more likely to be a newly emerging order whose signal qualities are complexity and diversity.

These changes now taking place in American society may well be compatible with—and perhaps call forth—metropolitan forms that are neither concentrated nor concentric nor contained. Sympathetic acceptance of this proposition might then lead us to new ways of seeing the metropolis, ways that are more sensitive to the environmental qualities that really matter. We might find new criteria for evaluating the changes in metropolitan spatial structure, suggesting that these changes are not as bad as we had thought. In turn, our approach to metropolitan spatial planning would be likely to shift from an ideological campaign to reconstruct the preconceived city forms that matched the social structures of past eras. Instead, we might see the emergence of a pragmatic, problem-solving approach in which the spatial aspects of the metropolis are viewed as continuous with and defined by the processes of urban society—in which space is distinguished from place, in which human interaction rather than land is seen as the fruitful focus of attention, and in which plans limited to the physical form of the urban settlement are no longer put forth as synoptic statements of our goals.

Metropolitan planning, then, would become the task of mutually accommodating changes in the spatial environment and changes in the social environment. And, because so much of the future is both unknowable and uncontrollable, the orientation of our efforts would shift from the inherently frustrating attempt to build the past in the future to the more realistic strategy of guiding change in desired directions—from a seeking after predesigned end-states to a continuing and much more complex struggle with processes of becoming.

So radical a revision of our thoughtways is not likely to come easily, for we are firmly devoted to the a priori values that we associate with land (especially with open land), with urban centers (especially with the more concentrated and culturally rich centers), and with certain visual attributes of the urban settlement (especially those features that result from the clean boundary line and the physical separation of different types of objects). And, above all, we are devoted to a unitary conception of order that finds expression in the separation of land uses, the classifiable hierarchy of centers, and the visual scene that conforms to classical canons.

So, let us briefly reconsider the idea of city and review some of the current and impending changes to see what their consequences are likely to be for future urbanization in the United States. We can then re-examine the idea of urban space to see how we might allocate it with some greater degree of rationality.

THE QUALITIES OF "CITYNESS"

In the literature and in the popular mind, the idea of city is imprecise: the terms "city," "urban," "metropolitan," and the various other synonyms are applied to a wide variety of phenomena. Sometimes we speak of the city as though it were simply an artifact—an agglomeration of buildings, roads, and interstitial spaces that marks the settlements of large numbers of people. On other occasions we refer not to physical buildings but to concentrations of physical bodies of humans, as they accumulate in nodal concentrations at higher densities than in "nonurban" places. At other times we refer to the spatial concentration of the places at which human activities are conducted. At still other times we mean a particular set of institutions that mark urban systems of human organization, where we mean to identify the organizational arrangements through which human activities are related to each other—the formal and the informal role allocating systems and the authority systems controlling human behavior. In turn, we sometimes refer to patterns of behavior, and sometimes we mean to distinguish the social value systems of those people and groups that are "urban" from those that are "nonurban."

The values, the ways of life, the institutional arrangements, and the kinds of activities that characterize people living in high-density clusters amidst large concentrations of buildings have been traditionally quite different from those of people living on farms or in small settlements. The large American city has been distinguished by a particular set of these characteristics, and yet, depending upon the specific purposes of our examination, not all these characteristics are necessary conditions of urbanness.

Large numbers of the people concentrated at the centers of New York, Chicago, and most other large metropolitan areas are recent migrants from "rural" areas. Their values, their life styles, their occupational skills, and their social institutions are certainly undergoing rapid change, but, nonetheless, these people are still rural villagers and are likely to retain many of their ways through at least another generation. After an intensive study of the residents of Boston's West End, Herbert Gans (1962) could best typify these second- and third-generation descendants of Italian immigrants as "urban villagers," whose way of life in the geographic center of a large metropolitan settlement has retained strong similarities to the patterns inherited from the villages of Italy. The cultural diversity typified by the West Enders living adjacent to Beacon Hill residents—rather than any particular social pattern—is one of the distinctive marks of the city.

The city also is frequently equated with the greatest variety of economic activities; modern urbanization is often conceived as the counterpart of industrialization. Industrialization carries with it an increasingly fine division of labor and, hence, an increasing interdependence among men having specialized skills, who exchange many types of goods and services with one another. As the industrial development process evolves, increasing varieties of goods and services are produced; purchasing power and hence consumer demands rise; and the economy moves ever further from the self-sufficiency of nonurban primitive societies.

Relatively few products and occupations are exclusively associated with urbanization. At an early date in history we might have been able to distinguish nonurban production from urban production by separating the extractive industries (agriculture, forestry, fishing, and mining) and their related occupations from all others. But this is no longer clear. When the skills of farmers and miners are so closely approximating those of men who work in factories and executive suites, the distinction is hard to retain. And when fishermen live on San Francisco's Telegraph Hill, when oil-workers are an industrial elite, and when farmers and foresters hold university degrees and maintain laboratories and research plots, it becomes very difficult indeed to avoid the conclusion that these men are more firmly integrated into the urban society than are Boston's West Enders.

To say this is not to extend the proposition that the amalgamation of the once-rural and once-urban societies is accompanying a movement to an "other-directed" "mass society." The opportunities for a diversity of choices are clearly much greater in the United States today than they were 150 years ago when industrialization and the opportunities for social mobility were just beginning to stir new ideas and new ways into a poorly educated and unskilled population. Despite some gloomy predictions of the impending impacts of the mass communications media and of the pressures for conformity, the American population is realizing expanding opportunities for learning new ways, participating in more diverse types of activities, cultivating a wider variety of interests and tastes, developing greater capacities for understanding, and savoring richer experiences.

In the next fifty years it is likely that the rate at which the opportunities for learning and for social mobility expand will be even greater than in the last sixty years, when millions of uneducated immigrants from all over the world were integrated into every stratum of American society. Urban life, the communications media, and the public education systems are not likely to reduce all to a lowest common mediocrity. They are more likely to open doors to new ideas, to increased opportunities for being different from one's parents and others in the subculture in which one was reared—as those who have enjoyed these benefits already know and as the American Negroes are coming to know. Rather than a "mass culture" in a "mass society" the long-term prospect is for a maze of subcultures within an amazingly diverse society organized upon a broadly shared cultural base. This is the important meaning that the American brand of urbanization holds for human welfare.

During the past half-century the benefits of urbanization have been extended to an ever-growing proportion of the population: differentials in income distribution have narrowed; formal and informal educational opportunities have spread; Americans have flooded into the middle class. Access to information and ideas has thereby been extended to larger and larger percentages of the population, and this has been greatly abetted by the increasing ease of communication and transportation, *across* space, bringing books, periodicals, lectures, music, and personal observation to more and more people. As the individual's interests develop, he is better able to find others who share these interests and with whom he can associate. The communities with which he associates and to which he "belongs" are no longer only the communities of place to which his ancestors were restricted; Americans are becoming more closely tied to various interest communities than to place communities, whether the interest be based on occupational activities, leisure pastimes, social relationships, or intellectual pursuits. Members of interest communities within a freely communicating society need not be spatially concentrated (except, perhaps, during the formative stages of the interest community's development), for they are increasingly able to interact with each other wherever they may be located. This striking feature of contemporary urbanization is making it increasingly possible for men of all occupations to participate in the national urban life, and, thereby, it is destroying the once-valid dichotomies that distinguished the rural from the urban, the small town from the metropolis, the city from the suburb.

THE SPATIAL CITY

Nothing that I have just said depends upon any specific assumption about the spatial patterns in which urbanites distribute themselves. I am contending that the essential qualities of urbanness are cultural in character, not territorial, that these qualities are not necessarily tied to the conceptions that see the city as a spatial phenomenon. But throughout all of human history these non-spatial qualities have indeed been typically associated with populations concentrated in high-density urban settlements.

Although, as some have suggested, there may be certain psychological propensities that induce people to occupy the same place, there seems to be almost universal agreement among urban theorists that population agglomeration is a direct reflection of the specialization of occupations and interests that is at the crux of urbanism and that makes individuals so dependent upon others. Dependency gets expressed as human interaction—whether through direct tactile or visual contact, face-to-face conversation, the transmission of information and ideas via written or electrical means, the exchange of money, or through the exchange of goods or services. In the nature of things, all types of interaction must occur through space, the scale of which depends upon the locations of the parties to the transaction. It is also in the nature of things that there are energy and time costs in moving messages or physical objects through space; and people who interact frequently with certain others seek to reduce the costs of overcoming space by reducing the spatial distances separating them. Population clusterings are the direct expression of this drive to reduce the costs of interaction among people who depend upon, and therefore communicate with, each other.

As the large metropolitan areas in the United States have grown ever larger, they have simultaneously become the places at which the widest varieties of specialists offer the widest varieties of specialized services, thus further increasing their attractiveness to other specialists in self-propelling waves. Here a person is best able to afford the costs of maintaining the web of communications that he relies upon and that, in turn, lies at the heart of complex social systems. Here the individual has an opportunity to engage in diverse kinds of activities, to enjoy the affluence that comes with diversity of specialized offerings; here cultural richness is not withheld simply because it is too costly to get to the place where it can be had.

The spatial city, and its high-density concentrations of people and buildings and its clustering of activity places, appears, then, as the derivative of the communications patterns of the individuals and groups that inhabit it. They have come here to gain accessibility to others and at a cost that they are willing and can afford to pay. The larger the number of people who are accessible to each other, the larger is the likely number of contacts among pairs, and the greater is the opportunity for the individual to accumulate the economic and cultural wealth that he seeks.

Having come to the urban settlement in an effort to lower its costs of communication, the household or the business establishment must then find that location within the settlement which is suitable to it. The competition for space within the settlement results in high land rents near the center, where communication costs are low, and low land rents near the edge of the settlement, where communication costs are high. The individual locator must therefore allocate some portion of his location budget to communication costs and some portion to rents. By choosing an outlying location with its typically larger space he substitutes communication costs (expended in out-of-pocket transportation payments, time, inconvenience, and lost opportunities for communication with others) for rents. And, since rent levels decline slowly as one leaves the built-up portions of the urban settlement and enters the agricultural areas, while communication costs continue to rise as an almost direct function of distance, very few have been wont to move very far out from the center of the urban settlement. The effect has traditionally been a compact settlement pattern, having very high population and employment densities at the center where rents are also highest, and having a fairly sharp boundary at the settlement's margin.

It is this distinctive form of urban settlement throughout history that has led us to equate urbanness with agglomerations of population. Some architects, some city planners, and some geographers would carry it still further, insisting that the essential qualities of the city are population agglomerations and the accompanying building agglomerations themselves; and they argue that the configurations and qualities of spatial forms are themselves objects of value. The city, as artifact or as locational pattern of activity places, has thus become the city planner's specific object of professional attention throughout the world; and certain canons have evolved that are held as guides for designers of spatial cities.

Sensitive to the cultural and economic productivity of populations residing in large and highly centralized urban settlements, some city planners have deduced that the productivity is caused by the spatial form; and plans for future growth of the settlement have therefore been geared to perpetuating or accentuating large, high-density concentrations. Other city planners, alert to a different body of evidence, have viewed the large, high-density city as the locus of filth, depravity, and the range of social pathologies that many of its residents are heir to. With a similar hypothesis of spatial environmental determinism and looking back with envy upon an idealization of the small-town life that predominated in the eighteenth and early nineteenth centuries, this group of planners has proposed that the large settlements be dismantled, that their populations and industries be redistributed to new small towns, and that all future settlements be prevented from growing beyond some predetermined, limited size.

Others have offered still other ideal forms. The metropolitan plan for the San Francisco Bay Area and Washington's Year 2000 plan propose star-like configurations surrounding a dominant center, with major subcenters along each of the radials (see Parsons et al., 1956; National Capital Planning Commission, 1961). The Greater London Plan calls for a somewhat similar pattern of subcenters surrounding central London, but these are to be spatially free-standing towns at the outer edge of a permanent greenbelt. Alert to the external economies that accompany large agglomerations, while sensitive to the problems that accompany high density and large size, Catherine Bauer Wurster (1960) has eschewed both the British New Towns doctrine and the American metropolitan growth patterns. She urges instead that major new settlements be separated from one another and limited to some half-million inhabitants each. Others have proposed slightly different modifications of the Bay Area–Washington, the Greater London, and the Wurster schemes in the official plans prepared for Detroit, Atlanta, and Denver.

Despite some important differences among these proposals, however, they all conform to two underlying conceptions from which they stem:

1. The settlement is conceived as a spatial *unit*, almost as though it were an independent artifact—an independent object separable from others of its kind. The unit is spatially delineated by a surrounding band of land which, in contrast to the unit, has foliage but few people or buildings. In some of the schemes subunits are similarly delineated by greenbelts; in others they are defined as subcenters, as subsidiary density peaks of resident and/or employed populations; but the unitary conception holds for all.

2. Whether the desired population size within the unit is to be large or small, whether subunits are to be fostered either as subsettlements within greenbelts or as subcenters within continuously built-up areas, the territorial extent of the "urbanized area" is to be deliberately contained, and a surrounding permanent greenbelt is to be maintained. The doctrine calls for distinct separation of land that is "urbanized" and land that is not. The editors of *Architectural Review* (1955) stated the contention with effective force, in "Outrage" and "Counter Attack," when they pleaded for sharply bounded separation of city, suburbs, and country:

The crime of subtopia is that it blurs the distinction between places. It does so by smoothing down the differences between types of environment—town and country, country and suburb, suburb and wild—rather than directly between one town and another. It doesn't deliberately set out to make Glen Shiel look like Helvellyn; it does so in fact by introducing the same overpowering alien elements —in this case blanket afforestation and the wire that surrounds it—into both. The job of this issue [of the magazine] is to get straight the basic divisions between types of environment, and to suggest a framework for keeping each true to itself and distinct from its neighbors.

Behind both ideas are the more fundamental beliefs that urban and rural comprise a dualism that should be clearly expressed in the physical and spatial form of the city, that orderliness depends upon boundedness, and that boundaries are in some way barriers. I have already indicated that the social and economic distinctions between urban and rural are weakening, and it is now appropriate that we examine the spatial counterparts of this blurring nonspatial boundary. I believe that the unitary conceptions of urban places are also fast becoming anachronistic, for the physical boundaries are rapidly collapsing; and, even where they are imposed by legal restraints, social intercourse, which has never respected physical boundaries anyway, is increasingly able to ignore them.

EMERGING SETTLEMENT PATTERNS

It is a striking feature of current, physical urbanization patterns that rapid growth is still occurring at the sites of the largest settlements and that these large settlements are to be found at widely scattered places on the continent. The westward population movement from the Atlantic Seaboard has not been a spatially homogeneous spread, but has leapfrogged over vast spaces to coagulate at such separated spots as the sites of Denver, Houston, Omaha, Los Angeles, San Francisco, and Seattle.

This is a very remarkable event. Los Angeles, San Francisco, San Diego, and Seattle, as examples, have been able to grow to their present proportions very largely as the result of a rapid expansion of industries that are located far from both their raw materials and their customers. The most

obvious of these, of course, are the producers of aircraft, missiles, and electronic equipment which use materials manufactured in the East, in Canada, and throughout the world, and then sell most of their products to firms and governments that are also spatially dispersed. They seem to have been attracted to the West by its climate, its natural amenities, and by a regional style of life that their employees seem to find attractive. Once there, they are highly dependent upon good long-distance transportation. And, since successful management of these industries depends upon good access to information about technical processes, about markets, and about finance, they are equally dependent upon good long-distance communication.

It seems clear that the scale of growth there would not have been possible without first the railroad, ocean freighters, and the telegraph and then the telephone, the highways, and the airlines. All of these changes, we must remember, are very recent occurrences in the history of urban man. (The centennial of the Pony Express was celebrated in 1961, and the Panama Canal is scarcely two generations old.) These technological changes have made it possible for individual establishments to operate efficiently thousands of miles away from the national business center at New York, the government center at Washington, and the industrial belt between Boston and Chicago, to which they are very intimately linked. At least at this territorial scale, it is apparent that economic and social propinquity is not dependent upon spatial propinquity.

These distant metropolitan areas continue to attract a wide variety of specialized firms and individuals, and most of them still prefer to locate *inside* these metropolitan settlements. It is impressive that the television industry, which requires such intricate coordination and split-second timing, has chosen to operate primarily out of two metropolitan areas at opposite ends of a continent, yet its establishments are located within the midst of each. Similarly, the financial institutions and administrative offices of corporations which also rely upon quick access to accurate information are attracted to locations within the midst of these settlements. The reasons are apparent.

Just as certain businesses must maintain rapid communications with linked establishments in other metropolitan areas throughout the nation and throughout the world, so too must they maintain easy communication with the vast numbers of local establishments that serve them and that in turn are served by them. The web of communication lines among interdependent establishments within the large urban settlements is extremely strong. Today it is possible to break off large chunks of urban America and place them at considerable distances from the national urban center in the East, but it does not yet seem possible for these chunks to be broken into smaller pieces and distributed over the countryside.

Nevertheless, the events that have marked the growth of widely separated metropolitan settlements force us to ask whether the same kinds of processes that induced their spatial dispersion might not also come to influence the spatial patterns of individual metropolitan settlements as well. A business firm can now move from Philadelphia to Los Angeles and retain close contact with the business world in the East while enjoying the natural amenities of the West; yet it has little choice but to locate within the Los Angeles Basin where it would be readily accessible to a large labor force, to suppliers, and to service establishments. It is attracted to the metropolitan settlement rather than the more pleasant Sierra Nevada foothills because here the costs of overcoming distance to linked establishments are lower. *The unique commodity that the metropolitan settlement has to offer is lower communication costs.* This is the paramount attraction for establishments and, hence, the dominant reason for high-density agglomeration.

The validity of this proposition would be apparent if we were to imagine a mythical world in which people or goods or messages could almost instantaneously be transported between any two establishments—say, in one minute of time and without other costs of any sort. One could then place his home on whichever mountaintop or lakeside he preferred and get to work, school, or shops anywhere in the world. Goods could be distributed to factories or homes without concern for their distances from the point of shipment. Decision-makers in industry and government could have immediate access to any available information and could come into almost immediate face-to-face contact with each other irrespective of where their offices were located, just as friends and relatives could visit in each other's livingrooms, wherever each might live. With transport costs between establishments reduced to nearly zero, few would be willing to suffer the costs of high density and high rent that are associated with high accessibility to the center of the metropolitan settlements. And yet, accessibility to all other establishments would be almost maximized, subject only to the one-minute travel time and to restraints of social distance. Under these assumptions, urban agglomerations would nearly disappear. Were it not that the immobility of certain landscape and climatic features would induce many household and business establishments to seek locations at places of high natural amenity, that some people may have attitudinal preferences for spatial propinquity to others, and that some industrial processes cannot tolerate even one-minute travel times between industrial establishments, we would expect a virtually homogeneous dispersion across the face of the globe.

Of course, zero communication costs are an impossibility, but the history of civilization has been marked by a continuous decline in the effective costs of communication. Time costs and the costs of inconvenience between any given pair of geographic points have declined consistently; and the financial capacity to bear high dollar-costs has tended to counterbalance the high expenses attached to high speed and high comfort. The concomitant effect of very high speeds between distant points and slower speeds between nearby points has been nearly to equate the travel times between pairs of points on the surface of the earth. Certain improvements in transportation equipment that are now becoming possible could gradually reduce differential time costs of travel to nearly zero. The effects of this potential change on the spatial patterns of settlements would be dramatic.

SOME POTENTIAL CHANGES IN TRANSPORTATION AND COMMUNICATION TECHNOLOGY

We are all aware of the fact that, within metropolitan areas in the United States, the widespread use of the automobile has freed the family's residence from the fixed transit lines that had induced the familiar star-like form of settlement. The pattern of residential scatteration at the growing edges of most metropolitan areas would clearly not have happened without the private car; indeed, this pattern was not apparent until the auto induced the suburban developments of the twenties. The telephone, the motor truck, and transportable water, fuels, and electricity have further abetted this lacy settlement boundary. And, of course, all these trends have been further nurtured by a rising level of average family income and by credit arrangements that have made it possible for the average family to choose— and get—one or more autos, telephones, and houses. Similarly the new communication devices, higher corporate incomes, and federal financial encouragement have made it possible for some foot-loose manufacturers and certain types of commercial establishments to locate in relatively outlying portions of metropolitan settlements.

To date, however, very few of these families and business establishments have chosen to locate very far from the metropolitan center, because the costs of maintaining the web of communications that are essential to their cultural and their economic well-being would simply be too high. Even though they might like to locate in a mountain setting, the benefits that would accrue from so pleasant a habitat seem to be far outweighed by the difficulties of maintaining contact with the various specialists they rely upon.

But today a great many of them are much farther away from the metropolitan center, in mileage distance, than they were even fifteen years ago, not to mention the differences that have occurred since the beginning of the century. Even so, a great many have chosen outlying locations without increasing their time distances to the center. Increased mileage distance carries a neces-

sary increase in dollar costs, but the more sensitive component of communications costs in the locator's calculus seems to be the time costs, as the recent traffic studies and the phenomenal rise in long-distance telephone usage indicate.

Increases in travel speeds within most of the metropolitan settlements have been relatively modest as compared to the changing speeds of intermetropolitan travel that the airlines have brought. In part because the potentials of the new freeway systems have been so severely restrained by the counter-effects of congestion and in part because the improvements in transit systems have been rare indeed, peak-hour travel speeds have not increased appreciably. But off-peak increases have been great in some places, and some changes are imminent that are likely to cause an emphatic change.

Where the urban freeway systems are uncongested, they have induced at least a doubling in speed and in some places a quadrupling—and the freeways do run freely in off-peak hours. As the urban freeway systems that are now under construction are extended farther out and connected to one another, an unprecedented degree of freedom and flexibility will be open to the traveler for moving among widely separated establishments in conducting his affairs. A network of freeways, such as that planned for the Los Angeles area, will make many points highly accessible, in direct contrast to the single high-access point that resulted from the traditional radial transit net. Even if new or improved high-speed fixed-route transit systems were to be superimposed on freeway networks, the freeway's leveling effect on accessibility would still be felt. And the positive advantages of automobiles over transit systems—affording, at their best, door-to-door, no-wait, no-transfer, private, and flexible-route service—make it inconceivable that they will be abandoned for a great part of intrametropolitan travel or that the expansion of the freeway systems on which they depend will taper off. We would do well, then, to accept the private vehicle as an indispensable medium of metropolitan interaction—more, as an important instrument of personal freedom.

There has been a great deal of speculation about characteristics of the evolutionary successor to the automobile, but it is probably too early to predict the exact form it will take. I would hazard some confident guesses, though, that it will not be a free-flight personal vehicle because the air-traffic control problems appear to be insoluble, that it will be automatically guided when on freeways and hence capable of traveling safely at much higher speeds, but that it will continue to be adaptable to use on local streets. If bumper-to-bumper movement at speeds of 150 miles per hour or more were to be attained, as current research-and-development work suggests is possible, greater per lane capacities and greater speeds would be realized than any rapid transit proposals now foresee for traditional train systems. When these on-route operating characteristics are coupled with the door-to-door, no-wait, no-transfer, privacy, and flexible route-end service of the personal vehicle, such a system would appear to be more than competitive with any type of rapid transit service now planned—with two important qualifications. The costs would have to be reasonable, and the land use patterns would have to be compatible with the operating characteristics of the transportation system.

A system that would be capable of moving large numbers of cars into a small area within a short period of time would face the parking dilemma in compounded form. Although unpublished reports of the engineers at The RAND Corporation suggest that it would be mechanically possible and perhaps even economically feasible to build sufficient underground parking facilities on Manhattan to store private cars for all employees and shoppers who arrive there daily, the problem of moving large numbers of cars into and out of the garages during brief periods would call for so elaborate and costly a maze of access ramps as to discourage any serious effort to satisfy a parking demand of such magnitude. Before such an all-out effort is made to accommodate the traditional central business district to the private motor car, the summary effect of thousands of locational decisions by individual entrepreneurs would probably have been to evolve a land use pattern that more readily

conforms to the auto's operating characteristics. With further increases in mass auto usage—especially if it could attain bumper-to-bumper, 150 mph movement—we are bound to experience a dispersion of many traditionally central activities to outlying but highly accessible locations. The dispersed developments accompanying the current freeways suggest the type of pattern that seems probable. Here, again, Los Angeles offers the best prototype available.

IN WHAT SENSE IS URBAN SPACE A RESOURCE?

I have been suggesting that the quintessence of urbanization is not population density or agglomeration but specialization, the concomitant interdependence, and the human interactions by which interdependencies are satisfied. Viewed from this orientation, the urban settlement is the spatial adaptation to demands of dependent activities and specialists for low communication costs. It is helpful, therefore, to view the spatial city as a communications system, as a vastly complex switchboard through which messages and goods of various sorts are routed.

Information, ideas, and goods are the very stuff of civilization. The degree to which they are distributed to all individuals within a population stands as an important indicator of human welfare levels—as a measure of cultural and economic income. Of course, the distribution of this income is determined predominantly by institutional rather than spatial factors—only the rare Utopian has even suggested that the way to "the good society" is through the redesign of the spatial city. And yet, space intervenes as a friction against all types of communication. Surely, salvation does not lie in the remodeled spatial city; but, just as surely, levels of cultural and economic wealth could be increased if the spatial frictions that now limit the freedom to interact were reduced. This is the important justification for city planning's traditional concern with space.

In the very nature of Euclidean geometry, the space immediately surrounding an urban settlement is limited. Given a transportation-communication technology and its accompanying cost structure, close-in space has greater value than distant space, since nearby inhabitants have greater opportunities to interact with others in the settlement.

But as the transportation-communication technologies change to permit interaction over greater distances at constant or even at falling costs, more and more outlying space is thereby brought into the market, and the relative value of space adjacent to large settlements falls. Urban space, as it has been associated with the economies of localization and agglomeration, is thus a peculiar resource, characterized by increasing supply and by ever-declining value.

These cost-reducing and space-expanding effects of transportation-communication changes are being reinforced by most of the technological and social changes we have recently seen. The patterns of social stratification and of occupations, the organizational structures of businesses and of governments, the goods and the ideas that are being produced, and the average individual's ranges of interests and opportunities are steadily becoming more varied and less tradition-bound. In a similar way, the repercussions of these social changes and the direct impacts of some major technological changes have made for increasing diversity in the spatial structures of urban settlements.

Projections of future change, and especially changes in the technologies of transportation and communication, suggest that much greater variation will be possible in the next few decades. It is becoming difficult to avoid the parallel prediction that totally new spatial forms are in the offing.

To date, very few observers have gone so far as to predict that the nodally concentric form, that has marked every spatial city throughout history, could give way to nearly homogeneous dispersion of the nation's population across the continent; but the hesitancy may stem mainly from the fact that a non-nodal city of this sort would represent such a huge break with the past. Yet, never before in human history has it been so easy to communicate across long distances. Never before have men been able to maintain intimate and continuing contact with others across thousands of miles; never has intimacy been so independent of spatial

propinquity. Never before has it seemed possible to build an array of specialized transportation equipment that would permit speed of travel to increase directly with mileage length of trip, thus having the capability of uniting all places within a continent with almost-equal time distance. And never before has it seemed economically feasible for the nodally cohesive spatial form that marks the contemporary large settlement to be replaced by drastically different forms, while the pattern of internal centering itself changes or, perhaps, dissolves.

A number of informed students have read the same evidence and have drawn different conclusions. Observing that the consequences of ongoing technological changes are spatially neutral, they suggest that increased ease of intercourse makes it all the more possible for households and business establishments to locate in the midst of high-density settlements. This was essentially the conclusion that Haig (1927) drew when he wrote, ". . . Instead of explaining why so large a portion of the population is found in urban areas, one must give reasons why that portion is not even greater. The question is changed from 'Why live in the city?' to 'Why not live in the city?' "

I am quick to agree that many of the recent and the imminent developments are ambiguous with respect to space. They could push urban spatial structure toward greater concentricity, toward greater dispersion, or, what I believe to be most likely, toward a very heterogeneous pattern. Since administrative and executive activities are so sensitive to the availability and immediacy of accurate information—and hence of good communications—they may be the bellwether of future spatial adjustments of other activities as well, and they therefore warrant our special attention.

The new electronic data-processing equipment and the accompanying procedures permit much more intensive use of downtown space than was ever possible with nonautomated office processes; but they can operate quite as effectively from an outlying location, far removed from the executive offices they serve. The sites adjacent to the central telephone exchange may offer competitive advantages over all others, and establishments relying upon computers, that in turn are tied to the long-distance telephone lines, seem to be clustering about the hub of those radial lines in much the manner that they once clustered about the hub of the radial trolley lines. At the same time we can already observe that outlying computer centers are attracting establishments that use their services.

The recent history of office construction in midtown New York, northwest Washington, and in the centers of most large metropolitan areas is frequently cited as clear evidence of the role that face-to-face contacts play in decision-making and of the importance of spatial propinquity in facilitating face-to-face contact. And yet, simultaneously, large numbers of executive offices have followed their production units to suburban locations, and some have established themselves in outlying spots, spatially separated from their production units and from all other establishments. The predominant movement in the New York area has been to the business center, but the fact that many have been able to move outside the built-up area suggests that a new degree of locational freedom is being added.

The patterns in Washington, Detroit, and Los Angeles clearly suggest that the walking-precinct type of central business district (CBD), with its restricted radius, compactness, and fixed-route transit service, is not the only effective spatial pattern for face-to-face communication. Washington's governmental and private offices are dispersed over so wide an area that few are within easy walking distance of each other. Meetings typically call for a short auto trip, either by taxi or private car. In Detroit and especially in Los Angeles, establishment types that have traditionally been CBD-oriented are much more dispersed throughout the settled area. Relying heavily upon the automobile, Los Angelenos seem to be able to conduct their business face-to-face, perhaps as frequently as do New Yorkers. Highly specialized firms employing highly specialized personnel are located in all parts of the Los Angeles Basin—in some places within fairly compact subcenters, in other places in quite scattered patterns. But the significant feature is this: few linked establishments are within walking distances of each other, and an auto trip is thus an adjunct to a face-to-face meeting.

Even with a moderate speed of automotive travel, considerable mileage can be covered within a short time. At door-to-door average speeds of only 15 mph, it takes but four minutes to get to another's office a mile away; and, especially for long-distance trips, average travel speeds are considerably higher, probably exceeding 50 mph door-to-door off-peak in Los Angeles. Although I know of no measurements of this sort having been made, I would guess that (after adjusting for the total number of establishments within the metropolitan area) an establishment on Wilshire Boulevard in Los Angeles has as many linked establishments within a given time-distance as does a similar establishment at Rockefeller Center.

Comparable studies of traffic patterns in New York and Los Angeles will be completed within a few years, and it will then be possible to compare travel-time costs to commuters and shoppers, as well as to men who need to transact business face-to-face. I think it is safe to predict, however, that large differences will not be found, that Los Angelenos are just about as accessible to their work places and to the various urban service establishments as are New Yorkers, and perhaps even more accessible. Moreover, I would expect to find that Los Angeles residents maintain as diverse a range of contacts, that they interact with others as frequently and as intensively, that they are participants in as broad and as rich a range of communications as the resident of any other metropolitan area. I believe the popular notion among outsiders that Los Angeles is a cultural desert is a myth whose basis lies in the ideology of metropolitan form. We have equated cultural wealth and urbanity with high-density cities; since Los Angeles is not spatially structured in the image of the culturally rich cities we have known, some have therefore inferred that life there must be empty and deprived of opportunity. It is strikingly apparent, however, that nearly seven million people and their employers seem to find this an amiable habitat and that Easterners continue to arrive at a rapid rate. It is also apparent that a considerable part of its attractiveness has been the natural setting and the opportunities to engage in activities outside the urban settlement itself.

If most of the social and technological changes I have mentioned were in fact neutral in their spatial impacts, this itself would represent a powerful new factor at work on the spatial organization of cities. Prior dominant modes of transportation and communication, traditional forms of organization of business and government, the older and more rigid patterns of economic and social stratification, and prior educational and occupational levels and opportunities all exerted positive pressures to population agglomeration around dominant high-density business-industrial-residential centers. If these pressures for concentration and concentricity are ebbing, the effects of counter processes will be increasingly manifest.

THE ASCENT OF AMENITY AS LOCATIONAL DETERMINANT

Throughout our history, the locations and the internal arrangements of our cities have been predominantly shaped by the efforts of individual establishments to lower the costs of transporting goods, information, and people. If our speculations concerning the secular declines in these costs should prove to be valid, we can expect that the nontransportable on-site amenities will come to predominate as locational determinants.

Population growth in California, Arizona, Florida, and other naturally favored places can be largely attributed to the favorable climate and landscape. At smaller scale, in turn, new residential accommodations and new industrial establishments are being developed at those sites whose natural conditions are most favored by groups of various types. This is a very remarkable development; the luxury of locational choice is now being extended to ever-increasing numbers within an increasingly diverse population.

During the past sixty years the work week of American manufacturing workers has fallen from about 59 hours to something under 40, while wages have risen from an average of about $450 per year to about $4,700 (in constant 1947–49 dollars from about $1,250 to about $4,000 per year). The prospects are for a continuing reduction in working hours and for a continuing rise in disposable income, perhaps accompanied by a narrowing of the extremes in income distribution. When compounded by the availability of credit, higher levels of education, lowering ages of retirement, and a further dispersion of middle-class ways to larger proportions of the population, the range of choice open to most people—including the range of locational choice—is certain to increase greatly.

Although it is undoubtedly true that the success of recent suburban developments to some extent reflects rather limited choices available within the contemporary metropolitan housing markets, it is also apparent that for most of their inhabitants these developments represent marked improvements in living standards. Most suburbanites in the upper-income brackets have made free locational choices, since they could afford more central sites. Even a recent disenchantment with suburban life has not refuted the compatibility of low-density housing developments with middle-class preferences for spaciousness, with middle-class attitudes about distance, with current status criteria, and with child-oriented family life.

Among certain professional groups that have recently been in high demand (most notably those specialists associated with research and development in the electronics, missiles, and petro-chemical industries) the preferences for suburban-type residential environments within pleasant natural settings seem to have been so strong as to have affected the locations of these industries in California, Long Island, and the suburbs of Boston. To attract these skilled persons, whole industries have moved. Very few have chosen locations very far removed from the universities and the business complexes to which they are closely linked, but it is significant that they have tended to select outlying spots. With increasing leisure time, increasing mobility via automobiles, and increased spending power, we can expect the average family to take much greater advantage of outdoor recreational activities available in the countryside accessible to its home. As transportation facilities are improved and week-ends lengthen, families will be able to travel longer distances than before. Some will prefer to locate their homes near recreational facilities, and the recreation place might even replace the work place as the major determinant of residential locations.

The range of locational choice is broadening at the same time that changing characteristics of the national population are breeding increasing diversity in people's locational preferences. Simultaneously, all segments of the national population are being woven into an increasingly complex social, political, and economic web, such that no person and no group is entirely independent of all other persons and all other groups. The growing pluralism in American society is more than a growing multiplicity of types of people and institutions. Each person, each group bound by a community of interests, is integrally related to each other person and group, such that each is defined by its relations to all others and that a change in one induces a change in all others.

The kinds of information that can be read from maps showing urbanized areas or land use patterns are therefore likely to be misleading. Suggesting that settlements of one size or another are in some way independent units, in some way separated from each other and from the spatial field in which they lie, maps of this sort miss the essential meaning of urbanization. Whether the maps represent existing patterns or plans for future patterns, they present static snapshots of locational patterns of people or buildings or activity places and say nothing (except as the reader may interpolate) about the human interaction patterns that are at the heart of complex social processes. When people can interact with others across great distances and when they can readily move themselves into face-to-face positions as the need to do so arises, it scarcely matters whether a greenbelt intervenes or whether the space between them and their associates is used for houses and factories. Surely Los Angeles is an integral part of the national urban system, despite the 2,500-mile-wide greenbelt that separates it from New York. Surely Bakersfield is as integral a part of the southern California urban system as is Pasadena, despite the intervention of the

Tehachapi Mountains and some 90 miles. Surely the researchers in Los Alamos are as much a part of the world-wide community of atomic physicists, as if they happened to be at Brookhaven or Berkeley or Argonne.

Spatial separation or propinquity is no longer an accurate indicator of functional relations; and, hence, mere locational pattern is no longer an adequate symbol of order. The task of the spatial planner is therefore considerably more difficult than we have traditionally thought. The normative guides that we have used have been oriented primarily to the form aspects that can be represented on maps and have applied static and simplistic concepts of order that are not consonant with the processes of growing and complex urban systems.

It is a fairly simple matter to prepare a land use plan for a territory, if its spatial organization is to follow any one of the simple universal models that city planners have promulgated. Sites for "self-contained and balanced" new towns are readily found, and site plans are readily made. It is quite another matter to get the townspeople to behave as though they comprised a "self-contained and balanced community"—nor would many of us really want them to be deprived of the enriched lives that come with free communication with the "outside world." Plans for increased centrality and higher density can also be portrayed readily within the traditional idiom of land use planning; but, again, it is hard to believe that the advocates would be willing to deprive the residents of the opportunities to choose outlying locations. Nevertheless, whether small town or large concentration, the rules are clear and simple; the variables to be accounted are limited in number and in complexity; and the solution is determined before the problem is attacked.

It is considerably more difficult, however, to plan for diversity in settlement and land use patterns, for here the formal rules of urban form are not very helpful. No single scheme can be taken as a rule to be applied to all establishments and to all places. Rather, the locational requirements of the many diverse groups of establishments must establish the rules, and the optimum pattern would then resemble none of the doctrinal models.

The optimum land use pattern of the future metropolis is likely to be highly diversified. Since transportation costs will never fall to zero, the external economies associated with clusterings of similar and dissimilar establishments will continue to induce certain types of establishments to seek centers and subcenters of many types. Some of these will be of the familiar employment and shopping-center types, whether in the CBD or in the unitary "regional center" molds. Other establishments, mutually linked to a third type of establishment, will undoubtedly continue to cluster about it wherever it may be, whether it be a stock exchange, a major university, an airport or a large manufacturer or retailer. Other establishments will form sub-centers, largely as a result of their mutual desire to occupy a particularly pleasant site, although such growth inducements are self-limiting, of course. Those establishments that depend upon good access to information will undoubtedly continue to seek locations that best facilitate easy communication. For some, formal meeting places that accommodate scheduled encounters will suffice, and for many of these the airports and the convention halls are already serving a large part of their requirements. Others, such as the ladies' garment industry and the securities exchanges, may be so sensitive to changes in styles and/or market conditions as to induce even more intensive business concentrations of the sort that Manhattan typifies.

Simultaneously, the optimum patterns would include scattered developments for a great variety of establishments in a great variety of land use mixes and density patterns. For those manufacturers who prefer to locate factories and workers' housing near mountain skiing and hiking areas, for those lone wolves who prefer solitude and possibly a part-time farm, and for all those for whom a high-speed auto drive is no commuting deterrent, we can expect (and should encourage) scattered developments of the type now becoming common east of Boston and north of New York.

The future land use pattern will certainly not be one of homogeneous dispersion. Transportation and communication costs will never permit that, and the very uneven distribution of favored climates and landscapes would strongly discourage it. But a much greater degree of dispersion is both likely and desirable, while centers and subcenters of various compositions and densities persist and grow in a range of sizes spanning the whole spectrum from "center" to "sprawl."

If we are willing to accept the idea that the optimum urban settlement and land use patterns are likely to be as pluralistic as society itself, then the conceptions of spatial order will follow from our conceptions of social order. Our spatial plans, then, will be plans for diversity, designed to accommodate the disparate demands upon land and space made by disparate individuals and groups that are bound up in the organized complexity of urban society.

PLANNED ALLOCATION OF URBAN SPACE

One of the planner's major tasks is to delineate the probable range of real future choice—the envelope within which goal-directed actions are likely to pay off. I read the evidence concerning the qualities and magnitudes of some uncontrollable aspects of future change to say that many of the spatial forms to which we have aspired are no longer within that envelope.

Moreover, I contend that we have been searching for the wrong grail, that the values associated with the desired urban structure do not reside in the spatial structure per se. One pattern of settlement and its internal land use form is superior to another only as it better serves to accommodate ongoing social processes and to further the nonspatial ends of the political community. I am flatly rejecting the contention that there is an overriding universal spatial or physical aesthetic of urban form.

Throughout this essay I have laid heavy emphasis upon the communication patterns that bring people into contact with others and that have created our traditional settlement patterns. I have done so because communication is a very powerful influence that has scarcely been studied. But it is not my view that this is the only important factor affecting urban spatial structure, or that the criteria for planning the spatial structure for complex urban communities stem from this relationship alone. No simple cause-and-effect relationships are likely to be uncovered in this field, for the maze of relationships within such complex open systems as urban societies are such that a change in one part of the web will reverberate to induce changes throughout all parts of the web. The problem of planning for the optimum utilization of urban space is far more complex than our present understanding permits us to even realize.

No attempt will be made here to catalogue the kinds of criteria that a rigorously conducted planning effort would need to weigh. I leave this omission not from modesty—only ignorance. But a few considerations can be mentioned, if only to suggest that my ignorance may not be complete.

I have chosen to deal with space, not with land, because, for the paramount purposes of men who engage in nonextractive industries, the surface of the earth has meaning as representation of communication distance rather than as inherent characteristics of the soil. I have contended that all space is urban space, since interaction among urbanites takes place through, or is inhibited by, all space. Space has significance for the urban planner primarily because of the implications that locational patterns have for fruitful interaction, hence for social welfare.

For some purposes, however, the surface of the earth does have meaning as soil or as minerals or as water storage; and in this context planners are indeed concerned with allocating *land* judiciously. With the prospect of increasing space utilization by urban activities, a growing conflict is inevitable between land users and space users. Fortunately the rate of increase in agricultural productivity continues to outpace the rate of population increase in the United States; and, in the face of embarrassing agricultural surpluses, the conflict is likely to thrive only in ideological disputes rather than in market competition.

Largely, I suspect, as vestige of our agrarian ancestry, many city planners and others hold to a rather fundamentalist belief in land. Land is seen as a scarce and sacred resource to be saved against those who would "encroach" upon and "desecrate" its natural features. To use good soils for housing is frequently decried as wasteful of a valuable natural resource, all the more objectionable because these changes are effectively irreversible. But the answer is surely not that simple. There may indeed be areas that would most profitably be retained in crops rather than in houses and factories, but in the places where the question arises the balance is probably more often in favor of the houses and factories. The values inherent in accessibility, that make those places attractive to the house buyer, are quite likely to weigh more heavily than the values to be derived from crops. But no answers can be found a priori. Each site must be evaluated for the relative costs and benefits implicit in the alternative purposes for which it might be used.

Similarly, lands that might provide the recreational opportunities that are increasingly in demand might also be used for other purposes. But, again, no doctrinaire answers are likely to be found supportable. Again, each site must be subjected to an analysis of the welfare implications implicit in the substitutable uses. The benefits from recreational use are quite as real as those deriving from farms and houses. Within the total spatial field, places for recreational activity need to be developed. But no ready solutions are in hand; certainly the greenbelt doctrine in itself is insufficient basis for the investments that are required.

Within any given territory at any given time, space is finite. Present and future demands for it are highly diverse in their requirements, but we can surely learn enough about the characteristics of each type of user to equip ourselves to make more rational allocations than would occur under unguided market conditions. The task is not to "protect our natural heritage of open space" just because it is natural, or a heritage, or open, or because we see ourselves as Galahads defending the good form against the evils of urban sprawl. This is a mission of evangelists, not planners.

Rather, and as the barest minimum, the task is to seek that spatial distribution of urban populations and urban activities that will permit greater freedom for human interaction while, simultaneously, providing freer access to natural amenities and effective management of the landscape and of mineral resources.

This is no mean task. And probably the meanest part of the task will be to disabuse ourselves of some deep-seated doctrine that seeks order in simple mappable patterns, when it is really hiding in extremely complex social organization, instead.

REFERENCES:

Counter attack. *Architectural Review,* 1955, 355–356.
Gans, H. J. *The urban villagers.* New York: The Free Press, 1962.
Haig, R. M. Toward an understanding of the metropolis. *New York Regional Survey, Regional Survey of New York and its Environs,* Vol. 1. New York: Regional Plan Association, 1927.
National Capital Planning Commission and the National Capital Regional Planning Council. *Policies plan for the year 2000.* Washington: Government Printing Office, 1961.
Parsons, Brinckerhoff, Hall, & Macdonald. *Regional rapid transit: Report to the San Francisco Bay Area Rapid Transit Commission.* San Francisco and New York: Parsons, Brinckerhoff, Hall, and Macdonald, 1956.
Wurster, C. B. Framework for an urban society, in *Goals for Americans: The report of the President's Commission on National Goals.* Englewood Cliffs, N.J.: Prentice-Hall, 1960.

54 The Built Environment: Its Creation, Motivations, and Control

Sir William Holford

The appearance of the urban and rural landscapes in which we live and work and learn and take our leisure is the reflection of two influences which are not always complementary: the conservation of natural re-

Tavistock pamphlet No. 11, London: Tavistock Publications Limited, 1965. Reprinted by permission of the author and publisher.
Author's note: The plan for a New Town between Bletchley and Wolverton is reproduced by permission of the Buckinghamshire County Council.

sources; and the development of man-made constructions, utilities, and services. This paper deals with the latter influence, which it is convenient—if slightly ambiguous—to describe as "the built environment."

Sir Hugh Beaver,[1] when he invited me to give this lecture, asked me to talk about the ways in which architects and planners work and communicate. A simple question; and perhaps I have made the answer sound pretentious by talking about environment. But the built environment is only the continually changing end-result of all the smaller designs and their co-ordination—or lack of it—which architects and engineers and owners and managers are responsible for. In discussing its creation, that is to say the positive process of designing it and building it up, and the reasons for our being socially self-conscious about it, and wanting to exercise some control over it—which I have loosely called its motivations—I am, in fact, discussing the broader and more challenging aspects of our work.

In fact, the architect today is more concerned with the design of environments than with the design of monuments. He is concerned with the ways in which space is used and conditioned: from indoor climates of sound and vision and movement, to external sites and services, and the layout of groups of buildings in the landscape. People are always saying to him, "Why can't you design rooms, buildings, streets, and towns which are economical to construct, a delight to use, and inspiring to look at?" So he is concerned with building methods and building economics on the one hand, and with social behaviour on the other; and all the time, if he is really good at his job, he is performing the function of an artist; he is helping to change that neutral thing "the environs" into something with character and personality—an environment.

In every part of this increasingly urban world this subject is under discussion. It excites the under-developed countries and the affluent ones; and it is very relevant to these islands, with their long history of industrial development, their small land area,

[1] Sir Hugh Beaver is Chairman of the Council of the Tavistock Institute of Human Relations.

and their high density of population, of vehicles per unit of road, and of power distribution per square mile.

OVERCROWDING AS A CRITICAL FACTOR

It is also important for us to know more about this subject, for there is now little doubt that adequate space is a natural good, while the lack of it, even when artificially compensated, leads very easily to neuroses, delinquency, and violence. A highly urban society has to adopt elaborate methods of easing social conflict. Julian Huxley (1923) described many years ago the "ritualized" behaviour of animals; and recently W. M. S. Russell (1964) gave two fascinating broadcast talks on "Violence, monkeys and man."

"The beautiful functioning of a wild primate society," he said, "is based on a number of automatic mechanisms. Group conflict is averted by the principle of territory, held in common by each band, and respected by its neighbour bands. . . . Order is maintained by a hierarchy of ranks, evolved peacefully as each generation grows up, and subject to re-arrangement in accordance with the performance of the leaders in guiding and protecting the rest. The monkey president and his establishment settle all quarrels within the band before they become violent. . . ." He went on to say that "when a monkey band grows unduly big, it splits without violence into two, and one of the daughter bands seeks its fortune elsewhere, like a band of colonists from a Neolithic village or a classical . . . Greek city"; and, he might have added, from a theoretical Garden City as advocated by Ebenezer Howard.

"But these mechanisms break down outside the conditions in which they evolved. If too many monkeys are confined together, hierarchy cannot be developed on a basis of individual recognition. Fighting is now the only means of establishing rank. But this brutal method does not even work. The wrong monkeys come to the top. They do not have to meet the test of useful performance in solving environmental problems . . . they are insecure and trigger-happy. Govern-ment by consent degenerates into an unstable sytem of 'absolute despotism tempered by assassination'."

All this is familiar to those of you who have read Mrs. Jane Jacobs's (1962) *Death and Life of Great American Cities*.

Environment also has its passive, picturesque aspects. As students, tourists, artists, or journalists we are apt to regard landscape from the point of view of spectators. As such we often find it wanting; and we cry havoc in consequence. But purely aesthetic views, however perceptive, are too weak to preserve all that is worth preserving and too detached to influence profoundly what is being created. Economic incentives and judgments are stronger; and it seems more useful to consider the built environment from the point of view of the participants—the planners and the planned.

THE LEGACY OF THE PAST

Examples of the built environment go back about 5000 years in recorded human history, rather more if the full Neolithic community at Jericho is claimed as a true town by 7000 B.C. Sir Leonard Woolley dated the birth of civilization to the Bronze Age and the fourth millennium. In the great UNESCO *History of Mankind* (1963) he wrote:

At the beginning man, like every other animal, has been forced to adapt himself to his environment. . . . But alone of the animals man in time adopted a different solution to the problem of existence, that of adapting his environment to himself . . . instead of having to live where food abounded he made it abound where he lived. . . . With the settlement of the two river valleys (the Tigris and the Euphrates) we see the emergence of civilized society . . . occupations became specialized, involving divisions of class, trade was organized, writing was invented, monumental architecture expressed the symbolic significance of public buildings, and representational art tended to replace the largely decorative art of Neolithic times.

This was the first urban revolution, and we are now facing another. I have no intention of dragging you back through history. I mention the span of man's influence on his surroundings to show how short it is in comparison with the slow evolution of the natural environment; how long in comparison with the ante-natal environment in which each of us is born. These comparative measurements are significant, because they indicate the rate of change. It is hard to imagine now that a Neolithic community could remain virtually the same for 500 years. Today, technology has whipped up the pace. On the other hand, the personal cycle, like a man's height and eyes, has changed very little since civilization began.

The past is, of course, an important factor in the built environment. In the cycle of his life the average individual comes sooner or later to regard it with emotion as a period of grace and ease and comparative stability. But the most comforting thing about the past is probably that it is dead; its decisions have been taken. Psychologists tell us that much of human conduct is governed by emotion, and that emotions are not controlled by argument and can only be acquired or extinguished by patient processes of conditioning. Therefore society needs to revise many of the methods by which it determines courses of action. Nevertheless the individual, while he has an autonomic nervous system which registers involuntary actions (like sweating or heart-beat), has also a central nervous system that *mediates* his perceptions. He can also contribute, by research and application, to the common fund of human experience and scientific knowledge. The collective mind can discard purely emotional reactions and retain what is necessary for its evolutionary purposes. In looking at the past, recorded social experience can draw from it something even more valuable for survival than recollections of former splendours and felicities—namely a guide to the measurement and anticipation of change. *This measuring rod is an essential instrument of planning.*

Scientists and artists and even the "beat groups" understand, in their different ways, that they must know what has happened before. And in architecture and landscape the most intelligent attitudes towards preservation do not seem to me to derive from love of the old or dread of the new; not even from a fashionable sensitivity to the picturesque. They derive from an understanding of what has been created in the past and handed down, on the part of those who are capable of creating in the present and handing on.

THE NEED TO FORECAST

As we swing away from the past to look at the future, and the sort of environment for which we are heading, one of the most essential techniques that we shall have to develop is that of forecasting. In the dark ages the bulk of the human race was still more or less *exposed* to environment, like the primates. Today we are modifying it rapidly. But at the same time we are increasing our numbers exponentially. Many scientists have pointed out that man's future now depends on predicting and providing for changes *that have not yet* occurred. Population growth is only one of these changes. The crisis on the roads, the crisis in higher technical education, the problems of automation and leisure, are among the others. Similarly the landscape resulting from these changes, actual and to come, can no longer be thought of as being in a process of slow evolution from forest clearing to city centre. The graphs of population, mobility, communication, and technological advance have all taken a sharp upward curve (Figures 54-1 and 54-2), and the rate of obsolescence—of "fallout," as it were—is rising along with the rate of change. The built environment must inevitably become less stable as a background to our lives, more subject to invasion, a field for operations new in character and unaccustomed in scale, with mounting problems of air and water pollution, detritus, and waste.

Now, change is of no particular value in itself; and although it is something to recognize that change is inevitable, intelligent forecasting has to be used to make a success of it. Perhaps it is the lack of response to this challenge which has so retarded professional discussion of planning and forecasting during the first half of this century.

One of the most stubborn difficulties in modernizing our outlook and methods, is to

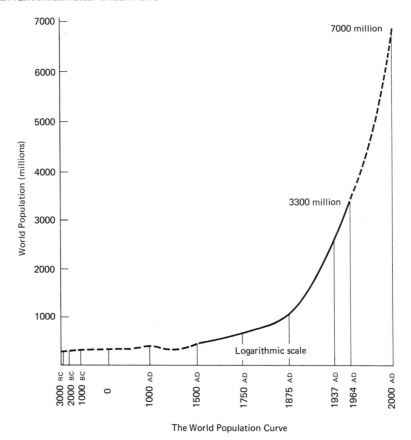

The World Population Curve

Figure 54–1

make people and politicians understand the *type* of forecasting that is possible and necessary. As Max Nicholson remarked in a PEP Broadsheet (1963): "So much of the forecasting that is currently attempted is done by technicians seeking to project trends and currents within their own narrow spheres regardless of the fact that such trends are bound to be affected, and often overridden, by broader developments which no one tries to forecast at all." Fuel policy, forestry policy, housing policy, and population policy in this country have all, until recently, been less effective because of dislike of social statistics and scepticism about analyses and forecasts that go beyond purely statistical computation. Nicholson also pointed out that during the second world war operational techniques, cybernetics, and communication theory owed much to biology, and in particular to that branch of it called ecology—the study of animals and

plants in their relations with one another and with their environment.

"Being limited," he said, "like the social sciences, in the use of experimental techniques and of exact laboratory measurements, and having to observe directly the working of vast and complex systems within a partly fixed and partly changing environment, ecology has been compelled to tackle problems technically analogous to those which confront the student and forecaster of pressures and trends in human societies. Training in and close links with other natural sciences has recently assisted ecologists in measuring biological productivity and rates of turnover of nutrients and energy in ecological systems functioning naturally without human interference. Such research must be done partly in the laboratory and partly in the field, and experimental techniques must be supplemented by descriptive observation, tested by prediction of the evolution

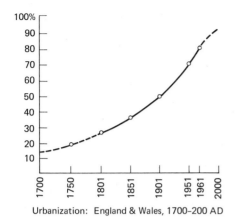

Urbanization: England & Wales, 1700–200 AD

Figure 54–2. Percentage of population living in urban communities: i.e.—those with a population over 5,000 in 1700, over 10,000 in 1851, over 20,000 in 1961.

of the system and by investigation to check departures from the predicted development. Evidently such an approach has analogies with the professional requirements of forecasting for use in planning."

Here is the case for research into human relations, not only in the natural but in the built environment; research which embraces building materials and methods and such techniques as modular co-ordination which we already know something about; and even more essentially the whole realm of social ecology of which we know very little.

THE ARCHITECTURAL FACULTY IN THE CREATION OF THE BUILT ENVIRONMENT

The central operation in the spectrum of activities that create the built environment can be broadly described as architectural: i.e. it consists of the organization of a number of constructional and developmental techniques, to a brief that is defined or definable, in such a way as to produce unity and significance. It is not contended that architecture always results; nor that it is the architect who necessarily shapes the environment. In fact, it is only too obvious that in many places he has conspicuously failed to do so. The motivations behind any man-made environment are, of course, human and social; its *new* elements are due to design and invention. Architectural design is another of the distinctively human faculties, not shared by animals. It involves calculation, forecasting, and planning; and the planning is more than the co-ordination of structure for the use and enclosure of space. It consists of dozens or hundreds of intuitive choices of forms, symbols, colours, textures, and proportions, *made at the same time as the process of calculation and combination is going on.*

Design is integral; it cannot be added afterwards: decoration, unfortunately, can. And decoration which does not form part of a larger design, but is applied independently, is seldom successful or significant.

Trained architects know this; but many of their clients do not. So it is often the case that far too little time is allowed for the really essential architectural procedures of tailoring the brief and preparing a design that is both elegant and economical. Intuitive processes in experienced hands can be fairly rapid; so can the "feed-back" process of a computer that has been fed the proper programme. But the making of the programme in either case can only be hurried at the risk of making faulty decisions; and the simplification and refinement of an original design idea is usually worth the time that has to be spent on this part of the process.

All sorts of expediting procedures are now being tried out. Analyses are being made of the decisions that have to be taken in the course of arriving at a design, and of the extent to which these decisions are compatible. Negotiated contracts and procedures for expediting tendering are being investigated. Prefabrication is developing into building systems. Critical path analysis is being applied to whole building operations. All these are moves in the direction of speed and efficiency; but if the design process is ignored altogether, or reduced to a formula for automatic selection and placement, then the results may not be worth having. (I recollect my mother returning, flushed with victory, from a visit to the New Year bargain sales and flourishing her purchase before my father, ending up with ". . . and George, it's so *cheap!*" To which my father only replied: "Nothing is cheap, Katie, if you don't need it.")

"NON-DESIGN"

"Non-design"—if I can give it such a name—has particularly unfortunate results on the built environment.

We all know office buildings, for example, where all the intelligence that went to their making was concentrated in the financial calculation of floor space, rental, and minimum cost; everything else such as external maintenance and cleaning, internal comfort and flexibility, good appearance, aspect, and recognition of their surroundings being organized just well enough to get by. Such buildings, if they do not ignore design altogether, regard it as an optional extra. An architect is employed with reluctance and—quite naturally in such circumstances—is grudged his 6 percent.

Another type of client impatient with design is the man or the manager with excellent motives, the reverse of speculative, who confuses the process of creating a building with the process of acquiring goods retail. In other words, he deals only in goods whose design has already been proved in a competitive market; he will not give time to creating something specially for its purpose, or even to combining existing designs in a new way. He changes his mind, as any customer has a right to, and tells his architect at a late stage in the contract to change a large space for two small spaces, or to take back the built-in furniture designed for the building, and replace it with some he has just seen in a catalogue.

Equally unsuccessful is the man, or more often the committee, who believes that a building designs itself, provided that full information is available on its requirements and that the democratic process is given full play in coming to decisions. We all know the wisecrack that . . . "a camel is a horse designed by a committee"; but the result is even more like one of these pantomime horses whose main impact on the spectator is a wonderful lack of co-ordination and consistency in its parts.

More serious than any of these human failings—which are, after all, susceptible to improvement and experience—is the limitation of design to mechanical objects and individual artifacts in themselves, *without applying it to the spaces in which they are set.* The setting may be a covered area or an open space, a town square, a street, an industrial complex, or a whole river valley.

Density, in the town planner's use of the word, is a relative term, and architects on the whole have been rather contemptuous of it as an instrument of measurement or control. Nevertheless, as the biologists have demonstrated with monkeys, there seems to be a critical point for humans too, at which over-crowding and space limitation start to produce neuroses. The social organism can no longer adapt to its environment. Signs of dilapidation and waste appear; and they remain, because natural regeneration no longer operates and artificial regeneration is seldom economic, and is thus nobody's business. The Civic Trust this year (1964) put the figure of derelict land in England and Wales at 150,000 acres, and its spread at 3,500 acres a year.

Dereliction must be at least partly due to an attitude of mind which is produced by over-mechanization, by the multiplication of unrelated objects in the street and the landscape, by a breakdown in the unity of design which governed, for example, a country house in its park, or mediaeval Edinburgh, or Georgian Bath. And one of the best defences against dereliction would be the extention of design techniques to cover what has been called *the main structure* of an environment, or its "grand design" as compared with the design of its details and components.

MAIN STRUCTURE PLANNING

The main structure is ". . . that aspect of its pattern which is most apparent. . . ."

> . . . Le Corbusier in his plan for Algiers had the idea of combining traffic, work and housing in a single linear thread. Within this complex he envisaged every type of activity. The road and the load-bearing elements constitute the main structure. As filler his drawings show Baroque, Moorish and modern houses jumbled together according to the whim

of the inhabitants, but always within the discipline of the main structure (Doshi and Alexander, 1962).

This discipline can be seen in a simple form in some of the best of the Italian hill towns; and a more recent illustration of the "main structure" concept is the Buckinghamshire County Council's plan, designed by their Planning Officer Mr F. B. Pooley and his colleagues, for a compact, linear, district-heated city between Bletchley and Wolverton, on the A5 (Figure 54-3). Sir Donald Gibson (1964) urged on the plan to an even more highly integrated form by suggesting that the monorail public transport system would itself be a good direct overhead route for the heating mains. But whether this is done or not, the plan is a design for the main structure of a new settlement for 250,000 people; the structure has shape and meaning; this is "the aspect of its pattern which is most apparent." The plan thus achieves two kinds of synthesis: first, it establishes a unified and comprehensible form and silhouette and circulation for the town, which is not heedless of the existing environment and its green spaces, but creates an environment which will be in time even richer. Secondly, it *combines* as economically as possible the main functions of the town—housing, employment, education, marketing, leisure opportunities, rapid transit, heat and power, and safe accessibility by pedestrians and cars. It sets out to achieve these two objects by avoiding built-in obsolescence and by inviting instead a great deal of variety and choice in the infilling of the main structure.

The Town Planning Department in University College, London, has carried out with its postgraduate Diploma students in the last ten years, a number of exercises for main structure design in new towns of 100,-000 to 300,000 population; but owing to the limited time and resources of students and

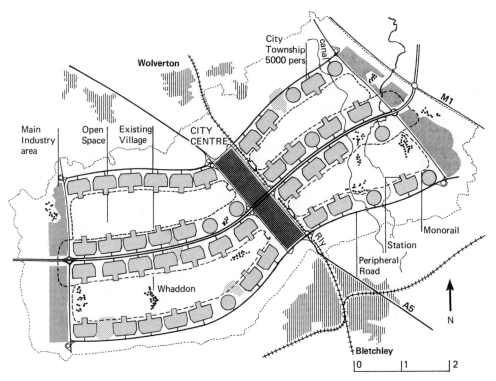

Figure 54-3. Plan for a new town between Bletchley and Wolverton. The residential townships are shown in black, linked by main roads on one side and by a monorail on the other. The city centre and two industrial areas are shown shaded; and existing development is shown hatched.

staff has produced nothing quite as simple, realistic, and fully integrated as this "live" project in Buckinghamshire, which has now reached the stage of a draft application for land purchase.

DESIGN ON A REGIONAL SCALE

The design principle behind these examples is also valid on a regional or sub-regional scale, where the built and the natural environments must either compete with or support each other. The recreational landscapes, the agricultural, industrial, and housing improvements, and the hydro-electric power generation which the TVA combined in the Tennessee Valley, is the most celebrated of pre-war examples (Huxley, 1943). The more recent achievements of the Snowy River Authority in Australia are equally interesting. In both instances the engineering and landscape design of the main structure is regional in scale; the contribution of architecture and farming more local in its impact. But the important thing is the unified approach.

In this small and already highly developed country the same kind of operation would be far more difficult. But the design principle behind it is one of our best hopes for conserving and renewing the somewhat raddled face of Britain. Historic villages and nature reserves are a part of our inheritance; but we also need modern accessible towns capable of higher social and industrial productivity. National Parks are a national asset; but so is the electricity grid. Without design for the main structure of such areas as the Solent, or Teesside, or the lower reaches of the Trent, it is difficult to see how administrative and political energies—which now so often tend towards compartmentalism and competition which is not always productive, between ministries, local authorities, private and public developers, industry, amenity, large companies and small—can be canalized and concentrated on wider and more inspiring objectives. Without a combined physical and economic plan, improvements in building components and methods, in vehicles and traction, in services and equipment, and in industrial

design generally, will only proliferate in clutter and litter.

And it is a sad fact that few organizations can be found these days to dispose of the fallen leaves, whether they take the form of industrial waste or old jalopies, or dirty unbreakable plastic cups.

INDUSTRIALIZATION WITHIN THE BUILT ENVIRONMENT

If we pass on from the main structure of regional planning, new town planning, urban redevelopment and the comprehensive layout of neighbourhoods, universities or hospitals, and if we leave aside for the moment the rich legacy of the past and our ability to maintain it, we have to consider not only the quality of the infilling that we should *like* to have, but the quality we can *afford* to have. In future the answer must depend largely on the level of industrial productivity and profit attained by the country as a whole, especially in exports. Part of this national product is the output of the building industry itself. It is in a special position compared with other industries in being hardly at all subjected to international competition, under-capitalized, composed of a very high proportion of small units, at a disadvantage in competing for skilled labour, and employed as to a full third of its resources in works of repair and maintenance. It is not surprising, therefore, that although a great deal of original development work is carried out by its constituent firms, as an industry it is not research-oriented. Nor is it surprising that its professional elements are criticized for remaining too much within their professional pitches instead of attacking bigger targets such as management, automation, commercial efficiency, and competition with other industries. Building has often taken refuge from such criticisms in the knowledge that it *is* different from other industries. But now that it is quickening its own pace towards industrialization, it is becoming more necessary to distinguish its industrial characteristics from those it has as a service or as a form of art.

The environment is not only created by

the *surplus* of wealth and resources, that is to say, by how much extra we can afford to spend on visual order and amenity, craftsmanship, high quality building materials, and the recreational landscape. It is also made up of standard industrial building products of the day. If these are poor of their kind, uncompetitive in price, unreliable in performance, outmoded in idea and appearance, then the architectural faculty of combination and selection, of deciding where the "one-off" is justified, and the "hundred-off" made acceptable by intelligent site-planning, will count for very little.

Some developments in this field have logically moved out of the traditional architectural skills altogether, including the design and erection of entire plants within buildings, and buildings and layouts designed entirely for plant. (An example of the first is the two-storey service unit designed by ICI for Basingstoke and shown at the IBSAC Exhibition; of the second, any largely automated chemical or oil-cracking plant, or an electrical switching station.) Here, if the architect acts centrally, he must become the industrial designer or the works manager; if he acts on the side he can only advise, or camouflage, or cover with an envelope of some sort when required.

When plant or services in a building are not entire but have to be co-ordinated with each other and designed integrally with the plan, section, and structure of the building, then the authentic architectural process is again involved. But the traditional methods of taking briefs and thinking up designs, tailoring the dimensions, specifying materials, and going out to open competitive tender, are now being modified in many ways. As a great deal has been said recently about industrialized building and the necessity for it, I need not add much to this lecture; it is a subject on its own. But I should like to make a brief reference to a very few of the new techniques of inquiry.

NEW PLANNING TECHNIQUES

Of these, research into user requirements is perhaps the most fundamental as it identifies the nature of the operation for which building is being proposed. If it is objective as well as thorough, it may even reveal that building—or at any rate new building—is *not* the right answer to a particular client's problem.

This is, incidentally, an additional reason why the boundaries of building and environmental research should not be drawn too tightly; why they should be subject to scientific inquiries from outside the industry itself; and why, above all, research should not be tied completely to executive departments. Both the Building Research Station and the Road Research Laboratory, for example, have lately been drawn, and inevitably so, into the consideration of the nature of urban development; and far from being diversionary this research is likely to inform their more specific and routine studies and make them more useful.

Social studies, including social surveys and statistics, urban sociology, demography, and the economics of land and building development, are intensely relevant here. New techniques of forecasting and measurement are only now being explored and tested. For example, the Building Industry Communications Research Project, directed by Gurth Higgin, Neil Jessop, and others, has carried "Critical Path" programming a stage further and evolved a technique (AIDA) for Analysing the Interconnected Decision Areas which are met with in the translation of a building brief into a building design with estimates of cost. The technique assists, checks, and may in some degree supersede the untested intuitive processes of designers. Another aid to decision-making in matters of preservation and development is the Cost Benefit analyses now being investigated, notably by Dr. Lichfield. Process diagrams, social and building-user studies, and environmental standards were ably demonstrated for hospital and research laboratory planning by the Nuffield Division of Architectural Studies directed by Richard Llewelyn Davies.

But the fact that all these can still be called pioneer studies shows how much more is still to be done to discover the nature and purposes of building projects, their optimum size, capacity, and location, the ways in which they change and become obsolete, and the means necessary to record and evaluate them, economically and socially.

PROFESSIONAL EFFICIENCY

On the professional side of the industry a good deal of heart-searching has been going on as to the meaning of efficiency. It is not just a matter of returning the regular answer to a building problem or a town planning problem—only more quickly and in a smarter package. It involves an analysis of the problem itself and the knowledge that enables one to question whether it is soluble in the terms suggested.

Since the publication by the RIBA in 1962, of *The Architect and His Office,* none of the professional members of the building industry can maintain the illusion that good design can any longer be carried out without efficiency in the whole process of its evolution, from briefing to site management. On the other hand, it is possible to be efficient in design without being good—in other words to fail to contribute anything original in idea, in method, or in significant form.

Functional efficiency in moveable objects and equipment forms a very high proportion of their value; one does not ask much more of a kettle or a typewriter or a stacking chair. But even here an original approach to design can make previous designs quite suddenly obsolete, however efficient they were. As you pass from moveable objects to fixed buildings and on to consideration of a multi-form environment, in which some features change quickly but most of them very slowly, and in which the static element is land and the dynamic element is the human being moving singly and in groups, then efficiency values grow comparatively less. The bigger the scale of operations, the quicker is the rejection of designs that do not look at the larger problem in comprehensive terms, and take in other values as well—aesthetic, social, cultural. Aluminium conductors carried overhead on lattice towers are at the moment the most *efficient* way of transmitting alternating current at, say, 400 kV around the country. What everyone is now looking for is a scientific break-through which will enable current to be transmitted by underground cables with equal efficiency. This would enable these other values to be taken into account. To put the Supergrid underground at present would not only distort the whole economy of the electricity supply industry, but would not by any means solve the problem of amenity.

In the middle ranges of the built environment, between, so to speak, the electric kettle and the electrified landscape, are structures of every kind, and the land formations, plantings, and pavings which surround and support them. These form the main internal and external spaces which we use and enjoy and it is with them, it seems to me, that most work needs to be done to keep unit efficiency in step with a larger design that means something in social and aesthetic terms. This is the key problem of urban development and of planning controls.

Town planning also has a time dimension, in that the individual designs that make up the environment are not simultaneous, as they are in a single building composition and to some extent in a new town. Moreover the different elements age and expand at different rates; and for qualitative as well as quantitative reasons. So we shall need to know much more than we do now about the relevant social purposes and limitations of a design, as well as its immediate functional requirements; and also about the rate of obsolescence and renewal that different types of environment exhibit.

UNCERTAINTY AND OPPORTUNITY

As to purposes, it seems essential in any large project to discover at what stage the briefing and design stage should be closed. Everyone who has planned a hospital knows that unless certain key decisions are held, it is hazardous to let a contract, and difficult to carry out an efficient construction programme. If lack of finance, for example, postpones construction for even a year or two you may as well make a fresh start, because the rate of change of ideas (sometimes a sign of progress, sometimes due to a change of personalities) creates an actual *opportunity* to think again. And no one coming onto the job and taking up new responsibilities can resist the temptation to do so.

On the other hand, there are building programmes which positively benefit from a reassessment of their value and correctness in the course of construction. It may happen during the redevelopment of a town centre, for example. It all depends on the purpose and the priorities, which therefore need very full discussion at the outset.

It also appears that planning and building programmes are often too specific about factors that are unpredictable. The Communications Research Project has already commented on the friction caused by exact building schedules based, for example, on deliveries, which are bound to be uncertain in the nature of things. On the other hand, action on information that is capable of being planned or computed is frequently left to human computers, who fail to co-ordinate it and to take the right decisions. Similarly a factory may be built too close to its limit of capacity; a nuclear physics laboratory may be superseded in the time it takes to build. "If it works, it's obsolete," as the Americans put it.

Therefore we need to look carefully into the ways in which construction programmes are affected by rates of change. And further research would be valuable on many problems connected with the life of buildings, singly and in groups—a subject tackled during the war in the report of the Uthwatt Committee. It could usefully take in a wider range of social factors than that Committee were called on to consider; for example, historic buildings retained or adapted because of their cultural significance, heavily mechanized buildings (like telephone exchanges) retained in central positions because of the cost and disturbance that would be caused by moving their plant and service connections.

THE PLANNED ENVIRONMENT

Taking all these points together, what is the outlook? My conclusion is that a high rate of technological advance seems unlikely to lead to a new and improved environment unless equal advances are made in the study of human ecology and social controls.

The ingredients are so diverse in type and timing, the motivations so various, the agents of change so many, that the architectural faculty will have to become more and more concerned with problems of *selection* and *combination*, on a scale ranging from the room to the region.

Selection will be needed to identify sites and locations, the economic and social elements of a design; the particular ways in which technical invention and processes can be put to work for human purposes of accommodation and circulation. Selection could also define the role of design in the total approach—*industrial* in the case of plant and utilities (which has its own aesthetic), *building* design and the organization of space, *urban* design, which has to take account both of preservation and of development, short- and long-life buildings, accessibility, and environmental quality. It is argued that maximization of choice is one of the objects of social *planning*; hence we have policies for mixed neighbourhoods, variety in housing types and in leisure opportunities, education in comprehensive schools, diversification of industry. But *design* is a process of selection among a host of variables, so as to produce unity, impact, symbolic significance, and permanent cultural value.

Combination is necessary to establish, among other things, the means by which standard components can be sensitively adjusted to the requirements of particular programmes, layouts, and landscapes; and to determine the "main structure" of a building group or a town. It is also a means of bringing together a number of physical assets and improvements with reasonable economy.

The environment can be "planned" only to a limited extent, but it would seem that what *is* plannable could be immensely improved by better methods of forecasting and control, and by the force of example that models and executed projects at full scale would provide. These are as essential to the future of urban and regional development as experimental rockets are for the future exploration of outer space.

Implicit in everything I have suggested about the built environment is the need for an Applied Research Council, drawing its membership to begin with from the existing research organizations in the construction industries, from DSIR, and from the associated professions, including those concerned with urban studies and with the use and development of land. It would stand in relation to this whole field of activity in the same way as other Research Councils do to agriculture and medicine, and will do—one hopes—to natural resources. It would not be divorced from industry; but on the other hand it would be a connector with all the sciences in which advances are being made that will affect our knowledge of what to build and how to build it. It would also be a connector with university and other institutions where research is supported. Nothing it did would diminish existing initiative in matters of research and development. Like a discriminating connoisseur, it would create a demand for new thinking at the same time as it encouraged and co-ordinated an increasing supply.

Obviously its relationship to any research council for the social sciences as a whole, which may be set up as a result of the report of Lord Heyworth's Committee, will need definition. As the Council of the Tavistock Institute has called them, there are "domains" in the social sciences which represent different and sometimes merging colours in a considerable spectrum. But if this definition were made, it would help very much to focus attention on the built environment as one of the great social and technical challenges of our time, ". . . lest we become swamped," as the Director of the Nature Conservancy said recently (Nicholson, 1964), ". . . in lost hordes of mini-citizens erupting, like bewildered human lemmings, from more and more mega-cities."

REFERENCES:

Civic Trust. *Derelict land.* September 1964.

Doshi, B. V., & Alexander, C. International design conference, Aspen, Colo., June 1962.

Gibson, D. Inaugural address as President of the Royal Institute of British Architects, November 3, 1964.

Huxley, J. S. *Essays of a biologist.* London: Chatto & Windus, 1923.

Huxley, J. S. *TVA: Adventure in planning.* Cheam: Architectural Press, 1943.

Jacobs, J. *Death and life of great American cities.* London: Cape, 1962.

Nicholson, M. PEP: Planning No. 47, *The shape of the sixties.* April 1963.

Nicholson, E. M. *Conservation and the next Renaissance.* The Albright Conservation Lectureship, University of California, March 1964.

Royal Institute of British Architects. *The architect and his office.* London: RIBA, 1962.

Russell, W. M. S. *Violence, monkeys and man: The affluent crowd.* BBC Third Programme; see *The Listener,* November 5 and 12, 1964.

Woolley, L., & Hawkes, J. *Prehistory and the beginnings of civilization.* History of mankind: Vol. 1. London: Allen and Unwin, 1963.

55 Function as the Basis of Psychiatric Ward Design

Humphry Osmond

The aim of this paper is twofold: to encourage psychiatrists to present the needs of institutionalized mentally ill people so that these needs can be understood by members of another profession—architecture; to encourage architects to question psychiatrists about the care of these sick people in a knowledgeable way so that they can derive a truer understanding of the architectural problem that is being presented. For where client and architect do not communicate freely and accurately, the architect cannot easily discover the real purpose of the building and his design must suffer. Hundreds of monstrous and unsatisfactory mental hospitals, cluttering the countryside and causing grave clinical and administrative difficulties, are an eloquent testimony to the failure in communication which has existed between architect and psychiatrist for much of the last century. This has not always been so and must not continue.

My thesis here hinges on certain assumptions. To avoid confusion I shall list these

A slightly condensed version from *Mental Hospitals* (Architectural Supplement), April 1957, 8, 23–30. Reprinted with the permission of the author and of *Hospital & Community Psychiatry* (formerly *Mental Hospitals*), a journal of the American Psychiatric Association.

so that the reader may challenge them if he wishes.

1. Structure will determine function, unless function determines structure.

2. The architect's task is to devise a structural expression of the functional requirements which have been communicated to him by his client.

3. Since mentally ill people have been studied far more closely and intensively and in a greater variety of ways than almost any other group of people, it follows that we should be able to define their needs very exactly. There are dozens of books giving detailed accounts of the sufferings of mentally ill individuals. No physical illnesses have been so extensively described. We are therefore peculiarly well placed to make a functional formulation of requirements for mentally ill people, and from this an architect should be able to devise an efficient structure.

In designing a particular ward, of course, the functional formulation should be worked out in the greatest detail. Since this is not possible here, I shall deal with principles rather than with particulars.

To make a functional formulation we must first delineate the problem. Luckily there is no difficulty in doing this, for the heart of the psychiatric hospital is, and must be, the ward on which patients spend most of their time. It is the sort of care given on the wards which determines the sort of buildings needed elsewhere in the hospital. That care, in its turn, is determined by the nature of the sick people for whose benefit it has been devised.

The mentally ill, like any other group of handicapped people, require surroundings which allow them to make the most of their assets and which aggravate their disabilities as little as possible. It would be heartless to house legless men in a building which could only be entered by ladders or very steep gradients. But so little thought has been given to the care of the mentally ill that buildings far more detrimental have been foisted on them.

These sick people have only one quality common to all of them without exception: *a rupture in interpersonal relationships resulting in alienation from the community, culminating in expulsion or flight.* They are to a greater or lesser extent socially isolated. The psychiatric ward then has to be designed to care for people whose capacity to relate to others has been gravely impaired.

This disturbance in interpersonal relationships is usually produced by primary changes in perception, thinking, feeling (affectivity) and sometimes motility. Such changes often produce, and when present always enhance, any existing difficulties in interpersonal relationships. These interpersonal difficulties frequently aggravate the difficulties in perception, thinking, and so on. The design of a psychiatric ward must incorporate ways of influencing this vicious circle for the better. In particular the staff must be placed so that they can provide the greatest amount of support, help and encouragement for the patients in their care. The patients too must have every opportunity to help each other by means of group activity such as we are now able to devise.

THE NATURE OF THE PATIENTS' DISABILITIES

Mentally ill people, particularly schizophrenic people, who fill rather more than half of the mental hospital beds in North America (say at least 500,000 beds out of about 800,000), suffer from a well defined group of symptoms whose effects are known. I shall give examples, not exhaustive, of the way in which these symptoms make the patients' life difficult. Clearly, in a major psychiatric architectural study these symptoms should be examined in great detail.

Though I have divided these changes up under headings of perception, feeling and thinking, these abstractions must not be taken too literally.

1. Disturbances in Perception: In spite of Bleuler's contrary opinion there is growing evidence that schizophrenic people have peculiarities in perception ranging from minor changes (which may and probably do have very extensive consequences), to illusions, distortions and hallucinations of a gross sort. These may affect every sensory modality, including the perceived body. Weckowicz (1957) has shown under test conditions that schizophrenic people have anomalies in visual perception. In my own clinical experience, changes in spatial perception are often accompanied by changes in perception of the body, which is only a special but very important aspect of general perception. So the huge corridors and unnecessarily enlarged spaces so often found in mental hospitals are liable to enhance one of the most harmful and distressing of schizophrenic experiences—uncertainty about the integrity of the self.

Other results of these perceptual changes are:

(a) Changes in visual perception so that familiar surroundings seem changed; the uncertainty which this generates may be frightening. Experimental evidence (and we have not nearly enough of this at the moment) suggests that small, reassuring, easily encompassed spaces are desirable.

People too can appear strange and threatening, or they may even seem to be others who possess these attributes. This danger can be reduced by having small groups of patients, who know each other well, living together in comfortable surroundings. Such groups of four to eight people cared for by someone trained in interpersonal skills will give each other empathic support and lessen fear.

(b) Changes in auditory sensation. The very frequent auditory hallucinations, voices and so on, are good examples of this. Very often these appear mostly when the sick person is tense. Disturbing echoes and auditory peculiarities should be avoided in design.

(c) Changes in time sense can make life very difficult and leave the patient puzzled and uncertain about where he is. The ample provision of clocks, calendars and up-to-date newspapers is necessary to remind patients that "world time" is "real time." Television, properly used, and internal broadcast systems can all help to focus the patients' attention on the socially recognized time.

(d) Changes in tactile sense occur also and an interest in texture which needs study and must be used constructively. The coarseness of institutional clothing and the lack of pleasantly-textured fabrics and surfaces in the surroundings have undoubtedly been harmful to the mentally ill. Indeed this was noted in the York Retreat, England, so that good linen, tableware, and so on, was provided by Samuel Tuke in the 1790s.

(e) Changes in the olfactory sense. Hypersensitivity and changes in this sense make properly functioning, well-ventilated and a sufficient number of toilets of even greater importance than in general hospitals.

(f) Changes in the perception of one's own body. This very alarming type of experience is probably instrumental in starting many schizophrenic delusions of the hypochondriacal variety. It is probable that good and congenial surroundings can reduce preoccupation with these changes. Experiments in perception show that our perceptual apparatus can easily be confused; such confusion must be avoided in psychiatric wards.

2. *Changes in Mood:* Changes in mood make interaction difficult. A small group of people who know and understand each other tend to stabilize mood changes. In a very large group, swings of mood can reverberate through many people, including the nurses, resulting in panic and social disintegration.

With mood change may be included that peculiar quality, empathy—feeling in or with other people. Few of us dare to be "involved in mankinde." At least some mentally ill people find themselves involuntarily in this heroic situation. For them, privacy and a place of their own is essential if they are to avoid being overwhelmed emotionally by the suffering of their companions.

3. *Changes in Thinking:* These can be of such extreme severity that even very simple actions become difficult. The ward must therefore make the patients' biological life easy to live. Washing arrangements and toilets must be close at hand and easily located. Clothing and personal possessions too must be stored so that they can be kept nearby and be under the patients' own control as far as possible. Where, as in older folk, memory failure plays an important part in asocial behavior, rooms must be clearly labeled in letters of a suitable size and color.

In some people, apart from difficulties in perception, the notion of self may be lost or impaired. Simple devices such as the patient's name being clearly written on the doors of rooms and lockers can help here. Mirrors in bedrooms and bathrooms can help to remind one who one is. (In bedrooms particularly these mirrors should be under the patients' own control. That is, it should be possible to cover them.)

RULES DERIVING FROM THE PATIENTS' NEEDS

An appreciation of the nature of the mentally ill person's disease and the sort of experience which he may be enduring allows an imaginative architect to evolve certain simple rules which can then be applied. Luckily today we can depend less on imagination and more on experience because, thanks to psychiatric tools such as LSD-25 and Mescalin, changes in perception resembling those found in some schizophrenic people can be produced experimentally. We also have evidence that mood and thought changes can be produced with adrenolution and adrenochrome.

1. Patients Must Not Be Overcrowded: Too many people must not be forced to live or sleep in a space intended for a lesser number. Overcrowding forces people, who do not wish or are unable to interact, literally to tread upon each other's toes. It has been shown that in animals, overcrowding alone can cause major changes in the adrenal glands (believed to play an important part in schizophrenia and known to be important in the physiology of the emotions). Some animals, if forced to live in overcrowded conditions from which they cannot escape, will die.

2. Patients Must Not Be Overconcentrated: Too many people must not be forced to interact together, regardless of whether the space provided is sufficient or not. A dayroom in which 100 patients have to congregate would be harmful even though its dimensions were very generous. We are not used to living in crowds and the attempt to do so is unpleasant even for healthy people. It can so damage the mentally ill that they lose all hope of recovery.

While overcrowding and overconcentration are often combined in our deplorable provincial and state mental hospitals, they can also occur separately. *Each is harmful, overconcentration probably being worse.* Architects and psychiatrists have a very high responsibility to design buildings which do not lend themselves to overcrowding and in which overconcentration cannot take place.

3. The Provision of a Path of Retreat: When patients feel threatened they must, if at all possible, have the opportunity to retreat physically rather than be forced to resist physically or, *what is more harmful, be forced into psychological withdrawal from reality.* Physical retreat can easily be reversed; it is less likely to harm the patient than psychological withdrawal, and less likely to be accompanied by psychosomatic disturbances. It is obvious that while physical resistance may do the patient less harm immediately, it is likely to involve him in interpersonal relationships with the staff and other patients which may, in the long run, force him into psychological withdrawal.

4. Need for Private Place: It follows that patients require a place of their own, as far as possible under their own control. Hediger (1955) has shown that for many wild animals incarcerated in zoos, the presence or absence of this nest or den makes the difference between the survival or death of the creature. He has also shown that the size of this place is much less important than that it should be *functionally rather than structurally* equivalent to the conditions found in nature. This would mean that for psychotic people a small room of perhaps only 50 square foot floor space is much to be preferred to twice that space in a dormitory with many people. (In his most valuable book on wild animals in zoos and circuses, Hediger frequently emphasizes the importance of providing the functional equivalent of the animal's natural living conditions rather than making futile attempts to reproduce its natural surroundings.)

5. *Opportunity To Form Beneficial Relationships:* Patients must have the opportunity implicit both in the organization and physical structure of the hospital to form relationships of a beneficial sort among themselves and with the hospital staff. There is evidence that groups of four to eight people are especially liable to form beneficial, supportive and constructive relationships, and that these can be enhanced by the presence of a nurse trained in group activity.

Conversely the structure must not encourage dangerous and unstable relationships. For gravely psychotic people, rooms having two or three together are nearly always objectionable and can be very harmful. If for some reason single rooms cannot be provided, then dormitories for from four to eight people with bed alcoves are the best substitute.

The relationship implied between two or three people sleeping in a single room is a highly complex one. In our culture, the only people who commonly sleep two to a room are siblings, spouses, lovers and some hotel guests. Psychotic people are very often muddled about their social and sexual status. It would seem unwise to muddle them even more.

6. *Psycho-Social Needs Must Be Met:* Illusory administrative conveniences such as security and supervision, must not be allowed to endanger the psycho-social needs of the patients. The "security" type of building is often necessary because the design of psychiatric wards wholly neglects the psycho-social needs of patients. When the building is itself an expression of those needs, both patients and staff will, I believe, feel so much more secure themselves that they will not have to rely as much on mechanical aids.

This does not mean that all security measures must be abandoned. It does mean that these measures must be scrutinized and their purpose analyzed. Many of them result from a combination of improper care and confused thinking, and so have no place in a modern building.

7. *The Reduction of Ambiguity and Uncertainty:* Well people respond to ambiguity with tension; and it is in consequence of this that ambiguity plays such a large part in humor of various sorts. Laughter releases the tension. If we meet someone who closely resembles an old friend or an old enemy, it can be difficult to relate to him in an appropriate manner. We know from conditioning experiments that animals become disturbed when asked to choose between objects which they have been trained to recognize, but which are presented to them in a manner that makes the animal unsure which test object is being shown. Children are notoriously upset by ambiguity, and it is often uncertainty caused by this rather than open unkindness and neglect which forms a focus for the development of habit patterns which dog them later in life. The most responsible tasks in society consist in choosing a course of action from a number of alternatives, not one of which is without danger.

Mentally sick people, especially schizophrenics and old folks, find ambiguity and the uncertainty which accompanies it hard to bear. This is a predictable consequence of illnesses which interfere with perception, thinking and affect. Mentally ill people find that aspects of living which are purely automatic for the well become filled with puzzlement, danger and distress for them. The sick person often has to make a heroic effort to cope with the most ordinary happenings. It is important not to add to this wretched condition by avoidable ambiguities in the function and structure of hospitals supposed to help the sick.

Gratuitous burdens are not uncommon. A famous British mental hospital welcomes its new arrivals in a richly painted and gilded hall. Among the intertwining leaves covering the walls, goblin-like creatures are concealed. Sometimes a whole head can be seen, sometimes only an eye gleams malevolently at the new arrival. While not all hospitals are as openly gruesome of their cultivation of the ambiguous, the whole matter of the enforced segregation of the mentally sick people in badly designed, poorly financed, understaffed and over-crowded places, ostensibly for their own good, is highly charged with ambiguity.

Another example of ambiguous structure found in the great majority of mental hospitals is the huge system of corridors which dominates old and new buildings. These thoroughfares, often serving no very obvious purpose, are unlike anything found in the lives of ordinary people. The extraordinary perspectives of these elongated corridors are disturbing even to the well and place a great strain on the perceptual apparatus of the psychotic. Anyone watching mentally ill people in these corridors can see how strange they find them. My colleague, Dr. M. Rejskind, drew my attention to how they crouch against the walls, or move slowly from line to line on the floor as if feeling their way along, or even lie on the floor as if hugging it to themselves.

8. The Preservation and Limitation of Choice: While this is closely linked to ambiguity it should, I think, be discussed separately. I was puzzled by comments from two of my colleagues who suggested that many difficulties in mental hospitals might spring from what seemed to be diametrically opposite causes. Dr. J. Cummings emphasized that patients in mental hospitals have far too few opportunities for choice; Dr. M. Rejskind suggested that they had too many. How could two perceptive and able men come to such very different conclusions? Yet on reflection it seems that both are right.

Choosing is a feature of all life, even the humblest, and survival often depends on making the right choice. Different social organizations impose different sorts of choice on their members. Choosing between many alternatives, even when these are pleasant, produces tension and even irritation in well people. In the most exclusive shops this is recognized by displaying very few goods because customers are likely to be hard put to discriminate between uniform excellence and elegance.

In our day to day life we make frequent choices in minor matters and so show our

preference for different sorts of food, clothing, entertainment, and to some extent, for the company of other people. Yet in major matters most of us exercise choice infrequently. For instance, we rarely choose with whom we should interact closely, because we live in one restricted group of people (our family) and work with another. Consequently we are far more restricted in our interpersonal transactions than we realize. In addition, we have means readily available for reducing these transactions with those people who are socially close to us, until the intensity of the relationship is one that we find congenial. We can close our office door. At home we can hide behind a book or newspaper. Or we can go into another room. We recognize that people have rights to privacy, although even in our culture this recognition is not universal. When we cannot reduce interaction then we are forced, as I have already suggested, to withdraw psychologically or to act out against our environment.

Ironically, the organizational and architectural structure of mental hospitals has managed, in the matter of exercising choice, to meet the patients' needs almost exactly in reverse. In mental hospitals as usually designed and in some social homologues such as jails, old folks' homes, and special schools, almost exactly opposite conditions obtain from those found in normal life. People incarcerated in these places have their everyday choices—food, clothing, recreation—limited, whereas they have to choose intimate companions from a mob of equally sick strangers—a choice we are seldom faced with in normal living.

Further, in most mental hospitals, not only is the patient exposed to an extraordinary number of potentially intimate interpersonal transactions, but he also has a variety of choices as to where and how to locate himself on the ward. Deprived of a room and frequently of a corner that he can call his own, he is forced to choose where he should sit or lie in the face of competition. In the huge dormitories he must seek out his bed among many anonymous beds.

The psychotic person needs surroundings which allow and encourage him to make the sort of choices which we all make regarding everyday matters, food, clothing, entertainment and our relationships with casual intruders. He should be limited strictly in the sort of choices which well people make infrequently, i.e. changing the group of people with whom he lives and works, and changing the location in his dwelling place.

9. *The Preservation of Personality and Individuality:* One of the most important objectives and one in which failure has been most conspicuous, is to preserve personality and to prevent the sick people being submerged in the hospital machine.

The hospital organization can do very little to preserve the patient's individuality if dormitories, day rooms, bathrooms, toilets and decorations are all clearly meant for mass living and herd existence. While it may well be that the general plan of wards will be very similar, the patient's personal living space must have something distinctive about it and the design should lend itself to placing furniture, small personal possessions, rugs, pictures, wall decorations and lighting so that patients can impress their personalities on their surroundings and be encouraged to do so.

For instance, thought should be given to see how suitable arrangements could be made for patients to have small animals as pets on and near their wards. This was done at the Retreat in York in the 1790's. It seems that people can form close affective relationships with animals even when it is not possible to do so with humans.

10. *Note on the Sexual Segregation of Patients:* One classification of mental hospital patients so widely used that it is hardly noticed is by sex. For the last 100 years or so, men and women have been more or less rigidly segregated, especially in state and provincial hospitals. Even Dr. Kirkbride (1880) was so moulded by the ideas of his age as to suggest separate hospitals for men and women, which is one of the very few stupid things in his great book.

Segregation of men and women sprang from the need to counter the depravity of the 18th century jails and mad houses. This was an age untrammeled by the sexual inhibitions and prudery of the succeeding Victorian era. The reformers feared that female patients would be debauched and abused if cared for by men and that women would seduce men. However, like many reforms, the cure, rigid segregation, was as bad as the disease; for mentally ill people are often forced to live in homosexual communities which are not suitable for them.

Schizophrenic people in particular are often quite unsure about their sexual status. Suggestions as to why this should be are:

(a) Regression to earlier stages in personality development.
(b) Eruption of complex determined material both of a personal and what Jung has called an archetypal sort.
(c) A need to repress an unrecognized homosexual urge.
(d) Disordered perception resulting in disturbances of the perceived body. With these changes may go uncertainty about sexual status.

Whatever the causes, the consequences are fairly clear. Like any other group of people, schizophrenics have sexual interests and since schizophrenia develops largely in young adults, in whom overt sexual behavior is expected, sexual difficulties occur. It is hardly surprising that where a strange and mysterious subject like sex combines with an equally mysterious illness, the victims of this joint puzzle are confused.

Schizophrenics, then, require surroundings where they meet people of the other sex, so that they can maintain those social skills which our culture and most others require for regulating relationships between the sexes. Interaction with both nurses and patients of the opposite sex is therefore of great importance.

The danger of sex segregation is that it encourages desocialization by allowing the development of carelessness in dress, uncouthness and lack of pride in one's appearance. In addition, as experience from the armed services in wartime shows, it assures an increase in ipsophilic (autoerotic) and isophilic (homoerotic) activities.

Psychiatric wards should allow for the

close proximity of male and female patients —without of course reducing the decorum found in other hospitals. While not subscribing to 18th century license, we do not have to be bound by 19th century prudery which no longer finds much support in our culture.

SOCIOPETAL AND SOCIOFUGAL BUILDINGS

This brief outline shows some of the snags awaiting the unwary who design mental hospitals without inquiring into the nature of schizophrenic experience. It is pleasanter not to guess how many patients have been irreparably damaged by unsuitable buildings and how many are presently being tortured by them.

I believe that there are some general qualities of buildings which can be called sociofugality and sociopetality. By *sociofugality* I mean a design which prevents or discourages the formation of stable human relationships. In urban society such buildings are clearly necessary. Railway stations are perhaps the apogee of sociofugality; hotels have this quality to a high degree, as do mental hospitals, general hospitals and jails.

Sociopetality is that quality which encourages, fosters and even enforces the development of stable interpersonal relationships such as are found in small, face-to-face groups. The tepee, the igloo, the Zulu kraal are examples of buildings that could be described as highly sociopetal. Merritt's design of a psychiatric ward, although aimed mainly at improving nursing supervision, shows a fair degree of sociopetality, as do some circular medical wards at the Liverpool Royal Infirmary in England, and most but not all private dwellings. General hospitals, mental hospitals, prisons and old folks' homes are often low in it.

I believe that the concepts of sociofugality and sociopetality are a means of analyzing the function and structure of buildings whose usefulness is not limited to psychiatry. Sociopetal buildings have as their objectives the fostering of those relationships found in the small, face-to-face groups of people. Where this sort of relationship is required,

the design must accord with the needs of these small groups. Sociofugal buildings do not encourage interpersonal relationships and when group relationships occur they are of the shoulder-to-shoulder type found in a crowd or, when modified by discipline, in the regimented group. From the old English word "shoulder" we derive such verbs as "to shun" and phrases such as "the cold shoulder." Language is a sensitive indicator of implied human relationships.

Corridors, which are high in sociofugality, are admirably suited for keeping people on the move, but ill-suited for developing interpersonal relationships. It follows from this that, quite apart from a saving in cost (as high as 15% in some buildings) which the elimination of corridors allows, we should attempt to reduce corridors to a minimum in buildings in which we wish to encourage the growth of interpersonal relationships.

DISCUSSION

It may seem arrogant to lay down principles for designing psychiatric wards when many ward plans appear in journals with felicitous descriptions of the luxurious accommodation that is being provided. Even the most expensive show little sign that thought has been given to the type of interaction implicit in the structure of the building. Those most sophisticated observers, Stanton and Schwartz (1954), in their critical description of the ward they studied at a private hospital, suggest that its shortcomings lay mainly in drab walls and shabby furniture; they give less attention to the random arrangements of the two-, three- and four-bed dormitories and their strange relationship to the dayroom spaces, which probably contributed much to the difficulties on the ward which they describe with such acuity.

Since the ward is in an old building, this is not surprising. But on the other hand, some of the luxury buildings found in private psychiatric hospitals seem to be derived not from psychiatirc principles but from an attempt to ape general hospitals and hotels—both highly sociofugal buildings. Such attempts can at best lead to a very unsatisfactory building which cannot make full use of modern psychiatric knowledge; at worst it is a disastrous waste of money.

In the less luxurious sphere of public mental hospitals, equal confusion prevails. In one Health Department, twenty-year plans carefully relabeled but not otherwise changed, are being used for a multi-million dollar hospital. Perhaps the timeless world of the psychotic has infected those who care for him! In the last year or so a single dormitory was built to contain about 100 chronic mentally ill men, and opened with great satisfaction by the legislators, in spite of the misgivings of the medical staff.

Yet psychiatrists must bear their share of the blame, for one of them showed me with pride a geriatric building completed only this year. In it ambulant old ladies slept in dormitories of 30 to 40 beds and inhabited a huge dayroom where patients from another dormitory foregathered. The old ladies fed in a huge, glittering and hygienic restaurant. Bedridden old ladies were shut up in small single rooms, alone. Not only did this make a great nursing problem, but naturally the isolated ladies were lonely and unhappy.

Old ladies don't sleep in groups of thirty and forty. They don't commonly eat in huge garish restaurants or sit about with 70 or 80 other old ladies. If they don't enjoy doing this when well and in the community, it is unlikely that they will like it any more in an old folks' home or a mental hospital. Permanently bedridden people like company and usually prefer to be with a small group of people rather than to be alone. While some single rooms are doubtless needed, four- to six-bed dormitories with draw curtains or sliding partitions make life far more tolerable for most old ladies. Incidentally, a design of this sort would have made nursing much easier, as the work done by the Nuffield Foundation has shown.

The old classification of wards continues to be employed mechanically in new buildings: chronic, semi-chronic, untidy, disturbed, etc., are the labels used, in spite of ample evidence that it is low-grade care and bad conditions on wards of poor design that produce these invidious distinctions. Show-piece blocks for new admissions are built with good intentions, but in fact make the lot of those whose illness exceeds some arbitrary time limits even worse than it need be. Kirkbride (1880) long ago recognized the folly and cruelty of this policy and noted that, in a properly run hospital those patients who were newly admitted were always the most difficult and dangerous because they were unknown quantities. Since no one would wish to give them any but the best care, there should be but one standard for all patients—the best known to medicine. He emphasized that only in this way could true economy and Christian decency be combined. The disasters of the last 70 years in hospital psychiatry confirm his views. Unhappily, the lesson has still to be learned.

Architect and psychiatrist must work together to see that the thousands of psychotic people who have to be rehoused in the coming decade are not simply transferred to barracks where radio, brass and linoleum have been replaced by stainless steel, vinyl and television. We must earnestly persuade state and provincial governments that it is no longer possible to build hospitals that will "last forever." Indeed, it is likely that the best that we can build now will be obsolescent in 15 to 20 years' time.

We must learn to think much more like plane designers who have, I believe, as their motto "Draw 'em, build 'em, test 'em, fly 'em, scrap 'em." The human and material organization of a ward in a mental hospital is as complicated as a modern jet plane and about as expensive. Yet our ways of attacking the problems involved are very different. The aircraft designers pay the very greatest attention to their prototype. After they have built a machine of the most up-to-date design, it is tested by a team of the most skilled experts. From what they learn, the production model is built. This is finally handed over to pilots who are specially trained to understand the ways of the new plane.

No psychiatric ward has, so far as I know, ever been subjected to such rigorous and logical enquiry. The Nuffield Foundation has made a study of this sort for general hospital wards. It is ironical that where the need is so much less, the effort is greater. Let us hope that someone will have the courage and enterprise to do what is obvious and logical—build a series of psychiatric wards on functional plans and then study them carefully and thoroughly with a trained team of architects, psychiatrists, sociologists, psychologists and nurses. Then at last we may have mental hospitals which fulfill Florence Nightingale's "first requirement of a hospital: to do the sick no harm."

REFERENCES:

Hediger, H. *Studies of the psychology and behavior of captive animals in zoos and circuses.* London: Butterworth & Company, 1955.

Kirkbride, T. S. *On the construction, organization, and general arrangements of hospitals for the insane.* (2nd ed.) London, 1880.

Stanton, A. H., & Schwartz, M. *The mental hospital.* New York: Basic Books, 1954.

Weckowicz, T. E. Notes on the perceptual world of schizophrenic patients. *Mental Hospitals* (Architectural Supplement). April 1957, 8, 25.

56 Psychosocial Phenomena and Building Design

Kiyoshi Izumi

Psychosocial considerations in architectural and building design are often misunderstood, ignored, or abused. They are, however, of great depth and scope. As the validity of, and need for concern about, these phenomena are frequently questioned, the scope of architectural and building design should be reviewed in order to establish a framework for discussion.

Imagine a rectangle with a diagonal drawn from top left to bottom right (see Figure 56-1). Let the rectangle represent the field of architectural design as related to buildings, and let the diagonal line separate the human from the nonhuman con-

From *Building Research*, the journal of the Building Research Institute, 1965, 2, 9–11. Reprinted by permission of the author and publisher.

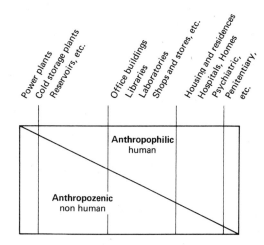

Figure 56–1. Field of design.

siderations. The term anthropophilic, meaning in part preferring human beings or attractive to man, may then be applied to the area to the upper right, and the term anthropozenic, meaning foreign to man, may be applied to the area at lower left. At the left end of the field are buildings designed primarily to contain objects, machinery, equipment and other inanimate things, with very few facilities for human beings. An extreme case would be a remotely controlled power plant, maintained electronically.

At the right end of the field are buildings used solely to contain human beings. Examples of these are nursing homes, penitentiaries, psychiatric hospitals, and housing in general, incorporating only the equipment necessary to serve the occupants. Between these extremes are a variety of building types which contain objects and human beings in varying proportions. These include libraries, laboratories, schools, stores, and offices, among others.

IMPORTANCE OF PSYCHOSOCIAL CONSIDERATIONS

The importance of psychosocial considerations increases as the buildings become more anthropophilic. For example, a toilet with privacy may be more important in a nursing home than at an airport. Importance is also determined by the number of choices available and the intensity of use. There is a difference between designing the only housing unit for Eskimos in Frobisher and a housing unit for Chicagoans in Chicago. In a buyers' market, even in the case of Chicago housing, an investor needs to concern himself with psychosocial considerations if he hopes to ensure the continued success of his venture. When there are several choices, there is less need for concern. This would not be the case if all the buildings available for a given use were to be designed exactly alike, ignoring these considerations.

The psychiatric hospital, the prison, the nursing home, homes for the aging, and in some circumstances, public housing, are comparable to the only housing unit for Eskimos in Frobisher. Because of conditions beyond the individual's control, many may be forced to live in a particular facility. The greater the degree of incarceration resulting from the conditions, the more important these limited environments become (see Figure 56-2). A person may even have to be confined to a single room and may also experience disability caused by changes in perception, as in the case of a person who is mentally ill or a child who is emotionally disturbed. There are many changes in perception. Some are slowly acquired and easily accommodated, such as myopia. However, others are related to mental and physical illnesses, experienced for very short durations under conditions of stress, and can cause severe difficulties. In such cases it is important to consider psychosocial phenomena.

AMBIGUOUS DESIGN

Such considerations are innumerable. Representative examples of situations that occur range from very complex to simple ones which seem obvious, but which in practice are often forgotten. It is not sufficient merely to recognize these situations, it is necessary to know when and where they are critical. Some familiar examples are related to ambiguity in visual perception.

Ambiguity may be created by glass doors, with or without frames, which have identically proportioned sidelights and few, if any, indications as to which is the door. Frequently, even if a person is able to find the door, he is confronted with identical push

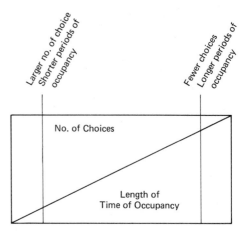

Figure 56–2. "Degree of incarceration."

and pull plates or, even more confusing, the bar type on both sides combined with concealed hinges so that he does not know which is the hinged side or in which direction the door swings. Yet these glass doors are found in airports, public buildings and institutions, even hospitals, where the users are often under stress and frequently are also experiencing changes in perception.

Another ambiguous situation occurs when what one sees appears illogical. An example is a simple, structural wood beam at the end of a cantilevered beam. Because of the nature of wood, the connection is best achieved by a tension bolt which hangs the beam from the end of the cantilever. The visual effect is that the beam is floating and insecure. Such a construction created enough concern among a church congregation that the joint had to be covered.

Another example of ambiguous design is the door hidden in a paneled wall. There is nothing wrong with this kind of design, but it should not be used in a school for emotionally disturbed children. Still another serious situation occurs when a transom over a door is designed without the horizontal mullion, so that it appears as a guillotine when the door is opened. This is particularly exaggerated when the top of the door and bottom of the transom are cut on a bevel.

Frequently, in public institutions such as hospitals, a glossy paint is selected, with the same color used for ceiling, walls, and sometimes the floor. The illusion that the walls and ceilings do not exist is further heightened by curved ceiling coves and bases. This is most disturbing in a room in which one is isolated.

② VISUAL SITUATIONS

More subtle, but still critical, visual situations occur when it is impossible to distinguish between the outdoors and indoors. This concept is thought to be based on examples of Japanese architecture where, presumably, a high quality of integration of outdoor-indoor space is achieved. The fact is that this space relationship in traditional Japanese architecture is achieved only when the translucent or opaque shoji or sliding doors are opened. There was never an invisible glass panel, as is prevalent in contemporary design, to interrupt the continuity of planes of similar material on the floor, walls, or ceiling. Even with the shoji open, one is aware of interior space as opposed to the exterior, because the opening is clearly defined. There is no illusory effect and no difficulty in ascertaining whether one is inside or outside. Again, the important consideration is to know how and when to design such a feature.

Feelings of insecurity in a tall building can result from many visual phenomena which relate to the law of gravity and create a fear that the person will fall. Other insecure situations relate to being lost, or to a feeling of being dislocated in space and time. For example, a white-out is very critical in the North, particularly during flight. Where does the sky begin and the land start? Or, where does the street end? Where does the corridor end? Where does the room end? All of these questions which come to mind in insecure physical situations are related to the question: "When do we come to the end?"

The architect, in his concern for spatial flow, spatial integration, open planning, continuity, plastic concept, and the like, must also concern himself with their psychological ramifications and realize that aesthetic concepts can be disturbing. In most situations the architectural environment is only a small segment of a person's total environment. However, at a specific time, it can be the critical environment. In this context, there are very few buildings which can be designed deliberately with ambiguity in mind. Buildings need not be dull, unexciting or uninteresting, however, and ambiguity may still be used consciously if it is in context with the purpose of the building.

When people are deprived of one of their senses of perception, such as their vision, unique situations occur. Blind persons claim that the right-angle change in direction is the most easily perceived by them, but many buildings designed for use by the blind do not reflect this.

The reaction of the blind to a building may also be illustrated by the experience of a musician who has been blind since the age of five and who has no conscious recall of sight. His world is the world of acoustics and, within it, a very narrow range related to music. A comfortable room to him is, in part, a musical room. In contrast, the writer, when influenced by LSD-25, has found a comfortable room to be a visually warm room.

Even to the sighted, what appears to be the simplest plan in a drawing can be quite complex when viewed in three dimensions. Many subdivision plans demonstrate this. A site plan may appear to be quite simple, yet, on the ground and experienced in three dimensions, the spaces between the buildings are not easily grasped visually. If other qualities of a psychosocial nature are introduced, the significance of identity is even more important. Most housing projects have a typical unit repeated, and the problem is how to give each a uniqueness so that each unit can be a home in the fullest sense of the word. In many cases, the architect does not permit this uniqueness, particularly on the exterior, and the enclosing elevations of similar units tend to negate any differences. Landscaping often increases this illusion, even in the smallest development. To many aging people, this can be very disturbing.

③ THE CONCEPT OF PRIVACY

A more complex psychosocial phenomenon relates to the concept of privacy. Architecturally, one may think of visual privacy, acoustical privacy, physical privacy and what might be called space-time privacy. The relationship of space and time is very complex. A distance covered, measured in miles or hours, is the element that provides a unique sense of privacy for some, and it is related to the sense of isolation. Isolation does not necessarily mean privacy. These phenomena are related to overcrowding and overconcentration and they become important considerations in institutional housing.

Privacy is related to cultural phenomena, to an individual's make-up, and to the task at hand. One example is the concept of privacy as it relates to toilet facilities. Public toilets consisting of a row of stalls with partitions open at top and bottom are not as efficient as fully enclosed toilets. Two toilets in separate rooms can serve as well as three divided only by standard stall partitions, and most people find the private toilet psychologically more comfortable and hence more effective. The effect of cultural influences is evident when this is compared with toilet practices in certain Oriental countries where there is no separation of toilet facilities for male and female. If there is more than one fixture, they are used concurrently.

There are many detailed design elements which visually convey the idea of privacy. An example, in addition to size and proportion, is the location and treatment of the opening between one room and another. Doors may swing in, or be solid as opposed to being glazed. A doorway may or may not have a frame. The depth and thickness of the frame, and the size, profile, and treatment of the trim around the opening may vary, and other elements may convey varying degrees of the sense of separation of space, and hence an element of privacy. The contrast of the visual elements beyond with those of the wall adjacent to the opening also affects this sense of separation.

In addition to the sense of privacy created by the design of an opening, it also affects the ease of entering a space. A situation may call for one's being able to enter unobtrusively, either to avoid disturbing people already in the room, or so the person entering will not feel on display. Often, the need for this is not recognized.

(4) SOCIAL RELATIONSHIPS

A more complex psychosocial situation which may be architecturally articulated is related to social groupings and relationships. The sociopetal concept of hospital planning is an illustration of this. This is a concept of space relationships which reflects in architectural form a psychosocial concept which is thought to be desirable in the care of the mentally ill. Such a plan, combined with some of the design elements mentioned before, can represent a high degree of architectural articulation of psychosocial phenomena.

Some persons feel that there is no need for architectural articulation of such phenomena, there being other ways to achieve psychosocial goals. This view is quite valid, as there are functional equivalents for many situations, and the problem is to establish when architectural articulation is the most effective technique.

(5) SAFETY AND WELFARE FACTORS

Many safety and welfare factors which are reflected in building codes are based on psychosocial considerations. Examples are the establishment of minimum ceiling heights and room sizes. These may be expensive, not only in the cost of construction, but also in human values which cannot be evaluated in dollars. For example, most housing codes do not permit bedrooms smaller than 80 sq ft for a single person and 120 sq ft for two, when it would often appear to be much more considerate of both the user's pocketbook and of his mental welfare to permit three spaces of 60 sq ft. The privacy provided may be the more important consideration. Another example is the prohibition of plumbing fixtures in bedrooms in a proposed housing code. This presents a considerable obstacle to any program of home care for incapacitated persons.

There is a danger in attempting to reduce these articulations of psychosocial phenomena to standards and specific guides. Any specific dimensional regulations not only become minimums, but are followed too literally even when other factors may negate the logic of a particular requirement. Many of the bad design features of hospitals are a result of an architect's simply following the standards established by various public health departments. A performance-type code and a well-written document in which the psychosocial considerations are explicitly stated for each situation are essential, if good design is to be expected.

An example of the seriousness of too rigid and piecemeal regulations stemming from the lack of a comprehensive understanding of psychosocial phenomena was seen recently in a hospital in which a minor fire resulted in loss of life. This loss was caused by toxic and hot gases. The patients who died were exposed because the smoke cut-off doors had been propped open, though they were equipped as required with closers and other fittings. This was because of convenience which stemmed from a desired functional efficiency of the area, including the psychosocial relationship of the staff to the patients. The smoke cut-off doors were placed in accordance with regulations prohibiting a floor area of more than a certain size without provision for horizontal fire and smoke separation. The area limitations presumably were based not only on certain technical considerations related to fire fighting, fire behavior, combustible contents, and other factors, but also on certain psychosocial considerations of occupancy and human behavior under emergency conditions. The location of these fire cut-off doors did not coincide with the function of the area. A greater understanding of psychosocial aspects is essential if this kind of disaster is to be minimized.

In the area of architectural articulation of psychosocial phenomena, there are literally thousands of conditions which have significant long-range implications. Documentation is essential, and there is a great need for everyone involved to participate in the necessary research. However, no attempt should be made to codify too stringently and in too much detail, as this is one of the major limitations to good and imaginative design. It is more desirable for everyone to become more aware of these considerations, and to understand the reasons for them, than for a few to become

experts. The architect and designer, in particular, must recognize that each human being perceives his environment differently and that some of the designer's aesthetic perceptions do not exist in others. Unlike the other arts, the art of architecture is seldom self-generated and is always an imposition. Compared to the other arts, it is more difficult to avoid architectural art. A major difficulty, and hence the reason for the need for documentation, is the fact that the designer deals with very subjective matters. Comfort, distress, elation, and other emotional and intellectual experiences are very personal, and the best designs only result from the understanding of many related considerations.

57 Factors which Determine Hospital Design

Roslyn Lindheim

There is a story attributed to Freud in which he tells of the famous surgeon whose students, during an autopsy, exclaimed over arteries, "as thick and hard as ropes . . . no wonder he died." "But gentlemen," the surgeon remonstrated, "you must remember that he was alive until yesterday." Hospitals with all their ills continue to survive and prosper. For one thing, many ailments are annoying but not crucial, while for those that might be fatal, some expedient solution is eventually devised. This fact so far has allowed those involved in the design of hospitals "to be let off the hook"—clients as well as architects because they too bear the responsibility for both good and bad hospitals.

A hospital is one of the most complex contemporary planning and design areas. It is in many ways a microcosm of the larger social context of which it is a part. It reflects within its own organization many of the

From the *American Journal of Public Health*, 1966, **56**, No. 10, 1668–1675. Reprinted by permission of the author and publisher.

larger unsolved complexities of urban life as a whole. The hospital client is multi-headed with many, often contradictory, goals. The patients come from varying socioeconomic groups and their evaluation of their surroundings is as vastly different as the culture and subcultures they come from. As different as are the hospital users so also are the biases of the medical and paramedical staff. The hospital is one of the building forms most resistant to change. The large capital outlays involved make hospital boards reluctant to scrap the old, and administrators, doctors, and architects fearful of recommending the new.

I wish to outline some of the factors which influence hospital design—some of the trends which are generating new needs and demanding new spatial solutions. And I would like also to discuss alternate and perhaps more effective ways of arriving at design decisions than are currently being practiced. It is the decisions made prior to the time that the architect sets pencil to paper which most affect the physical form.

Many obvious factors go into the determination of the design of a hospital—the technology, the requirements of medical practice, the concepts of organization, the standard of living, and the image of the hospital. More specifically and pertaining to an individual project the architect considers the site, orientation, building codes, costs, materials to be used, the ease of expansion, the relationship of the component parts. He must decide whether it is to be vertical or horizontal, the approach to the hospital, the view, the segregation of different types of traffic, the methods of moving goods and materials, to mention but a few of the necessary design considerations.

GOALS

Basic to every design decision is the need for clearly defined goals and objectives. A hospital designed primarily for teaching purposes requires a different type of plant than one where no teaching is done. An institution whose aim is to provide diagnostic services for an entire community will require a different facility from one which is to be devoted entirely to bed patients.

Sizes of hospitals vary, scope of service varies, the availability of personnel varies. Each hospital has its own design problem and the success or failure of that design can only be evaluated in terms of how the specific solution satisfies the particular objectives it sets out to accomplish.

Today's needs are forcing us to reanalyze many of our hospital ideas. New methods of diagnosis and care, changing patterns of illness, the increase in the number of geriatric patients, the growth of hospital insurance, new forms of medical organization, progressive patient care, to mention but a few, are placing new demands on our hospital buildings. Changes in medical care concepts and requirements are occurring at accelerated tempos. A building designed to satisfy one set of medical requirements becomes functionally obsolete while still structurally sound. Still worse is the fact that a hospital building takes about a year to plan and two years to build (minimally). In this three-year period the changes in medical practice and organization of the hospital may make the brand new hospital functionally obsolete even as it opens its doors.

Analytic and educated answers to the questions: who is to be served; what type of service is to be offered; what are the physical requirements for this service; how shall the service be organized; what is the prognosis for future developments; these are the best guards against premature obsolescence.

Usually because of force of habit the first question we ask of a hospital client is "how many beds" as somehow the clue to solving the remaining problems. The key to a hospital may well be how many ambulant patients it will serve. The answers to the questions: how many beds; how many ambulant patients; what types and scope of service; what you will do; establish the prime factor affecting hospital design, namely, the size. Once this is established the alternate methods for organizing service can be explored; decisions as to the size, scope, and method of organization of the service are prerequisites for planning. I cannot emphasize enough that the plan of operation, the plan of the physical facility, and the goals of the institution are totally interlocked. Design is usually considered to be the organization of the physical space. Design of the physical space and design of the methods of operation are two sides of the same coin and both meaningless unless associated with a specific goal. For example, consider a hospital organization like that of the Kaiser Health Plan on the west coast, which has a chain of 16 or so hospitals.

They have designed a food service system which requires no cooking on the premises. As a consequence of this concept, the kitchen facilities of the individual hospitals are small and are used only for putting the heat back in the food and assembling the trays. The physical form of the kitchen is a part of the design of the food system. The comparatively small area is adequate under the Kaiser Hospitals' food service plan. However, if the same spatial arrangements were to be copied for another hospital which required cooking on the premises, they would be totally inadequate.

If the function of the kitchen is to reheat and assemble food, the form will be one thing; if the function is to prepare and cook the food, the form will be something else. This is another way of saying the form must fit the function.

To date, the purpose of a hospital has been to isolate the sick from the community. This was true of the mental institutions built in the country—the now obsolete TB hospitals—as well as the city hospitals. They were all designed as fortresses.

The image of the hospital before 1880 was "an alms house, a place for the needy and the poor." A place "not to live in but to die in." The flophouse was the prototype of the ward. The goal was to take people away from society and let them die. With the influence of Florence Nightingale the image of the hospital as a place to die in was slowly transformed into the image of a place with nursing care. In her words, the "place should do no harm to the patient." The nursing hospital which should do no harm developed slowly into a hospital whose goal was to do some good. A complex array of technical services and equipment was added to the nursing center. The demands on the diagnostic and therapeutic departments of the hospital to be both expendable

and have proximity to each other—to serve both the bed patient and the ambulant patient—these, coupled with the technological developments of the elevator and air-conditioning, made possible the hospital form so common today—the large diagnostic base topped by the nursing tower. The motel room with private bath has become the prototype of the hospital bedroom.

Today there is a new hospital goal. You in the health field talk of the hospital as a dynamic force for health education and for preventive medicine as well as a place for curing the sick. The problem becomes how to weave the hospital into the surrounding urban fabric.

Many people believe that a change in the geometric form of a building is the solution to new problems. That somehow, if the round or the hexagonal shape is used, it comes closer to solving the needs of the new goals and the new problems. I do not believe it makes any difference if the nursing tower is round or square or rectangular or kidney-shaped. Of course it looks different, but just changing the shape of a building in no way alters the form of the organization. It harks back to the same model. It would still be referred to by the English journals as "a matchbox on a muffin." New forms are not generated by new geometry, but rather by new forms of spatial organization generally made possible by the advent of new technology. Spatial solutions to social processes develop over long periods of years and take on certain characteristic forms. A hospital begins to look a certain way; so does a school, a factory, or a radiology department. Spatial patterns have a very strong hold on thinking and on attitudes. They become habitual and are etched into the mind of the user. Solutions which are developed in response to specific needs are the exception rather than the rule.

Habits are formed in relation to existing activities. Habits, by definition, lag behind new technology. It is extremely difficult for an architect to free himself from these preconceived images and to approach a problem from an analytic point of view. It is even harder to convince a client who has been used to working in one set of spaces that there are alternative and possibly better possibilities of spatial organization and arrangement, unless an architect can really demonstrate a knowledge of his activities and problems as well as alternative methods to solve them.

ROLE OF THE ARCHITECT

There is considerable ambiguity in people's minds as to the exact role of the architect. There are some who believe that the best hospital plant will be developed if all of the preliminary decisions are made before the architect arrives on the scene, and that the architect should be provided with room sizes, even floor plans of departments, and that his function is to connect these elements, select the materials of construction and make the building look "nice." The end result of such an approach, even when scrupulously executed, often in no way resembles the image in the client's mind. The ability to visualize space and the movement of persons and materials within this space requires a specific type of skill and training not ordinarily available to doctors, nurses, or administrators, and the basic decisions may be wrong in the first place.

Others, and I include myself among them, believe that the architect has a more fundamental part to play in developing the hospital structure. But to make the maximum contribution in this development he requires an understanding of the objective, goals, and nature of the hospital organization—from the most mundane processes and procedures to the understanding of the most effective interrelationship of the respective parts.

Many architectural firms give a considerable amount of time to independent study of functional needs and requirements before arriving at their design decisions. Observations are made of how things work. Doctors, technicians, nurses, administrators, and other personnel are consulted about how they do things and how they think these things could be done in a better manner. The architect who has designed a number of hospitals acquires knowledge of the hospital organization. But even with conscientious effort, there are obvious limitations to the validity of the results obtained by such

methods. The answers an architect obtains by interviewing personnel about their needs and requirements are colored by both the background and scope of those being questioned. This does not mean that preferences and opinions are unimportant—they are very important—but a means has to be developed whereby opinions can be objectively assessed. Many a design decision has been reached on the basis of the statement "it will produce greater functional efficiency" without any basis for determining whether this statement is really true.

The problem that faces us is that visual patterns persist like vestigial characteristics long after their functional needs have changed. Vested interests in ideas are hard to eradicate. They are used as building directives. We have new goals, but old images. We need to find new ways to study the problems of the hospital—new ways to observe and record all the facets of these organizations—new methods of identifying the problems—of studying the processes—of freeing ourselves from preconceptions as to how the spaces should be arranged and of approaching the problem analytically. We must isolate prejudice from genuine and valid ideas.

STUDY OF A RADIOLOGY DEPARTMENT

We have just concluded the first phase of a research study of the organization of a diagnostic radiology department. This study was sponsored by the U. S. Public Health Service. I would like to report on this work because as a part of this study we "uncoupled the system of radiology" to allow for alternate spatial design decisions. Radiology was selected for study because it provided in capsule form many of the problems encountered in the design of other hospital departments. Its primary function is to render service, and consequently its operating efficiency ranks high as a basic criterion. It is undergoing constant technical change and a flexible design approach is required. It is utilized by patients in all states of sickness and health—the ambulant, the bed patient, the chronic patient, and both inpatients and outpatients. Most of the current guides to planning are designed by x-ray companies—the makers of the equipment used—whose advice is influenced by their own particular equipment rather than by the needs of a key department in the total hospital. Major capital outlay in terms of plant and equipment is required. There is a strong preconceived idea that a radiology department always has to be next to surgery, emergency, and laboratory facilities, as well as be accessible to both outpatients and inpatients. There is never enough room to accommodate radiology, along with everything else, in central priority location and still maintain flexibility and expansion potential.

In this study we selected three radiology departments to use as our experimental laboratories: one in a typical community hospital, one in a university hospital, and one in a hospital which operated a large prepayment plan. Our reason for choosing three vastly different types of departments was to see if there were indeed common denominators to the system of diagnostic radiology.

I use the word "system" advisedly because our bias was to approach the problem of analyzing diagnostic radiology from a systems point of view. I wish there were an alternate word which says the same thing. "Systems" has been both overworked and misused, but I have not come up with another one, so instead I shall quote Lewis Carroll and then define systems.

> "When I use a word," Humpty Dumpty said, in a rather scornful tone, "it means just what I choose it to mean, neither more nor less." "The question is," said Alice, "whether you can make words mean so many different things." "The question is," said Humpty Dumpty, "which is to be master, that is all."

By a systems approach I mean more a state of mind than any specific amalgam of mathematical, scientific, or technological methods. A system is a set of interrelated needs and activities linked together to accomplish a desired end. We approached the study of the activity system, radiology, by asking the questions—what is the desired end or function of the system—what are the sets of interrelated needs and activities which make up the system—what are the links in the system or the structure of the system—how are they interrelated—how are the parts or the subsystems put together? We further looked at a system as a method for the preliminary ordering of facts awaiting description, interpolation, and analysis. Any aspect of health must be looked at from an over-all view because the solution to the individual problem might lie not within the hospital itself but in the relationship to the greater health community.

Our first step was to uncouple or separate the various subsystems or sets that make up the total radiology system and then to identify those sets which required spatial proximity.

The sets of the system of radiology which required spatial proximity were:

1. The patient, the machine, and someone to both help the patient and run the machine (the technician) must come together. There is no way of taking a picture with the patient in one location and the machine in another; there has to be direct contact. The machines can be operated remotely, but someone must still help the patient on and off the machine.

2. The film and the film-processing must come into contact. If a film is to be developed, there is no way of developing it remotely. There are numerous alternate ways of developing film (Polaroid, manually, automatically), but contact must still be made between the film and the developing agent.

3. The radiologist in order to make a diagnosis needs the x-ray image of the patient as well as previous images and other pertinent information. He can get this image in a number of ways, but the image is essential as is previous information.

These then became the sets which required spatial proximity. Each of these sets had a series of secondary needs which demanded spatial solutions. Thus when a patient, a machine, and a technician were brought together, the patient needed toilet facilities, a place to dress and undress (if he was an outpatient), and so forth. The machine required a room with a lead lining (or the scatter of x-rays would become damaging), control booths to protect the technician, and space for the machine requirements (transformers, generators, tube stands), and so forth. The film and the film-processing unit required their own sets of spaces depending on the method of processing, and the radiologist in turn had to have his own set of space requirements for viewing the image.

If these were the only needs which had to be satisfied by spatial proximity, then by implication the other subsystems necessary to functionally satisfy the requirements of radiology did not demand spatial proximity to one another.

We found various forms of links, and linkages used to connect different activities are internally related to technological developments. It is now common practice to have verbal messages transmitted over intercom and telephone or written messages transmitted by teletype or pneumatic tube. Dumbwaiters, conveyors, and elevators are commonly used to transport material objects of varying sizes. All of these ways of communicating messages and materials have modified the physical requirements for proximity between activities. Now there is a new technological development, closed-circuit television, which could become an additional and very important new communication vehicle. The possibility of transmitting picture images through space gives increasing freedom for radiological spatial organization. An examination of the requirements necessary to link together the activities of radiology shows the following. The processing of the film does not require a location next to the diagnostic rooms. What is required is that a method of transporting the exposed film to the processing room be available. In some cases locating it directly adjacent will be the best solution. But it is also possible that, in certain circumstances, the processing may be on one floor and the diagnostic machines on another, and the connection between the two may be by means of dumbwaiter or other vertical conveyance.

The filing system certainly does not have to have physical proximity to the diagnostic rooms or the radiologist. All that is impor-

tant is that a method be developed whereby the image of the old films be at the required place at the declared time. In a like manner it is not an essential part of the system to locate the radiologist in close proximity to either the diagnostic rooms or the processing unit. The image of the developed film or the fluoroscopic image could be transmitted over closed-circuit television to a radiologist located in another part of the building or even in another building. Already image intensifiers and television are integral parts of fluoroscopy rooms. The video taping of fluoroscopic images is a real technical possibility. Since there is no film to develop, instant playback is possible.

From all of this we can see that uncoupling allows us to free ourselves from many of the preconceptions that freeze design decision. It does not follow from this method of analysis that one or another design decision is the only way. For example, our study of radiology in no way was intended to imply that a centralized radiology department is necessarily wrong or a decentralized radiology is necessarily right. It would depend on the department's size and relationship to other aspects of the hospital and the community.

The uncoupling of the hospital systems is already occurring on many fronts. Progressive patient care is an example. The patient system is no longer regarded as monolithic either organizationally or spatially. An acutely ill patient is placed in intensive care. A less sick patient is accommodated in less high-power facilities. The patient system includes the patient at home, the patient convalescing, the patient undergoing diagnostic procedures. It includes the ambulant as well as the bed patient.

Another example of uncoupling can be found in the industrial base of the hospital where food, laundry, and aspects of central supply are being provided away from the hospital site, resulting in changes in spatial form. It is technologically feasible to have a data center located in a city equipped with all information pertaining to the health of an individual or a family. Such information could be available at a moment's notice for use at all levels of a health complex. It also is technologically possible to have a doctor's paging system locate him at any point in a city and put him directly in contact with any health facility.

The acutely ill may be housed in a high-pressured facility designed with maximum flexibility to respond to changing mechanical and spatial needs. The less acutely sick, the old, the convalescent may well be placed in a totally different facility more intimately connected to a patient's normal environment.

I have no single prototype for the new hospital. I think there will be many. Methods of communication are such that we can begin to think of the hospital as spreading over the city with parts spatially separated but still functionally linked.

We will only find the right fit between our new medical needs, our social goals, our technological potential, if we approach the design of hospitals considering them as parts of a larger health system rather than as isolated buildings. Only by systematically uncoupling hospital spatial systems can we hope to break up the image blockade and allow ourselves to find alternative and perhaps better design possibilities.

REFERENCES:

Block, L. Hospital profiles: A decade of change, 1953–1962. *Modern Hospital,* 1964, **102,** 92–101.

Brown, W. T. Hospitals—designing the medical community. *Journal of the Royal Institute of British Architects,* February 1965.

Coughlin, Isard, & Schneider. *The activity structure and transportation requirements of a major university hospital.* Regional Science Institute, GPO Box 8776, Philadelphia, January 1964.

Cowan, P. Hospital in towns: Location and siting. *Architectural Review,* June 1965.

Falk, I. S. Group practice is pattern for the future. *Modern Hospital,* September 1963.

Greer, S. *The emerging city.* New York: The Free Press, 1962.

Ittelson, W. *Environmental psychology and architectural planning.* Presented at American Hospital Association Conference on Hospital Planning. New York: December 1964.

Jacobs, R. H. The architects' guide to surgical infection. *Journal of the American Institute of Architects,* November 1962.

Lindheim, R. The ambulant patient comes of age. *Modern Hospital,* March 1954.

Lubin, Drosnes, & Reed. The application of computer graphics to patient origin study techniques. *Public Health Reports,* January 1965.

Morss, S. Hospital design and construction. *Hospitals,* April 1965.

Pelletier, R. Search for a therapeutic environment. *Hospitals,* February 1965.

Research in community health. PHS Publ. No. 1225. Washington, D.C.: Government Printing Office, July 1964.

Rosenthal, F. D. The demand for general hospital facilities. *Hospital Monograph Serial No. 14,* Chicago: American Hospital Association, 1964.

Webber, M. *The urban place and the nonplace urban realm: Exploration into urban structure.* Philadelphia: University of Pennsylvania Press, 1964.

58 A Conceptual Framework for Hospital Planning

J. J. Souder, W. E. Clark, J. I. Elkind, and M. B. Brown

What is the role of architecture in our society? Is it art, or the engineering of shelter? How are the buildings of our time molded? What are the sources and requirements that determine the form and substance of hospital architecture? What rules are applied or what criteria weighed to decide plan arrangements, utilization, expression, character, or whether to build at all? Obviously, there are some satisfactory answers to these questions; otherwise the recurring patterns that we see in hospital design throughout the nation and over long periods of time could not exist.

Nevertheless, there are no explicit theories of hospital planning that serve to guide the process and to provide answers to the questions posed. You may ask, "Is such a theory either possible or desirable?" Architecture and planning are obviously arts more than sciences, and theories are generally the province of the sciences. Hospital planners are, after all, practical people making practical decisions. The practical decisions of our world are based on experience and common sense, or on intuition, if they are not grounded in significant theories.

From J. J. Souder, W. E. Clark, J. I. Elkind, M. B. Brown, *Planning for Hospitals: A Systems Approach Using Computer-Aided Techniques.* Chicago: American Hospital Association, 1964, pp. 31–37. Reprinted by permission of the authors and publisher.

The difficulties arise in a planning problem when new conditions or requirements have no parallel in past experience, or when a new factor makes the traditional solution inappropriate. This is indeed often the case in contemporary hospital architecture because changing and broadened concepts of patient care and highly specialized medical practices create demands for facilities that were unknown in the hospitals of the past. Further, the progress in building construction, especially in mechanical equipment systems for buildings (e.g., conveyor systems, air conditioning), allows a wider variety in forms of buildings to accommodate specific needs. All these complications suggest that some statement of guiding principles should be useful in planning, even though a full theory is not possible at present (or perhaps ever).

In this paper an attempt is made to outline portions of a conceptual framework for hospital planning and architecture. This framework is nothing more than a suggestion of lines of thoughts to be followed or hypotheses to be examined. It is only through a continuing process of formulating such hypotheses, checking them against the real world of experience, and reaching conclusions or alternative hypotheses that any useful body of hospital planning theory can ever be established. With this purpose in mind, let us proceed to examine: (1) an idealized model of the planning process; (2) the sources of information and decisions; (3) the functions of the architecture; and (4) some propositions that can be used as the elements of our framework for planning.

A MODEL OF THE PLANNING PROCESS

The process of planning a hospital involves the skills and experience of architects, administrators, and consultants in medicine and many allied fields. The success of the resulting hospital depends on the fusion of many dissimilar and complicated requirements into an organizational and operational pattern and a facility arrangement that provides reasonable satisfaction of a variety of important needs. In view of the variety of requirements and the number of partici-

pants, any attempt at abstracting and modeling this creative process may seem rash. Nevertheless, a common pattern or model can be found in the varied approaches and solutions. Such a model is advanced here as one part of a framework for hospital planning. The model is also discussed later in this report as the operational basis for a computer-oriented method of hospital planning.

It is useful and instructive to consider the planning process as having three distinct phases. These may be called:

Investigation
Synthesis
Evaluation

The first phase, *investigation*, involves acquiring and digesting information on requirements for functions of the hospital, prior successful solutions to problems, available materials and equipment, budget limitations, site limitations, and many other considerations. The second phase, *synthesis*, is the part normally considered as the creative effort. It involves the invention or discovery of physical arrangements and organizational and operational patterns to satisfy the requirements of the facility. The third phase, that of *evaluation*, might alternatively be called the decision process. It involves choosing between physical arrangements or operational patterns that have been synthesized, and deciding whether at any given point in the planning effort the relevant requirements have been satisfied.

It should be readily apparent that the model suggested above is idealized. Planning on one aspect of the hospital may be in the synthesis stage, while another is still in the investigation stage, and still another may have been satisfactorily consummated. This point leads to an important feature of the model—it represents an iterative process. This iterative aspect is illustrated in Figure 58-1, where the three phases are shown as separate blocks in a flow diagram of the planning process. Note the feedback loops. These suggest the disruption of creative *synthesis* for further *investigation*, the negative *evaluation* of the current scheme leading to further *synthesis*, and the negative

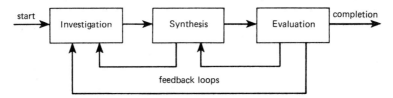

Figure 58–1. Diagram of a simple model of the planning process.

evaluation that leads to further *investigation* and *synthesis*.

Each phase of this process is dependent on the preceding phase. That is, the synthesis of organizational or physical arrangements to meet the needs of the hospital is assured only by providing enough information in the investigation phase to identify all relevant requirements and constraints. Similarly, the usefulness of the evaluation phase depends on the number and range of alternatives presented from the synthesis.

INFORMATION SOURCES AND DECISION GROUPS

It is obvious that, at least in the long run, society is the client or consumer of hospital planning. Various elements of society have a part in setting requirements for, utilizing, and paying for hospitals. An attempt to identify the information sources and decision groups by means of a description of the social organization and functional groupings in the hospital world should be useful in furthering a framework for planning.

Social Organization

A general theory of social organization has been formulated by Talcott Parsons (1958, 1959a, 1959b). He structures the organizations of our society into social units with three distinct levels: technical, managerial, and institutional. If we apply this structuring to the hospital situation we find at the *technical* level nursing, medical, and paramedical groups; at the *managerial* level administrative and executive officers; and at the *institutional* level the boards of directors and trustees. Essentially then, the technical level represents a direct working operation while the managerial level represents a control and service function. The institutional

level serves to relate the other levels of the specific organization to a larger society by explaining their operations, raising and handling funds for their support, shielding them, and guiding them insofar as broad objectives of community health care are involved. This function of the institutional level as intermediary between the community at large and the administrative and medical managerial levels is generally performed by "lay" boards of directors to provide perspective and generality, and to enhance communication with other segments of society.

An important point noted by Parsons is that the organizational structure is not simply a line-type chain of command; instead, particular areas of authority and independence of action are inherent at each level. For example, matters of technical substance and professional ethics are determined at the technical level and are subject to veto at the managerial and institutional levels only for reasons of incompatibility with overall goals of the organization. Similarly, the executive at the managerial level does not simply carry out the instructions of the next higher echelon, but instead independently "manages," subject only to policy decisions and goals established for his guidance.

Analysis of this concept of organizational structure can help identify the guiding forces for the establishment and operation of hospitals and the appropriate sources for various kinds of planning information. Thus, for questions of the relation of the hospital to other community facilities, of the type and extent of services to be provided, of long-range planning goals, and of the relation of the facility to its community physical environment, the institutional level is an appropriate source. For questions of daily operational procedures, staffing, balance between functions, and physical environment needs for staff satisfaction, the managerial level is appropriate. For detailed information on procedures, equipment and arrangements for patient care and supporting functions, the technical level is appropriate. This is not to say that other levels do not have legitimate interests in any specific topic, but rather that their interests are secondary to those noted.

Now, the foregoing suggests the social elements or levels having cognizance of particular areas of hospital operation. These are viewed as primary sources of information on hospital planning needs and as decision makers. It is obvious, however, that not all of these levels of the hospital social organization are actually accommodated in the hospital's physical facilities. In particular, the institutional level does not occupy space in the actual physical plant (except for minor office and board room facilities). Those parts of the social organization that do occupy the hospital are important to the planner in another way besides their usefulness as direct information and decision sources. To consider that part of the hospital social organization that physically occupies the buildings, it is convenient to refer to a *hospital system*.

Systems and Subsystems

The hospital system includes not only the part of the social organization that occupies the physical facilities, but also the facilities and other resources, and the patients who are the input and output of the system. Thus we might say that the hospital system includes the continuously active (lower) levels of the hospital social organization and their environment.[1]

The concept of systems and subsystems is a convenient frame of reference for our con-

[1] It is interesting to note, in parallel, that the next higher level of the organizational pattern, the institutional level, can be said to coexist, together with the institutional levels of other social organizations, in a common larger environment—the community. Thus the hospital system can be considered as a subsystem of a larger community system, which is part of a still larger system, etc.

sideration of hospital problems. The various services in a hospital can be defined as subsystems. Further, a separate subsystem can be defined that is concerned solely with the communication between elements of the hospital.

OBJECTIVES FOR THE HOSPITAL FACILITIES

A model of the planning process in general and some suggestions as to the nature of the client for hospital planning have been advanced. It remains, now, to discuss the functions that the architecture is expected to provide and to consider ways of assessing the performance of these functions or of the operations they shelter.

Functions

One important concept is the notion of the *functions* of the hospital facility. By functions is meant the broad purposes served, rather than the individual patient care operations. It appears useful to consider three kinds of functions which one may label *utility, amenity,* and *expression*. Now, what do we mean when we speak of utility, amenity, and expression as functions of the facility? These are common words with many shades of definition. For present purposes, let us assume a restricted definition for each function as follows:

Utility—The functioning of the hospital in providing health care services to its community.

Amenity—The satisfaction of individual or personal requirements of the people working and staying in the hospital, as distinct from the health care objectives of the hospital.

Expression—The symbolic function of the hospital facility as a public institution and a haven for the ill of the community; in other words, the impact of the hospital facility on the community at large, as distinct from its patients and personnel. In this sense, the esthetic spirit of elegance and quiet contemplation of an art museum, the air of sophistication or power (the corporate image) reflected in a Park Avenue headquarters building, and the suggestion of low overhead cost in the plain brick of a discount store are manifestations of design for expression.

These are still uncomfortably abstract notions. Several examples may serve to pin down the definitions that are sought after. The provision of special rooms, equipment, and a clean environment for surgery is an example of the utility function of the facility. As an example of the amenity function, consider the provision of an attractive and comfortable working environment for the skilled personnel that are a vital part of the hospital. Obviously, planning and design features that contribute to a pleasurable and comfortable working environment can also influence the ease of work performance; thus, an overlap between utility and amenity functions occurs to some extent. Accommodations for the public, the sense of repose in the environment, and the esthetic character of the hospital building and site enabling people to recognize it as a community institution are examples of expression.

In a slightly different sense we might say that utility relates to the hospital's main technical objective of patient care, amenity relates to individual satisfactions, and expression relates to the symbolic values of the hospital complex.

Properties and Measures

These notions of utility, amenity and expression are difficult to handle and far too general to be useful by themselves. There are, however, a number of specific requirements for any hospital facility, and it is useful to classify some of these as properties of the three general functions, as follows:

Some properties of utility:
    space sufficient for equipment, personnel
    internal arrangement of spaces
    communication between related spaces
    control of movement
    control of environment

Some properties of amenity:
    safety and health protection
    personal comfort
    ease of access and movement
    provision for privacy and relaxation
Some properties of expression:
    esthetic value
    conformity
    (advertising value)

The idea that a set of properties characterize architecture suggests that assessment of those properties is a way of answering the questions: How do we measure utility? amenity? expression? The concept of measurement is central to the theories of the sciences, and the ideas that have been evolved are useful for our present purpose.[2] One basic concept is that we measure the properties of things—the thickness of a beam, the floor area of a room, or the comfort of an office—rather than the *things* themselves. A subtle distinction is necessary at this point. We compare our measure, a yardstick, to the object we call a "beam" to assess directly the property of thickness. Floor area is a property determined from measurements with our yardstick of the fundamental properties of length and width of the room. In these cases we are actually measuring the property of interest, and we thus speak of the *measure* of thickness. However, in the case of comfort we have no way to measure the property directly. The best we can do is to identify one or more indirect measures—operationally defined notions such as the air temperature and humidity, noise level, brightness contrast—which are assumed to specify the theoretical, immeasurable property we term comfort. Stevens (1951) and Torgerson (1958) differentiate these indirect measures by calling them *indicants*.

We must, then, remember that for some of the properties of architecture we can expect to find direct measures that relate the concepts to data from the real world,

[2] Excellent discussions of the concepts and problems of measurement are found in Stevens (1951), Torgerson (1958) and Lazarsfeld (1959).

while for other properties we must be presently satisfied if we can come up with the indirect measures, rooted in the real world, which we have reason to believe are related to the theoretical notions. The staff manhours per day of interdepartmental travel in a hospital is thus a direct measure of that property called "relation between spaces." In contrast, the time in transit is only an indirect measure of the comfort of patients being transported in the hospital, and we have no direct measure. At the extreme, we are not even sure we can suggest indirect measures for the property called esthetic value.

Problem Solving

In a planning problem, as in a problem in mathematics, a solution represents a selection of values for the factors, or variables, involved. If there are only a few variables and these operate independently of one another, it is usually possible to vary them one at a time and, after a few trials, to decide in which direction to proceed for a "best," or optimum, solution. However, if there are many factors, and particularly if these are not all independent of one another —that is, if changes in one cause changes in another—it is usually not possible to arrive at an optimum solution by varying one at a time. One must either look at all possible combinations of values of all the factors, a prohibitively time-consuming and expensive task, or one must find other clues to help decide what combinations of factors should be investigated.

It is at this point that the planning practitioner can fall back on his experience and intuition as a guide. But perhaps there is another way of deciding where, in the tangle of relevant factors, to start searching for a good solution. Consider the factors themselves. They can be catalogued into three groups:

a. *Variables* that can take on measurable values along objective scales such as length or cost, or along subjective scales such as "comfortableness"

b. *Constraints* that have only two relevant values—acceptable and unacceptable

c. *As yet unmeasured quantities* such as esthetic value.

Now the search for good solutions is simplified somewhat. For the immeasurables, there is no other recourse but to accept the judgments of experienced practitioners. The constraints enter the problem-solving process only to indicate what areas of solution are acceptable, and the reduced set of remaining variables can now be explored for good solutions.

Assessment of Performance

The next concept we need consider is that of a measure of effectiveness. We have noted that an architectural function, such as utility, is measured in terms of a number of properties. Thus, a combination of values of these various properties can lead to a value of the total function, utility, so long as we can use a common measure for those properties. For example, if each of the properties of utility could be expressed in terms of dollar costs of construction or operation, then one measure for utility could be total dollar cost. Likewise, if all of the properties of amenity could be measured in terms of job tenure (which is unlikely), amenity might be measured by personnel turnover rate.

The important point is that a single measure is possible only if it can be used for all properties of interest. It is apparent, then, that a single measure of the "goodness" of architecture would be possible only if such disparate properties as internal arrangement and esthetic value were measurable in common terms. However—and this is important —if one function of the architecture, say expression, were of dominant importance in a particular social context, then a measure for expression could be used as a primary guide in design. Otherwise the three functions must be considered separately.

Optimization

One might say that a design solution for a building complex was *optimum* if all properties of interest were measurable in common terms and the solution resulted in a better value for this common measure than any other possible solution. An example that comes to mind is an uninhabited storage warehouse at a remote industrial site. The architectural function utility is important; amenity and expression are not. All relevant properties can probably be measured in terms of construction and maintenance costs.

Obviously it is not meaningful to talk of optimizing a hospital design in this sense; the architectural functions utility, amenity and expression are all of acknowledged relevance, and no universal measure is available that enables us to balance the provisions for these three disparate functions. It is possible, of course, to consider *suboptimization*— that is, to optimize one or more parts of the whole, each of which can be evaluated in terms of a single measure. Suboptimization of each part does not necessarily lead to an optimum solution for the whole, however.

A FRAMEWORK FOR HOSPITAL PLANNING

In the world of science and technology, theories often lead to computational procedures or design methods. For example, abstract theories of the strength of materials, or of column behavior, lead to practical techniques for designing trusses and determining column sizes for buildings. Our hope in this portion of the project work is to formulate an abstract outline or conceptual framework in which practical planning methods can be grounded. The analogy is far from complete because our conceptual framework is not neat, precise, and as thoroughly validated as the theories of materials and structures. The best we can do is to state rather loose and general hypotheses inferred from knowledge and observations of the art of planning. Imprecise and tentative as they are, however, these hypotheses should be amenable to some experimental corroboration. Further, even in their present form they provide a basis for new techniques of computer-aided planning.

The framework for planning we describe here is, as noted earlier, only a set of hypotheses to be examined. This set of hypotheses is founded on two assumptions or axioms:

a. The hospital planning process is basically an orderly, rational endeavor.

b. The planning process can be considered as a three-phase process of investigation, synthesis and evaluation.

The hypotheses that follow are labeled as propositions; that is, they are unproven statements that should be susceptible to proof at some future time, but that are an adequate basis for some conditional statements in the meantime.

Proposition 1: Architecture and operational patterns are conceived to satisfy requirements specified by various elements of social organizations. An item of architecture and an operational pattern may accommodate one, or several, levels of a particular social organization. The requirements are not entirely imposed by the particular level, or levels, accommodated, but rather by all levels.

Proposition 2: The different levels of an organization differ in the generality of their concern with the organization's activities, the technical level having the most detailed responsibilities and the institutional level the most general responsibilities. The functions of architecture range, in a parallel way, from the most detailed, utility, to the most general, expression. Partly as a consequence of this parallelism, the requirements for utility are most appropriately developed, in general, at the technical level, the requirements for amenity at the managerial level, and the requirements for expression at the institutional level.

Proposition 3: Some, but probably not all, major aspects of the performance of a hospital care system are measurable, either in objective terms or along subjective scales.

Proposition 4: Many important aspects of the performance of a hospital care system are functions of the arrangement of physical resources and of operational patterns. Thus, the performance can be affected by planning choices. Further, alternative planning choices can be evaluated in terms of their anticipated effects on the hospital system performance.

Proposition 5: If the various requirements for any one function (e.g., that of utility) can all be related or measured in common terms, then the performance of that function can be expressed by a single composite criterion, and suboptimization of the solution may be possible with respect to that one function. The requirements and measures of the three functions, utility, amenity and expression, are not mutually interrelatable in common terms, however, and thus no over-all optimization of a solution to the hospital planning problem is possible, in the mathematical sense.

Proposition 6: The utility, amenity and expression functions, in that order, represent increasing levels of abstraction and generality. The properties of the utility function appear to be directly measurable, for the most part, and in objective terms. The properties of the amenity function can be measured only in subjective terms, for the most part. Only a few aspects of the expression function are measurable even in subjective terms. Therefore, an approach to hospital planning might consist in establishing the broad requirements for and the desired level of provision of, first, expression, then amenity, and finally, utility. In this way the less well defined and less specific requirements could serve as constraints on the solution of the planning problem, rather than being included as explicit variables to be investigated. The danger in such an approach is that establishment of too rigid or ill-chosen requirements for expression and amenity may actually inhibit the development of appropriate designs for the utility function. This is, of course, the lesson learned from past periods of eclecticism in architecture.

Proposition 7: Increased access to background data on hospital operational patterns should result in improved effectiveness of the planning process. As an example, the use of detailed data on commerce patterns in typical hospitals as a starting point from which to project anticipated operational patterns in proposed hospitals appears likely to improve the realism and precision of planning decisions.

Proposition 8: Development and examination of a large number of architectural arrangements and operational patterns should improve the effectiveness of the planning process and the quality of the end product, even though the first arrangement synthesized may very well be the final choice.

Proposition 9: The large number of variables to consider and the individual nature of each hospital planning problem seriously limit the usefulness of simple guidelines and prototype arrangements in the synthesis and evaluation phases of the planning process, and make very desirable a technique for considering a large number of variables at once, and for evaluation of a large variety of possibilities.

Proposition 10: Construction budgets, site considerations, and patient care quality level may be variables in the planning problem, but are more often constraints that outline the acceptable limits for solutions.

Proposition 11: More freedom in searching out good solutions to the planning problem is available if the planning of organizational and operational patterns proceeds concurrently with the initial planning of architectural arrangements, rather than entirely beforehand.

One serious lack will be noted in this outline for a conceptual framework. No propositions are advanced that will help to determine the balance that is "proper" among performances of the three functions, utility, amenity and expression. Certainly the client has some part in the decision, for a particular project. It appears, however, that in general the balance for any given "type" of architecture (churches, schools, factories, etc.) is determined by consensus of society as a whole, based on suggestions (buildings) by architects and comments by their critics. Thus, the "proper" balance for our time and society could be determined from the public or from the architects or critics who sense the public reaction. No one "proper" balance can be meaningful in the absolute sense, although as we learn more of other cultures it may be possible to discover the balance they strike and to correlate these with other features of their cultures.

As a conclusion to this barrage of abstractions—social organization, amenity, properties, measures, etc.—let us pose, and attempt to answer, one last question: Is this whole planning problem actually so complex, or are we only confusing the issue with a fancy "theory"? Consider a hospital planning project as an example. The client and principal information source for the project is a community and its medical care facility—that is, a social organization. The hospital which the architecture will shelter or enclose is composed of groups of people and facilities that can best be described in terms of an operational organization; that is, as subsystems of an over-all medical care system. Finally, the buildings to be created must exhibit their own particular sort of architectonic organization (e.g., logic of structure, adaptation to site, etc.). Thus, the hospital planners are expected to juggle three different kinds of complicated "organizations" of things and ideas—the client organization, the process organization, and the building organization—and come up with a superbly functioning machine, a masterpiece of art, and an economical building, all in one!

The problem is complex, and the "theory" or conceptual framework suggested here should be a useful tool for coping with that complexity.

The descriptive model of the planning process and the hypotheses concerning aspects of hospital planning that have been stated as propositions will, we hope, provide food for thought to the planners who must manipulate many factors in arriving at decisions. Some of the hypotheses, plus the model of the planning process, serve as a basis for the computer-aided planning methodology described in a later section.[3] As noted earlier, these hypotheses should be susceptible to proof at some future time.

REFERENCES:

Lazarsfeld, P. F. Problems in methodology. In R. K. Merton, L. Broom, & L. A. Cottrell, Jr. (Eds.), *Sociology today*. New York: Basic Books, 1959.

Parsons, T. Some ingredients of a general theory of formal organization. In A. W. Halpin (Ed.), *Administrative theory in education*. Chicago: University of Chicago Press, 1958.

Parsons, T. *Structure and process in modern society*. New York: The Free Press, 1959a.

Parsons, T. A general theory of social organization. In R. K. Merton, L. Broom, & L. A. Cottrell, Jr. (Eds.), *Sociology today*. New York: Basic Books, 1959b.

Stevens, S. S. Mathematics, measurement, and psychophysics. *Handbook of experimental psychology*. New York: John Wiley, 1951.

Torgerson, W. S. *Theory and methods of scaling*. New York: John Wiley, 1958.

[3] See Article 59.

PART SIX
Methods in Environmental Research

A section devoted to special methods in environmental research probably does not need an introduction. The interrelationships between theory and technique have been too well discussed to be repeated here. The circular process has been documented in which problems lead to technology and technology in turn leads to new problems. No matter at what point the circle is entered, it is frequently difficult for the historian to identify whether technology or problem led the way. Well-documented examples of both cases abound in the history of science.

In Part Six we have chosen to present methodologies that have been developed to meet the demands of specific environmental problems. In general, the methodologies presented are somewhat of a departure from traditional approaches, in that the main focus is the environment, its use and impact, rather than individuals and objects in the environment. There are of course, in addition, many established procedures for investigation that have direct applications to environmental studies. These procedures are described in detail in standard works, and no useful purpose would be served by including them here. Like all areas of study, environmental psychology has its own procedural problems. As might be expected in a new field, the solutions to these problems are as yet relatively few and by no means of a magnitude comparable to that of the difficulties that need to be overcome.

Environments are extremely complex, and methods for studying environmental influences are ultimately of the same order of complexity. That important approaches in this direction have already been accomplished is indicated by the selections offered here, as well as by the procedures followed by many of the authors in other parts of this volume. The reader is likely, however, to conclude that this section, as much as any other, represents unfinished business and that techniques for environmental studies remain a vital area for future contributions. The problems are many, and the means for studying them will surely grow.

59 Computer-Aided Analyses of Interdepartmental Commerce

J. J. Souder, W. E. Clark, J. I. Elkind, and M. B. Brown

The intent of this chapter is to outline techniques for the hospital planning process. The concern of this project is with interdepartmental relations in hospitals, and the techniques developed relate primarily to the relationships between elements of the physical arrangement. One of our objectives in this part of the study is to develop a procedure for predicting the commerce activity in a future hospital situation. Another objective is to develop a procedure for evaluating the performance of a given pattern of commerce tasks in a given physical arrangement.

The procedures discussed in this paper are predicated on a new concept—*computer-aided planning*—involving close interaction between human planners and a versatile digital computer. In the last section of this paper, this concept is introduced and explained.

A PROCEDURE FOR PREDICTING INTERDEPARTMENTAL COMMERCE

Interdepartmental commerce—the movement of people, supplies and equipment, and information between departments of a hospital—has been shown to be important in the operation of the facility, and thus in the planning. It is our belief that the capability of simulating future commerce patterns is very useful in planning. Changing

From J. J. Souder, W. E. Clark, J. I. Elkind, M. B. Brown, *Planning for Hospitals: A Systems Approach Using Computer-Aided Techniques*. Chicago: American Hospital Association, 1964, pp. 115–118. Reprinted by permission of the authors and publisher.

concepts of patient care suggest arrangements and operational patterns that have no parallel in existing facilities, and neither direct observation in existing facilities nor over-all judgment based on the experience of the planners is entirely relevant.

Intensive observations of commerce activity in two hospitals have provided an inventory of basic data. From analysis of these data, a detailed picture of commerce patterns in the two hospitals emerges. These patterns in separate hospitals at opposite ends of the country are remarkably alike in many aspects. They show that an underlying consistency is present in the seemingly diverse traffic patterns of the hospitals.

Using the generalizations developed in our earlier work, hospital planners can estimate the volume of various kinds of commerce trips for estimated patient loads and anticipated hospital facilities. Further, for each kind of trip the time distribution, the origins and destinations, and the categories of persons involved can be estimated from our data and supplemented by the planners' experience and knowledge of the anticipated operations. By focusing attention on one component of the total traffic at a time, the planners can make a detailed appraisal of anticipated interdepartmental commerce.

The commerce characteristics are easy to express and to grasp in graphical form. Manipulation of these graphs by hand to determine the over-all commerce patterns would be a tedious, time-consuming job, especially to evaluate commerce patterns resulting from operational alternatives in, for example, shift changes, visiting hours, or patient-escort procedures. One of the fruitful applications for computer-aided planning is manipulation of these many graphs which together describe an over-all commerce pattern.

Manipulation of commerce estimates by computer makes feasible the simulation of realistic but hypothetical traffic "histories" for proposed future hospitals. This simulation serves two purposes. First, the simulated traffic data can be used to test the efficacy of alternative proposed plan arrangements. Second, the commerce patterns can be examined for activity peaks and coincidences that might lead to congestion, excessive elevator waiting times, etc.

A PROCEDURE FOR EVALUATING COMMERCE PERFORMANCE

In an earlier report some possible measures for evaluation of commerce in hospitals are stated and examined. These all involve, in one way or another, enumeration of trips required for various commerce tasks and calculation of the time required for these trips. In addition, the category of person involved in the trip can be taken into account to provide a measure of skill-weighted time for the commerce task.

If the set of commerce data to be used for performance computation represents actual observations from a hospital and includes information on routes of travel, the computation can be done directly, using those routes. Such a procedure requires a complete description of routes of travel for all trips and thus is unusable for a situation which has not been observed or for which these paths are not described.

For a proposed plan of a future hospital, therefore, we can only describe a model, or hypothesis, about the factors that determine the choice of routes for a given trip. From this model a procedure can be developed that will assign trips to the various routes with approximately the same probability as they would have in the real life situation.

A brief description of the computation of travel times in the COPLANNER system is presented here to illustrate the calculation procedure and the model for route assignments. Distances of travel are measured in a three-coordinate system: horizontal x and y coordinates, in feet, perpendicular to each other (and parallel to major building walls in a predominantly rectilinear plan), and vertical distances in terms of floors.

The computation of travel time for a single commerce trip is as follows: first, one must determine whether the trip takes place entirely on one floor or involves movement from a given floor to another floor of the hospital. If the trip takes place entirely on one floor, the travel distance is determined as the sum of the distances between origin

and destination points in the x direction and in the y direction.[1] This distance is divided by the unit travel rate (in feet per minute) to obtain the travel time for the trip.

Note that actual travel routes along corridors are not computed. The computation assumes the existence of a system of corridors parallel to the x and y coordinate axes. Origin and destination points are defined in COPLANNER as the *control centers* of the various departments, not their doorways to corridors. Thus, minor inaccuracies arise from computing point-to-point travel distances. These are not serious enough to warrant a more complicated computational procedure, since they are most apparent on short trips that contribute little to the overall commerce time.

If the commerce trip requires movement from one floor to another, the trip time is computed as described above for the horizontal travel from origin to vertical pathway (elevator, stair or dumb-waiter) and for the horizontal trip from vertical pathway to destination on the destination floor. The vertical trip time is computed by dividing the number of floors traversed by the rate (in floors per minute) and adding an expected value for the vertical conveyance waiting time, if any. Total trip time is then the sum of times of two horizontal trips and one vertical trip. A round trip would double the trip time as computed.

In the present version of COPLANNER one rate for horizontal travel, one rate for vertical travel by stairs, and one rate for vertical travel by elevator or dumb-waiter are used. These are essentially average values derived from observations. However, different rates for different conveyances, or types of trips, could be used. Trips via pneumatic tube are assumed to take a fixed time, regardless of distance, and to require no other travel. A dumb-waiter trip between

---

[1] It should be noted that the computational procedure for horizontal travel could also be programed to compute radial and circumferential distances in a circular plan, etc. The rectilinear coordinates system has been used in this first version of COPLANNER because of its widespread applicability.

floors, in contrast, may involve a horizontal trip by a person on each floor.

The foregoing description illustrates the computation of travel time for a specified route in the hospital. In general there is a multiplicity of routes available between any two hospital departments. The choice of a specific one of these for a given trip requires that two questions be resolved: (1) Is the route feasible for this type of trip? (2) Is the route the "best" of the feasible routes?

Feasibility is determined, in the co-PLANNER system, by ascertaining whether the *bulk* or *mode of travel* for the trip can be accommodated. Thus, patients in wheel chairs can be transported in elevators but not on stairways (mode of travel constraint) or in dumb-waiters (bulk constraint).

The criterion used in COPLANNER to determine the "best" route of those feasible is *least trip time*. That is, trip times are computed for all feasible routes, and the route for shortest time is selected. The rationale for this criterion is that, to a first approximation, people appear to use the pathway which provides least time in transit. Other constraints on the choice of paths, such as the familiar prohibition of elevator use by staff for one-floor trips, could be programed.

WHY CONSIDER COMPUTERS?

Hospital planning is a well-established field of endeavor for architects, administrators and consultants. Why, then, suggest "rocking the boat" by introducing a new and foreign concept of computer-aided planning? There are several reasons. One, that of the increasing complexity of hospital planning and the increasing influence of technical decisions in the planning process, has been discussed in earlier work (see Article 58). A second reason has to do with new capabilities and concepts for computer application.

Most computers in the past have been designed primarily for large-scale routine tasks such as accounting and information retrieval, or for scientific computation. However, computers are coming into use as partners of men in tasks such as traffic control, and as simulators for complicated gaming analyses. Heretofore, most versatile and powerful computers were large, costly, and difficult to maintain, but developments in electronic circuitry have made medium and small high-speed computers a practical reality. Advances in input-output equipment and in programing techniques can now provide communication between man and computer for useful and direct man-machine cooperation in solving problems.

A mechanism for the use of computers has been proposed by Licklider (1960) that is pertinent to the planning task. He calls this "man-computer symbiosis." The basic idea is that computers are not yet developed far enough to count as "artificial intelligences" in many real life situations, but are far enough developed to perform very efficiently and swiftly many functions that man performs only haltingly, such as quick retrieval of data, manipulation and display of simple patterns, and various sorts of mathematical calculations. Thus man and machine can complement each other.

This concept of man-computer cooperation leads to a possible assignment of jobs for human planners and a computer that should enable their effective interaction for planning tasks.

Assume that the hospital planning team includes architect, administrator and consultant. Assume further that these planners can convene in working conference sessions at the console of a computer rather than at a drafting board or conference table. Better still, the essential communication elements of the computer console can be installed in a conference room and remotely connected to the computer. The group of planners, or any one of their number, can now proceed with consideration of planning problems as before, but with an important difference. Immediate recourse is possible to background data and relationships; and various possible operational patterns (or policies) and physical arrangements can be formulated and evaluated or compared without tedious calculations and long delays.

The reader may pause and wonder, at this point, if the authors envision turning the whole planning process over to an "electronic brain" and adding planners to the ranks of the unemployed—victims of automation. *We do not!* The day may come when many of the planning functions which we regard as intuitive and creative will be accomplished better by computers than by humans. At present and in the foreseeable future, however, a planning machine which grinds out finished designs "untouched by human hands" does not seem feasible for a variety of reasons. The most compelling of these is that many of the decisions in the hospital planning process are subjective and hinge on traditions, personal experience, or the consensus of the judgments of an interested technical group, such as the medical profession, or of society in general.

The computer application suggested herein and implemented in the COPLANNER system is essentially the mechanization of only those parts of the planning task that are easily done by computer and not easily or willingly done by the human planners.

The following chart summarizes this discussion of computer-aided planning by suggesting the roles to be filled by human planners and the computer:

Planning Phase	Man Provides	Computer Provides
Investigation (development of requirements and programing)	Knowledge and experience	Storage, retrieval, and processing of information
Synthesis of physical and organizational arrangements	Imagination and design sense	Manipulation, simulation, and short-time memory
Evaluation of arrangements and anticipated performance	Judgment and assessment of intangibles	Calculation and display

It should be obvious that this assignment of roles does not tend to reduce the freedom of the planners, but rather extends their capabilities.

SUMMARY

In this paper a basis for prediction and evaluation of commerce performance has been traced, and models or procedures for predicting commerce patterns by simula-

tion, and for calculating some measures of commerce performance, have been discussed. The discussions about these models have mentioned computers, and in particular the COPLANNER system, from time to time. It should be emphasized here, however, that prediction and evaluation models are independent of the computer system and could be utilized in hand calculation except for the magnitude of clerical work it would entail. Indeed, simplified versions of these models might be developed that could provide quick, rough approximations without excessive clerical work. That approach has not been followed since the main hope in improvement in hospital planning methodology seems to lie in the direction of better manipulation of the many variables presented to the planners. The computer-aided approach offers, in our opinion, the best hopes for such improvement in hospital planning.

REFERENCE:

Licklider, J. C. R. Man-computer symbiosis. *Institute of Radio Engineers, Transactions on Human Factors in Electronics*, Vol. HFE-1, No. 1, March 1960.

60 Notes on the Description, Scaling, Notation, and Scoring of Some Perceptual and Cognitive Attributes of the Physical Environment[1]

Philip Thiel

This paper is a formulation of part of a study concerned with the description, scaling, notation, and scoring of some of the perceptual and cognitive attributes of the parameters of experienceable physical environments. In the model now under devel-

[1] This work was initiated by the author in 1952 in a thesis at the Massachusetts Institute of Technology and further developed in the course of a recent sabbatical from the University of Washington with support from the National Institute of Mental Health. Part of this material has been published earlier (Thiel, 1961a) and this present version presents revisions thereof and additions thereto.

opment, these parameters, or factors, are identified as the personality (P) participating in the physical environment (EN) and undergoing the concurrent multilevel experience (EX): the environment (EN) is composed of space (S), which is provided with furnishings (F) and peopled with humanity (H). P's mode of experience in S is in motion (M), and for this motion to be purposeful, P must be able to orient himself in S. This present note is limited to a summary discussion of selected aspects of M, S, and orientation in S.

This study is directed toward the development of a simple graphic sign system, analogous to musical [or dance (Hutchinson, 1954)] notation, as a means for the analysis and design of physical environments on the basis of sequential experience in real time. Since the conventional professions of "environmental design" have become established within the self-imposed boundaries of such discrete areas as "industrial," "interior," "architecture" (building), "urban," and "landscape" design, and whereas environmental *experience* is continuous across such conceptual boundaries, the word *envirotecture* has been coined to fill the need for a general reference to a purposeful act of intervention in the physical environment (including the provision of new facilities and the management of existing facilities) which transcends these artificial boundaries and is concerned with continuous environmental experience.

An envirotect then is a person engaged in environmental intervention on the basis of the continuous process of real-time experience, ultimately to enrich the quality of this experience and promote the development of individuals and groups experiencing this total environment. An envirotect does not design vehicles or rooms or buildings or gardens or cities; he designs *experiences* in any and all combinations of these parts of the environment. His chief tool for this work is the sequence notation and score with which he describes a proposed or an existing potential sequence of distal stimuli and/or signals, at the appropriate level of detail.

Motion (M) refers to a change of position in space over time and, given an initial spatial location (as in latitude, longitude, and elevation), can be described in terms of time, distance, and direction. Time and distance are related in rate, or velocity, of motion and in changes in velocity, or acceleration and deceleration. Time is recorded as clock time, as an objective reference, and/or as experienced time, as a subjective reference. Distance is measured here in orthographic terms; that is, in the lengths of tangents and circular arcs in a horizontal plane, and in vertical directions perpendicular to this plane. Directional changes are measured, in the horizontal plane, in terms of the angle turned through in turning to the left or right, and/or in terms of the compass heading at the completion of such turning movements. In the vertical dimension, direction is measured as positive (upward) or negative (downward) changes in elevation from the previous horizontal plane.

Figure 60-1 illustrates and defines a notation and scoring for motion that involves separate "channels" of information for time, horizontal distance, and rate, on one hand, and for direction, in terms of turns to the left or right and ascents or descents, on the other. It should be noted that time (objective and/or subjective, as noted) serves as the common reference, or base, for both these channels and for all additional channels of information. The scoring as presented here is to be read from the bottom upward [as in dance notation (see Hutchinson, 1954)] and may be thought of as analogous to a musical score for a symphony but rotated 90 degrees counterclockwise. In the present vertical scoring, any horizontal line intersecting all the vertical channels indicates a concurrent instant in time.

The rate channel denotes the average rate of speed over the interval of time and distance indicated. In the case where the rate is zero, a pause, stop, or rest in motion is indicated; time continues to pass, but distance does not change. In the case where horizontal distance does not change, but a change in elevation is occurring, then movement by elevator, hoistway, or vertical ladder is taking place; and the rate refers to this vertical motion. Likewise, when no motion in a vertical direction is indicated, the rate signifies movement in a horizontal plane only.

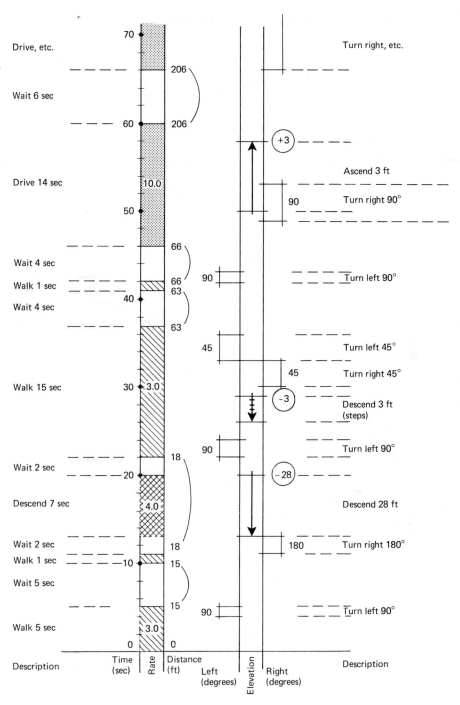

Figure 60–1. Motion channels. (Walk) (along a corridor) 5 seconds and turn 90 degrees left (to face an elevator). After 5 seconds wait, walk (enter) and turn 180 degrees clockwise in place. Descend 28 ft. in 7 seconds, wait 2 seconds (for doors to open), then walk, turning left 90 degrees, descending 3 ft. via steps, and move right and left 45 degrees. Wait 4 seconds, step forward (into a taxi) and turn 90 degrees left in place (to sit down). After a 4 second pause (the taxi) moves off, turns 90 degrees right, ascends a ramp for 3 ft., and stops (for traffic). After 6 seconds (it) moves again, making a right turn, and . . .

The point at which any uniform, or uniformly varying, attribute such as rate, direction, slope, curvature, or distance changes is called an "event," and a "duration" is defined as the interval of time between successive events. An event occurs when motion departs from, or returns to, movement in a straight and/or level path, or to any change in these changes. Note that compound motions can be notated; as is often the case, one may ascend on a turn to the left and slow down, or turn to the right while descending and accelerating. Turn indications to the left or right are shown by event lines at instants of time when motion departs from and returns to movement in a straight line, and the duration of turning by a line connecting the initial and final event lines. The angle turned through, or, alternately, the initial and final compass headings, may be indicated along this duration line. Ascents and descents are shown by duration-line arrows pointing either up or down, as appropriate, and connecting the initial and final event lines denoting the change from and return to movement in a horizontal plane. The net change above or below the former elevation at the initial event is noted alongside. Note that an event also occurs if the rate of ascent or descent changes and if a change in the radius of turn occurs in a horizontal curve. If the means of vertical movement is stairs or a ladder, this may be indicated by hatching the directional arrow.

In the case of a precisely engineered trajectory as on a highway or railroad, an alternate indication may be used. Here the reciprocal of the radius of curvature of the horizontal curve is plotted to scale on the left and right, and the transition spirals are indicated as sloping event lines out to the duration lines of constant radius. The area of the resulting rectangle or trapezoid is proportional to the angle turned through (for further details see Tunnard, 1963). Likewise, elevational changes may alternately be shown in terms of cross-hatched portions extending over the nonlevel part of the path, with grades above the initial reference elevation indicated alongside. Upgrades may be cross-hatched in one direction and downgrades in another for easier reading.

Turning next to orientation, reference is made to empirical studies by Lynch (1960), in which five physical, visual-form elements that appear to be generally relevant in environmental orientation are identified. They are grouped here in terms of conceptual dimensionality: two-dimensional elements are the districts and nodes, which one may enter or traverse; one-dimension linear elements are, for example, paths and edges, which one may follow or cross; and the nominal no-dimensional point elements with the attributes of position only, are, for example, landmarks and a sixth element here supplied by the writer, signs. Signs are explicit traffic or locational indications commonly found in urban districts and nodes and on most paths. Fuller definitions of the first five elements may be found in Lynch (1960).

It is important to note that these six elements may be used in various ways in environmental orientation. That is, landmarks and signs may be approached as goals or used as guides toward the attainment of other goals. Paths and edges may also be used in these ways, that is, as goals and guides, and in addition may be either followed or crossed. Nodes and districts in turn may be used as goals or guides, and in addition may be entered and traversed. Figure 60-2a illustrates and defines a notation for these elements, and Figure 60-2b, a scoring to be used in conjunction with the movement notation and scoring described previously.

It will be noticed that Figure 60-2 contains a graphic notation not yet discussed. This is a position indicator, based on a hemispherical projection which will now be described. For the present purposes it is assumed that P is moving along a trajectory in the manner described in the movement score. At any given instant in time his "line of sight" or "axis of vision" may be at some vertical angle, ϕ, and some horizontal angle, θ, with his instantaneous horizontal direction of motion or heading (the tangent to the horizontal projection of his trajectory). In the special case when ϕ and θ are zero, P's line of sight coincides with his heading, and this is assumed to be the case unless values for ϕ and/or θ are given.

The line of sight or visual axis is taken

as the reference axis of symmetry for a 180° concave hemisphere encompassing one-half of the visual world. This is somewhat more than the typical binocular field of human vision (Gibson, 1966). Referring to Figure 60-3, a line between p and a point, O, of any visible object in this hemisphere will make an angle, α, with the visual axis. (The point p is assumed to be at the exact eye-height of P at any given instant.) If angle α is zero, the point O is on the visual axis and therefore dead ahead of P at a given instant. If the angle α is 90°, then the point, O, is in the plane containing p, perpendicular to the visual axis. In Figure 60-3 a circle of convenient radius $\overline{R}$ is shown, representing a special projection of this hemisphere on this plane. The visual axis is at the center, p, of the circle and is perpendicular to the plane of the circle. The circumference of the circle then represents the locus of all points 90° off the visual axis, and when $\phi = \theta = O$, the vertical axis (ZN) and horizontal axis (LR) in the plane of this circle determine the cardinal points Z, 90° above p (the zenith), N, 90° below p (the nadir), and 90° to the left, L, and right, R, of p.

The plane containing the ray p'O and the visual axis will intersect the plane of the circle along some radius at some angle, β, with the horizontal axis, LR, or the vertical axis, ZN. (The position of this radius may be denoted as at 2 o'clock, 7 o'clock, etc.) The projected point O' may be located on this radius at a distance, r, from the center, where $r = \overline{R} (\alpha/90°)$. This then provides a positional indicator for any point within the forward visual hemisphere. This projection is identical to those 180° "fish-eye" camera lenses in which the projected radial distance of any point from the optical axis varies linearly with the angle, α. Note also that this projection is independent of the radial variation of acuity of the human eye. (Points in the rearward visual hemisphere may be also indicated on this plot, using a minus sign $(-)$ to signify this direction.)

This position indicator is shown in use in Figure 60-2 to locate the direction in which a goal or a guide first becomes visible, or when it appears in a new position. Used alongside this positional indicator are numbers indicating the range or distance, $\overline{pO}$,

between p and a characteristic point on the object in question, and the angular field of view of the element of orientation. The range may be expressed in terms of "distance zone" numbers, defined in Table 60-1 (from Thiel, 1961a), as a convenience in estimating, or it can be the exact distance. The angular extent or field of view of the element of orientation, as visible at a given moment from a given point, as defined above, may be denoted by the angle itself, or in a similar "scale of views," given in Table 60-2.

The anatomy of visual space (S), presented next, does not presume to be complete but, as far as it goes, is believed to be an improvement on the conventional mode of conceptualization. The fact that the experience of space involves sensory perceptions other than the visual is well appreciated. Auditory, olfactory, thermal, proprioceptive, and tactile stimuli all play their part in the establishment and qualification of a sense of space. Space experience, in the broadest sense, is a biological function necessary to the continual adaptation of any organism to its environment for the purposes of survival; consequently, it draws on a broad range of sensation. In the human species, however, vision plays the dominant role and thus requires our particular attention.

The spaces dealt with are limited to those that are humanly occupiable. Since it is possible to occupy more than one space at the same time, it is necessary to distinguish between such simultaneous spaces. (For example, one may be in the fifth seat of a bus, on a raised causeway lined with trees, crossing a lake set in a bowl of low hills which are surrounded by distant mountain ranges. Or one may be standing on a rug covering part of the floor area of a raised platform, located in a field surrounded by trees overlooked by the tops of flanking buildings.) For this reason the smallest space that is most explicitly established (as will be described later) is called the primary space. Smaller, less explicit spaces, and spaces larger than the primary space are called subspaces and secondary spaces, respectively. In any sequence experience, by definition, P moves directly from one primary space to the next, irrespective of the possible oc-

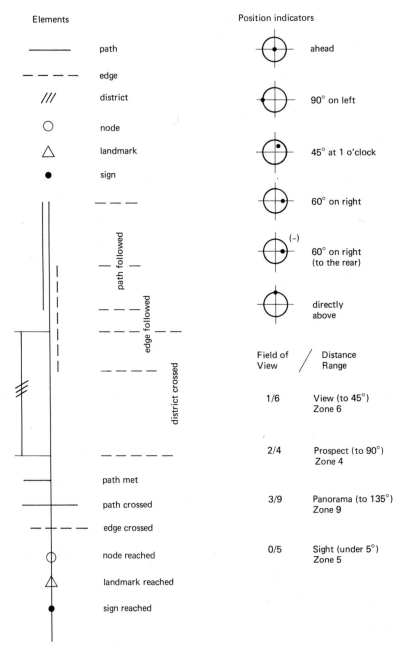

Elements

————	path
— — — —	edge
///	district
○	node
△	landmark
●	sign

Position indicators

⊕	ahead
⊕	90° on left
⊕	45° at 1 o'clock
⊕	60° on right
⊕ (–)	60° on right (to the rear)
⊕	directly above

Field of View / Distance Range

1/6	View (to 45°) Zone 6
2/4	Prospect (to 90°) Zone 4
3/9	Panorama (to 135°) Zone 9
0/5	Sight (under 5°) Zone 5

path followed

edge followed

district crossed

path met

path crossed

edge crossed

node reached

landmark reached

sign reached

Figure 60–2. (**a**) Orientation notation. (**b**) Orientation scoring (*facing page*). At time/distance 0, while following a path, an intersecting path is seen ahead, and a landmark (grove of trees) is visible off to the right. At t/d 5 the path ahead is crossed, and at t/d 7 the grove of trees is passed on the left. At that moment an edge (lake shore) is seen off to the right, and a landmark (standpipe) and an edge (low ridge) are seen up ahead. At t/d 10 the edge of the lake is reached and followed, and beyond that, at t/d 11 a path branches to the left. At t/d 13 the path is dropped, and the landmark disappears behind the ridge. At t/d 16 the ridge is reached and crossed, and the landmark is seen again atop a second ridge (edge) ahead.

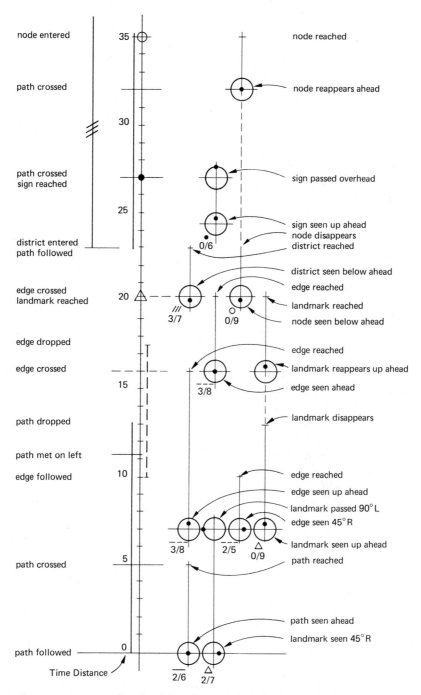

Figure 60–2 (*continued*). The lake edge is left behind at t/d 17½, and by t/d 20 the ridge and landmark are reached and passed. Here a district and a node are seen below. The district is reached at t/d 23, and a path is there followed: the node is no longer visible. At t/d 24½ a sign is seen up ahead, and this is passed under, at an intersecting path, at t/d 27. A second path is crossed at t/d 32, when the node reappears ahead. The node is reached and entered at t/d 35.

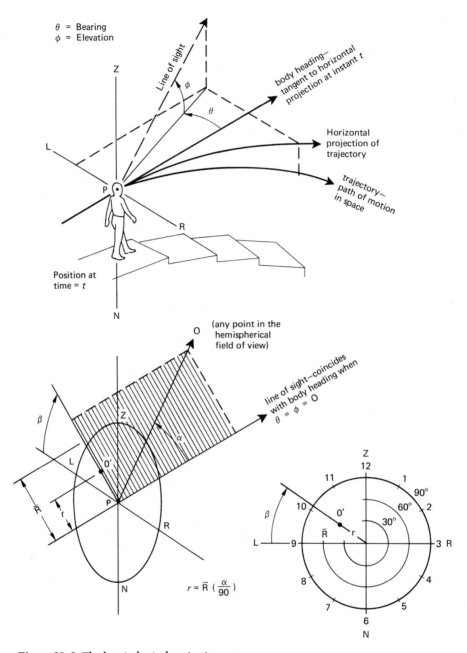

Figure 60–3. The hemispherical projection.

currence of sub-spaces and/or secondary spaces. At no time is P not in some space, and if at any time he is in more than one space, one of them will be primary. (These successive primary spaces may, of course, vary in their degree of explicitness.)

Care should be taken not to confuse a secondary space with a view. Secondary spaces, like subspaces and primary spaces, are by definition *occupied* by P (an in-space); the implication here is that in these cases P is able to see all the elements which establish these spaces. A view on the other hand (as an out-space) implies a partial visual relationship with a space. Refer again to Table 60-2.

Table 60-1 Distance Zones

Gibson (1947) divides the range of every-day space experience into two groups: aerial space and local space. He describes these as follows: "Aerial space may be defined as the visual surroundings extending away from the observer and bounded in any direction by the horizon, the surface of the earth and the sky. It may be distinguished from local space primarily by its voluminousness and long range of distances. Local space is the kind to which we are accustomed; it is enclosed by walls and restricted in range by them. Even out of doors in a civilized environment the spatial scene is cut up and confined to localized areas by buildings and other objects which obliterate the horizon. . . ." He also points out that "persons who are adapted to going about and making the ordinary judgements of distance in the city are usually misled by the extent of distances in the desert, mountains, on water or from a plane. Generally, aerial distances are poorly estimated by such persons because they are unfamiliar with the visual cues present in the situation for space perception. . . ."

In view of the difficulty of estimating distances accurately, especially larger distances, it is advantageous to have a means of denoting a dimension by bracketing it within a range with an upper and a lower limit. Such a system should possess narrow limits for the smaller, more easily estimated distances, and wider limits as the distances grow larger and more difficult to estimate precisely. As a matter of convenience a series of zones, identified 0, 1, 2, . . . 10 may be suggested, with the range limits for each zone as in the accompanying table.

These range dimensions are derived from a logarithmic scale based on points at 6 feet and 15,000 feet. The average ratio between successive dimensions is about 2.4. (The dimensions have been rounded off to the nearest whole number.) The reasons for the base points of 6 feet and 15,000 feet are obvious. It is curious to note that Sitte (1945) observes that the average dimensions of the great squares of the old cities are 190 × 465 feet. This is an interesting situation: 465 feet is roughly the distance that objects about ½ inch in size may be seen under reasonable daylight conditions (Moon and Spencer, 1948), and a dimension of ½ inch is of about the order of gross facial characteristics. Possibly the maximum size of these spaces, designed for static experience and pedestrian occupancy, may have been based on the condition of facial recognition—the "face-to-face" experience. Blumenfeld (1953) has some interesting comments on this matter.

Zone Number	Range Limits (feet)	Notes and References
Local space		
0	0–6	6 ft. is a minimum dimension for a habitable space.
1	6–15	7–12 ft. is a distant phase of social-consultative distance (Hall, 1963).
2	15–35	40 ft. is limit for discerning facial expression (Spreiregan, 1965).
3	35–80	Far phase of public distance begins near 30 ft. (Hall, 1963). 80 ft. is limit for facial recognition (Spreiregan, 1965).
4	80–200	
Transition space		
5	200–450	Medieval city squares average 190 × 465 ft. (Sitte, 1945). 450 ft. is limit for discerning action (Spreiregan, 1965).
Aerial space		
6	450–1,000	
7	1,000–2,500	
8	2,500–6,000	Maximum distance, for seeing people is 4,000 ft. (Spreiregan, 1965).
9	6,000–15,000	15,000 ft. is horizon distance for 5½ ft. eye height (U.S.H.O. Pub. 111B).
10	15,000 & over	

All this may be summarized as follows: We conceptualize a visual world, existing all around us in three dimensions. At a given moment our perceived visual field encompasses approximately half this visual world

Table 60-2 Scale of Views

Angular Extent of Field of View	Descriptive Designation	Code Number
up to 45 degrees	Sight	0
up to 90 degrees	View	1
up to 135 degrees	Prospect	2
up to 180 degrees	Panorama	3
over 180 degrees	Secondary Space —see text	–

and may be schematized as occupying a concave hemisphere symmetrical about our (usually nearly horizontal) line of sight. The differentiation of this field of view constitutes the "environmental display," or "scene." The scene, in turn, is seen to be composed of the in-spaces, or momentarily occupied sub-spaces, primary, secondary, and other spaces; and the out-spaces, or non-occupied spaces seen as views. Scenes are notated in a hemispherical projection: in-spaces by SEEPIs (to be described subsequently), and out-spaces (views) as part of the orientation scoring.

Any space is established by the perceived relationship between surfaces, screens, and objects. Objects may be thought of as three-dimensional forms existing as separate, isolated visual entities in a larger space than that smaller space which they help establish. [In the context of the *larger* space, the object no longer functions as a space-establishing element and consequently becomes a furnishing (F).] Surfaces are two-dimensional plane forms, limited in spatial effect to that space they help establish, although they may be part of a larger object when experienced in a larger context. Screens, as perforated surfaces, or as closely spaced objects, obviously are an intermediate condition between the above two limiting types.

To test whether a surface, screen, or object is in fact an element actually establishing a given space, one may try mentally removing the element from the situation and, if the space (as a finite, delimited volume) is not significantly affected by the removal, conclude that it is not a space-establishing element. This test is similar to that suggested by Hall (1959) for use in discriminating "isolates." Hall's "isolates,"

"sets," and "patterns" are analogous to SEEs, spaces, and sequences, respectively.

Surfaces, screens, and objects, as the Space-Establishing Elements (hereinafter for convenience identified as SEEs) may exist in natural or man-made forms and, as is the case with any visual form, may be described in terms of their number, position, shape, direction, size, color, and texture.

The position of the SEEs is specified with reference to the observer's place in the space they establish. Thus, SEEs generally in a horizontal plane at the top of a space are said to be in the over position and those similarly at the bottom, in the under position, while SEEs chiefly in a vertical plane are said to be in the side position. These latter are further qualified as to left, front, and right side. The position attributes of the SEEs are further qualified by indicating whether they occur above or below eye level, in the case of the side position, or on the left or right side of the observer in the case of the over, front, and under positions. Figure 60-4 illustrates a variety of common SEEs in these various positions.

The direction of a SEE refers to both the direction of its major dimension, as vertical, horizontal, or transverse, or as variations thereof and also its angular position relative to the horizontal and vertical axes of the space itself.

The shape of a SEE refers to the overall profile or contour, and to its surface configuration.[2] The texture of a SEE concerns the two- or three-dimensional patterning of a surface, screen, or object and will be discussed later, along with color. The meaning of the number and size (true, projected; apparent, real) of the SEEs should be obvious.

Having considered the SEEs, it is now necessary to describe the ways they may be associated. Figure 60-5 illustrates four basic categories of relationship: jointed, separated, continuous, and overlapped. The latter category is subdivided in terms of overlapping and overlapped elements.

From this consideration of some of the attributes of the SEEs we move next to

[2] Rose (1965) has developed a number of statistical indices to characterize these attributes.

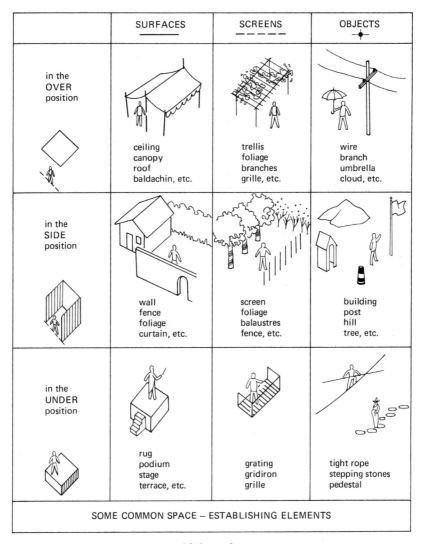

	SURFACES	SCREENS	OBJECTS
in the OVER position	ceiling canopy roof baldachin, etc.	trellis foliage branches grille, etc.	wire branch umbrella cloud, etc.
in the SIDE position	wall fence foliage curtain, etc.	screen foliage balaustres fence, etc.	building post hill tree, etc.
in the UNDER position	rug podium stage terrace, etc.	grating gridiron grille	tight rope stepping stones pedestal
SOME COMMON SPACE – ESTABLISHING ELEMENTS			

Figure 60–4. Some common space-establishing elements.

those of the established space itself. The first concerns the "degree of explicitness" of the established space. As diagrammed in Figure 60-6, it is seen to vary in a continuum from the ambiguous indefinite form of the vague, involving a few unconnected objects; through a suggest, established by a variety of surfaces, screens, and/or objects, in several positions; to a volume, a space explicitly defined by joined surfaces in all positions. Building interiors usually tend to be volumes, or strong suggests; exterior spaces in modern cities are usually suggests (medieval cities show a greater tendency toward volumes), while vagues are seen

chiefly in the natural landscape—but also in certain parts of modern cities.

Figure 60-7 illustrates this in terms of various combinations of joined surfaces in orthogonal relationships, as shown in the hemispherical projection. Zero explicitness is denoted by the absence of all SEEs; it is represented in the projection as a visual field consisting of half sky and half empty ground, as on the ocean or in a level uniform desert. Complete explicitness, on the other hand, is represented by the presence of SEEs in all five positions. Between these extremes other combinations are grouped in a tentative pattern proposed as a "base

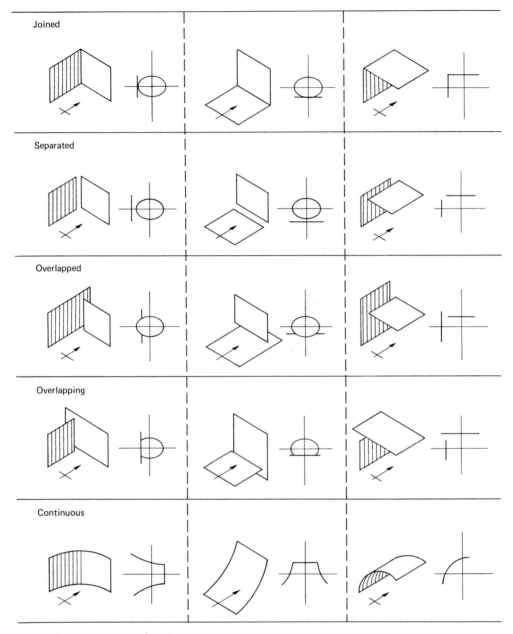

Figure 60–5. Typical SEE connections.

reference." A numerical index and a graphic notation are shown at 10 percent intervals. (The notation (SEEPI) is described later.) Corrections must be made to this base, reducing the degree of explicitness for openings in or between SEEs, as in separated surface SEEs or in the case of screen or object SEEs. In the numerical scale of Figure 60-7, spaces below an index of 30 may be referred to as vagues, and those above 70 as volumes, while those in between may be termed suggests.

A second concept is that of "degree of enclosure," producing a sense of confinement, which should not be confused with "degree of explicitness." The degree of en-

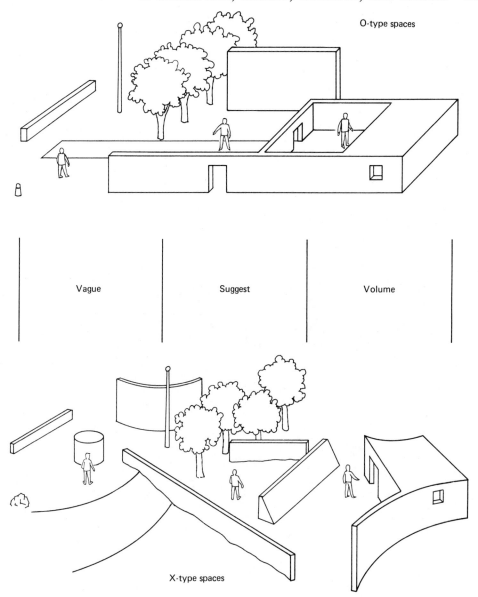

O-type spaces

Vague   Suggest   Volume

X-type spaces

Figure 60–6. Explicitness of establishment, I.

closure is postulated as a function of three factors: the degree of explicitness, the absolute volume of the space, and the relative proportions of the configuration of SEEs. A little reflection will illustrate this. Assuming a given configuration of SEEs, if the relative proportions remain constant, a large change in the volume of the space will obviously produce a different sense of confinement. Similarly, assuming a space of given volume

and degree of explicitness, if the proportions are varied (by raising the ceiling and closing in the walls, for example) while the volume and explicitness are kept constant, the degree of enclosure will again change.

Figure 60-8 suggests a tentative formulation of this relationship. Contours of equal degrees of enclosure (ranging from 0, claustrophobic, to 10, agoraphobic) are shown plotted on a grid of degree of explicitness

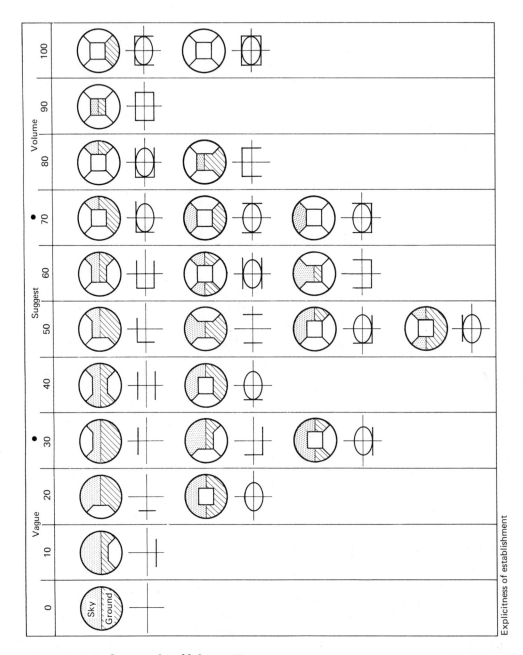

Figure 60–7. Explicitness of establishment, II.

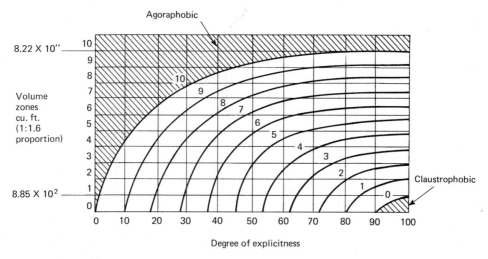

Figure 60–8. Contours of degrees of enclosure (hypothetical).

and volume zones. The latter are based on a space with proportions of length equal to 1.6 times the width, and width equal to 1.6 times the height.[3]

Given this tentative formulation, it still remains to plot additional series of contours of degree of enclosure for different proportions and, of course, to experimentally test the whole proposition.

Turning next to form, it should be noted that (as indicated in Figure 60-6) the form quality of a suggest or a volume is independent of the explicitness of establishment or degree of enclosure (a vague, being by definition of nebulous form, is to a degree excluded from these considerations). Assuming two polar form prototypes (exemplified in an egg, coded O, and a tree, coded X), a suggest or a volume may be characterized as to its form quality on a scale extending from O—characterized by regularity, closure, rest, completeness, cohesion, balance,

Table 60-3 Form Quality

Form Type	Notation	Code Number
Romantic, Dionysian	X	1
		2
		3
		4
Classical, Apollonian		5

or symmetry (the classical or Apollonian), on one hand, to X—characterized by irregularity, randomness, dissolution, unbalance, incompleteness, mobility, or expansion (the romantic or Dionysian) on the other.[4] A notation for this scale is shown in Table 60-3.

Space form may also be described in terms of gross proportion. If one dimension of a space is significantly larger (say two-and-a-half times larger) than either of the others, a space so proportioned may be termed a run (and the others, areas) and, depending on which dimension (relative to P's position) is the greater, may be a longitudinal run (streets, corridors), a transverse run (cross streets, corridors), or a vertical run (a well, or mineshaft).

Simple space-forms resulting from different combinations of uncomplicated SEEs in various positions may readily be indicated by a system of analogic notation. The frame

[3] The ratio 1:1.6 is approximately the "golden mean," and the space form so proportioned is proposed as a reference base. If 6 ft. is assumed as a minimum height, then the smallest volume on this scale becomes $6 \times 9.6 \times 15.36$, or 885 cubic feet. The upper limit on the scale may be assumed to be the similarly proportioned space whose length is the horizon distance for a 5½-ft. eye height—approximately 15,000 ft. The volume of this space is 8.23×10^{11} cubic feet. The intermediate volume zones are formulated on a logarithmic scale between these two limits, analogous to the distance zones presented earlier.

[4] This characterization is from Kepes (1956).

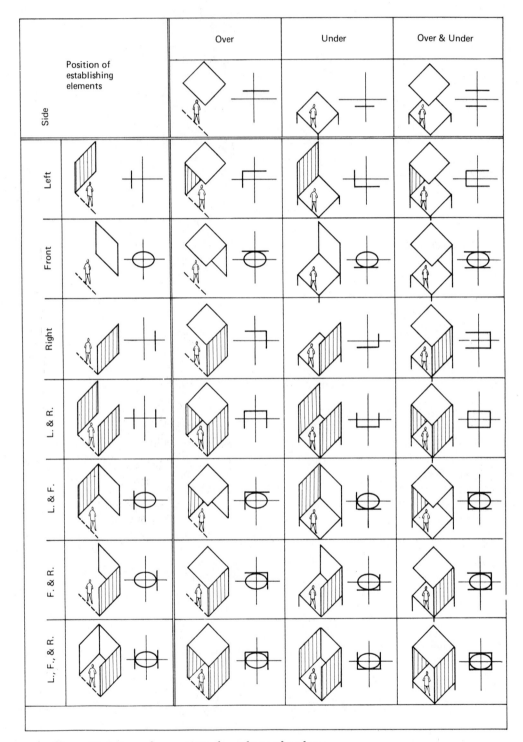

Figure 60–9. Space-form notation for orthogonal surfaces.

608

of reference is a cross of equal-length horizontal and vertical straight lines, intersecting at right angles at their midpoints. The vertical line represents the vertical axis of an upright participant and the horizontal line represents the transverse axis at the height of his eyes. Their intersection thus represents the location "right between the eyes." For the purposes of this notation, the *in-space* as experienced *at a given moment* is assumed to be limited to that which can be seen in a field of view extending 180 degrees horizontally and 180 degrees vertically. It thus coincides with the visual field covered by the hemispherical projection.

By means of isometric perspectives, Figure 60-9 illustrates the basic types of form-establishment resulting from all possible combinations of equal-sized (say 20-foot) joined square surfaces, in all possible vertical and horizontal positions parallel or perpendicular to the horizontal line of sight ahead. With each diagram is shown the corresponding notation for the particular space established. Since this notational diagram indicates the position of the space-establishing elements, it is called a Space-*E*stablishing *E*lement *P*osition *I*ndicator, or SEEPI for short. Figures 60-10 and 60-11 illustrate other types of simple space forms and the corresponding SEEPIs.

In the usual terrestrial case of space experience, the participant is always standing on something, usually a level surface. This may be assumed and omitted from the notation except in the special cases when the element in the under position is either not horizontal, not a surface, or is specially differentiated from the general surface, so that it acts as an element establishing a specific space. A change in level, texture, color, or even an outline may differentiate a part of the general surface and thus act to establish a specific space (a paved path or a roadway is one common example).

In the above diagrams surfaces were used as the SEEs. If screens act to establish spaces, the continuous line used in the notation would be replaced by a dashed or dotted line. In the case of objects acting as SEEs, a black dot is used.

If the SEEs in the side position exist only above or below eye level, they would then be shown only above or below the horizontal axis which represents eye height; and similarly, if the SEEs in the over or under position existed only to the left or right of the forward longitudinal axis, they would then be shown only on the left or right side of the vertical axis of the notation.

Figure 60-5 illustrated the variations in SEEPI notation to denote the basic types of possible connections between SEEs: joined, separated, continuous, overlapping, and overlapped.

The dimensions of an O-type space may be expressed in terms of its average height, width, and length. The SEEPI as discussed above may be qualified with these dimensions, as follows: the height dimension is written at the top of the vertical axis; the width dimension is written at the right of the horizontal axis; and the length dimension is written in the upper righthand quadrant formed by the two axes—all in consistent units such as feet or meters. Alternately the distance zone numbers may be used instead, if it is necessary to estimate the dimensions of the space. The length of a space is defined as that horizontal dimension parallel to the participant's line of sight ($\phi = 0$), and width and height are measured perpendicular to the length and each other. These dimensions, actual or estimated, are written for a given position on a trajectory at a given moment in time. The size of vagues may be recorded in terms of a diameter D of a circle of equivalent ground area, and using an average dimension for height.

The SEEPI may be further qualified to indicate the participant's lateral position within the space, by writing numbers on the left and right at the bottom of the vertical axis in proportional parts of the space width, reflecting this lateral position. The vertical position, if necessary, may similarly be described in terms of proportional parts of the space height, written at the left side of the horizontal axis.

As mentioned previously, the SEEPI represents the characterization of an occupied, or in-space, as it appears from a given point in space at a given moment in time. Ordinarily the angles ϕ and θ are both equal to zero—that is, the participant's line of sight is parallel to his instantaneous heading

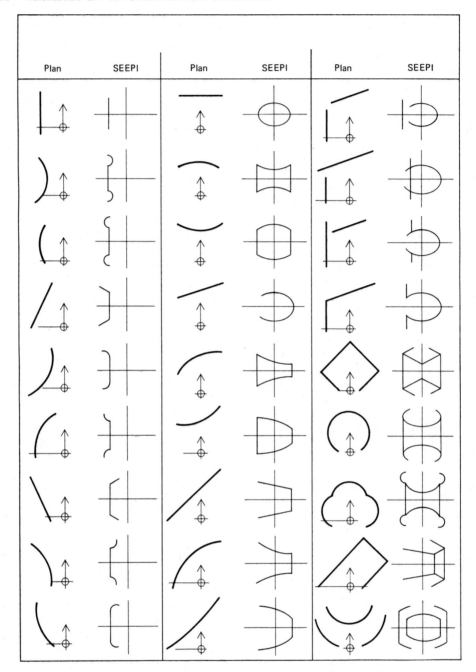

Figure 60–10. Various cases and combinations of vertical surfaces in side positions.

—and usually SEEPIs are written at a "space event," or the moment of entering any new space—subspace, primary, or secondary space. (They may, of course, be written at any other point too, if desired, but they will usually never be identical for any two different participant positions or headings.) It should be pointed out that SEEPIs are easier to formulate when the participant's line of sight is parallel to one of the main directions of a space, and either the trajectory may be adjusted or arranged to achieve this condition at each space-event or, alternately, the participant's line of sight may be so directed at that moment, and this head rotation indicated for that SEEPI by an appropriate notation of the angle θ and/or ϕ.

By writing the successive SEEPIs of a series of space events along a vertical line, reading upward, in association with the corresponding movement score representing the participant's path in space, an indication of a spatial sequence results. Separate parallel scores may be written for subspaces, primary spaces, secondary spaces, and so on, all in conjunction with the same movement score. Care must be taken that only the

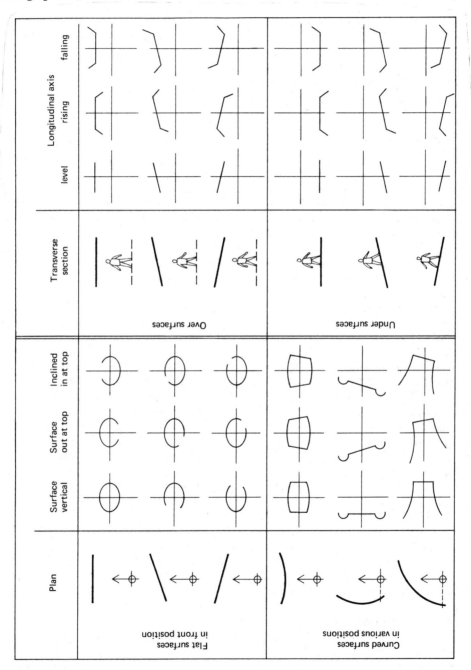

Figure 60–11

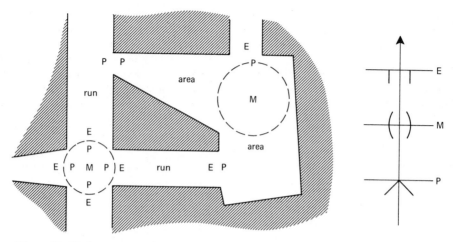

Figure 60–12. Space connections.

SEEs for the actual in-space are notated, in each case. Information concerning elements of out-spaces should be handled in a supplementary view channel (using the hemispherical projection) if desired, or included with the orientation scoring as described above.

Figure 60-12 illustrates how spaces themselves may be connected. There are three different categories: the *end*, the *port*, and the *merge*. A merge exists when two (or more) areas, runs, or vagues join in such a manner that there is no definite point of juncture, and one space merges or flows into the other. Usually a certain amount of space can be equivocally assigned to either space. A port exists when a constriction occurs when passing from one space into another. An end exists when the juncture of one space with another is neither a merge nor a port. Note that the same connection between two spaces may be both a port and an end, depending on the direction in which the participant moves. Figure 60-12 also presents a notation for these space connections.

The spaces as described, notated, and scored up to this point are considered to be established by SEEs with the attributes of number, position, direction, size, and shape only. At this point their attributes of color and texture will be taken up, along with the luminous aspects and "scale" of the spaces they establish, as part of the total scene.

The ordinary experience of our visual world is that of differentiated luminous space. That is, as we look and move around in our physical environment we act, consciously or unconsciously, with regard to information reaching us in the form of patterned light. If there were no light, or if the light was quite uniform (as in a heavy fog), our activities would be severely restricted, and to operate we would have to rely on other senses such as touch or hearing.

In moving about in a differentiated luminous environment we notice that as we change our position in space the scene changes. We may walk around in a space to investigate its various aspects, or we may try different positions to better "compose" a view we wish to photograph. Each point in space is the locus of a unique confluence of light rays. Generally, we orient ourselves in the physical environment by consciously or unconsciously keeping track of our location in space by the perceived differences in the patterns of light stimuli available to our eyes at a series of successive points. By successively sampling these signals over time we are able to probabilistically discriminate invariant and transient characteristics of our environment, and thus infer a visual "world."

For any participant moving on a trajectory in space, the general factors determining the experience of space with light are illuminants and modulators.

The illuminants provide radiant energy in the visible range of the spectrum. They may be natural (sun, moon, fire) or artificial (incandescent, fluorescent, sodium vapor, neon, etc.) and, of course, may exist in various combinations. The attributes of the illuminants (as specified for a given instant and position on a trajectory in space) are type, as just mentioned—implying spectral composition—"color temperature," and also whether they are "direct" (unshielded) or "indirect" (in which case the source is baffled by an opaque or translucent modulator). In addition, their size, in terms of wattage or foot-candles, and their number, position, and shape (as point, line, or area sources) are included.

The modulators consist of space-establishing elements (SEEs), sky and ground, and the furnishings and humanity occupying a specific space or spaces. At a given point in space, at a given instant in time, light may reach a participant directly from an illuminant. Usually, however, the light has been "modulated" and reaches the participant only indirectly from one or more sources. That is, it has been reflected, inter-reflected, filtered, diffused, absorbed, or refracted from, by, or in adjacent or surrounding elements, and/or scattered or dispersed in passing through smoke, mist, fog, or dust in the atmosphere intervening between the illuminant and modulator, and between the modulator and participant.

The light attributes of modulators may be described in the following terms, in addition to their position, number, size, direction, and shape. First is the articulation mode, referring to the means by which an element achieves legibility. This exists in terms of a characterization of form by shade and shadow (as in the case of three-dimensional monochromatic sculpture) or by an arrangement of pigmentation (as in two-dimensional decoration). Obviously combinations of these two modes also exist, in varying proportions (Kepes, 1968). Reflectance is a second characteristic, and may be specular, as from a mirror or polished surface, or diffuse, as from a matte or textured surface. The amount of light reflected is a function of both the surface and the illuminant: a red surface illuminated by a red light may reflect 90 percent of the incident red light, but if the same surface is illuminated by a

blue light, it may reflect hardly any light. Color as perceived is thus a consequence of the reflecting microstructure and absorptive pigmentation of the surface, *and* the incident light as reflected therefrom to the participant.[5] It may be described by means of a standardized color classification system such as the Munsell alphanumeric code, in terms of hue, value, and chroma.

It now remains to identify the luminous attributes of a given space as a whole, resulting from a particular association of illuminants and modulators, as experienceable at a given point in time and space. First is the level, or key, as described on a subjective, relative scale ranging from "glaring" through "bright," "dull," and "dim," to "dark," with an absolute reference of no light at all. A second attribute is temperature feeling, also a subjective interpretation depending on the relative quantitative distribution of specific colors and the association context of the experienced patterns. This may be characterized on a scale of "cold," "cool," "neutral," "warm," and "hot."

A third attribute is the shade and shadow pattern. A "shadow" is caused by the interception of illumination by an opaque body and is generally experienced as a darker figure on a lighter ground. The shape of the figures is characteristic of the intercepting object, the type of illuminant, and their positional relationship. The shadow may be illuminated by light from other sources, including reflected light. "Shade" refers to a condition of reduced illumination, as on that part of a form not directly exposed to an illuminant. In its pattern of gradual transitions or abrupt changes a shade serves to characterize the shape of the form (as an articulating mode). A given spatial experience may then be characterized in terms of the percentage areas of the modulators directly illuminated, in shade, or in shadow; in the latter case the shadows may be described as solid or (as occurs under trees in bright sunshine) as dappled or broken. In addition, there is the special case of a gen-

---

[5] Offsetting this somewhat is the phenomenon of "approximate color constancy," and complicating this considerably is the phenomenon of "successive" and "simultaneous color contrast." See Eastman Kodak (1956).

eral, even diffuse illumination producing an unshadowed or "flat" effect.

Finally, there is the significative attribute of the mood of the ambient luminous quality, which summarizes the overall subjective effect of the preceding attributes of key, temperature, and shade and shadow pattern. Mood results from the dialogue between the illuminants and modulators—but only as interpreted by a specific participant in the context of a specific sequential pattern of stimuli. Such words as "cheery," "somber," "bright," "ominous," "radiant," "dead," "clear," "bleak," "sparkling," "looming," and "intimate" will apply here, with the emphasis that any such use is a subjective characterization by a given participant in a specific experience context. Such characterization may be investigated by the use of the "semantic differential" (see Osgood, 1967).

The codification, notation, and scoring of the light channel of an environmental experience is next discussed. Illuminants are notated by means of the hemispherical projection, encompassing one half of the visual world, with position, number, and shape graphically indicated on the projection. Note that positions to the rear of the participant are shown with a (−) indication (one example of an "indirect" type). The illuminant type and size are indicated alongside their appropriate position indications. These illuminant characterizations are written at those points in time where their attributes change significantly: these are "illuminant events." Figure 60-13 illustrates an example of this notation.

Figure 60-14 shows a corresponding notation for the modulators, also using the hemispherical projection. These notations may be written at each "space event"—that is, at the moment of entering each successive space, or at each "illuminant event," if this changes within a given space.

For this purpose one may generalize the visual scene, as schematized in the hemispherical projection, into a number of discrete color areas. This schematization then graphically defines the number, position, size, and shape attributes of the elements constituting a luminous differentiation of the space. Whether this differentiation is done as an analysis of an existing situation or, alternately, represents a design proposal, one must report or specify the discrete color areas on either a "local color" or an "atmospheric color" basis. Local colors are "seen" as a consequence of "color constancy," as an intrinsic property of the modulator. In effect they refer to a label on a paint can. The atmospheric basis, on the other hand, includes the effects of illumination, simultaneous contrast, interreflections, shading, shadowing, or atmospheric modifications in the manner of detailed, illusionary, pictorial representation. Generalizations done on this basis obviously will tend to result in a greater number of discrete color areas, including many with gradations.

In any case the color of the areas themselves can be described by means of the Munsell alphanumeric hue/value/chroma system, in notations adjacent to the hemispherical projection. In addition, it should be clearly indicated whether local or atmospheric colors are specified, and if the notation is a design proposal or an environmental report. The latter case obviously is a subjective experience (EX), which will also theoretically include the effects of "successive color contrast," and can only be objectified into an environmental description (EN) by the use of mechanical spectrophotometric means of color reporting.

It should be apparent that an atmospheric color indication includes, or presumes, a specific illuminant composition—ostensibly that specified in the adjacent illuminant score —and as such combines illuminant and modulator characteristics. (A local color indication, of course, also implies an illuminant, but it is an unknown memory trace.) A tabulation of each color area in terms of percentage area (of the total hemispherical projection area) and in terms of numerical color attributes of the hue, value, and chroma then permits a succinct characterization of color key and temperature feeling. The summation of the product of the value of each color element and its percentage area of the hemispherical projection, divided by the total projected area, indicates the general level of scene brightness. This may be reported in the six-point scale mentioned above, and notated by the indication shown in Table 60-4. In a similar manner the tem-

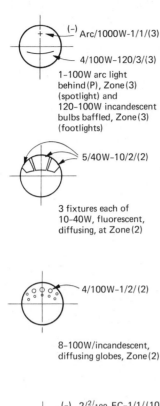

1–100W arc light
behind(P), Zone(3)
(spotlight) and
120–100W incandescent
bulbs baffled, Zone(3)
(footlights)

3 fixtures each of
10–40W, fluorescent,
diffusing, at Zone(2)

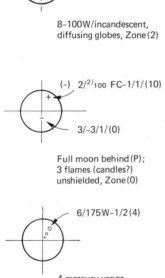

8–100W/incandescent,
diffusing globes, Zone(2)

Full moon behind(P);
3 flames (candles?)
unshielded, Zone(0)

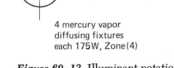

4 mercury vapor
diffusing fixtures
each 175W, Zone(4)

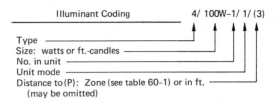

Type
Size: watts or ft.-candles
No. in unit
Unit mode
Distance to(P): Zone (see table 60-1) or in ft.
(may be omitted)

Example shown: one 100-watt bare
incandescent in Zone 3 (35–80 ft.)

Illuminant Types

Sun	1
Moon	2
Flame (fire, candle, etc.)	3
Incandescent	4
Fluorescent	5
Mercury vapor	6
Sodium vapor	7
Other: specify (neon, arc...)	8

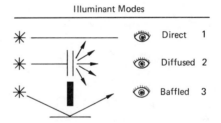

Illuminant Modes

Direct 1

Diffused 2

Baffled 3

Natural Source Sizes (Moon and Spencer, 1948)

Sun (Mode 1) 10,000 ft.-candles
Sun (Mode 2) 1,000 ft.-candles
Moon (Mode 1) 0.02 ft.-candles

Figure 60–13. Illuminant notation.

perature feeling may also be summarized. Table 60-4 suggests a codification for this procedure, too.[6]

Figure 60-14 also presents a further analysis/specification characterizing the

[6] This procedure may be facilitated by using a color photograph taken with a fish-eye lens, projected on a gridded screen, and color-matched with Munsell samples.

shade and shadow pattern of the scene, as color-notated in the previous figure. Directly illuminated, shaded, shadowed, and broken-shadowed areas, as shown in the hemispherical projection, are separately indicated. The percentage distribution of these areas then serves to characterize the EN.

The contribution of the above descriptions to the characterization of an EX can

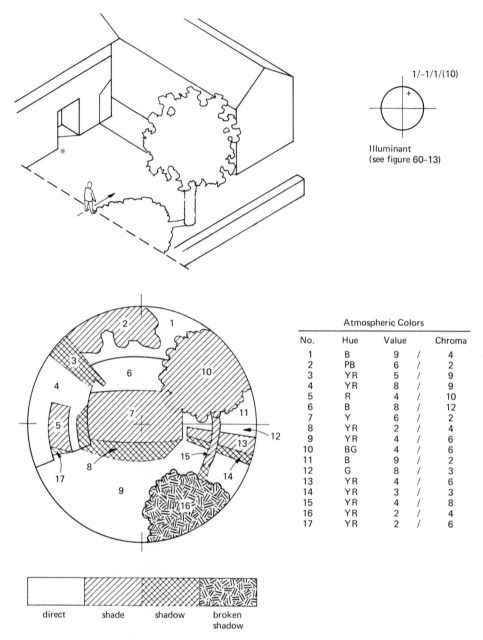

1/-1/1/(10)

Illuminant
(see figure 60–13)

Atmospheric Colors			
No.	Hue	Value	Chroma
1	B	9 /	4
2	PB	6 /	2
3	YR	5 /	9
4	YR	8 /	9
5	R	4 /	10
6	B	8 /	12
7	Y	6 /	2
8	YR	2 /	4
9	YR	4 /	6
10	BG	4 /	6
11	B	9 /	2
12	G	8 /	3
13	YR	4 /	6
14	YR	3 /	3
15	YR	4 /	8
16	YR	2 /	4
17	YR	2 /	6

direct   shade   shadow   broken
shadow

Figure 60–14. Modular notation.

be summarized, as suggested earlier, by a P mood description summarizing the cumulative effect of the ambient luminous quality as produced by illuminants and modulators at a given time/place in a sequence.

Finally, the attribute of texture and its consequence in terms of "scale" will be considered. The formulation presented here is

based on the work of Curtis (1967), in which "traditional," "contemporary," and "functional" differentiations are made in this elusive concept. In the latter case, "scale" is defined as the affect of a scene patterned by a specific proportion of various size elements of a spectrum of apparent sizes.

A hemispherical projection of a scene will

Table 60-4 Illumination Key and Temperature[a]

Element Number[b]	BTE Size[c]	% Total Area[d]	Warm Hues[e] +	Neutral Hues[e] 0	Cool Hues −	Value[f]	Chroma[f]	% Area × Value	% Area × Warm Chroma +	% Area × Cool Chroma −
1		3	R			4	14	12	42	
2		7	YR			7	10	49	70	
3		20		GY		7	10	140		
4		5			PB	4	4	20		20
5		5	R			5	8	25	40	
6		5	Y			9	6	45	30	
7		25			B	8	4	200		100
8		10	YR			7	6	70	60	
9		20	YR			6	4	120	80	
		Σ = 100						Σ = 681[g]	322[h]	120[h]

[a] Key scale:

Glaring	10	○
Bright	8	◉
Dull	6	◍
Dim	4	◕
Dark	2	◕
Black	0	◎

[b] As discriminated in the hemispherical projection.
[c] For scale calculation, see text.
[d] Of the hemispherical projection.
[e] Warm = RP, R, YR, Y; neutral = P, GY; cool = G, BG, B, PB.
[f] Munsell notation.
[g] Average value = 681/100 = 6.81 (dull–bright).
[h] Average chroma = (322 − 120)/100 = 2.02 (warm, low).

in general be characterized by a unique pattern of color patches (including value differences) of some variety of sizes. If these patches, as *Basic Texture Elements* (BTE), are ranked in order of apparent actual size,[7] and the percentage of the total area of the hemispherical projection occupied by each rank in this size scale plotted on a continuous scale-spectrum, the resulting profile will then characterize the "scale" of the scene.

Typically the scene has texture patterns in addition to those of its color patches. For example, a given monochromatic area may be textured by a pattern of lines (representing, for instance, the joints of the masonry elements comprising a wall). These superimposed patterns are also basic texture elements, and must also be included in the BTE size-use plot. This will obviously produce area totals over 100 percent.

[7] BTE size is expressed in terms of area, based on the apparent dimensions of each discriminable element. Thus, an element recognized as (apparently) a standard concrete block would have a BTE size of 8 in. × 16 in. = 128 sq. in., or 0.89 sq. ft.

A finite BTE spectrum may be used, ranging from a (tentative) lower end of 0.001 sq. ft. (about ⅜-inch square) to an upper limit of about 10^9 sq. ft. [Curtis (1967) suggests that this limit should be much lower, so as to include mirror-smooth surfaces.] This upper limit is based on a BTE of one-half the visual field (one-quarter the surface of a sphere) representing a clear field of sky. (For an eye height of 5½ ft., the horizon distance is about 15,000 ft., and the quarter area of a sphere of this radius is about 7×10^8 sq. ft.)

The BTE size-spectrum may be plotted in a compact polar coordinate form. Radii at 12 o'clock, 3 o'clock, 6 o'clock, 9 o'clock, and 12 o'clock represent BTE sizes of 10^{-3} sq. ft., 10^0 sq. ft., 10^3 sq. ft., 10^6 sq. ft., and 10^9 sq. ft., respectively. A distance in on any radius then represents a percentage of the total area of the hemispherical projection of the BTE size represented by that radius (with a point on the circumference representing 0 percent and at the center, 100 percent). This pattern then provides a unique graphic characterization of the

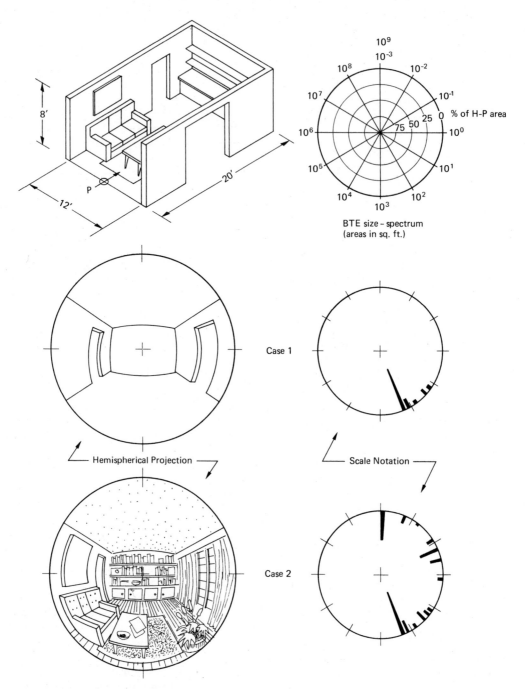

Figure 60–15. Scale notation.

"scale" of a particular scene. Figure 60-15 illustrates such a plot for two different cases. It should be noted that such a plot can be made for several conditions of any given space. That is, the scale of a scene can be calculated and plotted for a populated and furnished condition, for a furnished but un-populated condition, for an unfurnished and unpopulated condition, and also for an un-decorated condition equivalent to an un-painted stage set (as is implied in the ordinary SEEPI notation).

REFERENCES:

Blumenfeld, H. Scale in civic design. *Town Planning Review,* April 1953.

Boutourline, S. Notes on "object-oriented" and "signal-oriented" approaches to the definition of the physical world (mimeo). Department of Architecture, University of Washington, Seattle, 1968.

Curtis, J. W. A working definition of scale for environmental designers (mimeo). Department of Architecture, University of Washington, Seattle, 1967.

Eastman Kodak. *Color as seen and photographed.* Rochester, N.Y.: 1956.

Gibson, J. J. (Ed.). *Motion picture testing and research.* Report No. 7, A.A.F. Aviation Psychology Research Reports, Washington, D.C.: Government Printing Office, 1947.

Gibson, J. J. *The senses considered as perceptual systems.* Boston: Houghton Mifflin, 1966.

Hall, E. T. *The silent language.* Garden City, N.Y.: Doubleday, 1959.

Hall, E. T. Silent assumptions in social communication. In *Disorders of communication.* Vol. 42. Research Publications, Association for Research in Nervous and Mental Disease. Baltimore: Williams and Wilkins, 1964.

Huchinson, A. *Labannotation.* New York: New Directions, 1954.

Illuminating Engineering Society. *Color and the use of color by the illuminating engineer.* New York: 1961.

Illuminating Engineering Society. *Lighting fundamentals course.* New York: 1961.

Kepes, G. *The new landscape.* Chicago: Theobald, 1956.

Kepes, G. Design and light. *Design Quarterly,* 68. Minneapolis: Walker Art Center, 1968.

Lynch, K. *The image of the city.* Cambridge, Mass.: MIT Press and Harvard University Press, 1960.

Moon, P., & Spencer, D. E. *Lighting design.* Cambridge, Mass.: Addison-Wesley, 1948.

Mueller, C. G. *Light and vision.* New York: Time, Inc., 1966.

Osgood, C. E., et al. *The measurement of meaning.* Urbana, Ill.: University of Illinois, 1967.

Rose, S. A method for describing the physical qualities of an urban street space. Unpublished master's thesis, Department of Architecture, University of Washington, Seattle, 1965.

Rose, S. *A notation/simulation process for composers of space.* College of Education, Michigan State University, East Lansing, Michigan, 1968.

Sitte, C. *The art of building cities.* New York: Reinhold, 1945.

Spreiregan, P. *Urban design.* New York: McGraw-Hill, 1965.

Thiel, P. A sequence-experience notation. *Town Planning Review,* April 1961a.

Thiel, P. To the Kamakura station. *Landscape,* Fall 1961b.

Tunnard, C. *Man-made America: Chaos or control?* New Haven: Yale University Press, 1963.

U.S. Government Printing Office. *List of lights and fog signals.* H.O. Pub. No. 111B, Washington, D.C.

61 An Approach to an Objective Analysis of Behavior in Architectural Space[1]

Gary H. Winkel and Robert Sasanoff

INTRODUCTION

The design profession has long lacked a method for the objective analysis of behavior in architectural spaces. Architects continue to rely upon intuitive design concepts evolved from individual experiences even though increasing environmental complexity and rapid technological change place severe restrictions upon the human being's ability to encode this complexity and utilize it in a rational manner. There are a few architects, however, who have raised serious questions concerning continued reliance upon the "cult of the individual" (Alexander, 1964, and Van der Ryn, 1965). It is their feeling that architects must make a change toward the evolution of methods which will allow the decision-maker to approach environmental problems more rationally. This report concerns one step in a continuing series of related studies seeking to provide a laboratory

This article is condensed from *An Approach to an Objective Analysis of Behavior in Architectural Space.* Architecture/Development Series No. 5, Seattle, Wash.: University of Washington, College of Architecture and Urban Planning, August, 1966. Presented by permission of the authors and publisher. The authors acknowledge the support of the United States Steel Institute in carrying out this project.

[1] The authors are greatly indebted to the United States Steel Institute, part of whose grants made reproduction of this study possible. The authors also wish to acknowledge their indebtedness to Serge Boutourline, Jr. and Robert Weiss, who laid the theoretical and experimental foundation for this work; to Professor Robert Dietz, Dean of the College of Architecture and Urban Planning of the University of Washington, and Elizabeth Sutton Gustison, Director of the Museum of History and Industry in Seattle, Washington, for their support and cooperation.

tool for the *experimental* study of behavior in architectural environments.

The initial purpose of this project is to assess the feasibility of bringing a real world environment into the laboratory via what is termed "simulation." The ultimate objective is to develop a tool, here called the simulation booth, for the study of proposed, as yet unbuilt architectural, urban, or designed landscape environments, for use as a means of predicting certain aspects of user behavior in these environments before they are built.

Photographic representation was used to simulate a real world system. The real world system was the interior of a museum, and the user behavior studied in this environment was movement through the museum; as well as patterns of exhibit viewing. Color photographs of the interior of the museum were used to allow observers to report on how they would move through the museum and which exhibits they would view.

Observed patterns of user movement in the real world system were compared with patterns of user movement obtained in the simulated space.

Although this study involves a museum it is not concerned with museums *per se*. It is only concerned with how well a specific space in a specific museum could be simulated within a laboratory setting, using pedestrian traffic and patterns of exhibit viewing as the dependent variables to be cross-compared. A museum was selected as the setting for this study for reasons to be discussed later, but a supermarket, a shopping center, or a public park could have served just as well. The reader is therefore cautioned against using this report as a basis for decisions concerning the operation or design of museums.

THE REAL WORLD AND THE TRACKING STUDY

The real world system selected for simulation was the Museum of History and Industry in Seattle, Washington. This setting was chosen because the occasional change in exhibits would allow even regular visitors to find themselves in the position of a "tourist" rather than that of an "habitué" (Thiel, 1964), thus increasing the tendency of their behavior to reflect the influences of the perceived environment rather than that of habit. Other reasons for the selection of the museum included the opportunities it provided for a variety of experiences (due to the physical configuration of the building), the apparent heterogeneity of its visiting population in terms of socio-economic background, age, and education, and finally, for the shelter it provided from inclement weather.

Movement through the museum was selected as the user-behavior of interest because it was possible to obtain highly reliable estimates of movement patterns; because movement was one variable which appeared to be more easily amenable to study in a simulation setting; because movement is one variable which may be influenced by the form and content of any kind of space; and because movement in the museum situation represents an exceedingly crucial aspect of user behavior operating to define a complete "museum experience."

It should be noted that movement is not a single-dimensioned variable. In addition to specification of path, movement patterns will reveal the number of exhibits visited, the particular points on the floor which the visitor passes over, the elapsed time spent in motion or at rest, head movements and body orientation, etc. Thus movement can serve as a potentially rich user behavior.

Because the focus of this study is architectural, movement through space was chosen as the user behavior which seemed best suited to understanding how visitors utilize the Museum of History and Industry. Had the focus been upon the educational features of the museum, a greater amount of time might have been spent concentrating upon devices which measured the amount of information the visitor retained from his experience of the museum. It is important to note, however, that movement through the space can define the kinds of information available to the viewer and hence data on movement is fundamental to an understanding of the types of experiences assimilated by the visitor.

The space consists of the main exhibit hall, a rectangular room 60 feet by 88 feet with a ceiling height of 13 feet. There are four doors on three sides leading into either auxiliary exhibition spaces or passageways to other points in the museum. A floor plan of the space is shown in Figure 61-1. This hall is lined with illuminated glass cases on all sides, in which permanent displays are presented. In addition, the main hall was furnished with four temporary "island" displays, free-standing in the center of the space, composed of four different trucks or wagons.

A brief description of the auxiliary rooms

is necessary. The space on the plan labeled "animal wing" is a smaller rectangular room containing the stuffed heads and bodies of animals from various parts of the world. The heads are mounted on vertical panels arranged around the room so that the visitor must move around the entire room to view them. There are also side cases with animals arranged against naturalistic backgrounds.

The space on the plan labeled "maritime wing" contains exhibits representative of oceanographic research and industry.

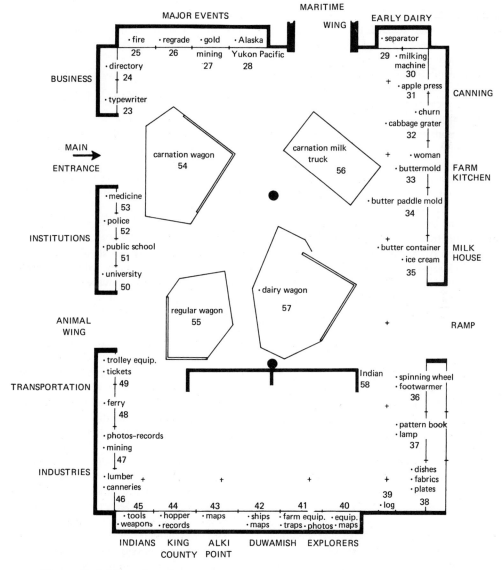

Figure 61–1. Floor plan of museum.

The space labeled "ramp" leads down from the main exhibition hall to exhibitions of various modes of transportation.

The space labeled "main entrance" is a wide corridor fitted with an information and souvenir counter and a variety of permanent exhibits. Most visitors to the museum enter through this hall.

THE TRACKING METHOD

The method of data-gathering employed is called "tracking" (Weiss & Boutourline, 1962). Plans of the main gallery of the museum were furnished each of the investigators (see Figure 61-2 for an example), along with a stopwatch. Using these plans the investigators could track and record the movement of subjects through the space by drawing a line on the plan corresponding to the movement of the subject in the actual space.

Movement was indicated by lines on the maps, with arrows interspersed to show direction of movement. If the subject moved to an exhibit, the line was drawn up to the exhibit and the time spent at that point recorded. If for some reason the subject stopped in the middle of the floor, not at an exhibit, the time spent at that point was also recorded (a stop being defined as an actual physical cessation of movement). Time spent in the ancillary galleries was also recorded, although the observer did not follow the subject into these spaces. Also noted was the amount of time elapsed between the time the subject entered and left the main gallery.

In addition to this information the observer recorded other user behavior in the space, such as "trouble with children," "family conference," "crowding about exhibits," "lack of access to auxiliary galleries" and "indecision as to where to go next."

After the subject left the main gallery for an "exit" (defined for our purposes as down the ramp, or out the entrance corridor) the observer interviewed him briefly to obtain information on his museum-visit patterns and significant memories of his visit, if any. The subject's sex, estimated age, and whether he visited the museum alone or with a group was also noted on a form provided for this purpose.

At all times the tracker attempted to remain inconspicuous. It was found that observation at an appropriate distance allowed the preservation of an anonymity consistent with careful data collecting.

Subjects were selected by the following procedure, designed to produce a random sample: the hand of the stopwatch was allowed to pass an arbitrary time point, and the first person thereafter passing an arbitrarily-selected mark at the entrance became the subject to be tracked.

Most of the tracking data was collected by five graduate students of the Department of Architecture of the College of Architecture and Urban Planning, of the University of Washington.

THE SIMULATED WORLD AND THE TRACKING STUDY

Having established patterns of user behavior from an analysis of the data collected in the real world, attention was next turned to the creation of a laboratory reconstruction of this real world, in which we could observe user behavior for comparison with that of the real world.

One of the most pervasive difficulties which a research worker encounters in environmental study is the sheer enormity of the systems under consideration. One solution to this difficulty involves abstracting parts of the system so that they may be more easily brought into the laboratory for controlled study. The process of abstracting elements of a system sometimes involves the danger that patterns which may exist among the elements of the fully intact system become lost or minimized as a consequence of the abstraction. Rather than ignore such patterns, it seems apparent that research must proceed with an appreciation of system characteristics and attempt to incorporate them into the research designs ultimately selected.

It is only recently that methodologies have been devised which take pattern relationships between or among elements of the system into account. Current work in the area of large-scale systems has led to the development of techniques which have been given the generic term "simulations." The most reasonable definition of this term is

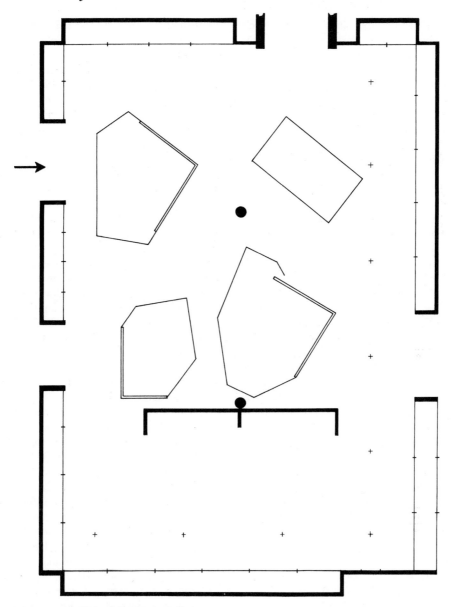

Figure 61–2. Plan of the Main Gallery.

given by Thomas and Deemer (1957). They suggest that "to simulate is to attain the essence of, without the reality." Inherent in this definition is the realization that complete realism is not necessary for successful simulation. Successful simulation requires only that one be able to reproduce the system under study as accurately as possible without actually employing the system itself. Such a specification tends to make simulation broader in scope than most of the "conventional" methods of experimentation.

As a matter of fact, experimentation represents one facet of simulation.

Harman (1961) presents one way of defining the simulation continuum while Larsen (1963) suggests a slightly different characterization. There are some areas of agreement between the definitions of these two workers, but Larsen appears to have provided a more exhaustive and possibly more fruitful set of definitions.

Harman has more clearly linked his definitions to a simulation continuum. At the lower end is "identity" simulation, in which the real world is used as the model to obtain knowledge about itself. The complexity of the system being studied, however, usually makes the use of "identity" simulations impractical. At the upper end of the simulation continuum is complete "analytical" simulation. This type represents the highest degree of abstraction from the real world and is exemplified by the use of a mathematical model descriptive of the system. The existence of systems involving relatively unknown sets of variables makes complete "analytical" simulation difficult to attain. Between these two types of simulation are found the "laboratory" simulations. In "laboratory" simulation, the replication of the "salient" aspects of the real world system is attempted within the laboratory.

In Larsen's (1963) system, simulation is classified according to the degree to which it resembles reality. In *isomorphic* simulations, all the operational features of the real situations are included and thus, in theory, they could replace the real situation. This type of simulation sounds quite like Harman's "identity" simulation discussed above. In *homomorphic* simulations, gross effects of interactions are reproduced in the real situation rather than the detailed effects. This type of simulation is similar to Harman's "laboratory" simulations. Larsen also classifies types of simulation in terms of their structuring characteristics, as follows: (1) *Iconic* simulation is one that "looks like" the subject of inquiry. It is characterized by the use of some metric transformation or scaling. It is of use in the description of static things, or of dynamic things at a point in time. Globes and still photographs are examples. (2) *Analogical* simulations are characterized by the use of a convenient transformation of one set of properties for another set of properties in accordance with specified rules. These types of simulations are used to describe dynamic systems or processes. Flow charts, schedule boards, plant layouts, and structural plans represent examples of this type of simulation. (3) *Symbolic* simulations are characterized by the fact that the components of the subject of inquiry and the interrelationships among them are represented by symbols, both

mathematical and logical. Such a simulation is similar to Harman's complete analytical simulation.

The approach taken in the present study does not clearly fit in any of the classifications discussed above. It is of course a "laboratory" simulation in Harman's sense, but this term seems uncomfortably broad. Because of the use of still photographs, the present method also has some similarity to Larsen's iconic simulations but there is a major characteristic of the present method which definitely lifts it out of the category of iconic simulations. This characteristic is that the present method is *not* static and is *not* a dynamic process frozen in time. The advantage (assumed at the present time) of the simulation booth is that it provides a technique for allowing the subject to make his experience dynamic (within the limits of the bulky slide mechanisms used). In this sense, the simulation booth is like Larsen's analogical simulations which are used to describe dynamic systems or processes. Again, however, the simulation booth transcends the analogical simulation because the "analogue" is a two-dimensional photographic collapse of a three-dimensional space which can be programmed by the subject to change in time (the present authors' restricted definition of a "dynamic" system). The analogue used in the simulation booth represents a less abstracted transformation than a detailed architectural plan, for example. It seems to the authors that the abstraction involved in such a plan leads to an ambiguity which the simulation booth attempts to overcome. Hence, its assumed advantage over most of the analogues used by those who purport to study systems.

One other advantage is present in the use of the present kind of simulation technique. *It provides a method for checking the results of the simulation booth against behavior in the "real" space.* This advantage should not be underestimated. At whatever level of abstraction at which the simulation booth operates, it is not so far removed from a working system that it ceases to be devoid of any "real world" meaning. Thus, the technique itself makes for a relatively easy transformation from one set of behavioral data (obtained from those operating in the "real world") to another set of behavioral data (obtained from the subjects who experienced and used the simulation booth). The choice of type of simulation must always make provision for an evaluation of the simulation data compared to data obtained from the working system. Without such a provision, the simulation effort might occupy the status of an interesting intellectual exercise, but not much more.

THE SIMULATION METHOD

The real world was simulated by means of the projection of photographs on screens within a "simulation booth." With a suitable "vocabulary" of photographs of the real world the attempt was made to recreate this real world in the laboratory, in terms of the user behavior of interest. The vocabulary of photographs of the real world presumably was such that it would be possible to enable a subject in the simulation booth to "move" through the simulated world as fully and spontaneously as he could in the real world.

The equipment used for this part of the study was as follows:

1 Nikon 35 mm. camera and f 1.4, 35 mm. lens (lens angular coverage ± 50 degrees horizontally)
1 Majestic tripod
1 Weston Master III exposure meter
2 50-foot tapes
2 wooden "t's"
2 levels
1 metal shim, ³⁄₃₂" thick
1 plumb bob
   Ektachrome high speed film (daylight) ASA 125

The floor of the main gallery of the museum was divided up on a 5-foot-square grid. This grid was set up by laying off 5-foot intervals along the base of walls of the main gallery. One of the two "t's" was placed at one of these 5-foot points. The other "t" was placed on a grid interval at a 90-degree angle to the first "t" on an adjacent wall. The 50-foot tapes were attached to the "t's" at the wall, and points on the floor were marked where the tapes crossed.

After all grid points had been marked on the floor, the camera was mounted on the tripod. The platform of the tripod was divided into 8 equal angular parts (at 45 degrees each). The plumb bob was attached to the tripod itself so that it hung from the center of the tripod platform. The tripod was then centered over each grid-point on the floor by means of the plumb bob.

The camera was attached to the tripod platform, with the ³⁄₃₂" metal shim placed between the bottom of the camera and the tripod platform, so that the camera was tilted about 3 degrees down from the horizontal. This was done so that more of the floor and less of the ceiling would be seen in the slides.

The tripod was positioned vertically so that the lens was at about eye height (5'-7"). Eight exposures at 45 degree increments (as marked on the tripod platform) were taken at each grid-point on the floor, with the first shot always taken in a specified direction. In the museum the first shot was perpendicular to the ramp side wall. All photographs were taken when there were no people in the gallery.

Close-ups were also taken of the exhibition cases along the side walls. In each case one photograph was taken in an "up" position and one in a "down" position, in such a way that the entire vertical dimension of the objects in the case was covered.

The exposures varied according to the local light conditions. The light was a mixture of yellow (tungsten), blue (fluorescent), and natural daylighting. Besides the variety of color there were intensity variations. The aperture of the lens was held constant at f.8 or f.16 (in order to attain a greater depth of field), and the shutter speed varied between 1 and 3 seconds, depending upon the light conditions.

The apparatus used for equipping the simulation booth was as follows:

3 Bell and Howell 2" × 2" manual projectors, with 4" lenses
3 Screens each 30" × 40", of white illustration board
3 Adjustable stands for the screens
2 Compartmented slide trays
3 Blank slides

Boxes of end tags
Platform, desks, chairs, pencils, papers,
tacks, etc.

The simulation booth was initially established in a building on the campus of the
University of Washington and, later, at the
museum. Figure 61-3 shows the disposition
of the equipment in the simulation booth.

The platform (36″ high) was located in one
corner, and positioned on it was a 30″ high
desk. The three projectors were arranged
on this desk, with their lenses about 6″ above
the top of the desk so that the total height
of the lenses was thus 6 feet above the floor.

A second sloping platform was arranged
18″ over the projectors for the sectioned
slide trays. These trays were compartmented

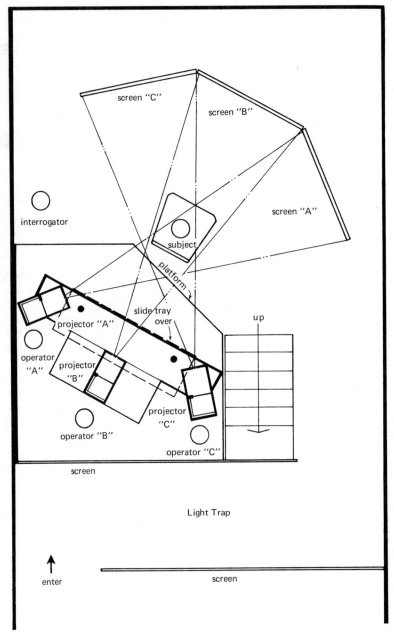

Figure 61–3. Floor plan, simulation booth

so that there were pigeon holes for each set of 8 slides taken in the museum. The placement of the sections in the slide trays was analogous to that of the points on the museum floor. Each slide was tagged with a flag showing its point on the museum floor and the direction of the photograph.

The screens were diagonally opposite the projector platform at a distance of 8'-6". Each of the three screens were placed together with their edges touching. The width of the projected image was 36". The projectors were adjusted so that the rays of the two outer projectors crossed, and so that the axis of each projector was perpendicular (90 degrees) to its screen. The images did not overlap.

The subjects were seated about 3'-6" from the screen. The distance from the ground to the top of the subject's head was about 4'-6". The subjects were invited into the booth and seated in front of the screens. They were told to adjust the position of the chair so that they could see the screens well. After they were seated they were given the following instructions:

We have taken some photographs of the main gallery at the Museum of History and Industry. We have arranged these photographs in such a way that you may go anywhere you wish in the Museum merely by telling us which way you wish to go. (At this time the experimenter pointed to each of the three screens and said to the subject that he could go "left," "straight," or "right" in the room.) It is important that you try to tell us as much as possible how you would act in the museum if you were actually there. If, for example, you would stop at some exhibits please tell us that. It is, however, important to realize that there are *no right or wrong answers* in this experiment. What is most important is that you do what you think you would do in the museum if you were there. The photographs will help you make your decisions.

We have the slides arranged so that the first photograph you will see will be the view of the museum as you walk into the main entrance. The next set of photographs will put you in the main hallway leading into the main gallery. We will walk you up to the gallery, put you inside the door, and from that point you tell us where you wish to go. If you want to stop at any time and look around the main gallery you may do so.

At this time the first photographs were shown to the observer. He was told that he was being walked up the hallway to the main gallery by the experimenter. After he was inside the door, the observer was shown the full view of the main gallery from the door. The first set of three photographs shown to him revealed the view from 90 degrees to his right and left and the next set showed the views from 45 degrees to his right and to his left. The order of presentation was randomized over the subjects. From that point on, the observer told the experimenter in which direction he wished to go, as well as what he wished to see.

During the time that the observer was in the simulation booth, the experimenter followed the course of the observer's "trip" in the gallery by marking it on a floor plan of the gallery along with a note on the particular exhibits "seen" by the observer.

At the end of the "trip" through the museum (that is, at the point at which the observer indicated that he wished to leave the main gallery and not return) the observer was given a blank map of the floorplan and was asked to mark on it his trip through the museum, and also to label, in a non-detailed manner, the things he remembered seeing. After this was completed, the observer was interviewed about his reactions to the simulation booth and the museum.

Two groups of subjects were used for the simulation study. One volunteer group consisted of 14 male and 14 female students at the University of Washington, 18–20 years old, most of whom were either architecture or interior design majors. The other group consisted of 43 actual museum visitors, randomly selected just before they entered the museum. Their mean age was 35, and 75 percent of the sample were males.

Since the observers used in the first simulation booth analysis were not entirely representative of the usual visitors to the museum, it seemed advisable to repeat the simulation using a second group of observers drawn from the population of individuals who actually visited the museum. In this phase of the study, the simulation booth was relocated at the Museum of History and Industry, and was arranged there according to the same specifications previously used at the University.

The subjects who were selected for participation in the museum study were chosen by the same randomizing procedure as those subjects who provided the original real-world data. The major difference was that these subjects were chosen *before* they entered the museum.[2]

METHODS OF DATA ANALYSIS

A number of analytic procedures suggested themselves for use with the data. There are advantages and disadvantages to each of these methods, but if used in combination they can provide a reasonable picture of the results.

The first analysis made consisted of collations of the separate tracking maps into composite maps, which give an overview of the paths which the subjects followed in their museum experience. Each of the individual tracking maps was combined into a single map representing the path behavior of the sample. The method of presentation which was utilized involved the breakdown of the composite maps in such a way that the path behavior of the sample becomes clearer. Thus separate maps were made for Saturday and Sunday. The justification for doing this was simply the assumption that possibly a different sample visited the museum on each of those two days. There may be more subtle differences between the groups than this, however, but in the absence of any information to the contrary, it was decided to make separate maps for those days. A second breakdown involved whether the person tracked turned right or left at the main entrance. This was done so that the visual presentation might be clearer on the maps.

One of the most immediately apparent advantages of composite maps is that they summarize a good deal of information which can be quickly grasped by inspection. The size of the sample taking a particular path can be assessed and the direction or the sequences of movement can be relatively easily evaluated.

For the purposes of this study, however, the composites do not provide complete information about the paths and in some cases obscure the relationships which actually exist between movement patterns and sequential experiences, for example, the diversity of paths taken by some of the samples who were tracked in the museum. Visual inspection of the composite maps alone does not provide any criteria for assessing the significance of path diversity when it is encountered. For the purposes of simulation it is necessary to provide the criteria which the composites lack.

More important, perhaps, is the fact that the composite maps do not possess any means for inducing the set of experiences enjoyed by those visitors who take a particular path through the main gallery. Unfortunately, it is not possible to assume that if the same path was taken by two different visitors that they then enjoyed the same set of experiences. Reflection on the point for a moment will easily suggest why this is so. The first visitor may have used a path to get from one point in the gallery to another, while the second visitor may have used the path to experience the set of exhibits which are available to him. Composite map path indicators obscure this kind of information.

To compensate for some of these disadvantages of the composite maps a more objective procedure was adopted. Factor analytic techniques were utilized with the data. The results of the factor analysis were studied to see if they would provide information on the relationships between particular paths taken and sets of exhibits which were visited by the sample. It was possible to subdivide the paths taken from each of the adjunct galleries (maritime, animal, and ramp area) as well as the main entrance, and relate the direction taken from each of these points (either right, straight, or left) with the set of exhibits seen by each visitor. Such information provided a more quantitative estimate of the behavior of our visitors to the museum. This estimate could be used later when comparisons were made

---

[2] A brief description of the methods of data analysis follows. For a more complete analysis and discussion of the results, the reader is referred to the original study.

between the behavior of our "vicarious visitors" to the museum and those who actually visited the museum.

CONCLUSIONS AND IMPLICATIONS

One of the goals of the present study was to evaluate an experimental technique for the simulation of selected environments. Ultimately, it is expected that the simulation technique can be developed into a practical design tool which will allow predictions of user behavior in certain kinds of architectural spaces.

The justification of any experimental tool lies in its ability to predict, with a minimum amount of error, phenomena observed in the "real" world. For this reason a great deal of attention has been devoted in this study to correspondences which exist between the simulated world and the real world. Without evidence of such correspondence, the simulation device remains experimental and can only be used in practical decision situations with caution. The results indicated that there are similarities between the real and the simulated world. It is not overly surprising that the similarity was not closer since any new technique usually contains unanticipated error components. The problem is simply to identify and remove those elements in the technique which are contributing to errors.

An initial identification of possible errors in the simulation probably can be traced to the "unreal" aspects of the simulation as currently used. Objective consideration of the simulation device indicates that in many ways it is a very arbitrary method for extracting and reproducing the essence of a space. Assuming the objectively "unreal" aspects of the simulation booth as a device which is designed to transport a viewer to the main gallery of a museum as an "actual" visitor, it is something short of miraculous that the results obtained from it are so encouraging. For the present, attention must be directed toward the refinement of the experimental techniques so that they will bring the simulated data into closer congruence with the real world data.

Briefly, there appear to be two sets of variables which should be more closely examined in any future simulation effort: (1) the freedom which the booth gives to the observer and (2) the clarity of the visual information presented to the simulation booth observer.

Attempts to account for the overestimation of path behavior shown by some of the simulation booth groups led to a suggestion that the booth cannot replicate some of the negative aspects of museum visiting. For example, walking a few steps cannot be considered to be an overly fatiguing experience, but there can be no doubt that the comfort entailed in "viewing" the museum while seated in a chair may increase the propensity of the observer to seek a broader range of experiences than might be the case in the real world experience. Combining the relative ease of movement with experimental instructions that there can be complete freedom of behavior while in the museum may contribute to the increased number of paths taken by the simulation booth observers. Alterations in either the instructions (e.g. a de-emphasis upon freedom of movement) or the manner in which the museum is visited (e.g. having the observer stand while he is shown the slides) may bring the simulation booth data into closer congruence with the observed real world.

A second factor which potentially might account for the observed path overestimation offers much greater possibilities for future study. This factor is concerned with the degree to which a comprehensive "image" of a space can be attained if it is experienced as an abstraction, as it is in the simulation booth.

As the observer "moves" about the main gallery the slides restrict his ability to visually scan his environment extensively. If the observer wishes to "get his bearings" (or clarify his "image" of the space) he must ask the experimenter to let him look around the museum. Although this option was available to the observers very few of them requested it. Two hypotheses suggest an explanation for this finding: (1) it does not "look good" if the observer becomes lost in the main gallery and must constantly ask for information concerning his present location, and (2) the waiting time required to simply turn an observer around in the space may convince him that the resulting information is not worth the effort. The net effect of inability to orient and establish the relationship between the "self" and the external space denies to the simulation booth observer an experience which is readily accessible to the actual museum visitor. Thus, it is quite likely that the actual museum visitor can form a better integrated visual image or picture of the main gallery than his simulation booth counterpart. If the actual museum visitor does possess a superior information base about the space there will be a corresponding decrease in any ambiguity or uncertainty about his environment. It is well known from information theory (Garner, 1960) that there is an inverse relationship between uncertainty and redundancy in information. One of the consequences of redundancy is that the rate of responsiveness decreases since no new information is forthcoming. Translating such an information processing model into the museum experience, it seems reasonable to suppose that the actual museum visitor moves about the main gallery less because his visual scanning of the environment quickly establishes the redundancy in the gallery. The simulation booth observer can do this visual scanning only if he is willing to pay the price of his time while slides are laboriously changed. Since most of the observers do not take the time, their uncertainty can only be reduced by actually "moving" through the main gallery.

Some evidence obtained from comments spontaneously made by the museum simulation booth sample indicated that some of the observers were uncertain about which parts of the gallery they had visited. Often a partitioned area appeared to be another room. The observers would then move into the partitioned area and seem disappointed that they had simply entered another section of the main gallery. Once committed to the area, however, the natural tendency was to continue in the path selected.

A more searching test of the hypothesis that the simulation booth observer had greater difficulty orienting himself could be obtained if he were given a blank piece of paper and requested to draw the gallery as well as the path he took through it. Such information was available from the student simulation sample, and it confirmed that most of them did have a reasonably good idea of where they were and where they had been. It is possible that being architecture majors, their ability to orient themselves spatially was more developed than the observers from the museum simulation sample. It might be added that the data from the student simulation sample was closer to the real world data than the data from the museum simulation sample. Unfortunately, due to time considerations it was impossible to give the same test to our museum sample. Unsolicited comments, however, did suggest that some of the visitors were just a little confused about their various locations in the simulated museum.

A testing device which might allow the simulation booth observer greater opportunities to scan his environment with a minimum of difficulty is television. Preliminary work in our laboratory has demonstrated the feasibility of utilizing closed-circuit television equipment in conjunction with a scale model environment. Currently this work is being extended to include study of a model of the main gallery of the museum which was used in the present study. Televised "visiting" might reveal patterns of movement which are in closer congruence with actual path behavior.

One of the ultimate goals of the simulation technique would be to allow both researchers and designers an opportunity to test alternate designs which have been proposed as solutions to architectural problems. The utilization of the technique for such a purpose will necessitate adaptations in the equipment depending upon the type of information the designer hopes to obtain. For example, in the present study our primary dependent variable was movement, inferred from patterns of exhibit viewing. If the designer were interested in those elements which the observer looked at as he moved about the gallery different equipment would be required (e.g. an eye movement camera). If he were concerned about the effects of other people in the space a device would have to be included which would allow the superimposition of crowds in the space.

The addition or deletion of equipment is an advantage to the simulation technique because it increases its generalizability. It should not be assumed, however, that the present simulation device will answer all kinds of questions of concern to the architect. But if the device can increase the information base even in limited areas its utility is apparent.

At a level of analysis other than movement the simulation method might be very useful in understanding those components of design which are related to potentially "rich" user behaviors, such as aesthetic preferences, attitudes, and affective responses to design, the relationship of design elements to the formation of coherent or incoherent mental images of the external world, and possibly an initial understanding of the role which the physical environment plays in human behavior.

From an educational point of view, the use of the simulation booth as an "experience generator" should not be overlooked. In the long run, the tendency of the simulation booth to overestimate the amount of movement on the part of observers may be one of its chief assets rather than liabilities. If the simulation booth can control the rate of information input (by restricting the amount of visual scanning which can be done) it may force the observer to look at things that otherwise might have been ignored. Hence, the use of the simulation technique as a "controlled information output device" might be closely connected to the development of *enriched* mental images which have many branches and cross connections. In many ways, this possibility is the most exciting of the many directions that research in this area might lead.

Any final evaluations of the simulation technique will depend upon the limits of the technique and the limits of those who use it. Hopefully the method will be useful enough so that it may be included in the architect's basic "tool kit."

REFERENCES:

Alexander, C. *Notes on the synthesis of form.* Cambridge, Mass.: MIT Press, 1964.
Garner, W. R. *Uncertainty and structure as psychological concepts.* New York: John Wiley, 1960.
Harman, H. Simulation as a tool for research. *Systems Development Corporation,* SP-565, September 25, 1961.
Larsen, J. W. Simulation—A tool for industrial engineers. In S. M. Selig and M. Ettelstein (Eds.), *New horizons in industrial engineering.* Baltimore, Md.: Spartan Books, 1963.
Thiel, P. *The tourist and the habitué.* Unpublished working paper, College of Architecture and Urban Planning, University of Washington, 1964.
Thomas, C., & Deemer, W., Jr. The role of operational gaming in operations research. *Operations Research,* 1957, **5**, 1–27.
Van der Ryn, S. *The ecology of student housing: A case study in environmental analysis and design.* Berkeley, Calif.: University of California, College of Environmental Design, 1965 (mimeo).
Weiss, R., & Boutourline, S. *Fairs, exhibits, pavilions and their audiences.* New York: IBM Corporation, 1962.

62 A Walk Around the Block

Kevin Lynch and Malcolm Rivkin

What does the ordinary individual perceive in his landscape? What makes the strongest impression on him and how does he react to it? In recent research at the Massachusetts Institute of Technology we have recorded the impressions of persons as they walked through the city streets. Other studies of urban perception have been made, but we believe this to be the first where responses have been recorded while actually moving through the city itself.

In this sample there were interesting agreements about what parts of the scene were most remarkable, and how these parts could be fitted together to make a whole. Spatial form seemed to be a fundamental impression. Spatially dominant buildings, of dominant use or association, also appear in the front rank. Of next importance was the quality of the city "floor," or pavement; and the contents and details of the various storefronts.

THE SEARCH FOR ORDER IN THE ENVIRONMENT

Most of these people felt strongly about their visual world, even if they found difficulty in being articulate about it. Emotions were associated with the spatial characteristics, in particular, and with the apparent coherence (or lack of it) in the whole scene.

From *Landscape,* 1959, 8, 24–34. Reprinted by permission of the publisher and author.

They seemed to search for, or try to create, a sense of order and continuity in what they saw. The look of the world about them did indeed make a difference in their lives.

The trip began at the corner of Berkeley and Boylston Streets in Boston, and each time the interviewer told his companion: "We are about to take a short walk. Don't look for anything in particular, but tell me about the things you see, hear, or smell; everything and anything you notice." A tiny microphone was attached to the subject's lapel, and the interviewer recorded his comments as they went around the block, through the alley, and into the park. (See Figure 62-1.)

The block itself is not an extraordinary one. It has many typical features of an American shopping street, but with some touches of Boston tradition, and much physical contrast in small compass. Boylston Street, on one side, has a wide range of offices and middle-income specialty stores, while Newbury Street, on the opposite side, caters to a wealthier class, with its elegant dress shops, decorators, beauticians and haberdashers. These shops occupy the ground floors of old, narrow-fronted, business buildings, which vary markedly in height. Traffic on both streets is one-way, and that on Boylston is quite heavy.

Between the streets is a narrow alley, neither meaner nor dirtier than most. At the eastern end, across Arlington Street, lie the Public Gardens, planted in the romantic style. At the corner of Arlington and Boylston stands the old brownstone Arlington Street Church, completed in 1861, and one of the first buildings to occupy the newly-filled Back Bay lands. At the western end of our block facing Berkeley Street is Bonwit Teller's, occupying the building built in 1864 for the Museum of Natural History. During the interviews the weather was cold, sometimes sunny. The trees were bare, and there were a few patches of old snow on the ground.

Twenty-seven subjects made this tour, which was an outgrowth of earlier tests along Copley Square, in Boston, and Brattle Street, in Cambridge. After the walk, the subjects were tested for their memories of the event, both verbally and through photo-

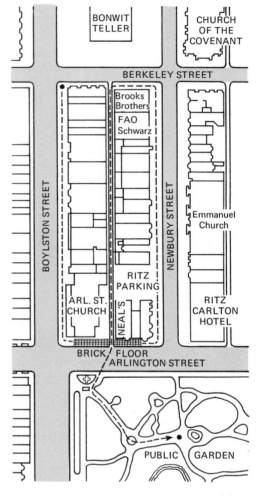

Figure 62–1. The Block itself: The dotted line shows the course of the walk, starting at the corner of Boylston and Berkeley Streets.

graphic recognition. Some of the subjects were very familiar with the area, and for others it was their first visit. They varied in age, sex, occupation and national background, but the group was too small to be truly representative of American city-dwellers.

Since the process of perception is so rapid and complex, often so difficult to verbalize, the findings must be regarded only as the perceptions which were "at the top of the heap" in the whole conscious-unconscious sensing of the environment. Furthermore, a recorded tour in itself is sufficiently abnormal as to intensify, and possibly distort, the usual day-by-day perception of the city.

Yet with all these qualifications, the results are a first clue as to how our cities affect us. Even aside from its value as a research tool, the method used has potential value in the training of designers, and as a device to make the layman more directly aware of the environment in which he lives.

THE WALK ITSELF

The walk proceeded first along the wide Boylston Street sidewalk. Two-thirds remarked almost immediately on the spatial quality of the street—its breadth, the width of the sidewalk, the height of the flanking buildings and the open vista at the Garden end.

> I like the openness, I like the width of the sidewalks, I like the feeling of uncrowded space. You can never feel at the bottom of a well on this spot.

One or two referred to the heights of the buildings along the street, with the remark that they were not so high as to be uncomfortable. This same sense of scale is implied in the word "house" which several people used, even though few of these business buildings could have been residences in the past. Some subjects were conscious of the general architectural disunity:

> Each individual building is almost ugly, and they don't seem to fit together at all.

A woman recalled after the walk:

> There were all different styles of houses, they didn't seem to match, especially the heights of the houses varied so much, with some houses you could see the sides and you could see that they were not really meant to be exposed.

One walker summed it up briefly:

> I think it is the hodge-podgeness of our streets, like down ahead of us, that is so sort of discouraging.

The majority of our walkers commented at one time or another on some sign they saw. However, there was little consensus of recognition of any particular one. Out of the vast number of signs strewn along the path, only a small minority were noticed at all, and

some subjects referred to this welter of communication with irritation:

> The first thing I notice are the signs along the street, a confusion of signs.

> They sort of reach out and grab you by the throat.

A large clock on a standard in the center of the wide sidewalk excited the comment of a third of the subjects, as did a sidewalk book stall, both because of their intrinsic interest as well as their position in space. But a mid-sidewalk sign farther down the street was blissfully ignored. Alongside the Arlington Street Church a number of newly-painted trash cans caught everyone's eye, no doubt because of their bright yellow and black colors, contrasting with the gray of the sidewalk and the brown of the façades.

All but one of the walkers commented at one time or another upon the stores themselves, and the contents of their windows. Window-shopping is undoubtedly a pleasant and absorbing occupation for many of them. Like the signs, the consensus of selection seemed weak, but the interest was real, and not marked by irritation.

At least half spoke of the parked cars along the sidewalk edge, most often in reference to the problem of parking itself. Almost as many remarked upon the moving traffic, although with little emotional connotation at this stage. But up to this point, of the multitude of other details to be seen or discussed, almost all were passed by in silence or with only scattered comment: street furniture, people, colors, smells, sounds, weather.

At the Arlington Street Church the subjects' animation once again matched that with which they first greeted Boylston Street. Only three failed to comment upon this church which, by its associations, position, material, form and landscaping, contrasts strongly with the remainder of the block. Their remarks conveyed pleasure as well as interest:

> Seems to be the most exciting thing on the street, the church.

> Every time I look up, I tend to look at our church steeple.

Being of sandstone, it has a much richer character, really, than most stone buildings.

As they approached this corner and remarked upon the church, they were struck even more forcibly by the space of the Public Gardens opening up across the street. Only one walker was so stubborn as not to mention it at all. The comments were precise and emphatic in their pleasure:

Well, the nicest part of this section is definitely the Public Gardens.

And the comments are often well-considered:

I often envy the people who are able to stay . . . [where] they can look out onto the Public Gardens, across the Common. . . . People don't realize what a beautiful thing, not only in the daytime, but at night. . . . Here you get the feeling of spaciousness and at the same time you don't feel lost.

Distant objects could now be appreciated:

Look at that dome on the State House. That certainly shines.

The space of the Public Gardens was one of the strongest experiences of the entire journey. It also called attention to details within itself: one-third of the subjects noticed the statue of Channing which faces the church, and several pointed out the old iron fence which encloses the Garden.

Around the corner on Arlington, the subway entrance, a low masonry box in the middle of the sidewalk, elicited diverse comments. To one women it was:

These ugly subway entrances—low, squat and dirty, black and cold-looking holes in the ground.

But to a little girl it held promise of adventure:

Why don't we go down there, and go out to another town?

Here the sidewalk material changed from patched cement slabs to brick. This drew a surprising amount of attention, mixing pleasure with the uneasiness of high-heeled women:

Brick sidewalks, hazardous, but very pleasant just to have a different texture for a sidewalk.

Over one-half spontaneously recalled the floor material in the post-walk interview:

I recall here the sidewalks seemed to be the major point of interest or the things that struck one most. It was a sidewalk which was in rather poor condition, extended for a great distance before the eye.

The mouth of the alley did not escape attention. Some were struck by its narrowness alone, others by a happy accident of the city—the view that opens up at the far end of the slot:

The spire of the New England Mutual Hall at the end of the alley—certainly dramatic—I've never noticed that before.

Particularly striking at night as you come along, to see the tower lighted as you glance up the alley.

Past the Arlington Church and across the mouth of the alley is one of the few stores in which there was common interest. "Neal's of California," with its gaudy display of women's apparel, stands in sharp feminine contrast to the church on one side and a dignified antique store on the other. Since the stores abut directly on the sidewalk, while the church is well set back, Neal's is also spatially prominent. Half of the observers seem impelled to pick it out.

A woman's shoe store with the whimsical address of "Zero Newbury" leads around the corner and into Newbury Street itself. Only one-third of the subjects referred to the Newbury space in comparison with the two-thirds who spoke up about Boylston Street, but among these there seemed to be a new enjoyment of the total composition:

I think looking down the street here, where the sun hits the buildings two blocks or so down, is a sort of unified loveliness. At least, all are approximately the same height, all built at approximately the same time, all have certain characteristics very definitely in common. . . . And I like the punctuation marks of church steeples here and there.

While another puts the feeling of harmony in a more prosaic way:

> There aren't any old signs sticking out.

Three separate buildings draw comments from one-half to two-thirds of the walkers on Newbury: the Ritz Carlton Hotel on the corner, with its connotations of luxury, its sheer cubical mass standing in contrast to the space of the Gardens; the Church of the Covenant at the Berkeley Street corner, whose tall spire is silhouetted against the sky; and the Emmanuel Church, which is also in architectural contrast to its surroundings, but which gets less mention, due probably to its more subordinate mid-block position. It is interesting to note that this is the only building in the entire walk to sustain any significant comment which is not spatially exposed on at least two sides.

One feature on Newbury Street roused more comment than any building: the Ritz-Carlton parking lot, which separates the corner stores from those further up the street, and whose cars project forward over the sidewalk itself. The spontaneous remarks expressed annoyance:

> An ugly little spot where they've cut out some buildings and provided parking . . . a gaping hole.

> This parking lot here has always annoyed me. It separates the shopping. I always hate to walk across the lot from one store to the next.

Newbury Street was impressive particularly for its social connotations and personal associations. The non-familiar subjects immediately picked up its class character:

> This seems to be the more fashionable sector. Seems to be more exclusive, since they don't have too much show and pomp in the windows, and no big signs.

The habitués found pleasure and many memories:

> Dear old Newbury Street . . . it's just the epitome of the top aristocratic Boston.

> I can walk in this area and never get tired of it. When I'm away, this is the only—not really the only place—but the place I think of most.

But some of the comments were uncomfortable:

> In an area like this, I've always felt sort of like a stranger . . . sort of like this wasn't particularly your street . . . where the stores sell expensive things not particularly useful to myself.

The small, select stores with their carefully chosen, unpriced displays all came in for comment. But only two, F. A. O. Schwarz and Brooks Bros., caught nearly as much attention as Neal's of California. Schwarz has windows full of attractive toys and Brooks Bros. is remarkable for its corner position, and for its social standing. It might be noted here that throughout the walk only three stores drew the attention of more than half the observers, and all of these had spatial position in which at least two sides of the store were exposed.

At this point another of the strong impressions of the walk appears—the Bonwit Teller store across Berkeley Street, occupying the entire narrow end of the block from Boylston to Newbury. Spatially isolated on three sides, set among trees and grass in a stony environment, it is an obvious period piece of warm red brick and carved stone trim set against the massive smooth backdrop of the New England Mutual building. It is particularly remarkable for its contrast of contemporary commercial use in a building symbolizing institutional values of another time, and for its mannered additions of awnings and show windows. More people chose to comment on this single structure than any other in the total walk, except for the Arlington Street Church.

> And I do like Mr. Bonwit. I like it largely because of space, the effect of non-crowding. I know it was an old M.I.T. building at one time [it wasn't]. It's very distinguished, it's done with taste, and mainly it's space, I think, that makes it largely attractive. If the front steps were level with the sidewalk, and there was a new building on each side, it would just be something else, another rather homely spot.

The attention may be captured just as handily, even if the feelings are quite different:

I hate that monstrous awning coming out, it's so affected . . . like a worm coming out of a hole. . . . I've never heard anything so silly as converting a museum into a women's dress store and then showing it from the outside.

Two spontaneous post-walk memories of this building are interesting:

Bonwit's . . . was the dominant thing. It filled your eyes . . . set the mood for the whole place.

I have never realised that it was a museum until the other day [i.e., during the walk], when I looked at it from across the street at Brooks Bros. and noticed that these columns went up the front of it and gave it this museum or post office-like, type of atmosphere. Suddenly I saw the building as a whole though I had passed by it a million times. I had noticed its very obvious distinctive qualities but not the whole building.

Half of the walkers looked up along Berkeley long enough to catch a glimpse of the towering silhouette of the John Hancock building, two blocks away. The majority opinion was unfavorable:

You are suddenly faced with a very ugly mass, the John Hancock, which rises much too high, much too out of shape.

Just as the tour seemed about to end, we turned abruptly down into the alley, which, though not spotless, was reasonably neat by alley standards. In emotional vigor, the comments on this alley and on the Public Gardens stand alone. Three-quarters of the subjects reacted strongly, particularly to the spatial constriction of the alley and to its real or imagined dirt. The tone of voice, the facial expression conveyed the impact as well as the actual words:

Do we have to walk down here? There is no place to walk. Oh, this is awful . . . if they did have a fire people would come down here and land on the garbage, and they'd be killed for sure. . . . I'll bet its stinky in the summer.

Heaven knows what we're going to get into, in the way of rats and trash . . . it's back alleys and they should all be done away with . . . they're horrible eyesores.

Seems like the alley wants to make you look down not up. Seems as the walls are closing in.

As they proceeded down the alley they were preoccupied with the confinement of space, the lack of light, the dirt and water on the ground, the trash barrels which line the way. In this constricted volume their eyes no longer moved freely about but were turned downwards to the floor, or were fixed on the spot of light at the alley's end. Yards, breaks in the side-walls or lighted windows caused them to turn their heads automatically. Smells were mentioned for the first time, not because the alley was actually very odorous, but because alleys are supposed to smell, and the subjects noticed the lack of them.

Little contrasts caught their attention, such as a small window with shelves of china displayed, or a "poor little weed tree" fighting for life in a storage yard. Their eyes went up to see such things as the tops of fire escapes, outlined against the sky.

But the principal impression, along with the space and the dirt, was the contrast between the backs of the shops lining the alley, and the memory of their fashionable façades on Newbury Street. To the strong physical impression was added the dramatic and human one—of the wealthy shoppers in front and the poor workers behind. Almost half of the tourists were moved to speak when they passed the windows of a basement workroom:

Isn't it amazing—you walk down one street with ladies in furs, and you go down the alley . . . tailor shops down there. Miserable place to work. . . . You forget how many people there are working out of sight.

Ah, this is the true life of the city with the false façade!

Yet despite the sense of drama many of them felt, they were glad to get out again:

The one thing that really saves this alley is the fact that you look out and see that very broad space which gives relief to it. Pigeons flying there, and the sun silhouetted by the buildings.

The spatial release at the end of the alley was correspondingly strong. The Ritz-

Carlton parking lot, which had been an irritation on Newbury Street, now became a window from the alley prison.

> What a relief! This parking lot with the open space. . . . It feels so good coming out of that dark alley!

And when they came to the end of the alley itself, with the space of the Gardens before them, they were full of joy. These moments of relief were vividly remembered later:

> When we finally came out into the Ritz parking lot, it was open, open space and the sunshine came in . . . everything looked so sunny and so clean and nice.

> Crossing that street into the park was like . . . a sense of freedom, really.

In all of these reactions to space, it is notable how closely interwoven was the perception with the sense of potential movement on the one hand, and the sense of light or sun on the other.

Before reaching the Gardens, however, they had one more trial; they must cross the traffic of Arlington Street. Until this spot their reaction to traffic and parked cars had been mild, primarily sympathetic with the problems of the driver. There had been little consciousness of traffic noise, and some even managed to call a street a "quiet" one, in the midst of sounds of auto horns. But at this crossing they were faced with the problem of fording the traffic stream, and each one betrayed the anxiety and tense care that this required:

> Cars keep coming around here. These cars keep coming around and I can't get by. They never stop—yes, here they come! Exactly what I'm talking about; they never stop going down the street!

During the crossing, there was no mention of any other feature of the environment.

It was with a sense of marked relaxation and pleasure that all entered the Public Gardens. The spatial liberation again came in for almost universal comment. For a second time a significant number of comments were made about other people in the scene: the moving, brightly dressed skaters, enjoying the last ice of the season. Half the walkers specifically mentioned the trees.

It seems like a very good idea to have a park in the middle of the city, if only for cars to go around as well as a place for a quiet walk in between the trees. . . . This is a place I'd like to explore more and look at in more detail. . . . The very idea of trees is pleasant, and there haven't been many on surrounding streets, if any at all.

Several people seemed to enjoy being able to see and hear the city from a little distance while in the park. They were particularly taken by the contrast of park and the city which visibly encloses it. Here they enjoyed two worlds simultaneously.

One man voiced his underlying anxiety that this open space may be one day swallowed up:

> Tremendous real estate value this area must be! I wonder if and when Boston will do away with it?

While another looked at it in terms of personal associations:

> A park has always been for me a sort of quiet ground from the battle of the city. As you walk along any of the avenues that lead to Central Park, this one also, the battle crowds on, and when you finally get to the park, all of a sudden things are quiet and it's a different world.

THE WALK ANALYZED

After the trip, in some cases within a few hours and in others in two or three days, the subjects were interviewed again. First they were asked:

> Try to put yourself back at the beginning of the walk, and describe to me in detail the sequences of things and events you noticed.

When they had completed this description they were then asked various questions; whether they remembered any particular buildings, features of buildings, people, sounds, smell, traffic signs or pavements. They were asked how many definite areas they had passed by; if they felt the areas had any order or continuity and why; and whether this part of the city seemed to fit into their pictures of Boston. Some were asked to describe their feelings on the walk, and to say what made the greatest impression on them. All subjects were given a set of photographs of buildings, street views, pavements, details, etc. They were asked to say which objects they had seen on the journey. In general the items noted in the walk interview and in the spontaneous recall of the post-walk interview coincided very well, and a lapse of two or three days versus a lapse of one or two hours made surprisingly little difference in what was mentioned.

The fundamental impressions for almost all our observers came from certain individual buildings and open spaces. Moreover, there is agreement on particular buildings or spaces, and this is consistent between walk and recall. The buildings noticed are remarkable for singularities of style, material, use or association, but particularly for their spatial quality. Only a few structures received significant mention which were not somehow prominent in space.

We might assert that open space is the most impressive feature of all in the cityscape. We might buttress this assertion by speculation that "building" is an expected element of city description, culturally what one "should" discuss; while space relations are seemingly more esoteric and more difficult to verbalize. Thus their frequency is all the more striking.

The spaces remembered afterwards seemed to be either those which were clearly defined in form, or which made evident breaks in the general continuity. In certain earlier (and less systematic) interviews for instance, the space of entering cross streets was ignored, except where heavy on-coming traffic forced recognition of the street as a break in continuity. There was a unanimous reaction of dislike to what was described as the "huge and formless" space of a railroad yard.

Somewhat less strong than spaces or structures, but still a dominant impression, was that of the city floor, the sidewalk pavement. Particularly evocative were the material and the state of repair. There was interest in variations of texture or color, but some irritation at rough surfaces, especially from women in high heels. As a footnote, it is surprising to find that 16 out of 27 people commented on the width of the Boylston

Street sidewalk in their spontaneous recall. Four described it in their first sentence, four more in the second, and six in the next few sentences.

Next in interest was the impact of storefronts and their window contents. For most of our subjects these were a pleasant and absorbing feature of the stroll. But there was little unanimity as to which particular stores were singled out for comment. Much depended on the particular interests of the observer.

Signs were also important during the walk itself, but we found only one sign which drew common remark. Some sense of this scatter of attention may be gleaned from the fact that 78 different signs were noted by some one of the walkers; yet only six signs received the attention of more than two people, and only three the attention of more than three. Of these latter three signs, two were associated with buildings or stores which had received overwhelming attention for other reasons, the third was the clock in the Boylston Street sidewalk. Ninety-five percent of the people commented on signs while walking, but only 25 percent later recalled them. The subjects seemed highly conscious of the visual clamor, and often irritated by it, but particular signs seemed to make only a scattered and transitory impression.

Succeeding in frequency of mention were the two categories of street detail and people. The former includes such a miscellany of smaller objects as street furniture, fences, fire escapes, waste containers, subway entrances and statues, and this makes generalization difficult. Specific reasons may usually be attached to the choice of specific items, such as the relation to the Gardens of the Channing statue and the iron fence; the spatial prominence of the book-stall, or the subway entrance; the association with dirt of the alley barrels and the Boylston waste paper container (although the latter was undoubtedly also characterized by its bright color); the spatial constriction of the alley which forced an upward view and thus the silhouetting of the fire escapes. It is interesting to note that one type of detail which has been the subject of some recent design discussion—the street furniture (parking meters, light poles, etc.)—was only rarely mentioned.

There was somewhat greater unanimity in regard to the people selected for comment, and usually the remark seemed to involve a class or group: the dramatic contrast of the seamstresses in the alley basement; the well-dressed women on Newbury who symbolised the street; the skaters in the Gardens, bright moving objects in a peaceful setting. Some of the subjects indicated that during a more normal walk they would be much more observant of others than they seemed to be in these experiments. It may be that there was something in the test situation which implied that their attention should be upon the inanimate environment, and that the rest was not "the city."

Traffic came in for some comment, with somewhat more focus on the parked cars than on the moving ones, until the street had to be crossed. Up to this point, the emotional reaction was low, except where the parked car protruded onto the sidewalk. Feelings were intense and anxious while crossing, however, and all other perceptions were momentarily shut out. These pedestrians seem to accept, or at least to be hardened to, the car, until it threatens their safety, view, or freedom of movement.

Vegetation also played a role of some significance; not only its presence but its absence was expressed. Comments ran toward wishful replantings of street trees, or sadness at "pathetic" grass islands in the vortex of traffic. In fact, there was not much vegetation to notice, but where it occurred, as in the Public Gardens, there was a universal, and very positive, reaction of pleasure. Curiously enough, as with the signs, the recall of this part of the environment seemed to be quite low, in contrast to its relatively high mention during the walk. Why it should be forgotten so easily is a puzzle.

Few people talked about the weather, although there was perhaps a significant unconscious impression which was not verbalized. Sounds and smells were both equally low in conscious awareness. Some sounds were recalled after direct questioning, but even then smells could not be remembered. In both cases, we are probably dealing with a level of habituation, so that the signal rarely receives attention unless it varies significantly from the normal level. Thus, many of the "mentions" of sound or smell were actually the lack of it, i.e., a "quiet" street or an "odorless" alley.

Several obvious elements drew almost no comment at all: color for example (which may nevertheless be important in making another object noticeable), or the sky; wall materials and textures, overhead wires, upper floor façades or doorways.

The recognition of photographs also agreed with the interview results, since people tended to recognize easily photographs of items which were mentioned frequently, and vice versa. Unfortunately, since the photographs did not always cover what later proved to be some of the key visual features of the environment, this particular test was not so useful as it might have been.

THE NEED FOR ORDER

But how were these perceptions fitted together? This was a fundamental point. Take the way in which our particular block was mentally organized. It is interesting to note that interviewees did not hesitate to try to discover whether the area possessed any sense of order for them. Some broke it down into many sub-areas, and others felt it was all one thing. In the "average" case, it was organized somewhat as follows: the three fundamental parts were Boylston Street, Newbury Street and the Public Gardens. Arlington and Berkeley Streets were considered as parts of one or the other of these. The alley was a puzzle, since it didn't "fit" well; usually it was considered either as a separate area or as something which occupied the "backs" of Boylston and Newbury and thus either sewed them together or belonged ambiguously to one or the other. In some cases it was simply forgotten; in one case even explicitly ignored as a part that was rarely seen and thus in a sense didn't exist. Here is a typical example from a foreign viewer:

I could make out three distinct, different impressions. There was the semigaudiness of Boylston Street and the sounds associated with that. There was the relative quiet, possibly even quaintness of the Gardens. Newbury Street was very distinctly on a different level than Boylston. . . . Then there was the alley, of course. . . . These areas stand off from each other, they don't go together. . . . Let's say, with any one of two impressions, Newbury or Boylston, the alley must be along with it; it's just necessary. So perhaps: the alley and Boylston; the alley and Newbury; and the Gardens.

This same agreement as to the organization of certain parts of the environment, coupled with indecision and disagreement as to other parts, could be detected in earlier exploratory studies. For example, the upper end of a certain street, with its large colonial houses, was easily organized as a distinct entity. This was contrasted to the lower end, a busy shopping district, by all observers. Between these two regions, lies another piece of the street which corresponds neither in use nor in physical form to either end. On the other hand, it has no sharp character of its own, being a mixture of apartments, offices, houses and irregular spaces. The observers found this to be a section that they could not easily attach to either the upper or the lower end, yet they were unwilling to give it a life of its own. Feeling compelled to organize their walk, and unable to leave their organization incomplete or to "forget" this section (as some were able to do with the Boylston alley), they responded by attaching it, half-heartedly, to one or the other of the strong "ends." The result was agreement on two classes into which the walk fell, separated by a weak, oscillating boundary.

Thus we have organizational consensus at one point, due to suggestions inherent in the physical form itself, coupled with disagreement in regard to the rest, where the unit into which a part is put depends primarily on past experience. Where this organizational indecision was strongest we found hints of feelings, not only of puzzlement, but of discomfort.

There was apparently a drive to organize the environmental impressions into meaningful patterns, which could be handled with

economy. Since the city environment is complex and fluid, this is a difficult operation. Since the present environment so often does not suggest links by its physical shape, the process becomes all the more difficult. Yet it persists, and the resulting mental organization, while apparently quite loose, ambiguous and even contradictory at points, is nevertheless clung to firmly. Certain elements seem particularly important in furnishing distinctions for area classifications in the city, such as people and activity; land use; and general physical form, spatial form in particular.

Native and newcomer agree surprisingly well as to *what* is worth their notice, but significant differences appear between them in the way they organize these things (see Figures 62-2 and 62-3). The more familiar observer tends to establish more connections, and not to break his environment down into as many isolated parts. Thus a stranger might divide the walk into six parts: the four sides of the block, the alley, and the Gardens. For an old hand, however:

> Brooks Bros. rounds the corner and Charles Antell rounds the other corner, and the Arlington Street Church rounds the third corner, and well, the fourth corner is a little bit broken up; there's two places there, but you sort of get this feeling like you never come to the end of the street and then make a sharp corner, you just sort of make a round corner there. This whole block therefore seems to be a very complete continuous compact tightly set-in block, and the stores such as Bonwit's, Peck and Peck, Schrafft's, and so forth, which are on the outer periphery of this square belong to the square, definitely.

Not only is the block considered as one, but the façades facing the block are also drawn into the unit. Even the rectangular shape with its sharp corners cannot be allowed, and the form is distorted towards the seamless circle. (Compare the previous quotation from a stranger: "these areas stand off from each other, they don't go together.") Note also in this quotation that the corner of Boylston and Berkeley is resistant to the neat organization, which puts a key use to mark each corner from both directions; but that

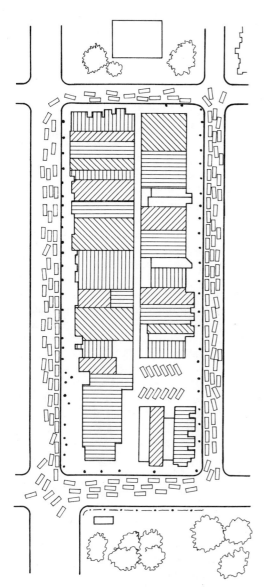

Figure 62–2. The stranger organizes his environment: He sees no overall uniformity in the buildings or the types of business; signs and street furniture break the block up into small confused areas; heavy traffic isolates him from the other side of streets.

the resistant material is forced into place anyhow.

No, this is definitely all a piece of one material as far as I am concerned. There is a distinction between Boylston and Newbury. . . . But the whole area has always been very much one grouping, one place.

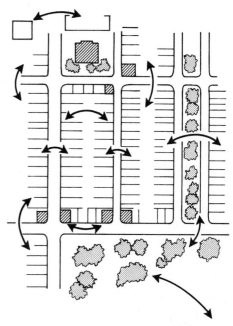

Figure 62–3. The native organizes his environment: Familiarity with the area enables him to see similarities (often imaginary) between streets, blocks, buildings and open spaces.

It is also true that these were the people who were less able to distinguish this block from its context in the larger Back Bay district. The streets are not boundaries for them. For the unfamiliar, however, this block seems to have no particular relation to the rest of the city.

These findings might be generalized in the following hypothesis: the individual must perceive his environment as an ordered pattern, and is constantly trying to inject order into his surroundings, so that all the relevant perceptions are jointed one to the other. Certain physical complexes facilitate this process through their own form, and are seen as ordered wholes by native and newcomer alike. Subsequent use and association simply strengthen this structure. Other complexes, however, do not encourage this fitting together, and they are seen as fundamentally disordered by the newcomer. For the native, this "disordered" complex may also seem to be an organized one, since habitual use and perception have allowed him to put the collection together by means of associated meanings, or by selection, simplification, distortion or even suppression of his perceptions. This progressive imputation of order is often alluded to, implicitly or explicitly:

> I don't feel any sense of real order and yet I didn't feel that everything was jumbled and I suppose that is because I am familiar with the area. To me it didn't seem confused, it seemed right.

> I've always liked this section, ever since I first became familiar with it about fourteen years ago. Although it has undergone some change, I feel the change has been a progressive one toward blending and uniformity of buildings rather than of strange contrasts and conflicts of colors, sizes and shapes.

Thus this sense of order can finally be achieved by familiarity despite physical chaos. Yet there is evidence that this organization is achieved only by real effort and by distortion of the pattern of reality, and that even after it is accomplished it is attended by emotions of insecurity where the required organization is particularly ruthless. Certainly it lacks the conviction and depth of a relationship which is backed up by physical pattern.

An "old hand" may recognize a shopping district as an organized entity where strangers say it is chaotic. Intensive use and association have satisfactorily overcome physical confusion, even if the satisfaction would be deeper were the spatial form more continuous. At least the physical continuities of land use and activity are there to back up the mental category.

But, even for the native, there is no satisfaction in the "fringe" of that shopping district. He can tell that it is more commercial than residential, and thus ought to go with the shopping, and he can hold it there in his mind when it is necessary for practical purposes, but the reality keeps wandering off, keeps contradicting him. It is like a restless animal which one must constantly correct. For the newcomer, moreover, the fringe makes no particular sense at all, and he is likely to recognize the fact, with some discomfort.

Some newcomers may ask for a very sweeping and rigid kind of physical organization:

> I had no idea that the town would be built up as it is, just on cow paths and up little hills. . . . I just supposed that the city would be beautiful, quite modern, that the stores would be in order, the dress shops together and the bridal shop with it and not off in a corner all by itself; the antiques would be together and the big business areas would be business areas.

Very possibly this observer might change her mind about such a "neat" city were she to live in it long, but the wish is indicative of the troubles she is facing. The native may be able to handle, and indeed find more pleasure in, a more intricate and complexly organized environment, but organized it must be, whether by city dwellers or by the sweat of his own brow.

Our study suggests one further remark. The method used may not only be useful for research purposes, but may be an educational tool as well. Such a recorded walk in itself tends to heighten the perception of the city. When combined with a discussion in the field of general interview results, along with the critique of the surrounding forms, it might prove to be an excellent way of awakening the citizen's interest in the form of his city, sharpening his critical abilities, and heightening his ultimate pleasure in a well-shaped environment.

63 Human Movement and Architecture

Robert B. Bechtel

"What other monumental interior in America produces such an overwhelming effect?" critic Lewis Mumford has asked of New York's Guggenheim Museum. "You may go to this building to see Kandinsky or Jackson Pollock; you remain to see Frank Lloyd Wright."

A construction worker on architect Wright's gigantic spiral expressed other ideas when the now-famous building was going up in 1957:

> The way I figure it is that this is the screwiest project I ever got tied up in. The whole joint goes round and round and round and where it comes out nobody knows. (*The New Yorker*)

Architects have long been interested in knowing how their designs affect the traffic pattern within a building and how utilization of available space may be made more effective by proper design. More recently, some behavioral scientists have also become interested in the ways people respond to architectural and spatial design. Do they find some buildings more comfortable, more appealing, or more stimulating than others? Do they move and behave differently in these different settings?

PERCEPTION AND LOCOMOTION

When a person moves around inside a building, he is responding to the building as architecture—as a particular definition of interior space—and not as a sketch on the drawing board or a monumental piece of sculpture to be viewed from the street. If the building is familiar territory, he moves through it in a *habitual* manner, scarcely aware of his architectural environment; if it is unfamiliar, he moves in an *exploratory* manner, looking in all directions, hesitating, and sometimes retracing his steps. Exploratory locomotion usually occurs in public buildings such as museums and art galleries. Habitual motion is far more common and generally occurs in homes and office buildings.

Psychologist James J. Gibson has suggested that human perception is dependent on locomotion possibilities. According to his view, perceiving space is the same as perceiving that an area is capable of being walked into; a space that does not look this way confuses spatial and distance judgment. Gibson even defines movement as any motion of the body that causes movement in the field of vision.

The emphasis on locomotion, both ex-ploratory and habitual, poses special problems for the architect as he works with interior space. How, for example, can he provide a layout that will minimize the visitor's confusion on first entering an unfamiliar public building? Or how can he design a home so as to maximize the family's use of available space as they go about their daily activities?

Most human behavior indoors does not involve locomotion, but rather such activities as sitting, talking, eating, and sleeping. Also, exploratory locomotion is less common than habitual. However, to begin to find answers to the architects' questions, it is easiest to study people in public buildings. The development of a new measuring device which can indirectly "observe" patterns of movement has helped considerably. It is called the "hodometer."

The hodometer is an electrical system for automatically recording the number and location of footsteps across a floor. The name hodometer comes from the Greek *hodos*, meaning pathways. The device consists of a cluster of electric switch mats covering an entire floor space with each mat connected to an electric counter. Each mat has two metal plates separated at the sides and center by resilient material. When the plates come together under four pounds per square inch pressure, an electrical contact is made.

The counters that keep score are housed in a cabinet placed out of sight in a closet or in the next room. A clock is mounted on the face of the counter cabinet to record the amount of time people spend in the room—the clock starts when someone steps on the first mat and stops with the last electrical impulse recorded, when the last person leaves the room.

While many interesting and useful kinds of information can be gained through the more usual techniques of interviews and questionnaires, some information is difficult to obtain simply by asking. Finding out how a person responds to architecture is a case in point, mainly because he is rarely consciously aware of his own reactions. Further, even if it were feasible for an observer to simply follow him around to record his reactions, these reactions would likely be altered by the knowledge that he was being observed. People who know they are being studied, observed, or evaluated generally act differently when the observer is present. The subject may be much more cooperative or show much higher verbal skills in an experiment than in real-life situations, because he wants to please or impress the experimenter. The museum visitor who feels he is being followed by someone, for whatever purpose, will likely move through the building in a different pattern and at a different speed than one who is not aware of being observed.

THE MUSEUM EXPERIMENT

The hodometer was constructed by the Environment Research Foundation of Topeka, Kansas, and installed in a room at the art museum of the University of Kansas. Seven prints were hung in the room. As far as anyone but the museum staff and the experimenter knew, the prints composed an ordinary exhibit of recent acquisitions.

Our first question was: Do people tend to stop more often in front of the pictures they like best? The results of our first study with the hodometer indicated that they do. We began by recording the movement pattern of 1,200 museum visitors. From this pattern the preferences for each of the seven prints were predicted in rank order, depending on how many visitors had stood in front of a particular print. For example, there were more footsteps recorded in front of a print of John F. Kennedy than any other, so it was ranked first. Then 241 new subjects were sent through the room one at a time and asked to write down their preferences. Only 161 of these subjects gave their preferences for the same set of prints. The average preferences of these people coincided very closely with those predicted from the movement patterns of the first group. Extra information on all 241 subjects was collected for a different kind of analysis that was done later.

The process was then repeated for an architecture exhibit. Three walls of the room were covered with drawings and photographs of the work of various architects. Movement patterns were recorded for 1,085 visitors, and a prediction of preferences

made. Fifty-eight architecture students who had seen the exhibit then gave their preferences. The prediction from the movement pattern corresponded 100 percent with the students' preferences.

The next study examined a fuller range of the hodometer's potentialities. The measures taken on all 241 experimental subjects were carefully analyzed. These subjects were divided into several roughly equal experimental groups. Each subject was ushered into the exhibit room individually.

Members of the first group were asked simply to go through and rank the prints according to preference; they were not aware of being observed.

Members of the second group were ushered into the room and asked to wait there without further instructions; they, too, were unaware of being observed.

The third group consisted of natural museum visitors; they were not asked to rank the pictures, nor were they aware that they were participating in a study or experiment of any sort.

Members of the fourth group, in contrast, were asked to rank the pictures and knew they were being observed as they walked around the exhibit.

The mean results for the four groups are summarized in Table 63-1. *Area* is the number of square feet the average person in each group used as he moved about the room. Since each mat was one square foot, a measure of area is simply the number of mats stepped on regardless of the number of times each was stepped on. *Elevation* is the total number of footsteps recorded during the time a person was in the room. *Time* is the number of seconds a person spent in the room. *Pace* is elevation divided by time,

Table 63-1 Mean Results for the Four Groups

	Group I	Group II	Group III	Group IV
Area	76.10	74.15	34.95	58.25
Elevation	158.28	160.76	47.68	110.85
Time (seconds)	313.70	300.00	71.15	220.48
Pace	2.08	2.12	1.46	2.15
Standard deviation	1.37	1.53	.54	1.12

or the number of footsteps per second. *Standard deviation* is how evenly the person distributes his footsteps among the mats. A good way to imagine this is to consider two possible extreme patterns, one where a person steps on only one mat 100 times, and the other where a person steps on 100 mats one time each. In the first case the standard deviation is 6.7, and in the second case it is 0.5. The smaller the standard deviation, the more evenly the footsteps are distributed among the mats.

Notice particularly the figures for Groups III and IV. Every measure in Group III was markedly different from all other groups. This means that knowledge of being in an experiment made subjects behave in a radically different manner from natural visitors. The differences in area, elevation, and time for Group IV indicate that knowledge of being watched and measured also made persons behave differently. An interesting sidelight is the sex differences (not shown in the table): Males were more active than females, using more footsteps and covering a greater amount of ground; however, they also paused more often, apparently to give the pictures closer scrutiny, so their standard deviation and pace scores were lower.

FUTURE RESEARCH PROSPECTS

A number of possible uses for the hodometer in future social research have already become evident. The first is in the study of social distance. Anthropologists (as well as American tourists and businessmen visiting Latin American countries) have noticed that Central and South Americans carry on conversations at uncomfortably close range for Northerners. A hodometer with smaller switch mats could easily measure these social distances under natural conditions and among groups as well as between two persons. This is the kind of information architects need for building for different cultures and ethnic groups and for laying out space appropriate for social activities in each.

A second area of research is color. Some experts maintain that warm colors tend to increase activity while cool colors depress it. The hodometer is a useful device for measuring these differences without the subject's awareness. It can measure not only the extent and rate of human movement in a room, but even the slight shifts from one foot to the other that a person makes when he appears to be standing still.

A third area of research is in the use of space. Do windows or light colors for the walls really increase the amount of space *used* in a room, or do they only make the room *look* larger? A preliminary study by Thomas Peel and Rajendra Srivastava has shown that, contrary to expectation, subjects used a larger part of the floor space in a chocolate-colored room even though they estimated a beige room of the same size to be larger. This finding may be due to the color factor, however. Chocolate may be a warmer color than beige, and the increased use of space in the chocolate room may be due to color-induced activity.

A fourth area of research is personality variables. This is a field of special interest to the architect who builds for the individual person or family. It has been shown that people who have a low tolerance for ambiguity in ideas do not like complexity as much as those with high tolerance for ambiguity. Since tolerance of ambiguity is a personality variable that can be independently measured by psychological tests, it would be interesting to determine whether such people would respond similarly to complexity in architectural design. Since it has already been shown that the hodometer can measure preferences for art objects, it would be equally feasible to measure art and design preferences of people who differ in personality characteristics. The possibilities of combining personality measures and architectural variables open up a new dimension for the creative architect. Will the day come when the architect gives personality tests to his client to help in the selection of spatial designs and color schemes?

The hodometer is a small but significant addition to our repertory of devices for observing human behavior without the subject's awareness. The kinds of research it makes possible will help the architect plan his building around human needs and behavior and help the social scientists understand more about man's behavioral responses to his architectural environment.

64 The Comprehension of the Everyday Physical Environment

Kenneth H. Craik

In 1965, Studer and Stea were able to compile a preliminary directory listing over 170 persons who are professionally interested in the relatoin of behavior to the physical environment. The directory is only one of several signs of the increasing attention being paid to the possible implications and significance of behavioral science research for the environmental planning and design professions. The source and potential of this awareness is broadly interdisciplinary in scope as is evidenced by the inclusion in the directory of persons in the fields of anthropology, architecture, city and regional planning, engineering, design, geography, landscape architecture, psychiatry, psychology, sociology, and zoology.

Psychologists, after an unduly tardy entry, seem now ready to review the directions they might take in advancing knowledge in this area. The recent year-long faculty seminar series devoted to the topic, "Psychology and the Form of the Environment," held in 1965 and 1966 at the M.I.T. Department of City and Regional Planning, and the second National Research Conference on Architectural Psychology, held at the University of Utah in May 1966, document the growing commitment among psychologists to explore, to foster, and even to undertake research approaches in environmental psychology.

Surprisingly, the initiative in the development of research in environmental psychology has been with the disciplines of environmental design and planning. A full understanding of the tardiness of psychology in attempting to study the behavioral implications of what have become constant,

Reprinted by permission of the *Journal of the American Institute of Planners,* Vol. 34, No. 1, January 1968, and the author.

extensive, and often massive transformations project itself. In professional practice, the _(?) [missing] in the structure of the everyday physical environment will require an enterprising and scholarly investigation into the history of ideas and the history of a science. In the meantime, it can be suggested that scientific psychology, since its beginnings in the 1870's, often has been willing to forfeit immediate attacks upon a whole range of significant and compelling aspects of human behavior (Sanford, 1965). It has tended to concentrate its energies upon the study of basic, if apparently simple and inconsequential, processes and, perhaps more importantly, upon the development of a repertory of quantitative methods and techniques appropriate to the phenomena it ultimately seeks to investigate and to understand. However, in recent years, particularly since World War II, scientific psychology has been emerging from its seclusion in the laboratory and more eagerly seeking problems in the "real" world upon which to test and to expand the usefulness of its methods and concepts.

During these same decades of psychological seclusion, man's physical environment has increasingly become man-made, man-influenced, and urban. The planning and design professions have occupied the best vantage points from which to observe this tendency and from which to absorb and gauge the dramatic implications it may have for human experience and behavior. Thus, as the psychologists somewhat timidly emerge from their laboratory retreats in search of phenomena of real human significance to study, the environmental planners and designers, with a sense of urgency—and perhaps a tinge of guilt—have attempted to attract their attention and efforts to the momentous trends and deeds that the planners and designers have witnessed—and sometimes wrought.

The selection of problems for study, and the sequence and timing of attack upon them, move according to quite different criteria in research and in practice. In research, strategy tends to be guided by the conceptual framework and techniques already at hand, by the relative likelihood that solutions to the problems will be attained, and by the general theoretical interest and feedback provided by the research structure of problems is seen in the context of social purposes, of the relative desirability that solutions be attained, and of the urgent necessity that judgments be rendered, decisions reached, and actions taken. Nevertheless, it might be valuable to select a simple yet central problem in environmental psychology and to sketch out the form and pathways that research directed to it would likely take. In doing so, some basis might be laid for an appraisal of the sort of contributions the environmental planning and design professions can reasonably expect environmental psychology, as well as related branches of the behavioral sciences, to make to their own endeavors.

THE EXPLORATION OF A PROBLEM

How do people come to grasp cognitively the everyday physical world in which they live and move? What terms and categories do they employ in talking and thinking about it? What aspects and qualities of it do they distinguish and attend to? What assumptions and expectations do they bring to it? What are the factors that influence the particular way a specific person comprehends his physical surroundings? These are surely some of the questions to which the environmental psychologist would be expected to turn his attention. How would he proceed in exploring the structure and ramifications of this problem from the point of view of research strategy and design?

In tracing the course of an environmental psychologist's exploration of a problem, it will be seen that the research strategy follows in a rather straightforward way from the necessary process of defining the terms of discourse, identifying the elements of the problem, and studying their interrelationships. Out of this basically commonsensical procedure, terminology is introduced, methods are developed, research projects are conceived, and some by-products of practical interest to the design and planning professions emerge. Often, as the exploration

of the main problem is pursued, subsidiary topics of investigation unexpectedly spin off, which also lead to scientific and practical gains.

I. A Unit of Discourse: "The Environmental Display"

In the long run, psychological research should yield an understanding of the manner in which any entity of the everyday physical environment is comprehended. The term "environmental display" will be adopted to signify generally "that which is comprehended"—that is, those units of the everyday physical environment, of which buildings, urban scenes, and forest glades are instances. Environmental displays may be considered to vary along at least two important dimensions: scale, and natural to man-influenced. As Figure 64-1 suggests, a flower would be small scale, natural; a tool, small scale, man-influenced; the Grand Canyon viewed from the air, large scale, natural; and Manhattan Island viewed from the air, large scale, man-influenced. A field of tulips growing upon reclaimed land in Holland would be intermediate on both dimensions. The term "display" has been chosen because of its flexible application along these continua and because of its connotation of something that is to be reacted to in perceptual-cognitive-affective modalities.

II. The Elements of the Problem: A Model for the Comprehension of Environmental Displays

The next step in the process is to consider the essential components of the problem. These structural elements are quickly revealed when the environmental psychologist attempts to design a simple study of the comprehension of a single environmental

Natural to man-influenced

		Natural	man-influenced
	small	a flower	a tool
Scale			
	large	Grand Canyon	Manhattan Island

Figure 64–1

display. He is immediately forced to make decisions about these issues: Whose comprehension am I to study (Observers)? By what means am I to present the environmental display to the observer (Presentation of Environmental Displays)? What behavioral reactions of the observer am I to elicit and record (Nature and Format of Judgments)? By what standards might I evaluate the observer's comprehension (Validational Criteria)? A review of the possibilities inherent in each of these issues serves to enrich our conception of the problem. They are presented in summary form in Table 64-1, and a brief discussion of them follows.

A. *Characteristics of the Observers.* At first glance, it would appear to be most appropriate to study the comprehensions of a representative sample of the general public. For some purposes, this approach would be the best method for selecting the observers. However, for other purposes, the observations of specific subgroups of the general population would warrant investigation.

Several groups come readily to mind, including:

1. Groups whose members are thought to possess special competence in the comprehension and description of environmental displays, such as architects, planners, real estate appraisers, stage designers, and "space managers"—persons who have practical knowledge of the ways people behave in and use space, for example, hotel and resort managers.

2. Groups whose modes of comprehension of the nonhuman environment are of particular interest to architects and planners. Elderly persons, migrant workers, physically disabled persons, psychiatric patients, and college students would constitute groups belonging to this category.

3. Groups formed according to personality dimensions that are thought to be theoretically relevant to individual variations in the comprehension of the nonhuman environment. The theory of C. G. Jung, for example, would lead to such hypotheses. Extravert sensing types, as an instance, would be predicted to react to the non-

Table 64-1 A Process Model for the Comprehension of Environmental Displays

Observers 1	Presentation of environmental displays 2	Nature and format of judgments 3	Validational criteria 4
Special competence groups: architects planners real estate appraisers stage designers "space" managers, i.e., hotel, theatre, resort managers, building superintendents, etc.	Direct experience: looking at walking around and through driving around and through aerial views living in	Free descriptions Adjective checklists Activity and mood checklists Q-sort descriptions Ratings Thematic potential analysis	Measures of objective characteristics of environmental displays Judgments by experts Any judgment-form in Column 3 based upon more
Special user-client groups: elderly persons migrant workers college students	Simulative exploration Cinematic and photographic studies Sketches and drawings Models and replicas Tachistoscopic views Laser beam presentations	Symbolic equivalents Multisensory equivalents Emphatic interpretations: "role" enactments "role" improvisations	extensive acquaintance with the environmental display
Groups formed on the basis of relevant personality measures Everyman, general public	No presentation	Social stereotypic cues Beliefs about human consequences Viewing time "Motational" systems	

human environment in a manner characteristically different from that of introvert intuitive types. A subclass of this category would be the formation of groups of observers on the basis of especially developed personality scales assessing persons according to their more enduring dispositions, attitudes, and beliefs concerning the nonhuman environment.

B. Presentation of Environmental Displays. Once a group of observers has been selected, the next step is to present to them the environmental display to be comprehended. The practical problem is this: how to present the environmental display to the group of observers within a reasonable and efficient time span, but in such a way that the full and complex character of the display is conveyed to them. A wide range of possible media of presentation is available. The appropriateness of the individual media to specific research purposes, of course, will vary. Some of the media of presentation of environmental displays may be briefly appraised as follows:

1. *Direct experience.* The direct experience of looking at environmental displays, walking or driving around and through them, and taking in aerial views of them has a certain epistemological priority. The site visit also has the advantage of conveying the environmental display through all the sense modalities it might be capable of stimulating. However, there are also limitations to the use of the site visit, in addition to the obvious one of costliness. For example, anyone who has watched architectural students on a house tour will realize the striking differences in exploratory and observational strategies that they employ compared with other groups. Thus the free exploration and observation of the site visit leaves indeterminate the precise nature of the environmental display which in fact has been presented to the observers, as well as the degree of equivalence of presentation which exists among the observers. Moreover, if one is willing to accept these limitations, it might be noted that an even more thorough presentation of the environmental display would consist in having the observer use or reside in it, in whatever sense that

might be appropriate to the specific nature of a given environmental display.

2. *Simulative exploration.* Attempts are being made to approximate the free exploration of an environmental display while maintaining fairly precise recordings of the specific explorations of each observer (see Weiss and Boutourline, 1962; Winkel and Sasanoff, 1966). Either through sequential presentations of photographic slides, with choice points that move the observer directionally through the display, or through observer-guided remote-controlled mobile television cameras at the environmental display, the observer is presented with a considerable amount of freedom to visually roam and explore the display, yet the sequence of his explorations is recorded, allowing a determination of what, in fact, has been presented to him. The limitation of this method, and of many of the following methods, is the degradation of the full nature and richness of the original environmental display. In this case, visual aspects of the display alone are being simulated. However, considerations are being made of the possibilities of simulating auditory and olfactory experiences within the context of this method (Stea, 1966).

3. *Cinematic and photographic studies.* Although again at some loss of the full richness of the original environmental display and of full monitoring of the observational sequences of the viewers, cinematic and photographic studies nevertheless can convey a great deal of information about an environmental display, with a high degree of verisimilitude. In addition, recent studies of cinematic presentations of environmental displays that have employed the eye-movement camera suggest that some monitoring of the attentional patterns of the observers can be achieved (Carr & Kurilko, 1964).

4. *Sketches and drawings; models and replicas.* Sketches, drawings, and models take on a certain importance as media of presentation due to their traditional use in architecture and planning. In addition, the development of miniaturized television cameras will soon allow the simulative exploration of models and replicas of environmental displays.

5. *Tachistoscopic views.* The very brief

exposures of photographic presentations of environmental displays afforded by the tachistoscope may be useful in investigating the salience of certain elements of such environmental displays as urban scenes (Vigier, 1965), as well as in establishing affective qualities of features of displays.

6. *Laser beam presentations.* The possible development of full dimensional presentations of objects through the use of Laser beam holograms (Leith & Upatnieks, 1965) may offer opportunities in the future for much more extensive and realistic presentation of environmental displays within the laboratory setting than is now feasible.

7. *No presentation.* In studies of enduring images of familiar environmental displays, it will be of interest to study the different descriptions given when the environmental display is identified only by name, and when it actually is presented.

C. The Nature and Format of Judgments. The kinds of descriptive judgments and other behavioral reactions requested of observers of environmental displays and the format provided for guiding and assisting them in making their responses are of central importance, for they are the signs by which the nature of the observer's comprehensions is made known to us.

Column 3 of Table 64-1 lists several possible kinds of response eliciting and recording procedures. Some of the methods stress the ease of recording the impressions and judgments in everyday language and highlight the advantage of obtaining standardized and comparable responses from observers. Other procedures listed in Column 3 are suggested in the light of an assumption that many reactions to the nonhuman environment are subtle and are neither customarily nor easily talked about in everyday discourse. These procedures, therefore, entail unusual modes of responding to environmental displays. If the subtlety of reactions to the everyday physical surroundings has been one factor in hampering the development of behavioral science research in this area, as it indeed appears to have been, then the psychologist, if anyone, should be able to make a contribution. Responses are, after all, the business of the psychologist.

Table 64-2 presents a brief description of each response format. This assortment of response formats that might be employed in studying the comprehension of environmental displays, while far from complete, does serve to illustrate the impressive variety of responses to the nonhuman environment that are potentially contained in the human repertory.

D. Validational Criteria. If a specific investigation were directed toward assessing the accuracy or quality of the observers' comprehensions of environmental displays, then some well-founded description and assessment of the displays would be required to serve as criterion. There is no simple basis upon which to select validational criteria. In some cases, objective measures of physical attributes of the environmental displays may be appropriate, especially if the original descriptive responses made by the observers were in those terms (such as the relative size of components of the environmental displays). In other investigations, the judgment of experts, that is, of observers with special competence or experience, would do. In some instances, responses of the same sort as those made by the observers whose accuracy is being assessed might serve as criteria, if the descriptive judgments made by the criterion observers were founded upon more extensive acquaintance with and surveillance of the environmental displays.

III. Directions in which Research Would Proceed

Commonsensical analysis of the problem has revealed four elements that must be considered in research on the comprehension of environmental displays (Figure 64-2).

By focusing upon each of these elements in turn, four domains of research are generated, each with distinctive methodological demands and conceptual and practical implications. It would be burdensome to treat the total structure of each domain here.

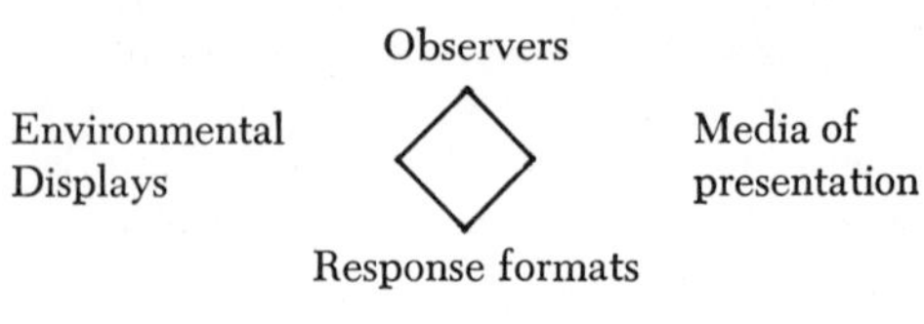

Observers

Environmental Displays

Media of presentation

Response formats

Figure 64–2

Table 64-2 Response Formats for the Descriptive Assessment of Environmental Displays

---

Free descriptions: Free descriptions of environmental displays made by the observers in either spoken or written form have the advantage of placing minimal constraints upon the natural, spontaneous manner of response, but the disadvantage of not easily allowing quantitative comparisons among responses.

Adjective checklists: Adjective checklists have been successfully used in the recording of staff impressions in personality assessment programs (see Gough & Heilbrun, 1965). An ACL may consist of 300 adjectives drawn from everyday usage, which the observer checks as applicable or not applicable to the person, object, or concept described. Special adjective checklists can be developed for use in environmental psychology. The advantages of the adjective checklist method are its use of everyday language, the brevity and ease with which judgments are made and recorded, and its wide and flexible application and forms of analysis.

Activity and mood checklists: Like the adjective checklist, mood checklists are simple, standard, and brief means of recording impressions (see Nowlis, 1965; Clyde, 1960). A special mood checklist for the assessment of environmental displays can be developed, with a special effort being made to embody in it "atmospheric" mood referents. In addition, an activity checklist, consisting of perhaps 300 verbs expressing a wide range of discrete human activities might be developed. The latter checklist would be useful in describing an environmental display in terms of both its observed and its potential capacity for human activity.

Q-sort descriptions: The Q-sort method is another procedure that is widely used in the field of personality assessment for the purpose of obtaining standardized, comparable, and quantifiable observer descriptions of persons and person-relevant concepts (see Block, 1961). A Q-sort deck typically consists of 50 or 100 statements, each on a separate card and each expressing an important characteristic, which are sorted by the observer into piles of specified number along a dimension ranging from "most characteristic" to "least characteristic" of the entity being described. Special Q-decks can be developed that would be appropriate to the description of environmental displays.

Ratings: Ratings are another standard and flexible technique for obtaining observer judgments. An especially sensitive form of the rating scale, the Semantic Differential, can be fruitfully employed in the descriptive assessment of environmental displays (see Osgood, Suci, Tannenbaum, 1957; Carroll, 1959; Lamm, 1965).

Thematic potential analysis: One subtle and relatively implicit reaction to environmental displays such as buildings, rooms, rural and urban scenes, and so forth, is likely to be an automatically functioning scanning response designed to answer the question, "What might go on here; what might occur here?" A method for assessing this response-characteristic of environmental displays is the thematic potential analysis. In this procedure, a series of environmental displays would be presented to a large number of observers. The observers would be requested to write a story about each display, with instructions to this effect: "Create a brief story that might fittingly take place here." Techniques for thematic analysis have been carefully developed in psychology, under the impetus of the Thematic Apperception Test (TAT), which could readily be adapted to the task of sensitively analyzing the protocols obtained from the suggested procedure (see Henry, 1956; Saarinen, 1966; Michelson, 1966). Individual differences among observers in the thematic potentials they ascribed to environmental displays would be studied. In addition, a method would be available for assessing the thematic potential of environmental displays such as urban scenes and for grouping them according to the results of the thematic analysis, for further study.

Symbolic equivalents: The study of metaphorical expression, either in terms of the production of metaphors or the preference for metaphors, has been profitably employed in personality research (see Barron, 1958; Knapp, 1960). An appropriate adaptation of these techniques would require of the observer the production of metaphorical expressions as the mode of reacting to environmental displays. The produced metaphors can be analyzed in terms of the individual styles

Table 64-2 Response Formats for the Descriptive Assessment of Environmental Displays (*Continued*)

of sensitivity of given observers and in terms of the typical metaphorical expressions elicited by given environmental displays. It would be possible, when sufficient research has been conducted, to establish multiple-choice preference procedures for metaphorical reactions to environmental displays which might assess meaningful individual consistencies among observers.

Multisensory equivalents: Another equivalence procedure that would be more exploratory in nature involves the presentation of a series of musical sequences, color sequences (perhaps projected upon a full-wall screen), and other sensory projections. The observer's task would be to select those phases of each such series that in some way represent some aspect of the experience of a given complex display (such as walking up Market Street in San Francisco on a Saturday afternoon). This expressive preference or equivalence procedure would help to elaborate the full response-characteristics of given environmental displays.

Empathic interpretations: Two methods for establishing empathic sets in observers are available. In the "role enactment" procedure, an anecdote would be recounted which illustrates the vivid enactment by a person of a physical object, in this particular case, a bathtub. After telling this story to the observers, the experimenter would then instruct them: "In the same way in which that person 'was' the bathtub, you 'be' the _____ (environmental display which is being comprehended) and 'being it' describe yourself." Using this procedure, it would be possible, for example, to compare descriptions of given environmental displays made by means of an adjective checklist under standard conditions with those made under "role enactment" conditions. Furthermore, if over a variety of environmental displays described by a variety of observer groups, certain adjectives are checked consistently more frequently under the empathic set, those adjectives could be constituted into a scale that would be scored for descriptions made under standard conditions. The resulting Empathic Set scale would provide useful information about both observers and environmental displays.

The "role" improvisations technique would also be exploratory in nature. The general method has been found to be valuable in personality assessment (see Moreno, 1934; Harris, 1955; Sarbin, 1954). Under these usages, the two assessees are assigned roles, such as doctor and patient, and instructed to improvise an interaction between themselves. As an appropriate adaptation, the two observers would be instructed to "be" two given environmental displays, such as the Eiffel Tower and the Statue of Liberty, and to personify them in an interaction. Many clues to the more subtle reactions to specific environmental displays and to the nonhuman environment in general might be gained by this exploratory procedure.

The two methods for obtaining empathic interpretations of environmental displays are somewhat akin to the techniques employed by the Synectics group (see Gordon, 1961).

Social stereotypic cues: In their comprehension of the everyday physical environment, persons make inferences about the kinds of people who will be associated with kinds of environmental displays. The Gough Adjective Check List would be an appropriate device for investigating the social stereotypic cues provided by environmental displays. In this procedure, the observers are presented with the environmental display and asked to record their judgments about the kinds of people who would probably live in, work in, or in general be found in and around the environmental display.

Beliefs about human consequences: Another class of inferences commonly made about environmental displays relates to their human consequences. For example, the observers might be asked to record their judgment of what the effect would be upon them if they were to live in, work in, or in some other way be associated with a given environmental display for two years (five years, ten years, and so forth). The format employed here could be a description of themselves on the Gough Adjective Check List conveying these effects upon themselves, which would be compared with their present self-description, or the format could be adapted from that employed by the Guilford Consequences Test (see Christensen, Merrifield & Guilford, 1958), in which the observer simply lists as many such consequences as he can.

Table 64-2 Response Formats for the Descriptive Assessment of Environmental Displays (*Continued*)

Viewing time: A gross indication of the course of attentional processes during the observation of environmental displays would be the amount of time the display, or elements of it, are held in view. Tracking the course of such fluctuating deployments of attention is a difficult task. Three methods are available. The portable eye-movement camera achieves noteworthy fullness of coverage but entails the use of a somewhat cumbersome and unnatural apparatus (see Carr & Kurilko, 1964). Methods for the simulated exploration of environmental displays would provide relevant data. Another, simpler method would be the serial presentation of environmental displays by means of photographic slides, in which the viewing time is under the option and control of the observer. Each of these methods has potential value in research on the deployment of attention, both as characterological or stylistic modes of observation or as response-characteristics of the environmental displays.

Motational systems: Motational systems have been developed as standardized methods, akin to choreographic notational systems, whereby trained observers may note the sequence of principal elements and features in the experience of moving through environmental displays, as in the movement along highways and pedestrian pathways (See Thiel, 1961; Appleyard, Lynch & Myer, 1964; Halprin, 1965; Abernathy & Noe, 1966; Casey, 1966; Rose, n.d.).

Instead, research on the media of presentation will be traced in some detail, and the nature of the remaining research domains will be sketched in broader strokes.

A. Study of the Media of Presentation. Establishing the effects of differences in the media of presentation upon the comprehension of the environmental displays has practical priority in research in environmental psychology. Consider a study of the comprehension of a sample of town squares and plazas by nursemaids. The experimenter would be faced with the decision to employ direct or indirect media of presentation—to send the nursemaids to the sites or to use some presentations such as photographs or models.

It is clear that knowledge of the degree of comparability of comprehensions of environmental displays evoked by the different media of presentation is fundamental to the planning of other research in this field. The paradigm for studies that would yield this kind of knowledge is straightforward. A series of existing environmental displays would be selected. Presentations of each display would be developed in a standard form, using, for example, these media:

1. Direct exploration (complete freedom to roam about the actual displays)

2. Viewing a model of the environmental displays

3. A photographic slide series

4. A complete set of architectural elevations, plans, and perspectives

Observers would be assigned to a given medium of presentation and instructed to describe the environmental displays as they are presented, by the use of the several developed response formats, such as the Environmental Display Adjective Checklist. (It should be noted that a major preliminary effort would be required to develop standardized and technically sound versions of the response formats suggested in Table 64-2, such as Environmental Display Adjective Checklists and Q-Decks, Mood and Activity Checklists, Thematic Potential Analysis procedures, and so forth.) Observers of media 2, 3, and 4 would try to describe the display as it would appear if it had been directly presented to them. The findings would be analyzed primarily in terms of the similarity of the descriptions based upon indirect media to those based upon direct exploration.

A research program that developed such empirical estimates of the comparability among media would be useful in determining the degree to which substantive research findings gained on the basis of one medium would be applicable to other media, especially to direct exploration. Such research would also provide interesting general information on the behavioral reactions to the different media. The research requirements in this area would be extensive, for it would be necessary to sample widely from classes of media, observers, response formats, and displays, before stable and reliable generalizations could be established.

Although this research endeavor follows directly from the nature of the problem and the requirements of research strategy, it would also have practical implications for the disciplines of environmental design and planning. A considerable amount of anecdotal evidence and folklore wisdom surrounds the issue of how best to convey a proposed project solution to clients, planning commissions, citizen groups, and others, through professional presentations. The research on the media of presentation would provide systematic baseline evidence concerning the relative equivalence of the various indirect media to direct-media presentations. This consideration leads to another research tactic altogether: the possibility of experimenting with basic innovations and alterations in the nature of each indirect medium, using as a target for improvement the degree of equivalence of the resulting descriptions to direct-media descriptions. Finally, it would be fitting to take heed of the traditional use of a *combination* of indirect media in professional presentations (for example, plans, sketches, elevations, and so forth) and to search systematically for optimal combinations of indirect media, again using as the target of improvement the approximation to direct-media descriptions. An assumption implicit in these considerations is that the chief purpose of professional presentations is to convey an accurate, veridical notion of the proposed design or planning solution to the audience. Of course, to the extent that the overriding purpose is persuasive rather than descriptive, the importance of achieving direct-media equivalence may be lessened.

Another direction of research will be briefly noted to further illustrate the close interplay between systematic research and practical by-products. A personality psychologist viewing this domain of research would immediately become interested in possible stable differences among individual observers in the ability to make direct-media descriptions upon the basis of indirect-media presentations. Even in the use of indirect media that evoke comprehensions that on the whole poorly approximate direct-media descriptions, it would probably be found that some individuals are consistently better than others in making this approximation. The personality psychologist would be interested in what other abilities, skills, traits, and dispositions are correlated with the ability to make this descriptive and comprehensive leap from the indirect-media presentation to a direct-media grasp of the nature of the environmental displays. That is, he would ask: what are individuals like, in terms of their personality as a whole, who perform this trick especially well or especially poorly? He would wonder whether the same personality syndrome appears with regard to all indirect media or whether there are further refinements in this constellation of abilities, skills, traits, and dispositions, depending upon which indirect medium is involved. He would be interested in whether certain groups display more of this capacity than others. He would attempt to determine which indirect media are most suitable for particular groups. There would be practical implications here for the choice of indirect media for professional presentations to varying audiences. Also at the practical level, it would be important to determine to what degree the capacity to make direct-media descriptions upon the basis of indirect-media presentations is possessed by students in the environmental design and planning disciplines and how essential this capacity is to effective performance in these fields. If the capacity were found to be either essential or especially helpful, quick, standard methods for assessing candidates on the degree to which they display this ability might be developed; and, taking an ameliorative approach, methods for training and improving performance in this skill might be explored.

B. Study of the Observers: Individual and Group Differences in the Comprehension of the Everyday Physical Environment. Individual and group differences can be observed in the comprehension of the non-human environment if the research design holds constant the media of presentation, the response formats, and the environmental displays, but varies systematically the criteria for selection of observers. For example, if the medium is photography, if the response format is the Environmental Display Adjective Checklist descriptions, and if the environmental display is a typical subway station under Manhattan Island, then, in what way would architects, corporate presidents, janitors, Sierra Club members, and opera singers differ in their comprehensions of the subway station? Would Democrats differ from Republicans in their descriptions? Or children from adults? Or males from females? If the contrasting observer groups were selected upon the basis of personality traits and dispositions, rather than upon the basis of membership in socially differentiated groups, then a different set of questions must be asked: Would extraverts differ from introverts? Dominant persons from submissive persons? Would groups who differ in their motivation for achievement, or their cognitive flexibility, or their level of anxiety also differ in their description of the subway station?

If differences among groups defined socially or according to social variables or personality traits did emerge, then interest would turn to the generality of the differences: would the differences hold up if the media of presentation were systematically varied? Over what range of response formats and of environmental displays would these differences among groups in the comprehension of the everyday physical environment be discovered?

The impetus for research in this domain comes from both scientific and practical sources. The full sociopsychological understanding of a subgroup of the human population, whether it be defined sociologically or in terms of personality, will remain strikingly incomplete if that group's distinctive style of comprehending the everyday physical environment remains unexplored and unknown. At the practical level, the need for systematic understanding of specific client groups for whom the increasingly total environmental transformations are being made is perhaps even more urgent. With the advent of massive urban renewal programs and the creation of entire new communities, the relationship between the planners and designers, on the one hand, and the user-clients and inhabitant-clients, on the other, has become increasingly attenuated and indirect. Some new, reliable, empirical means of providing the necessary information and understanding of client groups has become necessary.

C. Study of Human Responsiveness to Environmental Displays. The third domain of research arises out of an interest in the list of possible response formats presented in Table 64-2. As this already extensive list, which nevertheless is presently only suggestive and incomplete, becomes increasingly expanded, the following question will arise: Do these response formats, each and every one, elicit totally different, independent, and unrelated dimensions of responsiveness to given environmental displays? Or is there rather some structural ordering and overlapping among them? Let us explore how such structure in human responsiveness might show itself. Take the research design in which a constant group of observers, using the same medium of presentation, respond to a variety of environmental displays by means of a wide range of response formats. In the analysis of the data, it might be noticed that whenever a cluster of adjectives was checked as descriptive of an environmental display, a certain metaphorical image was also applied to that display. Or perhaps it is revealed that whenever a certain theme appeared in the Thematic Potential Analysis of an environmental display, a combination of items from the mood checklist and the verb checklist was also designated as descriptive of it. This kind of comprehensive overlap or semantic correlation among response forms would demonstrate order among them. The structure of responsiveness to environmental displays may be fairly constant or it may vary with the nature of the observers, the environmental displays, or certain observer-display combinations.

D. Study of Environmental Displays: The Assessment and Appraisal of the Everyday Physical Environment. If the research design holds constant the observer groups, the media of presentation, and the response formats, but varies the environmental displays, then a domain of research focused upon the behavioral characteristics of environmental displays is generated, which might take three forms:

1. *Descriptive assessments.* On some sensible basis, a team of observers is selected. A class of environmental displays is defined and chosen for assessment study, such as, for example, the class of shopping centers, movie theaters, nursery schools, or vest-pocket parks. A sample of actual, existing environmental displays is randomly drawn from this class for assessment. The team of observers is presented with the sample of environmental displays, perhaps forty of them, by means of all possible and useful media of presentation; and the members of the assessment team respond to each environmental display independently by means of a wide variety of response formats. From this data would emerge an empirical, wide-ranging psychological description of this class or type of environmental display. Psychologically defined subgroups within the sample of environmental displays might also be identified on the basis of the relative similarity of the descriptive assessments they evoke. It would also be possible to explore the degree of association of individual response variables with variations in objective, physical characteristics among the sample of displays.

2. *Evaluative assessments.* Evaluative assessments combine a full-range descriptive assessment of a sample drawn from a class of environmental displays with an appraisal of the relative success or goodness of the individual environmental displays. If a descriptive assessment were made of a sample of forty vestpocket parks, drawn randomly from the total nationwide class of vestpocket parks, it would also be possible to identify the degree to which each park had been successful in its function and purpose. It is quite likely that a group of persons with expert understanding of the requirements and functioning of vestpocket parks would show high agreement in their ratings of the relative success of the parks, if they were given an opportunity to observe and study them. Other evaluative indices might also

be employed, such as a measure of the relative use of the parks by their neighborhood population, the injury rate, and so forth. Any of these measures, which express an appraisal of the environmental displays in terms of the success in which they are considered to have met their purposes, can be employed as *criterion indices*. By correlating the *criterion indices* with the findings of the full-scale *descriptive assessment*, it would be possible to determine the psychological characteristics of successful and unsuccessful parks. A differentiated picture would emerge of the ways in which the excellent and the inadequate environmental displays are comprehended and systematically described by human observers.

3. *Preconstruction predictive assessments.* The practical, social limitation of evaluative assessments is that inadequate environmental displays have already been constructed or otherwise brought into being. Would it be feasible to attempt to predict the ultimate evaluative criterion indices of environmental displays before they are constructed or otherwise developed into actual form? In order to make diagnostic predictions of useful accuracy in the preconstruction stage, several prerequisites would have to be met. First, a fund of systematic empirical knowledge concerning stable relationships between descriptive characteristics of environmental displays and evaluative criterion indices would have to become available. Secondly, since at the preconstruction stage, only indirect media presentations are possible, the kind of research discussed earlier concerning improvement in the ability to make direct-media descriptive assessments upon the basis of indirect media presentations would have to have moved ahead. Given these two prerequisites, however, it might well become possible to predict at the preconstruction stage both how human observers, and even specific subgroups of observers, will most likely comprehend the environmental display and how the environmental display will be evaluated in terms of its success in fulfilling its function. The ability of environmental psychology to develop predictive power in this area can be expected to have important effects upon the development and selection of prototypical designs and plans

for man-influenced environmental transformations and to place the process of design and planning more directly under rational guidance.

CONCLUSION

If any lessons are contained in this case study of research strategy in environmental psychology, they are perhaps these:

Appropriate Time Perspectives Must Be Developed

When the intricacy and scope of the research possibilities uncovered by analysis of the present problem are considered, and when it is recognized that this problem is only one selected from the domain of environmental psychology, which in turn is only one field of environmental behavioral science, then it is evident that any expectation of immediate cognitive gratification must be destined to frustration. Even with the most generously financed, large-scale, crash program of research imaginable, the magnitude of the methodological and empirical groundwork that must be established as the basis for a mature branch of research makes it imperative to think in terms of decades rather than months or years, and makes it incumbent upon behavioral scientists in this field to be humble in their advice and proclamations as well as incumbent upon environmental planners and designers to be patient in their expectations.

The Claims of Science and the Claims of Practice Must Be Kept in Balance

There is a danger that environmental behavioral science will be mistakenly considered applied research, because of the valuable encouragement the field has been receiving in its beginning period from the environmental planning and design professions. However, what is true of the problem treated here—the comprehension of the everyday physical environment—will be true of the problems environmental behavioral science will be encountering generally: they will be basic, fundamental problems concerning human behavior and experience.

While it will be greatly beneficial to the research enterprise if the professions exert strong and steady pressure upon environmental behavioral scientists to speak to professional needs, and to carry on research appropriate to their needs, it will often be necessary and wise for the scientists to move in other directions. In the fullness of time, of course, all issues will be dealt with, but there will necessarily be sequential constraints upon the timing and ordering of the development of the field.

Scientists and Practitioners Should Share a Commonsensical Grasp of the Nature of the Problem

The review of possible directions of research on the comprehension of environmental displays has demonstrated the often overlapping but essentially tangential relationship between the inherent conceptual structure of a problem and the context of professional practice. Since the points of contact will inevitably be intermittent rather than constant, it will promote understanding on the part of the professional disciplines if they are aware of the more abstract and socially indifferent perspective scientists bring to bear upon the conceptual structure of problems. On the other hand, if the scientists are to be alert to the social significance of their research and to practical implications of their methods and findings, then they will always need to be familiar with developments within the environmental planning and design disciplines.

REFERENCES:

Abernathy, B. L., & Noe, S. Urbanography. *Progressive Architecture,* 1966, **47,** 184–190.
Appleyard, D., Lynch, K., & Myer, J. R. *The view from the road. Cambridge,* Mass.: MIT Press, 1964.
Barron, F. Psychology of imagination. *Scientific American,* 1958, **199,** 150–166.
Block, J. *The Q-sort method in personality assessment and psychiatric research.* Springfield, Ill.: Charles C Thomas, 1961.
Carr, S., & Kurilko, G. *Vision and memory in the view from the road: Progress report.* Cambridge, Mass.: MIT-Harvard Joint Center for Urban Studies, 1964.
Carroll, J. B. Review of: C. E. Osgood, G. Suci, & P. H. Tannenbaum, The measurement of meaning, *Language,* 1959, **35,** 58–77.
Casey, T. G. Proposed method for the descrip-

tion of urban form. M. Arch. thesis, College of Environmental Design, University of California, Berkeley, 1966.

Christensen, P. R., Merrifield, P. R., & Guilford, J. P. *Consequences test.* Beverly Hills, Calif.: Sheridan Supply Co., 1958.

Clyde, D. J. Self ratings. In L. Uhr & J. G. Miller (Eds.), *Drugs and behavior.* New York: John Wiley, 1960.

Gordon, W. J. J. *Synectics: The development of creative capacity.* New York: Harper & Row, 1961.

Gough, H. G., & Heilbrun, A. B., Jr. *The adjective checklist manual.* Palo Alto, Calif.: Consulting Psychologists Press, 1965.

Halprin, L. Motations. *Progressive Architecture,* 1965, **46,** 126–133.

Harris, R. E. The improvisations procedure as a device for the assessment of air force officers. *I.P.A.R. Research Bulletin,* Berkeley, Calif.: Institute of Personality Assessment and Research, University of California, 1955.

Henry, W. E. *The analysis of fantasy.* New York: John Wiley, 1956.

Knapp, R. H. A study of metaphor. *Journal of Projective Techniques,* 1960, **24,** 389–395.

Lamm, J. W. Wurster Hall: A case study of people's reactions to buildings. B. Arch. thesis, College of Environmental Design, University of California, Berkeley, 1965.

Leith, E. M., & Upatnieks, J. Photography by laser. *Scientific American,* 1965, **212,** 24–35.

Michelson, W. An empirical analysis of urban environmental preferences. *Journal of the American Institute of Planners,* 1966, **32,** 355–360.

Moreno, J. L. *Who shall survive?* New York: Beacon House, 1934.

Nowlis, B. Research with the mood adjective checklist. In S. S. Tomlins & C. E. Izard (Eds.), *Affect, cognition and personality.* New York: Springer, 1965.

Osgood, C. E., Suci, G., & Tannenbaum, P. H. *The measurement of meaning.* Urbana, Ill.: University of Illinois Press, 1957.

Rose, S. W. A notation/simulation process for composers of space. Lincoln, Nebr.: University of Nebraska, n.d., mimeographed.

Saarinen, T. F. *The perception of the drought hazard on the Great Plains.* Department of Geography Research Paper No. 106. Chicago: University of Chicago, Department of Geography, 1966.

Sanford, N. Will psychologists study human problems? *American Psychologist,* 1965, **20,** 192–202.

Sarbin, T. R. Role theory. In G. Lindzey (Ed.), *Handbook of social psychology.* Reading, Mass.: Addison-Wesley, 1954. Pp. 223–258.

Stea, D. Personal communication, April 1966.

Studer, R. G., & Stea, D. Directory of behavior and environmental design. Providence, R.I.: Brown University, 1965.

Thiel, P. A sequence-experience notation for architectural and urban space. *Town Planning Journal,* 1961, **32,** 33–52.

Vigier, F. C. An experimental approach to urban design. *Journal of the American Institute of Planners,* 1965, **31,** 21–30.

Weiss, R., & Boutourline, S. *Fairs, exhibits, pavilions and their audiences.* New York: IBM Corp., 1962.

Winkel, G., & Sasanoff, R. *Approaches to an objective analysis of behavior in architectural space.* University of Washington, Architecture/Development, Series No. 5, August 1966.

65 The Use of Behavioral Maps in Environmental Psychology

William H. Ittelson, Leanne G. Rivlin, and Harold M. Proshansky

Behavior always occurs someplace, within the limits of some physical surroundings. Recent recognition of the importance of this self-evident fact has led to a growing number of studies relating various aspects of behavior to the physical spaces in which they are observed. Any data of this kind can be thought of as constituting a *behavioral map.* The necessary features of such a map are descriptions of behavior and of participants and statements relating the behavior to its physical locus. Behavioral mapping as thus defined is a very general technique for studying environmental influences on behavior. As might be expected in any new field of inquiry, this technique has so far not been widely used, but those who have used it have found it extremely fruitful. We wish here to describe procedures for producing and using behavioral maps in the study of environmental psychology.

GENERAL CHARACTERISTICS OF BEHAVIORAL MAPS

The familiar architect's floor plan provides the prototype of all behavioral maps—a scale drawing of a physical space with each area labeled according to the kinds of behavior expected to occur there. It presents, in capsule form, the salient features encountered in any attempt at behavioral mapping: categories of behavior, physical locations, and a technique for relating one to the other. "Living room," "bedroom," "kitchen"; these labels represent, at the same time, physical areas and rather gross behavioral categories. Both aspects can on occasion be made more precise. An architect can, for example, divide a living room into separate areas for

"TV viewing," "reading," and "conversation."

The same information can be conveyed in other ways than labels on a floor plan. For the purpose of relating behavior to its physical locus, it may be more useful to use a table in which rows represent physical locations and columns represent behavior. An index mark at the intersection of a row and column then indicates whether that behavior occurs at that location. Other possible ways of presentation include graphs, pictures, and combinations in which, for example, tables may be superimposed on plans or graphs or pictures. The optimum presentation varies with the nature of the specific problem and the audience being addressed.

The behavioral maps discussed in this paper will be tabular in form for the most part, but it should be clear that in our terminology the floor plan, the table, and any other methods of data presentation are all equivalent behavioral maps that differ only in the manner in which they visually present the same information.

The information needed to use a behavioral map as a research tool differs in two significant ways from that provided by the prototypical architect's floor plan. First and most obvious is the nature of the behavior categories. The floor plan implies very broad groupings of behavior. For research purposes, however, the behavior categories must be explicit, precise, and relatively narrow, and in addition, relevant to the particular problem under consideration. Let us consider, for example, a room conventionally labeled "bathroom" on the plan. The behaviors implicitly associated with this label are bodily functions, washing, and grooming, and these are what the room presumably is designed for. Kira's study of the bathroom, however, clearly reveals that these are only a small sample of the total range of behaviors that characteristically go on in that area (see Article 28). The bathroom, according to Kira, also functions as a private telephone booth and as a refuge from family quarrels, among other things. These categories of behavior not only explicitly extend the types of behaviors expected to occur in the "bathroom" beyond

those implied by the label, they also are more relevant to an understanding of the problems related to the structure of family life than are the behaviors more conventionally associated with that area. Behavioral maps, therefore, require a detailed analysis of behavior into relevant categories.

The same study of the bathroom suggests the second characteristic of behavioral maps which sets them apart from the architect's floor plan. The behaviors ascribed to the bathroom were learned about empirically; they were not postulated on theoretical or *a priori* grounds. The bathroom is not intended to be a telephone booth; it is not designed as a telephone booth; and there is no reason to believe that anyone would assume that it would be used as a telephone booth, except for the very simple fact that it can be observed to function in that way. Behavioral maps, then, are empirical; they describe observed behavior. Since any complete description of observed behavior must be quantitative, it follows that behavioral maps also are quantitative; they deal with amounts of behavior in addition to qualitative descriptions. For example, to say that the bathroom may be used as a telephone booth is interesting but tells us relatively little about the actual functioning of the bathroom until we also have information such as how often it serves this purpose compared to its other functions and how much telephoning occurs there compared to other more conventional places in the home.

MAPPING THE PSYCHIATRIC WARD: AN ILLUSTRATIVE EXAMPLE

The two characteristics of behavioral maps —the analysis of behavior into relevant categories and the empirical observation of these behavior categories—constitute the two major technical problems of behavioral mapping. They will be discussed here in the context of specific procedures developed for the mapping of two psychiatric wards of a large, private, urban general hospital. The wards have a patient population of approximately 22 patients each, and are devoted to an active treatment program. A patient's stay rarely exceeds three months. During that time a variety of therapeutic techniques may be used, including drugs, electric shock, psychotherapy, and several activity therapies. The wards will not be described in any more detail here since the interest of this paper is in behavioral mapping techniques rather than in behavior on the psychiatric ward. Fuller descriptions of the wards and analysis of behavior on them have been presented elsewhere in this volume (Article 43).

Categories of Behavior

Presumably, any category or set of categories of behavior could be used in constructing a behavioral map. Before empirical work can be carried out, however, decisions have to be made as to what kinds of behavior are relevant to the problem being studied. A basic decision, even before the types of behaviors are considered, is whether the focus is to be the behavior of individuals or the behavior of groups. All behavioral maps reported here concentrate on individuals, but we are also developing approaches to the mapping of group activity.

In dealing with the psychiatric ward, it seemed desirable to look at behaviors that most nearly describe the daily round of activities of the patients. These would also presumably be most likely to be related to the physical surroundings in which they take place. Eating, sleeping, reading, talking, watching television—these are what the patients actually do. At the same time, they involve direct commerce with the environment. For these reasons, attention was focused on common-sense descriptive categories of the gross, overt, observable behaviors that, taken together, actually make up the daily routine of the patients.

Once the basic decision as to the kinds of behaviors to be studied is made, the development of the actual behavioral categories is a straightforward process applicable to any setting. It involves three steps: cataloguing observed behaviors, generalizing the behaviors into categories for observation, and combining observational categories into analytic categories.

Cataloguing the behavior on the psychiatric ward was carried out by having observers on the ward record, over extended periods of time, all specific examples of a particular behavior that they observed. This, of course, resulted in a very large list of detailed units of behavior. After observations had been conducted for a sufficiently extended period of time, so that major examples of behavior presumably had not been missed, the list was examined, and duplicate, trivial, or obviously totally idiosyncratic observations were eliminated. The resulting inventory was a list of some 300 descriptions of behavior, samples of which are listed in Table 65-1.

Clearly such a list is too long and too specific to be useful in the collection of data. Summary observational categories were therefore derived from this list. Trained judges sorted the list of behaviors into groups that were judged to be more or less homogeneous within themselves and distinct from the others in terms of some observational characteristic; that is, they represented sets of behaviors that could be readily described for the observers and in turn identified by them. Table 65-1 also indicates the list of observational categories and sample behaviors under each.

For the purpose of analysis, the observational categories were still further combined into analytic categories that were appropriate for the particular problems being studied. Analytic categories may vary from problem to problem. In the behavioral maps described below, six summary analytic categories are used: isolated-passive, isolated-active, social, mixed-active, miscellaneous, and traffic behavior. The observational categories comprising these analytic categories are indicated in Table 65-1.

It should be noted that the way in which behaviors are grouped into observational and analytic categories is crucial to interpreting the data. Clearly, different combinations could produce different results. The procedures for the categorization are of great importance. The use of trained judges is a well-accepted technique, although it is not the only one. We are presently investigating the use of multi-variate techniques for determining whether there is an underlying dimensional structure to the inventory of behaviors. The results of this approach are not available at the present time, but they

Table 65-1 Classifying Behavior into Categories

Behavior	Observational Categories	Analytic Category
Patient reclines on bench, hand over face, but not asleep Patient lies in bed awake	lie awake	
Patient sleeps on easy chair One patient sleeps while others are lined up for lunch	sleeping	Isolated Passive
Patient sits, smiling to self Patient sits, smoking and spitting	sitting alone	
Patient writes letter on bench Patient takes notes from a book	write	
Patient sets own hair Patient sits, waiting to get into shower	personal hygiene	
Patient reads newspaper and paces Patient reads a book	read	Isolated Active
Patient and nurse's aid stand next to alcove Patient stands in doorway smoking	stand	
Patient paces between room and corridor Patient paces from room to room saying hello to other patients	pacing	
Upon receiving lunch some patients take it to bedroom Patient sits at table and eats by self	eating	
Patient cleans tables with sponge Patient makes bed	housekeeping	
Two patients listen to record player Patient turns down volume on radio	phonograph- radio	Mixed Active
Patient knits, sitting down Patient paints (oils), sitting down	arts and crafts	
Patient and registered nurses watch TV together Patient watches TV, goes to get towel, returns	TV	
Patient stands and watches a card game Patient sits on cans in hall watching people go by	watching an activity	
Patients play soccer in corridor Patient and doctor play chess	games	
One patient talks to another in reassuring tones Four patients sit facing corridor, talk sporadically Patient fails to respond to doctor's questions	talk	Social
Patient introduces visitors to other patient Patient stands near room with visitors	talk (visitor)	Visit
Patient comes in to flick cigarette ashes Patients go to solarium	traffic	Traffic

may ultimately lead to a better technique for categorizing the inventoried behaviors.

Observational Techniques

The general methodological and technical problems involved in the use of observational procedures in the social sciences have been fully discussed in volumes devoted to those problems and need not be presented here. In any social-science study, alternative approaches are available to the investigator; in this section we will briefly indicate the specific procedures used.

All the data were collected through the

use of well-trained observers who spent considerable time on the ward becoming thoroughly familiar with the functioning of the ward and well known to the ward occupants. They were introduced to and accepted by all as students of "ward architecture." They were instructed to be friendly with ward personnel and patients, but to avoid direct involvement in ward activities. Whether the presence of the observers affected behavior on the ward cannot be directly answered. Ward personnel, however, reported no differences between periods with the observers present and periods without them.

The location and timing of observations typically involved complete coverage of all physical spaces of the ward on an instantaneous time-sampling basis. What this meant in practice was that all areas of the ward were observed every 15 minutes by enough observers so that the total observation time, while not actually instantaneous, did not exceed three or four minutes. This general procedure, which was used for all the maps reported in this paper, was varied in a number of ways for specific problems. On occasion, only a single area in the ward was observed, if that area was of particular relevance to a question raised. Similarly, the instantaneous time-sampling procedure occasionally was modified to include continuous observations over longer periods of time. This made it possible to record the duration of activities and patterns of flow of activities, which can be of more interest for certain problems than the instantaneous recording of behavior. The choice between instantaneous or continuous observation must be made in terms of the particular problems studied. It can be noted, however, that in this context time and space vary reciprocally; that is, if a complete coverage of spaces is required, a time-sampling procedure becomes necessary. On the other hand, if complete coverage over time is needed, spaces must be sampled or selected. The only alternative in either case is to flood the ward with so many observers that behavior must inevitably be altered.

Observations were recorded on data sheets designed for quick and easy use by the observers. The sheets permitted direct punching of the data. A sample sheet is given in Table 65-2. It will be noted that the observer recorded, in addition to data such as the location and time of observation, the number of participants engaged in each category of behavior described in the previous section. The participants themselves are identified in only the broadest terms—for example, male or female patient, staff, or visitor. Even so broad an identification required considerable training and familiarity on the part of the observers since, in the hospitals studied, patients, staff, and visitors alike wore street clothes. Specific identification of individual patients is obviously desirable for certain purposes, but it can be done only at the sacrifice of other forms of data.

In summary, then, the behavioral maps of the psychiatric ward described here were obtained from reports of observers, who recorded, on a time-sampling basis for every area of the ward, the number of patients, staff, and visitors engaged in each of a predetermined set of behavior categories.

The maps discussed below report only the data on the behavior of the patients. The behavioral map is presented as a table, the rows of which represent physical areas of the ward and the columns, behavior categories. The numbers at the intersections of rows and columns are the numbers or the percentages of patients engaged in the particular behavior at the particular place. A map presenting the actual number of individuals observed (in our terminology, an "observed map") is necessary and useful for a description of the actual uses to which the various locations on the ward are being put. For all practical questions of design, assignment of staff, requirements for facilities, and so on, the important determinant is the actual number of users. For most nonapplied research problems, however, the observed map is of limited value because it does not permit comparison of different situations involving different absolute numbers of individuals. For this purpose, a map showing percentages based on the observed number divided by the potential number of users (in our terminology an "adjusted map") is preferable. All of the maps discussed below are adjusted maps.

Table 65-2 Ward Observation Form

Date 7/15   Ward 10   Observer 3   Time M _____   Census M 4
                                            A _____   F 24
                                            E 8:15   T 28

Day	Talk				Games				Watching an Activity				Writing				Read				Stand				Pace			
Room	M	F	S	V	M	F	S	V	M	F	S	V	M	F	S	V	M	F	S	V	M	F	S	V	M	F	S	V
Ind																					1							
Group 1	1	1																										
Group 2	1		1																									
Group 3																												
Group 4																												
Group 5																												

	Personal Hygiene				Lie Awake				Sleep				Sitting Alone				Arts & Crafts				TV				House-keeping			
	M	F	S	V	M	F	S	V	M	F	S	V	M	F	S	V	M	F	S	V	M	F	S	V	M	F	S	V
Ind													1	1														
Group 1																					2							
Group 2																												
Group 3																												
Group 4																												
Group 5																												

	Phono-Radio				Eating				Hospital Routine				Traffic															
	M	F	S	V	M	F	S	V	M	F	S	V	M	F	S	V	M	F	S	V	M	F	S	V	M	F	S	V
Ind																												
Group 1																												
Group 2																												
Group 3																												
Group 4																												
Group 5																												

Reliability and Validity of Behavioral Maps

Table 65-3 represents a typical sample map of a hypothetical average psychiatric ward. It is hypothetical in the sense that the data represent average figures for a number of different wards observed on many different occasions. The columns represent the analytic behavior categories described earlier, that is, social, isolated-passive, isolated-active, mixed (mostly television watching), miscellaneous (mostly visiting), and traffic. The rows represent the entire ward divided into major areas, bedrooms, and public rooms. For present purposes, no finer discrimination of spatial locations is necessary. For other purposes, however, it is valuable to differentiate among bedrooms of different sizes and number of occupants, and also among public rooms of varying functions, such as the dayroom, the hallway, the dining room, and so on. The numbers in the

Table 65-3 Behavior on an Average Ward[a]

	Traffic	Visiting	Social	Mixed Active	Isolated Active	Isolated Passive	Total
Bedrooms	0.1	3.2	3.9	0.8	5.7	10.4	24.1
Public rooms	2.7	6.5	14.3	9.4	4.6	2.6	40.1
Total	2.8	9.7	18.2	10.2	10.3	13.0	64.2

[a] Unless otherwise indicated in this and subsequent tables, the numbers represent the percent of the patients assigned to the ward engaged in each activity, and the times of observations were 9:30 A.M.–12:30 P.M.; 1:30–4:30 P.M.; 6–9 P.M.

table represent the percentage of patients assigned to the ward who were actually observed to be engaged in the particular behavior at the particular location indicated.

The data in Table 65-3 were obtained from a number of different observers in a number of different locations at many different times. Clearly, this table is of use only if the data on which it is based are reliable. Since a number of different observers must necessarily be used in order to cover the times and spaces involved, a special check of interobserver reliability was conducted by having two observers independently report the same ward at the same times. Interobserver agreement was high. Of 693 physical areas observed, 583 or 84 percent were reported identically by the two observers; that is, the observers identified all participants and categorized all behaviors in each area in exactly the same way. Of 797 individuals observed, 83 percent were reported identically. When behavioral maps were constructed from the data for each observer, they were almost identical. The mean difference in the percentage of patients reported for each of the six analytic categories was less than 1 percent, and the range was from 0 to 2.2 percent.

The reliability of the instrument itself is more directly revealed by a split-half check, in which the data obtained from 50 percent

of the observations is compared with that obtained from the remaining 50 percent. In one such check, the percentage of patients assigned to each of the observational categories in one-half of the observations differed from that obtained from the other half by a mean of 0.55 percent, with a range from 0 to 2.7 percent. Behavioral maps constructed from these data differed by even smaller amounts.

Repeated observations represent another way of assessing the reliability of a measurement technique. Table 65-4 represents a comparison of the data obtained on three separate days of the week, and we find that repeated observations yield almost identical behavioral maps of the wards. Similarly, Table 65-5 presents data obtained on two separate wards in the same hospital. The wards are virtually identical in physical construction and very similar in patient and staff characteristics. They are, of course, both operated under the same general set of hospital administrative procedures. Clearly, the behavior on the two wards as reflected in the behavioral maps is virtually identical.

In summary then, interobserver reliability is high, split-half reliability is high, and reliability is high for repeated observations of the same situation at different times and also for repeated observations of different but similar situations. We feel relatively secure in concluding from these diverse ob-

Table 65-4 Comparison of Behavior on Three Different Days: Average Ward

	Traffic	Visiting	Social	Mixed Active	Isolated Active	Isolated Passive	Total
Monday	3.2	3.4	20.6	11.2	10.1	14.0	62.5
Wednesday	3.2	7.8	21.6	11.2	10.4	14.4	68.6
Friday	3.4	8.0	20.2	9.8	14.0	12.0	67.4

Table 65-5 Camparison of Behavior on Two Wards

	Traffic	Visiting	Social	Mixed Active	Isolated Active	Isolated Passive	Total
Bedrooms							
Ward 1	0.0	3.3	3.4	1.0	6.5	10.3	24.5
Ward 2	0.2	3.1	4.4	0.6	4.9	10.4	23.6
Public rooms							
Ward 1	2.5	4.7	14.5	10.0	4.1	2.3	38.1
Ward 2	2.9	8.3	14.1	8.8	5.1	3.0	42.2

servations that the behavioral maps produced by the techniques described above are indeed reliable within the limits of accepted scientific practice.

The question of assessing the validity of the behavioral mapping technique is much more complex. Indeed, the very meaning of validity in this context is not clear. The observational categories were designed to be directly and easily observed and identified. It has been argued that in dealing with this type of overt, easily observed behavior, high reliability is tantamount to high validity. This is probably the closest we can come to a rigorous assessment of the validity of the behavioral maps.

While the fact may not be directly related to the question of validity, however, it is interesting that the pictures of the wards derived from the behavioral maps agree quite well with descriptions obtained in other ways. For example, Table 65-6 compares estimates of the way patients distribute time spent in their bedrooms derived from their responses to items in an interview with the actually observed distribution of activities in the bedrooms. While such estimates should be evaluated with caution, it is remarkable to note an almost exact duplication between the observed distribution and the estimated one. Similarly, although they are not reducible to quantitative form, qualitative descriptions of the uses of various parts of the ward obtained from staff members agree in almost every detail with corresponding pictures drawn from the behavioral maps. In short, the description of behavior on the ward given by the behavioral map is in very close agreement with the picture reported by those most intimately familiar with the ward.

A number of objective conditions are readily translatable into expected behavioral differences that can be verified by examining the behavioral maps. For example, a fairly large amount of visiting would be expected on visiting days and a correspondingly small amount on nonvisiting days. Table 65-7 compares the distribution of activities on visiting and nonvisiting days and indeed reflects the expected differences. Other evidences of consistency with objective expectations can be found by examining almost any behavioral map. Table 65-3, for example, shows that traffic takes place primarily in the public rooms; in this case, halls are subsumed in the public rooms category. The same table shows that television viewing occurs exclusively in the public rooms, which indeed is where the television set is located. Less obvious but still internally consistent is the distribution of social and isolated-passive behavior; the public rooms are chosen primarily for social activities, while isolated-passive activities take place primarily in the bedrooms. In short, wherever fairly certain predictions can be made on the basis of objective differences in the situation, these differences are reflected in the behavior as recorded in the behavioral maps.

It seems fairly justifiable to conclude, therefore, that the behavioral mapping tech-

Table 65-6 Comparison between Observed Distribution of Activities in Bedrooms and Patients' Estimates of Their Activities

	Social (%)	Isolated Active (%)	Isolated Passive (%)
Observed	29	28	43
Estimated	29	31	40

Table 65-7 Comparison of Behavior on Visiting Day and Nonvisiting Day

	Traffic	Visiting	Social	Mixed Active	Isolated Active	Isolated Passive	Total
Bedrooms							
Nonvisiting	1.1	0.6	1.8	0.1	5.5	13.8	22.9
Visiting	0.9	6.7	2.1	0.0	5.0	11.3	26.0
Public rooms							
Nonvisiting	3.4	1.3	13.0	18.0	6.9	7.1	49.7
Visiting	3.5	6.0	8.6	14.0	7.7	5.4	45.2
Total							
Nonvisiting	4.5	1.9	14.8	18.1	12.4	30.9	72.6
Visiting	4.4	12.7	10.7	14.0	12.7	16.7	71.2

nique produces reasonably reliable and accurate descriptions of the quantitative distribution of behaviors in the various parts of the psychiatric wards studied.

Some Uses of Behavioral Maps

Behavioral maps were developed as a technique for studying the relationships between behavior and the physical space in which it occurs. Four general examples of ways in which they can be used for this purpose will be illustrated here from the studies of psychiatric wards. These types of uses are not limited to the psychiatric wards, however, but can be of value in studying any setting.

1. Description. Any of the behavioral maps already described provides a shorthand description of the distribution of behaviors throughout the ward. These descriptions, in terms of percentages, are the basic data on which most other uses of behavioral maps are based. However, for some purposes, distributions of actual numbers of patients, rather than percentages, are necessary. The designer of a specific facility, for example, needs to know the number of individuals for whom he is designing. Also

for the student of ward behavior it is useful to bear in mind at all times the meaning of the percentages in terms of actual numbers of patients. Table 65-8, an "observed" map, shows such a picture, at a particular moment in time, of the 24 patients assigned to one ward. Eight patients were off the ward; of the sixteen remaining, six were in the bedrooms and ten in the public rooms. In the bedrooms, three patients were lying in their beds, probably asleep, one was probably engaged in personal hygiene, one was entertaining a visitor, and one was talking to a staff member. In the public rooms, four patients were engaged in social conversation among themselves and with staff members. Two were entertaining visitors, two were watching television, and one was probably working on a craft project.

2. Comparison. For purposes of comparing two different situations or conditions, "adjusted" maps showing percentages rather than actual numbers must be used. As an example, Table 65-9 compares the use of spaces on the ward by male and female patients. Some interesting differences clearly emerge. The women tend to use their bedrooms more than the men, and this difference is reflected in all categories of behavior

Table 65-8 Distribution of Actual Numbers of Patients[a]

	Traffic	Visiting	Social	Mixed Active	Isolated Active	Isolated Passive	Total
Bedrooms	0	1	1	0	1	3	6
Public rooms	1	2	4	2	1	0	10

[a] Total $N = 24$.

Table 65-9 Comparison between Male and Female Patients on One Ward

	Traffic	Visiting	Social	Mixed Active	Isolated Active	Isolated Passive	Total
Bedrooms							
Male	0.0	3.0	4.1	0.6	5.2	9.0	21.9
Female	0.4	3.7	2.9	1.2	7.6	10.7	26.5
Public rooms							
Male	3.2	3.4	18.8	6.3	4.3	3.1	39.1
Female	2.0	5.8	11.2	13.0	4.0	1.7	37.7
Total							
Male	3.2	6.4	22.9	6.9	9.5	12.1	61.0
Female	2.4	9.5	14.1	14.2	11.6	12.4	64.2

except social. Here the overall trend toward much greater social activity by the males produces the only category in which male use of bedrooms exceeds female. The total use of the public rooms by men and women is approximately equal, but the distribution of activity is markedly different; the men devote almost half of their time in the public rooms to social activity, while the women spend less than one-third of the time there socializing. In contrast, the single most popular activity for the women in the public room is television watching which, together with visiting, accounts for 50 percent of their activity. These and similar examples illustrate the kinds of comparisons that can fruitfully be made with the use of behavioral maps.

3. General Principles in the Use of Space.
The major value of behavioral maps, as a research tool, lies in the possibility of developing general principles regarding the use of space that apply in a variety of settings. It is premature to attempt such generalizations at this time, but two examples will illustrate the way they may ultimately emerge.

Peaking is a descriptive generalization used to indicate the fact that certain areas consistently show a predominance of a single type of activity. In Table 65-9, for example, the bedrooms show a characteristic peaking at isolated-passive behavior. In some cases, peaking is a product of an interaction effect between space and occupants, as shown again in Table 65-9 by the marked peaking in the public rooms of social behavior for male patients only.

Constancy and reciprocity of behavior refer to two related observations. First, certain kinds of behavior tend to remain virtually constant over wide varieties of conditions, and second, spaces are used reciprocally for this behavior. When the behavior increases in one area, it decreases in another. Table 65-10 shows data derived from behavioral maps made at three different times of the day. Here all behavior (except traffic) is combined into two major analytic categories: nonsocial and social. Social behavior in this case is defined as all behavior that primarily involves interaction between two or more individuals, while nonsocial behavior is primarily not concerned with interactions among individuals. From Table

Table 65-10 Distribution of Behavior in Afternoon Compared to Morning and Evening

	Combined Non-social Behavior			Combined Social Behavior		
	Bedrooms	Public Rooms	Total	Bedrooms	Public Rooms	Total
Afternoon	18.9	13.2	32.1	6.5	13.9	20.4
Morning	15.3	19.2	34.5	6.1	23.1	29.2
Evening	13.6	19.8	33.4	10.9	23.6	34.5

65-10, clearly nonsocial behavior remains virtually constant at one-third of the total ward activity over the entire day. The bedrooms and public rooms function reciprocally for this behavior, which is higher in the bedrooms and lower in the public rooms in the afternoon and the opposite during morning and evening. In contrast, social behavior shows no such constancy or reciprocity. Once again it should be emphasized that this is offered as an illustration of the kinds of generalizations that may emerge through the use of behavioral maps and not as an established conclusion regarding social and nonsocial behavior on the ward.

4. Prediction. Behavioral maps showing quantitatively the predicted or expected distributions of behavior in a new facility can be prepared in advance of construction or occupancy. To the best of our knowledge, this application of behavioral maps has not yet been made, but it potentially offers a useful tool for quantitatively checking the validity of assumptions behind the design of spaces and facilities.

AUTHOR INDEX

SUBJECT INDEX

681